THE LETTERS OF
OSCAR WILDE

Drawing by Phil May, 1893

THE LETTERS OF
OSCAR WILDE

EDITED BY

RUPERT HART-DAVIS

HARCOURT, BRACE & WORLD, INC.

NEW YORK

Pool

PR
5823
A27

Library of Congress Catalog Card Number: 60-10942

Printed in Great Britain

Contents

Illustrations

ILLUSTRATIONS

ILLUSTRATIONS

Introduction

André Gide reported Oscar Wilde as saying: *"Voulez-vous savoir le grand drame de ma vie? C'est que j'ai mis mon génie dans ma vie; je n'ai mis que mon talent dans mes œuvres,"* and nobody who heard his conversation ever doubted the truth of the remark. But the art of the talker, like that of the actor, dies with the artist and can seldom be recaptured from the written word. Perhaps the nearest approach to it is by way of letters, particularly those written to intimate friends without thought of publication.

Moreover, unless a man has kept diaries and other papers, his biography is difficult to write without the countless facts, dates and corroborations that his collected letters provide. Oscar Wilde's many biographers—even the best of them, Mr Hesketh Pearson—hampered by the dispersal of his letters and papers, and the wholesale destruction in 1895 of what were thought to be incriminating documents, have constantly been forced to rely on vague dates and secondhand evidence.

Happily several batches of Wilde's most important letters have been preserved as collections; those to Robert Ross, More Adey and the surviving letters to Lord Alfred Douglas in the William Andrews Clark Memorial Library in California; those to Reginald Turner in the collection of Donald and Mary Hyde; those to William Ward at Magdalen College, Oxford; those to Reginald Harding and E. W. Godwin in the collection of Mr Harford Montgomery Hyde, and so on. On the other hand the letters to Leonard Smithers have been widely scattered and keep turning up in unexpected places, as do the letters to Ada Leverson and Frank Harris.

Wilde's letters[1] have never before been collected, though at least two attempts have been made. Before the first war Robert Ross planned a volume of the post-prison letters to himself and began to draft an introduction.[2] He died suddenly in 1918, and after the war two small volumes of selections from these letters were published: *After Reading* (1921) and *After Berneval* (1922). The first was introduced (anonymously) by Stuart Mason, the second by More Adey. They contain respectively

---

[1] Throughout this book the word "letters" is taken to include postcards, telegrams, letters to the press and incomplete letters.

[2] The manuscript of this fragment, which will be quoted later (see pp. 564–565), is in the William Andrews Clark Library.

twenty-seven and thirty letters, expurgated by the removal of the names of Lord Alfred Douglas, Constance Wilde and a few others.[1]

Four other small batches of Wilde's letters have appeared in limited editions as follows:

Resurgam (1917) contains six letters to Dalhousie Young, edited by Clement Shorter. Whether they are expurgated I cannot say, for the originals have eluded my search.

Some Letters from Oscar Wilde to Alfred Douglas (San Francisco, 1924) contains twenty-five letters, edited by A. C. Dennison and Harrison Post. They are printed in full, with facsimiles to prove it.

Sixteen Letters from Oscar Wilde [to William Rothenstein] (1930). These are printed in full, but there are some errors of transcription.

Letters to the Sphinx from Oscar Wilde: with Reminiscences of the Author by Ada Leverson (1930). Contains thirty letters, heavily cut and doctored without any indication that this has been done. Only eighteen of the originals have so far come to light.

One further pamphlet must be mentioned:

Oscar Wilde's Letters to Sarah Bernhardt (1924), edited by Sylvestre Dorian and published by the Haldeman-Julius Company of Girard, Kansas, as Little Blue Book No. 64. Embedded in its sixty-four pages of rambling gossip and quotation are what purport to be eight letters from Wilde to Sarah Bernhardt, translated from their original French. Prolonged study has convinced me that, though some of them may have been partially based on genuine originals, they are too spurious for inclusion here. One of them, for instance, includes a long *verbatim* passage from one of Wilde's much later essays.

Many other letters of Wilde's have appeared during this century, in books about him, new editions of his own books, in periodicals, booksellers' catalogues (notably Dulau & Co's catalogue 161, of 1928) and in books of memoirs, but the only other attempt to collect them was made by A. J. A. Symons between the wars. He was planning a biography of Wilde, three portions of which were published in *Horizon* (April, May and October 1941), and he collected many letters, but after his death in 1941 the main results of his work disappeared. Luckily Mr Vyvyan Holland had sent him carbon copies of all the transcripts of letters made by Stuart Mason. After Symons's death Mr Holland recovered them, and where I have been compelled to use these texts for lack of better, I have designated them TS. Holland. Comparison of typescripts with available originals shows, as one would expect, that Mason was a reliable transcriber.

Work on the present edition was begun in 1954 with Allan Wade as editor. He died suddenly in July 1955 and I took over the task. My original intention was to couple his name with mine on the title-page, but I later

---

[1] These letters, and thirty-three others to Ross (ninety in all), appeared in a German translation by Max Meyerfeld (*Letzte Briefe*, Berlin, S. Fischer Verlag, 1925). These versions are less expurgated, and Meyerfeld contributed useful notes.

realised that it would not be fair to saddle him with the responsibility for many hundreds of footnotes he never saw, and dating-decisions in which he had no part. All the early enquiring, collecting and transcribing were done by him with his customary care and skill. He was a rare scholar and a beloved friend. I salute his memory.

Of the 1298 letters which I have collected 1098 are here printed.[1] (The remaining 200 are brief notes, often to unidentified people, of no literary, biographical or other interest.) Of the 1098, the texts of 866 are from the original manuscripts or photostat copies, 4 from manuscript copies in another hand, 3 from manuscript translations, 12 from facsimiles, 50 from typescripts, and 163 from printed sources. Except for the last category, where the information is each time given in a footnote, the provenance of each letter is shown in the headnote, and a key to the locations is printed on pp. xix–xxi. A headnote reading 'MS. Private' means that I have seen the original but the present owner is unknown or prefers to remain anonymous. The texts of all letters to periodicals are taken from the periodicals. The manuscript of a telegram means the original post-office form which was delivered to the recipient. I have not considered it necessary to number the letters, and all cross-reference is to page-numbers, which seem to me easier to find quickly.

Several scholarly friends have urged me always to indicate exactly which letters, or parts of letters, have previously appeared in print, but I have decided that to do so would enormously complicate the notes without any great benefit. Those, comparatively few, letters which have already seen the light in public or semi-public print have generally been cut, expurgated or altered, and rather than laboriously record all these anomalies, I prefer to rely on presenting here the first full and accurate text of as many letters as possible.

Wilde's spelling was mostly good, but he often misspelled proper names, even of places like Babbacombe and Berneval where he stayed for several months. I have corrected these and other such slips everywhere. His punctuation consisted mainly of short dashes, which he used to represent every kind of stop. They make the letters difficult to read, and I have re-punctuated normally as the sense seems to demand. Similarly I have re-paragraphed freely: often Wilde wrote only a word or two on each line and it is difficult to follow his intention, whereas in prison he habitually wrote in a tiny hand and compressed his letters to save space. His use of capital letters was erratic: for instance he generally used an initial capital for words beginning with T and H, presumably because he enjoyed making those particular capitals more than their lower-case equivalents. To perpetuate this whim would only irritate the reader, and I have followed the standard usage wherever the capital clearly has no significance.

---

[1] I hope that the publication of this book will bring many more to light, including those which I am at present able to print only from catalogue extracts.

INTRODUCTION

Each address from which Wilde wrote is given in full the first time it occurs, and thereafter abbreviated to the essential minimum. No distinction has been made between printed and written addresses. For convenience the address is always printed on the right, and the date, in standardised form, on the left. To save space the beginning and ending of each letter have been run into the body of the letter. The varying squiggles which Wilde used to signify "Truly yours," "Ever yours," and so on I have interpreted to the best of my ability. Abbreviations in the text have been lengthened, and figures of small numbers written out in words. The printing of titles has been standardised: those of poems, stories and articles are printed in Roman type between quotation marks; those of books, plays, periodicals and ships in italics. All foreign words are printed in italics unless the whole letter is in French. All underlined words are italicised, but no indication is given of the occasional words which have more than one underlining.

Except for three unimportant omissions, made to avoid giving pain to descendants and clearly indicated, Wilde's letters are here printed exactly as he wrote them, repetitions and all. His letters have hitherto suffered such expurgation, and impropriety is so often believed to lurk behind dots, that the time has surely come to publish the *ipsissima verba*. Although Mr Vyvyan Holland does not wholly approve of this decision, he has nobly allowed me to carry it out.

Wilde seldom dated his letters. Postmarks have often helped (though occasionally letters have strayed into wrong envelopes), and other dates have been deduced from internal evidence or cross-reference. All dates editorially supplied are enclosed within square brackets: doubtful ones are preceded by a query. It might be thought that the extensive Wilde literature would answer most dating problems, but exactitude was not the leading quality of Wilde's early biographers. For instance, no fact, date or statement given by Frank Harris or Lord Alfred Douglas can be accepted without reliable corroborative evidence. R. H. Sherard is more trustworthy, but he scarcely saw Wilde during the busiest years and is hazy on most of the important dates. Later biographers have generally adopted the errors or evasions of their predecessors.

For sixty years readers have been surfeited with opinions about Wilde's life, character and work, but starved of exact dates and details, and I have included a number of otherwise trivial letters because they help to fix a fact, a date or an address. In the footnotes, which have been kept as factual as possible, I have included a modicum of cross-reference to assist the reader, but he will have to rely largely on the index, where the first page-number after each person's name indicates the position of his main biographical particulars. To give the sources of all the information in the footnotes would have increased their length intolerably. The reader should perhaps be reminded that the footnotes refer only to surviving letters, and can therefore supplement, but not replace, a biography.

Dear Mr. Ruskin,

I send you my little book, "The Happy Prince and Other Tales", and need hardly say how grateful I will be if you find in it any charm or beauty –

"My handwriting . . .

to none other, so
that your message
might come to us
with the fire &
passion, and the
marvel & music —
making the deaf
to hear, and the
blind to see. I wish
I had something
better to give you, but,
such as it is, take
it with my love.

Oscar Wilde

once Greek and gracious . . .

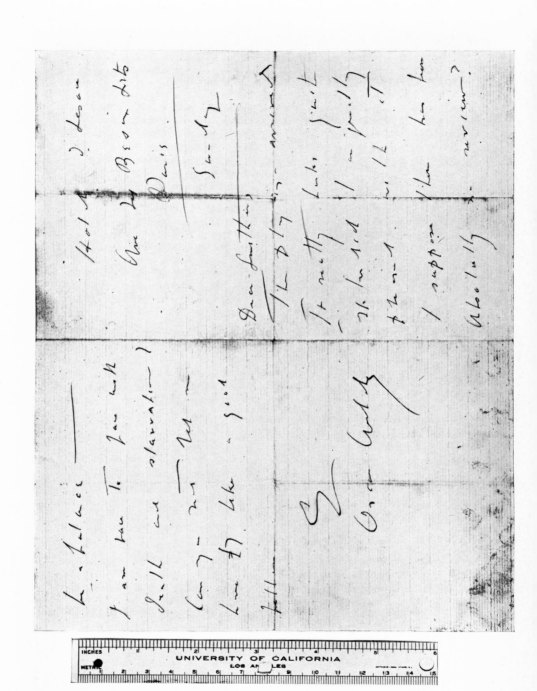

Example of forgery (see p. xiii)

INTRODUCTION

The following abbreviations are used in the footnotes:

Glaenzer	*Two Hundred Books from the Library of Richard Butler Glaenzer* (Anderson Auction Co., New York, 1911).
Harris	*Oscar Wilde, His Life and Confessions* by Frank Harris (New York, 1918).
Mason	*Bibliography of Oscar Wilde* by Stuart Mason [1914]. This book, although inadequately indexed and badly arranged, is packed with accurate and often out-of-the-way information.
Meyerfeld	Max Meyerfeld's notes to his translation of Wilde's *Letzte Briefe* (Berlin, 1925).
Miscellanies	Volume XIV of the Collected Edition of Wilde's works, edited by Robert Ross (1908).
O'Sullivan	*Aspects of Wilde* by Vincent O'Sullivan (1936).
Reviews	Volume XIII of the Collected Edition of Wilde's works, edited by Robert Ross (1908).
Rothenstein	*Men and Memories* by William Rothenstein (Vol. I, 1930).
Trials	*The Trials of Oscar Wilde*, edited with an introduction by H. Montgomery Hyde (1948).

Besides the printed examples already mentioned, there have been several attempts to circulate forged Wilde letters. A small number, together with forged Wilde manuscripts, were bought by Messrs Hodges Figgis, the Dublin booksellers, were first authenticated and then rightly repudiated by Stuart Mason, and are now safely in the William Andrews Clark Library. They are believed to have been the work of Fabian Lloyd, Wilde's nephew by marriage. Mr Owen Dudley Edwards contributed an article on these letters, entitled "The Wilde Goose Chase," to the *American Book Collector*, vol. vii, no. 5 (January 1957).

One or two obvious forgeries were reproduced in facsimile in a preposterous book called *Osrac the Self-Sufficient* by J. M. Stuart-Young (1905) and a third group is still in circulation. These letters are usually addressed to Leonard Smithers, are often on ruled or squared paper much folded and creased, purport to have been written in Paris between 1898 and 1900, mostly mention Arthur Clifton, and are easily recognisable as forgeries by comparison with genuine letters of the period. An example is reproduced opposite.

I have received much help and kindness in my work, and I am very grateful to all my benefactors. The first and greatest of them is Mr Vyvyan Holland, the son of Oscar Wilde and owner of the copyright in his letters. Mr Holland has throughout helped me with encouragement, information and forbearance. He has seen and checked my work, but the editorial responsibility is entirely mine.

INTRODUCTION

To all the owners of original letters whose names are listed on pp. xx–xxi I give warm thanks for sending me their letters, and to many of the private owners for the gift of photostat copies.

The finest collection of Wilde letters and other material in the world is in the William Andrews Clark Library. Without the ceaseless and ungrudging assistance of the Director, Dr Lawrence Clark Powell, and his staff my task would have been impossible. In particular I received much initial help from Mr John Charles Finzi, the compiler of the collection's catalogue (*Oscar Wilde and his Literary Circle*, 1957), and I have been continuously sustained by the kindness and efficiency of Mrs Edna C. Davis.

To the best of my knowledge the most comprehensive Wilde collection in private hands is that of Mr Harford Montgomery Hyde, and through his benevolence I have been able to consult and borrow many items otherwise unprocurable, and to draw repeatedly upon his extensive knowledge of the period.

For generous permission to publish copyright material I am grateful to the following: Sir Bronson Albery for two letters by Charles Wyndham; Mr Edward W. Colman for unpublished poems and letters by Lord Alfred Douglas; the executors of the late Campbell Dodgson for the letter which forms Appendix A; Messrs Methuen & Co. Ltd for the 1949 version of *De Profundis*; Mr Kerrison Preston for a passage from *Time Was* by W. Graham Robertson; Mr J. P. Ross for letters by Robert Ross; Dr Octavia Wilberforce for an unpublished passage by Elizabeth Robins; Mrs Violet Wyndham for quotations and a letter by Ada and Ernest Leverson; and to all the owners and copyright-holders of the pictures and photographs that form the illustrations.

In my quest for footnote-information I have had the benefit of an inner ring of expert researchers. Near at hand Mr Richard Garnett has persistently ransacked the British Museum and the London Library on my behalf. In Dublin and in London Mr Owen Dudley Edwards has time and again achieved astonishing results: he has now come to man's estate, but when he first began to help me he was almost an infant prodigy of research. From America Mr Dan H. Laurence has conducted much research and answered countless questions of great complexity, and Professor Roger Lhombreaud has done the same from France. Theatrical information has been expertly and generously supplied by Messrs Raymond Mander and Joe Mitchenson, ably seconded by Miss Freda Gaye, the editor of *Who's Who in the Theatre*. At the proof-stage my work has benefited beyond telling through the devoted assistance of two remarkable men, Mr Ernest Mehew and Mr Henry Maas. They are both busy professional men with little spare time, yet their contribution has been immense. Mr Mehew has unearthed several dozen letters unknown to me, besides doing the most acute detective work on behalf of the footnotes: any of them that seem particularly ingenious, amusing or recondite can safely be attributed to him, while Mrs Joyce Mehew's extensive knowledge of the

INTRODUCTION

Bible has proved invaluable. Mr Maas, far from the great libraries, has concentrated mainly on the problems of dating, where his knowledge of the period and penetrating analytical mind have saved me from countless blunders. All these helpers have laboured far beyond the call of friendship, duty or scholarship, and I am profoundly in their debt.

But my gratitude for personal reminiscences, family histories, the loan of books and papers, a mass of specialised information, and manifold favours to myself and Allan Wade, is also due to the following:

Mr John Alden of the Boston Public Library; Mr Alan Anderson; Miss R. V. Anderson; Mr William W. Appleton; Mrs W. M. Ashton of *Punch*; Professor L. J. Austin.

Lady Ruth Balfour; Miss Elizabeth Barber of the Society of Authors; Miss Doris Barfoot; the late Sir Kenneth Barnes; M. Gérard Bauër; Mr Clifford Bax; Mr Christopher Bean; Mr John Bebbington, City Librarian of Sheffield; the late Lady Beerbohm; Dr Doyne Bell and the Committee of the Savile Club; Mr George Bellord; the late Dr R. I. Best; Mr John Betjeman; Mr Oliver Morchard Bishop; Mr Charles W. Black, City Librarian of Derby; Wing Commander G. D. Blackwood; Mr Ernest Bletcher, Borough Librarian of Derby; Professor Edmund Blunden; Mr Christopher Blunt; Mr Wilfrid Blunt; Mr T. S. R. Boase; Mr Charles S. Boesen; Mr W. H. Bond of Harvard University Library; Mr Ernest Bradbury; Mr Christopher Bradshaw; Mr Boris Brasol; Mr G. R. F. Bredin, Bursar of Pembroke College, Oxford; Mrs Frances J. Brewer of the Detroit Public Library; Mr J. G. Broadbent; Mr Vincent Brome; Professor Julian Brown; Mr I. R. Browning, Librarian of Pembroke College, Oxford; Miss Lillian Browse; Mr John Bryson; Mr. T. F. Burns; the Rev. O. Mordaunt Burrows.

Mr Herbert Cahoon; the Rev. Philip Caraman, S.J.; Mr John Carter; Mr Aubrey Cartwright; The Countess of Cavan; Mr Terence Cawthorne; Professor Guy Chapman; the late Sir Marcus Cheke; Professor Kathleen Coburn; Mr John Connell; Mr Colin A. Cooke, Bursar of Magdalen College, Oxford; Mr Francis J. Cooper, Director of the Lincoln City Library; the Rev. Thomas Corbishly, S.J.; Mr Gordon Craig; Dr Macdonald Critchley; Mr John Crow; Mr Anthony Curtis.

The late Mr Henry Danielson; the late Dr Helen Darbishire; Madame Cecile Delhorbe; Mr Alan Dent; the Rev. C. Stephen Dessain; Mr William S. Dix of Princeton University Library; Mrs Vera Dobie; Mr J. H. Drake; Professor Fraser Drew; Lady Juliet Duff; Mr Barry Duncan.

Miss Nancy Eastwood; Professor Leon Edel; Mr C. Edwards, Borough Librarian of Chelsea; Mr H. C. W. Edwards of Christ's Hospital; Professor R. Dudley Edwards; Miss Doris Eldridge of the Chelsea Public Library; Miss Blanche B. Elliott; Sir Arthur Elton; Mr Elwyn Evans of the National Library of Wales; Dr Joan Evans.

Mr Jan Farquharson; Mr Robert Farquharson; Mr Gerard Fay; Dr

INTRODUCTION

W. R. Fearon; Mr John F. Fleming; Mr Ian Fletcher; Dr Desmond Flower; Mr R. A. C. Fothergill; Mr George Freedly of the New York Public Library.

Mr Donald Gallup of Yale University Library; Don Patricio Gannon; Mr Daniel George; Mr Val Gielgud; Mr Edwin Gilcher; Mr Thomas J. Gillcrist; Mr Karl Goedecke; Mr Robin Goodfellow; Dr John Gordan, Curator of the Berg Collection; Lord Gorell and the Committee of the Royal Literary Fund; Mr J. W. Gough, Librarian of Oriel College, Oxford; Mr David Gould; Sir Basil Goulding, Bart; Mr Leonard Green; Mr Edward Grierson; Lord Grimthorpe; The Rev. Professor Aubrey Gwynn, S.J.; Professor Denis Gwynn.

Mrs Beatrice Forbes-Robertson Hale; Sir William Haley; Mr Victor Hall; Mr Irving S. Halpern of the Carnegie Bookshop; Mr Tyrus G. Harmsen of the Huntington Library; Mr A. G. Harrison of the Jersey *Evening Post*; Sir Harold Hartley; Mr W. S. Haugh, City Librarian of Bristol; Mr John Hayward; Mr Richard J. Hayes, Director of the National Library of Ireland; Mr R. H. Helman of Tonbridge School; Mr Jocelyn Hillgarth; Mr E. Austin Hinton, City Librarian of Newcastle-upon-Tyne; Mrs Dulcie Holland; Mr John S. L. Holland; Mr Robert Holland; the late Mr Joseph Hone; Mrs Jacqueline Hope-Nicholson; Mr Reginald Horrox; Mr L. P. Hose; Mrs Madeline House; the late Mr Laurence Housman; Mr A. J. Hucker; Mr C. B. Hunt; Mr F. G. B. Hutchings, City Librarian of Leeds.

Admiral Sir William James; Mr Douglas Jerrold; Miss Marjorie Kate Jerrold; Mr L. Jolly of Glasgow University Library.

Mr E. A. F. Keen, City Librarian of Worcester; Sir Thomas Kendrick; Mr Neil Ker, Librarian of Magdalen College, Oxford; Mr R. W. Ketton-Cremer.

Mr Donald L. LaChance; the Very Rev. Mgr. Francis J. Lally of the Boston *Pilot*; Mrs Enid Lambart; Mr H. A. R. Langford of the Law Society; Mr Charles Lazenby; Dr E. Lehmann, Librarian of the Bodmer Library; Mr John A. Lester, Jr.; Mr Henry Lethbridge; Mr Harry A. Levinson; the late Miss Katherine Lewis; Mr O. St Clair Lloyd; Mr Edward Lockspeiser; Mrs Long of the Royal General Theatrical Fund; Mr Mark Longman; Mrs E. B. C. Lucas.

Mr Richard S. MacCarteney of the Reference Division of the Library of Congress; Mr William H. McCarthy of the Rosenbach Foundation; Mr Moray McLaren; Mr Daniel Macmillan; Mr R. C. Mackworth-Young, Royal Librarian at Windsor; Mrs Stanley V. Makower; Mr Thomas Mark; Mr H. Marley; Miss A. Martin of Maggs Bros; the Rev. F. X. Martin, O.S.A.; Mr Dudley Massey; Mr Paul F. Matheisen; Miss H. I. McMorran, Librarian of Girton College, Cambridge; Mr David C. Mearns of the Library of Congress; Mr I. D. Merry, Bursar of Clifton College; Mr Robert F. Metzdorf of Yale University Library; Mr Hamish Miles; Mr K. D. Miller, City Librarian of Stoke-on-Trent; Mr C. S. Millington;

INTRODUCTION

Mr C. S. Minto, City Librarian of Edinburgh; Professor T. W. Moody; Mr F. Peter Morgan of Romeike & Curtice Ltd; Mr C. D. Morley, Secretary to the Council of the Stock Exchange; Mr Leonard Mosley; Mr A. N. L. Munby; Mr John Grey Murray; Miss Winifred Myers.

Mr A. R. Newton of Bernard Quaritch Ltd; Mr Simon Nowell-Smith; Lt.-Col. Lord Nugent.

Mr Basil O'Connell; Mr T. O'Connor, Departmental Record Officer of the Home Office; Mr Eoin O'Mahony; Mr T. P. O'Neill; Mr Colin F. Osborn; the Rev. William O'Sullivan.

Mr George D. Painter; Mr Mike Papantonio of the Seven Gables Bookshop, New York; Professor Julian Park of the University of Buffalo; Mr Lynn Parsons; Miss Marjory Pegram; Captain Basil Peterson; Mr Sam Pierce of the Museum of the City of New York; Mr Malcolm Pinhorn; Mr Eric S. Pinker; Mr C. J. B. Pollitt; Lady Pooley; the Rev. R. St C. Pozzi; Miss Angela Preston; Mr A. W. Price; Mrs Eleanor G. Pyne of the Providence Public Library.

Mr Max Reinhardt; Mr Paul R. Reynolds; Mr A. N. G. Richards, Librarian of St Paul's School; Mr R. L. Rickard; Mrs Millicent Riddett; Professor F. Warren Roberts of the University of Texas; Mr Kenneth Rose; Mr Harold Rosenthal; Mr Bertram Rota; Mr George Rowell; Mrs Esmé Rowley; Mr Harold Rubinstein; Mr John H. Russell of the University of Rochester Library; Mr S. Rutherford, Town Clerk of Morpeth; Mr S. G. Ryall of the Foreign Office.

Lady Margaret Sackville; Mr N. C. Sainsbury of the Bodleian Library; the late Christopher St John; Mr Dennis L. Sandelson; Mr Marcie Lee Sandy; Dr Claudio Sartori; Mr Siegfried Sassoon; the Rev. Roland Burke Savage, S.J.; Mr Stanley Sawyer; Mr John Schroeder; Miss May Davenport Seymour; Mrs Muriel Sherard; Colonel E. A. Shipton; Mrs Oswald Sickert; Mr Frank Singleton; Mr H. S. A. Smith, Librarian of Stratford-on-Avon; Mr Kenneth Smith, City Librarian of Carlisle; Mr R. E. Snaith; Mr Philip Snow, Bursar of Rugby School; Dr Eileen Souffrin; Mr John Sparrow; Mr Robert Speaight; Mr David Stephens; Mr J. I. M. Stewart; Mr Noel Stoker; the late Mr William Stone; Mr George Stubbs; Mr H. A. C. Sturgess, Librarian of the Middle Temple; the late Mr Arthur Swann of the Parke-Bernet Galleries; Mr John L. Sweeney; Mr Forest H. Sweet; Mr Christopher Sykes; Miss Angel Symons.

Mr C. R. H. Taylor of the Alexander Turnbull Library, Wellington, N.Z.; Mr H. A. Taylor; Mr Giles Telfer; Professor Geoffrey Tillotson; Air Commodore G. N. E. Tindal-Carill-Worsley; Mr O. S. Tomlinson, City Librarian of York; Mr E. M. Trehern; Miss Joy Treherne; the late Prince Troubetzskoy.

Mr Richard Usborne; Mr J. D. Utley; Miss Marjorie Vernon, Librarian of Penrith; Mr E. H. Visiak.

Mr Alexander D. Wainwright of Princeton University Library; Mr R. A. Walker; the Rev. James Walsh, S.J.; Miss Cecil Ward; Professor

INTRODUCTION

Roberto Weiss; Professor George Whalley; Miss C. R. Wildhaber, Librarian of West Herts; Mr Edwin E. Williams of the Widener Library at Harvard; Mr T. Michael Williams; Mrs Owen Williams; Dr T. G. Wilson; Mrs Undine Wilson; Miss E. M. Woodfine; Mr Victor Woods, City Librarian of Birmingham; Miss Gertrude L. Woodward of the Newberry Library, Chicago; Mr Louis B. Wright of the Folger Shakespeare Library; Mr John Cook Wyllie of the University of Virginia; Miss Marjorie G. Wynne of Yale University Library; Mrs W. B. Yeats; Mr Kenneth Young; and Professor Morton D. Zabel.

The final proofs have benefited greatly from the expert scrutiny of Mr Nicolas Barker, Professor Bruce Dickins, Dr Lawrence Evans, the Hon. George Lyttelton, Dr Arthur Ransome and Mr Bertie van Thal.

If the names of any helpers have been inadvertently omitted from this list I beg their forgiveness and should like to thank them collectively, together with the staffs of the various libraries and institutions who have worked anonymously for the improvement of this book; in particular the staff of the London Library, to whom I have never yet applied in vain.

To Mrs Ruth Simon I owe more than can be expressed. She has transcribed and helped to check the great majority of the letters, typed and retyped all the footnotes and other editorial matter, controlled the flowing correspondence of years and conducted much individual research. No editor can ever have been blessed with an abler or more encouraging collaborator.

December 1961   RUPERT HART-DAVIS

xviii

Manuscript and Other Locations

1. *Manuscripts: Institutions*

Aberystwyth	National Library of Wales, Aberystwyth
Arents	Arents Tobacco Collection, New York Public Library
Berg	Henry W. and Albert A. Berg Collection, New York Public Library
B.M.	British Museum, London
Bodley	Bodleian Library, Oxford
Bodley Head	The Bodley Head Ltd
Boston	Boston Public Library
Buffalo	State University of New York, Buffalo
Clark	William Andrews Clark Memorial Library, University of California, Los Angeles
Congress	Library of Congress, Washington, D.C.
Doucet	Bibliothèque Doucet, Paris
Dublin	Library of Trinity College, Dublin
Edinburgh	National Library of Scotland, Edinburgh
Fales	Haliburton Fales Collection, New York University
Folger	Folger Shakespeare Library, Washington, D.C.
Glasgow	University of Glasgow Library
Harvard	Harvard University Library
H.O.	Home Office, London
Huntington	Henry E. Huntington Library, San Marino, California
Magdalen	Magdalen College, Oxford
Minnesota	University of Minnesota Library
Morgan	Pierpont Morgan Library, New York
New	New College, Oxford
Newberry	Newberry Library, Chicago
Paris	Bibliothèque Nationale, Paris
Princeton	Princeton University Library
R.L.F.	Royal Literary Fund, London
Russell	Annie Russell Papers, New York Public Library
Smallhythe	Ellen Terry Memorial Museum, Smallhythe, Tenterden, Kent
Sterling	Louis Sterling Library, University of London
Texas	University of Texas Library
Turnbull	Alexander Turnbull Library, Wellington, N.Z.
Watts	Watts Gallery, Compton, Surrey
Yale	Yale University Library

2. *Manuscripts: Private Owners*

Abrahams	Mrs Beth-Zion Abrahams
Albery	Sir Bronson Albery
Anderson	Mr Alan Anderson
Baird Smith	Mrs Jessica Baird Smith
Beange	Mrs Madeline Mary Beange
Beaverbrook	Lord Beaverbrook
Blacker	Dr C. P. Blacker
Bonniot	Madame Bonniot
Bridge	Mrs Ursula Bridge
Burke	The Rev. Edmund Burke, C.P.
Butler	Mr LaFayette Butler
Camrose	Viscount Camrose
Clark (R.)	Mr Roger Clark
Cobbold	Lady Hermione Cobbold
Cockerell	Sir Sydney Cockerell
Cortés	Dr Noel J. Cortés
Curtiss	Mrs Mina Curtiss
Davitt	Miss Eileen Davitt
Dickey	Mr Harry S. Dickey
Distin	Mrs Cyril Distin
Du Cann	Mr C. L. G. Du Cann
Dugdale	Mrs E. T. S. Dugdale
Edmiston	Mr Fred W. Edmiston
Feinberg	Mr Charles E. Feinberg
Flower	Sir Newman Flower
Gentry	Mr Bryen Gentry
Gielgud	Sir John Gielgud
Graham	Mrs Isabel Graham
Hart-Davis	Mr Rupert Hart-Davis
Hassall	Mr Christopher Hassall
Hedley	Mr Arthur Hedley
Hillyard	Mrs Fabienne Hillyard
Holland	Mr Vyvyan Holland
Houghton	Mr A. A. Houghton, Jr.
Hughes	Commander A. M. Hughes, R.N.
Hunt	Mrs Ethel Hunt
Hyde (D. & M.)	Mr Donald and Mrs Mary Hyde
Hyde (H. M.)	Mr H. Montgomery Hyde
Irving	Mr Laurence Irving
Johnston	Mr Denis Johnston
Kittleson	Mr Harold Kittleson
Knott	Miss Eleanor Knott
Lohman	Miss Helen Lohman
Marshall	Mr Norman Marshall
Martin	Mr H. Bradley Martin
Mayfield	Mr John S. Mayfield
Millar	Dr Eric G. Millar
Miller	Miss Irene Miller
Montefiore	Mr Leonard G. Montefiore

Morrison	Mr Murray D. Morrison
Navarro	Mrs D. H. de Navarro
O'Donohue	Mr Joseph J. O'Donohue IV
Paton	Mr John D. Paton
Pearson	Mr Hesketh Pearson
Philips	Captain H. V. Philips
Pratt	Mr Dallas Pratt
Prescott	Mrs Sherburne Prescott
Preston	Mr Kerrison Preston
Reichmann	Mrs Eva Reichmann
Roberts	Mr G. C. Roberts
Ross (A. L.)	Mr Arthur Leonard Ross
Ross (J. P.)	Mr J. P. Ross
Rothenstein	Sir John Rothenstein
Roughead	Mr W. N. Roughead
Satcher	The Rev. Herbert Boyce Satcher
Secker	Mr Martin Secker
Sharp	Mr Noel F. Sharp
Sowerby	Mrs Olivia Sowerby
Springarn	Mr Arthur B. Springarn
Taylor	Mr Robert H. Taylor
Thursfield	Mr Patrick Thursfield
Vander Poel	Mr H. B. Vander Poel
Wansbrough	Mrs Elizabeth Wansbrough
White	Mr Terence de Vere White
Whittington-Egan	Mr Richard Whittington-Egan
Wilberforce	Dr Octavia Wilberforce
Wilkinson	Mr Louis Wilkinson

3. *Facsimile Locations*

Brasol	*Oscar Wilde: The Man—The Artist—the Martyr* by Boris Brasol (1938)
Butterfly	The *Butterfly Quarterly* (Philadelphia), Autumn 1907
Cantel	*Opinions de Littérature et d'Art* by Oscar Wilde, translated by J. Cantel (Paris, 1914)
Keller	*Epigrams*, A volume of a collected edition of Wilde's works published by A. R. Keller & Co. (London and New York, 1907)
Le Gallienne	*The Romantic 90's* by Richard Le Gallienne (1926)
Traubel	*With Walt Whitman in Camden* by Horace Traubel (1908)

4. *Typescript Locations*

Congress	Library of Congress, Washington, D.C.
De Saix	M. Guillot de Saix
Harrod	Sir Roy Harrod
Holland	Mr Vyvyan Holland
Leslie	Sir Shane Leslie, Bart
Ross (A. L.)	Mr Arthur Leonard Ross
Sheppard	Mr James H. Sheppard
Zarnekah	Alexandre, Comtesse de Zarnekah

Biographical Table

1854	October 16	Oscar Wilde born at 21 Westland Row, Dublin
1855		Family moves to 1 Merrion Square North
1864–71		At Portora Royal School, Enniskillen
1871–74		At Trinity College, Dublin
1874	October	Goes up to Magdalen College, Oxford, as Demy
1875	June	Travels in Italy with Mahaffy
1876	April 19	Death of Sir William Wilde
	July 5	First in Mods
1877	March–April	Visits Greece with Mahaffy, returning *via* Rome
1878	June 10	Wins Newdigate Prize with *Ravenna*
	July 19	First in Greats
	November 28	B.A. degree
1879	Autumn	Takes rooms with Frank Miles at 13 Salisbury Street, London
1880	August	Moves with Miles to Keats House, Tite Street, Chelsea
1881	June ?30	*Poems* published
	December 24	Embarks for U.S.A.
1882		Lectures in U.S.A. and Canada all the year
1883	January–?May	In Paris, Hôtel Voltaire
	?July	Moves into rooms at 9 Charles Street, Grosvenor Square
	Aug–Sept	Visits New York briefly for production of *Vera*
	September 24	Begins lecture-tour in U.K., which lasts off and on for a year
	November 26	Engaged to Constance Lloyd
1884	May 29	Married to Constance Lloyd in London
	May–June	On honeymoon in Paris and Dieppe
1885	January 1	Moves into 16 Tite Street
	June 5	Cyril Wilde born

BIOGRAPHICAL TABLE

1886		Meets Robert Ross
	November 3	Vyvyan Wilde born
1887		Undertakes editorship of the *Woman's World*
1888	May	*The Happy Prince and other Tales* published
1889	July	"The Portrait of Mr W. H." published in *Blackwood's*. Gives up editorship of the *Woman's World*
1890	June 20	*The Picture of Dorian Gray* published in *Lippincott's*
1891	?January	Meets Lord Alfred Douglas
	January	*The Duchess of Padua* produced in New York as *Guido Ferranti*
	February	*The Soul of Man under Socialism* published in *Fortnightly*
	April	*The Picture of Dorian Gray* published in book form
	May 2	*Intentions* published
	July	*Lord Arthur Savile's Crime and Other Stories* published
	November	*A House of Pomegranates* published
	Nov–Dec	Writes *Salome* in Paris
1892	February 20	*Lady Windermere's Fan* produced
	May 26	Limited edition of *Poems* published
	June	*Salome* banned by Lord Chamberlain
	July	Takes cure at Homburg
	Aug–Sept	Writes *A Woman of No Importance* in Norfolk
	November	Takes Babbacombe Cliff, near Torquay
1893	February 22	*Salome* published in French
	March 5	Leaves Babbacombe
	April 19	*A Woman of No Importance* produced
	June–October	At The Cottage, Goring-on-Thames
	October	Takes rooms at 10 and 11 St James's Place. Writes *An Ideal Husband* there
	November 9	*Lady Windermere's Fan* published
1894	February 9	*Salome* published in English, illustrated by Beardsley
	May	In Florence with Douglas
	June 11	*The Sphinx* published
	Aug–Sept	Writes *The Importance of Being Earnest* at Worthing
	October 9	*A Woman of No Importance* published
	October	At Brighton with Douglas

xxiii

BIOGRAPHICAL TABLE

1895	January 3	*An Ideal Husband* produced
	Jan–Feb	Visits Algiers with Douglas
	February 14	*The Importance of Being Earnest* produced
	February 28	Finds Queensberry's card at Albemarle Club
	March 1	Obtains warrant for Queensberry's arrest
	March 9	Queensberry remanded at Bow Street for trial at Old Bailey
	March	Visits Monte Carlo with Douglas
	April 3	Queensberry trial opens
	April 5	Queensberry acquitted. Wilde arrested
	April 6–26	Imprisoned at Holloway
	April 26	First trial opens
	May 1	Jury disagree. New trial ordered
	May 7	Released on bail
	May 20	Second trial opens
	May 25	Sentenced to two years' hard labour and imprisoned (after two days in Newgate) at Pentonville
	July 4	Transferred to Wandsworth
	September 24	First examination in Bankruptcy
	November 12	Second examination in Bankruptcy
	November 20	Transferred to Reading
1896	February 3	Death of Lady Wilde
	February 11	*Salome* produced in Paris
1897	January–March	Writes *De Profundis*
	May 18	Transferred to Pentonville
	May 19	Released. Crosses to Dieppe by night boat
	May 26	Moves from Dieppe to Berneval-sur-Mer
	August ?28–29	Meets Douglas at Rouen
	September 4–11	At Rouen
	September 15	Leaves Dieppe for Paris
	September 20	Arrives at Naples
	September ?27	Moves to Villa Giudice, Posilippo
	October 15–18	Visits Capri with Douglas
	December	Visits Sicily
1898	January	Moves to 31 Santa Lucia, Naples
	February ?13	Moves to Hôtel de Nice, Paris
	February 13	*The Ballad of Reading Gaol* published
	March *c.* 28	Moves to Hôtel d'Alsace
	April 7	Death of Constance Wilde
	June–July	At Nogent-sur-Marne
	August	At Chennevières-sur-Marne
	December 15	Leaves for Napoule, near Cannes
1899	February	*The Importance of Being Earnest* published

BIOGRAPHICAL TABLE

1899	February	Leaves Napoule for Nice
	February 25	Leaves Nice for Gland, Switzerland
	April 1	Leaves Gland for Santa Margherita
	April–May	Returns to Paris, Hôtel de la Neva
	May	Moves to Hôtel Marsollier
	June 23–26	At Trouville and Le Havre
	July	*An Ideal Husband* published
	July	At Chennevières-sur-Marne
	August	Moves back to Hôtel d'Alsace
1900	April 2–10	At Palermo
	April 12–	
	May ?15	In Rome
	May	Ten days at Gland
	May–June	Returns to Paris
	October 10	Operated on
	November 30	Dies in Hôtel d'Alsace

PART ONE

OXFORD

1875-78

PART ONE

Oxford: 1875-78

Oscar Wilde was born on 16 October 1854 at 21 Westland Row, Dublin, and on 26 April 1855, in the neighbouring church of St Mark, he was christened Oscar Fingal O'Flahertie. In his youth he added the name Wills, which his father also used. His brother Willie was born in 1852 and his sister Isola in 1859. She died in 1867.

Their father, Sir William Wilde (born 1815), was a leading oculist and ear-surgeon who had built and equipped his own hospital in Dublin. He published books on aural surgery, topography, Dean Swift, and an immense medical report on the 1851 census. He was knighted in 1864.

In 1851 he married Jane Francesca Elgee (born about 1824), who had played a leading part in the Young Ireland movement of the 1840's, writing inflammatory poems and articles in the *Nation* under the name Speranza. She published books in prose and verse, including *Sidonia the Sorceress* (1849), a translation from the German of *Sidonia von Bork* (1847) by Wilhelm Meinhold (1797–1851), which William Morris reprinted at the Kelmscott Press in 1893.[1]

In 1855 the Wilde family moved to 1 Merrion Square North, and in 1864 Oscar was sent to Portora Royal School, Enniskillen, where he stayed until 1871. From Portora dates the first letter which has survived (if the writer had dated and addressed all his letters as scrupulously, his editor's task would have been lighter):

8 September 1868   *Portora School*
Darling Mama, The hamper came today, I never got such a jolly surprise, many thanks for it, it was more than kind of you to think of it . . . You never told me anything about the publisher in Glasgow, what does he say? And have you written to Aunt Warren on the green note paper?[2]

In 1871 he won an entrance scholarship at Trinity College, Dublin, and went there armed with an exhibition from Portora. During the next

[1] Lives of Oscar's parents have been published: *Victorian Doctor* by T. G. Wilson (1942), *Speranza* by Horace Wyndham (1951) and *The Wildes of Merrion Square* by Patrick Byrne (1953). Of *Sidonia the Sorceress* Edmund Gosse wrote: "It is hardly a paradox to say that this German romance did not begin to exist until an Irishwoman revealed it to a select English circle."

[2] Text from the Stetson sale catalogue (1920). I have been unable to trace the original further.

three years he won many prizes for classics, including a foundation scholarship and the Berkeley Gold Medal for Greek. He also came strongly under the influence of the Rev. John Pentland Mahaffy (1839–1919). This remarkable man (who later became Provost of the College, and was knighted in 1918) was then Professor of Ancient History. His passion for all things Greek, his study of the art of conversation, and his social technique all left their mark on his pupil.

In 1874, at the age of twenty, Wilde crowned his academic success by winning a Demyship at Magdalen College, Oxford. It was worth £95 a year for four years, and in October he took up residence in the rooms known as Chaplain's I (2 Pair Right). A year later he moved into Cloisters VIII (Ground Room Right). During his first summer vacation he travelled to Italy, where the letters begin.

To Sir William Wilde
MS. Clark

Tuesday [Postmark 15 June 1875]   *[Postmark Florence]*

Went in the morning to see San Lorenzo, built in the usual Florentine way, cruciform: a long aisle supported by Grecian pillars: a gorgeous dome in the centre and three small aisles leading off it. Behind it are the two Chapels of the Medici. The first, the Burial Chapel, is magnificent; of enormous height, octagonal in shape. Walls built entirely of gorgeous blocks of marble, all inlaid with various devices and of different colours, polished like a looking-glass. Six great sarcophagi of granite and porphyry stand in six niches: on top of each of them a cushion of inlaid mosaic bearing a gold crown. Above the sarcophagi are statues in gilded bronze of the Medici; on the dome, of course, frescoes and gilded carving.

The other chapel is very small, built simply of white marble. Two mausoleums in it to two great Medici; one bearing Michael Angelo's statues of Night and Morning and the other those of Evening and Dawn.

Then to the Biblioteca Laurenziana in the cloisters of San Lorenzo, where I was shown wonderfully illuminated missals and unreadable manuscripts and autographs. I remarked the extreme clearness of the initial letters in the Italian missals and bibles, so different from those in the Book of Kells etc., which might stand for anything. The early illuminations are very beautiful in design and sentiment, but the later are mere mechanical *tours de force* of geometrical scroll-work and absurd designs.

Then to the Etruscan Museum, which is in the suppressed monastery of San Onofrio and most interesting. You come first to a big tomb, transplanted from Arezzo; cyclopean stonework, doorway with sloping jambs and oblong lintel, roof slightly conical, walls covered with wonderfully beautiful frescoes, representing first the soul in the shape of a young man naked, led by a beautifully winged angel or genius to the two-horsed chariot which is to convey them to Elysium—and then represents the banquet which awaits him. This same idea of the resurrection of the

4

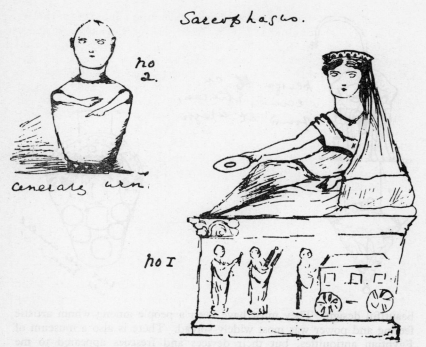

Sarcophagus.

no 2.

cenerary urn.

no 1

soul and a state of happiness after death pervades the whole system of Etruscan art. There were also wonderful sarcophagi which I have roughly drawn for you. On the top the figure of the dead man or woman holding a plate containing the obol for paying the ferryman over Styx. Also extraordinary jars with heads and arms—funeral of course—I have drawn them. The sarcophagi, of which there are over *a hundred and fifty* to be seen, are about two and a half feet long and about three feet high. The sides of the sarcophagi are sculptured with the achievements and adventures of the dead man, mostly in bas-relief which are sometimes coloured. There were some with frescoes instead of sculpture, beautifully done. Of course urns and vases of every possible shape, and all painted exquisitely.

A great collection of coins, from the old *as*, a solid pound weight of metal about as big as a large bun and stamped with a ship on one side and a double-faced Janus on the other, down to tiny little gold coins the same size as gold five-franc pieces. The goldsmiths' work for beauty of design and delicacy of workmanship exceeded anything I have ever seen. As I was kept there for a long time by an awful thunderstorm I copied a few which I send you. I cannot of course give you the wonderful grace and delicacy of workmanship, only the design. Goblets and bowls of jasper and all sorts of transparent pebbles—enamelled jars in abundance. Swords of the leaf shape, regular torques but somewhat same design, metal hand-mirrors, and household utensils of all kinds, and every thing, even the commonest plate or jug, done with greatest delicacy and of

5

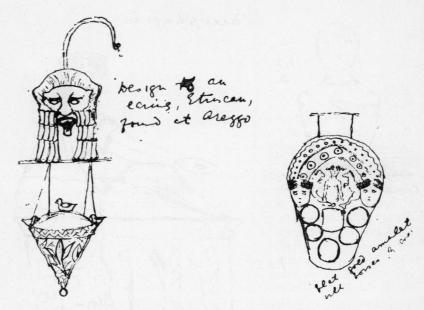

design for an earring, Etruscan, found at Arezzo

feet all gold amulet

beautiful design. They must have been a people among whom artistic feeling and power was most widely spread. There is also a museum of Egyptian antiquities, but their devices and frescoes appeared to me grotesque and uncouth after the purity and sentiment of the Etruscan. You would have been much interested in all the Etruscan work: I spent two delightful hours there.

In the evening I dined at a restaurant on top of San Miniato, air delightfully clear and cool after the thunderstorm. Coming back I met just opposite the Pitti Palace a wonderful funeral; a long procession of monks bearing torches, all in white and wearing a long linen veil over their faces— only their eyes can be seen. They bore two coffins and looked like those awful monks you see in pictures of the Inquisition.

Mahaffy is not come yet. I do hope he will arrive today, as I shan't be able to stay much longer away. Today is the anniversary of the birth of Michael Angelo: there will be great fêtes.[1]

Hope Abbotstown will turn out well. It certainly spoiled the look of the place, and that terrible large ditch between us and it will, I suppose, be bridged over. Yours ever truly affectionately OSCAR O'F. W. WILDE

---

[1] Michael Angelo was born on 6 March 1475, but the main quatercentenary celebrations seem to have taken place in September. I can find no record of any particular fêtes in Florence in June.

To Lady Wilde

MS. Clark

Wednesday [*23 June 1875. Postmark 24 June 1875*]

Albergo della Francia, Milan

So busy travelling and sight-seeing for last five days that I have had no time to write.

Diary. Left Florence with much regret on Saturday night; passed through the Apennines, beautiful Alpine scenery; train runs on side of mountains half-way up, above us pine-forests and crags, below us the valley, villages and swollen rivers. Supper at Bologna; about 5.30 in the morning came near Venice. Immediately on leaving the mountains a broad flat tableland (there are no hills in Italy—mountains or flat plains) cultivated like a rich garden. Within four miles of Venice a complete change; a black bog, exactly like Bog of Allen only flatter; crossed over a big *laguna* on a bridge and arrived at Venice 7.30. Seized on immediately by gondoliers and embarked with our luggage, into a *black* hearse-like barge, such as King Arthur was taken away in after the fatal battle. Finally through long narrow canals we arrived at our hotel, which was in the great Piazza San Marco—the only place in Venice except the Rialto anyone walks in. Plan of it. [*Rough Sketch*] The Church of San Marco is most gorgeous; a splendid *Byzantine* church, covered with gilding and mosaics, inside and out. The floor of inlaid marbles, of colour and design indescribable. and through the sinking of the piles undulates in big sweeping waves. Splendid gates of bronze, everything glorious. Next to it the Doge's Palace, which is beyond praise. Inside, giant council chambers; the walls painted with frescoes by Titian of the great battles of the Venetians; the ceiling crossed by gilded beams and rich in gilded carving; rooms fit for the noble-looking grave senators whose pictures are on the walls by Titian or Tintoretto.

Council Room of the celebrated " Three,"[1] black marble and gold. Two dismal passages lead from it across the *Ponte dei Sospiri*. In size and colour and dignity the rooms are beyond description, and the view from the windows across the sea wonderful. Beneath all this greatness are the most dismal dungeons and torture-rooms—most terrible.

Here we spent the morning; afterwards took a gondola and visited some of the islands off Venice; on one an Armenian monastery where Byron used to live. Went to another, the Lido, a favourite place on Sunday, and had oysters and shrimps. Returned home in the flood of a great sunset. Venice as a city just risen from the sea; a long line of crowded churches and palaces; everywhere white or gilded domes and tall campaniles; no opening in the whole city except at the Piazza San Marco. A great pink sunset with a long line of purple thunderclouds behind the city. After dinner went to the theatre and saw a good circus. Luckily a wonderful

---

[1] The three commissioners, appointed in 1171, who had laid down restrictions limiting membership of the Great Council of Venice to those who themselves, or whose ancestors, had already held office.

7

moon. We landed from our gondola coming from the theatre at the Lion of St Mark. The scene was so romantic that it seemed to be an "artistic" scene from an opera. We sat on the base of the pillar; on one side of us the Doge's Palace, on the other the King's Palace, behind us the Campanile. The water-steps crowded with black gondolas, and a great flood of light coming right up to us across the water. Every moment a black silent gondola would glide across this great stream of light and be lost in the darkness.

To Lady Wilde

MS. Clark

Thursday [and Friday, 24 and 25 June 1875]   *Milan*

I believe you left me last looking at the moon from the Piazza San Marco. With difficulty we tore ourselves away to the hotel. Next morning we went up the Grand Canal in a gondola. Great palaces on each side with huge steps leading down to the water, and all round big posts to moor the gondolas to, coloured with the arms of the family. Wonderful colour everywhere—windows hung with striped yellow awnings, domes and churches of white marble, campaniles of red brick, great gondolas filled with fruit and vegetables going to the Rialto where the market is. Stopped to see the picture gallery which, as usual, was in a suppressed monastery. Titian and Tintoretto in great force. Titian's *Assumption* certainly the best picture in Italy. Went to a lot of churches, all however in extravagant "baroque" style—very rich in worked metal and polished marble and mosaic but as a rule inartistic. In the picture gallery besides the Titians there are two great pictures; one a beautiful Madonna by Bellini, the other a picture of Dives and Lazarus by Bonifazio containing the only *lovely* woman's face I have seen in Italy.

Spent the day in gondolas and markets; in the evening a great band and promenade of all the swells of Venice in the Piazza San Marco. Every woman, nearly, over thirty powdered the front of her hair; most wore veils but I see that bonnets are now made with very high crowns and two wreaths, one under the diadem and one round the crown.

After marriage the Italian women degenerate awfully, but the boys and girls are beautiful. Amongst married women the general types are "Titiens" and an ugly sallow likeness of "Trebelli Bettini."[1]

In the morning breakfasted on board the P. & O. steamer *Baroda*. I was asked by the doctor, a young Dublin fellow called Fraser. Left for Padua at twelve o'clock. Believe me, Venice in beauty of architecture and colour is beyond description. It is the meeting-place of the Byzantine and Italian art—a city belonging to the *East* as much as to the West.

---

[1] Thérèse Tietjens or Titiens (1831–77) and Zélie Trebelli (1838–92), who married Alexander Bettini, an Italian tenor, were prima donnas of ample proportions who had regularly sung in Dublin with J. H. Mapleson's Italian Opera Company in the 1860's and 1870's.

Arrived at Padua at two o'clock. In the middle of a rich vineyard stands the Baptistery, the great work of Giotto; the walls covered entirely with frescoes by him; one wall the life of Mary, the other the life of Christ; the ceiling blue with gold stars and medallion pictures; the west wall a great picture of Heaven and Hell suggested to him by Dante who, weary of trudging up the steep *stairs*, as he says, of the *Scaligeri* when in exile at Verona, came to stay at Padua with Giotto in a house still to be seen there.[1] Of the beauty and purity of sentiment, the clear transparent colour, bright as the day it was painted, and the harmony of the whole building, I am unable to tell you. He is the first of all painters. We stayed over an hour in the Baptistery filled with wonder and reverence and above all love for the scenes he has painted.

Padua is a quaint town with good colonnades along each street, a university like a barracks, one charming church (Sant' Anastasia) and a lot of bad ones, and the best restaurant in Italy, where we dined.

Arrived at Milan in a shower of rain; went in the evening to the theatre and saw a good ballet.

This morning the Cathedral. Outside most elaborate in pinnacles and statues awfully out of proportion with the rest of the building. Inside most impressive through its huge size and giant pillars supporting the roof; some good old stained glass and a lot of hideous modern windows. These moderns don't see that the use of a window in a church is to show a beautiful massing together and blending of colour; a good old window has the rich pattern of a Turkey carpet. The figures are quite subordinate and only serve to show the sentiment of the designer. The modern fresco style of window has *suâ naturâ* to compete with painting and of course looks monstrous and theatrical.

The Cathedral is an awful failure. Outside the design is monstrous and inartistic. The over-elaborated details stuck high up where no one can see them; everything is vile in it; it is, however, imposing and gigantic as a failure, through its great size and elaborate execution.

From Padua I forgot to tell you we went to Verona at six o'clock, and in the old Roman amphitheatre (as perfect inside as it was in the old Roman times) saw the play of *Hamlet* performed—and certainly indifferently—but you can imagine how romantic it was to sit in the old amphitheatre on a lovely moonlight night. In the morning went to see the tombs of the Scaligeri—good examples of rich florid Gothic work and ironwork; a good market-place filled with the most gigantic umbrellas I ever saw—like young palm trees—under which sat the fruit-sellers. Of our arrival at Milan I have told you.

[1] Cf. Dante, *Paradiso*, xvii, 59–60:

com' è duro calle
Lo scendere e il salir per l'altrui scale

and the opening of Wilde's sonnet "At Verona," published in *Poems* (1881):

How steep the stairs within Kings' houses are
For exile-wearied feet as mine to tread.

He had already used the first line in his *Ravenna* (1878).

Yesterday (Thursday) went first to the Ambrosian Library where we saw some great manuscripts and two very good palimpsests, and a bible with Irish glosses of the sixth or seventh century which has been collated by Todd and Whitley Stokes and others;[1] a good collection of pictures besides, particularly a set of drawings and sketches in chalk by Raffaelli—much more interesting I think than his pictures—good Holbeins and Albrecht Dürers.

Then to the picture gallery. Some good Correggios and Peruginos; the gem of the whole collection is a lovely Madonna by Bernardino standing among a lot of trellised roses that Morris and Rossetti would love; another by him we saw in the library with a background of lilies.

Milan is a second Paris. Wonderful arcades and galleries; all the town white stone and gilding. Dined excellently at the Biffi Restaurant and had some good wine of Asti, like good cider or sweet champagne. In the evening went to see a new opera, *Dolores*, by a young maestro called Auteri; a good imitation of Bellini in some parts, some pretty rondos; but its general character was inharmonious shouting.[2] However, the frantic enthusiasm of the people knew no bounds. Every five minutes a terrible furore and yelling of *Bravas* from every part of the house, followed by a frantic rush of all the actors for the composer, who was posted at the side-scenes ready to rush out on the slightest symptom of approval. A weak-looking creature who placed his grimy hand on a shady-looking shirt to show his emotion, fell on the prima donna's neck in ecstasy, and blew kisses to us all. He came out no less than nineteen times, and finally three crowns were brought out, one of which, a green laurel one with green ribbons, was clapped on his head, and as his head was very narrow it rested partly on a very large angular nose and partly on his grimy shirt-collar. Such an absurd scene as the whole thing was I never saw. The opera except in two places is absolutely devoid of merit. The Princess Margherita was there, very high-bred and pale.[3]

I write this at Arona on the Lago Maggiore, a beautiful spot. Mahaffy and young Goulding[4] I left at Milan and they will go on to Genoa. As I had no money I was obliged to leave them and feel very lonely. We have had a delightful tour.

[1] This document is not a bible and has no Irish glosses. It is a service-book, known as the Antiphonary of Bangor, and is perhaps the oldest known Irish manuscript. James Henthorn Todd (1805–69) and Whitley Stokes (1830–1909), both of Trinity College, Dublin, were two of the ablest Irish antiquarian scholars of their time.

[2] *Dolores* by Salvatore Auteri-Manzocchi (1845–1924) was performed first in Florence earlier in 1875, and on 24 June at the Teatro dal Verme in Milan. It was revived at the Scala in 1878.

[3] Margherita Teresa Giovanna, Princess of Savoy-Genoa (1851–1926), married (1868) her cousin, the Prince of Piedmont, who became the second King of Italy as Humbert I (1878). Her only son became King Victor Emmanuel III.

[4] Possibly William Joshua Goulding (1856–1925), later director of many Irish companies, Baronet 1904, Privy Councillor 1917. He was certainly a friend of Mahaffy, but his descendants have no record of their travelling abroad together.

Tonight at twelve o'clock the *diligence* starts. We go over the Simplon Pass till near Lausanne; eighteen hours *en diligence*. Tomorrow night (Saturday) I get to Lausanne. Yours   OSCAR

To Lady Wilde
MS. Clark

[*? 26 June 1875*]   [*? Lausanne*]

Will be in Paris Monday. Have now £2 to bring me, after paying 38 francs for the *diligence* just this moment. I have only had *one* letter from you since I left, and one from Sir William. I suppose there are some at Florence since I left. If there is no money at Paris for me I will not know what to do, but I feel sure there will be the genial £5. Yours ever

OSCAR O'F. WILDE

To William Ward[1]
MS. Magdalen

Monday [*March 1876*] *S. Benedict of Siena* †[2]   *Magdalen College, Oxford*

Magd. Coll. Tea Club.

My dear Bouncer, I am very glad to hear from Mark[3] that you have come back safe out of the clutches of those barbarous Irish. I was afraid that the *potato-chips* that we live on over there would have been too much for you.

Some beastly old Evangelical parson about here has, I believe, been praying for snow, and his prayers have been quite successful, as the weather has been awful since you went away.

[1] William Welsford Ward (1854–1932) went up to Magdalen from Radley as a Classical Demy in 1873. First in Mods 1874. Everyone at Magdalen had a nickname (Wilde's was Hosky) and Ward's came from *Little Mr Bouncer and his Friend Verdant Green* (1873), the last of a series of comic Oxford novels by Cuthbert Bede (Edward Bradley, 1827–89). Wilde's drawing inscribed "Little Mr Bouncer" can still be seen scratched on the window of the room they successively occupied in the college. Ward went down at the end of 1876 and, after a five-months tour of the continent, followed his father as a solicitor in Bristol. His short "Oxford Reminiscence" of Wilde was published as an appendix to *Son of Oscar Wilde* by Vyvyan Holland (1954).
[2] I can find no mention of such a saint. Wilde must have been making a joke or a mistake.
[3] I can find no Magdalen undergraduate of the right date with this Christian name, but it may conceivably have been the nickname of Herbert Delamark Banks (1854–1931), an Etonian who was a Magdalen undergraduate 1873–76 and became a soldier. Wherever possible I have briefly identified Wilde's Oxford friends: those without footnotes I have failed to trace.

I heard once from the Kitten[1] about a gummy[2] hat-box he says he left in his little room. I was too much ashamed to ask Mrs Brewer[3] about it, so I suppose the poor Kitten has to go to church in a frock coat and *pot*-hat.

I have not done so much reading as I thought I would, but am going to turn over a new leaf this week. Mark has been out every night to see a Brasenose man, but I have just found out that *all* the men there have gone down, so I suppose he mistook the Lane for the College. He is working hard at scores of the lowest kind to be practised on Stubbs[4] next term.

I hope you will write soon. Your affectionate friend

OSCAR O'F. W. WILDE

Algy[5] was up last week and old Hammond[6] has written to me to say he will be up today, so our reading has been rather disturbed.

I am more than ever in the toils of the Scarlet Woman, and brought Mac and young Frank to S. Aloysius[7] last night to hear Father Coleridge— Mark as sick and costive (mentally) as possible about it—"I know what it all means."

To Reginald Harding

MS. Hyde (H. M.)

Wednesday [28 June 1876]   *Magdalen College*

My dear Kitten, Many thanks for your delightful letters; they were quite a pleasant relaxation to us to get your letters every morning at breakfast. (This is sarcasm.) I think you an awful wretch really for never writing to

[1] Richard Reginald Harding (1857–1932), Magdalen Commoner 1875–79. His nickname came from a popular music-hall song which began:

> "Beg your parding, Mrs Harding,
> Is my kitting in your garding?"

His elder brother James was known as Puss and his sister Amy as Miss Puss. Harding was a member of the London Stock Exchange from 1895 until his death.

[2] University slang for sweaty.

[3] A landlady at 76 High Street, Oxford, where presumably Harding had rooms.

[4] William Stubbs (1825–1901), author of *Select Charters* (1870) and *The Constitutional History of England* (1874–78), was Regius Professor of Modern History at Oxford 1866–84, but his lectures were not popular. He was made Bishop of Chester 1884, Bishop of Oxford 1889. There was, however, also a Magdalen Demy at this time called Thomas Walker Stubbs, and the allusion may be to him.

[5] Algernon Francis Peyton (1855–1916) succeeded his father as sixth Baronet 1888. His brother Thomas Thornhill Peyton (1856–1927) became Rector of St Mary's, March, Cambridgeshire 1882, Rural Dean 1909, Canon of Ely 1915.

[6] Robert Sharp Borgnis Hammond-Chambers (1855–1907) became a lawyer (Q.C. 1897).

[7] The Roman Catholic church in St Giles's, Oxford. It was built 1874–75; the architect was Joseph Aloysius Hansom (1803–82), who invented the hansom cab. Wilde was much interested in the church, and was present when Cardinal Manning preached at the dedication service on 23 November 1875. The Rev. Henry James Coleridge, S.J. (1822–93), a great-nephew of the poet and editor of the *Month* 1865–82, preached a course of Lenten sermons beginning on Sunday, 27 February 1876, and I have dated this letter accordingly. Gerard Manley Hopkins, the poet, was an assistant priest at St Aloysius 1878–79.

us, living all alone in this desolate college. However, we have been very pleasant notwithstanding, and have survived the loss of provincial gossip.

Bouncer's people stayed up till Monday, as I suppose you know from a stupid telegram Bouncer *would* send you. We were very pleasant and went to Radley and a lot of places together.

I like Mrs Bouncer immensely and the eldest Miss B. is very charming indeed. We brought them to All Souls and Worcester and a lot of colleges. I am more charmed than ever with Worcester Chapel. As a piece of simple decorative and beautiful art it is perfect, and the windows very artistic.

Monday we rode to Abingdon and dined there, and Tuesday we had tea at Radley and lawn tennis. Tonight we dined at the Mitre. We have been very jolly together indeed and Bouncer, you will be glad to hear, *most kind!*

Tomorrow I go down to Lincolnshire to stay with my uncle.[1] I suppose you are too much occupied with croquet and loafing and playing the organ to write to me. In case you have time, however, I will be at The Vicarage, West Ashby, Horncastle, Lincolnshire.

I will have to come up next week for *viva voce*—about Tuesday or Wednesday and all for nothing probably, as I think I have missed my First and will have to look cheerful under the doubtful honours of a Second.

I will be in Nottingham with the Mileses[2] for a week and then home till September. After the partridge comes the Pope, whom I hope to see about the 1st of October.

Please remember me to Mrs Harding and your sister. Yours ever

OSCAR O'F. W. WILDE

I hope Puss is reading hard for a First. Give him my love.

To William Ward

MS. Magdalen

Sunday [*2 July 1876*]   *The Vicarage, West Ashby*

My dear Bouncer, I am in terrible dread of reading a pathetic account in *Reynolds'* Police News of "the death by starvation of a *young man* on Lundy Island." The idea of *you* forgetting your food. I hope you got it safe. I sent it off by twelve o'clock on Thursday.

I arrived here in an awful storm; it came down as if the angels thought the earth was on fire and were pumping fire engines on us.

Luckily I met some people who live here in the Manor House in the train, so it was not so tedious after all, but two miles in a dogcart and a restive horse in pouring rain did not improve my temper.

I have been kissed and petted and made to examine schools in geography! and played lawn tennis and *talked* and *sang*, and made myself

[1] The Rev. John Maxwell Wilde, Sir William's elder brother. He was Vicar of West Ashby from 1866 to 1885.

[2] The family of the Rev. Robert Henry William Miles (1819–83), Rector of Bingham, Notts, 1845–83 and a Prebendary of Lincoln.

13

the "*bellus homo*" of a tea party. My uncle is milder than ever, says "Dear me now, wouldn't you have found the penny post more convenient than a telegram?" about six times a day. I have found out he had to pay half-a-crown for my enquiry—the whole transaction costing five shillings and sixpence, while as he [*the rest of this letter is missing*].

To Reginald Harding

MS. Hyde (H. M.)

Wednesday [*5 July 1876*]   *Magdalen College*

My dear Kitten, I am very sorry to hear you did not meet the poor Bouncer Boy; see what comes of having rowdy friends fond of practical jokes. I had an awful pencil scrawl from him yesterday, written sitting on the rocks at Lundy. I hope nothing will happen to him.

I had a very pleasant time in Lincolnshire, but the weather was so hot we did nothing but play lawn tennis, as probably Bouncer will tell you when you see him next (I wrote a full account to him). I examined schools in geography and history, *sang* glees, *ate* strawberries and argued fiercely with my poor uncle, who revenged himself on Sunday by preaching on Rome in the morning, and on humility in the evening. Both very " nasty ones" for me.

I ran up to town yesterday from Lincoln and brought Frank Miles[1] a great basket of roses from the Rectory. I found him sketching the most lovely and dangerous woman in London—Lady Desart. She is very fascinating indeed.[2]

I came down Monday night to read for *viva voce*, but yesterday morning at ten o'clock was woke up by the Clerk of the Schools, and found I was in already. I was rather afraid of being put on in Catullus, but got a delightful exam from a delightful man—not on the books at all but on Aeschylus *versus* Shakespeare, modern poetry and drama and every conceivable subject. I was up for about an hour and was quite sorry when it was over. In Divinity I was ploughed of course.

I am going down to Bingham with Frank Miles and R. Gower[3] on Saturday for a week. They have the most beautiful modern church in England, and the finest lilies. I shall write and tell you about it.

[1] George Francis Miles (1852–91), son of the rector, was a popular artist in the early 80's: his many drawings of Lily Langtry did much to enhance her popularity. After he had shared two sets of rooms with Wilde in London they quarrelled and separated. Miles spent the last four years of his life in an asylum.

[2] Maria Emma Georgina (Minnie) Preston married the fourth Earl of Desart (1845–98) in 1871 and was divorced by him in 1878. The co-respondent, whom she later married, was the actor Charles Sugden. See note 2, p. 359.

[3] Lord Ronald Sutherland-Gower (1845–1916), younger son of the second Duke of Sutherland, was sculptor, politician, author and art-critic. On 4 June 1876 he wrote in his diary: "By early train to Oxford with F. Miles . . . There I made the acquaintance of young Oscar Wilde, a friend of Miles's. A pleasant cheery fellow, but with his long-haired head full of nonsense regarding the Church of Rome. His room filled with photographs of the Pope and of Cardinal Manning."

Being utterly penniless I can't go up to town till Friday. It is very slow here—now that Bouncer is gone. But tonight the Mods list comes out so I will have some excitement being *congratulated*—really I don't care a bit (no one ever does now) and quite expect a Second *after* my Logic, though *of course much the cleverest man in.* (Such cheek!)

You will probably see the list on Thursday or Friday; if I get a Second mind you write and condole with me awfully, and if I get a First say it was only what you expected.

See the results of having nothing to do—ten pages of a letter! Yours ever
OSCAR F. O'F. WILLS WILDE

My address will be The Rectory, Bingham, Notts after Saturday. I hope you will write a line and tell me all extra news about Bouncer.

PS no. 2. The paper enclosed in Bouncer's letter was *not dirty*.

To William Ward

MS. Magdalen

[*Postmark 10 July 1876*]   *4 Albert Street, S.W.*

My dear Boy, I know you will be glad to hear I have got my First all right.[1] I came up from Lincolnshire to town on Monday and went down that night to Magdalen to read my Catullus, but while lying in bed on Tuesday morning with Swinburne (a copy of) was woke up by the Clerk of the Schools to know why I did not come up. I thought I was not in till Thursday. About one o'clock I *nipped* up and was ploughed immediately in Divinity and then got a delightful *viva voce*, first in the *Odyssey*, where we discussed epic poetry in general, *dogs*, and women. Then in Aeschylus where we talked of Shakespeare, Walt Whitman and the *Poetics*. He had a long discussion about my essay on Poetry in the Aristotle paper and altogether was delightful. Of course I knew I had got a First, so swaggered horribly.

The next day the B.C.'s and myself were dining with Nicols in Christ Church[2] and the list came out at seven, as we were walking up the High. I said I would not go up to the Schools, as I knew I had a First etc., and made them all very ill, absolutely. I did not know what I had got till the next morning at twelve o'clock, breakfasting at the Mitre, I read it in *The Times*. Altogether I swaggered horribly, but am really pleased with myself. My poor mother is in great delight and I was overwhelmed with telegrams on Thursday from everyone I know. My father would have been so pleased about it. I think God has dealt very hardly with us.[3] It has robbed me of any real pleasure in my First, and I have not sufficient faith in Providence to believe it is all for the best—I know it is not. I feel an awful dread of going home to our old house, with everything filled with

[1] Wilde's First in Classical Moderations (Mods) was announced on 5 July and listed in *The Times* on 6 July.

[2] Possibly Edward Richard Jeffereys Nicolls, Christ Church undergraduate 1876–79.   [3] Sir William Wilde had died on 19 April.

memories. I go down today for a week at Bingham with the Mileses. I have been staying here with Julia Tindal[1] who is in great form. Yesterday I heard the Cardinal at the Pro-Cathedral preach a charity sermon.[2] He is more fascinating than ever. I met MacCall[3] and Williamson there who greeted me with much *empressement*. I feel an impostor and traitor to myself on these occasions and must do something decided.

Afterwards I went to the Zoo with Julia and the two Peytons—Tom is nearly all right. Young Stewy dined with us on Saturday. He said he was afraid he must have jarred you by his indecencies and was going to reform. Altogether I found out we were right in thinking that set a little jarred about our carelessness about them. Next term I shall look them up.

I hope you will see the Kitten. I got a very nice letter from him about Mods. Miss Puss has fallen in my estimation if she is fetched with Swan[4]—who to men is irritable, but to women intolerable I think. Write soon to Bingham Rectory, Nottinghamshire. Ever yours

OSCAR O'F. W. WILDE

To Reginald Harding
MS. Hyde (H. M.)

[*Circa 13 July 1876*]   *Bingham Rectory, Notts*

My dear Boy, Thousand thanks for your letter. Half the pleasure of getting a First is to receive such delightful congratulations. I *am* really a little pleased at getting it, though I swaggered horribly and pretended that I did not care a bit. In fact I would not go up to the Schools on Wednesday evening—said it was a bore—and actually did not know certainly till Thursday at twelve o'clock when I read it in *The Times*. The really pleasant part is that my mother is so pleased. I got a heap of telegrams on Thursday from Ireland with congratulations.

I went up to town on Friday and stayed with Julia Tindal; we had a very pleasant time together. Sunday we went to the Zoo with Algy and Tom Peyton. Tom is all right now; he had got paralysis of his face.

I came down here Monday and had no idea it was so lovely. A wonderful garden with such white lilies and rose walks; only that there are no serpents or apples it would be quite Paradise. The church is very fine indeed. Frank and his mother, a very good artist, have painted wonderful windows,

---

[1] Nickname of Charles Harrison Tindal (1851–1930). He was a Magdalen undergraduate 1870–74, took his B.C.L. at Oxford 1877, and was called to the Bar, Lincoln's Inn, 1878.

[2] The Church of Our Lady of Victories in High Street, Kensington, was used as Pro-Cathedral until the consecration of Westminster Cathedral in 1903. Cardinal Manning preached there on Sunday, 9 July 1876.

[3] Archibald Noel Locke MacCall (1852–1926), Magdalen undergraduate 1874–76, became a Roman Catholic 1875. Member of the London Oratory 1876–91, Canon of Southwark 1916.

[4] Charles Arthur Swan (1854–1941), an Etonian, was a Magdalen Demy 1874–77. Became regular soldier, commanding the 3rd Battalion, the Lincolnshire Regiment.

and frescoed angels on the walls, and one of his sisters has carved the screen and altar. It is simply beautiful and everything done by themselves.

These horrid red marks are strawberries, which I am eating in basketfuls, during intervals of lawn tennis, at which I am awfully good.

There are four daughters, all very pretty indeed, one of them who is writing at the other side of the table quite lovely. My heart is torn in sunder with admiration for them all, and my health going, so I return to Ireland next week.

We are having a large garden party here today, and tomorrow one at the Duke of Rutland's who is quite close.

I make myself as charming as ever and am much admired. Have had some good arguments with Dean Miles who was a great friend of Newman, Pusey and Manning at Oxford and a very advanced Anglican.[1]

Write me a line soon like a good boy. Ever yours

OSCAR F. O'F. WILLS WILDE

I heard the Cardinal on Sunday preach a charity sermon at the Pro-Cathedral, Kensington. MacCall was there.

To William Ward

MS. Magdalen

Monday [Postmark 17 July 1876]   *Bingham*

Dear Boy, I have never heard from you except your scrawl written from the rocks on your arrival. However I hope to find some letters at home waiting for me.

I have had a delightful week here. The garden and house are very beautiful. I never saw such lilies—white and red and golden. Nearly all the family are good artists. Mrs Miles is really wonderful. I suppose you remember my showing you her drawings in Ruskin's School at Oxford when we went there to your sister.

Mr Miles *père* is a very advanced Anglican and a great friend of Newman, Pusey, Manning, Gladstone and all English theologians. He is very clever and interesting: I have learned a lot from him.

If you want an interesting book get *Pomponio Leto*—an account of the last Vatican Council—a really wonderfully dramatic book.[2] How strange

[1] The Rev. Edward Bouverie Pusey (1800–82), Fellow of Oriel, Professor of Hebrew at Oxford since 1828, had been one of the leaders of High Church, Trac-tarian, or Oxford Movement from 1833 to 1845, when the Rev. John Henry Newman (1801–90), also a Fellow of Oriel and Vicar of St Mary's, Oxford, the leader of the movement, turned Roman Catholic. He was not created Cardinal till 1879. Henry Edward Manning (1808–92) remained an Anglican clergyman till 1850, and in 1857 he too went over to Rome. He was created Archbishop 1865 and Cardinal 1875.

[2] *The Vatican Council. Eight months at Rome during the Vatican Council* by Pomponio Leto [The Marquis Francesco Nobili-Vitelleschi]. Translated from the original (John Murray, 1876). This Council, convoked by Pope Pius IX, sat from December 1869 till October 1870 and eventually issued the definition of Papal Infallibility, for which Manning had rigorously striven.

that on the day of the Pope publicly declaring that his Infallibility and that of the Church were identical a fearful storm broke over Rome *and two thunderbolts fell from heaven.* It reads like the talkative ox of Livy (*bos locutus est*) and the rain of blood, that were always happening.

I don't know what to think myself. I wish you would come to Rome with me and test the whole matter. I am afraid to go alone.

I never knew how near the English Church was to joining with Rome. Before the Promulgation of the Immaculate Conception Pusey and Liddon[1] and others were working hard for an Eirenicon and union with Rome, but now they look to the Greek Church. But I think it is a mere dream, and very strange that they should be so anxious to believe the Blessed Virgin conceived in sin.

As regards worldly matters, we have had some very pleasant garden parties and any amount of lawn tennis. The neighbourhood also boasts of a giant in the shape of the Honourable Lascelles who is sixteen years old and six foot eight in height! He is reading with a Mr Seymour near here, a clergyman (father of young Seymour of Balliol), to go up for *Magdalen.* What an excitement he will cause, but he is not going up for two years, so we won't see him there.[2]

I suppose you will see the Kitten, after you leave Lundy. Send me your address like a good boy. Mine will be 1 Merrion Square North, Dublin, till I go down to Galway, which I hope to do soon. Ever yours

OSCAR F. O'F. WILLS WILDE

To Reginald Harding

MS. Hyde (H. M.)

20 July 1876   *1 Merrion Square North, Dublin*

Dear Kitten, Thousand thanks for the testimonial. I have of course laid it up in the Family Archives. When found in two or three hundred years by some of the family devoted to Natural History and the habits of the Feline Race it will cause much discussion. In case I become bankrupt I suppose the autographs will fetch something, especially those of the "child Amy" and "Fräulein"?

I want Bouncer's address: will you send it like a good boy as soon as you can remember it?

I found a heap of congratulatory letters from all sorts of [*piece cut away*] telegrams from Hammond and the Boy, which Mamma had of course

---

[1] The Rev. Henry Parry Liddon (1829–90), Ireland Professor of Biblical Exegesis at Oxford 1870–82, Canon of St Paul's Cathedral from 1870, and last of the great pulpit orators of the English Church, was a strong defender of the Tractarians and wrote a four-volume biography of Pusey (1893–97).

[2] Brian Piers Lascelles (1859–1922), a grandson of the second Earl of Harewood, went up to Magdalen in 1879, was known as the Magdalen Giant and measured 6 ft 10⅝ in. in his socks. The Rev. Henry Seymour was Rector of Holme Pierrepont, Notts, and his son, Henry Sidney Seymour, was a Balliol undergraduate 1874–77.

opened and was very much troubled to know why a telegram should begin "Indeed Oscar" and whether S. Aloysius was one of the examiners.

Don't forget Bouncer's address. [*Signature cut away*]

To William Ward

MS. Magdalen

[*Circa 20 July 1876*] *1 Merrion Square North*

My dear Boy, I sent you two charming letters, one from Julia Tindal's lodgings in London, and one from Bingham. Did you get them? Or are they now used by the *literati* of Lundy Island as models of polite letter-writing? I hope they are not used to give *laxas tunicas* to *scombri*,[1] *as our friend Juvenal has it* (see what comes of Mods).

I came back home yesterday from Bingham. I had a delightful time there. The whole family are charming. Mr Miles knew your father when he was rector of S. Raphael's in Bristol and talked much of his great liberality and devotion to the Church. He was much interested to hear about you.

I got a delightful lot of letters congratulating me—the pleasantest part of Mods—from Mark and Jack Barrow[2] and a lot of fellows I hardly thought would take the trouble. Terribly absurd telegrams from Hammond and the Boy sent here and of course opened by Mamma, who was greatly troubled as to what S. Aloysius had to do with me, and why when only twenty words go for a shilling a telegram should begin "*Indeed Oscar*."

I go down to Mayo probably next week, and then to Galway to have some fishing. Illaunroe, Leenane, Co. Galway is our address,[3] but I am very uncertain about when I shall be there, so I hope you will write here and tell me all about the King's Close Cats.[4] I suppose they told you about the testimonial sent to me from the whole set including the Child Amy.

I am going to edit an unfinished work of my father's, the *Life of Gabriel Beranger, Artist*, for next Christmas, so between this and Newman will have no time for any reading for scholarship.[5]

[1] "Loose jackets for mackerel," the fate of the verses of bad poets according not to Juvenal, but to Catullus (xcv, 8).

[2] John Burton Barrow (b. 1855), Magdalen undergraduate 1874–78, became a barrister.

[3] For a description of the fishing lodge, see p. 65.

[4] Reginald Harding's home was at King's Close, Barnstaple, Devon, where his father was a solicitor.

[5] Most of Sir William Wilde's *Memoir of Gabriel Beranger* had been published in the *Journal of the Archaeological Association of Ireland* between 1871 and 1873. The book was in fact finished by Lady Wilde, and the final portion appeared in the same *Journal* in the autumn of 1876. The complete work was published in a single volume, with an introduction by Lady Wilde, in 1880. Beranger was an artist and archaeologist of Franco-Dutch parentage, who came to Ireland in 1750 and painted many water-colours of Irish landscapes and antiquities. Sir William was an eager collector of his works.

About Newman I think that his higher emotions revolted against Rome but that he was swept on by Logic to accept it as the only rational form of Christianity. His life is a terrible tragedy. I fear he is a very unhappy man. I bought a lot of his books before leaving Oxford.

Luckily the life of Beranger is three-quarters finished; so I will not have much trouble. Still it is a great responsibility: I will not be idle about it.

I hope your mother and sisters are well. Ever yours

OSCAR F. O'F. WILLS WILDE

To William Ward

MS. Magdalen

Wednesday [26 July 1876. Postmark 27 July 1876]

1 Merrion Square North

My dear Boy, I confess not to be a worshipper at the Temple of Reason. I think man's reason the most misleading and thwarting guide that the sun looks upon, except perhaps the reason of woman. Faith is, I think, a bright lantern for the feet,[1] though of course an exotic plant in man's mind, and requiring continual cultivation. My mother would probably agree with you. Except for the *people*, for whom she thinks dogma necessary, she rejects all forms of superstition and dogma, particularly any notion of priest and sacrament standing between her and God. She has a very strong faith in that aspect of God *we* call the Holy Ghost—the divine intelligence of which we on earth partake. Here she is very strong, though of course at times troubled by the discord and jarring of the world, when she takes a dip into pessimism.

Her last pessimist, Schopenhauer, says the whole human race ought on a given day, after a strong remonstrance *firmly but respectfully* urged on God, to walk into the sea and leave the world tenantless, but of course some skulking wretches would hide and be left behind to people the world again I am afraid.

I wonder you don't see the beauty and necessity for the *incarnation* of God into man to help us to grasp at the skirts of the Infinite. The atonement is I admit hard to grasp. But I think since Christ the dead world has woke up from sleep. Since him we have lived. I think the greatest proof of the Incarnation aspect of Christianity is its whole career of noble men and thoughts and not the mere narration of unauthenticated histories.

I think *you* are bound to account (psychologically most especially) for S. Bernard and S. Augustine and S. Philip Neri—and even in our day for Liddon and Newman—as being good philosophers and good Christians. That reminds me of Mallock's *New Republic* in *Belgravia*; it is decidedly

---

[1] "Thy word is a lantern unto my feet" are the opening words of the portion of the Psalm (CXIX, verse 105) for Morning Prayer on the twenty-sixth day of the month. It seems possible that Wilde had either been to Matins or had read the Prayer-book for the day.

20

clever—Jowett especially. If you have the key to all the actors please send it to me.[1]

I send you this letter and a book together. I wonder which you will open first. It is *Aurora Leigh*, which I think you said you had not read.[2] It is one of those books that, written straight from the heart—and from such a large heart too—never weary one: because they are sincere. We tire of art but not of nature after all our aesthetic training. I look upon it as much the greatest work in our literature.

I rank it with *Hamlet* and *In Memoriam*. So much do I love it that I hated the idea of sending it to you without marking a few passages I felt you would well appreciate—and I found myself marking the whole book. I am really very sorry: it is like being given a bouquet of plucked flowers instead of being allowed to look for them oneself. But I could not resist the temptation, as it *did* instead of writing to you about each passage.

The only fault is that she overstrains her metaphors till they snap, and although one does not like polished emotion, still she is inartistically rugged at times. As she says herself, she shows the mallet hand in carving cherry-stones.[3]

I hope you will have time to read it, for I don't believe your dismal forebodings about Greats.

I wrote to Kitten for your address, and his letter and yours arrived simultaneously. His thoughts and ink rarely last beyond one sheet.

I ride sometimes after six, but don't do much but bathe, and although always feeling slightly immortal when in the sea, feel sometimes slightly heretical when good Roman Catholic boys enter the water with little amulets and crosses round their necks and arms that the good S. Christopher may hold them up.

I am now off to bed after reading a chapter of S. Thomas à Kempis. I think half-an-hour's warping of the inner man daily is greatly conducive to holiness.

[1] William Hurrell Mallock (1849–1923), a nephew of J. A. Froude, the historian, and Newman's friend, Hurrell Froude, had come down from Balliol in 1874, having won the Newdigate Prize in 1871. His Peacockian novel *The New Republic, or Culture, Faith and Philosophy in an English Country House*, was serialised anonymously in *Belgravia* from June to December 1876. In book form it was published, still anonymously, in two volumes in March 1877. Clearly its authorship was known from the beginning, at any rate in Oxford. All the characters were portraits: the main ones Ruskin, Jowett, Matthew Arnold, Huxley and Walter Pater.

[2] A novel in verse by Elizabeth Barrett Browning (1857). This copy, inscribed "W. W. Ward from Oscar F. O'F. Wilde. 1 Merrion Square. July 25th '76," was until recently in the possession of Vyvyan Holland.

[3] I wrote tales beside,
Carved many an article on cherry-stones
To suit light readers,—something in the lines
Revealing, it was said, the mallet-hand,
But that, I'll never vouch for.

Aurora Leigh, Third Book

Pray remember me to your mother and sisters. Ever yours

OSCAR F. O'F. WILLS WILDE

Post Scriptum[1]

You don't deserve such a long letter, but I must tell you that I met Mr Rigaud (the gentleman who met with that sad accident in early youth) and his brother the General swaggering up Grafton Street here yesterday.[2] I had a long talk with them and the General told me yarns by the dozen about the time he was quartered here "with the 16th Battalion, sir! Damme, sir! We were the best corps in the Regiment! Service gone to the dogs! Not a well drilled soldier in the country, sir!"

To William Ward

MS. Magdalen

Sunday [*6 August 1876*]   *1 Merrion Square North*

My dear Bouncer, I feel quite sure you never could have got a book and letter I sent you about ten days ago. You couldn't have been such a complete Scythian as not to write how charmed you were with my delightful letter and book if you had got them. I sent them to Cliff Court.[3] If you did not get the book will you ask your post office about it as I should be very sorry if you did not get it. It was Mrs Browning's *Aurora Leigh*.

I have got three poems (and perhaps four!) coming out on the 1st of September in various magazines, and am awfully pleased about it. I will send you one of them which I would like you to read. I call it no name but put as a motto that great chaunt Αἴλινον αἴλινον εἰπέ, τὸ δ' εὖ νικάτω.[4]

I am with that dear Mahaffy every day. He has a charming house by the sea here, on a place called the Hill of Howth (one of the crescent horns that shuts in the Bay of Dublin), the only place near town with fields of yellow gorse, and stretches of wild myrtle, red heather and ferns. By dallying in the enchanted isle of Bingham Rectory, and eating the lotus flowers of Love and the *moly* of Oblivion I arrived just too late to go on a charming party to the North of Ireland—Mahaffy, Seyss[5] of Queen's, Appleton the

[1] This postscript has become detached from its letter, but it was clearly written from Dublin at the end of a comparatively long letter to Ward.

[2] Major-General Gibbes Rigaud (1821–85) had served in the Kaffir War (1851–1853) and in China (1860). His brother, the Rev. John Rigaud (1823–88), was at various times Fellow, Senior Dean of Arts, Bursar, Vice-President, Dean of Divinity, and Librarian, of Magdalen.

[3] The Wards' home at Frenchay, near Bristol.

[4] These words from the *Agamemnon* of Aeschylus ("Sing woe, woe, but let the good prevail") were the poem's only heading in the *Dublin University Magazine* for September 1876. It was reprinted in *Lyra Hibernica Sacra* (1878) and in *Poems* (1908); in 1913 its original manuscript title "Tristitiae" was restored to it. For the other poems mentioned here see notes 2 and 4, p. 26.

[5] Wilde's phonetic spelling of the Rev. Archibald Henry Sayce (1845–1933), who had been a Fellow of Queen's College, Oxford, since 1869 and was a family friend of the Wildes. He was Professor of Assyriology at Oxford 1891–1919.

editor of the *Academy*[1] and my brother.[2] They had a very royal time of it, but Circe and Calypso delayed me till it was too late to join them. Mahaffy's book of Travels in Greece will soon be out. I have been correcting his proofs and like it immensely.[3]

I want to ask your opinion on this psychological question. In our friend *Todd*'s[4] ethical barometer, at what height is his moral quicksilver? Last night I strolled into the theatre about ten o'clock and to my surprise saw Todd and young Ward the quire boy[5] in a private box together, Todd very much in the background. He saw me so I went round to speak to him for a few minutes. He told me that he and Foster Harter[6] had been fishing in Donegal and that he was going to fish South now. I wonder what young Ward is doing with him. Myself I believe Todd is extremely moral and only mentally spoons the boy, but I think he is foolish to go about with one, if he *is* bringing this boy about with him.

You are the only one I would tell about it, as you have a philosophical mind, *but don't tell anyone about it like a good boy—it would do neither us nor Todd any good.*

He (Todd) looked awfully nervous and uncomfortable. I thought of Mark.

I hope nothing is wrong with your people or yourself that you don't write. Ever yours   OSCAR F. O'F. WILLS WILDE

P.S. I hope you did not write to Illaunroe? They only get letters *once a week there.*

To Reginald Harding
MS. Hyde (H. M.)

Sunday [6 August 1876]   *1 Merrion Square North*

My dear Kitten, I suppose you are reading much too hard ever to write

[1] Charles Edward Cutts Birch Appleton (1841–79) founded the *Academy* in 1869 and edited it until his death.

[2] William Charles Kingsbury Wilde (1852–99). After coming down from Trinity College, Dublin, he was called to the Bar, but soon became a journalist. He wrote for the *World* and *Vanity Fair* and was for many years a leader-writer on the *Daily Telegraph*. He was once briefly engaged to the composer Ethel Smyth. He lived with his mother until he married Mrs Frank Leslie, a rich American widow and newspaper-owner. The marriage was not a success, and Willie turned to alcohol. Later he married an Irish girl, Sophie (Lily) Lees, who bore him a daughter, Dorothy Ierne (Dolly), who died in 1941. After Willie's death Lily married Alexander Teixeira de Mattos, the translator (see note 1, p. 340).

[3] Mahaffy's *Rambles and Studies in Greece* duly appeared in 1876. A second edition, containing "new observations and reflections," was published in 1878. Neither edition carries any acknowledgment to Wilde, but in the preface to an earlier book, *Social Life in Greece from Homer to Menander* (1874), Mahaffy expressed gratitude to his "old pupil Mr Oscar Wilde of Magdalen College, Oxford," who had "made improvements and corrections all through the book."

[4] Charles John Todd (1854–1939), Magdalen undergraduate 1874–77, Chaplain to the Royal Navy 1881–1909.

[5] Eric Richard Ward, Magdalen chorister 1874–78.

[6] George Loyd Foster Harter (1852–1920), Magdalen undergraduate 1871–75, became a barrister.

any letter now. It seems a long time since I heard from you, and as for Bouncer I have not heard anything about him for a fortnight.

In his last letter he complained terribly that his mother and sisters would not let him read. I hope your people are better, and encourage your industry in every way.

I have been waiting for my brother who is on circuit, and for Frank Miles who could not get away from home till we go down to Galway together. We expect them both tomorrow. I am rather tired of sea bathing and lawn tennis and shall be glad to be down for the 12th. After this rain too there will be a lot of fish up.

I am just going out to bring an *exquisitely pretty girl* to afternoon service in the Cathedral. She is just seventeen with the *most perfectly beautiful face I ever saw and not a sixpence of money*. I will show you her photograph when I see you next.[1]

Strutt and his wife, or rather Mrs Strutt and Mrs Strutt's husband, are in town. I am going to call and see them on my way.[2]

I hope you will write all about yourself and your belongings soon. Ever yours   OSCAR F. O'F. WILLS WILDE

To Reginald Harding
MS. Hyde (H. M.)

Wednesday [*?16 August 1876*]   *Moytura House*[3] [*Cong, Co. Mayo*]

Dear Kitten, Have you fallen into a well, or been mislaid anywhere that you never write to me? Or has one of your nine lives gone?

Frank Miles and I came down here last week, and have had a very royal time of it sailing. We are at the top of Lough Corrib, which if you refer to your geography you will find to be a lake thirty miles long, ten broad and situated in the most romantic scenery in Ireland. Frank has done some wonderful sunsets since he came down; he has given me some more of his drawings. Has your sister got the one he calls "My Little Lady"—a little girl's face with a lot of falling hair? If she has not got it I would like to send it to her in return for her autograph on the celebrated memorial.

Frank has never fired off a gun in his life (and says he doesn't want to) but as our proper sporting season here does not begin till September I have not taught him anything. But on Friday we go into Connemara to a charming little fishing lodge we have in the mountains where I hope to make him land a salmon and kill a brace of grouse. I expect to have very good sport indeed this season. Write to me there if your claws have not been clipped. Illaunroe Lodge, Leenane, Co. Galway.

Best love to Puss. I hope he is reading hard. Ever yours
OSCAR F. O'F. WILLS WILDE

[1] Almost certainly Florence Balcombe. See note 4, p. 36.
[2] George Herbert Strutt (1854–1928), Magdalen undergraduate 1874–76, married Edith Balguy 22 April 1876. Chairman of Derbyshire County Council 1902–14, High Sheriff of Derbyshire 1903–4.
[3] Built by Sir William Wilde, two miles from Cong, with a fine view over Lough Corrib, about which he published a successful book in 1867.

To William Ward

MS. Magdalen

[*Postmark 28 August 1876*] *Illaunroe Lodge, Connemara*

Dear Bouncer, I am very glad you like *Aurora Leigh*. I think it simply *"intense"* in every way. I am deep in a review of Symonds's last book whenever I can get time and the weather is too bright for fishing. Mahaffy has promised to look it over before publication.[1] Up to this however I am glad to say that I have been too much *occupied with rod and gun for the handling of the quill* (neat and Pope-like?).

I have only got one salmon as yet but have had heaps of sea-trout which give great play. I have not had a blank day yet. Grouse are few but I have got a lot of hares so have had a capital time of it. I hope next year that you and the Kitten will come and stay a (lunar) month with me. I am sure you would like this wild mountainous country, close to the Atlantic and teeming with sport of all kinds. It is in every way magnificent and makes me years younger than actual history records.

I hope you are reading hard; if you don't get your First the examiners ought to be sent down.

Write like a good boy to Moytura House, Cong, County Mayo, as I will be leaving here this week.

With kind regards to your mother and sisters, ever yours

OSCAR F. O'F. WILLS WILDE

I have Frank Miles with me. He is delighted with all.

To William Ward

MS. Magdalen

Wednesday [? *6 September 1876*] *1 Merrion Square North*

My dear Bouncer, Note paper became such a scarcity in the West that I had to put off answering your letter till I came home.

I had a delightful time, and capital sport, especially the last week, which I spent shooting, and got fair bags.

I am afraid I shall not cross to England via Bristol, as I hear the boats are rather of the "Ancient Mariner" type! but I may be down in Bristol with Frank Miles as I want to see S. Raphael's and the pictures at Cleve-don.[2]

[1] John Addington Symonds (1840–93) published the second and final volume of his *Studies of the Greek Poets* in 1876. Wilde's review is not known to have been published, but the manuscript was sold at the American Art Association on 25 April 1927. It is headed "The Women of Homer" (the title of a chapter in Symonds's first volume, 1873), and the catalogue quotes Wilde as saying that Symonds "has all the picturesqueness and loveliness of words that we admire so much in Mr Ruskin and Mr Pater."

[2] St Raphael's, Bristol, is a Victorian Gothic church, designed by Henry Woodyer (1816–96) and built in the 1850's. Attached to it was an almshouse for seamen,

I would like very much to renew my friendship with your mother and sisters so shall write to you if I see any hope of going down.

I have given up my pilgrimage to Rome for the present: Ronald Gower and Frank Miles were coming: (we would have been a great Trinity) but at the last hour Ronald couldn't get time, so I am staying in Dublin till the 20th, when I go down to Longford, and hope to have good sport.

I have heard from many people of your father's liberality and noble spirit, so I know you will take interest in the report I send you of my father's hospital, which he built when he was only twenty-nine and not a rich man. It is a great memorial of his name, and a movement is being set on foot to enlarge it and make it still greater.

I have got some charming letters lately from a great friend of my mother, Aubrey de Vere—a cultured poet (though sexless) and a convert to Catholicity.[1] I must show you them; he is greatly interested in me and is going to get one of my poems into the *Month*.[2] I have two this month out: one in the *Dublin University Magazine*,[3] one in the *Irish Monthly*.[4] Both are brief and Tennysonian.

I hope you are doing good work, but I suppose at home you are hardly allowed "to contemplate the abstract" (whatever that means) undisturbed.

I am bothered with business and many things and find the world an ἀναρχία[5] at present and a Tarpeian Rock[6] for honest men.

I hope you will write when you have time. Ever yours

OSCAR F. O'F. WILLS WILDE

I like signing my name as if it was to some document of great importance as "Send two bags of gold by bearer" or "Let the Duke be slain tomorrow and the Duchess await me at the hostelry."

I send you one of Aubrey de Vere's letters. I know you will be amused at them. Return it when you have committed it to memory.

To John Boyle O'Reilly[7]

F. Keller

[*September 1876*]   *1 Merrion Square North*

Dear Sir, Accept my thanks for your letter and its enclosure. I esteem

---

which was built at the expense of Frank Miles's father. Clevedon Court, some fifteen miles west of Bristol, is a fourteenth-century manor house, the home of the Elton family for 250 years. Thackeray's friend Mrs Brookfield was a daughter of Sir Charles Elton, and Clevedon Court was in part the original of Castlewood in *Esmond*. The pictures were mostly family portraits by West Country painters, and the house was open to the public one day a week.

[1] Sir Aubrey Thomas De Vere, Bart (1814–1902), prolific Irish poet and critic.

[2] "Graffiti D'Italia (Arona, Lago Maggiore)" in the September 1876 issue. Reprinted, with slight revisions and renamed "Rome Unvisited," in *Poems* (1881).

[3] See note 4, p. 22.

[4] "The True Knowledge" in the September 1876 issue. Reprinted in *Lyra Hibernica Sacra* (1878) and in *Poems* (1908).   [5] Chaos.

[6] A precipice on the Capitoline Hill in Rome, from which criminals were thrown.

[7] 1844–90. He had in 1868 been transported from Ireland to Australia for

it a great honour that the first American paper I appear in should be your admirable *Pilot*.[1]

I send you two magazines with contributions of mine which perhaps you might like to reprint, or notice; they are quite at your disposal.

I hope always to be able to keep up my connection with the *Pilot*. Lady Wilde sends you her compliments and best wishes. Believe me, truly yours   OSCAR WILDE

To Reginald Harding
MS. Hyde (H. M.)

Sunday 17 December [1876]   *85 Jermyn Street, S.W.*[2]

My dear Kitten, I have not had a line from you since you rushed away from Oxford leaving me on a bed of *broken neck-ness*; I suppose your Christmas anthem keeps you too much employed to write to anyone.

I have been having a delightful time here; any amount of theatres and dining out. On Thursday I brought young May[3] down to Windsor and we had a delightful day with Ronald Gower who has got a new house there (one of the most beautiful houses I ever saw). He brought us to St George's Chapel for afternoon service and I did not like the singing so well as our own.

We had just time after it was over to catch the 6.30 train and go to the Albert Hall to hear the *Creation*. Foli sang magnificently and the song about the "sinewy tiger and the horrid lion" was very fine, but Lemmens-Sherrington was rather horrid and affected.[4]

I have taken a great fancy to May, he is quite charming in every way and a beautiful artist. He dined with me last night and we went to see Henry Irving in *Macbeth*. I enjoyed it of course immensely.[5]

Fenian activities. He escaped to the United States in 1870, became an American citizen and devoted himself to journalism. As editor and part-proprietor of the *Boston Pilot* he did much for the cause of Irish Nationalism and encouraged many young Irish writers.

[1] Wilde's poem "Graffiti D'Italia (Arona, Lago Maggiore)" also appeared in the *Boston Pilot* for 23 September 1876.

[2] Furnished apartments.

[3] Almost certainly Arthur Dampier May, portrait and landscape painter, whose portrait of the first Lord Coleridge hangs in Trinity College, Oxford. Except that he is said to have worked in London from 1873 to 1914, and was reported as attending an "At Home" at the Wildes' in July 1887, I have failed to discover any more about him.

[4] A performance of Haydn's *Creation* was given at the Albert Hall on Thursday, 14 December 1876, with Foli and Lemmens-Sherrington singing solos. Foli was in fact an Irishman, Allan James Foley (1835–99). Helen Lemmens-Sherrington (1834–1906) was a Lancashire-born soprano.

[5] Henry Irving (stage-name of John Henry Brodribb, 1838–1905) had gone on the stage in 1855, and in 1871 joined the company at the Lyceum, where on 16 December 1876 *Macbeth* was revived, with Irving and Kate Bateman in the leading parts. Irving's triumphant management of the Lyceum began in 1878.

I have heard nothing from Bouncer, except a very incoherent telegram the day he got his degree. He promised to write however from "The Palace." I suppose you know I have got his rooms. I am awfully pleased about it.[1]

I am off to Ireland tonight, and intend *"nipping down"* to the Oratory for the 3.30 service. Dunskie[2] went off yesterday. We were at the Court Theatre on Friday together.[3] He tells me *Lang*[4] is going to become a Catholic. I must know him next term. You are not to tell anyone. Love to Puss. Ever yours   OSCAR F. O'F. W. WILDE

Remember Christmas is near, and that there is an old custom of giving presents. I gave you a lovely Arundel lately.[5]

To William Ward

MS. Magdalen

Saturday [*30 December 1876*]   *1 Merrion Square North*

My dear Bouncer, I was very glad indeed to hear from you and to find what I expected all along, that your philosophy in Greats was so good:[6] it is a great thing to do well in the subjects worth doing well in.

Except the Mark I think few people would set laborious industry on any footing with brilliant and original thought. It really was a great pity you did not make up your books. I suppose one ought to be a Gibeonite, a "wood-hewer and water-drawer of Literature," in order to make one's First safe.

I hope greatly you will stay and read for a Fellowship, not merely on selfish grounds of having you at any rate within reach if not at Oxford, but because I feel certain you would get one within a year: at least if *you* don't I don't know who will.

You would see Italy with greater pleasure after having gained what I certainly consider a great honour. After a year you might find yourself

[1] When Ward went down Wilde moved into his rooms on the Kitchen Staircase (1 Pair Left), overlooking the Cherwell.

[2] The nickname (from Dunskey, his Galloway home) of David Hunter-Blair (1853–1939), a contemporary and friend of Wilde at Magdalen. A Roman Catholic convert in 1875, he entered the Benedictine Order in 1878, was ordained priest in 1886, and was Abbot of Fort Augustus 1913–17. In 1896 he succeeded his father as fifth Baronet. He published several volumes of reminiscences, of which *In Victorian Days* (1939) contains a chapter "Oscar Wilde as I knew him."

[3] *New Men and Old Acres* by Tom Taylor and A. W. Dubourg had been revived at the Court Theatre on 2 December 1876, with Ellen Terry and her future husband Charles Kelly in the cast.

[4] Alexander Dennistoun Lang (1857–1908), Magdalen undergraduate 1876, became a soldier.

[5] The Arundel Society, founded by Ruskin and others in 1848, published from 1856 to 1897 a series of some two hundred chromo-lithographic reproductions of paintings by the old masters, which were much esteemed by the fashionable. A number of Arundel Society prints were included in the sale of Wilde's possessions in 1895.

[6] Ward got a Second in Literae Humaniores (Greats) in December 1876.

disinclined to read up your philosophy again, too tired to return on the road you have already travelled. The extreme beauty of Italy may ruin you, as I think it has done me, for hard work again: but I think that *now*, with your knowledge fresh, and your brain keen, you could work well and successfully.

However, you are much stronger that I am, and Italy may not unnerve you after all: and I don't think as a rule that people ever mind much what advice friends *of the same age* give them. After all, for effect and persuasion there is nothing like wrinkles and either grey hair or baldness.

I was very sorry you did not come up to town after term. I had a delightful week and saw everything from Nelly Bromley[1] and the Brompton Priest-Shop, down to Henry Irving and Gibson's *Tinted Hebe*: a lovely statue by the bye, quite Greek, and the effect of the colouring is most lifelike and beautiful.[2] I had a charming day at Windsor with Ronald Gower. I brought Arthur May with me and have not enjoyed myself so much for years.

We went to St George's Chapel for evening service after lunch, and just got up in time to hear the *Creation* at the Albert Hall. I saw a great deal of Arthur May; he is quite charming in every way and we have rushed into friendship.

Dublin is very gay but I have got tired of evening parties and go in for dining out now which is much more satisfactory, especially as the Dublin people all think I am a Fellow of Magdalen, and so listen to all I say with great attention.

I got a long letter from the Kitten asking me to go over for this Fancy Ball, but I have already refused the Mileses who want me to go to Bingham the same week. (page 12. *Ohé jam satis*.[3]) The fact is I have a lot of things to do in Dublin and cannot manage to leave home so early in the vac.

I am so glad your people liked the ring, and if the Greek lines you quoted to me would fit it would be charming. Perhaps however our initials inside and φιλίας μνημόσυνον outside would be all that would fit conveniently.[4]

[1] English actress (1850–1939). She scored a great success with Charles Wyndham in *Hot Water*, adapted by H. B. Farnie from *La Boule* by Meilhac and Halévy. She played the part of a burlesque actress, giving evidence in Court and undoing the twenty-four buttons of her glove to take the oath. The play opened at the Criterion Theatre on 13 November 1876 and ran until February 1877.

[2] The sculptor John Gibson, R.A. (1790–1866) bequeathed his fortune and the contents of his studio to the Royal Academy, where the Gibson Gallery, containing a selection of his works, was opened to the public on 27 November 1876. Commenting on the exhibition in the *Nation* of 15 March 1877, Henry James wrote: "As regards the 'tinting' I should say, on the evidence of the Hebe, that it matters little, one way or the other. It is so very vague and unimportunate that it neither spoils a good piece of sculpture nor makes a poor one better. Gibson's statues strike one not so much as interesting but as respectable."

[3] "Well! that's enough" (Martial, iv, 91).

[4] This ring, which was given by Wilde and Harding to Ward when he went down from Oxford, is now in Magdalen Library. It is a thick gold band in the form of a buckled strap engraved on the outside Μνημόσυνον φιλίας ἀντιφιλοῦντι φίλοι, which can be roughly translated "A memento of friendship, from two friends to a

I find I have written about twelve pages! poor boy! but as I have not heard from you for a long time I had a lot to write about.

It certainly would be a very charming surprise to find you back in Oxford; I need not tell you I shall miss you greatly if you go to Italy. In any case I hope you will come up (page 15. Ἀπόλλων ἀλεξίκακος¹) and see us next term and we will promise not to call you the Old Crust.²

Please give my best wishes for the New Year to your mother and sisters. Yours affectionately   OSCAR WILDE³

P.S. (16 pages) How can *you*, an aesthetic youth, dress yourself as a Chinaman and so exhibit yourself to some girl you are fond of? You ought to go as Pico della Mirandula with a Plato under your arm. Don't you think that "Puss in Boots" would be a good dress for King's Close?

To William Ward

MS. Magdalen

[*Week ending 3 March 1877*]   [*Oxford*]

[*A letter of four double sheets, the first of which is missing*]
Webbe and Jack Barrow, and is blossoming out into the fast man: however his career has been cut short by the Dean refusing to let him take his degree through his late hours in lodgings! *Wee! Wee!* is Mark's expression in consequence.

The freshmen *in it* are Gore,⁴ a great pal of Tom Peyton's lot, Grey a nice Eton boy⁵—and we have all suddenly woke to the idea that Wharton⁶ is charming. I like him very much indeed and ran him in for the Apollo lately. I also ran in Gebhardt⁷ with whom I have had several rows through his *drunken-noisy-Jewish ways*—and two freshmen Vinton⁸ and Chance⁹ both of them very casual fellows indeed. I have got rather keen on Masonry lately and believe in it awfully—in fact would be awfully sorry to have to give it up in case I secede from the Protestant Heresy.¹⁰ I now breakfast with Father Parkinson,¹¹ go to St Aloysius, talk sentimental religion to

---

third," and on the inside "O.F.F.W. & R.R.H. to W.W.W. 1876." See also note p. 61.

¹ "O Apollo, averter of evil."   ² University slang for impudence or cheek.

³ Wilde now dropped his other names and initials from his signature.

⁴ Frederick St John Gore (b. 1857), Magdalen undergraduate 1877–80.

⁵ John Chipchase Grey (1857–1946), Magdalen undergraduate 1877–80, became a clergyman.

⁶ John Henry Turner Wharton (1857–1944), Magdalen undergraduate 1876–80, rowed in university eight 1879–80; became a solicitor in Southampton.

⁷ Thomas Gebhardt (b. 1855), Magdalen undergraduate 1875–78.

⁸ Frank Jones Vinton (b. 1857), Magdalen undergraduate 1877–80.

⁹ Henry Featherstone Chance (b. 1859), Magdalen undergraduate 1877–80, became a member of Lloyd's.

¹⁰ Wilde was admitted to the thirty-third degree of the Scottish Masonic rite at the Oxford University chapter on 27 November 1876. His certificate of admission is in the collection of Mr Montgomery Hyde.

¹¹ The Rev. Thomas B. Parkinson, S.J., was the Superior at St Aloysius from 1875 to 1888.

Reginald Harding

William Ward

Oxford, 13 March 1876
A. F. Peyton, C. H. Tindal, C. H. Lindon, Oscar Wilde, T. T. Peyton

Dunlop[1] and altogether am caught in the fowler's snare, in the wiles of the Scarlet Woman—I may go over in the vac. I have dreams of a visit to Newman, of the holy sacrament in a new Church, and of a quiet and peace afterwards in my soul. I need not say, though, that I shift with every breath of thought and am weaker and more self-deceiving than ever.

If I *could hope* that the Church would wake in me some earnestness and purity I would go over *as a luxury*, if for no better reasons. But I can hardly hope it would, and to go over to Rome would be to sacrifice and give up my two great gods "Money and Ambition."

Still I get so wretched and low and troubled that in some desperate mood I will seek the shelter of a Church which simply enthrals me by its fascination.

I hope that now in the Sacred City you are wakened up from the Egyptian darkness that has blinded you. *Do* be touched by it, *feel* the awful fascination of the Church, its extreme beauty and sentiment, and let every part of your nature have play and room.

We have had our Sports and are now in the midst of Torpids[2] and tomorrow the pigeons are shot.[3] To escape I go up to town to see the Old Masters[4] *with the Kitten!* who is very anxious to come. Dear little Puss is up, and looks wretched, but as pleasant and bright as ever. He is rather keen on going to Rome for Easter with me, but I don't know if I can afford it, as I have been elected for the St Stephen's and have to pay £42. I did not want to be elected for a year or so but David Plunket ran me in in three weeks some way rather to my annoyance.[5]

I would give worlds to be in Rome with you and Dunskie. I know I would enjoy it awfully but I don't know if I can manage it. You would be a safeguard against Dunskie's attacks.

I am in for the "Ireland" on Monday.[6] God! how I have wasted my life up here! I look back on weeks and months of extravagance, trivial talk, utter vacancy of employment, *with feelings so bitter that I have lost faith in myself*. I am too ridiculously easily led astray. So I have idled and won't get it and will be wretched in consequence. I feel that if I had read I would have done well up here but I have not.

I enjoy your rooms awfully. The inner room is filled with china, pictures,

---

[1] Archibald Claude Dunlop (1858–1924) became a Catholic while a Magdalen undergraduate. Later he lived and worked in Southampton, where he acted as Consul for several foreign countries and built St Boniface's Catholic church, largely at his own expense. [2] The Lent Term rowing-races at Oxford.

[3] The shooting of pigeons in Oxford college gardens is not done at any particular time, but only when the birds become too great a nuisance.

[4] In January and February 1877 the Royal Academy held its usual exhibition of "Old Masters and Deceased Masters of the British School" at Burlington House.

[5] St Stephen's is a "Conservative and Constitutional" Club on Victoria Embankment, Westminster, established in 1870. Wilde's proposer was probably the Hon. David Robert Plunket (1838–1919), third son of the third Lord Plunket and Conservative M.P. for Dublin University from 1870 to 1895, when he was created Lord Rathmore.

[6] In 1877 the examination for the annual Ireland Scholarship in "classical learning and taste" began on Monday, 5 March.

a portfolio and a piano—and a grey carpet with stained floor. The whole get-up is much admired and a little made fun of on Sunday evenings. They are more delightful than I ever expected—the sunshine, the cawing rooks and waving tree-branches and the breeze at the window are too charming.

I do nothing but write sonnets and scribble poetry—some of which I send you—though to send anything of mine to Rome is an awful impertinence, but you always took an interest in my attempts to ride Pegasus.

My greatest chum, except of course the Kitten, is Gussy[1] who is charming though not educated well: however he is "*psychological*" and we have long chats and walks. The rest of Tom's set are capital good fellows but awful children. They talk nonsense and smut. I am quite as fond of the dear Kitten as ever but he has not enough power of character to be more than a pleasant affectionate boy. He never exerts my intellect or brain *in any way*. Between his mind and mine there is no *intellectual friction to rouse me up to talk or think*, as I used when with you—especially on those dear rides through the greenwood. I ride a good deal now and the last day rode an awful brute which by a skilful buckjump threw me on my head on Shotover. I escaped however unhurt and got home all safe.

The Dean comes sometimes and we talk theology, but I usually ride by myself, and have got such new trousers—quite the dog! I have written a very foolish letter; it reads very rambling and absurd, but it is so delightful writing to you that I just put down whatever comes into my head.

Your letters are charming and the one from Sicily came with a scent of olive-gardens, blue skies and orange trees, that was like reading Theocritus in this grey climate. Goodbye. Ever, dear boy, your affectionate friend

OSCAR WILDE

I have a vacant page.

I won't write to you theology, but I only say that for *you* to feel the fascination of Rome would to me be the greatest of pleasures: I think it would *settle me*.

And really to go to Rome with the bugbear of formal logic on one's mind is quite as bad as to have the "Protestant jumps."

But I know you are keenly alive to beauty, and do try and see in the Church not man's hand only but also a little of God's.

To William Ward

MS. Magdalen

[*Circa 14 March 1877*]   [*Oxford*]

My dear Bouncer, I sent you a long letter to the Poste Restante about a fortnight ago which I hope you got. I have been in for "the Ireland" and of course lost it: on six weeks' reading I could not expect to get a prize for which men work two and three years. What stumped me was Philology of which they gave us a long paper: otherwise I did rather well: it is horrid receiving the awkward commiserations of most of the College. I shall not

[1] Perhaps the nickname of Cresswell Augustus Cresswell (1856–1935), Magdalen undergraduate 1875–79, who became a London stockbroker.

be sorry when term ends: though I have only a year for Greats work, still I intend to reform and read hard if possible.

I am sorry to say that I will not see the Holy City this Easter at any rate: I have been elected for the St Stephen's Club and £42 is a lot to pay down on the nail, so I will go up to town for a week and then to Bingham and then home. I am going first to see Newman at Birmingham to burn my fingers a little more.[1] Do you remember young Wise of this place?[2] He is awfully caught with the wiles of the Scarlet Woman and wrote to Newman about several things: and received the most charming letters back and invitations to come and see him: I am awfully keen for an interview, not of course to argue, but merely to be in the presence of that divine man.

I will send you a long account of it: but perhaps my courage will fail, as I could hardly resist Newman I am afraid.

Oxford is much as usual and dining in Hall more horrid than ever. Now of course Jupp[3] and I are not on speaking terms, but when we were I gave him a great jar; the Caliban came into Hall beaming and sniggering and said "I'm very glad they've given the £15 Exhibition to *Jones*" (put in all the beastly pronunciation for yourself) so I maliciously said "What! the old Jugger[4] got an Exhibition! very hot indeed." He was *too sick* and said "Not likely, I mean Wansbrough Jones,"[5] to which I replied "I never knew there was such a fellow up here." Which confined Jupp to his gummy bed for a day and prevented him dining in hall for two days.

Some rather good demies have come up this term, Fletcher an Eton fellow,[6] and Armitage,[7] who has the most Greek face I ever saw, and Broadbent.[8] I have been doing my duty like a brick and keeping up the reputation of these rooms by breakfasts, lunches etc.: however I find it is rather a bore and that one gains nothing from the conversation of anyone. The Saturday before the Ireland I brought up the dear Kitten to town and saw the Old Masters, which brought out his little Popish tendencies very much.

Had afternoon tea with Frank Miles to meet Ronald Gower and his sister the Duchess of Westminster, who is the most fascinating, Circe-like, brilliant woman I have ever met in England: something too charming.[9]

[1] There is no evidence that this visit ever took place.
[2] Henry Edward Wise (1856–1923), Magdalen undergraduate 1876–80, became a country gentleman and amateur musician.
[3] Herbert Basil Jupp (b. 1853), Magdalen Demy 1873–77.
[4] Nickname of Edward Cholmeley Jones, Magdalen Bible Clerk 1873–76.
[5] William Wansbrough Jones (1853–1930), Magdalen Demy 1873–77, became a Major in the Royal Army Medical Corps.
[6] Charles Robert Leslie Fletcher (1857–1934), Magdalen undergraduate 1877–80. Fellow of All Souls 1881–88. Fellow and Tutor of Magdalen 1889–1906. Historian. Collaborated with Kipling in *A School History of England* (1911).
[7] Robert Armitage (1857–1954), Magdalen Demy 1877–80, won the D.S.O. as Chaplain to the Forces. Rural Dean of Ludlow 1930. Prebendary of Hereford 1932.
[8] George Broadbent (1857–1911), Magdalen undergraduate 1877–80, became a solicitor in London.
[9] Constance, daughter of the second Duke of Sutherland, married the third Marquess of Westminster 1852. He was created first Duke 1874. She died 1880.

Did I tell you that in consequence of Mark's late hours the Dean refused to let him take his degree? However he hopes to take it the boat race day.

Collins, Cooper and old Stewy are giving three dinners on three successive nights in town, for the Sports, Race etc., and we are all going to them.

Our Varsity Sports have just been on and were much as usual with the exception of Bullock-Webster's running which is the most beautiful thing I ever saw. Usually running men are so ungraceful and stiff-legged and pigeon-breasted, but he is lithe and exquisitely graceful and strides about *nine feet*: he is like a beautiful horse trotting, as regards his action. I never saw anything like it: he and Stevenson ran a three mile race, he keeping behind Stevenson about a yard the whole time till the last quarter when he rushed in before him amid awful cheers and shouting: you will see in Naples two bronze statues of two Greek boys running quite like Webster.[1]

We have had the Jugger down till we are very tired of him: he is coming up for all the summer term to coach (!) and give concerts.

I hope soon to get a long letter from you with all your Roman experiences in it. Ever affectionately OSCAR WILDE

To Reginald Harding
MS. Hyde (H. M.)

[*Late March 1877*]   *Magdalen College*

My dear Kitten, I start for Rome on Sunday; Mahaffy comes as far as Genoa with me: and I hope to see the golden dome of St Peter's and the Eternal City by Tuesday night.

This is an era in my life, a crisis. I wish I could look into the seeds of time and see what is coming.

I shall not forget you in Rome, and will burn a candle for you at the Shrine of Our Lady.

Write to me like a good boy, Hôtel d'Angleterre, Rome. Yours ever
OSCAR

Postcard: To Reginald Harding
MS. Hyde (H. M.)

2 April [*Postmark 1877*]   *Corfu*

I never went to Rome at all! What a changeable fellow you must think me, but Mahaffy my old tutor carried me off to Greece with him to see Mykenae and Athens. I am awfully ashamed of myself but I could not

---

[1] In the University Sports of 1877, which took place on 8, 9 and 10 March, F. Bullock-Webster (Hertford) won the three miles in 15 mins 23⅜ secs, beating W. R. H. Stevenson (New) by three yards.

34

help it and will take Rome on my way back.[1] We[2] went to Genoa, then to Ravenna and left Brindisi last night, catching sight of Greece at 5.30 this morning. We go tomorrow to Zante and land near Olympia and then ride through Arcadia to Mykenae. Write to Athens *Poste Restante*. Love to Puss.   OSCAR WILDE

To the Rev. H. R. Bramley[3]
MS. Princeton

2 April 1877   *Hotel St George, Corfu*

My dear Mr Bramley, My old tutor Mr Mahaffy, Fellow of Trinity College Dublin, met me on my way to Rome and insisted on my going with him to Mykenae and Athens. The chance of seeing such great places—and in such good company—was too great for me and I find myself now in Corfu. I am afraid I will not be able to be back at the beginning of term. I hope you will not mind if I miss ten days at the beginning: seeing Greece is really a great education for anyone and will I think benefit me greatly, and Mr Mahaffy is such a clever man that it is quite as good as going to lectures to be in his society.

We came first to Genoa, which is a beautiful marble city of palaces over the sea, and then to Ravenna which is extremely interesting on account of the old Christian churches in it of enormous age and the magnificent mosaics of the *fourth century*. These mosaics were very remarkable as they contained two figures of the Madonna enthroned and receiving adoration; they completely upset the ordinary Protestant idea that the worship of the Virgin did not come in till late in the history of the Church.

I read the book you kindly lent me with much interest; the Roman Catholics certainly do seem to confuse together Catholic doctrines which we may all hold and the supremacy of the Pope which we need not hold.

I hope your health has been good this Easter. We expect to be in Athens by the 17th and I will post back to Oxford immediately. Yours very truly
OSCAR WILDE

---

[1] Wilde carried out this plan, paying his first visit to Rome on his way home, and there meeting William Ward and Hunter Blair, who in his memoirs *In Victorian Days* (1939) wrongly ascribes the visit to 1876.

[2] Besides Mahaffy, the party consisted of his friend Goulding (see note 4, p. 10) and George Macmillan (1855–1936), a member of the publishing family and one of the founders of the Hellenic Society in 1879. His elder brother Malcolm disappeared from the top of Mount Olympus in 1889.

[3] Henry Ramsden Bramley (1833–1917) was a Tutor of Magdalen 1858–68 and 1871–83. He was also Dean of Arts 1871–82. A great favourite in the College, he was a Tractarian, a Jacobite, the editor of several collections of carols, and claimed to be "in favour of progress, but of progress backward." He was Canon and Precentor of Lincoln 1895–1902.

To Lady Wilde[1]
MS. Clark

[? *Early April 1877*]   [? *Corfu*]

The island is full of idyllic loveliness. Set in its olive woods. In Italy nearly all the olives are pollarded and stunted, but here one sees them in the fullness of their natural beauty.

What strikes one is extreme age, and the twisted broken writhing in pain such as Gustave Doré[2] loves to draw. The delicate grey-green and silver of their leaves, changing to silver when the wind blows on them.

To Reginald Harding
MS. Hyde (H. M.)

Tuesday [*May 1877*]   *1 Merrion Square North*

My dear Boy, Thanks for your letter: I had made out the facts by a careful study of the statutes going up to town, but it was comforting all the same to have it confirmed by such an authority as the Schools Clerk.[3]

I had a delightful time in town with Frank Miles and a lot of friends and came home on Friday. My mother was of course awfully astonished to hear my news and very much disgusted with the wretched stupidity of our college dons, while Mahaffy is *raging*! I never saw him so indignantly angry: he looks on it almost as an insult to himself.

The weather is charming, Florrie[4] more lovely than ever, and I am going to give two lectures on Greece to the Alexandra College girls here, so I am rapidly forgetting the Boeotian ἀναισθησία[5] of Allen[6] and the wretched time-serving of that old woman in petticoats, the Dean.

As I expected, all my friends here refuse to believe my story, and my brother who is down at Moytura at present writes me a letter marked

---

[1] This fragment or draft clearly refers to Corfu and was preserved with the other three surviving letters from Wilde to his parents.

[2] French painter, draughtsman, illustrator and sculptor (1832–83).

[3] As a punishment for coming up to Oxford a month late after his journey to Greece, Wilde was fined £47.10 (half his Demyship for the year) and rusticated, i.e. sent down for the rest of the term. The money was paid back to him in 1878. Years later Charles Ricketts reported his saying: "I was sent down from Oxford for being the first undergraduate to visit Olympia."

[4] Florence Anne Lemon Balcombe (1858–1937) daughter of a retired lieutenant-colonel living at 1 Marino Crescent, Clontarf, Dublin. He had fought in the Crimea, and it seems likely that Florence was named after Miss Nightingale. A drawing of her by Wilde is reproduced in Vyvyan Holland's *Son of Oscar Wilde* (1954). According to E. V. Lucas (*The Times*, 6 March 1934) George du Maurier considered her one of the three most beautiful women he had ever seen, the other two being Mrs John Hare (wife of the actor, *née* Mary Holmes) and Mrs Stillman (a Greek lady, *née* Marie Spartali, who sat to Rossetti).

[5] Boorish insensitiveness.

[6] The Rev. William Dennis Allen (1848–1923), Fellow of Magdalen 1871, Classical Tutor 1873–81, Vicar of Findon, Sussex, 1881.

"Private" to ask "what it *really* is all about and *why* have I been rusticated," treating my explanations as mere child's play.

I hope you will write and tell me all about the College, who is desecrating my rooms and what is the latest scandal.

When Dunskie comes tell him to write to me and remember me to Dick and Gussy and little Dunlop and everyone you like or I like. Ever yours

OSCAR

I am going down I hope for my May fishing soon, but I am overwhelmed with business of all kinds.

Get *Aurora Leigh* by Mrs Browning and read it carefully.

To W. E. Gladstone[1]

MS. B.M.

[*14 May 1877*][2]   *1 Merrion Square North*

Sir, Your noble and impassioned protests, both written and spoken, against the massacres of the Christians in Bulgaria have so roused my heart that I venture to send you a sonnet which I have written on the subject.

I am little more than a boy, and have no literary interest in London, but perhaps if *you* saw any good stuff in the lines I send you, some editor (of the *Nineteenth Century* perhaps or the *Spectator*) might publish them: and I feel sure that you can appreciate the very great longing that one has when young to have words of one's own published for men to read. I remain, in deepest admiration, your obedient servant   OSCAR WILDE

ON THE RECENT MASSACRES
OF THE CHRISTIANS IN BULGARIA

> Christ, dost thou live indeed? or are thy bones
>   Still straitened in their rock-hewn sepulchre?
>   And do we owe thy rising but to Her
> Whose love of thee for all her sin atones?
> For here the air is heavy with men's groans,
>   The priests that call upon thy name are slain;
>   Dost thou not hear the bitter wail of pain
> From those whose children lie upon the stones?
>
> Our prayers are nought: impenetrable gloom
>   Covers God's face: and in the starless night
>   Over thy Cross the Crescent Moon I see.

[1] William Ewart Gladstone (1809–98) had already once been Liberal Prime Minister (1868–74) and was to be three more times, but in 1877 the Liberals were in Opposition to Disraeli's Tory Government.
[2] So dated by Gladstone.

If thou in very truth didst burst the tomb,
Come down, O Son of Man, and show thy might
Lest Mahomet be crowned instead of Thee.[1]

Magdalen College, Oxford   OSCAR WILDE

To W. E. Gladstone
MS. B.M.

[*17 May 1877*][2]   *1 Merrion Square North*

Dear Mr Gladstone, I give you my most sincere thanks for your courtesy and kindness in what I feared was an intrusion on you.

A sympathetic word of interest from a man who has shown himself nobly great in deed and word gives a boy more real encouragement and pleasure than to see one's poems in every magazine published.

I have sent the sonnets to the editor of the *Spectator* and mentioned, as you allowed me, that you saw some promise in them.

The lines 3 and 4 are perhaps a little obscure, the allusion is of course to *Mary Magdalen* being the first to see our Lord after his Resurrection, and bringing the news to the Disciples; Renan says somewhere that this was the divinest lie ever told.[3]

The idea of *your* reading anything of mine has so delighted me, that I cannot help sending you a second sonnet. I am afraid you will think it a poor return for your courtesy to repeat the offence, but perhaps you may see some beauty in it. I remain, in sincere gratitude, your obedient servant

OSCAR WILDE

EASTER DAY

The silver trumpets rang across the dome:
     The people knelt upon the ground with awe,
     And borne upon the necks of men I saw,
Like some great God, the Holy Lord of Rome.
Priest-like he wore a robe more white than foam,
     And, King-like, swathed himself in royal red,
     Three crowns of gold rose high above his head,

In splendour and in light the Pope passed home.
My heart stole back across wide wastes of years
     To One who wandered by a lonely sea,

---

[1] This sonnet was apparently first published, slightly revised, in *Poems* (1881). The massacre took place in May 1876, but Gladstone's first pamphlet, *The Bulgarian Horrors and the Question of the East*, was not published till 6 September, and his second, *Lessons in Massacre*, on 13 March 1877.

[2] So dated by Gladstone.

[3] *Disons cependant que la forte imagination de Marie de Magdala joua dans cette circonstance un rôle capital. Pouvoir divin de l'amour! Moments sacrés où la passion d'une hallucinée donne au monde un Dieu ressuscité!* (*Vie de Jésus*, ch. xxvi).

38

And sought in vain for any place of rest:
"Foxes have holes, and every bird its nest.
   I, I alone, must travel wearily,
   And bruise my feet, and drink wine salt with tears."[1]

To Keningale Cook[2]

[*May–June 1877*]

I return proof.[3] What I meant by two proofs was one with your marginal corrections for my guide, the other plain, but of course both from the same type. Naturally, one of the great sorrows of youthful artists is that they always "expurgate" bits of their articles, the very bits that they think best. However, I am glad to get the article published in your July number before the Gallery closes. Please have all my corrections attended to. Some of them are merely "style" corrections, which, for an Oxford man, must be always attended to. As regards the additions, they are absolutely necessary, and as I intend to take up the critic's life, I would not wish the article published without them. I would sooner pay for the proof and publish elsewhere.

(1) I and Lord Ronald Gower and Mr Ruskin, and all artists of my acquaintance, hold that Alma Tadema's drawing of men and women is disgraceful. I could not let an article signed with my name state he was a powerful drawer.

(2) I always say I and not "we." We belongs to the days of anonymous articles, not to signed articles like mine. To say "we have seen at Argos" either implies that I am a Royal Personage, or that the whole staff of the *D.U.M.* visited Argos. And I always say clearly what I know to be true, such as that the revival of culture is due to Mr Ruskin, or that Mr Richmond[4] has not read Aeschylus's *Choephoroe*. To say "perhaps" spoils the remark.

(3) I have been obliged to explain what I mean by imaginative colour, and what Mr Pater means by it. We mean thought expressed by colour such as the sleep of Merlin being implied and expressed in the colour. I do not mean odd, unnatural colouring. I mean "thought in colour."

(4) I think Mr Legros's landscape very smudgy and the worst French style. I cannot say it is bold or original—and I wish my full remarks on Mr

[1] This sonnet was first published, slightly revised, in *Waifs and Strays*, vol. 1, no. 1, June 1879, and was reprinted, after further revision, in *Poems* (1881).

[2] Keningale Robert Cook (1846–86), Irish poet and writer, had been a Civil Servant in London and was now on the Stock Exchange. He had recently purchased and was now editing the *Dublin University Magazine* (which died in December). The text of this incomplete letter is taken from the American Art Association catalogue of 9 February 1927, where the last two paragraphs and the signature are reproduced in facsimile.

[3] Of Wilde's notice of the first exhibition at the Grosvenor Gallery in London, which opened on 1 May 1877. It appeared in the July issue of the *Dublin University Magazine,* and was reprinted in *Miscellanies.*   [4] See note 2, p. 233.

Whistler to be put in (as per margin). I know he will take them in good part, and besides they are really clever and amusing. I am sorry you left out my quotation from Pater at the end. However, I shall be glad to get a second proof before you go to press with my corrections. I am afraid you would find my account of our ride through Greece too enthusiastic and too full of metaphor for the *D.U.M.*

When I receive the second proof I am going to have small notes of the article appearing in *D.U.M.* by me sent to the Oxford booksellers. I know it would have a good sale there and also here if properly advertised, but for the past year the articles have been so terribly dull in the *D.U.M.* that people require to be told beforehand what they are to get for 2/6.

I hope we will come to terms about this article—and others. Believe me I am most anxious to continue my father's connection with the *D.U.M.* which, I am sure, under your brilliant guidance will regain its lost laurels.

Yours truly OSCAR WILDE

To the Rev. Matthew Russell, S.J.[1]

MS. Folger

[*15 or 16 June 1877*]   [*1 Merrion Square North*]

Dear Sir, I write in haste to say that my sonnet[2] must be printed in *full large type*: it looks and reads *bad* as it stands. Let the article begin on the *middle* of p. 473, and then 475 will begin, as I wished, with "As I stood beside the mean grave" and the *sonnet will end the page*. Please manage this for me, and send me second proof to look at. You might fill up the space with "winged words" which are always good wherever they come.

I have put "heart of hearts" in inverted commas; of course you remember "*cor cordium*" is the inscription on Shelley's tombstone.

Please see to the change.

I am sorry you object to the words "*our* English Land." It is a noble privilege to count oneself of the same race as Keats or Shakespeare. However I have changed it. I would not shock the feelings of your readers for anything.

I am glad Mr Walter Meynell[3] likes my sonnet. I have been surprised at the way it has touched the hearts of the Catholic priests I have met. It was recited nine times at the Glencree Reformatory the day it arrived

---

[1] 1834–1912. Younger brother of the first Lord Russell of Killowen. Editor of the *Irish Monthly* from its beginning in 1873. His answer to this letter (printed by Mason, p. 87) is dated 17 June 1877.

[2] "Heu Miserande Puer," which appeared in the *Irish Monthly* for July 1877, preceded by a short article entitled "The Tomb of Keats." The sonnet, revised and renamed "The Grave of Keats" (see next letter), was reprinted in *Poems* (1881).

[3] Almost certainly a slip for Wilfrid Meynell (1852–1948), who was beginning to make his name as a Catholic journalist. He married the poet Alice Thompson in April 1877.

there! Dr O'Leary tells me; and I have been, I fear, awfully overpraised
for it.

I hope soon to hear of Dr Russell's recovery to health.[1] Yours truly

OSCAR WILDE

I will await the second proof eagerly.

To Lord Houghton [2]

MS. Harvard

[*Circa 16 June 1877*]   *1 Merrion Square North*

Dear Lord Houghton, Knowing your love and admiration for John Keats
I venture to send you a sonnet which I wrote lately at Rome on him: and
should be very glad to know if you see any beauty or stuff in it.

Someway standing by his grave I felt that *he too* was a Martyr, and worthy
to lie in the City of Martyrs. I thought of him as a Priest of Beauty slain
before his time, a lovely Sebastian killed by the arrows of a lying and
unjust tongue.

Hence—my sonnet. But I really have other views in writing to you than
merely to gain your criticism of a boyish poem.

I don't know if you have visited Keats's grave since a marble tablet in his
memory was put up on the wall close to the tomb. There are some fairly
good lines of poetry on it, but what is really objectionable in it is the bas-
relief of Keats's head—or rather a *medallion profile*, which is *extremely ugly*,
exaggerates his facial angle so as almost to give him a hatchet-face and
instead of the finely cut nostril, and Greek sensuous delicate lips that he
had, gives him thick almost negro lips and nose.[3]

Keats we know was lovely as Hyakinthos, or Apollo, to look at, and this
medallion is a very terrible lie and misrepresentation. I wish it could be
removed and a tinted bust of Keats put in its place, like the beautiful
coloured bust of the Rajah of Koolapoor at Florence.[4] Keats's delicate

[1] Father Matthew's uncle, Dr Charles Russell (1812–80), Lord President of
Maynooth Training College, of whom Newman wrote: "My dear friend Dr
Russell . . . had perhaps more to do with my conversion than anyone else."

[2] Richard Monckton Milnes (1809–85), poet, politician and philanthropist. His
Life, Letters and Literary Remains of John Keats had appeared in 1848 and his
edition of the *Poetical Works*, with a memoir, in 1854. He had been created Lord
Houghton in 1863, and had visited Ireland in October and November 1876. Many
phrases in this letter occur in Wilde's article in the *Irish Monthly* (see last letter).

[3] The medallion by John Warrington Wood (1839–86) was unveiled on 21
February 1876 by Major-General Sir Vincent Eyre (1811–81), who also wrote the
acrostic poem engraved beneath:

Keats! if thy cherished name be "writ in water,"
Each drop has fallen from some mourner's cheek:
A sacred tribute, such as heroes seek,
Though oft in vain, for dazzling deeds of slaughter.
Sleep on! not honoured less, for epitaph so meek.

[4] A coloured and gilt bust of Rajaram Chuttraputti, Maharajah of Koolapoor,
who died in 1870, in his twenty-first year, while passing through Florence on his
way home to India. It forms part of an elaborate memorial marking the site of his
funeral pyre in the Cascine, the public park of Florence.

features and rich colour could not be conveyed I think in plain white marble.

In any case I do not think this very ugly thing ought to be allowed to remain: I am sure a photograph of it could easily be got, and you would see how horrid it is.

Your influence and great name could achieve anything and everything in the matter, and I think a really beautiful memorial might be erected to him. Surely if everyone who loves to read Keats gave even half-a-crown, a great sum of money could be got for it.

I know you always are engaged *in Politics and Poetry,* but I feel sure that with your name at the head of the list, a great deal of money would be got: in any case the ugly libel of Keats could be taken down.

I should be very glad to hear a line from you about it, and feel sure that you will pardon my writing to you on the subject. For you are fitted above all others to do anything for Keats's memory.

I hope we will see you again in Ireland: I have very pleasant memories of some delightful evenings passed in your society. Believe me yours truly

OSCAR WILDE

KEATS' GRAVE

Rid of the world's injustice and its pain
He rests at last beneath God's veil of blue;
Taken from life while life and love were new
The youngest of the Martyrs here is lain,
Fair as Sebastian and as foully slain.
No cypress shades his tomb, nor funeral yew,
But red-lipped daisies, violets drenched with dew,
And sleepy poppies, catch the evening rain.
O proudest heart that broke for misery!
O saddest poet that the world hath seen!
O sweetest singer of our English land!
Thy name was writ in water on the sand,
But our tears shall keep thy memory green,
And make it flourish like a Basil-tree.

Rome: 1877.   OSCAR WILDE

To Reginald Harding
MS. Hyde (H. M.)

[*Circa 16 June 1877*]   1 *Merrion Square North*

My dear Kitten, Many thanks for your delightful letter. I am glad you are in the midst of beautiful scenery and *Aurora Leigh.*

I am very much down in spirits and depressed. A cousin of ours to whom we were all very much attached has just died—quite suddenly from some chill caught riding. I dined with him on Saturday and he was dead

42

on Wednesday.[1] My brother and I were always supposed to be his heirs but his will was an unpleasant surprise, like most wills. He leaves my father's hospital about £8,000, my brother £2,000, and me £100 on condition of my being a Protestant!

He was, poor fellow, bigotedly intolerant of the Catholics and seeing me "on the brink" struck me out of his will. It is a terrible disappointment to me; you see I suffer a good deal from my Romish leanings, in pocket and mind.

My father had given him a share in my fishing lodge in Connemara, which of course ought to have reverted to me on his death; well, even this I lose "if I become a Roman Catholic for five years" which is very infamous.

Fancy a man going before "God and the Eternal Silences" [2] with his wretched Protestant prejudices and bigotry clinging still to him.

However, I won't bore you with myself any more. The world seems too much out of joint for me to set it right.

I send you a little notice of Keats's grave I have just written which may interest you. I visited it with Bouncer and Dunskie.

If you would care to see my views on the Grosvenor Gallery send for the enclosed, and write soon to me. Ever yours   OSCAR WILDE

I heard from little Bouncer from Constantinople lately: he said he was coming home. Love to Puss.

To William Michael Rossetti [3]
MS. B.M.

[*14 July 1877*][4]   *1 Merrion Square North*

Dear Sir, Knowing your love and admiration for John Keats I take the liberty of sending you a short monograph of mine on his grave at Rome; not indeed for any merit it may contain, for it is little more than a stray sheet from a boy's diary, but in hope that you might take up the question of having a suitable memorial erected to him.

I am only a boy, and could not of course originate anything of the kind, but you with your great literary influence and eloquent pen might, I think, easily gain the honour of raising a statue of this divine poet. Believe me, truly yours   OSCAR WILDE

[1] The "cousin" was in fact Wilde's half-brother, one of Sir William's many bastards. He was Dr Henry Wilson, Fellow of the Royal College of Surgeons of Ireland. He died of pneumonia on Wednesday, 13 June 1877, aged thirty-nine. Oscar and his brother Willie were the chief mourners at the funeral.

[2] Perhaps an echo of Alfred de Vigny's "*silence éternel de la Divinité*" (from '*Le Mont des Oliviers*' in *Les Destinées*, 1864) or of Carlyle's "brief Life-transit to all the Eternities, the Gods and Silences" (*Past and Present*, book iv. ch. iv).

[3] 1829–1919. Brother of Christina and Dante Gabriel. In the intervals of his life as a civil servant he published many literary and critical books (including a life of Keats, 1887) and editions of the English poets. He edited the Pre-Raphaelite paper, the *Germ*, in 1850, and in 1874 married a daughter of Ford Madox Brown.

[4] So dated by recipient.

43

To Harry Buxton Forman[1]

MS. B.M.

[? *July 1877*]   *1 Merrion Square North*

Dear Sir, In your beautiful edition of Shelley there is an etching of the
poet's grave, by W. B. Scott,[2] which I am very anxious to get a separate
copy of, to send to some friends in Rome.

Will you pardon my writing to you to know if you will allow me to write
to your publishers for one.

It is a place very dear to me, and I take the liberty of sending you a short
monograph of mine on the grave of John Keats: which is indeed only a
stray sheet from a boy's diary, but will, I think, show you that I love the
spot. Believe me, truly yours   OSCAR WILDE

To the Editor of Good Words[3]

MS. Clark

[? *July 1877*]   *1 Merrion Square North*

Mr Oscar Wilde begs to enclose two sonnets for publication in *Good Words*
if approved of.

If accepted Mr Wilde would be much obliged if they were printed on
a full half-page, *without the intersecting line*, which destroys the appearance
of a sonnet very much.

Mr Wilde would not like them both to appear in the same month, as
there is a slight similarity of rhyme in them.

EASTER DAY

[Text almost identical with that on p.38].

SONNET

(Written after hearing Mozart's *Dies Irae* sung in Magdalen Chapel)

Nay come not *thus*: white lilies in the spring,
 Sad olive-gardens, or a murmuring Dove,
 Teach me more clearly of thy life and love
Than terrors of red flame and thundering;
Fruit-laden vines dear memories of thee bring;
 A bird at evening flying to its nest
 Tells me of One who had no place of rest;
I think it is of thee the sparrows sing.

---

[1] 1842–1917. Civil servant and man of letters, edited the works of Shelley
(1876–80) and of Keats (1883).

[2] William Bell Scott, poet and painter (1811–90).

[3] The Very Rev. Donald Macleod (1832–1916) edited *Good Words* (which had
been started by his brother Norman in 1860) from 1872 till it ceased in 1906. He
was Moderator of the Assembly of the Church of Scotland 1895–96.

Come rather on some autumn afternoon
    When red and brown are burnished on the leaves,
    And the woods echo to the reapers' song:
Come when the splendid fullness of the moon
Looks down upon the rows of golden sheaves
    And reap thy Harvest; we have waited long.

Magdalen College, Oxford   OSCAR WILDE[1]
Proof to be sent to 1 Merrion Square North, Dublin.

To William Ward
MS. Magdalen

[*Postmark 19 July 1877*]   *1 Merrion Square North*

Dear old Boy, I hear you are back: did you get my telegram at the Lord Warden?[2] Do write and tell me about the Turks. I like their attitude towards life very much, though it seems strange that the descendants of the wild Arabs should be the Sybarites of our day.

I sent you two mags, to Frenchay: one with a memoir of Keats, the other religious.[3]

Do you remember our delightful visit to Keats's grave, and Dunskie's disgust. Poor Dunskie: I know he looks on me as a renegade; still I have suffered very much for my Roman fever in mind and *pocket* and happiness.

I am going down to Connemara for a month or more next week to try and read. I have not opened a book yet, I have been so bothered with business and other matters. I shall be quite alone. Will you come? I will give you fishing and scenery—and bring your books—*and some note-books for me*. I am in despair about "Greats."

It is roughing it, you know, but you will have
(1) bed
(2) table and chair
(3) knife and fork
(4) fishing
(5) scenery—sunsets—bathing—heather—mountains—lakes
(6) whisky and salmon to eat. Write and say when you can come, and also send me please *immediately* the name and address of Miss Fletcher whom I rode with at Rome, and of her stepfather. I have never sent her some articles of Pater's I promised her.[4]

---

[1] No poem of Wilde's ever appeared in *Good Words*. For "Easter Day" see note 1, p. 39. The second sonnet first appeared, revised, in *Lyra Hibernica Sacra* (1878), and then in *Poems* (1881).

[2] The hotel at Dover.

[3] Probably the sonnet, "Written during Holy Week," which appeared in the *Illustrated Monitor* for July 1876. Reprinted, with revisions, in *Poems* (1881).

[4] Julia Constance Fletcher (1858–1938) wrote six novels and a number of plays under the name George Fleming, including a dramatisation of Kipling's *The Light that Failed* (1903). Wilde had met her in Rome in the spring. He dedicated his

I want you to read my article on the Grosvenor Gallery in the *Dublin University Magazine* of July—my first art-essay.

I have had such delightful letters from many of the painters, and from Pater *such sympathetic praise*. I must send you his letter: or rather do so, but return it in *registered letter* by next post: don't forget. Ever yours

OSCAR

After all I can't trust my letter from Pater to the mercies of the postman, but I send you a copy:

Dear Mr Wilde, Accept my best thanks for the magazine and your letter. Your excellent article on the Grosvenor Gallery I read with very great

---

prize-winning Newdigate poem *Ravenna* to her in 1878. One of the minor characters in her novel *Mirage* (3 vols, 1877) may well have been based on Wilde. Claude Davenant, a young Oxford poet, aesthete and lover of the paganism of Greece, had a "face that was almost an anachronism. It was like one of Holbein's portraits; a pale, large-featured, individual; a peculiar, an interesting countenance, of singularly mild yet ardent expression. Mr Davenant was very young—probably not more than one or two and twenty; but he looked younger. He wore his hair rather long, thrown back, and clustering about his neck like the hair of a mediaeval saint. He spoke with rapidity, in a low voice, with peculiarly distinct enunciation; he spoke like a man who made a study of expression. He listened like one accustomed to speak."

Here he is in poetical mood:

"I wrote some verses for your fan, for your Japanese fan, the other day," he said dreamily; and after a moment, and as no one answered, he began to repeat himself, and in a low and singularly well modulated voice:

"A flowery fan for a white flower hand
(*White cranes flying across the moon*)—
A breath of wind from a windless land—
A breath in the breathless noon.

Flowers that blossom—a wind that blows
(*White cranes sailing across the sky*)—
A sigh for the light love, the love that goes,
A flower for the loves that die!"

"Very pretty," said Fanny, as he finished, "very pretty indeed. But I'm afraid you will think me sadly stupid for asking, and indeed it is hardly a fair question to ask, but what did you intend it to mean, Mr Davenant?"

"Ah, but I never explain things," said Davenant, in his most languid tone.

And on brothers-in-law:

"I don't object to mine particularly," said Davenant; "to be sure I don't see much of him. Their house is pure Elizabethan, and they have furnished it with Louis Quinze chairs—those gilt things, with legs, don't you know. I'm sorry, for I was very fond of my sister. . . . Still I do go down there every autumn for a few days, to shoot. Last year I shot the dog," he added mildly.

A copy of *Mirage* was among the books sold at the enforced sale of Wilde's belongings in 1895.

Walter Horatio Pater (1839–94), Fellow and Tutor of Brasenose College, had published his first book, *Studies in the History of the Renaissance*, in 1873. The book's six-page "Conclusion," a presentation of Epicureanism, caused such a stir that Pater omitted it from the second edition (1877). During 1876 he had published three essays: "Demeter and Persephone" and "A Study of Dionysus" in the *Fortnightly Review*, and "Romanticism" in *Macmillan's Magazine*.

46

pleasure: it makes me much wish to make your acquaintance, and I hope you will give me an early call on your return to Oxford.

I should much like to talk over some of the points with you, though on the whole I think your criticisms very just, and they are certainly very pleasantly expressed. The article shows that you possess some beautiful, and, for your age, quite exceptionally cultivated tastes: and a considerable knowledge too of many beautiful things. I hope you will write a great deal in time to come. Very truly yours   Walter Pater.[1]

You won't think me snobbish for sending you this? After all, it *is* something to be honestly proud of.   O. F. W.

To Reginald Harding

MS. Hyde (H. M.)

[*August 1877*]   *Illaunroe Lodge, Lough Fee*

My dear Kitten, So glad to hear from you again. I have been here fishing for the last three weeks. Jack Barrow and Dick Trench[2] are staying with me, so I find myself far from lonely, which is unfortunate as far as reading goes.

The fishing has not been so good as usual. I only got one salmon, about 7½ lbs. The sea-trout however are very plentiful; we get a steady average of over four a day and lots of brown trout, so it is not difficult to amuse oneself and as no fish are going in any of the neighbouring lakes I am fairly pleased. I have become an awful misanthrope however: you won't know me next term.

I had two jolly letters yesterday, one from Bouncer who is quill-driving or going to: the other from Dunskie who is a Captain now, he says.[3] Did I tell you of my wonderful letter from Pater of Brasenose about my "Grosvenor Gallery," which I am glad by the bye you like. Pater gives me great praise, so I am vainer than usual.

One week more of this delightful, heathery, mountainous, lake-filled region! Teeming with hares and trout! Then to Longford for the partridge, then home.

Love to Puss. Yours   OSCAR

Write to me at the Square.

---

[1] This letter (MS. Texas) is headed "Bradmore Road. Oxford. July 14." Wilde's transcription is correct except that in line 6 "criticisms . . . they are" should be "criticism . . . it is," in line 7 "The article" should be "It," and in line 9 "too" should be "also".

[2] Possibly Richard John le Poer Trench (b. 1843), son of the Rev. John Trench.

[3] Hunter-Blair had become a Captain in Prince Albert's Royal Ayrshire Militia in 1876.

To William Ward

MS. Magdalen

[*August 1877*]   *Illaunroe Lodge*

My dear Bouncer, So very glad to hear from you at last: I was afraid that you were still seedy.

I need not say how disappointed I was that you could not come and see this part of the world. I have two fellows staying with me, Dick Trench and Jack Barrow, who took a lodge near here for July and came to stay with me about three weeks ago. They are both capital fellows, indeed Dick Trench is I think my oldest friend, but I don't do any reading someway and pass my evenings in "Pool, Ecarté and Potheen Punch." I wish you had come; one requires sympathy to read.

I am however in the midst of two articles, one on Greece, the other on Art, which keep me thinking if not writing. But of Greats work I have done nothing. After all there are more profitable studies, I suppose, than the Greats course: still I would like a good Class awfully and want you to lend me your notes on Philosophy: I know your style, and really it would be a *very great advantage* for me to have them—Ethics, Politics (*Republic*) and general Philosophy. Can you do this for me? If you could send them to me in Dublin? Or at least to Oxford next term? And also *give me advice* —a thing I can't stand from my elders because it's like preaching, but I think I would like some from you "who have passed through the fire."

The weather is fair but not good for fishing. I have only got one salmon but our "bag" yesterday of "twelve white trout and twenty brown" was not bad. I have also had capital hare-shooting, but mountain-climbing is not my *forte*.

I heard, by the same post which brought me your letter, from Miss Fletcher, who is still in the Tyrol. She sends her best wishes to you of course, and writes as cleverly as she talks: I am much attracted by her in every way.

Please give my very best wishes to your sister on her approaching marriage. I remember Mr St John's *window* very well, and will hope to have the pleasure of knowing him some day.[1] He must be a very cultured artist. Will the wedding be soon? *What* form you *will* be in! Ever yours

OSCAR WILDE

I am going to Longford on Friday to shoot. Write me at Clonfin House, Granard, Co. Longford.

To William Ward

MS. Magdalen

Monday [*Autumn 1877*]   *Magdalen College*

My dear Bouncer, I hope you will come up soon: I am reading hard for a Fourth in Greats. (How are the mighty fallen!!)

---

[1] Ward's sister Gertrude Mary married the Rev. Harris Fleming St John of Dinmore Manor, Herefordshire.

I never remembered your kindness in lending me £5 in Rome till I met Grissell[1] the other day (Idea Association). I hope you don't think me very careless. Please cash enclosed cheque, if your bankers think the name of Wilde still valid for £5.

How much do I owe you for the Greek rugs? I hope you will bring them with you. Yours ever   OSCAR WILDE

Dunskie talks of coming up on Saturday.

To John T. Gilbert [2]

Sunday [30 December 1877]   *1 Merrion Square North*

Dear Mr Gilbert, In the *Saunders* of yesterday you will find a short article by me on the unfortunate author of *Irish Crosses*. I have put forward your point about the Cunningham Bequest as strongly as I could without being rude. I have just suggested it. I hope that the Academy will do something for this very learned and clever artist.[3]

Pray offer Miss Gilbert my best wishes for the New Year, and accept them yourself, from yours very truly   OSCAR WILDE

To William Ward

MS. Magdalen

[? March 1878]   *1 Merrion Square North*

My dear Willie, I am very sorry I cannot come down for your Ball, but I only go back to Oxford tomorrow, and much as I would like it I would not like to ask for leave, and indeed it would not be fair to Milner.[4] It is

---

[1] Hartwell de la Garde Grissell (1839–1907) had been a Chamberlain of Honour to the Pope since 1869. Wilde had met him in Rome.

[2] Irish historian and archivist (1828–98), Vice-President of the Royal Irish Academy, Secretary of the Public Record Office of Ireland. He was a friend of Sir William Wilde, who shared his antiquarian interests. The text of this letter is taken from *The Life of Sir John T. Gilbert* by his widow (1905).

[3] On 29 December 1877 the Dublin paper *Saunders's News-Letter* published an anonymous article headed "Mr Henry O'Neill, Artist." It described the artist's age and poverty; praised his book *The Sculptured Crosses of Ancient Ireland*, "which must always rank among the very first productions of modern Irish art;" told how "Mr Ruskin, whose flawless and exquisite taste is so well known, paid as much as fifty guineas some years ago for a small collection of his [O'Neill's] drawings;" and suggested that the Royal Irish Academy should give him £200 from the Cunningham Fund at their disposal. The article is not listed by Mason, and its authorship was not mentioned in any of the Wilde literature, until Mr Owen Dudley Edwards reprinted it with a commentary in the *Irish Book*, vol. 1, no. 1 (Spring 1959).

[4] Alfred Milner (1854–1925), afterwards famous as statesman and proconsul, was a friend of Wilde at Oxford, where he was a Balliol undergraduate 1872–76 and a Fellow of New College 1877–81. Created Baron 1901, Viscount 1902.

a great disappointment to me but I don't think I would be acting wisely in going away from Oxford after I got leave to come up and read.[1]

I hope that I will be able to come and see you in the summer, after I get my *Fourth*.

I find really that I can't read: I have too much to think about. Pray express to your mother how sorry I am to miss your kind invitation. And believe me very truly yours   OSCAR

To Reginald Harding
MS. Hyde (H. M.)

Tuesday [? *March 1878*]   *Magdalen College*

My dear Kitten, Many thanks for your kind note. I have a childish longing for some flowers—I don't care what—only *not* wallflowers. If you have any spare moments and can get me a few you will be doing as benevolent an action as giving groundsel to a starving canary would be!

I am very wretched and ill and as soon as possible I am to be sent away somewhere out of Oxford, so my Greats work has collapsed finally for ever.

Only that Tuckwell[2] and William are awfully kind to me I should jump into the muddy Cherwell. Ever yours   OSCAR

Could you steal a branch of that lovely red blossoming tree outside the new buildings for me? I am sick at heart for want of some freshness and beauty in life.

To Reginald Harding
MS. Hyde (H. M.)

[? *March 1878*]   *Magdalen College*

Dear Kitten, If there is anything that could console me for being ill it is your charming basket of flowers and delightful letter.

The roses have quite given me a sense of the swift beauty and light of the spring: they are most exquisite. And I heard your light quick step down the passage this morning and am awfully obliged for your theft of the pink and white blossoms.

I can bury my face in them and dream how nice it would be to be out again.

You are the nicest of kittens. Ever yours   OSCAR

[1] Wilde spent some or all of the Easter vacation of 1878 reading at Magdalen.
[2] Perhaps the Rev. Lewis Stacey Tuckwell, Chaplain and Precentor at Magdalen 1866–77.

To Florence Balcombe
MS. Clark

[April 1878]   *Royal Bath Hotel, Bournemouth*

My dear Florrie, I send you a line to wish you a pleasant Easter.[1] A year ago I was in Athens and you sent me I remember a little Easter card—over so many miles of land and sea—to show me you had not forgotten me.

I have been greatly disappointed in not being able to come over, but I could only spare four days and as I was not feeling well came down here to try and get some ozone. The weather is delightful and if I had not a good memory of the past I would be very happy.

I have a delightful friend (a *new* friend) with me and have written *one* sonnet, so am not so misanthropic as usual. I hope you are all well especially Gracie: Willie's success in the North is most encouraging.[2]

I send you an account of Bournemouth. Ever yours   OSCAR

To Marian Willett[3]
MS. Hunt

Monday, 13 May [1878]   *Magdalen College*

Dear Miss Willett, I send you the magazine you kindly wished to see. I have tried, in the metre as well as the words, to mirror some of the swiftness and grace of the springtime.[4]

And though I know but too well that in this, like in everything that I do, I have failed, yet after all Nature lies out of the reach of even the greatest masters of song. She cannot be described, she can only be worshipped: and there is more perfection of beauty, it seems to me, in a single white narcissus of the meadow than in all the choruses of Euripides, or even in the *Endymion* of Keats himself.

If you care to keep the magazine it will give me great pleasure—still more if my verses can recall to you any of the loveliness of that time of the year, which, though I have failed to describe, I at least have loved. Believe me, truly yours   OSCAR WILDE

---

[1] In 1878 Easter Sunday was on April 21.

[2] Gracie and Willie were Florence's sister and brother. Gracie married the novelist Frankfort Moore (1855–1931).

[3] Marian Fitzgerald Willett (1853–1916) was living in Oxford with her stepfather, the Rev. James Legge (1815–97), who had been appointed first Professor of Chinese in 1876. An undergraduate, Bertram Hunt (1856–95), fell in love with her in the train, but could find no means of being introduced to her until one day on the towpath he saw her talking to Wilde, who gave a tea-party for them both at Magdalen. They were married at Oxford in 1880. Hunt became a doctor and helped to discover the anti-diphtheria serum. Wilde sent Miss Willett an inscribed copy of *Ravenna*.

[4] In his poem "Magdalen Walks," which had appeared in the *Irish Monthly* of April 1878.

To Marian Willett

MS. Hunt

Thursday [? *May–June 1878*]   *Magdalen College*

Dear Miss Willett, I have much pleasure in sending you the photograph of *Hope*, which you were kind enough to accept yesterday.[1]

I am particularly pleased at *your* admiring it so much, as I myself think it the most entirely beautiful out of all my collection.

It seems to me to be full of infinite pathos and love, and to be a vision of what that hope is which comes "to those that sit in darkness."[2]

In so many of Burne-Jones's pictures we have merely the pagan worship of beauty: but in this one I seem to see more humanity and sympathy than in all the others.

If you have half the pleasure in receiving it that I have in offering it to you, I will be well repaid for any trouble I have had. Believe me, truly yours   OSCAR WILDE

To the Rev. Matthew Russell, S.J.

TS. Holland

[*June 1878*]   *Magdalen College*

My dear Sir, I am sure you will excuse my not thanking you before for verses which in their depth and their beauty are well worthy of the great mystery of your Church, but my recent success has quite plunged me in business of all kinds, and I have had no time to myself.[3]

I wish I could thank you personally. Why do we never meet? I would like to know you very much. Truly yours   OSCAR WILDE

To William Ward

MS. Magdalen

Thursday [? *11 July 1878*]   *St Stephen's Club, Westminster*

Dear Boy, Why don't you write to me? I don't know what has become of you.

As for me I am ruined. The law suit[4] is going against me and I am afraid I will have to pay costs, which means leaving Oxford and doing some horrid work to earn bread. The world is too much for me.

[1] *Spes*, a water-colour by Edward Burne-Jones (1833–98), companion-piece to *Temperantia* and *Fides*, was first shown at the opening of the Grosvenor Gallery in 1877.   [2] *Isaiah*, xlii, 7, and *Luke*, i, 79.

[3] The award of the Newdigate Prize to Wilde's poem *Ravenna* was announced on 10 June 1878, and its author recited parts of it before the Vice-Chancellor and other notables in the Sheldonian Theatre on 26 June. It was published on that day as a pamphlet by Thomas Shrimpton & Son of Oxford, price 1*s*. 6*d*.

[4] This case, which concerned some house property that Wilde had inherited from his father, was heard in Dublin on 8, 11 and 12 July 1878.

However, I have seen Greece and had some golden days of youth. I go back to Oxford immediately for *viva voce* and then think of rowing up the river to town with Frank Miles. Will you come? Yours   OSCAR

To William Ward
MS. Magdalen

[*Circa 20 July 1878*]   *Magdalen College*

My dear old Boy, You are the best of fellows to telegraph your congratulations: there were none I valued more.[1] It is too delightful altogether this display of fireworks at the end of my career. I cannot understand my First except for the essays which I was fairly good in. I got a very complimentary *viva voce*.

The dons are "astonied" beyond words—the Bad Boy doing so well in the end! They made me stay up for the Gaudy and said nice things about me. I am on the best terms with everyone including *Allen!* who I think is remorseful of his treatment of me.

Then I rowed to Pangbourne with Frank Miles in a birchbark canoe! and shot rapids and did wonders everywhere—it was delightful.

I cannot, I am afraid, yacht with you. I am so troubled about my law suit, which I have won but find my own costs heavy, though I was allowed them.[2] I have to be in Ireland.

Dear old boy, I wish I could see you again. Ever yours   OSCAR

To the Rev. Matthew Russell, S.J.
TS. Holland

[? *September 1878*]   *Illaunroe Lodge, Connemara*

Dear Father Russell, Thanks for the magazine. With regard to the Newdigate, if you look in the *Oxford Calendar* you will find the whole account of it. The subject is given out at the June Encaenia and is the same for all. There is besides the κῦδος a prize of twenty guineas. It was originally limited to fifty lines, and the subject used to be necessarily taken from some *classical* subject, either Greek or Latin, and generally a work of art. The metre is heroic couplets, but as you have seen perhaps from my poem, of late years laxity is allowed from the horrid Popeian jingle of regular heroics, and *now* the subject may be taken from any country or time and there is no limit to the length. I rather think it is very much older than 1841. There is a picture of the Founder hanging in the dining hall of University College, Oxford, which as well as I remember is very old. Besides I have an idea that Ruskin and Dean Stanley got it. You

[1] Wilde's First in Greats was announced on 19 July 1878 and listed in *The Times* on 20 July.
[2] Judgment in the lawsuit was given on 17 July.

might by looking at the *Oxford Calendar* get all information and make your article the *locus classicus* for the History of the Newdigate Prize.[1]

There was a strange coincidence about my getting it. On the 31st of March 1877 (long before the subject was given out) I entered Ravenna on my way to Greece, and on 31st March 1878 I had to hand my poem in. It is quite the blue ribbon of the Varsity and my college presented me with a marble bust of the "young Augustus" which had been bequeathed by an old Fellow of Magdalen, Dr Daubeny,[2] to the first undergraduate who should get the Newdigate.

I am resting here in the mountains—great peace and quiet everywhere—and hope to send you a sonnet as the result. Believe me, very truly yours

OSCAR WILDE

To Florence Balcombe

MS. Clark

Monday night [late 1878][3]   *1 Merrion Square North*

Dear Florrie, As I shall be going back to England, probably for good, in a few days, I should like to bring with me the little gold cross I gave you one Christmas morning long ago.

I need hardly say that I would not ask it from you if it was anything you valued, but worthless though the trinket be, to me it serves as a memory of two sweet years—the sweetest of all the years of my youth—and I should like to have it always with me. If you would care to give it to me yourself I could meet you any time on Wednesday, or you might hand it to Phil,[4] whom I am going to meet that afternoon.

Though you have not thought it worth while to let me know of your marriage, still I cannot leave Ireland without sending you my wishes that you may be happy; whatever happens I at least cannot be indifferent to your welfare: the currents of our lives flowed too long beside one another for that.

We stand apart now, but the little cross will serve to remind me of the bygone days, and though we shall never meet again, after I leave Ireland, still I shall always remember you at prayer. Adieu and God bless you.

OSCAR

[1] Father Matthew Russell may be presumed to have written the article "An Irish Winner of the Newdigate" which appeared anonymously in the *Irish Monthly* for November 1878. The Prize, founded by Sir Roger Newdigate, antiquary (1719–1806), was first awarded in 1806. Arthur Penrhyn Stanley (1815–81) won it in 1837 and Ruskin in 1839.

[2] Charles Giles Bridle Daubeny, F.R.S. (1795–1867), Fellow of Magdalen 1815, was consecutively Professor of Chemistry, Botany and Rural Economy at Oxford.

[3] Florence Balcombe was married on 4 December 1878 at St Anne's Church, Dublin, to Bram Stoker (1847–1912), a young Irish civil servant with literary and dramatic interests. He had done much to promote Irving's triumphal visit to Dublin two years earlier, and in October 1878 Irving appointed him business manager of the Lyceum Theatre, the management of which Irving had just taken over from Mrs Bateman. Stoker's horrific novel *Dracula* was published in 1897.

[4] Florence's sister Philippa (see p. 166), who did not marry till 1881.

To Florence Balcombe

MS. Clark

[*Late 1878*]   *1 Merrion Square North*

Dear Florence, I could not come to Harcourt Street:[1] it would be painful
for both of us: but if you would care to see me for the last time I will go
out to the Crescent on Friday at two o'clock. Perhaps it would be better
for us both if we saw one another once more.

Send me a line and I will be there. Very truly yours   OSCAR WILDE

I will send you back your letters when I go to Oxford. The enclosed scrap
I used to carry with me: it was written eighteen months ago: how strange
and out of tune it all reads now.

To Florence Balcombe

MS. Clark

Thursday [*late 1878*]   *1 Merrion Square North*

Dear Florence, As you expressed a wish to see me I thought that *your
mother's house* would be the only suitable place, and that we should part
where we first met. As for my calling at Harcourt Street, you know, my
dear Florence, that such a thing is quite out of the question: it would have
been unfair to you, and me, and to the man you are going to marry, had
we met anywhere else but under your mother's roof, and with your mother's
sanction. I am sure that you will see this yourself on reflection; as a man
of honour I could not have met you except with the full sanction of your
parents and in their house.

As regards the cross, there is nothing "exceptional" in the trinket except
the fact of my name being on it, which of course would have prevented
you from wearing it ever, and I am not foolish enough to imagine that you
care now for any memento of me. It would have been impossible for you
to keep it.

I am sorry that you should appear to think, from your postscript, that
I desired any clandestine "*meeting*:" after all, I find you know me very
little.

Goodbye, and believe me yours very truly   OSCAR WILDE

---

[1] The house there of Bram Stoker's brother Thornley (1845–1912), who became
a successful surgeon and was knighted in 1895.

PART TWO

LONDON I
1879-81

London I: 1879-81

After Wilde's academic triumphs in the summer of 1878 Magdalen renewed his Demyship for a further (fifth) year. On 22 November he satisfied the examiners in the Rudiments of Religion, and on 28 November took his degree as Bachelor of Arts. It is not known how much of the year he spent in Oxford—presumably in lodgings, since he no longer had rooms in college—but it seems probable that he was mostly in London, learning to charm Society with his conversation and developing his aesthetic tastes. In the records of Messrs Macmillan there is a copy of a letter of 24 March 1879 from George Macmillan to Wilde at Oxford, which discusses the possibility of Wilde's translating a selection from Herodotus for the firm, as well as the *Hercules* or the *Phoenissae* of Euripides. Both these projects, which seem to have originated with Wilde, came to nothing.

To Claude Montefiore[1]

MS. Montefiore

September 1879   *St Stephen's Club, Westminster*

My dear Montefiore, I am distressed beyond words to hear the fearful news from America: I have not yet recovered from the shock. I had the greatest love and admiration for Leonard as I am sure you know. We were in every way great friends. His death is a terrible loss to me, but what it must be to you all I hardly dare think. I know how you all loved him, and can only picture a desolate and sorrowful household.

Will you assure your people of my deepest sympathy in their terrible affliction.

If you are in town I should like to see you so much, to learn all that you can tell me about Leonard. I trust your mother is bearing up, though I know how crushing the blow must be.

I hardly can write about it, for I am in the deepest sorrow at the death of one whom I was always proud to call my friend.

With deepest sympathy, believe me, very truly yours   OSCAR WILDE

[1] Writer of books on biblical and Judaistic subjects (1858–1938). He had been a pupil of Jowett at Balliol, where his elder brother Leonard was a contemporary of Wilde's. Leonard died in America in September 1879, aged twenty-six.

To Charlotte Montefiore[1]
MS. Philips

[*September 1879*]   *St Stephen's Club*

I am so glad you are coming to town. I want to see you, though the memories you will bring with you will be most bitter. Yet often I think when a friend dies those who are left become very close to one another, just as when an oak falls in the forest the other trees reach out and join branches over the vacant place.

Alfred Milner has been with me all the morning. We talked together of Leonard—the first real talk I have had yet about him. I think we both loved him well. He tells me you are so brave. I knew you would be—it is what Leonard would have expected of you. You hold your mother's and your father's life so much now in your hands: while you bear up there will be left still some comfort for their hearts.

If I called in on Wednesday evening would you see me? But fix your own day. Your affectionate friend   OSCAR WILDE

To Helena Sickert[2]
TS. Clark

[*2 October 1879*]   *Thames House, 13 Salisbury Street*[3]

Dear Miss Nellie, Though you are determined to go to Cambridge, I hope you will accept this volume of poems by a purely *Oxford* poet. I am sure you know Matthew Arnold already but still I have marked just a few of the things I like best in the collection, in the hope that we may agree about them. "Sohrab and Rustum" is a wonderfully stately epic, full of the spirit of Homer, and "Thyrsis" and "The Scholar Gipsy" are exquisite

[1] Sister of Leonard and Claude (1855–1933). She married (1884) Lewis M'Iver (1846–1920), M.P. for Torquay 1885–86, for Edinburgh, W., 1895–1909, made a Baronet 1896. Lady M'Iver destroyed her other letters from Wilde, but told her son-in-law that Wilde once proposed marriage to her; she was much attached to him but not in love, so she refused him; that evening Wilde sent her a note: "Charlotte, I am so sorry about your decision. With your money and my brain we could have gone so far." Their friendship continued until 1895.

[2] Helena Maria Sickert (1864–1939), writer, lecturer and untiring advocate of women's rights. Younger sister of W. R. Sickert (see note 4, p. 62). She went up to Girton College, Cambridge, in 1882 and took a degree in Moral Science. In 1888 she married F. T. Swanwick, and always wrote as H. M. Swanwick. She was a prominent suffragist, the first president of the Women's International League (British Section) and was made C.H. in 1931. In her autobiography *I Have been Young* (1935) she described Wilde's friendship with her family: "He was the first of our friends to call me Miss Nellie . . . He discussed books with me and gave me my first volume of poetry, *Selected Poems of Matthew Arnold*, marking his favourites." She says it was inscribed "Nellie Sickert from her friend Oscar Wilde. 2 October 1879."

[3] Wilde and Frank Miles shared rooms at this address, off the Strand, till August 1880. I have been unable to discover when they went there.

idylls, as artistic as "Lycidas" or "Adonais:" but indeed I think all is good in it, and I hope you will accept it, *φιλίας μνημόσυνον*,[1] from your sincere friend   OSCAR WILDE

To Oscar Browning[2]
MS. Cortés

[? *November 1879*]   St Stephen's Club

Dear Mr Browning, I would have been only too happy to have the opportunity of doing any commission for you had I been in town, but I have been away for a week with friends. I shall see about your ties this afternoon. I am perhaps a better judge of neckties than of bibles, but I shall not fail to enquire about the latter.

Nothing would please me more than a visit to you: when are your festivities? Very truly yours   OSCAR WILDE

To Reginald Harding
MS. Hyde (H. M.)

[*28 November 1879*]   St Stephen's Club

Dear Reggie, I was only in Cambridge for the night with Oscar Browning (I wish he was *not* called Oscar) and left the next morning for the Hicks-Beach's in Hampshire, to kill time and pheasants and the *ennui* of not having set the world quite on fire as yet.

I will come some day and stay with you, though your letters are rather what boys call "Philippic."

I am going to night with *Ruskin* to see Irving as Shylock,[3] and afterwards to the *Millais* Ball.[4] How odd it is. Dear Reg, ever yours   OSCAR

Remember me to Tom Peyton.

[1] "As a memento of friendship." For Wilde's previous use of this phrase see p. 29.

[2] 1837–1923. Eton master 1860–75, Cambridge don and "character" 1876–1909 (George Curzon, Arthur Balfour and Austen Chamberlain were all his pupils). Author of many books, mainly historical. The date of this letter is conjectural, but Wilde had already stayed with Browning by 28 November, and the festivities may refer to the Founder's Feast at King's College on 6 December.

[3] Irving's production of *The Merchant of Venice* opened at the Lyceum on 1 November 1879. It is clear from Ruskin's letter to Irving of 30 November (quoted in Laurence Irving's *Henry Irving*, p. 346) that he first saw the production on the previous Friday (28 November) and this was perhaps when Wilde met Irving for the first time. "Portia," his sonnet to Ellen Terry, appeared in the *World* on 14 January 1880, and he was a guest at the Lyceum banquet to celebrate the hundredth performance on 14 February.

[4] On 28 November 1879 Millais's daughter Effie married Captain James of the Scots Greys. "Wisely and thoughtfully," according to *Vanity Fair* of 6 December, "Mr and Mrs Millais abstained from giving that most tiresome of all things, a wedding breakfast; they did much better by giving in its stead a ball in the evening . . . There were notable artists (with their wives in Grosvenor Gallery dresses), notable actors and actresses and notable persons of the smarter sort, all met together like a happy family." For Millais see note 2, p. 110.

To Harold Boulton[1]

23 December 1879   *Thames House*

My dear Harold, I very often have beautiful people to tea, and will always
be very glad to see you and introduce you to them. Any night you like to
go to the theatre I will give you a bed with great pleasure in this untidy
and romantic house.   OSCAR WILDE

To Frederick Locker[2]
MS. Texas

[? *23 December 1879*]   *13 Salisbury Street*

Dear Mr Locker, Will you come and see Frank Miles's picture which got
the Turner silver medal this year,[3] and have some "Tea and Beauties" at
3.30 tomorrow, when I shall also hope to have the pleasure of introducing
you to my mother Lady Wilde. Believe me truly yours   OSCAR WILDE

Tomorrow is Wednesday.

To Helena Sickert
TS. Clark

[? *23 December 1879*]   *13 Salisbury Street*

Dear Miss Nellie, I am really so annoyed about missing my skating lesson
with you, that I will think you have not forgiven me if you, and Walter,[4]
do not come to tea tomorrow, Wednesday, at 4.30, to see Frank Miles's
Turner medal picture and, I hope, some beautiful people.

Some future day I hope you will teach me skating, and a great many
other things. Believe me, your sincere friend   OSCAR WILDE

To Harold Boulton
MS. Clark

[? *Late December 1879*]   *St Stephen's Club*

Dear Harold, I was very sorry you did not come to tea as I could have
introduced you to some very beautiful people. Mrs Langtry[5] and Lady

---

[1] Harold Edwin Boulton (1859–1935). Undergraduate (1878–81) at Balliol College, Oxford, where he edited *Waifs and Strays* and Wilde probably met him. (A
copy of *Ravenna*, 1878, inscribed to him by Wilde, came up at the Kern sale, 1929.)
Editor of songs and author of song-lyrics, including "The Skye Boat Song" (1884).
Became a director of many charitable and artistic institutions. Succeeded his father
as second Baronet 1918. The text of this incomplete letter is taken from the
American Art Association catalogue, 5 and 6 November 1923.

[2] Civil servant, poet, anthologist and collector (1821–95). Published *London
Lyrics* (1857) and edited *Lyra Elegantiarum* (1867). Created the Rowfant Library.
In 1885 he added his second wife's surname Lampson to his own.

[3] This special medal (for a painting of an Ocean Coast) was presented to Miles
by the Royal Academy on 10 December 1879. It was extra to the annual Turner
Gold Medal. [4] Walter Richard Sickert (1860–1942), the painter. [5] See note 3, p. 65.

Florence Balcombe

Water-colour by Oscar Wilde
Inscribed on mount: "For Florrie. September 1876. View from Moytura House.
Oscar F. Wilde."

Mrs Bernard Beere

Helena Modjeska

Mary Anderson

Lily Langtry by Frank Miles

Lonsdale[1] and a lot of clever beings who were at tea with me: you ought to study the Choice of Hercules, though it *was* written by a sophist.[2]

I shall be at home tomorrow at four o'clock. Miss Graham, a beautiful creature, is coming to tea; if you can come to town I shall be glad to see you. Any Saturday you are in London I hope you will call and see my mother who is always at home from five to seven on Saturday. She is always glad to see my friends, and usually some good literary and artistic people take tea with her. Her address is Lady Wilde, 1 Ovington Square, S. Kensington.

I am so uncertain about my winter that I fear I must decline your kind invitation. It is better to do so than to disappoint you at the last as I might have to do. Ever yours   OSCAR

To Oscar Browning [3]

[? *January–February 1880*]

Will you do me a good service, and write me a testimonial of what you think my ability for a position in the Education Office or School Inspectorship would be? Rents being as extinct in Ireland as the dodo or moly, I want to get a position with an assured income, and any Education work would be very congenial to me, and I have here good opportunity of studying the systems of France and Germany. I think your name would carry a good deal of weight with it in a matter of this kind. The Duke of Richmond is the President of the Council in whose hands the appointments rest.[4]   OSCAR WILDE

To Oscar Browning [5]

[? *Mid-February 1880*]

Yes, I am twenty-five years old, and any testimonial from you will be very valuable. I saw Lord Houghton at Irving's supper.[6] He tells me the A.D.C. are having a great fête, but I don't think he is over pleased at Master Bobbie's devotion to the Drama.[7] Let me see you soon.

OSCAR WILDE

[1] See note 2, p. 65.

[2] The choice between Virtue and Pleasure, as recorded in the only surviving fable of Prodicus of Ceos (Xenophon's *Memorabilia*, II, i, 21–34).

[3] The text of this incomplete letter is taken from the American Art Association catalogue of 9 February 1927.

[4] The sixth Duke of Richmond (1818–1903) was President of the Council 1874–80.

[5] The text of this fragment is taken from the American Art Association catalogue of 9 February 1927.

[6] Probably that of 14 February 1880 (see note 3, p. 61), when Lord Houghton sat on Irving's right.

[7] Lord Houghton's son Robert Milnes (later Marquess of Crewe) was an undergraduate at Trinity College, Cambridge, 1874–79, and spent much time there in amateur acting. The Amateur Dramatic Club was started by F. C. Burnand and others in 1855.

To Mrs Alfred Hunt [1]

MS. Clark

[Postmark 1 March 1880]   13 Salisbury Street

Dear Mrs Hunt, I hope that you have not forgotten your promise to have
tea with me tomorrow (Tuesday) at five o'clock, and that your Violet—
the sweetest Violet in England I think her, though you must not tell her
so—will come too. I can hardly hope Mr Hunt will come, though I am
very anxious to introduce him to my mother who has so often heard of him.
Truly yours   OSCAR WILDE

To Norman Forbes-Robertson [2]

TS. Congress

[? Circa 16 March 1880][3]   St Stephen's Club

My dear Norman, I suppose you are engaged for Saturday and that there
is no chance of our going to the Boat Race together? If you have any
time do come and see me soon.

I don't know if I bored you the other night with my life and its troubles.
There seems something so sympathetic and gentle about your nature, and
you have been so charming whenever I have seen you, that I felt somehow
that although I knew you only a short time, yet that still I could talk to
you about things, which I only talk of to people whom I like—to those
whom I count my friends.

If you will let me count *you* as one of my friends, it would give a new
pleasure to my life.

I hope so much to see you again. Till I do, ever yours

OSCAR WILDE

[1] Margaret Raine (1831–1912), the original of Tennyson's "Margaret," married
the landscape painter Alfred William Hunt in 1861, and for many years they lived
at Tor Villas, Campden Hill. She was a voluminous and successful novelist under
her married name. Her daughter Violet Hunt (1862–1942), also the author of many
novels, wrote in her autobiography *The Flurried Years* (1926):

I remember Oscar, before America, when he was really still a slightly stuttering,
slightly lisping, long-limbed boy, sitting in the big arm-chair at Tor Villas, where
we lived then, lounging fatuously, tossing the long black lock on his forehead that
America swept away, and talking—talking—happening to talk about maps and
other things. We did—father, mother, Oscar and I—talk of anything we could
any of us lay a hand to; and this Sunday evening it was maps—the maps of the
Ancients that he had been seeing: Africa.
"Oh, Miss Violet," he exclaimed, drawing his breath through his teeth in a
sibilant whisper of intense appreciation, "think of a map drawn of a whole continent, and beside the names of an insignificant city or two a blank and: *Hic sunt
leones!* Miss Violet, let you and me go there."
"And get eaten by lions?" said I.

[2] 1859–1932. Younger brother of Johnston (see note 3, p. 87), acted under the
name Norman Forbes. He wrote several plays, including dramatisations of *The
Scarlet Letter* (1888) and *The Man in the Iron Mask* (1909).

[3] This letter may have been written in the spring of 1879, but 1880 seems
likelier. In that year the Oxford and Cambridge Boat Race was to have been rowed
on 20 March, but was postponed owing to dense fog.

To an Unidentified Correspondent

MS. Private

[*? Early 1880*]   *13 Salisbury Street*

Dear Sir, My Fishing Lodge is situated on Lough Fee near Leenane and the Killary Bay, and three miles from the sea: it is a small two-storied cottage, furnished in bachelor fashion for *three* persons, but would accommodate more. My servant, an excellent fisherman, and his wife, a good cook, are in charge of it. There are boats etc. belonging to the house.

The fishing extends over Lough Fee 2½ miles, Lough Muck 1 mile, River Calfin 2 miles, salmon and white trout.

A public car by which letters and provisions can be brought passes *every day* within one mile of the house. Leenane is 5 miles off, Westport 30 miles.

The rent is £40 for one month, £70 for two, £90 for season. Truly yours   OSCAR WILDE

To Genevieve Ward[1]

[*April–May 1880*]   *St Stephen's Club*

Dear Miss Ward, I suppose you are very busy with your rehearsals. If you are not too busy to stop and drink tea with a *great* admirer of yours, please come on Friday at half-past five to 13 Salisbury Street. The two beauties—Lady Lonsdale[2] and Mrs Langtry[3]—and Mamma, and a few

---

[1] Genevieve Teresa Ward (1838–1922), an American, began as an opera singer but lost her singing voice and became an actress. As a girl she was married in St Petersburg, almost at pistol-point, to a Russian Count, whom she never saw after the ceremony. She made her English début in 1873 as Lady Macbeth, which in 1878 she played in French in Paris. In August 1879 at the Lyceum she scored a great hit in *Forget-Me-Not* by Herman Merivale and F. D. Grove, which was revived at the Prince of Wales's Theatre in February 1880, and which she afterwards acted all over the world. In 1893–96 she appeared with Irving in *Henry VIII*, *Richard III* and Tennyson's *Becket*. Beerbohm Tree described her as "an old iron-clad." The text of this letter is taken from *Genevieve Ward* by Zadel Barnes Gustafson (1881).

[2] Constance Gladys (1859–1917), daughter of the first Baron Herbert of Lea and sister of the thirteenth Earl of Pembroke, married the fourth Earl of Lonsdale in 1878. After his death in 1882 she married Lord de Grey, who succeeded his father as second Marquess of Ripon in 1909. Wilde dedicated *A Woman of No Importance* to her.

[3] Emily Charlotte Le Breton (1852–1929), who came from Jersey and was considered the most beautiful woman in her generation, married in her teens Edward Langtry, an Irish widower of thirty. He brought her to London, where she quickly became a leading figure in Society and a friend of the Prince of Wales. She was painted by Whistler, Poynter, Watts, Burne-Jones, Leighton, and particularly Millais, whose portrait of her, called *The Jersey Lily*, was the origin of her nickname. Wilde's friend Frank Miles did many drawings of her. Wilde's poem to her, "The New Helen," appeared in *Time* for July 1879 and was reprinted, with revisions, in *Poems* (1881). In Mrs Langtry's copy of this book Wilde wrote: "To Helen, formerly of Troy, now of London." In 1899 she married Hugo Gerald de Bathe (1871–1940), who succeeded his father as fifth Baronet in 1907. Vincent O'Sullivan records Wilde as saying in 1899: "The three women I have most admired are Queen Victoria, Sarah Bernhardt, and Lily Langtry. I would have married any one of them with pleasure."

friends are coming. We are all looking forward to *L'Aventurière* so much: it will be a great era in our dramatic art.[1] Yours most sincerely

OSCAR WILDE

To Violet Fane[2]

MS. Clark

[*Postmark 28 April 1880*] *18 Pont Street, S.W.*[3]

Dear Mrs Singleton, Mrs Langtry has asked me to answer your nice letter, and to say that she is very ill, and not allowed to leave her room, and must put off her dinner—had indeed to put it off, as it was for last Sunday.

She would be very pleased if you would come and see her, either in the morning or afternoon, or let her know when you are coming, as her number of visitors is limited.

As she is tired, I am for the moment playing secretary.

I hope to find you at home some afternoon, and remain, truly yours

OSCAR WILDE

To Mrs Bancroft[4]

[*May 1880*] *St Stephen's Club*

Dear Mrs Bancroft, I am charmed with the photograph and with your

[1] During the run of her perennial *Forget-Me-Not* Genevieve Ward gave a performance in French of Emile Augier's *L'Aventurière* on 10 May 1880 at the Prince of Wales's Theatre. Two of the cast were French, the others (including Beerbohm Tree) English. The Prince and Princess of Wales were in the audience.

[2] Mary Montgomerie Lamb (1843–1905) married (1) in 1864 Henry Sydenham Singleton (d. 1893); (2) in 1894 the first Lord Currie (1834–1906), H.M. Ambassador in Constantinople 1893–98, in Rome 1898–1902. She wrote under the name Violet Fane, began publishing poems and essays in the 1870's and was the original of one of the characters in *The New Republic* (see note p. 21). Later she published novels and stories. There exists a copy of Wilde's *Poems* (1881) inscribed in his hand:

To V.F.
Through many loveless songless days
We have to seek the golden shrine,
But Venus taught you how to twine
Love's violets with Apollo's bays.
Oscar Wilde.

[3] Mrs Langtry's house. Besides acting as her amanuensis, Wilde also instructed and advised her on other matters, as this letter (MS. Holland) shows.

Sunday *Beaconsfield, Milehouse, Nr Plymouth*
Of course I'm longing to learn more Latin but we stay here till Wednesday night so I shan't be able to see my kind tutor before Thursday. Do come and see me on that afternoon about six if you can.

I called at Salisbury Street about an hour before you left. I wanted to ask you how I should go to a fancy ball here, but I chose a soft black Greek dress with a fringe of silver crescents and stars, and diamond ones in my hair and on my neck, and called it Queen of Night. I made it myself.

I want to write more but this horrid paper and pen prevent me so when we meet I will tell you more: (only don't tell Frank) LILLIE LANGTRY

[4] Marie Effie Wilton (1839–1921), English actress, married the actor-manager

kindness in sending it to me; it has given me more pleasure than any quill pen can possibly express, and will be a delightful souvenir of one whose brilliant genius I have always admired. Dramatic art in England owes you and your husband a great debt.

Since Tuesday I have had a feeling that I have never rightly appreciated the treasures hidden in a girls' school. I don't quite know what I shall do, but I think I must hold *you* responsible. Believe me, sincerely yours

OSCAR WILDE

To Mrs Alfred Hunt
MS. Clark

[*20 May 1880*] [1]   *St Stephen's Club*

Dear Mrs Hunt, I shall be *very glad* to come on Sunday evening.

How *could* you be too shy to ask me on Tuesday? I should have been delighted to stay: I always enjoy my evenings with you all so much: but you really must not write me such charming letters or I shall be coming a great deal too often.

I count it a very great privilege indeed to know anyone whose art I have always loved and admired so much as Mr Hunt's (though he *has* this terrible passion for barricades and revolutions!) and it is very nice of you to think of me as a friend—indeed I should like to be one. Believe me very sincerely yours   OSCAR WILDE

To the Printer of the World
MS. Clark

[*Postmark 19 August 1880*]   *Hurst Lodge, Twyford, Berks*

Mr Oscar Wilde requests that a proof of his poem "Ave Imperatrix" will be sent at once to him here.[2]

To Mrs Alfred Hunt
MS. Clark

25 August [*1880*]   *Tite Street, Chelsea*[3]

Dear Mrs Hunt, It was so good of you to take the trouble of sending me

---

Squire Bancroft (1841–1926) in 1867. They revived T. W. Robertson's comedy *School* at the Haymarket Theatre on 1 May 1880, with Johnston Forbes-Robertson and Marion Terry in the cast. Mrs Bancroft contributed an article on the Engadine to the first number of the *Woman's World* (November 1887). The text of this letter is taken from *The Bancrofts* (1909).

[1] So dated by recipient.

[2] "Ave Imperatrix," described as "A Poem on England," appeared in the *World* on 25 August 1880. It was reprinted with revisions and two additional stanzas, in *Poems* (1881).

[3] Wilde and Frank Miles had recently moved into rooms at No 1 Tite Street. This

such a long account of your little village.[1] I have been hoping to go every week, but have had so many engagements that it has been out of my power; which, believe me, is no small disappointment. I should like so much to be with you all.

And now I am trying to settle a new house, where Mr Miles and I are going to live. The address is *horrid* but the house very pretty. It is much nearer you than my old house, so I hope we shall often, if you let me, have "dishes of tea" at one another's houses.

I have broken a promise shamefully to Miss Violet about a poem I promised to send her. My only excuse is that nowadays the selection of colours and furniture has quite taken the place of the cases of conscience of the middle ages, and usually involves quite as much remorse. However I send her one I have just published. I hope she will see some beauty in it, and that your wonderful husband's wonderful radicalism will be appeased by my first attempt at political prophecy, which occurs in the last verse.[2] If she will send me a little line to say what she thinks of it, it will give me such pleasure.

I hope she has been writing herself. After all, the Muses are as often to be met with in our English fields as they ever were by Castaly, or Helicon, though I have always in my heart thought that the simultaneous appearance of *nine* (*unmarried*) sisters at a time must have been a little embarrassing.

Please remember me *most* kindly to your husband, and all yours, and believe me very truly yours   OSCAR WILDE

To G. F. Watts [3]

MS. Watts

[*August–September 1880*]   *1 Tite Street*

Dear Mr Watts, Will you accept from me a copy of a poem I have just published on England, as a very poor mark of homage to one whose pictures are great poems? Very truly yours   OSCAR WILDE

---

southern end of the street had been called Calthorpe Place until 1875, when it was renamed in honour of the architect Sir William Tite (1798–1873). (The northern end of the street, which Wilde was later to inhabit, was built between 1877 and 1887.) A Miss Elizabeth Skeates had lived in the southern part of the street from 1814 to 1821, and it was probably Skeates House that Wilde's poetic imagination quickly transformed into Keats House.

[1] Mrs Hunt was staying at Warkworth in Northumberland.

[2] The last stanza of "Ave Imperatrix" (which Wilde enclosed) runs:

Yet when this fiery web is spun,
    Her watchmen shall descry from far
The young Republic like a sun
    Rise from these crimson seas of war.

[3] George Frederick Watts, English painter and sculptor (1817–1904). R.A. 1867. In 1864 he married the seventeen-year-old Ellen Terry.

To Clement Scott[1]

MS. Clark

[Circa September 1880]   Keats House, Tite Street

Dear Mr Clement Scott, I send you the translation of Madame Modjeska's vision, which we have called *The Artist's Dream*:[2] I read it to her last night and she was good enough to say beautiful things about it, so she was satisfied fully.

Will you kindly be sure and let *me* have a proof, as I must go over it carefully. Believe me, yours truly   OSCAR WILDE

To Clement Scott

MS. Berg

[Circa September 1880]   Keats House, Tite Street

Dear Mr Clement Scott, Your letter has given me very great pleasure: whatever beauty is in the poem is due to the graceful fancy and passionate artistic nature of Madame Modjeska. I am really only the reed through which her sweet notes have been blown: yet slight as my own work has been, and of necessity hasty, I thank you very much for your praise, praise really welcome, and giving me much encouragement, as coming from a real critic.

Your own poems I know very well. You dare to do, what I hardly dare, to sing of the passion and joy and sorrow of the lives of the men and women among whom we live, and of the world which is the world of all of us.

When I read your poem some weeks ago on the clerks,[3] I remember thinking of the praise Wordsworth gave to Burns for having shown how "Verse may build itself a princely throne on humble truth."[4] For my own part I fear I too often "trundle back my soul five hundred years," as Aurora Leigh says,[5] and find myself more at home in the woods of Colonus

---

[1] Clement William Scott (1841–1904) was dramatic critic of the *Daily Telegraph* from 1872 until shortly before his death. He also edited a monthly magazine, the *Theatre*, 1877–97, wrote some plays and translated others, including Sardou's *Diplomacy* (1878). A violent opponent of Ibsen.

[2] "Sen Artysty; or The Artist's Dream," a poem "by Madame Helena Modjeska. Translated from the Polish by Oscar Wilde" was published in *The Green Room*, Routledge's Christmas Annual, edited by Clement Scott and published in October 1880. It was reprinted in *Poems* (1908). Helena Modjeska (1844–1909), Polish actress, scored her first success in San Francisco in 1877. She then toured America and Europe extensively and was considered one of the leading emotional actresses of the day. She made her London début at the Court Theatre on 1 May 1880 in *Heartsease*, an adaptation of *La Dame aux Camélias* by Dumas *fils*. The Prince of Wales was in the audience. There exists a letter from her to Wilde in which she says that it would be unwise to visit so young a man, even for tea.

[3] "The Cry of the Clerk" was included in Scott's volume of verse, *Lays of a Londoner* (1882).

[4] "At the Grave of Burns, 1803." Wilde has added the word "itself."

[5] "I do distrust the poet who discerns
No character or glory in his times,

or the glades of Arcady than I do in this little fiery-coloured world of ours. I envy you your strength. I have not got it.

With many thanks again. Very truly yours OSCAR WILDE

To Ellen Terry [1]
MS. Smallhythe

[*Circa September 1880*] *Tite Street*

Dear Miss Ellen Terry, Will you accept the first copy of my first play, a drama on modern Russia.[2] Perhaps some day I shall be fortunate enough to write something worthy of your playing.

We all miss you so much, and are so jealous that the provinces should see you in all the great parts you are playing before we do.[3]

So please come back quite soon. Believe me, yours sincerely

OSCAR WILDE

To Clara Morris [4]
MS. Berg

[*Circa September 1880*] *Keats House, Tite Street*

Dear Madam, Permit me to send you a copy of a new and original drama I have written: the character of the heroine is drawn in all those varying moods and notes of passion which you can so well touch. Your great fame, which has long ago passed over here, and a suggestion of my friend Mr Dion Boucicault[5] have emboldened me, being a very young writer, to

---

And trundles back his soul five hundred years
Past moat and drawbridge, into a castle-court.
(*Aurora Leigh*, book 5)

[1] Ellen Alice Terry (1847–1928), after making her stage début at the age of nine and acting with the Keans and the Bancrofts, had been engaged by Irving as his leading lady at the Lyceum in 1878. This partnership continued till 1902.

[2] A copy of the first, privately printed, edition (1880) of *Vera; or, The Nihilists*, a drama in four acts, which Wilde had had specially bound in dark red leather, with Ellen Terry's name stamped in gold on the binding. The book is inscribed "From her sincere admirer the Author." Letter and book are now in the Ellen Terry Memorial Museum at Smallhythe, Tenterden, Kent. Only two other copies are known to have survived, one in Clark and one in the collection of Mr Montgomery Hyde. This last is inscribed "To Genevieve Ward from her sincere friend and admirer the author, Sept. 1880," and the inscription was reproduced in Mason (p. 250) with the recipient's name omitted.

[3] Ellen Terry toured the provinces throughout the second half of 1880, reappearing at the Lyceum in January 1881.

[4] American actress (1848–1925). Wilde met her several times in New York in 1882 and saw her act there. In 1885 ill-health made her retire from the stage.

[5] Dionysius Lardner Boucicault, Irish dramatist and actor (1822–90). Among the best known of his 150 plays and adaptations are *The Corsican Brothers* (1852) and *The Colleen Bawn* (1860). Since 1876 he had lived in America.

send you my first play: and if you do not think it suitable for dramatic representation in America, at any rate accept it as a homage to your genius.

On account of its avowedly republican sentiments I have not been able to get permission to have it brought out here,[1] but with you there is more freedom, and though democracy is the note through which the play is expressed, yet the tragedy is an entirely human one. Believe me, Madam, your obedient servant OSCAR WILDE

In case you approve of the play I shall be so happy to correspond on the subject.

To Norman Forbes-Robertson [2]

[*Circa 1 October 1880*]   *Tite Street*

I have not yet finished furnishing my room, and have spent all my money over it already, so if no manager gives me gold for *The Nihilists* I don't know what I shall do; but then I couldn't really have anything but Chippendale and satinwood. I shouldn't have been able to write.

Modjeska has asked me to adapt some play for her—we have not yet settled what—probably *Luisa Miller*.[3] I am looking forward to her first night for which Barrett[4] has just sent me stalls . . . As for me I am lonely, *désolé* and wretched. I feel burned out.

To Hermann Vezin [5]

MS. Clark

[*4 October 1880*][6]   *Tite Street*

My dear Vezin, I send you a copy of my drama which you were kind enough to hear me read some months ago; any suggestions about situations or dialogue I should be so glad to get from such an experienced artist as yourself: I have just found out what a difficult craft playwriting is.

---

[1] See note 3, p. 110.   [2] The text of this incomplete letter is taken from Messrs Maggs's catalogue 568 (1931).

[3] An opera by Verdi (1849), with libretto by Salvatore Cammarano based on Schiller's play *Kabale und Liebe* (1782). This project came to nothing.

[4] Wilson Barrett (1846–1904), actor-manager and author, was at this time managing the Court Theatre. Later he was very successful in melodramas such as *The Silver King* by Henry Arthur Jones and Henry Herman (1882) and his own *The Sign of the Cross* (1895). His letter sending Wilde these tickets (MS. Hart-Davis) is dated 30 September.

[5] American actor (1829–1910) who appeared mostly in England. He had played Iago to the Othello of Neville Moritz at the Queen's Theatre, Long Acre, in March 1878. He later acted with Irving at the Lyceum. As a sideline he taught acting and elocution, and Wilde took lessons from him before his American lecture tour. Mrs Patrick Campbell was also his pupil and was on tour in his company when she first attracted the attention of the London managers. Vezin is said to have introduced greasepaint into the English theatre.   [6] So dated by recipient.

Will you let me tell you what immense pleasure your *Iago* gave me. It seems to me the most perfect example I have ever seen of that right realism which is founded on consummate art, and sustained by consummate genius: the man Iago walked and talked before us. Two points particularly delighted me—the enormous *character* you gave to otherwise trivial *details*: a rare and splendid art, to make all common things *symbolic* of the leading idea, as Albert Dürer loved to do in his drawings. The other is your delivery of asides, notably in Act II: I never knew how they ought to be given before—but perhaps you are saying in an aside now *"Ohé jam satis!"*,[1] so believe me your friend and admirer   OSCAR WILDE

To George Lewis Junior[2]

MS. Wansbrough

[*Postmark 1 November 1880*]   *Tite Street*

My dear George, I send you by this post a little pencil-case as a present, in order that you may take down everything that Mr Jacobs[3] says, and that when you go to the Lyceum you may be able to make notes in a wise manner on the side of your programme, like all the dramatic critics. I hope you will like it: if it gives you half as much pleasure to receive as it gives me to send it to you I feel sure you will. Believe me, your affectionate friend   OSCAR WILDE

Who is this?

To George Lewis Junior

MS. Wansbrough

[*November 1880*]   *Keats House, Tite Street*

My dear George, I am very pleased to have a letter from you indeed, particularly as I hear you are now the possessor of a certain drawing by a

---

[1] See note 3, p. 29.

[2] George James Graham Lewis (1868–1927) later succeeded his father (see note 2, p. 92) as second Baronet and head of the firm of Lewis & Lewis, solicitors.

[3] Joseph Jacobs (1854–1916), an Australian Jew, author and editor of many books on religion, folklore and other subjects, who occasionally gave lessons to the Lewis children.

certain eminent painter (whose name I for obvious reasons will not mention)[1] and that I am sure you spend a good deal of your time looking at it, and you could not spend your time better.

I had a very charming time in France, and travelled among beautiful vineyards all down the Loire, one of the most wonderful rivers in the world, mirroring from sea to source a hundred cities and five hundred towers. I was with a delightful Oxford friend[2] and, as we did not wish to be known, he travelled under the name of Sir Smith, and I was Lord Robinson. I then went to Paris—a large town, the capital of France—and enjoyed myself very much. Your sincere friend   OSCAR WILDE

To Mrs Alfred Hunt
MS. Clark

[*30 November 1880*][3]   *Keats House, Tite Street*

Dear Mrs Hunt, Will you accept a box for Madame Modjeska tomorrow (Wednesday) night, in *Marie Stuart*:[4] I should like you all to see her so much and the play is being changed next week for *Adrienne Lecouvreur*,[5] which I do not think is such a beautiful play. It is a large box and will hold you all, including I hope Mr Hunt whose republican sympathies will vanish before the misery of that lovely treacherous Queen of Scots.

Will you send me a line as soon as you conveniently can and I shall meet you at the theatre at 7.45.

With kind remembrances, believe me, truly yours   OSCAR WILDE

To Genevieve Ward

[*Early December 1880*]   *Keats House, Chelsea*

Dear Miss Ward, I *must* see the last night of *Anne-Mie!*[6] Might I ask for

---

[1] Wilde's own sketch of Henry Irving in the previous letter. The Lewis family were all great admirers of Irving.

[2] Almost certainly James Rennell Rodd (1858–1941), poet and diplomat (later British Ambassador to Italy, 1908–19, and first Lord Rennell of Rodd). He had been a friend of Wilde at Oxford, where he won the Newdigate Prize in 1880, two years after Wilde had done so. In his "envoi" to Rodd's *Rose Leaf and Apple Leaf* (1882) Wilde wrote: "I think that the best likeness to the quality of this young poet's work I ever saw was in the landscape by the Loire. We were staying there once, he and I, at Amboise . . ."

[3] So dated by recipient.

[4] An adaptation by the Hon. Lewis Wingfield of Schiller's play opened at the Court Theatre on 9 October 1880, with Madame Modjeska in the title-part.

[5] Madame Modjeska's production of this play by Scribe and Legouvé opened at the Court Theatre on 11 December 1880.

[6] *Anne-Mie*, adapted by Clement Scott from the Dutch of Rosier Faasen, opened at the Prince of Wales's Theatre on 1 November 1880, with Genevieve Ward and Johnston Forbes-Robertson in the principal parts. It was not well received, and was taken off on 10 December. The text of this letter is taken from *Genevieve Ward* by Zadel Barnes Gustafson (1881).

73

the same box Mamma and I had ? Or, if that is taken, any box will do. I should like to be there to show how much I appreciate your noble acting, and how much I admire a play the critics have so misunderstood. Your sincere friend and admirer   OSCAR WILDE

To Minnie Simpson[1]
MS. Aberystwyth

Monday night [? *20 December 1880*]   *1 Tite Street*

Dear Mrs Simpson, I caught a glimpse of you on Saturday night. Will you and your daughter come and meet "Cassandra," "Clytaemnestra" and some of the "Argive Elders" at tea tomorrow at five o'clock ?[2] I expect Madame Modjeska and a few friends. Believe me, very truly yours
                                                                          OSCAR WILDE

To Ellen Terry
MS. Anderson

[*3 January 1881*][3]   *Tite Street, Chelsea*

My dear Nellie, I write to wish you *every success* tonight. *You* could not do anything that would not be a mirror of the highest artistic beauty, and I am so glad to hear you have an opportunity of showing us that passionate power which *I know you have*. You will have a great success—perhaps one of your greatest.

I send you some flowers—two crowns. Will you accept one of them, whichever you think will suit you best. The other—don't think me treacherous, Nellie—but the other please give to Florrie *from yourself*. I should like to think that she was wearing something of mine the first night she comes on the stage, that anything of mine should touch her. Of course if you think—but you won't think she will suspect? How could she? She thinks I never loved her, thinks I forget. My God how could I!

[1] Mary Charlotte Mair (Minnie), 1825–1907, was the daughter of William Nassau Senior (1790–1864), the economist and poor-law reformer. She kept house for him in his later years and met many of the great and famous. In 1867 she married Charles Turner Simpson, a barrister.

[2] On 3 June 1880, by special permission of the Master, Dr Jowett, a performance of the *Agamemnon* of Aeschylus in Greek was given by Oxford undergraduates in Balliol Hall. Clytemnestra was played by F. R. Benson (New College), Cassandra by George Lawrence (Corpus), and the Watchman by W. L. Courtney (New). The chorus of fifteen Argive Elders had been trained by A. C. Bradley, the Shakespearean scholar. The performance caused a great stir, being the first of its kind anywhere in living memory, and three performances were given in the St George's Hall, London, on 16, 17 and 18 December (Saturday). George Eliot attended the last performance and died five days later.

[3] Tennyson's verse play *The Cup* was produced at the Lyceum on 3 January 1881, with Irving, Ellen Terry and William Terriss in the leading parts. One of the "Priestesses and Attendants in the Temple" was Florence Balcombe (see note 4, p. 36 and note 3, p. 54.) Wilde wrote a sonnet to Ellen Terry called "Camma" (her part in the play): it was published in *Poems* (1881).

Dear Nellie, if you can do this—in any case accept these flowers from your devoted admirer, your affectionate friend   OSCAR WILDE

To the Editor of Macmillan's Magazine[1]
MS. Hyde (H. M.)

[? *1881*]   *Keats House, Tite Street*

Mr Oscar Wilde begs to enclose a sonnet for the approval of the Editor of *Macmillan's Magazine*.[2]

To Mrs Alfred Hunt
MS. Clark

[*8 February 1881*][3]

Dear Mrs Hunt, I caught such a cold on Saturday night coming from the Corkrans[4] that I could not get to Tor Villas on Sunday as I hoped, to meet Arthur Severn.[5] I was so sorry, as Ruskin could not be so fond of anyone unless he was charming, and my evenings with you are always delightful.

I hope to get out soon and see you. Very truly yours   OSCAR WILDE

To Mrs Alfred Hunt
MS. Clark

[*17 February 1881*][6]   *Keats House, Tite Street*

Dear Mrs Hunt, Thank you so much for your kind invitations but I am in the "lion's den" on both days. Sunday I dine to meet Mr Lowell, a poet, statesman, and an American in one! A sort of three-headed Cerberus of civilization who barks when he is baited and is often mistaken for a lion, at a distance.[7]

And on Wednesday the 2nd I have a long-standing engagement to dine with Sir Charles Dilke, a lion who has clipped his radical claws and only roars through the medium of a quarterly review now—a harmless way of roaring.[8] So I cannot come to you, which *makes me very sad.*

[1] George Grove (1820–1900) was editor of *Macmillan's Magazine* 1868–83. His great *Dictionary of Music and Musicians* first appeared 1878–89. Knighted 1882. First Director of Royal College of Music 1883.

[2] No sonnet of Wilde's appeared in *Macmillan's Magazine*.

[3] So dated by recipient.

[4] The family of John Frazer Corkran (d. 1884), Irish author and journalist, who was for many years Paris correspondent of several London papers. Of his daughters, Henriette was a painter and Alice (see p. 232) a writer.

[5] English artist (1836–1931), son of Joseph Severn, the friend of Keats. Married (1871) Ruskin's cousin and ward Joan Agnew (1847–1924). Together they looked after Ruskin for the last twenty-seven years of his life, and to them he bequeathed Brantwood, his house on Coniston Water.   [6] So dated by recipient.

[7] James Russell Lowell (1819–1891), poet, editor and diplomat, was American Minister in London 1880–85.

[8] Sir Charles Wentworth Dilke, Bart (1843–1911), Liberal (Radical) M.P. for Chelsea 1868–86, Under-Secretary for Foreign Affairs 1880–82, President of the

I ought, like Sir Boyle Roche's bird, to be able to be in two places at once,[1] but in that case I should *always* be at Tor Villas. I hope to see you all soon again. Very truly yours   OSCAR WILDE

To Henry Irving

MS. Irving

[*Late April 1881*]   *Keats House, Tite Street*

Dear Mr Henry Irving, The Worshipful Company of Drapers in the City, having a great deal too much money, are anxious to give a donation and annual subscription to some institution which has for its object the support of old actors who have fallen on evil days, and have begged me to ask you what institution of the kind you would recommend as deserving of their charity. They are anxious to accept your recommendation in order that their money may go to the right channel.

If you would kindly send me a line giving your advice on this matter I will have it conveyed to them.

The meeting at which their charity is distributed is held on Monday morning, so perhaps you would let me hear from you as soon as possible.[2]

With best possible wishes for your success next week,[3] yours very sincerely   OSCAR WILDE

To David Bogue [4]

MS. Newberry

[*May 1881*][5]   *Keats House, Tite Street*

Dear Sir, I am anxious to publish a volume of poems immediately, and

---

Local Government Board 1882–85. His political career was ruined by his appearance as co-respondent in a divorce case in 1885. W. H. Chesson reported Wilde as saying in 1898: "I've only one fault to find with Dilke; he knows too much about everything. It is hard to have a good story interrupted by a fact. I admit accuracy up to a certain point, but Dilke's accuracy is almost a vice."

[1] Sir Boyle Roche (1743–1807) was an Irish politician famous for his "bulls" or ludicrous inconsistencies of speech. He is reputed to have said that "he regretted that he was not a bird, and could not be in two places at once."

[2] Wilde was never a member of the Drapers' Company, and it can only be supposed that he was misinformed, since in fact the Company had in 1881 more demands than it could satisfy. Wilde's sonnet "Fabien dei Franchi," addressed to Irving and ending "Thou trumpet set for Shakespeare's lips to blow," was published in *Poems* (1881). Irving doubled the parts of Lucien and Fabien dei Franchi in a revival of *The Corsican Brothers* from 18 September 1880 to 9 April 1881.

[3] Irving's production of *Othello*, in which he and the American tragedian Edwin Booth (1833–93) alternated in the roles of Othello and Iago, opened at the Lyceum on 2 May 1881. Wilde was at the first night.

[4] English publisher, son of publisher of same name, was now in business on his own at 3 St Martin's Place. He published, on commission, three books by Samuel Butler: *Evolution Old and New* (1879), *Unconscious Memory* (1880) and *Alps and Sanctuaries* (1882). He went bankrupt in June 1885, and was found dead on the beach at Folkestone in 1897. By his agreement with Wilde dated 17 May 1881 (MS. Hyde (H.M.), reproduced in Mason, p. 283) Wilde paid all the expenses of his *Poems*, of which five editions (each of 250 copies at 10/6) were issued within a year.   [5] So dated in another hand.

should like to enter into a treaty with your house about it. I can forward you the manuscript on hearing that you will begin negotiations.

Possibly my name requires no introduction. Yours truly

OSCAR WILDE

To May Morris[1]
MS. B.M.

[May–June 1881]   *Keats House, Tite Street*

Dear Miss May Morris, I have much pleasure in sending you Henry Irving's and Ellen Terry's autographs, to which I have ventured to add that of Mr Edwin Booth, to make the cast of *Othello* complete. But perhaps you don't care for Mr Booth? If so, pray tear up his bad writing at once! Yours very truly   OSCAR WILDE

To Oscar Browning

[June 1881]   *Keats House, Tite Street*

My dear Browning, If you get the opportunity, and would care for it, I wish you would review my first volume of poems just about to appear.[2] Books so often fall into stupid and illiterate hands that I am anxious to be really criticised: ignorant praise or ignorant blame is so insulting. Truly yours   OSCAR WILDE

To Robert Browning[3]

[June 1881]   *Keats House, Tite Street*

Dear Mr Browning, Will you accept from me the first copy of my poems —the only tribute I can offer you for the delight and the wonder which the strength and splendour of your work has given me from my boyhood.

Believe me, in all affectionate admiration, very truly yours

OSCAR WILDE

[1] 1862–1938. Younger daughter of William Morris (see note 3, p. 290). Expert embroiderer and maker of jewellery. Bernard Shaw fell in love with her, and it is believed she with him, but he made no proposal and she unsatisfactorily married H. Halliday Sparling, a disciple of her father's. She published a two-volume work on William Morris (1936) and edited a complete edition of his works (24 vols, 1910–15).

[2] The exact publication date of Wilde's *Poems* (1881) has not been established, though in his 1908 bibliography (in *Miscellanies*) Mason gives it as 30 June. An advertisement in the *Athenaeum* of 2 July describes the book as "just ready," and the *Lady's Pictorial* reviewed it on 9 July. The British Museum copy is stamped 28 July, and Oscar Browning's review (here solicited) appeared in the *Academy* of 30 July. The text of this letter is taken from Mason, p. 286.

[3] 1812–89. The text of this letter is taken from Mason, p. 149.

To Matthew Arnold[1]

[*June–July 1881*]   *Keats House, Tite Street*

Dear Mr Arnold, Will you accept from me my first volume of poems . . .
of the constant source of joy and wonder that your beautiful work was to
all of us at Oxford . . . for I have only now, too late perhaps, found out
how all art requires solitude as its companion, only now indeed know the
splendid difficulty of this great art in which you are a master illustrious
and supreme. Still, such as it is, let me offer it to you, and believe me in all
affectionate admiration, truly yours   OSCAR WILDE

To William Ward
MS. Magdalen

[*June–July 1881*]   *Keats House, Tite Street*

Dear Will, My volume is out: I wish you could review it: no one is more
qualified to be a critic than you with your keen insight and exquisite taste.

I wish in any case you would let me know what you think of it. But I
am very anxious to be read, and a review in a Bristol paper might cause a
sale in that lovely old town. Ever affectionately yours   OSCAR

To W. R. Paton[2]
MS. Paton

[*June–July 1881*]   *Keats House, Tite Street*

Dear Paton, Would you, or could you, kindly let me know if Browning's
review of my volume will appear next Saturday, as if so I will have an
advertisement in that number—a sure method, my publisher tells me, of
alluring those simple folk who prefer buying poetry to buying chimney-
pot hats, heavy black frock-coats, and the like. Yours very truly
                                                              OSCAR WILDE

To Aniela Gielgud[3]
MS. Gielgud

[? *Early July 1881*][4]   *Tite Street*

Dear Mrs Gielgud, It will give me great pleasure to dine with you on
Tuesday the 12th. Believe me, very truly yours   OSCAR WILDE

[1] 1822–88. The text of this incomplete letter is taken from a catalogue issued by
Henry Danielson, bookseller, in 1921.

[2] William Roger Paton (1858–1921) was at Magdalen with Wilde. He later
became a considerable Greek scholar and an authority on Plutarch. A close friend
of Oscar Browning, in whose house he was at Eton, and of Wilde's friend Carlos
Blacker (see note 2, p. 540).

[3] Aniela Aszperger, daughter of a well-known Polish actress, was born in Lvov
in 1841; she came to England and married Adam Gielgud, who was also of Polish
origin, in the 1860's. Grandparents of Sir John Gielgud.

[4] This letter must have been written before Wilde's marriage, and the Tite Street

I am filled with delight at the beauty of your name—Aniela! it has an exquisite forest simplicity about it, and sounds most sweetly out of tune with this fiery-coloured artificial world of ours—rather like a daisy on a railway bank!

To W. E. Gladstone
MS. B.M.

[*20 July 1881*][1]   *Keats House, Tite Street*

Dear Mr Gladstone, Will you do me the honour of accepting my first volume of poems—as a very small token of my deep admiration and loyalty to one who has always loved what is noble and beautiful and true in life and art, and is the mirror of the Greek ideal of the statesman.

I have the honour to remain in all things your most obedient servant

OSCAR WILDE

To Violet Hunt
MS. Clark

[*Postmark 22 July 1881*]   *Keats House, Tite Street*

Dear Miss Violet Hunt, I thank you very much for your kind letter, and am infinitely delighted that you have thought my poems beautiful. In an age like this when Slander, and Ridicule, and Envy walk quite unashamed among us, and when any attempt to produce serious beautiful work is greeted with a very tornado of lies and evil-speaking, it is a wonderful joy, a wonderful spur for ambition and work, to receive any such encouragement and appreciation as your letter brought me, and I thank you for it again and again.

The poem I like best is "The Burden of Itys" and next to that "The Garden of Eros." They are the most lyrical, and I would sooner have any power or quality of "song" writing than be the greatest sonnet writer since Petrarch.

I go to the Thanes[2] this afternoon with Mr Burne-Jones but will hope to see you when I return.

You have made me very happy. Believe me ever sincerely yours

OSCAR WILDE

---

address narrows down the years to 1880 (after August) and 1881. The only three months in that period with a Tuesday on the 12th were October 1880, April and July 1881. I have chosen the latest, when Wilde's circle of friends and acquaintances was largest.

[1] Endorsed by Gladstone "R. 21 July/81."

[2] Probably the family of George Dancer Thane (1850–1930), Professor of Anatomy at University College, London, from 1877 to 1919, when he was knighted.

To the Hon. Mrs Stanley[1]

MS. Hughes

[? *1881*]   *Keats House, Tite Street*

Dear Mrs Stanley, The fates are always against me! And on the night
when the only place in London worth going to is your brilliant salon I find
myself so engaged that I cannot escape.

Still, if you will allow me I will try and come. Who would not "venture
for such merchandise"?[2] Believe me, truly yours   OSCAR WILDE

To an Unidentified Correspondent

MS. Clark

October 1881   *Keats House, Tite Street*

My dear Madam, The only two arts which I work at are those of song and
of painting, and if I could play the organ I certainly would never play it in
a fashionable church. As for modern newspapers with their dreary records
of politics, police-courts, and personalities, I have long ago ceased to care
what they write about me—my time being all given up to the gods and
the Greeks. But your letter is full of charming and sweet words, and I
thank you for it.   O. W.

To James Knowles[3]

MS. Hyde (H. M.)

[? *Late 1881*]   *Keats House, Tite Street*

Dear Mr Knowles, I send you a—rather soiled—copy of my mother's
pamphlet on the reflux wave of *practical* republicanism which the return
of the Irish emigrants has brought on Ireland. It was written three years
ago nearly, and is extremely interesting as a political prophecy.[4] You
probably know my mother's name as the "Speranza" of the *Nation* newspaper in 1848. I don't think that age has dimmed the fire and enthusiasm
of that pen which set the young Irelanders in a blaze.

---

[1] Susan Mary Elizabeth Mackenzie (?1849–1931) married (1) Lieut.-Col. the
Hon. John Constantine Stanley (1837–78), second son of the first Lord Stanley of
Alderley; (2) in August 1881 Francis Jeune, a lawyer who was first knighted
and then created Lord St Helier. She was a leading society hostess.

[2] *Romeo and Juliet*, Act II, scene ii.

[3] Architect and editor (1831–1908), friend of Tennyson, with whom he started
the Metaphysical Society in 1869. Designed Tennyson's house, Aldworth, in
Surrey, and the gardens in Leicester Square, London. He was editor of the
Contemporary Review from 1870 to 1877, when he founded and edited the *Nineteenth
Century*. Knighted 1903.

[4] Probably *The American Irish*, which was published in New York *circa* 1879.

I should like so much to have the privilege of introducing you to my mother—all brilliant people should cross each other's cycles, like some of the nicest planets. In any case I am glad to be able to send you the article. It is part of the thought of the nineteenth century, and will I hope interest you. Believe me, truly yours OSCAR WILDE

PART THREE

AMERICA

1882

PART THREE

America: 1882

Gilbert and Sullivan's *Patience* was first produced by Richard D'Oyly Carte (1844-1901) at the Opera Comique, London, on 23 April 1881, and on 10 October was moved to the Savoy Theatre, which Carte had just built. The opera satirised contemporary aestheticism, and the character of Bunthorne, the Fleshly Poet, though perhaps intended for Rossetti, was generally taken as a caricature of Wilde. *Patience* opened in New York on 22 September, and Col. W. F. Morse, Carte's American representative, thought that the appearance of Wilde himself might provide useful publicity. He was accordingly booked to give a series of lectures, sailed on the *Arizona* on 24 December 1881, and landed at New York on 2 January 1882.

His first lecture, at the Chickering Hall, New York, on 9 January, was on "The English Renaissance." It was printed in *Miscellanies*. House decoration was the subject of his other principal lecture, which was published (its text taken from an American newspaper) as *Decorative Art in America* (edited by Richard Butler Glaenzer, New York, 1906) and reprinted in *Miscellanies*.

To Mrs George Lewis[1]
MS. Wansbrough

[*Between 3 and 7 January 1882*]   [*New York*]

... is blocked, and policemen wait for me to clear a way. I now understand why the Royal Boy[2] is in good humour always: it is delightful to be a *petit roi*. However if I am not a success on Monday I shall be very wretched. Without Mr Lewis to consult I feel a little at sea! They constantly ask me about him: he is quite a rival and I grow jealous. Very truly yours

OSCAR WILDE

---

[1] Betty Eberstadt (1844-1931) married (1867) George Lewis, the solicitor (see note 2, p. 92). This fragment is written on both sides of a correspondence card.
[2] Popular nickname for the Prince of Wales, later King Edward VII.

To Mrs George Lewis

MS. Wansbrough

[*Circa 15 January 1882*]   [*New York*]

My dear Mrs Lewis, I am sure you have been pleased at my success! The hall had an audience larger and more wonderful than even Dickens had. I was recalled and applauded and am now treated like the Royal Boy. I have several "Harry Tyrwhitts" as secretaries.[1] One writes my autographs all day for my admirers, the other receives the flowers that are left really every ten minutes. A third whose hair resembles mine is obliged to send off locks of his own hair to the myriad maidens of the city, and so is rapidly becoming bald.

I stand at the top of the reception rooms when I go out, and for two hours they defile past for introduction. I bow graciously and sometimes honour them with a royal observation, which appears next day in all the newspapers. When I go to the theatre the manager bows me in with lighted candles and the audience rise. Yesterday I had to leave by a private door, the mob was so great. Loving virtuous obscurity as much as I do, you can judge how much I dislike this lionizing, which is worse than that given to Sarah Bernhardt I hear.[2]

For this, and indeed for nearly all my successes, I have to thank your dear husband. Pray give Mr Lewis my most affectionate remembrances, also to the Grange,[3] and believe me, very sincerely yours   OSCAR WILDE

To Norman Forbes-Robertson

TS. Congress

15 January 1882   *New York*

My dear Norman, I have been to call on Ian[4] and his wife. She is so pretty and sweet and simple, like a little fair-haired Madonna, with a baby who already shows a great dramatic power and behaved during my visit (I stayed about an hour, breaking fifty-four engagements) like Macbeth, Hamlet, King John, and all the remarkable characters in Shakespeare. They seem very happy, and she is very loving to Ian, and unaffected.

I go to Philadelphia tomorrow.[5] Great success here: nothing like it since

---

[1] The Hon. Harry Tyrwhitt (1854–91), eldest son of Sir Henry Tyrwhitt, Bart., and Baroness Berners. Assumed the additional surname of Wilson in 1876. Equerry in Waiting to the Prince of Wales from 1881.

[2] The great French actress (1844–1923) had made her début at the Comédie Française in 1862, paid her first visit to London in 1879, when Wilde is said to have welcomed her with an armful of lilies, and to New York in 1880.

[3] The Burne-Jones's London house in Fulham, which the Lewis family often visited.

[4] Ian Forbes-Robertson (1857–1936), actor brother of Johnston and Norman. He married a daughter of Joseph Knight (see note 3, p. 109).

[5] Wilde arrived in Philadelphia on 16 January and lectured there next day at the Horticultural Hall.

Dickens, they tell me. I am torn in bits by Society. Immense receptions, wonderful dinners, crowds wait for my carriage. I wave a gloved hand and an ivory cane and they cheer. Girls very lovely, men simple and intellectual. Rooms are hung with white lilies for me everywhere. I have "Boy"[1] at intervals, also two secretaries, one to write my autograph and answer the hundreds of letters that come begging for it. Another, whose hair is brown, to send locks of his own hair to the young ladies who write asking for mine; he is rapidly becoming bald. Also a black servant, who is my slave —in a free country one cannot live without a slave—rather like a Christy minstrel, except that he knows no riddles. Also a carriage and a black tiger[2] who is like a little monkey. I give sittings to artists, and generally behave as I always have behaved—"*dreadfully*." Love to your mother and Forby[3] and all of them. Ever your affectionate friend   OSCAR

To J. M. Stoddart [4]
MS. Clark

[? *18 January 1882*]   [? *Philadelphia*]

Dear Mr Stoddart, Will you very kindly send *three* copies of today's *Press* and *three* of today's *Times* to Lady Wilde, and copies of the *Press* alone to the addresses I gave you yesterday, also to J. McN. Whistler, Tite Street, Chelsea, London; Comyns Carr,[5] Grosvenor Gallery, Bond Street, London; Hon. George Curzon, Balliol College, Oxford; Oscar Browning, King's College, Cambridge, England; Dr Shaw,[6] Fellow and Tutor, Trinity College, Dublin, Ireland. Very sincerely yours   OSCAR WILDE

---

[1] A slang word for champagne.   [2] i.e. a Negro groom in livery.

[3] The family nickname of Johnston Forbes-Robertson, actor-manager (1853–1937).

[4] Joseph Marshall Stoddart (1845–1921) was a native of Philadelphia, where he worked first for J. B. Lippincott & Co. In 1874 he began publishing under his own name, and in 1878 he acquired the U.S. publishing rights of the Gilbert and Sullivan operas. He gave a reception for Wilde after his Philadelphia lecture on 17 January. The other names (MS. Clark) to whom periodicals (the *Philadelphia Press, New York Times, Philadelphia Enquirer* and *North American Review*) were to be sent were Lady Wilde, Willie Wilde, Mrs Langtry, Mrs Millais, Edmund Yates, Lady Archibald Campbell, Mrs George Lewis, Norman Forbes-Robertson, Rennell Rodd, Mr Samuelson, Mrs Louise Jopling, Edwin Levy, Mrs Labouchere, Philip Burne-Jones, T. H. Warren, and the President of the Junior Common Room at Magdalen.

[5] Joseph William Comyns Carr, art critic and dramatist (1849–1916). Director and one of the founders of the New Gallery 1888. Founder and editor of the *English Illustrated Magazine* 1883.

[6] George Ferdinand Shaw (1821–99), a cousin of Bernard Shaw, who combined his Fellowship with the editing of the *Dublin Evening Mail*.

To Archibald Forbes[1]

MS. Wansbrough

[20 *January 1882*]   *Arlington Hotel, Washington*

Dear Mr Forbes, I felt quite sure that your remarks on me had been mis-represented. I must however say that your remarks about me *in your lecture* may be regarded as giving *some* natural ground for the report. I feel bound to say quite frankly to you that I do not consider them to be either in good taste or appropriate to your subject.

I have something to say to the American people, something that I know will be the beginning of a great movement here, and all foolish ridicule does a great deal of harm to the cause of art and refinement and civilisation here.

I do not think that your lecture will lose in brilliancy or interest by expunging the passage, which is, as you say yourself, poor fooling enough.

You have to speak of the life of action, I of the life of art. Our subjects are quite distinct and should be kept so. Believe me, yours truly

OSCAR WILDE

To Archibald Forbes

MS. Wansbrough

Monday [*23 January 1882*]   *Arlington Hotel, Washington*

Dear Mr Forbes, Colonel Morse,[2] who kindly manages for me a somewhat bulky correspondence, tells me that you feel yourself wronged by something I am supposed to have said of you in the papers, and that you have written to me in, natural I acknowledge, indignation on the subject. He has sent the letter to Mr Carte without my reading it, as he considers that Mr Carte can best answer those parts of it relating to my intended visit to

[1] British war correspondent and author (1838–1900). He was also lecturing in the States at this time, wearing all his medals, and had small sympathy with Wilde's ideas of aesthetics and dress reform. It had been reported that Wilde would attend Forbes's lecture at Baltimore on 19 January, but the two men quarrelled on the train from Philadelphia, and Wilde went straight on to Washington without stopping at Baltimore. Both Forbes and the leaders of Baltimore Society were offended. The passage in Forbes's lecture to which Wilde objected described a visit to the Czar in war-torn Bulgaria:

I glanced down at my clothes, which I had not changed for a fortnight, and in which I had ridden 150 miles. Now I wish it understood that I am a follower, an humble follower, of the aesthetic ecstasy, but I did not look much like an art object then. I did not have my dogskin knee breeches with me, nor my velvet coat, and my black silk stockings were full of holes. Neither was the wild, barren waste of Bulgaria congenial to the growth of sunflowers and lilies.

[2] D'Oyly Carte's representative in America. He contributed two chapters, "American Lectures" and "Lectures in Great Britain," to the otherwise anonymous volume called *His Life, with a Critical Estimate of his Writings* in the unauthorised "Uniform Edition" of Wilde's works published by A. R. Keller & Co. Inc., London and New York, 1907.

Baltimore. In any case let me assure you that I have neither spoken of you to anyone except as I would speak of a man whose chivalry, whose personal bravery, and whose pluck, have won him the respect and the admiration of all honest men in Europe and in America, and who has given to English journalism the new lustre of action, of adventure and of courage. I did not believe what I read in the papers about you, that you had spoken of me in a sneering way behind my back. I in fact denied it to a reporter who came here with the story on *Thursday* night late. I do not think you should have believed it of me. It is true you hardly know me at all personally, but at least you know me well enough to come and ask me personally if, after your generous letter to me, I had said of you things which seem to you ungenerous and unfair and untrue. The only papers I have seen about the subject are the *Herald* and *World*. Miss Meigs whom I had the honour of meeting last night tells me that some garbled interview appeared in the *Post* which contained certain foolish things supposed to have proceeded from me. I have not seen the paper at all, or I would have written to you at once about it. [*The rest of this letter is missing*]

To Richard D'Oyly Carte

MS. Private

[? *24 or 25 January 1882*]   [? *Washington*]

My dear Carte, Another such fiasco as the Baltimore business and I think I would stop lecturing. The little wretched clerk or office boy you sent to me in Col. Morse's place is a fool and an idiot. Do let us be quite frank with one another. I must have, according to our agreement, Morse or some responsible experienced man always with me. This is for your advantage as well as for mine. I will not go about with a young office boy, who has not even the civility to come and see what I want. He was here for five minutes yesterday, went away promising to return at eleven o'clock a.m. and I have not seen him since. I had nine reporters, seven or eight telegrams, eighteen letters to answer, and this young scoundrel amusing himself about the town. I must never be left again, and please do not expose me to the really brutal attacks of the papers. The whole tide of feeling is turned by Morse's stupidity.

I know you have been ill, and that it has not been your doing but we must be very careful for the future. Very sincerely yours OSCAR WILDE

To Oliver Wendell Holmes[1]

MS. Congress

[*26–27 January 1882*]   [? *Washington*][2]

Dear Sir, I have the honour to enclose you a letter of introduction from

---

[1] American writer and physician (1809–94). In 1856–57 he was a co-founder of the *Atlantic Monthly*, and made its name (as well as his own) with his series of papers, *The Autocrat of the Breakfast Table*, which were published as a book in 1858. Later the *Autocrat* was followed by the *Professor* and the *Poet*.

[2] This letter is on paper headed 1267 Broadway, New York, which was the

Mr Lowell. I arrive at the Vendome on Saturday and hope to be allowed the privilege of calling on one whose work was so delightful to us all at Oxford. I remain yours truly OSCAR WILDE

To Oliver Wendell Holmes
MS. Congress

Saturday [28 January 1882] *Vendome Hotel [Boston]*

Dear Mr Holmes, It will give me great pleasure to go with you to the Saturday Club: will you kindly let me know at what hour I can call on you. Will two o'clock do? Thanking you for your courtesy, truly yours
OSCAR WILDE

Or will I go direct to Parkers at 2.30?

To Oliver Wendell Holmes
MS. Congress

[? 29 January 1882] *Vendome Hotel, Boston*

Dear Doctor Holmes, Will you accept from me a copy of my poems as a small token of the pleasure and the privilege I had in meeting you. I will be in Boston for a few days and will look forward to the chance of finding you at home some afternoon.

Pray remember me most kindly to your son, and to that Penelope of New England whose silken pictures I found so beautiful, and believe me most truly yours OSCAR WILDE

To Archibald Forbes
MS. Boston

[Circa 29 January 1882] *[Boston]*

Dear Mr Forbes, I cannot tell you how surprised and grieved I am to think that there should have been anything in my first letter to you which seemed to you discourteous or wrong.[1]

---

headquarters of D'Oyly Carte's American enterprises, including Wilde's tour. Wilde was apt to use this headed paper wherever he was, so without corroboration it is worthless as evidence of his place of writing.

[1] Forbes had answered Wilde's letters of 20 and 23 January as follows (MS. Clark):

26 January 1882 *46 West 28 Street, New York*

Dear Mr Wilde, It has a tendency to create confusion when a man does not read important letters addressed to himself, and there is yet greater risk of this when he essays to reply to them on a summary given him apparently without a due realisation of their personal significance to him.

I accept your disclamation of the remarks in connection with me which your letter states to have been put into your mouth without warrant.

But it was not of these remarks which my letter complained. What that letter protested against was

First: the claim set up by you in your letter of Friday last, that I should trim

Believe me, I had intended to answer you in the same frank spirit in which you had written to me. Any such expressions however unintentional I most willingly retract.

As regards my motive for coming to America, I should be very disappointed if when I left for Europe I had not influenced in *however* slight a way the growing spirit of art in this country, very disappointed if I had not out of the many who listen to me made one person love beautiful things a little more, and very disappointed if in return for the dreadfully hard work of lecturing—hard to me who am inexperienced—I did not earn enough money to give myself an autumn at Venice, a winter at Rome, and a spring at Athens; but all these things are perhaps dreams.

Letter-writing seems to lead to grave misunderstandings. I wish I could have seen you personally: standing face to face, and man to man, I might have said what I wished to say more clearly and more simply. I remain yours truly   O. WILDE

To Mrs Julian Hawthorne[1]
F. Keller

8 February 1882   *Niagara*

Dear Mrs Hawthorne, I was so sorry not to see you when I was at Boston but I had so little time there I was unable to go over to Concord. When I return I must see you, and the Alcotts, if they will let me.[2] Mrs Hall was

---

a lecture of mine to suit your sensitiveness to an inoffensive effort at humour: and

Secondly and *chiefly*—with the knowledge I have, and which you know I have, of the utterly mercenary aim of your visit to America, the possibility of my accepting your pretensions put forward in the same letter as follows: "I have something to say to the American people, something that I know will be the beginning of a great movement; and all foolish ridicule does a great deal of harm to the cause of art, refinement and civilisation here."

It is no affair of mine to whom else you may choose to advance these pretensions; but I must utterly decline to allow you to address them to me, for the reasons given at length in my letter which you have not thought proper to read.

Your letter of Monday, with its irrelevant expressions of cordiality, cannot affect the situation. What I have to ask is that you withdraw, as obviously offensive to me, the whole of your letter of Friday, and that you do so categorically, and in so many words, with the exception of the first sentence of it.

As it is irksome to me that the matter should hang over, I must demand that you send me a letter containing the withdrawal specified, by Sunday next. In the event of my non-receipt thereof, I beg to intimate to you that I will print the whole correspondence in a New York paper of Monday morning. I am faithfully yours   ARCHIBALD FORBES

[1] Wife of Nathaniel Hawthorne's novelist son Julian (1846–1934), whom Wilde had met in London in 1879.

[2] The family of Amos Bronson Alcott (1799–1888), educationist, writer, and father of Louisa May Alcott (1832–88), author of *Little Women* (1868) and other popular novels. Wilde had met her in New York.

kind enough to ask me for Sunday evening but I could not go. On my return to New York I must visit her.[1]   OSCAR WILDE

To George Lewis [2]

MS. Wansbrough

[*9 February 1882*]   *Prospect House, Niagara Falls, Canada Side*

My dear Mr Lewis, Things are going on very well, and you were very kind about answering my telegrams. Carte blundered in leaving me without a manager, and Forbes through the most foolish and mad jealousy tried to lure me into a newspaper correspondence. His attack on me, entirely unprovoked, was one of the most filthy and scurrilous things I ever read—so much so that Boucicault and Hurlbert of the *World*[3] both

---

[1] Probably Mrs Florence Howe Hall, a daughter of Julia Ward Howe (see p. 122).

[2] George Henry Lewis (1833–1911) was knighted in 1893 and made a baronet in 1902. Head of the firm of Lewis & Lewis, solicitors. Elizabeth Robins reports Wilde's saying of him in 1888: "George Lewis is the best [solicitor] in London. Brilliant. Formidable. A man of the world. Concerned in every great case in England. Oh, he knows all about us—and forgives us all." See also p. 440.

[3] William Henry Hurlbert (1827–95). American journalist and author. Editor-in-chief of the *New York World* 1876–83. At his own dinner-table he had recently been insulted by Archibald Forbes. Boucicault had written to Mrs George Lewis from Boston on 29 January (MS. Wansbrough):

My dear Mrs Lewis, I am sure you will be gratified to hear about Oscar Wilde—his doings here and his progress. He has been much distressed; and came here last night looking worn and thin.

Mr Carte has not behaved well, and Mr Forbes—well, I do not wish to trust myself with an expression of opinion. But I cannot help feeling that so long as Carte and Forbes thought Oscar was only a puppet—a butt—a means of advertising the Opera Comique of *Patience*—they were charming, but when Oscar's reception and success threw Forbes into the shade, Forbes went into an ecstasy of rage, and "went back" on Wilde, behaving more like a wild bull than a gentleman. Carte escaped all responsibility, turned Oscar over to a subordinate and left him at the mercy of the Press, making a market of their caricatures to advertise him in connection with *Patience* and Bunthorne. (I sent you a paper with a portrait.)

On *Tuesday* he lectures here, on *Monday* Carte produces the "Ideal *Patience*" at the Globe Theatre. This is not fair, and you will see by the enclosed cutting from an interview published today that I have said so publicly.

Oscar is helpless, because he is not a practical man of business, so when I advised him to throw over Carte, and offered to see him through financially if he did so, he felt afraid. I offered him a thousand pounds or two if he required it, but he says he will play out his contract to April.

I do wish I could make him less Sybarite—less Epicurean. He said this morning "Let me gather the golden fruits of America that I may spend a winter in Italy and a summer in Greece amidst beautiful things." Oh dear—if he would spend the money and the time amongst six-per-cent bonds! I think I told him so, but he thinks I take "a painful view of life."

There is a future for him here, but he *wants management*.

Carte thought he had got hold of a popular fool. When he found that he was

92

entreated me to publish it, as it would have brought people over to my side, but I thought it wiser to avoid the garbage of a dirty-water-throwing in public. It was merely on Forbes's part that the whole thing began, I really declining always to enter into any disquisition. I will show you his letter —it was infamous. He has been a dreadful failure this year and thought he would lure me on to a public quarrel.[1]

I am hard at work, and I think making money, but the expenses seem very heavy. I hope to go back with £1000: if I do it will be delightful.

Your friend Whitelaw Reid,[2] to whom I brought two letters of introduction, has not been very civil—in fact has not helped me in any way at all. I am sorry I brought him any letters, and the *New York Herald* is most bitter. I wonder could you do anything for it? Pray remember me to Mrs Lewis, and with many thanks, yours most affectionately   OSCAR WILDE

---

astride of a live animal instead of a wooden toy, he was taken aback.

I write to you instead of to G. L. (although I know it is all the same) because you will make allowance for my chatter, and I know you both have a most affectionate regard for Oscar (as indeed I have).

I shall try and make him conclude his tour on March 31st for many reasons— one of which is: all the money that he can make will be made by that time, and before he leaves he should make engagements ahead for an autumn tour.

You will be glad to hear that my success here has been unprecedented. I think I shall "get away" with about eleven thousand pounds in April when I return to London—by far the most profitable sweep I have ever made in the same time.

I hope all your charming young people are well. I wonder if they will grow up as handsome as their mother.

I cannot tell you with what admiration and gratitude Wilde speaks of you both. Sincerely yours   DION BOUCICAULT
Postscript. Feb. 10.   *The Vendome, Boston*
My dear Mrs Lewis, I delayed this letter to give you fuller news of O. W. He continues to draw, but the *Patience* movement is directed to follow him, and to turn him into ridicule. I fear that he has no second visit here—those who undertake such enterprises tell me they would not be able to touch him. Still he might make a fair income—if better managed—and if he would reduce his hair and take his legs out of the last century.

I think he would do well in the provinces in England, and I have suggested to him an *illustrated* lecture—with paintings and drawings—including some reproductions on a large scale of the caricatures in *Punch* thirty years ago on the pre-Raphaelite craze—against Millais and Hunt. With kind regards to G. L. believe me, sincerely yours   D. B.

[1] According to Morse, the quarrel was ended by George Lewis's cabling to Forbes on 28 January: "Like a good fellow don't attack Wilde. I ask this personal favour to me."

[2] American journalist and diplomat (1837–1912). Principal proprietor and editor-in-chief of the New York *Tribune* (1872–1905). American Ambassador to the Court of St James's 1905–12.

To Mrs George Lewis

MS. Wansbrough

12 February 1882   *Grand Pacific Hotel, Chicago*

My dear Mrs Lewis, I sent you a letter this morning, but must write you a little line to tell you how delighted I was to get *your* letter. It touched me and pleased me more than I can tell you to receive such kindly words, I being so far away. It seemed a little touch and breath of home, and came with the sweet memory of people for whom I have the warmest affection, and most loving respect.

The English papers are too ridiculous. You know the Americans—they don't spend their money without a return. For lecturing in Chicago I received before I stepped on the platform a fee of 1000 dollars—£200: for one hour's work—that is answer enough. Of course in smaller places I get less, but never less than £40. Here I get £200, as at Boston. I could lecture from now till day of doom if I had strength and time to do it, and though the east has been horrid in the newspapers, the west is very good and simple. I have a sort of triumphal progress, live like a young sybarite, travel like a young god. At Boston I had an immense success: here I expect one. I am deluged with poems and flowers at every town, have a secretary writing autographs all day, and would be bald in half a week if I sent the locks of hair I am asked for through the post every morning. The whole bad reports of New York were got up by Whitelaw Reid and Clarence Stedman[1]—to both of whom I brought letters from *le bon*[2]—and to Reid from Yates,[3] and Stedman from Lowell also. Neither of them took any notice of these letters, but they have been entirely defeated. Nothing could exceed the entertaining at New York. At Boston I dined with Oliver W. Holmes, breakfasted with Longfellow,[4] lunched with Wendell Phillips,[5] and was treated gloriously.

I lecture again at New York, Boston, Philadelphia, and other cities, so you see they understand and like me. All this sounds egotistical, but I do not like my friends in England to be ignorant of the success of one they have been so kind and loyal to.

And your supper—I should have been there. It must have been most

---

[1] Edmund Clarence Stedman, American poet and critic (1833–1908), known as the "Wall Street poet."

[2] George Lewis.

[3] Edmund Hodgson Yates (1831–94), English journalist and novelist. In 1858 he had been expelled from the Garrick Club for writing a disparaging article on Thackeray which contained private information acquired in the club. He edited *Town Talk* (1858–59), *Temple Bar* (1863–67) and *Tinsley's Magazine* (1867–70). In 1874 he founded the *World*, which he edited and in which he published several of Wilde's early poems.

[4] Henry Wadsworth Longfellow, born in 1807, died on 24 March 1882, when Wilde was travelling to the west. Asked in Salt Lake City for a comment on the dead poet, he said: "Longfellow was himself a beautiful poem, more beautiful than anything he ever wrote."

[5] American orator, reformer and slavery abolitionist (1811–84).

dramatic. I am delighted about the Lily: she and I are facing great publics, and here I know she will succeed.[1]

Phil writes me wonderful news of Katie,[2] that she has ceased to be the modern Nero and is now angelic, and gives up to Gertie. If she does I no longer adore her: her fascinating villainy touched my artistic soul.

Please forgive my paper, and writing—they are characteristic of the country. But you were so good and kind to write. Pray remember me to Mr Lewis most affectionately, and believe me, ever sincerely yours

OSCAR WILDE

To Mrs Julian Hawthorne
MS. Clark

[*Postmark 12 February 1882*]   [*Chicago*]

Your letter has been following me from city to city. You should have asked me when I was at Boston. I would have come with greater pleasure than I can tell you, but now I am—how many hundred miles off—in Chicago. And the New England farm house, how I should have liked that. Yes: I must come in April: may I come then?   O. W.

[*This is written on a card embossed with a butterfly, against which Wilde has marked a cross and added as a postscript*:]

This is what you thought me in London.

To Colonel W. F. Morse[3]

[? *Circa 12 February 1882*]   *Grand Pacific Hotel, Chicago*

I hope you will arrange some more matinées: to lecture in the day does not tire me. I would sooner lecture five or six times a week, and travel, say, three or four hours a day than lecture three times and travel ten hours. I do not think I should ever lecture less than four times, and these matinées are a great hit. Let me know what we are to do after Cincinnati —is it Canada? I am ready to lecture till last week in April—25 April, say.

---

[1] Mrs Langtry, whose husband had lost his money, had gone on the stage and was planning an American tour. In an interview at Halifax, Nova Scotia, in October Wilde said: "I would rather have discovered Mrs Langtry than have discovered America," and when she arrived he met her with lilies at the boat. She opened at Wallack's Theatre on 6 November 1882 in *An Unequal Match* by Tom Taylor, and next day's *New York World* contained a glowing article by Wilde, praising her beauty and her clothes. It was reprinted in *Miscellanies*.

[2] Mrs Lewis's daughter Katherine (1878–1961). Gertie (later Mrs Theodore Burney) was her elder sister. Phil was the son of the painter Edward Burne-Jones, whose delightfully illustrated *Letters to Katie* were published in facsimile in 1925.

[3] The text of this fragment is taken from Glaenzer, supplemented by Morse's chapters (see note 2, p. 88).

To James McNeill Whistler[1]

MS. Glasgow

[? *February 1882*][2]

My dear Jimmy, They are "considering me *seriously*." Isn't it dreadful? What would you do if it happened to you? Yours   OSCAR

To J. M. Stoddart

TS. Holland

[? *19 February 1882*]   *Cincinnati*

Dear Mr Stoddart, I send you the volume of poems[3] and the preface. The preface you will see is most important, signifying my new departure from Mr Ruskin and the Pre-Raphaelites, and marks an era in the aesthetic movement. Please send proofs to *New York*: they will forward them to me as I race from town to town. I also wish to ask Mr Davis[4] a favour. I should like to be able to send Mr Rodd some money: if Mr Davis will advance £25 on the whole half-profits that fall to Mr Rodd and myself it would be to this young poet a great encouragement, and would give him good hope of success. If Mr Davis would do this he would be encouraging a young fellow of, as you know, great poetical promise: by sending me the whole draft I could forward it to Rennell Rodd—his £25. As for your paper it is charming.[5] I would undertake to be your art-correspondent for London and Paris—two articles a month—and in the summer letters from Italy on art.

You will think this over. Ever yours   OSCAR WILDE

Post Scriptum

Yes: *The Daisy* will be the title, *and Other Poems*. You can print the little poem on the daisy first. As regards the binding, have it a bound book—not in loose sheets like Tiffany's monstrosity.[6] Send me your ideas of a cover. Lathrop[7] could do a delightful thing for you.

Look at dedication.[8]

[1] American artist (1834–1903), after studying in Paris, in 1862 settled in England and spent the rest of his life there. His methods of painting and opinions on art roused a storm of protest from conservative critics (including Ruskin) and from the public. At the beginning of their friendship, he and Wilde got on very well.

[2] It is impossible to date this letter, but "they" may well refer to the Americans.

[3] In 1881 Rennell Rodd (see note 2, p. 73) had published in London a small book of poems called *Songs in the South*. It was substantially this same volume which Wilde now sent to Stoddart, with his own preface or "envoi."

[4] Robert Stewart Davis (1839–1911), "a disciple of aestheticism," had given a reception for Wilde in Philadelphia on 16 January. He was the publisher of a new paper, *Our Continent*, whose first issue (15 February 1882) contained two poems by Wilde ("Impressions—1. Le Jardin, 2. La Mer"). Davis was presumably associated with Stoddart in publishing Rodd's poems.

[5] *Stoddart's Review*, which appeared monthly from March 1880 till June 1882.

[6] Possibly the cover of *Our Continent*, which was designed by Louis C. Tiffany.

[7] Francis Lathrop (1849–1909), American artist and book-illustrator. Studied in England under Madox Brown, Burne-Jones and William Morris 1870–73.

[8] *Songs in the South* had been dedicated to Rodd's father, but Wilde removed the dedication and substituted :

To Colonel W. F. Morse

MS. Clark

[? *26 February 1882*]   *St Louis* [*Missouri*]

Dear Colonel Morse, Will you kindly go to a good costumier (theatrical)
for me and get them to make (you will not mention my name) two coats,
to wear at matinées and perhaps in evening. They should be beautiful;
tight velvet doublet, with large flowered sleeves and little ruffs
of cambric coming up from under collar. I send you design and
measurements. They should be ready at *Chicago* on Saturday for matinée
there—at any rate the black one. Any good costumier would know what
I want—sort of Francis I dress: only knee-breeches instead of long hose.
Also get me two pair of grey silk stockings to suit grey mouse-coloured
velvet. The sleeves are to be flowered—if not velvet then plush—stamped
with large pattern. They will excite a great sensation. I leave the matter
to you. They were dreadfully disappointed at Cincinnati at my not wearing
knee-breeches. Truly yours   OSCAR WILDE

To Joaquin Miller[1]

28 February 1882   *St Louis*

My dear Joaquin Miller, I thank you for your chivalrous and courteous
letter to me published in the *World*. Believe me, I would as lief judge of

TO
OSCAR WILDE
"HEART'S BROTHER"
THESE FEW SONGS AND MANY SONGS TO COME

Rodd later complained to Stoddart that the dedication was "too effusive," and
asked for it to be removed from all the remaining copies.

[1] Pen-name of American poet, playwright, lawyer and journalist, Cincinnatus
Hiner (or Heine) Miller (1837–1913). His best-known book of poems was *Songs of
the Sierras* (1869). He had lectured in London, dressed as a cowboy and very
much the literary backwoodsman. Rossetti took a fancy to him and he came to be
known as "the American Byron." Wilde had met him in New York, whence on 9
February he had written (MS. Clark):

> My dear Oscar Wilde, I read with shame about the behaviour of those ruffians
> at Rochester at your lecture there [on 7 February].
>
> Sir, when I see such things here in the civilised portion of my country and read
> the coarse comments of the Philistine Press, I feel like thanking God that my
> home lies three thousand miles farther on, and in what is called the wilderness.
> Should you get as far as Oregon in your travels, go to my father's. You will find
> rest there, and room. As much land as you can encompass in a day's ride. And,
> Sir, I promise you there the respect due a stranger to our shores, to your attain-
> ments, your industry and your large, generous and tranquil nature.
>
> Or should you decide to return here and not bear further abuse, come to my
> house-top and abide with me where you will be welcome and loved as a brother.
> And bear this in mind, my dear boy, the more you are abused the more welcome
> you will be. For I remember how kind your country was to me; and at your age
> I had not done one-tenth your work. May my right hand fail me when I forget
> this.
>
> But don't you lose heart or come to dislike America. For whatever is said or

97

the strength and splendour of sun and sea by the dust that dances in the beam and the bubble that breaks on the wave,[1] as take the petty and profitless vulgarity of one or two insignificant towns as any test or standard of the real spirit of a sane, strong and simple people, or allow it to affect my respect for the many noble men and women whom it has been my privilege in this great country to know.

For myself and the cause which I represent I have no fears as regards the future. Slander and folly have their way for a season, but for a season only; while, as touching either the few provincial newspapers which have so vainly assailed me, or that ignorant and itinerant libeller of New England who goes lecturing from village to village in such open and ostentatious isolation, be sure I have no time to waste on them. Youth being so glorious, art so godlike, and the very world about us so full of beautiful things, and things worthy of reverence, and things honourable, how should one stop to listen to the lucubrations of a literary *gamin*, to the brawling and mouthing of a man whose praise would be as insolent as his slander is impotent, or to the irresponsible and irrepressible chatter of the professionally unproductive?

" 'Tis a great advantage, I admit, to have done nothing, but one must not abuse even that advantage!"[2]

Who, after all, that I should write of him, is this scribbling anonymuncule in grand old Massachusetts who scrawls and screams so glibly about what he cannot understand?[3] This apostle of inhospitality, who delights to defile, to desecrate, and to defame the gracious courtesies he is unworthy to enjoy? Who are these scribes who, passing with purposeless alacrity from the police news to the Parthenon, and from crime to criticism, sway with such serene incapacity the office which they so lately swept? "Narcissuses of imbecility," what should they see in the clear waters of

---

done the real heart of this strong young world demands, and will have, fair play for all. This sentiment is deep and substantial and will shew itself when appealed to.

So go ahead, my brave youth, and say your say if you choose. My heart is with you; and so are the hearts of the best of America's millions. Thine for the Beautiful and True   JOAQUIN MILLER

The *New York World* published this letter on 10 February under the heading THE SINGER OF THE SIERRAS SMITES THE PHILISTINES, and Wilde's answer on 3 March. It was reprinted in *Miscellanies*. Text from the *New York World*.

[1] This sentence from "judge" to "wave" is a quotation from Wilde's lecture "The English Renaissance."

[2] *"C'est sans doute un terrible avantage que de n'avoir rien fait, mais il ne faut pas en abuser"* (*Le Petit Almanach de nos Grands-hommes*, 1788, by Antoine de Rivarol, 1753–1801).

[3] This was generally believed to refer to Thomas Wentworth Higginson (1823–1911) of Cambridge, Mass., who had been a prominent anti-slavery reformer, a Colonel in the Civil War, was a keen advocate of Women's Suffrage, and a prolific author. In an article in the *Woman's Journal* of 4 February 1882 he denounced Wilde's poems as "immoral" and suggested he be socially ostracised. Mrs Julia Ward Howe (see note 2, p. 122), who had entertained Wilde in Boston, defended him in the *Boston Daily Globe* of 15 February.

Beauty and in the well undefiled of Truth but the shifting and shadowy image of their own substantial stupidity? Secure of that oblivion for which they toil so laboriously and, I must acknowledge, with such success, let them peer at us through their telescopes and report what they like of us. But, my dear Joaquin, should we put them under the microscope there would be really nothing to be seen.

I look forward to passing another delightful evening with you on my return to New York, and I need not tell you that whenever you visit England you will be received with that courtesy with which it is our pleasure to welcome all Americans, and that honour with which it is our privilege to greet all poets. Most sincerely and affectionately yours   OSCAR WILDE

To Mrs George Lewis
MS. Wansbrough

Tuesday, 28 February [*1882*]   *Grand Pacific Hotel, Chicago*

Dear Mrs Lewis, I send you a line to say that since Chicago I have had two great successes: Cincinnati where I have been invited to lecture a second time—this time to the workmen, on the handicraftsman—and St Louis. Tomorrow I start to lecture eleven consecutive nights at eleven different cities, and return here on Saturday week for a second lecture. I go to Canada then, and also return to New England to lecture. Of course I have much to bear—I have always had that—but still as regards my practical influence I have succeeded beyond my wildest hope. In every city they start schools of decorative art after my visit, and set on foot public museums, getting my advice about the choice of objects and the nature of the building. And the artists treat me like a young god. But of this I suppose little reaches England. My play will probably come out, but this is not settled, and I will be back about May I hope.

Pray remember me most affectionately to Mr Lewis, and believe me very truly yours   OSCAR WILDE

To Walt Whitman [1]
F. Traubel

[*Postmark 1 March 1882*]   [*Postmark Chicago*]

My dear dear Walt, Swinburne has just written to me to say as follows. "I am sincerely interested and gratified by your account of Walt

[1] The great American poet (1819–92) was now living in Camden, New Jersey, a suburb of Philadelphia across the Delaware, where Wilde had been taken by Stoddart to see him in January. Although his *Leaves of Grass* had been published as long ago as 1855, the eighth edition was withdrawn by its publishers in 1882 on a threatened prosecution for indecency. Whitman's prose work *Specimen Days and Collect* was published later in 1882.

Whitman and the assurance of his kindly and friendly feeling towards me: and I thank you, no less sincerely, for your kindness in sending me word of it. As sincerely can I say, what I shall be freshly obliged to you if you will [—should occasion arise—] assure him of in my name, that I have by no manner of means [either 'forgotten him' or] relaxed my admiration of his noblest work—such parts, above all, of his writings, as treat of the noblest subjects, material and spiritual, with which poetry can deal. I have always thought it, and I believe it will hereafter be generally thought, his highest and surely most enviable distinction that he never speaks so well as when he speaks of great matters—liberty, for instance, and death. This of course does not imply that I do—rather it implies that I do not—agree with all his theories or admire all his work in anything like equal measure—a form of admiration which I should by no means desire for myself and am as little prepared to bestow on another: considering it a form of scarcely indirect insult."[1]

There! You see how you remain in our hearts, and how simply and grandly Swinburne speaks of you, knowing you to be simple and grand yourself.

Will you in return send me for Swinburne a copy of your *Essay on Poetry*[2]—the pamphlet—with your name and his on it: it would please him so much.

Before I leave America I must see you again. There is no one in this wide great world of America whom I love and honour so much.

With warm affection, and honourable admiration   OSCAR WILDE

[1] The original of this letter is in the collection of Mr Charles E. Feinberg. Written from The Pines, Putney, and dated 2 February 1882, it begins "Dear Mr Wilde," continues as Wilde quoted it (with the addition of the two phrases I have added in square brackets) and ends:

Jones has not yet sent me the portrait which should have accompanied your letter; but as the latter has come safe to hand, no doubt the former will also in due time: for which I do not wait before sending my thanks to Whitman and yourself. Yours very truly   A. C. SWINBURNE

Watts sends you his best remembrances. He reminds me that you have not as yet—owing to the negligence of my publishers—received a copy of any one of my books in return for your own *Poems*. I am now rectifying that omission.

The book Swinburne sent was probably the first edition of *Studies in Song* (1880), inscribed "To Oscar Wilde from Algernon Ch. Swinburne. *Amitiés et remerciements*," which is now in the collection of Mr John S. Mayfield. On 4 April 1882 Swinburne wrote to E. C. Stedman (MS. Huntington):

The only time I ever saw Mr Oscar Wilde was in a crush at our acquaintance Lord Houghton's. I thought he seemed a harmless young nobody, and had no notion he was the sort of man to play the mountebank as he seems to have been doing. A letter which he wrote to me lately about Walt Whitman was quite a modest, gentlemanlike, reasonable affair, without any flourish or affectation of any kind in matter or expression. It is really very odd. I should think you in America must be as tired of his name as we in London of Mr Barnum's and his Jumbo's.

[2] *The Poetry of the Future*, published in the *North American Review*, February 1881, and reissued in pamphlet form.

To Colonel W. F. Morse

MS. Clark

[? *Early March 1882*]

Dear Colonel Morse, I hope you will not let me lecture again without a proper guarantee, which in every case it would be easy to get. Such fiasco as the last ten days have given should be avoided.

Also I hope you are reserving time for my return lectures at Boston, New York and Philadelphia, where I am sure I would draw large audiences, instead of wearing my voice and body to death over the wretched houses here.

Thank you for ordering the clothes: I hope they will fit: and I wish letters would come a little oftener. Yours very truly   OSCAR WILDE

To Colonel W. F. Morse

MS. Clark

[? *Early March 1882*]

Dear Colonel Morse, Mr D'Oyly Carte writes to me that you feel hurt at some remarks of mine about my management. He will explain to you that I was referring in no sense to you but to the carelessness and the stupidity of the subordinate whom you, with the best intentions doubtless, employed to bring me to Baltimore. As far as you are concerned you have shown Napoleonic powers of arrangement. I sometimes wish that my tour could be arranged more according to geographical convenience, but I dare say you can't help that: and possibly also the New York papers are out of your influence, as the *Herald* is of course doing me a great deal of harm; their not publishing the Press Association telegram about Chicago was most cowardly.

As soon as the clothes come, please send them to me. The tour is working very well, and the big towns great successes. The new lecture is very brilliant. I will have to write a third for Chicago, which will be a bore. Please get me in New York *Art in the House* by Loftie (Macmillan) and *The Art of Dress* by Mrs Haweis and send them to me.[1]

And as far as your management of my tour goes, be quite sure that I appreciate your organization and power. Yours truly   OSCAR WILDE

[1] The Rev. William John Loftie (1839–1911) published *A Plea for Art in the House, with special reference to the Economy of collecting Works of Art and the importance of Taste in Education and Morals* in Philadelphia 1876, and in London (Macmillan) 1877. In 1888 Loftie proposed Wilde for the Savile Club (see p.224). According to Max Beerbohm (*Conversation with Max* by S. N. Behrman, 1960) Loftie was an authority on gravel and came to a sad end. Mrs Mary Eliza (Joy) Haweis (1852–98) published *The Art of Dress* in 1879.

To James McNeill Whistler

MS. Glasgow

[? *Early March 1882*]   *Chicago*

My dear Jimmy, Your abominable attempt at literature has arrived: I
don't believe that my lovely and *spirituelle* Lady Archie[1] ever signed it at all.
I was so enraged that I insisted on talking about you to a reporter. I send
you the result.   OSCAR WILDE

To Colonel W. F. Morse

MS. Berg

[*Early March 1882*]   *Bloomington, Illinois*

Dear Colonel Morse, The mail has just arrived: I hope California can be
arranged. These small towns should not be taken without guarantee: it's
so depressing and useless lecturing for a few shillings.

Kindly send enclosed telegram.[2]

---

[1] Janey Sevilla Callander (d. 1923) married (1869) Lord Archibald Campbell,
younger son of the eighth Duke of Argyll. She was a close friend of Whistler.

[2] In answer to a communication dated 4 February 1882, signed with Whistler's
butterfly, and reading (text from Stetson sale catalogue, 1920):

> Oscar! We of Tite Street and Beaufort Gardens joy in your triumphs, and delight in
> your success, but—we think that, with the exception of your epigrams, you talk
> like Sidney Colvin in the Provinces, and that, with the exception of your knee-
> breeches, you dress like 'Arry Quilter.
>   Signed J. McNeill Whistler, Janey Campbell, Mat Elden, Rennell Rodd
> New York papers please copy.

Both Lady Archie Campbell and Rennell Rodd lived in Beaufort Gardens,
Chelsea. This letter, with minor variations of wording (including S—C—for Sidney
Colvin), was printed in the *World* of 15 February, over Whistler's signature only.
In the issue of 22 February Whistler protested at the editor's caution: "My dear
Atlas, if I may not always call a spade a spade, may I not call a Slade Professor
Sidney Colvin?"
  Sidney Colvin (1845–1927), Slade Professor of Fine Arts at Cambridge (1873–
1885, Director of Fitzwilliam Museum 1876–84, Keeper of Prints and Drawings in
the British Museum 1884–1912, knighted 1911, friend and editor of Robert Louis
Stevenson, biographer of Keats. The origin of Wilde's dislike of him is not known.
In April or May 1883 Stevenson wrote from Hyères to Mrs Sitwell (who later
married Colvin): "We have just had Oscar Wilde's incredible letter to Colvin and
have roared over it, the bad child dancing to a T. I read his poems and found, with
disappointment, they were not even improper. This letter is his liveliest work—
what would not *Punch* give to publish it verbatim." Wilde's letter has disappeared.
  Harry Quilter (1851–1907), English barrister, author and art-critic, was Whistler's
"arch-enemy" and butt. In 1886 Wilde wrote of his book *Sententiae Artis*: "We
fully admit that it is extremely amusing and, no doubt, Mr Quilter is quite earnest
in his endeavours to elevate art to the dignity of manual labour, but the extraordinary vulgarity of the style alone will always be sufficient to prevent these
Sententiae Artis from being anything more than curiosities of literature. Mr
Quilter has missed his chance; for he has failed even to make himself the Tupper
of Painting."

Wilde, New York   Whistler, Tite Street, Chelsea, London

I admit knee-breeches, and acknowledge epigrams, but reject Quilter and repudiate Colvin.[1]

I hope I am to lecture again in New York—and in Boston. Yours truly

OSCAR WILDE

The most lying telegrams are being sent to the *Daily News* of London every day about me. Who does it? I can guess.[2]

To Mrs George Lewis
MS. Wansbrough

[*Early March 1882*]   *Griggsville* [*Illinois*]

Dear Mrs Lewis, I am sorry to say that an art-movement has begun at Griggsville, for I feel it will not last long and that Colvin will be lecturing about it. At present the style here is Griggsville rococo, and there are also traces of "archaic Griggsville," but in a few days the Griggsville Renaissance will blossom: it will have an exquisite bloom for a week, and then (Colvin's fourth lecture) become "debased Griggsville," and the Griggsville Decadence. I seem to hear the Slade Professor,[3] or dear Newton, on it.[4] As for myself I promise you never, never, to lecture in England, *not even* at dinner.

The Giottos of Griggsville are waiting in a deputation below, so I must stop. With kind remembrances to Mr Lewis, and remembrances to Katie, yours sincerely   OSCAR WILDE

To Richard D'Oyly Carte
MS. Minnesota

16 March 1882   *Metropolitan Hotel, St Paul, Minnesota*

Dear Mr Carte, I have received your letter about the play.[5] I agree to place it entirely in your hands for production on the terms of my receiving half-profits, and a guarantee of £200 paid down to me on occasion of its production, said £200 to be deducted from my share of subsequent profits if any. This I think you will acknowledge is fair. Of course for my absolute work, the play, I must have absolute certainty of some small kind.

As regards the cast: I am sure you see yourself how well the part will suit Clara Morris: I am however quite aware how *difficile* she is, and what practical dangers may attend the perilling of it on her. If you, exercising right and careful judgment, find it impossible to depend on her—then,

---

[1] Wilde followed this with an almost identically worded note to Whistler from Griggsville (MS. Glasgow.)   [2] Archibald Forbes.   [3] Ruskin.
[4] Sir Charles Thomas Newton (1816–94), archaeologist and author, was Keeper of Greek and Roman Antiquities in the British Museum 1861–85, and Professor of Classical Archaeology at University College London 1880–88. Wilde had taken Mrs Langtry to hear him lecture on Greek art.
[5] *Vera* (see note 2, p. 70). Carte arranged for a new, revised, edition (with the prologue added) to be printed in America while Wilde was there.

while the present excitement lasts, let us go to Rose Coghlan,[1] and Wallack's Theatre—they have a good company—and if Miss Morris cannot be really retained I am willing to leave it in your hands for Rose Coghlan. In case of producing it here, I will rely on you to secure a copyright for England also by some simultaneous performance. This however you can manage naturally without any advice of mine.

Please let me know your acceptance of my terms, and your decision of the cast by wire, as soon as possible. Yours very truly   OSCAR WILDE

Prologue follows soon: have been so tired—too tired to write.

To Richard D'Oyly Carte

MS. Berg

[*March 1882*]

Dear Mr Carte, I send you the prologue: if it is too long cut it. I have introduced Prince Paul Maraloffski in it as a simple Colonel: this will give a dramatic point to his meeting Vera among the Nihilists in the third act, where I will introduce a little speech about it. I will also give Vera a few sentences about her brother being sent to Siberia to show the connection of the prologue. This will be a matter of a few minutes only, when I get to New York.

The first act, which at present stands "Tomb of the Kings at Moscow," has too operatic a title: it is to be called "99 Rue Tchernavaza, Moscow," and the conspirators are to be *modern*, and the room a bare garret, painted crimson. It is to be realistic not operatic conspiracy. I am sure you will agree with me in that?

Let me hear soon about it. Truly yours   OSCAR WILDE

To Richard D'Oyly Carte

MS. Clark

[*March 1882*]

Dear Mr Carte, As regards any changes in the play, pray rest assured that any suggestions I will be only too glad to get. The play is meant, not to be read, but to be acted, and the actor has always a right to object and to suggest. No one could recognise the artist's right more than I do in the matter. The only reason, to speak honestly, that the play is as good an acting play as it is, is that I took every actor's suggestion I could get.

I am sorry you are going back to England, but suppose you would return for its production, which should not be at any matinée, or with any actress but Clara Morris—an evening theatre. I feel it will succeed, if she acts and you manage. Could you get Kyrle Bellew[2] or Johnston Forbes-Robertson for the Czarevitch?

---

[1] English actress (1851–1932) who worked mostly in America and was for many years leading lady at Wallack's Theatre in New York. In 1893 she produced *A Woman of No Importance* there.   [2] English actor (1855–1911).

Flockton[1] would be an able Prince Paul—and for the Czar a good character actor. But you know all the actors of course.

I hope Colonel Morse is arranging for a second New York lecture—I think it should go. Yours very truly   OSCAR WILDE

To Mrs George Lewis
MS. Wansbrough

[? *Circa 20 March 1882*]   [? *Sioux City*]

Dear Mrs Lewis, I am sure you will be interested to hear that I have met Indians. They are really in appearance very like Colvin, when he is wearing his professorial robes: the likeness is quite curious, and revived pleasant literary reminiscences. Their conversation was most interesting as long as it was unintelligible, but when interpreted to me reminded me strangely and vividly of the conversation of Mr Commissioner Kerr.[2]

I don't know where I am: somewhere in the middle of coyotes and cañons: one is a "ravine" and the other a "fox," I don't know which, but I think they change about. I have met miners: they are big-booted, red-shirted, yellow-bearded and delightful ruffians. One of them asked me if I was not "running an art-mill," and on my pointing to my numerous retinue, said he "guessed I hadn't need to wash my own pans," and his "pardner" remarked that "I hadn't need to sell clams neither, I could toot my own horn." I secretly believe they read up Bret Harte privately; they were certainly almost as real as his miners, and quite as pleasant. With my usual passion for personality I entertained them, and had a delightful time, though on my making some mention of early Florentine art they unanimously declared they could neither "trump or follow it."

Weary of being asked by gloomy reporters "which was the most beautiful colour" and what is the meaning of the word "aesthetic," on my last Chicago interview I turned the conversation on three of my heroes, Whistler, Labouchere,[3] and Irving, and on the adored and adorable Lily. I send you them all.

I hope you are all well. Pray remember me to your husband, and to the Grange when you visit there next.

Colvin in a blanket has just passed the window: he is decked out with feathers, and wants me to buy bead slippers; it is really most odd, and undoubtedly Colvin, I could hardly be mistaken.

Give my love to Katie please!!! and believe me, most sincerely and truly yours   OSCAR WILDE

[1] Charles P. Flockton (1828–1904), English actor who worked mostly in America.

[2] Robert Malcolm Kerr (1821–1902), Scottish judge of the City of London Court, 1859–1901. He was a strict teetotaller, and *Men and Women of the Time* (1895) comments: "Mr Commissioner Kerr is well known for his just administration of the law for the protection of the victims of unscrupulous usurers."

[3] Henry Du Pré Labouchere (1831–1912). Radical M.P. for Northampton 1880–1905. Founded *Truth* 1876. See note 1, p. 519.

To Colonel W. F. Morse

TS. Holland

[*21 March 1882*][1]   *Withnell House, Omaha, Nebraska*

Dear Colonel Morse, Six lectures a week for three weeks seem to me
enormous. I do not know if I can stand it. You should have communicated
with me first. However I will do my best, and if I feel Titan-like will do
matinées, but I do not think that possible: it depends of course on the
distances.

I did not revive any discussion on the Baltimore business at Chicago for
many reasons. First, the Chicago papers were particularly hostile at the
time, accusing me of encouraging the attack on me and of having "corrected
the proofs of the Washington attack and approved of the caricature before
it was published." These are the words of the *Chicago Herald*. It would
have been quite foolish to have gone back to an interview of a month old
which does not concern the public, when the paper had signified that it
would not have any more interviews, that I was seeking notoriety.

If Mr Carte wishes a public discussion on why I went to Washington
instead of to Baltimore I think he is very foolish. I will never be ready to
give any newspaper man all details about the bungling of the office-clerk
you sent down to take charge of me. Mr Carte should have (at the time I
was being so brutally assailed) written to say that the mistake arose through
a careless messenger from the office. It is intolerable to bore me about the
idiocy of an office-clerk. I have told Mr Carte the facts of the case, and that
is sufficient. I will lay the whole matter before my lawyer when I go back
to London. As regards my opinion of my management, that would be

---

[1] This letter is so dated by Mason (p. 255) and is certainly in answer to the
following (MS. Clark):

11 March 1882   *New York*

Dear Mr Wilde, This is the first day I have been out of bed for a week, and I am
still quite weak from a severe attack of malaria and neuralgia. I have tonight
wired both the applicants for the California trip, Seager of Lincoln and Fulton of
Kansas City, proposing terms for California: 60% of the gross, a guarantee of
$200 per night to be paid in advance, and fares for three to California and return.
If either one accepts they will meet you at Omaha prepared to go through. The
trip will take three weeks; ten lectures as a minimum, eighteen at the most. I
wired this to Vale tonight, and am in hopes to arrange by wire, which will save me
from coming to Chicago which I am in no condition to do.

If I fail with these men I shall arrange a tour back through Canada where I have
sold four nights and then into New England.

The business of last week was bad as the smaller towns are of no use. Mr Carte
has written fully about the play and I enclose his letter. He sailed today.

I have 100 artist's proofs of the etching [by J. E. Kelly] which I wish you would
kindly sign as it will increase their value greatly. Everything is being done that
can be to make the tour a success. I don't think the lithographs will be of
assistance since the season is so late. They are expensive and before we could get
them ready the tour will be nearly closed. Will you please advise Mr Vale of the
business arrangements proposed for California so he can complete should the
parties wire him. Fulton is the man if we can get him. Yours truly

W. F. MORSE

premature to declare now; at the close of my tour will be the time. Except for the Baltimore business, the Forbes business, I am quite satisfied, except as regards a few minor points, for which possibly the office may not be responsible.

I send you the play-prologue; please let me know latest particulars. I am very tired and worn out. Thank you for sending Lady Wilde the cheque. Did you send one to Edwin Levy[1] for £70 about the 5th February? Truly yours   OSCAR WILDE

I will lecture as long as the public stands being lectured—to middle of May certainly, or the end of it.[2]

---

[1] From this reference and the one on p. 462 it seems possible that Levy was some kind of money-lender or private inquiry agent. There are in Clark two letters from him to Wilde. The first was written from Elphinstone Lodge, Hastings, on 26 January 1883 and asks for an appointment in London. The second has no place of origin, is dated 17 April 1884 and runs: "Dear Mr Wilde, I am sorry that I have neglected attending to your business, but I have been suffering from a severe cold. I trust that the lace pleased Miss Lloyd. Enclosed please find cheque for £25. Yours truly, Edwin Levy." The Hastings directories show "E. Levy" as occupier of Elphinstone Lodge from 1883 to 1895, and "M. Levy" for the year 1896.

On 10 May 1895 *The Times* reported:

The gross amount has been entered as £261,518 of the personal estate of Mr Edwin Levy, chief proprietor of the business of refreshment contractors carried on as J. Lyons & Co. (Ltd) and one of the founders of Olympia (Ltd) who died [In West Hampstead] on February 26 last aged 55, intestate. Letters of administration have been granted to his widow Mrs Marion Levy.

The *Hampstead Record* further described him as "some years ago the confidential agent of the Emperor Napoleon III," though, according to Ivor Guest (*Napoleon III in England*, 1952), "the French Government were very concerned to know what was happening at Camden Place [Chislehurst], and employed a private detective called Edwin Levy to instal agents in the windmill on the other side of the cricket field and report the names of all the visitors to the house. But Mr Levy's spies were themselves spied upon, for every morning a copy of this report was placed on the Emperor's breakfast table!"

There is nothing to connect these Levys with the ones at Hastings, except the initials and the dates, which seem a little too exact to be coincidental.

[2] Morse answered from New York on 5 April (text from Mason, p. 257):

Dear Mr Wilde, I send herewith all letters received to date. None have been forwarded since 28th ult. to San Francisco. You will receive others at Kansas City.

I have the Prologue. There is no change in the present situation with regard to Miss Morris. She is announced for the leading part in an American adaptation of *Far from the Madding Crowd* at the Union Square Theatre to begin April 29, which probably was the reason why she was unwilling to consider the new play. It would seem to be best to postpone until next season the production, as the spring season here is very short and very unfavourable to the production of heavy pieces.

Your route will include lectures in Kansas for a week, then through Ohio to Pittsburgh, from where I propose to take the coal regions north into Canada and close the third week of May in New England, ending with a farewell lecture in New York which might be to a great extent a summary of your impressions—from an artistic standpoint—of America. Such a lecture would I think fill the house full.

There are received the copies of the *Poems* you sent for, which will have to pay a duty of $2.50. I have five copies of a medallion on plaster cast of an illustration

To Emma Speed[1]

MS. Pratt

21 March 1882   [*Omaha, Nebraska*]

What you have given me is more golden than gold, more precious than any treasure this great country could yield me, though the land be a network of railways, and each city a harbour for the galleys of the world.

It is a sonnet I have loved always, and indeed who but the supreme and perfect artist could have got from a mere colour a motive so full of marvel: and now I am half enamoured of the paper that touched his hand, and the ink that did his bidding, grown fond of the sweet comeliness of his charactery, for since my boyhood I have loved none better than your marvellous kinsman, that godlike boy, the real Adonis of our age, who knew the silver-footed messages of the moon, and the secret of the morning, who heard in Hyperion's vale the large utterance of the early gods, and from the beechen plot the light-winged Dryad, who saw Madeline at the painted window, and Lamia in the house at Corinth, and Endymion ankle-deep in lilies of the vale, who drubbed the butcher's boy for being a bully, and drank confusion to Newton for having analysed the rainbow. In my heaven he walks eternally with Shakespeare and the Greeks, and it may be that some day he will lift

> "his hymenaeal curls from out his amber gleaming wine,
> With ambrosial lips will kiss my forehead, clasp the hand of noble love in
>   mine."[2]

Again I thank you for this dear memory of the man I love, and thank you also for the sweet and gracious words in which you give it to me: it were strange in truth if one in whose veins flows the same blood as quickened into song that young priest of beauty, were not with me in this great renaissance

---

of a verse of one of your poems received from the designer. The copies of the etching were sent to England as you desired.

I have sent Mr Vale a sketch of the route and have made several good engagements which I think may bring in a good sum.

I shall do my best to make as successful a season as possible for the credit of all concerned. Very faithfully yours,   W. F. MORSE

[1] 1823–83. Wife of Philip Speed and daughter of George Keats, the poet's younger brother, who had emigrated to America in 1818 and made a fortune out of timber. She lived at Louisville, Kentucky, as her father had done, and after Wilde had lectured there on 21 February she invited him home and showed him her Keats letters and manuscripts. On 12 March she sent him the manuscript of Keats's "Sonnet on Blue," which he had quoted in his lecture. Wilde's account of this incident appeared in the *Century Guild Hobby Horse* for July 1886 (together with a facsimile of the manuscript) and was reprinted in *Miscellanies*. At the forced sale of Wilde's belongings on 24 April 1895 lot 122, "An etching of a lady, by Menpes after W. Graham Robertson, and a Manuscript Poem, by Keats, framed," was knocked down to a Mr Shaw for 38/-.

[2] A slightly altered quotation from Wilde's poem "Flower of Love," published in *Poems* (1881).

of art which Keats indeed would have so much loved, and of which he, above all others, is the seed.

Let me send you my sonnet on Keats's grave, which you quote with such courteous compliment in your note, and if you would let it lie near his own papers it may keep some green of youth caught from those withered leaves in whose faded lines eternal summer dwells.

I hope that some day I may visit you again at St Louis,[1] and see the little Milton and the other treasures once more: strange, you call your house "dingy and old," ah, dear Madam, fancy has long ago made it a palace for me, and I see it transfigured through the golden mists of joy. With deep respect, believe me, most truly yours   OSCAR WILDE[2]

To Norman Forbes-Robertson

TS. Congress

27 March 1882   *San Francisco*

My dear Norman, Here from the uttermost end of the great world I send you love and greeting, and thanks for your letters which delight me very much. But, dear boy, your hair will lose its gold and your cheek its roses if you insist on being such a chivalrous defender of this much abused young man. It is so brave and good of you! Of course I will win: I have not the slightest intention of failing for a moment, and my tour here is triumphal. I was four days in the train: at first grey, gaunt desolate plains, as colourless as waste land by the sea, with now and then scampering herds of bright red antelopes, and heavy shambling buffaloes, rather like Joe Knight[3] in manner and appearance, and screaming vultures like gnats high up in the air, then up the Sierra Nevadas, the snow-capped mountains shining like shields of polished silver in that vault of blue flame we call the sky, and deep cañons full of pine trees, and so for four days, and at last from the chill winter of the mountains down into eternal summer here, groves of orange trees in fruit and flower, green fields, and purple hills, a very Italy, without its art.

There were 4,000 people waiting at the "depot" to see me, open carriage, four horses, an audience at my lecture of the most cultivated people in 'Frisco, charming folk. I lecture again here tonight, also twice next week; as you see I am really appreciated—by the cultured classes.[4] The railway have offered me a special train and private car to go down the coast to

---

[1] A slip for Louisville.

[2] Enclosed was a handwritten copy of Wilde's sonnet "The Grave of Keats," its text substantially the same as that in *Poems* (1881) but with a few minor differences.

[3] Joseph Knight (1829–1907), English dramatic critic. Editor of *Notes and Queries* from 1883. Wilde slated his *Life of Dante Gabriel Rossetti* in the *Pall Mall Gazette* of 18 April 1887 under the heading "A Cheap Edition of a Great Man," describing the book as "just the sort of biography Guildenstern might have written of Hamlet," and Knight in his turn scoffed at *Lady Windermere's Fan* in 1892.

[4] On 5 April Wilde lectured in San Francisco on "The Irish Poets of '48." A manuscript of this lecture is in the collection of Mr Montgomery Hyde. It was published in the *University Review*, Dublin, spring 1955.

Los Angeles, a sort of Naples here, and I am fêted and entertained to my heart's content. I lecture here in California for three weeks, then to Kansas; after that I am not decided.

These wretched lying telegrams in the *Daily News* are sent by Archibald Forbes, who has been a fiasco in his lecturing this season and is jealous of me. He is a coward and a fool. No telegram can kill or mar a man with anything in him. The women here are beautiful. Tonight I am escorted by the Mayor of the city through the Chinese quarter, to their theatre and joss houses and rooms, which will be most interesting. They have "houses" and "persons."[1]

Pray remember me to all at home, also to that splendid fellow Millais and his stately and beautiful wife.[2]

Love to Johnston. Ever yours   OSCAR WILDE

(My new signature—specially for California)

To Helena Sickert

TS. Clark

[*Circa 10 April 1882*]   *Salt Lake City, Utah*

Dear Miss Nellie, Walter has told me in a charming letter of your chivalrous attempt to defend me against the *Daily News*. Those foolish and lying telegrams are sent by Archibald Forbes, who, merely because his lectures are now a failure, revenges himself on me because I am thought a greater attraction, but they do not in any way mirror the feeling of the people of America, who have received me with love and courtesy and hospitality. Nothing could be more generous than their treatment of me, or more attentive than my audiences. Even the papers, though venal and vile, and merely the mouthpieces of the slanderer, often report and write sensibly about me. I send you an extract from the last place I lectured at before this. It is full of common sense. I feel I am doing real good work here, and of course the artists have received me with enthusiasm everywhere. The excitement I cause would amuse you and amuses me, but the country is full of wonders—buffaloes, Indians, elks and the like. It all interests me very much.

I thank you very very sincerely for thinking of me, and trying to help me against my many foes, and with love to all at home, believe me, ever your sincere friend   OSCAR WILDE

To Mrs Bernard Beere[3]

[*17 April 1882*]   *Kansas City, Missouri*

My dear Bernie, I have lectured to the Mormons. The Opera House at

---

[1] Presumably brothels and their inhabitants.

[2] John Everett Millais, English painter (1829–96), R.A. 1863, Baronet 1885, P.R.A. 1895, married (1855) Euphemia Chalmers Gray, whose marriage to Ruskin had been annulled in 1854.

[3] English actress (1856–1915). Originally Fanny Mary Whitehead, she married

Salt Lake is an enormous affair about the size of Covent Garden, and holds with ease fourteen families. They sit like this

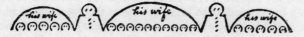

and are very, very ugly. The President, a nice old man, sat with five wives in the stage box. I visited him in the afternoon and saw a charming daughter of his.[1]

I have also lectured at Leadville, the great mining city in the Rocky Mountains. We took a whole day to get up to it on a narrow-gauge railway 14,000 feet in height. My audience was entirely miners; their make-up excellent, red shirts and blonde beards, the whole of the first three rows being filled with McKee Rankins of every colour and dimension.[2] I spoke to them of the early Florentines, and they slept as though no crime had ever stained the ravines of their mountain home. I described to them the pictures of Botticelli, and the name, which seemed to them like a new drink, roused them from their dreams, but when I told them in my boyish eloquence of the "secret of Botticelli" the strong men wept like children. Their sympathy touched me and I approached modern art and had almost won them over to a real reverence for what is beautiful when unluckily I described one of Jimmy Whistler's "nocturnes in blue and gold." Then they leaped to their feet and in their grand simple way swore that such things should not be. Some of the younger ones pulled their revolvers out and left hurriedly to see if Jimmy was "prowling about the saloons " or

---

three times, but always acted under her second married name. She made her début at the Opera Comique in London in 1877. All arrangements had been made for her to play the principal part in Wilde's *Vera* at the Adelphi Theatre on 17 December 1881, but three weeks beforehand the production was cancelled, "considering the present state of political feeling in England." The Czar Alexander II had been assassinated in March, and the new Czarina was the Prince of Wales's sister-in-law. The text of this letter, and facsimile of the drawing, are taken from *Oscar Wilde, Fragments and Memories* by Martin Birnbaum (1920).

[1] John Taylor (1808–1887). He accompanied Brigham Young on the mass migration to Utah, became acting President on Brigham Young's death in 1877, and officially third President of the Church of Jesus Christ of Latter-day Saints in October 1880. He had seven wives who bore him thirty-four children. He was forced into exile in 1884 to escape arrest by the U.S. Government following a Federal edict against polygamy. In Wilde's lecture "Personal Impressions of America" he said:

Salt Lake City contains only two buildings of note, the chief being the Tabernacle which is in the shape of a soup-kettle . . .

The building next in importance is called the Amelia Palace, in honour of one of Brigham Young's wives. When he died the present President of the Mormons stood up in the Tabernacle and said that it had been revealed to him that he was to have the Amelia Palace, and that on this subject there were to be no more revelations of any kind.

[2] Arthur McKee Rankin (1842–1914), American actor-manager, had appeared at Sadler's Wells in *The Danites in the Sierras*, a sensational melodrama about the Mormons by Joaquin Miller, in April 1880.

"wrestling a hash" at any eating shop. Had he been there I fear he would have been killed, their feeling was so bitter. Their enthusiasm satisfied me and I ended my lecture there. Then I found the Governor of the State[1] waiting in a bullock *wagon* to bring me down the great silver-mine of the world, the Matchless. So off we drove, the miners carrying torches before us till we came to the shaft and were shot down in buckets (I of course true to my principle being graceful even in a bucket) and down in the great gallery of the mine, the walls and ceilings glittering with metal ore, was spread a banquet for us.

The amazement of the miners when they saw that art and appetite could go hand in hand knew no bounds; when I lit a long cigar they cheered till the silver fell in dust from the roof on our plates; and when I quaffed a cocktail without flinching,[2] they unanimously pronounced me in their grand simple way "a bully boy with no glass eye"—artless and spontaneous praise which touched me more than the pompous panegyrics of literary critics ever did or could. Then I had to open a new vein, or lode, which with a silver drill I brilliantly performed, amidst unanimous applause. The silver drill was presented to me and the lode named "The Oscar." I had hoped that in their simple grand way they would have offered me shares in "The Oscar," but in their artless untutored fashion they did not. Only the silver drill remains as a memory of my night at Leadville.

I have had a delightful time all through California and Colorado and am now returning home, twice as affected as ever, my dear Bernie. Please remember me to dear Dot,[3] to Reggie and all our mutual friends including Monty Morris, who won't write to me or even criticise me. Goodbye. Your sincere friend   OSCAR WILDE

To Norman Forbes-Robertson
TS. Congress

19 April 1882   *St Joseph, Missouri*

My dear Norman, Outside my window about a quarter of a mile to the west there stands a little yellow house, with a green paling, and a crowd of

[1] Horace Austin Warner Tabor (1830–99), miner, politician and "bonanza king," made a fortune in silver-mining and real estate. He spent it lavishly as Lieutenant-Governor of Colorado (1879–83), buying a seat in the Senate (1883), building an opera house and otherwise developing Denver. He divorced his first wife to marry a dashing divorcée, secretly in 1882, and publicly with President Arthur as guest of honour in 1883. He became careless in his investments and went bankrupt in 1893. His second wife was found frozen to death in a shack beside the Matchless mine in 1935.

[2] Cf. R. L. Stevenson's American experience in 1880: "The playful innocuous American cocktail. I drank it, and lo! veins of living fire ran down my leg; and then a focus of conflagration remained seated in my stomach, not unpleasantly, for a quarter of an hour" (*The Silverado Squatters*, 1883).

[3] The nickname of Dionysius George Boucicault (1859–1929), actor and dramatist. Son of the playwright (see note 5, p. 70) and husband (1901) of the actress Irene Vanbrugh.

people pulling it all down. It is the house of the great train-robber and murderer, Jesse James, who was shot by his pal last week, and the people are relic-hunters.[1]

They sold his dust-bin and foot-scraper yesterday by public auction, his door-knocker is to be offered for sale this afternoon, the reserve price being about the income of an English bishop. The citizens of Kansas have telegraphed to an agent here to secure his coal-scuttle at all hazards and at any cost, and his favourite chromo-lithograph was disposed of at a price which in Europe only an authentic Titian can command, or an undoubted masterpiece.[2] The Americans are certainly great hero-worshippers, and always take their heroes from the criminal classes.

I still journey and lecture: it is a desperately exciting life. They want me now to go to Australia but I think I will refuse. I am not sure yet.

I hope you are better, dear old boy, and that Forby and all your people are well. *Don't yield to Eustacia.* I rely on you.

My night with the miners at Leadville was most exciting, down in the mine. I opened a new shaft called "The Oscar" in Governor Tabor's "Matchless mine." I had hoped that the miners in their simple, artless way would have given me shares in it, but in their childlike frankness they did not, but when they saw that I could smoke a long cigar, and drink a cocktail without winking, they called me in their simple language "a bully boy with no glass eye," spontaneous and artless praise far better in its unstudied frankness than the laboured and pompous panegyric of the literary critics. Ever yours   OSCAR

To an Unidentified Correspondent

MS. Clark

19 April [1882]   *The World's Hotel, St Joseph, Missouri*

Dear Hattie, Outside my window about a quarter of a mile to the west there is a small yellow house surrounded by people. This is Jesse James's house, and the people are relic-hunters. The door-knocker was sold yesterday by public auction and the man who sold it has retired on a large income in consequence. Today the foot-scraper and the dust-bin are to be raffled for, and his favourite chromo-lithograph has already been disposed of at a price which in Europe only a Titian or an authentic Michael Angelo can command. The Americans, if not hero-worshippers, are villain-worshippers. They interest me vastly, but when I think of America I only remember someone whose lips are like the crimson petals of a summer rose, whose eyes are two brown agates, who has the fascination of a panther, the pluck of a tigress, and the grace of a bird.

Darling Hattie, I now realise that I am absolutely in love with you, and for ever and ever your affectionate and devoted friend   OSCAR WILDE

[1] Jesse James (b. 1847) was in fact murdered by his friend Bob Ford on 3 April.
[2] So in the typescript, but "Mantegna" or even "Michael Angelo" seems more likely than "masterpiece" (see next letter and p. 115).

My kindest regards to Mr and Mrs Hobson, two of the most charming people in the world.

To Norman Forbes-Robertson
TS. Congress

[*Circa 20 April 1882*]   *The Windsor, Topeka, Kansas*

Dear Norman, The summer is just breaking in Kansas, and everything looks lovely. I took a long drive by myself yesterday afternoon and had a delightful time in what they call a "spider buggy and a fly-up trotter." No one knows the pleasure of driving till one drives an American trotter. They are absolutely perfect!

The local poet has just called on me with his masterpiece, a sanguinary lyric of 3000 lines on the Civil War. The most impassioned part begins thus:

"Here Mayor Simpson battled bravely with his Fifteenth Kansas Cavalry."

What am I to do? I enclose this morning's interview. Ever yours

OSCAR

To Helena Sickert
TS. Clark

25 April 1882   *Fremont, Nebraska*

My dear Miss Nellie, Since I wrote to you I have been to wonderful places, to Colorado which is like the Tyrol a little, and has great cañons of red sandstone, and pine trees, and the tops of the mountains all snow-covered, and up a narrow-gauge railway did I rush to the top of a mountain 15,000 feet high, to the great mining city of the west called Leadville, and lectured the miners on the old workers in metal—Cellini and others. All I told them about Cellini and how he cast his Perseus interested them very much, and they were a most courteous audience; typical too—large blonde-bearded, yellow-haired men in red shirts, with the beautiful clear complexions of people who work in silver-mines.

After my lecture I went down a silver-mine, about a mile outside the little settlement, the miners carrying torches before us as it was night. After being dressed in miner's dress I was hurled in a bucket down into the heart of the earth, long galleries of silver-ore, the miners all at work, looking so picturesque in the dim light as they swung the hammers and cleft the stone, beautiful motives for etching everywhere, and for Walter's impressionist sketches. I stayed all night there nearly, the men being most interesting to talk to, and was brought off down the mountain by a special train at 4.30 in the morning.

From there I went to Kansas where I lectured a week. At St Joseph the great desperado of Kansas, Jesse James, had just been killed by one of his followers, and the whole town was mourning over him and buying relics of his house. His door-knocker and dust-bin went for fabulous prices, two speculators absolutely came to pistol-shots as to who was to have his hearth-brush, the unsuccessful one being, however, consoled by being allowed to purchase the water-butt for the income of an English bishop, while his sole work of art, a chromo-lithograph of the most dreadful kind, of course was sold at a price which in Europe only a Mantegna or an undoubted Titian can command!

Last night I lectured at Lincoln, Nebraska, and in the morning gave an address to the undergraduates of the State University there: charming audience—young men and women all together in the same college, attending lectures and the like, and many young admirers and followers among them. They drove me out to see the great prison afterwards! Poor odd types of humanity in hideous striped dresses making bricks in the sun, and all mean-looking, which consoled me, for I should hate to see a criminal with a noble face. Little whitewashed cells, so tragically tidy, but with books in them. In one I found a translation of Dante, and a Shelley. Strange and beautiful it seemed to me that the sorrow of a single Florentine in exile should, hundreds of years afterwards, lighten the sorrow of some common prisoner in a modern gaol,[1] and one murderer with melancholy eyes—to be hung they told me in three weeks—spending that interval in reading novels, a bad preparation for facing either God or Nothing. So every day I see something curious and new, and now think of going to Japan and wish Walter would come or could come with me.

Pray give my love to everybody at home, and believe me your affectionate friend
OSCAR WILDE

To J. M. Stoddart
MS. Clark

[*Date of receipt 3 May 1882*]

Dear Mr Stoddart, I enclose final proof. I call it now "*L'*Envoi" and not "Envoi"—please see that the *headings* are right.

The poems seem correct, but let the printer be correct about his Greek. Ἔρωτος ἄνθος[2] (not αὔθος).

On page 11 please see that it is right:

"as swift and as sure as the beating of a bird's wing, *as* light and bright as"

I wish you could insert "The Sea-King's Grave" before "Tiber Mouth." It comes in well there. But it is not of much importance. Yours most truly
OSCAR WILDE

[1] Wilde himself read the whole of Dante in Reading Gaol.
[2] The flower of love.

115

To J. M. Stoddart

TS. Holland

[? *3 May 1882*]   *Columbus, Ohio*

Dear Mr Stoddart, Blank pages of themselves, being non-beautiful, could
not add anything to the charm of the book;[1] they must be ornamented.
You should get some young designer to do two good woodblocks of
delicate flower ornament, in treatment and in idea like a Japanese fan—just
a spray in blossom and a bird in flight, but put exactly in the right place,
and so giving one the right sense of ornament, the effect of the whole
surface being decorated. You might have one page of roses, and the other
page of apple blossoms and call the book *Rose leaf and Apple leaf,*[2] or
Narcissus and Daffodil, using those flowers—indeed all flowers would be
delightful—and out of any ordinary collection of Japanese fans or any book
of Japanese art any young artist will get the most perfect models, for while
the Japanese don't mind twisting the limbs of men and women into any
shape they are never grotesque in their flowers. I say wood engraving on
account of the superior texture wood gets as opposed to steel in the matter
of flowers, but no doubt you would have for printing purposes to get them
electrotyped or reproduced in some way.

Then the cover should be Japanese also, *not* grotesque, but beautiful.
This would be a delightful idea for book printing. I had intended to use
it for my own volume but it would have made it too large.

Of course the more varied the designs are the better, but two would do.
Yours ever   OSCAR WILDE

To J. M. Stoddart

MS. Clark

[*Date of receipt 5 May 1882*]

My young singer never wearies of singing. Here are two more poems—
quite beautiful. Send me proofs of them and of *the preface* also. I must get
a notice in somewhere of them—as they are so good.   OSCAR WILDE

To Norman Forbes-Robertson

F. Brasol

12 May 1882   [*Windsor Hotel, Montreal*]

My dear Norman, I am so delighted you are coming over. I will see that
you have some pleasant houses in Boston to go to. I hope I will be there.

---

[1] Rennell Rodd's poems (see note 3, p.96). The limited edition of the book was
eventually printed with the text and engravings in brown ink on one side of transparent buff paper, interleaved with blank sheets of apple-green paper. The ordinary
edition was printed normally in black on white paper.

[2] This title was eventually chosen, and the book was entered for copyright at the
Library of Congress, Washington, in Stoddart's name on 18 July 1882.

You and I will sit and drink "Boy" in our room and watch the large posters of our names. I am now six feet high (my name on the placards), printed it is true in those primary colours against which I pass my life protesting, but still it is fame, and anything is better than virtuous obscurity, even one's own name in alternate colours of Albert blue and magenta and six feet high.

This is my view at present from the Windsor Hotel, Montreal. I feel I have not lived in vain. My second lecture at New York was a brilliant success. I lectured at Wallack's Theatre in the afternoon, *not an empty seat*, and I have greatly improved in speaking and in gesture. I am really quite eloquent—at times. I was greatly congratulated.

Tomorrow night I lecture Lorne on dadoes at Ottawa.[1]

A nice friend of yours has just called—Murray Balfour—friend of Miller's. Ever yours   OSCAR

To Charles Godfrey Leland [2]

MS. Yale

[*Circa 15 May 1882*]   [*Montreal*]

My dear Mr Leland, Your letter was very very welcome to me, and indeed I do think that as regards that part of my lecture in which I spoke of the

[1] The Marquess of Lorne (1845–1914) was Governor-General of Canada 1878–83. In 1871 he married Princess Louise, the fourth daughter of Queen Victoria. He succeeded his father as ninth Duke of Argyll in 1900.

[2] American author (1824–1903). Authority on the language of the gipsies. His dialect ballads, *Hans Breitmann's Barty* (1868) and its sequels, were immensely popular. In 1882 he was working in his native Philadelphia trying to persuade the public schools to teach the industrial arts. Wilde had lectured there on "Decorative Art" on 10 May and repeated the lecture at Wallack's Theatre in New York on 11 May. The *New York Tribune* printed a full report on Friday, 12 May, including the following:

I would have a workshop attached to every school, and one hour a day given up to the teaching of simple decorative arts. It would be a golden hour to the

necessity of art as the factor of a child's education, and how all knowledge comes in doing something not in thinking about it, and how a lad who learns any simple art learns honesty, and truth-telling, and simplicity, in the most practical school of simple morals in the world, the school of art, learns too to love nature more when he sees how no flower by the wayside is too lowly, no little blade of grass too common but some great designer has seen it and loved it and made noble use of it in decoration, learns too to be kind to animals and all living things, that most difficult of all lessons to teach a child (for I feel that when he sees how lovely the little leaping squirrel is on the beaten brass, or the bird arrested in marble flight on the carven stone, he will never be cruel to them again), learns too to wonder and worship at God's works more, the carving round a Gothic cathedral with all its marvels of the animal and vegetable world always seeming to me a *Te Deum* in God's honour, quite as beautiful and far more lasting than that chanted *Te Deum* of the choir which dies in music at evensong— well, I felt my audience was with me there both in Philadelphia and in New York. When I showed them the brass work and the pretty bowl of wood with its bright arabesque at New York they applauded to the echo, and I have received so many letters about it and so many congratulations that your school will be known and honoured everywhere, and you yourself recognised and honoured as one of the great pioneers and leaders of the art of the future. If you come across the *Tribune* of last Friday you will see an account of my lecture, though badly reported.

For your kind words of confidence accept my thanks. I feel that I am gaining ground and better understood every day. Yes: I shall win, for the great principles are on our side, the gods are with us! Best regards to Mrs Leland. Very truly yours   OSCAR WILDE

---

children. And you would soon raise up a race of handicraftsmen who would transform the face of your country. I have seen only one such school in the United States, and this was in Philadelphia, and was founded by my friend Mr Leland. I stopped there yesterday, and have brought some of their work here this afternoon to show you. Here are two discs of beaten brass; the designs on them are beautiful, the workmanship is simple, and the entire result is satisfactory. The work was done by a little boy twelve years old. This is a wooden bowl decorated by a little girl of thirteen. The design is lovely and the colouring delicate and pretty. Here you see a piece of beautiful wood carving accomplished by a little boy of nine. In such work as this children learn sincerity in art.

On Monday, 15 May the *Montreal Daily Witness* published an interview with Wilde in which he said: "Here is a letter only received this morning, referring to the effect of my visit to Philadelphia last week." The interviewer goes on: "The letter was from Charles Leland, the famous 'Hans Breitmann', and a member of 'the school', thanking Mr Wilde for the good he had done in connection with the teaching of art principles to the young." Part of this letter from Leland, which is headed "Philadelphia, 11 May 82", runs (text from Stetson Sale Catalogue):

I can never thank you as you deserve for the good you have done the Great Cause of Art Education—and to me as one of its humble teachers . . . I have been a very sincere friend of yours from the first, and have even of old in London fought for you against odds—more both there and here than you ever supposed.

To Frances Richards[1]
MS. Distin

[*Circa 16 May 1882*]   [? *Ottawa*]

I send you with much pleasure a letter to Whistler. You will appreciate him, and he you. I wish I could be in London to show you a few houses and a few men and women, but I will be in Japan, sitting under an almond tree, drinking amber-coloured tea out of a blue and white cup, and contemplating a decorative landscape. Will you again give me the address of the best school at Paris for two young American girls, and any reference to *ateliers* etc. which would be of service. My address is 1267 Broadway, New York. Very truly yours   OSCAR WILDE

To James McNeill Whistler
MS. Distin

[*Circa 16 May 1882*]   *America* [? *Ottawa*]

My dearest Jimmy, I want you to know, and to know is to delight in, Miss Richards, who is an artist, and a little oasis of culture in Canada. She does really good work and has already civilised the Marquis of Lorne.

She is already devoted to your pictures, or rather to my descriptions of them, which are just as good, I often think better. She is quite worthy of your blue and white china, so I send her to you with this letter: I know you will be charming to her. *Toujours*   OSCAR

P.S. I have already civilised America—*il reste seulement le ciel !*

To Norman Forbes-Robertson
TS. Congress

[*25 May 1882*][2]   *Toronto*

My dear Norman, You are horrid not to write. Eustacia has you in her toils I see. I am as usual in high spirits. Your friend Murray is here and I have been able to be nice to him in some ways. Last night at Government House I met a girl, a Miss Burton, who talked of you a great deal. She is very pretty and sweet and calls you Norman. (Norman, you are an unscrupulous young flirt!)

I am just off to the Art Schools and the University. Tonight I lecture as

[1] Canadian artist (1852–1934). Her father was Lieutenant-Governor of British Columbia, and her uncle Chief Justice of Canada. She was a lifelong friend of Robert Ross. She later studied in Paris, where she made friends with Marie Bashkirtseff, who painted a portrait of her. She married William Edwin Rowley in London in 1888 and spent the rest of her life in England. Mason records (*Art and Morality*, p. 63) that she painted a portrait of Wilde. He signed her birthday book on 16 May 1882, giving his address as Government House, Ottawa.

[2] On this day Wilde lectured in the Art Schools at Toronto.

usual, will be home I don't know when. I must go to Japan, and live there with sweet little Japanese girls.

Love to dear Forby and all.   OSCAR

To Ian Forbes-Robertson

MS. Hyde (H. M.)

28 May 1882   *O'Neill House, Woodstock, Ontario*

My dear Ian, I have been obliged to alter my Boston lecture to next Friday: so will not be in New York till the next week: when I look forward to seeing you and your wife.

I have had a charming time here, and very large audiences.

Pray remember me to your wife and, believe me, your sincere friend

OSCAR WILDE

What paper!
What ink!!
What an envelope!!!

To Mrs George Lewis

MS. Wansbrough

3 June [Postmark 1882]   *Boston*

Dear Mrs Lewis, I have sent you a little present of an Indian fan, made by a Canadian tribe I visited in Canada. It is a fanciful thing of feathers, and being yellow will go delightfully with the sunflowers at the top of the long walk at Walton.[1] Please sit there once and fan yourself and entreat that masterly, that trenchant critic of life Katie to honestly acknowledge that she prefers me to the waggonette.

I have just lectured here again, and am now going to New Orleans.

They talk about yellow fever but I think that one who has survived the newspapers is impregnable. After that I don't know where I will go. I feel an irresistible desire to wander, and go to Japan, where I will pass my youth, sitting under an almond tree in white blossom, drinking amber tea out of a blue cup, and looking at a landscape without perspective.

I send you a little slip, this morning's interview. The papers are really very nice now and even the *New York Herald* is being converted, while as for Canada it was at my feet.

I often think of you and your charming house where I have passed so many delightful hours, and Phil and Mr Rodd give me little glimpses of you sometimes in their letters.

Pray remember me most kindly to your husband, and believe me most truly yours   OSCAR WILDE

[1] Walton-on-Thames, where the Lewises had a country house called Ashley Cottage. The Indian fan is now in the possession of Mrs Elizabeth Wansbrough.

To James McNeill Whistler[1]

[? June 1882]

You dear good-for-nothing old Dry-point! Why do you not write to me? Even an insult would be pleasant, and here am I lecturing on you, see penny rag enclosed, and rousing the rage of all the American artists by so doing. Of course the Salon is a success[2] ... The little pink lady ... I remember so well, tell me about them.[3] Also why "a wand," as I see in the *World*; it sounds charming.[4] And the Moon-Lady, the Grey Lady, the beautiful wraith with her beryl eyes, our Lady Archie, how is she?[5] Also when will you come to Japan? Fancy the book, I to write it, you to illustrate it. We would be rich.

OSCAR

To Colonel W. F. Morse

TS. Holland

[*Late June 1882*]

Dear Colonel Morse, It is very annoying to me to find that my Southern tour extends far beyond the three weeks you spoke of. It is now three weeks since I left New York,[6] and I am informed I have two weeks more. Five weeks for sixteen lectures—nothing could be worse in every way. It is quite stupid and gross and will do me much harm.

No mention should have been made of the cartoon at Washington.[7] I regard all caricature and satire as absolutely beneath notice. You, without consulting me, wrote a letter in which, as well as I recollect, you said it was an insult to Mr Carte to caricature anyone under his management. I regret you took any notice. The matter was mine and should have been left for me to decide on.

The Chicago affair is wretchedly told. Do you think I would notice an

---

[1] The text of this incomplete letter is taken from Maggs's catalogue 449 (1924).

[2] The Paris Salon of 1882, which opened on 1 May, was the first to which Whistler had contributed since 1867. He showed a portrait of Lady Meux entitled *Arrangement in Black and White*.

[3] At the Grosvenor Gallery exhibition of May 1882 Whistler exhibited several works, including another portrait of Lady Meux, called *Harmony in Flesh Colour and Pink*.

[4] According to the *World* of 3 May, "Mr Whistler's wand-like walking stick was one of the most striking objects at the private view of the Grosvenor Gallery. It was longer than himself, and even slimmer, and he balanced it delicately between finger and thumb. He explained that he intended it should become historical, and its appearance doubtless marks a new departure in the fashion of sticks."

[5] Whistler painted several portraits of Lady Archibald Campbell, including one called *The Grey Lady*, which he destroyed unfinished.

[6] Wilde left New York for the South on 9 June.

[7] Presumably in an article written by Morse in Wilde's defence. The cartoon in the *Washington Post* of 22 January showed a drawing of the Wild Man of Borneo above one of Wilde, captioned "How far is it from this to this?" See p. 106.

121

article comparing me to a prize-fighter?[1] Besides "decorated conscience" is pure nonsense.

No mention of Lady Wilde should have been made in connection with the money matter.

To say that I regarded my visit here as a mere speculation is grossly untrue and should not be said. I hope the article will not reach London.

As regards the rest, I hope to be allowed time to inspect them. The result you told me was very disappointing. Truly yours OSCAR WILDE

To Julia Ward Howe[2]
MS. Vander Poel

6 July [1882]   *Augusta, Georgia*

My dear Mrs Howe, My present plan is to arrive in New York from Richmond on Wednesday evening, and to leave that night for Newport, being with you Thursday morning and staying, if you will have me, till Saturday. I have an enormous trunk and a valet, but they need not trouble you. I can send them to the hotel. With what incumbrances one travels! It is not in the right harmony of things that I should have a hat-box, a secretary, a dressing-case, a trunk, a portmanteau, and a valet always following me. I daily expect a thunderbolt, but the gods are asleep, though perhaps I had better not talk about them or they will hear me and wake. But what would Thoreau have said to my hat-box! Or Emerson to the size of my trunk, which is Cyclopean! But I can't travel without Balzac and Gautier, and they take up so much room: and as long as I can enjoy talking nonsense to flowers and children I am not afraid of the depraved luxury of a hat-box.

I write to you from the beautiful, passionate, ruined South, the land of magnolias and music, of roses and romance: picturesque too in her failure to keep pace with your keen northern pushing intellect; living chiefly on credit, and on the memory of some crushing defeats. And I have been to Texas, right to the heart of it, and stayed with Jeff Davis at his plantation (how fascinating all failures are!)[3] and seen Savannah, and the Georgia

---

[1] When Wilde arrived in Chicago on 10 February he had to compete for publicity with the young heavyweight boxer John L. Sullivan, who had just beaten Paddy Ryan after nine rounds of a barefist fight.

[2] American author and reformer (1819–1910), author of " The Battle Hymn of the Republic" (1861). Married Samuel Gridley Howe, philanthropist, in 1843. When Wilde was attacked by Colonel Higginson during his first visit to Boston, Mrs Howe defended him in the press (see note 3, p. 98). When he read her letter Wilde sent the following undated note (quoted in *American Book Prices Current*, 1918): "Your letter is noble and beautiful. I have only just seen it, and shall not forget ever the chivalrous and pure-minded woman who wrote it."

[3] Jefferson Davis (1808–89), American soldier and statesman, was President and Commander-in-Chief of the Confederate States in the Civil War. After the defeat of the South he was imprisoned for two years, then pardoned, and retired to Beauvoir, on the Gulf of Mexico between New Orleans and Mobile, where Wilde visited him on 27 June.

forests, and bathed in the Gulf of Mexico, and engaged in Voodoo rites with the Negroes, and am dreadfully tired and longing for an idle day which we will have at Newport.

Pray remember me to Miss Howe, and believe me very truly yours

OSCAR WILDE

Would you send a line to me at 1267 Broadway to say if it is all right.

To Charles Eliot Norton[1]

MS. Harvard

[*Circa 15 July 1882*]   *Ocean House, Newport* [*Rhode Island*]

Dear Mr Norton, I send you the young Greek: a photograph of him: I hope you will admire him. I think it is very strong and right, the statue: and the slight asceticism of it is to me very delightful. The young sculptor's name is John Donoghue: pure Celt is he: and his address is Reaper Block, Chicago: any word of interest from you would be very cheering to him.[2] I feel sure he could do any one of your young athletes, and what an era in art that would be to have the sculptor back in the palaestra, and of much service too to those who separate athletics from culture, and forget the right ideal of the beautiful and healthy mind in a beautiful and healthy body. I can see no better way of getting rid of the mediaeval discord between soul and body than by sculpture. Phidias is the best answer to Thomas à Kempis, but I wish you could see the statue itself, and not the sun's libel on it.

When I had the privilege of dining with you you spoke to me, if I remember right, of Professor Morse, the Japanese traveller.[3] As I am going

---

[1] American scholar and man of letters (1827–1908). Friend of Longfellow, Emerson, Carlyle, Ruskin, FitzGerald and Henry James. Wilde had brought with him the following letter of introduction (MS. Houghton):

23 December 1881   *The Grange, North End Road, Fulham. S.W.*
My very very dear Norton, The gentleman who brings this little note to you is my friend Mr Oscar Wilde, who has much brightened this last of my declining years and I did promise him that if this scheme of a journey to America should ever come to pass I would give him some little message to carry from me to thee. So behold it: and any kindness shewn to him is shewn to me—and if some things in America should make him feel a bit that he has left home I know no antidote like your dear society—for he really loves the men and things you and I love—that is true of him. And so I leave him in the best hands I know. Yours very loving

EDWARD BURNE-JONES

[2] John Donoghue (1853–1903) was born of poor parents in Chicago. His career as a sculptor was largely made by Wilde's enthusiasm in 1882. Thereafter he worked in Paris and Rome. His greatest project, a colossal winged statue of "The Spirit," was designed for the Chicago World's Fair of 1892–93, but Donoghue was too poor to pay the freight charges from Europe, and after the statue had lain some time in the Brooklyn docks, it was dumped in the sea. The sculptor never recovered from this blow, but declined upon spiritualism and melancholia, and eventually drowned himself. He made a bas-relief based on Wilde's poem "Requiescat," and Wilde later had it fixed over the mantelpiece in the drawing-room at 16 Tite Street.

[3] Edward Sylvester Morse (1838–1925), American zoologist, museum director and Japanophile, had held a professorship in Tokyo 1877–80.

to Japan myself it would be of great service to me to get any instructions or letters from him which would enable me to see their method of studying art, their schools of design and the like. I hardly like to ask you to do this for me, knowing how busy your days are, but I am so anxious to see the artistic side of Japanese life that I have ventured to trespass on your courtesy. I have just returned from the South and have a three-weeks holiday now before Japan, and so find it not unpleasant to be in this little island where idleness ranks among the virtues. I suppose you are still among your beautiful trees. How rich you are to have a Rossetti and a chestnut tree. If I happen to be in Boston pray allow me to call on you, and believe me yours truly   OSCAR WILDE

To J. M. Stoddart
MS. Clark

7 August [1882]   *1267 Broadway [New York]*

Dear Mr Stoddart, The book is a *chef d'œuvre* of typography. I am more than delighted at its success. It is an era in American printing. Some of the drawings might be better, but as a whole they will be liked I feel sure. It has given me great pleasure to find such good workmen over here. Pray send Mr Rodd some copies: his address is 29 Beaufort Gardens, South Kensington, London.

There are some of your literary men of America to whom I am anxious to present some copies and will be much obliged if you will send me *half a dozen* addressed here.

Your name looks awkward printed *crookedly* on the back. Could you change this? I showed William Hurlbert of the *World* a copy last night at dinner: he was charmed, so you should send him a copy to review. He will write something delightful about it. He lives at University Buildings, Washington Square, New York. Believe me, truly yours OSCAR WILDE

To Mary Anderson[1]
MS. Navarro

[Early September 1882]   *Park Avenue Hotel, New York*

Dear Miss Anderson, Can I see you on Thursday at Long Branch?[2] I will come down in the morning, and sleep at the Elberon so as to have with you a long day. Pray *telegraph* to me here if you will be at home. I cannot

[1] American actress (1859–1940). After considerable success in England and America she retired from the stage in 1889, married Antonio de Navarro and settled at Broadway in Worcestershire, where she became the "dear enemy" of J. M. Barrie's cricket matches. The play Wilde wrote for her was his blank-verse tragedy *The Duchess of Padua*.

[2] A popular summer resort on the New Jersey coast where Mary Anderson had a country house.

write the scenario till I see you and talk to you. All good plays are a combination of the dream of a poet and that practical knowledge of the actor which gives concentration to action, which intensifies situation, and for poetic effect, which is description, substitutes dramatic effect, which is Life. I have much to talk to you about, having thought much since I saw you of what you could do in art and for art. I want you to rank with the great actresses of the earth. I desire your triumph to be for all time and not for the day merely, and having in you a faith which is as flawless as it is fervent I doubt not for a moment that I can and will write for you a play which, created for you, and inspired by you, shall give you the glory of a Rachel,[1] and may yield me the fame of a Hugo.[2] The dream of the sculptor is cold and silent in the marble, the painter's vision immobile on the canvas. I want to see my work return again to life, my lines gain new splendour from your passion, new music from your lips.

If I can do that, and see you in some creation of mine, a living poem yourself, I [*paper torn off at the bottom edge*] of shame and insult, of discourtesy and of dishonour.

I will look out for a *telegram*, if not Thursday, say Friday, but Thursday [*paper torn off*]

To Samuel Ward[3]

[*5 September 1882*]   [*New York*]

My dear Uncle Sam, I am much better—feel well and happy—and very little pain of any kind: slept well also. You are a magician, and a master of all things from finance to a dinner, and from lyrics to medicine . . . I have been sent a private box for tomorrow night at the *Standard*: first night of a new play . . . I have a charming young Englishman with me, friend of Ronald Powers, whom I want you to meet.   OSCAR

To Laura Don[4]

TS. Holland

[*7 September 1882*]   *Park Avenue Hotel* [*New York*]

Dear Miss Don, Will you permit me to write and tell you how charmed I was last night with your brilliantly written play, and your artistic and sensitive acting. I will not readily forget the joyousness and insouciance of

[1] Stage name of French tragic actress Elisa Félix (1821–58).

[2] Victor-Marie Hugo (1802–85), the great French poet, novelist and dramatist.

[3] American lobbyist, financier, talker and gastronome (1814–84). Elder brother of Julia Ward Howe. Described by Lord Rosebery as "the uncle of the human race." He had entertained Wilde lavishly in New York and the country. The text of this incomplete letter is taken from the American Art Association catalogue, 5 and 6 November 1923.

[4] *A Daughter of the Nile* by Laura Don was produced at the Standard Theatre, New York, on 6 September 1882, the authoress playing the chief part of "Egypt." It was withdrawn on 23 September.

your comedy, or the deeper chords of life and feeling which you struck in the fifth act, and to which the rich music of your voice and the appropriateness of your gesture gave full expression. Your dress, as the Princess, was quite delightful, and the silver bracelets you wore were very beautiful indeed. If you would allow me to suggest a change, I would ask you to consider whether the formal black and red horizontal stripes in the lining of your cloak in Act Five do not destroy by their over-definiteness the effect of your drapery and the long lines of your figure? Do you not think a plain dull red lining would give you the same colour-effect without the distraction of a commonplace pattern? But everything was a great success, and I warmly congratulate you. Believe me, very truly yours   OSCAR WILDE

To Mary Anderson

MS. Navarro

8 September [1882]   *Park Avenue Hotel, New York*

Dear Miss Anderson, I will be with you on Monday at ten o'clock, Fifth Avenue Hotel. It is very important I should see you and settle the scenario, if our idea is to become a reality. I think I have so conceived it that we shall simultaneously become immortal in one night!

Here in the city the streets seem paved with brass, and the air made of lead. I hope *you* are in your hammock, with the ripple and laughter of the leaves above you, and the light and laughter of the sea beyond you, and the crickets whirring in the grass—those shrill crickets who are as noisy as critics and quite as useless—and your greyhound keeping loyal guard over you. At any rate I shall imagine that you are. Very sincerely yours

OSCAR WILDE

To Mary Anderson

MS. Navarro

[September 1882]   *1267 Broadway, New York*

Dear Miss Anderson, I am very anxious to learn what decision you have come to as regards the production of my play. It is in our power to procure all the conditions of success by the beauty of costume, the dignity of scenery, the perfection of detail and dramatic order, without which, in England at any rate, you could not get your right position as an artist.

I will merely remind you of the complete fiasco made by Edwin Booth this summer in London merely through the inartistic style of the stage management, and the mediocre company.[1] If you desire, as I feel that you

[1] The American tragedian had had a disastrous season at the Princesses Theatre, London, from December 1880 to March 1881. He then played with Irving at the Lyceum (see note 3, p. 76) and from 26 June 1882 gave a six-weeks repertory season at the Adelphi Theatre, where the audience were said to be "sparse though friendly."

America, 1882

Oscar Wilde

Two Lecturers,
America, 1882

Archibald Forbes

at any rate do, to create an era in the history of American dramatic art, and to take your assured rank among the great artists of our time, here is the opportunity: and remember we live in an age when without art there is really no true success, *financial* or otherwise.

That I can create for you a part which will give your genius every scope, your passion every outlet, and your beauty every power, I am well assured. The bare, meagre outline I have given you is but a faint shadow of what Bianca Duchess of Padua will be.

Mr Lawrence Barrett[1] has made me a very large offer for the play, but I feel that it is for you to create the part and I have told him that the acceptance of the play rests at present with you.

Mr Steele Mackaye[2] has written to me estimating the cost of production at 10,000 dollars: you will appear in a more gorgeous frame than any woman of our day. This price I do not consider at all excessive, as, for your production of it in London, the properties, dresses, etc. will of course be available.

I will hope to hear from you soon on the matter. Mr Barrett is a good manager and actor, but for my Duchess I need you.

However there it lies. Think seriously and long about it. Perhaps for both of us it may mean the climacteric of our lives.   OSCAR WILDE

To Samuel Ward[3]

[*Late September 1882*]   *Boston*

My dear Uncle Sam, Thank you so much for the review.[4] It is very nicely done, and though literary discourtesy could go no further than to omit all mention of my name, still it is so marked as to be almost a compliment. I am surprised that Dana could have done such an ungracious and foolish act.[5] I am off to Nova Scotia and will be back . . . in three weeks.[6]

Your idea of a dinner to Mrs Langtry[7] is charming, but then everything you do from poetry to menus is perfect. You are the great authority on lyrics and Lafite. Ever affectionately yours   OSCAR

---

[1] American actor-manager (1838–91).

[2] James Morrison Steele Mackaye (1842–94). American actor, dramatist, designer and inventor. A childhood friend of Henry James.

[3] Text from Glaenzer.

[4] Of *Rose Leaf and Apple Leaf* in the New York *Sun* of 24 September. It was signed with the initials of the literary editor, Mayo Williamson Hazeltine (1841–1909).

[5] Charles Anderson Dana (1819–97), proprietor and editor of the *Sun*.

[6] Wilde lectured at Halifax, Nova Scotia, on or about 8 October.

[7] See note 1, p. 95.

To Mary Anderson

MS. Navarro

[*Circa 8 October 1882*]   *Halifax, Nova Scotia*

My dear Miss Anderson, Your letter has very much pleased me. Of course
one is impatient in one's youth, but I am quite ready to wait a year in
order to make our play the success it is entitled to be. Written by me,
acted by you, and set by Steele Mackaye, this tragedy will take the world
by storm.

Your plan of taking Booth's Theatre is excellent, and really necessary to
ensure the run of the piece, and in the interval we will all look out for a
young man to act with you. A mediocrity acting with a woman of such
noble presence as you are dwindles and shrivels into a mere nothing, and
becomes no better than a doublet and hose filled with sawdust.

I judge that it is now clearly settled that Steele Mackaye is to manage
the piece. I will have it so settled in our contract, and during my absence
from America he will represent me with full powers and be always at your
service in need. He is a man of great practical knowledge, of exquisite
taste, and sound experience. Except him there is no one can do it.

Mr Griffin[1] and I have not quite come to terms yet: but I hope we will.
I have written to him by this post. As soon as we do I shall begin hard at
work. I am having charming audiences, you will be glad to hear; the
Canadians are very appreciative people, but it is a great fight in this commercial age to plead the cause of Art. Still the principles which I represent
are so broad, so grand, so noble that I have no fear for the future. Some
day this [*piece torn off bottom edge of paper*] artistic nations, in spite of
its cast-iron stoves, and machine-made furniture, and whitewashed walls.

You of course are having a great success; you always have it, and you
[*piece torn off edge of paper.*]

To Steele Mackaye[2]

11 October 1882   *Halifax, Nova Scotia*

Mary Anderson has written to me, accepting you as director and supreme
autocrat (I think that over the "supers" you should have the power of life
and death: we will have no serious dramatic art until we hang a super),
offering to take Booth's Theatre for October, and to get a good young
actor for the hero, and indeed she seems most willing to do everything
requisite for our success. She is simple and nice, and the Griffin must have
his claws clipped.

I will see of course that in our contract you shall be named as the man
under whose direction the play shall walk the stage. I will be back in
about a fortnight; and we will settle matters about *The Duchess* and about

[1] Hamilton Griffin, Mary Anderson's stepfather and manager.
[2] The text of this letter is taken from *Oscar Wilde Discovers America* by Lloyd
Lewis and Henry Justin Smith (1936).

Vera. Any and all of your suggestions will be most valuable. I am glad you like it and if we can get Miss Mather[1] it will be a great thing.

Pray go over the play carefully, and note on the blank interleaf your changes, so that over the walnuts and the wine at some little Brunswick dinner we may settle everything.[2]

I long to get back to real literary work, for though my audiences are really most appreciative I cannot write while flying from one railway to another and from the cast-iron stove of one hotel to its twin horror in the next.

I will be at the Vendome Hotel, Boston, on Sunday next. Send me a line there to say how things are going with you.

Remember me to Frank Piersson, and believe me, very truly yours

OSCAR WILDE

To Colonel W. F. Morse
TS. Holland

[? *Circa 15 October 1882*]   *Boston*

Dear Colonel Morse, Mr Moore paid only 250 dollars, and *no expenses at all*. I did not like to stop lecturing as he entreated me to go on. I thought it best then that our side of the contract should be perfectly carried out. What to do now I leave to you. I think our only chance is to give him two weeks at 700 a week. He will do this in the large towns, but he brought me to wretched villages of 10,000 people where of course they did not come.

The business is bad but still his defalcation is too large. I think he should lose two weeks.

Hayman from Australia has not arrived yet. If Mary Anderson takes my play I could not go: this time year would be better, or in March, but I would sooner go this time year. Don't have many dates in November if possible. Moore I think should content himself with two weeks at 700.

Thank you for sending the play to Washington. I think to copyright under your name would be a very good plan.[3] I wish you would send one to the manager you spoke of here, Mr Field.[4] Also one to Rose Coghlan at Wallack's, and one to Wallack himself.[5] Also one to *Mr Henderson*: I think he might buy it.[6]

---

[1] Margaret Mather, American actress (1860–98).

[2] Mackaye was staying or living at the Hotel Brunswick in New York.

[3] *Vera* was entered for copyright at the Library of Congress, Washington, on 2 October 1882, in Wilde's name. This acting edition, which differed considerably from the 1880 version, consisted of some twenty-five copies only.

[4] R. M. Field of the Boston Museum Theatre.

[5] John Johnstone (Lester) Wallack (1820–88), American actor, had inherited the family theatre in New York from his father and uncle. The original theatre opened in 1837 and closed in 1881. On 4 January 1882 Lester Wallack opened a new Wallack's Theatre on Broadway at Thirtieth Street.

[6] Probably William Henderson, the manager of the Standard Theatre, New York, in 1882.

I hope this next week will be better than the other. I . . . brought to wretched place.

I wish you would tell Hayman that I accept his offer for next October, 1883. That would be equally good and more convenient. Yours truly

OSCAR WILDE

To Mary Anderson

MS. Navarro

[? *October 1882*]

Dear Miss Anderson, I do not wish that any business difficulties should interfere with our artistic project, so I have yielded to Mr Griffin's demands.

I do not know whether I have been right in doing so, but it is done, and now I hope the thing will be regarded as definitely settled: as regards the style of production, if it is not good and artistic a great wrong is done to both of us. Here is an opportunity of doing something fine in art and I think if you do not avail yourself of it to the full you will be missing a chance such as may not occur again, but remember that no dramatist and few actors can make any way against bad costumes, coarse scenery, faulty stage management, and the like. If the thing is worth doing at all, it is worth doing well. I know that *you* see all this as well as I do: we must take care that things are done as we want.

Write to me what you think of *Vera*, which from Mr Griffin's letter I understand you have received.[1]

I am glad to think that things are being settled. How long it seems to take one to get any business done! You and I could have done it all in five minutes. Believe me, your sincere friend   OSCAR WILDE

The terms I accept are the original terms—1000 dollars down: four thousand dollars on the acceptance of the manuscript and a royalty of twenty-five dollars in the big towns, and ten in the small ones.

OSCAR WILDE

Please telegraph me your acceptance of these, as I wish to have the matter definitely settled.

To Theodore Tilton[2]

F. *Butterfly*

[*Date of receipt 14 November 1882*]   48 West 11th Street [*New York*]

Dear Mr Tilton, You have done the only translation of Théophile Gautier

---

[1] In Mary Anderson's answering letter (sold at the Anderson Galleries, April 1923) she wrote: "*Vera* charms me; it is very mournful. I think I would like to play the part."

[2] American journalist and writer (1835–1907). In the 1870's he was one of the leading figures in the greatest scandal of the decade, when his wife was accused of adultery with Henry Ward Beecher of Brooklyn Heights, the most famous preacher in the country. The jury failed to agree, but all three lives and reputations were

which has the music and colour and form of the original. It is a little masterpiece, and there are very few who can pour the wine of song from the golden to the silver chalice, as you have done, without spilling a drop. I thank you for your most courteous present, and hope that I will soon have the opportunity of telling you in person what I think of your "Chant Celestial," and what of the little lyrical ecstasies which in a sort of sweet fitfulness break out here and there in your poem of "Thou and I," a poem which seems to me an exquisite combination of Gothic fancy and of Greek form. Pray remember me to Mr Moulton most kindly, and believe me, very truly yours   OSCAR WILDE

To William Wetmore Story[1]
MS. Clark

[? *November 1882*]   *48 West 11th Street* [*New York*]

My dear Mr Story, I thank you for your very courteous letter. The passage in question certainly bore an unlucky resemblance to the ordinary criticism my work has received in this country; and the use of the word "aesthetic" with the *soupçon* of a sneer, and the assonance between Osric and Oscar, seemed to clinch the matter in the minds of the audience. I was very glad however to be able to tell many of them, who spoke to me about it, that the allusion which they thought obvious did not really exist. Your complete unconsciousness of the matter was, to me, the best compliment my work or personality could have received, and for my own part I felt, even while you read the offending passage, that it must have been merely a curious coincidence, and that sneering satire of art was a thing impossible from one who has made marble musical in its harmony, and poetry in its perfection Parian.

Pray offer my compliments to Mrs Story, and believe me, yours very truly   OSCAR WILDE

---

ruined. Frank Moulton was a friend of all parties, but ended by siding with Tilton. In 1883 Tilton emigrated to Paris, where he spent the rest of his life writing poetry and romantic novels. Tilton's volume of poems *Thou and I* (1879) contained a poem called "Chant Celestial" and a translation of "*Affinités Secrètes*" from Gautier's *Émaux et Camées*. A copy of the book inscribed "To Oscar Wilde Esq from Theodore Tilton, New York, 4 Nov. 82" was sold at the Anderson Galleries on 2 November 1933. It contained also these words in Wilde's hand: "Theodore Tilton brought me to see the old room where Poe wrote 'The Raven,' on Friday, Nov. 10. An old wooden house over the Hudson, low rooms, fine chimney piece, very dull Corot day, clergyman with reminiscences of Poe, about chickens."

[1] American sculptor and poet (1819-95). He lived most of his life in Italy, where he was a friend of Landor and the Brownings. In 1882 he spent some months in America. His biography by Henry James appeared in 1903.

To Hamilton Griffin

MS. Navarro

[*Late November 1882*]   *1267 Broadway, New York*

Dear Sir, As I informed you by telegraph I accept your terms for writing
a play for Miss Anderson. Will you have an agreement drawn up with the
agreed-on terms: $1000 down: $4000 when it is finished: the play to be
ready by March 31st and played before a year from now.

On the question of dresses and mounting we are agreed: in that respect
I always found your views coinciding with mine.

In surrendering the customary author's royalty I have been actuated by
a wish not to allow a money matter to stand in the way of an artistic
success.

Will you give Miss Anderson my compliments and assure her from me
that I count it a pleasure to write for one whose capabilities as an artist are
so great. I am convinced that for both of us a great triumph is in waiting.
Believe me, yours truly   OSCAR WILDE[1]

---

[1] Griffin's answer (MS. Clark) reads:

1 December 1882   *Neil House, Columbus, Ohio*

Dear Sir, Your letter received. I am willing to risk the thousand dollars, so
strongly do I believe in your ability to write a superb play, but I will not agree to
pay the four thousand and to play the piece within a year unless it suits Miss
Anderson. When she received your telegram I thought that all our differences
were at an end but I see now that we are still apart.

If you sign the within contract and mail it to me at Pittsburg, Care Monongahela
House, I will send you an exact copy of it signed and witnessed and a check for
$1000. And will pay the four thousand immediately that Miss A. signifies that
she accepts the work and she will get it up grandly, costumes and scenes after
your drawings and paintings, within the year, and if it is a success in New York
will make it the principal feature of her repertory.

But if you do not sign and return she will consider the whole matter ended.

Miss Anderson returns the compliments and I believe with you that a glorious
future in *The Duchess of Padua* awaits you and her. Respectfully yours

HAMILTON GRIFFIN

LONDON II

1883-90

PART FOUR

London II: 1883-90

Wilde sailed home from New York on the *Bothnia* on 27 December 1882. After two or three weeks in London he used what was left of his American earnings to spend three months in Paris. There he met Verlaine and Victor Hugo, Mallarmé, Zola, Degas, Edmond de Goncourt and Alphonse Daudet. He had his hair curled in imitation of a bust of Nero in the Louvre and dressed in the height of fashion. "The Oscar of the first period is dead," he said.

To Waldo Story[1]

January 1883   *Hôtel Continental, Paris*

I saw a great deal of Jimmy in London *en passant*. He has just finished a second series of Venice Etchings—such water-painting as the gods never beheld. His exhibition opens in a fortnight in a yellow and white room (decorated by the master of colour) and with a catalogue which is amazing. He spoke of your art with more enthusiasm than I ever heard him speak of any modern work. For which accept my warm congratulations: praise from him is something.

To Mary Anderson
MS. Navarro

23 March 1883   *Paris*

My dear Miss Anderson, The play was duly forwarded some days ago: I

[1] American sculptor (1855-1915), son of William Wetmore Story. Whistler's exhibition, "Arrangement in Yellow and White," had its private view at the Fine Art Society's Rooms on 17 February 1883. The yellow-and-white decoration was carried on to the flowers, pots, chairs, assistants' neckties and Whistler's socks at the private view, which were all yellow. The catalogue mocked the critics, quoting their more ridiculous estimates of Whistler's work and, on its title-page, "Out of their own mouths shall ye judge them." The text of this incomplete letter is taken from Maggs's catalogue 445 (1923).

hope it arrived safe: I have no hesitation in saying that it is the master-piece of all my literary work, the *chef-d'œuvre* of my youth.[1]

As regards the characters, the Duke is a type of the Renaissance noble: I felt that to have made him merely a common and vulgar villain would have been "banal:" he is a cynic, and a philosopher: he has no heart, and his vileness comes from his intellect: it is a very strong acting part as you see, and must be given to an experienced actor. To write a comedy one requires comedy merely, but to write a tragedy, tragedy is not sufficient: the strain of emotion on the audience must be lightened: they will not weep if you have not made them laugh: so I proceeded in the following fashion.

At the beginning of the play I desired merely to place the audience in full possession of the facts, of the foundation of the play: comedy would have been disturbing, so with the exception of Ascanio's few prose speeches there is none: the action begins with the entrance of the Duke, whose comedy is bitter but comedy still, and the culmination of the act is the entrance of the Duchess: I have ended the act with the words

" The Duchess of Padua"

which strike the keynote of the play, and make a very novel and striking effect.

The comedy of Act II is the Duke's comedy, which is bitter, the citizens', which is grotesque, and the Duchess's comedy which is the comedy of Viola, and Rosalind; the comedy in which joy smiles through a mask of beauty.

Act III. Here there is no need of comedy: the act is short, quick, terrible: what we want is to impress the audience clearly with the two great speculations and problems of the play, the relations of Sin and Love: they must see that both Guido and the Duchess have rights on their side: Guido is cruel, and the Duchess has done wrong: but they represent great principles of Life and Love.

The Duchess's   *Sure it is the guilty*
       Who being very wretched need love most:

Guido's

     There is no love where there is any sin:

and the great speech of the Duchess that follows give to the audience exactly what one wants to produce: *intense emotion with a background of intellectual speculation.* Which is right? That is what they will ask.

The comedy of Act IV is elaborate, and necessary to relieve the audience: you must not think it too long: believe me it is vitally necessary to make our audience merry after the horror in the corridor. I have selected, as you see, the style of comedy which never fails to raise laughter: the unconscious comedy of stupidity, missing the meaning of words, yet in all its solemn ignorance stumbling now and then on a real bit of truth.

[1] According to the edition printed in 1883 (of which only five copies are known to survive), Wilde finished *The Duchess of Padua* in Paris on 15 March, though the manuscript (MS. Clark) is undated. For his later opinion of the play, see p. 757.

Act V. The comedy of the soldiers: this relieves the audience from the strain of the trial: and is a bit of realism not I think put before into a dungeon scene.

Well, there is my comedy: and I hope that you have laughed over it as you read it: for myself, I am devoted to the *"second citizen"* who seems to me an unconscious humorist of the highest order: he should get a great deal of fun out of his part.

To proceed with the characters:

Moranzone. He is the incarnate image of vengeance: the bird of evil omen: the black spectre of the past moving like Destiny through the scene.

Guido. Impulsive, ready to take oaths, to forget the past, to realise the moment only: full of noble ideas, but "Fortune's fool."[1]

As for the *Cardinal*, he is the polished pompous churchman of the time, and the *Lord Justice* the impassive image of justice, the rock against which the passion of the Duchess breaks like foam.

Lastly, *the Duchess.*

Her first effect is that of pure Beauty merely: she passes across the stage and says nothing: but it is not enough to make her stir the artistic sensibility of the audience, so in Act II she appears as the image of pity, and mercy: she comes with the poor about her: she stirs the sympathy of the gallery and pit. I do not know how it is in New York, but in London, where the misery is terrible among the poor, and where the sympathy for them is growing every day, such speeches as the one about the children dying in the lanes, or the people sleeping under the arches of the bridges, cannot fail to bring down the house: they will not expect to find in an Italian tragedy modern life: but *the essence of art is to produce the modern idea under an antique form.*

She is insulted by the Duke, left alone on the stage, when love comes into her life: she will not tell all at once, and like a girl plays in delicate comedy for a time. Then comes the passionate love-scene, the face at the window, the desertion of her lover, and her resolve to die. The act is long, but then she passes through so many emotions, and the act is so full of incident, that I don't think it is too long. The second entrance of the Duke, and the second appearance of Moranzone, are I think quite necessary to interrupt her soliloquy, which else might be to the actress, as well as to the audience, somewhat wearing.

Now to the third act: I remember what you talked to me about it: I think I have produced exactly what you desire.

She has left the audience under the impression that she would kill herself: she commits a murder under a momentary impulse, and a misunderstanding of her lover's words. Now murder is murder, a dreadful thing: we must not explain it away: it must produce a thrill of horror when she says *"I have just killed him:"* it becomes the bloody background of the play, and we must not dim its scarlet: but this horror is changed to

---

[1] *Romeo and Juliet*, Act III, scene i.

pity: the passionate cry of "*I did it all for you:*" the remorse shown in such
lines as:

> "Will we not sit beneath our vines and laugh?
> No, no, we will not laugh, but when we weep
> Well, we will weep together:"

Guido's sternness, which is right, but unsympathetic (and in judging of a
character it is *not by abstract morals but by living sympathy that an audience
is affected*), all this turns the tide towards the Duchess: and chiefly have I
tried to make her not merely an individual woman, but in some way the
incarnation of the lives of all women: *she is universal, and her cue is "we
women" always*: this note is first struck in Act II in her first soliloquy: in
Act III it is of course stronger:

> "the love of men
> Turns women into martyrs; for its sake
> We do and suffer anything."

or

> "O God, how little pity
> We women get in this untimely world"
> (and the following lines)

or

> "I see when men love women
> They give them but a little of their lives,
> But women when they love give everything."

or

> "Women grow mad when they are treated thus"
> (and the lines following)

and chiefly the passage on the relations of sin and love beginning:

> "There is many a woman here in Padua,
> Some workman's wife or ruder artisan's . . ."
> (and ending with the words)
> "*That is how women love.*"

Well, there is a speech which will wake such pity and such enthusiasm
that when her voice is heard saying

> "This way went he, the man who slew my lord"

every woman will say to herself "I would have done likewise." In London
(where the misery among the wives of our artisans has required special
legislation, so dreadful is it) this speech will produce an extraordinary
effect. (I should like it printed at length on some advertisements substituting for "*here in Padua*" the words "*in this city here*" which indeed if
you like you might speak.)

The keynote of Act IV is her saying to Guido:

> "I am what thou hast made me."

In a play the characters should create each other: no character must be ready made: the piteous cry of

"He has changed my heart into a heart of stone"

is the expression of this great truth of dramatic art: *but as the murder had to produce its horror, so revenge must create its terror*: the sympathy of the audience is a little suspended: but why? Well, for this reason, that in Act V when she drinks the poison, when she begs her lover to escape, when with wild words of self-condemnation she thrusts her lover's lips away, when the exclamation reiterated in many forms of

"I am not worthy, Guido, I am not worthy"

shows the depth of her remorse, then the sympathy of the audience returns in a great wave. An audience longs to be first out of sympathy, and ultimately in sympathy, with a character they have loved: they desire it; they demand it; without it they are not contented; but *this sympathy must not be merely emotional, it must have its intellectual basis*, above all it must be summed up for them briefly in the form of thought: audiences are well meaning but very stupid: they must have things told them clearly: they are nice children who need to have their vague emotions crystallised and expressed for them. They feel pity for Othello, but how incomplete the effect of that last dreadful scene would be if Othello did not say:

"speak of me as I am ...
then you must speak
Of one that loved not wisely but too well"

and the rest of the lines. He intellectually gives them the intellectual basis for their sympathy: it seems to me that in all Shakespeare's greatest plays he gives, in the last act, lines which the audience can quote to one another as they pass out, glad, very glad, to find the shield of intellect held over the newborn babe of pity.

This intellectual idea is the *health* of art, as the emotional idea is the *heart* of art: such a play for instance as *La Dame aux Camélias* is unhealthy: *Why?* Not because sympathy is asked for a fallen woman, but because it is only played on one string, an emotional string merely: so that in the last act the sympathy of the audience naturally excited for a woman who is dying young (and has a dreadful cough!) has no real intellectual basis: it would have had if Shakespeare, not Dumas, had written it.

Well, in this play of *The Duchess of Padua* and in the last act *Guido sums up intellectually for the audience their emotional sympathy*. Emotion lives in terror of ridicule, and the imputation of weakness, and is never happy unless it has got hold of its big brother Intellect by the hand. The Duchess in Act III defended her position: that was right: in Act V it would be horrible: so the places are changed: Guido defends her at that bar of judgment before which she passionately cries "I am guilty:" and to cry that one is guilty to God and man is to get the pardon of the one and the pity of the other.

Guido's speech:

> "Let those who have not loved
> Cast stones against thee"

down to:

> "My soul was murderous, but my hand refused;
> Your hand wrought murder, but your soul was pure"

and ending with the lines

> "let him
> Who has no mercy for your stricken head,
> Lack mercy up in heaven:"

this speech gives the audience the intellectual basis they want: emotion is momentary, ceases with the fall of the curtain, and cannot be remembered, or if remembered is thought a weakness, but intellect is eternal.

You remember what Hamlet says in the moment of his death:

> *"Horatio, I am dead;*
> *Thou livs't: report me and my cause aright*
> *To the unsatisfied."*

and so we have Horatio's noble speech to Fortinbras.

Well, this is what Guido does: he reports the Duchess and her cause aright to the unsatisfied: but not with the cold intellect of a philosopher, or the chilling plausibility of a pleader, but as a passionate lover: in the same way as Horatio speaks with the chivalry of a loving friend: but this again is not enough: the Duchess is to die: her death must be emphasised: its horror must intensify that sympathy which emotion has created, and which intellect has made invulnerable:

> *"Are there no rivers left in Italy to quench this fire within me?"*

She suffers pain, that is enough to make those eyes weep that held back their tears before. But it is not merely from life that Death takes her but from love:

> *"This is a wedding feast,*
> *You are out of place, sir,"*

she cries to Death himself: but she must not die with wandering mind, and diseased vision, and physical pain stifling her utterance. That would be too material, too physical an ending for a work of spiritual art: so a calm comes after the crisis, a little peace after the whirlwind, a little quiet before the eternal silence.

Do you think that love can cleanse my hands, and heal my wounds? she says. You have not sinned at all, says Guido. No, she answers, I have sinned, and yet:

> *"Perchance my sin will be forgiven me.*
> *I have loved much."*

140

Well, this is what I have meant by *The Duchess of Padua*. There are of course many points in the play I would like to write about more fully: Guido's soliloquy for instance at the close of Act III: why is this necessary? It is necessary I think for this reason: suspense is immensely important for the audience: Macbeth must hesitate at the door of Duncan's room, and Hamlet behind the praying King, and Romeo before Juliet's body. "What is going to happen?" is the question which every good situation makes the audience ask themselves. For suspense, time is necessary: it must not seem as if the guards were posted outside the door: the Duchess has to alarm the house, and when the house is up and the torches seen, and the feet of the soldiers heard, the audience must not know what is happening. "Pray God they have not seized her," says Guido: "You can escape" he cries to her: and the audience must fear with him that she has been taken. Then comes the great effect. But it must be preceded by suspense (as earlier in the act the Duchess does not say the moment she sees Guido "I have killed the Duke"): *suspense is the essence of situation, and surprise its climax*. Besides, and this point is equally necessary, the pity of the audience is aroused for the Duchess though she has done murder, but as long as Guido, cold, relentless, obdurate, rejects her, their pity is a little checked, but when he himself cries:

> "And yet she loved me:
> And for my sake has done this thing:
> I have been cruel,"

then they feel as if a barrier had been taken from the path where the steps of pity had before been checked: besides, his conduct in the court would appear paradoxical if he did not cry in the third act:

> "Beatrice I love you: come out."

and art should always surprise, but never be paradoxical.

Lastly, it produces on the audience the most tragical effect in the world: the effect of his speaking *too late*: the effect of Juliet waking *too late*: "if Guido had only spoken sooner:" "if Juliet had only sooner wakened:" "too late now" are in art and life the most tragical words.

I have written at a length which perhaps has been wearisome to you. I wanted to show you how scientifically I have thought out this matter in all details. I did it for two reasons: first, I was creating a work of art: secondly, I was creating it for a true artist.

As regards the scenery and the costumes I have already made drawings of both: I have indicated the scenery before each act briefly. I think you will be able to realise from the short scenarios what I desire. In the last act, the dungeon, about which I remember your talking to me, I have, I think, got rid of the depressing gloom of most such scenes: first by the gambling soldiers which will give a sort of "Salvator Rosa"[1] effect: secondly by the invention of the two gratings which open into the corridor. One of these gratings is small, the other large (almost a sort of gate), so that when

---

[1] Italian painter of romantic landscapes (1615–73).

141

the procession enters of the Lord Justice in his scarlet, and the headsman with his axe, as they pass through the corridor, first, at the first grating, their heads and shoulders are alone seen, then at the second grating they are full three-quarter lengths: this will be new and effective: and the Duchess taking the torch from the wall to look at Guido asleep is a good piece of business. I remember now that in Act III I said a "crimson *velvet* curtain over the door at top of staircase," an error I forgot to rectify from my designs: the curtain is of vermilion *silk*: for three reasons. First, it catches the light better in a dark scene: secondly, it is difficult to get such a good colour in velvet as one can get in silk: thirdly, as the torches cannot be seen at the window, or at the sides, the curtain must be transparent as the light shining through it will be most effective: it will suddenly become a door of crimson fire! Some other points I will write to you about, but as it takes some time to prepare designs for costumier and scene-painter I will ask you to telegraph to me your decision about the play. As I may have changed my rooms in Paris would you kindly telegraph to me at Lady Wilde's London address which is 116 Park Street, Grosvenor Square, London.

This letter has become a Titan: it should have been written in the mammoth age: but there is so much to say on a play: and all art must be capable of scientific analysis, if it is not merely prettiness.

Will you present my compliments to Mr and Mrs Griffin: and believe me that writing this play for you has been a task of pleasure, and a labour of love. I remain, dear Miss Anderson, most truly yours OSCAR WILDE

Post-Scriptum.

I have not forgotten your bell, Act V. We will have the most musical bell in the world.[1]

To Marie Prescott[2]

[? *March–April 1883*]   [? *Paris*]

My dear Miss Prescott, I have received the American papers and thank

[1] R. H. Sherard, in *The Real Oscar Wilde*, described how Wilde, in Paris, received Mary Anderson's telegram turning the play down: "Wilde opened it and read the disappointing news without giving the slightest sign of chagrin or annoyance. He tore a tiny strip off the blue form, rolled it up into a pellet, and put it into his mouth. Then he passed the cable over to me, and said: 'Robert, this is very tedious.' After that he never referred again to his disappointment." In a later letter (Stetson catalogue, 1920) Mary Anderson wrote: "The play in its present form, I fear, would no more please the public of today than would *Venice Preserved* or *Lucretia Borgia*." For the play's first production see p. 282.

[2] American actress (d. 1923), to whom Wilde had been introduced by Steele Mackaye. She had read *Vera* and agreed to play the leading part in it. The text of this letter is taken from the *New York Herald* of 12 August 1883, where it appeared as a puff for the play. Mason dates the letter December 1882, claiming that Marie Prescott's answer, in which she quotes from Wilde's letter, was written on 9 January 1883. It is perilous to disagree with Mason, but here I think he is wrong. Marie Prescott's letter (Mason, p. 259) seems to me to be March-April 1883, and I have dated Wilde's letter accordingly.

you for sending them. I think we must remember that no amount of advertising will make a bad play succeed, if it is not a good play well acted. I mean that one might patrol the streets of New York with a procession of vermilion caravans twice a day for six months to announce that *Vera* was a great play, but if on the first night of its production the play was not a strong play, well acted, well mounted, all the advertisements in the world would avail nothing. My name signed to a play will excite some interest in London and America. Your name as the heroine carries great weight with it. What we want to do is to have *all* the real conditions of success in our hands. Success is a science; if you have the conditions, you get the result. Art is the mathematical result of the emotional desire for beauty. If it is not thought out, it is nothing.

As regards dialogue, you can produce tragic effects by introducing comedy. A laugh in an audience does not destroy terror, but, by relieving it, aids it. Never be afraid that by raising a laugh you destroy tragedy. On the contrary, you intensify it. The canons of each art depend on what they appeal to. Painting appeals to the eye, and is founded on the science of optics. Music appeals to the ear and is founded on the science of acoustics. The drama appeals to human nature, and must have as its ultimate basis the science of psychology and physiology. Now, one of the facts of physiology is the desire of any very intensified emotion to be relieved by some emotion that is its opposite. Nature's example of dramatic effect is the laughter of hysteria or the tears of joy. So I cannot cut out my comedy lines. Besides, the essence of good dialogue is interruption. All good dialogue should give the effect of its being made by the reaction of the personages on one another. It should never seem to be ready made by the author, and interruptions have not only their artistic effect but their physical value. They give the actors time to breathe and get new breath power. I remain, dear Miss Prescott, your sincere friend   OSCAR WILDE

To Messrs Trübner & Co[1]

MS. Clark

2 April 1883   *Hôtel Voltaire, Quai Voltaire, Paris*

Mr Oscar Wilde begs to enclose a cheque for £1. 1. 6 for three copies of Mr Rodd's poems with his own preface, and will be much obliged if Messrs Trübner will forward them at once.[2]

---

[1] London publishing firm, founded 1851 by Nicholas Trübner (1817–84). Amalgamated with Kegan Paul 1884.

[2] An earlier note from Wilde to Messrs. Trübner (MS. Clark), also from the Hôtel Voltaire, runs: "Seeing you have republished the edition of Mr Rennell Rodd's poems with my preface, I would be much obliged if you would send me a copy." The British Museum has no copy of any Trübner edition of Rodd's *Rose Leaf and Apple Leaf*, and the firm's records have perished. Probably Trübner imported some copies of Stoddart's edition (see note 1, p. 116) and issued them with a Trübner stamp on the title-page, as he did with many other American books.

To R. H. Sherard[1]

MS. Congress

Wednesday [*early April 1883*]   *Hôtel Voltaire*

My dear Robert, I send you the volume of the true poet, and the false friend:[2] there are some new things in it, "Chartres Cathedral," and the "Viking's Grave," which have much beauty in them, the latter particularly and the "Envoi" I hope you will like. The rhythmical value of prose has never yet been fully tested; I hope to do some more work in that *genre*, as soon as I have sung my Sphinx to sleep, and found a trisyllabic rhyme for catafalque.[3] Ever affectionately yours   OSCAR WILDE

To Jacques-Emile Blanche[4]

5 Avril [*1883*]   *Hôtel Voltaire*

Cher Monsieur Blanche, Je vous remercie beaucoup pour ces trois charmants souvenirs de votre art. Quant à la petite fille qui lit mes poèmes, je l'adore déjà, mais hélas! elle ne veut pas lever ses yeux de mon livre, même pour un instant. Traître, vous l'avez fait préférer le poète à l'amant, et les vers aux baisers!

Cependant c'est intéressant de trouver une femme comme ça, car elle n'existe pas. À dimanche prochain, votre bien devoué   OSCAR WILDE

To Edmond de Goncourt[5]

MS. Paris

[? *April 1883*]   *Hôtel Voltaire*

Monsieur, Daignez recevoir mes poèmes, témoignage de mon admiration infinie pour l'auteur de *La Faustin*.

---

[1] Robert Harborough Sherard (1861–1943), author and journalist, great-grandson of Wordsworth, first met Wilde in Paris at this time. He spent most of his life in France and Corsica. His father was the Rev. B. Sherard Kennedy, but the son dropped his surname in youth and was thereafter always known as Sherard. Among other books he published biographies of Zola, Daudet and Maupassant (all of whom he had known) and four books about Wilde: *Oscar Wilde: the Story of an Unhappy Friendship* (1902), *The Life of Oscar Wilde* (1906), *The Real Oscar Wilde* (1915), and *Bernard Shaw, Frank Harris and Oscar Wilde* (1937), besides a proliferation of pamphlets.   [2] Rennell Rodd.

[3] It seems certain that Wilde began his long poem *The Sphinx* when he was still at Oxford and finished it now in Paris, though it was not published till 1894. For a rhyme to "catafalque" he had to be content with "Amenalk, the God of Heliopolis."

[4] French portrait-painter and writer (1862–1942). His father and grandfather were both doctors; they ran a *maison de santé* at Passy, in which at different times Gérard de Nerval, Baudelaire and Maupassant were patients. The text of this letter is taken from Blanche's *Portraits of a Lifetime* (1937).

[5] French diarist, novelist, historian and collector (1822–96). The first published mention of Wilde in his journal is on 21 April 1883 (see note 3, p. 303) and their first meeting may well have been earlier in the month. His novel *La Faustin* had been published in 1882, and *La Maison d'un Artiste*, a long two-volume description of the contents of his own house, in 1881.

Je serai bien content de penser qu'il y aura une place, peut-être, pour mes premières fleurs de poésies, près de vos Watteau, et de vos Boucher, et de ce trésor de laque, d'ivoire, et de bronze, que dans votre *Maison d'un Artiste* vous avez pour toujours immortalisé.

Acceptez, Monsieur, l'assurance de mes compliments les plus distingués.

OSCAR WILDE

To Maurice Rollinat[1]

TS. De Saix

[? *April 1883*]   *Hôtel Voltaire,*

Monsieur, J'aurai l'honneur de me présenter chez vous mardi prochain à l'heure indiquée.

Je viens, à ce moment (trois heures du matin), de relire "*La Vache au Taureau;*"[2] c'est un chef d'œuvre. Il y a dedans un vrai souffle de la Nature. Je vous en félicite. Depuis le *De Natura* de Lucretius, le monde n'a rien encore lu de pareil: c'est l'hymne le plus magnifique que la Vénus des Champs a jamais reçu, car c'est le plus simple.

Acceptez, Monsieur, mon hommage sympathique et, si vous me le permettez, mon amitié très sincère.   OSCAR WILDE

To Jacques-Emile Blanche[3]

[? *9–10 April 1883*]   *Hôtel Voltaire*

Cher Monsieur Blanche, Mille remerciements pour votre charmante lettre: cela me donnera beaucoup de plaisir de faire la connaissance de votre amie Madame Baignères. Je fixerai, avec votre permission, le rendezvous chez vous, dimanche prochain à quatre heures. J'aime tant voir votre atelier, avec sa porte bleue de paon, et la petite chambre verte et or, car c'est pour moi une fraîche oasis de beauté dans le désert de Louis seize que je trouve à Paris.

---

[1] French poet (1846–1903).

[2] A poem in Rollinat's book *Les Névroses* (1883).

[3] Text from *Portraits of a Lifetime* and clearly in answer to an undated letter from Auteuil (MS. Hart-Davis), in which Blanche says:

Une charmante dame de mes amies, Madame Baignères, a le plus vif désir de vous connaître et elle m'a demandé si je ne pourrais pas vous conduire chez elle dimanche prochain, vers cinq heures. Voulez-vous venir me prendre à Auteuil ou bien voulez-vous me fixer un rendez-vous dans le quartier de Saint Augustin *pour cette heure? Mes amis Arthur Baignères demeurent 4 rue du Général Foy...*

Pourrais-je plutôt vous rencontrer chez vous l'un des jours de cette semaine, vers la fin du jour, pour vous porter en même temps la photographie que je vous destine et un volume de vers encore inédit d'un ami?

Charlotte (*née* Borel), the wife of Arthur Baignères, was a wealthy hostess, whose *salon* was attended by André Gide and Marcel Proust. Arthur Baignères was said to be one of the wittiest men of his time, and Proust transferred at least one of his jokes to the great novel.

Vendredi, six heures, je serai chez moi, et je vous remercie d'avance pour la photographie de ma charmante petite esthétique Anglaise, et pour les vers de votre ami que vous avez la bonté de m'offrir: je serai plus charmé encore si je trouve que ces vers sont les vôtres.

Croyez, cher Monsieur Blanche, à mes meilleurs sentiments.

OSCAR WILDE

To Clarisse Moore[1]
MS. Clark

[? *April–May 1883*]   *Hôtel Voltaire*

Dear Mrs Moore, Thank you very much for your kind invitation to Rome, which, were I less busy, it would give me pleasure to accept. But at present I am deep in literary work, and cannot stir from my little rooms over the Seine till I have finished two plays. This sounds ambitious, but we live in an age of inordinate personal ambition and I am determined that the world shall understand me, so I will now, along with my art work, devote to the drama a great deal of my time. The drama seems to me to be the meeting place of art and life. [*The rest of this letter is missing*]

To R. H. Sherard
MS. Clark

[*Postmark 17 May 1883*][2]   *8 Mount Street, Grosvenor Square, London*

Dear Robert, Your letter was as loveable as yourself, and this is my first moment after channel-crossings, train-catchings, and my natural rage at the charges for extra luggage from Paris, for sitting down to tell you what pleasure it gave me, and what memories of moonlit meanderings, and sunset strolls, the mere sight of your handwriting brought.

As for the dedication of your poems, I accept it: how could I refuse a gift so musical in its beauty, and fashioned by one whom I love so much as I love you?[3]

To me the mirror of perfect friendship can never be dulled by any treachery, however mean, or disloyalty, however base. Individuals come

---

[1] A friend of Lady Wilde. She lived in Rome.

[2] Four letters from Sherard to Wilde written at this time have survived. They were all written from Eller Howe, Ambleside, Westmorland, the home of some friends, and dated according to the calendar of the French Revolution, of which Sherard was then a firm supporter (he recorded that some of Wilde's earliest letters to him were addressed to Citoyen Sherard). Those of 25 and 29 Floréal 91 (15 and 19 May 1883) refer to Sherard's forthcoming book of poems, the repayment of £8 which Wilde had lent him, and Wilde's return from Paris. In the library of Columbia University there is what appears to be a draft of the opening lines of this letter.

[3] The dedication to *Whispers, being The Early Poems of Robert Harborough Sherard* (1884) runs: "To Oscar Wilde, Poet and Friend, Affectionately and admiringly Dedicated." Willie Wilde, reviewing the book in *Vanity Fair*, said that it was well named.

and go like shadows but the ideal remains untarnished always: the ideal of lives linked together not by affection merely, or the pleasantness of companionship, but by the capacity of being stirred by the same noble things in art and song. For we might bow before the same marble goddess, and with hymns not dissimilar fill the reeds of her flutes: the gold of the night-time, and the silver of the dawn, should pass into perfection for us: and from each string that is touched by the fingers of the player, from each bird that is rapturous in brake or covert, from each hill-flower that blossoms on the hill, we might draw into our hearts the same sense of beauty, and in the House of Beauty meet and join hands.

That is what I think true friendship should be, like that men could make their lives: but friendship is a fire where what is not flawless shrinks into grey ashes, and where what is imperfect is not purified but consumed. There may be much about which we may differ, you and I, more perhaps than we fancy, but in our desire for beauty in all things we are one, and one in our search for that little city of gold where the flute-player never wearies, and the spring never fades, and the oracle is not silent, that little city which is the house of art, and where, with all the music of the spheres, and the laughter of the gods, Art waits for her worshippers. For we at least have not gone out into the desert to seek a reed shaken by the wind, or a dweller in kings' houses, but to a land of sweet waters, and to the well of life; for the nightingale has sung to both of us, and the moon been glad of us, and not to Pallas, or to Hera, have we given the prize, but to her who from the marble of the quarry and the stone of the mine can give us pillared Parthenon and glyptic gem, to her who is the spirit of Beauty, and who has come forth from her hollow hill into the chill evening of this old world, and walks among us visible.

That is, I think, what we are seeking, and that you should seek it with me, you who are yourself so dear to me, gives me faith in our futures, confidence in our love.   OSCAR

To R. H. Sherard
MS. Clark

[*May–June 1883*]   [*London*]

Dear Robert, Your letters are charming, they are iridescent, and everything you see or hear seems to become touched with colour, and tinged with joy. I think of you often, wandering in violet valleys with your honey-coloured hair, and meditating on the influence of paradoxes on the pastoral mind. But you should be here: one can only write in cities, the country hanging on one's walls in the grey mists of Corot, or the opal mornings that Daubigny has given us.

Not that I have written here—the splendid whirl and swirl of life in London sweeps me from my Sphinx. I am hard at work being idle; late midnights and famishing morrows follow one another. I wish I was back in Paris, where I did such good work. However, society must be amazed, and my Neronian coiffure has amazed it. Nobody recognises me, and everybody tells me I look young: that is delightful, of course.

Last night I went and dined with Miss Quen who talked of you very nicely: Johnnie Thompson was there, as charming as ever.

My book you will have next week: it is a great pleasure to give it to anyone so sympathetic as you. Poet to poet I give you my work because your joy in it makes it more dear to me.

Who is your young man who likes what I said of the primrose?[1]

My pen is horrid, my ink bad, my temper worse. Write soon, and come soon to London.   OSCAR

To Marie Prescott[2]

[*?July 1883*]   *9 Charles Street, Grosvenor Square*[3]

My dear Miss Prescott, It is with great pride and pleasure that I look forward to seeing you in the character of the heroine of my play—a character which I entrust to you with the most absolute confidence, for the first night I saw you act I recognised in you a great artist.

I do not mean only that there was strength, music and melody in your voice, and in every pose and gesture, as you walked the stage, the infinite grace of perfect expressiveness, but that behind all these things, which are merely the technique of acting, there lay the true artistic nature which alone can conceive a part, and the true artistic power which alone can create one.

As regards the play itself, I have tried in it to express within the limits of art that Titan cry of the peoples for liberty, which in the Europe of our day is threatening thrones, and making governments unstable from Spain to Russia, and from north to southern seas. But it is a play not of politics but of passion. It deals with no theories of government, but with men and women simply; and modern Nihilistic Russia, with all the terror of its tyranny and the marvel of its martyrdoms, is merely the fiery and fervent

---

[1] In his letter of 6 Prairial 91 (26 May 1883) Sherard wrote: "Will you send me your book? My copy I want then to give to a young man here, who when I had read him your 'Garden of Eros,' vowed austere Milton out of date as far as observation of flowers goes. He particularly admired and often repeats:

to see
The early primrose with shy footsteps run
From the gnarled oak-tree roots till all the wold,
Spite of its brown and trampled leaves, grew bright
with shimmering gold."

In his letter of 22 Prairial 91 (11 June 1883) Sherard answered: "The name of the young man who liked your lines on the primrose is James Carter Shepherd. He is the only friend I have here."

[2] Text from the *New York World* of 12 August 1883, where it appeared as a puff for *Vera*.

[3] In the early summer of 1883 Wilde moved into furnished rooms kept by a retired butler and cook at this address. He stayed there until after his marriage in 1884, when he moved to his own house, 16 Tite Street, Chelsea.

background in front of which the persons of my dream live and love. With this feeling was the play written, and with this aim should the play be acted.

I have to thank you for the list of your company which you have sent me; and congratulate you, as well as myself, on the names of the many well-known and tried actors which I see it includes.

I am very much pleased to know that my directions as regards scenery and costume have been carried out. The yellow satin council-chamber is sure to be a most artistic scene, and as you have been unable to match in New York the vermilion silk of which I sent you a pattern, I hope you will allow me to bring you over a piece large enough for your dress in the last act.

I look forward with much interest to a second visit to America, and to having the privilege of presenting to the American people *my first drama*.[1] There is, I think, no country in the world where there are such appreciative audiences as I saw in the United States.

I hope that by the time I arrive, the play will be in good rehearsing order, and I remain, dear Miss Prescott, your sincere friend and admirer

OSCAR WILDE

To Rebecca Smith[2]

MS. Princeton

[? *July 1883*][3]

Dear Miss Smith, Thank you for your prettily bound little volume which I feel sure must be interesting to all your mother's friends. There is no doubt something gracious always in the simple record of a blameless life, however far from the march of intellect, the clash of science, and the visions and wonders of art, that life may have been passed. Of course now, new and larger ideals have come to us; to us existence is more many-sided and more varied: we burn with a hundred flames: and culture is a

[1] On his second and last visit to America Wilde sailed from Liverpool on 2 August 1883 in the *Britannic* and reached New York on 11 August. *Vera* opened at the Union Square Theatre on 20 August but ran for only a week. It was described as "a foolish, highly-peppered story of love, intrigue and politics" (*New York Tribune*), "unreal, long-winded and wearisome" (*New York Times*) and "long-drawn dramatic rot" (*New York Herald*). Wilde sailed for home in the *Arizona* on 11 September.

[2] Mary Rebecca Darby Smith issued in 1882 *Brief Memorials of Departed Worth: being sketches of the character, life and death of Hannah Logan Smith, by her daughter . . . written when very young.* She had previously published (Philadelphia, 1878) a study of the Marquise de Boissy (Byron's "last attachment," the former Countess Guiccioli), which had inspired Lady Wilde to write a poem, but was described by Byron's biographer Ethel Colburn Mayne as "the silliest book that has ever been written."

[3] Since Wilde was in America all 1882, and the copy of *Brief Memorials* which the author presented to the British Museum is stamped 28 July 1883, I have tentatively dated this letter accordingly.

gem that reflects light from a myriad facets, of which religious piety is of course one, but one only, and to me one of the less fine, contenting itself usually, by some strange perversity, with all that is inferior in art and song.

Such systems of life and thought as that of the Philadelphia Friends we have long ago left behind: they are no longer vital factors in civilisation. As a daughter's memorial to her mother however there is much that is charming in your little book, much that springs from the tenderest love. Truly yours   OSCAR WILDE

To John Everett Millais
MS. Morgan

[? *July 1883*]   *9 Charles Street*

Dear Mr Millais, I am very anxious to have the privilege of being present at your Academy soirée, and not having had the honour of receiving an invitation would esteem it a great kindness if you would give me a card for it.

I know how many calls there must be on you of the same kind, so if I am too late in my request pray accept my excuses for troubling you. And believe me, most truly yours   OSCAR WILDE

To Violet Fane
MS. Clark

[? *July 1883*]   *9 Charles Street*

Of course I am coming! How could one refuse an invitation from one who is a poem and a poet in one, an exquisite combination of perfection and personality, which are the keynotes of modern art.

It was horrid of me not to answer before, but a nice letter is like a sunbeam and should not be treated as an epistle needing a reply. Besides your invitations are commands.

I look forward to meeting Proteus very much: his sonnets are the cameos of the decadence.[1] Very sincerely yours   OSCAR WILDE

To Wilfrid Scawen Blunt[2]
MS. Cockerell

[? *July 1883*]   *9 Charles Street*

Dear Mr Blunt, It will give me great pleasure to come down to you on Saturday week, and look at your horses, and talk about sonnets.

Please present my compliments to Lady Anne, and believe me most truly yours   OSCAR WILDE

[1] *The Love Sonnets of Proteus* by Wilfrid Scawen Blunt was first published, anonymously, in 1881.

[2] Poet, anti-Imperialist, champion of lost causes (most of them since won) and breeder of Arab horses (1840–1922). He married (1869) Byron's grand-daughter, Lady Anne Noel.

To the Hon. George Curzon[1]

MS. Beaverbrook

16 July 1883   *9 Charles Street*

My dear George Curzon, I have been so busy—too busy to answer any nice letters—but I hope to see you soon. When are you at home? I will come round one morning and smoke a cigarette with you. You must tell me about the East. I hope you have brought back strange carpets and stranger gods. Very truly yours   OSCAR WILDE

To John McInnes[2]

MS. Clark

[Late October 1883]   *9 Charles Street*

Dear Mr McInnes, I thank you very sincerely for the beautiful example of English-made and English-decorated china which you have so courteously sent me. In the exquisite delicacy of its material, and the loveliness, as well as the right principles, of its decoration, it will always be to me one of the little masterpieces of my collection.

I will hope some time again to visit the Derby works, and to have the opportunity of renewing my acquaintance with you. Believe me, yours very truly   OSCAR WILDE

To William Davenport Adams[3]

F. Keller

[? October–November 1883]   *9 Charles Street*

Dear Mr Davenport Adams, I have been too busy, and really said my say in my lecture at Derby.

But some day I will be very glad to send you some notes of the artistic qualities—or want of them—in English manufactories and their work.

I was very pleased to have the opportunity of meeting you. I hope not the last time. Yours very truly   OSCAR WILDE

The Hon. George Nathaniel Curzon (1859–1925), eldest son of the fourth Lord Scarsdale, had been an undergraduate (1878–82) at Balliol College, Oxford, where Wilde met him. In 1882–83 he travelled widely in Europe, Egypt and the Near East. He was Conservative M.P. for Southport from 1886 till 1898, when he was created Baron Curzon of Kedleston. Viceroy of India 1898–1905, Foreign Secretary 1919–24, created Marquess 1921.

[2] Chairman of the Royal Crown Derby Porcelain Co. Ltd. Wilde had lectured on "The House Beautiful" in the Lecture Hall, Derby, on 25 October 1883. His British lecture tour had opened at Wandsworth on 24 September, and altogether he delivered more than 150 lectures within a year. The tour was organised by Col. W. F. Morse, who was now London manager for J. M. Stoddart and the *Encyclopaedia Americana*. On 18 August Morse had written to Wilde (MS. Clark): "I can foresee a good season's work and fair prices—not large. From ten to twenty-five guineas per night is all they will pay."

[3] English author and journalist (1851–1904).

151

Telegram: To James McNeill Whistler[1]

[*Circa 10 November 1883*]   *Exeter*

Punch too ridiculous. When you and I are together we never talk about anything except ourselves.[2]   OSCAR WILDE

Constance Lloyd to Otho Holland Lloyd[3]
MS. Holland

23 November 1883   *1 Ely Place, Dublin*

Dearest Otho, . . . It occurred to our brilliant minds that perhaps O. W. would be in town that evening, so we left a note at the Shelbourne asking him to come in, and he accordingly did, and though decidedly extra affected, I suppose partly from nervousness, he made himself very pleasant. Cenie and Stanhope went to the lecture yesterday afternoon and brought O. W. back to four o'clock tea.[4] He was dining with the Fellows of Trinity College at six o'clock. Stanhope and Cenie were so delighted with

[1] On 10 November 1883 *Punch* published an article headed "Counter Criticism," in which occurred this passage:

> Referring to the Annual Meeting of the Hogarth Club, held a few evenings since, a contemporary states that it has received the subjoined communication from a Correspondent present on the occasion: "I was standing," says the gentleman in question, "at the buffet, when I suddenly heard the voice of Mr Oscar Wilde discussing with Mr Whistler and others the attributes of two well-known actresses. The criticism is at least expressive. 'Sarah Bernhardt,' he said, 'is all moonlight and sunlight combined, exceedingly terrible, magnificently glorious. Miss Anderson is pure and fearless as a mountain daisy. Full of change as a river. Tender, fresh, sparkling, brilliant, superb, placid.' "

[2] To this Whistler replied by telegram: "No, no, Oscar, you forget. When you and I are together, we never talk about anything except me."
Both telegrams were published in the *World* of 14 November, and reprinted by Whistler in his book *The Gentle Art of Making Enemies* (1890).

[3] Constance Mary Lloyd (b. 1857) was the daughter of Horace (Horatio) Lloyd, Q.C. (1828–74). At this time she was staying with her maternal grandmother, Mrs Atkinson. Constance had first met Wilde in London two years earlier, and on 7 June 1881 had written to her brother from her home at 100 Lancaster Gate (MS. Holland):

> O.W. came yesterday at about 5.30 (by which time I was shaking with fright!) and stayed for half an hour, begged me to come and see his mother again soon, which little request I need hardly say I have kept to myself. I can't help liking him, because when he's talking to me alone he's never a bit affected, and speaks naturally, excepting that he uses better language than most people. I'm glad they didn't duck him though *you* would have enjoyed it!

Otho Holland Lloyd (1856–1943) was Constance's only brother. Educated at Clifton and Oriel College, Oxford, he read for the Bar but never practised, preferring to spend his life reading and translating the classics. He was twice married and had five children. Like his sister he changed his name to Holland. He died as a result of a fall in the blackout. I have included only the relevant parts of this letter and the next.

[4] On 22 November 1883 Wilde lectured on "The House Beautiful" in the Gaiety Theatre, Dublin, and next day on "Personal Impressions of America."

the lecture that they were seized with the idea of going to the American one today, and some of us intend going to 2/- places today. Ella is coming if she can. He (Oscar) has taken a box at the Gaiety for the performance of *The Merry Duchess* this evening.[1]

Saturday [24 November] . . . We three went again to the lecture, which none of us thought as interesting as the former one. We also went to Oscar's box in the evening to see *The Merry Duchess* (stupid and somewhat vulgar thing!). He could not come himself as he was dining out. They all think him so improved in appearance, and he is certainly very pleasant. Stanhope has started on a new tack and chaffs my life out of me about O. W., such stupid nonsense . . . Ever your loving sister

CONSTANCE M. LLOYD

I have just read *Vera* through again, and I really think it very fine. Oscar says he wrote it to show that an abstract idea such as liberty could have quite as much power and be made quite as fine as the passion of love (or something of that sort).

Constance Lloyd to Otho Holland Lloyd

MS. Holland

26 November 1883   *1 Ely Place, Dublin*

My dearest Otho, Prepare yourself for an astounding piece of news! I am engaged to Oscar Wilde and perfectly and insanely happy. I am sure you will be glad because you like him, and I want you now to do what has hitherto been my part for you, and make it all right. Grandpapa will, I know, be nice, as he is always so pleased to see Oscar. The only one I am afraid of is Aunt Emily. Oscar will write to Grandpapa and to Mama when he arrives at Shrewsbury today, and probably to you at the same time, and he will call next Sunday (he is going up to town on purpose) so you must be at home and be nice to him. I shall probably be there myself, but I shall let you know in a day or two about that. I want to go because otherwise I shall not see him until Christmas . . . Now that he is gone, I am so dreadfully nervous over my family; they are so cold and practical. Everyone in this house is quite charmed, especially Mama Mary who considers me very lucky. Mind you write to me soon, dear old boy, and congratulate me. I am longing to know how you will all take it. I won't stand opposition, so I hope they won't try it. Ever your loving sister

CONSTANCE M. LLOYD[2]

[1] *The Merry Duchess*, a comic opera by George R. Sims and Frederic Clay, was performed at the Gaiety Theatre, Dublin, from 19 to 24 November.

[2] Otho wrote to Wilde on 27 November (text from Stetson sale catalogue, 1920): "I am pleased indeed: I am sure that for my own part I welcome you as a new brother . . . if Constance makes as good a wife as she has been a good sister to me your happiness is certain; she is staunch and true."

To Lily Langtry[1]

[*Circa 16 December 1883*]

... I am really delighted at your immense success; the most brilliant telegrams have appeared in the papers here on your performance in *Peril*.[2] You have done what no other artist of your day has done, invaded America a second time and carried off new victories. But then, you are made for victory. It has always flashed in your eyes and rung in your voice.

And so I write to tell you how glad I am at your triumphs—you, Venus Victrix of our age—and the other half to tell you that I am going to be married to a beautiful girl called Constance Lloyd, a grave, slight, violet-eyed little Artemis, with great coils of heavy brown hair which make her flower-like head droop like a blossom, and wonderful ivory hands which draw music from the piano so sweet that the birds stop singing to listen to her. We are to be married in April. I hope so much that you will be over then. I am so anxious for you to know and to like her.

I am hard at work lecturing and getting rich, though it is horrid being so much away from her, but we telegraph to each other twice a day, and I rush back suddenly from the uttermost parts of the earth to see her for an hour, and do all the foolish things that wise lovers do.[3]

Will you write me and wish me all happiness, and believe me, ever your devoted and affectionate   OSCAR WILDE

To Samuel Smith[4]
MS. Clark

[*Postmark 31 December 1883*]   *9 Charles Street, Grosvenor Square*

Dear Mr Smith, I regret extremely that I have no photograph at present of myself, but as soon as I get one taken will have much pleasure in sending you a copy.

I have most pleasant memories of my morning in Worcester with you, and of all the lovely things you showed me from the blue and white Worcester china down to the gilded King before the altar.

[1] Text from Mrs Langtry's autobiography, *The Days I Knew* (1925).

[2] An English adaptation of Sardou's *Nos Intimes*, originally produced in London in 1876, which Mrs Langtry first played at Ford's Opera House, Washington, D.C., on 15 December 1883, in the course of her second American tour. She later played in it at the Fifth Avenue Theatre, New York from 7 to 26 January 1884.

[3] On 21 December 1883 Constance Lloyd wrote to her brother's future wife Nellie Hutchinson (MS. Holland): "I am with Oscar when he is in town, and I am too miserable to do anything while he is away. He and I are going to Norwood to lunch today as he lectures at the Crystal Palace, and after that he has a week's holiday, which will be much joy for me."

[4] Librarian at the Worcester Public Library. Wilde had lectured on "The House Beautiful" in the Theatre at Worcester on 18 December. He was obviously taken to the Royal Porcelain works and to the Cathedral, where the effigy of King John before the High Altar had been gilded in 1874.

I will hope to lecture at Worcester again and hope you will do me the honour of arranging it for me. Most truly yours   OSCAR WILDE

To Waldo Story[1]

22 January 1884   *Royal Victoria Hotel, Sheffield*

Yes! my dear Waldino, yes! Amazing of course—that was necessary.

Naturally I did not write—the winds carry tidings over the Apennines better than the 2½d post: of course it accounts for the splendid sunsets about which science was so puzzled . . . Well, we are to be married in April, as you were, and then go to Paris, and perhaps to Rome—what do you think? Will Rome be nice in May? I mean, will you and Mrs Waldo be there, and the Pope, and the Peruginos? . . .

Her name is Constance and she is quite young, very grave, and mystical, with wonderful eyes, and dark brown coils of hair: quite perfect except that she does not think Jimmy the only painter that ever really existed:[2] she would like to bring Titian or somebody in by the back door: however, she knows I am the greatest poet, so in literature she is all right: and I have explained to her that you are the greatest sculptor: art instruction cannot go further.

We are, of course, desperately in love. I have been obliged to be away nearly all the time since our engagement, civilising the provinces by my remarkable lectures, but we telegraph to each other twice a day, and the telegraph clerks have become quite romantic in consequence. I hand in my messages, however, very sternly, and try to look as if "love" was a cryptogram for "buy Grand Trunks"[3] and "darling" a cypher for "sell out at par." I am sure it succeeds.

To G. W. Appleton[4]
MS. Berg

Thursday [7 or 14 February 1884]

Dear Mr Appleton, See to enclosed. I leave tomorrow. The lectures you have sent to me are Friday, Saturday, Monday, *Wednesday*. Is this all right? Thursday and Friday I keep to myself but *Tuesday* might have been filled. I look forward with some apprehension to Carlisle and Penrith.[5]

[1] The text of this incomplete letter is taken from Sotheby's catalogue of 10 April 1924. Wilde lectured at Firth College, Sheffield, on 21 January 1884 on "The House Beautiful" and next day on "Personal Impressions of America."

[2] The *World* of 26 December 1883 had reported that "Mr Whistler's last Sunday breakfast of the year was given in honour of two happy couples, Lord Garmoyle and his fairy queen, and Oscar and the lady whom he has chosen to be the *châtelaine* of the House Beautiful."   [3] Canadian railway shares.

[4] George Webb Appleton, American novelist and dramatist (1845–1909), was at this time working with Colonel Morse in Stoddart's London office.

[5] Wilde lectured on "The House Beautiful" in the County Hall, Carlisle, on Monday, 18 February. I would confidently date this letter 14 February but for the fact that Wilde lectured on "America" in the Public Hall at Cockermouth, Cumberland, on Wednesday, 13 February.

Fifty per cent usually means something less than my hotel bill. However we will have nothing except fees for the future. OSCAR WILDE

To J. S. Wood [1]

MS. Yale

[Early 1884] 9 Charles Street

Dear Sir, It will give me much pleasure to contribute to the *Shakespeare Show Book* in aid of an object so deserving. Pray let me know how soon the book is to be put in type. Yours truly OSCAR WILDE

To Alfred Milner

MS. New

[28 May 1884]

My dear Milner, I am going to be married tomorrow—quite privately— but would be so glad to see you at the church and afterwards at 100 Lancaster Gate. Enclosed ticket.[2] Yours OSCAR WILDE

Constance Wilde to Otho Holland Lloyd

MS. Holland

3 June 1884 Hôtel Wagram, Rue de Rivoli, Paris

My dearest Otho, I had of course forgotten your address so could not write to you until Auntie sent it to me this morning. I hope you arrived all safe, Tisie not dead tired.

I have had letters from Mama and Auntie today and from Lady Wilde. The wedding seems to me to have gone off very well and Paris is charming: lovely weather till yesterday evening when a sudden storm of wind and rain broke over us in the afternoon and passed in the night. We have been to the Salon, to the Meissonnier exhibition, to see Judic in *Lili*,[3] above all to see Sarah in *Macbeth*, the most splendid acting I ever saw: only Donalbain was bad. The witches were charmingly grotesque, the Macbeth very good, Sarah of course superb, she simply stormed the part.[4]

[1] Secretary of the Chelsea Hospital for Women, for the benefit of which he edited an anthology called *Shaksperean Show Book*, containing "original literary contributions, illustrations and music." It was published on Wilde's wedding day, 29 May 1884. Tennyson and Browning were among the contributors. Wilde gave his poem "Under the Balcony." It was reprinted in *Poems* (1908).

[2] The printed card reads: "Admit to St James's Church, Sussex Gardens, Thursday, May 29 1884 at 2.30 p.m."

[3] Anne Judic (1850–1911) was one of the stars of the *café-concert*, but she was also successful in light operas such as *Lili* by Florimondo Hervé (pseudonym of Florimond Ronger, 1825–92), which was first produced at the Variétés on 10 January 1882.

[4] This new version by Jean Richepin opened at the Matin theatre in May, with Marais as Macbeth.

Yesterday went to breakfast with a Miss Reubell, a very ugly and very amusing "American French" person here, great friend of Mr Whistler's.[1] Today we had a young Mr Sherard here to breakfast; he has a romantic story and a romantic face: I thought Chatterton was walking in when he appeared. When I knew him a little I remarked on this resemblance and he told me he had so many traits of character like him. His father is a millionaire (English) and he starves here in a garret and lives in dreamland always: he interests me. Very different but also interesting is the young sculptor Donoghue whom I have seen several times, very handsome Roman face but with Irish blue eyes. He has done a lovely bronze bas-relief for the Salon, a seraph: a nude figure full profile of a boy playing a harp, perfectly simple and quite exquisite in line and expression. Everything else in the Salon horrid except, of course, Mr Whistler's two pictures, one very interesting,[2] the Carlyle that Boehm copied for his statue, and which I have only seen before in a print.[3] I hope Nellie liked her things that Aunt Carrie sent her. Find a few moments to write to me before you are married, and when you do write send me the address of your lodgings which I have forgotten and the name of the landlady.

We have an *appartement* here of three rooms, twenty francs a day: not dear for a Paris hotel: we are *au quatrième* and have a lovely view over the gardens of the Tuileries: the ruins of the palace are, alas, no more.[4] I have heard from Mama, so conclude that Mr H. has not yet written?

Of course I need not tell you that I am very happy, enjoying my liberty enormously.

Tomorrow we are giving a dinner-party and as everything is sure to go right in a hotel I am rather looking forward to it. Miss Reubell, Mr Sargent (an American artist),[5] Mr Donoghue and M. Bourget, a French critic,[6] that is the party: I don't know yet whether the latter is coming.

---

[1] Henrietta Reubell (born *c.* 1849) was a wealthy American spinster who kept a *salon* at 42 Avenue Gabriel in Paris. Rothenstein described her as "a striking figure, with her bright red hair crowning an expressive but unbeautiful face, her fingers and person loaded with turquoise stones. In face and figure she reminded me of Queen Elizabeth—if one can imagine an Elizabeth with an American accent and a high, shrill voice like a parrot's." Henry James affectionately called her "the shepherdess of the studios."

[2] At the Salon of 1884 Whistler exhibited his *Arrangement in Grey and Black, No 2: Thomas Carlyle* (now in the Glasgow Art Gallery) and *Harmony in Grey and Green: Miss Cicely Alexander* (now in the National Gallery).

[3] Joseph Edgar Boehm (1814–90), English sculptor of Hungarian extraction, made a statuette of Carlyle (1874) and a full-sized statue (1875), which stands on Chelsea Embankment. Boehm was elected R.A. 1881 and made a Baronet 1889.

[4] The palace of the Tuileries was burnt down by the Communards in 1871, but the ruins were not removed till 1883.

[5] John Singer Sargent (1856–1925), American painter. Lived mostly in France and England, where he was a neighbour of Wilde's in Tite Street. R.A. 1897.

[6] Paul Bourget (1852–1935), French novelist and critic. Violet Paget (1856–1935), who lived mostly in Italy and published many books under the name Vernon Lee, wrote in a letter on 8 June: "Mrs Barstow and I lunched at John [Sargent]'s house. Had we announced ourselves the previous day we should have had the honour of lunching with Paul Bourget and Oscar Wilde and his bride, of whom Bourget says,

My dress creates a sensation in Paris. Miss R, who is, as I said frightful, fair, *white*-faced and forty, wants me to get Mrs Nettleship to make a dress for her exactly like one of mine.[1] Of course I promised: imagine Oscar's horror!

Writing is a labour, and I have still to send to Lady Wilde a few lines, so *addio*. Much love to Nellie. Send me news of her. Your loving sister

CONSTANCE WILDE

Oscar is out, so I can give you no message from him.

Constance and Oscar Wilde to Otho Holland Lloyd[2]

MS. Holland

25 *June 1884*   *The Brunswick, Jermyn Street, St James's*

Dearest Otho, I only got your letter last night, as we had left Paris when it arrived there, so it was sent back to Park Street. I am glad you are so happy, but I felt quite sure that you would be.[3]

We came back yesterday, arrived at 5.30 and came here for the night, the only place that Willie could find for us, London is so crammed. It is two guineas a day for rooms, scarcely suitable for our purse, so we went and dined at Lancaster Gate and gave them hints to ask us there, which they did not take, so I had to ask Auntie if we might! However she met my suggestion half way and suggested our staying for a few days till we found lodgings! London seems very horrid after Dieppe where we spent a delightful week.

I hear that Mr King won't let Mama have a dog that you bought for her, which I think perfectly horrid. I read your letter to her, and thought the description of the parasites must have affected him, but I understand that he did not see the letter. I am going this afternoon to see Mama. Tonight we dine with Mme Gabrielli[4] and go to the Avenue Theatre.[5] She seems smitten with Willie; in fact it is an extraordinary friendship and it's a pity there is an ancient nonentity called Mr Gabrielli in the background some-

---

'*J'aime cette femme—j'aime la femme annulée et tendre*'." In the previous year Vernon Lee had written from London on 11 July: "Oscar Wilde, who is lecturing here at 10/6 the seat, calls John [Sargent]'s art vicious and meretricious. I wonder what we should call Rossetti's."

[1] Ada, daughter of James Hinton, married (1876) John Trivett Nettleship (1841–1902), animal-painter and friend of Browning. For many years Ellen Terry's stage dresses were designed by Mrs J. Comyns Carr and made by Mrs Nettleship. Her daughter Ida married Augustus John.

[2] Only the envelope and the final postscript of this letter are in Wilde's hand.

[3] Otho Lloyd had married Nellie Hutchinson on 10 June.

[4] Henriette Gabrielli, an eccentric hostess (d. 1898). Willie Wilde is said to have worn a bangle she gave him, explaining: "I wear it because it's the gift of the Gab." See article on her by Alexander Michaelson (pseudonym of André Raffalovich) in *Blackfriars* for December 1928.

[5] Where *Gammon*, a farce by James Mortimer, adapted from *La Poudre aux Yeux* by Labiche, and *The Arrivals, or A Trip to Margate* by "J. M. Barrero and A. D. Pincroft," were then running.

Constance Wilde

E. W. Godwin

where. She sends W. a horse every morning and they ride in the row together; she sends him wine, cigarettes, even *tonics* I believe.

I hear you won't be home for nearly a fortnight: tell me when you are coming and I will go and see your rooms are all right: I quite forget the name of the place and the name of the landlady also.

Mr Whistler's etchings are beautiful: *en revanche* I opened a parcel of yours from Dublin, which contained a silver fish-slice. How horrid of the cake never to arrive: however the top part of ours is being kept for Aunt Carrie's party in honour of you: I think it is the most disgusting stuff!

I am thinking of becoming correspondent to some paper, or else of going on the stage: *qu'en pensez vous*? I want to make some money: perhaps a novel would be better. At present I am deep in *Les Misérables*, which is wonderful.

Look out for squalls at the Custom House when you return: they were brutal to us, wanted to make me pay for the silver fittings of my dressing case, bagged all Oscar's Tauchnitz which they had to give back because none of them were copyright.[1] They turned over everything and I am sure they have ruined my clothes. They might at least have clean hands if they insist on rummaging one's things.

Write and tell me how you are getting on and don't take any more waters!!! The cholera at Toulon seems rather awful.

Much love to Nellie, and thanks for writing. Your loving sister

CONSTANCE WILDE

P.S. Oscar is out, and I never send imaginary messages from people.

Am so glad you are enjoying yourselves, am quite anxious to meet Nellie.

O. W.

To E. W. Godwin[2]

MS. Hyde (H. M.)

[*19 July 1884*][3]   *7 Great College Street, Westminster, S.W.*

Dear G, I suppose you are as busy as you like it (or don't like it).[4] When can I see you *Monday* at Tite Street?

---

[1] Bernhard, Baron Tauchnitz (1816–95) founded his publishing house at Leipzig in 1837 and started his paperback edition of British authors in 1841. They were intended to circulate only on the Continent. Tauchnitz was ennobled as a result of his publishing career.

[2] Edward William Godwin, F.S.A., F.R.I.B.A. (1833–86), architect and theatrical designer, was a native of Bristol, where in 1861 he met Kate and Ellen Terry when they were performing there as children. At the age of twenty-five he built the Town Hall at Northampton, and later (for his friend Whistler) the White House in Chelsea. (When Whistler was forced by poverty to leave the house, he wrote above the front door: "Except the Lord build the house, they labour in vain that build it. E. W. Godwin, F.S.A., built this one.") Godwin's first wife died young, and in 1868 he set up house in Hertfordshire with the twenty-year-old Ellen Terry, whose child-marriage with the painter G. F. Watts had ended in separation, though not divorce, in 1866. Ellen Terry bore Godwin two children, Gordon and Edith Craig,

I want to press on the laggards. If you like, of course, after the play will have to do—i.e. *Thursday*, but Monday would be best. Ever yours

OSCAR WILDE

To Henry Irving

MS. Irving

[? *mid-August 1884*]   *9 Charles Street, Grosvenor Square*

Dear Mr Irving, Being dramatic critic of *Vanity Fair* during Willie's absence I have to open all letters that come for him to the office, among which I find an invitation from you for him for tomorrow.[1]

He is now in Savoy and will be much disappointed to have missed the opportunity of dining with you. I fear that my privileges as his understudy only extend to a necessary presence at dull farces and stupid burlesques, but pray let me wish you every success again in the States. You carry with you the sympathy of all who love art. Truly yours

OSCAR WILDE

To E. W. Godwin

MS. Hyde (H. M.)

[*Postmark 13 September 1884*][2]   *9 Charles Street*

My dear Godwin, I have missed you twice. When can I see you? Will you

---

but after six years of domesticity she returned to the stage. Godwin designed the scenery and costumes for the Bancrofts' production of *The Merchant of Venice* (in which Ellen Terry played Portia) at the Prince of Wales's Theatre in 1875. Later that year Godwin left her, and soon afterwards married Beatrix, the schoolgirl daughter of John Birnie Philip, the sculptor responsible for the frieze on the podium of the Albert Memorial. After Godwin's death she married Whistler. For fuller details of Godwin's designs for the decoration of Wilde's house in Tite Street and the subsequent difficulties see "Oscar Wilde and his Architect" by H. Montgomery Hyde (*Architectural Review*, March 1951) and *Cases that Changed the Law* by the same author (1951). Green was the first contractor employed. Wilde quarrelled with him and got rid of him only after legal actions, affidavits and distraint. He was succeeded by Sharpe.   [3] So noted by Godwin.

[4] Godwin was directing, or helping to direct, Lady Archibald Campbell's open-air production of the woodland scenes from *As You like It* in the grounds of Dr McGragh's hydropathic establishment at Coombe Wood, near Kingston-on-Thames, which took place in July. Lady Archie (see note 1, p. 102) was a pioneer of the production of pastoral plays in Victorian England. Besides *As You Like It* she produced Fletcher's *Faithful Shepherdess* (1885) and *Fair Rosamund*, specially adapted for her by Godwin from Tennyson's *Becket* (1886). On the first page of his first number of the *Woman's World* (November 1887) Wilde published an article of hers called "The Woodland Gods," in which she described the experiment and eulogised Godwin. See note 1, p. 205.

[1] The dramatic criticisms in *Vanity Fair* were unsigned, and since Wilde was doubtless imitating his brother Willie's style, it has proved impossible either to identify these hitherto unknown writings of Wilde's or to date this letter exactly. On the other hand, the criticism published on 16 August contains a quotation from Whistler on an aspect of art, which Willie would have been less likely to use, so I have tentatively dated this letter accordingly. Irving's second American tour opened on 30 September 1884.   [2] So dated by Godwin.

be at the club at ten o'clock tonight? Or will you be at my mother's, 116 Park Street, between five and seven? Let me see you somewhere. Ever yours   OSCAR WILDE

To an Unidentified Correspondent

MS. Clark

[9 October 1884][1]   Harker's York Hotel, York

Dear Sir, I regret extremely that your letter was not handed to me till the close of my lecture, as it would have given me much pleasure to have had some seats reserved for the members of your company. It is always a privilege to number any artists in one's audience.

After my evening lecture I will be very glad to visit the theatre. I have heard so much of Miss Dene's genius and beauty that I am extremely anxious to see her. Believe me, yours truly   OSCAR WILDE

To the Editor of the Pall Mall Gazette [2]

[Circa 13 October 1884]

The "Girl Graduate" must of course have precedence, not merely for her sex but for her sanity: her letter is extremely sensible. She makes two points: that high heels are a necessity for any lady who wishes to keep her dress clean from the Stygian mud of our streets, and that without a tight corset "the ordinary number of petticoats and etceteras" cannot be properly or conveniently held up. Now it is quite true that as long as the lower garments are suspended from the hips, a corset is an absolute necessity; the mistake lies in not suspending all apparel from the shoulders. In the latter case a corset becomes useless, the body is left free and unconfined for respiration and motion, there is more health, and consequently more beauty. Indeed all the most ungainly and uncomfortable articles of dress that fashion has ever in her folly prescribed, not the tight corset merely, but the farthingale, the vertugadin, the hoop, the crinoline, and that modern monstrosity the so-called "dress-improver" also, all of them have owed their origin to the same error, the error of not seeing that it is from the shoulders, and from the shoulders only, that all garments should be hung.

[1] On this day Wilde lectured twice in the Exhibition Hall at York as part of a festival week. At 3 p.m. he spoke on "The Value of Art in Modern Life" and at 8 p.m. on "Dress." All that week Dorothy Dene (who also won fame as one of Leighton's models) was appearing at the Theatre Royal, York, with Lewis Waller in Called Back!, a dramatisation by Hugh Conway and Comyns Carr of Hugh Conway's novel. Dorothy Dene was the stage-name of Ada Alice Pullen (1861–99). She played Mrs Arbuthnot in a tour of A Woman of No Importance in the autumn of 1894.

[2] Wilde's lecture on "Dress," given at Ealing on 1 October, had been reported in the Pall Mall Gazette next day. Mr Wentworth Huyshe's letter appeared on 3 October, and a "Girl Graduate's" on 7 October. Wilde's letter was published on 14 October. It was reprinted in Miscellanies.

And as regards high heels, I quite admit that some additional height to the shoe or boot is necessary if long gowns are to be worn in the street; but what I object to is that the height should be given to the heel only, and not to the sole of the foot also. The modern high-heeled boot is, in fact, merely the clog of the time of Henry VI, with the front prop left out, and its inevitable effect is to throw the body forward, to shorten the steps, and consequently to produce that want of grace which always follows want of freedom.

Why should clogs be despised? Much art has been expended on clogs. They have been made of lovely woods, and delicately inlaid with ivory, and with mother-of-pearl. A clog might be a dream of beauty, and, if not too high or too heavy, most comfortable also. But if there be any who do not like clogs, let them try some adaptation of the trouser of the Turkish lady, which is loose round the limb, and tight at the ankle.

The "Girl Graduate," with a pathos to which I am not insensible, entreats me not to apotheosise "that awful, befringed, beflounced, and bekilted divided skirt." Well, I will acknowledge that the fringes, the flounces, and the kilting do certainly defeat the whole object of the dress, which is that of ease and liberty; but I regard these things as mere wicked superfluities, tragic proofs that the divided skirt is ashamed of its own division. The principle of the dress is good, and, though it is not by any means perfection, it is a step towards it.

Here I leave the "Girl Graduate," with much regret, for Mr Wentworth Huyshe. Mr Huyshe makes the old criticism that Greek dress is unsuited to our climate, and the, to me, somewhat new assertion, that the men's dress of a hundred years ago was preferable to that of the second part of the seventeenth century, which I consider to have been the exquisite period of English costume.

Now, as regards the first of these two statements, I will say, to begin with, that the warmth of apparel does not depend really on the number of garments worn, but on the material of which they are made. One of the chief faults of modern dress is that it is composed of far too many articles of clothing, most of which are of the wrong substance; but over a substratum of pure wool, such as is supplied by Dr Jaeger[1] under the modern German system, some modification of Greek costume is perfectly applicable to our climate, our country, and our century. This important fact has already been pointed out by Mr E. W. Godwin in his excellent, though too brief, handbook on Dress, contributed to the Health Exhibition.[2] I call it an important fact because it makes almost any form of lovely costume perfectly practicable in our cold climate. Mr Godwin, it is true, points out that the English ladies of the thirteenth century abandoned after some time the flowing garments of the early Renaissance in favour of a

[1] Gustav Jaeger (1832–1917), German naturalist, hygienist and clothing reformer. In his *Die Normalkleidung als Gesundheitsschutz* (1880) he advocated a system of sanitary woollen clothing which was popularised by Bernard Shaw.

[2] *Dress, and its relation to health and culture*, one of a series of books published for the International Health Exhibition, 1884.

tighter mode, such as northern Europe seems to demand. This I quite admit, and its significance; but what I contend, and what I am sure Mr Godwin would agree with me in, is that the principles, the laws of Greek dress may be perfectly realised, even in a moderately tight gown with sleeves: I mean the principle of suspending all apparel from the shoulders, and of relying for beauty of effect, not on the stiff ready-made ornaments of the modern milliner—the bows where there should be no bows, and the flounces where there should be no flounces—but on the exquisite play of light and line that one gets from rich and rippling folds. I am not proposing any antiquarian revival of an ancient costume, but trying merely to point out the right laws of dress, laws which are dictated by art and not by archaeology, by science and not by fashion; and just as the best work of art in our days is that which combines classic grace with absolute reality, so from a continuation of the Greek principles of beauty with the German principles of health will come, I feel certain, the costume of the future.

And now to the question of men's dress, or rather to Mr Huyshe's claim of the superiority, in point of costume, of the last quarter of the eighteenth century over the second quarter of the seventeenth. The broad-brimmed hat of 1640 kept the rain of winter and the glare of summer from the face; the same cannot be said of the hat of one hundred years ago, which, with its comparatively narrow brim and high crown, was the precursor of the modern "chimney-pot:" a wide turned-down collar is a healthier thing than a strangling stock, and a short cloak much more comfortable than a sleeved overcoat, even though the latter may have had "three capes:" a cloak is easier to put on and off, lies lightly on the shoulder in summer, and, wrapped round one in winter, keeps one perfectly warm. A doublet, again, is simpler than a coat and waistcoat; instead of two garments we have one; by not being open, also, it protects the chest better.

Short loose trousers are in every way to be preferred to the tight knee-breeches which often impede the proper circulation of the blood; and, finally, the soft leather boots, which could be worn above or below the knee, are more supple, and give consequently more freedom, than the stiff Hessian which Mr Huyshe so praises. I say nothing about the question of grace and picturesqueness, for I suppose that no one, not even Mr Huyshe, would prefer a macaroni to a cavalier, a Lawrence to a Vandyke, or the third George to the first Charles; but for ease, warmth and comfort this seventeenth-century dress is infinitely superior to anything that came after it, and I do not think it is excelled by any preceding form of costume. I sincerely trust that we may soon see in England some national revival of it.

To E. W. Godwin

MS. Hyde (H. M.)

[*15 October 1884*][1]   *The Royal Hotel, Bristol*

Dear Godwin, I write to you from your own city to say that Allport estimates work to be done by Green at £72 ! ! ! Amazing. Now let us for heaven's sake move on. Is Sharpe in? And can I see you on *Friday* anywhere: it is my first day in town.

I want if possible Sharpe to be in and doing. I am so overwhelmed with expenses. I will be in town Friday afternoon, will you send a line to Charles Street? Ever yours   O. W.

To E. W. Godwin

MS. Hyde (H. M.)

[*26 October 1884*][2]

Dear Godwino, So sorry to miss you. I will be back on *Friday*. Can I see you Friday night? I fear I could hardly manage Oxford: when do you go however? What shall I do about Green? He is too horrid.

My letters will be forwarded. Hope you are well. Ever yours   O. W.

If you don't go Saturday to *Romeo and Juliet*, Lyceum, give me your stall.[3]

To E. W. Godwin

MS. Hyde (H. M.)

[*4 November 1884*][4]   *9 Charles Street, Grosvenor Square*

In case of no hurry a line here is safer.

Dear Godwin, My address for Thursday morning will be c/o Mr Keary, Oakhill, Stoke-on-Trent.[5] I will be at Tite Street at four o'clock on Thursday afternoon if you would be there also. Arthur[6] might be invited, to get your directions. Will you ask him?

---

[1] So dated by Godwin. On this day Wilde lectured twice on "Dress" in the Lesser Victorian Rooms, Clifton, Bristol. The *Bristol Times and Mirror* of next day described him as "a well-built, good-looking gentleman dressed in perfectly-fitting black frock coat and light trousers, with a naturally dignified yet withal easy and graceful manner, and who delivers his lecture in a resonant and musical voice, and in a highly interesting style."   [2] So dated by Godwin.

[3] The revival of *Romeo and Juliet*, which opened at the Lyceum on 1 November 1884, with William Terriss and Mary Anderson in the leading parts.

[4] So dated by Godwin.

[5] Wilde lectured on "The Value of Art in Modern Life" in the Town Hall, Stoke-on-Trent, on 5 November.

[6] Possibly Arthur May (see note 3, p. 27), who was a friend of Godwin's.

Don't you think a vermilion band in the front room—ground floor, in the recess—to continue the moulding would do for the present, till the bookcase is arranged?

I am in much distress over Green seizing the furniture. You alone can comfort me. Ever yours   OSCAR

To E. W. Godwin

MS. Hyde (H. M.)

[*Postmark 4 December 1884*][1]   *Station Hotel, Leeds*[2]

Dear Godwino, Your letter to *The Times* is excellent.[3] I must see you. I arrive tomorrow (Friday) and will be with you on Saturday morning. I wish you would choose the colours—the red for the drawing-room—as the thing is at a standstill: is it to be vermilion? is it not?

The universe pauses for an answer! Don't keep it waiting. Let us go to the Lyceum and see this thing. Also what shall I do about Kyrle?[4] Ever yours   OSCAR

Will Granger tell Sharpe about the window-lattice?

To Constance Wilde [5]

MS. Morgan

Tuesday [*Postmark 16 December 1884*]   *The Balmoral, Edinburgh*[6]

Dear and Beloved, Here am I, and you at the Antipodes. O execrable facts, that keep our lips from kissing, though our souls are one.

What can I tell you by letter? Alas! nothing that I would tell you. The messages of the gods to each other travel not by pen and ink and indeed your bodily presence here would not make you more real: for I feel your fingers in my hair, and your cheek brushing mine. The air is full of the music of your voice, my soul and body seem no longer mine, but mingled in some exquisite ecstasy with yours. I feel incomplete without you. Ever and ever yours   OSCAR

Here I stay till Sunday.

[1] So dated by Godwin.

[2] Wilde lectured on "Beauty, Taste and Ugliness in Dress" at the Albert Hall, Leeds, on 4 December.

[3] Printed 4 December 1884, in refutation of the architect William Butterfield, who wanted to "preserve" Westminster Hall by raising the roof and heightening the walls. Butterfield replied, and on 10 December Godwin wrote another letter, beginning: "What I want, in common with other antiquaries and artists, is that this building shall not be meddled with by any architect whatsoever."

[4] Kyrle Bellew (see note 2, p. 104).

[5] Except for the brief notes on pp. 384 and 386 this is the only letter from Wilde to his wife which is known to have survived. The rest were almost certainly destroyed by her or her family.

[6] Wilde lectured twice in the Queen Street Hall, Edinburgh, on Saturday, 20 December. At 3 p.m. his subject was "Dress," and at 8 p.m. (when the *Scotsman* reported "a meagre attendance") "The Value of Art in Modern Life."

To J. S. Blackie[1]
MS. Edinburgh

[*Circa 16 December 1884*]   *The Balmoral, Edinburgh*

My dear Professor, I am in Edinboro' for three days, and the man who comes to Scotland without scenting the heather on the mountain, or talking to you among your books, misses what is best in the land. So as I can see no glory of purple on the hillside, may I come and see you, when you have, if you ever have, an idle hour?

My excuse must be that all Celts gravitate towards each other. Believe me, in any case, your sincere admirer   OSCAR WILDE

To E. W. Godwin
MS. Hyde (H. M.)

[*19 December 1884*][2]   *The Balmoral, Edinburgh*

My dear Godwin, I cannot understand Sharpe's account, enclosed. What is (1) extra painting? What is (2) 14 gas brackets? What is deal shelf overmantel and case in dining-room etc? Sharpe has been paid first £40 for the overmantel in bedroom and drawing-room, and the sideboard—which by the bye I thought very dear—then £120 for his contract, but this new £100 takes me by surprise. I thought the £120 was for everything. Surely Green fixed the gas stoves? I may be wrong, but would you look over it again?

I hope you have been able to choose the stuffs. I don't think the oriental blue and red hanging is big enough for two curtains on landing at drawing-room. Would you choose something for that place, and see my wife about them? I do hope to see things nearly ready when I come home—the coverings for settees especially.

I wish you were in Edinboro' with me: it is quite lovely—bits of it. The house *must* be a success: do just add the bloom of colour to it in curtains and cushions. Ever yours   OSCAR

To Philippa Knott[3]
MS. Knott

[*Postmark 2 January 1885*]   *16 Tite Street, Chelsea*

My dear Phil, Thank you so much for your charming letter. It will be a

---

[1] John Stuart Blackie (1809–1905), Scottish professor and man of letters, Professor of Greek at Edinburgh University 1852–82. He was much loved, famous for his eccentricities and said to teach his pupils everything except Greek. In *The Letters of John Stuart Blackie to his Wife* (1910) he describes meeting Sir William and Lady Wilde in Dublin in June 1874.   [2] So dated by Godwin.

[3] Elder sister of Florence (Balcombe) Stoker. This letter was addressed to her in Dublin (see note 4, p. 36). Wilde lectured at the Gaiety Theatre, Dublin, on the afternoons of Monday, 5 January (on "Dress), and Tuesday, 6 January (on "The Value of Art in Modern Life").

great pleasure for me to come to you on Tuesday evening. I fear I could hardly manage an afternoon as my lectures rather tire me.

I am sorry Constance cannot come with me, but we have only just moved into our house, and she is busy over embroideries and housemaids: some day you must come and see us.

Pray remember me to your husband and to all at the Crescent: I will be delighted to see them and Florrie again. Very sincerely   OSCAR WILDE

To Edward Heron-Allen[1]
TS. Holland

9 January 1885   *16 Tite Street*

Dear Mr Heron-Allen, I have just returned from Ireland, and find waiting for me your beautiful book, and your kind invitation: both of which I have much pleasure in accepting.

I am greatly struck with the loveliness of the violin curves, and delighted to find that grasshoppers are fiddlers.

I hope you will often come and see us: in the interim I am glad to have your photograph, violin and all.   OSCAR WILDE

To Mary Anderson
MS. Navarro

[? January 1885]   *16 Tite Street*

Dear Miss Anderson, I had not seen your Juliet, since New York, till last night: will you allow me to send you my warm congratulations on the marvellous development of your art. There were, in your acting, moments of absolutely perfect beauty, in fact your method seems to me to have changed. What was a bud has grown to a blossom, and those who admired you as a woman must reverence you now as an artist.

Your own dresses were charming, and Tybalt's *second* dress a master-piece of colour, but oh! the guests!!!!! Very sincerely your admirer
OSCAR WILDE

---

[1] Writer, polymath and eccentric (1861–1943). A man of means, he practised as a solicitor in London but spent much of his later life at Selsey in Sussex, pursuing his recreations, which he described in *Who's Who* as "Persian Literature; Marine Zoology; Meteorology; Heraldry; Bibliography; Occasional Essays and Scientific Romances; Auricula and Asparagus Culture." He published many books on these subjects and a variety of others, including *Violin-making* (1882). He was made a Fellow of the Royal Society for his researches on Foraminifera.

To W. H. Pollock[1]

MS. Private

[? *Early January 1885*]   *16 Tite Street*

My dear Pollock, Let me thank you for your charming little book of poems. Many of the songs in it are old favourites, and it has been a real delight to read again your version of Musset's *"Nuits"* with your own fine introduction. Your portrait does not, I think, do you justice, but then one always sees a poet best in his music. Believe me, truly yours   OSCAR WILDE

To the Rev. J. Page Hopps[2]

14 January 1885

Dear Mr Hopps, I am very sorry to say that I am confined to the house with a severe cold, caught by lecturing in a Lincolnshire snowstorm, and am not allowed by my doctor to travel. It is with much regret that I find myself unable to join in the meeting tomorrow, as I sympathise most strongly with the object in question. The present style of burying and sorrowing for the dead seems to me to make grief grotesque, and to turn mourning to a mockery. Any reform you can bring about in these customs would be of value quite inestimable. The present ostentation and extravagance of burial rites seems to me to harmonise but ill with the real feeling of those at the doors of whose house the Angel of Death has knocked. The ceremony by which we part from those whom we have loved should not merely be noble in its meaning, but simple in its sincerity. The funeral of Ophelia does not seem to me "a maimed rite" when one thinks of the flowers strewn on her grave. I regret exceedingly that I cannot hear the actual suggestions on the matter which will be made at your meeting. I have always been of opinion that the coffin should be privately conveyed at night-time to the churchyard chapel, and that there the mourners should next day meet. By these means the public procession through the streets would be avoided; and the publicity of funerals is surely the real cause of

---

[1] Walter Herries Pollock (1850–1928), poet, author and journalist, was editor of the *Saturday Review* 1883–94. His *Verse of Two Tongues* (1884) contained English versions of three poems by Alfred de Musset—"*La Nuit de Mai*," "*La Nuit d'Août*," and "*La Nuit d'Octobre*." There is no portrait in the only copy of the book that I have seen.

[2] John Page Hopps (1834-1911) was first a Baptist and then a Unitarian minister. He was also a religious author and editor. Wilde had been one of the speakers billed to address a meeting "in support of the principles of Funeral and Mourning Reform" in the Temperance Hall, Leicester, on 15 January. At the meeting this letter was read out by Hopps. The text is taken from the report in the *Leicester Daily Post* of 16 January. The inauguration of the Church of England Funeral and Mourning Reform Association, under the joint presidency of the Archbishops of Canterbury and York, had been announced the previous January and there had been a conference in London in July. The secretary, the Rev. F. Lawrence, and another representative of the Association were on the platform at Leicester.

their expense. As regards dress, I consider that white and violet should be recognised as mourning, and not black merely, particularly in the case of children. The habit of bringing flowers to the grave is now almost universal, and is a custom beautiful in its symbolism; but I cannot help thinking that the elaborate and expensive designs made by the florist are often far less lovely than a few flowers held loose in the hand. There are many other points on which I should have liked to listen, and one point on which I had hoped to have the privilege of speaking. I mean the expression of sorrow in art. The urns, pyramids and sham sarcophagi—ugly legacies from the eighteenth century to us—are meaningless as long as we do not burn or embalm our dead. If we are to have funeral memorials at all, far better models are to be found in the beautiful crosses of Ireland, such as the cross at Monasterboice, or in the delicate bas-reliefs on Greek tombs. Above all, such art, if we are to have it, should concern itself more with the living than the dead—should be rather a noble symbol for the guiding of life than an idle panegyric on those who are gone. If a man needs an elaborate tombstone in order to remain in the memory of his country, it is clear that his living at all was an act of absolute superfluity. Keats's grave is a hillock of green grass with a plain headstone, and is to me the holiest place in Rome. There is in Westminster Abbey a periwigged admiral in a nightgown hurried off to heaven by two howling cherubs, which is one of the best examples I know of ostentatious obscurity.

Pray offer to the committee of the society my sincere regrets at my inability to be present, and my sincere wishes for the success of your movement. Believe me, sincerely yours   OSCAR WILDE

To A. P. T. Elder[1]
MS. Clark

[*January-February 1885*]   *16 Tite Street*[2]

Dear Sir, I have received the two copies of your new magazine, and thank you for your courtesy in sending them to me.

The literary activity of America is to me something marvellous absolutely, no year seems to pass without your giving us new poets, and new thinkers. I see no limit to the future in art of a country which has already given us Emerson, that master of moods, and those two lords of romance, Poe and Bret Harte.

You ask me for my opinion of your magazine, and I suppose you mean my candid opinion. I myself have always felt that there is much to be learned from the candid opinions of others, provided of course that they are

[1] American publisher and "book-promoter." His new magazine was a monthly called *Literary Life*, which he began to publish in 1884 at Cleveland, Ohio, but moved almost immediately to Chicago. The two issues he sent to Wilde were those of December 1884 and January 1885.

[2] Wilde began this address with "Keats House," presumably from force of habit or love of Keats.

complimentary, but in the case of *Literary Life* no such proviso seems to be necessary. It is exceedingly well printed, and the paper is excellent: the aim of the magazine seems to me lofty enough to be fine, and yet not too ambitious: its tone is the tone of cultivated appreciation of the best things, and its cover is execrable: you must not libel Sappho in Chicago.

I am glad to see you have given a haven to so many young poets: I call them young poets, because whoever is a poet grows not old; that is reserved for prose writers only. Cecil Harcourt's "Sea Foam" is very graceful and musical, though he should not rhyme "dawn" and "gone," and the "Winter Evening" by Franklin Denton is a really powerful bit of work: the third and fourth lines are absolutely beautiful, and absolutely new, and for their sake much shall be forgiven to others, even the appearance of Horace's charming Lalage, not merely as a page, but rhyming to one, even Achïlles with the penultimate short, and Cybēle with the penultimate long: trifles, do you say? No. It is the poets of a country who make its language; let them see that they keep it perfect.

Then as regards your prose writers: I like the College Professor best, but the standard is good everywhere. Still, if I might say so, a little more care, both as regards style and substance, should be taken. Rossetti is not living (p. 190), and *"in medias res"* (p. 192) could not pass, even at a Fancy Ball, for *"in medio tutissimus:"* that a book "will be *read* with interest by the *illiterate*" (p. 151) is too charming to alter, but that no man was more fortunate than Carlyle was in his marriage, is a somewhat too painful paradox (p. 134). Still, there is much that is good, and the advice to read the daily papers as a method of acquiring judgment and good sense (p. 183) is an excellent bit of American humour, on which you must allow me to congratulate the author.

In conclusion, let me say that with the large amount of new material in the shape of young writers which you have, it is in your power to make your magazine an influence for culture in your city: you have at any rate my best wishes for your success. I have not forgotten the pleasant week I spent in Chicago, and I am sure you will be glad to hear that one of the most beautiful things in last year's Salon was a bas-relief by your marvellous fellow-townsman, and my dear friend, young Donoghue.

OSCAR WILDE

To James McNeill Whistler[1]
MS. Glasgow

[*Circa 23 February 1885*]

Dear Butterfly, By the aid of a biographical dictionary I discovered that there were once two painters, called Benjamin West and Paul Delaroche, who recklessly took to lecturing on Art.

---

[1] On 20 February 1885 Whistler delivered his famous Ten O'Clock lecture on art in the Prince's Hall, London. Next day the *Pall Mall Gazette* published Wilde's account of it (reprinted in *Miscellanies*), in which he praised Whistler's "really

As of their works nothing at all remains, I conclude that they explained themselves away. Be warned in time, James; and remain, as I do, incomprehensible: to be great is to be misunderstood.[1] *Tout à vous*   OSCAR

Private

Jimmy! You must *stamp* your letters—they are dear at twopence—and also do send them in proper time. 2.30 on Monday! *Ciel!*

To E. W. Godwin

MS. Hyde (H. M.)

Friday [? *February or March 1885*]   *16 Tite Street*

Dear Godwino, We are very much annoyed at your being away, and not constantly dining with us.

There is also a question of another board in dining-room, and some kind of shelf, bracket, or little cupboard over it, a sort of Japanese arrangement of shelves—but very tiny.

---

marvellous eloquence," described him as "a miniature Mephistopheles, mocking the majority" and the lecture as a masterpiece. Wilde went on:

That an artist will find beauty in ugliness, *le beau dans l'horrible*, is now a commonplace of the schools, the *argot* of the atelier, but I strongly deny that charming people should be condemned to live with magenta ottomans and Albert blue curtains in their rooms in order that some painter may observe the side lights on the one and the values of the other. Nor do I accept the dictum that only a painter is a judge of painting. I say that only an artist is a judge of art; there is a wide difference. As long as a painter is a painter merely, he should not be allowed to talk of anything but mediums and megilp, and on those subjects should be compelled to hold his tongue; it is only when he becomes an artist that the secret laws of artistic creation are revealed to him. For there are not many arts, but one art merely: poem, picture and Parthenon, sonnet and statue—all are in their essence the same, and he who knows one knows all. But the poet is the supreme artist, for he is the master of colour and of form, and the real musician besides, and is lord over all life and all arts; and so to the poet beyond all others are these mysteries known; to Edgar Allan Poe and to Baudelaire, not to Benjamin West and Paul Delaroche.

Whistler responded with the following letter, dated 21 February, which was printed in the *World* of 25 February:

I have read your exquisite article in the *Pall Mall*. Nothing is more delicate, in the flattery of "the Poet" to "the Painter," than the *naïveté* of "the Poet," in the choice of his Painters—Benjamin West and Paul Delaroche!

You have pointed out that "the Painter's" mission is to find "*le beau dans l'horrible*," and have left to "the Poet" the discovery of "*l'horrible*" dans "*le beau*"!

To which Wilde's letter is an answer. There is another manuscript version (MS. Berg), lacking the postscript; with "Jimmy" erased at the beginning and "Dear Butterfly" superimposed; "made the discovery" for "discovered;" and "rashly lectured upon" for "recklessly took to lecturing on." This manuscript shows signs of having been marked up for press, and its text appeared in the *World* on 25 February 1885, and (with the rest of the controversy) in *The Gentle Art of Making Enemies* (1890). It was clearly a copy which Wilde wrote out from memory for publication, and I have preferred to print from the original letter, which reached Glasgow with Whistler's papers.

[1] These seven words are a quotation from Emerson's essay "Self-Reliance."

I enclose your pattern, and by the bye my wife has a huge bill against you—for your meat safe, and the buttercloth! something gigantic. Mary has never been here! Ever yours   O. W.

To E. W. Godwin
MS. Hyde (H. M.)

[*Late February or March 1885*]

My dear Godwin, I enclose a cheque and thank you very much for the beautiful designs of the furniture. Each chair is a sonnet in ivory, and the table is a masterpiece in pearl. Will you let me know what I owe you for the plan of the new room? I fear I cannot build it yet: money is as scarce as sunlight, but when I do I will look for your aid. I don't know what you owe Constance, but she will write to you. I was so sorry to miss you. Do come and dine any day this week, and will you come to my wife's box at *The Hunchback*, Lyceum, on Saturday evening?[1] Ever yours   OSCAR

To John Hollingshead[2]
MS. Huntington

[*March 1885*]   *16 Tite Street*

Dear Hollingshead, I regret very much that I had not the opportunity of reading you before I wrote my article, as I should like to have quoted the opinion of a practical manager, and high authority, on the subject.[3]

I am glad however to find you agree with me so thoroughly in the matter, and I hope that the sacred lamp of Burlesque may burn brightly and beautifully in the shrine of the scene-painter. Believe me, very truly yours
                                                                    OSCAR WILDE

To the Editor of the Pall Mall Gazette[4]

30 March 1885

Sir, I am deeply distressed to hear that tuberose is so called from its being a "lumpy flower." It is not at all lumpy, and, even if it were, no poet

---

[1] Mary Anderson's revival of Sheridan Knowles's verse drama *The Hunchback*, in which she played the part of Julia, opened at the Lyceum on 24 February 1885 and ran until April.

[2] Author, journalist and impresario (1827–1904). Worked on *Household Words* under Dickens and on the *Cornhill* under Thackeray. Helped to found the Alhambra Theatre 1866, founded the Gaiety Theatre 1868. Lessee of many London theatres and director of music hall companies. Claimed to have introduced electric light to the London theatre 1878. Sponsored first London season of the Comédie Française 1879.

[3] Wilde's article "Shakespeare on Scenery" appeared in the *Dramatic Review* of 14 March 1885. It was reprinted in *Reviews*.

[4] In the *Pall Mall Gazette* of 27 March Wilde had reviewed four books of verse,

should be heartless enough to say so. Henceforth there really must be two derivations for every word, one for the poet and one for the scientist. And in the present case the poet will dwell on the tiny trumpets of ivory into which the white flower breaks, and leave to the man of science horrid allusions to its supposed lumpiness and indiscreet revelations of its private life below ground. In fact, tuber as a derivation is disgraceful. On the roots of verbs Philology may be allowed to speak, but on the roots of flowers she must keep silence. We cannot allow her to dig up Parnassus. And, as regards the word being a trisyllable, I am reminded by a great living poet that another correctly wrote:

> And the jessamine faint, and the sweet tuberose,
> The sweetest flower for scent that blows;
> And all rare blossoms from every clime
> Grew in that garden in perfect prime.[1]

In justice to Shelley, whose lines I quote, your readers will admit that I have good authority for making a dissyllable of tuberose. I am, sir, your obedient servant
THE CRITIC
WHO HAD TO READ FOUR VOLUMES OF MODERN POETRY

---

including *Tuberose and Meadowsweet* by Mark André Raffalovich. On 30 March this letter appeared under the title THE ROOT OF THE MATTER:

Sir, I am sorry not to be able to accept the graceful etymology of your reviewer who in Friday's *Pall Mall* calls me to task for not knowing how to pronounce the title of my book *Tuberose and Meadowsweet*. I insist, he fancifully says, "on making tuberose a trisyllable always, as if it were a potato blossom and not a flower shaped like a tiny trumpet of ivory." Alas! tuberose is a trisyllable if properly derived from the Latin *tuberosus*, the lumpy flower, having nothing to do with roses or with trumpets of ivory in name any more than in nature. I am reminded by a great living poet that another correctly wrote:

> Or as the moonlight fills the open sky,
> Struggling with darkness, as a tuberose
> Peoples some Indian dell with scents which lie
>
> Like clouds above the flower from which they rose.

In justice to Shelley, whose lines I quote, your readers will admit that I have good authority for making a trisyllable of tuberose. I am, sir, your obedient servant
ANDRÉ RAFFALOVICH

Wilde's letter was printed on 1 April entitled PARNASSUS VERSUS PHILOLOGY. Raffalovich (1864–1934) was a rich Russian who had been educated in France and England. Wilde is reported to have said that he came to London to found a *salon* and only succeeded in founding a saloon. He is believed to have revenged himself by breaking up Wilde's friendship with John Gray (see note 3, p. 311), with whom Raffalovich remained close friends for the rest of his life. During Beardsley's last years he was largely supported by Raffalovich.

[1] "The Sensitive Plant." Raffalovich's quotation is from "The Woodman and the Nightingale".

To Edwin Palmer[1]

MS. Clark

[*March–April 1885*][2]   *16 Tite Street*

Dear Sir, I beg to acknowledge receipt of your cheque for £2. 2. o for my article on Shakespeare. If you would like a poem I will send you one, but I would ask you not to include any other poem in the number in which it appears, particularly no parody of any poet. Parodies are a legitimate form of art—and those in your paper I think exceedingly clever—but the art that appeals to laughter and the art that appeals to beauty are different things. Also a poem should be printed across a page: there should be no column line. So you see there are difficulties. Write to me how you propose to print it. Yours very truly   OSCAR WILDE

The poem is in twelve stanzas of three lines each. It is called "The Harlot's House."[3]

To E. W. Godwin

MS. Hyde (H. M.)

[*April 1885*][4]   *16 Tite Street*

Dear Godwino, I am glad you are resting.[5] Nature is a foolish place to look for inspiration in, but a charming one in which to forget one ever had any. Of course we miss you, but the white furniture reminds us of you daily, and we find that a rose leaf can be laid on the ivory table without scratching it—at least a white one can. That is something. We look forward to seeing you robust, and full of vigour. My wife sends her best wishes for your health. Ever yours   OSCAR WILDE

To W. A. S. Benson[6]

MS. Clark

[*16 May 1885*]   [*16 Tite Street*]

My dear Benson, I don't at all agree with you about the decorative value of Morris's wallpapers. They seem to me often deficient in real beauty of colour: this may be due as you say to his workmen, but Art admits of no

[1] Editor of the *Dramatic Review*.

[2] Someone has dated the original of this letter 15 April 1885, but it must obviously have been written earlier.

[3] This poem of Wilde's appeared in the *Dramatic Review* of 11 April 1885. It was reprinted in *Poems* (1908).   [4] So dated by Godwin.

[5] Godwin had begun to suffer from the illness which was to kill him a year later.

[6] William Arthur Smith Benson (1854–1924), elder brother of F. R. Benson the actor, was an architect and designer in metal-work. He was the model for the "Pygmalion" of his friend Burne-Jones, whose house at Rottingdean he "improved" and enlarged. He married Violet Hunt's sister Venetia. His answer to this letter (MS. Clark) is also dated 16 May 1885, from No. 1 Studio, Campden Hill Road.

excuses of that kind. Then as regards the design, he is far more successful with those designs which are meant for textures which hang in folds, than for those which have to be seen flat on a stretched material: a fact which may be due to the origin of many of his patterns, but which is a fact still.

Setting aside however a point on which we were sure for obvious reasons to disagree, I am surprised to find we are at such variance on the question of the value of pure colour on the walls of a room. No one I think would paint a room in distemper entirely: for the ceiling and the upper part of the wall distemper is excellent, for the lower part (as for the woodwork) one uses oil paint which has the great advantage of being cleanable, if there is such a word.

Nor are the colours one gets in distemper and oils necessarily spoiled by the introduction of silk embroideries or oil pictures. These things depend entirely on the scheme of colour one selects for the room, and on one's own knowledge of colour harmonies. I have for instance a dining-room done in different shades of white, with white curtains embroidered in yellow silk: the effect is absolutely delightful, and the room is beautiful.

I have seen far more rooms spoiled by wallpapers than by anything else: when everything is covered with a design the room is restless and the eye disturbed. A good picture is always improved by being hung on a coloured surface that suits it, or by being placed in surroundings which are harmonious to it, but the delicacy of line in an etching for instance is often spoiled by the necessarily broad, if not coarse, pattern on a block-printed wallpaper.

My eye requires in a room a resting-place of pure colour, and I prefer to keep design for more delicate materials than papers, for embroidery for instance. Paper in itself is not a lovely material, and the only papers which I ever use now are the Japanese gold ones: they are exceedingly decorative, and no English paper can compete with them, either for beauty or for practical wear. With these and with colour in oil and distemper a lovely house can be made.

Some day if you do us the pleasure of calling I will show you a little room with blue ceiling and frieze (distemper), yellow (oil) walls, and white woodwork and fittings, which is joyous and exquisite, the only piece of design being the Morris blue-and-white curtains, and a white-and-yellow silk coverlet. I hope, and in my lectures always try and bring it about, that people will study the value of pure colour more than they do. The ugly ceilings of modern houses are often due to the excessive use of wallpapers, and I do not think Morris himself sets the exaggerated value on wall-papers which you do.

Anybody with a real artistic sense must see the value and repose of pure colour, and even taking the matter in a practical light, wallpapers collect dirt and dust to a great extent and cannot be cleaned. They are economical and often pretty and charming but they are not the final word of Art in decoration by any means. I hope they will be used much less frequently than they are, and that Morris will devote his time, as I think he is doing, to textile fabrics, their dyes and their designs, and not so much to a form of wall decoration which has its value of course, but whose value has been overestimated, and whose use is often misunderstood.

I saw Frank at Oxford: there was a charming performance, and lovely costumes: he seemed very pleased at it and so was I.[1] Believe me, very truly yours   OSCAR WILDE

How can you see socialism in *The Earthly Paradise*?[2] If it is there it is an accident not a quality—there is a great difference.

To E. W. Godwin

MS. Hyde (H. M.)

[*20 May 1885*][3]

> I was in mourning for my uncle, and lo! he speaketh.
> *Revised Version.*[4]

Dear Godwino, I am delighted to know you are somewhere. We thought you were nowhere, and searched for you everywhere, but could not find you anywhere.

Thanks for your praise of my article.[5] The reason I spoke of "Lady Archie's" production was this. I had spoken before of you in *Claudian*, and was afraid that a second mention would look as if you had put me up to praise you. But everyone knows you did it all. The glory is yours entirely.

Do come to town. At Oxford you were mourned with lamentation. The play was charming. See next Saturday's *Dramatic Review* for my account of it. An amazing criticism! with views of archaeology enough to turn Lytton into a pillar of salt.[6]

[1] Frank Robert Benson (1858–1939) had just started his first Shakespearean tour, with Janet Achurch as his leading lady. Wilde must have seen him on 15 May (see next letter).

[2] A series of tales in verse by William Morris, published in four volumes 1868–70.

[3] So dated by Godwin.

[4] The complete Revised Version of the Bible (begun 1870) was first published on 19 May 1885. The New Testament had appeared separately in 1881, but this was the first appearance of the Old Testament, and of the complete work.

[5] "Shakespeare and Stage Costume," which appeared in the *Nineteenth Century* for May 1885. It was later reprinted, with some revision, and renamed "The Truth of Masks," in *Intentions* (1891). In it Wilde referred to the scenery and costumes which Godwin had designed for W. G. Wills's play *Claudian* (1883): "Mr E. W. Godwin, one of the most artistic spirits of this century in England, created the marvellous loveliness of the first act of *Claudian*, and showed us the life of Byzantium in the fourth century, not by a dreary lecture and a set of grimy casts, not by a novel which requires a glossary to explain it, but by the visible presentation before us of all the glory of that great town," and much more in the same vein. Apparently Godwin considered he should also have been given full credit for Lady Archibald Campbell's open-air production of *As You Like It* (see note 4, p. 160).

[6] Wilde's review of *Henry IV, Part I*, the first production of the newly founded Oxford University Dramatic Society at the Town Hall, Oxford, on 15 May, in which Cosmo Lang spoke a prologue specially written by George Curzon, Arthur Bourchier played Hotspur, Gilbert Coleridge Falstaff, and Margaret L. Woods

" My wife has a cold" but in about a month will be over it. I hope it is a boy cold, but will love whatever the gods send.

How about Coombe this year? I must criticise it somewhere.[1] Ever yours
                                                                    O. W.

To Edward Heron-Allen
MS. Hyde (H. M.)

[*Postmark 12 June 1885*]   [*16 Tite Street*]

My dear E. H. A., Thank you for your letter. Will you cast the child's horoscope for us? It was born at a quarter to eleven last Friday morning.[2] My wife is very anxious to know its fate, and has begged me to ask you to search the stars. Ever yours   OSCAR WILDE

To Norman Forbes-Robertson
MS. Clark

[*Early June 1885*]   [*16 Tite Street*]

Dear Norman, Thanks for your congratulations. Yes, come tomorrow. The baby is wonderful: it has a bridge to its nose! which the nurse says is a proof of genius! It also has a superb voice, which it freely exercises: its style is essentially Wagnerian.

Constance is doing capitally and is in excellent spirits.

I was delighted to get your telegram. You must get married *at once*! Ever yours   OSCAR

To E. W. Godwin
MS. Hyde (H. M.)

[*22 June 1885*][3]

Dear Godwin, I am so sorry, I am dining out, but I will call at the club at seven o'clock. There is a compromise proposed, but it means my paying £125! I cannot do that: but am ill with apprehension. It really rests on your evidence. If you cannot come my case is lost.[4]

Lady Percy, appeared in the *Dramatic Review* of 23 May 1885. In the *Nineteenth Century* of December 1884 in an article on "Mary Anderson's Juliet" Lord Lytton had, in Wilde's words, "laid it down as a dogma of art that archaeology is entirely out of place in the presentation of any of Shakespeare's plays, and the attempt to introduce it one of the stupidest pedantries of an age of prigs."

[1] Wilde published a review of the 1885 revival of Lady Archibald Campbell's production of *As You Like It* in the *Dramatic Review* of 6 June. It was reprinted in *Reviews*.

[2] Wilde's elder son Cyril was born at 16 Tite Street on 5 June 1885.

[3] So dated by Godwin. See note p. 160.

[4] Godwin noted: "Answered that my evidence was his always."

I hope to see you and will also look in after *Gringoire* is over—five to six.[1] I have not got my ticket for Coombe yet. I wish you would make it for two—it is nicer to have a companion. Ever yours   o. w.

To Norman Forbes-Robertson
TS. Holland

Tuesday [*23 June 1885*]

My dear Norman, I must write to congratulate you. The whole afternoon was charming and artistic: and your *Gringoire* was full of grace and pathos and naturalness.

I was quite delighted, and so indeed was everyone. Ever yours OSCAR

To the Hon. George Curzon
MS. Beaverbrook

20 July 1885   *16 Tite Street*

Dear Curzon, I want to be one of Her Majesty's Inspectors of Schools! This is ambition—however, I want it, and want it very much, and I hope you will help me. Edward Stanhope[2] has the giving away and, as a contemporary of mine at Oxford, you could give me great help by writing him a letter to say (if you think it) that I am a man of some brains. I won't trouble you with the reasons which make me ask for this post—but I want it and could do the work, I fancy, well.

If you could give me and get me any help you can I will be so much obliged to you, and I know how the party think of you—you brilliant young Coningsby![3]

I hope to get this and to get it with your approval and your good word. I don't know Stanhope personally and am afraid he may take the popular idea of me as a real idler. Would you tell him it is not so? In any case, ever yours   OSCAR WILDE

---

[1] Norman Forbes-Robertson gave a matinée performance of W. G. Wills's adaptation of Théodore de Banville's *Gringoire* at the Prince's Theatre on Monday 22 June 1885.

[2] The Rt Hon. Edward Stanhope (1840–93), second son of the fifth Earl Stanhope. Conservative politician. Vice-President of the Council on Education June 1885. President of the Board of Trade August 1885. Later Secretary of State for the Colonies and for War.

[3] Like the hero of Disraeli's novel (1844) Curzon, newly down from the university, where he had been President of the Union and a Fellow of All Souls, seemed destined to be the bright new star of the Tory Party.

To an Unidentified Correspondent[1]

[? *1885*]   *16 Tite Street*

I have been laid up with a severe attack of asthma, and have been unable to answer your letter before this. I return you your manuscript, as you desire, and would advise you to prune it down a little and send it to either *Time* or *Longman's*. It is better than many magazine articles, though, if you will allow me to say so, it is rather belligerent in tone.

As regards your prospects in literature, believe me that it is impossible to live by literature. By journalism a man may make an income, but rarely by pure literary work.

I would strongly advise you to try and make some profession, such as that of a tutor, the basis and mainstay of your life, and to keep literature for your finest, rarest moments. The best work in literature is always done by those who do not depend upon it for their daily bread, and the highest form of literature, poetry, brings no wealth to the singer. For producing your best work also you will require some leisure and freedom from sordid care.

It is always a difficult thing to give advice, but as you are younger than I am, I venture to do so. Make some sacrifice for your art, and you will be repaid; but ask of Art to sacrifice herself for you, and a bitter disappointment may come to you. I hope it will not, but there is always a terrible chance.

With your education you should have no difficulty in getting some post which should enable you to live without anxiety, and to keep for literature your most felicitous moods. To attain this end, you should be ready to give up some of your natural pride; but loving literature as you do, I cannot think that you would not do so.

Finally, remember that London is full of young men working for literary success, and that you must carve your way to fame. Laurels don't come for the asking. Yours   OSCAR WILDE

To the Hon. George Curzon

MS. Beaverbrook

23 October 1885   *16 Tite Street*

My dear Curzon, Since you were kind enough to write to Stanhope about me I see he has been succeeded by Sir Henry Holland as Vice-President of the Council of Education.[2] I suppose you are hard at work at your

---

[1] The text of this letter is taken from *Twenty Years in Paris* by R. H. Sherard (1905). It must have been written between 1885 (when Wilde moved to 16 Tite Street) and 1891 (when *Time* ended), but the year I have chosen is purely arbitrary.

[2] Sir Henry Thurstan Holland, Bart (1825–1914). Conservative M.P. for Midhurst 1874–85, for Hampstead 1885–88. Created Lord Knutsford 1888, Viscount 1895.

election so do not like bothering you,[1] but if you know Holland well or come across him, perhaps you would say something about me.

I hope you will be successful. Though I believe I am a Radical I should be sorry not to see Coningsby in the House. Ever yours   OSCAR WILDE

To H. C. Marillier[2]

[Postmark 5 November 1885]

Of course I remember the blue-coat boy, and am charmed to find he has not forgotten me.

Your letter gave me great pleasure and if possible I will come down to see the *Eumenides*—which I suppose will look like Hamlet surrounded by the witches of *Macbeth*—but you have not told me the date of the production yet, so I cannot say if I will be really free.[3]

I have a very vivid remembrance of the bright enthusiastic boy who used to bring me my coffee in Salisbury Street, and am delighted to find he is devoted to the muses, but I suppose you don't flirt with all nine ladies at once? Which of them do you really love? Whether or not I can come and see you, you must certainly come and see me when you are in town, and we will talk of the poets and drink Keats's health. I wonder are you all Wordsworthians still at Cambridge, or do you love Keats, and Poe, and Baudelaire? I hope so.

Write and tell me what things in art you and your friends love best. I do not mean what pictures, but what moods and modulations of art affect you most.

Is it five years ago really? Then I might almost sign myself an old friend, but the word old is full of terror.   OSCAR WILDE

To H. C. Marillier[4]

[Postmark 8 November 1885]   *Station Hotel, Newcastle-on-Tyne*

Harry, why did you let me catch my train? I would have liked to have

[1] Curzon had been chosen as a Conservative candidate for Parliament in 1884, but he was defeated in the General Election of 1885 and first elected in 1886.

[2] Henry Currie Marillier (1865–1951) was a Bluecoat Boy (i.e. pupil at Christ's Hospital, then still in London) 1875–84 and lodged at 13 Salisbury Street, Strand, when Wilde was living there (1880–81). Classical scholar of Peterhouse, Cambridge, 1884–87. Became an engineer: for some years partner in W. A. S. Benson's metal works. Took to literary and art journalism: wrote for *Pall Mall Gazette* from 1893. Edited *The Early Work of Aubrey Beardsley* (1899) and published books on various subjects, particularly tapestry, on which he became a great expert. The text of this letter is taken from *All That I Have Met* by Mrs Claude Beddington (1929).

[3] Seven performances of Aeschylus's tragedy in the original Greek were given by undergraduates at the Theatre Royal, Cambridge, 1–5 December 1885, with music by C. V. Stanford and an acting edition with an English translation by A. W. Verrall to help the audience.

[4] Text from *All That I Have Met* by Mrs Claude Beddington. Wilde lectured on "The Mission of Art in the Nineteenth Century" in the Town Hall, Newcastle,

gone to the National Gallery with you, and looked at Velasquez's pale evil King, at Titian's Bacchus with the velvet panthers, and at that strange heaven of Angelico's where everyone seems made of gold and purple and fire, and which, for all that, looks to me ascetic—everyone dead and decorative! I wonder will it really be like that, but I wonder without caring. *Je trouve la terre aussi belle que le ciel, et le corps aussi beau que l'âme.*[1] If I do live again I would like it to be as a flower—no soul but perfectly beautiful. Perhaps for my sins I shall be made a red geranium!!

And your paper on Browning? You must tell me of it. In our meeting again there was a touch of Browning—keen curiosity, wonder, delight.

It was an hour intensely dramatic and intensely psychological, and, in art, only Browning can make action and psychology one. When am I to see you again? Write me a long letter to Tite Street, and I will get it when I come back. I wish you were here, Harry. But in the vacation you must often come and see me, and we will talk of the poets and forget Piccadilly!! I have never learned anything except from people younger than myself and you are infinitely young.   OSCAR WILDE

To Isabel Harris[2]

MS. Graham

[*Postmark 18 November 1885*]   *16 Tite Street*

Dear Isabel, I am really delighted at the result of the investigation. I cannot understand anyone believing you capable of doing what you were accused of. I send you my warmest congratulations, and an autograph for the young lady who has asked for it. Your sincere friend   OSCAR WILDE

To H. C. Marillier[3]

[*Postmark 27 November 1885*]   *16 Tite Street*

Does it all seem a dream, Harry? Ah! what is not a dream? To me it is, in a fashion, a memory of music. I remember bright young faces, and grey misty quadrangles, Greek forms passing through Gothic cloisters, life playing among ruins, and, what I love best in the world, Poetry and Paradox dancing together!

---

on 10 November 1885. He had lectured at North Shields on the 8th and at Sunderland on the 9th.

[1] "*Mon corps rebelle ne veut point reconnaître la suprématie de l'âme, et ma chair n'entend point qu'on la mortifie. Je trouve la terre aussi belle que le ciel, et je pense que la correction de la forme est la vertu.*" (Théophile Gautier, *Mademoiselle de Maupin*, ch. ix).

[2] The sixteen-year-old daughter of some friends, who had been accused of inflicting minor cruelties and injuries on another girl at school. The affair reached ridiculous proportions: handwriting experts were called in, and Isabel's father was threatened with a libel action for suggesting that the victim had herself been responsible for everything, to which in the end she confessed.

[3] Text from *All That I Have Met* by Mrs Claude Beddington.

Only one evil omen—your fire! You are careless about playing with fire, Harry.

And my book? Where is it? I must have it now. How delightful it would be were everything in one's house a gift! However, one's friends are always a gift—θεόδωροι. It seems to me you were rather horrid to *your* friend, the poet in exile. Ever yours   OSCAR

To William Sharp[1]

[*November–December 1885*]   *16 Tite Street*

Dear Sir, It will give me much pleasure to see the sonnets you mention included in your selection.[2] Of the two, I much prefer "Libertatis Sacra Fames," and if only one is taken, would like to be represented by that. Indeed I like the sonnets on p. 3 and p. 16 of my volume better than the one written in Holy Week at Genoa. Perhaps however this is merely because Art and Liberty seem to me more vital and more religious than any Creed. I send you a sonnet I wrote at the Sale of Keats's love letters some months ago. What do you think of it? It has not yet been published. I wonder are you including Edgar Allan Poe's sonnet to Science. It is one I like very much.[3] I will look forward with much interest to the appearance of your book. I remain truly yours   OSCAR WILDE

ON THE SALE BY AUCTION
OF KEATS'S LOVE LETTERS

These are the letters which Endymion wrote
  To one he loved in secret, and apart.
  And now the brawlers of the auction mart
Bargain and bid for each poor blotted note.
Ay! for each separate pulse of passion quote
  The merchant's price: I think they love not art,
  Who break the crystal of a poet's heart
That small and sickly eyes may glare and gloat!

---

[1] Scottish poet, biographer and journalist (1856–1905). He also published extremely successful Celtic romances under the name Fiona Macleod. On 27 February 1890 W. B. Yeats wrote to Katharine Tynan: "Have you heard Oscar's last good thing? He says that Sharp's motto should be *Acutus descensus averni* (Sharp is the descent into Hell)." Le Gallienne records Wilde's saying, *à propos* of two speedily produced books about Rossetti, "Whenever a great man dies, Hall Caine and William Sharp go in with the undertakers." The text of this letter is taken from *William Sharp, a Memoir* by Elizabeth Sharp (1910).

[2] *Sonnets of This Century*, edited and arranged by William Sharp, was published on 25 January 1886. The first edition included two of Wilde's sonnets, "Libertatis Sacra Fames" (from *Poems*, 1881) and "On the Sale by Auction of Keats's Love Letters" (first published in the *Dramatic Review*, 23 January 1886, and included in *Poems*, 1908) The manuscript of the latter is dated 1 March 1885, the day before the letters to Fanny Brawne were sold at Sotheby's.

[3] Sharp included no sonnet by Poe in the first edition, but in the large-paper edition, issued later in the year, he added Poe's sonnet "Silence." This may have been what Wilde suggested, but Poe also wrote a "Sonnet to Science."

Is it not said that many years ago,
  In a far Eastern town, some soldiers ran
  With torches through the midnight, and began
To wrangle for mean raiment, and to throw
  Dice for the garments of a wretched man,
Not knowing the God's wonder, or his woe?

I wish I could grave my sonnets on an ivory tablet. Quill pens and notepaper are only good enough for bills of lading. A sonnet should always *look* well. Don't you think so?   O. W.

To the Editor of the Pall Mall Gazette[1]

[January 1886]

I am very much pleased to see that you are beginning to call attention to the extremely slipshod and careless style of our ordinary magazine-writers. Will you allow me to refer your readers to an article on Borrow, in the current number of *Macmillan*, which exemplifies very clearly the truth of your remarks? The author of the article is Mr George Saintsbury, a gentleman who has recently written a book on Prose Style, and here are some specimens of the prose of the future according to the *système Saintsbury*:

1. He saw, the rise, and, *in some instances, the death, of Tennyson,* Thackeray, Macaulay, Carlyle, Dickens.
2. *See* a *place* which Kingsley, *or* Mr Ruskin, *or* some other master of our decorative school, *have* described—*much more* one which has fallen into the hands of the small fry of their imitators—and you are almost sure to find that *it has been overdone.*
3. The great mass of his translations, published and unpublished, and the smaller mass of his early hackwork, no doubt *deserves* judicious excerption.
4. "The Romany Rye" *did not appear* for six years, *that is to say, in* 1857.
5. The elaborate apparatus which most prose tellers of fantastic tales *use,* and generally *fail in using.*
6. The great writers, whether they try to be like other people or try not to be like them (*and sometimes in the first case most of all*), succeed *only* in being themselves.
7. If he had a slight *overdose* of Celtic blood and Celtic peculiarity, it was *more than made up* by the readiness of literary expression which it gave him. He, if any one, bore an English heart, though, *as there often has been,* there

---

[1] This letter was published in the *Pall Mall Gazette* on 15 January 1886, under the heading HALF HOURS WITH THE WORST AUTHORS, and an editorial note reading: "A well-known literary man who signs himself 'Oxoniensis' sends us the following energetic protest against certain 'atrocities' recently perpetrated upon the English language." Mason accepted it as Wilde's, and Ross included it in *Reviews.* The article discussed was one on George Borrow by George Saintsbury (1845–1933), which had appeared in *Macmillan's Magazine* for January 1886. Saintsbury combined an encyclopaedic knowledge of French and English literature with a rebarbative prose style.

was something perhaps more than English as well as less than it in his fashion of expression.

8. His flashes of ethical reflection, which, though like *all* ethical reflections *often* one-sided.

9. He certainly was an *unfriend* to Whiggery.

10. *That it contains* a great deal of quaint and piquant writing *is only to say* that its writer wrote it.

11. *Wild Wales*, too, because of *its* easy and direct *opportunity* of comparing its description with the originals.

12. The capital *and* full-length portraits.

13. His attraction is *one* neither mainly nor in any very great degree one of pure form.

14. *Constantly* right *in general*.

These are merely a few examples of the style of Mr Saintsbury, a writer who seems quite ignorant of the commonest laws both of grammar and of literary expression, who has apparently no idea of the difference between the pronouns "this" and "that," and who has as little hesitation in ending the clause of a sentence with a preposition, as he has in inserting a parenthesis between a preposition and its object, a mistake of which the most ordinary schoolboy would be ashamed. And why cannot our magazine writers use plain, simple English? *Unfriend*, quoted above, is a quite unnecessary archaism, and so is such a phrase as "*with this Borrow could not away*," in the sense of "this Borrow could not endure." "Borrow's *abstraction* from general society" may, I suppose, pass muster. Pope talks somewhere of a hermit's "abstraction,"[1] but what is the meaning of saying that the author of *Lavengro* "*quartered* Castile and Leon in the most interesting manner, riding everywhere with his servant"? And what defence can be made for such an expression as "Scott, and other *black beasts* of Borrow's"? Black beast for *bête noire* is really abominable.

The object of my letter, however, is not to point out the deficiencies of Mr Saintsbury's style, but to express my surprise that his article should have been admitted into the pages of a magazine like *Macmillan's*. Surely it does not require much experience to know that such an article is a disgrace even to magazine literature.

To H. C. Marillier[2]

[? *January–February 1886*][3]   *Central Station Hotel, Glasgow*

Dear Harry, I am away in the region of horrible snow and horrible notepaper! Lecturing and wandering—a vagabond with a mission! But your letter has reached me, like a strain of music wind-blown from a far land.

---

[1] *An Essay on Man*, iv, 40–43.

[2] The text of this letter is taken from *All That I Have Met* by Mrs Claude Beddington.

[3] This date is almost certainly wrong. I can find no record of Wilde's lecturing in or near Glasgow after 1884, but the letter of 5 November 1885 (see p. 180) is surely the first to Marillier, and I have invented a date for this one.

You too have the love of things impossible—ἔρως τῶν ἀδυνάτων—
l'amour de l'impossible (how do men name it?). Sometime you will find,
even as I have found, that there is no such thing as a romantic experience;
there are romantic memories, and there is the desire of romance—that is
all. Our most fiery moments of ecstasy are merely shadows of what somewhere else we have felt, or of what we long some day to feel. So at least
it seems to me. And, strangely enough, what comes of all this is a curious
mixture of ardour and of indifference. I myself would sacrifice everything
for a new experience, and I know there is no such thing as a new experience
at all. I think I would more readily die for what I do not believe in than
for what I hold to be true. I would go to the stake for a sensation and be a
sceptic to the last! Only one thing remains infinitely fascinating to me,
the mystery of moods. To be master of these moods is exquisite, to be
mastered by them more exquisite still. Sometimes I think that the artistic
life is a long and lovely suicide, and am not sorry that it is so.

And much of this I fancy you yourself have felt: much also remains for
you to feel. There is an unknown land full of strange flowers and subtle
perfumes, a land of which it is joy of all joys to dream, a land where all
things are perfect and poisonous. I have been reading Walter Scott for
the last week: you too should read him, for there is nothing of all this in
him.

Write to me at Tite Street, and let me know where you will be. Ever
yours   O. W.

To the Editor of the Pall Mall Gazette[1]

[*Early February 1886*]

Books, I fancy, may be conveniently divided into three classes:

1. Books to read, such as Cicero's *Letters*, Suetonius, Vasari's *Lives of
the Painters*, the *Autobiography of Benvenuto Cellini*, Sir John Mandeville,
Marco Polo, St Simon's *Memoirs*, Mommsen, and (till we get a better one)
Grote's *History of Greece*.

2. Books to re-read, such as Plato and Keats: in the sphere of poetry,
the masters not the minstrels; in the sphere of philosophy, the seers not
the *savants*.

3. Books not to read at all, such as Thomson's *Seasons*, Rogers's *Italy*,
Paley's *Evidences*, all the Fathers except St Augustine, all John Stuart Mill
except the *Essay on Liberty*, all Voltaire's plays without any exception,
Butler's *Analogy*, Grant's *Aristotle*, Hume's *England*, Lewes's *History of
Philosophy*, all argumentative books and all books that try to prove any-
thing.

[1] The *Pall Mall Gazette* had been running a series on "The Best Hundred Books"
by "The Best Hundred Judges." Although this piece of Wilde's was reprinted in
the collected volume of *Reviews* and was originally printed without epistolary
beginning or end, it is clearly more like a letter than an article. It appeared on
8 February under the heading TO READ, OR NOT TO READ, with an editorial note:
"As we have published so many letters advising what to read, the following advice
'what not to read' from so good an authority as Mr Oscar Wilde may be of service."

The third class is by far the most important. To tell people what to read is, as a rule, either useless or harmful; for the appreciation of literature is a question of temperament not of teaching; to Parnassus there is no primer and nothing that one can learn is ever worth learning. But to tell people what not to read is a very different matter, and I venture to recommend it as a mission to the University Extension Scheme.

Indeed, it is one that is eminently needed in this age of ours, an age that reads so much that it has no time to admire, and writes so much that it has no time to think. Whoever will select out of the chaos of our modern curricula "The Worst Hundred Books," and publish a list of them, will confer on the rising generation a real and lasting benefit.

After expressing these views I suppose I should not offer any suggestions at all with regard to "The Best Hundred Books," but I hope that you will allow me the pleasure of being inconsistent, as I am anxious to put in a claim for a book that has been strangely omitted by most of the excellent judges who have contributed to your columns. I mean the *Greek Anthology*. The beautiful poems contained in this collection seem to me to hold the same position with regard to Greek dramatic literature as do the delicate little figurines of Tanagra to the Pheidian marbles, and to be quite as necessary for the complete understanding of the Greek spirit.

I am also amazed to find that Edgar Allan Poe has been passed over. Surely this marvellous lord of rhythmic expression deserves a place? If, in order to make room for him, it be necessary to elbow out someone else, I should elbow out Southey, and I think that Baudelaire might be most advantageously substituted for Keble. No doubt, both in *The Curse of Kehama* and in *The Christian Year* there are poetic qualities of a certain kind, but absolute catholicity of taste is not without its dangers. It is only an auctioneer who should admire all schools of art.

To Violet Fane[1]

13 February 1886   *16 Tite Street*

I hate our sunless, loveless winter, and in Tite Street there are no terracotta Caesars! However, some little swallow-flight of song may come to me ... The Oxford theatre opens tomorrow[2] and I am going to see our "young barbarians all at play."[3] Young Oxonians are very delightful, so Greek and graceful and uneducated. They have profiles but no philosophy.

---

[1] The text of this fragment is taken from a 1940 catalogue of Messrs Francis Edwards.

[2] The New Theatre, Oxford, opened its doors for the first time on 14 February 1886 with an O.U.D.S. production of *Twelfth Night* in which Arthur Bourchier played Feste. Wilde's notice of it appeared in the *Dramatic Review* for 20 February and was reprinted in *Reviews*.

[3] Byron: *Childe Harold*, canto 4, stanza cxli. Applied to Oxford by Matthew Arnold in the preface to his *Essays in Criticism* (1865).

To J. P. Mahaffy

MS. Yale

[*Late February 1886*]   *16 Tite Street*

Dear Mahaffy, Your letter in the *Pall Mall* is delightful. Though I should fight with you over some of the matter of it, the manner of it is most brilliant.[1]

I want you, if you would do it for me, to write to your friend Lord Spencer,[2] who is now Lord President of the Council, to make a recommendation of me as a suitable person to hold an Inspectorship of Schools. My name has been on the Education List for some time but a word from you as to my capabilities would go far towards getting me what I want. I know Spencer has a great admiration for your powers and judgment.

Archie[3] had tea with us at Christmas and looked delightful. He seems very clever. Very sincerely yours   OSCAR WILDE

To Clement Scott

[? *Early May 1886*][4]   *Tite Street*[5]

My dear Clement Scott, I think your ode very fine and spirited indeed, with vastly more colour than Lord T's. The Indian welcome, and the Canadian "Pine branch nestling with the English Rose" are specially good, but I think you might correct the one very Irish oversight, or slip (was it to give local Hibernian colour to the stanza?). Erin can do most things, but she can't, bless her! "*remember the days to come.*" Let her "look out to" or "rejoice in" or "greet kindly" the days etc. or "bethink her of days," but I fear that you must sacrifice the word "remember" in respect of the future.

I think the work so good that I fancy you will accept this kindly meant suggestion of correction.

We *do* say "remember next Tuesday, eight o'clock sharp," but we *mean*

[1] On 23 February 1886, as part of the controversy still raging over "The Best Hundred Books," the *Pall Mall Gazette* printed "a few stray reflections" on the subject, which purported to be by Mahaffy. Three days later he wrote to say that the contribution had been an undergraduate hoax: "I do not pretend to the knowledge, I have not yet acquired the assurance, and I shall never attain to the style displayed in that document."

[2] The fifth Earl Spencer (1835–1910). Liberal politician. Viceroy of Ireland 1882–85. Lord President of the Council 1880–83 and 1886. First Lord of the Admiralty 1892–95.

[3] Presumably Mahaffy's son Arthur, though he was generally known as Arty.

[4] I have failed to trace Scott's ode. It may have celebrated Queen Victoria's Golden Jubilee in June 1887, but Wilde's references point rather to the Queen's opening of the Indian and Colonial Exhibition at South Kensington on 4 May 1886. Tennyson (raised to the peerage in 1884) contributed odes on both occasions. The text of this letter is taken from *Old Days in Bohemian London* by Mrs Clement Scott (1919).

[5] Wilde again apparently headed his address "Keats House." See note 2, p. 169.

remember a bargain we have *just* made to dine on that date, and please do not forget it. Sincerely yours OSCAR WILDE

To Douglas Ainslie[1]
MS. Beange

[? *May–June 1886*] *Albemarle Club*[2]

Dear Douglas, I have lost your note. What is your address, and what day have you asked me for? I am really "impossible" about letters: they vanish from my room. I don't think Constance will be able to come, but I will certainly manage some day. I hope you and Osborne are reading hard. He is quite charming, with his low musical voice, and his graceful incapacity for a career. He is a little like the moon.

You were very sweet to come and see us; we must have many evenings together and drink yellow wine from green glasses in Keats's honour. Ever yours OSCAR

To Herbert P. Horne[3]
MS. Dugdale

[*Postmark 16 August 1886*] *16 Tite Street*

My dear Horne, Thank you for the copy of your letter. I am afraid it reads as if we wanted to entirely renovate the school,[4] and the more I think of that little grey building the more I feel we should proceed cautiously, and not do anything in a hurry.

[1] Poet, translator of Benedetto Croce, and sometime diplomat (1865–1948). One of his friends at Eton and Oxford was Lord Albert Edward Godolphin Osborne (1866–1914), fourth son of the ninth Duke of Leeds. They shared lodgings at Oxford and were both founder-members of the O.U.D.S. Ainslie in his *Adventures Social and Literary* (1922) quotes Wilde's saying " 'I will turn you to stone,' said Pallas Athene, 'if you harken not to the words of my wisdom.' 'Ah, but I am marble already,' said Osborne, little Osborne, and passed on."

[2] A mixed club of 600 members, established in 1879, to which both Wilde and his wife belonged.

[3] Architect, writer and connoisseur (1865–1916). Built the Church of the Redeemer, Bayswater Road. From 1886 to 1892 he edited a quarterly magazine called the *Century Guild Hobby Horse*, in which he printed some of his own poems. Before the end of the century he went to live in Florence, where he wrote a biography of Botticelli (1908) and set up the Museo Horne in the Via dei Benci. Rothenstein records Reggie Turner's saying: "Dear Herbert Horne! poring over Botticelli's washing bills—and always a shirt missing!"

[4] Colston's School, Stapleton, Bristol, at which the poet Thomas Chatterton (1752–70) was a pupil. Despite the efforts of Wilde, Horne and others, there is still no memorial to Chatterton in the school. A note in the *Century Guild Hobby Horse*, No 4, October 1886, reads: "Mr Oscar Wilde's article on Chatterton has been unavoidably postponed until the January number," but it never appeared, though Mason (p. 13) quotes an introductory passage from the manuscript, of which some seventy pages are in Clark. Wilde did, however, lecture on Chatterton (see p. 192).

We must not have William Morris down on us to begin with, and we must not alter the tone of the room.

Perhaps after all, cleaning, repairing, and a tablet would be enough. I wish you were in town to talk it over. But do not send circulars out till after the magazine appears, nor commit us to anything definite.

I am sure you regret that the muniment room is not as the "marvellous boy"[1] saw it; there may be others who would have the same view about the school.

Or course we will do something, and put up a tablet, but more than this we should seriously think about. And above all things let us not rashly commit ourselves: there is lots of time before us.

Write to me soon, and believe me, truly yours   OSCAR WILDE

To Herbert P. Horne

MS. Dugdale

[*Postmark 23 August 1886*]   *16 Tite Street*

My dear Horne, I am very glad we are in agreement on this matter. We must not spoil by new gauds the ancient spirit of the place. As for repairs don't you think that these should be done by the Trustees? I think the public would object to their money being spent on repairs of a Church school with a grant. Please think over this.

The tablet is excellent, so is the wainscot and fireplace idea; beyond that I feel we should not go.

Think over the point of repairs: it seems to me that the Trustees should do it. I don't fancy we will get very much money, and a memorial should be permanent.

Of course the whole place should be a Chatterton museum. I wish you were here to talk over it. Truly yours   OSCAR WILDE

To Herbert P. Horne

MS. Dugdale

[*Postmark 31 August 1886*]   *16 Tite Street*

My dear Horne, We must clearly wait till Christmas, as there should be no rash hurry, and I would like to have a long talk with you about the whole matter before any *pronunciamento*. Believe me, truly yours

OSCAR WILDE

---

[1] I thought of Chatterton, the marvellous Boy,
The sleepless Soul that perish'd in its pride.
Wordsworth: "Resolution and Independence"

189

To F. Pilcher[1]

MS. Private

[*Postmark 8 November 1886*]   *16 Tite Street*

Dear Sir, I can lecture for you on December 14th. My fee in this case will
be seven guineas. Faithfully yours   OSCAR WILDE

To F. Pilcher

MS. Private

[*Postmark 9 November 1886*]   *16 Tite Street*

Dear Sir, As you have mentioned to me the name of my friend Mr Edwards
of Merton[2] I am anxious to try and meet the wishes of your committee.
My lecture fee is £10. 10., but I will lecture for you for £5. 5. should that
be within the means of your society. Yours faithfully   OSCAR WILDE

To E. Nesbit[3]

[*November 1886*]   *16 Tite Street*

Dear Mrs Bland, Thank you so much for sending me your volume of
poems. I have been turning over the leaves, tasting as one tastes wine,
and am fascinated by the sonnets on pages 64–65 and 96–97, but I am
keeping the book as a whole for study in the Clumber woods next week.[4]
"The Last Envoy" seems a really beautiful piece of work. You see I am
getting to know you, petal by petal, but I will not touch the longer poems
just now.

Any advice I can give you is of course at your disposal. With regard to
your next volume—but you do not need to be taught how to tune your
many-chorded lyre, and you have already caught the ear of all lovers of
poetry. I hope, however, we may meet again soon.   OSCAR WILDE

---

[1] Unidentified. This letter and the next one are addressed to him at 18 Beer
Lane, E.C.

[2] Herbert Edward Osman Edwards (1864–1936), reviewer, lecturer, translator,
and amateur of the theatre, was a Postmaster (Scholar) of Merton College, Oxford,
1883–87. He was later a master at St Paul's School.

[3] Edith Nesbit (1858–1924), poet, Fabian, novelist and incomparable writer for
children, had married Hubert Bland in 1880. Her first book of poems, *Lays and
Legends*, here referred to, was published by Longman on 3 November 1886. She
contributed two poems to the *Woman's World*. The text of this letter is taken from
E. Nesbit: a Biography by Doris Langley Moore (1933).

[4] Clumber Park, near Worksop in Nottinghamshire, was the seat of Henry
Pelham Archibald Douglas Pelham-Clinton, seventh Duke of Newcastle (1864–
1928).

To the Editor of the World[1]

[*November 1886*]

Atlas, this is very sad! With our James "vulgarity begins at home," and should be allowed to stay there. *À vous*   OSCAR[2]

To Herbert P. Horne

MS. Dugdale

[*By hand. 7 December 1886*][3]   *16 Tite Street*

My dear Horne, Of course we will have the tablet. I thought we had fully settled that at Bristol. The little classical façade of the school-house is just the place for it, and it will add historic interest to the building without marring its antiquarian value or eighteenth-century look. I remember your telling me in the train that one of your friends had promised to design one, and I was talking the other day about it to an ardent Chattertonian.

Do you think we should have a bas-relief of T. C.? It seems to me that there is really no picture of the poet extant. What do you say to a simple inscription

To the Memory
of
Thomas Chatterton
One of England's greatest poets and sometime pupil at this school.

I prefer the inscription, though a symbolic design might accompany it.

I was very nearly coming to fetch you the night of the fog to come and

---

[1] On 17 November 1886 Whistler had published in the *World* this letter to the Committee of the National Art Exhibition:

> Gentlemen, I am naturally interested in any effort made among Painters to prove that they are alive, but when I find, thrust in the van of your leaders, the body of my dead 'Arry, I know that putrefaction alone can result. When, following 'Arry, there comes on Oscar, you finish in farce, and bring upon yourselves the scorn and ridicule of your *confrères* in Europe.
>
> What has Oscar in common with Art? except that he dines at our tables and picks from our platters the plums for the pudding he peddles in the provinces. Oscar—the amiable, irresponsible, esurient Oscar—with no more sense of a picture than of the fit of a coat, has the courage of the opinions—of others!
>
> With 'Arry and Oscar you have avenged the Academy.
>
> I am, Gentlemen, yours obediently.

According to Whistler's comment in *The Gentle Art of Making Enemies*, he sent Wilde a copy of the letter with the comment: "Oscar, you must really keep outside 'the radius'! " Wilde's reply appeared in the *World* on 24 November. Atlas was the name under which the editor, Edmund Yates, conducted a general editorial column. For 'Arry Quilter, see note 2, p. 102.

[2] On this Whistler commented (MS. Hart-Davis, printed in *The Gentle Art*): " 'A poor thing,' Oscar—but, for once, I suppose, 'your own'!"

[3] So endorsed by Horne.

hear my lecture on Chatterton at the Birkbeck, but did not like to take you out on such a dreadful night. To my amazement I found 800 people there! And they seemed really interested in the marvellous boy.[1]

You must come in for a cigarette some night soon. Sincerely yours
OSCAR WILDE

To Herbert P. Horne
MS. Dugdale

[Postmark 13 December 1886]   16 Tite Street

My dear Horne, I was very pleased indeed to receive your letter, as I felt sure that it was only an ardent enthusiasm for the success of my scheme of a Chatterton memorial that led you to overstep, even for a moment, the limits of right judgment, and remembering the pleasure I had in showing you the little school-house, and the many charming discussions we held over the poet of Ælla, I should be sorry to think that you had given up all your former interest in the movement, because I felt that it was necessary for its artistic success that it should be placed on its proper footing. Mackmurdo[2] and I propose to have a small meeting next week, and your absence from it would be the absence of one of Chatterton's best lovers.

I am sure you will be pleased to hear that Theodore Watts[3] is very much interested in the memorial, and has promised to attend. I also intend to invite Stopford Brooke to join.[4]

Believe me yours now, as before, most sincerely   OSCAR WILDE

To Norman Forbes-Robertson
TS. Congress

15 December 1886   16 Tite Street

My dear Norman, I will dine with pleasure with Stephen Coleridge[5] on

[1] Wilde lectured on Chatterton at Birkbeck College, London, on 24 November 1886.

[2] Arthur Heygate Mackmurdo (1851–1942), architect, designer of furniture etc. Founded the Century Guild in 1882, and assisted Horne in editing the *Century Guild Hobby Horse*. The river-range of the Savoy Hotel was designed by him.

[3] Walter Theodore Watts (1832–1914), critic, novelist and poet. Controlled the life and affairs of A. C. Swinburne 1879–1909. O'Sullivan records Wilde as saying: "You know, Watts is a solicitor and the business of a solicitor is to conceal crime. Swinburne's genius has been killed, and Watts is doing his best to conceal it." Watts changed his name to Watts-Dunton in 1897, when Whistler is reputed to have sent him a telegram: "Theodore What's Dunton?"

[4] The Rev. Stopford Augustus Brooke (1832–1916), clergyman and writer, was an Irishman and had been educated at Trinity College, Dublin. Chaplain to the Empress Frederick in Berlin 1863–65. In 1880 he left the Church of England and became a Unitarian minister. He wrote many books on literary subjects.

[5] The Hon. Stephen Coleridge (1854–1936), artist and author, son of the first Lord Coleridge, who was Lord Chief Justice and a great-nephew of the poet. Stephen Coleridge contributed a story, "The Man with the Broken Arm," to the *Woman's World* in November 1888.

Sunday. Will you tell him so? How agitated little André[1] was last night! His introducing Eric to Frankie was a masterpiece.[2]

I had a long talk with George Lewis last night. He is very nervous about Marlborough's cross-examination.[3]

Augusta's[4] party was a great success, but there was a virgin of some ninety winters who hid haggard blushes behind a tattered fan! She was quite dreadful, and must not be asked again. Ever yours   OSCAR

To Gleeson White[5]

MS. Harvard

[? Early 1887]   16 Tite Street

Dear Sir, You are quite at liberty to include the villanelle you allude to in your collection, to which I look forward. Yours truly   OSCAR WILDE

To J. S. Little[6]

MS. Berg

[29 April 1887][7]   16 Tite Street

Dear Mr Little, It will give me great pleasure to become a Fellow of the Society of Authors, and I hope we will have some more meetings. I hope also that for the future no one who is not a man of letters will be invited on the platform. Brett's speech was a gross impertinence at Gosse's lecture, and we should keep clear of the journeymen painters who usurp the name of artist.[8]

---

[1] Perhaps André Raffalovich (see p. 173).

[2] Eric and Frankie (Frances) were Norman Forbes-Robertson's brother and sister.

[3] Lady Colin Campbell had petitioned for divorce on account of her husband's adultery with a housemaid. He counter-petitioned, naming the Duke of Marlborough and three other co-respondents. After a hearing which lasted for three weeks the jury found none of the parties guilty and dismissed both petitions.

[4] Possibly Augusta Mary Anne Holmes (1847–1903), Irish-born, naturalised French, composer and musician, who had been a child prodigy as singer and pianist.

[5] Joseph William Gleeson White, author and journalist (1851–98). First editor of the Studio (1893), author of English Illustration: The Sixties, editor of the Pageant (1896 and 1897). His Ballades and Rondeaus, Chants Royal, Sestines, Villanelles, Etcetera (1887) included Wilde's villanelle on Theocritus (from Poems, 1881). In September 1889 White contributed an article on "The Kakemono Frame" to the Woman's World, and his anthology Book-Song (1893) gave first publication to Wilde's poems "To my wife: with a copy of my poems" and "With a copy of The House of Pomegranates."

[6] James Stanley Little (1856–1940), prolific journalist and committee man, was Executive Secretary of the Society of Authors 1887–88. Wilde was elected a Fellow of the Society on 17 July 1887.   [7] So dated by recipient.

[8] Edmund Gosse (see note 1, p. 331) had lectured on "The Profession of Authorship" at a Society of Authors conference in Willis's Rooms on 9 March 1887, under

Why not have a *soirée*? The artists have their *fêtes*, let us have ours, and try to get the thinkers and the men of style, not merely the scribblers and second-rate journalists. I enclose you a cheque for £1. 1. I think you could work up the Society into something very good. You have the qualifications and the opportunity. Truly yours   OSCAR WILDE

To Whitelaw Reid[1]
MS. Congress

[*April 1887*][2]   16 Tite Street

Dear Mr Reid, Some time ago I sent you a story of mine called "The Canterville Ghost." I have as yet received no acknowledgement for it, though I hear it has been published in your paper.

The *Tribune* has always pleaded the rights of authors with such eloquence and reason that I feel sure that it is only too anxious to put its theories into practice.

I look forward to hearing from you, and remain, truly yours
                                                                OSCAR WILDE

To Wemyss Reid[3]
MS. Flower

[*April 1887*]   16 Tite Street

Dear Mr Wemyss Reid, I have read very carefully the numbers of the *Lady's World* you kindly sent me, and would be very happy to join with you in the work of editing and to some extent reconstructing it. It seems to me that at present it is too feminine, and not sufficiently womanly. No one appreciates more fully than I do the value and importance of Dress, in its relation to good taste and good health: indeed the subject is one that I have constantly lectured on before Institutes and Societies of various kinds, but it seems to me that the field of the *mundus muliebris*, the field of mere millinery and trimmings, is to some extent already occupied by such papers as the *Queen* and the *Lady's Pictorial*, and that we should take a wider range, as well as a high standpoint, and deal not merely with what women wear, but with what they think, and what they feel. The *Lady's*

---

the chairmanship of Sir Frederick Pollock. Their remarks were printed in *The Grievances Between Authors and Publishers* (1887). The speaker who annoyed Wilde was John Brett (1832–1902), Pre-Raphaelite painter, A.R.A. 1881.
    [1] See note 2, p. 93. *The Canterville Ghost* appeared in the New York *Tribune* on 27 March 1887.   [2] So dated in another hand.
    [3] Thomas Wemyss Reid (1842–1905), journalist and biographer, was general manager of Cassell's publishing firm 1887–1905. He founded the *Speaker* in 1890 and edited it till 1897. He was knighted in 1894. The *Lady's World*, a shilling monthly, first appeared in November 1886.

World should be made the recognised organ for the expression of women's opinions on all subjects of literature, art, and modern life, and yet it should be a magazine that men could read with pleasure, and consider it a privilege to contribute to. We should get if possible the Princess Louise and the Princess Christian to contribute to it: an article from the latter on needlework for instance in connection with the Art School of which she is President would be very interesting. Carmen Sylva and Madame Adam should be got to write: Mrs Julia Ward Howe of Boston should be invited to contribute, as well as some of the other cultured women of America, while our list should include such women as Lady Archibald Campbell, a charming writer, Lady Ardilaun, who might give us some of her Irish experiences, Mrs Jeune, Miss Harrison, Miss Mary Robinson, Miss Olive Schreiner, the author of *South African Farm*; Lady Greville, whose life of Montrose is a very clever monograph, Miss Dorothy Tennant, Lady Verney, Lady Dilke, Lady Dufferin, Lady Constance Howard, Matthew Arnold's daughter, Lady Brassey, Lady Bective, Lady Rosebery, Lady Dorothy Nevill, who could write on the Walpoles, Mrs Singleton (Violet Fane), Lady Diana Huddleston, Lady Catherine Gaskell, Lady Paget, Miss Rosa Mulholland, Hon. Emily Lawless, Lady Harberton, Mrs Charles MacClaren, Lady Pollock, Mrs Fawcett, Miss Pater (sister of the author of *Marius*) and others too numerous to name in a letter.[1]

We should try to get such articles as Mrs Brookfield's on Thackeray's Letters, Miss Stoker's on the Letters of Sheridan, both of which appear this month in two magazines,[2] and though many of our charming women have not had much literary experience they could write for us accounts of great collections of family pictures and the like. Lady Betty Lytton might give us an account of Knebworth (illustrated), or Lady Salisbury a description of Hatfield House: these last have of course written and published, but I don't see why many who have not done so should not make an essay. All women are flattered at being asked to write. Mrs Proctor also would be invaluable if she would give us some of her recollections, and an article by Lady Galway if we could get it would be delightful. But we should not rely exclusively on women, even for signed articles: artists have sex but art has none, and now and then an article by some man of letters would be of service.

Literary criticism I think might be done in the form of paragraphs: that is to say, not from the standpoint of the scholar or the pedant, but from the standpoint of what is pleasant to read: if a book is dull let us say nothing about it, if it is bright let us review it.

From time to time also we must have news from Girton and Newnham Colleges at Cambridge, and from the Oxford colleges for women, and invite articles from the members: Mrs Humphry Ward and Mrs Sidgwick should not be forgotten, and the wife of the young President of Magdalen,

---

[1] It seems unnecessary to provide notes for this regiment of literary ladies.

[2] Mrs Brookfield's articles began to appear in *Scribner's* for April 1887, and Matilda Stoker's "Sheridan and Miss Linley" was printed in the *English Illustrated Magazine* for April. I have dated this letter accordingly.

Oxford,[1] might write on her own college, or, say, on the attitude of Universities towards women from the earliest times down to the present—a subject never fully treated of.

It seems to me also that just at present there is too much money spent on illustrations, particularly on illustrations of dress. They are also extremely unequal; many are charming, such as that on page 224 of the current number, but many look like advertisements and give an air to the magazine that one wants to avoid, the air of directly puffing some firm or modiste. A new cover also would be an improvement: the present one is not satisfactory.

With the new cover we should start our new names, and try and give the magazine a cachet at once: let dress have the end of the magazine; literature, art, travel and social studies the beginning. Music in a magazine is somewhat dull, no one wants it; a children's column would be much more popular. A popular serial story is absolutely necessary for the start. It need not be by a woman, and should be exciting but not tragic.

These are the outlines which for the moment suggest themselves to me, and in conclusion let me say that I will be very happy indeed to give any assistance I can in reconstructing the Lady's World, and making it the first woman's paper in England. To work for Messrs Cassell is a privilege which I fully recognize, to work with you a pleasure and a privilege that I look forward to. Believe me, dear Mr Reid, truly yours OSCAR WILDE

To Wemyss Reid
MS. Flower

[April–May 1887]   16 Tite Street

Dear Mr Wemyss Reid, The agreement seems to me to be right in every particular except that the preliminary salary should begin from May 1st, not June 1st. It is absolutely necessary to start at once, and I have already devoted a great deal of time to devising the scheme, and having interviews with people of position and importance.

Yesterday for instance I spent the whole afternoon with Mrs Jeune,[2] who was very delighted with the idea of our project, and I drew up with her our list of names. Tonight I am sending her a letter to put before the Princess Christian, who will I think aid us. Tomorrow I start for Oxford to arrange about the Lady Margaret's article, and to meet some women of ability. We must have the Universities on our side. On Monday I have a meeting at Mrs Jeune's, about which she will write to you. I hope that Lady Salisbury will be there and I shall deliver a brief address.

I have already engaged Lady Greville and some others, and will go to

[1] Mrs T. Herbert Warren, but Wilde may conceivably have confused her with the wife of the newly appointed President of Trinity, Mrs Margaret L. Woods (1856–1945), whose novel A Village Tragedy was published later in 1887, and favourably noticed by Wilde in the Woman's World.
[2] See note 1, p. 80. She contributed two articles to the Woman's World.

Cambridge before the end of the month. All this and innumerable letters take up time and money, and to defer operations till June would be a mistake. I am resolved to throw myself into this thing, and have already had to give up work for several papers. I feel you will recognize this, and see that the salary should begin when the work begins. June, as you know, will be for the aristocracy a very busy month, so I want to complete our arrangements now. To start well is half the race. I also wish to go to Paris to see Madame Adam about a letter every two months. I find personal interviews necessary. And though I do not expect to make much till the magazine is started, I feel sure Messrs Cassell would not wish me to be at a loss however small. I am to see Lady Dilke soon, and though I do not propose to have her *till next year*, I feel we *should* have her. I hope to call on you soon and have another talk: I think I am sure of Lady Tweeddale, Lady Malmesbury, and Maud Stanley. With the exception of the date I accept the agreement, and the date I leave to you.

I grow very enthusiastic over our scheme, and *with your assistance* will make it a success. Truly yours   OSCAR WILDE

To Joseph Hatton[1]
MS. Clark

[*Late May 1887*]   *16 Tite Street*

My dear Hatton, I am charmed with your book, and thank you very much for sending it to me.[2] Its method seems to me very true in its effect: it shows the fact "in the round," as one might say, and does not limit the reader to one point of view.

I must see about the *Pall Mall*. Boycotting in literature is detestable, and I can hardly believe that Stead[3] intends it.

How horribly dull *The Langworthy Marriage* is! Don't you think so? Here is Zola's *procès verbal* with a vengeance, and what a failure it is![4] Believe me, my dear Hatton, very truly yours   OSCAR WILDE

To Helena Sickert
TS. Clark

[*27 May 1887*][5]   *16 Tite Street*

Dear Miss Nellie, I am going to become an Editor (for my sins or my

---

[1] Prolific English journalist and author (1841–1907). Sometime editor of the *Sunday Times* and the *People*. His novel *By Order of the Czar* (1890) was an immense success.

[2] Probably Hatton's novel *The Old House at Sandwich* (1887), in which the story is told by several narrators.   [3] See note 2, p. 519.

[4] *The Langworthy Marriage: or, A Millionaire's Shame*, a "Strange True Story of Today," was published on 25 May 1887 as *Pall Mall Gazette Extra*, No 35. It was a sixty-four-page double-column pamphlet, price sixpence, and told of Mrs Langworthy's vain attempts to obtain legal redress against her rich, cruel and unscrupulous husband.   [5] So dated in another hand.

virtues?) and want you to write me an article. The magazine will try to be representative of the thought and culture of the women of this century, and I am very anxious that those who have had university training, like yourself, should have an organ through which they can express their views on life and things.

As for the subject—a review of the change of Political Economy during the last few years? Or on the value of Political Economy in education? But choose *your own aspect* of the question. About eight pages of printed matter in length, the honorarium a guinea a page, which is the same as the *Nineteenth Century* pays, and more than most of the magazines. I hope you will do this for me, but let me know what subject you like best to write on.

My wife is at home the first and third Thursdays in each month. Do come next Thursday with your mother, and talk over the matter. Believe me, very sincerely yours   OSCAR WILDE

The magazine will be published by *Cassell's*. It is of course a secret just at present.

To Louise Chandler Moulton[1]
MS. Congress

[? *June 1887*]   *16 Tite Street*

Dear Mrs Moulton, I have been asked to become literary adviser to one of the monthly magazines, and am anxious to make it an organ through which women of culture and position will be able to express their views.

Will you write me a short article, about seven or eight pages, on any subject you like? Would American poetesses please you? With illustrations, as the magazine will be illustrated. Or "Boston Literary Society"? With anecdotes of men like Longfellow, and Emerson. I think the last should make a charming article. The magazine will not make its new departure for some months, so you will have lots of time. Do Boston for me.

The honorarium will be the same as that paid by the *Fortnightly* and *Nineteenth Century*—a pound a page. Believe me, ever yours
                                                                      OSCAR WILDE

To Julia Ward Howe
MS. Berg

[? *June 1887*]   *16 Tite Street*

Dear Mrs Howe, I have been asked by Messrs Cassell & Co. the publishers

---

[1] American poet, author and journalist (1835–1908). She was at school with Whistler in America, and remained a lifelong friend. Wilde had met her during his American tour. She later lived alternately in Boston and London and formed a channel of literary communication. She did not contribute to the *Woman's World*.

to edit one of their monthly magazines and am anxious to make it the recognised organ through which women of culture and position will express their views, and to which they will contribute. There is at present no such magazine in England, though America can boast of many.

Will you allow me to add your name to my list of contributors, and write me a short article—about 5000 or 6000 words—on any subject you may like to speak on?

Some account of the remarkable development of the intellectual life of women in America would be most interesting, though as one of the leaders in the movement you may perhaps feel some difficulty about such a subject. Still, if you would not object, it is what would interest English women immensely. The position taken up by the women of America in the matter of slavery, of education, of social morals, of culture, of religion, and of politics, is one of the most interesting possible as a subject for an article— or would you prefer a purely literary subject? Whatever you write is sure to be most suggestive, and valuable.[1]

I trust your daughter also will write me a short story. I should be so gratified if she would.

It is very unkind of you never coming over to England: you have so many friends and admirers here, among the latter none more enthusiastic than my mother. Mrs Moulton brings us news of you from time to time, but we would prefer to see you *in propriâ personâ*, and you would receive a very warm welcome.

Pray remember me most kindly to your daughter. Believe me, very sincerely yours   OSCAR WILDE

To an Unidentified Correspondent
MS. Huntington

[*30 June 1887*][2]   *16 Tite Street*

Dear Sir, I do not think that the fashionable life in the Colonies is sufficiently interesting to warrant my asking you for a series of letters, but I should be glad to receive an article on Colonial Society generally, giving an account of the mode of life, the amusements, the *social grades and distinctions*, the intellectual and artistic *coteries*, if any. The DRESS of the Colonial ladies should also be treated of, and as the magazine is illustrated, you might send some photographs of the best houses and the like. The Theatre also should be treated of, and the Churches. This I think would make a very attractive article about seven or eight pages in length, and I hope you will write it. Yours very truly   OSCAR WILDE

[1] Mrs Howe did not contribute to the *Woman's World*.
[2] So dated in another hand.

To Phoebe Allen
MS. Hyde (H. M.)

[? *June–July 1887*]   *16 Tite Street*

Dear Madam, I think the idea of your *Playing at Botany* so excellent that I should be glad if you would do me a short article on the whole of your system. The article will be illustrated as you may direct.

It is for a magazine of Messrs Cassell's to which I am a sort of literary adviser, and which I am anxious should be the organ through which women of culture and position will be able to express their views.

If you have not done it before, an article on "How to Teach Children Botany" would I think prove attractive. The honorarium will be a guinea a page.[1] Believe me, Madam, yours truly   OSCAR WILDE

To Kate Terry Lewis[2]
MS. Butler

[? *July 1887*]   *16 Tite Street*

Dear Mrs Lewis, I have been asked to become literary adviser to one of the monthly magazines, and hope to make it the organ through which women of culture and position will be able to express their views. The Princess Christian, Lady Salisbury, and others have promised to write for me, and I should like to add your name to the list of contributors.

Could you write me a short article on your own experience of the Stage —the plays you acted in, the actors you knew, their method, manner and the like? It would be most interesting, and would be illustrated in any way you desire.

Anything you would write on the change and alteration in the style of modern acting would also be full of interest and suggestion—or any anecdotes of what you yourself saw and heard during your stage-career, a career, alas! far too brief. If you would write just as you talk, it would be all one could desire. Believe me, yours truly   OSCAR WILDE

To Minnie Simpson
MS. Aberystwyth

[*July 1887*]   *16 Tite Street*

Dear Mrs Simpson, I am so sorry, but my letter must have miscarried in the post. I wrote to you to express our regret that we were unable to be

---

[1] Phoebe Allen, whose *Playing at Botany* had just appeared, contributed an article "On Teaching Botany to Children" to the July 1889 number of the *Woman's World*.

[2] Kate Terry (1844–1924), leading actress and elder sister of Ellen Terry, retired from the stage in 1867 on her marriage to Arthur Lewis, a wealthy silk-mercer who had founded the Arts Club in 1863. Grandmother of Sir John Gielgud. She did not contribute to the *Woman's World*.

present at your daughter's marriage,[1] and to say how pleased I should be to have the articles you spoke of. They will be most interesting, and I hope you will let me have them as soon as you can conveniently. Indeed I should like to call on you and talk the matter over. Would you be at home Saturday morning? If so, I could come at twelve o'clock. There are, I think you said, illustrations? If so, these should be put in hand at once.[2]

I hear your daughter's wedding was most brilliant. I hope she will be happy, and that her husband is worthy of so fine a nature and so stately a presence.

I am quite distressed about the post.

I remain, truly yours   OSCAR WILDE

To the Hon. St John Brodrick[3]
MS. Clark

[? *Summer 1887*]   *16 Tite Street*

Dear Brodrick, I have been asked by Cassell's to edit one of their monthly magazines for them, and am anxious to make it the organ for women of culture and position. Mrs Jeune, Miss Thackeray, Mrs Fawcett, Lady Archibald Campbell, Lady Pollock, Lady Dorothy Nevill, and many others have promised to write for it and I should like to number your sister amongst my contributors.

Would you ask her to interest herself in the scheme, and to write something for the magazine? I see a notice of a book of hers in the catalogue of the Literary Society.[4]

Pray remember me to Lady Hilda, and believe me, truly yours

OSCAR WILDE

[1] Henrietta Mary Amy Simpson (1866–1957) was married on 13 July 1887 to John St Loe Strachey (1860–1927), who later became proprietor and editor of the *Spectator*. Wilde commissioned Amy Strachey to write an article on "The Child-Players of the Elizabethan Age," which appeared in the *Woman's World* for September 1888.

[2] Mrs Simpson had come into possession of manuscript material concerning Antoine-François Sergent (1751–1847), French engraver and Revolutionary politician, who married Emira Marceau (1753–1834), half-sister of the Revolutionary General. Eventually, after several efforts to abbreviate her manuscript (see p. 216), Mrs Simpson published an account of Emira, called "A Provincial Bourgeoise in the Eighteenth Century," illustrated from engravings by Sergent, in the *Woman's World* for February 1889.

[3] Politician and author (1856–1942). Conservative M.P. (1880–1906). Married (1880) Lady Hilda Charteris, daughter of the ninth Earl of Wemyss. Secretary of State for War 1900–3, for India 1903–5. Succeeded his father as ninth Viscount Midleton 1907. Created Earl of Midleton 1920.

[4] Brodrick had six sisters, but only one of them, Albinia Lucy (1862–1955), seems to have written. She published a short story *Linked Lives* (1896) and *Verses of Adversity* (1904).

To Georgina Weldon [1]
MS. Paris

3 August 1887   *16 Tite Street*

Dear Mrs Weldon, The little note in the *Lady's Pictorial* on the Irving Benefit was written not by me, but by my wife. She is very much flattered at your liking it. [2]

I am so sorry we missed your Jubilee party, but we never received your kind invitation. Believe me, truly yours   OSCAR WILDE

To Mrs Alfred Hunt
MS. Clark

[*29 August 1887*] [3]   *16 Tite Street*

Dear Mrs Hunt, I have been asked by Cassell to reconstruct the *Lady's World*, and am anxious to make it the recognised organ through which women of culture and position will express their views, and to which they will contribute.

I hope you will allow me to add your name to my list, and that you will send me either a short story or a short article.

Would you do me an article on "Some Old Fashion Books," that could be illustrated? I don't know if there are any Fashion Books earlier than this century, or the end of the last, but I know you have written on such things.

I do not know if Miss Violet cares for prose-writing, but I hope she will send me a short poem at any rate. A sonnet on Whitby, with an illustration of one of Mr Hunt's pictures, would be delightful. [4] Believe me, truly yours
OSCAR WILDE

---

[1] 1837–1914. Born Georgina Thomas, but in 1856 her father changed the family's name to Treherne. Singer and friend of the composer Charles Gounod, whom she virtually kidnapped. In 1860 she married William Henry Weldon, a lieutenant in the 18th Hussars. In the 1880's she became a popular figure as a litigant in person. At one time she had seventeen actions in hand, all conducted by herself. Her most famous and successful fight was against the "mad doctors" who on the instructions of her estranged husband had examined her disguised as spiritualists and attempted to consign her to a private asylum. She was twice imprisoned for criminal libel (in 1880 and 1885), but her agitations helped to secure the reform of the lunacy laws and the establishment of the Court of Criminal Appeal.

[2] Irving's 1887 benefit was on 16 July, when *The Merchant of Venice* was given on the last night of the Lyceum season. After the performance there was a party on the stage, at which the Wildes were present. In Constance's note, which appeared in the *Lady's Pictorial* on 23 July, she wrote: "The palm of beauty was perhaps borne off by Mrs Weldon, radiant and young-looking as ever."

[3] So dated by recipient.

[4] Neither Mrs Hunt nor her daughter contributed to the *Woman's World*.

To Mrs Hamilton King[1]

MS. Clark

1 September 1887   *16 Tite Street*

Mr Oscar Wilde presents his compliments to Mrs Hamilton King, and would be very much gratified if Mrs King would allow him to add her name to the list of contributors to an illustrated monthly magazine he has been asked to edit for Messrs Cassell's & Co. the publishers.

Mr Wilde is anxious to make the magazine the recognised organ through which women of culture and position will express their views, and to which they will contribute.

The Princess Christian has kindly promised to write, and so have Miss Thackeray, Mrs Fawcett, Miss Olive Schreiner, Lady Portsmouth, Lady Zetland, Lady Meath, Mrs Craik, Lady Archibald Campbell, Mrs Pfeiffer, Lady Tweeddale, Miss Edith Simcox, and many others.

A short poem, or sonnet, from Mrs King's pen would add a charm and distinction to the magazine, and Mr Wilde ventures to hope that Mrs King will send him something for one of the early numbers.

To Wemyss Reid

MS. Camrose

[5 September 1887][2]   *16 Tite Street*

Dear Mr Wemyss Reid, I am very anxious that you should make a final appeal to the Directors to alter the name of the magazine I am to edit for them from the *Lady's World* to the *Woman's World*. The present name of the magazine has a certain taint of vulgarity about it, that will always militate against the success of the new issue, and is also extremely misleading. It is quite applicable to the magazine in its present state; it will not be applicable to a magazine that aims at being the organ of women of intellect, culture, and position.

This is not merely my view, but is undoubtedly the view of those whom we want to contribute. In writing to the various women whose names stand now on the contributors' list I carefully avoided mentioning the name of the magazine, but in certain cases I have been obliged to tell it, and on every occasion of this kind the name has met with the strongest opposition.

Miss Thackeray[3] has spoken to me more than once on the subject, and

[1] Harriet Eleanor Baillie Hamilton (1840–1920), poet and author, married (1863) the publisher Henry Samuel King (1817–78). She was a friend of Mazzini and an ardent supporter of Italian independence, which formed the theme of many of her poems. Her *Letters and Recollections of Mazzini* were edited by G. M. Trevelyan (1912).   [2] So dated by recipient.

[3] Anne Isabella (1837–1919), eldest daughter of W. M. Thackeray, married (1877) Richmond Ritchie (1854–1912). He was made K.C.B. 1907. She published (mostly under the name of Miss Thackeray) novels, essays and memoirs, and edited an edition of her father's works. She contributed an article on "Madame de Sévigné's Grandmother" to the *Woman's World* of November 1887.

has told me very candidly that she does not care about having her name connected with a magazine that has so vulgar a title, and that had I not been the editor she would have definitely refused. Lady Verney first consented to write an article, but on hearing the name of the magazine withdrew her promise; "I have not the courage," she writes, "to contribute to a magazine with such a title," so I have been obliged to remove her name from the list. Miss Fletcher, the author of the serial,[1] has spoken and written to me on the subject in the strongest terms. Some days ago I received the enclosed post-card from Lady Margaret Magendie, which I beg you will read to the Directors: Lady Lindsay writes to the same effect: the same view has been expressed by Miss Agnes Giberne, Miss Edmonds, Mrs Frederika MacDonald, and Miss Orne, and I feel quite sure that the retention of the present name will be a serious bar to our success. It would also be impossible to ask any prominent man of letters to contribute to the magazine under its present title, and I see quite clearly that it will not be possible to rely entirely on women for our contributions.

From the commercial point of view I see that the slight change demanded by the contributors will be of no small advantage in emphasising the new departure: I may mention that the *Girls' Own Magazine* by altering its name to *Atalanta* has succeeded in gaining a staff of writers of a very distinguished order, including men like Ruskin, Walter Besant, Andrew Lang, Rider Haggard, Anstey and others, and I have no doubt that it will be a great success[2] For our magazine there is a definite opening and a definite mission, but without an alteration in the title it will not be able to avail itself of its opportunity. Its name should definitely separate itself from such papers as the *Lady* and the *Lady's Pictorial*.[3] I remain, yours truly   OSCAR WILDE

To Alice Meynell[4]

MS. Sowerby

[? *September 1887*]

Dear Mrs Meynell, I hope you will allow me to count you among the contributors to the *Woman's World*, and write me a short article on some literary or artistic subject. I prefer subjects that admit of illustrations.

---

[1] *The Truth about Clement Ker* by George Fleming (see note 4, p. 45) was the only serial published by Wilde in the *Woman's World*. It ran through twelve issues from November 1887 to October 1888 and was published in book form by Arrowsmith in 1889.

[2] *Atalanta*, edited by L. T. Meade and A. A. Leith, ran from 1887 till 1898, but I can find no record of the *Girls' Own Magazine*.

[3] Wilde had his way, and in the November 1887 issue, the first under his editorship, the name was changed to the *Woman's World*, with Wilde's name on the cover. He resigned his editorship after the October 1889 issue, and the paper died a year later.

[4] Poet and essayist (1847–1922). She did not contribute to the *Woman's World*.

When you have settled what you would like to write on, pray let me know, so that your article may not clash with any other. I hope to make the magazine the organ through which women of culture and position will express their views and my list would be quite incomplete without your name.

I hope your husband is well. Pray give him my kind regards and believe me, truly yours   OSCAR WILDE

To Edwin Bale[1]
MS. Hyde (H. M.)

[? *September 1887*]   *La Belle Sauvage, Ludgate Hill*[2]

Dear Mr Bale, I send you the photographs of Lady Archibald Campbell— one for frontispiece, two for setting into the article. Also three drawings by Godwin to be set into the text—like marginal sketches.

I also want a portrait of *Madame d'Épinay*, Rousseau's friend. Truly yours   OSCAR WILDE

To Mrs Hamilton King
MS. Clark

[? *September 1887*]   *16 Tite Street*

Dear Madam, I am very sorry that you have been unable to allow the poem to appear, but I hope that you will send me a sonnet for the magazine.

I think you will find that the *Woman's World* will be a really intellectual and cultured magazine. It will be quite different from the *Lady's World*, which seems to me to have been a very vulgar, trivial, and stupid production, with its silly gossip about silly people, and its social inanities.

I have just been reading again your poem about Nicotera.[3] What a wonderful picture of the sea it holds! *Keats* even would have envied you your

"... purple barge,
in purple shadow on the seas"[4]

---

[1] Water-colour artist (1838–1923). Art Director of Cassell & Co. Ltd 1882–1907. He introduced Wilde to W. E. Henley, who had edited the *Magazine of Art* for Cassell 1881–86. The first six illustrations mentioned in this letter duly appeared in the first issue of the *Woman's World*. (See note 4, p. 160).

[2] The offices of Messrs Cassell and of the *Woman's World*.

[3] Mrs King's book of poems *The Disciples*, which was published in 1873 and ran through twelve editions by 1890, contained a poem called "Baron Giovanni Nicotera." Italian patriot and politician, he was one of the leaders of the unsuccessful attempt in 1857 to liberate the Kingdom of the Two Sicilies from the Bourbons. He was captured, tried after an interval of nine months, condemned to death, reprieved and chained in the under-sea dungeons of the island of Favignana. He was released in 1860 by Garibaldi's victorious troops.

[4] The complete stanza reads:

The fishing-fleet at anchor-hold
Leans over, every purple barge,

Such colour and music together are rare. I have the honour to remain, faithfully yours   OSCAR WILDE

To Blanche Medhurst[1]
MS. Clark

[? *September 1887*]   *16 Tite Street*

Dear Mrs Medhurst, Thank you very much for the article on the Children's League, which is *most* interesting, and for the pretty song. I have no doubt that the League will do a *great* deal of good, and I wish it every possible success.

Lady Meath has promised to write a short article on it for a magazine I am going to edit for Messrs Cassell's the publishers in November, and this will no doubt bring you many members, and draw public attention.

I remember our meeting in Salt Lake City very well. I suppose you have written about it?* If not would you do me a short descriptive article (about 3000 words) to be illustrated? I think it would be an interesting subject. Believe me, truly yours   OSCAR WILDE

* I mean the city, of course.

To Bernard Partridge[2]

[*Postmark 24 September 1887*]

I send you two short poems, suitable for illustration.[3] One is a suggestion for a design for a Japanese panel, the other is a description of children flying balloons in the Tuileries Gardens in Paris. They should be set on a full page, and around them and through them should be the decorative design. Perhaps, as the girl under the rose tree is Japanese, the children who are playing with the balloons should be Japanese also. They would give a unity to the composition. Round the verses of the first poem should be fluttering rose leaves, and round the verses of the second the balloons should float, the children holding the strings from the side of the page.

OSCAR WILDE

Its purple shadow on the seas;
—In sweeps of silver outward rolled,
Till points of pearl upon the marge
Set sail for the Hesperides.

[1] Blanche Medhurst contributed an article on "Playgrounds and Open Spaces" to the September 1888 issue of the *Woman's World*.

[2] John Bernard Partridge (1862–1945), artist and book-illustrator. On the staff of *Punch* from 1892. The text of this incomplete letter is taken from the American Art Association catalogue of 9 February 1927.

[3] "*Fantaisies Décoratives*. I. *Le Panneau*. II. *Les Ballons*." They appeared, illustrated by Partridge, in the 1887 Christmas number of the *Lady's Pictorial*, and were reprinted in *Poems* (1908). Partridge also illustrated Wilde's fairy story "The Young King" in the 1888 Christmas number of the *Lady's Pictorial*.

To Emily Faithfull [1]
MS. Hyde (H. M.)

[*Circa October 1887*]   *16 Tite Street*

Dear Miss Faithfull, I will ask Cassell to put your name on the Free List with pleasure, and will send you the prospectus in a few days. I wish you would do me a short article on "Printing and Book-binding as a Profession for Women," giving some account of what a woman can earn at such an employment, and how she can find an opening: 2500 words would be quite sufficient.

If you don't care for this subject pray suggest one, but I am having a series of articles on what women can earn, and how they can make a livelihood, and should like you to do the one on Printing, etc.

Thank you very much for your promise to draw the public attention to the magazine: but for a few women like yourself such a magazine would have been an impossibility.

I have altered its title to the *Woman's World*, which is a great improvement. Truly yours   OSCAR WILDE

To Violet Fane [2]

[? *October 1887*]   *16 Tite Street*

A capital essay might be written on "The Demoralising Influence of Nature." However, as she has suggested a sonnet to you much will be forgiven her. Besides, *you* live between Parnassus and Piccadilly: it is those who live in the country whom Nature deteriorates.

To Helena Sickert
TS. Clark

[*October 1887*]   *16 Tite Street*

Dear Miss Nellie, I am very glad you have done the article. I hope that it is not more than 4000 words, as I find that my space is very limited. Should it be more please cut it before you send it to me, as I should like the condensation to come from your own pen. I look forward to reading it with great pleasure.[3]

---

[1] English writer, lecturer and pioneer of women's rights (1835–95). She founded and ran a monthly paper, the *Victoria Magazine* (1863–81), and was on the staff of the *Lady's Pictorial*. She contributed an article on "The Endowment of the Daughter" to the *Woman's World* of June 1888.

[2] The text of this fragment is taken from Sotheby's catalogue of 12 March 1920, supplemented by W. T. Spencer's *Forty Years in my Bookshop* (1923).

[3] The only article by Helena Sickert (H. M. Swanwick) which appeared in the *Woman's World* was on "The Evolution of Economics" in the issue of February 1889.

I enclose you a prospectus of the *Woman's World*. I hope I will be able to make it a success, but I am not allowed as free a hand as I would like. However, in the first number there is a real literary gem: a story, one *page* long! sent to me by a girl whom I have never seen, but who has a touch of genius in her work.[1]

Pray remember me to your mother, and believe me, very sincerely yours

OSCAR WILDE

To Amy Levy[2]

MS. Clark

[*October 1887*][3]   *16 Tite Street*

Dear Madam, I see that photographs of Rossetti's drawing of his sister can be procured—I suppose from Mr William Rossetti. If you would write to Christina Rossetti herself, I am sure she would give leave for their reproduction. I would see that the work was done by the best artists.

I hope you will send me another short story. I think your method as admirable as it is unique. I am having your article on Clubs illustrated, at least I am looking out for an artist who could do little life-like sketches of the various types to which you allude—not, of course, portraits of any individual.

Hoping to receive another short story from you, I remain, yours faithfully

OSCAR WILDE

To Florence Fenwick-Miller[4]

MS. Miller

7 October 1887   *La Belle Sauvage, Ludgate Hill*

Dear Mrs Fenwick-Miller, I find that the question of Education as a Profession for Women has been already dealt with by Miss Edith Simcox,[5] so I hope you will send me instead a monograph on some remarkable women. It should be short, vivid, and concentrated. But no one knows better than you do what the qualities of a good article are. Very truly yours

OSCAR WILDE

[1] "The Recent Telepathic Occurrence at the British Museum" by Amy Levy.

[2] English novelist and poet (1862–89). After her story in the first number of the *Woman's World* she contributed articles on "The Poetry of Christina Rossetti" (March 1888), "Women and Club Life" (June 1888), and two poems and a story during 1889. She committed suicide by inhaling fumes of charcoal.

[3] Christina Rossetti's answer to Amy Levy (MS. Abrahams) is dated 18 October 1887.

[4] Author, journalist and suffragist (1854–1935). Married Frederick A. Ford 1877.

[5] Edith Jemima Simcox (1844–1901), writer, social worker and passionate admirer of George Eliot. Her article on "Elementary School Teaching as a Profession" and Florence Fenwick-Miller's on "A Woman's Friendship: Mary Stuart and Mary Seton" both appeared in the October 1888 issue of the *Woman's World*.

To Richard le Gallienne[1]

[*Postmark 17 October 1887*]

So I have to thank you again, this time for the charming little printed edition of your poems.[2] With its stately brother it shall stand on my shelves, and be a delight to me. You ask me for a manuscript. Yes, I will give you one certainly, but which one would you like? I have written some since I saw you—and dreamed many. Today has been lovely—a stray day of summer that somehow got entangled in the red net of autumn. I suppose she loitered to listen to some poet singing, or fell asleep by the roadside till October overtook her. Let me see you soon—letters are not enough.

OSCAR WILDE

To Edward Heron-Allen[3]

[*Postmark 17 October 1887*]   *16 Tite Street*

My dear Heron-Allen, We are all charmed at your success, but of course we want you at home. When do you come back?

My wife tells me she has sent you a copy of "Lord Arthur Savile's Crime."[4] I was going myself to send it to McClure, the newspaper syndicate man in Philadelphia, as I want to have it published in the States.[5] If you can sell it for me to any enterprising editor pray do so, and you can write a short preface on the cheiromancy of the story![6]

I think I should get between fifty and a hundred dollars for it. Try McClure: he commands about fifty papers. I was at Molloy's[7] the other

---

[1] Poet, journalist and littérateur (1866–1947). His father, a Liverpool brewery-manager, had taken him to hear Wilde lecture on "Personal Impression of America" at Birkenhead on 10 December 1883. He had spent a holiday in London in September 1887 and probably paid his first visit to Wilde then. The text of this incomplete letter is taken from the American Art Association catalogue of 9 February 1927.

[2] *My Ladies Sonnets*, Le Gallienne's first book, was privately printed in Liverpool in August 1887. Its "stately brother" was presumably an earlier manuscript collection.

[3] Text from Mason, pp. 40–41, and the date is his, corroborated by the Spoor sale catalogue (1939).

[4] This short story was first published in three instalments in the *Court and Society Review* on 11, 18 and 25 May 1887 with two illustrations by F. H. Townsend. It later gave its name to a book of stories published by Osgood McIlvaine (1500 copies at 2/- in July 1891 and 1000 large-paper copies at 21/- in November).

[5] Samuel Sidney McClure (1857–1949) was an Irish emigrant who made good in the U.S.A. as a pioneer of newspaper syndication. His syndicate, founded in 1884, published works by Stevenson, Conan Doyle, Kipling and other popular British authors. He founded *McClure's Magazine* (1893) and was the original of Pinkerton in Stevenson and Lloyd Osbourne's *The Wrecker* (1892).

[6] This was one of Heron-Allen's many interests (see note p. 167); in 1885 he had published a *Manual of Cheirosophy*, and he may well have suggested to Wilde the idea for "Lord Arthur Savile's Crime."

[7] Joseph Fitzgerald Molloy (1858–1908), author of many popular biographies and quasi-historical works. One of the few meetings between Wilde and Bernard Shaw took place at his house in Red Lion Square.

night: it was very pleasant, and Bernard Partridge was charming. He talked about you a great deal. Believe me, very truly yours OSCAR WILDE

To Emilia Aylmer Gowing[1]
MS. Clark

[23 October 1887]   16 Tite Street

Dear Mrs Gowing, It will give me very great pleasure if you will write something for the *Woman's World*. The first number, which appears on Wednesday, will show you the lines on which I propose to conduct the magazine.

I do not propose to have much poetry, if any, but a short prose-article from your pen would I am sure be very attractive.

Is there any French man of letters you would like to write on? any one you knew, or know, personally. Personal reminiscences are always interesting.

The article should be about 3000 words in length.

Mamma was so sorry to have missed you yesterday but she came with me to see a production of Coppée's *Le Passant*. The translation was very mediocre, so you missed little by not seeing it.[2]

When you have decided on a subject pray let me know, and I will let no one else touch it. With kind regards to your husband, believe me, very truly yours OSCAR WILDE

To Violet Fane
MS. Clark

[Postmark 24 October 1887]   16 Tite Street

My dear Mrs Singleton, I think the sonnet[3] is quite clear as it stands. No

---

[1] Emilia Aylmer Gowing contributed a memoir of Lamartine to the *Woman's World* in September 1889.

[2] A matinée performance of *The Stroller*, a poetic idyll in one act from François Coppée's *Le Passant*, versified by Mrs Olive Logan, was given at the Princess's Theatre on Saturday, 22 October 1887, with Grace Hawthorne and Mary Rorke in the cast.

[3] "Hazely Heath," which appeared in the first issue of the *Woman's World*, November 1887. The sestet reads:

> Here all is light and song, with odorous breath
>   Of briar and pine, whilst ever, early and late,
> The yellow gorse, like kissing-time—or death—
>   Abides with us. It were a worthier fate
> To crawl, methinks, a worm on Hazely Heath,
>   Than strut, a peacock, at a palace gate!

The sonnet was reprinted in Violet Fane's *Autumn Songs* (1889). She also contributed another poem and an article to the paper in 1888.

lover could possibly miss the allusion to the old proverb about the gorse and kissing time,[1] and it is only for lovers that poets write. Anything approaching an explanation is always derogatory to a work of art. If the *public* cannot understand the line, well—they cannot understand it.

It is a beautiful gem, and you will receive the first copy of the magazine next week.

Are you coming back to town? I hope so. Very truly yours

OSCAR WILDE

To Mrs Bernard Beere
TS. Ross

[? *Late October 1887*][2]   *Beaufort Club, 32 Dover Street*

My dear Bernie, I am sure you will be very sorry to hear that I have been in great trouble. Our youngest boy[3] has been so ill that we thought he could never recover, and I was so unhappy over it that all my duties and letters escaped me, otherwise I would have been delighted to have had the chance of seeing you.

I am afraid as it is ten years since I lived in Dublin that all my friends have vanished—all that is who would have appreciated you, and whom you would have liked, but I have no doubt that by this time you are the idol of Hibernia, and all the College boys are in love with you. If they are not, at least they must have lost their old admiration for wit and beauty.

I hope you drive about on outside cars: there are several Dion Boucicaults on the stand opposite the Shelbourne who are delightful creatures.

How nice of the Earthquake to wait till you had left. *Après vous—le tremblement de terre!* Poor Edmund! I hope he had not to run about *en déshabille*.

When do you come back? Why should the cottage be left lonely? Your last dinner was a marvel, one of the pleasantest I was ever at. We have no *lionne* now but Ouida.[4] With best wishes, believe me, ever yours OSCAR

[1] "When gorse is out of bloom, kissing is out of favour."

[2] The only time that Mrs Bernard Beere seems to have acted in Ireland was 24–29 October 1887, when, with much success and "supported by the entire company from the Opera Comique, London," she played the leading parts in *As in a Looking Glass, Masks and Faces* and *Jim the Penman* at the Gaiety Theatre, Dublin. I cannot explain the reference to an earthquake.

[3] Wilde's second son Vyvyan was born on 3 November 1886. His parents usually spelt his name Vivian, but he was christened, and prefers, Vyvyan, which I have adopted throughout this book.

[4] Pen-name of the prolific novelist Maria Louise Ramé or, as she preferred, de la Ramée (1839–1908). Max Beerbohm called her "that unique, flamboyant lady, one of the miracles of modern literature." She contributed four articles to the *Woman's World* between March 1888 and May 1889.

To Helena Sickert

MS. Private

31 October 1887   *La Belle Sauvage*

Dear Miss Nellie, Thank you very much for the article.[1] I have just glanced at it, and it seems most brightly and pleasantly written.

Has your mother an At Home Day? I should like not to miss her the next time I call. Believe me, your sincere friend   OSCAR WILDE

To William Sharp

MS. Sharp

[*October–November 1887*]

Dear Mr Sharp, I am very much pleased that you like the magazine. The work of reconstruction was very difficult, as the *Lady's World* was a most vulgar trivial production, and the doctrine of heredity holds good in literature as in life. Would you kindly tell your wife that there will be no difficulty about getting photographs of Shortlands: at least I think now, as they are already published. I want her article for the January number, so should have it by 10 November.[2]

Thank you for Miss Blind's letter. She had promised to write something for me, and the subject she suggests seems excellent.[3] Would it be troubling you too much to write her present address on a postcard, and send it to me? Very truly yours   OSCAR WILDE

To Violet Fane

MS. Hyde (H. M.)

8 November 1887   *La Belle Sauvage, Ludgate Hill*

Dear Mrs Singleton, I am charmed that you like the magazine. Your sonnet is admired by everyone, and is quite the gem of the first number, from the literary point of view.[4] As for the copyright, that will of course

---

[1] See note 3, p. 207.

[2] Mrs Sharp's article duly appeared in the January 1888 issue of the *Woman's World*. It was a short account of the life and work of Mrs Craik (1826–87), entitled "The Author of *John Halifax, Gentleman*." It was illustrated with two engravings of the Corner House, Shortlands, Kent, which William Morris designed for Mrs Craik. In the previous number of the *Woman's World* (December 1887) Mrs Craik's last article, on "Miss Mary Anderson in *The Winter's Tale*," was posthumously published.

[3] Mathilde Blind (1841–96), poet, biographer and editor. She contributed a long article on Marie Bashkirtseff which appeared in two parts in the *Woman's World* for June and August 1888. In 1891 she published a translation of Marie Bashkirtseff's Journal.

[4] See note 4, p. 210. Violet Fane's book *The Edwin and Angelina Papers* had appeared in 1878.

remain with you, so pray draw your pen through that portion of the receipt that refers to it. The clause was inserted without my sanction.

Has the *Edwin and Angelina* spirit been killed by vegetarianism? Or will you write me a short prose article some day? I still think that the Philistine side of the country, of nature, would be a capital peg. Very truly yours   OSCAR WILDE

To Julia Ward Howe
MS. Harvard

6 December 1887   Woman's World, *La Belle Sauvage*

Dear Mrs Howe, I am charmed at the prospect of counting you among my contributors. Would you write me an article about 4000 words on Concord, with sketches of Thoreau, the faun, and Alcott, the mystic, and Emerson, with his bright Attic mind, made happy by a phrase, and finding comfort in an aphorism, and Margaret Fuller, to whom Venus gave everything except beauty, and Pallas everything except wisdom.[1]

I should like the article to be illustrated by views of Concord—from photographs—and by pictures of those you mention. I suppose I can easily get these?

I often look back to our charming days with Uncle Sam, and have the pleasantest memories of Newport.

Pray remember me to your daughter. Believe me, very truly yours
OSCAR WILDE

To W. Graham Robertson[2]
MS. Preston

[Postmark 12 December 1887]   *16 Tite Street*

Dear Mr Robertson, I am so sorry but neither my wife or I ever go to dances: I am not sure whether we are too old or too young, but we never tread measures now.

Pray thank your mother for her kindness all the same: I hope to have the pleasure of introducing my wife to her some day.

[1] Henry David Thoreau (1817–62), the author of *Walden: or Life in the Woods;* Amos Bronson Alcott (see note 2, p. 91); Ralph Waldo Emerson (1803–82), poet and essayist; and Margaret Fuller (1810–50), author, were all natives or inhabitants of Concord, Massachusetts. When Margaret Fuller said to Carlyle "I accept the Universe," he replied "Gad, you'd better!"

[2] Artist and writer (1866–1948). Painted by Sargent 1894. Formed important collection of Blake drawings. Designed many stage costumes. His successful children's play *Pinkie and the Fairies* was produced by Tree in 1908, though written in the 1890's, for which his autobiography *Time Was* (1931) is a valuable source-book.

When shall I see you again? The star-child is lovely: it is clear you have seen him: of course he is not an ordinary baby.[1]

We are always at home on Thursday. Very truly yours OSCAR WILDE

To J. S. Little

MS. Berg

[*15 January 1888*][2]   *16 Tite Street*

My dear Little, Thank you very much for your charming book, which I have read with great pleasure.[3] You ask me to give you a criticism of it, but Gil Blas is plucking my sleeve and reminding me of the Archbishop.[4] However, here *is* my opinion.

The book is a little too crowded: the motive is hardly clear enough: if Gwendoline is the heroine we should hear more of her: if she is not, the last chapters emphasise her too much. Captain Breutnall is not a success: his death is merely the premature disappearance of a shell-jacket: I decline to mourn with Gwendoline over someone who is not properly introduced.

Upon the other hand Ralph, Grace, and Mrs Landford are all admirable: they are your real characters: Gwendoline seems to me unnecessary. Your descriptions are excellent, whether of scenery or of women, and I wish that I could write a novel, but I can't! Give my love to Grace, who is very adorable, and believe me, truly yours   OSCAR WILDE

(A rash letter)

To Violet Fane

MS. Clark

[*Circa 1 February 1888*]   *16 Tite Street*

Dear Mrs Singleton, I think the idea of the article quite excellent, and I hope you will do it for me. It need not be more than 3500 words, as the illustrations will take up so much room. As to the latter, your suggestions are admirable; perhaps we might add a portrait of Flora Macdonald. Have you got one? If not, I suppose it can be found somewhere.[5]

[1] Wilde's fairy story "The Star-Child" was published in *A House of Pomegranates* (1891).

[2] So dated by recipient.

[3] Little's novel *Whose Wife Shall She Be?* published in 1888 and dedicated to Rider Haggard.

[4] In Le Sage's picaresque novel one of Gil Blas's many jobs was to copy out the homilies of an Archbishop, who made Gil promise to tell him when they showed signs of degenerating in quality. The Archbishop had a stroke, Gil told him the homilies were deteriorating, was sacked for his pains, and thus learned the folly of being too truthful.

[5] Violet Fane's illustrated article on the Stuarts, "Records of a Fallen Dynasty," appeared in the May 1888 issue of the *Woman's World*.

The March number is now going to press, but in April or May yours might appear. We should set about the illustrations at once.

I hope to find you at home some afternoon. I remain, very truly yours

OSCAR WILDE

To Violet Fane

MS. Clark

[*Postmark 15 March 1888*]   *16 Tite Street*

Dear Mrs Singleton, Your article is being set up, and you will get a proof, I hope, this week. I am charmed that Dorothy Tennant is going to make a drawing for your lovely little poem. It will make the whole thing very perfect.[1]

I am delighted also to hear that the ubiquitous young Jacobite who sat me out so successfully has returned to the Land o' Cakes. Perhaps now I may be asked to tea on Friday? Believe me, very truly yours

OSCAR WILDE[2]

To Jacomb Hood[3]

MS. Princeton

[*Early 1888*]   *16 Tite Street*

My dear Hood, Crane's little boy has nothing on, as well as I remember, but your children can be just as you like: perhaps clothes might be advisable.

I forgot one story: the illustration might be of a young Prince kissing the hand of a lovely Princess, who is in a long ermine cloak, with a little cap. She has come from the North Pole to marry him. There are courtiers and *a young page*, looking on.[4] In great haste, yours truly OSCAR WILDE

[1] Violet Fane's poem "The Mer-Baby" appeared, with Dorothy Tennant's illustration, in the August 1888 issue of the *Woman's World*. It was reprinted in Violet Fane's *Autumn Songs* (1889). Dorothy Tennant married the explorer H. M. Stanley in 1890.

[2] A little later this year Wilde, greatly daring, wrote to Queen Victoria to ask whether she had any early verses of her own which he might publish in the *Woman's World*. His letter has disappeared, but the Queen's Minute has been preserved. It is dated 1888 on the back and has been inserted in the record after a Minute of 8 April 1888. It is here printed by gracious permission of Her Majesty the Queen:

Really what will people not say and invent. Never cd the Queen in her whole life write *one line* of *poetry* serious or comic or make *a Rhyme* even. This is therefore all *invention* & a *myth*.

[3] Professional name of George Percy Jacob-Hood (1857–1929), artist and original member of the New English Art Club. He and Walter Crane (1845–1915) illustrated Wilde's book of fairy stories *The Happy Prince* (1888).

[4] Jacomb Hood faithfully carried out this suggestion in the headpiece-drawing for "The Remarkable Rocket" in *The Happy Prince*.

To Minnie Simpson

MS. Aberystwyth

[? *March–April 1888*]   *16 Tite Street*

Dear Mrs Simpson, I think the papers *most fascinating*; the only question
is the *length*.[1] Could you make out of them *three* articles of 7000 words
each? If so, I would set about reproducing the pictures at once. The
first article would be the youth of Sergent Marceau, and his arrival at
Paris. The second his experiences in Paris, the third the fall of Robespierre
and his own death.

I should be so sorry not to have the chance of publishing such interesting papers that I hope you will consider the question of *condensation*.

Very truly yours   OSCAR WILDE

To Minnie Simpson

MS Aberystwyth

[*Circa April 1888*]   *16 Tite Street*

Dear Mrs Simpson, The difficulty I am in about the articles is this. It
would be unfair to cut them any farther, as they are valuable bits of history; upon the other hand I don't see how I can get them in as long as
my serial lasts. Would you object to my holding them over till my serial
is finished, which however will not be for seven months? If you would
I think I had better resign them in favour of *Harper* or *Scribner*. I hate
parting with them, as I think they are quite fascinating in their vividness
and picturesqueness, but I could not use them for some time. Out of the
forty-eight pages of the magazine, twenty pages are permanently given up
to the serial, dress, and literary notes, so I have only twenty-eight pages
to dispose of. How limited this space is I am only now realising.

Pray let me know what you decide, and believe me, very truly yours

                                                         OSCAR WILDE

To W. Graham Robertson

MS. Princeton

[? *Early 1888*]   *16 Tite Street*

Dear Mr Robertson, I have got a little drawing of Sarah for you. Will you
come and fetch it on Thursday at tea-time? After I left you I tried to
invent a fairy tale for you to illustrate. I kept looking at the moon, and
beseeching her to tell me a story. At last she did. Very truly yours

                                                         OSCAR WILDE

[1] See note 2, p. 201.

To W. Graham Robertson

MS. Preston

[? *Early 1888*]   *16 Tite Street*

Thank you so much for the drawings. They are a real source of delight
to me. By the time you return I hope to have finished the story. I wish
I could draw like you, for I like lines better than words, and colours more
than sentences.

However, I console myself by trying now and then to put 'The Universe'
into a sonnet.

Some day you must do a design for the sonnet: a young man looking
into a strange crystal that mirrors all the world. Poetry should be like a
crystal, it should make life more beautiful and less real. I am sorry you
are going away, but your narcissus keeps you in my memory.

What do you allow your friends to call you? "W"? or "Graham"?
I like my friends to call me   OSCAR

To R. H. Sherard

MS. Clark

[? *1888*][1]   *16 Tite Street*

My dear Robert, If you send me your play I will forward it to Wilson
Barrett. His address changes every week as he is on tour.

I have been so busy that your letter escaped me. I hope you are well;
that you are brilliant your letters and stories in the *Table* assure me. You
certainly have the clever touch and caustic satire of the man of the world.

How is your pretty, romantic looking wife with her lovely eyes? No one
plays dominoes with me now. I hope you will come over to London soon.
Ever yours   OSCAR

To John Ruskin

MS. Berg

[? *May 1888*]   *16 Tite Street*

Dear Mr Ruskin, I send you my little book, *The Happy Prince and Other
Tales,* and need hardly say how gratified I will be if you find in it any charm
or beauty.[2]

---

[1] It is impossible to date this letter exactly. The *Table,* a weekly paper "social and
gastronomical," ran from 1886 to 1930. To it Sherard contributed sixty-seven
anonymous "Romances of the Table" between 10 December 1887 and 30 March
1889. He had married a Polish girl called Martha Lips in 1886.

[2] *The Happy Prince and Other Tales* was published by David Nutt (see note 1,
p. 219) in May 1888. It was dedicated to Carlos Blacker (see note 2, p. 540). The
edition consisted of 1000 copies at 5/- and 75 signed large-paper copies at 21/-.

It was a great pleasure to me to meet you again: the dearest memories of my Oxford days are my walks and talks with you, and from you I learned nothing but what was good.[1] How else could it be? There is in you something of prophet, of priest, and of poet, and to you the gods gave eloquence such as they have given to none other, so that your message might come to us with the fire of passion, and the marvel of music, making the deaf to hear, and the blind to see. I wish I had something better to give you, but, such as it is, take it with my love.   OSCAR WILDE

To Thomas Hutchinson [2]

[7 May 1888]   *16 Tite Street*

I am afraid that I don't think as much of the young Student as you do. He seems to me a rather shallow young man and almost as bad as the girl he thinks he loves. The nightingale is the true lover, if there is one. She, at least, is Romance, and the Student and the girl are, like most of us, unworthy of Romance. So, at least, it seems to me, but I like to fancy that there may be many meanings in the tale, for in writing it I did not start with an idea and clothe it in form, but began with a form and strove to make it beautiful enough to have many secrets and many answers.

To W. E. Gladstone

MS. B.M.

[June 1888][3]   *16 Tite Street*

Dear Mr Gladstone, Will you do me the honour of accepting a copy of a little book I have just brought out, called *The Happy Prince*? It is only a collection of short stories, and is really meant for children, but I should like to have the pleasure of presenting it, such as it is, to one whom I, and all who have Celtic blood in their veins, must ever honour and revere, and to whom my country is so deeply indebted. Believe me, dear Mr Gladstone, most faithfully and sincerely yours   OSCAR WILDE

---

[1] John Ruskin (1819–1900) was Slade Professor of Art at Oxford 1869–79 and 1883–84.

[2] 1856–1938. Headmaster of Pegswood Voluntary Board School, Northumberland, for more than forty years. Author of *Ballades and other Rhymes of a Country Bookworm* (1888), which contained a parody of one of Wilde's early poems; *Jolts and Jingles: a Book of Poems for Young People* (1889), which was dedicated to Wilde; and *Fireside Flittings: A Book of Homely Essays* (1890). This fragment, which is taken from Mason (p. 335), quoting Glaenzer, supplemented by the Anderson Galleries catalogue of 2 November 1933, where the date is given, concerns Wilde's story "The Nightingale and the Rose" in *The Happy Prince*.

[3] So dated by Gladstone.

218

To Alfred Nutt[1]

MS. Clark

[*Circa 13 June 1888*]   *16 Tite Street*

Dear Mr Nutt, I will try and arrange with Miss Terry: it certainly would
be charming to hear her read "The Happy Prince."

I find I have forgotten the *Century Guild Hobby Horse*. Will you kindly
send them a copy for review—at 28 Southampton Street, Strand, W.C.
The *Irish Times* I suppose has got its copy? Also, would it not be well
to have a *card* for the booksellers to hang up in their shops? It may show
Crane's frontispiece as well as the title etc. of the book. And is it not
time for a few advertisements? *Punch* and the *World* are capital papers to
advertise in—*once*. Mr Pater has written me a wonderful letter about my
prose, so I am in high spirits.[2] Yours faithfully   OSCAR WILDE

To G. H. Kersley[3]

F. Hyde (H. M.)

[*15 June 1888*]   *16 Tite Street*

Dear Mr Kersley, I am very pleased that you like my stories. They are
studies in prose, put for Romance's sake into a fanciful form: meant partly
for children, and partly for those who have kept the childlike faculties of
wonder and joy, and who find in simplicity a subtle strangeness.

If you come to tea some Wednesday about 5.30 o'clock I will be charmed
to write your name in the book.

I hope your painting is going on all right. Truly yours   OSCAR WILDE

---

[1] Alfred Trübner Nutt (1856–1910), head of the publishing business started in
1829 by his father David Nutt (d. 1863). Published the works of W. E. Henley, the
Tudor Translations series and other finely produced books. President of the Folk-
Lore Society 1897. In the van of the Celtic Revival. Drowned rescuing his invalid
son from the Seine.

[2] Pater's letter, written from Brasenose College, Oxford, and dated 12 June (text
from Mason, p. 334), reads:

> My dear Wilde, I am confined to my room with gout, but have been consoling
> myself with *The Happy Prince*, and feel it would be ungrateful not to send a line
> to tell you how delightful I have found him and his companions. I hardly know
> whether to admire more the wise wit of "The Wonderful [Remarkable] Rocket,"
> or the beauty and tenderness of "The Selfish Giant": the latter certainly is
> perfect in its kind. Your genuine "little poems in prose," those at the top of pages
> 10 and 14, for instance, are gems, and the whole, too brief, book abounds with
> delicate touches and pure English.
>
> I hope to get away in a day or two, and meantime am a debtor in the matter
> of letters. Ever, very sincerely yours   WALTER PATER

[3] George Herbert Kersley published five volumes of verse between 1885 and
1897. The first of these, *Early Flight* (1885), included a frontispiece drawing by the
author and was dedicated to Wilson Barrett. In his preface Kersley wrote: "For the
idea of writing simple impressions, I am partly indebted to my noted friend Mr
Oscar Wilde, who, I think, agrees with me in only meaning them to appear to the
reader short descriptions of any things that have fleeting charms for the poet."

To Harry Melvill[1]
MS. Private

[? *June 1888*]   *16 Tite Street*

My dear Harry, I am going down to my publisher to tell him to send you a copy of my little book. It contains some studies in prose: the best I think being the first, though "The Nightingale and the Rose" is the most elaborate.

What a charming time we had at Abbots Hill.[2] I have not enjoyed myself so much for a long time, and I hope that we will see much more of each other, and be often together.

We are always at home on Wednesday afternoons, when you will always be *le bienvenu*. On Friday I am paying a visit in Beaufort Gardens. Will you be in about 5.30? Ouida has just sent me a clever article. Your affectionate friend   OSCAR WILDE

To Lady Monckton[3]
MS. Edmiston

[? *June–July 1888*]   *16 Tite Street*

Dear Lady Monckton, I hope your son is better and that he won't go on reckless yachting tours again.

With regard to the article, if you did not care to write about acting as an art, you might still write on acting as a profession—on the advisability of training actors: on the advantages of learning by *experience* in the provinces, as opposed to the French method of teaching the *principles* in a *conservatoire*: or on modern plays? melodrama, farcical comedy, high comedy, drama, poetical tragedy, which is the best suited for our stage: why the French write, as a rule, better plays than the English.

Any subject of this kind treated by you in an article of four or five pages would be most attractive. When you get your holiday think it over—it would only take you a few days to write.

We look forward to seeing you on the 13th. Truly yours OSCAR WILDE

[1] Dandy and relentless *raconteur* (1861–1936). Then living with his parents at 32 Beaufort Gardens. Known, according to Jacques-Emile Blanche, as Mr Chatterbox. The central character of Osbert Sitwell's short story "The Machine Breaks Down" in *Triple Fugue* (1924). Caricatured as Mr Cherry-Marvel in *The Green Hat* by Michael Arlen (1924).

[2] The country home, near Hemel Hempstead in Hertfordshire, of John Dickinson (1860–96), the grandson of the founder of the paper-making firm. He had aesthetic tastes and deplored his family's connection with trade. Two of Wilde's books, inscribed by him to Dickinson, were sold at Sotheby's in October 1910.

[3] Maria Louisa, wife of Sir John Monckton (1832–1902), Town Clerk of London 1873. She acted for many years as an amateur, and for the first time as a professional in *Jim the Penman* at the Haymarket Theatre in 1886. She did not contribute to the *Woman's World*.

To the Librarian of Toynbee Hall[1]

MS. Clark

[*Postmark 4 July 1888*]   *16 Tite Street*

Dear Sir, I send you by this post a copy of a little book I have just published called *The Happy Prince*, for the library of Toynbee Hall. I hope that it will give pleasure to some of your readers, and remain, yours faithfully   OSCAR WILDE

To Leonard Smithers[2]

MS. Private

[*Postmark 13 July 1888*]   *16 Tite Street*

My dear Sir, I must very sincerely thank you for your charming letter, and am glad to think that "The Happy Prince" has found so sympathetic an admirer, so gracious a lover. The story is an attempt to treat a tragic modern problem in a form that aims at delicacy and imaginative treatment: it is a reaction against the purely imitative character of modern art—and now that literature has taken to blowing loud trumpets I cannot but be pleased that some ear has cared to listen to the low music of a little reed. So I thank you again, and remain, faithfully yours   OSCAR WILDE

To John Ruskin

MS. Baird Smith

[*? July 1888*]   *16 Tite Street*

Dear Mr Ruskin, I sent you my little book of fairy stories some time ago to the care of your publisher, but fear they may have gone astray. If you did *not* receive them would you send me a line, as I should like you to have a copy so much.

   Whether they will please you or not, I hardly dare to think, but it is a dear privilege to offer anything to one to whom I am so indebted as I am to you. Believe me, ever affectionately yours   OSCAR WILDE

To J. S. Little

MS. Berg

[*1 August 1888*][3]   *16 Tite Street*

My dear Little, Thank you for your most charming and complimentary letter. I know that you were not in the slightest degree responsible for the

---

[1] A social settlement in Whitechapel, erected in memory of the social reformer and economist Arnold Toynbee (1852–1883), who had been a contemporary of Wilde at Oxford.
[2] Leonard Charles Smithers (1861–1909), who was to figure largely in Wilde's last years, had been born in Sheffield, and was now working there as a solicitor. Wilde later gave him the manuscript of "The Happy Prince."
[3] So dated by recipient.

gross mismanagement, and can only hope that if the Society gives another banquet the arrangement of the guests will not be left to a person like Gosse, though it would perhaps be too much to expect that the universal benevolence of Besant should condescend to details. For philanthropy so wide as his, fiction is the proper place.[1] I must apologise for not sending enclosed sooner, but I thought it would be collected at dinner. Believe me, very sincerely yours   OSCAR WILDE

To Elizabeth Robins[2]

MS. Wilberforce

[*Postmark 12 September 1888*]

I have just received enclosed. If you bring it to the theatre[3] they will give

[1] On 25 July 1888 at the Criterion Restaurant the Society of Authors gave a banquet to American authors in recognition of their efforts to gain international copyright. The Rt Hon. James Bryce M.P. presided, and the guests included James Russell Lowell, Louise Chandler Moulton, Frances Hodgson Burnett, Wilkie Collins and G. R. Sims. Whistler, Henry James, Bret Harte and Marion Crawford were invited but apparently did not accept. Lord Tennyson, the Society's President, sent a telegram of greeting. Edmund Gosse was on the committee, but seems to have had nothing to do with the seating arrangements, which had given Little some concern: "The guests proper, i.e. the American authors," he wrote to William Black, "must be seated at the Top Table together, in order that the waiters may not make unpleasant mistakes regarding the wine etc." His last-minute instructions to the restaurant were: "All seated at Top Table to have wine, also everybody with red cross against on dinner chart." Wilde's complaint was that he had been placed next to Lady Colin Campbell (see note 3, p. 193), with whom he was not on speaking terms since she had referred to him as "The Great White Slug." Little reported afterwards that the food "left much to be desired." Walter Besant, the novelist (1836–1901) had been one of the founders of the Society of Authors in 1884 and was now Chairman of its Committee of Management. He was knighted in 1895.

[2] American actress and writer (1862–1952). She had acted in America with Edwin Booth, Lawrence Barrett and James O'Neill (father of Eugene O'Neill). In 1885 she married a young American actor called George Richmond Parks, who died in 1887. In July 1888 she came to England and stayed in London with Louise Chandler Moulton. There she met Wilde, of whom she wrote in her diary: "His smooth-shaven, rather fat face, rather weak; the frequent smile showed long crowded teeth, a rather interesting presence in spite of certain objectionable points." Many years later, in an unpublished appreciation (MS. Wilberforce) she wrote of him:

He was then at the height of his powers and fame and I utterly unknown on this side of the Atlantic. I could do nothing for him; he could and did do everything in his power for me.

He introduced me to Beerbohm Tree and others, encouraged me to cancel an American engagement and try my fortunes here. He warned me against a shady theatre manager, advised me about a reliable agent and solicitor, when I needed their help, and suggested plays for matinée production to introduce the unknown actress to London managers and public.

He was generous, too, in coming to see me act; and in sending or giving me afterwards his valuable opinion on play, production and acting. Busy as he then was with his own creative work and social engagements, he even came to see me in plays which were not at all in his line, such as the sugar-coated *Little Lord Fauntleroy* in which I played Dearest under Mrs Kendal's direction.

[3] The Haymarket, where Beerbohm Tree's production of *Captain Swift* by C.

Bournemouth, 1887

Robert Ross

you seats for yourself and any friend you may care to bring. You should see
Mr Tree. Truly yours   O. W.
In such haste.

To Elizabeth Robins
MS. Wilberforce

[*12 or 13 September 1888*]   *16 Tite Street*
Dear Mrs Parks, I could not have my name mentioned. These things get
about and make mischief, but you might ask Miss Calhoun[1] to enquire
from any of her theatrical friends, as they will I think speak in the same
way as I did.

I am glad you are going to see Tree—in any case he will be useful to
you next year.

I look forward to seeing you next year, and hope you will let me know
when you arrive. Faithfully yours   OSCAR WILDE

To Elizabeth Robins
MS. Wilberforce

[*21 or 22 September 1888*]   *16 Tite Street*
Dear Miss Robins, I hope that you have looked at the criticisms on *A Fair
Bigamist*. It has been the fiasco I prophesied and no acting could have
saved it.[2] You can tell Miss Calhoun, if you see her, that it was I who dissuaded you from accepting the part, but don't say anything about my views
on Sir R.R.[3]

I spoke to Tree about you on Friday, and I think he will devise something for a matinée. Truly yours   OSCAR WILDE

To Elizabeth Robins
MS. Wilberforce

[*Postmark 27 September 1888*]   *16 Tite Street*
The Royalty collapsed suddenly on Tuesday night and closed its doors.
                                                                      O. W.

Haddon Chambers had been running since 1 September, after a preliminary
matinée in June.

[1] Eleanor Calhoun, American actress (1865–1957), to whom Wilde had sent an
inscribed copy of *Vera* (1882). She had given up her part in a forthcoming play
called *A Fair Bigamist* by U. Burford and was anxious to recommend Elizabeth
Robins as substitute. She longed to accept, but Wilde persuaded her to refuse.

[2] *A Fair Bigamist* opened at the Royalty Theatre on 20 September, with Rose
Murray and Eille Norwood in leading parts.

[3] Sir Randal Roberts (1837–99), the "shady theatre manager". In *Both Sides of
the Curtain* (1940) Elizabeth Robins refers to him as Sir Mervyn Owen.

To W. E. Henley[1]
MS. Morgan

[? *September 1888*]   *16 Tite Street*

My dear Henley, It will give me great pleasure to lunch with you at the Savile on Saturday, though I am afraid that I shall be like a poor lion who has rashly intruded into a den of fierce Daniels. As for proposing me for the Savile, that is of course one of your merry jests.[2]

I am still reading your volume, preparatory to a review which I hope will be ready by the year 1900. I have decided that a great deal of it is poetry, and that, of the rest, part is poesy, and part . . . .[3]

The weather here is rather cloudy this morning, but I hope it will clear up, though I am told that dampness is good for agriculture. Pray remember me to Mrs Henley, and believe me, ever yours   OSCAR WILDE

To Bernard Partridge
MS. Clark

[*Postmark 12 October 1888*]   *16 Tite Street*

My dear Partridge, I was away at Clumber and unable to come and see you while you were at work on my story, but Gibbons[4] yesterday showed me some of the drawings and I cannot help writing to you to tell you how

---

[1] William Ernest Henley (1849–1903), poet, journalist and editor. A courageous but aggressive cripple, who quarrelled with most of his best friends, including R. L. Stevenson. His friendship with Wilde was short-lived. Wilde is reported (in the New York *Bookman* for December 1911) as having said in 1898:

> Have you noticed that if a man has once been an editor he can always be an editor? The fact that a paper has a way of dying when he is on it is of the smallest importance. He is in demand before the corpse is buried. Here is Henley. He kills the *Scots Observer*. Hey presto! he is made editor of the *New Review*. Then the *New Review* dies.

Mason points out that Wilde might have added that, after the death of the *New Review*, Henley became editor of the *Outlook*.

[2] Wilde was in fact put up for the Savile Club on 13 October 1888. His proposer was the Rev. W. J. Loftie, F.S.A., an old Trinity College, Dublin, man and Assistant Chaplain at the Chapel Royal, Savoy (see also note p. 101). Thirty-one other members of the Club backed Wilde's candidature, including Henley, Henry James, Edmund Gosse, Rider Haggard, R. A. M. Stevenson, W. H. Pollock, A. G. Ross, Walter Besant, J. K. Stephen, T. H. Warren, George Macmillan and J. W. Mackail, but he was never elected. Candidates for the Savile are not blackballed, but if there is opposition to their election, their names are simply postponed indefinitely. The Club possesses no records of those years except the Candidates Book.

[3] Wilde's dots. Henley's first collection of poems, *A Book of Verses*, had been published some months earlier (the British Museum copy is stamped 25 May 88). Wilde's review eventually appeared in the December issue of the *Woman's World*. It was reprinted in *Reviews*.

[4] Alfred Gibbons (d. 1900) was the editor of the *Lady's Pictorial*, which he had founded in 1880.

224

charmed I am by them. You have seen the Young King just as I hoped you would see him, and made him by delicate line and graceful design the most winsome and fascinating lad possible. I thank you very much for your beautiful and poetic work, and I can only hope that I may again have you to illustrate some story of mine. Crane, whom I admire very much, is always haunted by a touch of formal mannerism: you have perfect freedom and grace in all you do. Believe me, very sincerely yours

OSCAR WILDE

To Robert Ross[1]
MS. Marshall

[*Circa 13 October 1888*]   *16 Tite Street*
My dear Bobbie, I congratulate you. University life will suit you admirably, though I shall miss you in town. Enclosed is the praise of the Philistines. Are you in College or lodgings? I hope in College; it is much nicer. Do you know Oscar Browning? You will find him everything that is kind and pleasant.

I have been speaking at Stratford about Shakespeare, but in spite of that enjoyed my visit immensely. My reception was semi-royal, and the volunteers played God Save the Queen in my honour.[2] Ever yours

OSCAR WILDE

To A. J. Hipkins[3]
MS. B.M.

15 October 1888   Woman's World, *La Belle Sauvage*
Dear Sir, I have read with very great interest your fascinating article in

[1] Robert Baldwin Ross (1869–1918) was a Canadian. His grandfather Robert Baldwin was the first Prime Minister of Upper Canada; his father John Ross Attorney General. At the age of two, after the death of his father, he was brought to England by his mother to be educated. His schooling is unchronicled, but on 13 October 1888 he went up to King's College, Cambridge, as an undergraduate, to read History. Although he rowed in the college second boat, he was quickly in trouble for publishing in undergraduate periodicals some highly critical remarks about the election of college Fellows, was thrown into the Fountain, contracted pneumonia and left Cambridge abruptly in 1889 (see "Robert Ross at King's" by Bruce Dickins in the *Cambridge Review* of 23 January 1960). He then became a literary journalist and art-critic. He first met Wilde in 1886. For details of his later career and correspondence, see *Robert Ross: Friend of Friends*, edited by Margery Ross (1952).

[2] Wilde had spoken at Stratford on 10 October, proposing the health of his old friend Lord Ronald Gower (see note 3, p. 14) at the unveiling of Gower's statue of Shakespeare and four of his characters in the gardens of the Memorial Theatre.

[3] Alfred James Hipkins (1828–1903) was on the Council of the Royal College of Music, worked in Broadwood's piano business, and wrote much about such matters. His contribution to the *Century Guild Hobby Horse* of October 1888 was "On Some Obsolete Musical Instruments." Nothing of his appeared in the *Woman's World*. None of this letter is in Wilde's hand. It is written in copperplate on headed paper and was either Messrs Cassell's official copy or the original dictated but not signed by Wilde.

the *Hobby Horse* of this month and should be very much obliged if you would write a somewhat similar article for my magazine that could be illustrated.

The article need not be more than 2500 words in length and it would add greatly to its charm if you would make a selection of some old musical instruments, either spinets or viols, that could be reproduced. South Kensington has I know some and others might be got out of French books such as "Delacroix."[1] We might also have for the frontispiece of the magazine an engraving of a good Jan Steen or any other picture you might care to select.

If you think it would be advisable to have two articles, one on the spinet and the other on the lute and viol, I should be very pleased to count you among my contributors. I remain, yours faithfully   OSCAR WILDE

To John Williams[2]
MS. Gentry

[*Postmark 19 October 1888*]   *16 Tite Street*

Dear Mr Williams, I hope that the Board will authorise my closing with Tillotson for Mrs Burnett's story: it is a very pretty picturesque thing, and her name would do a great deal of good to the magazine.[3] Will you kindly tell them how very anxious I am to have it, especially as, under the new regime, most of the articles will be written by regular contributors whose names are not of much value, though their work will be very good. I find that without a staff of some kind a magazine with special illustrated articles cannot get on. Believe me, truly yours   OSCAR WILDE

I send you a little leaflet about my fairy tales.

To Wemyss Reid
MS. Gentry

[? *October 1888*][4]   *16 Tite Street*

Dear Mr Reid, I have read the report of the editor,[5] and must say that I am quite in accordance with him on nearly every point. I am, however,

---

[1] Probably a reference to Paul Lacroix, French scholar and littérateur (1806–84), whose *Les Arts au Moyen Age et à l'époque de la Renaissance* (1868) contained illustrations of early musical instruments.

[2] Assistant chief editor of Cassell's for some years before 1888; chief editor 1888–91.

[3] Mrs Frances Hodgson Burnett, novelist and dramatist (1849–1924), had scored a huge success with *Little Lord Fauntleroy* (1886) and was now in much demand. She never contributed to the *Woman's World*. Tillotson & Son Ltd, the owners of the *Bolton Evening News* (founded 1867), for many years ran an agency for syndicating serial fiction in the national and provincial press.

[4] Someone has pencilled "June '89" on the original, but it seems likely to have been written earlier.   [5] John Williams.

strongly of opinion that the first thing necessary is to reduce the price of the magazine to sixpence or sevenpence; at present it is too dear.

With regard to my own notes, I think that it would be better to have four pages of paragraphs on current topics every month from the pen of some well known woman such as Mrs Fenwick-Miller. There are many things in which women are interested about which a man really cannot write; and the commercial value of such notes should, I fancy, be considerable. I mention Mrs Fenwick-Miller as her notes in the *London News* are so admirable.[1]

With regard to the serial, I quite agree with the editor: short stories would be much better. In fact the editor's report seems to me quite admirable in every respect, except as regards my own notes. Literary subjects are the only subjects on which I care to write, and even in this sphere I have always felt myself hampered by my name being attached to the article: criticism of contemporary work should always be anonymous.

Should the price of the magazine be reduced, and its tone altered, in the sense of more prominence being given to distinctly feminine subjects, on the lines suggested by the editor, I think that it should turn out a great success. I need hardly say that my best endeavour will be directed to making it so. I remain, truly yours   OSCAR WILDE

To Felix Moscheles[2]
MS. Princeton

[? *October 1888*]   *16 Tite Street*

My dear Moscheles, Thank you so much for your charming present. I have read the letters with the greatest pleasure and they certainly reveal a most fascinating artistic nature. It seems to have been a beautiful nature from the human side of things too, and the friendship with your father is a most pleasant thing to read of. One thing strikes me forcibly as I read the volume, and that is that music has no subject matter; the letters might have been written in any century. Friendship and art are its only themes.

Do come back soon. We all miss you and your wife, to whom we send our kindest remembrances and regards. Sincerely yours   OSCAR WILDE

To Llewellyn Roberts[3]
MS. R.L.F.

[*October 1888*]   *16 Tite Street*

My dear Roberts, Thank you very much for the form of application: it is

---

[1] Mrs Fenwick-Miller (see p. 208) wrote the notes in the Ladies' Column of the *Illustrated London News* from 1886 to 1918.

[2] Artist (1833–1917). He translated and edited *Letters of Felix Mendelssohn to Ignaz and Charlotte Moscheles* (1888). The British Museum copy is stamped 6 October, and I have dated this letter accordingly.

[3] Secretary of the Royal Literary Fund. At their meeting in November 1888 the

quite right as it is for a literary woman. Could you send me a list of your council and supporters, as I wish to get hold of some good names? Very truly yours   OSCAR WILDE

To Llewellyn Roberts
MS. R.L.F.

[*October 1888*]   *16 Tite Street*

Dear Roberts, Thank you very much for the Report, but is there not one for 1888? Or is it not out yet? I want to see who exactly are the people before whom all applications come, and by whom they are considered.

I fear I am giving you a great deal of trouble. Very truly yours
                                                           OSCAR WILDE

To Theodore Watts
MS. Cortés

[? *October 1888*]   *16 Tite Street*

My dear Watts, Thank you for your kind letter, and tell Swinburne how gratified my mother is at his prompt and generous response to her request. I hope to be able to get my mother on the Civil List, but it takes a long time and there are many applicants, though few I think with my mother's claims.[1]

Wednesday is our day. You will always be most welcome if you come. I want to talk to you about a lot of things from the moon down to Henley, my last pet lunatic and hers. Ever yours   OSCAR WILDE

To Edward Dowden[2]
MS. Dublin

[*October 1888*]   *16 Tite Street*

Dear Professor Dowden, I write to ask you to do my mother a favour. For the last seven years her jointure, which is entirely fixed on a small

---

Committee of the Fund awarded Lady Wilde a grant of £100. Her sponsors included Swinburne, Mahaffy, Lords Lytton and Spencer, Lord Chief Justice Coleridge, Sir Theodore and Lady Martin, Sir George Otto Trevelyan, Sir John Lubbock, Professors A. H. Sayce and Edward Dowden. Gladstone's letter refusing to sign the memorial is dated 1 November 1888, so I have dated this letter accordingly.

[1] On 24 May 1890 Lady Wilde was awarded a Civil List Pension of £70 a year. Swinburne was again one of her sponsors (together with Lord Lytton and Sir Theodore Martin), so this letter may refer to that occasion rather than the appeal to the Royal Literary Fund.

[2] Irish scholar and critic (1843–1913), editor and biographer of Shelley, Professor of English Literature in Dublin University from 1867.

Irish property, has been unpaid, and as the widow of a literary man and a writer herself she has determined to apply to the Royal Literary Fund. She would [*The rest of this letter is missing*]

To Edward Dowden

MS. Harvard

[*October 1888*]   *16 Tite Street*

My dear Dowden, My mother is very much gratified by your kind letter, and by your readiness in signing the memorial. I am trying to get her name added to the Civil List, and have some hopes of success.

Am I mistaken? or did you in an article some time ago mention Pope's lines "O thou great Anna ... etc."[1] as an example of the pronunciation of the word tea = "tay" in Anne's reign? Would it not be possible that "obey" was pronounced = "obēe" as in 'obeisance,' 'obleege' and other words? The rhymes in the passage are so loose, and so lacking in any real correspondence of sound, that I do not see why Pope should not have rhymed obey = "obay" to tea = "tee." But is it impossible that obey was pronounced = obee? The early pronunciation of tea seemed to have been dissyllabic, = tëa, so I find it in the advertisement of an old newspaper, and this could have changed more easily into "tea" (*tee*) than into "tay." The point is quite a small one, but I know you like small points; so do I. But perhaps the article was not yours? If so, pay no attention to my letter. Believe me, truly yours   OSCAR WILDE

To A. G. Ross[2]

MS. Private

[*October 1888*]   *16 Tite Street*

Dear Ross, Henley writes to me that his mother is so ill that he will not be able to see us on Saturday night. So we will have to put off our expedition to the Chiswick poet. I have just finished a review of his poems for my own magazine. When it appears he will roar like the Bull of Bashan, though I think it is very complimentary.

The notice of *The Happy Prince* in the *Saturday*, which I only saw yesterday, fully explains Walter Pollock's guilty and agitated manner at

---

[1] Here thou, Great ANNA! whom three realms obey,
Dost sometimes counsel take—and sometimes tea.
The Rape of the Lock, canto 3, ll. 7–8.

[2] Alexander Galt Ross (1860–1927), elder brother of Robert Ross. A founder and secretary of the Society of Authors. Accompanied Rider Haggard to Iceland in 1888. After a brief period of literary work he became a partner in a bill-broking firm. It has been suggested that this letter is to Robert Ross, but Wilde was already writing to him as "Dear Bobbie" (see p. 225) and he had just gone up to Cambridge. Moreover Alec Ross was a close friend of W. H. Pollock (see note 1, p. 168).

the Savile.[1] No wonder he looked pale and, with the reckless courage of despair, invited me to contribute largely and frequently to the pages of his wicked and Philistine paper. Ever yours   OSCAR WILDE

To W. E. Henley

MS. Morgan

[? October 1888]   16 Tite Street

My dear Henley, I am so sorry to hear about your trouble. All poets love their mothers, and as I worship mine I can understand how you feel. I hope there is still some chance.[2] Ever yours affectionately   OSCAR

To Richard Le Gallienne

MS. Princeton

[Postmark 25 October 1888]   16 Tite Street

My dear Le Gallienne, The lovely little book has just arrived, and I must send you a line to thank you for so charming a gift. Written by your own hand it has the very quintessence of grace and beauty, and the page on which I find my own name set daintily in dainty music is a real delight to me, for I think often of the young poet who came here so wonderfully and so strangely, and whose memory is always with me.[3]

I hope to see you in London soon. I often think of your visit. Tomorrow

---

[1] See note 1, p. 168. The anonymous review of *The Happy Prince*, which appeared in the *Saturday Review* on 20 October 1888, was in fact written by A. G. Ross himself.

[2] Henley's mother died on 25 October 1888, aged sixty.

[3] Le Gallienne had visited Wilde again in June 1888 and this manuscript volume of poems contained one commemorating the occasion (MS. Whittington-Egan):

With Oscar Wilde
A Summer-day in June '88

With Oscar Wilde, a summer-day
Passed like a yearning kiss away,
The kiss wherewith so long ago
That little maid who loved me so
Called me her Lancelot—for aye!
Called me who whilom did but pray
To touch her rippling gown of gray.
Such accolade that day to know
            With Oscar Wilde.

That little maid has gone the way
Of all sweet flowers, alack-a-day!
And whatso'er shall come or go
She comes no more; but summer-glow
May find me once again—(O! say!)—
            With Oscar Wilde.

230

I hope to read your book over. It shall be a day of gold and marked with a white pearl. But the singer should be here also. Bother space and time! they spoil life by allowing such a thing as distance. Ever yours

OSCAR WILDE

To W. E. Gladstone

MS. B.M.

[*2 November 1888*]¹   *16 Tite Street*

Dear Mr Gladstone, I have to thank you for your very kind letter. I quite understand how difficult, how impossible indeed it is for you to lend your name to memorials of this kind, as many claims must be made upon it, and in the present day, as in olden times, everyone calls upon Achilles.

I can only assure you that though the absence of your name is, I will admit, a disappointment, it does not in the smallest iota alter the deep admiration that I along with my countrymen feel for the one English statesman who has understood us, who has sympathised with us, whom we claim now as our leader, and who, we know well, will lead us to the grandest and justest political victory of this age. I remain, dear Mr Gladstone, most faithfully yours   OSCAR WILDE

To Gerald Maxwell²

MS. Texas

[*Postmark 2 November 1888*]   *16 Tite Street*

My dear Gerald, Thanks so much for your letter. I was very sorry that I was not able to come down to Bournemouth, but I am terribly busy at present. You seem to have thrilled the great Bournemouth school of criticism. Will you send me your dates, and if you are nearer town I will certainly come and see you play.

Willie came up from the forest yesterday. We dined together, and played euchre afterwards, my skill enabling me to retire at midnight with seven shillings in my pocket to the good.

I am afraid little Coleman has not made the public rush to *The Dean's Daughter* but it is a capital play, and Olga Nethersole is quite wonderful.³

Remember me to Tryan, and believe me, truly yours   OSCAR WILDE

¹ So dated by Gladstone. See note 3, p. 227.
² Actor and dramatic critic (1862–1930). Son of Henry Maxwell and Miss Braddon (author of *Lady Audley's Secret* and many other novels) and elder brother of W. B. (Willie) Maxwell (1866–1928), who was also a prolific novelist.
³ *The Dean's Daughter*, by Sydney Grundy and F. C. Phillips, was produced at the St James's Theatre on 13 October 1888, with Lewis Waller, Allan Aynesworth and Olga Nethersole in the cast. George Coleman was the business manager of the theatre. Olga Nethersole, actress and manager (1867–1951), was an Australian.

To Alice Corkran[1]

[*Circa November 1888*]   *16 Tite Street*

My dear Alice, The non-appearance of the review makes no matter, and my letter was merely a bit of nonsense. I think I have got quite as much praise as is good for me, as you will see from the enclosed leaflet, and America has exhausted itself in complimentary adjectives. I have been reading your charming and clever story, *Meg's Friend,* and have said a few words about it in my Christmas number, which is now being printed. You have certainly a most sympathetic touch, and a very graceful style.

I am hard at work at some new stories, which I think you will like. Why don't you send something to the *Woman's World*? I want an article on Spinets and Harpsichords, with references to the South Kensington collection, for illustrations. Love to your mother. Ever sincerely yours

OSCAR WILDE

To James Nicol Dunn[2]
MS. Hyde (H. M.)

[*November–December 1888*]   *16 Tite Street*

My dear Sir, It will give me great pleasure to write for you, but as I am very busy I think it would be better not to advertise my name as a contributor. Besides I hear your paper is anti-Home Rule, and I am a most recalcitrant patriot.

As regards subject, my work at present is chiefly reviewing; any books you send me I will be happy to do for you. Would you like an article on Alexander Smith? He is one of the Scotch poets whom I admire very much, and he is, I fear, forgotten.[3]

I would also like to write on the Scotch poets between Chaucer and Shakespeare. They are so Keats-like.

No doubt other subjects will suggest themselves. In the meantime I send you a poem. If you don't have room for it kindly send it back. Truly yours   OSCAR WILDE

To W. E. Henley[4]

[*November–December 1888*]   *16 Tite Street*

My dear Henley, I am charmed you like my article. I tried to express as

---

[1] Author and journalist (d. 1916). Lived for many years with the novelist Richard Whiteing. Wilde's brief note on *Meg's Friend* appeared in the *Woman's World* for January 1889, but Alice Corkran did not contribute to the paper. The text of this letter is taken from *Bruno's Weekly* of 16 December 1916.

[2] Scottish journalist (1856–1919), managing editor of Henley's *Scots Observer,* which first appeared on 24 November. (He was later editor of the *Morning Post.*) The poem Wilde sent him was "Symphony in Yellow," which he declined. It first appeared in the *Centennial Magazine* (Sydney) in February 1889, and was reprinted in *Poems* (1908).   [3] Cf. note 2, p. 504.

[4] Text from *W. E. Henley* by John Connell (1949).

nicely as I could my feelings about the Marsyas of the early part of your book, and the Apollo of the latter, to me the lovelier portion.[1] I hope you have read what I say about poor Sharp. I think I have been fair all round— as fair as an Irishman with a temperament ever wants to be. I am dining with Willie Richmond[2] at Hammersmith on Saturday, but if I can come in late will try to do so. I have sent Dunn a wicked little symphony in yellow, suggested by seeing an omnibus (yellow omnibus) crawl across Blackfriars Bridge one foggy day about a week ago. He expresses himself "quite charmed" but says, not unwisely, that he is uncertain about publishing poetry! So I have produced my effect. Ever yours OSCAR

To W. E. Henley

MS. Morgan

[? *December 1888*]

Quite right, my dear "Marsyas et Apollo;" to learn how to write English prose I have studied the prose of France. I am charmed that *you* recognise it: that shows I have succeeded. I am also charmed that no one else does: that shows I have succeeded also.

Yes! Flaubert is my master, and when I get on with my translation of the *Tentation* I shall be Flaubert II, *Roi par grâce de Dieu*, and I hope something else beyond.[3]

Where do you think I am not so good? I want very much to know. Of course it is, to me, a new *genre*. Ever yours OSCAR

To W. E. Henley

MS. Morgan

[? *December 1888*]   *16 Tite Street*

My dear Henley, Your distinction is admirable. Flaubert did not write French prose, but the prose of a great artist who happened to be French. As for your critics, when a book has so much of life and so much of beauty

---

[1] In his long-delayed review of Henley's *A Book of Verses* (see p. 224) Wilde had written: "To me there is more of the cry of Marsyas than of the singing of Apollo in the early poems of Mr Henley's volume, 'Rhymes and Rhythms in Hospital' as he calls them. But it is impossible to deny their power." Marsyas was a mortal who challenged Apollo to a musical competition and was flayed alive for his pains. References to this myth recur in most of Wilde's writings. Later in the same article Wilde criticised severely William Sharp's *Romantic Ballads and Poems of Phantasy*.

[2] William Blake Richmond (1842–1921), painter. Son of George Richmond R.A. (1809–96), who was a friend of Blake. Slade Professor at Oxford 1878–83, R.A. 1895, knighted 1897. Designed the mosaics in St Paul's.

[3] In an undated letter to Alfred Nutt, sold at Sotheby's on 17 March 1916, Wilde wrote: "Do you think (this is private) that a translation of that amazing book of Flaubert's, *La Tentation de St Antoine*, would be a success? I want to do it." See also p. 715.

as yours has, it must inevitably appeal differently to different temperaments.

Beauty of form produces not one effect alone, but many effects. Surely you do not think that criticism is like the answer to a sum? The richer the work of art the more diverse are the true interpretations. There is not one answer only, but many answers. I pity that book on which critics are agreed. It must be a very obvious and shallow production. Congratulate yourself on the diversity of *contemporary* tongues. The worst of posterity is that it has but one voice. *À vous*   OSCAR

To T. J. Cobden-Sanderson[1]
MS. Morgan

3 December 1888   Woman's World, *La Belle Sauvage*

Dear Mr Sanderson, Thank you very much for your letter. I see now how my misapprehension arose. Will you take a noble revenge and write me a short article for my magazine on Bookbinding as a Craft?

I know that your lecture is to be reprinted, but as you said little in it about decoration itself, there would be ample room for an article confining itself specially to that side of bookbinding. The article need not be more than 3000 words in length but I should like to reproduce some of your own work and any fine bindings you may care to select at the South Kensington or British Museums.

The photographer of the Art Department here is quite accustomed to photographing delicate works of art.

About five specimens would be quite sufficient, and if you will allow me to include amongst them your *Atalanta* I should esteem it an honour.[2] Believe me, yours faithfully   OSCAR WILDE

P.S. I had an admirable article lately by Mr A. C. Bickley on "Embroidered Books," but have had none at all dealing with leather binding.

To James Nicol Dunn
MS. Hyde (H. M.)

[? *December 1888*]   *16 Tite Street*

Dear Mr Dunn, If you are *not* going to publish poetry in your paper will you kindly return my little "Symphony in Yellow" as I have been asked to send it elsewhere. Truly yours   OSCAR WILDE

[1] English printer and binder of fine books (1840–1922). Founded the Doves Press 1900. His lecture on bookbinding, given at the Arts and Crafts Exhibition in the New Gallery on 22 November 1888, had been anonymously reviewed by Wilde in next day's *Pall Mall Gazette*. A. C. Bickley's article appeared in the November 1888 issue of the *Woman's World*, to which Cobden-Sanderson never contributed.

[2] At the Exhibition, Cobden-Sanderson showed examples of his binding, including a copy of Swinburne's *Atalanta in Calydon* (1865), which is now in the British Museum.

To Henry Irving

MS. Irving

[? *30 December 1888*]   *16 Tite Street*

My dear Irving, My best congratulations on your magnificent production, and your magnificent performance. The murder-scene and the banquet-scene remain in my memory as two of the finest, most imaginative bits of acting I have ever seen.[1] They were instances of the highest *style*, and of the most subtle psychological insight; and the true temper of tragedy never left you all through the play. It was a really wonderful night of expectation, and wonder, and true artistic delight.

With best wishes for a great success, sincerely yours   OSCAR WILDE

To Arthur Clifton[2]

MS. Texas

8 January 1889   Woman's World, *La Belle Sauvage*

Dear Sir, I have to thank you for your pretty Roundel, which I hope to use in my March number.

A proof shall be sent to you before we go to press. Yours faithfully
                                                        OSCAR WILDE

To Violet Fane

MS. Clark

[*Postmark 15 January 1889*]   *16 Tite Street*

Dear Mrs Singleton, My February number went to press a fortnight ago, and I fear that in March a poem on the New Year would, as you suggest, look positively *unpunctual*.

I would have written before, but I have only just returned from Deepdene,[3] where I spent Sunday.

---

[1] Irving's revival of *Macbeth* opened at the Lyceum on 29 December 1888, with Ellen Terry as Lady Macbeth. Graham Robertson records Wilde's saying of this production: "Judging from the banquet, Lady Macbeth seems an economical housekeeper and evidently patronises local industries for her husband's clothes and the servants' liveries, but she takes care to do all her own shopping in Byzantium."

[2] Arthur Bellamy Clifton (1862–1932), son of the Professor of Experimental Philosophy at Oxford, was a solicitor who gradually became an art-dealer. In 1898, together with John Fothergill (see note 2, p. 623), he started the Carfax Gallery in Ryder Street and acted as business manager. In 1900 Robert Ross and More Adey joined the gallery, which exhibited early works by Conder, John, Max Beerbohm, Sickert and Rothenstein. This letter, which was addressed to the Albemarle Club, is not in Wilde's hand (see note 4, p. 225). "Roundel" by Arthur Marvell (a pseudonym of Clifton's) duly appeared in the March 1889 issue of the *Woman's World*.

[3] An eighteenth-century mansion near Dorking in Surrey which had been inherited, together with its art collections and the famous Hope diamond, by Lord Henry Francis Pelham-Clinton Hope (1866–1941), younger son of the sixth Duke of Newcastle. He succeeded his brother as eighth Duke in 1928.

I am sorry I did not see you at the Private View.[1] The Jacobites in the afternoon were rather dingy. Truly yours   OSCAR WILDE

Very nice of you to like my article in the *Nineteenth Century*.[2] It is meant to bewilder the masses by its fantastic form; *au fond* it is of course serious.

To W. H. Pollock[3]

MS. Butler

[? *January 1889*]   *16 Tite Street*

My dear Pollock, I am very pleased indeed that you like my article: the public so soon vulgarise any artistic idea that one gives them that I was determined to put my new views on art, and particularly on the relations of art and history, in a form that they could not understand, but that would be understood by the few who, like yourself, have a quick artistic instinct. I cannot however agree with you about your critic. If he admired my stories he certainly concealed his love, and I claim that any imaginative or fanciful writer can make nightingales build in any tree under heaven, or in any tree that heaven knows not, for that matter. It was an irresistible opportunity—*riposte pour riposte*. Besides I don't mind telling you (in the *strictest confidence*) that I thought that the holm-oak tree was to the nightingale what the Albany is to a man of letters. Very truly yours

OSCAR WILDE

To W. L. Courtney[4]

MS. Johnston

[? *January 1889*]   *16 Tite Street*

My dear Courtney, Thank you very much for your admirable little book

[1] Of the Winter Exhibition of the Royal Academy on 5 January.

[2] "The Decay of Lying," which appeared in the issue for January 1889. It was reprinted, revised, in *Intentions* (1891).

[3] See note 1, p. 168. In the *Saturday Review*'s notice of *The Happy Prince* (see note 1, p. 230) the story "The Nightingale and the Rose" was described as "the only place in the book where his artistic sense had stumbled a little along with his natural history." In "The Decay of Lying" Wilde wrote:

No doubt there will always be critics who, like a certain writer in the *Saturday Review*, will gravely censure the teller of fairy-tales for his defective knowledge of natural history, who will measure imaginative work by their own lack of any imaginative faculty, and will hold up their ink-stained hands in horror if some honest gentleman, who has never been farther than the yew-trees of his own garden, pens a fascinating book of travels like Sir John Mandeville, or, like great Raleigh, writes a whole history of the world, without knowing anything whatsoever about the past.

[4] William Leonard Courtney (1850–1928) author and journalist. Edited *Fortnightly Review* from 1894. Contributed an article on "The Women Benefactors of Oxford" to the *Woman's World* of June 1888. The prefatory note to his short *Life of John Stuart Mill* is dated November 1888 and the British Museum copy is stamped 20 December 1888, but the title-page is dated 1889, so I have presumed January publication.

on Mill, which I have read with great pleasure. It seems to me to be excellently done, and its conciseness and directness are excellent examples for others to follow. The whole account of Mrs Taylor (who I suppose is the representative of the *Seductive* Method in thought) interests me very much.[1] As for Mill as a thinker—a man who knew nothing of Plato and Darwin gives me very little. His reputation is curious to me. I gain nothing, I have gained nothing from him—an arid, dry man with moods of sentiment—a type that is poor, and, I fancy, common. But Darwinism has of course shattered many reputations besides his, and I hope that individual liberty has had its day, for a time. His later religious views show an astounding silliness and sentimentality. But your book is admirable. Many thanks for it. Ever yours   OSCAR WILDE

To Amelie Rives Chanler[2]

MS. Boston

[*January 1889*]   *16 Tite Street*

Dear Mrs Chanler, I send you my fairy tales and a copy of the *Nineteenth Century*.[3] The former are an attempt to mirror modern life in a form remote from reality—to deal with modern problems in a mode that is ideal and not imitative: I hope you will like them: they are, of course, slight and fanciful, and written, not for children, but for childlike people from eighteen to eighty!

The article is written only for artistic temperaments: the public are not allowed a chance of comprehension, so you will know what I mean by it.

When may I call and see you? Sincerely yours   OSCAR WILDE

To Kate Terry Lewis

TS. Holland

[*January 1889*]   *16 Tite Street*

My dear Mrs Lewis, Thank you so much for your charming and welcome letter. I am delighted you like the article: underneath the fanciful form it hides some truths, or perhaps some half-truths, about art, which I think require to be put forward, and of which some are, I think, quite new, and none the worse for that. I have blown my trumpet against the gate of dullness, and I hope some shaft has hit *Robert Elsmere* between the joints

[1] Mrs John Taylor was the lady with whom Mill (1806–73) fell in love at first sight in 1831, married in 1851 and mourned in the dedication to his essay *On Liberty* (1859). The Deductive Method was part of Mill's system of Logic.

[2] Amelie Rives (1863–1945), American novelist, playwright and poet, married (1) John Armstrong Chanler of New York (2) Prince Pierre Troubetzkoy.

[3] Containing "The Decay of Lying."

237

of his nineteenth edition.[1] It was delightful work writing the article, and it is equally delightful to know that Lady Betty[2] enjoyed it. Ever yours

OSCAR WILDE

To Violet Fane

MS. Clark

[? *January 1889*]   *16 Tite Street*

Dear Mrs Singleton, Miss Wynne's "Sea-gulls" is pretty and full of promise, but not finished, not perfected, too lax in metre, too vague in metrical treatment, too spasmodic.[3]

Let her try to write a short poem as good as the first half, and I will look at it. But she must remember that in the case of loose metres we require the most wonderful music.

I always suggest the sonnet-form to young poets: it is admirable as an exercise and trial of strength.

We miss you so much in town. Do come back soon and delight us. Will you tell Chapman and Hall to send me your book and I will review it.[4] Believe me, truly yours   OSCAR WILDE

To W. Graham Robertson

MS. Preston

[*Postmark 28 January 1889*]   *16 Tite Street*

My dear Graham, Come and dine here on Wednesday night at 7.30. I have asked Arthur Clifton. We will see *Dr Cupid* when you come back.[5] Ever yours   OSCAR WILDE

---

[1] In "The Decay of Lying" Wilde wrote of Mrs Humphry Ward's best-selling novel (3 vols, February 1888): "*Robert Elsmere* is of course a masterpiece—a masterpiece of the *genre ennuyeux*, the one form of literature that the English people seem to thoroughly enjoy. A thoughtful young friend of ours once told us that it reminded him of the sort of conversation that goes on at a meat tea in the house of a serious Nonconformist family, and we can quite believe it."

[2] Almost certainly Lady Elizabeth Edith (1867–1942), eldest daughter of the first Earl of Lytton (see note 1, p. 293). She married (1887) Gerald William Balfour (1853–1945), who succeeded his brother Arthur as second Earl Balfour 1930.

[3] Frances Wynne, an Irish girl, died in 1893 at the age of twenty-seven. "Seagulls" was included in her only book of poems, *Whisper!* (1890).

[4] Wilde reviewed Violet Fane's novel *The Story of Helen Davenant* (3 vols, 1889) in the February 1889 issue of the *Woman's World*.

[5] *That Doctor Cupid*, a fantastic comedy by Robert Buchanan, opened at the Vaudeville Theatre on 14 January 1889, with Cyril Maude and Winifred Emery in the cast.

To Walter Hamilton[1]

[*Postmark 29 January 1889*]   *16 Tite Street*

I have never collected the parodies of my poetry. Collecting contemporaneous things is like trying to hold froth in a sieve ... As most of my poems are long and lyrical, they have not, I fancy, been good models ... Parody, which is the Muse with her tongue in her cheek, has always amused me; but it requires a light touch, ... and, oddly enough, a love of the poet whom it caricatures. One's disciples can parody one—nobody else.

To Minnie Simpson
MS. Aberystwyth

[*January–February 1889*]   *16 Tite Street*

Dear Mrs Simpson, I will ask Cassell if they would undertake the publication of "Sergent."[2] What length would it be? About a small volume, I suppose?

Your article reads charmingly in the *Woman's World*. I am much obliged to you for it.

Any *short* article from your pen would be very welcome at any time. I prefer subjects that admit of illustration, but that is not essential at all: about *3000* words is the length I like. Can you suggest a subject?

I hope you are all well at home, and I remain, truly yours

OSCAR WILDE

To the Rev. T. Walker[3]
MS. Princeton

[*Postmark 6 February 1889*]   *16 Tite Street*

My dear Sir, I have to thank you for your courtesy in sending me the two epigrams, which have interested me very much. I fear that we have no authority in the Latin of either the golden or the silver age for applying such a term as *carmen* or *poema* to a woman, in the sense in which we talk of a beautiful person as a poem, but I do not see how the epigram could be otherwise rendered, and thank you for allowing me to see your versions. Believe me, yours faithfully   OSCAR WILDE

[1] English writer and book-collector (1844–99). His book *The Aesthetic Movement in England* (1882) discussed Wilde's early life and theories, and his *Parodies of English and American Authors* (6 vols, 1884–89), for which he was now collecting material, included several parodies of Wilde's work. The text of this fragment is taken from Mason (p. 93), quoting Glaenzer.   [2] See note 2, p. 201.

[3] This letter is addressed to the Oxford Union Society, Oxford, and the only possible recipient seems to be the Rev. Thomas Walker (d. 1918), who was an undergraduate of Queen's College 1872–76, a master at Tonbridge School 1884–1901, and from 1903 Vicar of Hougham, near Dover, but I can find no record of his having published anything.

To J. S. Little

MS. Berg

[*6 February 1889*][1]   *16 Tite Street*

My dear Little, Thank you very much for your book,[2] which I have read
with great interest, though it stops where the tragedy begins to develop.
I want to know more about Tim and Eva, and care less for the jealous
husband. The style is I think better than anything you have done yet. I
don't like the term "upholstery" (page 2)—*upholstery of the sixteenth
century* seems to be a wrong phrase—there is no such thing, besides; we
have tapestries of the time and hangings, but upholstery? No. Upon the
other hand "walls and terraces of fog . . ." (p. 130) is *delightful*, and as a
whole the book shows a great stride onward, on which I warmly congratulate you, and with best wishes for its success remain very truly yours

OSCAR WILDE

To Alice Meynell

MS. Sowerby

[*February 1889*]   *16 Tite Street*

Dear Mrs Meynell, Henley had already sent me the article, though without
telling me the name of the author.[3] I was very much interested in it, and
am delighted to know that it is from your graceful and clever pen. Yes:
there is super-human art as there is infra-human nature, but the highest
art is for our service, as the grandest nature is for her own service.

The Tower of Babel, that dreadful structure by whose monstrous walls
the German language was first heard, was the beginning of the art that did
not accept our proportions—a lurid origin!

I am much pleased that you enjoyed my article, and remain, truly yours

OSCAR WILDE

To A. G. Ross

MS. Ross (P.W.)

[? *Early 1889*]   *16 Tite Street*

Dear Ross, I have just finished "Mr Latimer:" it is admirable—just one
of the few, the very few stories that Hoffmann forgot to write.[4] I always

---

[1] So dated by recipient.   [2] Little's novel *Doubt* (1889).

[3] Mrs Meynell's essay "The Unit of the World," in which she refers to Wilde and
"The Decay of Lying," appeared anonymously in Henley's *Scots Observer* for
2 February 1889. It was reprinted in her book *The Rhythm of Life* (1893).

[4] "An Episode in the life of Mr Latimer" was a story in *A Picture's Secret* by
W. H. Pollock (1883). Ernst Theodor Wilhelm Hoffmann (1776–1822) was a
German novelist and short-story writer of the Romantic school.

felt that Walter Pollock could do something as good, but I did not know that he had done anything as good.

If I can get Sarrazin[1] to come and dine on Wednesday, would you and Bobbie come too? We dine at 7.30. There will be no one else. Truly yours   OSCAR WILDE

To Marie-Anne de Bovet [2]
MS. Yale

[*Early 1889*]   16 Tite Street

Dear Madame de Bovet, I am quite charmed by your delicate and subtle article on "*L'Esthéticisme en Angleterre*," and thank you so much for sending it to me.

The admirable English are still much bewildered by "The Decay of Lying," but even here there are a few who can decipher its paradoxes. It is a pleasure for me to think that I am presented to Paris by so clever a pen as yours, and *je vous baise les mains*.

I look forward to seeing you in London soon, and remain, very truly yours   OSCAR WILDE

By a printer's error on p. 581, second line from the bottom, "Dickens" is put instead of "Charles Reade."

To Louise Chandler Moulton
MS. Congress

[? *March 1889*]   16 Tite Street

Your pen drops honey, my dear Poetess, and what you have written of me is charming. Thanks so much for it.[3]

Do come and have tea with us on Wednesday next, at five o'clock. Sincerely yours   OSCAR WILDE

[1] Gabriel Sarrazin, French critic (b. 1853), who wrote reports on French literature for the *Athenaeum* and had in 1885 published *Poètes Modernes en Angleterre*. He contributed an article on Georges Ohnet to the March 1889 issue of the *Woman's World*.

[2] French journalist and translator (1855–1943). According to Harris she "was a writer of talent and knew English uncommonly well; but in spite of masses of fair hair and vivacious eyes she was certainly very plain . . . When [Wilde] caught sight of her, he stopped short: seeing his astonishment, she cried to him in her quick, abrupt way:

'*N'est-ce pas, M. Wilde, que je suis la femme la plus laide de la France?*'
Bowing low, Oscar replied with smiling courtesy:
'*Du monde, Madame, du monde.*' "

[3] This may well refer to a notice of "The Decay of Lying," which Mrs Moulton published in the Boston *Sunday Herald* on 3 March 1889. In it she wrote, "Oscar Wilde is not one of those selfish and grudging friends who decline to take the trouble to romance for us. I recall him, in long English twilights, standing with his back to an early English fire, and wasting—oh, no, it was not wasted—on a little

241

To an Income-tax Inspector[1]

[? *April 1889*]   [*Woman's World, La Belle Sauvage*]

Sir, It was arranged last year that I should send in my income-tax return from Chelsea where I reside, as I am resigning my position here and will not be with Messrs Cassell after August. I think it would be better to continue that arrangement. I wish your notices were not so agitating and did not hold out such dreadful threats. A penalty of fifty pounds sounds like a relic of mediæval torture. Your obedient servant   OSCAR WILDE

To Richard Le Gallienne
MS. Clark

[*Postmark 16 April 1889*]   *16 Tite Street*

Thank you so much for the sonnet, which I greatly like; it is very subtle, and very sweet—one of your best things.[2] London, for all its gloom, is not killing but making the poet.[3]

The *Academy* article is really very clever, so lightly touched and yet so pungent. Thanks for it too.[4]

I go away for Easter—after that let us meet and make music. Ever yours   OSCAR WILDE

---

audience of two or three, such wit, such brightness, such waggish drollery, such merry exaggeration as, printed in a book, would make an unknown man's fortune. Prodigal and charming talker, with him there is no danger that romance will be strangled to death by realism."

[1] Text from *Cassell's Weekly*, 2 May 1923.

[2] The sonnet (MS. Whittington-Egan) reads:

> To Oscar Wilde, for his Fairy Tale in the *Paris Illustré*
> "The Birthday of the Little Princess"
> (of which he gave me the first MS.)

> As one, the secret lover of a queen,
> Watches her move within the people's eye,
> Hears their poor chatter as she passes by,
> And smiles to think of what his eyes have seen;
> The little room where Love did 'shut them in',
> The fragrant couch whereon they twain did lie,
> And rests his hand where on his heart doth die
> A bruisèd daffodil of last night's sin.

> So, Oscar, as I read your tale once more
> Here where a thousand eyes may read it too,
> I smile your own sweet 'secret smile' at those
> Who deem the outer petals of the rose
> The rose's heart—I who through grace of you
> Have known it for my own so long before.

[3] Le Gallienne had come to London at the beginning of the year to seek his literary fortune, and was now working as secretary to Wilson Barrett at the Princess Theatre, Oxford Street, to which this letter was addressed.   [4] Untraced.

To William Blackwood[1]

MS. Edinburgh

[*April 1889*]   *16 Tite Street*

Dear Sir, I remember reading some interesting articles on Shakespeare's Sonnets in *Blackwood*, and would be very pleased if you would care to publish a story on the subject of the Sonnets which I have written. It is called "The Portrait of Mr W. H." and contains an entirely new view on the subject of the identity of the young man to whom the sonnets are addressed. I will ask you to return me the manuscript in case you decide not to publish it. Truly yours   OSCAR WILDE

To W. Graham Robertson

MS. Preston

[*Postmark 11 May 1889*]   *16 Tite Street*

Do you really live at Sandhills, Witley?[2] Surely not Sandhills! You are made for olive-groves, and for meadows starred with white narcissi. I am sure this letter will be returned to me by the post office.

I have written to you at Rutland Gate to tell you how sorry I am you have missed Paris, and how much more sorry I am that I did not keep you to your promise. I should have loved to have been with you—Sandhills or no Sandhills.

I send this letter into the air! Will you ever get it? I suppose not. Ever yours   O. W.

To William Blackwood

MS. Edinburgh

[*18 May 1889*][3]   *16 Tite Street*

Dear Sir, Will you kindly let me know by return if you have received my manuscript.

I wrote to you some weeks ago to ask the question, but have received no answer. Pray let me hear from you at once. Faithfully yours

OSCAR WILDE[4]

---

[1] Scottish publisher and editor (1836–1912). Head of William Blackwood & Sons, Edinburgh, and editor of *Blackwood's Magazine* 1879–1912.

[2] In 1888 Graham Robertson and his mother had bought a house in this Surrey hamlet from William Allingham, the poet. They lived there for the rest of their lives. Mrs Robertson died in 1907.

[3] So dated by recipient.

[4] Blackwood answered from 45 George Street, Edinburgh, on 20 May:

Dear Sir, The manuscript of your story "The Portrait of Mr W. H." was duly received, but from your letter accompanying the manuscript, and which I enclose, you will see no answer was required from me until I wrote you whether I was able to publish it or not. Your story I am pleased to say is a most powerful

To William Blackwood

MS. Edinburgh

[*Circa 22 May 1889*]   *16 Tite Street*

Dear Sir, I am very pleased you like the story. Could it be published in your July part? I am anxious to have it out as soon as possible.

I should like to retain the copyright myself. Have you any objection to this? If so, what arrangement do you propose? Yours faithfully

OSCAR WILDE[1]

To William Blackwood

MS. Edinburgh

[*30 May 1889*][2]   *16 Tite Street*

Dear Sir, I will agree to your publishing my story in your new series of *Tales from Blackwood* after it has appeared in the Magazine. It would be very convenient to me if you would kindly send me a cheque for the story now. Faithfully yours   OSCAR WILDE[3]

---

and fascinating one, charmingly told, and the Shakespearean theory possesses much playful ingenuity. I have pleasure in accepting it for my Magazine, and shall endeavour to find an opening for it as soon as I can. Yours truly

WILLIAM BLACKWOOD

[1] Blackwood answered on 29 May:

Dear Sir, In reply to your enquiry as to when I may be able to use your story in the Magazine I am afraid my previous engagements for July will prevent my being able to include it in that number. But should I see a possibility of doing so I shall gladly endeavour to meet your wishes. With regard to the Copyright, *Maga's* honorarium is based on the understanding that the Copyright of articles is conveyed to the publishers for the usual period unless otherwise arranged. I have no objection however to make some such departure in your case and have no doubt we shall be able to arrange matters.

Would you have any objection to our using your "Portrait of Mr W. H." in our new series of *Tales from Blackwood*? The use of it in this way might be considered as an equivalent for the Copyright which would thus remain your property. Yours truly   WILLIAM BLACKWOOD

[2] So dated by recipient.

[3] Blackwood answered on 4 June:

Dear Sir, I am glad you are agreeable to my publishing your story "The Portrait of Mr W. H." in our new series of *Tales from Blackwood* after it has appeared in *Maga*. I am having it set up, and am endeavouring to arrange for using it in my July number.

As you are desirous of having the honorarium now, I have the pleasure of enclosing you cheque £25 in acknowledgement of it, which in the circumstances is somewhat beyond *Maga's* usual scale. The printers estimate it will run to about 18 pages, and I expect to send you proof in a few days. Yours truly

WILLIAM BLACKWOOD

Maga is slang for *Blackwood's Magazine*.

To William Blackwood

MS. Edinburgh

[*Circa 6 June 1889*]   *16 Tite Street*

My dear Sir, I have to acknowledge the receipt of your cheque for £25, for which accept my best thanks. I shall be glad to receive a proof as soon as convenient, as I will have to verify all my references very carefully. Faithfully yours   OSCAR WILDE

To William Blackwood

MS. Edinburgh

[*Circa 12 June 1889*][1]   *16 Tite Street*

Dear Sir, I enclose corrected proof of my story. As for a paragraph for the *Athenaeum* I think something of this kind would be quite sufficient:

> "The July number of *Blackwood* will contain a story by Mr Oscar Wilde on the subject of Shakespeare's sonnets. We hear that Mr Wilde will put forward an entirely new theory as to the identity of the mysterious Mr W. H. of the famous preface."

Yes: I see that the story is somewhat longer than you calculated when you sent me your cheque.

I am very much gratified at what you say about the story, and remain, faithfully yours   OSCAR WILDE

To Herbert Vivian[2]

26 *June 1889*   *16 Tite Street*

Dear Mr Vivian, "Good wine needs no bush"—at least somebody in

[1] In answer to Blackwood's letter of 10 June:

My dear Sir, The printers sent you off proof of "The Portrait of Mr W. H." on Friday evening. I hope it reached you in due course and that you will be able to return it to me corrected for press in two or three days, as I am arranging to use it in my July number. I think it reads extremely well in type, and I shall be very disappointed if it does not excite considerable interest amongst the press critics, as the story is powerfully told, and the working out of the Shakespearean theory full of playful ingenuity.

We must set some newspaper paragraphs afloat about it. Perhaps you could draw out an ingenious and attractive one for the *Athenaeum* and such like and send it to me? But you must not reveal too much in it.

I observe that the article runs to a couple of pages more than the printers calculated, so that I am still a little in your debt. Believe me, Yours very truly
                                                  WILLIAM BLACKWOOD

[2] Journalist and author of travel books (1865–1940). Mr Vyvyan Holland reports that in his whole life the only person who refused to shake hands with him on hearing that he was the son of Oscar Wilde was Herbert Vivian. The text of this letter is taken from the *Sun* of 17 November 1889.

Shakespeare says so,[1] and certainly good reminiscences require no preface. And did I really say I would write one? I don't think one at all necessary. As for indiscretions, pray be indiscreet. If I can help you by reviews I shall certainly do so. Sincerely yours   OSCAR WILDE

To William Blackwood

MS. Edinburgh

[7 July 1889][2]   Tite Street

Dear Sir, I don't think that my story will really do for republishing in Stories from Maga: it is too literary.

Will you compromise and bring it out in a special volume of essays and studies by me? As a frontispiece we will have an etching of the fictitious portrait of Mr W. H. The other studies will be things that have appeared in the Nineteenth Century and the Fortnightly,[3] and that excited much interest.

You mentioned after you sent me my cheque that the story was longer than you had calculated for. Are you not a little in my debt? Truly yours
OSCAR WILDE[4]

[1] Rosalind in the Epilogue to As You Like It.

[2] So dated by recipient.

[3] "The Decay of Lying" and "Pen, Pencil, and Poison" a study of the life of Thomas Griffiths Wainewright (1794–1852) which appeared in the Fortnightly Review for January 1889. It was reprinted, revised, in Intentions (1891).

[4] Blackwood answered on 9 July:

My dear Sir, As you seem to be somewhat disinclined for the republication of your "Portrait of Mr W. H." in the new series of Tales from B I am quite willing to fall in with your wishes in the matter and to waive any claims on the story for this purpose.

With respect to your proposal that I should bring out a special volume of your Essays and Studies with a frontispiece portrait of the said Mr W. H. I shall be glad to consider it when you have given me an opportunity of looking over the material you propose to include along with your contributions to the Magazine. But I must warn you that as a rule these volumes of reprinted stories and essays are not remunerative to either publisher or author. It is only as a series such as Tales from Blackwood that, except in a very few cases, we have found them worth doing. Nevertheless as I have said I shall be very happy to consider your proposal and have no doubt we shall be able to arrange matters.

You are quite right regarding the length of your paper and as I had remarked in my previous letter it did exceed my printers' calculation by 2½ pages. The cheque for £25 I had the pleasure of sending you was calculated as for 18 pp. at £1–5–0 per page and the balance was thrown in to cover the right of reprinting in The Tales. The extra pages at this rate would amount to £3–15 about, less the Tales honorarium now cancelled leaving a small balance in your favour and herewith I have the pleasure of enclosing you cheque for Two Guineas.

I shall be glad to see the material for your proposed new volume at your convenience and believe me Yours very truly   WILLIAM BLACKWOOD
PS. I hope you have been pleased with the reaction your story has had, and on the whole I think it has taken well.   W.B.

To William Blackwood

MS. Edinburgh

[*10 July 1889*][1]   *16 Tite Street*

My dear Sir, Thank you for your letter and its enclosure. The articles I
thought of including are in the *Nineteeenth Century* and the *Fortnightly* for
January last. The former is quite out of print, but at your club no doubt
you will be able to see both.

What would you say to a dainty little volume of "Mr W. H." by itself?
I could add to it, as I have many more points to make, and have not yet
tackled the problem of the "dark woman" at the end of the sonnets. The
price should be not more than 5/-. This should, I think, sell fairly well.
I could add about 3000 words to the story. Personally I should prefer it
to be separate. Truly yours   OSCAR WILDE

To Oscar Browning

MS. Clark

[? *July 1889*]   *16 Tite Street*

My dear O. B., I am so disappointed, but I must put off my visit to
Cambridge. One of our little boys is not at all well, and my wife, who is
very nervous, has begged me not to leave town. You are so fond of children
that I am sure you will understand how one feels about things of this kind,
and I think it would be rather horrid of me to go away. I hope you will
let me know when you come to town. I want you and Bobbie at dinner.
Ever yours   OSCAR

To Robert Ross

MS. Clark

[*July 1889*][2]   *16 Tite Street*

Dear Bobbie, Your telegram (of course it was *yours*) has just arrived. So
many thanks for it: it was really sweet of you to send it, for indeed the
story is half yours, and but for you would not have been written.[3] Are
you well again? Terror for Cyril kept me away, but now I may come, may
I not?

Write to me a letter. Now that Willie Hughes has been revealed to the
world, we must have another secret. Ever yours, dear Bobbie   O. W.

---

[1] So dated by recipient.   [2] So dated by recipient.
[3] "The Portrait of Mr W. H." had duly appeared in *Blackwood's* for July 1889
(having been declined by Frank Harris for the *Fortnightly*). In it Wilde sought to
identify the dedicatee of Shakespeare's sonnets as a boy-actor called Willie Hughes.
The essay was reprinted in *Lord Arthur Savile's Crime and Other Prose Pieces*
(1908).

To W. E. Henley
MS. Morgan

[*July 1889*]   *16 Tite Street*

My dear Henley, To be exiled to Scotland to edit a Tory paper in the wilderness is bad enough, but not to see the wonder and beauty of my discovery of the real Mr W. H. is absolutely dreadful. I sympathise deeply with you, and can only beg you to return to London where you will be able to appreciate a real work of art.

The Philistines in their vilest forms have seized on you. I am so disappointed. [1]

Still, when you return you will be welcome; all is not lost. Ever yours

OSCAR

To Robert Ross
MS. Hyde (H. M.)

[? *mid-July 1889*][2]   *Kreuznach*

Dear Bobbie, I am actually in Germany! I had an invitation to come here to see somebody about a play, and I thought it would be a superb opportunity for forgetting the language. So I arrived on Saturday after a day's journey from Cologne by steamer.

The Rhine is of course tedious, the vineyards are formal and dull, and as far as I can judge the inhabitants of Germany are American.

I return this week, via Wiesbaden and Ostend. Somebody I used to like is at Ostend, and I have promised to stay a day.

I am charmed with what you say about the little Princess—the Infanta: in style (in *mere* style as honest Besant would say) it is my best story. The *Guardian* on Mr W. H. you must send to me at Tite Street. Write to me there: I shall be home on Saturday. And oh! Bobbie, let us have an evening together. What ages since we had a talk! Yours, with much love

OSCAR

To G. H. Kersley
MS. Clark

[*Postmark 6 August 1889*]   *16 Tite Street*

My dear Kersley, Of course you should have come to see me before you

---

[1] An unsigned notice in the *Scots Observer* of 6 July 1889 had said: "With the exception of one article which is out of place in *Maga*—or, indeed, in any popular magazine—the July number of *Blackwood* is particularly good."

[2] Nothing else is known of this visit to Germany, but the letter can be dated approximately. "The Birthday of the Little Princess" was first published in *Paris Illustré* on 30 March 1889, simultaneously in French and English. (It was reprinted, as "The Birthday of the Infanta", in *A House of Pomegranates*, 1891.) The *Guardian* printed a brief notice of "The Portrait of Mr W. H." (by Emily Thursfield) on 10 July 1889.

left town. I wanted to hear all about you, and what art you are now devoted to. As for the art of money-making I know nothing about it. I wish I did, but it is not in my temperament.

If I see Charlie Hawtrey I will speak to him about you.[1] Are you writing anything now? Sincerely yours   OSCAR WILDE

To W. Graham Robertson
MS. Preston

[? *August 1889*]   *16 Tite Street*

My dear Graham, I am so sorry you are going away. Don't let the olives and the myrtles keep you too long. I called to see you on Saturday, and will try my chance tomorrow between five and six.

I saw Mr Ricketts on Saturday, and he is most grateful for your cheque. He seems very cultivated and interesting.[2] Yours very sincerely

OSCAR WILDE

To Emily Thursfield[3]
MS. Thursfield

Sunday [*1 September 1889*]   *16 Tite Street*

Dear Mrs Thursfield, I must write and thank you for your great kindness to Constance, who has come back perfectly charmed with her visit, enchanted with you all, and looking extremely well—much better than when she went away. She is, of course, a little spoiled; in fact she has

---

[1] Charles Hawtrey (1858–1923), English actor and manager. Knighted 1922. See also note 6, p. 316.

[2] Charles De Sousy Ricketts (1866–1931), artist, writer, book and stage designer, lived for many years with Charles Hazlewood Shannon (1863–1937), first in a house (which had belonged to Whistler) in a Chelsea cul-de-sac called The Vale. Ricketts was elected R.A. in 1928, Shannon in 1921. Ricketts designed the title-page and binding of *The Picture of Dorian Gray* (1891) and of the limited edition of Wilde's *Poems* (1892), the binding of *Intentions* (1891) and *Lord Arthur Savile's Crime* (1891). Ricketts and Shannon jointly designed and decorated *A House of Pomegranates* (1891). Ricketts designed *The Sphinx* (1894) and the binding for the Collected Edition of 1908. Shannon designed the binding for *Lady Windermere's Fan* (1893), *A Woman of No Importance* (1894), *The Importance of Being Earnest* (1899) and *An Ideal Husband* (1899). Together they ran a privately printed magazine called the *Dial* from 1889 to 1897. They sent a copy of the first issue (the British Museum copy is stamped 21 August 1889) to Wilde, and this brought about their first meeting with him.

[3] Emily Herbert (1851–1949) married (1880) James Richard Thursfield (1840–1923), Fellow of Jesus College, Oxford. He later wrote much on naval matters and was on the staff of *The Times*. He was knighted 1920. Mrs Thursfield did a good deal of reviewing, particularly in the *Athenaeum* and the *Guardian*, in which she had noticed *The Portrait of Mr W. H.* on 10 July. Harry was the Thursfields' son, and their London home was at 4 Montague Place. Constance Wilde had just been staying with them in a rented rectory on the Yorkshire moors, and her bread-and-butter letter (MS. Thursfield) is dated 1 September.

already complained of the lack of a picturesque view in Tite Street, and has more than once spoken slightingly of town eggs. These moods, however, will I hope soon pass away.

I have been reading your husband's article on signalling with great interest, and am now quite capable of flashing messages to Montague Place, so you must be prepared with a winter code.[1]

Pray remember me to Mr Thursfield, and give my love to Harry. Sincerely yours   OSCAR WILDE

To Charles Ricketts[2]

[? *Autumn 1889*]   *16 Tite Street*

My dear Ricketts, It is not a forgery at all; it is an authentic Clouet of the highest authentic value. It is absurd of you and Shannon to try and take me in! As if I did not know the master's touch, or was no judge of frames![3]

Seriously, my dear fellow, it is quite wonderful, and your giving it to me is an act so charming that, in despair of showing you any return, I at once call upon the gods to shower gold and roses on the Vale, or on that part of the Vale where the De Morgans do not live.[4] I am really most grateful (no! that is a horrid word: I am never grateful) I am flattered and fascinated, and I hope we shall always be friends and see each other often.

I must come round and enjoy the company of the Dialists—*par nobile*[5] as they are. Sincerely yours   OSCAR WILDE

To J. M. Stoddart[6]

30 September [*1889*]   *16 Tite Street*

You ask me to try and send you my story "early in October"; surely you mean "early in November"? If you could be content with 30,000 words

---

[1] Thursfield's article appeared, anonymously, in *The Times* of 30 August, as a long pendant to a description of the Naval Manoeuvres. It was headed "H.M.S. *Northumberland*, Queenstown, August 28."

[2] Text from Ricketts's *Recollections of Oscar Wilde* (1932).

[3] Wilde had asked Ricketts to paint a small Elizabethan picture of Willie Hughes, such as the one in the story which was "quite in Clouet's style," to act as frontispiece to an enlarged edition of "The Portrait of Mr W. H." Ricketts painted it on "a decaying piece of oak and framed it in a fragment of worm-eaten moulding, which my friend Shannon pieced together." The edition did not appear in Wilde's lifetime (but see note p. 366), and at the sale of Wilde's effects on 24 April 1895 the painting was sold for a guinea. François Clouet (d. 1572) was a French painter of miniatures.

[4] William Frend De Morgan (1839–1917), the Pre-Raphaelite artist and potter, had married in 1888 and lived near Ricketts and Shannon in Chelsea. In his late sixties and seventies he achieved considerable success with *Joseph Vance* (1906) and other novels.   [5] Noble pair (Horace, *Satires*, II, iii, 243).

[6] The text of this incomplete letter is taken from the Anderson Galleries catalogue of 19 November 1931.

I might be able to post the manuscript to you the first week in November, but October is of course out of the question.

To Herbert Vivian

TS. Holland

[*Postmark 22 November 1889*]   *Albemarle Club*
    Private

Dear Mr Vivian, I have just seen a copy of the *Sun* with your spot on it.[1] I'm afraid I could not possibly be godfather to so ill-bred a child. Believe me, your style is quite impossible, and vulgarity is the worst début a man can make in life. The sad thing is that I see you have been actuated by the very best intentions all through. Good intentions are dangerous things. Truly yours   OSCAR WILDE

To Mrs Bernard Beere

MS. Clark

[? *December 1889*][2]   *Lyric Club, Piccadilly East*

My dear Bernie, I am so sorry to hear you are tired and worn out. Remember that Sarah never really *acts* more than twice a week, if so often. You must be careful, and yet I know your intense artistic conscientiousness, and your dislike of merely sauntering through a part. I long to see you. Last Sunday I was with the Abbot of Abbots Hill. If possible, I will come tomorrow.

Do take care of yourself, and believe me, ever affectionately yours
                                                                                OSCAR

To J. M. Stoddart[3]

17 December 1889   *16 Tite Street*

I have invented a new story which is better than "The Fisherman and his Soul," and I am quite ready to set to work at once on it.

[1] In the *Sun* of 17 November 1889 there appeared the first chapter of *The Reminiscences of a Short Life* by Herbert Vivian. In it he printed (without permission) Wilde's letter of 26 June (see p. 245), reported private conversations, and patronisingly discussed Wilde as a plagiarist. Further chapters appeared in subsequent issues of the *Sun*, but they were never published in book form.

[2] On 28 November 1889 Mrs Bernard Beere opened at the Garrick Theatre in an adaptation of Sardou's *La Tosca*, in which Sarah Bernhardt had created the title-part. According to the *Green Room Book* (1907) the strain of appearing in this play resulted in a severe illness and Mrs Beere was not able to appear on the stage again until the autumn of 1890. For Abbots Hill, see note 2, p. 220.

[3] The text of this fragment is taken from *American Book Prices Current*, 1918.

To an Unidentified Correspondent[1]

19 December 1889   *16 Tite Street*

I have been ill for some weeks and have been obliged to give up my
literary work, amongst which is a story for *Lippincott's Magazine* ...
Will you telegraph at once to Mr Stoddart and say that the story cannot
be ready for some months.

To Otho Stuart[2]

MS. Princeton

[Postmark 20 December 1889]   *16 Tite Street*

My dear Otho, I must send you a line to congratulate you warmly and
sincerely on your beautiful and poetic rendering of Oberon last night. Of
course you looked quite wonderful—like a marvellous Dionysos—and you
moved with infinite grace, but it was your treatment of the verse that really
fascinated me. To speak poetry well is so rare an accomplishment that it
was a delight to listen to your lovely voice, with its fine sense of music and
cadence and rhythmical structure. You certainly have a delicate artistic
sense of the way in which imaginative work should be treated, and I have
not enjoyed anything so much as "Otho's Oberon" for a long time. Ever
yours   OSCAR WILDE

To Aubrey Richardson[3]

MS. Clark

[? 1889]   *16 Tite Street*

My dear Aubrey Richardson, There is no poem called "The Nightingale
and the Rose:" there is simply a fairy-tale in a volume called *The Happy
Prince* published by David Nutt. If you come across it I hope you will
like it.

What a pretty name you have! it is worthy of fiction. Would you mind
if I wrote a book called *The Story of Aubrey Richardson*? I won't, but I
should like to. There is music in its long syllables, and a memory of
romance, and a suggestion of wonder. Names fascinate me terribly. Come
and see me some Wednesday. Sincerely yours   OSCAR WILDE

---

[1] The text of this fragment is taken from *American Book Prices Current*, 1930.
[2] English actor (1865–1930). The F. R. Benson production of *A Midsummer
Night's Dream* opened at the Globe Theatre on 19 December 1889.
[3] Unidentified, but possibly Aubrey Richardson (1863–1912), son of Sir Benjamin
Richardson (1828–96), physician and sanitary reformer. Aubrey became a solicitor
in 1888, but eventually took to drink and committed suicide.

To the Editor of Truth[1]

[*Early January 1890*]   *16 Tite Street*

Sir, I can hardly imagine that the public are in the very smallest degree interested in the shrill shrieks of "Plagiarism" that proceed from time to time out of the lips of silly vanity or incompetent mediocrity.

However, as Mr James Whistler has had the impertinence to attack me with both venom and vulgarity in your columns, I hope you will allow me

---

[1] An answer to this letter of Whistler's, which had appeared in *Truth* on 2 January 1890:

Dear Truth, Among your ruthless exposures of the shams of today, nothing, I confess, have I enjoyed with keener relish than your late tilt at that arch-impostor and pest of the period—the all-pervading plagiarist!

I learn, by the way, that in America he may, under the "Law of '84," as it is called, be criminally prosecuted, incarcerated, and made to pick oakum, as he has hitherto picked brains—and pockets!

How was it that, in your list of culprits, you omitted that fattest of offenders —our own Oscar?

His methods are brought again freshly to my mind, by the indefatigable and tardy Romeike, who sends me newspaper cuttings of "Mr Herbert Vivian's Reminiscences," in which, among other entertaining anecdotes, is told at length the story of Oscar simulating the becoming pride of author, upon a certain evening, in the club of the Academy students, and arrogating to himself the responsibility of the lecture, with which, at his earnest prayer, I had in good fellowship crammed him, that he might not add deplorable failure to foolish appearance, in his anomalous position as art expounder, before his clear-headed audience.

He went forth, on that occasion, as my St John—but, forgetting that humility should be his chief characteristic, and unable to withstand the unaccustomed respect with which his utterances were received, he not only trifled with my shoe, but bolted with the latchet!

Mr Vivian, in his book, tells us, further on, that lately, in an article in the *Nineteenth Century* on "The Decay of Lying," Mr Wilde has deliberately and incautiously incorporated, "without a word of comment," a portion of the well-remembered letter in which, after admitting his rare appreciation and amazing memory, I acknowledge that "Oscar has the courage of the opinions—of others!"

My recognition of this, his latest proof of open admiration, I send him in the following little note, which I fancy you may think *à propos* to publish, as an example to your readers, in similar circumstances, of noble generosity in sweet reproof, tempered, as it should be, to the lamb in his condition:

"Oscar, you have been down the area again, I see!

I had forgotten you, and so allowed your hair to grow over the sore place. And now, while I looked the other way, you have stolen *your own scalp*! and potted it in more of your pudding.

Labby has pointed out that, for the detected plagiarist, there is still one way to self-respect (besides hanging himself, of course), and that is for him boldly to declare, '*Je prends mon bien là où je le trouve.*'

You, Oscar, can go further, and with fresh effrontery, that will bring you the envy of all criminal *confrères*, unblushingly boast, '*Moi, je prends* son *bien là où je le trouve!* '"

Wilde's lecture was given to the Art Students of the Royal Academy on 30 June 1883. This answer of Wilde's appeared in *Truth* on 9 January 1890. Henry Romeike had established his press-cutting agency in London in 1881.

to state that the assertions contained in his letter are as deliberately untrue as they are deliberately offensive.

The definition of a disciple as one who has the courage of the opinions of his master is really too old even for Mr Whistler to be allowed to claim it, and as for borrowing Mr Whistler's ideas about art, the only thoroughly original ideas I have ever heard him express have had reference to his own superiority over painters greater than himself.

It is a trouble for any gentleman to have to notice the lucubrations of so ill-bred and ignorant a person as Mr Whistler, but your publication of his insolent letter left me no option in the matter. I remain, sir, faithfully yours   OSCAR WILDE[1]

To Gerald Maxwell

MS. Kittleson

[Postmark 4 February 1890]   Lyric Club

My dear Gerald, I had no idea you were the "G. Maxwell" of the Criterion.[2] Why suppress your beautiful name? Of course, if I can do anything for you I will. I am writing to George Alexander about you by this post. Charlie Hawtrey I fear has nothing to give at present unless you want a provincial engagement.

I hope to see you soon. Come to the matinée of *Clarissa* at the Vaudeville on Thursday; a great friend of mine is playing Lovelace.[3]

I hope you are all well, and that the next time you write you will remember that I have a Christian name. Ever yours   OSCAR WILDE

To Lionel Johnson[4]

MS. Secker

[Circa 16 February 1890]   Lyric Club

Dear Mr Johnson, I was so sorry I could not get back, to see you again, but I was dragged to the theatre to see the realisation of some suggestions I had made, and could not get away till just before my train started.

[1] Whistler replied with another letter in *Truth* on 16 January, and reprinted all three letters in *The Gentle Art of Making Enemies* later in the year.

[2] *Cyril's Success* by H. J. Byron was revived at the Criterion Theatre on 25 January 1890 but ran for only a fortnight. Gerald Maxwell was in the cast.

[3] *Clarissa*, a new drama in four acts by Robert Buchanan, founded on Samuel Richardson's novel, opened at the Vaudeville Theatre on Thursday, 6 February 1890, with Cyril Maude and Winifred Emery in the cast. The part of Lovelace was played by T. B. Thalberg.

[4] Poet and critic (1867–1902). At this time he was still an undergraduate of New College, Oxford. He was a friend and great admirer of Walter Pater. This was his first meeting with Wilde, and on 18 February he wrote to his friend Arthur Galton:

> On Saturday at mid-day, lying half asleep in bed, reading Green, I was roused by a pathetic and unexpected note from Oscar: he plaintively besought me to get up and see him. Which I did: and I found him as delightful as Green is not. He

I hope you will let me know when you are in town. I like your poetry—the little I have seen of it—so much, that I want to know the poet as well.

It was very good of you getting up to see me. I was determined to meet you before I left Oxford. Believe me, yours very truly   OSCAR WILDE

To Mrs Allhusen[1]

TS. Holland

[? *Early 1890*]   *16 Tite Street*

Dear Mrs Allhusen, It is most kind of you to ask me to Bournemouth. I am so busy at present I cannot get away, but if I can manage it a little later I will certainly ask you to take me in for a couple of nights. Bournemouth is delightful, and we would have long talks, on the things of Life and Art. I have just finished my first long story,[2] and am tired out. I am afraid it is rather like my own life—all conversation and no action. I can't describe action: my people sit in chairs and chatter. I wonder what you will think of it. I will send you a copy. You are quite right to assail me about letters being unanswered. My only excuse is that I am incorrigible. With many thanks, believe me yours   OSCAR WILDE

To Herbert Vivian

TS. Holland

[*Postmark 17 May 1890*]   *16 Tite Street*

Dear Mr Vivian, I am so sorry that you do not appreciate the courtesy of the form I used in addressing you on Wednesday night. I was not asking you to do me a favour: I was asserting my right to prevent my name being

---

discoursed, with infinite flippancy, of everyone: lauded the *Dial*: laughed at Pater: and consumed all my cigarettes. I am in love with him. He was come to visit Pater; and to see *Strafford*.

From 12 to 18 February 1890 the O.U.D.S. gave eight performances of Browning's *Strafford* in the New Theatre, Oxford, with H. B. Irving in the chief part. Lionel Johnson reviewed the production in the *Century Guild Hobby Horse*.

Later in 1890 Johnson wrote a Latin poem in praise of *The Picture of Dorian Gray* and its author, beginning:

> *Benedictus sis, Oscare!*
> *Qui me libro hoc dignare*
> *Propter amicitias:*
> *Modo modulans Romano*
> *Laudes dignas Doriano,*
> *Ago tibi gratias.*

The whole poem was first printed in Mason's *Art and Morality* (1912), and is in *The Complete Poems of Lionel Johnson* (1953). In 1891 Johnson introduced Wilde to Lord Alfred Douglas, and Johnson's poem "The Destroyer of a Soul" (1892) is believed to have been addressed to Wilde. It begins:

> "I hate you with a necessary hate."

[1] Beatrice May, *née* Butt (1857–1918), poet and novelist, wife of William Hutt Allhusen (1845–1923).   [2] *The Picture of Dorian Gray*.

in any way associated with a book that, from the extracts I have read of it, I must admit I consider extremely vulgar and offensive.[1] No one has the right to make one godfather to a dirty baby against one's will, or to put forward as a result of a suggestion of one's own a book with which no gentleman would wish to have his name associated. You may say you refuse to recognise this right: that is possible: but by doing so you make a very wilful surrender of that position you hold as a gentleman, a position for which your birth and culture give you the fullest qualifications. Believe me, it would be an ungentlemanly thing to do, and I should be sorry to think that any Cambridge man could be wilfully guilty of such conduct, conduct which combines the inaccuracy of the eavesdropper with the method of the blackmailer. Meeting you socially, I, in a moment which I greatly regret, happened to tell you a story about my little boy. Without asking my permission you publish this in a vulgar newspaper and in a vulgar, inaccurate and offensive form, to the great pain of my wife, who naturally does not wish to see her children paraded for the amusement of the uncouth. As a gentleman you had no right to do that, any more than you had to publish a letter of mine without my permission. You wrote of me personally with gross and impertinent familiarity. You may not be conscious of this, but you did so. It was an error of taste on your part. When you are older you will recognise it. As you cannot or will not understand the courtesy and form of address, pray understand that you have no right to make use of my name in connection with your book, or to report any private conversation I may have had with you, or to publish any letter of mine without my permission, and I must insist that you do not do so. Truly yours   OSCAR WILDE

To Herbert Vivian
TS. Holland

[*Postmark 20 May 1890*]   *16 Tite Street*
  Private

Dear Mr Vivian, I cannot possibly compete in abuse with you. Nor has it anything to do with the point at issue, which is this: you have no right to associate my name with a book of whose method and manner I disapprove. The fact of my disapproving of it is of course nothing to you. Your work is your own, the best you can do at the present, I suppose. But to associate my name with it is wrong. Believe me, when you think over the matter quietly, you will see that either from a gentleman's point of view, or from the point of view of literary honour, or from the point of view of mere honesty, such a proceeding would be unjustifiable. Nor have you the right to publish my private letters, or to report private conversations you may have had with me, without my permission. And when you reflect that you have given pain to a lady, to whom you have had the honour of being introduced, I think, my wife, by writing about our children in the public press,

[1] See note 1, p. 251.

I am sure you will see that such an error should not be repeated. If you still think I am taking up an unwarrantable position, ask any man of letters, say Wilfrid Blunt, whom I think you know well, and he will tell you I am right. You really have no position to go on. It would be a gross thing to do. I cannot believe you will do it. Truly yours   OSCAR WILDE

To the Editor of the St James's Gazette[1]

25 June [1890]   *16 Tite Street*

Sir, I have read your criticism of my story, *The Picture of Dorian Gray*, and I need hardly say that I do not propose to discuss its merits or demerits, its personalities or its lack of personality. England is a free country, and ordinary English criticism is perfectly free and easy. Besides, I must admit that, either from temperament or from taste, or from both, I am quite incapable of understanding how any work of art can be criticised from a moral standpoint. The sphere of art and the sphere of ethics are absolutely distinct and separate; and it is to the confusion between the two that we owe the appearance of Mrs Grundy, that amusing old lady who represents the only original form of humour that the middle classes of this country have been able to produce. What I do object to most strongly is that you should have placarded the town with posters on which was printed in large letters: MR OSCAR WILDE'S LATEST ADVERTISEMENT; A BAD CASE.

Whether the expression "A Bad Case" refers to my book or to the present position of the Government, I cannot tell. What was silly and unnecessary was the use of the term "advertisement."

I think I may say without vanity—though I do not wish to appear to run vanity down—that of all men in England I am the one who requires least advertisement. I am tired to death of being advertised. I feel no thrill when I see my name in a paper. The chronicler does not interest me any more. I wrote this book entirely for my own pleasure, and it gave me very great pleasure to write it. Whether it becomes popular or not is a matter of absolute indifference to me. I am afraid, sir, that the real advertisement is your cleverly written article. The English public, as a mass, takes no interest in a work of art until it is told that the work in question is immoral, and your *réclame* will, I have no doubt, largely increase the sale of the magazine; in which sale, I may mention with some regret, I have no pecuniary interest.

I remain, sir, your obedient servant   OSCAR WILDE

---

[1] Sidney James Mark Low (1857–1932, knighted 1918) was editor of the *St James's Gazette* 1888–97. Wilde's only novel, *The Picture of Dorian Gray*, was first published on 20 June 1890, in the July number of *Lippincott's Monthly Magazine*, where it occupied pp. 3–100. It was extensively reviewed. The *St James's Gazette* printed a scurrilous notice on 24 June, under the heading "A Study in Puppydom." Its anonymous author was Samuel Henry Jeyes (1857–1911). The full text of all the important reviews of, and letters about, *Dorian Gray* is given in Stuart Mason's *Art and Morality* (1912). This letter of Wilde's was published on 26 June, under the heading MR OSCAR WILDE'S "BAD CASE."

To the Editor of the St James's Gazette[1]

26 June [1890]   *16 Tite Street*

In your issue of today you state that my brief letter published in your columns is the "best reply" I can make to your article upon *Dorian Gray*. This is not so. I do not propose to fully discuss the matter here, but I feel bound to say that your article contains the most unjustifiable attack that has been made upon any man of letters for many years. The writer of it, who is quite incapable of concealing his personal malice, and so in some measure destroys the effect he wishes to produce, seems not to have the slightest idea of the temper in which a work of art should be approached. To say that such a book as mine should be "chucked into the fire" is silly. That is what one does with newspapers.

Of the value of pseudo-ethical criticism in dealing with artistic work I have spoken already. But as your writer has ventured into the perilous grounds of literary criticism I ask you to allow me, in fairness not merely to myself but to all men to whom literature is a fine art, to say a few words about his critical method.

He begins by assailing me with much ridiculous virulence because the chief personages in my story are "puppies." They *are* puppies. Does he think that literature went to the dogs when Thackeray wrote about puppy-dom? I think that puppies are extremely interesting from an artistic as well as from a psychological point of view. They seem to me to be certainly far more interesting than prigs; and I am of opinion that Lord Henry Wotton is an excellent corrective of the tedious ideal shadowed forth in the semi-theological novels of our age.

He then makes vague and fearful insinuations about my grammar and my erudition. Now, as regards grammar, I hold that, in prose at any rate, correctness should always be subordinate to artistic effect and musical cadence; and any peculiarities of syntax that may occur in *Dorian Gray* are deliberately intended, and are introduced to show the value of the artistic theory in question. Your writer gives no instance of any such peculiarity. This I regret, because I do not think that any such instances occur.

As regards erudition, it is always difficult, even for the most modest of us, to remember that other people do not know quite as much as one does oneself. I myself frankly admit I cannot imagine how a casual reference to Suetonius and Petronius Arbiter can be construed into evidence of a desire to impress an unoffending and ill-educated public by an assumption of superior knowledge. I should fancy that the most ordinary of scholars is perfectly well acquainted with the *Lives of the Caesars* and with the *Satyricon*. The *Lives of the Caesars*, at any rate, forms part of the curriculum at Oxford for those who take the Honour School of *Literæ Human-*

---

[1] The editorial note which accompanied Wilde's letter of the 25th was so offensive that it called forth this further letter, which appeared on the 27th, under the heading MR OSCAR WILDE AGAIN.

iores; and as for the *Satyricon*, it is popular even among passmen, though I suppose they are obliged to read it in translations.

The writer of the article then suggests that I, in common with that great and noble artist Count Tolstoi, take pleasure in a subject because it is dangerous. About such a suggestion there is this to be said. Romantic art deals with the exception and with the individual. Good people, belonging as they do to the normal, and so, commonplace, type, are artistically uninteresting. Bad people are, from the point of view of art, fascinating studies. They represent colour, variety and strangeness. Good people exasperate one's reason; bad people stir one's imagination. Your critic, if I must give him so honourable a title, states that the people in my story have no counterpart in life; that they are, to use his vigorous if somewhat vulgar phrase, "mere catchpenny revelations of the non-existent." Quite so. If they existed they would not be worth writing about. The function of the artist is to invent, not to chronicle. There are no such people. If there were I would not write about them. Life by its realism is always spoiling the subject-matter of art. The supreme pleasure in literature is to realise the non-existent.

And finally, let me say this. You have reproduced, in a journalistic form, the comedy of *Much Ado about Nothing*, and have, of course, spoilt it in your reproduction. The poor public, hearing, from an authority so high as your own, that this is a wicked book that should be coerced and suppressed by a Tory Government, will, no doubt, rush to it and read it. But, alas! they will find that it is a story with a moral. And the moral is this: All excess, as well as all renunciation, brings its own punishment. The painter, Basil Hallward, worshipping physical beauty far too much, as most painters do, dies by the hand of one in whose soul he has created a monstrous and absurd vanity. Dorian Gray, having led a life of mere sensation and pleasure, tries to kill conscience, and at that moment kills himself. Lord Henry Wotton seeks to be merely the spectator of life. He finds that those who reject the battle are more deeply wounded than those who take part in it. Yes; there is a terrible moral in *Dorian Gray*—a moral which the prurient will not be able to find in it, but which will be revealed to all whose minds are healthy. Is this an artistic error? I fear it is. It is the only error in the book.

To the Editor of the St James's Gazette[1]

27 June [1890]   *16 Tite Street*

Sir, As you still keep up, though in a somewhat milder form than before, your attacks on me and my book, you not merely confer on me the right, but you impose upon me the duty, of reply.

You state, in your issue of today, that I misrepresented you when I said

---

[1] Once again the editor of the *St James's Gazette* had added an abusive note to Wilde's previous letter. This one appeared on 28 June, under the heading MR OSCAR WILDE'S DEFENCE.

that you suggested that a book so wicked as mine should be "suppressed and coerced by a Tory Government." Now you did not propose this, but you did suggest it. When you declare that you do not know whether or not the Government will take action about my book, and remark that the authors of books much less wicked have been proceeded against in law, the suggestion is quite obvious. In your complaint of misrepresentation you seem to me, sir, to have been not quite candid. However, as far as I am concerned, the suggestion is of no importance. What is of importance is that the editor of a paper like yours should appear to countenance the monstrous theory that the Government of a country should exercise a censorship over imaginative literature. This is a theory against which I, and all men of letters of my acquaintance, protest most strongly; and any critic who admits the reasonableness of such a theory shows at once that he is quite incapable of understanding what literature is, and what are the rights that literature possesses. A Government might just as well try to teach painters how to paint, or sculptors how to model, as attempt to interfere with the style, treatment and subject-matter of the literary artist; and no writer, however eminent or obscure, should ever give his sanction to a theory that would degrade literature far more than any didactic or so-called immoral book could possibly do.

You then express your surprise that "so experienced a literary gentleman" as myself should imagine that your critic was animated by any feeling of personal malice towards him. The phrase "literary gentleman" is a vile phrase; but let that pass. I accept quite readily your assurance that your critic was simply criticising a work of art in the best way that he could; but I feel that I was fully justified in forming the opinion of him that I did. He opened his article by a gross personal attack on myself. This, I need hardly say, was an absolutely unpardonable error of critical taste. There is no excuse for it, except personal malice; and you, sir, should not have sanctioned it. A critic should be taught to criticise a work of art without making any reference to the personality of the author. This, in fact, is the beginning of criticism. However, it was not merely his personal attack on me that made me imagine that he was actuated by malice. What really confirmed me in my first impression was his reiterated assertion that my book was tedious and dull. Now, if I were criticising my book, which I have some thoughts of doing, I think I would consider it my duty to point out that it is far too crowded with sensational incident, and far too paradoxical in style, as far, at any rate, as the dialogue goes. I feel that from a standpoint of art these are two defects in the book. But tedious and dull the book is not. Your critic has cleared himself of the charge of personal malice, his denial and yours being quite sufficient in the matter; but he has only done so by a tacit admission that he has really no critical instinct about literature and literary work, which, in one who writes about literature, is, I need hardly say, a much graver fault than malice of any kind.

Finally, sir, allow me to say this. Such an article as you have published really makes one despair of the possibility of any general culture in England. Were I a French author, and my book brought out in Paris, there is not a single literary critic in France, on any paper of high standing, who would think for a moment of criticising it from an ethical standpoint. If he did so, he would stultify himself, not merely in the eyes of all men of letters, but in the eyes of the majority of the public. You have yourself often spoken against Puritanism. Believe me, sir, Puritanism is never so offensive and destructive as when it deals with art matters. It is there that its influence is radically wrong. It is this Puritanism, to which your critic has given expression, that is always marring the artistic instinct of the English. So far from encouraging it, you should set yourself against it, and should try to teach your critics to recognise the essential difference between art and life. The gentleman who criticised my book is in a perfectly hopeless confusion about it, and your attempt to help him out by proposing that the subject-matter of art should be limited does not mend matters. It is proper that limitations should be placed on action. It is not proper that limitations should be placed on art. To art belong all things that are and all things that are not, and even the editor of a London paper has no right to restrain the freedom of art in the selection of subject-matter.

I now trust, sir, that these attacks on me and on my book will cease. There are forms of advertisement that are unwarranted and unwarrantable.

I am, sir, your obedient servant,   OSCAR WILDE

To Ward, Lock & Co.

MS. Edmiston

[*Circa 28 June 1890. Date of receipt 2 July 1890*]   *16 Tite Street*

Gentlemen, Kindly do not send out any more copies of Messrs Lippincott's puff of my book. It is really an insult to the critics. Also, will you kindly let me know if I can have an interview with you on Thursday morning at twelve o'clock. Yours truly   OSCAR WILDE

To the Editor of the St James's Gazette[1]

28 June [*1890*]   *16 Tite Street*

Sir, In your issue of this evening you publish a letter from "A London Editor" which clearly insinuates in the last paragraph that I have in some way sanctioned the circulation of an expression of opinion, on the part of the proprietors of *Lippincott's Magazine*, of the literary and artistic value of my story of *The Picture of Dorian Gray*.[2]

Allow me, sir, to state that there are no grounds for this insinuation. I was not aware that any such document was being circulated; and I have written to the agents, Messrs Ward & Lock—who cannot, I feel sure,

[1] This letter appeared on 30 June, under the same heading as its predecessor.
[2] "A London Editor" had quoted a glowing advertisement of the book which he had received through the post from Messrs Ward, Lock, the English publishers of *Lippincott's Monthly Magazine*, and commented: "For a man who does not want advertisement this is not bad."

261

be primarily responsible for its appearance—to ask them to withdraw it at once. No publisher should ever express an opinion of the value of what he publishes. That is a matter entirely for the literary critic to decide. I must admit, as one to whom contemporary literature is constantly submitted for criticism, that the only thing that ever prejudices me against a book is the lack of literary style; but I can quite understand how any ordinary critic would be strongly prejudiced against a work that was accompanied by a premature and unnecessary panegyric from the publisher. A publisher is simply a useful middle-man. It is not for him to anticipate the verdict of criticism.

I may, however, while expressing my thanks to the "London Editor" for drawing my attention to this, I trust, purely American method of procedure, venture to differ from him in one of his criticisms. He states that he regards the expression "complete," as applied to a story, as a specimen of the "adjectival exuberance of the puffer!" Here, it seems to me, he sadly exaggerates. What my story is, is an interesting problem. What my story is not, is a "novelette," a term which you have more than once applied to it. There is no such word in the English language as novelette. It should never be used. It is merely part of the slang of Fleet Street.

In another part of your paper, sir, you state that I received your assurance of the lack of malice in your critic "somewhat grudgingly." This is not so. I frankly said that I accepted that assurance "quite readily," and that your own denial and that of your own critic were "sufficient." Nothing more generous could have been said. What I did feel was that you saved your critic from the charge of malice by convicting him of the unpardonable crime of lack of literary instinct. I still feel that. To call my book an ineffective attempt at allegory that, in the hands of Mr Anstey, might have been made striking, is absurd. Mr Anstey's sphere in literature and my sphere are different—very widely different.[1]

You then gravely ask me what rights I imagine literature possesses. That is really an extraordinary question for the editor of a newspaper such as yours to ask. The rights of literature, sir, are the rights of intellect.

I remember once hearing M. Renan say that he would sooner live under a military despotism than under the despotism of the Church, because the former merely limited the freedom of action, while the latter limited the freedom of mind. You say that a work of art is a form of action. It is not. It is the highest mode of thought.

In conclusion, sir, let me ask you not to force on me this continued correspondence, by daily attacks. It is a trouble and a nuisance. As you assailed me first, I have a right to the last word. Let that last word be the present letter, and leave my book, I beg you, to the immortality that it deserves.

I am, sir, your obedient servant,   OSCAR WILDE

[1] Thomas Anstey Guthrie (1856–1934), writing under the name F. Anstey, had scored a great success with his first novel, *Vice Versa, or a Lesson to Fathers* (1882) and followed it with other novels, each of which exploited some fantastic contingency.

To the Editor of the Daily Chronicle

30 June [1890]   *16 Tite Street*

Sir, Will you allow me to correct some errors into which your critic has fallen in his review of my story, *The Picture of Dorian Gray*, published in today's issue of your paper?[1]

Your critic states, to begin with, that I make desperate attempts to "vamp up" a moral in my story. Now, I must candidly confess that I do not know what "vamping" is. I see, from time to time, mysterious advertisements in the newspapers about "How to Vamp," but what vamping really means remains a mystery to me—a mystery that, like all other mysteries, I hope some day to explore.

However, I do not propose to discuss the absurd terms used by modern journalism. What I want to say is that, so far from wishing to emphasise any moral in my story, the real trouble I experienced in writing the story was that of keeping the extremely obvious moral subordinate to the artistic and dramatic effect.

When I first conceived the idea of a young man selling his soul in exchange for eternal youth—an idea that is old in the history of literature, but to which I have given new form—I felt that, from an aesthetic point of view, it would be difficult to keep the moral in its proper secondary place; and even now I do not feel quite sure that I have been able to do so. I think the moral too apparent. When the book is published in a volume I hope to correct this defect.[2]

As for what the moral is, your critic states that it is this—that when a man feels himself becoming "too angelic" he should rush out and make a "beast of himself!" I cannot say that I consider this a moral. The real moral of the story is that all excess, as well as all renunciation, brings its punishment, and this moral is so far artistically and deliberately suppressed that it does not enunciate its law as a general principle, but realises itself purely in the lives of individuals, and so becomes simply a dramatic element in a work of art, and not the object of the work of art itself.

Your critic also falls into error when he says that Dorian Gray, having a "cool, calculating, conscienceless character," was inconsistent when he destroyed the picture of his own soul, on the ground that the picture did not become less hideous after he had done what, in his vanity, he had considered his first good action. Dorian Gray has not got a cool, calculating, conscienceless character at all. On the contrary, he is extremely impulsive, absurdly romantic, and is haunted all through his life by an exaggerated sense of conscience which mars his pleasures for him and warns him that

---

[1] Part of the review runs: "Dulness and dirt are the chief features of *Lippincott's* this month. The element in it that is unclean, though undeniably amusing, is furnished by Mr Oscar Wilde's story . . . It is a tale spawned from the leprous literature of the French *Décadents*—a poisonous book, the atmosphere of which is heavy with the mephitic odours of moral and spiritual putrefaction." Wilde's letter appeared on 2 July.

[2] When *The Picture of Dorian Gray* was published in book form by Ward, Lock in April 1891, it contained some revision, a new preface and six additional chapters.

youth and enjoyment are not everything in the world. It is finally to get rid of the conscience that had dogged his steps from year to year that he destroys the picture; and thus in his attempt to kill conscience Dorian Gray kills himself.

Your critic then talks about "obtrusively cheap scholarship." Now, whatever a scholar writes is sure to display scholarship in the distinction of style and the fine use of language; but my story contains no learned or pseudo-learned discussions, and the only literary books that it alludes to are books that any fairly educated reader may be supposed to be acquainted with, such as the *Satyricon* of Petronius Arbiter, or Gautier's *Émaux et Camées*. Such books as Alphonso's *Clericalis Disciplina*[1] belong not to culture, but to curiosity. Anybody may be excused for not knowing them.

Finally, let me say this—the aesthetic movement produced certain colours, subtle in their loveliness and fascinating in their almost mystical tone. They were, and are, our reaction against the crude primaries of a doubtless more respectable but certainly less cultivated age. My story is an essay on decorative art. It reacts against the crude brutality of plain realism. It is poisonous if you like, but you cannot deny that it is also perfect, and perfection is what we artists aim at.

I remain, sir, your obedient servant   OSCAR WILDE

To Arthur Fish[2]

[? *Early July 1890*]

Dear Arthur Fish, I am very glad to hear you are going to be married, and I need hardly say I hope you will be very happy.[3] Lord Henry Wotton's views on marriage are quite monstrous, and I highly disapprove of them. I am delighted you like *Dorian Gray*—it has been attacked on ridiculous grounds, but I think it will be ultimately recognised as a real work of art with a strong ethical lesson inherent in it. Where are you going for your honeymoon? Believe me, sincerely yours   OSCAR WILDE

---

[1] The *Daily Chronicle* misprinted Alphonso as Le Conso, but cf. *The Picture of Dorian Gray*, chap. xi: "In Alphonso's *Clericalis Disciplina* a serpent was mentioned with eyes of real jacinth." Petrus Alphonsus was a Spanish Jew who, early in the twelfth century, compiled a collection of Jewish and Arabic fables, which he called *Clericalis Disciplina* and intended as seasoning for sermons. Some of them were included in *The Fables of Aesop etc., as first printed by Caxton in 1484* . . . edited and introduced by Joseph Jacobs (see note 3, p. 72), London, David Nutt, 2 vols, 1889. This edition however does not mention the serpent, and Wilde may well have been directed, by Jacobs's notes, to a French edition of 1824, in which there was "*un serpent d'or à yeux de pierres précieuses que l'on appelle jagonces.*"

[2] Journalist (1860–1940). Spent his whole working life as an editor for Messrs Cassell and was Wilde's assistant editor on the *Woman's World*. The text of this letter is taken from his article, "Memories of Oscar Wilde," in *Cassell's Weekly* of 2 May 1923.

[3] Arthur Fish was married to Ada Maria Turner at Barnet on 19 August 1890.

264

To Mrs Lathbury[1]

MS. Berg

[? *Summer 1890*]   *16 Tite Street*

Dear Mrs Lathbury, I don't think I like the Plymouth *Bothers*! But the Saint and the artistic Hedonist certainly meet—touch in many points. Right and wrong are not qualities of actions, they are mental attitudes relative to the incompleteness of the ordinary social organism. When one contemplates, all things are good.

For myself, I look forward to the time when aesthetics will take the place of ethics, when the sense of beauty will be the dominant law of life: it will never be so, and so I look forward to it.

I drove past your cottage on Sunday from the Graham Robertsons. It looked quite lovely, and I thought of the charming evening I passed there. The flowers were delightful, and more instructive than the Decalogue I had been listening to, or should have been listening to. Walking home from the Muirs we trespassed in your own pinewood. That was a real pleasure.

With kind regards to your husband, believe me, truly yours

OSCAR WILDE

To the Editor of the Scots Observer[2]

9 July 1890   *16 Tite Street, Chelsea*

Sir, You have published a review of my story, *The Picture of Dorian Gray*. As this review is grossly unjust to me as an artist, I ask you to allow me to exercise in your columns my right of reply.

---

[1] Probably Bertha Penrose (1846–1934), wife of Daniel Conner Lathbury (1831–1922), editor of the *Guardian* 1883–99. I have found no means of dating this letter. Wilde's visit to Graham Robertson and his mother was presumably to Sandhills, Witley (see note 2, p. 243).

[2] The *Scots Observer's* anonymous notice of *Dorian Gray* on 5 July read:

Why go grubbing in muck heaps? The world is fair, and the proportion of healthy-minded men and honest women to those that are foul, fallen, or unnatural is great. Mr Oscar Wilde has again been writing stuff that were better unwritten; and while *The Picture of Dorian Gray*, which he contributes to *Lippincott's*, is ingenious, interesting, full of cleverness, and plainly the work of a man of letters, it is false art—for its interest is medico-legal; it is false to human nature—for its hero is a devil; it is false to morality—for it is not made sufficiently clear that the writer does not prefer a course of unnatural iniquity to a life of cleanliness, health, and sanity. The story—which deals with matters only fitted for the Criminal Investigation Department or a hearing *in camerâ*—is discreditable alike to author and editor. Mr Wilde has brains, and art, and style; but if he can write for none but outlawed noblemen and perverted telegraph-boys, the sooner he takes to tailoring (or some other decent trade) the better for his own reputation and the public morals.

Although it was for long thought to have been written by W. E. Henley, the paper's editor, the author was in fact his henchman Charles Whibley (1860–1930). The outlawed nobleman and perverted telegraph-boys refer to Lord Arthur Somerset and the Cleveland Street scandal of 1889. This letter of Wilde's appeared on 12 July, under the heading MR WILDE'S REJOINDER. It was reprinted in *Miscellanies*.

Your reviewer, sir, while admitting that the story in question is "plainly the work of a man of letters," the work of one who has "brains, and art, and style," yet suggests, and apparently in all seriousness, that I have written it in order that it should be read by the most depraved members of the criminal and illiterate classes. Now, sir, I do not suppose that the criminal and illiterate classes ever read anything except newspapers. They are certainly not likely to be able to understand anything of mine. So let them pass, and on the broad question of why a man of letters writes at all let me say this. The pleasure that one has in creating a work of art is a purely personal pleasure, and it is for the sake of this pleasure that one creates. The artist works with his eye on the object. Nothing else interests him. What people are likely to say does not even occur to him. He is fascinated by what he has in hand. He is indifferent to others. I write because it gives me the greatest possible artistic pleasure to write. If my work pleases the few, I am gratified. If it does not, it causes me no pain. As for the mob, I have no desire to be a popular novelist. It is far too easy.

Your critic then, sir, commits the absolutely unpardonable crime of trying to confuse the artist with his subject-matter. For this, sir, there is no excuse at all. Of one who is the greatest figure in the world's literature since Greek days Keats remarked that he had as much pleasure in conceiving the evil as he had in conceiving the good.[1] Let your reviewer, sir, consider the bearings of Keats's fine criticism, for it is under these conditions that every artist works. One stands remote from one's subject-matter. One creates it, and one contemplates it. The further away the subject-matter is, the more freely can the artist work. Your reviewer suggests that I do not make it sufficiently clear whether I prefer virtue to wickedness or wickedness to virtue. An artist, sir, has no ethical sympathies at all. Virtue and wickedness are to him simply what the colours on his palette are to the painter. They are no more, and they are no less. He sees that by their means a certain artistic effect can be produced, and he produces it. Iago may be morally horrible and Imogen stainlessly pure. Shakespeare, as Keats said, had as much delight in creating the one as he had in creating the other.

It was necessary, sir, for the dramatic development of this story to surround Dorian Gray with an atmosphere of moral corruption. Otherwise the story would have had no meaning and the plot no issue. To keep this atmosphere vague and indeterminate and wonderful was the aim of the artist who wrote the story. I claim, sir, that he has succeeded. Each man sees his own sin in Dorian Gray. What Dorian Gray's sins are no one knows. He who finds them has brought them.

In conclusion, sir, let me say how really deeply I regret that you should have permitted such a notice as the one I feel constrained to write on to have appeared in your paper. That the editor of the *St James's Gazette* should have employed Caliban as his art-critic was possibly natural. The

[1] "The poetical character . . . has as much delight in conceiving an Iago as an Imogen. What shocks the virtuous philosopher delights the cameleon poet." John Keats to Richard Woodhouse, 27 October 1818.

editor of the *Scots Observer* should not have allowed Thersites to make mows in his review. It is unworthy of so distinguished a man of letters. I am, etc.   OSCAR WILDE

To Henry Lucy[1]

Saturday evening [26 July 1890][2]   *16 Tite Street*

My dear Lucy, Of course you intended to pain me by your manner to me last night, and pain me you certainly did. I think it was harsh and unnecessary of you.

You are no doubt hurt at what you consider a lack of courtesy on my part in not writing to tell you why I could not join your party at Boulogne. Well, I ask you to accept my apology, my really sincere and full apology, for that breach of etiquette. The fact is that I only saw *Punch* on Saturday night, when I was shown it in the Bachelors' Club, and I confess I was so annoyed at its offensive tone and horridness that I felt that I could not possibly meet Burnand,[3] and was afraid he might be one of your party. On expeditions of that kind any coolness or rudeness on the part of any of the guests is, of course, offensive to the host, and hostess, so I gave up what I knew was going to be a very pleasant party. Of course, I was foolish to let myself be annoyed; but so it was. Since Sunday I have ascertained that —— wrote it and not Burnand. I don't mind so much. I quite understand why —— should write like that. He can't help it.

I wanted to explain this to you in person, but you gave me no opportunity and I am sorry to have to write it, which is what I wanted to avoid. However, whether I was hurt at being offensively and vulgarly attacked in *Punch* or not, is nothing to you. I know now I should have written to say I missed the train, or had a cold, or to give some social excuse. I didn't; and I am sorry I didn't. Believe me that I intended no discourtesy to you by not doing so. In fact I am very sorry I missed the party, and still more sorry that I seemed to be discourteous to you.

Pray accept this apology, and believe me   OSCAR WILDE

---

[1] English parliamentary journalist and author (1845–1924). On the staff of *Punch* (1881–1916), where he wrote as "Toby M.P." Published many books on parliamentary subjects and several volumes of reminiscences. Knighted 1909. The text of this letter is taken from his *Nearing Jordan* (1916), where he explains that in July 1890 Wilde had accepted an invitation to accompany a number of the *Punch* staff and others on a day-trip to Boulogne, but had failed to turn up. Some days later Lucy cut him at a dinner party.

[2] The *Punch* review of *The Picture of Dorian Gray* appeared on 19 July. I have been unable to discover the identity of its author, which Lucy concealed by dashes.

[3] Francis Cowley Burnand (1836–1917), journalist and prolific writer of plays, burlesques and light literature, was editor of *Punch* 1862–1906. Knighted 1902.

To the Editor of the Scots Observer[1]

[? *31*] *July 1890*   *16 Tite Street*

Sir, In a letter dealing with the relations of art to morals recently published in your columns—a letter which I may say seems to me in many respects admirable, especially in its insistence on the right of the artist to select his own subject-matter—Mr Charles Whibley suggests that it must be peculiarly painful for me to find that the ethical import of *Dorian Gray* has been so strongly recognized by the foremost Christian papers of England and America that I have been greeted by more than one of them as a moral reformer!

Allow me, sir, to reassure, on this point, not merely Mr Charles Whibley himself but also your no doubt anxious readers. I have no hesitation in saying that I regard such criticisms as a very gratifying tribute to my story. For if a work of art is rich, and vital, and complete, those who have artistic instincts will see its beauty, and those to whom ethics appeal more strongly than aesthetics will see its moral lesson. It will fill the cowardly with terror, and the unclean will see in it their own shame. It will be to each man what he is himself. It is the spectator, and not life, that art really mirrors.

And so, in the case of *Dorian Gray*, the purely literary critic, as in the *Speaker* and elsewhere, regards it as a "serious and fascinating work of art:" the critic who deals with art in its relation to conduct, as the *Christian Leader* and the *Christian World*, regards it as an ethical parable. *Light*, which I am told is the organ of the English mystics, regards it as "a work of high spiritual import." The *St James's Gazette*, which is seeking apparently to be the organ of the prurient, sees or pretends to see in it all kinds of dreadful things, and hints at Treasury prosecutions; and your Mr Charles Whibley genially says that he discovers in it "lots of morality." It is quite true that he goes on to say that he detects no art in it. But I do not think that it is fair to expect a critic to be able to see a work of art from every point of view. Even Gautier had his limitations just as much as Diderot had, and in modern England Goethes are rare. I can only assure Mr Charles Whibley that no moral apotheosis to which he has added the most modest contribution could possibly be a source of unhappiness to an artist.

I remain, sir, your obedient servant   OSCAR WILDE

To the Editor of the Scots Observer[2]

13 August 1890   *16 Tite Street*

Sir, I am afraid I cannot enter into any newspaper discussion on the

---

[1] Since Wilde's last letter the *Scots Observer* had printed on the same subject a letter signed Charles Whibley and citing Maupassant, Dostoievsky, Flaubert, Daudet and Marlowe; another from Whibley in the guise of the original reviewer, signed "Thersites;" and one signed "H" and written by Sir Herbert Stephen (1857–1932), Clerk of Assize for the Northern Circuit. This letter of Wilde's appeared on 2 August under the heading ART AND MORALITY. It was reprinted in *Miscellanies*.

[2] The correspondence had now been swollen by two further signed letters from

subject of art with Mr Whibley, partly because the writing of letters is always a trouble to me, and partly because I regret to say that I do not know what qualifications Mr Whibley possesses for the discussion of so important a topic. I merely noticed his letter because, I am sure without in any way intending it, he made a suggestion about myself personally that was quite inaccurate. His suggestion was that it must have been painful to me to find that a certain section of the public, as represented by himself and the critics of some religious publications, had insisted on finding what he calls "lots of morality" in my story of *The Picture of Dorian Gray*.

Being naturally desirous of setting your readers right on a question of such vital interest to the historian, I took the opportunity of pointing out in your columns that I regarded all such criticisms as a very gratifying tribute to the ethical beauty of the story, and I added that I was quite ready to recognise that it was not really fair to ask of any ordinary critic that he should be able to appreciate a work of art from every point of view. I still hold this opinion. If a man sees the artistic beauty of a thing, he will probably care very little for its ethical import. If his temperament is more susceptible to ethical than to aesthetic influences, he will be blind to questions of style, treatment, and the like. It takes a Goethe to see a work of art fully, completely, and perfectly, and I thoroughly agree with Mr Whibley when he says that it is a pity that Goethe never had an opportunity of reading *Dorian Gray*. I feel quite certain that he would have been delighted by it, and I only hope that some ghostly publisher is even now distributing shadowy copies in the Elysian fields, and that the cover of Gautier's copy is powdered with gilt asphodels.

You may ask me, sir, why I should care to have the ethical beauty of my story recognised. I answer, simply because it exists, because the thing is there. The chief merit of *Madame Bovary* is not the moral lesson that can be found in it, any more than the chief merit of *Salammbô* is its archaeology; but Flaubert was perfectly right in exposing the ignorance of those who called the one immoral and the other inaccurate; and not merely was he right in the ordinary sense of the word, but he was artistically right, which is everything. The critic has to educate the public; the artist has to educate the critic.

Allow me to make one more correction, sir, and I will have done with Mr Whibley. He ends his letter with the statement that I have been indefatigable in my public appreciation of my own work. I have no doubt that in saying this he means to pay me a compliment, but he really overrates my capacity, as well as my inclination for work. I must frankly confess that, by nature and by choice, I am extremely indolent. Cultivated idleness seems to me to be the proper occupation for man. I dislike newspaper

Whibley; and one each from T. E. Brown, the Manx poet-schoolmaster (1830–97), containing much reference to Zola; J. Maclaren Cobban (1849–1903); Vernon Blackburn (1867–1907), the Catholic music-critic; and William Archer, the dramatic critic. Although this letter, which appeared on 16 August under the same heading as its predecessor (and was reprinted in *Miscellanies*), was the last Wilde wrote to the *Scots Observer*, the correspondence continued for another three weeks.

controversies of any kind, and of the two hundred and sixteen criticisms of *Dorian Gray* that have passed from my library table into the waste-paper basket I have taken public notice of only three. One was that which appeared in the *Scots Observer*. I noticed it because it made a suggestion, about the intention of the author in writing the book, which needed correction. The second was an article in the *St James's Gazette*. It was offensively and vulgarly written, and seemed to me to require immediate and caustic censure. The tone of the article was an impertinence to any man of letters. The third was a meek attack in a paper called the *Daily Chronicle*. I think my writing to the *Daily Chronicle* was an act of pure wilfulness. In fact, I feel sure it was. I quite forget what they said. I believe they said that *Dorian Gray* was poisonous, and I thought that, on alliterative grounds, it would be kind to remind them that, however that may be, it is at any rate perfect. That was all. Of the other two hundred and thirteen criticisms I have taken no notice. Indeed, I have not read more than half of them. It is a sad thing, but one wearies even of praise.[1]

As regards Mr Brown's letter, it is interesting only in so far as it exemplifies the truth of what I have said above on the question of the two obvious schools of critics. Mr Brown says frankly that he considers morality to be the "strong point" of my story. Mr Brown means well, and has got hold of a half-truth, but when he proceeds to deal with the book from the artistic standpoint he, of course, goes sadly astray. To class *Dorian Gray* with M. Zola's *La Terre* is as silly as if one were to class Musset's[2] *Fortunio* with one of the Adelphi melodramas. Mr Brown should be content with ethical appreciation. There he is impregnable.

Mr Cobban opens badly by describing my letter, setting Mr Whibley right on a matter of fact, as an "impudent paradox." The term "impudent" is meaningless, and the word "paradox" is misplaced. I am afraid that writing to newspapers has a deteriorating influence on style. People get violent, and abusive, and lose all sense of proportion, when they enter that curious journalistic arena in which the race is always to the noisiest. "Impudent paradox" is neither violent nor abusive, but it is not an expression that should have been used about my letter. However, Mr Cobban makes full atonement afterwards for what was, no doubt, a mere error of manner, by adopting the impudent paradox in question as his

[1] Some of the most welcome praise came later. Pater's review of *Dorian Gray* did not appear until after publication in book form. In the November 1891 issue of the *Bookman* he wrote:

There is always something of an excellent talker about the writing of Mr Oscar Wilde; and in his hands, as happens so rarely with those who practise it, the form of dialogue is justified by its being really alive.

And in *United Ireland* of 26 September 1891 W. B. Yeats wrote:

Dorian Gray, with all its faults, is a wonderful book. *The Happy Prince* is a volume of as pretty fairy tales as our generation has seen; and *Intentions* hides within its immense paradox some of the most subtle literary criticism we are likely to see for many a long day.

[2] A slip for Gautier, as another correspondent was quick to point out.

own, and pointing out that, as I had previously said, the artist will always look at the work of art from the standpoint of beauty of style and beauty of treatment, and that those who have not got the sense of beauty, or whose sense of beauty is dominated by ethical considerations, will always turn their attention to the subject-matter and make its moral import the test and touchstone of the poem, or novel, or picture, that is presented to them, while the newspaper critic will sometimes take one side and sometimes the other, according as he is cultured or uncultured. In fact, Mr Cobban converts the impudent paradox into a tedious truism, and, I dare say, in doing so does good service. The English public like tediousness, and like things to be explained to them in a tedious way. Mr Cobban has, I have no doubt, already repented of the unfortunate expression with which he has made his *début*, so I will say no more about it. As far as I am concerned he is quite forgiven.

And finally, sir, in taking leave of the *Scots Observer* I feel bound to make a candid confession to you. It has been suggested to me by a great friend of mine, who is a charming and distinguished man of letters, and not unknown to you personally,[1] that there have been really only two people engaged in this terrible controversy, and that those two people are the editor of the *Scots Observer* and the author of *Dorian Gray*. At dinner this evening, over some excellent Chianti, my friend insisted that under assumed and mysterious names you had simply given dramatic expression to the views of some of the semi-educated classes in our community, and that the letters signed "H" were your own skilful, if somewhat bitter, caricature of the Philistine as drawn by himself. I admit that something of the kind had occurred to me when I read "H's" first letter—the one in which he proposed that the test of art should be the political opinions of the artist, and that if one differed from the artist on the question of the best way of misgoverning Ireland, one should always abuse his work. Still, there are such infinite varieties of Philistines, and North Britain is so renowned for seriousness, that I dismissed the idea as one unworthy of the editor of a Scotch paper. I now fear that I was wrong, and that you have been amusing yourself all the time by inventing little puppets and teaching them how to use big words. Well, sir, if it be so—and my friend is strong upon the point—allow me to congratulate you most sincerely on the cleverness with which you have reproduced that lack of literary style which is, I am told, essential for any dramatic and life-like characterisation. I confess that I was completely taken in; but I bear no malice; and as you have no doubt been laughing at me in your sleeve, let me now join openly in the laugh, though it be a little against myself. A comedy ends when the secret is out. Drop your curtain, and put your dolls to bed. I love Don Quixote, but I do not wish to fight any longer with marionettes, however cunning may be the master-hand that works their wires.[2] Let them go, sir,

[1] According to Mason, this was Robert Ross.
[2] In Chapter 26 of the Second Part of the novel, Don Quixote, watching a puppet-show at an inn, gets so carried away by the plot that he draws his sword, intervenes in the play and cuts the puppets to pieces.

on the shelf. The shelf is the proper place for them. On some future occasion you can re-label them and bring them out for our amusement. They are an excellent company, and go well through their tricks, and if they are a little unreal, I am not the one to object to unreality in art. The jest was really a good one. The only thing that I cannot understand is why you gave your marionettes such extraordinary and improbable names. I remain, sir, your obedient servant   OSCAR WILDE

To Arthur Fish
TS. Holland

8 August 1890   *16 Tite Street*

My dear Arthur Fish, You said you would like a photograph of me. I have got one for you. Will you come and get it, either tomorrow (Saturday) at six o'clock or Sunday at twelve o'clock. I fear you may be engaged, but should like to see you before your marriage, and give you my best wishes in person. If you can't come I will send it to you. Believe me, your sincere friend   OSCAR WILDE

To Michael Field[1]
MS. Bodley

[Postmark 13 August 1890]   *16 Tite Street*

I have only just come back from France, and your lovely book is the most gracious of welcomes. Thank you so much for it. Your Queen is a splendid creature, a live woman to her finger-tips. I feel the warmth of her breath as I listen to her. She is closer to flesh and blood than the Mary of Swinburne's *Bothwell*, who seems to me less real than the Mary of his *Chastelard*. Indeed I thank you very much, though by comparison my own little gift of little fairy tales shows but poorly. Yet I like such inequality, for it keeps me your debtor, and since I read *Callirrhoë* I have been that without hope of repayment. Sincerely and with gratitude yours   OSCAR WILDE

To James Knowles[2]
MS. Private

[Date of receipt 16 August 1890]   *16 Tite Street*

Dear Mr Knowles, I have received no corrected proof, nor indeed any-

[1] The joint pen-name of Katherine Bradley (1846–1914) and her niece Edith Cooper (1862–1913). They published many books of poems and verse-plays, none of which ever reached the stage. Among them were *Callirrhoë* (1884) and *The Tragic Mary* (1890), to which Wilde is here referring.

[2] See note 3, p. 80. In the *Nineteenth Century* for July 1890 he had published the first part of Wilde's essay "The True Function and Value of Criticism; with some

thing from you. Will you kindly let me have one, as I want to be off to Scotland. It is still a great source of regret to me that the dialogue has been interrupted. You will not, of course, let it be later than September. Believe me, truly yours   OSCAR WILDE

To Norman Forbes-Robertson

MS. Clark

[*18 August 1890*][1]   *Springwood Park, Kelso*[2]

My dear Norman, Thanks for your letter. I will now think over the scenario of the play.[3]

I am going on tomorrow to Bamff near Alyth, to stay with some friends. Are you at all near there I wonder? My Scottish geography is very bad indeed.

Hoping you are enjoying yourself. Ever yours   OSCAR

Remarks on the Importance of Doing Nothing: a Dialogue." The second part did not appear until the September issue. Both parts were reprinted, revised and renamed "The Critic as Artist," in *Intentions* (1891).

[1] This letter was addressed to 22 Bedford Square, London, and redirected to Brahan Castle, Conon Bridge, Scotland. The London postmark is dated 19 August 1890.

[2] The seat of Sir George Brisbane Scott-Douglas, Bart (1856–1935), country gentleman and poet. On 4 March 1905 he wrote to Robert Ross from Springwood Park (MS. Ross):

I can scarcely say that Wilde was ever a friend of mine—if he was, our friendship was of short duration, and died a natural death. Still I cannot but have an interest in him still, a warm regard for his memory, and the deepest sympathy for his terrible sorrow.

I had met him two or three times in Town, and very soon after the publication of *Dorian Gray* he spent four or five days with me here. They were delightful days to me, for he was in a most genial and light-hearted frame of mind, and his conversation—always more remarkable than his writing, as I thought—was at its best and most brilliant. We spent most of the time in driving about together to call on my neighbours, lunch with them, and so on, and everybody was delighted with him. When I saw him off at the station and said I hoped he would return, his answer was "I should *love* to." But he never did—in fact I never asked him. The fact was that he regarded me, however mistakenly, as a type of old-fashioned propriety, and I believe that soon after this he felt that I should not have the same pleasure in his society as I had had before. So he steered clear of me. This at any rate is my view of the matter, and I think it is one creditable to his delicacy. But indeed in the relations of ordinary society, Wilde was always I believe a perfect, and even I should say a high-bred, gentleman. And I shall always think of him as I knew him—rather than in connexion with his aberrations.

[3] Norman Forbes-Robertson managed the Globe Theatre for the first three months of 1891, and was now in search of plays.

To Wilfrid Meynell
MS. Sowerby

29 August 1890   *Bamff, Alyth, Perthshire*[1]

My dear Meynell, I am far away from the *Athenaeum* in the midst of purple heather and silver mist—such a relief to me, Celt as I am, from the wearisome green of England. I only like green in art. This is one of my many heresies.

When I am back in a few days I must look up the point at issue. In what a fine "temper" Newman always wrote! the temper of the scholar. But how subtle was his simple mind![2]

Pray give my kind regards to your wife. Believe me, truly yours

OSCAR WILDE

To James Knowles
MS. Clark

[Postmark 9 September 1890]   16 *Tite Street*

Dear Mr Knowles, I have only just returned from Scotland, where your letter has been following me about, or I would have answered you before.

The passage I was so anxious to retain was the *entire* Dante passage, showing the progress of a soul from horror to Heaven, through the medium of a book. However, as the article has appeared, I will say no more about it. It seemed to me that the passage was essential.[3]

I am sorry you seem to think my letter to you too strongly expressed. Of course as an editor you have to consider space, to preserve a balance of contents, but no one should be better able than yourself to understand how really painful it is to have one's work touched. I certainly belong to the *genus irritabile*, though when the thing is over I don't vex myself. In any case I need hardly say I intended no discourtesy to you. Truly yours

OSCAR WILDE

---

[1] The seat of Sir James Henry Ramsay, Bart (1832–1925), landowner, historian and mountaineer. His daughter Katharine (1874–1960) became, as Duchess of Atholl, one of the first women to hold a ministerial post in a British Government.

[2] Cardinal Newman had died on 11 August, and in the *Athenaeum* of 23 August Wilfrid Meynell published "Afterthoughts on Cardinal Newman as a Man of Letters." Among other matters he discussed the grammar of Newman's sentence (from *Lectures on the Present Position of Catholics in England*, 1851): "To Wesley you must go, and such as him," saying that Matthew Arnold had supported the accusative.

[3] It was restored when the essay was reprinted in *Intentions*.

To Edgar Saltus[1]
MS. Springarn

[? *September 1890*]

Have just returned from Scotland, and found your strange book, so pessimistic, so poisonous and so perfect. You have given me that *nouveau frisson* I am always looking for. If this is "in the green wood what shall be done in the old?"[2]

Why are you out? I wanted tea and talk—but talk first.

Will you come down and see me Thursday evening about 8.30 or nine o'clock if you have nothing better to do. I will be quite alone, and will you lunch on Sunday at 1.30?

But let me see you before then. I am so glad you have come over. Ever yours   OSCAR WILDE

To Clyde Fitch[3]

[? *September 1890*]   *16 Tite Street*

Dear Clyde, Just a line to tell you how sorry I am that you have left town, and how much I shall miss you.

When you return we must make merry over a flagon of purple wine, and invent new tales with which to charm the world.   o. w.

To Norman Forbes-Robertson
MS. Clark

[? *September 1890*]   *16 Tite Street*

Dear Norman, I have carefully considered the whole question, and am afraid that I could not afford to let my work be quite speculative. If you want a play from me I would require £100 down on the scenario being drawn out and approved of, and £100 on the completion of the manuscript.

[1] American novelist, essayist and poet (1855–1921). This letter cannot be dated with certainty, but Saltus was in London in 1890, and Wilde came back from Scotland early in September. "Pessimistic, poisonous and perfect" are just the adjectives Saltus would have liked applied to any of his books. He certainly gave Wilde a copy of his *Mary Magdalen* (1891). In 1917 he published a pamphlet, *Oscar Wilde: An Idler's Impression*, and later wrote a brief introduction to an American selection of Wilde's plays in the Modern Library.

[2] "For if they do these things in a green tree, what shall be done in the dry?" (*Luke*, xxiii, 31).

[3] William Clyde Fitch (1865–1909) later became a prolific and successful American dramatist. The date of this letter is uncertain, but there is record of a copy of *The Happy Prince* (1888) inscribed "Clyde Fitch from his friend Oscar Wilde. Faëry-stories for one who lives in Faëry-Land. Sept. '90." Several emotionally hero-worshipping letters from Fitch to Wilde are preserved in Clark. The text of this letter is taken from *Oscar Wilde, Fragments and Memories* by Martin Birnbaum (1920).

Then royalties of course to follow. If you can give these terms, well and good. If not, I fear I could not give up paying work for speculative. I am always in need of money, and have to work for certainties. If I were rich I would of course gladly do it for you, but, as it is, it would not be fair to others who are in a large measure dependent on me.

Speaking quite generally, I think that as a manager you will find it good economic policy to pay a good price for good plays: the play is always "the thing." Everything else is nothing. Ever yours   OSCAR

To Arthur Fish[1]

[*Circa 16 October 1890*]

My dear Arthur, I was charmed to get your letter, and it was delightful of you to remember my birthday. Though we see each other so rarely, I always think of you as one of my real friends, as I hope you will always think of me.

Ricketts has just done for me a lovely cover for *Dorian Gray*—grey pastel-paper with a white back and tiny gold marigolds. When it appears I will send you a copy.

How happy you must be in your little house; there are only two things in the world of any importance, Love and Art; you have both; they must never leave you.

Let me send my kindest regards to your wife; I like to think that the wives of my friends are my friends also; and believe me, sincerely yours
OSCAR WILDE

To Arthur Symons[2]
MS. Berg

[*Postmark 22 October 1890*]   *16 Tite Street*

Dear Mr Symons, We have no day just at present, as my wife is going away for a fortnight, but I hope you will come and dine with us some night. It was a great pleasure meeting you, as I had admired your work for a long time. I look forward to an evening together, and to a talk about French art, the one art now in Europe that is worth discussing—Verlaine's art especially.

Who has parodied our dear Pater in the *Cornhill*? It is clever and horrid. The parody on Kipling is excellent: one had there merely to reproduce a caricature of life and literature. Do you think Barrie wrote it?[3] Truly yours   OSCAR WILDE

[1] Text from *Cassell's Weekly*, 2 May 1923.
[2] Poet and critic (1865–1945). At this date, apart from many critical articles, he had published only *An Introduction to the Study of Browning* (1886) and a book of poems, *Days and Nights* (1889), which was dedicated "to Walter Pater in all gratitude and affection." He had contributed to the *Woman's World* a poem and an article on Villiers de l'Isle-Adam.
[3] Not Barrie but Barry Pain (1864–1928). He contributed anonymous parodies

276

To Richard Le Gallienne[1]

[*Postmark 1 December 1890*]   *16 Tite Street*

It is a wonderful book,[2] full of exquisite intuitions, and bright illuminating thought-flashes, and swift, sudden, sure revelations, a book behind which there is a soul-temperament, and thought shows itself stained by colour and passion, rich and Dionysiac and red-veined, while the aesthetic instinct is immediate in its certainty, and has that true ultimate simplicity that comes, like the dawn, out of a complex night of many wandering worlds. I knew the book would be excellent, but its fine maturity amazes me; it has a rich ripeness about it. You have realised yourself in it.

I want so much to see you: when can that be? Friendship and love like ours need not meetings, but they are delightful. I hope the laurels are not too thick across your brow for me to kiss your eyelids.   OSCAR

---

of Kipling, Ruskin, R. D. Blackmore, Pater and Tolstoy to the *Cornhill* for October 1890. They were reprinted in his book *Playthings and Parodies* (1892).

[1] Text from the American Art Association catalogue of 9 February 1927.

[2] *George Meredith: Some Characteristics*, first published on 19 November 1890.

LONDON III

1891-95

PART FIVE

London III: 1891-95

It was almost certainly in the year 1891 that there entered Wilde's life the man who was to be in some sense his inspiration and in every sense his evil genius. Lord Alfred Bruce Douglas, the third son of the eighth Marquess of Queensberry, had been born in 1870, educated at Winchester, and was now a second-year undergraduate at Magdalen College, Oxford. Lionel Johnson, a Winchester contemporary and Oxford friend, brought him to see Wilde at Tite Street. Douglas says this momentous meeting took place in 1891, and in the vacation, which seems likely. In his letter to More Adey of 7 April 1897 (see p. 525) Wilde wrote:

> The friendship began in May 1892 by his brother appealing to me in a very pathetic letter to help him in terrible trouble with people who were blackmailing him. I hardly knew him at the time. I had known him eighteen months, but had only seen him four times in that space.

Eighteen months would put the first meeting back to November 1890, but two months' grace to Wilde's figures would bring it to January 1891, during the Christmas vacation.

There exists a copy of the Large Paper edition of *The Picture of Dorian Gray* (published 1 July 1891) inscribed "Alfred Douglas from his friend who wrote this book. July 91. Oscar," and in an unpublished letter to Frank Harris (MS. Ross, A. L.), dated 20 March 1925, Douglas wrote "the second time he saw me (when he gave me a copy of *Dorian Gray* which I took back with me to Oxford)."

This does not necessarily conflict with the possibility of a first meeting in January, and it is therefore possible that the extra material for the book-edition of *Dorian Gray* was written after the meeting. On the other hand, this material consists mainly of elaboration, and the main characters and episodes in the story were certainly written before Douglas entered Wilde's life.

To George Alexander[1]
MS. Arents

[2 February 1891]   16 Tite Street

My dear Aleck, I am not satisfied with myself or my work. I can't get a grip of the play[2] yet: I can't get my people real. The fact is I worked at it when I was not in the mood for work, and must first forget it, and then go back quite fresh to it. I am very sorry, but artistic work can't be done unless one is in the mood; certainly my work can't. Sometimes I spend months over a thing, and don't do any good; at other times I write a thing in a fortnight.

You will be interested to hear that the *Duchess of Padua* was produced in New York last Wednesday, under the title of *Guido Ferranti*, by Lawrence Barrett.[3] The name of the author was kept a dead secret, and indeed not revealed till yesterday when at Barrett's request I acknowledged the authorship by cable. Barrett wires to me that it was a huge success, and that he is going to run it for his season. He seems to be in great delight over it.

With regard to the cheque for £50 you gave me, shall I return you the money, and end the agreement, or keep it and when the play is written let you have the rights and refusal of it? That will be just as you wish.

I am delighted to hear you had a brilliant opening at the St James's.[4]
Ever yours   OSCAR WILDE

To Edward Lawson[5]
MS. Private

[2 February 1891]   16 Tite Street

Dear Mr Lawson, The delightful article in your issue of this morning has inspired the enclosed letter. I don't wish to sign my name, though I am afraid everybody will know who the writer is: one's style is one's signature always.

[1] Stage name of George Alexander Gibb Samson, English actor and manager (1858–1918). He acted with Irving from 1881 with one brief interval until 1889, when he entered into management on his own. His tenancy of the St James's Theatre lasted from 1891 until his death. He was knighted in 1911.

[2] *Lady Windermere's Fan.*

[3] Mason gives Monday, 26 January 1891 as the date of the play's opening, and clearly Wilde thought it had occurred on Wednesday, 28 January, but Odell (*Annals of the New York Stage*, vol. 14, p. 539) gives Wednesday, 21 January, and this is confirmed by the *New York Dramatic Mirror* of 31 January 1891. All are agreed that the run ended on 14 February. The part of Beatrice, which Wilde had written for Mary Anderson, was played by Minna K. Gale.

[4] Alexander's long tenancy of the St James's Theatre began on 31 January 1891, when he transferred R. C. Carton's *Shadow and Sunlight* there from the Avenue Theatre.

[5] 1833–1916. Principal proprietor and in practice editor of the *Daily Telegraph*. Born Edward Levy, he assumed the surname of Lawson in 1875, was created a baronet in 1892 and the first Lord Burnham in 1903. The second leading article in the *Daily Telegraph* of 2 February 1891 was on the subject of modern dress.

I think, however, that the subject of modern dress is worth discussing, and of course yours is the paper that is in quickest touch with the public, and to which the public look for a topic to write on. Believe me, truly yours   OSCAR WILDE

I know you like news of the stage. This will be news. On Wednesday last a blank-verse romantic drama in five acts, called *Guido Ferranti*, was produced in New York by Mr Lawrence Barrett. The name of the author was kept a profound secret. The play achieved an immense success and excited much curiosity. At Mr Barrett's request the author revealed himself on Sunday by cable. It was Mr Oscar Wilde. He was anxious to have the play judged entirely on its own merits. The result has justified his expectations. The play is running to crowded houses.[1]

To the Editor of the Daily Telegraph[2]

2 February 1891   *London*

Sir, With reference to the interesting article on men's dress and the fashions for next season that appears in today's issue of your paper, will you allow me to point out that the costume worn now by Mr Wyndham in *London Assurance* might be taken as the basis for a new departure, not in the style, but in the colour of modern evening dress.[3] The costume in question belongs to 1840 or 1841, and its charm resides in the fact that the choice of the colour of the coat is left to the taste and fancy and inclination of the wearer. Freedom in such selection of colour is a necessary condition of variety and individualism of costume, and the uniform black that is worn now, though valuable at a dinner-party, where it serves to isolate and separate women's dresses, to frame them as it were, still is dull and tedious and depressing in itself, and makes the aspect of club-life and men's dinners monotonous and uninteresting. The little note of individualism that makes dress delightful can only be attained nowadays by the colour and treatment of the flower one wears. This is a great pity. The colour of the coat should be entirely for the good taste of the wearer to decide. This would give pleasure, and produce charming variety of colour effects in modern life.

Another important point in Mr Wyndham's very graceful and elegant costume is that the decorative value of buttons is recognised. At present we all have more than a dozen useless buttons on our evening coats, and by always keeping them black and of the same colour as the rest of the costume we prevent them being in any way beautiful. Now, when a thing is useless

[1] The substance of this paragraph, slightly cut and altered, duly appeared in the *Daily Telegraph* of 6 February.
[2] This letter, which was published in the *Daily Telegraph* of 3 February 1891 under the heading FASHIONS IN DRESS, has not hitherto been recognised as Wilde's.
[3] Dion Boucicault's comedy *London Assurance* (originally produced in 1841) had been revived at the Criterion Theatre on 27 November 1890, with Charles Wyndham, Arthur Bourchier, Cyril Maude, Mary Moore and Mrs Bernard Beere in the cast.

it should be made beautiful, otherwise it has no reason for existing at all. Buttons should be either gilt, as in Mr Wyndham's costume, or of paste, or enamel, or inlaid metal, or any other material that is capable of being artistically treated. The handsome effect produced by servants' liveries is almost entirely due to the buttons they wear.

Nor would these suggested changes be in any way violent, or abrupt, or revolutionary; or calculated to excite terror in the timid, or rage in the dull, or fury in the honest Philistine. For the dress of 1840 is really the same in design and form as ours. Of course, the sleeves are tighter and the cuffs turn each over them, as sleeves should be and as cuffs should do. The trousers, also, are tighter than the present fashion, but the general cut of the dress is the same. It consists, as ours does, of tail-coat, open waistcoat, and trousers.

Two other points may be noticed. The first is that the use of a frill to the shirt prevents the tediousness of a flat polished surface of stiff linen—breaks it up very pleasantly in fact. Modern English evening shirts are too monotonous. In France—or perhaps I should say in Paris—shirts are made much more charming than with us. The second point is the beauty and utility of the cloaks in which Mr Wyndham and Mr Arthur Bourchier make their appearance. They are dark in colour, as, on the whole, cloaks in constant service should be. Their folds are ample, picturesque and comforting. Their bright-coloured linings are delightful, and fanciful and gay. Their capes give warmth and suggest dignity and serve to make the lines of the cloaks richer and more complex. A cloak is an admirable thing. Our nearest approach to it is the Inverness cape, which, when its wings are lined with black satin, is very charming in its way. Still it has, though not sleeves, yet sleeve openings. A cloak can be put on, or thrown off, far more easily. A cloak is also warmer, and can be wrapped round one, if there is a chill wind. We must wear cloaks with lovely linings. Otherwise we shall be very incomplete.

The coat, then, of next season, will be an exquisite colour-note, and have also a great psychological value. It will emphasise the serious and thoughtful side of a man's character. One will be able to discern a man's views of life by the colour he selects. The colour of the coat will be symbolic. It will be part of the wonderful symbolistic movement in modern art. The imagination will concentrate itself on the waistcoat. Waistcoats will show whether a man can admire poetry or not. That will be very valuable. Over the shirt-front Fancy will preside. By a single glance one will be able to detect the tedious. How the change is to be brought about it is not difficult to see. In Paris the Duc de Morny has altered the colour of coats.[1] But the English dislike individualism. Nothing but a resolution on the subject passed solemnly by the House of Commons will do with us. Surely there are some amongst our legislators who are capable of taking a serious interest in serious things? They cannot all be absorbed in the county-

[1] Auguste-Charles-Louis, Duc de Morny (1859–1920), French sportsman and dandy. Son of the famous Duc, who was a bastard half-brother of Napoleon III.

court collection of tithes.[1] I sincerely hope that a motion of some kind will be brought forward on the question, and that the First Lord of the Treasury will assign some day for discussion of a topic that is of really national importance. When the motion has been agreed to, servants will, of course, be asked to dress as their masters do now. As a slight compensation to them, their wages should be increased, if not doubled.

Of the moral value and influence of such a charming costume I think I had better say nothing. The fact is that when Mr Wyndham and Mr Arthur Bourchier appear in their delightful dresses they have been behaving very badly. At least Mr Arthur Bourchier has, and Mr Wyndham's conduct seems to me to justify some moral censure at any rate. But if one is to behave badly, it is better to be bad in a becoming dress than in one that is unbecoming, and it is only fair to add that at the end of the play Mr Wyndham accepts his lecture with a dignity and courtesy of manner that can only result from the habit of wearing delightful clothes. I am, sir, your obedient servant

o.

To Charles Cartwright[2]
MS. Private

[? *2 February 1891*]   *16 Tite Street*

Dear Mr Cartwright, I suppose a

> Blank verse
> Five Act
> Romantic
> Costume
> Tragedy

as performed in the States by Lawrence Barrett with great success—I am obliged to add—would not suit you? *The Duchess of Padua* is its name.

It requires

> One quite beautiful heroine
> One passionate *jeune premier*
> One evil old man.

But it would cost a lot of money.

I am so glad you are going to take a theatre. Truly yours

OSCAR WILDE

To Henry Irving
MS. Irving

[*Circa 3 February 1891*]   *16 Tite Street*

My dear Irving, On Wednesday last a poetic tragedy of mine called *Guido Ferranti* was produced in New York by Lawrence Barrett, the name of the

---

[1] The Tithe Rent-Charge Recovery Bill was then being considered in Committee by the House of Commons.   [2] English actor and manager (1855-1916.)

author being concealed. It achieved, Barrett cabled to me, an immense success, which, of course, pleased me very much, as it was entirely on its own merits. On Sunday, at Barrett's request, I acknowledged authorship by cabling my thanks to the public for their reception of my play.

Now, of course, you are the one artist in England who can produce poetic blank-verse drama, and as I have pointed out in this month's *Fortnightly*[1] you have created in the theatre-going public both taste and temperament, so that there is an audience for a poet inside a theatre, though there is no or but a small audience for a poet outside a theatre. The public as a class don't read poetry, but you have made them listen to it.

You have my play already under its first title *The Duchess of Padua*. Why not produce it? I should be quite content to have it produced for one performance, to be put regularly in the bills if you and the public take pleasure in it. I need not say what a delight it would be to me to have my work produced by you. You know that you have no warmer and sincerer admirer than myself, and your theatre has always been to me the one link between our stage and our literature.

If you wish I will send you a copy of the play, and Barrett will send the acting version I have no doubt, if I ask him. Or you may like to make your own. In the copy I have there is no cutting, and the play is long—too long—but in his version it plays three hours.

In any case, believe me, always yours   OSCAR WILDE

To Grant Allen[2]

MS. Clark

[*Circa 7 February 1891*]   *16 Tite Street*

Dear Mr Grant Allen, I beg you will allow me to express to you my real delight in your article in the *Fortnightly*, with its superb assertion of that

---

[1] In *The Soul of Man Under Socialism*, which first appeared in the *Fortnightly Review* for February 1891, Wilde had written:

> With his marvellous and vivid personality, with a style that has really a true colour-element in it, with his extraordinary power, not over mere mimicry but over imaginative and intellectual creation, Mr Irving, had his sole object been to give the public what they wanted, could have produced the commonest plays in the commonest manner, and made as much success and money as a man could possibly desire. But his object was not that. His object was to realise his own perfection as an artist, under certain conditions and in certain forms of Art. At first he appealed to the few: now he has educated the many. He has created in the public both taste and temperament. The public appreciate his artistic success immensely. I often wonder, however, whether the public understand that that success is entirely due to the fact that he did not accept their standard, but realised his own. With their standard the Lyceum would have been a sort of second-rate booth, as some of the popular theatres in London are at present.

[2] Man of letters and rationalist (1848–99). Wrote many books on evolution and kindred topics, as well as much fiction, including *The Woman Who Did* (1895). His essay "The Celt in English Art" appeared in the *Fortnightly Review* of February

Celtic spirit in Art that Arnold divined, but did not demonstrate, at any rate in the sense of scientific demonstration, such as yours is.

I was dining at the House of Commons on Thursday, and proposed to some Scotch and Welsh members, who had read your article with pride and pleasure, that as to break bread and drink wine together is, as Christ saw, the simplest and most natural symbol of comradeship, *all* of us who are Celts, Welsh, Scotch, and Irish, should inaugurate a Celtic Dinner, and assert ourselves, and show these tedious Angles or Teutons what a race we are, and how proud we are to belong to that race. You are, of course, a Celt. You must be. What do you think of the idea? It is the outcome of your article, so I want you to join in getting our gorgeous banquet up. Think over it. In any case, we all owe you a debt.

My mother is fascinated and delighted by your article, and begs me to tell you so. Truly yours   OSCAR WILDE

To Frances Forbes-Robertson[1]
MS. Princeton

[*Postmark 16 February 1891*]   *16 Tite Street*

My dear Frankie, My play has been an immense success. A thousand thanks for your congratulations. I hope to bring it out here soon, at some good theatre. Why do you never come to see us on Wednesdays? I go to Paris tomorrow for a week but will be in town afterwards for ages as I have much to do.

My novel is coming out next month in volume form, also a book of essays, so I am hard at work, or should be.[2] Believe me always your sincere friend   OSCAR WILDE

To Stéphane Mallarmé[3]
MS. Bonniot

Mercredi [*Postmark 25 February 1891*]   *Hôtel de l'Athénée* [*Paris*]

Cher Maître, Comment dois-je vous remercier pour la gracieuse façon avec

---

1891, alongside Wilde's *The Soul of Man Under Socialism*. There exists (MS. Clark) a letter from Allen to Wilde, dated 6 February, which must have crossed this one in the post. In it Allen wrote: "Will you allow me to thank you most heartily for your noble and beautiful essay in this month's *Fortnightly*? I would have written every line of it myself—if only I had known how."

[1] Novelist (1866–1956), sister of Johnston, Norman, Eric and Ian.

[2] *The Picture of Dorian Gray* was in fact published in volume form by Ward Lock at 6/- in April 1891, though the large-paper edition of 250 signed copies at 21/- did not appear till 1 July. Wilde received £125 on account of a 10 per cent royalty. In 1895 Ward Lock bought the book outright from the Official Receiver for £10, and in 1905 resold it "for a small sum" to Charles Carrington (see note 2, p. 758). The book of essays, *Intentions* (900 copies at 7/6), was published by Osgood McIlvaine on 2 May 1891.

[3] French symbolist poet (1842–98). He earned his living as a schoolmaster, but lived only for poetry. His Paris flat in the Rue de Rome became a centre of literary talk and inspiration.

laquelle vous m'avez présenté la magnifique symphonie en prose que vous a inspiré les mélodies du génie du grand poète celtique, Edgar Allan Poe.[1] En Angleterre nous avons de la prose et de la poésie, mais la prose française et la poésie dans les mains d'un maître tel que vous deviennent une et la même chose.

Le privilège de connaître l'auteur de *L'Après-midi d'un Faune* est on ne peut plus flatteur, mais de trouver en lui l'accueil que vous m'avez montré est en vérité inoubliable.

Ainsi, cher maître, veuillez agréer l'assurance de ma haute et très parfaite considération OSCAR WILDE

To Cyril Wilde
TS. Clark

Tuesday, 3 March [1891]   *Hôtel de l'Athénée, 15 Rue Scribe [Paris]*

My dearest Cyril, I send you a letter to tell you I am much better. I go every day and drive in a beautiful forest called the Bois de Boulogne, and in the evening I dine with my friend, and sit out afterwards at little tables and see the carriages drive by. Tonight I go to visit a great poet, who has given me a wonderful book about a Raven. I will bring you and Vyvyan back some chocolates when I return.

I hope you are taking great care of dear Mamma. Give her my love and kisses, and also love and kisses to Vyvyan and yourself. Your loving Papa
OSCAR WILDE

To Coulson Kernahan[2]
MS. B.M.

[Postmark 7 March 1891]   *Hôtel de l'Athénée, Rue Scribe, Paris*

My dear Kernahan, Thank you for your charming letter. I have been very ill, and unable to correct my proofs, but have sent them now.

I have changed my mind about correcting the passage about temptation. One can't pull a work of art about without spoiling it. And after all it is merely Luther's *Pecca Fortiter*[3] put dramatically into the lips of a character. Just explain this to Ward & Lock. I am responsible for the book: they are not. If they really feel deeply about it I will try in the revise and invent something else, but don't tell them I said so. It has bothered me terribly, their suggesting changes, etc. One can't do it.

[1] *Le Corbeau*, Mallarmé's prose translation of Poe's poem "The Raven" (1875, second edition 1889).

[2] English author and journalist (1858–1943). He was at this time and for many years literary adviser to Messrs Ward, Lock, the publishers of *The Picture of Dorian Gray*. His *In Good Company* (1917) contains a chapter on Wilde.

[3] *"Esto peccator et pecca fortiter"* (Be a sinner and sin in earnest). Martin Luther, in a letter to Melanchthon (*Lutheri Epistolae*, Jena, 1556, i, 345).

The preface will be as it stands in the *Fortnightly* with a few corrections. I will send it to you tomorrow.[1]

Do you think I should add to the preface the definition of "morbid" and "unhealthy" art I give in the *Fortnightly* for February? The one on morbidity is really good.[2]

Will you also look after my "wills" and "shalls" in proof. I am Celtic in my use of these words, not English.

As soon as I get the revise, and pass it, the book may go to press, but I must pass it first. *This is essential.* Please tell them so.

You are excellent on Rossetti. I read you with delight.[3] Your sincere friend   OSCAR WILDE

To Coulson Kernahan

MS. Edmiston

Monday [Postmark 16 March 1891]   *Hotel Metropole, Brighton*

My dear Kernahan, I am still very ill, but Brighton is doing me good. I have to return tomorrow, to town.

Your telegram was most welcome—the proposal of alterations really had vexed and worried my nerves to a point beyond bearing.

With regard to the preface, let it stand as in *Fortnightly*—except, after "No artist has ethical sympathies etc," insert "No artist is ever morbid. The artist can express everything." as a separate aphorism. Also in aphorism "Those who read the symbol do so at their peril *also*," strike out "*also*." It is unnecessary. Will you do this for me? I have not got a proof of the preface. Your friend   OSCAR WILDE

---

[1] The preface to *The Picture of Dorian Gray* (which consists of twenty-five aphorisms) appeared for the first time (as twenty-three aphorisms) in the March 1891 issue of the *Fortnightly Review*.

[2] The two passages from *The Soul of Man Under Socialism* are:

What is morbidity but a mood of emotion or a mode of thought that one cannot express? The public are all morbid, because the public can never find expression for anything. The artist is never morbid. He expresses everything. He stands outside his subject, and through its medium produces incomparable and artistic effects. To call an artist morbid because he deals with morbidity as his subject-matter is as silly as if one called Shakespeare mad because he wrote *King Lear*.

An unhealthy work of art . . . is a work whose style is obvious, old-fashioned, and common, and whose subject is deliberately chosen, not because the artist has any pleasure in it, but because he thinks that the public will pay him for it. In fact, the popular novel that the public call healthy is always a thoroughly unhealthy production; and what the public call an unhealthy novel is always a beautiful and healthy work of art.

[3] Kernahan's essay "A Note on Rossetti" first appeared as "Rossetti and the Moralists" in the *Fortnightly Review* for March 1891 and was reprinted in his book *Sorrow and Song* (1894).

To J. S. Little
MS. Berg

[*21 March 1891*][1]   *16 Tite Street*

My dear Little, I have been ill, and away in Paris to recruit, or I would have answered your charming letter before. Let me thank you now for it. I am very glad you liked the article. The attempt made by the journalists to dictate to the artist and to limit his subject matter is of course quite monstrous, and everyone who cares at all for Art must strongly protest against it.

My novel appears in volume form next month, and I am curious to see whether these wretched journalists will assail it so ignorantly and pruriently as they did before. My preface should teach them to mend their wicked ways. Believe me, sincerely yours   OSCAR WILDE

To Elizabeth Robins
MS. Wilberforce

[*Late March 1891*]   *16 Tite Street*

Dear Miss Robins, I have been very ill—overworked at any rate—and away for rest. But now that I am back I should very much like to have the pleasure of calling on you, and will do so at four o'clock tomorrow.

I should much like to be present at *Hedda Gabler*.[2] Perhaps your acting manager will kindly reserve a stall for me. It is a most interesting play, nor could there be any [better] exponent of its subtlety and tragedy than yourself. Believe me, truly yours   OSCAR WILDE

To William Morris[3]
MS. B.M.

[? *March–April 1891*]   *16 Tite Street*

Dear Mr Morris, The book has arrived! And I must write you a line to tell you how gratified I am at your sending it. How proud indeed so beautiful a gift makes me. I weep over the cover which is not nearly lovely

---

[1] So dated by recipient.
[2] The first production of Ibsen's play in English was at the Vaudeville Theatre on 20 April 1891, with Elizabeth Robins in the title-rôle.
[3] English poet, artist, manufacturer and Socialist (1834–96). Started the Kelmscott Press at Hammersmith 1890. The book mentioned here may conceivably have been *News from Nowhere*: the covers of either the first American edition (1890) or the paper-backed issue of the first English edition (1891) might easily have made Wilde weep. When Morris published the Kelmscott edition of *Sidonia the Sorceress*, Wilde suggested Aubrey Beardsley as illustrator, but his rough drawings were rejected by Morris. The oft-repeated story that when Morris was dying the only person he could bear to see was Wilde seems to have been invented by Bernard Shaw. Wilde had been almost eighteen months in prison when Morris died.

enough, not nearly rich enough in material, for such prose as you write. But the book itself, if it is to have suitable raiment, would need damask sewn with pearls and starred with gold. I have always felt that your work comes from the sheer delight of making beautiful things: that no alien motive ever interests you: that in its singleness of aim, as well as in its perfection of result, it is pure art, everything that you do. But I know you hate the blowing of trumpets. I have loved your work since boyhood: I shall always love it. That, with my thanks, is all I have to say. Sincerely yours   OSCAR WILDE

To Miss Marion Lea[1]
MS. Wilberforce

[*March–April 1891*]   *Lyric Club*

Dear Miss Lea, I should esteem it a great privilege to come to *Hedda Gabler*. It is most plucky of you and Miss Robins to produce this new and fascinating play, and I feel sure you will have a great success, and you are certain to have the sympathy and admiration of all who are interested in the development of the Drama. Truly yours   OSCAR WILDE

Telegram: *to Elizabeth Robins*
MS. Wilberforce

23 April 1891   *London*

Can I have a box or two stalls for tomorrow? I must see your great performance again. It is a real masterpiece of art.   OSCAR WILDE

To Arthur Conan Doyle[2]

[? *April 1891*]

Between me and life there is a mist of words always. I throw probability out of the window for the sake of a phrase, and the chance of an epigram

[1] American actress (1861–1944).

[2] 1859–1930. The text of this fragment is taken from his *Memories and Adventures* (1924). The original letter seems to have disappeared from the voluminous Conan Doyle papers. He introduced the fragment with these words:

Stoddart, the American, proved to be an excellent fellow, and had two others to dinner. They were Gill, a very entertaining Irish M.P., and Oscar Wilde, who was already famous as the champion of aestheticism. It was indeed a golden evening for me. Wilde to my surprise had read *Micah Clarke* and was enthusiastic about it, so that I did not feel a complete outsider.

The result of the evening was that both Wilde and I promised to write books for *Lippincott's Magazine*—Wilde's contribution was *The Picture of Dorian Gray*, a book which is surely upon a high moral plane, while I wrote *The Sign of Four*, in which Holmes made his second appearance.

When his little book came out I wrote to say what I thought of it. His letter

makes me desert truth. Still I do aim at making a work of art, and I am really delighted that you think my treatment subtle and artistically good. The newspapers seem to me to be written by the prurient for the Philistine. I cannot understand how they can treat *Dorian Gray* as immoral. My difficulty was to keep the inherent moral subordinate to the artistic and dramatic effect, and it still seems to me that the moral is too obvious.

To R. Clegg[1]
TS. Holland

[? *April 1891*]   *16 Tite Street*

My dear Sir, Art is useless because its aim is simply to create a mood. It is not meant to instruct, or to influence action in any way. It is superbly sterile, and the note of its pleasure is sterility. If the contemplation of a work of art is followed by activity of any kind, the work is either of a very second-rate order, or the spectator has failed to realise the complete artistic impression.

A work of art is useless as a flower is useless. A flower blossoms for its own joy. We gain a moment of joy by looking at it. That is all that is to be said about our relations to flowers. Of course man may sell the flower, and so make it useful to him, but this has nothing to do with the flower. It is not part of its essence. It is accidental. It is a misuse. All this I fear is very obscure. But the subject is a long one. Truly yours

OSCAR WILDE

To Henry Irving
MS. Irving

[*Circa April 1891*]   *16 Tite Street*

My dear Irving, I am of course very much pleased at your wishing to recite something of mine on the occasion of Sims Reeves's retirement, but I am afraid that I could not do anything for such an occasion that would be worthy of either you or myself.

Sims Reeves is merely to me a vague name, and he seems to me, though perhaps I am wrong, to have stood quite apart from the development of modern music. In fact I find no *motif* in the occasion; which, believe me, disappoints me very much indeed.[2]

---

is worth reproducing, as showing the true Wilde. I omit the early part in which he comments on my own work in too generous terms.

J. M. Stoddart (see note 4, p. 87) had in 1890 abandoned publishing on his own and returned to Lippincott. Thomas Patrick Gill (1858–1931), Irish Nationalist M.P. for South Louth 1885–92, had American connections in journalism and was an associate editor of the *North American Review* 1883–85.

[1] Unidentified. The last of the aphorisms which form the preface to *The Picture of Dorian Gray* is "All art is quite useless."

[2] A farewell concert to Sims Reeves the singer (1822–1900) on his retirement took place in the Albert Hall on 11 May 1891. During the performance Irving recited some laudatory verses written by W. H. Pollock.

Thanking you for your suggestion, however, I remain, very sincerely
yours   OSCAR WILDE

To the Earl of Lytton[1]
MS. Cobbold

[? *May 1891*]   *16 Tite Street*

My dear Lord Lytton, I have not been able to come over to Paris this
week—are you free next week? If so, a few days with you in Paris would
be a real privilege, and a great delight. But I fear your house may be
crowded. Will you let me know? A wire on Saturday would enable me
to fix my plans.

I was so pleased to find you were at one with me about the Ibsen play—
I felt pity and terror, as though the play had been Greek. Very sincerely
yours   OSCAR WILDE

To Roland Atwood[2]
TS. Holland

[*Postmark 25 June 1891*]   *16 Tite Street*

Dear Roland, I was so sorry not to see you yesterday: I hope you will come
and dine with me some night next week.

I send you your necktie, in which I know you will look Greek and
gracious. I don't think it is too dark for you.

Since I saw you I have heard so much of your Silvius, and how romantic
it was, and how beautifully that rich musical voice of yours rendered the
poetry and the passion of Shakespeare's verse, so I am not surprised that
you have had many offers. Do stay in town, and act for us. Affectionately
yours   OSCAR

Has Gerald Gurney forgiven me yet for talking to no one but you that
afternoon? I suppose not. But who else was there for me to talk to?

[1] Edward Robert Bulwer, first Earl of Lytton (1831–91). Only son of Bulwer
Lytton. Published much verse as Owen Meredith. Viceroy of India 1876–80.
Ambassador in Paris from 1887 until his death there on 24 November 1891. Wilde
dedicated *Lady Windermere's Fan* (1893) TO THE DEAR MEMORY OF ROBERT EARL
OF LYTTON IN AFFECTION AND ADMIRATION.
[2] English actor. On 18 June 1891 a matinee performance of *As You Like It*,
produced by Ben Greet, was given at the Shaftesbury Theatre. Mrs Patrick
Campbell (still an amateur) played Rosalind, Roland Atwood Silvius, and Gerald
Gurney Le Beau. *The Era* wrote: "Mr Roland Atwood filled the role of Silvius
with satisfaction."

To Herbert P. Horne

MS. Dugdale

[*Date of receipt 2 July 1891*]   *16 Tite Street*

My dear Horne, A thousand thanks. What a lovely little book! And what dainty delightful verse![1] The notes of passion so vivid and scarlet, and yet conveyed with such subtlety and fine reticence. I am rejoiced to see again your "Paradise Walk" with its marvellous third stanza, so large and simple:[2] and I love "Amico Suo" and "The Measure" and "If she be made of white and red," and indeed the whole book is full of honey and very sweet to taste, and just touched with that sadness which is inseparable from modern art, and gives a preciousness to beauty, as of a thing one might lose, and so loves overmuch: and you are a perfect player of a little lovely reed. And so, more thanks, and always sincerely yours   OSCAR WILDE

To William Heinemann[3]

MS. Berg

[*Summer 1891*]   *16 Tite Street*

Dear Mr Heinemann, I have sent you a copy of *Intentions*, the copyright of which belongs to me. In case you thought it too large a book for your series, the last essay might be left out.

Pray let me know at your convenience what you propose doing in the matter. The book has been very successful here, and I think should do well abroad.

A copy of *Lord Arthur Savile's Crime* has also been sent by my publishers. Yours very truly   OSCAR WILDE

To Jules Cantel[4]

F. Cantel

[? *Summer 1891*]

Avec beaucoup de plaisir j'autorise M. J. Cantel à faire la traduction en

---

[1] *Diversi Colores*, Horne's only volume of poems, was published by the author in 1891.

> [2] And the magical reach of her thigh
> Is the measure, with which God began
> To build up the peace of the sky,
> And fashion the pleasures of man.

[3] English publisher (1863–1920). Founded his own firm 1890. *Intentions* appeared in October in the paperback English Library, which Heinemann and Wolcott Balestier issued from Leipzig, in imitation of Tauchnitz. *Lord Arthur Savile's Crime* (which had been published in London by Osgood McIlvaine in July, 1500 copies at two shillings), though announced as "in the press," never appeared in the series.

[4] French writer and translator (b. 1873). This letter may not have been addressed to him, since the facsimile makes it look as though there may have been a preceding

français d'*Intentions*. Le droit de donner cette autorisation appartient à moi seul. Seulement je ne veux pas qu'il traduise le dernier essai, "La Vérité des Masques;" je ne l'aime plus. Au lieu de cela, on pourra mettre l'essai paru dans le *Fortnightly Review* de février dernier sur "L'Ame de l'Homme," qui contient une partie de mon esthétique.   OSCAR WILDE

To Coulson Kernahan
MS. Edmiston

[? *August 1891*][1]   *16 Tite Street*

My dear Kernahan, Thank you so much for your kind and charming letter. Of course I knew you had nothing at all to do with the very gross insult put on me by Mr Bowden: it has been followed by another. I sent them a cheque on the Friday: no acknowledgment was made of it: on the following Wednesday evening I got a letter from a solicitor to say that he was instructed by the firm to accept my cheque "provided that it was not dishonoured"! This is quite the climax of everything.

I feel it all the more, I mean the whole transaction, as, not knowing the proper price of books, I let them have *Dorian Gray* for ten per cent royalty: they assured me nothing larger was ever given! I know better now. But your letter has consoled and pleased me more than I can say. Sincerely yours   OSCAR WILDE

To the Editor of the Pall Mall Gazette [2]

27 August [*1891*]   *Albemarle Chambers, Piccadilly*

Sir, I have read with much astonishment the letter signed "S" that appears in your issue of this evening, and hope that you will allow me to assure the writer of the letter and the public in general that there is no truth whatsoever in the statement made in one of my essays that "Providence and Mr Walter Besant have exhausted the obvious." The public need be under no misapprehension. One has merely to read the ordinary English newspapers and the ordinary English novels of our day to become conscious of the fact that it is only the obvious that occurs, and only the

---

page. Cantel's translations followed Wilde's intructions, but did not appear until 1914, when they were published as *Opinions de Littérature et d'Art* by Oscar Wilde.

[1] This date is conjectural, but James Bowden did not join Ward Lock & Co. as a partner till August 1891.

[2] An anonymous review of Besant's novel *Armorel of Lyonnesse* in the *Pall Mall Gazette* of 26 August had described the book as "a masterpiece of dull extravagance" and disputed Wilde's epigram in "The Critic as Artist," maintaining that Besant was "all for the far-fetched and unnatural." This provoked a long letter from "S,' who defended both Wilde and Besant, remarking that "Mr Wilde . . . was referring to Mr Besant's novels of East-End life . . . In those stories Mr Besant was splendidly obvious." Wilde's letter was published on August 29.

obvious that is written about. Both facts are much to be regretted. I
remain, sir, your obedient servant   OSCAR WILDE

To Augustin Daly[1]
MS. Harvard

[*Autumn 1891*]   *16 Tite Street*

Dear Mr Daly, I send my play *A Good Woman* (four acts). I should so
much like you to read it and let Miss Rehan see it also.[2] I would sooner
see her play the part of Mrs Erlynne than any English-speaking actress we
have, or French actress for that matter.

Anderson tells me you have kindly promised to let me have it back on
Monday morning. Would you, if it would not too much trouble you, let
me have it by a *messenger*. I will be at home at twelve o'clock and receive
it from him.

Accept my warmest congratulations on the great success of your season,
and with kind regards to Miss Rehan, believe me truly yours
                                                     OSCAR WILDE

To the Editor of The Times[3]

25 September [*1891*]

Sir, The writer of a letter signed "An Indian Civilian" that appears in
your issue of today makes a statement about me which I beg you to allow
me to correct at once.

He says I have described the Anglo-Indians as being vulgar. This is
not the case. Indeed, I have never met a vulgar Anglo-Indian. There may
be many, but those whom I have had the pleasure of meeting here have been
chiefly scholars, men interested in art and thought, men of cultivation;
nearly all of them have been exceedingly brilliant talkers; some of them have
been exceedingly brilliant writers.

What I did say—I believe in the pages of the *Nineteenth Century*—was
that vulgarity is the distinguishing note of those Anglo-Indians whom Mr
Rudyard Kipling loves to write about, and writes about so cleverly.[4] This

[1] American dramatist and manager (1839–99). He first brought his company to
London in 1884, with Ada Rehan and John Drew heading the cast, returning in
1886, 1888 and 1890–91, when he took the Lyceum. He eventually had his own
theatre, named after him, in both London and New York. *A Good Woman* was the
original title of *Lady Windermere's Fan*.

[2] Ada Rehan (1860–1916), American actress who became a great favourite in
London and New York. All her best work was done under Daly's management, and
her failure after his death inspired the belief that she had depended on him as
Trilby on Svengali.

[3] Published on 26 September, under the heading AN ANGLO-INDIAN'S
COMPLAINT.

[4] In the *Nineteenth Century* for September 1890 (see note 2, p. 272) Wilde had
written:

As one turns over the pages of his *Plain Tales from the Hills*, one feels as if one
were seated under a palm-tree reading life by superb flashes of vulgarity. The

is quite true, and there is no reason why Mr Rudyard Kipling should not select vulgarity as his subject-matter, or as part of it. For a realistic artist, certainly, vulgarity is a most admirable subject. How far Mr Kipling's stories really mirror Anglo-Indian society I have no idea at all, nor, indeed, am I ever much interested in any correspondence between art and nature. It seems to me a matter of entirely secondary importance. I do not wish, however, that it should be supposed that I was passing a harsh and *saugrenu* judgment on an important and in many ways distinguished class, when I was merely pointing out the characteristic qualities of some puppets in a prose-play.

I remain, sir, your obedient servant   OSCAR WILDE

To Arthur Fish
TS. Holland

17 October 1891   *Albemarle Club*

My dear Arthur, Many thanks for your cheering letter; it was so sweet of you remembering my birthday. I hear my photograph and biography have appeared in one of Cassell's magazines.[1] I have not received my copies. Will you have half a dozen sent to me at Tite Street in wrappers for the post? How are your wife and child? I wish we could meet and see each other again. Your sincere friend   OSCAR WILDE

To Stéphane Mallarmé
MS. Bonniot

[*Early November 1891*]   *Hôtel de Normandie, Rue de l'Échelle, Paris*

Cher Maître, Je suis à Paris pour quelques semaines, et je compte avoir l'honneur de me présenter chez vous mardi prochain.

En attendant, permettez-moi de vous offrir un exemplaire de mon roman *Le Portrait de Dorian Gray* comme témoignage de mon admiration pour votre noble et sévère art.[2] En France la poésie a beaucoup de laquais mais un seul maître.

---

bright colours of the bazaars dazzle one's eyes. The jaded, commonplace Anglo-Indians are in exquisite incongruity with their surroundings. The mere lack of style in the storyteller gives an odd journalistic realism to what he tells us. From the point of view of literature Mr Kipling is a man of talent who drops his aspirates. From the point of view of life he is a reporter who knows vulgarity better than anyone has ever known it. Dickens knew its clothes. Mr Kipling knows its essence. He is our best authority on the second-rate. He terrifies us by his truth, and makes his sordid subject-matter marvellous by the brilliancy of its setting.

In the essay as reprinted in *Intentions* (1891) the last two sentences were revised.

[1] *The Cabinet Portrait Gallery*, vol. II, part 24 (August 1891.)

[2] It is inscribed "*A Stéphane Mallarmé, Hommage d'Oscar Wilde, Paris '91.*"

Agréez, cher maître, l'assurance de mes sentiments les plus distingués.

OSCAR WILDE[1]

Petit-Bleu:[2] To Constant-Benoît Coquelin[3]

MS. Hart-Davis

[Postmark 6 November 1891]   Grand Hotel [Post Office]
                                   [Boulevard des Capucines] Paris

Mon cher ami, À 9.30 demain matin je serai chez vous! Je vous remercie infiniment de l'interêt que vous avez porté dans cette affaire.[4] Tous mes compliments   OSCAR WILDE

To Pierre Louÿs[5]

28 November 1891   29 Boulevard des Capucines, Paris

Cher Monsieur Louÿs, J'accepte avec le plus vif plaisir la gracieuse et charmante invitation que vous et M. Gide[6] ont eu la bonté de m'adresser. Vous m'indiquerez, n'est-ce-pas, l'endroit et l'heure.

Je garde un souvenir délicieux de notre petit déjeuner de l'autre jour, et de l'acceuil sympathique que vous m'avez fait.

J'espère que les jeunes poètes de France m'aimeront un jour, comme moi à ce moment je les aime.

[1] Mallarmé answered on 10 November (text from an article by Guillot de Saix in Paris, les Arts et les Lettres, 12 July 1946, supplemented by the Stetson sale catalogue, 1920).

J'achève le livre, un des seuls qui puissent émouvoir, vu que d'une rêverie essentielle et des parfums d'âme les plus étranges s'est fait son orage.

Redevenir poignant à travers l'inouï raffinement d'intellect, et humain, et une pareille perverse atmosphère de beauté, est un miracle que vous accomplissez et selon quel emploi de tous les arts de l'écrivain!

"It was the portrait that had done everything." *Ce portrait en pied, inquiétant, d'un Dorian Gray, hantera, mais écrit, étant devenu livre lui-même.*

[2] Carte Pneumatique, or express letter, transmitted by pneumatic tube in Paris.

[3] French actor (1841–1909) known as Coquelin *aîné* to distinguish him from his younger brother. Rostand wrote *Cyrano de Bergerac* (1898) for him.

[4] Perhaps the translation into French of *Lady Windermere's Fan* (cf. p. 306).

[5] French poet and writer (1870–1925). In 1889 he founded the review *La Conque*, to which Swinburne, Leconte de Lisle, Heredia, Verlaine, Mallarmé, Maeterlinck, André Gide and Moréas were contributors. His first book, *Astarte*, was published in 1892. The text of this letter is taken from the catalogue of a French bookseller, L. Carteret, *Manuscrits de Pierre Louÿs et de divers Auteurs contemporains* (1926).

[6] André Paul Guillaume Gide (1869–1951) the French writer, appears to have met Wilde for the first time on 27 November, when he wrote to Paul Valery:

Quelques lignes de quelqu'un d'abruti, qui ne lit plus, qui n'écrit plus, qui ne dort plus, ni ne mange, ni ne pense—mais court avec ou sans Louÿs dans les cafés ou les salons serrer des mains et faire des sourires. Heredia, Régnier, Merrill, l'esthète Oscar Wilde, ô admirable, admirable celui-là.

According to his letters he saw Wilde almost every day till 15 December, but the pages in his journal covering those days have been torn out. Later he recalled:

A Paris, sitôt qu'il y vint, son nom courut de bouche en bouche; on rapportait sur

298

La poésie française a toujours été parmi mes maîtresses les plus adorées, et je serai très content de croire que parmi les poètes de France je trouverai de véritables amis.

Veuillez présenter à M. Gide l'assurance de mes sentiments les plus distingués. Veuillez, cher Monsieur Louÿs, l'agréer   OSCAR WILDE[1]

To Lady Dorothy Nevill[2]

[*Circa 30 November 1891*]   *29 Boulevard des Capucines, Paris*

My dear Lady Dorothy, I would have answered your charming letter before, but the death of poor dear Lytton has quite upset me. We had become during the last year very great friends, and I had seen him only a few days before he died, lying in Pauline Borghese's lovely room at the Embassy, and full of charm and grace and tenderness.

His funeral, in spite of the hideous Protestant service, was most impressive; the purple-covered bier with its one laurel wreath being a solemn note of colour and sadness in the midst of the gorgeous uniforms of the Ambassadors.[3]

He was a man of real artistic temperament. I had grown to be very fond of him, and he was most kind always to me.

By all means send your book: I will get Zola's name. Poor Maupassant is dying, I fear.[4] Believe me, dear Lady Dorothy, sincerely yours

OSCAR WILDE

To the Editor of the Speaker

[*Early December 1891*]   [*29*] *Boulevard des Capucines, Paris*

Sir, I have just, at a price that for any other English sixpenny paper I

---

lui quelques absurdes anecdotes: Wilde n'était encore que celui qui fumait des cigarettes à bout d'or et qui se promenait dans les rues une fleur de tournesol à la main. Car, habile à piper ceux qui font la mondaine gloire, Wilde avait su créer, par devant son vrai personnage, un amusant fantôme dont il jouait avec esprit.

Jean Delay, in *La Jeunesse d'André Gide* (vol. 2, 1957), publishes some uncollected notes on Wilde which Gide wrote during the next few years.

[1] Louÿs's answer (MS. Clark) is dated 29 November and reads:

Cher Maître, Ce sera, si vous le voulez bien, au café d'Harcourt, place de la Sorbonne, et vers huit heures du soir. Permettez-moi de vous remercier de l'honneur et du plaisir que vous nous faites en acceptant.

Veuillez agréer, cher maître, l'assurance nouvelle de notre affectueux respect.

PIERRE LOUŸS

[2] Authoress (1826–1913), daughter of the third Earl of Orford (of the second creation) and widow of Reginald Harry Nevill. She contributed "Some Recollections of Cobden" to the *Woman's World* in June 1888. The text of this letter is taken from her *Reminiscences* (1906). She wanted Zola's signature for her birthday book.

[3] Lytton was in fact buried in England at his home at Knebworth on 1 December. What Wilde describes was the funeral service in Paris in the English church in the Rue d'Aguesseau, opposite the British Embassy, on 28 November.

[4] Maupassant's mind had already begun to give way, but he lived until July 1893.

would have considered exorbitant, purchased a copy of the *Speaker* at one of the charming kiosks that decorate Paris; institutions, by the way, that I think we should at once introduce into London. The kiosk is a delightful object, and, when illuminated at night from within, as lovely as a fantastic Chinese lantern, especially when the transparent advertisements are from the clever pencil of M. Chéret.[1] In London we have merely the ill-clad newsvendors, whose voice, in spite of the admirable efforts of the Royal College of Music to make England a really musical nation, is always out of tune, and whose rags, badly designed and badly worn, merely emphasise a painful note of uncomely misery, without conveying that impression of picturesqueness which is the only thing that makes the spectacle of the poverty of others at all bearable.

It is not, however, about the establishment of kiosks in London that I wish to write to you, though I am of opinion that it is a thing that the County Council should at once take in hand. The object of my letter is to correct a statement made in a paragraph of your interesting paper.

The writer of the paragraph in question states that the decorative designs that make lovely my book *A House of Pomegranates*,[2] are by the hand of Mr Shannon, while the delicate dreams that separate and herald each story are by Mr Ricketts. The contrary is the case. Mr Shannon is the drawer of dreams, and Mr Ricketts is the subtle and fantastic decorator. Indeed, it is to Mr Ricketts that the entire decorative design of the book is due, from the selection of the type and the placing of the ornamentation, to the completely beautiful cover that encloses the whole. The writer of the paragraph goes on to state that he does not "like the cover." This is, no doubt, to be regretted, though it is not a matter of much importance, as there are only two people in the world whom it is absolutely necessary that the cover should please. One is Mr Ricketts, who designed it, the other is myself, whose book it binds. We both admire it immensely! The reason, however, that your critic gives for his failure to gain from the cover any

[1] Jules Chéret (1836–1932) was a leading French poster-artist. He lived in England 1859–66.

[2] *A House of Pomegranates*, Wilde's second collection of fairy stories (containing "The Young King," "The Birthday of the Infanta," "The Fisherman and his Soul," and "The Star-child"), dedicated to his wife, was published by Osgood McIlvaine & Co in November 1891 (1000 copies at 21/-). The paragraph in the *Speaker* of November 28 (apparently the book's first notice in the press) reads as follows:

> We do not like the outside of the cover of Mr Oscar Wilde's *House of Pomegranates* (Osgood). The Indian club with a house-painter's brush on the top which passes muster for a peacock, and the chimney-pot hat with a sponge in it, which is meant to represent a basket containing a pomegranate, or a fountain, or something of that kind, are grotesque, but not ideally so. The inside of the cover, however, with its olive sheaves of corn falling apart, its fluttering quails, and crawling snails, delights the eye. So do the pictures and the type and the paper. Mr Ricketts has learned the art of drawing dreams and visions, and Mr Shannon can make decorative designs full of charming detail. We can well believe that the book is as delightful as it looks.

Wilde's letter appeared on 5 December.

impression of beauty seems to me to show a lack of artistic instinct on his part, which I beg you will allow me to try to correct.

He complains that a portion of the design on the left-hand side of the cover reminds him of an Indian club with a house-painter's brush on top of it, while a portion of the design on the right-hand side suggests to him the idea of "a chimney-pot hat with a sponge in it." Now, I do not for a moment dispute that these are the real impressions your critic received. It is the spectator, and the mind of the spectator, as I pointed out in the preface to *The Picture of Dorian Gray*, that art really mirrors. What I want to indicate is this: the artistic beauty of the cover of my book resides in the delicate tracing, arabesques, and massing of many coral-red lines on a ground of white ivory, the colour-effect culminating in certain high gilt notes, and being made still more pleasurable by the overlapping band of moss-green cloth that holds the book together.

What the gilt notes suggest, what imitative parallel may be found to them in that chaos that is termed Nature, is a matter of no importance. They may suggest, as they do sometimes to me, peacocks and pomegranates and splashing fountains of gold water, or, as they do to your critic, sponges and Indian clubs and chimney-pot hats. Such suggestions and evocations have nothing whatsoever to do with the aesthetic quality and value of the design. A thing in Nature becomes much lovelier if it reminds us of a thing in Art, but a thing in Art gains no real beauty through reminding us of a thing in Nature. The primary aesthetic impression of a work of art borrows nothing from recognition or resemblance. These belong to a later and less perfect stage of apprehension. Properly speaking, they are not part of a real aesthetic impression at all, and the constant preoccupation with subject-matter that characterises nearly all our English art-criticism is what makes our art-criticism, especially as regards literature, so sterile, so profitless, so much beside the mark, and of such curiously little account.

I remain, sir, your obedient servant,   OSCAR WILDE

To the Editor of the Pall Mall Gazette

[*Early December 1891*]   *Boulevard des Capucines, Paris*

Sir, I have just had sent to me from London a copy of the *Pall Mall Gazette* containing a review of my book *A House of Pomegranates*.[1] The writer of this review makes a certain suggestion about my book which I beg you will allow me to correct at once.

He starts by asking an extremely silly question, and that is, whether or not I have written this book for the purpose of giving pleasure to the British child. Having expressed grave doubts on this subject, a subject on which I cannot conceive any fairly-educated person having any doubts at all, he proceeds, apparently quite seriously, to make the extremely limited vocabulary at the disposal of the British child the standard by which the

[1] This appeared on 30 November 1891, and Wilde's letter on 11 December.

prose of an artist is to be judged! Now in building this *House of Pome-granates* I had about as much intention of pleasing the British child as I had of pleasing the British public. Mamilius[1] is as entirely delightful as Caliban is entirely detestable, but neither the standard of Mamilius nor the standard of Caliban is my standard. No artist recognises any standard of beauty but that which is suggested by his own temperament. The artist seeks to realise in a certain material his immaterial idea of beauty, and thus to transform an idea into an ideal. That is the way an artist makes things. That is why an artist makes things. The artist has no other object in making things. Does your reviewer imagine that Mr Shannon, for instance, whose delicate and lovely illustrations he confesses himself quite unable to see, draws for the purpose of giving information to the blind?[2]

I remain, sir, your obedient servant,   OSCAR WILDE

To Elkin Mathews[3]
MS. Princeton

[*December 1891*]   *29 Boulevard des Capucines, Paris*

Dear Mr Elkin Mathews, I have been in Paris for the last month, and will not be in London for some weeks longer. With regard to Mr Ricketts, of course he must be paid for his design on its completion.[4] I mention this as I do not know whether it is on the question of money that he has written to you. Pray let me know by return what he wanted done.

This settled, I will ask Osgood & McIlvaine to hand you over the copies, and the book could be got out after the rush of Christmas books is over.

I think that as the edition will be limited each copy should be signed by the author. This will give a special character to the edition. I remain truly yours   OSCAR WILDE

To William Rothenstein[5]
MS. Rothenstein

[? *Early December 1891*]   *29 Boulevard des Capucines* [*Paris*]

My dear Will, I send you my novel, with my best wishes. It was a great

---

[1] The boy-prince in *A Winter's Tale*.

[2] In fact some of Shannon's illustrations, which were reproduced by a new process that failed, were and are almost invisible.

[3] Charles Elkin Mathews (1851–1921) opened his first bookshop at Exeter in 1885. In 1887 he joined John Lane (see note 3, p. 318) in starting a bookselling business under the sign of the Bodley Head in Vigo Street, London.

[4] Ricketts designed the title-page, half-title and cover of a new edition of Wilde's *Poems*. The rest of the book consisted of unsold sheets of the fifth Bogue edition, which had presumably been taken over by Osgood McIlvaine after Bogue's bankruptcy (though Mason, p. 316, says that Chatto & Windus did so). The new edition, limited to 220 copies at 15/-, each signed by Wilde, was eventually published on 26 May 1892. It was the first book to carry the joint imprint of Elkin Mathews & John Lane. Wilde received the proceeds less five guineas for Ricketts, five guineas for advertising and 20 per cent for the publishers.

[5] English artist (1872–1945). The son of a Bradford wool-merchant, he had

pleasure to see you last night, and it will be a great pleasure to see you tomorrow. Sincerely yours   OSCAR WILDE

To H.S.H. the Princess of Monaco[1]

MS. Private

[? *December 1891*]   *29 Boulevard des Capucines* [*Paris*]

In such a horrid hurry
with such a horrid pen!

My dear Princess, I am so pleased you like the book, and am charmed to think your name is in it to adorn it and make it lovely.

I will call for the Ranee[2] on Saturday at 4.30 and go with her to Madame Straus,[3] and am at her orders while she is in Paris.

Pray give her my kindest regards, and tell her how delighted I am at the prospect of seeing her, and believe me always your devoted friend

OSCAR WILDE

To Edmond de Goncourt[4]

MS. Paris

[*17 December 1891*]   *29 Boulevard des Capucines*

Cher Monsieur de Goncourt, Quoique la base intellectuelle de mon

---

already been a student at the Slade School and was now studying art in Paris. The first volume of his *Men and Memories* (1931) contains much valuable information about Wilde and his friends. Rothenstein was knighted 1931.

[1] Alice, *née* Heine (1858–1925), widow of the Duc de Richelieu and a grand-niece of the poet Heine, married Prince Albert Honoré Charles of Monaco (1848–1922) in 1889. She was a great patron of art and artists. In "The Diner-Out" (*Horizon*, October 1941) A. J. A. Symons gave an imaginative account of an apparently actual dinner-party given in 1891 at Claridge's by Frank Harris for the Princess, at which Wilde with his conversation charmed everyone, even George Moore, who disliked him. Wilde dedicated his story "The Fisherman and his Soul" (in *A House of Pomegranates*) to the Princess.

[2] Margaret de Windt (1849–1936) married in 1869 Sir Charles Johnson Brooke, second Rajah of Sarawak (1829–1917). Wilde dedicated his story "The Young King" (in *A House of Pomegranates*) to her.   [3] See note 5, p. 306.

[4] See p. 144. Goncourt's journal for 1883 was being serialised in the *Echo de Paris*, and on 17 December 1891 there appeared in the entry for 21 April 1883:

Le Poète anglais Wilde me disait, ce soir, que le seul Anglais qui avait lu Balzac à l'heure actuelle était Swinburne. Et ce Swinburne, il me le montre comme un fanfaron du vice, qui avait tout fait pour faire croire ses concitoyens à sa pédérastie, à sa bestialité, sans être le moins du monde pédéraste ni bestialitaire.

Wilde's letter of protest was printed in the *Echo de Paris* of 19 December with these prefatory words:

Dans son très intéressant 'Journal,' notre éminent collaborateur et ami, Edmond de Goncourt, avait incidemment relaté une conversation avec le poète anglais Swinburne. Une des plus curieuses personnalités de la littérature anglaise contemporaine, l'esthète Oscar Wilde, qui est en ce moment notre hôte, et le 'great event' des salons

303

esthétique soit la Philosophie de l'Irréalité, ou peut-être à cause de cela, je vous prie de me permettre une petite rectification à vos notes sur la conversation où je vous ai parlé de notre cher et noble poète anglais M. Algernon Swinburne et que vous avez insérés dans ces Mémoires qui ont, non seulement pour vos amis, mais pour le public tout entier, une valeur psychologique si haute.

Les soirées qu'on a eu le bonheur de passer avec un grand écrivain comme vous l'êtes sont inoubliables, et voilà pourquoi j'en ai gardé un souvenir très précis. Je suis surpris que vous en ayez reçu une impression assez différente.

Vous proposiez ce matin d'extraire l'hydrogène de l'air pour faire de notre atmosphère une terrible machine de destruction.[1] Ce serait un chef-d'œuvre, sinon de science, au moins d'art. Mais extraire de ma conversation sur M. Swinburne une sensation qui pourrait le blesser, voilà qui m'a causé quelque peine. Sans doute c'était de ma faute. On peut adorer une langue sans bien la parler, comme on peut aimer une femme sans la connaître. Français de sympathie, je suis Irlandais de race, et les Anglais m'ont condamné à parler le langage de Shakespeare.

Vous avez dit que je représentais M. Swinburne comme un fanfaron du vice. Cela étonnerait beaucoup le poète, qui dans sa maison de campagne mène une vie bien austère, entièrement consacrée à l'art et à la littérature.

Voici ce que j'ai voulu dire. Il y a aujourd'hui plus de vingt-cinq ans, M. Swinburne a publié ses *Poèmes et Ballades*, une des œuvres qui ont marqué le plus profondément dans notre littérature une ère nouvelle.

Dans Shakespeare, et dans ses contemporains Webster et Ford, il y a des cris de nature. Dans l'œuvre de Swinburne, on rencontre pour la première fois le cri de la chair tourmentée par le désir et le souvenir, la jouissance et le remords, la fécondité et la stérilité. Le public anglais, comme d'ordinaire hypocrite, prude et philistin, n'a pas su trouver l'art dans l'œuvre d'art: il y a cherché l'homme. Comme il confond toujours l'homme avec ses créations, il pense que pour créer Hamlet il faut être un peu mélancholique, pour imaginer Lear absolument fou. Ainsi on a fait autour de M. Swinburne une légende d'ogre et de mangeur d'enfants. M. Swinburne, aristocrate de race et artiste de tempérament, n'a fait que

---

littéraires parisiens, lui adresse à ce sujet la très curieuse lettre qui suit. M. O. Wilde s'y excuse de ne point parler suffisamment notre langue, on verra du moins qu'il l'écrit en toute élégance.

When the 1883 journal was published (as volume vi) in 1892 the whole of the second sentence about Swinburne was omitted, as was Goncourt's description of Wilde (entry of 5 May 1883) as "*cet individu au sexe douteux, au langage de cabotin, aux récits blagueurs.*"

In his journal for 17 December 1891 Goncourt wrote: "*Vers les six heures, quand je suis couché, dépêche de Mendès, qui me demande à faire passer une réclamation de Oscar Wilde sur ce que je lui ai fait dire sur Swinburne.*" Catulle Mendès (1842–1909), French poet, novelist, man of letters and son-in-law of Gautier, was at this time on the staff of the *Echo de Paris*.

[1] Goncourt referred to this notion in his journal for 25 August 1883.

rire de ces absurdités. Une telle attitude me semble éloignée de celle qu'aurait un fanfaron de vice.

Pardonnez-moi cette simple rectification; je suis sûr, puisque vous aimiez les poètes et que les poètes vous aiment, que vous serez heureux de la recevoir. J'espère que lorsque j'aurai l'honneur de vous rencontrer de nouveau, vous trouverez ma manière de m'exprimer en français moins obscure que le 21 avril 1883.

Veuillez agréer, cher Monsieur de Goncourt, l'assurance de toute mon admiration.   OSCAR WILDE

To Pierre Louÿs
MS. Clark

[*December 1891*]   [*Paris*]

Mon cher ami, Voilà le drame de *Salomé*.[1] Ce n'est pas encore fini ou même corrigé, mais ça donne l'idée de la *construction*, du motif et du

---

[1] There has been much speculation as to when, where, and in what language *Salome* was originally written. Wilde had certainly begun work on it by 27 October 1891, when Wilfrid Blunt wrote in his diary:

> I breakfasted with him [George Curzon], Oscar Wilde and Willy Peel, on which occasion Oscar told us he was writing a play in French to be acted in the Français. He is ambitious of being a French Academician. We promised to go to the first representation, George Curzon as Prime Minister.

Three manuscripts of *Salome* exist, all in Wilde's hand and all written in French. What appears to be the first draft (MS. Bodmer Library, Cologny, Geneva) is lightly corrected in Wilde's hand only. It is not dated, but is written in a half-leather notebook bearing the ticket of a stationer in the Boulevard des Capucines.

The presumed second draft (MS. Texas), which is dated "Paris, November '91," is in a similarly ticketed notebook and is lightly corrected in Wilde's hand.

The third and apparently final draft (MS. Rosenbach Museum, Philadelphia) was the one here submitted to Louÿs, and contains his interlinear corrections and suggested improvements. Where these were on points of grammar Wilde adopted them, but most of Louÿs's other remarks he deleted or ignored. There may how-ever have been still another intermediate version, since two other French writers helped to some extent. The Symbolist Adolphe Retté (1863–1910) recorded in his book *Le Symbolisme, Anecdotes et Souvenirs* (1903) that he was asked to remove

> les anglicismes trop formels ... J'indiquai quelques corrections en marge du drame. Je fis supprimer à Wilde une trop longue énumeration de pierreries mise dans la bouche d'Hérode. De son côté, Merrill lui proposa quelques retouches. Puis Salomé passa entre les mains de Pierre Louÿs qui modifia également quelques phrases. C'est ce texte qui a été imprimé.

Stuart Merrill (see note 2, p. 390), in his *'Souvenirs sur le Symbolisme"* (*Prose et Vers*, *Œuvres Posthumes*, 1925) corroborated this:

> Je confirme en passant ce que raconte Retté au sujet de la composition de Salomé. Un jour Oscar Wilde me remit son drame qu'il avait écrit très rapidement, de premier jet, en français, et me demanda d'en corriger les erreurs manifestes. Ce ne fut pas chose facile de faire accepter à Wilde toutes mes corrections. Il écrivait le français comme il le parlait, c'est-à-dire avec une fantaisie qui, si elle était savoureuse dans la conversation, aurait produit, au théâtre, une déplorable impression ... Je corrigeai donc comme je pus Salomé. Je me rappelle que la plupart des tirades de ses personnages commençaient par l'explétif: enfin. En ai-je assez biffé des enfin. Mais je m'aperçus bientôt que le bon Wilde n'avait en mon goût qu'une confiance relative,

mouvement dramatique. Ici et là, il y a des lacunes, mais l'idée du drame est claire.

Je suis encore très enrhumé et je me porte assez mal. Mais je serai tout à fait bien lundi et je vous attendrai à une heure chez Mignon pour déjeuner, vous et M. Fort.[1]

Je vous remercie beaucoup, mon cher ami, pour l'intérêt que vous daignez prendre à mon drame. À toi   OSCAR

To H.S.H. the Princess of Monaco

MS. Private

[? December 1891]   29 Boulevard des Capucines [Paris]

My dear Princess, It was a great pleasure seeing you in Paris, though I was so sorry you were ill. I must come south in February, and have charming days, if you will allow me, with you. By that time, of course I shall have become a French author![2]

Coquelin has recommended me to have my play translated by Delair, who has done La Mégère for the Français.[3] I have had an interview with him, and he is fascinated by the plot, but I don't know if he understands society-English sufficiently well, I mean the English of the salon and the boudoir, the English one talks. I am sending him the manuscript tomorrow.

Madame Straus was quite charming to me. What delightful friends you have. But of Le Roux I have seen nothing, which I regret.[4] Votre ami dévoué et sincère   OSCAR WILDE

To Madame Emile Straus [5]

MS. Curtiss

[? December 1891]   29 Boulevard des Capucines [Paris]

Chère Madame Straus, Je regrette beaucoup que je n'ai pas pu me

---

et je le recommandai aux soins de Retté. Celui-ci continua mon travail de correction et d'émendation. Mais Wilde finit par se méfier de Retté autant que de moi, et ce fut Pierre Louÿs qui donna le dernier coup de lime au texte de Salomé.

Professor Clyde de L. Ryals of the University of Pennsylvania (see Notes & Queries, February 1959) has compared the Rosenbach manuscript with the published version of the play and finds them virtually identical. It is clear therefore that the proof-corrections of Marcel Schwob (see note p. 325) were probably confined to two (see Adam, 241–43, 1954). There is in Berg a complete forged manuscript, probably the work of Fabian Lloyd (see p. xiii). Wilde often accented Salome, but not always, and I have omitted the accent except when he was writing in French.

[1] Paul Fort, French poet (1872–1960). Founded the Théâtre d'Art 1890.

[2] By virtue of Salome, though the next sentence must refer to Lady Windermere's Fan (see note 5, p. 298).

[3] Paul Delair (1842–94), French dramatist, novelist and poet. His translation of The Taming of the Shrew, entitled La Mégère Apprivoisée, was first performed at the Comédie Française on 19 November 1891, and was published in 1894.

[4] Robert-Henri (dit Hugues) Le Roux, French author and journalist (1860–1925).

[5] Géneviève Halévy (1846–1926), daughter of the composer Fromenthal Halévy,

présenter chez vous hier soir, mais j'étais avec des amis que je ne pouvais pas quitter.

Permettez moi de vous remercier du charmant accueil que vous m'avez fait, et de vous assurer que je suis on ne peut plus touché de votre bonté en m'accordant l'entrée de votre salon si célèbre, si artistique.

Agréez, chère Madame, l'assurance de mes sentiments les plus distingués   OSCAR WILDE

To An Unidentified Correspondent[1]
MS. Hyde (H. M.)

[? *December 1891*]   *16 Tite Street*

Dear Sir, I have to acknowledge the receipt of two drafts, for £20 each, for eight performances of *The Duchess of Padua*.

As I understood that my play was to be the principal feature of Miss Gale's tour, the amount of performances has both surprised and annoyed me. It was in order to have my play played, not in order to have my play suppressed, that I assigned my American rights to Miss Gale. This, however, I suppose is not a matter that lies within your province. I have written to Miss Gale on the subject.

I hear my play was played on a Saturday night at Harlem lately. No doubt you have already forwarded what is due. My play should be the opening production in each important city. To keep it for the last night is to show a want of recognition of the value and importance of the play. I remain, sir, your obedient servant   OSCAR WILDE

To Elkin Mathews
MS. Princeton

[? *January 1892*]   *16 Tite Street*

Dear Sir, I enclose you an order for the delivery of the copies of my book of poems (unbound).

I will show Mr Ricketts a bound copy of the book so that he can see its exact size.[2] Truly yours   OSCAR WILDE

---

married in 1869 the composer Georges Bizet (1838–73). After his death she married Emile Straus, a successful commercial barrister. She had a *salon* in the Rue de Miromesnil, much frequented by the writers of the 80's and 90's, and a centre of the supporters of Dreyfus. She corresponded with Marcel Proust until his death in 1922, and it is said that the witty remarks which he put into the mouth of the Duchesse de Guermantes (Oriane) were mostly taken from her.

[1] Presumably a dramatic agent in New York or London. Minna Gale, the leading lady of the abortive production of *Guido Ferranti* (*The Duchess of Padua*) in January (see note 3, p. 282), had put the play into her touring repertory under its proper name. She opened her tour with it on 31 August at the Chestnut Street Theatre, Philadelphia, with Creston Clarke in the part created by Lawrence Barrett (who had died on 20 March), but thereafter gave it less often than the other five plays in her repertory—*Romeo and Juliet*, *As You Like It*, Lytton's *The Lady of Lyons*, Knowles's *The Hunchback* and Lovell's *Ingomar*. The Harlem performance was given at Oscar Hammerstein's Harlem Opera House on 14 November.   [2] See note 4, p. 302.

To George Alexander[1]
Part MS. Hyde (H. M.)[2]

[Mid-February 1892]   *Hotel Albemarle*

With regard to the speech of Mrs Erlynne at the end of Act II, you must remember that until Wednesday night Mrs Erlynne rushed off the stage leaving Lord Augustus in a state of bewilderment. Such are the stage directions in the play. When the alteration in the business was made I don't know, but I should have been informed at once. It came on me with the shock of a surprise. I don't in any degree object to it. It is a different effect, that is all. It does not alter the psychological lines of the play. . . . To reproach me on Wednesday for not having written a speech for a situation on which I was not consulted and of which I was quite unaware was, of course, a wrong thing to do. With regard to the new speech written yesterday, personally I think it adequate. I want Mrs Erlynne's whole scene with Lord Augustus to be a "tornado" scene, and the thing to go as quickly as possible. However, I will think over the speech, and talk it over with Miss Terry. Had I been informed of the change I would of course have had more time and when, through illness caused by the worry and anxiety I have gone through at the theatre, I was unable to attend the rehearsals on Monday and Tuesday, I should have been informed by letter.

With regard to your other suggestion about the disclosure of the secret of the play in the second act, had I intended to let out the secret, which is the element of suspense and curiosity, a quality so essentially dramatic, I would have written the play on entirely different lines. I would have made Mrs Erlynne a vulgar horrid woman and struck out the incident of the fan. The audience must not know till the last act that the woman Lady Windermere proposed to strike with her fan was her own mother. The note would be too harsh, too horrible. When they learn it, it is after Lady Windermere has left her husband's house to seek the protection of another man, and their interest is concentrated on Mrs Erlynne, to whom dramatically speaking belongs the last act. Also it would destroy the dramatic wonder excited by the incident of Mrs Erlynne taking the letter and opening it and sacrificing herself in the third act. If they knew Mrs Erlynne was the mother, there would be no surprise in her sacrifice—it would be expected. But in my play the sacrifice is dramatic and unexpected. The cry with which Mrs Erlynne flies into the other room on

---

[1] *Lady Windermere's Fan* was first produced at the St James's Theatre on 20 February 1892, with Alexander as Lord Windermere, Marion Terry as Mrs Erlynne, H. H. Vincent as Lord Augustus Lorton, and Lily Hanbury as Lady Windermere. It ran until 29 July, was then taken on tour, and returned to the St James's on 31 October. This letter was clearly written during rehearsal.

[2] The text of the first part of this letter (down to 'adequate' in line eleven) is taken from *Sir George Alexander and the St James's Theatre* by A. E. W. Mason (1935), the rest from the original in the possession of Mr Montgomery Hyde. There is no proof that these two fragments come from one letter, but it seems probable that they do.

hearing Lord Augustus's voice, the wild pathetic cry of self-preservation, "Then it is I who am lost!" would be repulsive coming from the lips of one known to be the mother by the audience. It seems natural and is very dramatic coming from one who seems to be an adventuress, and who while anxious to save Lady Windermere thinks of her own safety when a crisis comes. Also it would destroy the last act: and the chief merit of my last act is to me the fact that it does not contain, as most plays do, the explanation of what the audience knows already, but that it is the sudden explanation of what the audience desires to know, followed immediately by the revelation of a character as yet untouched by literature.

The question you touch on about the audience misinterpreting the relations of Lord Windermere and Mrs Erlynne depends entirely on the acting. In the first act Windermere must convince the audience of his absolute sincerity in what he says to his wife. The lines show this. He does not say to his wife "there is nothing in this woman's past life that is against her;" he says openly, "Mrs Erlynne years ago sinned. She now wants to get back. Help her to get back." The suggestions his wife makes he doesn't treat trivially and say, "Oh, there is nothing in it. We're merely friends, that is all." He rejects them with horror at the suggestion.

At the ball his manner to her is cold, courteous but somewhat hard— not the manner of a lover. When they think they are alone Windermere uses no word of tenderness or love. He shows that the woman has a hold on him, but one he loathes and almost writhes under.

What is this hold? That is the play.

I have entered at great length into this matter because every suggestion you have made to me I have always carefully and intellectually considered. Otherwise it would have been sufficient to have said, what I am sure you yourself will on reflection recognise, and that is that a work of art wrought out on definite lines, and elaborated from one definite artistic standpoint, cannot be suddenly altered. It would make every line meaningless, and rob each situation of its value. An equally good play could be written in which the audience would know beforehand who Mrs Erlynne really was, but it would require completely different dialogue, and completely different situations. I have built my house on a certain foundation, and this foundation cannot be altered. I can say no more.

With regards to matters personal between us, I trust that tonight will be quite harmonious and peaceful. After the play is produced and before I leave for the South of France where I am obliged to go for my health, it might be wise for us to have at any rate one meeting for the purpose of explanation. Truly yours   OSCAR WILDE

To Frances Forbes-Robertson
TS. Holland

[*Circa 18 February 1892*]   *Hotel Albemarle*

Dear Frankie, Will you come to my first night? I should like you and your mother, or you and Ian, to come.

I wish I could offer you more seats, but I have been given hardly any myself, and there is such a rush on them. Your sincere friend

OSCAR WILDE

To Richard Le Gallienne[1]

[Circa 18 February 1892]

Dear Poet, Here are two stalls for my play. Come, and bring your poem to sit beside you.

To the Editor of the Daily Telegraph

19 February [1892]   *London*

Sir, I have just been sent an article that seems to have appeared in your paper some days ago, in which it is stated that, in the course of some remarks addressed to the Playgoers' Club on the occasion of my taking the chair at their last meeting, I laid it down as an axiom that the stage is only "a frame furnished with a set of puppets."[2]

Now it is quite true that I hold that the stage is to a play no more than a picture-frame is to a painting, and that the actable value of a play has nothing whatsoever to do with its value as a work of art. In this century, in England, to take an obvious example, we have had only two great plays— one is Shelley's *Cenci*, the other Mr Swinburne's *Atalanta in Calydon*, and neither of them is in any sense of the word an actable play. Indeed, the mere suggestion that stage representation is any test of a work of art is quite ridiculous. In the production of Browning's plays, for instance, in London and at Oxford, what was being tested was obviously the capacity of the modern stage to represent, in any adequate measure or degree, works of introspective method and strange or sterile psychology. But the artistic value of *Strafford*, or *In a Balcony*, was settled when Robert Browning wrote their last lines. It is not, sir, by the mimes that the muses are to be judged.

So far, the writer of the article in question is right. Where he goes wrong is in saying that I describe this frame—the stage—as being furnished "with a set of puppets." He admits that he speaks only by report; but he should have remembered, sir, that report is not merely a lying jade, which I

---

[1] Text from *The Romantic 90's* by Richard Le Gallienne (1926). His "poem" was his wife, Mildred Lee, whom he had married in October 1891. She died in 1894.

[2] The *Daily Telegraph* of 12 February in its column "The Drama of the Day" had, in a paragraph about the forthcoming production of *Lady Windermere's Fan*, referred to some remarks said to have been made by Wilde at a meeting of the Playgoers' Club on 7 February. John Gray (see note 3, p. 311) had spoken on the Modern Actor, and the *Telegraph* quoted some of his remarks in illustration of what it felt was the perverse attitude of modern critics. Wilde's letter was published, with the heading PUPPETS AND ACTORS, on 20 February.

personally would readily forgive her, but a jade who lies without lovely invention—a thing that I, at any rate, can forgive her never.

What I really said was that the frame we call the stage was "peopled with either living actors or moving puppets," and I pointed out briefly, of necessity, that the personality of the actor is often a source of danger in the perfect presentation of a work of art. It may distort. It may lead astray. It may be a discord in the tone or symphony. For anybody can act. Most people in England do nothing else. To be conventional is to be a comedian. To act a particular part, however, is a very different thing, and a very difficult thing as well. The actor's aim is, or should be, to convert his own accidental personality into the real and essential personality of the character he is called upon to impersonate, whatever that character may be; or perhaps I should say that there are two schools of actors—the school of those who attain their effect by exaggeration of personality, and the school of those who attain it by suppression. It would be too long to discuss these schools, or to decide which of them the dramatist loves best. Let me note the danger of personality, and pass on to my puppets.

There are many advantages in puppets. They never argue. They have no crude views about art. They have no private lives. We are never bothered by accounts of their virtues, or bored by recitals of their vices; and when they are out of an engagement they never do good in public or save people from drowning; nor do they speak more than is set down for them. They recognise the presiding intellect of the dramatist, and have never been known to ask for their parts to be written up. They are admirably docile, and have no personalities at all. I saw lately, in Paris, a performance by certain puppets of Shakespeare's *Tempest*, in M. Maurice Bouchor's translation.[1] Miranda was the image of Miranda, because an artist had so fashioned her; and Ariel was true Ariel, because so had she been made. Their gestures were quite sufficient, and the words that seemed to come from their little lips were spoken by poets who had beautiful voices.[2] It was a delightful performance, and I remember it still with delight, though Miranda took no notice of the flowers I sent her after the curtain fell. For modern plays, however, perhaps we had better have living players, for in modern plays actuality is everything. The charm— the ineffable charm—of the unreal is here denied us, and rightly.

Suffer me one more correction. Your writer describes the author of the brilliant fantastic lecture on "The Modern Actor" as "a *protégé*" of mine. Allow me to state that my acquaintance with Mr John Gray is, I regret to say, extremely recent, and that I sought it because he had already a perfected mode of expression both in prose and verse.[3] All artists in this vulgar age

[1] From 1889 to 1894 Maurice Bouchor (1855–1929) ran the Petit Théâtre des Marionnettes in the Galérie Vivienne. His biographer describes the project as "*si applaudi des lettres, si encouragé par la critique, mais hélas d'un si infructueux résultat.*" Bouchor's translation of *The Tempest* was published in 1888.

[2] Jean Richepin, Raoul Ponchon, Coquelin *cadet* and Bouchor himself were among the speakers.

[3] John Gray (1866–1934). His book of poems *Silverpoints* (Mathews & Lane, 1893), which was entirely paid for by Wilde, was designed by Ricketts, and in the

need protection certainly. Perhaps they have always needed it. But the nineteenth-century artist finds it not in Prince, or Pope, or patron, but in high indifference of temper, in the pleasure of the creation of beautiful things, and the long contemplation of them in disdain of what in life is common and ignoble, and in such felicitous sense of humour as enables one to see how vain and foolish is all popular opinion, and popular judgment, upon the wonderful things of art. These qualities Mr John Gray possesses in a marked degree. He needs no other protection, nor, indeed, would he accept it.

I remain, sir, your obedient servant,   OSCAR WILDE

To Pierre Louÿs
MS. Buffalo

[*Circa 20 February 1892*]   *Lyric Club*

Cher Pierre, Avant que vous voyez *Lady Windermere* pour la première fois —c'est à dire avec moi—peut-être vous consentirez à le voir sans moi.

Je vous envoie un billet pour ce soir (evening dress). Vous serez à coté d'Edouard Shelley.[1]   OSCAR

To the Editor of the St James's Gazette

26 February 1892[2]

Sir, Allow me to correct a statement put forward in your issue of this evening, to the effect that I have made a certain alteration in my play in consequence of the criticism of some journalists who write very recklessly and very foolishly in the papers about dramatic art. This statement is entirely untrue, and grossly ridiculous.

The facts are as follows. On last Saturday night, after the play was over, and the author, cigarette in hand, had delivered a delightful and immortal

---

same year *The Blackmailers*, a play written in collaboration with his close friend André Raffalovich (see note p. 173), was produced at the Prince of Wales Theatre in June. There is no evidence for the persistent suggestion that he was the original of Dorian Gray. In 1904 he edited and published *Last Letters of Aubrey Beardsley*, which were written to Raffalovich. He became a Roman Catholic in boyhood and at thirty-five was ordained priest. His later years were spent in Edinburgh, where Raffalovich built St Peter's Church for him.

[1] Edward Shelley, a young employee of Elkin Mathews & John Lane whom Wilde had recently met, was to be one of the witnesses brought against him in court. See also p. 355. On 8 April 1895 Mathews wrote to *The Times*: "You mention in your report that the young man Shelley was introduced to Mr Oscar Wilde by one of the partners of the publishing firm of Mathews and Lane, Vigo Street. Allow me to say that I know nothing of Mr Oscar Wilde except in a business capacity by publishing his *Lady Windermere's Fan* etc., and never introduced Shelley or any person to him in my life, nor knew that he had been introduced. I may mention that for several months I have ceased to be the publisher of any of Mr Oscar Wilde's books."

[2] Published 27 February, and reprinted in *Miscellanies*.

speech, I had the pleasure of entertaining at supper a small number of personal friends: and, as none of them was older than myself, I naturally listened to their artistic views with attention and pleasure. The opinions of the old on matters of Art are, of course, of no value whatsoever. The artistic instincts of the young are invariably fascinating; and I am bound to state that all my friends, without exception, were of opinion that the psychological interest of the second act would be greatly increased by the disclosure of the actual relationship existing between Lady Windermere and Mrs Erlynne—an opinion, I may add, that had previously been strongly held and urged by Mr Alexander. As to those of us who do not look on a play as a mere question of pantomime and clowning, psychological interest is everything, I determined consequently to make a change in the precise moment of revelation. This determination, however, was entered into long before I had the opportunity of studying the culture, courtesy, and critical faculty displayed in such papers as the *Referee*, *Reynolds*, and the *Sunday Sun*.

When criticism becomes in England a real art, as it should be, and when none but those of artistic instinct and artistic cultivation is allowed to write about works of art, artists will no doubt read criticisms with a certain amount of intellectual interest. As things are at present, the criticisms of ordinary newspapers are of no interest whatsoever, except in so far as they display in its crudest form the extraordinary Bœotianism of a country that has produced some Athenians, and in which other Athenians have come to dwell.

I am, sir, your obedient servant   OSCAR WILDE

To E. W. Pratt[1]
MS. Berg

[*Postmark 15 April 1892*]   *16 Tite Street*

Dear Sir, The book in *Dorian Gray* is one of the many books I have never written, but it is partly suggested by Huysmans's *À Rebours*, which you will get at any French bookseller's. It is a fantastic variation on Huysmans's over-realistic study of the artistic temperament in our inartistic age. Faithfully yours   OSCAR WILDE

To Oswald Sickert[2]
MS. Hassall

[*Early May 1892*]   *16 Tite Street*

My dear Oswald, Thank you for your charming letter, and for the new

---

[1] Unidentified. The letter is addressed to High Road, Lower Clapton, N.E.

[2] Oswald Valentine Sickert (1871–1923) was a younger brother of the painter. At this time he was an undergraduate at Trinity College, Cambridge, where on 3 May

venture as well. I wish that in the latter there had been more about that delicate artist in language Robert Louis Stevenson, and less about mysterious things called Boating and Billiards and Cricket. However, even these may be subjects for criticism if you take grace of movement and gesture as your standpoint. From the point of view of art the athlete may be criticized, but from no other.

Come and see me when term is over, and bring your friend Edward Marsh, who has a charming name—for fiction.[1] Sincerely yours

OSCAR WILDE

To Robert Ross
MS. Clark

[? *May-June 1892*][2] *Royal Palace Hotel, Kensington*

My dearest Bobbie, Bosie[3] has insisted on stopping here for sandwiches. He is quite like a narcissus—so white and gold. I will come either Wednesday or Thursday night to your rooms. Send me a line. Bosie is so tired: he lies like a hyacinth on the sofa, and I worship him.

You dear boy. Ever yours OSCAR

To Grant Richards [4]

[*June 1892*] *16 Tite Street*

Dear Sir, The new edition of my poems is limited to 200 copies, and these are meant not for reviewers, but merely for lovers of poetry, a small and quite unimportant sect of perfect people, so I fear I cannot bid my book wander towards Mowbray House. Its raiment, gold smeared on tired purple, might attract attention in the Strand, and that would annoy it, books being delicate and most sensitive things, and, if they are books worth reading, having a strong dislike of the public.

So you see I must perforce refuse your request. Yours truly

OSCAR WILDE

1892 he had produced and edited the first number of an undergraduate journal, the *Cambridge Observer*. It contained an article on Zola by the editor and a review of Robert Louis Stevenson's new book *Across the Plains*, by Edward Marsh. After coming down from Cambridge, Sickert published a novel called *Helen*; he then became an overseas traveller for the *Encyclopaedia Britannica* and wrote little more.

[1] Edward Marsh (1872–1953), civil servant, patron of the arts, friend and editor of Rupert Brooke. Edited five volumes of *Georgian Poetry* (1912–22), translated Horace and La Fontaine. Knighted 1937.

[2] This letter cannot be dated exactly, but it seems likely to have been written fairly soon after May 1892 (see p. 281).

[3] The nickname (a contraction of Boysie) by which Lord Alfred Douglas was known to his family and friends from early childhood.

[4] English publisher and author (1872–1948). He was at this time working for W. T. Stead on the *Review of Reviews*, which was edited at Mowbray House, Norfolk Street. The text of this letter is taken from his *Memories of a Misspent Youth* (1932).

To Coulson Kernahan[1]

MS. B.M.

[? *June 1892*]   *16 Tite Street*

My dear Kernahan, I should have thanked you long ago for sending me your charming fairy tale, but the season with its red roses of pleasure has absorbed me quite, and I have almost forgotten how to write a letter. However I know you will forgive me, and I must tell you how graceful and artistic I think your story is; full of delicate imagination, and a symbolism suggestive of many meanings, not narrowed down to one moral, but many-sided as, I think, symbolism should be. But your strength lies not in such fanciful, winsome work. You must deal directly with Life—modern terrible Life—wrestle with it, and force it to yield you its secret. You have the power and the pen. You know what passion is, what passions are; you can give them their red raiment, and make them move before us. You can fashion puppets with bodies of flesh, and souls of turmoil: and so, you must sit down, and do a great thing. It is all in you. Your sincere friend

OSCAR WILDE

To Pierre Louÿs

MS. Yale

[? *June 1892*]

Cher Pierre, Je ne peux pas déjeuner ici ce matin: j'ai des affaires très importantes et très ennuyeuses. Je serai au théâtre à quatre heures, pas avant.

Je vous ai télégraphié hier à 301 King's Road, mais le Post Office vient de me dire qu'on disait que vous n'étiez pas là.

Vous êtes le plus charmant de tous mes amis, mais vous ne mettez jamais votre adresse sur vos lettres. Tout à toi   OSCAR

To Pierre Louÿs [2]

[*June 1892*]

Mon très cher Ennemi, Pourquoi pas d'adresse sur ta carte? Voilà deux jours que je te cherche!! Enfin, voulez-vous dîner avec moi ce soir? Rendez-vous Café Royal, Regent Street, 7.45, habit de matin. Je serai

---

[1] In Kernahan's *In Good Company* (1917) he prints an earlier undated note from Wilde: "Dear Kernahan, I am only too pleased that any little phrase of mine will find a place in any title you may give to any story. Use it, of course. I am sure your story will be delightful. Hoping to see you soon. Your friend, Oscar Wilde." The story was "The Garden of God," subtitled (after Wilde) "A Story for children from Eight to Eighty." It was included in Kernahan's *A Book of Strange Sins* (1893).
[2] Text from Carteret catalogue (1926). See note 5, p. 298.

charmé naturellement si Madame[1] vous accompagne. Et j'inviterai John Gray.

Vous savez les nouvelles, n'est-ce-pas? Sarah va jouer *Salomé*!! Nous répétons aujourd'hui.[2]

Envoyez-moi un télégramme au Lyric Club, Coventry Street, W. immédiatement. Aussi, je serai à une heure au Café Royal jusqu'à deux déjeuner. Venez. Votre ami   OSCAR

To William Rothenstein
MS. Rothenstein

[*Early July 1892*]   *51 Kaiser-Friedrich's Promenade, Bad-Homburg*[3]

My dear Will, The *Gaulois*, the *Echo de Paris*, and the *Pall Mall* have all had interviews.[4] I hardly know what new thing there is to say. The licenser of plays is nominally the Lord Chamberlain, but really a commonplace official—in the present case a Mr Pigott,[5] who panders to the vulgarity and hypocrisy of the English people, by licensing every low farce and vulgar melodrama. He even allows the stage to be used for the purpose of the caricaturing of the personalities of artists, and at the same moment when he prohibited *Salome*, he licensed a burlesque of *Lady Windermere's Fan* in which an actor dressed up like me and imitated my voice and manner!!![6]

[1] Louÿs married a daughter of the poet José-Maria de Heredia, but not till 1899, so this must refer to another lady.

[2] Rehearsals for this production at the Palace Theatre, London, with Sarah Bernhardt as Salome, Albert Darmont as Herod, and costumes by Graham Robertson, were in full swing when the Lord Chamberlain, towards the end of June, banned the play on the ground that it contained biblical characters. There exists a copy of the limited edition of Wilde's *Poems* (1892) inscribed by him: "*A Sarah Bernhardt, hommage d'Oscar Wilde. 'Comme la Princesse Salomé est belle ce soir.' Londres, '92.*"

[3] On 7 July 1892 Constance Wilde wrote to her brother Otho (MS Holland): "Oscar is at Homburg under a régime, getting up at 7.30, going to bed at 10.30, smoking hardly any cigarettes and being massaged, and of course drinking waters. I only wish I was there to see it."

[4] About the banning of *Salome*. In at least one of these interviews Wilde was reported as announcing his departure for France, where it was possible to have works of art produced. This caused a storm of comment, and in the *Spectator* of 9 July William Watson published "Lines to our new Censor" (reprinted in his *Lachrymae Musarum*, 1892), which began:

> And wilt thou, Oscar, from us flee,
> And must we, henceforth, wholly sever?
> Shall thy laborious *jeux-d'esprit*
> Sadden our lives no more for ever?

Wilde commented: "There is not enough fire in William Watson's poetry to boil a tea-kettle." (See also note 1, p. 323).

[5] Edward F. Smyth Pigott (1826–95) was Examiner of Plays for the Lord Chamberlain from 1875 to 1895. After his death Bernard Shaw described him as "a walking compendium of vulgar insular prejudice."

[6] *The Poet and the Puppets*, a musical travesty by Charles Brookfield (1860–1912) and J. M. Glover (1861–1931), produced at the Comedy Theatre on 19 May 1892,

The curious thing is this: all the arts are free in England, except the actor's art; it is held by the Censor that the stage degrades and that actors desecrate fine subjects, so the Censor prohibits not the publication of *Salome* but its production. Yet not one single actor has protested against this insult to the stage—not even Irving, who is always prating about the Art of the Actor. This shows how few actors are artists. All the *dramatic* critics, except Archer of the *World*,[1] agree with the Censor that there should be a censorship over actors and acting! This shows how bad our stage must be, and also shows how Philistine the English journalists are.

I am very ill, dear Will, and can't write any more. Ever yours

OSCAR WILDE

---

in which Charles Hawtrey burlesqued Wilde as "The Poet." Brookfield was the son of Thackeray's friend (see note p. 26), and wrote her biography. He also produced several other books and plays. Although he and Hawtrey were given parts in *An Ideal Husband*, they are believed to have been the ringleaders in collecting evidence against Wilde, and they celebrated his conviction by giving a dinner to Lord Queensberry. Brookfield was made Examiner of Plays 1912.

[1] Scottish critic, translator and playwright (1856–1924). Dramatic critic of the *World* (1884–1905). Ibsen's champion and translator in England. His letter of protest against the banning of *Salome*, which was written on 30 June, appeared in the *Pall Mall Gazette* on 1 July 1892, and ran:

Sir, Ever since Mr Oscar Wilde told me, a fortnight ago, that his *Salome* had been accepted by Madame Sarah Bernhardt, I have been looking forward, with a certain malign glee, to the inevitable suppression of the play by the Great Irresponsible. Quaint as have been the exploits of that gentleman and his predecessors in the past, the record of the Censorship presents nothing quainter than the present conjuncture. A serious work of art, accepted, studied, and rehearsed by the greatest actress of our time, is peremptorily suppressed, at the very moment when the personality of its author is being held up to ridicule, night after night, on the public stage, with the full sanction and approval of statutory Infallibility. But it is surely unworthy of Mr Wilde's lineage to turn tail and run away from a petty tyranny which lives upon the disunion and apathy of English dramatic authors. Paris does not particularly want Mr Wilde. There he would be one talent among many, handicapped moreover, in however slight a degree, by having to use an acquired idiom. I am not aware that anyone has produced work of the highest artistic excellence in a living language which was not his mother tongue. Here, on the other hand, Mr Wilde's talent is unique. We require it and we appreciate it—those of us, at any rate, who are capable of any sort of artistic appreciation. And especially we require it to aid in the emancipation of art from the stupid meddling of irresponsible officialism. As soon as the English drama attains to anything like intellectual virility, the days of the Censorship will be numbered; but how is it ever to attain virility if men of talent, on their first brush with the enemy, "succumb to the temptation to seek out another nation"? "I can resist anything except temptation," says Lord Darlington in *Lady Windermere's Fan*. But this is a case for an exception within the exception. For a man like Mr Wilde the temptation to an act of cowardice should surely not be irresistible. I am, sir, your obedient servant   WILLIAM ARCHER

Before the Select Committee of the House of Commons which sat in 1892 to hear evidence on stage censorship Archer (who was heard on 16 May) was the only witness who advocated the abolition of the censorship. Irving, Clement Scott, Comyns Carr and all the other witnesses spoke strongly in its favour.

Postcard: To Pierre Louÿs[1]

Pourquoi pas de lettre? Écris-moi quelques mots. Je m'ennuie ici énormément, et les cinq médicins m'ont défendu de fumer des cigarettes! Je me porte très bien et je suis horriblement triste.   OSCAR

To Arthur Fish[2]

[*Postmark 11 July 1892*]   *Homburg*

My dear Arthur, I was charmed to get your letter, but so sorry to hear your wife has been ill. As regards the idea of my becoming a French citizen, I have not yet decided. I am very much hurt not merely at the action of the Licenser of Plays, but at the pleasure expressed by the entire Press of England at the suppression of my work. However, the Press only represents the worst side of English life—there are a few like yourself, who love and have sympathy with the artist. I confess I should be sorry to separate from them. When I return I hope to see you, and am ever your affectionate friend   OSCAR WILDE

To John Lane[3]
MS. Dickey

[*July 1892*]   *Homburg*

Dear Mr Lane, I return you the agreement signed and witnessed. I have made some alterations in it. The maker of a poem is a "poet," not an "author": author is misleading.

Also the selection of reviews to which the book[4] is sent must be a matter of arrangement between you and your partner and me. A book of this kind —very rare and curious—must not be thrown into the gutter of English journalism. No book of mine, for instance, ever goes to the *National Observer*. I wrote to Henley to tell him so, two years ago. He is too coarse, too offensive, too personal, to be sent any work of mine. I hope that the

---

[1] Text from Carteret catalogue (1926). See note 5, p. 298.

[2] Text from *Cassell's Weekly*, 2 May 1923, corroborated by Parke-Bernet catalogue 1061 (1949), where the postmark is given.

[3] English publisher (1854–1925). Born in Devon. Came to London 1868 and worked as a railway clerk at Euston station. Founded the Bodley Head with Elkin Mathews (see note 3, p. 302) in 1887, though his name did not appear in it until 1892. He and Wilde never liked each other, and Wilde called the manservant in *The Importance of Being Earnest* after him to show his contempt. In 1895 Lane speedily withdrew Wilde's books from circulation.

[4] *The Sphinx*, which was published by Mathews & Lane in 1894. In the contract (MS. Bodley Head) which is simply dated 1892, Wilde twice substituted "poet" for "author." He received a 10% royalty, and Ricketts was paid £75 for his decorations.

Pierre Louÿs

R. H. Sherard

Charles Conder, Charles Ricketts, Llewellyn Hacon, C. H. Shannon

John Gray

book will be subscribed for before publication, and that as few as possible will be sent for review. Where in a magazine of art, either French or English, we know that an important appreciation will be written, we can send a copy, but ordinary English newspapers are not merely valueless, but would do harm, just as they are trying in every way to harm *Salome*, though they have not read it. The *St James's Gazette*, again, I would not have a copy sent to. They are most scurrilous.

With regard to the copies given to other than reviewers, I will have six myself. You and Mr Mathews will of course have a copy each, besides a copy to be kept in your place of business, and Mr Ricketts will have a copy.

I did not contemplate assigning to you the copyright of so important a poem for so small an honorarium as ten per cent, but will do so, it being clearly understood that no new edition is to be brought out without my sanction: I mean no such thing as a popular or cheap edition is to be brought out: nor are you to be able to assign the right of publishing the poem to any other firm. You will see that this is a quite reasonable demand on my part.

I hope *The Sphinx* will be a great success. Will you have a type-written copy made for me, so that I can correct the text before Ricketts writes it out: it would be a saving of time and money. Truly yours

OSCAR WILDE

To William Archer

MS. B.M.

[Postmark of receipt 22 July 1892]   *Homburg*

Dear Archer, I am here taking the waters, and have not a copy of *Salome* with me, or would gladly lend it to you, though the refusal of the Licenser to allow the performance of my tragedy was based entirely on his silly vulgar rule about no Biblical *subject* being treated. I don't fancy he ever *read* the play, and if he did, I can hardly fancy even poor Pigott objecting to an artist *treating* his subject in any way he likes. To object to that would be to object to Art entirely—a fine position for a man to adopt, but a little too fine for Pigott, I should imagine.

I want to tell you how gratified I was by your letter in the *P.M.G.*, not merely for its very courteous and generous recognition of my work, but for its strong protest against the contemptible official tyranny that exists in England in reference to the drama. The joy of the ordinary dramatic critic that such tyranny should exist is to me perfectly astounding. I should have thought there would be little pleasure in criticising an art where the artist was not free. The whole affair is a great triumph for the Philistine, but only a momentary one. We must abolish the censure. I think we can do it. When I come back I must see you. Ever yours

OSCAR WILDE

To Frank Harris[1]

MS. Texas

[July–August 1892] [*London*]

My dear Frank, I have just come back from Homburg, and was charmed to hear from John Gray you were in town. I am going down to the Lyric Club, and should like to see you in the course of the evening. I hope the poet will be dining with me, but thought to find him here.

Your last story had a most delicate ending—honey in the lion's mouth; most subtle and suggestive.[2]

Here is the poet—we are off. Ever yours   OSCAR

To Herbert Beerbohm Tree[3]

MS. Pearson

[Circa 1 September 1892]   *Grove Farm, Felbrigg, Cromer*[4]

My dear Tree, My wife and I were much shocked to read of your father's death. I remember having had the pleasure of meeting him at supper at the Haymarket, and how proud he was of your success in art. Pray accept our sincere sympathies.

As regards the play: I have written two acts, and had them set up by the type-writer: the third is nearly done, and I hope to have it all ready in ten days or a fortnight at most. I am very pleased with it so far.

The American rights I have already sold the refusal of. I fancy they want to produce at the Chicago Exhibition two new plays, one by Sardou, and one by me.[5] But the English rights are quite free. If you will send me your dates I would read it to you somewhere about the end of this month.

I find Cromer excellent for writing, and golf still better. Yours

OSCAR WILDE

---

[1] James Thomas (Frank) Harris (?1856–1931), author, editor and adventurer. Having spent much of his youth in America he returned to England and in 1883 became editor of the *Evening News*. Since 1886 he had been editor of the *Fortnightly Review*. He was in many ways a scoundrel, and his gifts as an imaginative romancer are now more apparent in his biographies and autobiography than in his fiction. Nevertheless his *Oscar Wilde, His Life and Confessions* (1916), though factually unreliable, has considerable impressionistic merit, and the nicest thing about him was his almost unfailing kindness and generosity to Wilde.

[2] Harris's story "A Straight Flush," which appeared in the *Fortnightly Review* for August 1892.

[3] English actor-manager (1853–1917), and half-brother of Max Beerbohm. Their father Julius Beerbohm died on 30 August 1892.

[4] It is not known for exactly how long Wilde rented this house, but he certainly wrote a great part of *A Woman of No Importance* there. Two families of friends lived nearby: the Batterseas at The Pleasaunce, Overstrand, and the Locker-Lampsons at Newhaven Court, Cromer. Lord Alfred Douglas came to stay for ten days (see p. 427).

[5] The World's Fair was held in Chicago from July to October 1893, but Wilde's next play, *A Woman of No Importance*, was not produced in America until 11 December 1893, when Rose Coghlan presented it at the Fifth Avenue Theatre, New York. Victorien Sardou (1831–1908) was a prolific and very successful French playwright.

To Sydney Barraclough[1]

MS. Clark

[? *28 October 1892*]   *16 Tite Street*

My dear Sydney, I enclose you tickets for Monday night—St James's—
and hope you will like the play as much as you did before. I must someday
have you in a play of mine: your Ferdinand in *The Duchess of Malfi*[2] was a
really fine performance, with such rare qualities as style and distinction
wedded to power and passion, and mastering them. You brought with
you the atmosphere of romance as you came on the stage, and the Italy of
the Renaissance in its pride and cruelty moved gorgeously before us, and
became mad and monstrous in its insolence of sin and its sudden horror of
its sin. You have a great future before you, Sydney. Let me help you.
Sincerely yours   OSCAR WILDE

Café Royal 1.30 tomorrow (Saturday).

To Lady Mount-Temple[3]

MS. Clark

[*October–November 1892*]   *16 Tite Street*

Dear Lady Mount-Temple, I need hardly say how grateful Constance and
I are to you for your kindness in promising to let us your lovely house at
Babbacombe, where Constance has passed such beautiful days. I hope you
will not mind my writing to you on business matters. If you would allow
us to have it for three months for £100, we would both feel very grateful
to you, and I need not say we will take the greatest care possible of your
lovely home, and remember always who its *châtelaine* is, and how gracious
is her courtesy in permitting us to sojourn for a season in her own house.

If you would let us carry out the scheme we propose, we would have the
great joy of being still more in your debt for many kindnesses and gracious
acts. Believe me, truly yours   OSCAR WILDE

---

[1] English actor and vocalist (1871–1930).

[2] Two performances of Webster's tragedy, "re-arranged for the modern stage by
William Poel," were given by the Independent Theatre Society at the Opera
Comique, London, on 21 and 25 October 1892. The Duchess was played by Mary
Rorke, Bosola by Murray Carson, and Castruccio by G. H. Kersley. Of Barra-
clough's performance the *Theatre* wrote: "The arrogance and uncontrolled impulse
of the Ferdinand degenerated into want of discipline in his actor."

[3] Georgina Tollemache (1822–1901), sister of the first Lord Tollemache and
widow of William Francis Cowper-Temple, first Lord Mount-Temple (1811–88),
politician and heir of both Lord Melbourne and Lord Palmerston. She was a
distant cousin of Constance Wilde and was unfailingly kind to her and her children.
Presuming that she accepted Wilde's offer, his tenancy of Babbacombe Cliff may
have lasted from mid-November to mid-February, with an additional fortnight
added (see p. 328).

To Sydney Barraclough

TS. Holland

[? *November 1892*] *New Lyric Club, 63 St James's Place*

My dear Sydney, I am not very well, and am going to Bournemouth for four or five days. Royal Bath Hotel is the address. I will see you early next week and introduce you to Tree. I shall insist on your acting the boy's part. I believe in your power absolutely. Always your affectionate friend OSCAR

To Lady Mount-Temple[1]

[? *November 1892*] *Royal Bath Hotel Bournemouth*

Dear and gracious Lady, With the children of the gods one dare not argue, and so I submit to your decision without a murmur save one of thanks and gratitude.

. . . I want to write two plays, one in blank verse, and I know the peace and beauty of your home will set me in tune, so that I can hear things that the ear cannot hear and see invisible things.

To Lord Alfred Douglas[2]

[? *November 1892*]

Dearest Bosie, I am so glad you are better. I trust you like the little card-case. Oxford is quite impossible in winter. I go to Paris next week—for ten days or so. Are you really going to the Scilly Isles?

I should awfully like to go away with you somewhere where it is hot and coloured.

I am terribly busy in town. Tree running up to see me on all occasions, also strange and troubling personalities walking in painted pageants.

Of the poem I will write tomorrow. Ever yours OSCAR

Love to Encombe.[3]

---

[1] The text of this incomplete letter is taken from the American Art Association catalogue of 19 November 1931. There is no direct evidence that it was addressed to Lady Mount-Temple.

[2] The text of this letter is taken from *Oscar Wilde and the Black Douglas* by the Marquess of Queensberry in collaboration with Percy Colson (1949). Its date is problematical.

[3] John Scott, Viscount Encombe (1870–1900), eldest son of the third Earl of Eldon, was Douglas's friend and contemporary at Winchester and Magdalen. They shared rooms in the High Street at Oxford.

To Lady Mount-Temple

MS. Clark

[? *November 1892*]   *Babbacombe Cliff*
                                                     [*near Torquay, South Devon*]

Dear Lady Mount-Temple, I beg to enclose cheque for the first half of my tenancy here, with many thanks to you for your kindness in allowing us to enjoy your lovely place. The last few days have been wonderfully bright and sunny, and the children are so well and happy here.

With many thanks to you for letting us be the tenants of so gracious a place, believe me, sincerely yours   OSCAR WILDE

To Robert Ross

MS. Du Cann

[*November–December 1892*]   *Babbacombe Cliff*

My dearest Bobbie, Thank you so much for the *New Review*.[1] Gosse's mention of me is most charming and courteous. Pray tell him from me what pleasure it gave me to receive so graceful a recognition from so accomplished a man of letters. As a rule, journalists and literary people write so horribly, and with such gross familiarity, and virulent abuse, that I am rather touched by any mention of me that is graceful and civil.

How are you? Are there beautiful people in London? Here there are none; everyone is so unfinished. When are you coming down? I am lazy and languid, doing no work. I need stirring up. With best love. Ever yours   OSCAR

To Sydney Barraclough

MS. Clark

[*December 1892*]   [*Babbacombe Cliff*][2]

My dear Sydney, I don't think it makes any matter your not being in *Hypatia*, if you really are not. I want you down here: it is a lovely place,

---

[1] In the *New Review* for December 1892 Edmund Gosse, reviewing William Watson's book of poems *Lachrymae Musarum* (see note 4, p. 316), had written:

> There is one piece in this volume which Mr Watson, I am convinced, will allow himself to be persuaded to omit in his second edition. This is his lyrical gibe (not a very funny gibe, dear Mr Watson) against Mr Oscar Wilde. To peck at one another is not the business of humming-birds and nightingales. Daws do it best, and are kept for that very purpose, in large numbers, in the aviaries of Grub Street. Mr Oscar Wilde (with whom I seldom find myself in agreement) is an artist, and claims from his fellow-artists courteous consideration.

[2] This letter is on Tite Street paper, but was clearly written at Babbacombe. *Hypatia*, a play by Stuart Ogilvie based on Kingsley's novel, was produced by Beerbohm Tree at the Haymarket Theatre on 2 January 1893, with Julia Neilson, Fred Terry, Lewis Waller and Tree himself in the cast. It ran until 15 April.

and you need rest and quiet, and I need you too, and we will devise schemes and undermine the foolish Tree, who *must* engage you for my play.

It is absurd that I can't have the boy I want in the part, and there is no one but you. The other young men are dreadful: you are an artist. I saw Fuller Mellish play Charles Surface the other day here. He was *terrible*— really terrible.[1]

Don't be upset, dear Sydney. Everything must come right. Affectionately yours   OSCAR

To Sydney Barraclough

MS. Clark

[*December 1892*]   *Babbacombe Cliff*

My dear Sydney, It was the fact of your ending your Tuesday telegram with the words "all bosh" that made me so angry with Tree, who is slippery and deceptive. I have written him a strong letter insisting on you, but nicely and with compliments. I still think there is a strong chance. Esmond is obviously unsuited. He is, as you say, a clever character actor.[2] But Tree is most annoying. He is not to be relied on.

I return to town on Thursday or Friday and will of course see you, at once.

You know you are my ideal Gerald, as you are my ideal friend.[3] Ever yours   OSCAR

To W. E. Combe[4]

MS. Princeton

[*Postmark 15 December 1892*]   [*Babbacombe Cliff*]

It is only shallow people who do not judge by appearances. The mystery of the world is the visible, not the invisible.   OSCAR WILDE

To E. Bailly[5]

MS. Morgan

[? *Circa 16 December 1892*]   *16 Tite Street*

Monsieur, Je vous envoie les épreuves, sauf les trois dernières pages, que

---

[1] Fuller Mellish (1865–1936), son of actress Rose Leclercq, appeared with Miss Fortescue's company at the Theatre Royal, Torquay, on 12, 13 and 14 December 1892. They opened with *The Hunchback*, so Wilde probably saw *The School for Scandal* on the 13th or 14th.

[2] Henry V. Esmond, stage-name of Henry V. Jack (1869–1922), English actor-manager and dramatist.

[3] The part of Gerald Arbuthnot in *A Woman of No Importance* was played by Fred Terry.

[4] Unidentified. This letter is on Tite Street paper, but is postmarked Torquay. It is addressed to Oaklands, Battle, Sussex.

[5] The Manager of the Librairie de l'Art Indépendant, who were to publish

j'ai perdues. Après que les corrections ont été faites, vous m'enverrez des autres, n'est-ce-pas, et aussi à M. Marcel Schwob, et à M. Pierre Louÿs. Je pense que ce serait mieux de ne pas publier avant le quinze janvier. L'édition sera de 600 exemplaires, n'est-ce-pas, et 50 sur papier de luxe.

Recevez mes compliments et mes remerciements   OSCAR WILDE

To Alfred H. Miles[1]

[? *1892–93*]   *16 Tite Street*

You are quite at liberty to make any use of the poems you mention, with the exception of "The Dole of the King's Daughter;" the "Ballade de Marguerite," the "Serenade," and the "La Bella Donna." These four I do not consider very characteristic of my work. In the first edition of Sharp's *Sonnets of This Century* (Walter Scott, publisher) there is a sonnet on the sale by auction of Keats's love-letters, which I think is one of the best sonnets I have written. It is quite at your disposal.

To Gerald Maxwell

MS. Roughead

[*Postmark 4 January 1893*]   *Babbacombe Cliff*

My dear Gerald, Thank you so much for your letter. I am greatly distressed to hear you are no longer Lord Darlington. What has really happened? I fear the tour was horribly mismanaged. I wish I had seen you in the part; I feel sure you were admirable.[2] The amateur performance here I have not yet seen, as an east wind, not knowing, I suppose, who I was, has given me a cold. Nutcombe Gould played Darlington.[3] What are you going to do now in acting? Pray remember me to your people and to Willie. Sincerely yours   OSCAR WILDE

Salome (see note 4, p. 326). Mason prints (p. 374) a letter from Bailly to Wilde, dated 23 December 1892, which begins: "*J'ai remis à M. Marcel Schwob, qui vous les fera parvenir après corrections de sa main, les épreuves nouvelles de 'Salomé'.*" Schwob (1867–1905) was a French symbolist writer (see note p. 306). Wilde dedicated *The Sphinx* (1894) TO MARCEL SCHWOB IN FRIENDSHIP AND IN ADMIRATION.

[1] Alfred Henry Miles (1848–1929), author, editor and journalist, compiled many anthologies, particularly *The Poets and the Poetry of the Century*, which appeared in ten volumes 1891–97. Vol. viii (1893) contained seven of Wilde's poems, including the sonnet he suggested. The text of this incomplete letter is taken from Maggs's catalogue 492 (1927).

[2] A provincial tour of *Lady Windermere's Fan* had been sent out during the autumn of 1892 by J. Pitt Hardacre (1856–1933), a theatrical manager who specialised in tours.

[3] Wilde had supervised some rehearsals of a production of *Lady Windermere's Fan*, which opened at the Theatre Royal, Torquay, on 2 January 1893. The cast was composed of local amateurs (led by the Mayoress, Mrs Splatt, who directed the play and took the part of Mrs Erlynne), reinforced by the professionals Lily Hanbury and Nutcombe Gould.

To Lord Alfred Douglas[1]

[? *January 1893*]   [*Babbacombe Cliff*]

My Own Boy, Your sonnet[2] is quite lovely, and it is a marvel that those red rose-leaf lips of yours should have been made no less for music of song than for madness of kisses. Your slim gilt soul walks between passion and poetry. I know Hyacinthus, whom Apollo loved so madly, was you in Greek days.

Why are you alone in London, and when do you go to Salisbury?[3] Do go there to cool your hands in the grey twilight of Gothic things, and come here whenever you like. It is a lovely place—it only lacks you; but go to Salisbury first. Always, with undying love, yours   OSCAR

To John Lane
MS. Prescott

[*Early February 1893*]   *Babbacombe Cliff*

Dear Mr Lane, I expect *Salome*[4] will be ready in a fortnight—at any rate before the end of the month. I am printing 50 on large paper, of which you can have 25 if you like; they will be 10/- each, sale price. Of course you will have them at a proper reduction. But kindly let me have, as you promised, a formal note about the whole thing, so as to have no misunderstanding about the agreement. Pray do this at once.

Also, there are a large number of my poems still unpaid for. Will you kindly close the account and let me have a cheque for them.

With regard to Mr Gray's poems, if you wish to take the book yourself, you should give Mr Ricketts his honorarium, should you not?[5]

I should be glad to hear how *The Sphinx* is progressing, and what date it is likely to come out on.[6]

I hear there is some chance of your coming to Torquay—is it so? I hope I shall be here when you do. Believe me, truly yours   OSCAR WILDE

---

[1] This letter, the exact date of which is conjectural, was later stolen, used as material for attempted blackmail of Wilde, and finally read out in court during the Queensberry and later trials. Wilde stated in evidence that it was written at Babbacombe. In the *Spirit Lamp* (see note 1, p. 327) of 4 May 1893 there appeared an anonymous sonnet in French based on this letter and written by Pierre Louÿs. The text of the letter is taken from *Trials*, p. 112.

[2] Possibly "In Praise of Shame," which is dated 1893.

[3] Where Lady Queensberry had a house called St Ann's Gate in the Close.

[4] The original (French) edition (see note p. 325). It consisted of 600 copies at 10 francs or 5/-, and fifty on Dutch hand-made paper at 10/6. It was published on 22 February 1893 in Paris by the Librairie de l'Art Indépendant and in London by Elkin Mathews & John Lane. The names of both firms appeared on the title-page.

[5] See note 3, p. 311.

[6] *The Sphinx*, with decorations by Ricketts, was published by Mathews & Lane on 11 June 1894. There were 250 copies at two guineas, and twenty-five large-paper copies at five guineas, issued later.

To Lord Alfred Douglas

MS. Clark

[? *February 1893*]   *Babbacombe Cliff*

My dearest Bosie, I have written to your man, and have received no reply from him, which is most annoying, as things are the wrong colour without gold to light them up. Are you working? I hope so. Do get a good crammer.

I am rather unhappy as I can't write—I don't know why. Things are all wrong. Have you been writing lovely sonnets? I never got the *Spirit Lamp*, nor ever a cheque![1] My charge for the sonnet is £300. Who on earth *is* the editor? He must be rented.[2] I hear he is hiding at Salisbury.

With best love, ever yours   OSCAR

To John Lane

MS. Morgan

[*February 1893*]   *Babbacombe Cliff*

Dear Mr Lane, Your letter has not yet arrived, but I have received your telegram, which I will now regard as a formal record of our agreement. You see now, I feel sure, how right I was in continually pressing you for a written agreement, and I cannot understand why you would not do so. I spoke to you on the subject at your own place; you promised to forward the agreement next day; this was in November last; I spoke to you twice about it at the Hogarth Club, you made the same promise. I wrote to you endless letters—a task most wearisome to me—on this plain business matter. I received promises, excuses, apologies, but no agreement. This has been going on for three months, and the fact of your name being on the title-page was an act of pure courtesy and compliment on my part: you asked me to allow it as a favour to you; just as my increasing the numbers printed from 250 to 600 was done to oblige you. I make no profit from the transaction, nor do I derive any benefit. As you are interested in literature and curious works of art I was ready to oblige you. The least return you might have made would have been to have spared me the annoyance of writing endless business letters. I can only tell you that when I did not hear from you in Paris last week I very nearly struck your name off the title-page of the book, and diminished the edition. As you had advertised it, however, I felt this would have been somewhat harsh and unkind to you.

I will now look on the incident as over, and accept the regrets expressed in your telegram. I hope that we may publish some other book of mine, but it must clearly be understood that the business matters are to be attended to by your firm properly and promptly: my sphere is that of art, and of art merely.

[1] The *Spirit Lamp* was an Oxford undergraduate periodical, which was edited by Lord Alfred Douglas from November 1892 to June 1893. Wilde's sonnet "The New Remorse" was published in vol. II, no. 4, on 6 December 1892.

[2] A "renter" is a slang term for a man who participates in male homosexual affairs for a reward (originally perhaps for his rent).

With regard to the edition on Dutch paper, I am only putting twenty-five on the market. Of these I have reserved ten for you. Yours very truly

OSCAR WILDE

In the advertisements at the end of Mr Symonds's book,[1] I observe you state of *Salome*, "This is the play the Lord Chamberlain refused to license etc." Please do not do this again. The interest and value of *Salome* is not that it was suppressed by a foolish official, but that it was written by an artist. It is the tragic beauty of the work that makes it valuable and of interest, not a gross act of ignorance and impertinence on the part of the censor.

Also pray remember that it was agreed that no copy of *Salome* is to be sent either to the *National Observer* or to Mr O'Connor's *Sunday Sun*.[2]

To Lady Mount-Temple

MS. Clark

[*8-11 February 1893*]   *Babbacombe Cliff*

Dear Lady Mount-Temple, As I suppose Constance has told you, I have returned to your lovely house in order to be with the children while she is away, and if you still allow me I will gladly and gratefully accept your kind invitation to stay on for a couple of weeks more—till March 1st if it will not inconvenience you, as I find the peace and beauty here so good for troubled nerves, and so suggestive for new work.

Indeed, Babbacombe Cliff has become a kind of college or school, for Cyril studies French in the nursery, and I write my new play in Wonderland,[3] and in the drawing-room Lord Alfred Douglas—one of Lady Queensberry's sons—studies Plato with his tutor[4] for his degree at Oxford in June. He and his tutor are staying with me for a few days, so I am not lonely in the evenings.

Constance seems very happy in Florence. No doubt you hear from her.

I venture to enclose the formal tribute due to the Lady of The Manor, and with many thanks for your kindness remain most sincerely yours

OSCAR WILDE

---

[1] *In the Key of Blue and other Essays* by John Addington Symonds, published by Mathews & Lane in 1893.

[2] Thomas Power O'Connor (1848–1929), journalist and politician, was Nationalist M.P. for the Scotland Division of Liverpool 1885–1929. Founded and was first editor of the *Star*, the *Sun*, the *Sunday* (later the *Weekly*) *Sun*, *M.A.P.* and *T.P.'s Weekly*. Made a Privy Councillor 1924.

[3] All the rooms at Babbacombe Cliff had names, the bedrooms names of flowers to match the wallpaper. Lady Mount-Temple's boudoir, which had windows on three sides, was called Wonderland. It was hung with works by Rossetti and Burne-Jones.

[4] Campbell Dodgson, who was coaching Douglas for Greats at Oxford. See note 2, p. 333. For his description of life at Babbacombe, see Appendix A, p. 867.

To John Lane

TS. Holland

[February 1893]   *Babbacombe Cliff*

Dear Mr Lane, The Dutch papers are in your consignment, of course: you can easily recognise them. Let me know how many more you want, and I will try and get them for you, but I don't know if I can. Bailly has not marked the numbers of the editions, which is a mistake, but it allows me to print more.

Can you say if you wish more of the ordinary copies? Also, kindly send me a cheque for £35 by return. Yours ever   OSCAR WILDE

To John Lane

TS. Holland

[February 1893]   *Babbacombe Cliff*

Dear Mr Lane, I beg to acknowledge the receipt of your cheque for £17. There seems to be an error about the amount, which you will kindly rectify.

You have, I believe, received 15 copies on Dutch paper at 5/- a copy, which I believe represents a sum of £3. 15. 0. This added to the £15 (already due as balance of the £35) would make—would it not?—£18. 15. 0.

Will you kindly reply by return, and I will see about the 150 copies you wish to have, on receipt of your answer. Yours very truly

OSCAR WILDE

To Albert Marshman Palmer[1]

MS. Harvard

[February 1893]   *16 Tite Street*

Dear Mr Palmer, I beg you to accept my sincere thanks for the admirable company of actors you have secured for the presentation of *Lady Windermere's Fan* in America, and for the artistic care and taste with which you have put my play on the stage.

My American friends—and I am fortunate enough to have many—have written to me such charming accounts of the performances in Boston and New York that I regret extremely I have no opportunity of seeing the new interpretation of my work.

I see by the papers that you purpose visiting London this season with your own company. I hope the report is true, and I know that in London there is, as far as the stage is concerned, always a high appreciation of new

---

[1] American theatre manager (1838–1905). His production of *Lady Windermere's Fan* at Palmer's (late Wallack's) Theatre, New York, opened on 6 February 1893, with Maurice Barrymore (father of Ethel, John and Lionel) as Lord Darlington.

art and new methods. There is, I feel certain, a great success in store for you.

Believe me, dear Mr Palmer, very truly yours   OSCAR WILDE

To Edward Hamilton Bell[1]

MS. Millar

[? *February 1893*]   *16 Tite Street*

My dear Bell, Thank you so much for your friendly congratulations, which I value very much not merely on account of our old acquaintance, but because they come from one who is himself doing very beautiful and artistic work. I often hear of you, and the lovely costumes you design, and the distinction of your taste. The next play I produce in America I hope you will costume for me. It would give me very great pleasure.

Tell Johnny Sturges[2] that when poets send him life-sized photographs of themselves, he should write them charming letters, and send them some of his brilliant, vivid, jewelled stories. He seems to me to be as bad a correspondent as I am—and I am the worst in the whole world.

Thanking you again for the nice things you say of my play, believe me, your sincere friend   OSCAR WILDE

Telegram: To Elizabeth Robins

MS. Wilberforce

18 February 1893   *Torquay*

Your letter forwarded to me here. So sorry cannot be present at your première but wish the amazing Hedda every possible success. I count Ibsen fortunate in having so brilliant and subtle an artist to interpret him.[3]

          OSCAR WILDE

To Florence Balcombe Stoker

TS. Sheppard

[*Postmark 21 February 1893*]   *Babbacombe Cliff*

My dear Florence, Will you accept a copy of *Salome*—my strange venture

---

[1] English artist, actor, writer and stage designer (1857–1929). Nephew of Sir Edward Poynter, P.R.A. Studied at the Slade. Went on the stage in early 80's. Went to America in 1885 to play the boy's part in Pinero's *The Magistrate* and stayed there. Toured with Modjeska, who in her memoirs described him as "the dainty Mr Bell," and then worked as a stage designer for Augustin Daly, Lawrence Barrett, Irving and other managers. Ended as a museum curator in Philadelphia.

[2] Jonathan Sturges (1864–1911), American writer, was a cripple from childhood. Lived mostly in England. Friend of Whistler and Henry James. In some sense the original of Little Bilham in *The Ambassadors*. His book of stories *The First Supper and Other Episodes* was published in 1893.

[3] The first English performance of Ibsen's *The Master Builder* took place at the Trafalgar Square Theatre on 20 February 1893, with Elizabeth Robins as Hilda Wangel and Herbert Waring as Solness.

in a tongue that is not my own, but that I love as one loves an instrument of music on which one has not played before. You will get it, I hope, tomorrow, and I hope you will like it. With kind regards to Bram, believe me, always your sincere friend   OSCAR WILDE

To Edmund Gosse[1]
MS. B.M.

[*Date of receipt 23 February 1893*][2]   *Babbacombe Cliff*

My dear Gosse, Will you accept a copy of *Salome*, my first venture to use for art that subtle instrument of music, the French tongue. Accept it as a slight tribute of my admiration of your own delicate use of English. Very truly yours   OSCAR WILDE

The charming house in which I am staying contains many Burne-Joneses but not one Blue Book! So I send this to your club, along with the play. But I have no fear but that Salome will find her way to that delightful library you have let us know of, and if she be not too Tyrian in her raiment be suffered to abide there for a season. I could desire for her no pleasanter place to live in, and I know that you have a welcome always for things that aim at beauty. Should she try to dance, a stern look from a single tome by an eighteenth-century writer will quell her, for common sense she has none, and reason, a faculty which I am glad to say is rapidly dying out, affrights her terribly.

To an Unidentified Correspondent
MS. Berg

[*Postmark 23 February 1893*]   [*Postmark Torquay*]

My dear Sir, Pray let me very sincerely thank you for your charming letter, and for your graceful praise of my play.[3] The newspapers seemed to me not to understand the form or spirit of the work, and some of the criticisms sent to me seemed to me unnecessarily vulgar, even for newspapers, but I have received from New York many letters of delicate and generous appreciation, none of which has pleased me more than yours.

The psychological idea that suggested to me the play is this. A woman who has had a child, but never known the passion of maternity (there are such women), suddenly sees the child she has abandoned falling over a precipice. There wakes in her the maternal feeling—the most terrible of all emotions—a thing that weak animals and little birds possess. She rushes to rescue, sacrifices herself, does follies—and the next day she feels "This passion is too terrible. It wrecks my life. I don't want to know it again. It makes me suffer too much. Let me go away. I don't want to be a mother

---

[1] Civil servant, critic and author (1849–1928). Librarian to the House of Lords 1904–14. Knighted 1925.   [2] So annotated by Gosse.
[3] The New York production of *Lady Windermere's Fan*. (See note p. 329.)

any more." And so the fourth act is to me the psychological act, the act that is newest, most true. For which reason, I suppose, the critics say "There is no necessity for Act IV." But the critics are of no importance. They lack instinct. They have not the sense of Art. You have it, and I thank you again for your courteous and charming letter. Truly yours

OSCAR WILDE

To Bernard Shaw[1]
MS. Pearson

[*Postmark 23 February 1893*]   *Babbacombe Cliff*

My dear Shaw, You have written well and wisely and with sound wit on the ridiculous institution of a stage-censorship: your little book on Ibsenism and Ibsen is such a delight to me that I constantly take it up, and always find it stimulating and refreshing: England is the land of intellectual fogs but you have done much to clear the air: we are both Celtic, and I like to think that we are friends: for these and many other reasons Salome presents herself to you in purple raiment.

Pray accept her with my best wishes, and believe me, very truly yours

OSCAR WILDE[2]

To William Archer
MS. B.M.

[*Circa 23 February 1893*]   *Babbacombe Cliff*

My dear Archer, I hope you have received *Salome* in her Tyrian purple and fading silver. I have not forgotten that you were, with the exception of George Bernard Shaw, the only critic of note who upheld me at all against the Censorship. The others were grotesque in their antics of vulgar and ignoble delight at an occurrence which they regarded as an insult to me, but which was, in truth, merely an insult to the art of acting. Believe me, my dear Archer, sincerely yours   OSCAR WILDE

To Frances Forbes-Robertson
MS. Prescott

[*Circa 23 February 1893*]   *Babbacombe Cliff*

My dear Frankie, I fear I shall not be in town on the fourth, as I am here

---

[1] At this time G. B. S. (1856–1950) was music critic of the *World*. His book *The Quintessence of Ibsenism* had been published in 1891, and his first play, *Widowers' Houses*, performed in December 1892 (see note 3, p. 345).

[2] On 28 February Shaw answered from 29 Fitzroy Square (text from Stetson sale catalogue, 1920): "Salome is still wandering in her purple raiment in search of me, and I expect her to arrive a perfect outcast, branded with inky stamps, bruised by flinging from hard hands into red prison vans, stuffed and contaminated . . . I hope soon to send you my play *Widowers' Houses* which you will find tolerably amusing." (See letter p. 339.)

with my two boys who are devoted to the sea. Constance is in Rome with her aunt, and we don't like the children to be quite alone.

This is a lovely house, belonging to Lady Mount-Temple whom Norman knows, and has Rossetti drawings, and a Burne-Jones window, and many lovely things.

But today the sea is rough, and there are no dryads in the glen, and the wind cries like a thing whose heart is broken, so I am consoling myself by reading *Salome*, that terrible coloured little tragedy I once in some strange mood wrote. A copy in Tyrian purple and tired silver is on its way to you.[1] Pray accept it from me as a token of our old friendship, and believe me, always yours   OSCAR WILDE

To Campbell Dodgson[2]

[Postmark 23 February 1893]   *Babbacombe Cliff*

My dear Dodgson, We are charmed you like the paper-knife and hope it really brings a pleasant memory to you. For myself, I can only assure you how much I enjoyed your visit. I look forward to seeing you in town, either guarding marvellous Rembrandt etchings, or simply existing beautifully, which is even better, and we must talk of purple things and drink of purple wine.

I am still conducting the establishment on the old lines and really think I have succeeded in combining the advantages of a public school with those of a private lunatic asylum, which, as you know, was my aim. Bosie is very gilt-haired and I have bound *Salome* in purple to suit him. That tragic daughter of passion appeared on Thursday last, and is now dancing for the head of the English public. Should you come across her, tell me how you like her. I want you to like her.

All the boys of the school send their best love, and kindest wishes.
Sincerely yours   OSCAR WILDE
                                                                Headmaster Babbacombe School.

Babbacombe School

Headmaster—Mr Oscar Wilde
Second Master—Mr Campbell Dodgson
Boys—Lord Alfred Douglas

Rules.

Tea for masters and boys at 9.30 a.m.
Breakfast at 10.30.

---

[1] Now in the possession of Mrs Sherburne Prescott, it is inscribed "Frances Forbes-Robertson from her friend the author. Feb '93."

[2] Author and iconographer (1867–1948). Scholar of Winchester and New College, where he was a contemporary and friend of Lionel Johnson. Keeper of Prints and Drawings, British Museum 1912–32. The text of this letter is taken from a manuscript copy in his hand (MS. Clark).

Work. 11.30–12.30.

At 12.30 Sherry and biscuits for headmaster and boys (the second master objects to this).

12.40–1.30. Work.

1.30. Lunch.

2.30–4.30. Compulsory hide-and-seek for headmaster.

5. Tea for headmaster and second master, brandy and sodas (not to exceed seven) for boys.

6–7. Work.

7.30. Dinner, with compulsory champagne.

8.30–12. Écarté, limited to five-guinea points.

12–1.30. Compulsory reading in bed. Any boy found disobeying this rule will be immediately woken up.

At the conclusion of the term the headmaster will be presented with a silver inkstand, the second master with a pencil-case, as a token of esteem, by the boys.[1]

To Mrs Schuster[2]

MS. Princeton

[? *24 February 1893*]   *Babbacombe Cliff*

My dear Mrs Schuster, I am in despair! I have just been telegraphed for to go to town, on important business about my new play, and am obliged to go up by the 12.26 this afternoon, so we will not be able to come and dine with you tomorrow as we had hoped, which is a great disappointment.

We will be back on Monday, and will come and see you on Tuesday if we may. Lord Alfred comes with me to town, as the journey is so tedious, and to travel with sunbeams a real necessity. Will you excuse us then? Nothing but the destiny of affairs could drag me to town.

I hope Miss Tiny is better: it was a great disappointment not seeing her the other day. Very sincerely yours   OSCAR WILDE

To Pierre Louÿs[3]

[*Postmark 27 February 1893*]   [*Postmark Torquay*]

My dear Pierre, Is the enclosed really all that you have to say to me in

[1] Here Dodgson added: "As a matter of fact the second master was presented with an enormous paper-weight, with suitable inscriptions, by headmaster and boys."

[2] Wife of Leo Schuster, a wealthy Frankfurt banker who had settled in a large villa called Cannizaro at Wimbledon. Their daughter Adela (ironically nicknamed Miss Tiny on account of her size) was a woman of great perception and generosity.

[3] Text from Carteret catalogue (1926), where the last page is reproduced in facsimile.

return for my choosing you out of all my friends to whom to dedicate *Salome*?[1] I cannot tell you how hurt I am.

Those to whom I merely gave copies have written me charming letters coloured with delicate appreciation of my work. You alone—you whose name I have written in gold on purple—you say nothing, and I don't understand what your telegram means; some trivial jest I suppose; a drop of froth without wine. How you disappoint me! Had you wired "*Je vous remercie*" it would have been enough.

It is new to me to think that friendship is more brittle than love is.

OSCAR WILDE

To Oswald Yorke[2]
MS. Russell

[*Late February 1893*]   *Babbacombe Cliff*

My dear Oswald, In my new play[3] there are very few men's parts—it is a woman's play—and I am of course limited to some degree to the stock company at the Haymarket. I fear there would be no chance of a part suitable to you in it.

I am surprised to hear you are out of engagements—you made many successes lately, and I often heard your name mentioned, and read nice things of you. With your versatility and power you are sure to be engaged soon.

I am here in a lovely house in a glen over the sea; there are Rossetti drawings, and a window by Burne-Jones, and many lovely things and colours. I hear London like some grey monster raging over the publication of *Salome*, but I am at peace for the moment: all I desire is that the wind would cry like a thing whose heart is broken. I hate its gusts of rage and loud roaring.

When I come to town, we must dine together. Ever yours

OSCAR WILDE

To the Editor of The Times[4]

[*Circa 1 March 1893*]

Sir, My attention has been drawn to a review of *Salome* which was published in your columns last week. The opinions of English critics on a

---

[1] The original (French) edition of *Salome* was dedicated "*À mon ami Pierre Louÿs.*"

[2] English actor (1866–1943). After 1896 he acted mostly in the United States and married the American actress Annie Russell (1864–1936).

[3] *A Woman of No Importance.*

[4] *The Times* review of *Salome* on 23 February had run:

This is the play, written for Mme Sarah Bernhardt, which the Lord Chamberlain declined to license for performance in this country. It is an arrangement in blood and ferocity, morbid, *bizarre*, repulsive, and very offensive in its adaptation of scriptural phraseology to situations the reverse of sacred. It is not ill-suited to

French work of mine have, of course, little, if any, interest for me. I write simply to ask you to allow me to correct a misstatement that appears in the review in question.

The fact that the greatest tragic actress of any stage now living saw in my play such beauty that she was anxious to produce it, to take herself the part of the heroine, to lend the entire poem the glamour of her personality, and to my prose the music of her flute-like voice—this was naturally, and always will be, a source of pride and pleasure to me, and I look forward with delight to seeing Mme Bernhardt present my play in Paris, that vivid centre of art, where religious dramas are often performed. But my play was in no sense of the words written for this great actress. I have never written a play for any actor or actress, nor shall I ever do so. Such work is for the artisan in literature, not for the artist.

I remain, sir, your obedient servant   OSCAR WILDE

To Mr Iredale[1]
MS. Princeton

[March 1893]   Savoy Hotel, London[2]

Dear Mr Iredale, A great many of the *Salomes* have never arrived. Neither Mr Le Gallienne, Mr Swinburne, Mr William Archer, Mr Bernard Shaw, nor Mr Pater has received a copy. Can they have been mislaid?

Thanking you for your kind courtesy to me always, I remain yours truly
        OSCAR WILDE

To Lord Alfred Douglas[3]

[March 1893]   Savoy Hotel, London

Dearest of all Boys, Your letter was delightful, red and yellow wine to me; but I am sad and out of sorts. Bosie, you must not make scenes with me. They kill me, they wreck the loveliness of life. I cannot see you, so Greek and gracious, distorted with passion. I cannot listen to your curved lips saying hideous things to me. I would sooner [be blackmailed by every renter in London][4] than have you bitter, unjust, hating. I must see you

---

some of the less attractive phases of Mme Bernhardt's dramatic genius, and it is vigorously written in some parts. As a whole, it does credit to Mr Wilde's command of the French language, but we must say that the opening scene reads to us very like a page from one of Ollendorff's exercises [see note 2, p. 416].

Wilde's letter was published on 2 March.

[1] An employee of Elkin Mathews & John Lane.

[2] On his return from Babbacombe, Wilde took rooms at the Savoy, and stayed there for most of the month of March.

[3] Text from *Trials* (pp. 133–34 and 313), supplemented by letter on p. 457. For Wilde's later reference to this letter, see p. 457.

[4] These words, which were apparently thought too shocking or too obscure to be read out in court, are here supplied from the letter on p. 457.

soon. You are the divine thing I want, the thing of grace and beauty; but I don't know how to do it. Shall I come to Salisbury? My bill here is £49 for a week. I have also got a new sitting-room over the Thames. Why are you not here, my dear, my wonderful boy? I fear I must leave; no money, no credit, and a heart of lead.   YOUR OWN OSCAR

To Lord Alfred Douglas
MS. Clark

[?*12–15 April 1893*][1]

Dearest Boy—
   We have only just finished Act *2*!! *Don't wait*. Order, of course, what you want. Lunch 1.30 tomorrow: at Albemarle. I do not rehearse tomorrow at all. Ever yours   OSCAR

To W. Graham Robertson
MS. Preston

[*Postmark 14 April 1893*]   *Albemarle Club*

My dear Graham, I send you a stall for the first night of my play. I wish I could send another for your mother, but the rush for seats has been so enormous that we have had to refuse Royalties and bigwigs, and for my own friends I have only had very few stalls, and have been obliged to refuse many dear and delightful people.
   I hope you will like my new work, and am always yours
                                        OSCAR WILDE

To John Lane
MS. O'Donohue

[*Sent by messenger and marked Important.*]
[? *19 April 1893*]   *Hotel Albemarle*

Dear Mr Lane, Here is your seat; front row of dress-circle; I think the best in the house. Next you, you will find Pierre Louÿs, the young poet to whom I dedicated *Salome*. Pray introduce yourself to him. He is a perfect English scholar. In haste   OSCAR WILDE

To William Archer
MS. B.M.

[? *26 April 1893*]   *Hotel Albemarle*

My dear Archer, I must send you a line to tell you with what pleasure I

----
[1] It is impossible to date this letter accurately, but it may well have been written during rehearsals of *A Woman of No Importance*.

have read your luminous, brilliant criticism of my play.[1] There are points of course where I differ from you, but to be criticised by an artist in criticism is so keen a delight, and one so rare in England, that I love our modes of difference. They are, to me at any rate, so suggestive, so stimulating. Believe me, truly yours   OSCAR WILDE

To J. P. Mahaffy [2]
MS. Dublin

[? *April 1893*]   *Haymarket Theatre*

My dear Mahaffy, I am so pleased you like the play, and thank you for your charming letter, all the more flattering to me as it comes not merely from a man of high and distinguished culture, but from one to whom I owe so much personally, from my first and my best teacher, from the scholar who showed me how to love Greek things.

Let me sign myself, in affection and admiration, your old pupil and your old friend   OSCAR WILDE

To William Rothenstein
MS. Rothenstein

[? *April–May 1893*]   *Hotel Albemarle*

My dear Will, I have always been fond of you, and your art is always dear to me. I had been told that you wanted to take sides—that was all—and foolish as it is to take sides in a one-sided quarrel, or attack rather, still charming people are foolish often.[3] So I did not go to see you in Paris. But when I saw you in St James's Street, I had to jump from my hansom and shake hands with my friend.

When I go to Paris I shall wait your coming, and we shall be merry, as of old, at Sylvain's. Always affectionately yours   OSCAR

---

[1] *A Woman of No Importance* was produced at the Haymarket Theatre on 19 April 1893, with Beerbohm Tree, Mrs Bernard Beere, Fred Terry, Julia Neilson and Mrs Tree in the cast. It ran till 16 August, with a break of three nights in the middle. Archer's notice appeared in the *World* on 26 April. In it he wrote: "The one essential fact about Mr Oscar Wilde's dramatic work is that it must be taken on the very highest plane of modern English drama, and furthermore, that it stands alone on that plane. In intellectual calibre, artistic competence—ay, and in dramatic instinct to boot—Mr Wilde has no rival among his fellow-workers for the stage."

[2] It is impossible to date this letter accurately, but it seems more likely to have been written during the run of *A Woman of No Importance* (April–August 1893) than during that of *An Ideal Husband* (January–April 1895).

[3] Sir John Rothenstein thinks that this may refer to his father's continued friendship with Whistler.

To A. W. Pinero[1]

MS. Morgan

[*May 1893*]   *Hotel Albemarle*

My dear Pinero, I don't know if I shall be in town on the 25th. I fear I shall be in Paris, but it will be a great pleasure to me to be a Steward on so remarkable an occasion. I fancy that it is rarely that a theatrical dinner is presided over by a brilliant dramatist.

I enclose a small donation to the Fund, and remain sincerely yours

OSCAR WILDE

To Bernard Shaw

MS. Pearson

[*Postmark 9 May 1893*]   *16 Tite Street*

My dear Shaw, I must thank you very sincerely for Op. 2 of the great Celtic School.[2] I have read it twice with the keenest interest. I like your superb confidence in the dramatic value of the mere facts of life. I admire the horrible flesh and blood of your creatures, and your preface is a masterpiece—a real masterpiece of trenchant writing and caustic wit and dramatic instinct. I look forward to your Op. 4. As for Op. 5, I am lazy, but am rather itching to be at it. When are you coming to the Haymarket? Sincerely yours   OSCAR WILDE

---

[1] Arthur Wing Pinero, English dramatist (1855–1934). On 25 May 1893, two days before the production of his greatest success, *The Second Mrs Tanqueray*, he presided at a dinner of the Royal General Theatrical Fund in the Whitehall Rooms of the Hotel Metropole in London. Irving closed the Lyceum for the night so as to speak at the dinner. Other speakers included Comyns Carr, John L. Toole and Squire Bancroft. There is no record of Wilde's having been present, but he contributed two guineas a year to the Fund.

[2] Mr Hesketh Pearson has brilliantly interpreted the numbers in this letter as follows:

Op. 1 was obviously *Lady Windermere's Fan*; Op. 2 *Widowers' Houses*; Op. 3 *A Woman of No Importance*, then running at the Haymarket Theatre; Op. 4, Shaw's next play, *The Philanderer*; Op. 5, Wilde's next play, *An Ideal Husband*. And so on. Wilde thus paid Shaw the compliment of ranking their works together in the dramatic literature of the age, though he had just scored his second huge success with *A Woman of No Importance*, while Shaw's *Widowers' Houses* had practically been hooted from the stage the previous December. (*G.B.S. A Postscript*, 1951, p. 132.)

This is confirmed by Shaw's copy of *Lady Windermere's Fan* (now in the possession of Mrs Chaworth Musters), which is inscribed in Wilde's hand "Op. 1 of the Hibernian School, London '93."

To A. Teixeira de Mattos[1]

[? *May 1893*]

My dear Teixeira, There are difficulties about the bust being placed in the Haymarket . . . in the daytime there are the middle classes crowding in, who might break it; in the evening there are the aristocracy crowding out, who might steal it, and I could not sit just now, as I am going to Oxford tomorrow.

To William Rothenstein
MS. Rothenstein

[? *May 1893*]   *34 High Street, Oxford*

Dear Will, I should like Bosie to be framed.[2] I think a black and white frame with *no* margin or mounting.

The lovely drawing is complete in itself. It is a great delight to me to have so exquisite a portrait of a friend done by a friend also, and I thank you very much for letting me have it.

Enclosed is an absurdly coloured thing, which foolish bankers take in exchange and for which they give, in reckless moments, gold, both yellow and red. Ever yours   OSCAR

To Lord Alfred Douglas
MS. Clark

[? *May 1893*][3]   *16 Tite Street*

My dear Boy, No letter from you yet. But I hope to find a line when I go home. I lunched with Prince Troubetzkoy[4] and Mrs Chanler this afternoon. He has done a lovely picture of her, and would do a beautiful one of you. I talked to him about you. He is going down to the Batterseas

[1] Alexander Louis Teixeira de Mattos (1865–1921) was of Portuguese–Jewish origin, though his father was Dutch and his mother English. He spent most of his life in England, where he worked first as a journalist, and then as one of the most successful translators of his time. Maeterlinck, Fabre and Couperus were among the many authors whose works he translated into English. In 1900 he married Willie Wilde's widow Lily. His brother Henri Teixeira de Mattos (1856–1908) was a sculptor, and it may have been he who was to make the bust. The text of this incomplete letter is taken from the George D. Smith sale catalogue (Anderson Galleries, March 1921).

[2] Rothenstein made several drawings of Lord Alfred Douglas during 1893. This one, entitled "The Editor of the *Spirit Lamp* at work," showed him in profile, wearing flannels and lying back in an armchair. It was commissioned by Wilde, and later came into the possession of More Adey. Its present whereabouts are unknown. See also plate facing p. 351.

[3] This date is problematical.

[4] Prince Pierre Troubetzkoy (1864–1936), Russian-American portrait-painter. See note 2, p. 237.

to finish his portrait of Cyril[1] but will be back in the autumn. You really must be painted, and also have an ivory statue executed.

Willard, the actor,[2] lunches with me on Thursday to talk business. I hope to lure him to give me some of "the gold the gryphon guards in rude Armenia."[3]

Are you coming up on Wednesday? If so, do dine with me. Ever yours

OSCAR

To Charles Ricketts
MS. Private

[? *June 1893*]   *The Cottage, Goring-on-Thames*[4]

My dear Ricketts, I return proof of *The Sphinx*. Will you kindly have a corrected proof sent to me, as I want to see if I could make the whole poem longer. I do not know the name of the printers, or I would write to them direct.

Tell Shannon I am quite charmed with the setting of *Lady Windermere*; it looks delightful and is exquisitely placed. It seems to be however too late in the season to publish now. What do you think?[5]

I have done no work here. The river-gods have lured me to devote myself to a Canadian canoe, in which I paddle about. It is curved like a flower.

When are we to think about "Mr. W. H."?[6] Ever yours OSCAR WILDE

To Lady Randolph Churchill[7]

[? *June 1893*]   *The Cottage, Goring-on-Thames*

Dear Lady Randolph, "The only difference between the saint and the sinner is that every saint has a past, and every sinner has a future!" That, of course, is the quotation.[8] How dull men are! They should listen to

---

[1] Cyril Flower (1843–1907). Liberal M.P. from 1880 to 1892, when he was created first Lord Battersea. Collector of pictures and patron of the arts. At Harrow he was taught by F. W. (afterwards Dean) Farrar, who based on him the hero of *Eric, or Little by Little* (1858).

[2] Edward Smith Willard (1853–1915) was an English actor famous for his villains in melodrama.   [3] *The Duchess of Padua*, Act II.

[4] Wilde took this house from June to October 1893.

[5] *Lady Windermere's Fan*, having been declined by Macmillan in May 1892, was published by Elkin Mathews & John Lane on 9 November 1893. The binding was designed by Shannon. There were 500 copies at 7/6 and 50 large-paper at 15/-.

[6] The enlarged edition, with Ricketts's frontispiece (see note 3, p. 250).

[7] Jennie Jerome (1854–1921) married (1874) Lord Randolph Spencer Churchill, third son of the seventh Duke of Marlborough, and was the mother of Sir Winston. The text of this letter is taken from her *Reminiscences* (1908), in which she explained that she had been accused of misquoting him and had backed her memory with a bet, promising to present Wilde with "a beautiful penholder" if she won.

[8] *A Woman of No Importance*, Act III.

brilliant women, and look at beautiful ones, and when, as in the present case, a woman is both beautiful and brilliant, they might have the ordinary common sense to admit that she is verbally inspired.

I trust your bet will be promptly paid, as I want to begin writing my new comedy, and have no pen! Believe me, yours sincerely   OSCAR WILDE

To an Unidentified Correspondent[1]

[*June 1893*]   *The Cottage, Goring-on-Thames*

Dear Stuart, I am so sorry I am not in town but I am away in the country by the river—divided in interest between paddling a canoe and planning a comedy—and finding that life in meadow and stream is far more complex than is life in streets and salons. I may come to town for the Royal marriage;[2] if so will certainly let you know. Truly yours   OSCAR WILDE

To Henri Bauër[3]
MS. Fales

[*Postmark 24 June 1893*]   *The Cottage, Goring-on-Thames*

My dear Bauër, I am so sorry I have not been able to be of any service to your charming friend Madame Roger-Miclos,[4] but I am away from London in the country, working at a new comedy, and am not going to town at all, except for the Royal marriage.

I hope some day to have the honour of being presented to so distinguished an artist as Madame Roger-Miclos.

I hope you are quite well and that if you come to England you will come down and see me. Truly yours   OSCAR WILDE

Telegram: To Ada Leverson[5]
MS. Harvard

28 June 1893   *Paddington*

The author of *The Sphinx* will on Wednesday at two eat pomegranates with the Sphinx of Modern Life.

[1] Possibly Stuart Merrill (see note 2, p. 390). The text of this incomplete letter is taken from the George D. Smith sale catalogue (Anderson Galleries, 1928).

[2] The Duke of York and Princess May of Teck (later King George V and Queen Mary) were married in the Chapel Royal, St James's Palace, on 6 July 1893.

[3] French literary and dramatic critic (1851–1915). See p. 400.

[4] French pianist and harpsichord-player.

[5] Ada Esther Beddington (1862–1933) married Ernest David Leverson, the son of a diamond merchant. She contributed witty pieces to *Punch* and other periodicals, and later published successful novels. She was one of Wilde's closest woman friends and he always called her The Sphinx. From the following fragment, found among her papers, they appear to have met in 1892:

Old legends heard in the schoolroom still hung like a mist over Oscar Wilde

To William Wilde

MS. Clark

[? *Circa 10 July 1893*]   *The Cottage, Goring-on-Thames*

My dear Willie, This Saturday is, I fear, impossible, as people are staying here, and things are tedious. You and Dan should have come down for the regatta,[1] even in the evening; there were fireworks of surpassing beauty.

I am greatly distressed to hear you and the fascinating Dan are smoking American cigarettes. You really must not do anything so horrid. Charming people should smoke gold-tipped cigarettes or die, so I enclose you a small piece of paper, for which reckless bankers may give you gold, as I don't want you to die. With best love, ever yours   OSCAR

To Ada Leverson

[? *Circa 15 July 1893*]   *Albemarle Club*

Your sketch is brilliant, as your work always is. It is quite tragic for me to think how completely *Dorian Gray* has been understood on all sides![2]

Why don't you collect your wonderful, witty, delightful sketches—so slight, so suggestive, so full of *esprit* and intellectual sympathy?

You are one of those who, in art, are always, by intuition, behind the scenes, so you see how natural art is.   OSCAR WILDE

To Ada Leverson

[? *Summer 1893*][3]   *16 Tite Street*

Might it be Wednesday or Thursday or Friday? I am just told that there are to be feasters here on Tuesday. Do let me know. All my other days in the week belong to you.

How wilful and wonderful you are! Ever yours   OSCAR

---

when I met him, and I was half surprised not to see him "wan and palely loitering" in knee-breeches, holding that lily on the scent of which he had been said to subsist. But he had long given up the "aesthetic" pose of the eighties, the period so well described, when he grew up, by Max Beerbohm. Strange time of sunflowers and peacock's feathers, "Art needlework" and Japanese fans, when the poet first lectured on decoration, reformed dress, and, in reaction from Albert Memorials and rep curtains, "fired by the fervid words of the young Oscar, people threw their mahogany into the streets."

It was now '92, and he was in the full bloom of his second period when I saw him at Oswald Crawfurd's at a party given just after the success of *Lady Windermere's Fan*. There was no trace of his "earlier manner" in the genial. . . .

[1] Probably Henley Regatta, which in 1893 was held on July 5–7.

[2] Probably refers to "An Afternoon Party" by Ada Leverson, which appeared anonymously in *Punch* on 15 July 1893 and included a brief skit on *Dorian Gray*. The text of this letter is taken from *Letters to the Sphinx*.

[3] This letter and the one that follows it are impossible to date. Texts from *Letters to the Sphinx*.

343

To Ada Leverson

[? *Summer 1893*]

Dear Sphinx, This quite wrong rose-coloured paper was left here by some-one else, and I am using it by mistake.[1]

You are one of those—alas, too few—who are always followed by the flutes of the pagan world. Yours   OSCAR

To Lord Alfred Douglas
MS. Clark

Saturday [*9 September 1893*]   *Hotel Albemarle*

My dear Bosie, Thanks for your telegram which I got last night on my arrival from Jersey, where I had been for a night, on my way over, to see a performance of my play by Miss Lingard and the South Company.[2] It was rather good, and I had a great reception from a crowded house. The Gerald Arbuthnot was excellent, and very nice. I entertained the actors afterwards at supper. I am off to Goring now, to try and settle up things. I don't know what to do about the place—whether to stay there or not—and the servants are a worry. I went round to see Lane just now, but he is in Paris with Rothenstein. I hope you will get proofs soon.[3] I suppose you are in Devon for your brother's marriage. Give him my best wishes.[4] Ever yours   OSCAR

---

[1] It was headed FLORENCE.

[2] Tree's southern touring company gave two performances of *A Woman of No Importance* in the Theatre Royal, Jersey, on Thursday and Friday, 7 and 8 September 1893. Wilde was at the first performance. Alice Lingard, *née* Dunning (1847–97), was the wife of W. H. Lingard, actor and manager.

[3] Of the English translation of *Salome*, which was illustrated by Aubrey Beardsley and published by Elkin Mathews & John Lane on 9 February 1894. It was dedicated "To my friend Lord Alfred Bruce Douglas, the translator of my play." It is not known how much Wilde revised the translation before it was published (see p. 432), but, despite the dedication, Douglas's name did not appear on the title-page as translator. Some of Beardsley's drawings were thought indecent, and in a letter (MS. Ross) dated "Nov? [1893]" Beardsley wrote to Ross:

> I suppose you've heard all about the *Salome* Row. I can tell you I had a warm time of it between Lane and Oscar and Co. For one week the numbers of telegraph and messenger boys who came to the door was simply scandalous. I really don't quite know how the matter really stands now. Anyhow Bosie's name is not to turn up on the title. The book will be out soon after Xmas. I have withdrawn three of the illustrations and supplied their places with three new ones (simply beautiful and quite irrelevant).

Beardsley received fifty guineas for his illustrations; Wilde a royalty of a shilling a copy on the ordinary edition (500 copies at 15/-) and three shillings a copy on the large paper edition (100 copies at 30/-).

[4] Douglas's elder brother Percy Sholto, Lord Douglas of Hawick (1868–1920), was married to Hannah Maria Walters at Boyton, Launceston, Cornwall, on 11 September 1893. He succeeded his father as ninth Marquess of Queensberry in 1900.

To H. H. Morell[1]

[*September 1893*]   *The Cottage, Goring-on-Thames*

Dear Harry, The Company I saw at Jersey was, on the whole, very good. The Hester Worsley wants decision, and strength. She is not strong enough in Act 4, but she is very pretty and sweet.

Why is Miss Olliffe going?[2] She is quite excellent, and a great success in the part. I could not wish it better acted; it will be a great loss if she goes; she is the life and brightness of the piece.

Will you let me have a list of the dates of the South Company? . . . I hope the Lewis Waller one is doing well.

Don't send away Miss Olliffe, it would be a great and serious loss.

To Michael Field

MS. Princeton

[? *September 1893*]   *The Cottage, Goring-on-Thames*

Dear Michael Field, In the case of the Independent Theatre you have to rely chiefly on actors who are out of an engagement, those who have engagements being occupied or away. Tell Grein to select only *young* actors—there are possibilities of poetry and passion in the young—and picturesqueness also, a quality so valuable on the stage.[3] Shun the experienced actor; in poetic drama he is impossible. Choose graceful personalities—young actors and actresses who have charming voices—that is enough. The rest is in the hands of God and the poet.

I look forward to listening to your lovely play recited on a rush-strewn platform, before a tapestry, by gracious things in antique robes, and, if you can manage it, in gilded masks.

So, you see I have nothing to tell you, except that I am your sincere admirer   OSCAR WILDE

---

[1] Stage name of Henry Harvey Morell Mackenzie (1865–1916), eldest son of Sir Morell Mackenzie (1837–92), the throat specialist who treated the Crown Prince (afterwards Emperor Frederick III) of Prussia in 1887. At this time Morell was Tree's general manager, but the following January he presented *An Ideal Husband* in partnership with Lewis Waller. The text of this incomplete letter is taken from Maggs's catalogue 301 (1912).

[2] From Tree's No. 1 or northern touring company of *A Woman of No Importance*, which had opened at Birmingham on 14 August with Mr and Mrs Lewis Waller in the cast. Geraldine Olliffe opened as Mrs Allonby, but was soon superseded by Beryl Faber.

[3] Jack Thomas Grein (1862–1935), dramatic critic, playwright and manager, was a Dutchman naturalised in 1895. In 1891, following Antoine and his *Théâtre Libre* (see note 2, p. 749), he started the Independent Theatre in London. As Max Beerbohm wrote, "The Ibsen movement became more mobile later on, when a very dynamic and fervent little Dutchman, J. T. Grein, who was not at all content with being 'something in the City' and being also Consul for Bolivia, rushed in, founded the Independent Theatre and produced *Ghosts*." In 1892 the Independent Theatre produced *Widowers' Houses* (the first of Bernard Shaw's plays to be seen in London), and on 27 October 1893 *A Question of Memory*, a prose drama in four acts by Michael Field, at the Opera Comique, London.

To Michael Field

MS. Clark

[? *Late October 1893*]   *Albemarle Club*

Dear Michael Field, Write to Miss Elisabeth Marbury, c/o Low's Exchange, New York City, U.S.A. She manages all my plays.[1] I have written to her.

I am a wretch not to have answered sooner, but I have no excuse; so you will forgive me.

Your third act was quite admirable—a really fine piece of work—with that touch of terror our stage lacks so much. I think the theatre should belong to the Furies. Caliban and Silenus, one educated and the other sober, seem now to dominate, in their fallen condition, our wretched English drama. Ever yours   OSCAR WILDE

To Lady Queensberry[2]

TS. Holland

[*8 November 1893*][3]   *16 Tite Street*

Dear Lady Queensberry, You have on more than one occasion consulted me about Bosie. Let me write to you now about him.

Bosie seems to me to be in a very bad state of health. He is sleepless, nervous, and rather hysterical. He seems to me quite altered.

He is doing nothing in town. He translated my French play last August. Since then he has really done nothing intellectual. He seems to me to have lost, for the moment only I trust, his interest even in literature. He does absolutely nothing, and is quite astray in life, and may, unless you or Drumlanrig[4] do something, come to grief of some kind. His life seems to me aimless, unhappy and absurd.

All this is a great grief and disappointment to me, but he is very young, and terribly young in temperament. Why not try and make arrangements of some kind for him to go abroad for four or five months, to the Cromers in Egypt if that could be managed, where he would have new surroundings, proper friends, and a different atmosphere?[5] I think that if he stays in

[1] Elisabeth Marbury (1856–1933) was a leading play-agent in New York. She first met Wilde during his lecture-tour in 1882, and handled all his plays in America. In her autobiography, *My Crystal Ball* (1923), she gives a short, sympathetic and largely inaccurate record of Wilde.

[2] Sybil Montgomery (1845–1935), grand-daughter of the first Lord Leconfield, married (1866) John Sholto Douglas, eighth Marquess of Queensberry (1844–1900) and divorced him 1887. Lord Alfred Douglas was her third son. This letter certainly helped to send him abroad for some months (see pp. 427 and 433).

[3] So dated by Douglas (presumably from the original) in a letter to A. J. A. Symons dated 24 August 1937 (MS. Clark).

[4] Francis Archibald Douglas, Viscount Drumlanrig (1867–94) was Lady Queensberry's eldest son.

[5] Evelyn Baring (1841–1917) was created Lord Cromer 1892, Viscount 1899 and Earl 1901. He was Agent and Consul-General in Egypt 1883–1907.

London he will not come to any good, and may spoil his young life irretrievably, quite irretrievably. Of course it will cost money no doubt, but here is the life of one of your sons—a life that should be brilliant and distinguished and charming—going quite astray, being quite ruined.

I like to think myself his greatest friend—he, at any rate, makes me think so—so I write to you quite frankly to ask you to send him abroad to better surroundings. It would save him, I feel sure. At present his life seems to be tragic and pathetic in its foolish aimlessness.

You will not, I know, let him know *anything about my letter*. I can rely on you, I feel sure. Sincerely yours   OSCAR WILDE

Telegram: To Ada Leverson

MS. Harvard

18 November 1893   *St James's Street*

Your dialogue is brilliant and delightful and dangerous. I am quite charmed with it. What the Comtesse Gyp has done in France for Life you have done in England for Art.[1] No one admires your clever witty subtle style more than I do. Nothing pains me except stupidity and morality.

OSCAR WILDE

Telegram: To More Adey[2]

TS. Holland

23 November 1893   *St James's Street*

Bosie has influenza and is very pale. The wicked Lane has been routed with slaughter. I have begun a mystery play.   OSCAR

To Lord Alfred Douglas

MS. Clark

[? *December 1893*]   *10 & 11 St James's Place,*[3] *S.W.*

My dearest Boy, Thanks for your letter. I am overwhelmed by the wings of vulture creditors, and out of sorts, but I am happy in the knowledge that we are friends again, and that our love has passed through the shadow and

[1] Gyp was the pen-name of Sibylle Gabrielle Marie Antoinette Riqueti de Mirabeau, Comtesse de Martel de Janville (1849–1932). She published more than seventy volumes of social sketches and dialogues, many of which first appeared in the *Vie Parisienne* and the *Revue des Deux Mondes*.

[2] William More Adey (1858–1942). Published in 1891, under the pseudonym William Wilson, the first English translation of Ibsen's *Brand*. Close friend of Robert Ross, with whom he later ran the Carfax picture gallery. Joint editor of the *Burlington Magazine* 1911–19. For a description of him in later years, see *Siegfried's Journey* by Siegfried Sassoon (1945).

[3] Wilde rented rooms at this address from October 1893 until the end of March 1894, and went there daily to work. Most of *An Ideal Husband* was written there.

the night of estrangement and sorrow and come out rose-crowned as of old. Let us always be infinitely dear to each other, as indeed we have been always.

I hear Bobbie is in town, lame and bearded! Isn't it awful? I have not seen him yet. Lesly Thomson[1] has appeared; he is extremely anxious to devote his entire life to me. Tree has written a long apologetic letter. His reasons are so reasonable that I cannot understand them: a cheque is the only argument I recognise. Hare[2] returns to town early next week. I am going to make an effort to induce him to see that my new play is a masterpiece, but I have grave doubts. This is all the news. How horrid news is. I think of you daily, and am always devotedly yours   OSCAR

To Aubrey Beardsley[3]
MS. Yale

[? *December 1893*]   *10 & 11 St James's Place*

My dear Aubrey, I am charmed to find you are in town. Will you join Bobbie and me at dinner tonight at *Kettner's* (Church St, Soho) at *7.30*. We are not going to dress. Ever yours   OSCAR

To John Lane
MS. Dickey

[*Circa December 1893*]   *10 & 11 St James's Place*

Dear Mr Lane, The cover of *Salome* is quite dreadful.[4] Don't spoil a lovely book. Have simply a folded vellum wrapper with the design in scarlet—much cheaper, and much better. The texture of the present cover is coarse and common: it is quite impossible and spoils the real beauty of the interior. Use up this horrid Irish stuff for stories, etc: don't inflict it on a work of art like *Salome*. It really will do you a great deal of harm. Everyone will say that it is coarse and inappropriate. I loathe it. So does Beardsley. Truly yours   OSCAR WILDE.

    [1] English actor (see note 1, p. 377).

    [2] John Hare, English actor-manager (1844–1921). He eventually turned down *An Ideal Husband* because he considered the last act unsatisfactory. He had already declined Pinero's *The Second Mrs Tanqueray* as too daring.

    [3] English artist (1872–98). He worked in an insurance office 1889–92, and his drawings were first published in the *Pall Mall Budget* in February 1893. He was later art-editor of the *Yellow Book* (1894–95) and the *Savoy* (1896). This letter cannot be dated accurately within six months, but I have included it as apparently the only surviving letter from Wilde to Beardsley. The word Aubrey has been erased but is still legible. In the Sterling Library in the University of London there is a copy of the original edition of *Salome* (1893) inscribed "March '93. For Aubrey: for the only artist who, besides myself, knows what the dance of the seven veils is, and can see that invisible dance. Oscar."

    [4] The English translation (see note 3, p. 344). The ordinary edition was issued in coarse-grained blue canvas, the *édition de luxe* in green silk.

To William Harnett Blanch[1]

[January 1894]

Dear Mr Blanch, I have to thank the members of your club for their kind invitation, for which convey to them, I beg you, my sincere thanks. But I love superstitions. They are the colour element of thought and imagination. They are the opponents of common sense. Common sense is the enemy of romance.

The aim of your society seems to be dreadful. Leave us some unreality. Don't make us too offensively sane.

I love dining out; but with a society with so wicked an object as yours I cannot dine. I regret it. I am sure you will all be charming; but I could not come, though thirteen is a lucky number.   OSCAR WILDE

To Lewis Waller[2]

MS. Boston

[Mid-January 1894]   *16 Tite Street*

My dear Waller, What would you give me for a Triple Bill? I would require a certain sum of money down, and a certain sum on completion; the money down to be returned if you don't like the plays. Royalties on a triple bill which would be played at most two nights a week would not be anything important. I would sell you the plays right out—for Great Britain.

I have finished three acts of the play for Hare, and will do the fourth in the next fortnight, so I could not begin to write till the end of the month, but I could have them ready by the middle of March. Make me an offer, if you care to, and be sure that it is a temptation, for I never resist temptation. Truly yours   OSCAR WILDE

To George Alexander

MS. Private

[? January 1894]   *16 Tite Street*

My dear Aleck, I dare say you have seen in the papers that I have given

---

[1] Journalist. Founder and President of the Thirteen Club. This letter was read out by the Chairman (Harry Furniss) at a dinner of the Club at the Holborn Restaurant on 13 January 1894. The text is taken from *To-Day* of 13 January. It was reprinted in *Miscellanies*. Mason reports (p. 215):

> The dinner of 13 courses was held in Room No. 13, each of the 13 tables holding 13 guests, who wore bright green neckties and Japanese skeleton buttonholes. Each guest passed under a ladder to his seat; all knives were crossed; the saltspoons were shaped like sextons' spades. At the end of the dinner there was a general smashing of mirrors and Mr Harry Furniss presented each guest with a knife.

[2] English romantic actor (1850–1915). The idea of the triple bill came to nothing, but Waller produced and acted in *An Ideal Husband*, after Hare had turned it down.

Hare the refusal of my next play, and I am anxious to send you a few lines to explain to you my reasons in doing so.

I shall always remember with pride and with pleasure the artistic manner in which you produced my first play, and the artistic care you showed, down to the smallest detail of production, that my work should be presented in the best manner possible, and it would be a great delight to me to have some other play of mine produced by you at your charming theatre, but I have always been anxious to have some work of mine produced by Hare, whose wonderful stagecraft no one appreciates more than you do, and as he [*The rest of this letter is missing*]

To Lewis Waller

MS. Butler

[*Postmark 31 January 1894*]　　　　　*Royal Albion Hotel, Brighton*

My dear Waller, Have you not settled yet about *Lady Windermere's Fan*? I was in hopes it was all arranged. I do not think Alexander's terms by any means extravagant, as you have the play for two years, and, of course, unless you have *Lady Windermere*, there would be no use in my even thinking about letting you have a triple bill. The latter idea is an exotic one; one night a week would be the most one could play it. If you have *A Woman of No Importance* and *Lady Windermere* I would certainly let you have a triple bill, if I do one really suitable for theatric presentation, but otherwise—that is to say if you have someone else's play instead of *Lady Windermere*—I would not dream of doing anything of the kind. *Lady Windermere* has not been played in the big towns since 1892,[1] and I feel sure would be a great success. George Alexander personally would like to keep it, as in case *Mrs Tanqueray* runs to the end of the season,[2] which it may, he would require a play to run with it in the provinces, and *The Idler* and *Liberty Hall* are played out.[3] However, as I wanted to have you and your wife play a complete repertoire of me, he consented to let you have it.

Kindly settle, one way or the other, about *Lady Windermere*, as soon as possible. After my talk with Harry Morell I really thought it was settled.

I have still a very bad cold, and will not be in town for some days.

With kind regards to Mrs Waller, believe me, truly yours

OSCAR WILDE

To Aimée Lowther [4]

MS. Hillyard

[*Postmark 1 February 1894*]　　　　　*Royal Albion Hotel, Brighton*

My dear Aimée, How could you? Of course I have rushed down here to

---

[1] See note 2, p. 325.　　　　[2] See note p. 353.

[3] Two of Alexander's successes at the St James's Theatre. *The Idler*, a melodrama by C. Haddon Chambers, ran from February to July 1891, and *Liberty Hall*, a comedy by R. C. Carton, from December 1892 to May 1893.

[4] 1871–1935. One of the three children of Captain Francis William Lowther,

350

Oscar Wilde and Lord Alfred Douglas

Lord Alfred Douglas, 1893
by William Rothenstein

escape. I always want to kill people who bring me letters of introduction. Indeed everybody in the world should be either killed or kissed.

I am coming back to see you act at Lady De La Warr's, and know you will be wonderful.[1] What a great thing for dear Lady De La Warr to have you to act, and me for the audience. I hope it won't turn her head or make her give herself airs. She is a clever charming woman, so I think she will be able to carry it off, but what jealousy she will excite!

Of course you are going to wear a lovely frock. Love to Claude. Your sincere friend   OSCAR

To Gerald Duckworth[2]
MS. Wilberforce

[Early February 1894]   Royal Albion Hotel, Brighton

Dear Sir, I forget what I received back. I think about £1. 1. I enclose a cheque for it. Miss Robins deserves an offering indeed: a very imaginative artist, who has done very real work. The English stage is in her debt. I am one of her warmest admirers. Faithfully yours   OSCAR WILDE

To Gerald Duckworth
MS. Wilberforce

[February 1894]   16 Tite Street

Dear Sir, Kindly enter me as a subscriber to the gift to Miss Robins.

I am so sorry I can only give you 6/10. I will send it tomorrow. Faithfully yours   OSCAR WILDE

R.N. (1841–1908), an illegitimate son of the third Earl of Lonsdale. Her brother Claude, diplomat and politician, owned Hurstmonceux Castle. Her sister Toupie was the world's greatest woman fencer, also a first-class tennis-player, and a composer, who set to music these lines which Wilde wrote to Aimée:

> Your eyes are deep green pools
> In which the sun has gazed,
> And passing left a golden ray.

Aimée told Lady Juliet Duff that when she was a young girl Wilde said to her: "Aimée, Aimée, if you had been a boy you'd have wrecked my life."

[1] The Hon. Constance Mary Elizabeth Cochrane (1846–1929), eldest daughter of the first Lord Lamington, married the seventh Earl De La Warr in 1867. Her daughter, Lady Margaret Sackville, remembers amateur performances in their home at 66 Pont Street, including one of The Highwayman, a one-act play by J. M. Morton (1811–91).

[2] English publisher (1871–1937). Half-brother of Virginia Woolf. In May and June 1893 Elizabeth Robins had given twelve performances of plays by Ibsen at the Opera Comique in London. They were financed by subscription, and it was agreed that any profit should be divided equally between Miss Robins and the subscribers. This came to pass, and Duckworth was detailed to return 6/10 to each subscriber. Soon after these tiresome sums had been despatched, someone suggested that the money would be better spent on a presentation to Miss Robins, so Duckworth wrote round asking for the 6/10 back. Eventually on 10 March a silver tea-service was presented to Miss Robins at a party at Mrs W. K. Clifford's.

To W. E. Henley[1]

[Circa 12 February 1894]   *16 Tite Street*

My dear Henley, I am very sorry indeed to hear of your great loss.[2] I hope you will let me come down quietly to you one evening and over our cigarettes we will talk of the bitter ways of fortune, and the hard ways of life.

But, my dear Henley, to work, to work; that is your duty; that is what remains for natures like ours. Work never seems to me a reality, but a way of getting rid of reality. You asked me about Degas.[3] Well, he loves to be thought young, so I don't think he would tell his age. He disbelieves in art-education, so I don't think he will name a Master. He despises what he cannot get, so I am sure he will not give any information about prizes or honours. Why say anything about his person? His pastels are himself.
Ever yours   OSCAR

To Ralph Payne[4]
MS. Turnbull

[Postmark 12 February 1894]   *16 Tite Street*

Dear Mr Payne, The book that poisoned, or made perfect, Dorian Gray does not exist; it is a fancy of mine merely.[5]

I am so glad you like that strange coloured book of mine: it contains much of me in it. Basil Hallward is what I think I am: Lord Henry what the world thinks me: Dorian what I would like to be—in other ages, perhaps.

Will you come and see me?

I am writing a play, and go to St James's Place, number *10*, where I have rooms, every day at 11.30. Come on Tuesday about 12.30, will you? But perhaps you are busy? Still, we can meet, surely, some day. Your hand-writing fascinates me, your praise charms me. Truly yours

OSCAR WILDE

To Philip Houghton[6]
F. Keller

[? Late February 1894]   *16 Tite Street*

Dear Sir, I will send you a manuscript copy of my play, a little incomplete,

---

[1] Text from *W. E. Henley* by John Connell (1949).
[2] Henley's daughter Margaret, his only child, died on 11 February 1894, aged six.
[3] Presumably Henley wanted to get a statement from Edgar Degas, the French painter (1834–1917), for publication in the *National Observer*.
[4] Unidentified. This letter is addressed to 50 Ennismore Gardens, London.
[5] But see p. 313.
[6] An artist. The play Wilde sent him was almost certainly *An Ideal Husband*, of which the typescript was stamped 19 February 94 by Mrs Marshall's typing agency in the Strand.

but still enough to give you an idea of its ethical scheme. Your letter has deeply moved me. To the world I seem, by intention on my part, a dilettante and dandy merely—it is not wise to show one's heart to the world—and as seriousness of manner is the disguise of the fool, folly in its exquisite modes of triviality and indifference and lack of care is the robe of the wise man. In so vulgar an age as this we all need masks.

But write to me about yourself; tell me your life and loves, and all that keeps you wondering. Who are you? (what a difficult question for any one of us to answer!) I, at any rate, am your friend   OSCAR WILDE

To Philip Houghton
F. Keller

[? *February 1894*]   *10 & 11 St James's Place*

My dear friend, Thank you so much. I wish I could have heard your lecture.

I am sending you some photographs. Pray keep one for yourself, and return the others to the photographer.

Do publish your lecture. I want to read it.

Why don't you come to London? I want to talk to you—to see you—to know you. To really know a brother I must touch his hand. Not Christ alone, but all the gods, have to become incarnate before they can reveal themselves.

I think often of you, and am always with affection your friend and brother   OSCAR WILDE

To Mrs Patrick Campbell[1]

[*February 1894*]   *Box F. [St James's Theatre]*

Dear Mrs Campbell, Mr Aubrey Beardsley, a very brilliant and wonderful young artist, and like all artists a great admirer of the wonder and charm of your art, says that he must once have the honour of being presented to you, if you will allow it. So, with your gracious sanction, I will come round after Act III with him, and you would gratify and honour him much if you would let him bow his compliments to you. He has just illustrated my play of *Salome* for me, and has a copy of the *édition de luxe* which he wishes to lay at your feet. His drawings are quite wonderful. Very sincerely yours
OSCAR WILDE

[1] Beatrice Stella Tanner, English actress (1865–1940). Married Patrick Campbell 1884. She created the title-role in *The Second Mrs Tanqueray* by A. W. Pinero at the St James's Theatre on 27 May 1893. The play ran until 28 July, went on a provincial tour, and returned to the St James's on 11 November. It was taken off on 21 April 1894. Beardsley's drawing of Mrs Campbell appeared in the first number of the *Yellow Book*. The text of this letter is taken from the Kern sale catalogue (1929).

353

To Bernard Quaritch[1]

MS. Holland

[? *Early April 1894*] 16 Tite Street

Dear Mr Quaritch, I have just returned from France, and your beautiful and interesting catalogue charmingly welcomed me. It is a delightful book and the facsimiles of the book illuminations are real works of art, and a joy to look at. I need hardly say that the book has an additional value to me, coming, as it does, from so distinguished a scholar and lover of books as yourself, and I beg you to accept my most sincere thanks for it. I wish I were rich enough to rob you of your treasures, but console myself with the knowledge that they are in the keeping of one to whom all English men of letters are indebted, and so are worthily kept. Believe me, sincerely yours

OSCAR WILDE

To Lord Alfred Douglas

MS. Clark

[*Circa 16 April 1894*] 16 Tite Street

My dearest Boy, Your telegram has just arrived; it was a joy to get it, but I miss you so much. The gay, gilt and gracious lad has gone away—and I hate everyone else: they are tedious. Also I am in the purple valleys of despair, and no gold coins are dropping down from heaven to gladden me. London is very dangerous: writters come out at night and writ one, the roaring of creditors towards dawn is frightful, and solicitors are getting rabies and biting people.

How I envy you under Giotto's Tower, or sitting in the loggia looking at that green and gold god of Cellini's. You must write poems like apple blossom.

The *Yellow Book* has appeared. It is dull and loathsome, a great failure. I am so glad.[2]

Always, with much love, yours OSCAR

[1] Bookseller and bibliophile (1819–99). Born in Saxony, he came to London to work for H. G. Bohn, and started his own business in 1859, in which year he published FitzGerald's *Omar Khayyám*. The catalogue mentioned in this letter was *Palaeography; Notes upon the History of Writing and the Mediaeval Art of Illumination.* It was privately printed, dedicated to the Sette of Odd Volumes (a dining club of which Quaritch was a founder) and dated 31 March 1894.

[2] The first volume of the *Yellow Book* was published on 16 April 1894, and since it seems likely that Wilde saw it immediately, I have suggested the same date for this letter. Douglas, after returning from Egypt, was now paying his first visit to Florence, where, according to his *Autobiography*, he stayed about a month. Wilde joined him there in May, and on 28 May André Gide wrote from there to his mother: "*Qui rencontrai-je ici?—Oscar Wilde!!—Il est vieilli et laid, mais toujours extraordinaire conteur, un peu je pense comme Baudelaire a dû être, mais peut-être moins aigu et plus charmant. Il n'était plus ici que pour un jour, et quittant un appartement qu'il avait loué pour un mois et dont il n'avait profité que quinze jours, il m'en offrait aimablement la succession.*" Gide further reported to Paul Valéry that Wilde was "*fort peu flatté m'a-t-il semblé de la rencontre, car il se croyait clandestin.*"

To Lord Alfred Douglas

MS. Clark

[? *20 April 1894*]   *16 Tite Street*

My dearest Boy, Life here is much the same. I find a chastened pleasure in being shaved in Air Street: you are always enquired after, and sonnet-like allusions made to your gilt silk hair.

I saw an emissary from Mansfield, the actor, this morning. I think of writing *The Cardinal of Avignon* at once. If I had peace, I would do it. Mansfield would act it splendidly.[1]

Max on Cosmetics in the *Yellow Book* is wonderful: enough style for a large school, and all very precious and thought-out: quite delightfully wrong and fascinating.[2]

I had a frantic telegram from Edward Shelley, of all people! asking me to see him. When he came he was of course in trouble for money. As he betrayed me grossly I, of course, gave him money and was kind to him. I find that forgiving one's enemies is a most curious morbid pleasure; perhaps I should check it. With love, ever yours   OSCAR

To Mrs Bernard Beere

MS. Clark

[? *April 1894*]   *16 Tite Street*

My dear Bernie, Of course: *we* must fly to Australia: I could not let you go alone. I have written to Cartwright—a bald genius who is dear Dot's[3] agent—to ask him if it can be arranged. They have also *Mrs Tanqueray*, in which I long to see you.

I have also asked Cartwright if Dot is coming over—or I suppose I should say coming *up* from Australia. I believe that absurdly shaped country lies right underneath the floor of one's coal-cellar.

Why rusticate in this reckless way? You are wanted in town. *Once Upon a Time* was dreadful.[4] Since the appearance of Tree in pyjamas there has

[1] Richard Mansfield, American actor (1857–1907), had played *Richard III* in London in 1889. Wilde's rough scenario written in April 1894 for a play called *The Cardinal of Avignon* is printed by Mason (p. 583), but Wilde never carried the plan any further.

[2] Henry Maximilian Beerbohm (1872–1956) was still an undergraduate at Merton College, Oxford. Vincent O'Sullivan records Wilde's saying: "The gods bestowed on Max the gift of perpetual old age." This essay, "A Defence of Cosmetics," appeared in the first number of the *Yellow Book*. Revised and renamed "The Pervasion of Rouge," it was reprinted in *The Works of Max Beerbohm* (1896). But what Beerbohm originally wrote for the first number of the *Yellow Book* was the gently satirical portrait of Wilde, "A Peep into the Past."

[3] See note 3, p. 112. Presumably Mrs Bernard Beere was contemplating a tour in Australia, and wanted to include one of Wilde's plays in her repertory. Dot Boucicault ran the Bijou Theatre in Melbourne 1886–96, and also the Criterion in Sydney. He gave performances of *Lady Windermere's Fan* and *The Importance of Being Earnest*, as well as *The Second Mrs Tanqueray*.

[4] *Once Upon a Time*, a children's play, freely adapted from Ludwig Fulda's

been the greatest sympathy for Mrs Tree. It throws a lurid light on the difficulties of their married life.

Who is the fortunate mortal who has the honour of entertaining you? I dislike him more than I can tell you. Ever yours OSCAR

To William Rothenstein

MS. Rothenstein

[*Postmark 26 April 1894*] *New Travellers Club, Piccadilly*

Dear Will, I am off to Paris tomorrow. On my return I should love to sit to you, *mais cette fois un vrai portrait, pas un paysage.*[1] Ever yours OSCAR

To William Rothenstein

MS. Rothenstein

[*Postmark 6 May 1894*] *Hôtel des Deux Mondes,*
22 Avenue de l'Opéra, Paris

Dear Will, By all means, if you like.[2] Truly yours OSCAR
Love to the Valistes.

To Reginald Turner[3]

MS. Hyde (D. & M.)

[? *June 1894*] *16 Tite Street*

Dear Reggie, What a dear fellow you are! It is a great boon to have the number, as I am going to publish it in the *Fortnightly* next week.[4]

Could you come and dine with Bosie and me tonight? at Kettner's *eight o'clock*. Ever yours OSCAR

Send answer about dinner if possible. O.W.

Der Talisman by Louis N. Parker and H. Beerbohm Tree, was produced at the Haymarket Theatre on 28 March 1894, with Tree, Fred Terry, Julia Neilson and Mrs Tree in the cast. It was withdrawn on 21 April.

[1] In 1891 in Paris Rothenstein had done a pastel drawing of Wilde, which its subject never liked, saying that the red waistcoat and gold background made it look more like a landscape than a portrait, though he bought it and kept it until it was stolen in Naples in 1897.

[2] Rothenstein had asked permission to show his pastel of Wilde at a joint exhibition of work by himself and Shannon, who with Ricketts constituted the Valistes (see note 2, p. 249).

[3] 1869–1938. Illegitimate son of the first Lord Burnham (see note 5, p. 282). Journalist and wit. Lived mostly abroad. Published a number of novels. Oxford and lifelong friend of Max Beerbohm.

[4] The "number" was probably the *Spirit Lamp* for 17 February or 6 June 1893. Each contained a prose-poem, which Wilde revised and reprinted, with four others, in the *Fortnightly Review* for July 1894.

356

To Ada Leverson[1]

[*July 1894*]

Dear Sphinx, Your letter was wonderful and delightful.

The "Minx" I long to read. It is a brilliant title. Your feast was rose-like. Quite soon I hope to meet.   OSCAR

To Ada Leverson

MS. Clark

[*20 July 1894*][2]   *16 Tite Street*

Alas! dear Sphinx, I believe we are going to *La Femme de Claude* tonight; otherwise I would eat honey cakes with you at Willis's.[3]

Punch is delightful and the drawing a masterpiece of clever caricature. I am afraid she really was a minx after all. You are the only Sphinx.[4] Ever yours   OSCAR

Telegram: To Ada Leverson

MS. Harvard

25 July 1894   *Regent Street*

Pomegranates at Willis eight o'clock Friday with much joy.   OSCAR

To Lord Alfred Douglas

MS. Clark

[? *July 1894*]   *New Travellers Club*

My own dear Boy, I hope the cigarettes arrived all right. I lunched with

[1] Text from *Letters to the Sphinx*.

[2] Two performances of *La Femme de Claude* by Alexandre Dumas *fils* were given in French at Daly's Theatre on Tuesday 17 July 1894 (evening) and Wednesday 18 July (matinée) as part of the repertory season of the Renaissance Theatre company from Paris. Sarah Bernhardt and Lucien Guitry played the leading parts. A third performance was announced for the evening of Friday 20 July, but eventually another play was substituted. Ada Leverson's skit on *The Sphinx* appeared in *Punch* on 21 July, but was almost certainly available on the previous day. I have therefore dated this letter accordingly.

[3] Willis's Rooms in King Street, St James's, the most famous and fashionable restaurant of the decade. The building later became an auctioneer's saleroom and was destroyed by bombs in 1941.

[4] Ada Leverson's parody of *The Sphinx* in *Punch*, which did not name the poem or its author, was headed "The Minx—a Poem in Prose" and took the form of a dialogue between Poet and Sphinx. It ended:

"*Poet* In my opinion you are not a Sphinx at all.
Sphinx (*indignantly*) What am I, then?
Poet A Minx."

It was illustrated by a caricature of Ricketts's cover-design by E[dward] T[ennyson] R[eed].

357

Gladys de Grey, Reggie and Aleck Yorke there.[1] They want me to go to Paris with them on Thursday: they say one wears flannels and straw hats and dines in the Bois, but, of course, I have no money, as usual, and can't go. Besides I want to see you. It is really absurd. *I can't live without you.* You are so dear, so wonderful. I think of you all day long, and miss your grace, your boyish beauty, the bright sword-play of your wit, the delicate fancy of your genius, so surprising always in its sudden swallow-flights towards north or south, towards sun or moon—and, above all, you yourself. The only thing that consoles me is what the Sibyl of Mortimer Street (whom mortals term Mrs Robinson) said to me.[2] If I could disbelieve her I would, but I can't, and I know that early in January you and I will go away together for a long voyage, and that your lovely life goes always hand in hand with mine. My dear wonderful boy, I hope you are brilliant and happy.

I went to Bertie, today I wrote at home, then went and sat with my mother. Death and Love seem to walk on either hand as I go through life: they are the only things I think of, their wings shadow me.

London is a desert without your dainty feet, and all the buttonholes have turned to weeds: nettles and hemlock are 'the only wear.'[3] Write me a line, and take all my love—now and for ever.

Always, and with devotion—but I have no words for how I love you.

OSCAR

To Mrs Robinson
TS. Leslie

[? *July 1894*]   *16 Tite Street*
Dear Mrs Robinson, As I feared, Goodwood Races interfere, and my two friends will be obliged to defer their visit to you till another time.[4]

I have been deeply impressed by what you told me. It has made me very happy, but the thing is so serious that I must see you again. Believe me truly yours   OSCAR WILDE

---

[1] Gladys de Grey was the former Lady Lonsdale (see note 2, p. 65). Reggie was the Hon. Reginald Lister (1865–1912), son of the third Lord Ribblesdale, Minister in Tangier from 1908, K.C.M.G. 1911. Aleck Yorke was the Hon. Alexander Grantham Yorke (1847–1911), son of the fourth Earl of Hardwicke; he was Groom-in-Waiting to Queen Victoria and King Edward VII.

[2] Mrs Robinson was the fashionable fortune-teller of the time. (See also pp. 385 and 389.) Her prophecy was fulfilled, since Wilde and Douglas travelled together to Algiers in January 1895. O'Sullivan records her saying to Wilde: "I see a very brilliant life for you up to a certain point. Then I see a wall. Beyond the wall I see nothing."

[3] *As You Like It*, Act ii, scene 7.

[4] In 1894 Goodwood Races took place during the first week of August, and there is no evidence that Wilde consulted Mrs Robinson in earlier years.

To George Alexander[1]

[? *July 1894*]

The real charm of the play, if it is to have a charm, must be in the dialogue. The plot is slight, but, I think, adequate. . . . Well, I think an amusing thing with lots of fun and wit might be made. If you think so too, and care to have the refusal of it, do let me know, and send me £150. If when the play is finished, you think it too slight—not serious enough— of course you can have the £150 back. I want to go away and write it, and it could be ready in October, as I have nothing else to do. . . . In the meanwhile, my dear Aleck, I am so pressed for money that I don't know what to do. Of course I am extravagant. You have always been a good wise friend to me, so think what you can do.

To Charles Sugden[2]

MS. Hyde (H. M.)

[? *July–August 1894*]   16 Tite Street

Dear Sugden, I leave town tomorrow. I should like to have you in my play: but I question whether there is a part to suit you. Of the two big parts, Waller plays one, and the other has been offered already—and accepted, if the actor in question can cancel another engagement. I will of course let you know if the part should become vacant.[3]

What a pity one sees you act so rarely! I thought your Judge Brack the best thing I saw you in, a most perfect performance.[4] Truly yours

OSCAR WILDE

To Lord Alfred Douglas

MS. Clark

[*July–August 1894*]   16 Tite Street

Dearest Boy, I hope to send you the cigarettes, if Simmonds will let me have them. He has applied for his bill. I am overdrawn £41 at the bank: it really is intolerable the want of money. I have not a penny. I can't stand it any longer, but don't know what to do. I go down to Worthing tomorrow. I hope to do work there. The house, I hear, is very small, and I have no writing room. However, anything is better than London.

---

[1] The text of this fragment, which clearly refers to *The Importance of Being Earnest*, is taken from *Sir George Alexander and the St James's Theatre* by A. E. W. Mason.

[2] English actor (1850–1921). See note 2, p. 14.

[3] The casting of *An Ideal Husband* may well have been in progress by July–August 1894, and the first sentence of the letter may refer to Wilde's departure for Worthing.

[4] Sugden had played the part of Judge Brack in the first English performance of Ibsen's *Hedda Gabler* (see note 2, p. 290).

Your father is on the rampage again—been to Café Royal to enquire for us, with threats etc. I think now it would have been better for me to have had him bound over to keep the peace, but what a scandal! Still, it is intolerable to be dogged by a maniac.

When you come to Worthing, of course all things will be done for your honour and joy, but I fear you may find the meals, etc, tedious. But you will come, won't you? at any rate for a short time—till you are bored.

Ernesto[1] has written to me begging for money—a very nice letter—but I really have nothing just now.

What purple valleys of despair one goes through! Fortunately there is one person in the world to love. Ever yours   OSCAR

To Lord Alfred Douglas
MS. Clark

[*August 1894*]   [*The Haven, 5 Esplanade, Worthing*][2]
Letter—No. II.

Dearest Bosie, I have just come in from luncheon. A horrid ugly Swiss governess has, I find, been looking after Cyril and Vyvyan for a year. She is quite impossible.

Also, children at meals are tedious.

Also, you, the gilt and graceful boy, would be bored.

Don't come here. I will come to you. Ever yours   OSCAR

To George Alexander[3]

[*August 1894*]   *The Haven, 5 Esplanade, Worthing*

Dear Aleck, What do you think of this for a play for you? A man of rank and fashion marries a simple sweet country girl—a lady—but simple and ignorant of fashionable life. They live at his country place and after a time he gets bored with her, and invites down a lot of fashionable *fin-de-siècle* women and men. The play opens by his lecturing his wife on how to behave—not to be prudish, etc—and not to mind if anyone flirts with her. He says to her, "I have asked Gerald Lancing who used to admire you so much. Flirt with him as much as you like."

The guests arrive, they are horrid to the wife, they think her dowdy and dull. The husband flirts with Lady X. Gerald is nice and sweet and friendly to the wife.

Act II. The same evening, after dinner. Love scene between the husband and Lady X: they agree to meet in the drawing-room after everyone

[1] Possibly Ernest Scarfe, a valet (see *Trials*, pp. 148–49).

[2] Wilde took rooms for himself and his family at this address for the months of August and September, and there wrote the greater part of *The Importance of Being Earnest*.

[3] Text from *Sir George Alexander and the St James's Theatre* by A. E. W. Mason.

has retired. The guests bid good-night to the wife. The wife is tired and falls half asleep on a sofa. Enter husband: *he lowers the lamps*: then Lady X arrives: *he locks the door*. Love scene between them: wife hears it all. Suddenly violent beating on the door. Voice of Lady X's husband outside, desiring admittance. Terror of Lady X! Wife rises, turns up the lamp and goes to the door and unlocks it. Lady X's husband enters! Wife says "I am afraid I have kept Lady X up too late; we were trying an absurd experiment in thought reading" (anything will do). Lady X retires with her husband. Wife then left alone with her own husband. He comes towards her. She says "Don't touch me." He retires.

Then enter Gerald, says he has been alarmed by noises, thought there were robbers. Wife tells him everything; he is full of indignation; it is evident he loves the wife. She goes to her room.

Act III. Gerald's rooms. Wife comes to see him: it is clear that they love each other. They settle to go away together. Enter servant with card. The husband has called. The wife is frightened, but Gerald consents to see him. Wife retires into another room.

Husband is rather repentant. He implores Gerald to use his influence with the wife to make her forgive him. (Husband is a gross sentimental materialist.) Gerald promises that he will do so. It is evident that it is a great act of self-sacrifice for him. Exit husband with maudlin expressions of gratitude.

Enter wife: Gerald asks her to go back to her husband. She refuses with scorn. He says "You know what it costs me to ask you to do that. Do you not see that I am really sacrificing myself?" Etc. She considers: "Why should you sacrifice me? I love you. You have made me love you. You have no right to hand my life over to anyone else. All this self-sacrifice is wrong, we are meant to live. That is the meaning of life." Etc. She forces him by her appeals and her beauty and her love to take her away with him.

Three months afterwards: Act IV. Gerald and wife together. She is reading Act IV of *Frou-Frou*.[1] They talk about it. A duel between Gerald and the husband is fixed for the day on which the scene takes place. She is confident he will not be killed. He goes out. Husband enters. Wife proclaims her love for her lover. Nothing would induce her to go back to her husband. Of the two she wishes him to die. "Why?" says husband. "Because the father of my child must live." Husband goes out. Pistols are heard. He has killed himself.

Enter Gerald, the husband not having appeared at the duel. "What a coward," says Gerald. "No," she answers, "not at the end. He is dead." "We must love one another devotedly now." Curtain falls with Gerald and the wife clinging to each other as if with a mad desire to make love eternal. *Finis.*

What do you think of this idea?

I think it extremely strong. *I want the sheer passion of love to dominate everything.* No morbid self-sacrifice. No renunciation. A sheer flame of

---

[1] In the fourth act of *Frou-Frou* by Meilhac and Halévy (1869) the heroine's husband and lover fight a duel off-stage, in which the lover is mortally wounded.

love between a man and a woman. That is what the play is to rise to—from the social chatter of Act I, through the theatrical effectiveness of Act II, up to the psychology with its great *dénouement* in Act III, till love dominates Act IV and accepts the death of the husband as in a way its proper right, leaving love its tragedy, and so making it a still greater passion.

Of course I have only scribbled this off. I only thought of the plot this morning, but I send it to you. I see great things in it, and, if you like it when done, you can have it for America.[1] Ever yours   OSCAR

To William Rothenstein
MS. Rothenstein

[? *August 1894*]   *5 Esplanade, Worthing*

Dear Will, At 8 Glebe Place resides a very sweet and lovely girl, a Miss Marion Grey. She has been on the stage, but is anxious to also sit as a model to painters. Will you ask her to come and see you and, if you like her, give her some *recommendations* and advice.[2]

I am away by the seaside, bathing and sailing and amusing myself. How are you? Ever yours   OSCAR

To Lord Alfred Douglas
MS. Clark

[? *August 1894*]   *5 Esplanade, Worthing*

My own dearest Boy, How sweet of you to send me that charming poem.[3] I can't tell you how it touches me, and it is full of that light lyrical grace that you always have—a quality that seems so easy, to those who don't understand how difficult it is to make the white feet of poetry dance lightly among flowers without crushing them, and to those "who know" is so rare and so distinguished. I have been doing nothing here but bathing and playwriting. My play is really very funny: I am quite delighted with it.[4] But it is not shaped yet. It lies in Sibylline leaves about the room, and Arthur[5] has twice made a chaos of it by "tidying up." The result, however, was rather dramatic. I am inclined to think that Chaos is a stronger evidence for an Intelligent Creator than Kosmos is: the view might be expanded.

Percy[6] left the day after you did. He spoke much of you. Alphonso[7] is

[1] This scenario was eventually written up by Frank Harris as *Mr and Mrs Daventry*. See note 4, p. 829.

[2] Marion Grey sat to Rothenstein for several years. She was the subject of his *Porphyria* and of the drawing called *Chloe*, which was reproduced in the first number of the *Savoy* (January 1896).

[3] Possibly "Jonquil and Fleur-de-Lys" (see note 5, p. 394), which is dated 1894.

[4] *The Importance of Being Earnest.*   [5] The Wildes' butler and factotum.

[6] Not Douglas's brother but an unidentified boy.

[7] Alphonse Conway, a newspaper boy whom Wilde had met on the beach at Worthing. Wilde later took him to Brighton and bought him a new suit. All this was brought up in the Queensberry trial.

still in favour. He is my only companion, along with Stephen. Alphonso always alludes to you as "the Lord," which however gives you, I think, a Biblical Hebraic dignity that gracious Greek boys should *not* have. He also says, from time to time, "Percy was the Lord's favourite," which makes me think of Percy as the infant Samuel—an inaccurate reminiscence, as Percy was Hellenic.

Yesterday (Sunday) Alphonso, Stephen, and I sailed to Littlehampton in the morning, bathing on the way. We took five hours in an awful gale to come back! did not reach the pier till eleven o'clock at night, pitch dark all the way, and a fearful sea. I was drenched, but was Viking-like and daring. It was, however, quite a dangerous adventure. All the fishermen were waiting for us. I flew to the hotel for hot brandy and water, on landing with my companions, and found a letter for you from dear Henry, which I send you: they had forgotten to forward it. As it was past *ten* o'clock on a Sunday night the proprietor could not *sell* us any brandy or spirits of any kind! So he had to *give* it to us. The result was not displeasing, but what laws! A hotel proprietor is not allowed to sell 'necessary harmless' alcohol to three shipwrecked mariners, wet to the skin, because it is Sunday! Both Alphonso and Stephen are now anarchists, I need hardly say.

Your new Sibyl is really wonderful. It is most extraordinary. I must meet her.

Dear, dear boy, you are more to me than any one of them has any idea; you are the atmosphere of beauty through which I see life; you are the incarnation of all lovely things. When we are out of tune, all colour goes from things for me, but we are never really out of tune. I think of you day and night.

Write to me soon, you honey-haired boy! I am always devotedly yours

OSCAR

To Charles Spurrier Mason[1]

MS. Roberts

[*Circa 13 August 1894*]   *5 Esplanade, Worthing*

My dear Charlie, I was very sorry to read in the paper about poor Alfred Taylor.[2] It is a dreadful piece of bad luck, and I wish to goodness I could

[1] 1868–1940. In Wilde's first trial it was suggested that Mason had gone through a burlesque ceremony of marriage with Alfred Taylor (*Trials*, 281), which explains Wilde's references to marriage.

[2] On 12 August 1894 the police raided a club at 46 Fitzroy Street, London, and arrested eighteen men, including two in female dress. Among them was Alfred Waterhouse Somerset Taylor, who was subsequently discharged. Born *circa* 1862 and well educated, he was said to have run through a fortune of £45,000, and his house in Westminster was used as a meeting-place for male homosexuals. When Wilde was asked at his first trial whether it was in a rough neighbourhood, he said "That I don't know. It was near the Houses of Parliament." Wilde first met Taylor in 1892. Although he refused to turn Queen's Evidence against Wilde, and so shared the same fate, his indictment and trial alongside Wilde certainly prejudiced Wilde's chances of acquittal. After his release he lived in Canada and the U.S.A.

do something for him, but, as I have had occasion to write to him many times lately, as I have no play going on this season I have no money at all, and indeed am at my wits' end trying to raise some for household expenses and such tedious things. I should think that *now* his people would do something for him, when he is in real trouble. I know he is not on good terms with them, but still a family should stick together. Let me know, if you have time, what Alfred intends doing after next Monday is over, and how you yourself are going on in your married life. Your sincere friend

OSCAR WILDE

To Charles Spurrier Mason

MS. Roberts

[*August 1894*]   *5 Esplanade, Worthing*

My dear Charlie, Thanks for your letter. I am in a very much worse state for money than I told you. But am just finishing a new play which, as it is quite nonsensical and has no serious interest, will I hope bring me in a lot of red gold.

When I come back to town do come and dine. What fun our dinners were in the old days! I hope marriage has not made you too serious? It has never had that effect on me.

Do tell me all about Alfred. Was he angry or amused? What is he going to do?

Hoping, dear boy, you are gay and happy, yours   OSCAR

Telegram: To Elkin Mathews & John Lane

MS. Clark

17 August 1894   *Worthing*

My wife is compiling a small anthology of phrases from my works. You will have no objection I hope to her quoting from my plays.[1]

OSCAR WILDE

To Arthur L. Humphreys[2]

MS. Hyde (H. M.)

[? *August 1894*]   *5 Esplanade, Worthing*

Dear Mr Humphreys, I enclose you the permissions. In no case have I

[1] *Oscariana* (see next note). On the telegram is pencilled: "Telegraphed no objection whatever."

[2] Bookseller, author and publisher (1865–1946). For many years head of Hatchard's bookshop in Piccadilly. In January 1895 he produced fifty copies of *Oscariana*, a collection of epigrams from Wilde's work chosen by Constance Wilde, and in May a further edition of 200. In May 1895 he issued a privately printed edition (50 copies) of Wilde's *The Soul of Man under Socialism*.

parted with the copyright of my books: they are all mine. I wish you had
sent the £50 yesterday. I did not return here from Brighton till late last
night. Truly yours   OSCAR WILDE

To W. B. Yeats[1]
MS. Hyde (H. M.)

[? *August–September 1894*]   *5 Esplanade, Worthing*
Dear Yeats, With pleasure. I don't know that I think "Requiescat"[2] very
typical of my work. Still, I am glad you like it.

I have just finished a play, so my handwriting is abominable.

Personally, I would sooner you chose a sonnet: that one on the sale of
Keats's love letters: or the one beginning "Not that I love thy children"
with which my book opens, but the garden—such as it is—is yours to
pluck from. Truly yours   OSCAR WILDE

To John Lane
MS. Morgan

[*3 September 1894*][3]   *5 Esplanade, Worthing*
Dear Mr Mathews,[4] Certainly: I have no objection at all to your having the
plays. Let Mr Mathews have "Mr W. H." I am very pleased you like the
plays, and hope they will be a success in your hands. We could bring out
The Duchess of Padua in February.

I hope the notice of American copyright is duly inserted into *A Woman
of No Importance*: it is most important.

I have not yet received my copies of the *édition de luxe* of *The Sphinx*.
What *has* happened to them? Truly yours   OSCAR WILDE

To Elkin Mathews & John Lane
MS. Folger

[*September 1894*]   *5 Esplanade, Worthing*
Gentlemen, I have received your letters.

I am informed by Mr Lane that Mr Mathews declines to publish my

---

[1] Yeats was compiling *A Book of Irish Verse*, which was published by Methuen
in March 1895. The second sonnet suggested by Wilde is the "Sonnet to Liberty,"
the opening poem in *Poems* (1881). Yeats, however, adhered to his original choice.
In his later anthology, *The Oxford Book of Modern Verse* (1936), Wilde is represented
by thirty-nine stanzas of *The Ballad of Reading Gaol*.

[2] This poem, written in memory of Wilde's sister Isola, was first published in
Poems (1881).   [3] So endorsed in another hand.

[4] Clearly a slip for Lane, who published *A Woman of No Importance* on 9 October

365

story on Shakespeare's sonnets "at any price:" and that he himself will not publish it (at any price, I presume) unless he "approves" of it!

Eighteen months ago nearly—at any rate considerably more than a year ago—Mr Lane on behalf of the firm, and using the firm's name, entered into an agreement with me to publish "The Portrait of Mr W. H.".: the number of copies to be printed, the royalties to be paid to me, the selection of the artist to whom the style of presentation of the work was to be confided, were all agreed upon[1]: the book was subsequently advertised in the list of the coming publications of the firm: and notices to that effect have appeared in the literary columns of many newspapers. The agreement was stamped in my presence by Mr Lane, and signed by him on behalf of the firm. I do not suggest for a moment that he had not the authority to do so. He acted, I am quite sure, with the full authority of the firm of which he is, or was, a partner. If he did not, it is his affair, not mine.

It is the duty of the firm to publish my book, which they have now advertised for about sixteen months, and which they agreed with me to publish. I have a right to insist upon their doing so: and that right I retain. For the firm to break their agreement with me would be dishonourable, dishonest, and illegal.

Upon the other hand I am quite ready to enter into a compromise. You made an agreement to publish my book on certain terms: you have advertised the book as being about to appear: you have had the rights over the book since last July year. The delay in its publication has been very annoying to me, but I have always behaved towards your firm with perfect courtesy and kindness. Even now, when I am calmly told that one member of the firm refuses, after his stamped agreement nearly eighteen months old, to publish the book "at any price:" and the other calmly tells me that his publication of the book depends on his approval of it: I am not really angry: I am simply amused. However, I am quite ready to let you off your agreement, on condition that you send me a cheque for £25, by return. I think you will agree with me that under the circumstances I am acting with great consideration towards your firm. If you do not think so I shall feel

---

(500 copies at 7/6 and 50 large-paper at 15/-). This letter, like the three that follow it, was occasioned by a printed document announcing the termination of the Mathews–Lane partnership on 29 September. The recipient author was asked to say which partner he would like to follow. In the event Lane remained Wilde's publisher, but the longer version of *The Portrait of Mr W. H.* (see note 3, p. 250) never appeared, although at the end of 1893 Mathews and Lane had announced it as "in rapid preparation." The manuscript (105 pages in Wilde's hand, almost twice as long as the original *Blackwood's* version) came to light many years later among the effects of Lane's office manager, Frederick Chapman, was sold to the American dealer Rosenbach, and is now in the Museum of the Rosenbach Foundation in Philadelphia. Mitchell Kennerley published the full text in a limited edition in New York in 1921, and ten copies of his edition were issued in London by Duckworth with a new title-page. The first regular English edition appeared in 1958, edited by Vyvyan Holland.

[1] A draft letter concerning this agreement has been preserved in the Bodley Head: it is dated May 1893.

that I have been wrong in the estimate I have formed of your desire to act in an honourable and straightforward manner in your business relations with men of letters. Yours faithfully OSCAR WILDE

To Elkin Mathews & John Lane
MS. Dickey

[*September 1894*]   *5 Esplanade, Worthing*

Gentlemen, I have received your letter, in which it is stated that Mr Lane will "accept all responsibility assumed by the firm" in the matter of "Mr. W. H." It is always best to write quite plainly in business matters. If this phrase means that Mr Lane is going to publish the book, well and good. *If it means anything else, pray let me know.*

The suggestion that the delay in the production of the book is in any way to be attributed to me can hardly be seriously made. Mr Lane is quite aware that at his urgent solicitation and desire, repeatedly expressed both in London and at Goring, where the agreement was, I believe, finally signed and stamped, the manuscript was handed over by me to Mr Ricketts that he might select the type and form and suitable setting for the book, and convey the manuscript to the printers. The manuscript has been in Mr Ricketts's hands for *more than a year*, during which time I have waited very patiently, as I did not wish to interfere with the production of *The Sphinx*, or to cause any trouble.

Personally, I regret that the firm did not accept my offer for the sum of £25 to be paid over to me for the cancelling of the agreement. It is never pleasant to deal with a publisher who is not really interested in one's work at the moment. That, however, was for the firm to decide. I am pleased to note that in the last letter received by me no absurd statements are made about the members of the firm not having read the work, and so being relieved from any honourable responsibility to publish it. There is no objection to publishers reading the works they produce before publication, but if they enter into an agreement with an author to publish his work, they, if they desire to be considered an honest and honourable firm, cannot plead their own carelessness, or lack of intellectual interest, as an excuse for the non-performance of their agreement. The plea, in the present case, seems intentionally insincere. The firm is under an obligation to me to publish my five-act tragedy, *The Duchess of Padua*, the manuscript of which they have never seen, nor expressed any desire to see. Nor was the manuscript of *Salome* submitted to them beforehand: any desire on the part of Mr Lane to have the manuscript of my French play submitted to him for his approval would I fear have excited considerable amusement in myself and in others.

I note in your letter that you say it has now been arranged that all my works are to be handed over to Mr Lane. I think that it should be left to me to decide with which partner I will place my work. I have received the firm's circular on the subject, and am considering the point. There is after all no reason why I should not be treated with the same courtesy that is extended to obscure and humble beginners in the difficult art of Literature.

Personally I am at present in favour of entrusting my plays to Mr Mathews, whose literary enthusiasm about them has much gratified me, and to leave to Mr Lane the incomparable privilege of publishing *The Sphinx, Salome*, and my beautiful story on Shakespeare's sonnets.

I would be obliged by a reply to this letter being sent by return. Yours faithfully   OSCAR WILDE

To Elkin Mathews & John Lane
MS. Clark

[*September 1894*]   *5 Esplanade, Worthing*

Gentlemen, I should regret extremely to cause you any inconvenience in your publishing arrangements. The proposal I made to divide my works between the two partners was, I need hardly say, dictated by a desire to be fair and courteous to both. I am equally content that Mr Lane should have all my books, if such an arrangement is more convenient to you. It is of course clearly understood that the arrangement to publish "Mr W. H." is to be honourably and strictly kept: in case of Mr Lane not doing this I would of course regard Mr Mathews as equally responsible with him.

Mr Lane had better communicate with Mr Ricketts at once, and get him to make his final selection of type, format, etc. and the book can be proceeded with at once. Yours faithfully   OSCAR WILDE

Is it arranged in my *Sphinx* agreement that I am to have some of the *édition de luxe*? The document is with my lawyer, so I can't verify it at present. In any case send me a copy.

To George Alexander
MS. Arents

[? *September 1894*]   *5 Esplanade, Worthing*

My dear Aleck, I can't make out what could have become of your letter. I thought from your silence that you thought the play[1] too farcical in incident for a comedy theatre like your own, or that you didn't like my asking you to give me some money. I thought of telegraphing to you, but then changed my mind.

[1] *The Importance of Being Earnest.*

368

As regards the American rights: when you go to the States, it won't be to produce a farcical comedy. You will go as a romantic actor of modern and costume pieces. My play, though the dialogue is sheer comedy, and the best I have ever written, is of course in idea farcical: it could not be made part of a repertoire of serious or classical pieces, except for fun—once—as Irving plays Jeremy Diddler to show the Bostonians how versatile he is, and how a man who can realise Hamlet for us, can yet hold his own with the best of fantastic farce-players.[1]

I would be charmed to write a modern comedy-drama for you, and to give you rights on both sides of the disappointing Atlantic Ocean, but you, of all our young actors, should not go to America to play farcical comedy. You might just as well star at Philadelphia in *Dr Bill*.[2] Besides, I hope to make at least £3000 in the States with this play, so what sum could I ask you for, with reference to double rights? Something that you, as a sensible manager, would not dream of paying. No: I want to come back to you. I would like to have my play done by you (I must tell you candidly that the two young men's parts are equally good), but it would be neither for your artistic reputation as a star in the States, nor for my pecuniary advantage, for you to produce it for a couple of nights in each big American town. It would be throwing the thing away.

I may mention that the play is an admirable play. I can't come up to town, I have no money. (Why doesn't Hardacre give us something more?) Write me your views—about this whole business. Ever yours   OSCAR

To Lord Alfred Douglas
MS. Clark

[*September 1894*][3]   *5 Esplanade, Worthing*

My own dear Boy, Your sweet letter arrived this morning, and this moment I have received your delightful telegram—delightful because I love you to think of me. What do you think of three days at Dieppe? I have a sort of longing for France, and with you, if you can manage to come (I could only manage three days, as I am so busy).

I went yesterday up to town for the afternoon, lunched with George Alexander at the Garrick, got a little money from him, and returned by the 4.30 for dinner, so I can pay my rent, and Cyril's (little wretch and darling) school-fees. I dare not lodge the money in the bank, as I have overdrawn £40, but I think of hiding gold in the garden.

[1] Jeremy Diddler is the leading character in *Raising the Wind*, a farce by James Kenney (1780–1849), originally produced at Covent Garden in 1803. Irving often introduced it into his repertory for comic relief.

[2] A farcical comedy adapted by Hamilton Aidé from the French of Albert Carré. Originally put on by Alexander at the Avenue Theatre on 1 February 1890 (his first venture into management) with Fred Terry in the leading part, the play was an immense success, and was revived at the Court Theatre on 8 December 1894.

[3] 15 September 1894 was a Saturday, and this letter may well have been written some days earlier.

369

Could you meet me at Newhaven on the 15th? Dieppe is very amusing and bright. Or would you come down here first? Say on Thursday: and we could go on?

I saw Gatby, by chance, as I was driving through Pall Mall. He stopped my cab and we had a long chat about *you*, of course. He is one of your many admirers. Last night (see other letter) you, and I, and the Mayor figured as patrons of the entertainment given by the vagabond singers of the sands. They told me that our names, which have been placarded all over the town, excited great enthusiasm, and certainly the hall was crammed. I was greeted with loud applause, as I entered with Cyril. Cyril was considered to be you.

Dear boy, this is a scrawl, is it not? I find farcical comedies admirable for style, but fatal to handwriting.

Do write to me, and do come to France. Is Basil *here*? If so, of course come here. With fondest love, ever devotedly yours   OSCAR

To Arthur L. Humphreys
MS. Fales

[? *September 1894*]   *5 Esplanade, Worthing*

Dear Mr Humphreys, Would you kindly send *Cyril*, at 16 Tite Street, a copy of Butcher and Lang's translation of *The Odyssey*—from me. I am very anxious he should read the best book for boys, and those who keep the wonder and joy of boyhood, ever written.

How about *Oscariana*? Let me see some specimen pages, will you? Truly yours   OSCAR WILDE

To the Editor of the Pall Mall Gazette

18 September [*1894*][1]   [*Worthing*]

Sir, Will you allow me to draw your attention to a very interesting example of the ethics of modern journalism, a quality of which we have all heard so much and seen so little?

About a month ago Mr T. P. O'Connor published in the *Sunday Sun* some doggerel verses entitled "The Shamrock," and had the amusing impertinence to append my name to them as their author. As for some years past all kinds of scurrilous personal attacks had been made on me in Mr O'Connor's newspapers,[2] I decided to take no notice at all of the incident.

Enraged, however, by my courteous silence, Mr O'Connor returns to the charge this week. He now solemnly accuses me of plagiarising the poem he had the vulgarity to attribute to me.[3]

---

[1] Published on 20 September, under the heading THE ETHICS OF JOURNALISM.
[2] Cf. The *Sunday Sun* of 17 May 1891: "At worst Mr Wilde's *Intentions* may go to pave some Philistine Hell."
[3] The verses called "The Shamrock" were printed in the *Sunday Sun* on 5 August, and the charge of plagiarism was made in the issue of 16 September.

This seems to me to pass beyond even those bounds of coarse humour and coarser malice that are, by the contempt of all, conceded to the ordinary journalist, and it is really very distressing to find so low a standard of ethics in a Sunday newspaper.

I remain, sir, your obedient servant OSCAR WILDE

To the Editor of the Pall Mall Gazette

22 September [1894][1]   *Worthing*

Sir, The assistant editor of the *Sunday Sun*, on whom seems to devolve the arduous duty of writing Mr T. P. O'Connor's apologies for him, does not, I observe with regret, place that gentleman's conduct in any more attractive or more honourable light by the attempted explanation that appears in the letter published in your issue of today.[2] For the future it would be much better if Mr O'Connor would always write his own apologies. That he can do so exceedingly well no one is more ready to admit than myself. I happen to possess one from him.

The assistant editor's explanation, stripped of its unnecessary verbiage, amounts to this: It is now stated that some months ago, somebody, whose

---

[1] Published on 25 September.

[2] This letter, which was also headed THE ETHICS OF JOURNALISM, read:

Sir, Mr Oscar Wilde's letter in your issue of yesterday calls for a few words of explanation from me. Let me in the first place say that we regret exceedingly the suggestion of plagiarism.

The story of the association of Mr Wilde's name with the poem is a curious and perplexing one. Our own part in the matter is, however, easily explained. Some three months ago one of our correspondents sent to us in manuscript a poem entitled "The Shamrock." The name "Oscar Wilde" was appended to it. Accompanying the poem was a letter in which our correspondent said, "I have copied this poem on 'The Shamrock' from an old Irish newspaper which I happened on by accident. It is so beautiful and its sentiment is so fine and tender, that it came to me as a revelation. Oscar Wilde may be a *flâneur* and a cynic, but it is quite evident from this poem that deep down in his heart he has kept the fire of patriotism burning with something of a white purity. I think the poem is one which the *Weekly Sun* might well rescue from oblivion."

This, then, sir, was the way in which we came to give the poem publicity in the *Weekly Sun*, and this is the spirit in which the name of the elegant ornament of polite society came to be connected with it in our pages.

Mr Oscar Wilde places our ascription of the poem to himself on the level of certain mythical 'scurrilous attacks' which haunt his imagination. The suggestion is characteristic. I am not concerned here to defend the poem. It may be, and doubtless is, assailable; but even the most fastidious critic cannot deny that it is full of melodic charm and breathes a spirit of pure and exalted patriotism.

So conspicuous, indeed, was its elevation of tone that we were reluctant to believe that it could have been the product of a mind like Mr Oscar Wilde's, and were driven to take refuge in the charitable belief that it belonged to the period of a forgotten and generous youth. Faithfully yours, THE ASSISTANT EDITOR.

It subsequently transpired that the real author of "The Shamrock" was an inmate of the Cork Blind Asylum called Helena Callanan.

name, observe, is not given, forwarded to the office of the *Sunday Sun* a manuscript in his own handwriting, containing some fifth-rate verses with my name appended to them as their author. The assistant editor frankly admits that they had grave doubts about my being capable of such an astounding production. To me, I must candidly say, it seems more probable that they never for a single moment believed that the verses were really from my pen. Literary instinct is, of course, a very rare thing, and it would be too much to expect any true literary instinct to be found among the members of the staff of an ordinary newspaper; but had Mr O'Connor really thought that the production, such as it is, was mine, he would naturally have asked my permission before publishing it. Great licence of comment and attack of every kind is allowed nowadays to newspapers, but no respectable editor would dream of printing and publishing a man's work without first obtaining his consent.

Mr O'Connor's subsequent conduct in accusing me of plagiarism, when it was proved to him on unimpeachable authority that the verses he had vulgarly attributed to me were not by me at all, I have already commented on. It is perhaps best left to the laughter of the gods and the sorrow of men. I would like, however, to point out that when Mr O'Connor, with the kind help of his assistant editor, states, as a possible excuse for his original sin, that he and the members of his staff "took refuge" in the belief that the verses in question might conceivably be some very early and youthful work of mine, he and the members of his staff showed a lamentable ignorance of the nature of the artistic temperament. Only mediocrities progress. An artist revolves in a cycle of masterpieces, the first of which is no less perfect than the last.

In conclusion, allow me to thank you for your courtesy in opening to me the columns of your valuable paper, and also to express the hope that the painful *exposé* of Mr O'Connor's conduct that I have been forced to make will have the good result of improving the standard of journalistic ethics in England.

I remain, sir, your obedient servant   OSCAR WILDE

Telegram: To Ada Leverson

MS. Harvard

22 September 1894   *Worthing*

Esmé and Reggie[1] are delighted to find that their Sphinx is not a minx after all, but are somewhat disappointed to learn that. Esmé feels a little jealous but hopes the Sphinx will remember that Sunday should be no

---

[1] Esmé Amarinth [Wilde] and Lord Reginald Hastings [Douglas] were the names of the leading characters in *The Green Carnation*, a witty skit which was first published anonymously by Heinemann on 15 September 1894, and Ada Leverson had been suggested as its author. It was in fact the first book of Robert Smythe Hichens (1864–1950), who later became a prolific novelist, and his name was printed in the fourth impression (1895). He had met Douglas in Cairo.

exception to the general rule. Reggie goes up to town tonight—Cadogan Place. He proposes to call on the dear and rarely treacherous Sphinx tomorrow. The doubting disciple who has written the false gospel is one who has merely talent unrelieved by any flashes of physical beauty.

To Ada Leverson

MS. Clark

[? *23 September 1894*]   [? *Worthing*]

Dear Sphinx, Of course you have been deeply wronged. But there are many bits not unworthy of your brilliant pen: and treachery is inseparable from faith. I often betray myself with a kiss.

Hichens I did not think capable of anything so clever. It is such a bore about journalists, they are so very clever.

I suppose you heard about our telegrams.[1]

How sweet of you to have *Intentions* bound for me for your birthday! I simply love that book.[2]

I shall be in town soon, and must come and charm the Sphinx with honey-cakes. The trouble is I left my flute in a railway carriage—and the fauns take so long to cut new reeds. Ever yours   OSCAR

To the Editor of the Pall Mall Gazette

1 October [*1894*][3]   *Worthing*

Sir, Kindly allow me to contradict, in the most emphatic manner, the suggestion, made in your issue of Thursday last, and since then copied into many other newspapers, that I am the author of *The Green Carnation*.

I invented that magnificent flower. But with the middle-class and mediocre book that usurps its strangely beautiful name I have, I need hardly say, nothing whatsoever to do. The flower is a work of art. The book is not.

I remain, sir, your obedient servant   OSCAR WILDE

---

[1] In the Introduction to a new edition of *The Green Carnation* (1949) Robert Hichens wrote: "He [Wilde] sent me a bogus telegram about it though it came out anonymously, showing that he had guessed I had written it. Alfred Douglas at the same time sent me a comic telegram, telling me I was discovered, and had better at once flee from the vengeance to come."

[2] On the first page of an incomplete telegram (MS. Harvard), despatched from Piccadilly on 27 October 1894, Wilde wrote: "Dear Sphinx, the copy of *Intentions* is quite beautiful. It is more green than the original even, and I read it as a new work with wonder and joy."

[3] Published on 2 October, and reprinted in *Miscellanies*.

373

To Grace Hawthorne[1]

MS. Boston

[Postmark 4 October 1894][2]   5 Esplanade, Worthing

Dear Miss Hawthorne, My plays are difficult plays to produce well: they require artistic setting on the stage, a good company that knows something of the style essential to high comedy, beautiful dresses, a sense of the luxury of modern life, and unless you are going out with a management that is able to pay well for things that are worth paying for, and to spend money in suitable presentation, it would be much better for you not to think of producing my plays. The very nominal sum I said I would accept in advance of fees I would not, I need hardly say, have accepted from anyone else: but as you said you were in some difficulty I was ready to take a nominal sum in advance. A management that could not pay that could not, I fear, give anything better than a travesty of my work. Some day you must find a brilliant manager who can produce things well for you. I will be charmed then to have a talk with you over some play of mine.

Bon voyage, and best wishes for a most successful tour. Sincerely yours

OSCAR WILDE

To Ada Leverson

Friday [5 October 1894]   Hotel Metropole, Brighton

Dear Sphinx, I hope to be in London on the 15th. Will you be there?

Your article in *Punch*[3] I read with joy, and detected you, of course, before you sent it to me.

My friend is not allowed to go out today:[4] I sit by his side and read him passages from his own life. They fill him with surprise. Everyone should keep someone else's diary; I sometimes suspect you of keeping mine.

Is your birthday really the 10th? Mine is the 16th! How tragic: I fear that looks like brother and sister. Perhaps it is better so. Ever yours

OSCAR

Telegram: To Ada Leverson

MS. Harvard

6 October 1894   Brighton

Much better, temperature gone down, is to be allowed chicken to the sound of flutes at 7.30. Many thanks for kind enquiries.   OSCAR

---

[1] English actress (1860–1922).

[2] So recorded in the American Art Association catalogue of 9 February 1927. The envelope must since have been lost.

[3] Probably "Letters from a Debutante", which appeared anonymously in *Punch* on 6 October 1894. Ada Leverson's last contribution before that was on 4 August. The text of this letter is taken from *Letters to the Sphinx*.

[4] For Wilde's later account of this illness of Lord Alfred Douglas, see p. 436.

374

To George Ives[1]

MS. Princeton

[*Postmark 22 October 1894*]   *16 Tite Street*

Dear George, I have been so upset by the terrible tragedy of poor Drumlanrig's death that I have not been able to answer your letter.[2] It is a great
blow to Bosie: the first noble sorrow of his boyish life: the wings of the
angel of Death have almost touched him: their purple shadow lies across
his way, for the moment: I am perforce the sharer of his pain.

The attack on you I have not read: I can't find it in the *Review of
Reviews*: but congratulate you on it. When the prurient and the impotent
attack you, be sure you are right.[3]

Let me see you soon. Ever yours   OSCAR

To an Unidentified Correspondent [4]

MS. Harvard

[? *24 October 1894*]   *Albemarle Club*

My dear Hugh, On Thursday with great pleasure: that is tomorrow week:
where do we dine? If Alfred Douglas is in town then he will come with
pleasure. I will let you know. At present he is rather uncertain, as his
mother is of course anxious for him to be with her. But I think he will stay
on in town for ten days. Poor boy, he has been greatly upset by the horror
of the tragedy that has come on his house.

Of course you shall have a photograph. Ever yours   OSCAR WILDE

To George Alexander

MS. Arents

[*Circa 25 October 1894*][5]   *16 Tite Street*

My dear Aleck, I have been ill in bed for a long time, with a sort of

[1] Author and criminologist (1867–1950).

[2] Lord Drumlanrig was killed by the explosion of his gun on 18 October 1894.

[3] The *Review of Reviews* for October 1894 attacked Ives for an article in the
Humanitarian in which he had expressed disappointment that Grant Allen's essay
"The New Hedonism" shied off the problem of homosexuality. "A dissertation in
praise of unnatural vice," thundered the *Review of Reviews*; "the New Morality
which is seeking for a new heaven and a new earth might, I should have thought,
have gone elsewhere for its ideal than to Sodom and Gomorrah."

[4] Possibly Hugh Bryans, to whom another brief note has survived (MS. Clark),
addressed to him at 34 Fitzroy Square, which housed the Romilly Working Men's
Club, of which Bryans was treasurer 1892–93.

[5] The revised typescript of the play, in four acts and entitled *Lady Lancing*, was
stamped "3–25 October 94" by Mrs Marshall's typewriting agency. On 24 October
Alexander, entertained to lunch by the Birmingham Arts Club, had spoken on "The
Future of the Stage." The playwright Henry Arthur Jones (1857–1929) was as well

malarial fever, and have not been able to answer your kind letter of invitation. I am quite well now, and, as you wished to see my somewhat farcical comedy, I send you the first copy of it. It is called *Lady Lancing* on the cover: but the real title is *The Importance of Being Earnest*. When you read the play, you will see the punning title's meaning. Of course, the play is not suitable to you at all: you are a romantic actor: the people it wants are actors like Wyndham and Hawtrey. Also, I would be sorry if you altered the definite artistic line of progress you have always followed at the St James's. But, of course, read it, and let me know what you think about it. I have very good offers from America for it.

I read charming accounts of your banquet at Birmingham, and your praise of the English dramatist. I know and admire Pinero's work, but *who is Jones?* Perhaps the name as reported in the London papers was a misprint for something else. I have never heard of Jones. Have you?

Give my kind regards to Mrs Aleck, and believe me, sincerely yours

OSCAR WILDE

To Lord Alfred Douglas
MS. Clark

[5 or 6 November 1894]   16 Tite Street

My dearest Bosie, I suppose you won't come up now, it is so late. Perhaps I shall hear tomorrow. I can't bear your sadness and unhappiness: because I cannot cure it. But you know what a joy it will be to see you again. I have been staying at Cannizaro[1] from Saturday to Monday. Noel Holland, one of Knutsford's sons, was there: he is partner with Edward Arnold the publisher.[2] I told him of our idea of writing a book *How to Live Above one's Income: for the Use of the Sons of the Rich*: he was charmed: he seems very mad, but is quite brilliant. One of the Ameses with his fiancée was there also: there were many affectionate enquiries after you. Tiny was sweet as usual. Mrs Schuster had a black eye! a fall from her donkey-chaise. She was swathed in lace, jewels, and flowers: quite extraordinary to look at.

I heard all the details of the divorce of the Scarlet Marquis the other day: quite astonishing:[3] Arthur Pollen[4] told me all about it: he came to tea one afternoon.

---

known to Wilde as to everyone else. Jones had scored a number of great successes, and Alexander had produced *The Masqueraders* in April 1894 with Mrs Patrick Campbell as leading lady. They were even now touring with this play and *The Second Mrs Tanqueray*.

[1] The Wimbledon home of the Schuster family (see note 2, p. 334).

[2] The Hon. Lionel Raleigh Holland (1865–1936), fifth son of the first Viscount Knutsford (see note 2, p. 179) and through his mother a great-nephew of Lord Macaulay.

[3] Queensberry, having been divorced by his first wife in 1887, remarried in 1893 a Miss Ethel Weeden, who obtained a decree of nullity against him on 24 October 1894.

[4] Arthur Joseph Hungerford Pollen (1866–1937), business man and writer on naval affairs.

Surely your mother intends to give you a good allowance now. When she is a little better I feel certain she will: it should be about £400 or £500 a year. It is absurd you should not have an allowance suitable to your position. I think you should speak to your mother about it, before you come up.

On Thursday night I am going to the first night of Tree's new play:[1] so if you are in town I suppose you will dine with Robbie: or some other friend. I am sending you a copy of *Hafiz* the divinest of poets.[2] I hope the honey of his verse may charm you.

London is dripping with rain: a loathsome day. Ever, with much love, yours   OSCAR

To Lord Alfred Douglas
MS. Clark

[*Circa 9 November 1894*]   *Albemarle Club*
My dearest Boy, I have been very lonely without you: and worried by money matters. Today is golden enough, but rain has dripped monotonously on all other days.

I went to Haddon Chambers's play: it was not bad, but oh! so badly written! The bows and salutations of the lower orders who thronged the stalls were so cold that I felt it my duty to sit in the Royal Box with the Ribblesdales, the Harry Whites, and the Home Secretary:[3] this exasperated the wretches. How strange to live in a land where the worship of beauty and the passion of love are considered infamous. I hate England: it is only bearable to me because you are here.

Last night I supped at Willis's: there were respectful enquiries after "Lord Douglas." Always yours   OSCAR

To G. H. Kersley
TS. Holland

21 November 1894   *16 Tite Street*
Dear George, I fear that comic footmen do not come into my sphere of art,

[1] *John-a-Dreams* by Haddon Chambers was produced by Tree at the Haymarket Theatre on Thursday 8 November 1894, with Tree himself, Mrs Patrick Campbell, Charles Cartwright, Nutcombe Gould and Lesly Thomson in the cast. It ran until 27 December.

[2] Perhaps *Ghazels from the Divan of Hafiz*, done into English by J. H. M'Carthy (David Nutt, 1893).

[3] Sir Henry White (1849–1922) was Private Solicitor to the Queen. The fourth Lord Ribblesdale (1854–1925) was Lord-in-Waiting 1880–85 and Master of Buckhounds 1892–95. His portrait by Sargent is in the Tate Gallery. The Home Secretary was Herbert Henry Asquith (1852–1928), who was Liberal Prime Minister 1908–16. Created Earl of Oxford and Asquith 1925. In 1894 he married as his second wife Margot Tennant (1864–1945), to whom Wilde had dedicated "The Star-Child" in *A House of Pomegranates*.

and the two minor parts of my play—two young dandies—do not come into the possibility of an offer: they are both cast already.[1]

But I am cheered to know that you will at any rate be a part of my play, so that I shall have an opportunity of seeing you. You must not think that I have forgotten you: friends who are also poets are never forgotten: memory keeps them in rose-leaves: but Life—coloured, turbulent Life—rushes like a river between oneself and those whom one likes, too often. Sincerely yours   OSCAR WILDE

To Arthur L. Humphreys
MS. Clark

[Late November 1894]   16 Tite Street

Dear Mr Humphreys, The book[2] is, as it stands, so bad, so disappointing, that I am writing a set of new aphorisms, and will have to alter much of the printed matter. The plays are particularly badly done. Long passages are quoted, where a single aphorism should have been extracted.

The book, well done, should be a really brilliant thing: no English writer has for years ever published aphorisms. But to do it well requires time, and I am busy, with heaps of things, but I work a little at it every morning. I enclose Copeland & Day's[3] letter.

I think the book should be dearer than 2/6—all my books are dear—and it would look like underselling the other publishers, who have given their consent for extracts. I think also it should be bound in cloth, and look dainty and nice. I don't want a "railway bookstall" book. In England a paper-covered book gets so dirty and untidy: I should like a book as dainty as John Gray's poems by Ricketts. I think also there should be fifty large paper at a guinea: the book could be five shillings.

After the *Green Carnation* publication, this book of "real Oscar Wilde" should be refined and distinguished: else, it will look like a bit of journalism.

Besides, *your* first book should be a work of art—something to be proud of. Please think over all this.

The *Saturday* was of course mine.[4] Truly yours   OSCAR WILDE

I should prefer Copeland & Day to bring it out themselves separately, following our lines.

---

[1] The Vicomte de Nanjac (Cosmo Stuart) and Mr Montford (Harry Stanford) in *An Ideal Husband*. I have been unable to discover what part, if any, Kersley played, presumably off-stage or as an understudy, in the production.

[2] *Oscariana*. See note 2, p. 364.

[3] A firm of Boston publishers who had issued American editions of *Salome* and *The Sphinx*. They did not publish *Oscariana*.

[4] In September 1894 Frank Harris had bought the *Saturday Review*, and in the issue of 17 November there appeared, anonymously, nineteen aphorisms, headed "A Few Maxims for the Instruction of the Over-Educated." They were not recorded by Mason, and have never been included in the Wilde canon, but they certainly belong there, and they are now printed as Appendix B. on pp. 869–870.

To R. H. Sherard

MS. Clark

[*Postmark 30 November 1894*]   *Albemarle Club*

My dear Robert, If McClure wishes me to be interviewed he must pay me.[1]
I dislike the tone of his letter, and I never allow myself to be interviewed.
For you, as we are old friends and I appreciate and admire you, I don't
mind allowing an interview: but McClure, after his letter, must understand
that I must be paid: the classical sum I believe is £20. Of course he won't
do this: why on earth should he? But I certainly won't give him a column
of conversation to amuse his readers for nothing. Besides, I am sick of my
name in the papers.

It was charming seeing you so well and so delightful the other night.
Truly yours   OSCAR

To Ada Leverson

MS. Clark

[*Early December 1894*][2]   *Albemarle Club*

Dear Sphinx, Your aphorisms must appear in the second number of the
Chameleon: they are exquisite. "The Priest and the Acolyte" is not by
Dorian: though you were right in discerning by internal evidence that the
author has a profile. He is an undergraduate of strange beauty.

The story is, to my ears, too direct: there is no nuance: it profanes a
little by revelation: God and other artists are always a little obscure. Still,
it has interesting qualities, and is at moments poisonous: which is something.
Ever yours   OSCAR

Telegram: To Ada Leverson

MS. Harvard

8 January 1895   *Piccadilly*

Am so pleased, my dear Sphinx. No other voice but yours is musical

---

[1] See note 5, p. 209. In *The Real Oscar Wilde* Sherard writes:

The McClures of *McClure's Magazine* had asked me to give them an article
about him, "with as many Oscariana as possible." I had sent their letter to Wilde.
In the old days he would have been glad of the publicity, and still more glad to
give me the opportunity of doing some highly remunerated work which would
have attracted great attention in America.

[2] Thirty-five aphorisms of Wilde's, clearly intended as successors to those already
published in the *Saturday Review* and now printed on pp. 869–870, were published
as "Phrases and Philosophies for the Use of the Young" in the first (and only) issue
of the *Chameleon*, an Oxford undergraduate magazine issued in December 1894.
They were reprinted in *Miscellanies*. Much play was made with them at Wilde's
trial, and also with two other items in the magazine—a poem of Douglas's called
"Two Loves" (see note 3, p. 441) and an anonymous story called "The Priest and
the Acolyte," which was attributed to Wilde but was in fact written by the
magazine's editor, John Francis Bloxam, an undergraduate of Exeter College.

enough to echo my music. Your article will be worthy of you and of me.[1]
Have you a box tomorrow night? If so I will come, as I am still forbidden
to go out.   OSCAR

Telegram: To Ada Leverson
MS. Harvard

10 January 1895   *Piccadilly*
Your flowers are so lovely that they have made me well again. You are
the most wonderful Sphinx in the world.   OSCAR

To Ada Leverson
F. Le Gallienne

[*Circa 13 January 1895*]   *Hotel Albemarle*
Dear Sphinx, You are more than all criticisms. I have merely to thank you
again and again for your desire to sound in my honour a daffodil-shaped
horn. "Elder Harris" is of course a traitor.[2] But Sphinxes are true. Ever
yours   OSCAR
Bosie sends sweet words, and so does our Scotch friend Ross.

To R. Golding Bright[3]
MS. White

[*Postmark 14 January 1895*]   *Hotel Albemarle*
Sir, I have read your letter, and I see that to the brazen everything is brass.
Your obedient servant   OSCAR WILDE

---

[1] *An Ideal Husband* was produced at the Haymarket Theatre on 3 January 1895,
with Lewis Waller as Sir Robert Chiltern and Charles Hawtrey as Lord Goring.
Ada Leverson's short skit appeared anonymously in *Punch* on 12 January 1895,
entitled "Overheard Fragment of a Dialogue."

[2] Frank Harris's book *Elder Conklin and other Stories* had just been published.

[3] Reginald Golding Bright (1874–1941) was at this time a journalist on the *Sun*,
who habitually wrote to playwrights and actors, conscientiously criticising their
work and asking for an interview and a photograph. Although this technique failed
with Wilde, it was so successful elsewhere that Bright was soon able to abandon
journalism for theatrical agency, and ultimately became agent for Barrie, Maugham
and other leading dramatists. Elisabeth Marbury was his partner in America. In
1901 he married Mrs Chavelita Clairmonte (1859–1945), who wrote as George
Egerton. Her book of stories *Keynotes* (1893), published by Mathews & Lane with
a Beardsley title-page and cover, gave its name to a series and almost to a whole
decade.

To Ada Leverson

MS. Clark

[*Circa 16 January 1895*]   *Hotel Albemarle*

Dear Sphinx, Oh! how rash of you to trust me with your brilliant article. I had put it into a casket and thrown the key into the waters. But, now I have shattered the casket, I send you the purple papyrus of your perfect panegyric, so full of instinct, of subtlety, of charm—a real model of appreciation. I hope it will be published—in an edition de luxe.

Yes: I fly to Algiers with Bosie tomorrow.[1] I begged him to let me stay to rehearse, but so beautiful is his nature that he declined at once.

Poste Restante *Algiers*

Do write. Ever yours   OSCAR

To Ada Leverson

MS. Prescott

[? *10 February 1895*]   *Hotel Avondale, Piccadilly*

My dear Sphinx, You were kind enough to say I might bring someone to dinner tonight, so, after carefully going over the list, I have selected a young man, tall as a young palm tree (I mean "tall as two young palm trees"). His Christian name is "Tom"—a very rare name in an age of Algies and Berties—and he is the son of Colonel Kennion, and lives at Oxford in the hopes of escaping the taint of modern education. I met him on Tuesday, so he is quite an old friend.[2]

I could not get away last night. I am delighted to hear that the piece[3] was tedious, but want to know what sort of dialogue you spoke between the acts. The critics say nothing about it. Why is this? Ever yours   OSCAR

To Arthur L. Humphreys

MS. Hyde (H. M.)

[*Circa 12 February 1895*]   *Hotel Avondale, Piccadilly*

My dear Humphreys, I enclose you a stall for Thursday—the last to be got!

[1] The exact dates of this visit to Algiers are not known, but it certainly began during the rehearsals of *The Importance of Being Earnest*. On 22 January Constance Wilde wrote to her brother: "Did I tell you that Oscar has gone for a fortnight to Algiers?" and on 27 January André Gide ran into Wilde and Douglas at Blidah. Gide spent most of the next few days with Wilde in Algiers, and reported Wilde's leaving there on 3 February, presumably for London. Douglas stayed on at Biskra till 18 February.

[2] Thomas W. Kennion (1876–1955), in partnership with Courtenay Thorpe (see note 2, p. 579) and the actress May Pardoe, later ran an antique shop called Parkenthorpe in Ebury Street, London.

[3] Possibly *A Leader of Men* by Charles Ward produced at the Comedy Theatre on 9 February 1895, with Fred Terry, H. B. Irving and Marion Terry in the cast.

I hope you will enjoy my "trivial" play. It is written by a butterfly for butterflies.[1] Ever yours OSCAR WILDE

Telegram: To Ada Leverson
MS. Harvard

12 February 1895 *Piccadilly*

Come tonight to theatre 7.45 dress rehearsal without scenery. Will send you manuscript. Bring Bobbie or someone with you. Have secured small box for you for first night. OSCAR

Telegram: To Ada Leverson
MS. Harvard

[? *13*] *February 1895* *Piccadilly*

Thank you dear Sphinx for your two charming and kind letters. The rehearsals were dreary. The uncultured had caught colds. OSCAR

To Mrs Bernard Beere [2]

[? *13 February 1895*] *Hotel Avondale, Piccadilly*

I am hard at work rehearsing and everybody has been ill . . . However *you* are coming, so I hope all will go well. You are very necessary to me as you keep up the dramatic interest between the acts.

To R. V. Shone [3]
MS. Mayfield

[*13 February 1895*]

Dear Mr Shone, Lord Queensberry is at Carter's Hotel, Albemarle Street. Write to him from Mr Alexander that you regret to find that the seat given to him was already sold, and return him his money.

This will prevent trouble, I hope. Truly yours OSCAR WILDE

[1] *The Importance of Being Earnest* opened at the St James's Theatre on Thursday, 14 February 1895, with Alexander as John Worthing, Allan Aynesworth as Algernon Moncrieff, Irene Vanbrugh as Gwendolen Fairfax and Rose Leclercq as Lady Bracknell.

[2] The text of this fragment is taken from Sotheby's Catalogue of 3 December 1915.

[3] Robert V. Shone, business manager of the St James's Theatre. Queensberry had been planning to create a disturbance during the first night of *The Importance of Being Earnest*, but when he was unable to get a seat he contented himself with having a bouquet of vegetables, addressed to Wilde, delivered at the stage door. This letter is written in pencil.

Ada Leverson

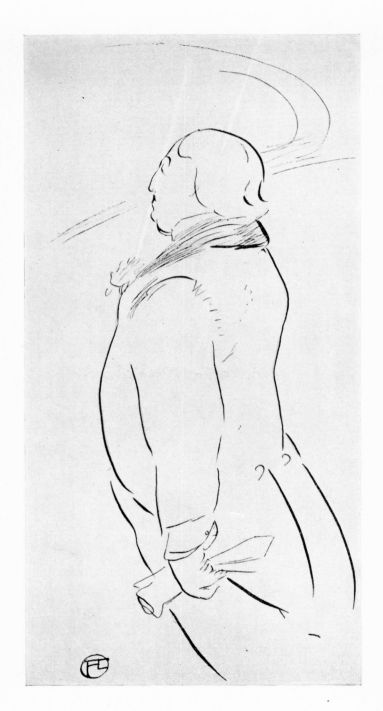

Drawing by Toulouse-Lautrec

Telegram: To Ada Leverson

MS. Harvard

15 February 1895   *Piccadilly*

Title for *Punch* quite charming.[1]   Rely on you to misrepresent me.   Your
flowers are lovely.   Will see you tonight.   OSCAR

To Lord Alfred Douglas

MS. Clark

[Circa 17 February 1895]   *Thos Cook & Son, 33 Piccadilly*

Dearest Boy, Yes: the Scarlet Marquis made a plot to address the audience
on the first night of my play! Algy Bourke[2] revealed it, and he was not
allowed to enter.

He left a grotesque bouquet of vegetables for me! This of course makes
his conduct idiotic, robs it of dignity.

He arrived with a prize-fighter!! I had all Scotland Yard—twenty police
—to guard the theatre. He prowled about for three hours, then left chattering like a monstrous ape. Percy[3] is on our side.

I feel now that, without your name being mentioned, all will go well.

I had not wished you to know. Percy wired without telling me. I am
greatly touched by your rushing over Europe. For my own part I had
determined you should know nothing.

I will wire to Calais and Dover, and you will of course stay with me till
Saturday. I then return to Tite Street, I think.

Ever, with love, all love in the world, devotedly your   OSCAR

To George Alexander

MS. Du Cann

[February 1895]   *St James's Theatre*

Dear Aleck, I am much obliged to you for your cheque for £300.

If it is possible could you let me have the balance as soon as possible. I
am already served with writs for £400, rumours of prosperity having
reached the commercial classes, and my hotel is loathsome to me. I want
to leave it.

On Sunday I hope to send you, or read you, the vital parts of my
Florentine play.[4] I think you will like it. In any case, some day soon I

---

[1] Ada Leverson published a brief anonymous skit on *The Importance of Being
Earnest* in *Punch* on 2 March 1895. It was headed THE ADVISABILITY OF NOT
BEING BROUGHT UP IN A HANDBAG: A TRIVIAL TRAGEDY FOR WONDERFUL
PEOPLE.

[2] The Hon. Algernon Henry Bourke (1854-1922), younger son of the sixth Earl
of Mayo.   [3] Lord Douglas of Hawick (see note 4, p. 344).

[4] *A Florentine Tragedy*, a play in blank verse which Wilde originally intended for
Lewis Waller, but never finished. The surviving fragments of manuscript were
published in Volume II of the Collected Edition of 1908.

would like to talk to you about it. I am sorry my life is so marred and maimed by extravagance. But I cannot live otherwise. I, at any rate, pay the penalty of suffering. Ever yours OSCAR

To Constance Wilde
MS. Magdalen

[? *February 1895*][1]   *Hotel Avondale, Piccadilly*

Dear Constance, I think Cyril better *not* come up. I have so telegraphed to Mr Badley.

I am coming to see you at nine o'clock. Please be in—it is important. Ever yours OSCAR

To Robert Ross
MS. Clark

[*28 February 1895*]   *Hotel Avondale, Piccadilly*

Dearest Bobbie, Since I saw you something has happened. Bosie's father has left a card at my club with hideous words on it.[2] I don't see anything now but a criminal prosecution. My whole life seems ruined by this man. The tower of ivory is assailed by the foul thing. On the sand is my life spilt. I don't know what to do. If you could come here at 11.30 please do so tonight. I mar your life by trespassing ever on your love and kindness. I have asked Bosie to come tomorrow. Ever yours OSCAR[3]

Ada Leverson
MS. Private

[*Circa 13 March 1895*]

My dear Friend, A thousand thanks. For a week I go away with Bosie: then return to fight with panthers.[4] OSCAR

Kind regards to dear Ernest.

---

[1] It is impossible to date this letter exactly, but Wilde was certainly staying at the Avondale Hotel in February 1895, and may even have written this note on the fatal 28th. It is in pencil, as is the following letter.

[2] Lord Queensberry's card, on which he had written "To Oscar Wilde posing as a somdomite [*sic*]," was left by him with the porter of the Albemarle Club on 18 February. The porter put it in an envelope and handed it to Wilde when he next came to the club, which was on 28 February.

[3] Ross appended this note: "I cannot find Queensberry's original card, but the enclosed was Wilde's letter telling me of it. He sent note by hand, about 6.40, to 24 Hornton Street. I went up that evening at 11.30. Douglas was there. Date Feb 28, 1895."

[4] On 1 March Wilde obtained a warrant for the arrest of Queensberry, who on the following day was arrested and charged with criminal libel. Soon after this Wilde and Douglas went to Monte Carlo for a short holiday (see p. 429.) Mason says (*Oscar Wilde Three Times Tried*, p. 41) that they left on 13 March.

To Ernest Leverson

TS. Zarnekah

[*Printed Letter-heading, Cadogan Hotel, Sloane Street*]
[*March 1895*]   *16 Tite Street*

Dear Ernest, Can you do me a very great favour? Can you advance me
£500 for my legal expenses, in this tedious and dreadful trial? Lord
Douglas of Hawick, the eldest son, has promised to pay half my costs, and
Lady Queensberry has promised to pay any amount required, but Lord
Douglas is in Devonshire and Lady Queensberry in Florence, and the sum
is required by my lawyers at once. If you would do this for me you would
be repaid, as far as the money is concerned, within a week or ten days at
most. My own indebtedness to you could never be repaid in any way. Will
you kindly let me have your answer tomorrow morning by messenger. If
you can do it I feel sure you will. Sincerely yours   o. w.

To Ernest Leverson

TS. Zarnekah

[*March 1895*]   *16 Tite Street*

Dear Ernest, Bosie and I cannot sufficiently thank you for your great
kindness to us: we shall never forget it, but shall always cherish in affection
and gratitude the friend who at a moment's notice came forward to help us.

In a few days we hope to be free of our monetary obligation; the other
obligation of gratitude and *reconnaissance* we would like to always keep.

Our homage to the dear and wonderful Sphinx, and believe me, dear
Ernest, your sincere and grateful friend   o. w.

Telegram: To Ada Leverson

MS. Harvard

25 March 1895   *Charles Street, Haymarket*

Thanks for charming letter. We have been to the Sibyl Robinson. She
prophesied complete triumph and was most wonderful.[1]   OSCAR

Telegram: To Ada Leverson

MS. Harvard

3 April 1895[2]   *Holborn Viaduct*

Pray excuse us from dining tonight as we have a lot of very important
business to do. Everything is very satisfactory. Best love from
                                                    OSCAR AND BOSIE

[1] See note 2, p. 358.

[2] The Queensberry trial opened at the Old Bailey on 3 April.

385

To Constance Wilde
MS. Holland

[? *5 April 1895*]¹

Dear Constance, Allow no one to enter my bedroom or sittingroom—except servants—today. See no one but your friends. Ever yours

OSCAR

To the Editor of the Evening News

*5 April 1895*²   *Holborn Viaduct Hotel*

It would have been impossible for me to have proved my case without putting Lord Alfred Douglas in the witness-box against his father.

Lord Alfred Douglas was extremely anxious to go into the box, but I would not let him do so.

Rather than put him in so painful a position I determined to retire from the case, and to bear on my own shoulders whatever ignominy and shame might result from my prosecuting Lord Queensberry.³   OSCAR WILDE

To Lord Alfred Douglas
MS. Hyde (H. M.)

[*5 April 1895*]   [*Cadogan Hotel*]

My dear Bosie, I will be at Bow Street Police Station tonight—no bail possible I am told. Will you ask Percy, and George Alexander, and Waller, at the Haymarket, to attend to give bail.

Would you also wire Humphreys to appear at Bow Street for me.⁴ Wire to 41 Norfolk Square, W.

Also, come to see me. Ever yours   OSCAR⁵

¹ This letter, which is in an envelope addressed to Mrs Oscar Wilde, 16 Tite Street, was clearly delivered by hand. It cannot be dated with confidence, but the morning of the last day of the Queensberry trial, when Wilde knew he could not win, seems a likely time.

² On the morning of this day the prosecution was forced to withdraw and Queensberry was acquitted.

³ Douglas maintained to his dying day that, if he had been allowed to give evidence, his revelations of his father's conduct would have discredited Queensberry and won the case for Wilde. But, since the matter at issue was Queensberry's charge against Wilde, no court could possibly have considered Douglas's evidence relevant.

⁴ Charles Octavius Humphreys (1828–1902), of the firm of Humphreys, Son & Kershaw, was Wilde's solicitor throughout his trials.

⁵ When the police came in the evening to arrest Wilde at the Cadogan Hotel, Douglas had gone to the House of Commons to try and discover from his kinsman George Wyndham whether there was to be a prosecution. When he returned he found Wilde gone and this letter waiting for him.

READING

1895-97

Reading: 1895-97

On 6 April 1895 Wilde was charged at Bow Street Police Court with offences under Section Eleven of the Criminal Law Amendment Act, 1885. The magistrate, Sir John Bridge, refused bail, and Wilde was imprisoned at Holloway until his first trial began at the Old Bailey on 26 April before Mr Justice Charles. On 1 May the jury disagreed and a new trial was ordered. On 7 May Wilde was released on bail, and on 20 May his second trial began at the Old Bailey before Mr Justice Wills. On 25 May Wilde was found guilty and sentenced to two years' imprisonment with hard labour. The first six months of his sentence were served in Pentonville and Wandsworth prisons, the rest at Reading. For a full account of his trials, see *The Trials of Oscar Wilde*, edited by H. Montgomery Hyde (1948).

To Ada and Ernest Leverson
MS. Hyde (D. & M.)

9 April 1895   *H.M. Prison, Holloway*

Dear Sphinx and Ernest, I write to you from prison, where your kind words have reached me and given me comfort, though they have made me cry, in my loneliness. Not that I am really alone. A slim thing, gold-haired like an angel, stands always at my side. His presence overshadows me. He moves in the gloom like a white flower.

With what a crash this fell! Why did the Sibyl[1] say fair things? I

---

[1] Mrs Robinson, the fortune-teller. On 19 April 1895 Constance Wilde wrote to her from Babbacombe (TS. Leslie):

My dear Mrs Robinson, What is to become of my husband who has so betrayed and deceived me and ruined the lives of my darling boys? Can you tell me anything? You told me that after this terrible shock my life was to become easier, but will there be any happiness in it, or is that dead for me? And I have had so little. My life has all been cut to pieces as my hand is by its lines.

As soon as this trial is over I have to get my judicial separation, or if possible my divorce in order to get the guardianship of the boys. What a tragedy for him who is so gifted.

Do write to me and tell me what you can. Very sincerely yours
                                                CONSTANCE WILDE
I have not forgotten that I owe you a guinea.

thought but to defend him from his father: I thought of nothing else, and now—

I can't write more. How good and kind and sweet you and Ernest are to me.   OSCAR

To More Adey and Robert Ross
MS. Clark

9 April 1895   *H.M. Prison, Holloway*

Dear More and Bobbie, Will you tell the Sphinx, Ernest Leverson, Mrs Bernard Beere (Church Cottage, Marylebone Road) how deeply touched I am by their affection and kindness.

Inform the committee of the New Travellers Club, and also of the Albemarle, that I resign my membership (Piccadilly and Dover Street).

Bosie is so wonderful. I think of nothing else. I saw him yesterday.

They are kind in their way here, but I have no books, nothing to smoke, and sleep very badly. Ever yours   OSCAR

Ask Bobbie to go to Tite Street and get a type-written manuscript, part of my blank-verse tragedy, also a black book containing *La Sainte Courtisane*[1] in bedroom.

To R. H. Sherard
MS. Clark

13 April 1895   *H.M. Prison, Holloway*

My dear Robert, I cannot tell you how your letters have cheered and comforted me in this awful, terrible position in which I am placed, and how glad I am that Sarah, and Goncourt, and other artists are sympathising with me. Pray assure Louÿs, Stuart Merrill,[3] Moréas,[2] and all others how

[1] When Ross published a fragment of a first draft of this play in *Miscellanies* he wrote: "At the time of Wilde's trial the nearly completed drama was entrusted to Mrs Leverson, who in 1897 [?1898] went to Paris on purpose to restore it to the author. Wilde immediately left the manuscript in a cab. A few days later he laughingly informed me of the loss, and added that a cab was a very proper place for it."   [2] Jean Moréas, Graeco-French poet (1856–1910).

[3] Stuart Fitzrandolph Merrill (1863–1915), American poet who wrote in French and lived in Paris. He had met Wilde in 1890, when he visited London with Jonathan Sturges. In November 1895 he drew up a petition to Queen Victoria begging for Wilde's release from prison, but it came to nothing, since scarcely any of the leading French writers agreed to sign it. Sardou, the dramatist, wrote: "*C'est une boue trop immonde pour que je m'en mêle, de quelque façon que soit,*" and Jules Renard wrote in his journal: "*Je veux bien signer la pétition pour Oscar Wilde, à la condition qu'il prenne l'engagement d'honneur . . . de ne jamais plus écrire.*"

On 27 November 1895 Jonathan Sturges wrote to Merrill from London (MS. Princeton):

Henry James came in to see me yesterday, and I communicated to him that part of your letter which concerned him. He will write to you himself in a few days,

touched—touched beyond words—I am. I am sending you a telegram to ask you if you think Sarah would buy *Salome* from me. I am so pressed by my creditors that I don't know where to turn. I would repay her of course, when all comes well, but perhaps if you mentioned to her the need I was in of 10,000 francs (£400) she might do it. Ever, with deepest affection and gratitude   OSCAR

To R. H. Sherard

MS. Du Cann

16 April 1895   *H.M. Prison, Holloway*

My dear Robert, You good, daring reckless friend! I was delighted to get your letter, with all its wonderful news. For myself, I am ill—apathetic. Slowly life creeps out of me. Nothing but Alfred Douglas's daily visits quicken me into life, and even him I only see under humiliating and tragic conditions.

Don't fight more than six duels a week! I suppose Sarah is hopeless; but your chivalrous friendship—your fine, chivalrous friendship—is worth more than all the money in the world. Ever yours   OSCAR

---

but I do not think he will sign the petition, though I know that he feels sorry for Oscar . . . James says that the petition would not have the slightest effect on the *authorities* here who have the matter in charge, and in whose nostrils the very name of Zola and even of Bourget is a stench, and that the document would only exist as a manifesto of personal loyalty to Oscar by his friends, of which he was never one.

In a letter to André Gide written from Paris on 6 May 1896 (MS. Doucet) Douglas enclosed this:

> Sonnet, dedicated to those French men of letters
> (Messrs Zola, Coppée, Sardou and others)
> who refused to compromise their spotless reputations
> or imperil their literary exclusiveness
> by signing a merciful petition in favour of Oscar Wilde.
>
> Not all the singers of a thousand years
> Can open English prisons. No. Though hell
> Opened for Thracian Orpheus, now the spell
> Of song and art is powerless as the tears
> That love has shed. You that were full of fears,
> And mean self-love, shall live to know full well
> That you yourselves, not he, were pitiable
> When you met mercy's voice with frowns or jeers.
>
> And did you ask who signed the plea with you?
> Fools! It was signed already with the sign
> Of great dead men, of God-like Socrates,
> Shakespeare and Plato and the Florentine
> Who conquered form. And all your petty crew
> Once, and once only, might have stood with these!
>
>   Alfred Douglas

Douglas printed the sestet from memory in his *Without Apology* (1938).

To Ada Leverson[1]

17 April 1895   *H.M. Prison, Holloway*

I hear that wonderful things are being done for me—by people of noble beautiful souls and natures.

Of course I cannot thank you. Words may not bear such burdens. I cannot even try. I merely say that you will always remain in a niche of a heart—half broken already—as a most dear image of all that in life has love and pity in it.

As for me, the wings of great love encompass me: holy ground.

With deep affection and gratitude. Ever yours   OSCAR

To R. H. Sherard
MS. Clark

20 April 1895   *H.M. Prison, Holloway*

Dear Robert, Many thanks for your letter. Sarah, of course, did not keep her appointment—she never does.[2]

Thank Hugues Rebell[3] *very much* from me. I need not say how deeply touched I am by any kindness from an artist.

Dear old Robert. Ever affectionately yours   OSCAR

To Ada Leverson
MS. Clark

23 April 1895   *H.M. Prison, Holloway*

My dear Sphinx, I have just had a charming note from you, and a charming note from Ernest. How good you both are to me!

Willie has been writing me the most monstrous letters. I have had to beg him to stop.[4]

Today Bosie comes early to see me. My counsel seem to wish the case to be tried at once. I don't, nor does Bosie. Bail, or no bail, I think we had better wait.

[*Later*]

I have seen counsel, and Bosie. I don't know what to do. My life seems to have gone from me. I feel caught in a terrible net. I don't know where to turn. I care less when I think that he is thinking of me. I think of nothing else. Ever yours   OSCAR

---

[1] Text from *Letters to the Sphinx*.

[2] Sherard described in *Oscar Wilde: The Story of an Unhappy Friendship* how Sarah Bernhardt received him graciously, wept at the thought of Wilde's plight, and said she could not buy *Salome* but would lend Wilde some money. She made a series of appointments with Sherard, but kept none of them, and sent Wilde nothing.

[3] Pseudonym of Georges Grassal, French novelist (1868-1905). His French translation of *Intentions* was published in 1906.

[4] W. B. Yeats reports Wilde's saying: "My poor brother writes to me that he is defending me all over London; my poor, dear brother, he could compromise a steam-engine."

To Lord Alfred Douglas[1]

Monday Evening [29 April 1895]   *H.M. Prison, Holloway*

My dearest boy, This is to assure you of my immortal, my eternal love for you. Tomorrow all will be over. If prison and dishonour be my destiny, think that my love for you and this idea, this still more divine belief, that you love me in return will sustain me in my unhappiness and will make me capable, I hope, of bearing my grief most patiently. Since the hope, nay rather the certainty, of meeting you again in some world is the goal and the encouragement of my present life, ah! I must continue to live in this world because of that.

Dear ———[2] came to see me today. I gave him several messages for you. He told me one thing that reassured me: that my mother should never want for anything. I have always provided for her subsistence, and the thought that she might have to suffer privations was making me unhappy. As for you (graceful boy with a Christ-like heart), as for you, I beg you, as soon as you have done all that you can, leave for Italy and regain your calm, and write those lovely poems which you do with such a strange grace. Do not expose yourself to England for any reason whatsoever. If one day, at Corfu or in some enchanted isle, there were a little house where we could live together, oh! life would be sweeter than it has ever been. Your love has broad wings and is strong, your love comes to me through my prison bars and comforts me, your love is the light of all my hours. Those who know not what love is will write, I know, if fate is against us, that I have had a bad influence upon your life. If they do that, you shall write, you shall say in your turn, that it is not so. Our love was always beautiful and noble, and if I have been the butt of a terrible tragedy, it is because the nature of that love has not been understood. In your letter this morning you say something which gives me courage. I must remember it. You write that it is my duty to you and to myself to live in spite of

---

[1] In August 1895, at Sorrento, Douglas wrote an article in passionate defence of Wilde. It was intended for the *Mercure de France*, but when Wilde heard that it included some of his letters to Douglas from Holloway Prison, he told Sherard to prevent its appearance. This he did, and the article was never published (see p. 453 et seq). Douglas wrote it in English and friends put it into French. A manuscript of this translation is at Princeton, with the main text in the hand (I believe) of Henry D. Davray. There are extensive corrections in a second hand (probably some editor of the *Mercure de France*), and the translations of the three Wilde letters are in a third. All three hands are clearly those of Frenchmen or people accustomed to writing in French. Stuart Mason somehow saw this document and translated it back into English (TS. Clark). I have based my text of this letter, and of the ones on pp. 396 and 397, on Mason's version, but have not hesitated to alter words and phrases, following the French, into what seems more like Wilde's language, and I have followed the versions of several sentences given by Douglas in his *Autobiography* (1929). All this may well have slightly distorted Wilde's words, but their substance need not be doubted. Douglas says that he later destroyed 150 of Wilde's letters to him, including those from Holloway.

In the article Douglas records that on the envelope of this letter Wilde wrote: "To be sent after the jury's verdict," and that it was not in fact despatched until after the second jury's verdict on 25 May.   [2] Name omitted by Douglas.

everything. I think that is true. I shall try and I shall do it. I want you to keep Mr Humphreys informed of your movements so that when he comes he can tell me what you are doing. I believe solicitors are allowed to see the prisoners fairly often. Thus I could communicate with you.

I am so happy that you have gone away![1] I know what that must have cost you. It would have been agony for me to think that you were in England when your name was mentioned in court. I hope you have copies of all my books. All mine have been sold.[2] I stretch out my hands towards you. Oh! may I live to touch your hair and your hands. I think that your love will watch over my life. If I should die, I want you to live a gentle peaceful existence somewhere, with flowers, pictures, books, and lots of work. Try to let me hear from you soon. I am writing you this letter in the midst of great suffering; this long day in court has exhausted me. Dearest boy, sweetest of all young men, most loved and most lovable. Oh! wait for me! wait for me! I am now, as ever since the day we met, yours devoutly and with an immortal love   OSCAR

To Ada Leverson

MS. Clark

3 May 1895   *H.M. Prison, Holloway*

Dear and wonderful Sphinx, If I do not get bail today[3] will you send me some books ? I would like some Stevensons—*The Master of Ballantrae* and *Kidnapped*. Now that he[4] is away I have no one who brings me books, so I come to you, for you and Ernest are so good to me that I am glad to think that I never can repay you. Life is not long enough to allow of it. Always, always, I shall be in your debt.

Your letter cheered me very much. I do hope to see you soon. I have had no letter as yet today from Fleur-de-Lys.[5] I wait with strange hunger for it.

My warmest thanks to Ernest. Always yours in gratitude and affection
                                                                              OSCAR

---

[1] Douglas had left the country on 25 April, the eve of Wilde's first trial. He went unwillingly but at the urgent request of Wilde's lawyers. He stopped in Calais, Rouen and Paris.

[2] The contents of 16 Tite Street, including all Wilde's books and papers, had been forcibly sold on 24 April, at the insistence of his creditors.

[3] The jury at Wilde's first trial had disagreed on 1 May, and on 3 May a judge in Chambers (Baron Pollock) agreed to Wilde's being released on bail. Lord Douglas of Hawick and the Rev. Stewart Headlam (see note p. 556) stood surety.

[4] Lord Alfred Douglas.

[5] Fleur-de-Lys and Jonquil (see next letter) were two of Wilde's nicknames for Lord Alfred Douglas, who had written a ballad, called "Jonquil and Fleur-de-Lys," about a king's son and a shepherd boy who changed clothes. It was published in his *Poems* (1896).

To Ada Leverson

MS. Clark

[*4 or 5 May 1895*]   [*H.M. Prison, Holloway*]

My dear Sphinx, Ernest's Shakespeare has arrived safe, and I hear your books are below. I hope I shall be allowed to have them, as Sunday is such a long day here.

I had two letters from Jonquil today—to make up—and I saw Frank Harris. He was very pleasant and I think will be able to help in the way of the press. I have just written to Calais to say how sweet you and Ernest are to me. I believe I come out on Tuesday next. I must see you, of course. Ever with great affection yours   OSCAR

To Ada Leverson

MS. Clark

6 May 1895   *H.M. Prison, Holloway*

My dear Sphinx, I have not had a line today from Fleur-de-Lys. I suppose he is at Rouen. I am so wretched when I don't hear from him, and today I am bored, and sick to the death of imprisonment.

I am reading your books, but I want to be out, and with people I love. The days seem endless.

Your kindness and Ernest's make things better for me. I go on trespassing on it more and more. Oh! I hope all will come well, and that I can go back to Art and Life. Here I sicken in inanition. Ever with great affection yours   OSCAR

Letter from Bosie, at Rouen, just arrived. Please wire my thanks to him. He has cured me of sorrow today.

Telegram: To Ada Leverson

MS. Harvard

8 May 1895[1]   *Sloane Square*

Am staying at 146 Oakley Street for a few days. Can I call this evening?
                                                                       OSCAR

To Ada Leverson

MS. Clark

[*Early May 1895*]   [*146 Oakley Street, Chelsea*]

My dear Sphinx, Thank you again and again, but I fear I can make no

---

[1] When Wilde was released from Holloway on bail on 7 May, he could find no hotel willing to accept him, and was forced to take refuge with his mother in Oakley Street.

definite promise about tomorrow, as I am not well today.[1] I have nervous prostration, so perhaps I had better do nothing till my Sunday evening with you. To that I look forward, I need hardly say, with all deep feeling towards you and Ernest. I heard today from Rouen.[2]

No more at present, as I am ill. Your affectionate and devoted friend

OSCAR

To Ada Leverson

MS. Clark

[? *Early May 1895*]   [? *146 Oakley Street*]

My dear Sweet Kind Friend, I have no words to thank you for all you do for me, but for you and Ernest Bosie and I have deepest love.

I hope to be in better spirits tonight. Your sweetness last night was wonderful. Your flowers are like him—your sending them like yourself. Dear, dear Friend, tonight I see you at 7.45. Ah! you are good and gentle and wonderful. Always devotedly yours   OSCAR

To Lord Alfred Douglas[3]

[*May 1895*]   [? *2 Courtfield Gardens*]

As for you, you have given me the beauty of life in the past, and in the

---

[1] After Wilde had been a few days at Oakley Street, the Leversons took him into their home at 2 Courtfield Gardens, and he stayed with them until his second trial opened on 20 May and through it till his conviction on 25 May. Stewart Headlam recorded that, during the second trial, "each morning I met Mr Wilde and went with him to the court, and in the evening took him back."

[2] One of the only three letters from Douglas to Wilde which have been recovered (MS. Clark) reads as follows:

Wednesday, 15 May 1895   Hôtel des Deux Mondes
                                                22 Avenue de l'Opéra, Paris

My darling Oscar, Have just arrived here. It seems too dreadful to be here without you, but I hope you will join me next week. Dieppe was too awful for anything; it is the most depressing place in the world, even Petits Chevaux was not to be had, as the Casino was closed. They are very nice here, and I can stay as long as I like without paying my bill, which is a good thing as I am quite penniless. The proprietor is very nice and *most* sympathetic; he asked after you at once and expressed his regret and indignation at the treatment you had received. I shall have to send this by a cab to the Gare du Nord to catch the post as I want you to get it first post tomorrow.

I am going to see if I can find Robert Sherard tomorrow if he is in Paris.

Charlie is with me and sends you his best love. I had a long letter from More this morning about you. Do keep up your spirits, my dearest darling. I continue to think of you day and night, and send you all my love.

I am always your own loving and devoted boy   BOSIE

"I had with me young Charlie Hickey (a charming boy about a couple of years younger than myself and well known to Oscar, a son of Colonel Hickey)" (Lord Alfred Douglas, *Autobiography*, 1929).

[3] For the provenance of the text of this incomplete letter, see note, p. 393.

future if there is any future. That is why I shall be eternally grateful to you for having always inspired me with adoration and love. Those days of pleasure were our dawn. Now, in anguish and pain, in grief and humiliation, I feel that my love for you, your love for me, are the two signs of my life, the divine sentiments which make all bitterness bearable. Never has anyone in my life been dearer than you, never has any love been greater, more sacred, more beautiful . . .

Dear boy, among pleasures or in prison, you and the thought of you were everything to me. Oh! keep me always in your heart; you are never absent from mine. I think of you much more than of myself, and if, sometimes, the thought of horrible and infamous suffering comes to torture me, the simple thought of you is enough to strengthen me and heal my wounds. Let destiny, Nemesis, or the unjust gods alone receive the blame for everything that has happened.

Every great love has its tragedy, and now ours has too, but to have known and loved you with such profound devotion, to have had you for a part of my life, the only part I now consider beautiful, is enough for me. My passion is at a loss for words, but you can understand me, you alone. Our souls were made for one another, and by knowing yours through love, mine has transcended many evils, understood perfection, and entered into the divine essence of things.

Pain, if it comes, cannot last for ever; surely one day you and I will meet again, and though my face be a mask of grief and my body worn out by solitude, you and you alone will recognize the soul which is more beautiful for having met yours, the soul of the artist who found his ideal in you, of the lover of beauty to whom you appeared as a being flawless and perfect. Now I think of you as a golden-haired boy with Christ's own heart in you. I know now how much greater love is than everything else. You have taught me the divine secret of the world.

To Lord Alfred Douglas[1]

[20 May 1895]   *[? 2 Courtfield Gardens]*

My child, Today it was asked to have the verdicts rendered separately. Taylor is probably being judged at this moment, so that I have been able to come back here. My sweet rose, my delicate flower, my lily of lilies, it is perhaps in prison that I am going to test the power of love. I am going to see if I cannot make the bitter waters sweet by the intensity of the love I bear you. I have had moments when I thought it would be wiser to separate. Ah! moments of weakness and madness! Now I see that that would have mutilated my life, ruined my art, broken the musical chords which make a perfect soul. Even covered with mud I shall praise you, from the deepest abysses I shall cry to you. In my solitude you will be with me. I am determined not to revolt but to accept every outrage through devotion to love, to let my body be dishonoured so long as my soul

[1] For the provenance of the text of this letter, see note, p. 393.

may always keep the image of you. From your silken hair to your delicate feet you are perfection to me. Pleasure hides love from us but pain reveals it in its essence. O dearest of created things, if someone wounded by silence and solitude comes to you, dishonoured, a laughing-stock to men, oh! you can close his wounds by touching them and restore his soul which unhappiness had for a moment smothered. Nothing will be difficult for you then, and remember, it is that hope which makes me live, and that hope alone. What wisdom is to the philosopher, what God is to his saint, you are to me. To keep you in my soul, such is the goal of this pain which men call life. O my love, you whom I cherish above all things, white narcissus in an unmown field, think of the burden which falls to you, a burden which love alone can make light. But be not saddened by that, rather be happy to have filled with an immortal love the soul of a man who now weeps in hell, and yet carries heaven in his heart. I love you, I love you, my heart is a rose which your love has brought to bloom, my life is a desert fanned by the delicious breeze of your breath, and whose cool springs are your eyes; the imprint of your little feet makes valleys of shade for me, the odour of your hair is like myrrh, and wherever you go you exhale the perfumes of the cassia tree.

Love me always, love me always. You have been the supreme, the perfect love of my life; there can be no other.

I decided that it was nobler and more beautiful to stay. We could not have been together. I did not want to be called a coward or a deserter. A false name, a disguise, a hunted life, all that is not for me, to whom you have been revealed on that high hill where beautiful things are transfigured.

O sweetest of all boys, most loved of all loves, my soul clings to your soul, my life is your life, and in all the worlds of pain and pleasure you are my ideal of admiration and joy.   OSCAR

To Robert Ross
MS. Clark

10 March 1896   [*H.M. Prison, Reading*][1]

My dear Robbie, I want you to have a letter written at once to Mr Hargrove, the solicitor,[2] stating that as my wife has promised to settle one third on me in the case of her predeceasing me I do not wish any opposition to

[1] Wilde had been moved from Pentonville to Wandsworth on 4 July 1895, and from there to Reading on 20 November. To begin with he was allowed to write only one letter every three months, and the first ones were certainly to his wife and his lawyers (see Appendix C, p. 871). On 29 August 1895 Lady Wilde wrote to Ernest Leverson (text from Maggs's catalogue 608, 1935):

Accept my grateful thanks for your kind attention in bringing me news of dear Oscar, as I am myself very poorly and unable to see friends or to leave my room . . . I thought that Oscar might perhaps write to me after the three months, but I have not had a line from him, and I have not written to him as I dread my letters being returned.

[2] Messrs Hargrove & Co were the solicitors of Constance Wilde's family, the Lloyds.

be made to her purchasing my life-interest.[1] I feel that I have brought such unhappiness on her and such ruin on my children that I have no right to go against her wishes in anything. She was gentle and good to me here, when she came to see me.[2] I have full trust in her. Please have this done *at once*, and thank my friends for their kindness. I feel I am acting rightly in leaving this to my wife.

Please write to Stuart Merrill in Paris, or Robert Sherard, to say how gratified I was at the performance of my play: and have my thanks conveyed to Lugné-Poe;[3] it is something that at a time of disgrace and shame I should be still regarded as an artist. I wish I could feel more pleasure: but I seem dead to all emotions except those of anguish and despair. However, please let Lugné-Poe know that I am sensible of the honour he has done me. He is a poet himself. I fear you will find it difficult to read this, but as I am not allowed writing materials I seem to have forgotten how to write: you must excuse me.

Thank More for exerting himself for books: unluckily I suffer from headaches when I read my Greek and Roman poets, so they have not been of much use, but his kindness was great in getting them sent.[4] Ask him to express also my gratitude to the lady who lives at Wimbledon.[5] Write to me please in answer to this, and tell me about literature—what new books etc: also about Jones's play and Forbes-Robertson's management:[6] about any new tendency in the stage of Paris or London. Also, try and see what

---

[1] In his marriage-settlement (see note p. 415).

[2] Lady Wilde had died on 3 February 1896, and Constance travelled specially from Genoa to Reading to break the news to him. Her visit was on 19 February. It was their last meeting. "I went to Reading on Wednesday and saw poor O," she wrote to her brother. "They say he is quite well, but he is an absolute wreck compared with what he was."

[3] Aurélien-Marie Lugné-Poe (1869–1940), the French actor-manager, had produced Wilde's *Salome* at the Théâtre de L'Œuvre in Paris (which he had founded in 1893) on 11 February 1896, with himself as Herod and Lina Munte as Salome. This was the play's first production. Stuart Merrill was the manager of the theatre.

[4] By courtesy of the Home Office I have been able to examine the lists of books sent to Wilde in prison. First, through the kindness of R. B. Haldane (see note 3, p. 706), fifteen volumes were sent to Wandsworth in July 1895: the *Confessions* and *De Civitate Dei* (2 vols) of St Augustine, Pascal's *Pensées* and *Provincial Letters*, Pater's *Renaissance*, Mommsen's *History of Rome* (5 vols), and Newman's *Grammar of Assent*, *Apologia*, *Two Essays on Miracles* and *The Idea of a University*. In September 1895 Pater's *Greek Studies*, *Appreciations* and *Imaginary Portraits* were added, and in January 1896 More Adey arranged with the Home Office to send Dante's *Divina Commedia*, Liddell and Scott's Greek Lexicon, Lewis and Short's Latin Dictionary, and the *Corpus Poetarum Latinorum*, followed on 3 February by *Poetae Scenici Graeci*, an Italian dictionary and an Italian grammar.

[5] Adela Schuster. See note 2, p. 234. While Wilde was out on bail she gave him £1000 for his personal use. Wilde handed the money to Ernest Leverson to hold as trustee, and was later much upset by its use. See pp. 526–527 and 551–552.

[6] *Michael and his Lost Angel* by Henry Arthur Jones had been produced at the Lyceum on 15 January 1896 by Johnston Forbes-Robertson (who had just gone into management for the first time), with himself and Marion Terry in the leading parts. The play ran for only ten days.

Lemaître, Bauër, and Sarcey said of *Salome* and give me a little résumé:[1] please write to Henri Bauër and say I am touched at his writing nicely. Robert knows him. It was sweet of you to come and see me:[2] you must come again next time. Here I have the horror of death with the still greater horror of living: and in silence and misery [*Some lines cut out by prison officials*][3] but I won't talk more of this. I always remember you with deep affection. Ever your friend   O. W.

I wish Ernest would get from Oakley Street my portmanteau, fur coat, clothes, and the books of *my own writing* I gave my dear mother. Ask Ernest in whose name the burial-ground of my mother was taken. Goodbye.

To Robert Ross

MS. Clark

Saturday, [*? 23 or 30 May 1896*][4]   [*? H.M. Prison, Reading*]

Dear Robbie, I could not collect my thoughts yesterday, as I did not expect you till today. When you are good enough to come and see me will you always fix the day? Anything sudden upsets me.

You said that Douglas was going to dedicate a volume of poems to me. Will you write at once to him and say he must not do anything of the kind. I could not accept or allow such a dedication. The proposal is revolting and grotesque.[5] Also, he has unfortunately in his possession a number of letters of mine. I wish him to at once hand all these without exception over to you; I will ask you to seal them up. In case I die here you will destroy them. In case I survive I will destroy them myself. They must not be in existence. The thought that they are in his hands is horrible to me, and though my unfortunate children will never of course bear my name, still they know whose sons they are and I must try and shield them from the possibility of any further revolting disclosure or scandal.

Also, Douglas has some things I gave him: books and jewellery. I wish these to be also handed over to you—for me. Some of the jewellery I know has passed out of his possession under circumstances unnecessary to detail, but he has still some, such as the gold cigarette-case, pearl chain and enamelled locket I gave him last Christmas. I wish to be certain that he

[1] Jules François Elie Lemaître (1854–1914), Henri Bauër (see p. 342) and Francisque Sarcey (1827–99) were three of the leading French dramatic critics. Bauër had reviewed the production of *Salome* favourably in the *Echo de Paris*.

[2] Ross and Leverson had visited Wilde on 25 February 1896.

[3] See pp. 413 and 418.

[4] This letter is difficult to date. The reference to "last Christmas" suggests 1895, but Wilde later placed the dedication incident in May 1896 (see p. 458) and it seems best to follow him. His ignorance of Irving's movements and Stevenson's letters is easily understood. Sherard says that he and Ross visited Wilde on 25 May, but if the Saturday is correct, their visit must have been on the 22nd or the 29th.

[5] When Douglas's *Poems* was published by the *Mercure de France* at the end of 1896 it contained no dedication.

has in his possession nothing that I ever gave him. All these are to be sealed up and left with you. The idea that he is wearing or in possession of anything I gave him is peculiarly repugnant to me. I cannot of course get rid of the revolting memories of the two years I was unlucky enough to have him with me, or of the mode by which he thrust me into the abyss of ruin and disgrace to gratify his hatred of his father and other ignoble passions. But I will not have him in possession of my letters or gifts. Even if I get out of this loathsome place I know that there is nothing before me but a life of a pariah—of disgrace and penury and contempt—but at least I will have nothing to do with him nor allow him to come near me.

So will you write at once to him and get these things: until I know they are in your possession I will be more miserable than usual. It is I know an ungracious thing to ask you to do, and he will perhaps write to you in terms of coarse abuse, as he did to Sherard when he was prevented publishing more of my letters, but I earnestly beg of you not to mind. *As soon* as you have received them please write to me, and make part of your letter just like your other, with all its interesting news of literature and the stage. Let me know why Irving leaves Lyceum etc, what he is playing[1]: what at each theatre: who did Stevenson criticise severely in his letters:[2] anything that will for an hour take my thoughts away from the one revolting subject of my imprisonment.

In writing to Douglas you had better quote my letter fully and frankly, so that he should have no loophole of escape. Indeed he cannot possibly refuse. He has ruined my life—that should content him.

I am deeply touched by the Lady of Wimbledon's kindness. You are very good to come and see me. Kind regards to More, whom I would so like to see.   O. W.

[*Ten words omitted*][3] The Sphinx has some letters of D's to me: they should be returned to him at once, or destroyed.   O. W.

To the Home Secretary[4]
MS. H.O.

2 July 1896   *H.M. Prison, Reading*

To the Right Honourable Her Majesty's Principal Secretary of State for the Home Department.

The Petition of the above-named prisoner humbly sheweth that he does not desire to attempt to palliate in any way the terrible offences of which

---

[1] Irving, whose knighthood had been announced on the day of Wilde's conviction, had ended his Lyceum season on 27 July 1895 and then toured America for ten months. He reappeared at the Lyceum in *Cymbeline* on 22 September 1896.

[2] Robert Louis Stevenson had died in Samoa on 3 December 1894, and his *Vailima Letters*, edited by their recipient Sidney Colvin, had been published on 2 November 1895.

[3] A piece of unimportant gossip which might give pain to descendants.

[4] This petition and those on pp. 406, 411 and 528 are here printed for the first time, having recently been made available by the Home Office. They are all written

he was rightly found guilty, but to point out that such offences are forms of sexual madness and are recognised as such not merely by modern pathological science but by much modern legislation, notably in France, Austria, and Italy, where the laws affecting these misdemeanours have been repealed, on the ground that they are diseases to be cured by a physician, rather than crimes to be punished by a judge. In the works of eminent men of science such as Lombroso and Nordau,[1] to take merely two instances out of many, this is specially insisted on with reference to the intimate connection between madness and the literary and artistic temperament, Professor Nordau in his book on "Degenerescence" published in 1894 having devoted an entire chapter to the petitioner as a specially typical example of this fatal law.

The petitioner is now keenly conscious of the fact that while the three years preceding his arrest were from the intellectual point of view the most brilliant years of his life (four plays from his pen having been produced on the stage with immense success, and played not merely in England, America, and Australia, but in almost every European capital, and many books that excited much interest at home and abroad having been published), still that during the entire time he was suffering from the most horrible form of erotomania, which made him forget his wife and children, his high social position in London and Paris, his European distinction as an artist, the honour of his name and family, his very humanity itself, and left him the helpless prey of the most revolting passions, and of a gang of people who for their own profit ministered to them, and then drove him to his hideous ruin.

It is under the ceaseless apprehension lest this insanity, that displayed itself in monstrous sexual perversion before, may now extend to the entire nature and intellect, that the petitioner writes this appeal which he earnestly entreats may be at once considered. Horrible as all actual madness is, the terror of madness is no less appalling, and no less ruinous to the soul.

For more than thirteen dreadful months now, the petitioner has been subject to the fearful system of solitary cellular confinement: without human intercourse of any kind; without writing materials whose use might

---

on official forms, on which the opening words as far as "sheweth" are printed. The Home Secretary was Sir Matthew White Ridley, Bart (1842–1904). He was created Viscount 1900. If this appeal seems a little desperate and exaggerated, the reader should remember that Wilde had already been in prison for more than a year, a shattering experience for one of his temperament and circumstances, and had begun to suffer from the painful ear-disease which was to kill him four years later.

[1] Cesare Lombroso (1836–1909) was an Italian criminologist, several of whose books had been translated into English. Max Simon Nordau (1849–1923) was a German author and sociologist. *Degeneration* (1895) was the English translation of the second edition of his book *Entartung* (1893). In Chapter 3 ("Decadents and Aesthetes") of Book Three ("Ego-Mania") Wilde was unfavourably discussed in these contexts, but his trials quickly rendered such judgments obsolete, and in the third German edition of the book (1896) Nordau added a long, up-to-date footnote. Bernard Shaw's attack on the book, which was headed A DEGENERATE'S VIEW OF NORDAU, filled almost a whole issue of the American Anarchist paper *Liberty* on 27 July 1895, and was reprinted with revisions as *The Sanity of Art* (1908).

help to distract the mind: without suitable or sufficient books, so essential to any literary man, so vital for the preservation of mental balance: condemned to absolute silence: cut off from all knowledge of the external world and the movements of life: leading an existence composed of bitter degradations and terrible hardships, hideous in its recurring monotony of dreary task and sickening privation: the despair and misery of this lonely and wretched life having been intensified beyond words by the death of his mother, Lady Wilde, to whom he was deeply attached, as well as by the contemplation of the ruin he has brought on his young wife and his two children.

By special permission the petitioner is allowed two books a week to read: but the prison library is extremely small and poor: it hardly contains a score of books suitable for an educated man: the books kindly added at the prisoner's request he has read and re-read till they have become almost meaningless to him: he is practically left without anything to read: the world of ideas, as the actual world, is closed to him: he is deprived of everything that could soothe, distract, or heal a wounded and shaken mind: and horrible as all the physical privations of modern prison life are, they are as nothing compared to the entire privation of literature to one to whom Literature was once the first thing of life, the mode by which perfection could be realised, by which, and by which alone, the intellect could feel itself alive.

It is but natural that living in this silence, this solitude, this isolation from all human and humane influences, this tomb for those who are not yet dead, the petitioner should, day and night in every waking hour, be tortured by the fear of absolute and entire insanity. He is conscious that his mind, shut out artificially from all rational and intellectual interests, does nothing, and can do nothing, but brood on those forms of sexual perversity, those loathsome modes of erotomania, that have brought him from high place and noble distinction to the convict's cell and the common gaol. It is inevitable that it should do so. The mind is forced to think, and when it is deprived of the conditions necessary for healthy intellectual activity, such as books, writing materials, companionship, contact with the living world, and the like, it becomes, in the case of those who are suffering from sensual monomanias, the sure prey of morbid passions, and obscene fancies, and thoughts that defile, desecrate and destroy. Crimes may be forgotten or forgiven, but vices live on: they make their dwelling house in him who by horrible mischance or fate has become their victim: they are embedded in his flesh: they spread over him like a leprosy: they feed on him like a strange disease: at the end they become an essential part of the man: no remorse however poignant can drive them out: no tears however bitter can wash them away: and prison life, by its horrible isolation from all that could save a wretched soul, hands the victim over, like one bound hand and foot, to be possessed and polluted by the thoughts he most loathes and so cannot escape from.

For more than a year the petitioner's mind has borne this. It can bear it no longer. He is quite conscious of the approach of an insanity that will not be confined to one portion of the nature merely, but will extend over all alike, and his desire, his prayer is that his sentence may be remitted now, so that he may be taken abroad by his friends and may put himself under medical care so that the sexual insanity from which he suffers may be cured. He knows only too well that his career as a dramatist and writer is ended, and his name blotted from the scroll of English Literature never to be replaced: that his children cannot bear that name again, and that an obscure life in some remote country is in store for him: he knows that, bankruptcy having come upon him, poverty of a most bitter kind awaits him, and that all the joy and beauty of existence is taken from him for ever: but at least in all his hopelessness he still clings to the hope that he will not have to pass directly from the common gaol to the common lunatic asylum.

Dreadful as are the results of the prison system—a system so terrible that it hardens their hearts whose hearts it does not break, and brutalises those who have to carry it out no less than those who have to submit to it —yet at least amongst its aims is not the desire to wreck the human reason. Though it may not seek to make men better, yet it does not desire to drive them mad, and so, earnestly does the petitioner beg that he may be allowed to go forth while he has still some sanity left: while words have still a meaning, and books a message: while there is still some possibility that, by medical science and humane treatment, balance may be restored to a shaken mind and health given back to a nature that once knew purity: while there is still time to rid the temperament of a revolting madness and to make the soul, even for a brief space, clean.

Most earnestly indeed does the petitioner beg the Home Secretary to take, if he so desires it, the opinion of any recognised medical authorities on what would be the inevitable result of solitary confinement in silence and isolation on one already suffering from sexual monomania of a terrible character.

The petitioner would also point out that while his bodily health is better in many respects here than it was at Wandsworth, where he was for two months in the hospital for absolute physical and mental collapse caused by hunger and insomnia, he has, since he has been in prison, almost entirely lost the hearing of his right ear through an abscess that has caused a perforation of the drum. The medical officer here has stated that he is unable to offer any assistance, and that the hearing must go entirely. The petitioner, however, feels sure that under the care of a specialist abroad his hearing might be preserved to him. He was assured by Sir William Dalby,[1] the great aurist, that with proper care there was no reason at all why he should lose his hearing. But though the abscess has been running now for the entire time of his imprisonment, and the hearing getting worse every week, nothing has been done in the way even of an attempted cure. The ear has been syringed on three occasions with plain water for the purpose of examination, that is all. The petitioner is naturally apprehensive lest, as often happens, the other ear may be attacked in a similar way, and to the

[1] William Bartlett Dalby (1840–1918). Knighted 1886.

misery of a shattered and debilitated mind be added the horrors of complete deafness.

His eyesight, of which like most men of letters he had always been obliged to take great care, has also suffered very much from the enforced living in a whitewashed cell with a flaring gas-jet at night: he is conscious of great weakness and pain in the nerves of the eyes, and objects even at a short distance become blurred. The bright daylight, when taking exercise in the prison-yard, often causes pain and distress to the optic nerve, and during the past four months the consciousness of failing eyesight has been a source of terrible anxiety, and should his imprisonment be continued, blindness and deafness may in all human probability be added to the certainty of increasing insanity and the wreck of the reason.

There are other apprehensions of danger that the limitation of space does not allow the petitioner to enter on: his chief danger is that of madness, his chief terror that of madness, and his prayer that his long imprisonment may be considered with its attendant ruin a sufficient punishment, that the imprisonment may be ended now, and not uselessly or vindictively prolonged till insanity has claimed soul as well as body as its prey, and brought it to the same degradation and the same shame.   OSCAR WILDE[1]

[1] This petition was forwarded to the Home Office by the Governor of Reading Prison, Major Isaacson, together with a short medical report from the prison doctor, saying that Wilde had put on weight in prison and showed no signs of insanity. Four Prison Visitors were sent to Reading to carry out an enquiry, and on 10 July they reported in much the same terms as the prison doctor. The Home Office then referred the papers to Dr Nicholson, the medical officer at Broadmoor who had examined Wilde at Wandsworth. As a result of Dr Nicholson's recommendations the Home Office on 27 July ordered the Governor to allow Wilde to have writing materials in his cell and a larger supply of books. A list of his requests, written in his own hand, is in the Home Office files. The titles in angled brackets were struck out by the new Governor, who wrote at the bottom "Erased by me. 29.7.96. J. O. Nelson." The list reads:

A Greek Testament
Milman's *History of the Jews* ⟨and *Latin Christianity*⟩
⟨Stanley's *Jewish Church*⟩
Farrar's *St Paul*
Tennyson's Poems (complete in one volume)
Percy's *Reliques* (the collection of old ballads)
Christopher Marlowe's Works
⟨Buckle's *History of Civilization*⟩
Carlyle's *Sartor Resartus* and Life of *Frederick the Great*
⟨Froude's *Short Studies on Great Subjects*⟩
A Prose translation of Dante's *Divine Comedy*
Keats's Poems
Chaucer's Poems
Spenser's Poems
⟨Letters of R. Louis Stevenson (edited by Sidney Colvin)⟩
⟨Walter Pater's posthumous volume of essays⟩
Renan's *Vie de Jésus* and *Les Apôtres* (The chaplain sees no objection to these if they are in the original French) ["In French" wrote Nelson in the margin]
⟨[E. B.] Tylor's *Primitive Culture* [1871]⟩
Ranke's *History of the Popes*
Critical and Historical Essays by Cardinal Newman   [*Footnote continues overleaf.*

To The Home Secretary
MS. H.O.

4 July 1896   *H.M. Prison, Reading*

To the Right Honourable Her Majesty's Principal Secretary of State for the Home Department.

The Petition of the above-named prisoner humbly sheweth[1] that the petitioner has been informed by the Governor of the Prison that Mr More Adey is anxious to see him on behalf of Mrs Oscar Wilde with reference to coming to some agreement with regard to the guardianship, education, and future of their children, and also with regard to financial arrangements connected with their marriage-settlements, which in consequence of the petitioner's bankruptcy require serious consideration.

The petitioner is naturally anxious to meet his wife's wishes, whatever they may be, in every possible way. But while perfectly ready to see Mr Adey on her behalf would earnestly beg that the interview be in the Solicitors' Room and for the space of one hour, and not in the cage for half-an-hour and in presence of a warder.

It would be impossible to discuss delicate and private matters from behind a cage and with a warder present. Mr Adey has no doubt written instructions of some kind from Mrs Wilde, who is now in Germany, which the petitioner should see or be made acquainted with. The petitioner has full confidence in Mr Adey and would gladly avail himself of his advice. In a matter so important as the guardianship and education of his children an hour is but barely sufficient time even for scant consideration. There are also difficult financial matters that require settlement. The petitioner has also to settle the question of his having access to his children, and other still more domestic questions. Hurried interviews from behind a cage in a warder's presence are necessarily of a painful and distressing character: the petitioner is anxious that he should be able to have this important business interview, so vital for his wife and children, under conditions that allow of judgment, reflection, and, if possible, wise and rational decision.   OSCAR WILDE[2]

⟨*En Route* [by J. K. Huysmans]. Translation from the French by C. Kegan Paul. I would of course prefer it in the French if it would be allowed. If not I would like to read it in the translation. It is a book on modern Christianity.⟩
⟨Lecky's *History of Rationalism*⟩
Emerson's Essays (if possible in one volume).
⟨Cheap Edition of Dickens's Works. The Library here contains no example of any of Thackeray's or Dickens's novels. I feel sure that a complete set of their works would be as great a boon to many amongst the other prisoners as it certainly would be to myself.⟩ ["Cheap Edition of Dickens's Works", wrote Nelson in the margin]

The amended list was approved by the Home Office, with the proviso that the total net cost of the books must not exceed £10, which was the prison's allotment for 1896–97.   [1] As before, the words up to here are printed.
[2] On 6 July the Home Office ruled that the interview might take place in the Solicitors' Room, its length being left to the Governor's discretion.

To R. H. Sherard

MS. Hyde (H. M.)

Wednesday [26 August 1896][1]　　　　　　　　　　[*H.M. Prison, Reading*]

My dear Robert, The Governor has told me that you have written to ask to see me. It is most kind and affectionate of you, but an order has already been sent to More Adey and Arthur Clifton (whom I have not seen yet) and, as you know, I am only allowed two visitors. I did not think there would have been any chance of your being in town. I hope you are well and writing a great deal. I often think of you and of our uninterrupted friendship, of twelve years' standing, and while I bitterly regret the sorrow that I have brought on you and others of my friends, I remember with pride and gratitude your chivalry and courage on my behalf. Should the end of my terrible punishment ever come, you are one of the few people I would like to see, and be with from time to time.

Please remember me very kindly to George Ives. I was greatly touched at hearing of his desire to come and see me. In the terrible solitude and silence in which one lives a message or a memory means a great deal. I hope he is hard at work writing books. I am very glad you know him. He is such a good fellow and so clever.

Should you have anything special to communicate to me—something separate from the sympathy and affection you have, I know, for me—More Adey, who is to write to me in the course of the next fortnight, will communicate it in his letter. He has to write to me on business.

I was so disappointed at not seeing you that I have been allowed as a favour to write this letter to you. Pray remember me to any of my friends who may ask after me, and believe me, dear Robert, sincerely yours

OSCAR

To More Adey

MS. Clark

Friday [25 September 1896]
[Postmark 28 September 1896]　　　　　　　　[*H.M. Prison, Reading*]

My dear More, I was greatly delighted to get your letter.[2] I was afraid that

---

[1] So dated by prison official.

[2] Part of a draft of Adey's letter of 23 September (MS. Clark) runs:

Robbie is still at the sea, with his brother and mother, who has taken a house there for him. She sends you kind messages saying she often thinks of you and prays for your welfare. Robbie is going on well, the doctors say, but he suffers a great deal from dyspepsia which affects his spirits very much. You know how much he thinks of and feels for you. He looks very ill still. He had his hair cut very short while he was at his worst and, owing to his continued weakness, it has not yet grown again and is very thin. This makes him look different. He has had a photograph taken which I hope to have an opportunity of showing you before long. He amuses himself by reading Dickens and has become quite enthusiastic over *Barnaby Rudge* and *Our Mutual Friend*, etc. They just serve to amuse him without tiring his head.

Miss Schuster says "Could not Mr Wilde now write down some of the lovely

Bobbie might have been ill, and that that was the cause of the delay. It was a real pleasure to hear from him at such length, and to see his old wit and pleasant satire running through his budget: I do hope he will be quite well soon. Please thank his mother for her kind messages. I am very glad she has been spared to watch over Bobbie in his illness.

I thank you very much for writing to the Home Secretary.[1] I do hope it will have some effect. But pity seems to beat in vain at the doors of officialism; and power, no less than punishment, kills what else were good and gentle in a man: the man without knowing it loses his natural kindli-

---

tales he used to tell me? Remind him of one about a nursing-sister who killed the man whom she was nursing. And there was one about the two souls on the banks of the Nile. Were there time I could mention others, but I think the mere reminder of some of his tales may set his mind in that direction and stir the impulse to write. He told me also a beautiful play (just two years ago) that he has not written, about a husband, a wife and her lover, with a plot rather in the style of *Frou-frou*." [see note p. 361]

Perhaps you could jot down the plots of some of those splendid stories you told us from time to time; Robbie knows more than I do, but I remember the Moving Sphere story [see note 1, p. 732], and the one about the Problem and the Lunatic. To make a little résumé from memory of what you have already invented might put you in the vein for fresh invention.

Poor Miss Schuster has to leave her beautiful house. She cannot manage to keep it on now that her mother is dead. She is expecting Lady Brooke [the Ranee of Sarawak] to stay with her in October. Lady Brooke has been with your wife during the last nine months. I will try to see her, or if that is impossible, will learn from Miss Schuster all about your children, and will then try to obtain permission to visit you to tell you all about them. I should ask for permission towards the middle or end of October.

Acting on advice I have just written to the Home Secretary, undertaking, if you are released before May, to accompany you abroad at once, and promising that you will remain there until after the end of May. I hope I did right.

I have also written to your wife saying you are better, as I gave her a very bad account of you after I saw you in July. I think it would be well if you obtained leave to write to her; if you were inclined to consent to her appointing a guardian of whom you approved for your children in case of her death it would be well to tell her so, but I think a letter to her in any case would be a good thing.

If you should hear of anything that I have done on your behalf without your knowledge of which you do not approve, I trust you will repudiate it in as strong terms as you please. If you should have changed your mind about the clothes, let me know when you write, otherwise I will order you a travelling suit from your tailors Doré. I think on the whole my suggestion was the better one, but it really does not matter if you prefer my getting them at Doré's. I shall not go abroad until I am quite certain I cannot be of any use to you here. I hope you do not think I have any feeling against Sherard. I am on perfectly friendly terms with all your friends and get on particularly well with Sherard. I merely object to his frightful indiscretion, which is a positive mania with him and, contrary to his affectionate intentions, does you harm.

[1] Adey's petition to the Home Secretary (which is believed to have been drafted by Bernard Shaw) urging a remission of Wilde's sentence, though printed and ready, was never sent, since almost immediately Adey received a letter from the Home Office saying that "the case of this prisoner has been the subject of careful inquiry and consideration" and that therefore the Home Secretary "has come to the conclusion that no grounds, medical or other, exist which would justify him in advising any mitigation of the sentence." See also note 3, p. 789.

ness, or grows afraid of its exercise. Still, I hope something may be done. I admit that I look forward with horror to the prospect of another winter in prison: there is something terrible in it: one has to get up long before daybreak and in the dark cold cell begin one's work by the flaring gas-jet; through the small barred window only gloom seems to find an entrance: and days often go over without one's being once even in the open air: days on which one stifles: days that are endless in their dull monotony of apathy or despair. If I could be released before the winter comes, it would be everything. On November 19th I will have had eighteen months of this black loathsome life: perhaps then something may be done. I know you will do your best: I have no words for my sense of your great wonderful kindness to me.

With regard to my children, I feel that for their own sake as well as for mine they should not be bred up to look on me with either hatred or contempt: a guardian amongst my wife's relations would be for this reason impossible. Of course I would like Arthur Clifton if he would undertake the charge. And so, would you ask Arthur to be my solicitor now: Humphreys is of course of no use: though paid an enormous fee through Leverson he never once came to see me about my Bankruptcy: so I was allowed to become insolvent when there was no reason.[1] If Arthur will be my solicitor he can on application to the Home Secretary come and see me in the Solicitors' Room here for one hour without the presence of a warder, and with him I could discuss the whole affair, and then write to my wife on the whole subject. I would feel quite safe if Arthur was my children's guardian. And as a solicitor his advice would be of great service. If he could come within the next fortnight it would be a great thing.[2]

[1] Wilde had been taken from prison for his public examination in the Bankruptcy Court on 24 September 1895. The examination was adjourned until 12 November, when he was again brought up. The *Labour Leader* of 16 November reported: "They have cut his hair in a shocking way and parted it down the side and he wears a short, scrubby, unkempt beard."

[2] On 8 October 1896 Arthur Clifton wrote to Carlos Blacker (MS. Blacker):

I was very much shocked at Oscar's appearance, though scarcely surprised. Fortunately he had his ordinary clothes on: his hair was rather long and he looked dreadfully thin. You can imagine how painful it was to meet him: and he was very much upset and cried a good deal: he seemed quite broken-hearted and kept on describing his punishment as savage. Of course I talked as much as possible about the future, about the friendship of his friends, about his plays and everything I could think of to cheer him up. He was very eager for news and I told him as much as possible of what had happened lately and really I suppose I did most of the talking.

As to business matters, he did not express any decided opinion, but thought he ought to be left something out of the settlement if possible, and I told him what I thought would be a good plan—namely that he should retain about a third of his life-interest: and I told him I would do my best to see that that was arranged.

As I told you, Mrs Wilde, whom I saw immediately after, quite agreed, so there ought to be little difficulty.

He has been reading Pater and Newman lately, one book a week. I do not know what work he does.

He was terribly despondent and said several times that he did not think he would be able to last the punishment out. [*Footnote continues overleaf.*

I was greatly touched by the extract from the letter of the Lady of Wimbledon. That she should keep a gracious memory of me, and have trust or hope for me in the future, lightens for me many dreadful hours of degradation or despair. I have tried to remember and write down the *Florentine Tragedy*: but only bits of it remain with me, and I find that I cannot invent: the silence, the utter solitude, the isolation from all humane and humanising influences, kill one's brain-power: the brain loses its life: becomes fettered to monotony of suffering. But I take notes of books I read, and copy lines and phrases in poets: the mere handling of pen and ink helps me: the horror of prison is the horror of complete brutalisation: that is the abyss always in front of one, branding itself on one's face daily, and the faces of those one sees. I cling to my notebook: it helps me: before I had it my brain was going in very evil circles.

I am so glad you are friends with Robert Sherard: I have no doubt he is very indiscreet, but he is very true, and saved my letters from being published. I know there was nothing in them but expressions of foolish, misplaced, ill-requited, affection for one of crude and callous nature, of coarse greed, and common appetites, but that is why their publication would have been so shameful. The gibbet on which I swing in history now is high enough. There is no need that he of all men should for his own vanity make it more hideous.

I am so glad Pierre Louÿs has made a great name for himself.[1] He was most cultivated, refined, and gentle. Three years ago he told me I would have to choose between his friendship and my fatal connection with A.D. I need hardly say I chose at once the meaner nature and the baser mind. In what a mire of madness I walked! . . .[2] From your silence I see he still refuses to return my presents and letters . . . It is horrible he should still have the power to wound me and find some curious joy in doing so . . . I won't write about him any more today. He is too evil, and there is a storm outside. . . .

Poor Aubrey: I hope he will get all right.[3] He brought a strangely new personality to English art, and was a master in his way of fantastic grace, and the charm of the unreal. His muse had moods of terrible laughter. Behind his grotesques there seemed to lurk some curious philosophy . . .

As for my clothes, my fur coat is all I need really; the rest I can get

---

I was very fortunate in being allowed to see him, as his trustee, about his bankruptcy. He was in the care of two warders who were in the room all the time but I was able to sit quite close to him and talk quietly: a very different arrangement to any visits allowed at the prison. The Prison Commissioners refused my application to see him about six weeks ago and gave me leave to write to him: however they returned my letter at once as not being about business.

I wish I could give you a better account of what he said but really the conversation was very desultory and he wanted news much more than he wanted to talk.

[1] Louÿs's book *Aphrodite* (1896) was a phenomenal success in France.
[2] All the dots in this letter are Wilde's.
[3] Aubrey Beardsley had already begun to suffer from consumption.

abroad. Don't bother yourself. I hope Arthur will come and bring me good news of you and Robbie. Ever yours   OSCAR

To the Home Secretary
MS. H.O.

10 November 1896   *H.M. Prison, Reading*

To the Right Honourable Her Majesty's Principal Secretary of State for the Home Department.

The Petition of the above-named prisoner humbly sheweth[1] that in the month of June last the petitioner, having been at that time a prisoner for more than a year, addressed to the Secretary of State a petition praying for his release on the grounds chiefly of mental health.

That the petitioner has received no answer to his petition, and would earnestly beg that it be taken into consideration, as on the 19th inst the petitioner will have completed eighteen months of solitary confinement, a sentence of terrible severity in any case, and, in the case of the petitioner, rendered all the more difficult to bear, as it has been inflicted for offences which are in other countries of Europe more rightly recognised as tragic forms of madness coming chiefly on those who overtax their brain, in art or science.

Some alleviations have been granted to the petitioner since the date of his former petition: his ear, that was in danger of total deafness, is now attended to daily: spectacles have been provided for the protection of his eyes: he is allowed a manuscript-book to write in, and out of a list of books, selected by himself and approved of by the Prison Commissioners, a few have been added to the Prison Library: but these alleviations, for which the petitioner is naturally very grateful, count for but little in relieving the terrible mental stress and anguish that the silence and solitude of prison-life intensify daily.

Of all modes of insanity—and the petitioner is fully conscious now, too conscious it may be, that his whole life, for the two years preceding his ruin, was the prey of absolute madness—the insanity of perverted sensual instinct is the one most dominant in its action on the brain. It taints the intellectual as well as the emotional energies. It clings like a malaria to soul and body alike. And while one may bear up against the monotonous hardships and relentless discipline of an English prison: endure with apathy the unceasing shame and the daily degradation: and grow callous even to that hideous grotesqueness of life that robs sorrow of all its dignity, and takes from pain its power of purification; still, the complete isolation from everything that is humane and humanising plunges one deeper and deeper into the very mire of madness, and the horrible silence, to which one is, as it were, eternally condemned, concentrates the mind on all that one longs to loathe, and creates those insane moods from which one desires to be free, creates them and makes them permanent.

[1] As before, the words up to here are printed.

411

Under these circumstances the petitioner prays for his release on the expiration of his term of eighteen months' confinement, or at any rate before Christmas comes. Some friends have promised to take him abroad at once, and to see that he has the treatment and care that he requires. There is of course before him no public life: nor any life in literature any more: nor joy or happiness of life at all. He has lost wife, children, fame, honour, position, wealth: poverty is all that he can look forward to: obscurity all that he can hope for: yet he feels that, if released now, some-where, unknown, untormented, at peace, he might be able to recreate the life of a student of letters, and find in literature an anodyne from pain, first, and afterwards a mode by which sanity and balance and wholesomeness might be restored to the soul. But the solitary confinement, that breaks one's heart, shatters one's intellect too: and prison is but an ill physician: and the modern modes of punishment create what they should cure, and, when they have on their side Time with its long length of dreary days, they desecrate and destroy whatever good, or desire even of good, there may be in a man.

To be at length, after these eighteen months of lonely sorrow and despair, set free, for whatever brief space of time health of mind or body may allow, is the earnest prayer of the petitioner.　　　　　　OSCAR WILDE[1]

To Robert Ross[2]
MS. Clark

[November 1896]　　　　　　　　　　　　　[H.M. Prison, Reading]
France by Lina Munte. Could nothing be done, in improving the company and getting fees? I would be quite ready to give for the time the complete acting rights of Salome to Lugné-Poe. I think Robert Sherard might help with advice. Or Stuart Merrill.

(6) I brought out Salome at my own expense with the Librairie de l'Art Indépendant. So it is mine. I have had no accounts from them of any kind. I wonder would not a new edition be advisable as it is being played? This might be arranged for, and some fees or money got. Sherard or Merrill will do it I am sure.

(7) To these purely business matters perhaps More Adey will kindly reply. His letter dealing purely with business I will be allowed to receive. It will not, I mean, interfere with your literary letter, with regard to which the Governor has just now read me your kind message.

For myself, dear Robbie, I have little to say that can please you. The refusal to commute my sentence has been like a blow from a leaden sword. I am dazed with a dull sense of pain. I had fed on hope, and now Anguish,

---

[1] This petition, like its predecessor, was forwarded to the Home Office with a medical report. It was rejected almost immediately.

[2] Attached to this letter is a note in Ross's hand: "The front sheet of this letter which dealt with business matters was forwarded to Hansell [see note 2, p. 537] or Humphreys and was not returned to me."

grown hungry, feeds her fill on *me* as though she had been starved of her proper appetite. There are, however, kinder elements in this evil prison air than there were before: sympathies have been shown to me, and I no longer feel entirely isolated from humane influences, which was before a source of terror and trouble to me. And I read Dante, and make excerpts and notes for the pleasure of using a pen and ink. And it seems as if I were better in many ways. And I am going to take up the study of German: indeed this seems to be the proper place for such a study. There is a thorn, however—as bitter as that of St Paul, though different—that I must pluck out of my flesh in this letter. It is caused by a message you wrote on a piece of paper for me to see. I feel that if I kept it secret it might grow in my mind (as poisonous things grow in the dark) and take its place with other terrible thoughts that gnaw me. . . .[1] Thought, to those that sit alone and silent and in bonds, being no "winged living thing," as Plato feigned it,[2] but a thing dead, breeding what is horrible, like a slime that shows monsters to the moon.

I mean, of course, what you said about the sympathies of others being estranged from me, or in danger of being so, by the deep bitterness of the feelings I expressed about Alfred Douglas: and I believe that my letter was lent and shown to others with the part about him cut out by a pair of scissors.[3] Now I don't like my letters shown about as curiosities: it is most distasteful to me: I write to you freely as to one of the dearest friends I have, or have ever had: and, with a few exceptions, the sympathy of others touches me, as far as its loss goes, very little. No man of my position can fall into the mire of life without getting a great deal of pity from his inferiors; and I know that when plays last too long, spectators tire. *My* tragedy has lasted far too long: its climax is over: its end is mean; and I am quite conscious of the fact that when the end *does* come I shall return an unwelcome visitant to a world that does not want me; a *revenant*, as the French say, as one whose face is grey with long imprisonment and crooked with pain. Horrible as are the dead when they rise from their tombs, the living who come out from tombs are more horrible still.

Of all this I am only too conscious. When one has been for eighteen terrible months in a prison cell, one sees things and people as they really are. The sight turns one to stone. Do not think that I would blame *him* for my vices. He had as little to do with them as I had with his. Nature was in this matter a stepmother to each of us. I blame him for not appreciating the man he ruined. An illiterate millionaire would really have suited him better. As long as my table was red with wine and roses, what did he care? My genius, my life as an artist, my work, and the quiet I needed for it, were nothing to him when matched with his unrestrained and coarse appetites for common profligate life: his greed for money: his incessant and violent scenes: his unimaginative selfishness. Time after time I tried, during those two wasted weary years, to escape, but he always brought me back, by threats of harm to himself chiefly. Then when his

[1] All the dots in this letter are Wilde's.
[2] *Phaedrus*, 246 A–249 B.   [3] See pp. 400 and 418.

413

father saw in me a method of annoying his son, and the son saw in me the chance of ruining his father, and I was placed between two people greedy for unsavoury notoriety, reckless of everything but their own horrible hatred of each other, each urging me on, the one by public cards and threats, the other by private, or indeed half-public scenes, threats in letters, taunts, sneers . . . I admit I lost my head. I let him do what he wanted. I was bewildered, incapable of judgment. I made the one fatal step. And now . . . I sit here on a bench in a prison cell. In all tragedies there is a grotesque element. He is the grotesque element in mine. Do not think I do not blame myself. I curse myself night and day for my folly in allowing him to dominate my life. If there was an echo in these walls it would cry "Fool" for ever. I am utterly ashamed of my friendship with him. For by their friendships men can be judged. It is a test of every man. And I feel more poignant abasement of shame for my friendship with Alfred Douglas . . . fifty thousand times more . . . than I do, say, for my connection with Charley Parker[1] of which you may read a full account in my trial. The former is to me a daily source of mental humiliation. Of the latter I never think. It troubles me not. It is of no importance . . . Indeed my entire tragedy sometimes seems to me grotesque and nothing else. For as a result of my having suffered myself to be thrust into the trap Queensberry had laid for me—the trap he openly betted in the Orleans Club he would lure me into—as a result of that, the father ranks in history with the good parents of moral tales: the son with the Infant Samuel: and I, in the lowest mire of Malebolge,[2] sit between Gilles de Retz and the Marquis de Sade.[3] In certain places no one, except those actually insane, is allowed to laugh: and, indeed, even in their case it is against the regulations for conduct: otherwise I think I would laugh at that . . . For the rest, do not let Alfred Douglas suppose that I am crediting him with unworthy motives. He really had no motives in his life at all. Motives are intellectual things. He had passions merely. And such passions are False Gods that *will* have victims at all costs, and in the present case have had one wreathed with bay. He himself cannot but choose to feel *some* remorse. That he should really realise what he has done would be a burden too heavy for him to bear. But he must sometimes think of it. So in your letter tell me how he lives, what his occupations are, his mode of life.

And so now I have in my letter plucked the thorn out. That little scrawled line of yours rankled terribly. I *now* think merely of you getting quite well again, and writing at last the wonderful story of the little restaurant with the strange dish of meat served to the silent clients. Pray remember me, with my thanks, to your dear mother, and also to Aleck.[4]

[1] One of the young men who gave evidence at Wilde's trials.

[2] The eighth circle of Dante's *Inferno*.

[3] Gilles de Laval, Sire de Retz or Raiz (1404–40), the comrade-in-arms of Joan of Arc and a Marshal of France, turned to debauchery, devil-worship and child-murder, for which he was finally executed. The Marquis de Sade (1740–1814), author of *Justine* (1791) and other novels of cruelty which gave rise to the words Sadism and Sadistic, was sentenced to death for various offences but escaped the scaffold and died in a lunatic asylum.   [4] Ross's brother (see note 2, p. 229).

More Adey

This photograph was taken by Vyvyan Holland at Wotton-
under-Edge in 1920, but Adey is said to have looked much
the same in the 1890's

Frank Harris
by William Rothenstein

The gilded Sphinx is I suppose wonderful as ever. And send from me all that in my thoughts and feelings is good, and whatever of remembrance and reverence she will accept, to the Lady of Wimbledon, whose soul is a sanctuary for those who are wounded, and a house of refuge for those in pain. Do not show this letter to others, nor discuss what I have written, in your answer. Tell me about that world of shadows I loved so much. And about his life and soul tell me also. I am curious of the thing that stung me: and in my pain there is pity.   OSCAR

To More Adey

MS. Clark

Wednesday Evening, 16 December [1896]   [*H.M. Prison, Reading*]

My dear More, I have received a letter from Mr Hargrove informing me that the Official Receiver has determined to sell half of my interest to my friends, and that under these circumstances, unless your offer is at once withdrawn, my wife's offer contained in the letters handed to Arthur Clifton will be withdrawn too.[1]

I feel that I had better trust myself entirely to your judgment, and I am now of opinion that your course was a wise one. I know you and others have carefully considered the whole case, and my wife's proposal that in case of my surviving her I was to have £150 a year was, I think, a cruel and heartless one, and as inconsiderate of the children's interest as of my existence.

What Hargrove's next move will be I do not know. If my wife leaves me absolutely without a penny I can only trust that for a year at any rate I will be looked after, and I may be able to write again. Business matters, such as the present, of course upset me, and make me weak in mind and body, with the hysteria of shattered nerves, sleeplessness, and the anguish in which I walk; but Art is different. *There* one makes one's own world. It is with shadows that one weeps and laughs. A mirror will give back to one one's own sorrow. But Art is not a mirror, but a crystal. It creates its own shapes and forms.

(2) It would be a great thing for me to see you (or Arthur Clifton) some-time next month, and at intervals, on my affairs. I hope permission will be granted. I suggested, on the last occasion, *Arthur*, as through his being a *solicitor* I felt it gave some chance of the interview being *private*. You remember how abortive and painful and useless was my interview with you, with the Prison Officer seated between us to note the subject and character of our conversation; I could not discuss anything with you to any purpose, and finally cut short the interview. I was unable to go through with it. I would sooner see *you*, as you are more thoroughly acquainted with all the various difficulties in my way. Were the matter in the hands of the

---

[1] Constance Wilde's advisers were anxious for her to buy Wilde's half-share of their marriage settlement from the Official Receiver. Despite Wilde's requests that this should be allowed to happen (see pp. 398–99), his friends had offered the Receiver £50 for Wilde's share.

Governor I would have no fear of the result. *But the matter is entirely one for the Commissioners.* In case they prove obdurate, would your solicitor, Mr Holman,[1] act for me, if Mr Hargrove tries to force legal proceedings? Nothing would induce me to see Humphreys. His advice would, I think, be worthless. This, for your consideration. His fees to be managed through Leverson.

(3) With regard to the books, there has been a little misunderstanding. The list was sent to you that you should add whatever *new* books *you* could think of, such as Stevenson's memoirs etc: books published since my imprisonment. To save time and trouble, it was considered more politic to have no further delay. So *my* list will have to suffice. And, indeed, will be a very great boon to me—of incalculable service—even Ollendorff priceless:[2] I find that to study a language one had forgotten is a good mental tonic: the mere mechanical side having its value. Of the kindness of my good friend Arthur[3] Humphreys, the publisher, I cannot trust myself to write. It is a very dear remembrance on his part of a pleasant literary friendship. Give him my warmest thanks. When I read Walter Pater I shall have two friends to think of.[4] The books, however, remain behind. They are sentenced to perpetual imprisonment. But they may soothe and heal other troubled minds and breaking hearts. Those not on Humphreys's really lavish list, pray provide. Perhaps in February a few *new* books may be got. But these are, now, more than most welcome. I wait them eagerly.[5]

[1] Martin Holman of the firm of Parker, Garrett & Holman.

[2] Heinrich Gottfried Ollendorff (died 1865) produced a "new method of learning to read, write and speak a language in six months," adapted to the French, the German, the Italian and the English. These works, which achieved immense popularity, appeared between 1840 and 1860.

[3] Wilde accidentally wrote "Charles," with his now-despised solicitor in mind.

[4] Humphreys (see note p. 364) had sent Wilde a present of books.

[5] This list in the Home Office files, which was submitted by the Prison Governor on 3 December 1896 and approved on 10 December (after Adey had assumed responsibility for providing the books), is not in Wilde's or Adey's hand. It reads:

Gaston de Latour by Walter Pater, M.A. (Macmillan)
Milman's *History of Latin Christianity*
Wordsworth's Complete Works in one volume with preface by John Morley (Macmillan. 7/6)
Matthew Arnold's Poems. One volume complete (Macmillan. 7/6)
Dante and Other Essays by Dean Church (Macmillan. 5/-)
Percy's *Reliques*
Hallam's *Middle Ages* (*History of*)
Dryden's Poems (1 vol. Macmillan. 3/6)
Burns's Poems   ,,   ,,
Morte d'Arthur   ,,   ,,
Froissart's Chronicles   ,,
Buckle's *History of Civilization*
Marlowe's Plays
Chaucer's *Canterbury Tales* (Edited by A. Pollard. 2 vols. 10/-) ⎫
Introduction to Dante by John Addington Symonds   ⎬ Macmillan
Companion to Dante by A. J. Butler   ⎪
Miscellaneous Essays by Walter Pater   ⎪
An English Translation of Goethe's *Faust*   ⎭

(4) I feel that my wife does not realise my mental state, or the suffering, both mental and physical, she is inflicting on me. I wish she could be brought to see that she should let me alone now for the next five months. When I reflect that the only two people who have, since my imprisonment, tried to distress me by terrible letters are my wife and Lord Queensberry, I feel fixed on some shrill pinnacle of horror. Lady Brooke has influence with my wife. Could she be asked from me to suggest to my wife not to trouble me or distress me any more till my release? We were great friends once.

(5) As my affairs are apparently being wound up I am anxious that the French translator of my novel should be considered.[1] I was under the impression that the French copyright was mine. It seems that, *subject to a ten-per-cent royalty*, it is Ward & Lock's. Of course, their having it is absurd. But I am entitled to ten per cent on every copy sold, which of course should go to the translator. Would you see Kernahan, the author, who is one of Ward & Lock's readers, and a friend of mine. The nominal sum of £10 was paid for the French rights to Humphreys: but it is monstrous that Ward & Lock should be making money before the translator is paid. The French are so nice to me, I am horrified at the position of the translator. I propose to refund the £10, through Leverson, and then to have the translator considered. His honorarium should be not less than £50. If I, through Leverson, have half of this paid, would Ward & Lock pay the rest? Also what of my ten per cent?

(6) The French rights of all my plays are mine. The mischief of *Lady Windermere's Fan* has been done. I suppose there is no use bothering.[2]

(7) A matter of great seriousness was alluded to by Arthur Clifton, and written about by Robbie, to me: but in both cases with such delicacy that it is still quite unintelligible to me. I refer to my feelings with regard to Alfred Douglas. I have not mentioned the subject to anyone but Robbie: I am horrified to think that newspapers should busy themselves with it: I don't know what they say, or who writes the things. Eighteen months ago I asked Robert Sherard to stop the publication of any more of my letters: since then, I have said nothing to him on the matter. If *he* writes on me,

---

Educational

Ollendorff's *German Method.* 5/6
Key to the same. 3/6
Wilhelm Tell. Hamiltonian System. 5/-
German-English Dictionary
Faust by Goethe (in the original)
Key to Mariotti's *Italian Grammar.* 1/-
Guide to the Italian Language by A. Biaggi. 5/-
Biaggi's *Prosatori Italiani.* 5/-
Italian-English Dictionary

F. Norgate
44 Shaftesbury Avenue
London, W

[1] In 1895 Albert Savine had published a French translation of *The Picture of Dorian Gray* by Eugène Tardieu (1851-1920). His prose translations of Lord Alfred Douglas's poems appeared opposite their originals in Douglas's first book, *Poems* (1896).

[2] Presumably a reference to the French translation rights, but see later reference to a possible translation on p. 605.

pray beg him *from me* never to mention in conjunction with mine that ill-omened and most unfortunate name, so fatal to me and to my house. Also, I would *like you* to see all my letters to Robbie. I find that I accused him of a mutilation, done here under the old régime, without my knowledge.[1] I am very sorry. I have been unjust to Robbie. In this life we lead, we become ungracious. Tell him all this.

(8) In case of my copyrights being sold I hope the Receiver will let me know what terms are offered. There are some I consider of value still: *Dorian Gray, Lady Windermere, The Importance of Being Earnest,* have still money-making chances. I fear it is only by putting *all* my troubles on to your shoulders that I can show you my gratitude to you and my trust in you. In such a strange plight Fate places one. Ever yours   OSCAR

To More Adey
MS. Clark

18 February 1897   [*H.M. Prison, Reading*]

My dear More, The Governor has kindly allowed me to see your letter, and to answer it at once.

(1) With what pleasure I have read it I need not say. On Saturday the 27th I hope to see you with Robbie and Ernest Leverson. The interview, by special permission, is to be of an hour's duration and in a private room. A warder will be present, but this need not incommode us. The visiting order is for three. We shall then surely be able to discuss all business matters. Business with you, seriousness with Ernest, nonsense with Robbie.

(2) I enclose the authorisation for Lugné-Poe. Pray thank him from me for his kindness. To be represented by so distinguished a poet charms me.

(3) With regard to what I will call the "deposit-fund," that is a sum of money left for my disposal, not for the paying of my debts, but for my own help, and support, and the help of those I love like my mother, there will, I feel sure, be, after what has been expended on my dear mother, a certain sum left, perhaps not small. Out of this I propose to pay in instalments at first my debts of honour, after I have seen that enough is forthcoming to give me at least eighteen months of free life to collect myself. To Charles Wyndham, to take merely one instance out of alas! too many, I owe £300 for literary work never done: my trial of course prevented it. I must pay him half, if possible.[2] But I want to do it myself

---

[1] See pp. 400 and 413.

[2] On 18 February 1895 the actor-manager Charles Wyndham (1837–1919) had written to Henry Arthur Jones (MS. Albery):

You are probably aware that *The Importance of Being Earnest* was mine for production later on. You may remember my asking you once when you were likely to have another piece ready for me, and I had this in view at the time. *Guy Domville* failed so utterly and Alexander was in a "hole." Oscar Wilde came to me and asked whether I would let Alexander have *The Importance of Being Earnest*, which would benefit Alexander and also enable Wilde to realise earlier

when I go out of prison. Also with regard to Miss Napier,[1] the money was advanced to my wife (£50) and I will pay it myself when I go out. I forget if Mrs Napier lent my wife anything. The debt of £50 to my old friend please have paid at once *from me* through Ernest Leverson. I am sure Ernest will see that I must begin by paying half to people and then gradually all. Of this when we meet. It is only a week off. I may say that I would like to wait and see what my wife proposes to do before I come forward as having kind and generous friends. She has no right to take technical advantage of our marriage-settlement to leave me without anything.

(4) I told you I was going to write to Alfred Douglas. I am still at work at the letter.[2] It is the most important letter of my life, as it will deal ultimately with my future mental attitude towards life, with the way in which I desire to meet the world again, with the development of my character: with what I have lost, what I have learned, and what I hope to arrive at. At last I see a real goal towards which my soul can go simply, naturally, and rightly. Before I see you and Robbie I must finish the letter, that you may understand what I have become, or rather desire to become in nature and aim. My whole life depends on it. I will send the letter to Robbie, who must read it carefully and *copy it out carefully* every word, for me. Then you, having read it and seen that it is copied rightly, will send it for me to A. D. I don't know his address. I hope to have it finished by Tuesday.

To dear Frank Harris my kindest regards and thanks. To you always my best of thanks and gratitude OSCAR WILDE

To the Société des Auteurs[3]

19 Février 1897 *H.M. Prison, Reading*

Je prie, étant absent de France et ne pouvant faire enregistrer cette signature pendant tout le temps de mon internement, la Société des

---

than he could with me. I did so, hoping that our piece would run through the season. By one of those odd coincidences, however, from the day that I promised to cede the piece our business fell; of course I kept my word.

In a further, undated, letter, probably of March 1895 (MS. Albery), Wyndham said that he had transferred *The Importance of Being Earnest* to George Alexander "without ever suggesting a premium, which one manager asks another for parting with an acquired property, but also without suggesting a return of the money advanced to the author on signing." It further appears, from a letter from Wyndham to Alexander (quoted in *Sir George Alexander and the St James's Theatre* by A. E. W. Mason, p. 74) that one of the conditions of his surrendering the play was that he should have Wilde's next play. The £300 may therefore have been for this unwritten play, or Wyndham's original payment for *The Importance of Being Earnest*.

[1] Mary Eliza Napier was Constance Wilde's first cousin. After Constance's death she became in some sense a foster-mother to Cyril and Vyvyan.

[2] The long letter commonly known as *De Profundis* and here printed on pp. 423–511.

[3] This was the enclosure referred to in the previous letter. The text is taken from *Acrobaties* (1931), the second volume of Lugné-Poe's memoirs.

Auteurs et Compositeurs, rue Hippolyte-Lebas, à Paris, de veiller à mes intérêts, et charge M. Lugné-Poe d'être mon conseil et de la sauvegarde de mes affaires en France. Ceci, jusqu'à nouvel ordre.   OSCAR WILDE

To More Adey
MS. Clark

8 March 1897   *H.M. Prison, Reading*

My dear More, I am very much obliged to you for your letter, which the Governor has kindly allowed me to have and to answer. My business is I know unpleasant, but then it was not for pleasure that you took its burden on you, so I will write quite frankly to you.

Your news has distressed me a good deal. The claims of my own trustees and my brother-in-law would of course be easily withdrawn, and I thought I could, if the Queensberry debt was paid, as it should have been, by the Queensberry family, have made an effort at any rate to pay off my own personal creditors, who are really very few in number. I see, however, that this cannot be. I will now have to think of how to retain or buy my interest in my books and plays. I do not think they will be valued high. As £150 has been already paid to Humphreys who did nothing to help me (beyond of course forcing me to put in two appearances at the Bankruptcy Court where one would have been sufficient, and engaging their own relative Mr Grain to appear as counsel where no counsel was required) I am reluctant to even write to them.[1] I am very anxious however to know how I can be kept informed of the state of things, so that if my copyrights are to be sold I may have a chance of bidding for them. I am also anxious about my claim to the place in Ireland: it is now in utter rack and ruin, but I am reluctant to see it pass to a stranger: could Mr Holman, already in communication with the Receiver, let you know if anything happens? In the case of my brother's death, without male issue, the Irish property should fetch something: £4000 or £5000 at least.

As regards the Queensberry family, I of course feel very strongly about their allowing me to be made bankrupt by their father for the costs of the trial, and for such an absolutely contemptible sum; less than half, as I told you, of what in three wasted summer months I spent on Bosie at Goring—less than one half! Their idea that it would be a sort of "score" off their father not to pay him his paltry claim showed how utterly blind they were to my feelings. As for Queensberry, I suppose nobody ever had such intense pleasure of a low order at such a low cost as he had. It was in the cheapest of markets that he bought his triumph. Indeed it was the only occasion in his life that he found his pleasures economical. To send a man like myself to prison for £900, and then to take him out and make him an insolvent for £700 more, was a piece of good fortune he

---

[1] John Peter Grain (1839–1916), barrister brother of Corney Grain, the entertainer, was C. O. Humphreys's brother-in-law. He appeared as counsel for Alfred Taylor in both Wilde's trials, and for Wilde in the Bankruptcy Court.

never looked for. As regards my own debts, they were hardly anything. Their letting their father triumph a second time over me, rather than pay so petty, so abject a sum as £700, cut me very deeply. And people who live in the world of action don't understand that there is another world in which they who are not free live: a world in which nothing happens but emotions, and in which consequently emotions have a power, a proportion, a permanence that is beyond the possibility of description.

I was told, on Percy's behalf, that he had laid aside the sum of £600 for me, as the equivalent of his father's costs, to be used I suppose in buying back for me the property the Bankruptcy Receiver had seized, and possibly in other ways. I conveyed to him my thanks. I consider Percy a very good-hearted fellow, kind and considerate. I would very much like to see him again sometime. He should of course have paid the costs, and left me then if necessary to settle my other debts. But he, I have no doubt, acted under advice. If he had realised matters a little more he would have seen that he merely doubled his father's delight and exultation by not interfering to prevent my insolvency. It was the only thing Queensberry was afraid of. He need not have been . . .[1] With regard to the whole question the Queensberry family must remember that through them I am in prison, through them a bankrupt, and that they can hardly allow people whom they ruined so completely to go to the workhouse.

I was touched and helped immeasurably by your telling me that some friends of mine have arranged that for eighteen months I am to have enough to live on: that gives me breathing space. But of course I cannot trespass for a lifetime on those on whom I have no more claim than any other of the poor and wretched and homeless people of whom God's world is so full. I couldn't do it. And I may live longer than eighteen months. A heart may be broken and yet fulfil its natural functions. The soul may sit in the shadow of death, and yet the body walk in the ways of life, and breathe and eat and know the sun and rain. I have no organic disease of any kind. I am troubled with insomnia, but I get my four or five hours of sleep every night. Supposing I live on? I should not be at all surprised if I did. I come of a long-lived race. The Queensberry family had better consider the point, the Douglases we will call them, as the other name is loathsome. There are debts of dishonour in a family as well as debts of honour. If the Douglas estates have to be burdened with a prospective claim of some paltry life-interest, let them be so burdened. A family cannot ruin a man like me, and look on the whole thing merely as a subject for sentiment or reminiscence over the walnuts and the wine. People, as somebody in one of Ibsen's plays says, don't do these things.[2] It is dreadful that it should fall on me to remind them. They should consult their family solicitor, and let him communicate the result to my solicitor. That is all that is necessary.

You say in your letter that Bosie is so anxious to make "some little return" to me for all I "spent on him." Unfortunately, I spent on him my life, my genius, my position, my name in history; for these no little, or big

---

[1] Wilde's dots.

[2] The last line of *Hedda Gabler*, spoken by Judge Brack after Hedda's suicide.

return is possible. But as regards the mere wretched pounds, shillings, and pence side of my ruin—the workhouse aspect—he must seriously consider the whole point. It is his duty to do so. His duty to himself as much, far more indeed, than to me. When people play a tragedy they should play it in the "grand style." All smallness, pettiness, meagreness of mood or gesture is out of place. If the Douglases don't recognise this, let me be informed. But I don't doubt that they will. It is a perfectly obvious matter. And as for me, my life will of course necessarily be one of great retirement, simplicity and economy of living, and many modes of self-denial, imposed and accepted. But a certain small permanence is requisite even for the practice of the virtues of thrift and economy. Bosie must consider the matter. I will be much obliged if you will copy out all that I have written, from the bottom of page one,[1] and send it off to him. It will relieve my own letter to him of a very unpleasing duty, one that a little thought on his part would have spared me.

As regards my children, I sincerely hope I may be recognised by the Court as having some little, I won't say right, but claim to be allowed to see Cyril from time to time: it would be to me a sorrow beyond words if I were not. I do hope the Court will see in me something more than a man with a tragic vice in his life. There is so much more in me, and I always was a good father to both my children. I love them dearly and was dearly loved by them, and Cyril was my friend. And it would be better for them not to be forced to think of me as an outcast, but to know me as a man who has suffered. Pray let everything be done on my behalf that is possible. A little recognition by the Court would help me so much. And it is a terrible responsibility for the Law to say to a father that he is unfit to see his own children: the consciousness of it often makes me unhappy all day long.

As regards my life-interest, should Mr Hargrove make any proposal about it, it of course will be communicated to me by you *at once*. It will require grave consideration. The advances cannot come from me, can they? Should my own solicitor come to see me, pray let it be the last week in this month. I am quite distressed at the idea of his only charging £1. 1 and expenses. I think he should have at least £3. 3. Let the money be got from Leverson, and whatever Mr Stoker[2] is owed be paid to him from the same fund in Leverson's hands.

I fear you see traces of bitterness in my business letters. Yes, that is so. It is very terrible. In the prison in which my body is I am shown much kindness, but in the prison in which my soul is I can show myself none. I hope that neither in your heart nor in Robbie's, nor in the heart of any that have been good to me, will bitterness of any kind ever find a place. It makes one suffer very deeply. Your affectionate friend   OSCAR WILDE

I quite see that I must accept, gratefully indeed, my discharge as a bankrupt, when I get it, and then set to work to try and pay off some of the debts. I suppose it won't be done till I go out of prison? I would like

[1] i.e. from "As regards the Queensberry family" on p. 420.
[2] Presumably a partner in Messrs Stoker & Hansell, solicitors.

things held over, on account of the sale of copyrights etc. At present I receive no communication at all from the Receiver. That is, I suppose, right.

For the list of books, so many thanks. I am going to ask for a Bible in French: *la Sainte Bible*.[1]

[1] The following list of books, from the Home Office files, was submitted by the Prison Governor on 10 March 1897. It is in Adey's hand, except for the last title and the starred note at the bottom, which are in Wilde's. With the exception of the *Nineteenth Century*, which the Governor thought unsuitable, the list was approved on 13 March:

A French Bible
German Grammar
German Conversation Book
French-Italian Conversation Book
Dante: *Vita Nuova*
    „   *Vita Nuova*. English Translation
Goldoni. *Commedie*
Augustin Filon. *L'Art Dramatique en Angleterre* [*Le Théâtre Anglais*, 1896]
Journal des Goncourt. Latest volume
[Francis de] Pressensé. *Vie du Cardinal Manning* [1896]
Huysmans. *En Route** [1895]
Letters of Dante Gabriel Rossetti [1895]
Robert Louis Stevenson. *Vailima Letters* [1895]
George Meredith. *Essay on Comedy* [1897]
    „   „   *Amazing Marriage* [1895]
Thomas Hardy. *The Well-Beloved*. [1897]
Harold Frederic. *Illumination* [1896]
Nineteenth Century for 1896
Robert Louis Stevenson. *Treasure Island*.

* This is the religious novel of which Mr Gladstone wrote in terms of such high commendation.

To Lord Alfred Douglas[2]
MS. B.M.

[*January–March 1897*]   *H.M. Prison, Reading*

Dear Bosie, After long and fruitless waiting I have determined to write to

[2] This long letter was not posted from Reading (see note p. 512), but on the day after Wilde left prison he handed it to Robert Ross (see p. 564), who had two typed copies made. Ross then sent Douglas, not the original manuscript, as Wilde had instructed (see p. 513), but one of the typed copies, which Douglas always denied having received.

In 1905 Ross published extracts, amounting to less than half the letter, under the title *De Profundis*, and a slightly fuller version appeared in the Collected Edition of 1908. Neither of these contained any references to Douglas. In 1909 Ross presented the original manuscript to the British Museum, on condition that no one be allowed to see it for fifty years.

The second typescript, kept by Ross and eventually bequeathed by him to Vyvyan Holland, supplied the text for the "first complete and accurate version" which Mr Holland published, again as *De Profundis*, in 1949. Everyone naturally assumed that typescript and manuscript were identical, and that this edition was

you myself, as much for your sake as for mine, as I would not like to think that I had passed through two long years of imprisonment without ever having received a single line from you, or any news or message even, except such as gave me pain.

Our ill-fated and most lamentable friendship has ended in ruin and public infamy for me, yet the memory of our ancient affection is often with me, and the thought that loathing, bitterness and contempt should for ever take that place in my heart once held by love is very sad to me: and you yourself will, I think, feel in your heart that to write to me as I lie in the loneliness of prison-life is better than to publish my letters without my permission or to dedicate poems to me unasked, though the world will know nothing of whatever words of grief or passion, of remorse or indifference you may choose to send as your answer or your appeal.

I have no doubt that in this letter in which I have to write of your life and of mine, of the past and of the future, of sweet things changed to bitterness and of bitter things that may be turned into joy, there will be much that will wound your vanity to the quick. If it prove so, read the letter over and over again till it kills your vanity. If you find in it something of which you feel that you are unjustly accused, remember that one should be thankful that there is any fault of which one can be unjustly accused. If there be in it one single passage that brings tears to your eyes, weep as we

---

indeed complete and accurate, but in fact it was neither. It contained several hundred errors, which can be divided into four main categories:

1. Misreadings of Wilde's hand.
2. Aural misprints, probably caused by Ross's dictating to an ill-educated typist.
3. Ross's "improvement" of Wilde's grammar and syntax.
4. The inexplicable shifting of passages and whole paragraphs from one part of the letter to another.

In addition, Ross removed in all more than a thousand words, almost all of them fiercely critical of Douglas and his father: the description of Lord Queensberry in court (see p. 492) is a striking example. Now at last this longest and most important of all Wilde's letters is printed exactly as he wrote it, except that I have broken it up into rather more paragraphs than his scanty ration of paper allowed him.

The letter is written on twenty folio sheets (each of four pages) of blue ruled prison paper, with the Royal Arms blind-stamped at the head of each sheet. The sheets are numbered 1 to 18 (including 3A and 5A) in Wilde's hand. On 4 April 1897 the Governor of Reading Gaol, explaining how the letter had been written, wrote to the Prison Commissioners (MS. Home Office): "Each sheet was carefully numbered before being issued and withdrawn each evening at locking and placed before me in the morning with the usual papers." Careful study of the manuscript makes this statement hard to believe, and I suspect that Major Nelson had been much more considerate to Wilde than his official position allowed him to admit to his superiors. My reasons for this belief are:

(a) Sheets 1, 2 and 13 have every appearance of being fair copies. The writing on them is more ordered, neat and compact than anywhere else, and they contain scarcely a correction or second thought, whereas all the other seventeen sheets are heavily corrected.

(b) Only two of the twenty sheets (apart from the last one) finish at the end of a sentence.

(c) In Wilde's covering letter of 1 April 1897 (see p. 513) he quotes from several different sheets at once—"from memory" he says, but his accuracy makes this claim scarcely credible.

weep in prison where the day no less than the night is set apart for tears. It is the only thing that can save you. If you go complaining to your mother, as you did with reference to the scorn of you I displayed in my letter to Robbie,[1] so that she may flatter and soothe you back into self-complacency or conceit, you will be completely lost. If you find one false excuse for yourself, you will soon find a hundred, and be just what you were before. Do you still say, as you said to Robbie in your answer, that I *"attribute unworthy motives"* to you? Ah! you had no motives in life. You had appetites merely. A motive is an intellectual aim. That you were *"very young"* when our friendship began? Your defect was not that you knew so little about life, but that you knew so much. The morning dawn of boyhood with its delicate bloom, its clear pure light, its joy of innocence and expectation you had left far behind. With very swift and running feet you had passed from Romance to Realism. The gutter and the things that live in it had begun to fascinate you. That was the origin of the trouble in which you sought my aid, and I, so unwisely according to the wisdom of this world, out of pity and kindness gave it to you. You must read this letter right through, though each word may become to you as the fire or knife of the surgeon that makes the delicate flesh burn or bleed. Remember that the fool in the eyes of the gods and the fool in the eyes of man are very different. One who is entirely ignorant of the modes of Art in its revolution or the moods of thought in its progress, of the pomp of the Latin line or the richer music of the vowelled Greek, of Tuscan sculpture or Elizabethan song may yet be full of the very sweetest wisdom. The real fool, such as the gods mock or mar, is he who does not know himself. I was such a one too long. You have been such a one too long. Be so no more. Do not be afraid. The supreme vice is shallowness. Everything that is realised is right. Remember also that whatever is misery to you to read, is still greater misery to me to set down. To you the Unseen Powers have been very good. They have permitted you to see the strange and tragic shapes of Life as one sees shadows in a crystal. The head of Medusa that turns living men to stone, you have been allowed to look at in a mirror merely. You yourself have walked free among the flowers. From me the beautiful world of colour and motion has been taken away.

I will begin by telling you that I blame myself terribly. As I sit here in this dark cell in convict clothes, a disgraced and ruined man, I blame myself. In the perturbed and fitful nights of anguish, in the long monotonous days of pain, it is myself I blame. I blame myself for allowing an unintellectual friendship, a friendship whose primary aim was not the creation and contemplation of beautiful things, to entirely dominate my life. From the very first there was too wide a gap between us. You had been idle at your school, worse than idle at your university. You did not realise that an artist, and especially such an artist as I am,[2] one, that is to say, the quality of whose work depends on the intensification of personality, requires for the development of his art the companionship of ideas, and intellectual atmosphere, quiet, peace, and solitude. You admired my work

[1] See pp. 400–401.   [2] Wilde originally wrote "was."

425

when it was finished: you enjoyed the brilliant successes of my first nights, and the brilliant banquets that followed them: you were proud, and quite naturally so, of being the intimate friend of an artist so distinguished: but you could not understand the conditions requisite for the production of artistic work. I am not speaking in phrases of rhetorical exaggeration but in terms of absolute truth to actual fact when I remind you that during the whole time we were together I never wrote one single line. Whether at Torquay, Goring, London, Florence or elsewhere, my life, as long as you were by my side, was entirely sterile and uncreative. And with but few intervals you were, I regret to say, by my side always.

I remember, for instance, in September '93, to select merely one instance out of many, taking a set of chambers, purely in order to work undisturbed, as I had broken my contract with John Hare for whom I had promised to write a play, and who was pressing me on the subject. During the first week you kept away. We had, not unnaturally indeed, differed on the question of the artistic value of your translation of *Salome*, so you contented yourself with sending me foolish letters on the subject. In that week I wrote and completed in every detail, as it was ultimately performed, the first act of *An Ideal Husband*. The second week you returned and my work practically had to be given up. I arrived at St James's Place every morning at 11.30, in order to have the opportunity of thinking and writing without the interruptions inseparable from my own household, quiet and peaceful as that household was. But the attempt was vain. At twelve o'clock you drove up, and stayed smoking cigarettes and chattering till 1.30, when I had to take you out to luncheon at the Café Royal or the Berkeley. Luncheon with its *liqueurs* lasted usually till 3.30. For an hour you retired to White's. At tea-time you appeared again, and stayed till it was time to dress for dinner. You dined with me either at the Savoy or at Tite Street. We did not separate as a rule till after midnight, as supper at Willis's had to wind up the entrancing day. That was my life for those three months, every single day, except during the four days when you went abroad. I then, of course, had to go over to Calais to fetch you back. For one of my nature and temperament it was a position at once grotesque and tragic.

You surely must realise that now? You must see now that your incapacity of being alone: your nature so exigent in its persistent claim on the attention and time of others: your lack of any power of sustained intellectual concentration: the unfortunate accident—for I like to think it was no more—that you had not yet been able to acquire the "Oxford temper" in intellectual matters, never, I mean, been one who could play gracefully with ideas but had arrived at violence of opinion merely—that all these things, combined with the fact that your desires and interests were in Life not in Art, were as destructive to your own progress in culture as they were to my work as an artist? When I compare my friendship with you to my friendship with such still younger men as John Gray and Pierre Louÿs I feel ashamed. My real life, my higher life was with them and such as they.

Of the appalling results of my friendship with you I don't speak at present. I am thinking merely of its quality while it lasted. It was intellectually degrading to me. You had the rudiments of an artistic temperament in its germ. But I met you either too late or too soon, I don't know which. When you were away I was all right. The moment, in the early December of the year to which I have been alluding, I had succeeded in inducing your mother to send you out of England,[1] I collected again the torn and ravelled web of my imagination, got my life back into my own hands, and not merely finished the three remaining acts of *An Ideal Husband*, but conceived and had almost completed two other plays of a completely different type, the *Florentine Tragedy* and *La Sainte Courtisane*, when suddenly, unbidden, unwelcome, and under circumstances fatal to my happiness you returned. The two works left then imperfect I was unable to take up again. The mood that created them I could never recover. You now, having yourself published a volume of verse, will be able to recognise the truth of everything I have said here. Whether you can or not it remains as a hideous truth in the very heart of our friendship. While you were with me you were the absolute ruin of my Art, and in allowing you to stand persistently between Art and myself I give to myself shame and blame in the fullest degree. You couldn't know, you couldn't understand, you couldn't appreciate. I had no right to expect it of you at all. Your interests were merely in your meals and moods. Your desires were simply for amusements, for ordinary or less ordinary pleasures. They were what your temperament needed, or thought it needed for the moment. I should have forbidden you my house and my chambers except when I specially invited you. I blame myself without reserve for my weakness. It was merely weakness. One half-hour with Art was always more to me than a cycle with you. Nothing really at any period of my life was ever of the smallest importance to me compared with Art. But in the case of an artist, weakness is nothing less than a crime, when it is a weakness that paralyses the imagination.

I blame myself again for having allowed you to bring me to utter and discreditable financial ruin. I remember one morning in the early October of '92 sitting in the yellowing woods at Bracknell with your mother. At that time I knew very little of your real nature. I had stayed from a Saturday to Monday with you at Oxford. You had stayed with me at Cromer for ten days and played golf. The conversation turned on you, and your mother began to speak to me about your character. She told me of your two chief faults, your vanity, and your being, as she termed it, "*all wrong about money.*" I have a distinct recollection of how I laughed. I had no idea that the first would bring me to prison, and the second to bankruptcy. I thought vanity a sort of graceful flower for a young man to wear; as for extravagance—for I thought she meant no more than extravagance—the virtues of prudence and thrift were not in my own nature or my own race. But before our friendship was one month older I began to see what your mother really meant. Your insistence on a life of reckless profusion: your

[1] See letter p. 346.

427

incessant demands for money: your claim that all your pleasures should be paid for by me whether I was with you or not: brought me after some time into serious monetary difficulties, and what made the extravagances to me at any rate so monotonously uninteresting, as your persistent grasp on my life grew stronger and stronger, was that the money was really spent on little more than the pleasures of eating, drinking, and the like. Now and then it is a joy to have one's table red with wine and roses, but you outstripped all taste and temperance. You demanded without grace and received without thanks. You grew to think that you had a sort of right to live at my expense and in a profuse luxury to which you had never been accustomed, and which for that reason made your appetites all the more keen, and at the end if you lost money gambling in some Algiers Casino you simply telegraphed next morning to me in London to lodge the amount of your losses to your account at your bank, and gave the matter no further thought of any kind.

When I tell you that between the autumn of 1892 and the date of my imprisonment I spent with you and on you more than £5000 in actual money, irrespective of the bills I incurred, you will have some idea of the sort of life on which you insisted. Do you think I exaggerate? My ordinary expenses with you for an ordinary day in London—for luncheon, dinner, supper, amusements, hansoms and the rest of it—ranged from £12 to £20, and the week's expenses were naturally in proportion and ranged from £80 to £130. For our three months at Goring my expenses (rent of course included) were £1340. Step by step with the Bankruptcy Receiver I had to go over every item of my life. It was horrible. *"Plain living and high thinking"*[1] was, of course, an ideal you could not at that time have appreciated, but such extravagance was a disgrace to both of us. One of the most delightful dinners I remember ever having had is one Robbie and I had together in a little Soho café, which cost about as many shillings as my dinners to you used to cost pounds. Out of my dinner with Robbie came the first and best of all my dialogues.[2] Idea, title, treatment, mode, everything was struck out at a 3 franc 50 c. *table-d'hôte*. Out of the reckless dinners with you nothing remains but the memory that too much was eaten and too much was drunk. And my yielding to your demands was bad for you. You know that now. It made you grasping often: at times not a little unscrupulous: ungracious always. There was on far too many occasions too little joy or privilege in being your host. You forgot—I will not say the formal courtesy of thanks, for formal courtesies will strain a close friendship—but simply the grace of sweet companionship, the charm of pleasant conversation, that τερπνὸν κακόν as the Greeks called it, and all those gentle humanities that make life lovely, and are an accompaniment to life as music might be, keeping things in tune and filling with melody the harsh or silent places. And though it may seem strange to you that one in the terrible position in which I am situated should find a difference between one disgrace and another, still I frankly admit that the folly of

---

[1] Wordsworth, "Sonnet written in London, September 1802."
[2] Almost certainly "The Decay of Lying."

throwing away all this money on you, and letting you squander my fortune to your own hurt as well as to mine, gives to me and in my eyes a note of common profligacy to my Bankruptcy that makes me doubly ashamed of it. I was made for other things.

But most of all I blame myself for the entire ethical degradation I allowed you to bring on me. The basis of character is will-power, and my will-power became absolutely subject to yours. It sounds a grotesque thing to say, but it is none the less true. Those incessant scenes that seemed to be almost physically necessary to you, and in which your mind and body grew distorted and you became a thing as terrible to look at as to listen to: that dreadful mania you inherit from your father, the mania for writing revolting and loathsome letters: your entire lack of any control over your emotions as displayed in your long resentful moods of sullen silence, no less than in the sudden fits of almost epileptic rage: all these things in reference to which one of my letters to you, left by you lying about at the Savoy or some other hotel and so produced in Court by your father's Counsel, contained an entreaty not devoid of pathos, had you at that time been able to recognise pathos either in its elements or its expression:[1]—these, I say, were the origin and causes of my fatal yielding to you in your daily increasing demands. You wore one out. It was the triumph of the smaller over the bigger nature. It was the case of that tyranny of the weak over the strong which somewhere in one of my plays I describe as being "the only tyranny that lasts."[2]

And it was inevitable. In every relation of life with others one has to find some *moyen de vivre*. In your case, one had either to give up to you or to give you up. There was no other alternative. Through deep if misplaced affection for you: through great pity for your defects of temper and temperament: through my own proverbial good-nature and Celtic laziness: through an artistic aversion to coarse scenes and ugly words: through that incapacity to bear resentment of any kind which at that time characterised me: through my dislike of seeing life made bitter and uncomely by what to me, with my eyes really fixed on other things, seemed to be mere trifles too petty for more than a moment's thought or interest—through these reasons, simple as they may sound, I gave up to you always. As a natural result, your claims, your efforts at domination, your exactions grew more and more unreasonable. Your meanest motive, your lowest appetite, your most common passion, became to you laws by which the lives of others were to be guided always, and to which, if necessary, they were to be without scruple sacrificed. Knowing that by making a scene you could always have your way, it was but natural that you should proceed, almost unconsciously I have no doubt, to every excess of vulgar violence. At the end you did not know to what goal you were hurrying, or with what aim in view. Having made your own of my genius, my will-power, and my fortune, you required, in the blindness of an inexhaustible greed, my entire existence. You took it. At the one supremely and tragically critical moment of all my life, just before my lamentable step of

[1] See letter p. 326.   [2] *A Woman of No Importance*, Act III.

429

beginning my absurd action, on the one side there was your father attacking me with hideous cards left at my club, on the other side there was you attacking me with no less loathsome letters. The letter I received from you on the morning of the day I let you take me down to the Police Court to apply for the ridiculous warrant for your father's arrest was one of the worst you ever wrote, and for the most shameful reason. Between you both I lost my head. My judgment forsook me. Terror took its place. I saw no possible escape, I may say frankly, from either of you. Blindly I staggered as an ox into the shambles. I had made a gigantic psychological error. I had always thought that my giving up to you in small things meant nothing: that when a great moment arrived I could reassert my will-power in its natural superiority. It was not so. At the great moment my will-power completely failed me. In life there is really no small or great thing. All things are of equal value and of equal size. My habit—due to indifference chiefly at first—of giving up to you in everything had become insensibly a real part of my nature. Without my knowing it, it had stereotyped my temperament to one permanent and fatal mood. That is why, in the subtle epilogue to the first edition of his essays, Pater says that "Failure is to form habits."[1] When he said it the dull Oxford people thought the phrase a mere wilful inversion of the somewhat wearisome text of Aristotelian *Ethics*, but there is a wonderful, a terrible truth hidden in it. I had allowed you to sap my strength of character, and to me the formation of a habit had proved to be not Failure merely but Ruin. Ethically you had been even still more destructive to me than you had been artistically.

The warrant once granted, your will of course directed everything. At a time when I should have been in London taking wise counsel, and calmly considering the hideous trap in which I had allowed myself to be caught—the booby-trap as your father calls it to the present day—you insisted on my taking you to Monte Carlo, of all revolting places on God's earth, that all day, and all night as well, you might gamble as long as the Casino remained open. As for me—baccarat having no charms for me—I was left alone outside to myself. You refused to discuss even for five minutes the position to which you and your father had brought me. My business was merely to pay your hotel expenses and your losses. The slightest allusion to the ordeal awaiting me was regarded as a bore. A new brand of champagne that was recommended to us had more interest for you.

On our return to London those of my friends who really desired my welfare implored me to retire abroad, and not to face an impossible trial. You imputed mean motives to them for giving such advice, and cowardice to me for listening to it. You forced me to stay to brazen it out, if possible, in the box by absurd and silly perjuries. At the end, I was of course arrested and your father became the hero of the hour: more indeed than

[1] In the "Conclusion" to his *Studies in the History of the Renaissance* (1873). See note p. 46. The "Conclusion" was omitted from the second edition (1877) but restored in the third (1888), where this sentence is altered to "In a sense it might even be said that our failure is to form habits."

the hero of the hour merely: your family now ranks, strangely enough, with the Immortals: for with that grotesqueness of effect that is as it were a Gothic element in history, and makes Clio the least serious of all the Muses, your father will always live among the kind pure-minded parents of Sunday-school literature, your place is with the Infant Samuel, and in the lowest mire of Malebolge I sit between Gilles de Retz and the Marquis de Sade.

Of course I should have got rid of you. I should have shaken you out of my life as a man shakes from his raiment a thing that has stung him. In the most wonderful of all his plays[1] Æschylus tells us of the great Lord who brings up in his house the lion-cub, the λέοντος ἷνιν, and loves it because it comes bright-eyed to his call and fawns on him for its food: φαιδρωπός ποτὶ χεῖρα, σαίνων τε γαστρὸς ἀνάγκαις. And the thing grows up and shows the nature of its race, ἦθος τὸ πρόσθε τοκήων, and destroys the lord and his house and all that he possesses. I feel that I was such a one as he. But my fault was, not that I did not part from you, but that I parted from you far too often. As far as I can make out I ended my friendship with you every three months regularly, and each time that I did so you managed by means of entreaties, telegrams, letters, the interposition of your friends, the interposition of mine, and the like to induce me to allow you back. When at the end of March '93 you left my house at Torquay I had determined never to speak to you again, or to allow you under any circumstances to be with me, so revolting had been the scene you had made the night before your departure. You wrote and telegraphed from Bristol to beg me to forgive you and meet you. Your tutor,[2] who had stayed behind, told me that he thought that at times you were quite irresponsible for what you said and did, and that most, if not all, of the men at Magdalen were of the same opinion. I consented to meet you, and of course I forgave you. On the way up to town you begged me to take you to the Savoy. That was indeed a visit fatal to me.

Three months later, in June, we are at Goring. Some of your Oxford friends come to stay from a Saturday to Monday. The morning of the day they went away you made a scene so dreadful, so distressing that I told you that we must part. I remember quite well, as we stood on the level croquet-ground with the pretty lawn all round us, pointing out to you that we were spoiling each other's lives, that you were absolutely ruining mine and that I evidently was not making you really happy, and that an irrevocable parting, a complete separation was the one wise philosophic thing to do. You went sullenly after luncheon, leaving one of your most offensive letters behind with the butler to be handed to me after your departure. Before three days had elapsed you were telegraphing from London to beg to be forgiven and allowed to return. I had taken the place to please you. I had engaged your own servants at your request. I was always terribly sorry for the hideous temper to which you were really a prey. I was fond of you. So I let you come back and forgave you. Three months later still, in September, new scenes occurred, the occasion

[1] *Agamemnon.* The words quoted occur in lines 717–728.
[2] Campbell Dodgson. See note p. 333.

431

of them being my pointing out the schoolboy faults of your attempted translation of *Salome*.[1] You must by this time be a fair enough French scholar to know that the translation was as unworthy of you, as an ordinary Oxonian, as it was of the work it sought to render. You did not of course know it then, and in one of the violent letters you wrote to me on the point you said that you were under *"no intellectual obligation of any kind"* to me. I remember that when I read that statement, I felt that it was the one really true thing you had written to me in the whole course of our friendship. I saw that a less cultivated nature would really have suited you much better. I am not saying this in bitterness at all, but simply as a fact of companionship. Ultimately the bond of all companionship, whether in marriage or in friendship, is conversation, and conversation must have a common basis, and between two people of widely different culture the only common basis possible is the lowest level. The trivial in thought and action is charming. I had made it the keystone of a very brilliant philosophy expressed in plays and paradoxes. But the froth and folly of our life grew often very wearisome to me: it was only in the mire that we met: and fascinating, terribly fascinating though the one topic round which your talk invariably centred was, still at the end it became quite monotonous to me. I was often bored to death by it, and accepted it as I accepted your passion for going to music-halls, or your mania for absurd extravagances in eating and drinking, or any other of your to me less attractive characteristics, as a thing, that is to say, that one simply had to put up with, a part of the high price one paid for knowing you. When after leaving Goring I went to Dinard for a fortnight you were extremely angry with me for not taking you with me, and, before my departure there, made some very unpleasant scenes on the subject at the Albemarle Hotel, and sent me some equally unpleasant telegrams to a country house I was staying at for a few days. I told you, I remember, that I thought it was your duty to be with your own people for a little, as you had passed the whole season away from them. But in reality, to be perfectly frank with you, I could not under any circumstances have let you be with me. We had been together for nearly twelve weeks. I required rest and freedom from the terrible strain of your companionship. It was necessary for me to be a little by myself. It was intellectually necessary. And so I confess I saw in your letter, from which I have quoted, a very good opportunity for ending the fatal friendship that had sprung up between us, and ending it without bitterness, as I had indeed tried to do on that bright June morning at Goring, three months before. It was however represented to me—I am bound to say candidly by one of my own friends[2] to whom you had gone in your difficulty—that you would be much hurt, perhaps almost humiliated at having your work sent back to you like a schoolboy's exercise; that I was expecting far too much intellectually from you; and that, no matter what you wrote or did, you were absolutely and entirely devoted to me. I did not want to be the first to check or discourage you in your beginnings in literature: I knew quite well that no

[1] See note 3, p. 344.   [2] Wilde originally wrote "Robbie."

432

translation, unless one done by a poet, could render the colour and cadence of my work in any adequate measure: devotion seemed to me, seems to me still, a wonderful thing, not to be lightly thrown away: so I took the translation and you back. Exactly three months later, after a series of scenes culminating in one more than usually revolting, when you came one Monday evening to my rooms accompanied by two of your friends, I found myself actually flying abroad next morning to escape from you, giving my family[1] some absurd reason for my sudden departure, and leaving a false address with my servant for fear you might follow me by the next train. And I remember that afternoon, as I was in the railway-carriage whirling up to Paris, thinking what an impossible, terrible, utterly wrong state my life had got into, when I, a man of world-wide reputation, was actually forced to run away from England, in order to try and get rid of a friendship that was entirely destructive of everything fine in me either from the intellectual or ethical point of view: the person from whom I was flying being no terrible creature sprung from sewer or mire into modern life with whom I had entangled my days, but you yourself, a young man of my own social rank and position, who had been at my own college at Oxford, and was an incessant guest at my house. The usual telegrams of entreaty and remorse followed: I disregarded them. Finally you threatened that unless I consented to meet you, you would under no circumstances consent to proceed to Egypt. I had myself, with your knowledge and concurrence, begged your mother to send you to Egypt away from England, as you were wrecking your life in London. I knew that if you did not go it would be a terrible disappointment to her, and for her sake I did meet you, and under the influence of great emotion, which even you cannot have forgotten, I forgave the past; though I said nothing at all about the future.

On my return to London next day I remember sitting in my room and sadly and seriously trying to make up my mind whether or not you really were what you seemed to me to be, so full of terrible defects, so utterly ruinous both to yourself and to others, so fatal a one to know even or to be with. For a whole week I thought about it, and wondered if after all I was not unjust and mistaken in my estimate of you. At the end of the week a letter from your mother is handed in. It expressed to the full every feeling I myself had about you. In it she spoke of your blind exaggerated vanity which made you despise your home, and treat your elder brother —that *candidissima anima*—"as a Philistine:" of your temper which made her afraid to speak to you about your life, the life she felt, she knew, you were leading: about your conduct in money matters, so distressing to her in more ways than one: of the degeneration and change that had taken place in you. She saw, of course, that heredity had burdened you with a terrible legacy, and frankly admitted it, admitted it with terror: he is "the one of my children who has inherited the fatal Douglas temperament," she wrote of you. At the end she stated that she felt bound to declare that your friendship with me, in her opinion, had so intensified your vanity

[1] Wilde originally wrote "wife."

that it had become the source of all your faults, and earnestly begged me not to meet you abroad. I wrote to her at once, in reply, and told her that I agreed entirely with every word she had said. I added much more. I went as far as I could possibly go. I told her that the origin of our friendship was you in your undergraduate days at Oxford coming to beg me to help you in very serious trouble of a very particular character. I told her that your life had been continually in the same manner troubled. The reason of your going to Belgium you had placed to the fault of your companion in that journey, and your mother had reproached me with having introduced you to him. I replaced the fault on the right shoulders, on yours. I assured her at the end that I had not the smallest intention of meeting you abroad, and begged her to try to keep you there, either as an honorary *attaché*, if that were possible, or to learn modern languages, if it were not; or for any reason she chose, at least during two or three years, and for your sake as well as for mine.

In the meantime you are writing to me by every post from Egypt. I took not the smallest notice of any of your communications. I read them, and tore them up. I had quite settled to have no more to do with you. My mind was made up, and I gladly devoted myself to the Art whose progress I had allowed you to interrupt. At the end of three months, your mother, with that unfortunate weakness of will that characterises her, and that in the tragedy of my life has been an element no less fatal than your father's violence, actually writes to me herself—I have no doubt, of course, at your instigation—tells me that you are extremely anxious to hear from me, and in order that I should have no excuse for not communicating with you, sends me your address in Athens, which, of course, I knew perfectly well. I confess I was absolutely astounded at her letter. I could not understand how, after what she had written to me in December, and what I in answer had written to her, she could in any way try to repair or to renew my unfortunate friendship with you. I acknowledged her letter, of course, and again urged her to try and get you connected with some Embassy abroad,[1] so as to prevent your returning to England, but I did not write to you, or take any more notice of your telegrams than I did before your mother had written to me. Finally you actually telegraphed to my wife begging her to use her influence with me to get me to write to you. Our friendship had always been a source of distress to her: not merely because she had never liked you personally, but because she saw how your continual companionship altered me, and not for the better: still, just as she had always been most gracious and hospitable to you, so she could not bear the idea of my being in any way unkind—for so it seemed to her—to any of my friends. She thought, knew indeed, that it was a thing alien to my character. At her request I did communicate with you. I remember the wording of my telegram quite well. I said that time healed every wound but that for many months to come I would neither

---

[1] When Douglas left Egypt in March 1894 he was appointed Honorary Attaché to Lord Currie, the Ambassador at Constantinople, but did not take up the appointment.

write to you nor see you. You started without delay for Paris, sending me passionate telegrams on the road to beg me to see you once, at any rate. I declined. You arrived in Paris late on a Saturday night, and found a brief letter from me waiting for you at your hotel stating that I would not see you. Next morning I received in Tite Street a telegram of some ten or eleven pages in length from you. You stated in it that no matter what you had done to me you could not believe that I would absolutely decline to see you: you reminded me that for the sake of seeing me even for one hour you had travelled six days and nights across Europe without stopping once on the way: you made what I must admit was a most pathetic appeal, and ended with what seemed to me a threat of suicide, and one not thinly veiled. You had yourself often told me how many of your race there had been who had stained their hands in their own blood; your uncle certainly, your grandfather possibly; many others in the mad, bad line from which you come.[1] Pity, my old affection for you, regard for your mother to whom your death under such dreadful circumstances would have been a blow almost too great for her to bear, the horror of the idea that so young a life, and one that amidst all its ugly faults had still promise of beauty in it, should come to so revolting an end, mere humanity itself—all these, if excuses be necessary, must serve as my excuse for consenting to accord you one last interview. When I arrived in Paris, your tears, breaking out again and again all through the evening, and falling over your cheeks like rain as we sat, at dinner first at Voisin's, at supper at Paillard's afterwards: the un-feigned joy you evinced at seeing me, holding my hand whenever you could, as though you were a gentle and penitent child: your contrition, so simple and sincere, at the moment: made me consent to renew our friend-ship. Two days after we had returned to London, your father saw you having luncheon with me at the Café Royal, joined my table, drank of my wine, and that afternoon, through a letter addressed to you, began his first attack on me.[2]

It may be strange, but I had once again, I will not say the chance, but the duty of separating from you forced on me. I need hardly remind you that I refer to your conduct to me at Brighton from October 10th to 13th, 1894. Three years ago is a long time for you to go back. But we who live in prison, and in whose lives there is no event but sorrow, have to measure time by throbs of pain, and the record of bitter moments. We have nothing else to think of. Suffering—curious as it may sound to you—is the means by which we exist, because it is the only means by which we become conscious of existing; and the remembrance of suffering in the past is necessary to us as the warrant, the evidence, of our continued identity. Between myself and the memory of joy lies a gulf no less deep than that between myself and joy in its actuality. Had our life together been as the world fancied it to be, one simply of pleasure, profligacy and laughter, I would not be able to recall a single passage in it. It is because it was full of

[1] The seventh Marquess of Queensberry (1818–58) died in a shooting accident. His youngest son, Lord James Edward Sholto Douglas (1855–91), cut his own throat in the Euston Hotel. [2] *Circa* 1 April 1894.

moments and days tragic, bitter, sinister in their warnings, dull or dreadful in their monotonous scenes and unseemly violences, that I can see or hear each separate incident in its detail, can indeed see or hear little else. So much in this place do men live by pain that my friendship with you, in the way through which I am forced to remember it, appears to me always as a prelude consonant with those varying modes of anguish which each day I have to realise; nay more, to necessitate them even; as though my life, whatever it had seemed to myself and to others, had all the while been a real Symphony of Sorrow, passing through its rhythmically-linked movements to its certain resolution, with that inevitableness that in Art characterises the treatment of every great theme.

I spoke of your conduct to me on three successive days, three years ago, did I not? I was trying to finish my last play at Worthing by myself. The two visits you had paid to me had ended. You suddenly appeared a third time bringing with you a companion whom you actually proposed should stay in my house. I (you must admit now quite properly) absolutely declined. I entertained you, of course; I had no option in the matter: but elsewhere, and not in my own home. The next day, a Monday, your companion returned to the duties of his profession, and you stayed with me. Bored with Worthing, and still more, I have no doubt, with my fruitless efforts to concentrate my attention on my play, the only thing that really interested me at the moment, you insist on being taken to the Grand Hotel at Brighton. The night we arrive you fall ill with that dreadful low fever that is foolishly called the influenza, your second, if not third attack.[1] I need not remind you how I waited on you, and tended you, not merely with every luxury of fruit, flowers, presents, books, and the like that money can procure, but with that affection, tenderness and love that, whatever you may think, is not to be procured for money. Except for an hour's walk in the morning, an hour's drive in the afternoon, I never left the hotel. I got special grapes from London for you, as you did not care for those the hotel supplied, invented things to please you, remained either with you or in the room next to yours, sat with you every evening to quiet or amuse you.

After four or five days you recover, and I take lodgings in order to try and finish my play. You, of course, accompany me. The morning after the day on which we were installed I feel extremely ill. You have to go to London on business, but promise to return in the afternoon. In London you meet a friend, and do not come back to Brighton till late the next day, by which time I am in a terrible fever, and the doctor finds I have caught the influenza from you. Nothing could have been more uncomfortable for anyone ill than the lodgings turn out to be. My sitting-room is on the first floor, my bedroom on the third. There is no manservant to wait on one, not even anyone to send out on a message, or to get what the doctor orders. But you are there. I feel no alarm. The next two days you leave me entirely alone without care, without attendance, without anything. It was not a question of grapes, flowers, and charming gifts: it was a question of mere necessaries: I could not even get the milk the doctor had

[1] See p. 374.

ordered for me: lemonade was pronounced an impossibility: and when I begged you to procure me a book at the bookseller's, or if they had not got whatever I had fixed on to choose something else, you never even take the trouble to go there. And when I was left all day without anything to read in consequence, you calmly tell me that you bought me the book and that they promised to send it down, a statement which I found out by chance afterwards to have been entirely untrue from beginning to end. All the while you are of course living at my expense, driving about, dining at the Grand Hotel, and indeed only appearing in my room for money. On the Saturday night, you having left me completely unattended and alone since the morning, I asked you to come back after dinner, and sit with me for a little. With irritable voice and ungracious manner you promise to do so. I wait till eleven o'clock and you never appear. I then left a note for you in your room just reminding you of the promise you had made me, and how you had kept it. At three in the morning, unable to sleep, and tortured with thirst, I made my way, in the dark and cold, down to the sitting-room in the hopes of finding some water there. I found *you*. You fell on me with every hideous word an intemperate mood, an undisciplined and untutored nature could suggest. By the terrible alchemy of egotism you converted your remorse into rage. You accused me of selfishness in expecting you to be with me when I was ill; of standing between you and your amusements; of trying to deprive you of your pleasures. You told me, and I know it was quite true, that you had come back at midnight simply in order to change your dress-clothes, and go out again to where you hoped new pleasures were waiting for you, but that by leaving for you a letter in which I had reminded you that you had neglected me the whole day and the whole evening, I had really robbed you of your desire for more enjoyments, and diminished your actual capacity for fresh delights. I went back upstairs in disgust, and remained sleepless till dawn, nor till long after dawn was I able to get anything to quench the thirst of the fever that was on me. At eleven o'clock you came into my room. In the previous scene I could not help observing that by my letter I had, at any rate, checked you in a night of more than usual excess. In the morning you were quite yourself. I waited naturally to hear what excuses you had to make, and in what way you were going to ask for the forgiveness that you knew in your heart was invariably waiting for you, no matter what you did; your absolute trust that I would always forgive you being the thing in you that I always really liked the best, perhaps the best thing in you to like. So far from doing that, you began to repeat the same scene with renewed emphasis and more violent assertion. I told you at length to leave the room: you pretended to do so, but when I lifted up my head from the pillow in which I had buried it, you were still there, and with brutality of laughter and hysteria of rage you moved suddenly towards me. A sense of horror came over me, for what exact reason I could not make out; but I got out of my bed at once, and bare-footed and just as I was, made my way down the two flights of stairs to the sitting-room, which I did not leave till the owner of the lodgings— whom I had rung for—had assured me that you had left my bedroom, and promised to remain within call, in case of necessity. After an interval of an hour, during which time the doctor had come and found me, of course, in a state of absolute nervous prostration, as well as in a worse condition of fever than I had been at the outset, you returned silently, for money: took what you could find on the dressing-table and mantelpiece, and left the house with your luggage. Need I tell you what I thought of you during the two wretched lonely days of illness that followed? Is it necessary for me to state that I saw clearly that it would be a dishonour to myself to continue even an acquaintance with such a one as you had showed yourself to be? That I recognised that the ultimate moment had come, and recognised it as being really a great relief? And that I knew that for the future my Art and Life would be freer and better and more beautiful in every possible way? Ill as I was, I felt at ease. The fact that the separation was irrevocable gave me peace. By Tuesday the fever had left me, and for the first time I dined downstairs. Wednesday was my birthday.[1] Amongst the telegrams and communications on my table was a letter in your handwriting. I opened it with a sense of sadness over me. I knew that the time had gone by when a pretty phrase, an expression of affection, a word of sorrow would make me take you back. But I was entirely deceived. I had underrated you. The letter you sent to me on my birthday was an elaborate repetition of the two scenes, set cunningly and carefully down in black and white! You mocked me with common jests. Your one satisfaction in the whole affair was, you said, that you retired to the Grand Hotel, and entered your luncheon to my account before you left for town. You congratulated me on my prudence in leaving my sickbed, on my sudden flight downstairs. *"It was an ugly moment for you,"* you said, *"uglier than you imagine."* Ah! I felt it but too well. What it had really meant I did not know: whether you had with you the pistol you had bought to try and frighten your father with, and that, thinking it to be unloaded, you had once fired off in a public restaurant in my company:[2] whether your hand was moving towards a common dinner-knife that by chance was lying on the table between us: whether, forgetting in your rage your low stature and inferior strength, you had thought of some specially personal insult, or attack even, as I lay ill there: I could not tell. I do not know to the present moment. All I know is that a feeling of utter horror had come over me, and that I had felt that unless I left the room at once, and got away, you would have done, or tried to do, something that would have been, even to you, a source of lifelong shame. Only once before in my life had I experienced such a feeling of horror at any human being. It was when in my library at Tite Street, waving his small hands in the air in epileptic fury, your father, with his bully, or his friend, between us, had stood uttering every foul word his foul mind could think of, and screaming the loathsome threats he afterwards with such cunning carried out. In the latter case he, of course, was the one who had to leave the room first. I drove him out.

[1] In 1894 Wilde's birthday (16 October) was a Tuesday, and Ross changed this sentence accordingly.
[2] The Berkeley, in Piccadilly.

In your case I went. It was not the first time I had been obliged to save you from yourself.

You concluded your letter by saying: "*When you are not on your pedestal you are not interesting. The next time you are ill I will go away at once.*" Ah! what coarseness of fibre does that reveal! What an entire lack of imagination! How callous, how common had the temperament by that time become! "*When you are not on your pedestal you are not interesting. The next time you are ill I will go away at once.*" How often have those words come back to me in the wretched solitary cell of the various prisons I have been sent to. I have said them to myself over and over again, and seen in them, I hope unjustly, some of the secret of your strange silence. For you to write thus to me, when the very illness and fever from which I was suffering I had caught from tending you, was of course revolting in its coarseness and crudity; but for any human being in the whole world to write thus to another would be a sin for which there is no pardon, were there any sin for which there is none.

I confess that when I had finished your letter I felt almost polluted, as if by associating with one of such a nature I had soiled and shamed my life irretrievably. I had, it is true, done so, but I was not to learn how fully till just six months later on in life. I settled with myself to go back to London on the Friday,[1] and see Sir George Lewis personally and request him to write to your father to state that I had determined never under any circumstances to allow you to enter my house, to sit at my board, to talk to me, walk with me, or anywhere and at any time to be my companion at all. This done I would have written to you just to inform you of the course of action I had adopted; the reasons you would inevitably have realised for yourself. I had everything arranged on Thursday night, when on Friday morning, as I was sitting at breakfast before starting, I happened to open the newspaper and saw in it a telegram stating that your elder brother, the real head of the family, the heir to the title, the pillar of the house, had been found dead in a ditch with his gun lying discharged beside him.[2] The horror of the circumstances of the tragedy, now known to have been an accident, but then stained with a darker suggestion; the pathos of the sudden death of one so loved by all who knew him, and almost on the eve, as it were, of his marriage; my idea of what your own sorrow would, or should be; my consciousness of the misery awaiting your mother at the loss of the one to whom she clung for comfort and joy in life, and who, as she told me once herself, had from the very day of his birth never caused her to shed a single tear; my consciousness of your own isolation, both your other brothers being out of Europe, and you consequently the only one to whom your mother and sister could look, not merely for companionship in their sorrow, but also for those dreary responsibilities of dreadful detail that Death always brings with it; the mere sense of the *lacrimae rerum*, of the tears of which the world is made, and of the sadness of all human things—out of the confluence of these thoughts and emotions crowding into my brain came infinite pity for you and your family. My

[1] 19 October 1894.   [2] See note 2, p. 375.

439

own griefs and bitternesses against you I forgot. What you had been to me in my sickness, I could not be to you in your bereavement. I telegraphed at once to you my deepest sympathy, and in the letter that followed invited you to come to my house as soon as you were able. I felt that to abandon you at that particular moment, and formally through a solicitor, would have been too terrible for you.

On your return to town from the actual scene of the tragedy to which you had been summoned, you came at once to me very sweetly and very simply, in your suit of woe, and with your eyes dim with tears. You sought consolation and help, as a child might seek it. I opened to you my house, my home, my heart. I made your sorrow mine also, that you might have help in bearing it. Never, even by one word, did I allude to your conduct towards me, to the revolting scenes, and the revolting letter. Your grief, which was real, seemed to me to bring you nearer to me than you had ever been. The flowers you took from me to put on your brother's grave were to be a symbol not merely of the beauty of his life, but of the beauty that in all lives lies dormant and may be brought to light.

The gods are strange. It is not of our vices only they make instruments to scourge us.[1] They bring us to ruin through what in us is good, gentle, humane, loving. But for my pity and affection for you and yours, I would not now be weeping in this terrible place.

Of course I discern in all our relations, not Destiny merely, but Doom: Doom that walks always swiftly, because she goes to the shedding of blood. Through your father you come of a race, marriage with whom is horrible, friendship fatal, and that lays violent hands either on its own life or on the lives of others. In every little circumstance in which the ways of our lives met; in every point of great, or seemingly trivial import in which you came to me for pleasure or for help; in the small chances, the slight accidents that look, in their relation to life, to be no more than the dust that dances in a beam, or the leaf that flutters from a tree, Ruin followed, like the echo of a bitter cry, or the shadow that hunts with the beast of prey. Our friendship really begins with your begging me in a most pathetic and charming letter to assist you in a position appalling to anyone, doubly so to a young man at Oxford: I do so, and ultimately through your using my name as your friend with Sir George Lewis, I begin to lose his esteem and friendship, a friendship of fifteen years' standing. When I was deprived of his advice and help and regard I was deprived of the one great safeguard of my life.

You send me a very nice poem, of the undergraduate school of verse, for my approval: I reply by a letter of fantastic literary conceits:[2] I compare you to Hylas, or Hyacinth, Jonquil or Narcisse, or someone whom the great god of Poetry favoured, and honoured with his love. The letter is like a passage from one of Shakespeare's sonnets, transposed to a minor key. It can only be understood by those who have read the *Symposium* of Plato, or caught the spirit of a certain grave mood made beautiful for us in Greek marbles. It was, let me say frankly, the sort of letter I would, in a

---

[1] *King Lear*, Act V, scene iii.   [2] See letter p. 326.

440

happy if wilful moment, have written to any graceful young man of either University who had sent me a poem of his own making, certain that he would have sufficient wit or culture to interpret rightly its fantastic phrases. Look at the history of that letter! It passes from you into the hands of a loathsome companion: from him to a gang of blackmailers: copies of it are sent about London to my friends, and to the manager of the theatre where my work is being performed:[1] every construction but the right one is put on it: Society is thrilled with the absurd rumours that I have had to pay a huge sum of money for having written an infamous letter to you: this forms the basis of your father's worst attack: I produce the original letter myself in Court to show what it really is: it is denounced by your father's Counsel as a revolting and insidious attempt to corrupt Innocence: ultimately it forms part of a criminal charge: the Crown takes it up: the Judge sums up on it with little learning and much morality: I go to prison for it at last. That is the result of writing you a charming letter.

While I am staying with you at Salisbury you are terribly alarmed at a threatening communication from a former companion of yours: you beg me to see the writer and help you: I do so: the result is Ruin to me. I am forced to take everything you have done on my own shoulders and answer for it. When, having failed to take your degree, you have to go down from Oxford, you telegraph to me in London to beg me to come to you. I do so at once: you ask me to take you to Goring, as you did not like, under the circumstances, to go home: at Goring you see a house that charms you: I take it for you: the result from every point of view is Ruin to me. One day you come to me and ask me, as a personal favour to you, to write something for an Oxford undergraduate magazine, about to be started by some friend of yours, whom I had never heard of in all my life, and knew nothing at all about. To please you—what did I not do always to please you?—I sent him a page of paradoxes destined originally for the *Saturday Review*.[2] A few months later I find myself standing in the dock of the Old Bailey on account of the character of the magazine. It forms part of the Crown charge against me. I am called upon to defend your friend's prose and your own verse. The former I cannot palliate; the latter I, loyal to the bitter extreme, to your youthful literature as to your youthful life, do very strongly defend, and will not hear of your being a writer of indecencies. But I go to prison, all the same, for your friend's undergraduate magazine, and "the Love that dares not tell its name."[3] At Christmas I give you a "very pretty present," as you described it in your letter of thanks, on which

---

[1] Beerbohm Tree.   [2] See note 2, p. 379.

[3] Lord Alfred Douglas's poem "Two Loves" appeared in the *Chameleon* (see note 2, p. 379) and was quoted in court. Its last lines run:

"I am true Love, I fill
The hearts of boy and girl with mutual flame."
Then sighing said the other, "Have thy will,
I am the Love that dare not speak its name."

Douglas reprinted the poem in his first volume, *Poems* (1896), but not in *The City of the Soul* (1899), though it reappeared, with an apologia, in his *Lyrics* (1935).

I knew you had set your heart, worth some £40 or £50 at most. When the crash of my life comes, and I am ruined, the bailiff who seizes my library, and has it sold, does so to pay for the "very pretty present." It was for that the execution was put into my house. At the ultimate and terrible moment when I am taunted, and spurred-on by your taunts, to take an action against your father and have him arrested, the last straw to which I clutch in my wretched efforts to escape is the terrible expense. I tell the solicitor in your presence that I have no funds, that I cannot possibly afford the appalling costs, that I have no money at my disposal. What I said was, as you know, perfectly true. On that fatal Friday[1] instead of being in Humphreys's office weakly consenting to my own ruin, I would have been happy and free in France, away from you and your father, unconscious of his loathsome card, and indifferent to your letters, if I had been able to leave the Avondale Hotel. But the hotel people absolutely refused to allow me to go. You had been staying with me for ten days: indeed you had ultimately, to my great and, you will admit, rightful indignation, brought a companion of yours to stay with me also: my bill for the ten days was nearly £140. The proprietor said he could not allow my luggage to be removed from the hotel till I had paid the account in full. That is what kept me in London. Had it not been for the hotel bill I would have gone to Paris on Thursday morning.

When I told the solicitor I had no money to face the gigantic expense, you interposed at once. You said that your own family would be only too delighted to pay all the necessary costs: that your father had been an incubus to them all: that they had often discussed the possibility of getting him put into a lunatic asylum so as to keep him out of the way: that he was a daily source of annoyance and distress to your mother and to everyone else: that if I would only come forward to have him shut up I would be regarded by the family as their champion and their benefactor: and that your mother's rich relations themselves would look on it as a real delight to be allowed to pay all costs and expenses that might be incurred in any such effort. The solicitor closed at once, and I was hurried to the Police Court. I had no excuse left for not going. I was forced into it. Of course your family don't pay the costs, and, when I am made bankrupt, it is by your father, and *for* the costs—the meagre balance of them—some £700.[2] At the present moment my wife, estranged from me over the important question of whether I should have £3 or £3. 10 a week to live on, is preparing a divorce suit, for which, of course, entirely new evidence and an entirely new trial, to be followed perhaps by more serious proceedings, will be necessary. I, naturally, know nothing of the details. I merely know the name of the witness on whose evidence my wife's solicitors rely. It is your own Oxford servant, whom at your special request I took into my service for our summer at Goring.

[1] 1 March 1895.
[2] This (or rather £677) was the amount of Queensberry's taxed costs in Wilde's unsuccessful action against him. The total of Wilde's debts was £6000, but Queensberry was the petitioning creditor whose action made Wilde a bankrupt.

But, indeed, I need not go on further with more instances of the strange Doom you seem to have brought on me in all things big or little. It makes me feel sometimes as if you yourself had been merely a puppet worked by some secret and unseen hand to bring terrible events to a terrible issue. But puppets themselves have passions. They will bring a new plot into what they are presenting, and twist the ordered issue of vicissitude to suit some whim or appetite of their own. To be entirely free, and at the same time entirely dominated by law, is the eternal paradox of human life that we realise at every moment; and this, I often think, is the only explanation possible of your nature, if indeed for the profound and terrible mysteries of a human soul there is any explanation at all, except one that makes the mystery more marvellous still.

Of course you had your illusions, lived in them indeed, and through their shifting mists and coloured veils saw all things changed. You thought, I remember quite well, that your devoting yourself to me, to the entire exclusion of your family and family life, was a proof of your wonderful appreciation of me, and your great affection. No doubt to you it seemed so. But recollect that with me was luxury, high living, unlimited pleasure, money without stint. Your family life bored you. The "cold cheap wine of Salisbury," to use a phrase of your own making, was distasteful to you. On my side, and along with my intellectual attractions, were the fleshpots of Egypt. When you could not find me to be with, the companions whom you chose as substitutes were not flattering.

You thought again that in sending a lawyer's letter to your father to say that, rather than sever your eternal friendship with me, you would give up the allowance of £250 a year which, with I believe deductions for your Oxford debts, he was then making you, you were realising the very chivalry of friendship, touching the noblest note of self-denial. But your surrender of your little allowance did not mean that you were ready to give up even one of your most superfluous luxuries, or most unnecessary extravagances. On the contrary. Your appetite for luxurious living was never so keen. My expenses for eight days in Paris for myself, you, and your Italian servant were nearly £150: Paillard alone absorbing £85. At the rate at which you wished to live, your entire income for a whole year, if you had taken your meals alone, and been especially economical in your selection of the cheaper form of pleasures, would hardly have lasted you for three weeks. The fact that in what was merely a pretence of bravado you had surrendered your allowance, such as it was, gave you at last a plausible reason for your claim to live at my expense, or what you thought a plausible reason: and on many occasions you seriously availed yourself of it, and gave the very fullest expression to it: and the continued drain, principally of course on me, but also to a certain extent, I know, on your mother, was never so distressing, because in my case at any rate, never so completely unaccompanied by the smallest word of thanks, or sense of limit.

You thought again that in attacking your own father with dreadful letters, abusive telegrams, and insulting postcards you were really fighting your mother's battles, coming forward as her champion, and avenging the no doubt terrible wrongs and sufferings of her married life. It was quite an illusion on your part; one of your worst indeed. The way for you to have avenged your mother's wrongs on your father, if you considered it part of a son's duty to do so, was by being a better son to your mother than you had been: by not making her afraid to speak to you on serious things: by not signing bills the payment of which devolved on her: by being gentler to her, and not bringing sorrow into her days. Your brother Francis[1] made great amends to her for what she had suffered, by his sweetness and goodness to her through the brief years of his flower-like life. You should have taken him as your model. You were wrong even in fancying that it would have been an absolute delight and joy to your mother if you *had* managed through me to get your father put into prison. I feel sure you were wrong. And if you want to know what a woman really feels when her husband, and the father of her children, is in prison dress, in a prison cell, write to my wife and ask her. She will tell you.

I also had my illusions. I thought life was going to be a brilliant comedy, and that you were to be one of many graceful figures in it. I found it to be a revolting and repellent tragedy, and that the sinister occasion of the great catastrophe, sinister in its concentration of aim and intensity of narrowed will-power, was yourself, stripped of that mask of joy and pleasure by which you, no less than I, had been deceived and led astray.

You can now understand—can you not?—a little of what I am suffering. Some paper, the *Pall Mall Gazette* I think, describing the dress-rehearsal of one of my plays, spoke of you as following me about like my shadow: the memory of our friendship is the shadow that walks with me here: that seems never to leave me: that wakes me up at night to tell me the same story over and over till its wearisome iteration makes all sleep abandon me till dawn: at dawn it begins again: it follows me into the prison-yard and makes me talk to myself as I tramp round: each detail that accompanied each dreadful moment I am forced to recall: there is nothing that happened in those ill-starred years that I cannot recreate in that chamber of the brain which is set apart for grief or for despair: every strained note of your voice, every twitch and gesture of your nervous hands, every bitter word, every poisonous phrase comes back to me: I remember the street or river down which we passed, the wall or woodland that surrounded us, at what figure on the dial stood the hands of the clock, which way went the wings of the wind, the shape and colour of the moon.

There is, I know, one answer to all that I have said to you, and that is that you loved me: that all through those two and a half years during which the Fates were weaving into one scarlet pattern the threads of our divided lives you really loved me. Yes: I know you did. No matter what your conduct to me was I always felt that at heart you really did love me. Though I saw quite clearly that my position in the world of Art, the interest my personality had always excited, my money, the luxury in which I lived, the thousand and one things that went to make up a life so charmingly, so wonderfully improbable as mine was, were, each and all of them,

[1] Drumlanrig.

elements that fascinated you and made you cling to me: yet besides all this there was something more, some strange attraction for you: you loved me far better than you loved anybody else. But you, like myself, have had a terrible tragedy in your life, though one of an entirely opposite character to mine. Do you want to learn what it was? It was this. In you Hate was always stronger than Love. Your hatred of your father was of such stature that it entirely outstripped, o'erthrew, and overshadowed your love of me. There was no struggle between them at all, or but little; of such dimensions was your Hatred and of such monstrous growth. You did not realise that there is no room for both passions in the same soul. They cannot live together in that fair carven house. Love is fed by the imagination, by which we become wiser than we know, better than we feel, nobler than we are: by which we can see Life as a whole: by which, and by which alone, we can understand others in their real as in their ideal relations. Only what is fine, and finely conceived, can feed Love. But anything will feed Hate. There was not a glass of champagne you drank, not a rich dish you ate of in all those years, that did not feed your Hate and make it fat. So to gratify it, you gambled with my life, as you gambled with my money, carelessly, recklessly, indifferent to the consequence. If you lost, the loss would not, you fancied, be yours. If you won, yours, you knew, would be the exulta-tion, and the advantages of victory.

Hate blinds people. You were not aware of that. Love can read the writing on the remotest star, but Hate so blinded you that you could see no further than the narrow, walled-in, and already lust-withered garden of your common desires. Your terrible lack of imagination, the one really fatal defect of your character, was entirely the result of the Hate that lived in you. Subtly, silently, and in secret, Hate gnawed at your nature, as the lichen bites at the root of some sallow plant, till you grew to see nothing but the most meagre interests and the most petty aims. That faculty in you which Love would have fostered, Hate poisoned and paralysed. When your father first began to attack me it was as your private friend, and in a private letter to you. As soon as I had read the letter, with its obscene threats and coarse violences, I saw at once that a terrible danger was looming on the horizon of my troubled days: I told you I would not be the catspaw between you both in your ancient hatred of each other: that I in London was naturally much bigger game for him than a Secretary for Foreign Affairs at Homburg:[1] that it would be unfair to me to place me even for a moment in such a position: and that I had something better to do with my life than to have scenes with a man drunken, *déclassé*, and half-witted as he was. You could not be made to see this. Hate blinded you. You insisted that the quarrel had really nothing to do with me: that you would not

[1] In 1893 Queensberry's eldest son, Drumlanrig, who was then private secretary to Lord Rosebery (Foreign Secretary in Gladstone's last Government), was created Baron Kelhead in the Union peerage (all Queensberry's titles being Scottish). Queensberry approved this action and wrote to thank Gladstone, but within a month he was sending abusive letters to the Queen, Gladstone, Rosebery, and his own son. He followed Rosebery to Homburg, threatening to horsewhip him, and was only persuaded to desist by the Prince of Wales.

allow your father to dictate to you in your private friendships: that it would be most unfair of me to interfere. You had already, before you saw me on the subject, sent your father a foolish and vulgar telegram, as your answer.[1] That of course committed you to a foolish and vulgar course of action to follow. The fatal errors of life are not due to man's being unreasonable: an unreasonable moment may be one's finest moment. They are due to man's being logical. There is a wide difference. That telegram conditioned the whole of your subsequent relations with your father, and consequently the whole of my life. And the grotesque thing about it is that it was a telegram of which the commonest street-boy would have been ashamed. From pert telegrams to priggish lawyers' letters was a natural progress, and the result of your lawyer's letters to your father was, of course, to urge him on still further. You left him no option but to go on. You forced it on him as a point of honour, or of dishonour rather, that your appeal should have the more effect. So the next time he attacks me, no longer in a private letter and as your private friend, but in public and as a public man. I have to expel him from my house. He goes from restaurant to restaurant looking for me, in order to insult me before the whole world, and in such a manner that if I retaliated I would be ruined, and if I did not retaliate I would be ruined also. *Then* surely was the time when *you* should have come forward, and said that you would not expose me to such hideous attacks, such infamous persecution, on your account, but would, readily and at once, resign any claim you had to my friendship? You feel that now, I suppose. But it never even occurred to you then. Hate blinded you. All you could think of (besides of course writing to him insulting letters and telegrams) was to buy a ridiculous pistol that goes off in the Berkeley, under circumstances that create a worse scandal than ever came to *your* ears. Indeed the idea of your being the object of a terrible quarrel between your father and a man of my position seemed to delight you. It, I suppose very naturally, pleased your vanity, and flattered your self-importance. That your father might have had your body, which did not interest me, and left me your soul, which did not interest him, would have been to you a distressing solution of the question. You scented the chance of a public scandal and flew to it. The prospect of a battle in which you would be safe delighted you. I never remember you in higher spirits than you were for the rest of that season. Your only disappointment seemed to be that nothing actually happened, and that no further meeting or fracas had taken place between us. You consoled yourself by sending him telegrams of such a character that at last the wretched man wrote to you and said that he had given orders to his servants that no telegram was to be brought to him under any pretence whatsoever. That did not daunt you. You saw the immense opportunities afforded by the open postcard, and availed yourself of them to the full. You hounded him on in the chase still more. I do not suppose he would ever really have given it up. Family instincts were strong in him. His hatred of you was just as persistent as

[1] This telegram (which was dated 2 April 1894) read: "WHAT A FUNNY LITTLE MAN YOU ARE."

your hatred of him, and I was the stalking-horse for both of you, and a mode of attack as well as a mode of shelter. His very passion for notoriety was not merely individual but racial. Still, if his interest had flagged for a moment your letters and postcards would soon have quickened it to its ancient flame. They did so. And he naturally went on further still. Having assailed me as a private gentleman and in private, as a public man and in public, he ultimately determines to make his final and great attack on me as an artist, and in the place where my Art is being represented. He secures by fraud a seat for the first night of one of my plays, and contrives a plot to interrupt the performance, to make a foul speech about me to the audience, to insult my actors, to throw offensive or indecent missiles at me when I am called before the curtain at the close, utterly in some hideous way to ruin me through my work. By the merest chance, in the brief and accidental sincerity of a more than usually intoxicated mood, he boasts of his intention before others. Information is given to the police, and he is kept out of the theatre. You had your chance then. Then was your opportunity. Don't you realise now that you should have seen it, and come forward and said that you would not have my Art, at any rate, ruined for your sake? You knew what my Art was to me, the great primal note by which I had revealed, first myself to myself, and then myself to the world; the real passion of my life; the love to which all other loves were as marsh-water to red wine, or the glow-worm of the marsh to the magic mirror of the moon. Don't you understand now that your lack of imagination was the one really fatal defect of your character? What you had to do was quite simple, and quite clear before you, but Hate had blinded you, and you could see nothing. I could not apologise to your father for his having insulted me and persecuted me in the most loathsome manner for nearly nine months. I could not get rid of you out of my life. I had tried it again and again. I had gone so far as actually leaving England and going abroad in the hope of escaping from you. It had all been of no use. You were the only person who could have done anything. The key of the situation rested entirely with yourself. It was the one great opportunity you had of making some slight return to me for all the love and affection and kindness and generosity and care I had shown you. Had you appreciated me even at a tenth of my value as an artist you would have done so. But Hate blinded you. The faculty "by which, and by which alone, we can understand others in their real as in their ideal relations"[1] was dead in you. You thought simply of how to get your father into prison. To see him "in the dock," as you used to say: that was your one idea. The phrase became one of the many *scies* of your daily conversation. One heard it at every meal. Well, you had your desire gratified. Hate granted you every single thing you wished for. It was an indulgent Master to you. It is so, indeed, to all who serve it. For two days you sat on a high seat with the Sheriffs, and feasted your eyes with the spectacle of your father standing in the dock of the Central Criminal Court. And on the third day I took his place. What had occurred? In your hideous game of hate together, you

[1] Cf. p. 445, line 13.

had both thrown dice for my soul, and you happened to have lost. That was all.

You see that I have to write your life to you, and you have to realise it. We have known each other now for more than four years. Half of the time we have been together: the other half I have had to spend in prison as the result of our friendship. Where you will receive this letter, if indeed it ever reaches you, I don't know. Rome, Naples, Paris, Venice, some beautiful city on sea or river, I have no doubt, holds you. You are surrounded, if not with all the useless luxury you had with me, at any rate with everything that is pleasurable to eye, ear, and taste. Life is quite lovely to you. And yet, if you are wise, and wish to find Life much lovelier still, and in a different manner, you will let the reading of this terrible letter—for such I know it is—prove to you as important a crisis and turning-point of your life as the writing of it is to me. Your pale face used to flush easily with wine or pleasure. If, as you read what is here written, it from time to time becomes scorched, as though by a furnace-blast, with shame, it will be all the better for you. The supreme vice is shallowness. Whatever is realised is right.

I have now got as far as the House of Detention, have I not? After a night passed in the Police Cells I am sent there in the van. You were most attentive and kind. Almost every afternoon, if not actually every afternoon till you go abroad, you took the trouble to drive up to Holloway to see me. You also wrote very sweet and nice letters. But that it was not your father but you who had put me into prison, that from beginning to end you were the responsible person, that it was through you, for you, and by you that I was there, never for one instant dawned upon you. Even the spectacle of me behind the bars of a wooden cage could not quicken that dead unimaginative nature. You had the sympathy and the sentimentality of the spectator of a rather pathetic play. That you were the true author of the hideous tragedy did not occur to you. I saw that you realised nothing of what you had done. I did not desire to be the one to tell you what your own heart should have told you, what it indeed would have told you if you had not let Hate harden it and make it insensate. Everything must come to one out of one's own nature. There is no use in telling a person a thing that they don't feel and can't understand. If I write to you now as I do it is because your own silence and conduct during my long imprisonment have made it necessary. Besides, as things had turned out, the blow had fallen upon me alone. That was a source of pleasure to me. I was content for many reasons to suffer, though there was always to my eyes, as I watched you, something not a little contemptible in your complete and wilful blindness. I remember your producing with absolute pride a letter you had published in one of the halfpenny newspapers about me.[1] It was a very

---

[1] In April 1895, when Wilde was in Holloway awaiting trial, the *Star* ran a lengthy correspondence about his case. On 15 April Robert Buchanan (author and dramatist, 1841–1901) wrote:

Sir, Is it not high time that a little charity, Christian or anti-Christian, were imported into this land of Christian shibboleths and formulas? . . . I for one,

prudent, temperate, indeed commonplace production. You appealed to the *"English sense of fair play,"* or something very dreary of that kind, on behalf of *"a man who was down."* It was the sort of letter you might have written had a painful charge been brought against some respectable person with whom personally you had been quite unacquainted. But you thought it a wonderful letter. You looked on it as a proof of almost quixotic chivalry. I am aware that you wrote other letters to other newspapers that

---

at any rate, wish to put on record my protest against the cowardice and cruelty of Englishmen towards one who was, until recently, recognised as a legitimate contributor to our amusement, and who is, when all is said and done, a scholar and a man of letters . . . His case still remains *sub judice* . . . Even if one granted for a moment that the man was guilty, would that be any reason for condemning work which we know in our hearts to be quite innocent? . . . Let us ask ourselves, moreover, who are casting these stones, and whether they are those "without sin amongst us" or those who are themselves notoriously corrupt.
Yours etc   ROBERT BUCHANAN

On 18 April Lord Queensberry replied:

I have received many anonymous letters . . . One this morning called my attention to this letter of Mr Buchanan. Can it possibly have come from himself? Or was it inspired by him? I have not the pleasure of Mr Buchanan's acquaintance, but he seems to address a question to myself in this letter . . . where he says "who are casting these stones?" and are they without sin or those "who are notoriously corrupt." Is Mr Buchanan himself without sin?

                                                             QUEENSBERRY

On 20 April the following appeared:

19 April   *Chalcott House, Long Ditton*
Sir, When the great British public has made up its great British mind to crush any particular unfortunate whom it holds in its power, it generally succeeds in gaining its object, and it is not fond of those who dare to question its power, or its right to do as it wishes. I feel, therefore, that I am taking my life in my hands in daring to raise my voice against the chorus of the pack of those who are now hounding Mr Oscar Wilde to his ruin; the more so as I feel assured that the public has made up its mind to accept me, as it has accepted everybody and everything connected with this case, at Mr Carson's valuation. I, of course, am the undutiful son who, in his arrogance and folly, has kicked against his kind and affectionate father, and who has further aggravated his offence by not running away and hiding his face after the discomfiture of his friend. It is not a pleasant position to find oneself in with regard to the public, but the situation is not without an element of grim humour, and it is no part of my intention to try and explain my attitude or defend my position. I am simply the *vox in solitudine clamantis* raising my feeble protest; not in the expectation of making head against the wave of popular or newspaper clamour, but rather dimly hoping to catch the ear and the sympathy of one or two of those strong and fearless men and women who have before now defied the shrieks of the mob. To such as these I appeal to interfere and stay the hand of "Judge Lynch." And I submit that Mr Oscar Wilde has been tried by the newspapers before he has been tried by a jury, that his case has been almost hopelessly prejudiced in the eyes of the public from whom the jury who must try his case will be drawn, and that he is practically being delivered over bound to the fury of a cowardly and brutal mob. Sir John Bridge, in refusing bail today, stated that he knew of no graver offence than that with which Mr Wilde is charged. Mr Wilde, as a matter of fact, is charged with a "misdemeanour" punishable by two years' imprisonment with or without hard labour *as a maximum penalty*; therefore, the offence with which he is charged is, in the eye of the law, which Sir John Bridge is supposed to represent, comparatively trifling. I should

they did not publish.[1] But then they were simply to say that you hated your father. Nobody cared if you did or not. Hate, you have yet to learn, is, intellectually considered, the Eternal Negation. Considered from the point of view of the emotions it is a form of Atrophy, and kills everything but itself. To write to the papers to say that one hates someone else is as if one

---

very much like to know how, in view of this fact, Sir John Bridge can reconcile what he said with his conscience, and with his position as the absolutely impartial exponent of the law, and whether it is not obvious that, in saying what he did, he allowed his personal feelings on a particular point to override his sense of abstract justice, to the prejudice of the man charged before him. If a police magistrate of twenty years' experience shows such flagrant prejudice, what can be expected from the men who will at the Old Bailey form the jury of what the law humorously terms Mr Oscar Wilde's "peers"?

There are a thousand other things that might be said, but I am not the person to say them, nor is it my place to make any reply to the precious bit of cant and bad grammar which appears over Lord Queensberry's signature in your issue of today, and which I feel I may safely leave to the tender mercies of Mr Robert Buchanan, whom I hereby beg to thank, in the name of justice, of sanity, and of Christian charity, for his noble letter. Your obedient servant

ALFRED DOUGLAS

The correspondence continued, with further letters from Buchanan and Douglas, until 25 April (the day before Wilde's first trial opened), when Queensberry wrote:

Were I the authority that had to mete out to him his punishment, I would treat him with all possible consideration as a sexual pervert of utterly diseased mind, not as a sane criminal. If this is sympathy Mr Wilde has it from me to this extent.

[1] On 13 June 1895 Labouchere's *Truth*, which had been violently anti-Wilde during and after his trials, printed the following:

I have received a long letter from Lord Alfred Douglas, in which he says, after explaining that he will not enter into discussion with me on a subject upon which I am "quite bigotted", and deploring "the cruelty and prejudice" which condemns Oscar Wilde "to the treatment of felons", that I am unfair on him in terming him a coward. He continues:

I stayed for three weeks after Mr Wilde's arrest, and visited him every day, and I did everything my mind could devise to help him, and I left on the day before his trial at his own most urgent request, and at the equally urgent request of his legal advisers, who assured me that my presence in the country could only do him harm, and that if I were called as a witness I should infallibly destroy what small chance he had of acquittal. Mr Wilde's own counsel absolutely declined to call me as a witness, fearing the harm I might do him in cross-examination, so that had I been called as a witness at all, it would have only been under a subpœna from the prosecution. Now, sir, you must give the devil his due, and granting, for the sake of argument, that I am an exceptional young scoundrel, you have no right to call me a coward. Perhaps you will pause to consider whether or not it is consistent with cowardice to do what I did—remain for three weeks in London with the daily and momentary expectation of being arrested and consigned to a fate like Mr Wilde's, receiving every day letters of warning, implored by all my friends and relations to go and save myself, and held up to execration by every catchpenny rag in England.

Certainly this exceptional moralist has the courage of his opinions but, these opinions being what they are, it is to be regretted that he is not afforded an opportunity to meditate on them in the seclusion of Pentonville.

On 28 June Douglas also wrote a long letter to W. T. Stead, editor of the *Review of Reviews* (printed in *Trials*, pp. 360–362), and on 1 June 1896 published an article on *L'affaire Wilde* in the *Revue Blanche*.

were to write to the papers to say that one had some secret and shameful malady: the fact that the man you hated was your own father, and that the feeling was thoroughly reciprocated, did not make your Hate noble or fine in any way. If it showed anything it was simply that it was an hereditary disease.

I remember again, when an execution was put into my house, and my books and furniture were seized and advertised to be sold, and Bankruptcy was impending, I naturally wrote to tell you about it. I did not mention that it was to pay for some gifts of mine to you that the bailiffs had entered the home where you had so often dined. I thought, rightly or wrongly, that such news might pain you a little. I merely told you the bare facts. I thought it proper that you should know them. You wrote back from Boulogne in a strain of almost lyrical exultation. You said that you knew your father was "hard up for money," and had been obliged to raise £1500 for the expenses of the trial, and that my going bankrupt was really a "splendid score" off him, as he would not then be able to get any of his costs out of me! Do you realise now what Hate blinding a person is? Do you recognise now that when I described it as an Atrophy destructive of everything but itself, I was scientifically describing a real psychological fact? That all my charming things were to be sold: my Burne-Jones drawings: my Whistler drawings: my Monticelli: my Simeon Solomons: my china: my Library with its collection of presentation volumes from almost every poet of my time, from Hugo to Whitman, from Swinburne to Mallarmé, from Morris to Verlaine; with its beautifully bound editions of my father's and mother's works; its wonderful array of college and school prizes, its *éditions de luxe*, and the like; was absolutely nothing to you. You said it was a great bore: that was all. What you really saw in it was the possibility that your father might ultimately lose a few hundred pounds, and that paltry consideration filled you with ecstatic joy. As for the costs of the trial, you may be interested to know that your father openly said in the Orleans Club that if it had cost him £20,000 he would have considered the money thoroughly well spent, he had extracted such enjoyment, and delight, and triumph out of it all. The fact that he was able not merely to put me into prison for two years, but to take me out for an afternoon and make me a public bankrupt was an extra-refinement of pleasure that he had not expected. It was the crowning-point of my humiliation, and of his complete and perfect victory. Had your father had no claim for his costs on me, you, I know perfectly well, would, as far as words go, at any rate have been most sympathetic about the entire loss of my library, a loss irreparable to a man of letters, the one of all my material losses the most distressing to me. You might even, remembering the sums of money I had lavishly spent on you and how you had lived on me for years, have taken the trouble to buy in some of my books for me. The best all went for less than £150: about as much as I would spend on you in an ordinary week. But the mean small pleasure of thinking that your father was going to be a few pence out of pocket made you forget all about trying to make me a little return, so slight, so easy, so inexpensive, so obvious, and so enormously welcome to me, had you brought it about. Am I right in saying that Hate blinds people? Do you see it now? If you don't, try to see it.

How clearly I saw it then, as now, I need not tell you. But I said to myself: "*At all costs I must keep Love in my heart. If I go into prison without Love what will become of my Soul?*" The letters I wrote to you at that time from Holloway were my efforts to keep Love as the dominant note of my own nature. I could if I had chosen have torn you to pieces with bitter reproaches. I could have rent you with maledictions. I could have held up a mirror to you, and shown you such an image of yourself that you would not have recognised it as your own till you found it mimicking back your gestures of horror, and then you would have known whose shape it was, and hated it and yourself for ever. More than that indeed. The sins of another were being placed to my account. Had I so chosen, I could on either trial have saved myself at his expense, not from shame indeed but from imprisonment. Had I cared to show that the Crown witnesses—the three most important—had been carefully coached by your father and his solicitors, not in reticences merely, but in assertions, in the absolute transference, deliberate, plotted, and rehearsed, of the actions and doings of someone else on to me, I could have had each one of them dismissed from the box by the Judge, more summarily than even wretched perjured Atkins was.[1] I could have walked out of Court with my tongue in my cheek, and my hands in my pockets, a free man. The strongest pressure was put upon me to do so. I was earnestly advised, begged, entreated to do so by people whose sole interest was my welfare, and the welfare of my house. But I refused. I did not choose to do so. I have never regretted my decision for a single moment, even in the most bitter periods of my imprisonment. Such a course of action would have been beneath me. Sins of the flesh are nothing. They are maladies for physicians to cure, if they should be cured. Sins of the soul alone are shameful. To have secured my acquittal by such means would have been a life-long torture to me. But do you really think that you were worthy of the love I was showing you then, or that for a single moment I thought you were? Do you really think that at any period in our friendship you were worthy of the love I showed you, or that for a single moment I thought you were? I knew you were not. But Love does not traffic in a marketplace, nor use a huckster's scales. Its joy, like the joy of the intellect, is to feel itself alive. The aim of Love is to love: no more, and no less. You were my enemy: such an enemy as no man ever had. I had given you my life, and to gratify the lowest and most contemptible of all human passions, Hatred and Vanity and Greed, you had thrown it away. In less than three years you had entirely ruined me from every point of view. For my own sake there was nothing for me to do but to love you. I knew, if I allowed myself to hate you, that in the dry

[1] Frederick Atkins was at times a billiard-marker and a bookmaker's clerk. When he gave evidence for the Crown at Wilde's first trial, he perjured himself so flagrantly that the judge described him in his summing up as "a most reckless, unreliable, unscrupulous, and untruthful witness." Wilde, who admitted having taken Atkins with him on a trip to Paris, was acquitted of the charges brought in respect of this witness.

desert of existence over which I had to travel, and am travelling still, every rock would lose its shadow, every palm tree be withered, every well of water prove poisoned at its source. Are you beginning now to understand a little? Is your imagination wakening from the long lethargy in which it has lain? You know already what Hate is. Is it beginning to dawn on you what Love is, and what is the nature of Love? It is not too late for you to learn, though to teach it to you I may have had to go to a convict's cell.

After my terrible sentence, when the prison-dress was on me, and the prison-house closed, I sat amidst the ruins of my wonderful life, crushed by anguish, bewildered with terror, dazed through pain. But I would not hate you. Every day I said to myself, *"I must keep Love in my heart today, else how shall I live through the day."* I reminded myself that you meant no evil, to me at any rate: I set myself to think that you had but drawn a bow at a venture, and that the arrow had pierced a King between the joints of the harness.[1] To have weighed you against the smallest of my sorrows, the meanest of my losses, would have been, I felt, unfair. I determined I would regard you as one suffering too. I forced myself to believe that at last the scales had fallen from your long-blinded eyes. I used to fancy, and with pain, what your horror must have been when you contemplated your terrible handiwork. There were times, even in those dark days, the darkest of all my life, when I actually longed to console you. So sure was I that at last you had realised what you had done.

It did not occur to me then that you could have the supreme vice, shallowness. Indeed, it was a real grief to me when I had to let you know that I was obliged to reserve for family business my first opportunity of receiving a letter: but my brother-in-law had written to me to say that if I would only write once to my wife she would, for my own sake and for our children's sake, take no action for divorce. I felt my duty was to do so. Setting aside other reasons, I could not bear the idea of being separated from Cyril, that beautiful, loving, loveable child of mine, my friend of all friends, my companion beyond all companions, one single hair of whose little golden head should have been dearer and of more value to me than, I will not merely say you from top to toe, but the entire chrysolite of the whole world:[2] was so indeed to me always, though I failed to understand it till too late.

Two weeks after your application, I get news of you. Robert Sherard, that bravest and most chivalrous of all brilliant beings, comes to see me, and amongst other things tells me that in that ridiculous *Mercure de France,* with its absurd affectation of being the true centre of literary corruption, you are about to publish an article on me with specimens of my letters. He asks me if it really was by my wish. I was greatly taken aback, and much annoyed, and gave orders that the thing was to be stopped at once.[3] You had left my letters lying about for blackmailing companions to steal, for hotel servants to pilfer, for housemaids to sell. That was simply your careless want of appreciation of what I had written to you. But that you should seriously propose to publish selections from the balance was almost

[1] *Kings,* xxii, 34.   [2] Cf. *Othello,* Act II, scene i.   [3] See note p. 393.

incredible to me. And which of my letters were they? I could get no information. That was my first news of you. It displeased me.

The second piece of news followed shortly afterwards. Your father's solicitors had appeared in the prison, and served me personally with a Bankruptcy notice, for a paltry £700, the amount of their taxed costs. I was adjudged a public insolvent, and ordered to be produced in Court. I felt most strongly, and feel still, and will revert to the subject again, that these costs should have been paid by your family. You had taken personally on yourself the responsibility of stating that your family would do so. It was that which had made the solicitor take up the case in the way he did. You were absolutely responsible. Even irrespective of your engagement on your family's behalf you should have felt that as you had brought the whole ruin on me, the least that could have been done was to spare me the additional ignominy of bankruptcy for an absolutely contemptible sum of money, less than half of what I spent on you in three brief summer months at Goring. Of that, however, no more here. I did through the solicitor's clerk, I fully admit, receive a message from you on the subject, or at any rate in connection with the occasion. The day he came to receive my depositions and statements, he leant across the table—the prison warder being present—and having consulted a piece of paper which he pulled from his pocket, said to me in a low voice: "Prince Fleur-de-Lys[1] wishes to be remembered to you." I stared at him. He repeated the message again. I did not know what he meant. "The gentleman is abroad at present," he added mysteriously. It all flashed across me, and I remember that, for the first and last time in my entire prison-life, I laughed. In that laugh was all the scorn of all the world. Prince Fleur-de-Lys! I saw— and subsequent events showed me that I rightly saw—that nothing that had happened had made you realise a single thing. You were in your own eyes still the graceful prince of a trivial comedy, not the sombre figure of a tragic show. All that had occurred was but as a feather for the cap that gilds a narrow head, a flower to pink the doublet that hides a heart that Hate, and Hate alone, can warm, that Love, and Love alone, finds cold. Prince Fleur-de-Lys! You were, no doubt, quite right to communicate with me under an assumed name. I myself, at that time, had no name at all. In the great prison where I was then incarcerated I was merely the figure and letter of a little cell in a long gallery, one of a thousand lifeless numbers, as of a thousand lifeless lives. But surely there were many real names in real history which would have suited you much better, and by which I would have had no difficulty at all in recognising you at once? I did not look for you behind the spangles of a tinsel vizard only suitable for an amusing masquerade. Ah! had your soul been, as for its own perfection even it should have been, wounded with sorrow, bowed with remorse, and humble with grief, such was not the disguise it would have chosen beneath whose shadow to seek entrance to the House of Pain! The great things of life are what they seem to be, and for that reason, strange as it may sound to you, are often difficult to interpret. But the little things of

[1] See note 5, p. 394.

454

life are symbols. We receive our bitter lessons most easily through them. Your seemingly casual choice of a feigned name was, and will remain, symbolic. It reveals you.

Six weeks later a third piece of news arrives. I am called out of the Hospital Ward, where I was lying wretchedly ill, to receive a special message from you through the Governor of the Prison. He reads me out a letter you had addressed to him in which you stated that you proposed to publish an article "on the case of Mr Oscar Wilde," in the *Mercure de France* ("a magazine," you added for some extraordinary reason, "corresponding to our English *Fortnightly Review*") and were anxious to obtain my permission to publish extracts and selections from—what letters? The letters I had written to you from Holloway Prison! The letters that should have been to you things sacred and secret beyond anything in the whole world! These actually were the letters you proposed to publish for the jaded *décadent* to wonder at, for the greedy *feuilletoniste* to chronicle, for the little lions of the *Quartier Latin* to gape and mouth at! Had there been nothing in your own heart to cry out against so vulgar a sacrilege you might at least have remembered the sonnet he wrote who saw with such sorrow and scorn the letters of John Keats sold by public auction in London and have understood at last the real meaning of my lines

> I think they love not Art
> Who break the crystal of a poet's heart
> That small and sickly eyes may glare or gloat.[1]

For what was your article to show? That I had been too fond of you? The Paris *gamin* was quite aware of the fact. They all read the newspapers, and most of them write for them. That I was a man of genius? The French understood that, and the peculiar quality of my genius, much better than you did, or could have been expected to do. That along with genius goes often a curious perversity of passion and desire? Admirable: but the subject belongs to Lombroso rather than to you. Besides, the pathological phenomenon in question is also found amongst those who have not genius. That in your war of hate with your father I was at once shield and weapon to each of you? Nay more, that in that hideous hunt for my life, that took place when the war was over, he never could have reached me had not your nets been already about my feet? Quite true: but I am told that Henri Bauër had already done it extremely well.[2] Besides, to corroborate his view, had such been your intention, you did not require to publish my letters; at any rate those written from Holloway Prison.

Will you say, in answer to my questions, that in one of my Holloway

---

[1] The closing lines of the octave of Wilde's sonnet "On the Sale by Auction of Keats's Love Letters" (see p. 182.)

[2] On 3 June 1895 Bauër published a powerful article in the *Echo de Paris*, attacking the barbarity of Wilde's sentence, the stupidity of punishing homosexuals, and the hypocrisy of the English. Queensberry he described as *"type de brute sportive malfaisante, mauvais mari, méchant père,"* typical of England and her reputation for *"pudibonderie menteuse."*

letters I had myself asked you to try, as far as you were able, to set me a little right with some small portion of the world? Certainly, I did so. Remember how and why I am here, at this very moment. Do you think I am here on account of my relations with the witnesses on my trial? My relations, real or supposed, with people of that kind were matters of no interest to either the Government or Society. They knew nothing of them, and cared less. I am here for having tried to put your father into prison. My attempt failed of course. My own Counsel threw up their briefs. Your father completely turned the tables on me, and had *me* in prison, has me there still. That is why there is contempt felt for me. That is why people despise me. That is why I have to serve out every day, every hour, every minute of my dreadful imprisonment. That is why my petitions have been refused.

You were the only person who, and without in any way exposing yourself to scorn or danger or blame, could have given another colour to the whole affair: have put the matter in a different light: have shown to a certain degree how things really stood. I would not of course have expected, nor indeed wished you to have stated how and for what purpose you had sought my assistance in your trouble at Oxford: or how, and for what purpose, if you had a purpose at all, you had practically never left my side for nearly three years. My incessant attempts to break off a friendship that was so ruinous to me as an artist, as a man of position, as a member of society even, need not have been chronicled with the accuracy with which they have been set down here. Nor would I have desired you to have described the scenes you used to make with such almost monotonous recurrence: nor to have reprinted your wonderful series of telegrams to me with their strange mixture of romance and finance; nor to have quoted from your letters the more revolting or heartless passages, as I have been forced to do. Still, I thought it would have been good, as well for you as for me, if you had made some protest against your father's version of our friendship, one no less grotesque than venomous, and as absurd in its reference to you as it was dishonouring in its reference to me. That version has now actually passed into serious history: it is quoted, believed, and chronicled: the preacher has taken it for his text, and the moralist for his barren theme: and I who appealed to all the ages have had to accept my verdict from one who is an ape and a buffoon. I have said, and with some bitterness, I admit, in this letter that such was the irony of things that your father would live to be the hero of a Sunday-school tract: that you would rank with the infant Samuel: and that my place would be between Gilles de Retz and the Marquis de Sade. I dare say it is best so. I have no desire to complain. One of the many lessons that one learns in prison is that things are what they are, and will be what they will be. Nor have I any doubt but that the leper of mediævalism, and the author of *Justine*, will prove better company than *Sandford and Merton*.[1]

But at the time I wrote to you I felt that for both our sakes it would be a

[1] *The History of Sandford and Merton*, an improving and immensely popular book for children by Thomas Day (1748–89), was originally published 1783–89.

good thing, a proper thing, a right thing *not* to accept the account your father had put forward through his Counsel for the edification of a Philistine world, and that is why I asked you to think out and write something that would be nearer the truth. It would at least have been better for you than scribbling to the French papers about the domestic life of your parents. What did the French care whether or not your parents had led a happy domestic life? One cannot conceive a subject more entirely uninteresting to them. What did interest them was how an artist of my distinction, one who by the school and movement of which he was the incarnation had exercised a marked influence on the direction of French thought, could, having led such a life, have brought such an action. Had you proposed for your article to publish the letters, endless I fear in number, in which I had spoken to you of the ruin you were bringing on my life, of the madness of moods of rage that you were allowing to master you to your own hurt as well as to mine, and of my desire, nay, my determination to end a friendship so fatal to me in every way, I could have understood it, though I would not have allowed such letters to be published: when your father's Counsel desiring to catch me in a contradiction suddenly produced in Court a letter of mine, written to you in March '93,[1] in which I stated that, rather than endure a repetition of the hideous scenes you seemed to take such a terrible pleasure in making, I would readily consent to be "blackmailed by every renter in London,"[2] it was a very real grief to me that that side of my friendship with you should incidentally be revealed to the common gaze: but that you should have been so slow to see, so lacking in all sensitiveness, and so dull in apprehension of what is rare, delicate and beautiful, as to propose yourself to publish the letters in which, and through which, I was trying to keep alive the very spirit and soul of Love, that it might dwell in my body through the long years of that body's humiliation—this was, and still is to me, a source of the very deepest pain, the most poignant disappointment. Why you did so, I fear I know but too well. If Hate blinded your eyes, Vanity sewed your eyelids together with threads of iron. The faculty "by which, and by which alone, one can understand others in their real as in their ideal relations,"[3] your narrow egotism had blunted, and long disuse had made of no avail. The imagination was as much in prison as I was. Vanity had barred up the windows, and the name of the warder was Hate.

All this took place in the early part of November of the year before last. A great river of life flows between you and a date so distant. Hardly, if at all, can you see across so wide a waste. But to me it seems to have occurred, I will not say yesterday, but today. Suffering is one long moment. We cannot divide it by seasons. We can only record its moods, and chronicle their return. With us time itself does not progress. It revolves. It seems to circle round one centre of pain. The paralysing immobility of a life, every circumstance of which is regulated after an unchangeable pattern, so that we eat and drink and walk and lie down and pray, or kneel at least for prayer, according to the inflexible laws of an iron formula: this immobile

[1] See letter p. 336.   [2] Cf. note 4, p. 336.   [3] Cf. p. 445.

quality, that makes each dreadful day in the very minutest detail like its brother, seems to communicate itself to those external forces the very essence of whose existence is ceaseless change. Of seed-time or harvest, of the reapers bending over the corn, or the grape-gatherers threading through the vines, of the grass in the orchard made white with broken blossoms, or strewn with fallen fruit, we know nothing, and can know nothing. For us there is only one season, the season of Sorrow. The very sun and moon seem taken from us. Outside, the day may be blue and gold, but the light that creeps down through the thickly-muffled glass of the small iron-barred window beneath which one sits is grey and niggard. It is always twilight in one's cell, as it is always midnight in one's heart. And in the sphere of thought, no less than in the sphere of time, motion is no more. The thing that you personally have long ago forgotten, or can easily forget, is happening to me now, and will happen to me again to-morrow. Remember this, and you will be able to understand a little of why I am writing to you, and in this manner writing.

A week later,[1] I am transferred here. Three more months go over and my mother dies. You knew, none better, how deeply I loved and honoured her. Her death was so terrible to me that I, once a lord of language, have no words in which to express my anguish and my shame. Never, even in the most perfect days of my development as an artist, could I have had words fit to bear so august a burden, or to move with sufficient stateliness of music through the purple pageant of my incommunicable woe. She and my father had bequeathed me a name they had made noble and honoured not merely in Literature, Art, Archæology and Science, but in the public history of my own country in its evolution as a nation. I had disgraced that name eternally. I had made it a low byword among low people. I had dragged it through the very mire. I had given it to brutes that they might make it brutal, and to fools that they might turn it into a synonym for folly. What I suffered then, and still suffer, is not for pen to write or paper to record. My wife, at that time kind and gentle to me, rather than that I should hear the news from indifferent or alien lips, travelled, ill as she was, all the way from Genoa to England to break to me herself the tidings of so irreparable, so irredeemable a loss. Messages of sympathy reached me from all who had still affection for me. Even people who had not known me personally, hearing what a new sorrow had come into my broken life, wrote to ask that some expression of their condolence should be conveyed to me. You alone stood aloof, sent me no message, and wrote me no letter. Of such actions, it is best to say what Virgil says to Dante of those whose lives have been barren in noble impulse and shallow of intention: "*Non ragioniam di lor, ma guarda, e passa.*"[2]

Three more months go over. The calendar of my daily conduct and labour that hangs on the outside of my cell-door, with my name and sentence written upon it, tells me that it is Maytime. My friends come to see me again. I enquire, as I always do, after you. I am told that you are in

[1] Wilde originally wrote "On the 13th of November."
[2] "Let us not speak of them, but look, and pass on." (*Inferno*, iii, 51.)

your villa at Naples, and are bringing out a volume of poems. At the close of the interview it is mentioned casually that you are dedicating them to me. The tidings seemed to give me a sort of nausea of life. I said nothing, but silently went back to my cell with contempt and scorn in my heart. How could you dream of dedicating a volume of poems to me without first asking my permission? Dream, do I say? How could you dare to do such a thing? Will you give as your answer that in the days of my greatness and fame I had consented to receive the dedication of your early work? Certainly, I did so; just as I would have accepted the homage of any other young man beginning the difficult and beautiful art of literature. All homage is delightful to an artist, and doubly sweet when youth brings it. Laurel and bay leaf wither when aged hands pluck them. Only youth has a right to crown an artist. That is the real privilege of being young, if youth only knew it. But the days of abasement and infamy are different from those of greatness and of fame. You have yet to learn that Prosperity, Pleasure and Success may be rough of grain and common in fibre, but that Sorrow is the most sensitive of all created things. There is nothing that stirs in the whole world of thought or motion to which Sorrow does not vibrate in terrible if exquisite pulsation. The thin beaten-out leaf of tremulous gold that chronicles the direction of forces that the eye cannot see is in comparison coarse.[1] It is a wound that bleeds when any hand but that of Love touches it and even then must bleed again, though not for pain.

You could write to the Governor of Wandsworth Prison to ask my permission to publish my letters in the *Mercure de France*, "*corresponding to our* English *Fortnightly Review*." Why not have written to the Governor of the Prison at Reading to ask my permission to dedicate your poems to me, whatever fantastic description you may have chosen to give of them? Was it because in the one case the magazine in question had been prohibited by me from publishing letters, the legal copyright of which, as you are of course perfectly well aware, was and is vested entirely in me, and in the other you thought that you could enjoy the wilfulness of your own way without my knowing anything about it till it was too late to interfere? The mere fact that I was a man disgraced, ruined, and in prison should have made you, if you desired to write my name on the fore-page of your work, beg it of me as a favour, an honour, a privilege. That is the way in which one should approach those who are in distress and sit in shame.

Where there is Sorrow there is holy ground. Some day you will realise what that means. You will know nothing of life till you do. Robbie, and natures like his, can realise it. When I was brought down from my prison to the Court of Bankruptcy between two policemen, Robbie waited in the long dreary corridor, that before the whole crowd, whom an action so sweet and simple hushed into silence, he might gravely raise his hat to me, as handcuffed and with bowed head I passed him by. Men have gone to heaven for smaller things than that. It was in this spirit, and with this mode of love that the saints knelt down to wash the feet of

[1] Perhaps a reference to the Gold-Leaf Electroscope, invented in 1787, to detect charges of static electricity, though "direction" makes no sense.

the poor, or stooped to kiss the leper on the cheek. I have never said one single word to him about what he did. I do not know to the present moment whether he is aware that I was even conscious of his action. It is not a thing for which one can render formal thanks in formal words. I store it in the treasury-house of my heart. I keep it there as a secret debt that I am glad to think I can never possibly repay. It is embalmed and kept sweet by the myrrh and cassia of many tears. When Wisdom has been profitless to me, and Philosophy barren, and the proverbs and phrases of those who have sought to give me consolation as dust and ashes in my mouth, the memory of that little lowly silent act of Love has unsealed for me all the wells of pity, made the desert blossom like a rose, and brought me out of the bitterness of lonely exile into harmony with the wounded, broken and great heart of the world. When you are able to understand, not merely how beautiful Robbie's action was, but why it meant so much to me, and always will mean so much, then, perhaps, you will realise how and in what spirit you should have approached me for permission to dedicate to me your verses.

It is only right to state that in any case I would not have accepted the dedication. Though, possibly, it would under other circumstances have pleased me to have been asked, I would have refused the request for *your* sake, irrespective of any feelings of my own. The first volume of poems that in the very springtime of his manhood a young man sends forth to the world should be like a blossom or flower of spring, like the white thorn in the meadow at Magdalen, or the cowslips in the Cumnor fields. It should not be burdened by the weight of a terrible, a revolting tragedy, a terrible, a revolting scandal. If I had allowed my name to serve as herald to the book it would have been a grave artistic error. It would have brought a wrong atmosphere round the whole work, and in modern art atmosphere counts for so much. Modern life is complex and relative. Those are its two distinguishing notes. To render the first we require atmosphere with its subtlety of *nuances*, of suggestion, of strange perspectives: as for the second we require background. That is why Sculpture has ceased to be a representative art; and why Music *is* a representative art; and why Literature is, and has been, and always will remain the supreme representative art.

Your little book should have brought with it Sicilian and Arcadian airs, not the pestilent foulness of the criminal dock or the close breath of the convict cell. Nor would such a dedication as you proposed have been merely an error of taste in Art; it would from other points of view have been entirely unseemly. It would have looked like a continuance of your conduct before and after my arrest. It would have given people the impression of being an attempt at foolish bravado: an example of that kind of courage that is sold cheap and bought cheap in the streets of shame. As far as our friendship is concerned Nemesis has crushed us both like flies. The dedication of verses to me when I was in prison would have seemed a sort of silly effort at smart repartee, an accomplishment on which in your old days of dreadful letter-writing—days never, I sincerely hope for your sake, to return—you used openly to pride yourself and about which it was your joy to boast. It would not have produced the serious, the beautiful effect which I trust—I believe indeed—you had intended. Had you consulted me, I would have advised you to delay the publication of your verses for a little; or, if that proved displeasing to you, to publish anonymously at first, and then when you had won lovers by your song—the only sort of lovers really worth the winning—you might have turned round and said to the world "These flowers that you admire are of my sowing, and now I offer them to one whom you regard as a pariah and an outcast, as my tribute to what I love and reverence and admire in him." But you chose the wrong method and the wrong moment. There is a tact in love, and a tact in literature: you were not sensitive to either.

I have spoken to you at length on this point in order that you should grasp its full bearings, and understand why I wrote at once to Robbie in terms of such scorn and contempt of you,[1] and absolutely prohibited the dedication, and desired that the words I had written of you should be copied out carefully and sent to you. I felt that at last the time had come when you should be made to see, to recognise, to realise a little of what you had done. Blindness may be carried so far that it becomes grotesque, and an unimaginative nature, if something be not done to rouse it, will become petrified into absolute insensibility, so that while the body may eat, and drink, and have its pleasures, the soul, whose house it is, may, like the soul of Branca d'Oria in Dante, be dead absolutely.[2] My letter seems to have arrived not a moment too soon. It fell on you, as far as I can judge, like a thunderbolt. You describe yourself, in your answer to Robbie, as being "deprived of all power of thought and expression." Indeed, apparently, you can think of nothing better than to write to your mother to complain. Of course, she, with that blindness to your real good that has been her ill-starred fortune and yours, gives you every comfort she can think of, and lulls you back, I suppose, into your former unhappy, unworthy condition; while as far as I am concerned, she lets my friends know that she is "very much annoyed" at the severity of my remarks about you. Indeed it is not merely to my friends that she conveys her sentiments of annoyance, but also to those—a very much larger number, I need hardly remind you—who are not my friends: and I am informed now, and through channels very kindly-disposed to you and yours, that in consequence of this a great deal of the sympathy that, by reason of my distinguished genius and terrible sufferings, had been gradually but surely growing up for me, has been entirely taken away. People say "Ah! he first tried to get the kind father put into prison and failed: now he turns round and blames the innocent son for his failure. How right we were to despise him! How worthy of contempt he is!" It seems to me that, when my name is mentioned in your mother's presence, if she has no word of sorrow or regret for her share—no slight one—in the ruin of my house, it would be more seemly if she remained silent. And as for you—don't you think now that, instead of writing to *her* to complain, it would have been better for you, in every way, to have written to *me* directly, and to have had the courage to say to me whatever

[1] See pp. 400–401. [2] Wilde originally wrote "was."

461

you had or fancied you had to say? It is nearly a year ago now since I wrote that letter. You cannot have remained during that entire time "deprived of all power of thought and expression." Why did you not write to me? You saw by my letter how deeply wounded, how outraged I was by your whole conduct. More than that; you saw your entire friendship with me set before you, at last, in its true light, and by a mode not to be mistaken. Often in old days I had told you that you were ruining my life. You had always laughed. When Edwin Levy[1] at the very beginning of our friendship, seeing your manner of putting me forward to bear the brunt, and annoyance, and expense even of that unfortunate Oxford mishap of yours, if we must so term it, in reference to which his advice and help had been sought, warned me for the space of a whole hour against knowing you, you laughed, as at Bracknell I described to you my long and impressive interview with him. When I told you how even that unfortunate young man who ultimately stood beside me in the Dock had warned me more than once that you would prove far more fatal in bringing me to utter destruction than any even of the common lads whom I was foolish enough to know, you laughed, though not with such sense of amusement. When my more prudent or less well-disposed friends either warned me or left me, on account of my friendship with you, you laughed with scorn. You laughed immoderately when, on the occasion of your father writing his first abusive letter to you about me, I told you that I knew I would be the mere catspaw of your dreadful quarrel and come to some evil between you. But every single thing had happened as I had said it would happen, as far as the result goes. You had no excuse for not seeing how all things had come to pass. Why did you not write to me? Was it cowardice? Was it callousness? What was it? The fact that I was outraged with you, and had expressed my sense of the outrage, was all the more reason for writing. If you thought my letter just, you should have written. If you thought it in the smallest point unjust, you should have written. I waited for a letter. I felt sure that at last you would see that, if old affection, much-protested love, the thousand acts of ill-requited kindness I had showered on you, the thousand unpaid debts of gratitude you owed me—that if all these were nothing to you, mere duty itself, most barren of all bonds between man and man, should have made you write. You cannot say that you seriously thought I was obliged to receive none but business communications from members of my family. You knew perfectly well that every twelve weeks Robbie was writing to me a little budget of literary news. Nothing can be more charming than his letters, in their wit, their clever concentrated criticism, their light touch: they are real letters: they are like a person talking to one: they have the quality of a French *causerie intime*: and in his delicate modes of deference to me, appealing at one time to my judgment, at another to my sense of humour, at another to my instinct for beauty or to my culture, and reminding me in a hundred subtle ways that once I was to many an arbiter of style in Art, the supreme arbiter to some, he shows how he has the tact of love as well as the tact of literature. His letters have been the little

1 See note 1, p. 107.

messengers between me and that beautiful unreal world of Art where once I was King, and would have remained King, indeed, had I not let myself be lured into the imperfect world of coarse uncompleted passions, of appetite without distinction, desire without limit, and formless greed. Yet, when all is said, surely you might have been able to understand, or conceive, at any rate, in your own mind, that, even on the ordinary grounds of mere psychological curiosity, it would have been more interesting to me to hear from *you* than to learn that Alfred Austin was trying to bring out a volume of poems,[1] or that Street was writing dramatic criticisms for the *Daily Chronicle*,[2] or that by one who cannot speak a panegyric without stammering Mrs Meynell had been pronounced to be the new Sibyl of Style.[3]

Ah! had *you* been in prison—I will not say through any fault of mine, for that would be a thought too terrible for me to bear—but through fault of your own, error of your own, faith in some unworthy friend, slip in sensual mire, trust misapplied, or love ill-bestowed, or none, or all of these —do you think that I would have allowed you to eat your heart away in darkness and solitude without trying in some way, however slight, to help you to bear the bitter burden of your disgrace? Do you think that I would not have let you know that if you suffered, I was suffering too: that if you wept, there were tears in my eyes also: and that if you lay in the house of bondage and were despised of men, I out of my very griefs had built a house in which to dwell until your coming, a treasury in which all that men had denied to you would be laid up for your healing, one hundredfold in increase? If bitter necessity, or prudence, to *me* more bitter still, had prevented my being near you, and robbed me of the joy of your presence, though seen through prison-bars and in a shape of shame, I would have written to you in season and out of season in the hope that some mere phrase, some single word, some broken echo even of Love might reach you. If you had refused to receive my letters, I would have written none the less, so that you should have known that at any rate there were always letters waiting for you. Many have done so to me. Every three months people write to me, or propose to write to me. Their letters and communications are kept. They will be handed to me when I go out of prison. I know that they are there. I know the names of the people who have written them. I know that they are full of sympathy, and affection, and kindness. That is sufficient for me. I need to know no more. Your silence has been horrible. Nor has it been a silence of weeks and months merely,

[1] Alfred Austin (1835–1913) eventually succeeded Tennyson as Poet Laureate in 1896, after a four-year interregnum. In 1887 Wilde had written in the *Pall Mall Gazette*: "Mr Austin is neither an Olympian nor a Titan, and all the puffing in Paternoster Row cannot set him on Parnassus." In 1895, when asked who he thought should be the next Laureate, Wilde wrote (in the *Idler* for April): "Mr Swinburne is already the Poet Laureate of England. The fact that his appointment to this high post has not been degraded by official confirmation renders his position all the more unassailable. He whom all poets love is the Poet Laureate always."

[2] George Slythe Street (1867–1936), journalist and author of *The Autobiography of a Boy* (1894) and other books.

[3] In December 1895 Coventry Patmore (1823–96) had written to the *Saturday Review*, advocating the claims of Mrs Meynell to the vacant Laureateship.

but of years; of years even as they have to count them who, like yourself, live swiftly in happiness, and can hardly catch the gilt feet of the days as they dance by, and are out of breath in the chase after pleasure. It is a silence without excuse; a silence without palliation. I knew you had feet of clay. Who knew it better? When I wrote, among my aphorisms, that it was simply the feet of clay that made the gold of the image precious,[1] it was of you I was thinking. But it is no gold image with clay feet that you have made of yourself. Out of the very dust of the common highway that the hooves of horned things pash into mire you have moulded your perfect semblance for me to look at, so that, whatever my secret desire might have been, it would be impossible for me now to have for you any feeling other than that of contempt and scorn, for myself any feeling other than that of contempt and scorn either. And setting aside all other reasons, your indifference, your worldly wisdom, your callousness, your prudence, whatever you may choose to call it, has been made doubly bitter to me by the peculiar circumstances that either accompanied or followed my fall.

Other miserable men, when they are thrown into prison, if they are robbed of the beauty of the world, are at least safe, in some measure, from the world's most deadly slings, most awful arrows. They can hide in the darkness of their cells, and of their very disgrace make a mode of sanctuary. The world, having had its will, goes its way, and they are left to suffer undisturbed. With me it has been different. Sorrow after sorrow has come beating at the prison doors in search of me. They have opened the gates wide and let them in. Hardly, if at all, have my friends been suffered to see me. But my enemies have had full access to me always. Twice in my public appearances at the Bankruptcy Court, twice again in my public transferences from one prison to another, have I been shown under conditions of unspeakable humiliation to the gaze and mockery of men. The messenger of Death has brought me his tidings and gone his way, and in entire solitude, and isolated from all that could give me comfort, or suggest relief, I have had to bear the intolerable burden of misery and remorse that the memory of my mother placed upon me, and places on me still. Hardly has that wound been dulled, not healed, by time, when violent and bitter and harsh letters come to me from my wife through her solicitor. I am, at once, taunted and threatened with poverty. That I can bear. I can school myself to worse than that. But my two children are taken from me by legal procedure.[2] That is and always will remain to me a source of infinite distress, of infinite pain, of grief without end or limit. That the law should decide, and take upon itself to decide, that I am one unfit to be with my own children is something quite horrible to me. The disgrace of prison

---

[1] *The Picture of Dorian Gray*, ch. xv. This chapter first appeared in the book-edition of April 1891. Cf. p. 281.

[2] Constance Wilde's summons had been heard by Mr Justice Kekewich in the Chancery Division on 12 February 1897. The resulting order gave Constance custody of the children, with herself and Adrian Hope (see note p. 499) as their guardians.

is as nothing compared to it. I envy the other men who tread the yard along with me. I am sure that their children wait for them, look for their coming, will be sweet to them.

The poor are wiser, more charitable, more kind, more sensitive than we are. In their eyes prison is a tragedy in a man's life, a misfortune, a casualty, something that calls for sympathy in others. They speak of one who is in prison as of one who is "*in trouble*" simply. It is the phrase they always use, and the expression has the perfect wisdom of Love in it. With people of our rank it is different. With us prison makes a man a pariah. I, and such as I am, have hardly any right to air and sun. Our presence taints the pleasures of others. We are unwelcome when we reappear. To revisit the glimpses of the moon[1] is not for us. Our very children are taken away. Those lovely links with humanity are broken. We are doomed to be solitary, while our sons still live. We are denied the one thing that might heal us and help us, that might bring balm to the bruised heart, and peace to the soul in pain.

And to all this has been added the hard, small fact that by your actions and by your silence, by what you have done and by what you have left undone, you have made every day of my long imprisonment still more difficult for me to live through. The very bread and water of prison fare you have by your conduct changed. You have rendered the one bitter and the other brackish to me. The sorrow you should have shared you have doubled, the pain you should have sought to lighten you have quickened to anguish. I have no doubt that you did not mean to do so. I know that you did not mean to do so. It was simply that "one really fatal defect of your character, your entire lack of imagination."[2]

And the end of it all is that I have got to forgive you. I must do so. I don't write this letter to put bitterness into your heart, but to pluck it out of mine. For my own sake I must forgive you. One cannot always keep an adder in one's breast to feed on one, nor rise up every night to sow thorns in the garden of one's soul. It will not be difficult at all for me to do so, if you help me a little. Whatever you did to me in old days I always readily forgave. It did you no good then. Only one whose life is without stain of any kind can forgive sins. But now when I sit in humiliation and disgrace it is different. My forgiveness should mean a great deal to you now. Some day you will realise it. Whether you do so early or late, soon or not at all, my way is clear before me. I cannot allow you to go through life bearing in your heart the burden of having ruined a man like me. The thought might make you callously indifferent, or morbidly sad. I must take the burden from you and put it on my own shoulders.

I must say to myself that neither you nor your father, multiplied a thousand times over, could possibly have ruined a man like me: that I ruined myself: and that nobody, great or small, can be ruined except by his own hand. I am quite ready to do so. I am trying to do so, though you may not think it at the present moment. If I have brought this pitiless indictment against you, think what an indictment I bring without pity against

---

[1] *Hamlet*, Act I, scene iv.   [2] Cf. pp. 445 and 447.

myself. Terrible as what you did to me was, what I did to myself was far more terrible still.

I was a man who stood in symbolic relations to the art and culture of my age. I had realised this for myself at the very dawn of my manhood, and had forced my age to realise it afterwards. Few men hold such a position in their own lifetime and have it so acknowledged. It is usually discerned, if discerned at all, by the historian, or the critic, long after both the man and his age have passed away. With me it was different. I felt it myself, and made others feel it. Byron was a symbolic figure, but his relations were to the passion of his age and its weariness of passion. Mine were to something more noble, more permanent, of more vital issue, of larger scope.

The gods had given me almost everything. I had genius, a distinguished name, high social position, brilliancy, intellectual daring: I made art a philosophy, and philosophy an art: I altered the minds of men and the colours of things: there was nothing I said or did that did not make people wonder: I took the drama, the most objective form known to art, and made it as personal a mode of expression as the lyric or the sonnet, at the same time that I widened its range and enriched its characterisation: drama, novel, poem in rhyme, poem in prose, subtle or fantastic dialogue, whatever I touched I made beautiful in a new mode of beauty: to truth itself I gave what is false no less than what is true as its rightful province, and showed that the false and the true are merely forms of intellectual existence. I treated Art as the supreme reality, and life as a mere mode of fiction: I awoke the imagination of my century so that it created myth and legend around me: I summed up all systems in a phrase, and all existence in an epigram.

Along with these things, I had things that were different. I let myself be lured into long spells of senseless and sensual ease. I amused myself with being a *flâneur*, a dandy, a man of fashion. I surrounded myself with the smaller natures and the meaner minds. I became the spendthrift of my own genius, and to waste an eternal youth gave me a curious joy. Tired of being on the heights I deliberately went to the depths in the search for new sensations. What the paradox was to me in the sphere of thought, perversity became to me in the sphere of passion. Desire, at the end, was a malady, or a madness, or both. I grew careless of the lives of others. I took pleasure where it pleased me and passed on. I forgot that every little action of the common day makes or unmakes character, and that therefore what one has done in the secret chamber one has some day to cry aloud on the housetops. I ceased to be Lord over myself. I was no longer the Captain of my Soul, and did not know it. I allowed you to dominate me, and your father to frighten me. I ended in horrible disgrace. There is only one thing for me now, absolute Humility: just as there is only one thing for you, absolute Humility also. You had better come down into the dust and learn it beside me.

I have lain in prison for nearly two years. Out of my nature has come wild despair; an abandonment to grief that was piteous even to look at: terrible and impotent rage: bitterness and scorn: anguish that wept aloud:

misery that could find no voice: sorrow that was dumb. I have passed through every possible mood of suffering. Better than Wordsworth himself I know what Wordsworth meant when he said:

> Suffering is permanent, obscure, and dark
> And has the nature of Infinity.[1]

But while there were times when I rejoiced in the idea that my sufferings were to be endless, I could not bear them to be without meaning. Now I find hidden away in my nature something that tells me that nothing in the whole world is meaningless, and suffering least of all. That something hidden away in my nature, like a treasure in a field, is Humility.

It is the last thing left in me, and the best: the ultimate discovery at which I have arrived: the starting-point for a fresh development. It has come to me right out of myself, so I know that it has come at the proper time. It could not have come before, nor later. Had anyone told me of it, I would have rejected it. Had it been brought to me, I would have refused it. As I found it, I want to keep it. I must do so. It is the one thing that has in it the elements of life, of a new life, a *Vita Nuova* for me. Of all things it is the strangest. One cannot give it away, and another may not give it to one. One cannot acquire it, except by surrendering everything that one has. It is only when one has lost all things, that one knows that one possesses it.

Now that I realise that it is in me, I see quite clearly what I have got to do, what, in fact, I must do. And when I use such a phrase as that, I need not tell you that I am not alluding to any external sanction or command. I admit none. I am far more of an individualist than I ever was. Nothing seems to me of the smallest value except what one gets out of oneself. My nature is seeking a fresh mode of self-realisation. That is all I am concerned with. And the first thing that I have got to do is to free myself from any possible bitterness of feeling against you.

I am completely penniless, and absolutely homeless. Yet there are worse things in the world than that. I am quite candid when I tell you that rather than go out from this prison with bitterness in my heart against you or against the world I would gladly and readily beg my bread from door to door. If I got nothing at the house of the rich, I would get something at the house of the poor. Those who have much are often greedy. Those who have little always share. I would not a bit mind sleeping in the cool grass in summer, and when winter came on sheltering myself by the warm close-thatched rick, or under the penthouse of a great barn, provided I had love in my heart. The external things of life seem to me now of no importance at all. You can see to what intensity of individualism I have arrived, or am arriving rather, for the journey is long, and "where I walk there are thorns."[2]

Of course I know that to ask for alms on the highway is not to be my lot, and that if ever I lie in the cool grass at night–time it will be to write sonnets to the Moon. When I go out of prison, Robbie will be waiting for me on

---

[1] *The Borderers*, Act III; "has" should be "shares."
[2] *A Woman of No Importance*, Act IV.

the other side of the big iron-studded gate, and he is the symbol not merely of his own affection, but of the affection of many others besides. I believe I am to have enough to live on for about eighteen months at any rate, so that, if I may not write beautiful books, I may at least read beautiful books, and what joy can be greater? After that, I hope to be able to re-create my creative faculty. But were things different: had I not a friend left in the world: were there not a single house open to me even in pity: had I to accept the wallet and ragged cloak of sheer penury: still as long as I remained free from all resentment, hardness, and scorn, I would be able to face life with much more calm and confidence than I would were my body in purple and fine linen, and the soul within it sick with hate. And I shall really have no difficulty in forgiving you. But to make it a pleasure for me you must feel that you want it. When you really want it you will find it waiting for you.

I need not say that my task does not end there. It would be comparatively easy if it did. There is much more before me. I have hills far steeper to climb, valleys much darker to pass through. And I have to get it all out of myself. Neither Religion, Morality, nor Reason can help me at all.

Morality does not help me. I am a born antinomian. I am one of those who are made for exceptions, not for laws. But while I see that there is nothing wrong in what one does, I see that there is something wrong in what one becomes. It is well to have learned that.

Religion does not help me. The faith that others give to what is unseen, I give to what one can touch, and look at. My Gods dwell in temples made with hands, and within the circle of actual experience is my creed made perfect and complete: too complete it may be, for like many or all of those who have placed their Heaven in this earth, I have found in it not merely the beauty of Heaven, but the horror of Hell also. When I think about Religion at all, I feel as if I would like to found an order for those who cannot believe: the Confraternity of the Fatherless one might call it, where on an altar, on which no taper burned, a priest, in whose heart peace had no dwelling, might celebrate with unblessed bread and a chalice empty of wine. Everything to be true must become a religion. And agnosticism should have its ritual no less than faith. It has sown its martyrs, it should reap its saints, and praise God daily for having hidden Himself from man. But whether it be faith or agnosticism, it must be nothing external to me. Its symbols must be of my own creating. Only that is spiritual which makes its own form. If I may not find its secret within myself, I shall never find it. If I have not got it already, it will never come to me.

Reason does not help me. It tells me that the laws under which I am convicted are wrong and unjust laws, and the system under which I have suffered a wrong and unjust system. But, somehow, I have got to make both of these things just and right to me. And exactly as in Art one is only concerned with what a particular thing is at a particular moment to oneself, so it is also in the ethical evolution of one's character. I have got to make everything that has happened to me good for me. The plank-bed, the loathsome food, the hard ropes shredded into oakum till one's finger-tips grow dull with pain, the menial offices with which each day begins and finishes, the harsh orders that routine seems to necessitate, the dreadful dress that makes sorrow grotesque to look at, the silence, the solitude, the shame—each and all of these things I have to transform into a spiritual experience. There is not a single degradation of the body which I must not try and make into a spiritualising of the soul.

I want to get to the point when I shall be able to say, quite simply and without affectation, that the two great turning-points of my life were when my father sent me to Oxford, and when society sent me to prison. I will not say that it is the best thing that could have happened to me, for that phrase would savour of too great bitterness towards myself. I would sooner say, or hear it said of me, that I was so typical a child of my age that in my perversity, and for that perversity's sake, I turned the good things of my life to evil, and the evil things of my life to good. What is said, however, by myself or by others matters little. The important thing, the thing that lies before me, the thing that I have to do, or be for the brief remainder of my days one maimed, marred, and incomplete, is to absorb into my nature all that has been done to me, to make it part of me, to accept it without com-plaint, fear, or reluctance. The supreme vice is shallowness. Whatever is realised is right.

When first I was put into prison some people advised me to try and forget who I was. It was ruinous advice. It is only by realising what I am that I have found comfort of any kind. Now I am advised by others to try on my release to forget that I have ever been in a prison at all. I know that would be equally fatal. It would mean that I would be always haunted by an intolerable sense of disgrace, and that those things that are meant as much for me as for anyone else—the beauty of the sun and the moon, the pageant of the seasons, the music of daybreak and the silence of great nights, the rain falling through the leaves, or the dew creeping over the grass and making it silver—would all be tainted for me, and lose their healing power and their power of communicating joy. To reject one's own experiences is to arrest one's own development. To deny one's own experiences is to put a lie into the lips of one's own life. It is no less than a denial of the Soul. For just as the body absorbs things of all kinds, things common and unclean no less than those that the priest or a vision has cleansed, and con-verts them into swiftness or strength, into the play of beautiful muscles and the moulding of fair flesh, into the curves and colours of the hair, the lips, the eye: so the Soul, in its turn, has its nutritive functions also, and can transform into noble moods of thought, and passions of high import, what in itself is base, cruel, and degrading: nay more, may find in these its most august modes of assertion, and can often reveal itself most perfectly through what was intended to desecrate or destroy.

The fact of my having been the common prisoner of a common gaol I must frankly accept, and, curious as it may seem to you, one of the things I shall have to teach myself is not to be ashamed of it. I must accept it as a punishment, and if one is ashamed of having been punished, one might just as well never have been punished at all. Of course there are many things of which I was convicted that I had not done, but then there are many things of which I was convicted that I had done, and a still greater number of things in my life for which I never was indicted at all. And as for what I have said in this letter, that the gods are strange, and punish us for what is good and humane in us as much as for what is evil and perverse, I must accept the fact that one is punished for the good as well as for the evil that one does. I have no doubt that it is quite right one should be. It helps one, or should help one, to realise both, and not to be too conceited about either. And if I then am not ashamed of my punishment, as I hope not to be, I shall be able to think, and walk, and live with freedom.

Many men on their release carry their prison along with them into the air, hide it as a secret disgrace in their hearts, and at length like poor poisoned things creep into some hole and die. It is wretched that they should have to do so, and it is wrong, terribly wrong, of Society that it should force them to do so. Society takes upon itself the right to inflict appalling punishments on the individual, but it also has the supreme vice of shallowness, and fails to realise what it has done. When the man's punishment is over, it leaves him to himself: that is to say it abandons him at the very moment when its highest duty towards him begins. It is really ashamed of its own actions, and shuns those whom it has punished, as people shun a creditor whose debt they cannot pay, or one on whom they have inflicted an irreparable, an irredeemable wrong. I claim on my side that if I realise what I have suffered, Society should realise what it has inflicted on me: and that there should be no bitterness or hate on either side.

Of course I know that from one point of view things will be made more difficult for me than for others; must indeed, by the very nature of the case, be made so. The poor thieves and outcasts who are imprisoned here with me are in many respects more fortunate than I am. The little way in grey city or green field that saw their sin is small: to find those who know nothing of what they have done they need go no further than a bird might fly between the twilight before dawn and dawn itself: but for me "the world is shrivelled to a handsbreadth,"[1] and everywhere I turn my name is written on the rocks in lead. For I have come, not from obscurity into the momentary notoriety of crime, but from a sort of eternity of fame to a sort of eternity of infamy, and sometimes seem to myself to have shown, if indeed it required showing, that between the famous and the infamous there is but one step, if so much as one.

Still, in the very fact that people will recognise me wherever I go, and know all about my life, as far as its follies go, I can discern something good for me. It will force on me the necessity of again asserting myself as an artist, and as soon as I possibly can. If I can produce even one more beautiful work of art I shall be able to rob malice of its venom, and cowardice of its sneer, and to pluck out the tongue of scorn by the roots. And if life be, as it surely is, a problem to me, I am no less a problem to Life.

[1] *A Woman of No Importance*, Act IV.

People must adopt some attitude towards me, and so pass judgment both on themselves and me. I need not say I am not talking of particular individuals. The only people I would care to be with now are artists and people who have suffered: those who know what Beauty is, and those who know what Sorrow is: nobody else interests me. Nor am I making any demands on Life. In all that I have said I am simply concerned with my own mental attitude towards life as a whole: and I feel that not to be ashamed of having been punished is one of the first points I must attain to, for the sake of my own perfection, and because I am so imperfect.

Then I must learn how to be happy. Once I knew it, or thought I knew it, by instinct. It was always springtime once in my heart. My temperament was akin to joy. I filled my life to the very brim with pleasure, as one might fill a cup to the very brim with wine. Now I am approaching life from a completely new standpoint, and even to conceive happiness is often extremely difficult for me. I remember during my first term at Oxford reading in Pater's *Renaissance*[1]—that book which has had such a strange influence over my life—how Dante places low in the Inferno those who wilfully live in sadness, and going to the College Library and turning to the passage in the *Divine Comedy* where beneath the dreary marsh lie those who were "sullen in the sweet air," saying for ever through their sighs:

> *Tristi fummo*
> *nell' aer dolce che dal sol s'allegra.*[2]

I knew the Church condemned *accidia*, but the whole idea seemed to me quite fantastic, just the sort of sin, I fancied, a priest who knew nothing about real life would invent. Nor could I understand how Dante, who says that "sorrow remarries us to God,"[3] could have been so harsh to those who were enamoured of melancholy, if any such there really were. I had no idea that some day this would become to me one of the greatest temptations of my life.

While I was in Wandsworth Prison I longed to die. It was my one desire. When after two months in the Infirmary I was transferred here, and found myself growing gradually better in physical health, I was filled with rage. I determined to commit suicide on the very day on which I left prison. After a time that evil mood passed away, and I made up my mind to live, but to wear gloom as a King wears purple: never to smile again: to turn whatever house I entered into a house of mourning: to make my friends walk slowly in sadness with me: to teach them that melancholy is the true secret of life: to maim them with an alien sorrow: to mar them with my own pain. Now I feel quite differently. I see it would be both ungrateful and unkind of me to pull so long a face that when my friends came to see me they would have to make their faces still longer in order to

---

[1] In the essay on "The Poetry of Michelangelo."
[2] Sad once were we,
In the sweet air made gladsome by the sun.
(*Inferno*, vii, 121-22, H. F. Cary's translation.)
[3] *Purgatorio*, xxiii, 81.

show their sympathy, or, if I desired to entertain them, to invite them to sit down silently to bitter herbs and funeral baked meats. I must learn how to be cheerful and happy.

The last two occasions on which I was allowed to see my friends here I tried to be as cheerful as possible, and to show my cheerfulness in order to make them some slight return for their trouble in coming all the way from town to visit me. It is only a slight return, I know, but it is the one, I feel certain, that pleases them most. I saw Robbie for an hour on Saturday week, and I tried to give the fullest possible expression to the delight I really felt at our meeting.[1] And that, in the views and ideas I am here shaping for myself, I am quite right is shown to me by the fact that now for the first time since my imprisonment I have a real desire to live.

There is before me so much to do that I would regard it as a terrible tragedy if I died before I was allowed to complete at any rate a little of it. I see new developments in Art and Life, each one of which is a fresh mode of perfection. I long to live so that I can explore what is no less than a new world to me. Do you want to know what this new world is? I think you can guess what it is. It is the world in which I have been living.

Sorrow, then, and all that it teaches one, is my new world. I used to live entirely for pleasure. I shunned sorrow and suffering of every kind. I hated both. I resolved to ignore them as far as possible, to treat them, that is to say, as modes of imperfection. They were not part of my scheme of life. They had no place in my philosophy. My mother, who knew life as a whole, used often to quote to me Goethe's lines—written by Carlyle in a book he had given her years ago—and translated, I fancy, by him also:

Who never ate his bread in sorrow,
    Who never spent the midnight hours
Weeping and waiting for the morrow,
    He knows you not, ye Heavenly Powers.[2]

They were the lines that noble Queen of Prussia, whom Napoleon treated with such coarse brutality, used to quote in her humiliation and exile:[3] they were lines my mother often quoted in the troubles of her later life: I absolutely declined to accept or admit the enormous truth hidden in them. I could not understand it. I remember quite well how I used to tell her that I did not want to eat my bread in sorrow, or to pass any night weeping and watching for a more bitter dawn. I had no idea that it was one of the special

[1] This probably refers to Saturday, 27 February 1897, when Ross and Adey paid Wilde a visit.

[2] Carlyle's translation of Goethe's *Wilhelm Meister's Apprenticeship*, Bk. ii, ch. 13, where "midnight" is "darksome," "waiting" is "watching," and "Heavenly" is "gloomy."

[3] Louisa (1776–1810), wife of King Frederick William III. She is said to have copied these lines when she and her husband were in flight after the Battle of Jena (1806). After the total defeat of Prussia in 1807 she went to Tilsit to plead unavailingly for generous terms from Napoleon, who had consistently but vainly tried to blacken her character.

things that the Fates had in store for me; that for a whole year of my life, indeed, I was to do little else. But so has my portion been meted out to me; and during the last few months I have, after terrible struggles and difficulties, been able to comprehend some of the lessons hidden in the heart of pain. Clergymen, and people who use phrases without wisdom, sometimes talk of suffering as a mystery. It is really a revelation. One discerns things that one never discerned before. One approaches the whole of history from a different standpoint. What one had felt dimly through instinct, about Art, is intellectually and emotionally realised with perfect clearness of vision and absolute intensity of apprehension.

I now see that sorrow, being the supreme emotion of which man is capable, is at once the type and test of all great Art. What the artist is always looking for is that mode of existence in which soul and body are one and indivisible: in which the outward is expressive of the inward: in which Form reveals. Of such modes of existence there are not a few: youth and the arts preoccupied with youth may serve as a model for us at one moment: at another, we may like to think that, in its subtlety and sensitiveness of impression, its suggestion of a spirit dwelling in external things and making its raiment of earth and air, of mist and city alike, and in the morbid sympathy of its moods, and tones and colours, modern landscape art is realising for us pictorially what was realised in such plastic perfection by the Greeks. Music, in which all subject is absorbed in expression and cannot be separated from it, is a complex example, and a flower or a child a simple example of what I mean: but Sorrow is the ultimate type both in life and Art.

Behind Joy and Laughter there may be a temperament, coarse, hard and callous. But behind Sorrow there is always Sorrow. Pain, unlike Pleasure, wears no mask. Truth in Art is not any correspondence between the essential idea and the accidental existence; it is not the resemblance of shape to shadow, or of the form mirrored in the crystal to the form itself: it is no Echo coming from a hollow hill, any more than it is the well of silver water in the valley that shows the Moon to the Moon and Narcissus to Narcissus. Truth in Art is the unity of a thing with itself: the outward rendered expressive of the inward: the soul made incarnate: the body instinct with spirit. For this reason there is no truth comparable to Sorrow. There are times when Sorrow seems to me to be the only truth. Other things may be illusions of the eye or the appetite, made to blind the one and cloy the other, but out of Sorrow have the worlds been built, and at the birth of a child or a star there is pain.

More than this, there is about Sorrow an intense, an extraordinary reality. I have said of myself that I was one who stood in symbolic relations to the art and culture of my age. There is not a single wretched man in this wretched place along with me who does not stand in symbolic relations to the very secret of life. For the secret of life is suffering. It is what is hidden behind everything. When we begin to live, what is sweet is so sweet to us, and what is bitter so bitter, that we inevitably direct all our desires towards pleasure, and seek not merely for "a month or twain to feed on honeycomb,"[1] but for all our years to taste no other food, ignorant the while that we may be really starving the soul.

I remember talking once on this subject to one of the most beautiful personalities I have ever known:[2] a woman, whose sympathy and noble kindness to me both before and since the tragedy of my imprisonment have been beyond power and description: one who has really assisted me, though she does not know it, to bear the burden of my troubles more than anyone else in the whole world has: and all through the mere fact of her existence: through her being what she is, partly an ideal and partly an influence, a suggestion of what one might become, as well as a real help towards becoming it, a soul that renders the common air sweet, and makes what is spiritual seem as simple and natural as sunlight or the sea, one for whom Beauty and Sorrow walk hand in hand and have the same message. On the occasion of which I am thinking I recall distinctly how I said to her that there was enough suffering in one narrow London lane to show that God did not love man, and that wherever there was any sorrow, though but that of a child in some little garden weeping over a fault that it had or had not committed, the whole face of creation was completely marred. I was entirely wrong. She told me so, but I could not believe her. I was not in the sphere in which such belief was to be attained to. Now it seems to me that Love of some kind is the only possible explanation of the extraordinary amount of suffering that there is in the world. I cannot conceive any other explanation. I am convinced that there is no other, and that if the worlds have indeed, as I have said, been built out of Sorrow, it has been by the hands of Love, because in no other way could the Soul of man for whom the worlds are made reach the full stature of its perfection. Pleasure for the beautiful body, but Pain for the beautiful Soul.

When I say that I am convinced of these things I speak with too much pride. Far off, like a perfect pearl, one can see the city of God. It is so wonderful that it seems as if a child could reach it in a summer's day. And so a child could. But with me and such as I am it is different. One can realise a thing in a single moment, but one loses it in the long hours that follow with leaden feet. It is so difficult to keep "heights that the soul is competent to gain."[3] We think in Eternity, but we move slowly through Time: and how slowly time goes with us who lie in prison I need not speak again, nor of the weariness and despair that creep back into one's cell, and into the cell of one's heart, with such strange insistence that one has, as it were, to garnish and sweep one's house for their coming, as for an unwelcome guest, or a bitter master, or a slave whose slave it is one's chance or choice to be. And, though at present you may find it a thing hard to believe, it is true none the less that for you, living in freedom and idleness and comfort, it is more easy to learn the lessons of Humility than it is for me, who begin the day by going down on my knees and washing the floor of my cell. For prison-life, with its endless privations and restrictions, makes

[1] Swinburne: "Before Parting" (*Poems and Ballads*, 1866): "feed" should be "live." [2] Adela Schuster. See note 2, p. 334
[3] Wordsworth: *The Excursion*, iv, 139.

474

one rebellious. The most terrible thing about it is not that it breaks one's heart—hearts are made to be broken—but that it turns one's heart to stone. One sometimes feels that it is only with a front of brass and a lip of scorn that one can get through the day at all. And he who is in a state of rebellion cannot receive grace, to use the phrase of which the Church is so fond—so rightly fond, I dare say—for in life, as in Art, the mood of rebellion closes up the channels of the soul, and shuts out the airs of heaven. Yet I must learn these lessons here, if I am to learn them anywhere, and must be filled with joy if my feet are on the right road, and my face set towards the "gate which is called Beautiful,"[1] though I may fall many times in the mire, and often in the mist go astray.

This new life, as through my love of Dante I like sometimes to call it, is, of course, no new life at all, but simply the continuance, by means of development, and evolution, of my former life. I remember when I was at Oxford saying to one of my friends—as we were strolling round Magdalen's narrow bird-haunted walks one morning in the June before I took my degree—that I wanted to eat of the fruit of all the trees in the garden of the world, and that I was going out into the world with that passion in my soul. And so, indeed, I went out, and so I lived. My only mistake was that I confined myself so exclusively to the trees of what seemed to me the sun-gilt side of the garden, and shunned the other side for its shadow and its gloom. Failure, disgrace, poverty, sorrow, despair, suffering, tears even, the broken words that come from the lips of pain, remorse that makes one walk in thorns, conscience that condemns, self-abasement that punishes, the misery that puts ashes on its head, the anguish that chooses sackcloth for its raiment and into its own drink puts gall—all these were things of which I was afraid. And as I had determined to know nothing of them, I was forced to taste each one of them in turn, to feed on them, to have for a season, indeed, no other food at all. I don't regret for a single moment having lived for pleasure. I did it to the full, as one should do everything that one does to the full. There was no pleasure I did not experience. I threw the pearl of my soul into a cup of wine. I went down the primrose path to the sound of flutes. I lived on honeycomb. But to have continued the same life would have been wrong because it would have been limiting. I had to pass on. The other half of the garden had its secrets for me also.

Of course all this is foreshadowed and prefigured in my art. Some of it is in "The Happy Prince:" some of it in "The Young King," notably in the passage where the Bishop says to the kneeling boy, "Is not He who made misery wiser than thou art?" a phrase which when I wrote it seemed to me little more than a phrase: a great deal of it is hidden away in the note of Doom that like a purple thread runs through the gold cloth of *Dorian Gray*: in "The Critic as Artist" it is set forth in many colours: in *The Soul of Man* it is written down simply and in letters too easy to read: it is one of the refrains whose recurring *motifs* make *Salome* so like a piece of music and bind it together as a ballad: in the prose-poem of the man who from the bronze of the image of the "Pleasure that liveth for a Moment" has to

[1] *Acts*, iii, 2.

475

make the image of the "Sorrow that abideth for Ever" it is incarnate.[1] It could not have been otherwise. At every single moment of one's life one is what one is going to be no less than what one has been. Art is a symbol, because man is a symbol.

It is, if I can fully attain to it, the ultimate realisation of the artistic life. For the artistic life is simple self-development. Humility in the artist is his frank acceptance of all experiences, just as Love in the artist is simply that sense of Beauty that reveals to the world its body and its soul. In *Marius the Epicurean* Pater seeks to reconcile the artistic life with the life of religion in the deep, sweet and austere sense of the word. But Marius is little more than a spectator: an ideal spectator indeed, and one to whom it is given "to contemplate the spectacle of life with appropriate emotions," which Wordsworth defines as the poet's true aim:[2] yet a spectator merely, and perhaps a little too much occupied with the comeliness of the vessels of the Sanctuary to notice that it is the Sanctuary of Sorrow that he is gazing at.

I see a far more intimate and immediate connection between the true life of Christ and the true life of the artist, and I take a keen pleasure in the reflection that long before Sorrow had made my days her own and bound me to her wheel I had written in *The Soul of Man* that he who would lead a Christ-like life must be entirely and absolutely himself, and had taken as my types not merely the shepherd on the hillside and the prisoner in his cell but also the painter to whom the world is a pageant and the poet for whom the world is a song. I remember saying once to André Gide, as we sat together in some Paris café, that while Metaphysics had but little real interest for me, and Morality absolutely none, there was nothing that either Plato or Christ had said that could not be transferred immediately into the sphere of Art, and there find its complete fulfilment. It was a generalisation as profound as it was novel.

Nor is it merely that we can discern in Christ that close union of personality with perfection which forms the real distinction between classical and romantic Art and makes Christ the true precursor of the romantic movement in life, but the very basis of his nature was the same as that of the nature of the artist, an intense and flamelike imagination. He realised in the entire sphere of human relations that imaginative sympathy which in the sphere of Art is the sole secret of creation. He understood the leprosy of the leper, the darkness of the blind, the fierce misery of those who live for pleasure, the strange poverty of the rich. You can see now—can you not?—that when you wrote to me in my trouble, "When you are not on your pedestal you are not interesting. The next time you are ill I will go

---

[1] A slight misquotation of Wilde's prose poem "The Artist," which first appeared in the *Fortnightly Review* for July 1894 (see note 4, p. 356). It was reprinted in *Lord Arthur Savile's Crime and Other Prose Pieces* (1908)).

[2] Wilde must have been thinking of Pater's essay on Wordsworth in *Appreciations* (1889). After quoting Wordsworth on "the operations of the elements and the appearances of the visible universe, on storm and sunshine, on the revolutions of the seasons, on cold and heat, on loss of friends and kindred, on injuries and resentments, on gratitude and hope, on fear and sorrow," Pater comments: "To witness this spectacle with appropriate emotions is the aim of all culture."

away at once," you were as remote from the true temper of the artist as you were from what Matthew Arnold calls "the secret of Jesus."[1] Either would have taught you that whatever happens to another happens to oneself, and if you want an inscription to read at dawn and at night-time and for pleasure or for pain, write up on the wall of your house in letters for the sun to gild and the moon to silver "*Whatever happens to another happens to oneself,*" and should anyone ask you what such an inscription can possibly mean you can answer that it means "Lord Christ's heart and Shakespeare's brain."

Christ's place indeed is with the poets. His whole conception of Humanity sprang right out of the imagination and can only be realised by it. What God was to the Pantheist, man was to him. He was the first to conceive the divided races as a unity. Before his time there had been gods and men. He alone saw that on the hills of life there were but God and Man, and, feeling through the mysticism of sympathy that in himself each had been made incarnate, he calls himself the Son of the One or the son of the other, according to his mood. More than anyone else in history he wakes in us that temper of wonder to which Romance always appeals. There is still something to me almost incredible in the idea of a young Galilean peasant imagining that he could bear on his own shoulders the burden of the entire world: all that had been already done and suffered, and all that was yet to be done and suffered: the sins of Nero, of Cæsar Borgia, of Alexander VI., and of him who was Emperor of Rome and Priest of the Sun:[2] the sufferings of those whose name is Legion and whose dwelling is among the tombs,[3] oppressed nationalities, factory children, thieves, people in prison, outcasts, those who are dumb under oppression and whose silence is heard only of God: and not merely imagining this but actually achieving it, so that at the present moment all who come in contact with his personality, even though they may neither bow to his altar nor kneel before his priest, yet somehow find that the ugliness of their sins is taken away and the beauty of their sorrow revealed to them.

I have said of him that he ranks with the poets. That is true. Shelley and Sophocles are of his company. But his entire life also is the most wonderful of poems. For "pity and terror"[4] there is nothing in the entire cycle of Greek Tragedy to touch it. The absolute purity of the protagonist raises the entire scheme to a height of romantic art from which the sufferings of "Thebes and Pelops' line"[5] are by their very horror excluded, and shows how wrong Aristotle was when he said in his treatise on the Drama that it would be impossible to bear the spectacle of one blameless in pain.[6] Nor in Æschylus or Dante, those stern masters of tenderness, in Shakespeare, the most purely human of all the great artists, in the whole of Celtic myth and legend where the loveliness of the world is shown

---

[1] "But there remains the question what righteousness really is. The method and secret and sweet reasonableness of Jesus." (*Literature and Dogma*, ch. xii.)
[2] The Emperor Heliogabalus.   [3] *Mark*, v, 5 and 9.
[4] Aristotle, *Poetics*, ch. xiii.   [5] Milton: *Il Penseroso*. "and" should be "or."
[6] *Poetics*, ch. xiii.

through a mist of tears, and the life of a man is no more than the life of a flower, is there anything that for sheer simplicity of pathos wedded and made one with sublimity of tragic effect can be said to equal or approach even the last act of Christ's Passion. The little supper with his companions, one of whom had already sold him for a price: the anguish in the quiet moonlit olive-garden: the false friend coming close to him so as to betray him with a kiss: the friend who still believed in him and on whom as on a rock he had hoped to build a House of Refuge for Man denying him as the bird cried to the dawn: his own utter loneliness, his submission, his acceptance of everything: and along with it all such scenes as the high priest of Orthodoxy rending his raiment in wrath, and the Magistrate of Civil Justice calling for water in the vain hope of cleansing himself of that stain of innocent blood that makes him the scarlet figure of History: the coronation-ceremony of Sorrow, one of the most wonderful things in the whole of recorded time: the crucifixion of the Innocent One before the eyes of his mother and of the disciple whom he loved: the soldiers gambling and throwing dice for his clothes: the terrible death by which he gave the world its most eternal symbol: and his final burial in the tomb of the rich man, his body swathed in Egyptian linen with costly spices and perfumes as though he had been a King's son—when one contemplates all this from the point of view of Art alone one cannot but be grateful that the supreme office of the Church should be the playing of the tragedy without the shedding of blood, the mystical presentation by means of dialogue and costume and gesture even of the Passion of her Lord, and it is always a source of pleasure and awe to me to remember that the ultimate survival of the Greek Chorus, lost elsewhere to art, is to be found in the servitor answering the priest at Mass.

Yet the whole life of Christ—so entirely may Sorrow and Beauty be made one in their meaning and manifestation—is really an idyll, though it ends with the veil of the temple being rent, and the darkness coming over the face of the earth, and the stone rolled to the door of the sepulchre. One always thinks of him as a young bridegroom with his companions, as indeed he somewhere describes himself, or as a shepherd straying through a valley with his sheep in search of green meadow or cool stream, or as a singer trying to build out of music the walls of the city of God, or as a lover for whose love the whole world was too small. His miracles seem to me as exquisite as the coming of Spring, and quite as natural. I see no difficulty at all in believing that such was the charm of his personality that his mere presence could bring peace to souls in anguish, and that those who touched his garments or his hands forgot their pain: or that as he passed by on the highway of life people who had seen nothing of life's mysteries saw them clearly, and others who had been deaf to every voice but that of Pleasure heard for the first time the voice of Love and found it as "musical as is Apollo's lute:" [1] or that evil passions fled at his approach, and men whose dull unimaginative lives had been but a mode of death rose as it were from the grave when he called them: or that when he taught on the hillside

[1] Milton: *Comus*, 478.

the multitude forgot their hunger and thirst and the cares of this world, and that to his friends who listened to him as he sat at meat the coarse food seemed delicate, and the water had the taste of good wine, and the whole house became full of the odour and sweetness of nard.

Renan in his *Vie de Jésus*—that gracious Fifth Gospel, the Gospel according to St Thomas one might call it—says somewhere that Christ's great achievement was that he made himself as much loved after his death as he had been during his lifetime.[1] And certainly, if his place is among the poets, he is the leader of all the lovers. He saw that love was that lost secret of the world for which the wise men had been looking, and that it was only through love that one could approach either the heart of the leper or the feet of God.

And, above all, Christ is the most supreme of Individualists. Humility, like the artistic acceptance of all experiences, is merely a mode of manifestation. It is man's soul that Christ is always looking for. He calls it "God's Kingdom"—$\dot{\eta}$ $\beta a\sigma\iota\lambda\epsilon ia$ $\tau o\tilde{v}$ $\theta\epsilon o\tilde{v}$—and finds it in everyone. He compares it to little things, to a tiny seed, to a handful of leaven, to a pearl. That is because one only realises one's soul by getting rid of all alien passions, all acquired culture, and all external possessions be they good or evil.

I bore up against everything with some stubbornness of will and much rebellion of nature till I had absolutely nothing left in the world but Cyril. I had lost my name, my position, my happiness, my freedom, my wealth. I was a prisoner and a pauper. But I had still one beautiful thing left, my own eldest son. Suddenly he was taken away from me by the law. It was a blow so appalling that I did not know what to do, so I flung myself on my knees, and bowed my head, and wept and said "The body of a child is as the body of the Lord: I am not worthy of either." That moment seemed to save me. I saw then that the only thing for me was to accept everything. Since then—curious as it will no doubt sound to you—I have been happier.

It was of course my soul in its ultimate essence that I had reached. In many ways I had been its enemy, but I found it waiting for me as a friend. When one comes in contact with the soul it makes one simple as a child, as Christ said one should be. It is tragic how few people ever "possess their souls" before they die.[2] "Nothing is more rare in any man," says Emerson, "than an act of his own."[3] It is quite true. Most people are other people. Their thoughts are someone else's opinions, their life a mimicry, their passions a quotation. Christ was not merely the supreme Individualist, but he was the first in History. People have tried to make him out an ordinary Philanthropist, like the dreadful philanthropists of the nineteenth

[1] "*S'être fait aimer,* '*à ce point qu'après sa mort on ne cessa pas de l'aimer,*' *voilà le chef-d'œuvre de Jésus et ce qui frappa le plus ses contemporains.*" (Ch. xxviii).

[2] And see all sights from pole to pole,
And glance, and nod, and bustle by—
And never once possess our soul
Before we die.
Matthew Arnold, "A Southern Night."

[3] In his lecture "The Preacher," published posthumously in *Lectures and Biographical Sketches* (1883).

century, or ranked him as an Altruist with the unscientific and sentimental. But he was really neither one nor the other. Pity he has, of course, for the poor, for those who are shut up in prisons, for the lowly, for the wretched, but he has far more pity for the rich, for the hard Hedonists, for those who waste their freedom in becoming slaves to things, for those who wear soft raiment and live in Kings' houses. Riches and Pleasure seemed to him to be really greater tragedies than Poverty and Sorrow. And as for Altruism, who knew better than he that it is vocation not volition that determines us, and that one cannot gather grapes off thorns or figs from thistles?

To live for others as a definite self-conscious aim was not his creed. It was not the basis of his creed. When he says "Forgive your enemies," it is not for the sake of the enemy but for one's own sake that he says so, and because Love is more beautiful than Hate. In his entreaty to the young man whom when he looked on he loved, "Sell all that thou hast and give it to the poor," it is not of the state of the poor that he is thinking but of the soul of the young man, the lovely soul that wealth was marring. In his view of life he is one with the artist who knows that by the inevitable law of self-perfection the poet must sing, and the sculptor think in bronze, and the painter make the world a mirror for his moods, as surely and as certainly as the hawthorn must blossom in Spring, and the corn burn to gold at harvest-time, and the Moon in her ordered wanderings change from shield to sickle, and from sickle to shield.

But while Christ did not say to men, "Live for others," he pointed out that there was no difference at all between the lives of others and one's own life. By this means he gave to man an extended, a Titan personality. Since his coming the history of each separate individual is, or can be made, the history of the world. Of course Culture has intensified the personality of man. Art has made us myriad-minded. Those who have the artistic temperament go into exile with Dante and learn how salt is the bread of others and how steep their stairs:[1] they catch for a moment the serenity and calm of Goethe, and yet know but too well why Baudelaire cried to God:

> O Seigneur, donnez-moi la force et le courage
> De contempler mon corps et mon cœur sans dégoût.[2]

Out of Shakespeare's sonnets they draw, to their own hurt it may be, the secret of his love and make it their own: they look with new eyes on modern life because they have listened to one of Chopin's nocturnes, or handled Greek things, or read the story of the passion of some dead man for some dead woman whose hair was like threads of fine gold and whose mouth was as a pomegranate. But the sympathy of the artistic temperament is necessarily with what has found expression. In words or in colour, in music or in marble, behind the painted masks of an Æschylean play or through some Sicilian shepherd's pierced and jointed reeds the man and his message must have been revealed.

[1] See note p. 9. [2] From "*Un Voyage à Cythère*" in *Les Fleurs du Mal* (1857).

To the artist, expression is the only mode under which he can conceive life at all. To him what is dumb is dead. But to Christ it was not so. With a width and wonder of imagination, that fills one almost with awe, he took the entire world of the inarticulate, the voiceless world of pain, as his kingdom, and made of himself its eternal mouthpiece. Those of whom I have spoken, who are dumb under oppression and "whose silence is heard only of God,"[1] he chose as his brothers. He sought to become eyes to the blind, ears to the deaf, and a cry on the lips of those whose tongue had been tied. His desire was to be to the myriads who had found no utterance a very trumpet through which they might call to Heaven. And feeling, with the artistic nature of one to whom Sorrow and Suffering were modes through which he could realise his conception of the Beautiful, that an idea is of no value till it becomes incarnate and is made an image, he makes of himself the image of the Man of Sorrows, and as such has fascinated and dominated Art as no Greek god ever succeeded in doing.

For the Greek gods, in spite of the white and red of their fair fleet limbs, were not really what they appeared to be. The curved brow of Apollo was like the sun's disk crescent over a hill at dawn, and his feet were as the wings of the morning, but he himself had been cruel to Marsyas and had made Niobe childless: in the steel shields of the eyes of Pallas there had been no pity for Arachne: the pomp and peacocks of Hera were all that was really noble about her: and the Father of the Gods himself had been too fond of the daughters of men. The two deep suggestive figures of Greek mythology were, for religion, Demeter, an earth-goddess, not one of the Olympians, and, for art, Dionysus, the son of a mortal woman to whom the moment of his birth had proved the moment of her death also.

But Life itself from its lowliest and most humble sphere produced one far more marvellous than the mother of Proserpina or the son of Semele. Out of the carpenter's shop at Nazareth had come a personality infinitely greater than any made by myth or legend, and one, strangely enough, destined to reveal to the world the mystical meaning of wine and the real beauty of the lilies of the field as none, either on Cithaeron or at Enna, had ever done it.[2]

The song of Isaiah, "*He is despised and rejected of men, a man of sorrows and acquainted with grief: and we hid as it were our faces from him*,"[3] had seemed to him to be a prefiguring of himself, and in him the prophecy was fulfilled. We must not be afraid of such a phrase. Every single work of art is the fulfilment of a prophecy. For every work of art is the conversion of an idea into an image. Every single human being should be the fulfilment of a prophecy. For every human being should be the realisation of some ideal, either in the mind of God or in the mind of man. Christ found the type, and fixed it, and the dream of a Virgilian poet, either at Jerusalem or at Babylon, became in the long progress of the centuries

---

[1] Cf. p. 477.
[2] Mount Cithaeron was the scene of the Bacchic orgies in honour of Dionysus, son of Semele. It was from the flower-filled meadows of Enna that Proserpina was seized by Pluto and carried off to the underworld.   [3] *Isaiah*, liii, 3.

incarnate in him for whom the world was waiting.[1] *"His visage was marred more than any man's, and his form more than the sons of men,"*[2] are among the signs noted by Isaiah as distinguishing the new ideal, and as soon as Art understood what was meant it opened like a flower at the presence of one in whom truth in Art was set forth as it had never been before. For is not truth in Art, as I have said, "that in which the outward is expressive of the inward; in which the soul is made flesh, and the body instinct with spirit: in which Form reveals"?[3]

To me one of the things in history the most to be regretted is that the Christ's own renaissance which had produced the Cathedral of Chartres, the Arthurian cycle of legends, the life of St Francis of Assisi, the art of Giotto, and Dante's *Divine Comedy*, was not allowed to develop on its own lines but was interrupted and spoiled by the dreary classical Renaissance that gave us Petrarch, and Raphael's frescoes, and Palladian architecture, and formal French tragedy, and St Paul's Cathedral, and Pope's poetry, and everything that is made from without and by dead rules, and does not spring from within through some spirit informing it. But wherever there is a romantic movement in Art, there somehow, and under some form, is Christ, or the soul of Christ. He is in *Romeo and Juliet*, in the *Winter's Tale*, in Provençal poetry, in "The Ancient Mariner," in "La Belle Dame sans Merci," and in Chatterton's "Ballad of Charity."

We owe to him the most diverse things and people. Hugo's *Les Misérables*, Baudelaire's *Fleurs du Mal*, the note of pity in Russian novels, the stained glass and tapestries and quattrocento work of Burne-Jones and Morris, Verlaine and Verlaine's poems, belong to him no less than the Tower of Giotto, Lancelot and Guinevere, Tannhäuser, the troubled romantic marbles of Michael Angelo, pointed architecture, and the love of children and flowers—for both of whom, indeed, in classical art there was but little place, hardly enough for them to grow or play in, but who from the twelfth century down to our own day have been continually making their appearance in art, under various modes and at various times, coming fitfully and wilfully as children and flowers are apt to do, Spring always seeming to one as if the flowers had been hiding, and only came out into the sun because they were afraid that grown-up people would grow tired of looking for them and give up the search, and the life of a child being no more than an April day on which there is both rain and sun for the narcissus.

And it is the imaginative quality of Christ's own nature that makes him this palpitating centre of romance. The strange figures of poetic drama and ballad are made by the imagination of others, but out of his own imagination entirely did Jesus of Nazareth create himself. The cry of Isaiah had really no more to do with his coming than the song of the nightingale has to do with the rising of the moon—no more, though perhaps no less. He was the denial as well as the affirmation of prophecy. For every expectation that he fulfilled, there was another that he destroyed. In all beauty,

---

[1] Cf. Virgil's fourth Eclogue: *"Jam redit et virgo."*
[2] *Isaiah*, lii, 14.   [3] Cf. p. 473.

says Bacon, there is "some strangeness of proportion,"[1] and of those who are born of the spirit, of those, that is to say, who like himself are dynamic forces, Christ says that they are like the wind that "bloweth where it listeth and no man can tell whence it cometh or whither it goeth."[2] That is why he is so fascinating to artists. He has all the colour-elements of life: mystery, strangeness, pathos, suggestion, ecstasy, love. He appeals to the temper of wonder, and creates that mood by which alone he can be understood.

And it is to me a joy to remember that if he is "of imagination all compact,"[3] the world itself is of the same substance. I said in *Dorian Gray*[4] that the great sins of the world take place in the brain, but it is in the brain that everything takes place. We know now that we do not see with the eye or hear with the ear. They are merely channels for the transmission, adequate or inadequate, of sense-impressions. It is in the brain that the poppy is red, that the apple is odorous, that the skylark sings.

Of late I have been studying the four prose-poems about Christ with some diligence. At Christmas I managed to get hold of a Greek Testament, and every morning, after I have cleaned my cell and polished my tins, I read a little of the Gospels, a dozen verses taken by chance anywhere. It is a delightful way of opening the day. To you, in your turbulent, ill-disciplined life, it would be a capital thing if you would do the same. It would do you no end of good, and the Greek is quite simple. Endless repetition, in and out of season, has spoiled for us the *naïveté*, the freshness, the simple romantic charm of the Gospels. We hear them read far too often, and far too badly, and all repetition is anti-spiritual. When one returns to the Greek it is like going into a garden of lilies out of some narrow and dark house.

And to me the pleasure is doubled by the reflection that it is extremely probable that we have the actual terms, the *ipsissima verba*, used by Christ. It was always supposed that Christ talked in Aramaic. Even Renan thought so. But now we know that the Galilean peasants, like the Irish peasants of our own day, were bilingual, and that Greek was the ordinary language of intercourse all over Palestine, as indeed all over the Eastern world. I never liked the idea that we only knew of Christ's own words through a translation of a translation. It is a delight to me to think that as far as his conversation was concerned, Charmides[5] might have listened to him, and Socrates reasoned with him, and Plato understood him: that he really said ἐγώ εἰμι ὁ ποιμὴν ὁ καλός:[6] that when he thought of the lilies of the field, and how they neither toil nor spin, his absolute expression was καταμάθετε τὰ κρίνα τοῦ ἀγροῦ πῶς αὐξάνει· οὐ κοπιᾷ οὐδὲ νήθει,[7] and that his last

---

[1] "Of Beauty."   [2] *John*, iii, 8.

[3] *A Midsummer Night's Dream*, Act V, scene i.   [4] Chapter 2.

[5] The central character of Plato's dialogue *Charmides*, where he appears as a beautiful young man typifying the central theme of σωφροσύνη or moderation. Wilde's long poem of the same name is about an imaginary character.

[6] "I am the Good Shepherd" (*John*, X, 11 and 14).

[7] "Consider the lilies of the field, how they grow; they toil not, neither do they spin" (*Matthew*, vi, 28).

word when he cried out "My life has been completed, has reached its fulfilment, has been perfected," was exactly as St John tells us it was: τετέλεσται:[1] no more.

And while in reading the Gospels—particularly that of St John himself, or whatever early Gnostic took his name and mantle—I see this continual assertion of the imagination as the basis of all spiritual and material life, I see also that to Christ imagination was simply a form of Love, and that to him Love was Lord in the fullest meaning of the phrase. Some six weeks ago I was allowed by the Doctor to have white bread to eat instead of the coarse black or brown bread of ordinary prison fare. It is a great delicacy. To you it will sound strange that dry bread could possibly be a delicacy to anyone. I assure you that to me it is so much so that at the close of each meal I carefully eat whatever crumbs may be left on my tin plate, or have fallen on the rough towel that one uses as a cloth so as not to soil one's table: and do so not from hunger—I get now quite sufficient food—but simply in order that nothing should be wasted of what is given to me. So one should look on love.

Christ, like all fascinating personalities, had the power not merely of saying beautiful things himself, but of making other people say beautiful things to him; and I love the story St Mark tells us about the Greek woman —the γυνὴ Ἑλληνίς—who, when as a trial of her faith he said to her that he could not give her the bread of the children of Israel, answered him that the little dogs—κυνάρια, "little dogs" it should be rendered—who are under the table eat of the crumbs that the children let fall.[2] Most people live *for* love and admiration. But it is *by* love and admiration that we should live.[3] If any love is shown us we should recognise that we are quite unworthy of it. Nobody is worthy to be loved. The fact that God loves man shows that in the divine order of ideal things it is written that eternal love is to be given to what is eternally unworthy. Or if that phrase seems to you a bitter one to hear, let us say that everyone is worthy of love, except he who thinks that he is. Love is a sacrament that should be taken kneeling, and *Domine, non sum dignus* should be on the lips and in the hearts of those who receive it. I wish you would sometimes think of that. You need it so much.

If I ever write again, in the sense of producing artistic work, there are just two subjects on which and through which I desire to express myself: one is "Christ, as the precursor of the Romantic movement in life:" the other is "the Artistic life considered in its relation to Conduct." The first is, of course, intensely fascinating, for I see in Christ not merely the essentials of the supreme romantic type, but all the accidents, the wilfulnesses even, of the romantic temperament also. He was the first person who ever said to people that they should live "flower-like" lives. He fixed the phrase. He took children as the type of what people should try to become. He held them up as examples to their elders, which I myself have always thought the chief use of children, if what is perfect should have a use.

[1] "It is finished" (*John*, xix, 30).   [2] *Mark*, vii, 26–30.
[3] Cf. "We live by admiration, hope and love" (Wordsworth, *The Excursion*, iv, 763).

Dante describes the soul of man as coming from the hand of God "weeping and laughing like a little child," and Christ also saw that the soul of each one should be "*a guisa di fanciulla, che piangendo e ridendo pargoleggia.*"[1] He felt that life was changeful, fluid, active, and that to allow it to be stereotyped into any form was death. He said that people should not be too serious over material, common interests: that to be un- practical was a great thing: that one should not bother too much over affairs. "The birds didn't, why should man?" He is charming when he says, "Take no thought for the morrow. Is not the *soul* more than meat? Is not the *body* more than raiment?"[2] A Greek might have said the latter phrase. It is full of Greek feeling. But only Christ could have said both, and so summed up life perfectly for us.

His morality is all sympathy, just what morality should be. If the only thing he had ever said had been "Her sins are forgiven her because she loved much," it would have been worth while dying to have said it. His justice is all poetical justice, exactly what justice should be. The beggar goes to heaven because he had been unhappy. I can't conceive a better reason for his being sent there. The people who work for an hour in the vineyard in the cool of the evening receive just as much reward as those who had toiled there all day long in the hot sun. Why shouldn't they? Probably no one deserved anything. Or perhaps they were a different kind of people. Christ had no patience with the dull lifeless mechanical systems that treat people as if they were things, and so treat everybody alike: as if anybody, or anything for that matter, was like aught else in the world. For him there were no laws: there were exceptions merely.

That which is the very keynote of romantic art was to him the proper basis of actual life. He saw no other basis. And when they brought him one taken in the very act of sin and showed him her sentence written in the law and asked him what was to be done, he wrote with his finger on the ground as though he did not hear them, and finally, when they pressed him again and again, looked up and said "Let him of you who has never sinned be the first to throw the stone at her." It was worth while living to have said that.

Like all poetical natures, he loved ignorant people. He knew that in the soul of one who is ignorant there is always room for a great idea. But he could not stand stupid people, especially those who are made stupid by education—people who are full of opinions not one of which they can understand, a peculiarly modern type, and one summed up by Christ when he describes it as the type of one who has the key of knowledge, can't use it himself, and won't allow other people to use it, though it may be made to open the gate of God's Kingdom. His chief war was against the Philistines. That is the war every child of light has to wage. Philistinism was the note of the age and community in which he lived. In their heavy inaccessibility to ideas, their dull respectability, their tedious orthodoxy, their worship of vulgar success, their entire preoccupation with the gross materialistic side of life, and their ridiculous estimate of themselves and their importance,

---

[1] *Purgatorio*, xvi, 86–87.   [2] *Matthew*, vi, 34 and 25.

the Jew of Jerusalem in Christ's day was the exact counterpart of the British Philistine of our own. Christ mocked at the "whited sepulchres" of respectability, and fixed that phrase for ever. He treated worldly success as a thing to be absolutely despised. He saw nothing in it at all. He looked on wealth as an encumbrance to a man. He would not hear of life being sacrificed to any system of thought or morals. He pointed out that forms and ceremonies were made for man, not man for forms and ceremonies. He took Sabbatarianism as a type of the things that should be set at nought. The cold philanthropies, the ostentatious public charities, the tedious formalisms so dear to the middle-class mind, he exposed with utter and relentless scorn. To us, what is termed Orthodoxy is merely a facile unintelligent acquiescence, but to them, and in their hands, it was a terrible and paralysing tyranny. Christ swept it aside. He showed that the spirit alone was of value. He took a keen pleasure in pointing out to them that though they were always reading the Law and the Prophets they had not really the smallest idea of what either of them meant. In opposition to their tithing of each separate day into its fixed routine of prescribed duties, as they tithed mint and rue, he preached the enormous importance of living completely for the moment.

Those whom he saved from their sins are saved simply for beautiful moments in their lives. Mary Magdalen, when she sees Christ, breaks the rich vase of alabaster that one of her seven lovers had given her and spills the odorous spices over his tired, dusty feet, and for that one moment's sake sits for ever with Ruth and Beatrice in the tresses of the snow-white Rose of Paradise.[1] All that Christ says to us by way of a little warning is that *every* moment should be beautiful, that the soul should *always* be ready for the coming of the Bridegroom, *always* waiting for the voice of the Lover. Philistinism being simply that side of man's nature that is not illumined by the imagination, he sees all the lovely influences of life as modes of Light: the imagination itself is the world-light, τὸ φῶς τοῦ κοσμοῦ: the world is made by it, and yet the world cannot understand it: that is because the imagination is simply a manifestation of Love, and it is love, and the capacity for it, that distinguishes one human being from another.

But it is when he deals with the Sinner that he is most romantic, in the sense of most real. The world had always loved the Saint as being the nearest possible approach to the perfection of God. Christ, through some divine instinct in him, seems to have always loved the sinner as being the nearest possible approach to the perfection of man. His primary desire was not to reform people, any more than his primary desire was to relieve suffering. To turn an interesting thief into a tedious honest man was not his aim. He would have thought little of the Prisoners' Aid Society and other modern movements of the kind. The conversion of a Publican into a Pharisee would not have seemed to him a great achievement by any means. But in a manner not yet understood of the world he regarded sin and suffering as being in themselves beautiful, holy things, and modes of perfection. It *sounds* a very dangerous idea. It is so. All great ideas *are* dangerous.

[1] Cf. Dante, *Paradiso*, xxx–xxxii.

That it was Christ's creed admits of no doubt. That it is the true creed I don't doubt myself.

Of course the sinner must repent. But why? Simply because otherwise he would be unable to realise what he had done. The moment of repentance is the moment of initiation. More than that. It is the means by which one alters one's past. The Greeks thought that impossible. They often say in their gnomic aphorisms "Even the Gods cannot alter the past."[1] Christ showed that the commonest sinner could do it. That it was the one thing he could do. Christ, had he been asked, would have said—I feel quite certain about it—that the moment the prodigal son fell on his knees and wept he really made his having wasted his substance with harlots, and then kept swine and hungered for the husks they ate, beautiful and holy incidents in his life. It is difficult for most people to grasp the idea. I dare say one has to go to prison to understand it. If so, it may be worth while going to prison.

There is something so unique about Christ. Of course, just as there are false dawns before the dawn itself, and winter-days so full of sudden sunlight that they will cheat the wise crocus into squandering its gold before its time, and make some foolish bird call to its mate to build on barren boughs, so there were Christians before Christ. For that we should be grateful. The unfortunate thing is that there have been none since. I make one exception, St Francis of Assisi. But then God had given him at his birth the soul of a poet, and he himself when quite young had in mystical marriage taken Poverty as his bride; and with the soul of a poet and the body of a beggar he found the way to perfection not difficult. He understood Christ, and so he became like him. We do not require the *Liber Conformitatum*[2] to teach us that the life of St Francis was the true *Imitatio Christi*: a poem compared to which the book that bears that name is merely prose. Indeed, that is the charm about Christ, when all is said. He is just like a work of art himself. He does not really teach one anything, but by being brought into his presence one becomes something. And everybody is predestined to his presence. Once at least in his life each man walks with Christ to Emmaus.

As regards the other subject, the relation of the artistic life to conduct, it will no doubt seem strange to you that I should select it. People point to Reading Gaol, and say "There is where the artistic life leads a man." Well, it might lead one to worse places. The more mechanical people, to whom life is a shrewd speculation dependent on a careful calculation of ways and means, always know where they are going, and go there. They start with the desire of being the Parish Beadle, and, in whatever sphere they are placed, they succeed in being the Parish Beadle and no more. A man whose desire is to be something separate from himself, to be a Member of Parliament, or a successful grocer, or a prominent solicitor, or a judge, or

[1] Cf. Aristotle, *Ethics*, vi, 2 and Pindar, *Olympia*, ii, 17.
[2] A massive compilation illustrating the similarities in the lives of Christ and St Francis, written by Fr. Bartholomaeus de Pisa in the fourteenth century and first printed in 1510.

something equally tedious, invariably succeeds in being what he wants to be. That is his punishment. Those who want a mask have to wear it.

But with the dynamic forces of life, and those in whom those dynamic forces become incarnate, it is different. People whose desire is solely for self-realisation never know where they are going. They can't know. In one sense of the word it is, of course, necessary, as the Greek oracle said, to know oneself.[1] That is the first achievement of knowledge. But to recognise that the soul of a man is unknowable is the ultimate achievement of Wisdom. The final mystery is oneself. When one has weighed the sun in a balance, and measured the steps of the moon, and mapped out the seven heavens star by star, there still remains oneself. Who can calculate the orbit of his own soul? When the son of Kish went out to look for his father's asses, he did not know that a man of God was waiting for him with the very chrism of coronation, and that his own soul was already the Soul of a King.

I hope to live long enough, and to produce work of such a character, that I shall be able at the end of my days to say, "Yes: this is just where the artistic life leads a man." Two of the most perfect lives I have come across in my own experience are the lives of Verlaine and of Prince Kropotkin: both of them men who passed years in prison: the first, the one Christian poet since Dante, the other a man with the soul of that beautiful white Christ that seems coming out of Russia.[2] And for the last seven or eight months, in spite of a succession of great troubles reaching me from the outside world almost without intermission, I have been placed in direct contact with a new spirit working in this prison through men and things, that has helped me beyond any possibility of expression in words; so that while for the first year of my imprisonment I did nothing else, and can remember doing nothing else, but wring my hands in impotent despair, and say "What an ending! What an appalling ending!" now I try to say to myself, and sometimes when I am not torturing myself do really and sincerely say, "What a beginning! What a wonderful beginning!" It may really be so. It may become so. If it does, I shall owe much to this new personality that has altered every man's life in this place.[3]

Things in themselves are of little importance, have indeed—let us for once thank Metaphysics for something that she has taught us—no real existence. The spirit alone is of importance. Punishment may be inflicted in such a way that it will heal, not make a wound, just as alms may be given in such a manner that the bread changes to a stone in the hands of the giver. What a change there is—not in the regulations, for they are fixed by iron

[1] γνῶθι σεαυτόν (know thyself) was inscribed over the entrance to the temple of Apollo at Delphi.

[2] Paul Marie Verlaine (1844–96) was imprisoned for wounding Rimbaud with a revolver shot. Prince Peter Alexeievitch Kropotkin, Russian author, geographer and anarchist (1842–1921) was imprisoned for his political views and actions. For Kropotkin's opinion of *De Profundis* (1905), see *Robert Ross, Friend of Friends* (1952), pp. 112–14.

[3] Major James Osmond Nelson, who had taken over the Governorship of Reading Prison in July 1896.

rule, but in the spirit that uses them as its expression—you can realise when I tell you that had I been released last May, as I tried to be, I would have left this place loathing it and every official in it with a bitterness of hatred that would have poisoned my life. I have had a year longer of imprisonment, but Humanity has been in the prison along with us all, and now when I go out I shall always remember great kindnesses that I have received here from almost everybody, and on the day of my release will give my thanks to many people and ask to be remembered by them in turn.

The prison-system is absolutely and entirely wrong. I would give anything to be able to alter it when I go out. I intend to try. But there is nothing in the world so wrong but that the spirit of Humanity, which is the spirit of Love, the spirit of the Christ who is not in Churches, may make it, if not right, at least possible to be borne without too much bitterness of heart.

I know also that much is waiting for me outside that is very delightful, from what St Francis of Assisi calls *"my brother the wind"* and *"my sister the rain,"* lovely things both of them, down to the shop-windows and sunsets of great cities. If I made a list of all that still remains to me, I don't know where I should stop: for, indeed, God made the world just as much for me as for anyone else. Perhaps I may go out with something I had not got before. I need not tell you that to me Reformations in Morals are as meaningless and vulgar as Reformations in Theology. But while to propose to be a better man is a piece of unscientific cant, to have become a *deeper* man is the privilege of those who have suffered. And such I think I have become. You can judge for yourself.

If after I go out a friend of mine gave a feast, and did not invite me to it, I shouldn't mind a bit. I can be perfectly happy by myself. With freedom, books, flowers, and the moon, who could not be happy? Besides, feasts are not for me any more. I have given too many to care about them. That side of life is over for me, very fortunately I dare say. But if, after I go out, a friend of mine had a sorrow, and refused to allow me to share it, I should feel it most bitterly. If he shut the doors of the house of mourning against me I would come back again and again and beg to be admitted, so that I might share in what I was entitled to share in. If he thought me unworthy, unfit to weep with him, I should feel it as the most poignant humiliation, as the most terrible mode in which disgrace could be inflicted on me. But that could not be. I have a right to share in Sorrow, and he who can look at the loveliness of the world, and share its sorrow, and realise something of the wonder of both, is in immediate contact with divine things, and has got as near to God's secret as anyone can get.

Perhaps there may come into my art also, no less than into my life, a still deeper note, one of greater unity of passion, and directness of impulse. Not width but intensity is the true aim of modern Art. We are no longer in Art concerned with the type. It is with the exception we have to do. I cannot put my sufferings into any form they took, I need hardly say. Art only begins where Imitation ends. But something must come into my work, of fuller harmony of words perhaps, of richer cadences, of more curious colour-effects, of simpler architectural-order, of some æsthetic quality at any rate.

When Marsyas was "torn from the scabbard of his limbs"—*dalla vagina delle membre sue*,[1] to use one of Dante's most terrible, most Tacitean phrases —he had no more song, the Greeks said. Apollo had been victor. The lyre had vanquished the reed. But perhaps the Greeks were mistaken. I hear in much modern Art the cry of Marsyas.[2] It is bitter in Baudelaire, sweet and plaintive in Lamartine, mystic in Verlaine. It is in the deferred resolutions of Chopin's music. It is in the discontent that haunts the recurrent faces of Burne-Jones's women. Even Matthew Arnold, whose song of Callicles tells of "the triumph of the sweet persuasive lyre," and the "famous final victory," in such a clear note of lyrical beauty—even he, in the troubled undertone of doubt and distress that haunts his verse, has not a little of it.[3] Neither Goethe nor Wordsworth could heal him, though he followed each in turn, and when he seeks to mourn for "Thyrsis" or to sing of "the Scholar Gipsy," it is the reed that he has to take for the rendering of his strain. But whether or not the Phrygian Faun[4] was silent, I cannot be. Expression is as necessary to me as leaf and blossom are to the black branches of the trees that show themselves above the prison wall and are so restless in the wind. Between my art and the world there is now a wide gulf, but between Art and myself there is none. I hope at least that there is none.

To each of us different fates have been meted out. Freedom, pleasure, amusements, a life of ease have been your lot, and you are not worthy of it. My lot has been one of public infamy, of long imprisonment, of misery, of ruin, of disgrace, and I am not worthy of it either—not yet, at any rate. I remember I used to say that I thought I could bear a real tragedy if it came to me with purple pall and a mask of noble sorrow,[5] but that the dreadful thing about modernity was that it put Tragedy into the raiment of Comedy, so that the great realities seemed commonplace or grotesque or lacking in style. It is quite true about modernity. It has probably always been true about actual life. It is said that all martyrdoms seemed mean to the looker-on.[6] The nineteenth century is no exception to the general rule.

Everything about my tragedy has been hideous, mean, repellent, lacking in style. Our very dress makes us grotesques. We are the zanies of sorrow. We are clowns whose hearts are broken. We are specially designed to appeal to the sense of humour. On November 13th 1895 I was brought down here from London.[7] From two o'clock till half-past two on that day

---

[1] Dante, *Paradiso*, i, 20.　　　　[2] Cf. note 1, p. 233.
[3] Oh, that Fate had let me see
　　That triumph of the sweet persuasive lyre,
　　That famous, final victory,
　　When jealous Pan with Marsyas did conspire.
　　　　　　　　　　　　　　　　　(Empedocles on Etna.)

[4] "Marsyas, that unhappy Faun" (*Empedocles on Etna*).
[5] "Some noble grief that we think will lend the purple dignity of tragedy to our days" ("The Critic as Artist," Part II, in *Intentions*).
[6] Emerson: "Essay on Experience."　　[7] Actually 20 November.

I had to stand on the centre platform of Clapham Junction in convict dress and handcuffed, for the world to look at. I had been taken out of the Hospital Ward without a moment's notice being given to me. Of all possible objects I was the most grotesque. When people saw me they laughed. Each train as it came up swelled the audience. Nothing could exceed their amusement. That was of course before they knew who I was. As soon as they had been informed, they laughed still more. For half an hour I stood there in the grey November rain surrounded by a jeering mob. For a year after that was done to me I wept every day at the same hour and for the same space of time. That is not such a tragic thing as possibly it sounds to you. To those who are in prison, tears are a part of every day's experience. A day in prison on which one does not weep is a day on which one's heart is hard, not a day on which one's heart is happy.

Well, now I am really beginning to feel more regret for the people who laughed than for myself. Of course when they saw me I was not on my pedestal. I was in the pillory. But it is a very unimaginative nature that only cares for people on their pedestals. A pedestal may be a very unreal thing. A pillory is a terrific reality. They should have known also how to interpret sorrow better. I have said that behind Sorrow there is always Sorrow. It were still wiser to say that behind sorrow there is always a soul. And to mock at a soul in pain is a dreadful thing. Unbeautiful are their lives who do it. In the strangely simple economy of the world people only get what they give, and to those who have not enough imagination to penetrate the mere outward of things and feel pity, what pity can be given save that of scorn?

I have told you this account of the mode of my being conveyed here simply that you should realise how hard it has been for me to get anything out of my punishment but bitterness and despair. I have however to do it, and now and then I have moments of submission and acceptance. All the spring may be hidden in a single bud, and the low ground-nest of the lark may hold the joy that is to herald the feet of many rose-red dawns, and so perhaps whatever beauty of life still remains to me is contained in some moment of surrender, abasement and humiliation. I can, at any rate, merely proceed on the lines of my own development, and by accepting all that has happened to me make myself worthy of it.

People used to say of me that I was too individualistic. I must be far more of an individualist than I ever was. I must get far more out of myself than I ever got, and ask far less of the world than I ever asked. Indeed my ruin came, not from too great individualism of life, but from too little. The one disgraceful, unpardonable, and to all time contemptible action of my life was my allowing myself to be forced into appealing to Society for help and protection against your father. To have made such an appeal against anyone would have been from the individualist point of view bad enough, but what excuse can there ever be put forward for having made it against one of such nature and aspect?

Of course once I had put into motion the forces of Society, Society turned on me and said, "Have you been living all this time in defiance of my laws, and do you now appeal to those laws for protection? You shall have those laws exercised to the full. You shall abide by what you have appealed to." The result is I am in gaol. And I used to feel bitterly the irony and ignominy of my position when in the course of my three trials, beginning at the Police Court, I used to see your father bustling in and out in the hopes of attracting public attention, as if anyone could fail to note or remember the stableman's gait and dress, the bowed legs, the twitching hands, the hanging lower lip, the bestial and half-witted grin. Even when he was not there, or was out of sight, I used to feel conscious of his presence, and the blank dreary walls of the great Court-room, the very air itself, seemed to me at times to be hung with multitudinous masks of that apelike face. Certainly no man ever fell so ignobly, and by such ignoble instruments, as I did. I say, in *Dorian Gray* somewhere,[1] that "a man cannot be too careful in the choice of his enemies." I little thought that it was by a pariah that I was to be made a pariah myself.

This urging me, forcing me to appeal to Society for help, is one of the things that make me despise you so much, that make me despise myself so much for having yielded to you. Your not appreciating me as an artist was quite excusable. It was temperamental. You couldn't help it. But you might have appreciated me as an Individualist. For that no culture was required. But you didn't, and so you brought the element of Philistinism into a life that had been a complete protest against it, and from some points of view a complete annihilation of it. The Philistine element in life is not the failure to understand Art. Charming people such as fishermen, shepherds, ploughboys, peasants and the like know nothing about Art, and are the very salt of the earth. He is the Philistine who upholds and aids the heavy, cumbrous, blind mechanical forces of Society, and who does not recognise the dynamic force when he meets it either in a man or a movement.

People thought it dreadful of me to have entertained at dinner the evil things of life, and to have found pleasure in their company. But they, from the point of view through which I, as an artist in life, approached them, were delightfully suggestive and stimulating. It was like feasting with panthers. The danger was half the excitement. I used to feel as the snake-charmer must feel when he lures the cobra to stir from the painted cloth or reed-basket that holds it, and makes it spread its hood at his bidding, and sway to and fro in the air as a plant sways restfully in a stream. They were to me the brightest of gilded snakes. Their poison was part of their perfection. I did not know that when they were to strike at me it was to be at your piping and for your father's pay. I don't feel at all ashamed of having known them. They were intensely interesting. What I do feel ashamed of is the horrible Philistine atmosphere into which you brought me. My business as an artist was with Ariel. You set me to wrestle with Caliban. Instead of making beautiful coloured, musical things such as *Salome*, and the *Florentine Tragedy*, and *La Sainte Courtisane*, I found myself forced to send long lawyer's letters to your father and constrained to appeal to the

---

[1] Chapter I.

very things against which I had always protested. Clibborn and Atkins were wonderful in their infamous war against life.[1] To entertain them was an astounding adventure. Dumas *père*, Cellini, Goya, Edgar Allan Poe, or Baudelaire, would have done just the same. What is loathsome to me is the memory of interminable visits paid by me to the solicitor Humphreys in your company, when in the ghastly glare of a bleak room you and I would sit with serious faces telling serious lies to a bald man, till I really groaned and yawned with *ennui*. *There* is where I found myself after two years' friendship with you, right in the centre of Philistia, away from everything that was beautiful, or brilliant, or wonderful, or daring. At the end I had to come forward, on your behalf, as the champion of Respectability in conduct, of Puritanism in life, and of Morality in Art. *Voilà où mènent les mauvais chemins!*[2]

And the curious thing to me is that you should have tried to imitate your father in his chief characteristics. I cannot understand why he was to you an exemplar, where he should have been a warning, except that whenever there is hatred between two people there is bond or brotherhood of some kind. I suppose that, by some strange law of the antipathy of similars, you loathed each other, not because in so many points you were so different, but because in some you were so like. In June 1893 when you left Oxford, without a degree and with debts, petty in themselves, but considerable to a man of your father's income, your father wrote you a very vulgar, violent and abusive letter. The letter you sent him in reply was in every way worse, and of course far less excusable, and consequently you were extremely proud of it. I remember quite well your saying to me with your most conceited air that you could beat your father "at his own trade." Quite true. But what a trade! What a competition! You used to laugh and sneer at your father for retiring from your cousin's house where he was living in order to write filthy letters to him from a neighbouring hotel. You used to do just the same to me. You constantly lunched with me at some public restaurant, sulked or made a scene during luncheon, and then retired to White's Club and wrote me a letter of the very foulest character. The only difference between you and your father was that after you had dispatched your letter to me by special messenger, you would arrive yourself at my rooms some hours later, not to apologise, but to know if I

---

[1] Clibborn, referred to in the Queensberry trial as Cliburn, was a professional blackmailer who failed to extort any money from Wilde in respect of the letter to Lord Alfred Douglas (printed on p. 326), which had been stolen from Douglas by another member of the blackmailing gang. Clibborn was later sentenced to seven years' penal servitude for blackmailing offences.

Atkins (for whom see note p. 452) is here probably a slip for Allen, a blackmailing associate of Clibborn's.

[2] The last five words are the title of the third part of Balzac's *Splendeurs et Misères des Courtisanes*, in which the misguided life of Lucien de Rubempré comes to its pitiful and tragic end. O'Sullivan records Wilde's saying: "When I was a boy my two favourite characters were Lucien de Rubempré and Julien Sorel [in Stendhal's *Le Rouge et le Noir*]. Lucien hanged himself, Julien died on the scaffold, and I died in prison."

493

had ordered dinner at the Savoy, and if not, why not. Sometimes you would actually arrive before the offensive letter had been read. I remember on one occasion you had asked me to invite to luncheon at the Café Royal two of your friends, one of whom I had never seen in my life. I did so, and at your special request ordered beforehand a specially luxurious luncheon to be prepared. The *chef*, I remember, was sent for, and particular instructions given about the wines. Instead of coming to luncheon sent me at the Café an abusive letter, timed so as to reach me after we had been waiting half an hour for you. I read the first line, and saw what it was, and putting the letter in my pocket, explained to your friends that you were suddenly taken ill, and that the rest of the letter referred to your symptoms. In point of fact I did not read the letter till I was dressing for dinner at Tite Street that evening. As I was in the middle of its mire, wondering with infinite sadness how you could write letters that were really like the froth and foam on the lips of an epileptic, my servant came in to tell me that you were in the hall and were very anxious to see me for five minutes. I at once sent down and asked you to come up. You arrived, looking I admit very frightened and pale, to beg my advice and assistance, as you had been told that a man from Lumley, the solicitor, had been enquiring for you at Cadogan Place, and you were afraid that your Oxford trouble or some new danger was threatening you. I consoled you, told you, what proved to be the case, that it was merely a tradesman's bill probably, and let you stay to dinner, and pass your evening with me. You never mentioned a single word about your hideous letter, nor did I. I treated it as simply an unhappy symptom of an unhappy temperament. The subject was never alluded to. To write to me a loathsome letter at 2.30, and fly to me for help and sympathy at 7.15 the same afternoon, was a perfectly ordinary occurrence in your life. You went quite beyond your father in such habits, as you did in others. When his revolting letters to you were read in open Court he naturally felt ashamed and pretended to weep. Had your letters to him been read by his own Counsel still more horror and repugnance would have been felt by everyone. Nor was it merely in style that you "beat him at his own trade," but in mode of attack you distanced him completely. You availed yourself of the public telegram, and the open postcard. I think you might have left such modes of annoyance to people like Alfred Wood whose sole source of income it is.[1] Don't you? What was a profession to him and his class was a pleasure to you, and a very evil one. Nor have you given up your horrible habit of writing offensive letters, after all that has happened to me through them and for them. You still regard it as one of your accomplishments, and you exercise it on my friends, on those who have been kind to me in prison like Robert Sherard and others. That is disgraceful of you. When Robert Sherard heard from me that I did not wish you to publish any article on me in the *Mercure de France*, with or without letters, you should have been grateful to him for having ascertained my wishes on the point, and for having saved you from, without intending it, inflicting more pain on me than you had done already.

---

[1] A blackmailer who gave evidence at Wilde's trials.

You must remember that a patronising and Philistine letter about "fair play" for a "man who is down" is all right for an English newspaper. It carries on the old traditions of English journalism in regard to their attitude towards artists. But in France such a tone would have exposed me to ridicule and you to contempt. I could not have allowed any article till I had known its aim, temper, mode of approach and the like. In art good intentions are not of the smallest value. All bad art is the result of good intentions.

Nor is Robert Sherard the only one of my friends to whom you have addressed acrimonious and bitter letters because they sought that my wishes and my feelings should be consulted in matters concerning myself, the publication of articles on me, the dedication of your verses, the surrender of my letters and presents, and such like. You have annoyed or sought to annoy others also.

Does it ever occur to you what an awful position I would have been in if for the last two years, during my appalling sentence, I had been dependent on you as a friend? Do you ever think of that? Do you ever feel any gratitude to those who by kindness without stint, devotion without limit, cheerfulness and joy in giving, have lightened my black burden for me, have visited me again and again, have written to me beautiful and sympathetic letters, have managed my affairs for me, have arranged my future life for me, have stood by me in the teeth of obloquy, taunt, open sneer or insult even? I thank God every day that he gave me friends other than you. I owe everything to them. The very books in my cell are paid for by Robbie out of his pocket-money. From the same source are to come clothes for me, when I am released. I am not ashamed of taking a thing that is given by love and affection. I am proud of it. But do you ever think of what my friends such as More Adey, Robbie, Robert Sherard, Frank Harris, and Arthur Clifton, have been to me in giving me comfort, help, affection, sympathy and the like? I suppose that has never dawned on you. And yet —if you had any imagination in you—you would know that there is not a single person who has been kind to me in my prison-life, down to the warder who may give me a good-morning or a good-night that is not one of his prescribed duties—down to the common policemen who in their homely rough way strove to comfort me on my journeys to and fro from the Bankruptcy Court under conditions of terrible mental distress—down to the poor thief who, recognising me as we tramped round the yard at Wandsworth, whispered to me in the hoarse prison-voice men get from long and compulsory silence: "*I am sorry for you: it is harder for the likes of you than it is for the likes of us*"—not one of them all, I say, the very mire from whose shoes you should not be proud to be allowed to kneel down and clean.

Have you imagination enough to see what a fearful tragedy it was for me to have come across your family? What a tragedy it would have been for anyone at all, who had a great position, a great name, anything of importance to lose? There is hardly one of the elders of your family—with the exception of Percy, who is really a good fellow—who did not in some way contribute to my ruin.

I have spoken of your mother to you with some bitterness, and I strongly advise you to let her see this letter, for your own sake chiefly. If it is painful to her to read such an indictment against one of her sons, let her remember that *my* mother, who intellectually ranks with Elizabeth Barrett Browning, and historically with Madame Roland,[1] died broken-hearted because the son of whose genius and art she had been so proud, and whom she had regarded always as a worthy continuer of a distinguished name, had been condemned to the treadmill for two years. You will ask me in what way your mother contributed to my destruction. I will tell you. Just as you strove to shift onto me all your immoral responsibilities, so your mother strove to shift on to me all her moral responsibilities with regard to you. Instead of speaking directly to you about your life, as a mother should, she always wrote privately to me with earnest, frightened entreaties not to let you know that she was writing to me. You see the position in which I was placed between you and your mother. It was one as false, as absurd, and as tragic as the one in which I was placed between you and your father. In August 1892, and on the 8th of November in the same year, I had two long interviews with your mother about you. On both occasions I asked her why she did not speak directly to you herself. On both occasions she gave the same answer: "*I am afraid to: he gets so angry when he is spoken to.*" The first time, I knew you so slightly that I did not understand what she meant. The second time, I knew you so well that I understood perfectly. (During the interval you had had an attack of jaundice and been ordered by the doctor to go for a week to Bournemouth, and had induced me to accompany you as you hated being alone.) But the first duty of a mother is not to be afraid of speaking seriously to her son. Had your mother spoken seriously to you about the trouble she saw you were in in July 1892 and made you confide in her it would have been much better, and much happier ultimately for both of you. All the underhand and secret communications with me were wrong. What was the use of your mother sending me endless little notes, marked "Private" on the envelope, begging me not to ask you so often to dinner, and not to give you any money, each note ending with an earnest postscript "*On no account let Alfred know that I have written to you*"? What good could come of such a correspondence? Did you ever wait to be asked to dinner? Never. You took all your meals as a matter of course with me. If I remonstrated, you always had one observation: "*If I don't dine with you, where am I to dine? You don't suppose that I am going to dine at home?*" It was unanswerable. And if I absolutely refused to let you dine with me, you always threatened that you would do something foolish, and always did it. What possible result could there be from letters such as your mother used to send me, except that which did occur, a foolish and fatal shifting of the moral

[1] Manon Jeanne Phlipon, bluestocking and hostess (1754–93), married (1781) Jean Marie Roland (1734–93), who later held office in the Revolutionary Government. Eventually they fell foul of Marat, Madame Roland was arrested, wrote her *Mémoires* in the Conciergerie, and was guillotined, after exclaiming "O Liberty! What crimes are committed in thy name!" Her husband killed himself two days later.

responsibility on to my shoulders? Of the various details in which your mother's weakness and lack of courage proved so ruinous to herself, to you, and to me, I don't want to speak any more, but surely, when she heard of your father coming down to my house to make a loathsome scene and create a public scandal, she might then have seen that a serious crisis was impending, and taken some serious steps to try and avoid it? But all she could think of doing was to send down plausible George Wyndham[1] with his pliant tongue to propose to me—what? That I should "gradually drop you"!

As if it had been possible for me to gradually drop you! I had tried to end our friendship in every possible way, going so far as actually to leave England and give a false address abroad in the hopes of breaking at one blow a bond that had become irksome, hateful, and ruinous to me. Do you think that I *could* have "gradually dropped" you? Do you think that would have satisfied your father? You know it would not. What your father wanted, indeed, was not the cessation of our friendship, but a public scandal. That is what he was striving for. His name had not been in the papers for years. He saw the opportunity of appearing before the British public in an entirely new character, that of the affectionate father. His sense of humour was roused. Had I severed my friendship with you it would have been a terrible disappointment to him, and the small notoriety of a second divorce suit, however revolting its details and origin, would have proved but little consolation to him.[2] For what he was aiming at was popularity, and to pose as a champion of purity, as it is termed, is, in the present condition of the British public, the surest mode of becoming for the nonce a heroic figure. Of this public I have said in one of my plays that if it is Caliban for one half of the year, it is Tartuffe for the other,[3] and your father, in whom both characters may be said to have become incarnate, was in this way marked out as the proper representative of Puritanism in its aggressive and most characteristic form. No gradual dropping of you would have been of any avail, even had it been practicable. Don't you feel now that the only thing for your mother to have done was to have asked me to come to see her, and had you and your brother present, and said definitely that the friendship must absolutely cease? She would have found in me her warmest seconder, and with Drumlanrig and myself in the room she need not have been afraid of speaking to you. She did not do so. She was afraid of her responsibilities, and tried to shift them on to me. One letter she did certainly write to me. It was a brief one, to ask me not to send the lawyer's letter to your father warning him to desist. She was

[1] The Rt Hon. George Wyndham (1863–1913), son of the Hon. Percy Scawen Wyndham and grandson of the first Lord Leconfield. He had been M.P. for Dover since 1889, and private secretary to Mr Balfour 1887–92. He later reached the Cabinet. He wrote a number of books on literary subjects and was a kinsman of Lord Alfred Douglas.   [2] See note 3, p. 376.

[3] There is no such remark in any of Wilde's plays, but in a manuscript notebook (MS. Clark) containing aphorisms and short speeches, many of which were later used in the plays, occurs the phrase: "England—Caliban for nine months of the year—Tartuffe for the other three."

quite right. It was ridiculous my consulting lawyers and seeking their protection. But she nullified any effect her letter might have produced by her usual postscript: "*On no account let Alfred know that I have written to you.*"

You were entranced at the idea of my sending lawyers' letters to your father, as well as yourself. It was your suggestion. I could not tell you that your mother was strongly against the idea, for she had bound me with the most solemn promises never to tell you about her letters to me, and I foolishly kept my promise to her. Don't you see that it was wrong of her not to speak directly to you? That all the backstairs-interviews with me, and the area-gate correspondence were wrong? Nobody can shift their responsibilities on anyone else. They always return ultimately to the proper owner. Your one idea of life, your one philosophy, if you are to be credited with a philosophy, was that whatever you did was to be paid for by someone else: I don't mean merely in the financial sense—that was simply the practical application of your philosophy to everyday life—but in the broadest, fullest sense of transferred responsibility. You made that your creed. It was very successful as far as it went. You forced me into taking the action because you knew that your father would not attack your life or yourself in any way, and that I would defend both to the utmost, and take on my own shoulders whatever would be thrust on me. You were quite right. Your father and I, each from different motives of course, did exactly as you counted on our doing. But somehow, in spite of everything, you have not really escaped. The "infant Samuel theory," as for brevity's sake one may term it, is all very well as far as the general world goes. It may be a good deal scorned in London, and a little sneered at in Oxford, but that is merely because there are a few people who know you in each place, and because in each place you left traces of your passage. Outside of a small set in those two cities, the world looks on you as the good young man who was very nearly tempted into wrong-doing by the wicked and immoral artist, but was rescued just in time by his kind and loving father. It sounds all right. And yet, you know you have not escaped. I am not referring to a silly question asked by a silly juryman, which was of course treated with contempt by the Crown and by the Judge.[1] No one cared

---

[1] On 25 May 1895, the sixth and last day of Wilde's final trial, during the Judge's summing-up, the following dialogue took place:

The Foreman of the Jury In view of the intimacy between Lord Alfred Douglas and Wilde, was a warrant ever issued for the apprehension of Lord Alfred Douglas?

Mr Justice Wills I should think not. We have not heard of it.

The Foreman of the Jury Was it ever contemplated?

Mr Justice Wills Not to my knowledge. A warrant would in any case not be issued without evidence of some fact, of something more than intimacy. I cannot tell, nor need we discuss that, because Lord Alfred Douglas may yet have to answer a charge. He was not called. There may be a thousand considerations of which we may know nothing that might prevent his appearance in the witness-box. I think you should deal with the matter upon the evidence before you.

The Foreman of the Jury But it seems to us that if we are to consider these letters as evidence of guilt, and if we adduce any guilt from these letters, it applies as much to Lord Alfred Douglas as to the defendant.

Mr Justice Wills Quite so. But how does that relieve the defendant? Our present

about that. I am referring perhaps principally to yourself. In your own eyes, and some day you will have to think of your conduct, you are not, cannot be quite satisfied at the way in which things have turned out. Secretly you must think of yourself with a good deal of shame. A brazen face is a capital thing to show the world, but now and then when you are alone, and have no audience, you have, I suppose, to take the mask off for mere breathing purposes. Else, indeed, you would be stifled.

And in the same manner your mother must at times regret that she tried to shift her grave responsibilities on someone else, who already had enough of a burden to carry. She occupied the position of both parents to you. Did she really fulfil the duties of either? If I bore with your bad temper and your rudeness and your scenes, she might have borne with them too. When last I saw my wife—fourteen months ago now—I told her that she would have to be to Cyril a father as well as a mother. I told her everything about your mother's mode of dealing with you in every detail as I have set it down in this letter, only of course far more fully. I told her the reason of the endless notes with "Private" on the envelope that used to come to Tite Street from your mother, so constantly that my wife used to laugh and say that we must be collaborating in a society novel or something of that kind. I implored her not to be to Cyril what your mother was to you. I told her that she should bring him up so that if he shed innocent blood he would come and tell her, that she might cleanse his hands for him first, and then teach him how by penance or expiation to cleanse his soul afterwards. I told her that if she was frightened of facing the responsibility of the life of another, though her own child, she should get a guardian to help her. That she has, I am glad to say, done. She has chosen Adrian Hope, a man of high birth and culture and fine character, her own cousin, whom you met once at Tite Street, and with him Cyril and Vyvyan have a good chance of a beautiful future.[1] Your mother, if

---

inquiry is whether guilt is brought home to the man in the dock. We have got the testimony of his guilt to deal with now. I believe that to be the recipient of such letters and to continue the intimacy is as fatal to the reputation of the recipient as to the sender, but you have really nothing to do with that at present.

There is a natural disposition to ask, "Why should this man stand in the dock, and not Lord Alfred Douglas?" But the supposition that Lord Alfred Douglas will be spared because he is Lord Alfred Douglas is one of the wildest injustice—the thing is utterly and hopelessly impossible. I must remind you that anything that can be said for or against Lord Alfred Douglas must not be allowed to prejudice the prisoner; and you must remember that no prosecution would be possible on the mere production of Wilde's letters to Lord Alfred Douglas. Lord Alfred Douglas, as you all know, went to Paris at the request of the defendant, and there he has stayed, and I know absolutely nothing more about him. I am as ignorant in this respect as you are. It may be that there is no evidence against Lord Alfred Douglas—but even about that I know nothing. It is a thing we cannot discuss, and to entertain any such consideration as I have mentioned would be a prejudice of the worst possible kind.

[1] Adrian Charles Francis Hope (1858–1904) remained the official guardian of the children after Wilde and his wife were dead. He was a connection by marriage of Constance Wilde, and was Secretary to the Hospital for Sick Children, Great Ormond Street, from 1888.

she was afraid of talking seriously to you, should have chosen someone amongst her own relatives to whom you might have listened. But she should not have been afraid. She should have had it out with you and faced it. At any rate, look at the result. Is she satisfied and pleased?

I know she puts the blame on me. I hear of it, not from people who know you, but from people who do not know you, and do not desire to know you. I hear of it often. She talks of the influence of an elder over a younger man, for instance. It is one of her favourite attitudes towards the question, and it is always a successful appeal to popular prejudice and ignorance. I need not ask you what influence I had over you. You know I had none. It was one of your frequent boasts that I had none, and the only one indeed that was well-founded. What was there, as a mere matter of fact, in you that I could influence? Your brain? It was undeveloped. Your imagination? It was dead. Your heart? It was not yet born. Of all the people who have ever crossed my life you were the one, and the only one, I was unable in any way to influence in any direction. When I lay ill and helpless in a fever caught from tending on you, I had not sufficient influence over you to induce you to get me even a cup of milk to drink, or to see that I had the ordinary necessaries of a sickroom, or to take the trouble to drive a couple of hundred yards to a bookseller's to get me a book at my own expense. When I was actually engaged in writing, and penning comedies that were to beat Congreve for brilliancy, and Dumas *fils* for philosophy, and I suppose everybody else for every other quality, I had not sufficient influence with you to get you to leave me undisturbed as an artist should be left. Wherever my writing room was, it was to you an ordinary lounge, a place to smoke and drink hock-and-seltzer in, and chatter about absurdities. The "influence of an elder over a younger man" is an excellent theory till it comes to my ears. Then it becomes grotesque. When it comes to your ears, I suppose you smile—to yourself. You are certainly entitled to do so. I hear also much of what she says about money. She states, and with perfect justice, that she was ceaseless in her entreaties to me not to supply you with money. I admit it. Her letters were endless, and the postscript "*Pray do not let Alfred know that I have written to you*" appears in them all. But it was no pleasure to me to have to pay every single thing for you from your morning shave to your midnight hansom. It was a horrible bore. I used to complain to you again and again about it. I used to tell you—you remember, don't you?—how I loathed your regarding me as a "*useful*" person, how no artist wishes to be so regarded or so treated; artists, like art itself, being of their very essence quite useless. You used to get very angry when I said it to you. The truth always made you angry. Truth, indeed, is a thing that is most painful to listen to and most painful to utter. But it did not make you alter your views or your mode of life. Every day I had to pay for every single thing you did all day long. Only a person of absurd good nature or of indescribable folly would have done so. I unfortunately was a complete combination of both. When I used to suggest that your mother should supply you with the money you wanted, you always had a very pretty and graceful answer. You said that the income allowed her by your father—some £1500 a year I believe—was quite inadequate to the wants of a lady of her position, and that you could not go to her for more money than you were getting already. You were quite right about her income being one absolutely unsuitable to a lady of her position and tastes, but you should not have made that an excuse for living in luxury on me: it should on the contrary have been a suggestion to you for economy in your own life. The fact is that you were, and are I suppose still, a typical sentimentalist. For a sentimentalist is simply one who desires to have the luxury of an emotion without paying for it. To propose to spare your mother's pocket was beautiful. To do so at my expense was ugly. You think that one can have one's emotions for nothing. One cannot. Even the finest and the most self-sacrificing emotions have to be paid for. Strangely enough, that is what makes them fine. The intellectual and emotional life of ordinary people is a very contemptible affair. Just as they borrow their ideas from a sort of circulating library of thought—the *Zeitgeist* of an age that has no soul—and send them back soiled at the end of each week, so they always try to get their emotions on credit, and refuse to pay the bill when it comes in. You should pass out of that conception of life. As soon as you have to pay for an emotion you will know its quality, and be the better for such knowledge. And remember that the sentimentalist is always a cynic at heart. Indeed sentimentality is merely the bank holiday of cynicism. And delightful as cynicism is from its intellectual side, now that it has left the Tub for the Club, it never can be more than the perfect philosophy for a man who has no soul.[1] It has its social value, and to an artist all modes of expression are interesting, but in itself it is a poor affair, for to the true cynic nothing is ever revealed.

I think that if you look back now to your attitude towards your mother's income, and your attitude towards my income, you will not feel proud of yourself, and perhaps you may some day, if you don't show your mother this letter, explain to her that your living on me was a matter in which my wishes were not consulted for a moment. It was simply a peculiar, and to me personally most distressing, form that your devotion to me took. To make yourself dependent on me for the smallest as well as the largest sums lent you in your own eyes all the charm of childhood, and in the insisting on my paying for every one of your pleasures you thought that you had found the secret of eternal youth. I confess that it pains me when I hear of your mother's remarks about me, and I am sure that on reflection you will agree with me that if she has no word of regret or sorrow for the ruin your race has brought on mine it would be better if she remained silent. Of course there is no reason she should see any portion of this letter that refers to any mental development I have been going through, or to any point of departure I hope to attain to. It would not be interesting to her. But the parts concerned purely with your life I should show her if I were you.

If I were you, in fact, I would not care about being loved on false

[1] Diogenes, the Cynic philosopher (419–324 B.C.), lived in a tub.

pretences. There is no reason why a man should show his life to the world. The world does not understand things. But with people whose affection one desires to have it is different. A great friend of mine—a friend of ten years' standing[1]—came to see me some time ago and told me that he did not believe a single word of what was said against me, and wished me to know that he considered me quite innocent, and the victim of a hideous plot concocted by your father. I burst into tears at what he said, and told him that while there was much amongst your father's definite charges that was quite untrue and transferred to me by revolting malice, still that my life had been full of perverse pleasures and strange passions, and that unless he accepted that fact as a fact about me and realised it to the full, I could not possibly be friends with him any more, or ever be in his company. It was a terrible shock to him, but we are friends, and I have not got his friendship on false pretences. I have said to you that to speak the truth is a painful thing. To be forced to tell lies is much worse.

I remember as I was sitting in the dock on the occasion of my last trial listening to Lockwood's[2] appalling denunciation of me—like a thing out of Tacitus, like a passage in Dante, like one of Savonarola's indictments of the Popes at Rome—and being sickened with horror at what I heard. Suddenly it occurred to me, *"How splendid it would be, if I was saying all this about myself!"* I saw then at once that what is said of a man is nothing. The point is, who says it. A man's very highest moment is, I have no doubt at all, when he kneels in the dust, and beats his breast, and tells all the sins of his life. So with you. You would be much happier if you let your mother know a little at any rate of your life from yourself. I told her a good deal about it in December 1893, but of course I was forced into reticences and generalities. It did not seem to give her any more courage in her relations with you. On the contrary. She avoided looking at the truth more persistently than ever. If you told her yourself it would be different. My words may perhaps be often too bitter to you. But the facts you cannot deny. Things were as I have said they were, and if you have read this letter as carefully as you should have done you have met yourself face to face.

I have now written, and at great length, to you in order that you should realise what you were to me before my imprisonment, during those three years' fatal friendship: what you have been to me during my imprisonment, already within two moons of its completion almost: and what I hope to be to myself and to others when my imprisonment is over. I cannot reconstruct my letter, or rewrite it. You must take it as it stands, blotted in many places with tears, in some with the signs of passion or pain, and make it out as best you can, blots, corrections and all. As for the corrections and *errata*, I have made them in order that my words should be an absolute expression of my thoughts, and err neither through surplusage nor through

[1] Frank Harris, according to himself, but more likely Sherard, who records a similar confession.

[2] The Solicitor-General, Sir Frank Lockwood (1847–97), who led for the prosecution in Wilde's second trial.

being inadequate. Language requires to be tuned, like a violin: and just as too many or too few vibrations in the voice of the singer or the trembling of the string will make the note false, so too much or too little in words will spoil the message. As it stands, at any rate, my letter has its definite meaning behind every phrase. There is in it nothing of rhetoric. Wherever there is erasion or substitution, however slight, however elaborate, it is because I am seeking to render my real impression, to find for my mood its exact equivalent. Whatever is first in feeling comes always last in form.

I will admit that it is a severe letter. I have not spared you. Indeed you may say that, after admitting that to weigh you against the smallest of my sorrows, the meanest of my losses, would be really unfair to you, I have actually done so, and made scruple by scruple the most careful assay of your nature. That is true. But you must remember that you put yourself into the scales.

You must remember that, if when matched with one mere moment of my imprisonment the balance in which you lie kicks the beam, Vanity made you choose the balance, and Vanity made you cling to it. *There* was the one great psychological error of our friendship, its entire want of proportion. You forced your way into a life too large for you, one whose orbit transcended your power of vision no less than your power of cyclic motion, one whose thoughts, passions and actions were of intense import, of wide interest, and fraught, too heavily indeed, with wonderful or awful consequence. Your little life of little whims and moods was admirable in its own little sphere. It was admirable at Oxford, where the worst that could happen to you was a reprimand from the Dean or a lecture from the President, and where the highest excitement was Magdalen becoming head of the river, and the lighting of a bonfire in the quad as a celebration of the august event. It should have continued in its own sphere after you left Oxford. In yourself, you were all right. You were a very complete specimen of a very modern type. It was simply in reference to me that you were wrong. Your reckless extravagance was not a crime. Youth is always extravagant. It was your forcing me to pay for your extravagances that was disgraceful. Your desire to have a friend with whom you could pass your time from morning to night was charming. It was almost idyllic. But the friend you fastened on should not have been a man of letters, an artist, one to whom your continual presence was as utterly destructive of all beautiful work as it was actually paralysing to the creative faculty. There was no harm in your seriously considering that the most perfect way of passing an evening was to have a champagne dinner at the Savoy, a box at a Music-Hall to follow, and a champagne supper at Willis's as a *bonne-bouche* for the end. Heaps of delightful young men in London are of the same opinion. It is not even an eccentricity. It is the qualification for becoming a member of White's. But you had no right to require of me that I should become the purveyor of such pleasures for you. It showed your lack of any real appreciation of my genius. Your quarrel with your father, again, whatever one may think about its character, should obviously have remained a question entirely between the two of you. It should have been carried on in a backyard. Such quarrels, I believe, usually are. Your mistake was in insisting on its being played as a tragi-comedy on a high stage in History, with the whole world as the audience, and myself as the prize for the victor in the contemptible contest. The fact that your father loathed you, and that you loathed your father, was not a matter of any interest to the English public. Such feelings are very common in English domestic life, and should be confined to the place they characterise: the home. Away from the home-circle they are quite out of place. To translate them is an offence. Family-life is not to be treated as a red flag to be flaunted in the streets, or a horn to be blown hoarsely on the housetops. You took Domesticity out of its proper sphere, just as you took yourself out of your proper sphere.

And those who quit their proper sphere change their surroundings merely, not their natures. They do not acquire the thoughts or passions appropriate to the sphere they enter. It is not in their power to do so. Emotional forces, as I say somewhere in *Intentions*, are as limited in extent and duration as the forces of physical energy.[1] The little cup that is made to hold so much can hold so much and no more, though all the purple vats of Burgundy be filled with wine to the brim, and the treaders stand knee-deep in the gathered grapes of the stony vineyards of Spain. There is no error more common than that of thinking that those who are the causes or occasions of great tragedies share in the feelings suitable to the tragic mood: no error more fatal than expecting it of them. The martyr in his "shirt of flame"[2] may be looking on the face of God, but to him who is piling the faggots or loosening the logs for the blast the whole scene is no more than the slaying of an ox is to the butcher, or the felling of a tree to the charcoal-burner in the forest, or the fall of a flower to one who is mowing down the grass with a scythe. Great passions are for the great of soul, and great events can be seen only by those who are on a level with them.

I know of nothing in all Drama more incomparable from the point of view of Art, or more suggestive in its subtlety of observation, than Shakespeare's drawing of Rosencrantz and Guildenstern. They are Hamlet's college friends. They have been his companions. They bring with them memories of pleasant days together. At the moment when they come across him in the play he is staggering under the weight of a burden intolerable to one of his temperament. The dead have come armed out of the grave to impose on him a mission at once too great and too mean for him. He is a dreamer, and he is called upon to act. He has the nature of the poet and he is asked to grapple with the common complexities of cause and effect, with life in its practical realisation, of which he knows nothing, not with life in its ideal essence, of which he knows much. He has no conception of what to do, and his folly is to feign folly. Brutus used madness as a cloak to conceal the sword of his purpose, the dagger of his will,[3]

[1] "The Critic as Artist," Part II.

[2] "Like a pale martyr in his shirt of fire" (Alexander Smith: *A Life-Drama*, scene ii). Cf. p. 232.

[3] Not the Brutus of Shakespeare's *Julius Caesar*, but Junius Brutus who expelled Tarquin, the last King of Rome.

but to Hamlet madness is a mere mask for the hiding of weakness. In the making of mows and jests he sees a chance of delay. He keeps playing with action, as an artist plays with a theory. He makes himself the spy of his proper actions, and listening to his own words knows them to be but "words, words, words." Instead of trying to be the hero of his own history, he seeks to be the spectator of his own tragedy. He disbelieves in everything, including himself, and yet his doubt helps him not, as it comes not from scepticism but from a divided will.

Of all this, Guildenstern and Rosencrantz realise nothing. They bow and smirk and smile, and what the one says the other echoes with sicklier iteration. When at last, by means of the play within the play and the puppets in their dalliance, Hamlet "catches the conscience" of the King, and drives the wretched man in terror from his throne, Guildenstern and Rosencrantz see no more in his conduct than a rather painful breach of court-etiquette. That is as far as they can attain to in "the contemplation of the spectacle of life with appropriate emotions."[1] They are close to his very secret and know nothing of it. Nor would there be any use in telling them. They are the little cups that can hold so much and no more. Towards the close it is suggested that, caught in a cunning springe set for another, they have met, or may meet with a violent and sudden death. But a tragic ending of this kind, though touched by Hamlet's humour with something of the surprise and justice of comedy, is really not for such as they. They never die. Horatio who, in order to "report Hamlet and his cause aright to the unsatisfied,"

> Absents him from felicity a while
> And in this harsh world draws his breath in pain,

dies, though not before an audience, and leaves no brother. But Guildenstern and Rosencrantz are as immortal as Angelo and Tartuffe, and should rank with them. They are what modern life has contributed to the antique ideal of friendship. He who writes a new *De Amicitia* must find a niche for them and praise them in Tusculan prose. They are types fixed for all time. To censure them would show a lack of appreciation. They are merely out of their sphere: that is all. In sublimity of soul there is no contagion. High thoughts and high emotions are by their very existence isolated. What Ophelia herself could not understand was not to be realised by "Guildenstern and gentle Rosencrantz," by "Rosencrantz and gentle Guildenstern." Of course I do not propose to compare you. There is a wide difference between you. What with them was chance, with you was choice. Deliberately and by me uninvited you thrust yourself into my sphere, usurped there a place for which you had neither right nor qualifications, and having by curious persistence, and by the rendering of your very presence a part of each separate day, succeeded in absorbing my entire life, could do no better with that life than break it in pieces. Strange as it may sound to you, it was but natural that you should do so. If one gives to a child a toy too wonderful for its little mind, or too beautiful for its

[1] See note 2, p. 476.

505

but half-awakened eyes, it breaks the toy, if it is wilful; if it is listless it lets it fall and goes its way to its own companions. So it was with you. Having got hold of my life, you did not know what to do with it. You couldn't have known. It was too wonderful a thing to be in your grasp. You should have let it slip from your hands and gone back to your own companions at their play. But unfortunately you were wilful, and so you broke it. That, when everything is said, is perhaps the ultimate secret of all that has happened. For secrets are always smaller than their manifestations. By the displacement of an atom a world may be shaken. And that I may not spare myself any more than you I will add this: that dangerous to me as my meeting with you was, it was rendered fatal to me by the particular moment in which we met. For you were at that time of life when all that one does is no more than the sowing of the seed, and I was at that time of life when all that one does is no less than the reaping of the harvest.

There are some few things more about which I must write to you. The first is about my Bankruptcy. I heard some days ago, with great disappointment I admit, that it is too late now for your family to pay your father off, that it would be illegal, and that I must remain in my present painful position for some considerable time to come. It is bitter to me because I am assured on legal authority that I cannot even publish a book without the permission of the Receiver to whom all the accounts must be submitted. I cannot enter into a contract with the manager of a theatre, or produce a play without the receipts passing to your father and my few other creditors. I think that even you will admit now that the scheme of "scoring off" your father by allowing him to make me a bankrupt has not really been the brilliant all-round success you imagined it was going to turn out. It has not been so to me at any rate, and my feelings of pain and humiliation at my pauperism should have been consulted rather than your own sense of humour, however caustic or unexpected. In point of actual fact, in permitting my Bankruptcy, as in urging me on to the original trial, you really were playing right into your father's hands, and doing just what he wanted. Alone, and unassisted, he would from the very outset have been powerless. In you—though you did not mean to hold such a horrible office —he has always found his chief ally.

I am told by More Adey in his letter that last summer you really did express on more than one occasion your desire to repay me "a little of what I spent" on you. As I said to him in my answer, unfortunately I spent on you my art, my life, my name, my place in history, and if your family had all the marvellous things in the world at their command, or what the world holds as marvellous, genius, beauty, wealth, high position and the like, and laid them all at my feet, it would not repay me for one tithe of the smallest things that have been taken from me, or one tear of the least tears that I have shed. However, of course everything one does has to be paid for. Even to the Bankrupt it is so. You seem to be under the impression that Bankruptcy is a convenient means by which a man can avoid paying his debts, a "score off his creditors" in fact. It is quite the other way. It is the method by which a man's creditors "score off" him, if we are to continue your favourite phrase, and by which the Law by the confiscation of all his property forces him to pay every one of his debts, and if he fails to do so leaves him as penniless as the commonest mendicant who stands in an archway, or creeps down a road, holding out his hand for the alms for which, in England at any rate, he is afraid to ask. The Law has taken from me not merely all that I have, my books, furniture, pictures, my copyright in my published works, my copyright in my plays, everything in fact from *The Happy Prince* and *Lady Windermere's Fan* down to the stair-carpets and door-scraper of my house, but also all that I am ever going to have. My interest in my marriage-settlement, for instance, was sold. Fortunately I was able to buy it in through my friends. Otherwise, in case my wife died, my two children during my lifetime would be as penniless as myself. My interest in our Irish estate, entailed on me by my own father, will I suppose have to go next. I feel very bitterly about its being sold, but I must submit.

Your father's seven hundred pence—or pounds is it?—stand in the way, and must be refunded. Even when I am stripped of all I have, and am ever to have, and am granted a discharge as a hopeless Insolvent, I have still got to pay my debts. The Savoy dinners—the clear turtle-soup, the luscious ortolans wrapped in their crinkled Sicilian vine-leaves, the heavy amber-coloured, indeed almost amber-scented champagne—Dagonet 1880, I think, was your favourite wine?—all have still to be paid for. The suppers at Willis's, the special *cuvée* of Perrier-Jouet reserved always for us, the wonderful *pâtés* procured directly from Strasburg, the marvellous *fine champagne* served always at the bottom of great bell-shaped glasses that its bouquet might be the better savoured by the true epicures of what was really exquisite in life—these cannot be left unpaid, as bad debts of a dishonest *client*. Even the dainty sleeve-links—four heart-shaped moonstones of silver mist, girdled by alternate ruby and diamond for their setting—that I designed, and had made at Henry Lewis's as a special little present to you, to celebrate the success of my second comedy—these even—though I believe you sold them for a song a few months afterwards—have to be paid for. I cannot leave the jeweller out of pocket for the presents I gave you, no matter what you did with them. So, even if I get my discharge, you see I have still my debts to pay.

And what is true of a bankrupt is true of everyone else in life. For every single thing that is done someone has to pay. Even you yourself—with all your desire for absolute freedom from all duties, your insistence on having everything supplied to you by others, your attempts to reject any claim on your affection, or regard, or gratitude—even you will have some day to reflect seriously on what you have done, and try, however unavailingly, to make some attempt at atonement. The fact that you will not be able really to do so will be part of your punishment. You can't wash your hands of all responsibility, and propose with a shrug or a smile to pass on to a new friend and a freshly spread feast. You can't treat all that you have brought upon me as a sentimental reminiscence to be served up occasionally with the cigarettes and *liqueurs*, a picturesque background to a modern life of pleasure like an old tapestry hung in a common inn. It may for the moment have the charm of a new sauce or a fresh vintage, but the scraps of a banquet grow stale, and the dregs of a bottle are bitter. Either today, or tomorrow, or some day you have got to realise it. Otherwise you may die without having done so, and then what a mean, starved, unimaginative life you would have had. In my letter to More I have suggested one point of view from which you had better approach the subject as soon as possible. He will tell you what it is. To understand it you will have to cultivate your imagination. Remember that imagination is the quality that enables one to see things and people in their real as in their ideal relations. If you cannot realise it by yourself, talk to others on the subject. I have had to look at my past face to face. Look at your past face to face. Sit down quietly and consider it. The supreme vice is shallowness. Whatever is realised is right. Talk to your brother about it. Indeed the proper person to talk to is Percy. Let him read this letter, and know all the circumstances of our friendship. When things are clearly put before him, no judgment is better. Had we told him the truth, what a lot would have been saved to me of suffering and disgrace! You remember I proposed to do so, the night you arrived in London from Algiers. You absolutely refused. So when he came in after dinner we had to play the comedy of your father being an insane man subject to absurd and unaccountable delusions. It was a capital comedy while it lasted, none the less so because Percy took it all quite seriously. Unfortunately it ended in a very revolting manner. The subject on which I write now is one of its results, and if it be a trouble to you, pray do not forget that it is the deepest of my humiliations, and one I must go through. I have no option. You have none either.

The second thing about which I have to speak to you is with regard to the conditions, circumstances, and place of our meeting when my term of imprisonment is over. From extracts from your letter to Robbie written in the early summer of last year I understand that you have sealed up in two packages my letters and my presents to you—such at least as remain of either—and are anxious to hand them personally to me. It is, of course, necessary that they should be given up. You did not understand why I wrote beautiful letters to you, any more than you understood why I gave you beautiful presents. You failed to see that the former were not meant to be published, any more than the latter were meant to be pawned. Besides, they belong to a side of life that is long over, to a friendship that somehow you were unable to appreciate at its proper value. You must look back with wonder now to the days when you had my entire life in your hands. I too look back to them with wonder, and with other, with far different, emotions.

I am to be released, if all goes well with me, towards the end of May, and hope to go at once to some little seaside village abroad with Robbie and More Adey. The sea, as Euripides says in one of his plays about Iphigenia, washes away the stains and wounds of the world. Θάλασσα κλύζει πάντα τ'ανθρώπων κακά.[1]

---

[1] *Iphigenia in Tauris*, 1193.

I hope to be at least a month with my friends, and to gain, in their healthful and affectionate company, peace, and balance, and a less troubled heart, and a sweeter mood. I have a strange longing for the great simple primeval things, such as the Sea, to me no less of a mother than the Earth. It seems to me that we all look at Nature too much, and live with her too little. I discern great sanity in the Greek attitude. They never chattered about sunsets, or discussed whether the shadows on the grass were really mauve or not. But they saw that the sea was for the swimmer, and the sand for the feet of the runner. They loved the trees for the shadow that they cast, and the forest for its silence at noon. The vineyard-dresser wreathed his hair with ivy that he might keep off the rays of the sun as he stooped over the young shoots, and for the artist and the athlete, the two types that Greece gave us, they plaited into garlands the leaves of the bitter laurel and of the wild parsley which else had been of no service to man.

We call ourselves a utilitarian age, and we do not know the uses of any single thing. We have forgotten that Water can cleanse, and Fire purify, and that the Earth is mother to us all. As a consequence our Art is of the Moon and plays with shadows, while Greek art is of the Sun and deals directly with things. I feel sure that in elemental forces there is purification, and I want to go back to them and live in their presence. Of course, to one so modern as I am, *enfant de mon siècle*, merely to look at the world will be always lovely. I tremble with pleasure when I think that on the very day of my leaving prison both the laburnum and the lilac will be blooming in the gardens, and that I shall see the wind stir into restless beauty the swaying gold of the one, and make the other toss the pale purple of its plumes so that all the air shall be Arabia for me. Linnæus fell on his knees and wept for joy when he saw for the first time the long heath of some English upland made yellow with the tawny aromatic blossoms of the common furze, and I know that for me, to whom flowers are part of desire, there are tears waiting in the petals of some rose. It has always been so with me from my boyhood. There is not a single colour hidden away in the chalice of a flower, or the curve of a shell, to which, by some subtle sympathy with the very soul of things, my nature does not answer. Like Gautier I have always been one of those *pour qui le monde visible existe*.[1]

Still, I am conscious now that behind all this Beauty, satisfying though it be, there is some Spirit hidden of which the painted forms and shapes are but modes of manifestation, and it is with this Spirit that I desire to become in harmony. I have grown tired of the articulate utterances of men and things. The Mystical in Art, the Mystical in Life, the Mystical in Nature—this is what I am looking for, and in the great symphonies of Music, in the initiation of Sorrow, in the depths of the Sea I may find it. It is absolutely necessary for me to find it somewhere.

All trials are trials for one's life, just as all sentences are sentences of

[1] "*Critiques et louanges me louent et m'abiment sans comprendre un mot de ce que je suis. Toute ma valeur, ils n'ont jamais parlé de cela, c'est que je suis un homme pour qui le monde visible existe*" (Gautier, as reported in the Goncourt Journal for 1 May 1857.) Wilde used the phrase in Chapter ix of *Dorian Gray*, describing Dorian.

death, and three times have I been tried. The first time I left the box to be arrested, the second time to be led back to the House of Detention, the third time to pass into a prison for two years. Society, as we have constituted it, will have no place for me, has none to offer; but Nature, whose sweet rains fall on unjust and just alike, will have clefts in the rocks where I may hide, and secret valleys in whose silence I may weep undisturbed. She will hang the night with stars so that I may walk abroad in the darkness without stumbling, and send the wind over my footprints so that none may track me to my hurt: she will cleanse me in great waters, and with bitter herbs make me whole.

At the end of a month, when the June roses are in all their wanton opulence, I will, if I feel able, arrange through Robbie to meet you in some quiet foreign town like Bruges, whose grey houses and green canals and cool still ways had a charm for me, years ago. For the moment you will have to change your name. The little title of which you were so vain—and indeed it made your name sound like the name of a flower—you will have to surrender, if you wish to see *me*; just as *my* name, once so musical in the mouth of Fame, will have to be abandoned by me, in turn. How narrow, and mean, and inadequate to its burdens is this century of ours! It can give to Success its palace of porphyry, but for Sorrow and Shame it does not keep even a wattled house in which they may dwell: all it can do for *me* is to bid me alter my name into some other name, where even mediaevalism would have given me the cowl of the monk or the face-cloth of the leper behind which I might be at peace.

I hope that our meeting will be what a meeting between you and me should be, after everything that has occurred. In old days there was always a wide chasm between us, the chasm of achieved Art and acquired culture: there is a still wider chasm between us now, the chasm of Sorrow: but to Humility there is nothing that is impossible, and to Love all things are easy.

As regards your letter to me in answer to this, it may be as long or as short as you choose. Address the envelope to "The Governor, H.M. Prison, Reading." Inside, in another, and an open envelope, place your own letter to me: if your paper is very thin do not write on both sides, as it makes it hard for others to read. I have written to you with perfect freedom. You can write to me with the same. What I must know from you is why you have never made any attempt to write to me, since the August of the year before last, more especially after, in the May of last year, eleven months ago now, you knew, and admitted to others that you knew, how you had made me suffer, and how I realised it. I waited month after month to hear from you. Even if I had not been waiting but had shut the doors against you, you should have remembered that no one can possibly shut the doors against Love for ever. The unjust judge in the Gospels rises up at length to give a just decision because Justice comes knocking daily at his door; and at night-time the friend, in whose heart there is no real friendship, yields at length to his friend "because of his importunity."[1] There is no prison in any world into which Love cannot force an entrance. If you

[1] *Luke,* xi, 5–8.

did not understand that, you did not understand anything about Love at all. Then, let me know all about your article on me for the *Mercure de France*. I know something of it. You had better quote from it. It is set up in type. Also, let me know the exact terms of your Dedication of your poems. If it is in prose, quote the prose; if in verse, quote the verse. I have no doubt that there will be beauty in it. Write to me with full frankness about yourself: about your life: your friends: your occupations: your books. Tell me about your volume and its reception. Whatever you have to say for yourself, say it without fear. Don't write what you don't mean: that is all. If anything in your letter is false or counterfeit I shall detect it by the ring at once. It is not for nothing, or to no purpose, that in my lifelong cult of literature I have made myself

> Miser of sound and syllable, no less
> Than Midas of his coinage.[1]

Remember also that I have yet to know you. Perhaps we have yet to know each other.

For yourself, I have but this last thing to say. Do not be afraid of the past. If people tell you that it is irrevocable, do not believe them. The past, the present and the future are but one moment in the sight of God, in whose sight we should try to live. Time and space, succession and extension, are merely accidental conditions of Thought. The Imagination can transcend them, and move in a free sphere of ideal existences. Things, also, are in their essence what we choose to make them. A thing *is*, according to the mode in which one looks at it. "Where others," says Blake, "see but the Dawn coming over the hill, I see the sons of God shouting for joy."[2] What seemed to the world and to myself my future I lost irretrievably when I let myself be taunted into taking the action against your father: had, I dare say, lost it really long before that. What lies before me is my past. I have got to make myself look on that with different eyes, to make the world look on it with different eyes, to make God look on it with different eyes. This I cannot do by ignoring it, or slighting it, or praising it, or denying it. It is only to be done by fully accepting it as an inevitable part of the evolution of my life and character: by bowing my head to everything that I have suffered. How far I am away from the true temper of soul, this letter in its changing, uncertain moods, its scorn and bitterness, its aspirations and its failure to realise those aspirations, shows you quite clearly. But do not forget in what a terrible school I am sitting at my task. And incomplete, imperfect, as I am, yet from me you may have still much to gain. You came to me to learn the Pleasure of Life and the Pleasure of Art. Perhaps I am chosen to teach you something much more wonderful, the meaning of Sorrow, and its beauty. Your affectionate friend   OSCAR WILDE

[1] Keats: "Sonnet on the Sonnet."

[2] "What," it will be Questioned, "When the Sun rises, do you not see a round disk of fire somewhat like a Guinea?" O no, no, I see an Innumerable company of the Heavenly host crying, "Holy, Holy, Holy is the Lord God Almighty" ("A Vision of the Last Judgment").

To Robert Ross

MS. Clark

1 April 1897   *H.M. Prison, Reading*

My dear Robbie, I send you, in a roll separate from this, my letter to Alfred Douglas, which I hope will arrive safe.[1] As soon as you, and of course More Adey whom I always include with you, have read it, I want you to have it carefully copied for me. There are many reasons why I wish this to be done. One will suffice. I want you to be my literary executor in case of my death, and to have complete control over my plays, books and papers. As soon as I find I have a legal right to make a will I will do so. My wife does not understand my art, nor could be expected to have any interest in it, and Cyril is only a child. So I turn naturally to you, as indeed I do for everything, and would like you to have all my works. The deficit that their sale will produce may be lodged to the credit of Cyril and Vyvyan.

Well, if you are my literary executor, you must be in possession of the only document that really gives any explanation of my extraordinary behaviour with regard to Queensberry and Alfred Douglas. When you have read the letter you will see the psychological explanation of a course of conduct that from the outside seems a combination of absolute idiocy with vulgar bravado. Some day the truth will have to be known: not necessarily in my lifetime or in Douglas's: but I am not prepared to sit in the grotesque pillory they put me into, for all time: for the simple reason that I inherited from my father and my mother a name of high distinction in literature and art, and I cannot, for eternity, allow that name to be the shield and catspaw of the Queensberrys. I don't defend my conduct. I explain it.

Also there are in the letter certain passages which deal with my mental development in prison, and the inevitable evolution of character and intellectual attitude towards life that has taken place: and I want you, and others who still stand by me and have affection for me, to know exactly in what mood and manner I hope to face the world. Of course from one point of view I know that on the day of my release I shall be merely passing from one prison into another, and there are times when the whole world seems to me no larger than my cell, and as full of terror for me. Still I believe that at the beginning God made a world for each separate man, and in that world which is within us one should seek to live. At any rate, you will read those parts of my letter with less pain than the others. Of course I need not remind *you* how fluid a thing thought is with me—with us all— and of what an evanescent substance are our emotions made. Still, I do see a sort of possible goal towards which, through art, I may progress. It is not unlikely that you may help me.

[1] On 2 April the Governor wrote to the Prison Commission to ask whether the preceding letter, "written during the last three or four months," might be sent out. On 6 April the Commission wrote to say this was impossible, but the letter could be kept and handed to the prisoner on his release. This was done on 19 May and Wilde handed it to Ross at Dieppe when he landed there next morning.

As regards the mode of copying: of course it is too long for any amanuensis to attempt: and your own handwriting, dear Robbie, in your last letter seems specially designed to remind me that the task is not to be yours. I may wrong you, and hope I do, but it really looks as if you were engaged in writing a three-volume novel on the dangerous prevalence of communistic opinions among the rich, or some dreadful subject of vital interest, or in some other way wasting a youth that I cannot help saying has always been, and will always remain, quite full of promise. I think that the only thing to do is to be thoroughly modern, and to have it typewritten. Of course the manuscript should not pass out of your control, but could you not get Mrs Marshall to send down one of her type-writing girls—women are the most reliable, as they have no memory for the important—to Hornton Street or Phillimore Gardens to do it under your supervision?[1] I assure you that the type-writing machine, when played with expression, is not more annoying than the piano when played by a sister or near relation. Indeed many, among those most devoted to domesticity, prefer it.

I wish the copy to be done not on tissue paper but on good paper such as is used for plays, and a wide rubricated margin should be left for corrections. The copy done and verified from the manuscript, the original should be despatched to A. D. by More, and another copy done by the typewriter so that *you* should have a copy as well as myself.[2] Also I would wish two typewritten copies to be made from the fourth page of sheet 9 to the last page of sheet 14: from "and the end of it . . . I must forgive you" down to "Between art and myself there is none" (I quote from memory). Also on page 3 of sheet 18 from "I am to be released if all goes well" to "bitter herbs . . . whole" on page 4.[3] These welded together with anything else you may extract that is good and nice in intention, such as first page of sheet 15, I wish sent, one copy to the Lady of Wimbledon—whom I have spoken of, without mentioning her name—the other to Frankie Forbes-Robertson. I know both these sweet women will be interested to know something of what is happening to my soul—not in the theological sense, but merely in the sense of the spiritual consciousness that is separate from the actual occupations of the body. It is a sort of message or letter I send them—the only one, of course, I dare send. If Frankie wishes she can show it to her brother Eric, of whom I was always fond, but of course it is a strict secret from the general world. The Lady of Wimbledon will know that too.

If the copying is done at Hornton Street the lady type-writer might be fed through a lattice in the door like the Cardinals when they elect a Pope, till she comes out on the balcony and can say to the world "*Habet Mundus Epistolam;*" for indeed it is an Encyclical Letter, and as the Bulls of the Holy Father are named from their opening words, it may be spoken of as the *Epistola: In Carcere et Vinculis.*

There is no need to tell A. D. that a copy has been taken, unless he should

---

[1] More Adey lived at 24 Hornton Street, Kensington, and Robert Ross nearby at 11 Upper Phillimore Gardens.   [2] See note p. 423.
[3] Most of these two passages were included in *De Profundis* (1905).

write and complain of injustice in the letter or misrepresentation: then he should be told that a copy has been taken. I earnestly hope the letter will do him good. It is the first time anyone has ever told him the truth about himself. If he is allowed to think that the letter is merely the result of the influence of a plank-bed on style, and that my views are distorted by the privations of prison-life, no good will follow. I hope someone will let him know that the letter is one he thoroughly deserves, and that if it is unjust, he thoroughly deserves injustice. Who indeed deserves it more than he who was always so unjust to others?

In point of fact, Robbie, prison-life makes one see people and things as they really are. That is why it turns one to stone. It is the people outside who are deceived by the illusion of a life in constant motion. They revolve with life and contribute to its unreality. We who are immobile both see and know. Whether or not the letter does good to his narrow nature and hectic brain, to me it has done great good. I have "cleansed my bosom of much perilous stuff,"[1] to borrow a phrase from the poet whom you and I once thought of rescuing from the Philistines.[2] I need not remind you that mere expression is to an artist the supreme and only mode of life. It is by utterance that we live. Of the many, many things for which I have to thank the Governor there is none for which I am more grateful than for his permission to write fully to A. D. and at as great length as I desired. For nearly two years I had within me a growing burden of bitterness, much of which I have now got rid of. On the other side of the prison-wall there are some poor black soot-smirched trees that are just breaking out into buds of an almost shrill green. I know quite well what they are going through. They are finding expression.

There is another very serious thing about which I have to write to you, and I address myself to you because I have got to blame you, and I am far too fond of you to blame you to anyone else. On the 20th March 1896,[3] more than a year ago now, I wrote to you in the very strongest terms telling you that I could not bear the idea of any discord being made between myself and my wife on such a subject as money, after her sweetness in coming here from Italy to break to me the news of my mother's death, and that I desired my friends to withdraw their proposal to purchase my life-interest against her wishes. You should have seen that my wishes were carried out. You were very wrong not to do so. I was quite helpless in prison and I relied on you. You thought that the thing to do was the clever thing, the smart thing, the ingenious thing. You were under a mistake. Life is not complex. We are complex. Life is simple, and the simple thing is the right thing. Look at the result! Are you pleased with it?

Again, a complete error was made in the estimate formed of Mr Hargrove.

---

[1] *Macbeth*, Act V, scene iii.
[2] Meyerfeld says that this refers to Ross's joking suggestion of founding an Anti-Shakespeare Society to combat exaggerated Bardolatry, and that Douglas's sonnet "To Shakespeare" (published in *The City of the Soul*, 1899) was written in anger at the suggestion.   [3] Actually 10 March. See p. 398.

He was regarded as a solicitor of the Humphreys class, one who would threaten to gain an end, bluster, extort, and the like. Quite the contrary. He is a man of very high character, and extremely good social position. Whatever he said he meant. The idea of putting me—a wretched prisoner and pauper—up to fight Mr Hargrove and Sir George Lewis was grotesque. The idea of bidding against them absurd. Mr Hargrove—the family solicitor of the Lloyds for thirty years—would advance my wife £10,000 if she wanted it, and not feel it. I asked Mr Holman whether in case of a divorce a settlement was not *ipso facto* broken. I received no answer. I find that it is as I suspected.

Again, how silly the long serious letters advising me "not to surrender my rights over my children," a phrase that occurs seven times in the correspondence. My rights! I had none. A claim that a formal appeal to a Judge in Chambers can quash in ten minutes is not a right. I am quite astounded at the position I have been placed in. How much better if you had done as I asked you, as at that time my wife was kind and ready to let me see my two children and be with them occasionally.[1] A. D. put me into a false position with regard to his father, forced me into it, and held me there. More Adey, with the best intentions, forced me into a false position with regard to my wife. Even had I any legal rights—and I have none—how much more charming to have privileges given to me by affection than to extort them by threats. My wife was very sweet to me, and now she, very naturally, goes right against me. Of her character also a wrong estimate was made. She warned me that if I let my friends bid against her she would proceed to a certain course, and she will do so.

Again, Swinburne says to Marie Stuart in one of his poems,

> But surely you were something better
> Than innocent![2]

and really my friends must face the fact that (setting aside such details in my indictment as belonged to my bosom-friend, three in number) I am not in prison as an innocent man. On the contrary, my record of perversities of passion and distorted romances would fill many scarlet volumes. I think it right to mention this—however surprising, and no doubt shocking, it will sound to many—because More Adey in his letter tells me that the opposite side will be obliged to furnish strict details of the dates and places and exact circumstances of the terrible charges to be

---

[1] On 26 March Constance Wilde had written from Italy to her brother (MS. Holland):

I have again had pressure put upon me to persuade me to go back to Oscar, but I am sure you will agree that it is impossible. I am told that I would save a human soul, but I have no influence over Oscar. I have had none, and though I think he is affectionate I see no reason for believing that I should be able now to perform miracles, and I must look after my boys and not risk their future. What do you think I should do? The Ranee thinks that he has fallen and cannot rise. That is rather like Humpty Dumpty, but then I think his fate is rather like Humpty Dumpty's, quite as tragic and quite as impossible to put right.

[2] From "Adieux à Marie Stuart," published in *Tristram of Lyonesse and other Poems* (1882).

brought against me. Does he seriously imagine that if I submitted to more cross-examination I would be believed? Does he propose I should do so, and repeat the Queensberry fiasco? It is the case that the charges are not true. But that is a mere detail. If a man gets drunk, whether he does so on white wine or red is of no importance. If a man has perverse passions, their particular mode of manifestation is of no importance either.

I said from the first that I relied entirely on my wife's condonation. I now learn that no condonation is of any value where more than one offence may be charged. My wife has simply to say that she condoned X, but knew nothing of Y, and would not hear of condoning Z. There is a little shilling book—ninepence for cash—called *Every Man his own Lawyer*. If my friends had only sent it to me, or even read it themselves, all this trouble, expense, and worry would have been saved. However, while I blame you *ab initio*, I am now in a mood of mind that makes me think that everything that happens is for the best, and that the world is not a mere chaos in which chance and cleverness clash. What I have to do is simply this. I have got to submit to my divorce. I don't think that the Government could possibly prosecute me again. Even for a British Government it would be too brutal a procedure. I have also, before that, to restore to my wife my interest in the settlement-money before it is taken from me. I have thirdly to state that I will accept nothing from her at all in the way of income or allowance. This seems to be the simple, straightforward, and gentlemanly thing to do. It is a great blow to me. I feel the legal deprivation of my children poignantly.

My friendship with A. D. brought me first to the dock of the Criminal Court, then to the dock of the Bankruptcy Court, and now to the dock of the Divorce Court. As far as I can make out (not having the shilling primer on the subject) there are no more docks into which he can bring me. If so, I can draw a breath of relief. But I want you to seriously consider my proposal, to ask More to do so, and his lawyer, and to write to me, and to get More to write to me, as soon as possible about it. I think my wife will have no objection to refunding the £75 paid for the *damnosa hæreditas* of my life-interest. She is quite just on money matters. But personally I hope there will be no bargaining. A grave mistake has been made. Submission has to follow. I propose that my life-interest should be restored to my wife, its rightful owner, as a parting gift from me. It will render my exit from marriage less ignominious than to wait for its being done by legal coercion. Whether I am married or not is a matter that does not concern me. For years I disregarded the tie. But I really think that it is hard on my wife to be tied to me. I always thought so. And, though it may surprise some of my friends, I am really very fond of my wife and very sorry for her. I sincerely hope she may have a happy marriage, if she marries again. She could not understand me, and I was bored to death with the married life. But she had some sweet points in her character, and was wonderfully loyal to me. On this point of my surrendering everything, pray let More and yourself write at once, after you have considered the point.

Also, I would take it as a great favour if More would write to the people who pawned or sold my fur coat since my imprisonment,[1] and ask them from me whether they would be kind enough to state where it was sold or pawned as I am anxious to trace it, and if possible get it back. I have had it for twelve years, it was all over America with me, it was at all my first nights, it knows me perfectly, and I really want it. The letter should be quite courteous, addressed first to the man: if he doesn't answer, to the woman. As it was the wife who pressed me to leave it in her charge, it might be mentioned that I am surprised and distressed, particularly as I paid out of my own pocket *since my imprisonment* all the expenses of her confinement, to the extent of £50 conveyed through Leverson. This might be stated as a reason for my being distressed. Their letters must be kept. I have a most particular reason for wishing it to be done—in fact, one vitally important. And the letter being one of civil request, with the reasons set forth, cannot involve argument or denial. I just require documentary evidence for my protection.

I hope to see Frank Harris on Saturday week, or soon. The news of the copying of my letter will be welcome, when I hear from you about my divorce. If Arthur Clifton would like to see the copy show it to him, or your brother Aleck. Ever yours   OSCAR WILDE

To Robert Ross [2]
MS. Clark

6 April [1897]   *H.M. Prison, Reading*

My dear Robbie, I am going to delay for a short time my letter to Alfred Douglas for certain reasons, some of which, though not all, are suggested in a letter I am sending to More Adey at the same time as this.[3]

I write to you now, partly for the pleasure of writing to you and getting from you in return one of your delightful literary letters, and partly because I have to blame you, and I cannot bear the idea of doing that indirectly, or in a letter addressed to another.

It is now more than a year—a year and one month to be exact—since I wrote to you telling you that I wished my friends to withdraw completely all opposition to my wife buying my life-interest in my marriage-settlement, as I did not desire anything to be done that could make an estrangement between my wife and myself. My wife had come all the way from Genoa to break to me personally the news of my dear mother's death. She had been very sympathetic and sweet to me. Her offer of a third of the interest in case of her death was ample and right.

I wrote strongly to you, because I trusted that you would see that to make an estrangement between my wife and myself over a paltry money

---

[1] This must refer to Wilde's brother and sister-in-law, since Mrs Willie Wilde was the only recipient of £50 from Leverson (see note p. 552).

[2] Although this letter repeats much of the preceding one (which may well have been withheld by the prison authorities) it is included for the extra matter which it contains.   [3] See next letter, p. 524.

517

question would be wrong, unseemly, and unjust to both of us: you knew my wife better than any of my friends did. You were fond of her, and she was excessively fond of you. I felt sure I could rely on you to see that my wishes and hers were carried out. I was mistaken. Seven months later—on October 22nd—I found out through a violent and insulting letter from her lawyer, enraged at what seemed like double-dealing on my part, that my wishes had not been regarded.

I was at once thrust into a false position. Just as Alfred Douglas forced me into a false position with his father, and made me, with my life behind me, take action against the entire forces of Society, the Bar, and the Government, so my friends forced me, an isolated and pauper prisoner in an English gaol, to fight Sir George Lewis and Mr Hargrove. I was told again and again how important it was that I should not "surrender" any of my "rights" over my children. The phrase occurs in three letters now lying before me. As if I had any rights! I had none. The formal application to a Judge in Chambers by a solicitor's clerk deprived me of Cyril and Vyvyan in less than ten minutes. It was a mere matter of form.

I wrote to Mr Holman to ask him if a divorce would not break my marriage-settlement. I felt sure it would. I received no answer. But the purchase of a small shilling book—ninepence for cash—entitled *Every Man his own Lawyer* would have informed my friends that when a divorce is granted a settlement is annulled unless it is specified to the contrary.

I also let my friends know that my only chance of resisting a divorce was the fact of *condonation* by my wife. I now hear that condonation counts as nothing where more than one offence may be alleged. My solicitor told me it was a commonplace in law, the sort of thing an office-boy would know. More Adey gravely writes to tell me that details and dates of each separate offence will have to be given, so that I may prepare my defence!

In one of his poems to Marie Stuart, Swinburne says to his heroine

> But surely you were something better
> Than innocent!

and so, though the particular offence required by the law did not find part amongst my perversities of passion, still perversities there were, or else why am I here? It may be a terrible shock to my friends to think that I had abnormal passions, and perverse desires, but if they read history they will find I am not the first artist so doomed, any more than I shall be the last. To talk of my defending the case against Sir George Lewis is childish. How can I expect to be believed on a mere detail? What limit is there to the amount of witnesses he can produce? None. He and Queensberry can sweep Piccadilly for them. It makes me sick with rage when I am told about the opportunities I shall have of defending the case. What commonsense have my friends got to write such twaddle to me?

However, we must accept facts as they are. My wife is now going for a divorce. She has been forced to do so. The purchase of my life-interest against her wishes and interests has left her no option. From the first she was advised by Sir George Lewis to divorce me. She resisted out of affection for me. Now she has been forced to do so. And I feel that the only thing now for me to do is to make my wife a present of my life-interest, and to submit to the divorce. It is bitter to me, but I think it is the right thing for me to do, and it would I think be more seemly and generous of me to make my full submission and leave her perfectly free. I don't think that even a British Government with Labouchere,[1] Stead,[2] and the Social Purity League to back them would re-arrest me and send me to prison again. It would be a ridiculous thing to do. I must live in England, if I am to be a dramatist again, so I must face it if they do. But it would be a bestial infamy to again send me to a prison for offences that in all civilized countries are questions of pathology and medical treatment if their cure is desired.

You see, Robbie, how wrong you were to pretend to me that you were carrying out my wishes and my wife's, when really you were doing the exact opposite. We all make the mistake of thinking life is complex. It is not. It is we who are complex, and people think that clever, smart, round-about schemes are the best. They are the worst. Life is quite simple. One should do the straightforward thing. Complex people waste half their strength in trying to conceal what they do. Is it any wonder they should always come to grief?

Consider now, dear Robbie, my proposal. I think my wife, who in money-matters is most honourable and high-minded, will refund the £75 paid for my share. I have no doubt she will. But I think it should be offered from me, and that I should not accept anything in the way of in-come from her. I can accept what is given in love and affection to me, but I could not accept what is doled out grudgingly, or with conditions. I would sooner let my wife be quite free. She may marry again. In any case I think that if free she would allow me to see my children from time to time. That is what I want. But I must set her free first, and had better do it as a gentleman by bowing my head and accepting everything.

You must consider the whole question, as it is through you and your ill-advised action it is due: and let me know what you and others think. Of course you acted for the best. But you were wrong in your view. I may say candidly that I am gradually getting to a state of mind when I think that everything that happens is for the best. This may be philosophy, or a broken heart, or religion, or the dull apathy of despair. But, whatever

[1] Labouchere (see note 3, p. 105) was responsible for inserting into the Criminal Law Amendment Act (1885) the clause under which Wilde was convicted. After Wilde's conviction Labouchere wrote in *Truth* that he was sorry his original maximum penalty had been reduced from seven to two years.

[2] William Thomas Stead (1849–1912), editor of the *Pall Mall Gazette* 1883–89, had in 1885 organised a campaign against the white slave traffic and organised vice, in a series of articles called "Maiden Tribute of Modern Babylon." This landed him in Holloway Prison but probably helped the passing of the Criminal Law Amendment Act (1885), which raised the age of consent from 13 to 16 and was sometimes popularly known as Stead's Act. In 1890 he started the *Review of Reviews*, which was surprisingly generous about Wilde in 1895, though Wilde may not have known this. Stead later became an ardent spiritualist. He was drowned in the *Titanic*.

its origin, the feeling is strong with me. To tie my wife to me against her will would be wrong. She has a full right to her freedom. And not to be supported by her would be a pleasure to me. It is an ignominious position to be a pensioner on her. Talk over this with More Adey. Get him to show you the letter I have written to him. Ask your brother Aleck to give me his advice. He has excellent wisdom on things.

Now to other points.

I have never had the chance of thanking you for the books. They were most welcome. Not being allowed the magazines was a blow, but Meredith's novel charmed me.[1] What a sane artist in temper! He is quite right in his assertion of sanity as the essential in romance. Still, up to the present only the abnormal have found expression in life and literature.

Rossetti's letters are dreadful. Obviously forgeries by his brother.[2] I was interested however to see how my grand-uncle's *Melmoth*[3] and my mother's *Sidonia* had been two of the books that fascinated his youth. As regards the conspiracy against him in later years I believe it really existed, and that the funds for it came out of Hake's bank. The conduct of a thrush in Cheyne Walk seems to me most suspicious, though William Rossetti says, "I could discern nothing in the thrush's song at all out of the common."[4]

Stevenson letters most disappointing also.[5] I see that romantic surroundings are the worst surroundings possible for a romantic writer. In Gower Street Stevenson could have written a new *Trois Mousquetaires*. In Samoa he wrote letters to *The Times* about Germans. I see also the traces of a terrible *strain* to lead a natural life. To chop wood with any advantage to oneself, or profit to others, one should not be able to describe the process. In point of fact the natural life is the unconscious life. Stevenson merely extended the sphere of the artificial by taking to digging. The whole dreary book has given me a lesson. If I spend my future life reading Baudelaire in a *café* I shall be leading a more natural life than if I take to hedger's work or plant cacao in mud-swamps.

En Route is most over-rated.[6] It is sheer journalism. It never makes one hear a note of the music it describes. The subject is delightful, but the style is of course worthless, slipshod, flaccid. It is worse French than

---

[1] *The Amazing Marriage*, first published, in two volumes, on 15 November 1895.

[2] *Dante Gabriel Rossetti, his Family-Letters, with a Memoir by William Michael Rossetti* (2 vols., 1895).   [3] See note p. 555.

[4] This incident in fact took place at Broadlands in Hampshire. W. M. Rossetti wrote (*op. cit.*, i, 339):

> I remember there was once a thrush hard by, which, to my hearing, simply trilled its own lay on and off. My brother discerned a different note, and conceived that the thrush had been trained to ejaculate something insulting to him. Such is perverted fantasy—or I may rather infer such is an outcome of chloral-dosing.

The poet Dr Thomas Gordon Hake (1809–95) was one of D. G. Rossetti's closest friends. His son Alfred Egmont Hake, author of *Free Trade in Capital* (1891) and other books, invented a new system of banking which had amused Wilde.

[5] *Vailima Letters* (1895). See note 2, p. 401.

[6] This novel by Joris-Karl Huysmans (1848–1907) was first published in 1895.

Ohnet's.[1] Ohnet tries to be commonplace and succeeds. Huysmans tries not to be, and is . . .[2] Hardy's novel[3] is pleasant, and Frederic's very interesting in matter. . . .[4] Later on, there being hardly any novels in the prison library for the poor imprisoned fellows I live with, I think of presenting the library with about a dozen good novels: Stevenson's (none here but *The Black Arrow*!), some of Thackeray's (none here). Jane Austen (none here), and some good *Dumas-père-like* books, by Stanley Weyman for instance, and any modern young man.[5] You mentioned Henley had a *protégé*?[6] Also the "Anthony Hope" man.[7] After Easter, you might make out a list of about fourteen, and apply to let me have them. They would please the few who do not care about Goncourt's journal. Don't forget. I would pay myself for them.

I have a horror myself of going out into a world without a single book of my own. I wonder would there be any of my friends who would give me a few books, such as Cosmo Lennox,[8] Reggie Turner,[9] Gilbert Burgess,[10] Max,[11] and the like? You know the sort of books I want: Flaubert, Stevenson, Baudelaire, Maeterlinck, Dumas *père*, Keats, Marlowe, Chatterton, Coleridge, Anatole France, Gautier, Dante and all Dante literature; Goethe and ditto: and so on. I would feel it a great compliment to have books waiting for me, and perhaps there may be some friends who would like to be kind to me. One is really very grateful, though I fear I often seem not to be. But then remember I have had incessant worries besides prison-life.

In answer to this you can send me a long letter all about plays and books.

---

[1] Georges Ohnet, prolific and popular French novelist (1848–1918).

[2] All dots in this letter are Wilde's.

[3] *The Well-Beloved* (published 16 March 1897).

[4] *Illumination* by the American novelist Harold Frederic (1856–98). See note 1, p. 423.

[5] Stanley John Weyman (1855–1928) had already published nine historical novels, including *Under the Red Robe* (1894) and *Memoirs of a Minister of France* (1895).

[6] Probably H. G. Wells, whose first novel, *The Time Machine* (1895), had been serialised by Henley in the *New Review*.

[7] Pen-name of Anthony Hope Hawkins (1863–1933), author of many books. In 1894 he had scored a double success with *The Dolly Dialogues* and *The Prisoner of Zenda*.

[8] Cosmo Charles Gordon-Lennox (1869–1921), son of Lord and Lady Alexander Gordon-Lennox and grandson of the fifth Duke of Richmond. Actor (as Charles Stuart), playwright and successful adaptor of French plays. His greatest success was *The Marriage of Kitty* (1902). Played the part of the Vicomte de Nanjac in the original production of *An Ideal Husband.*   [9] See note 3, p. 356.

[10] English author and journalist (1868–1911). On 9 January 1895, six days after the first night of *An Ideal Husband*, he published in the *Sketch* a long interview entitled "A Talk with Mr Oscar Wilde." It also appeared in the New York *Daily Tribune* on 27 January. Mason prints long extracts (pp. 439–42). It ends with Wilde's saying:

"I am sure that you must have a great future in literature before you."

"*What makes you think so?*" I asked, as I flushed with pleasure at the prediction. "Because you seem to be such a very bad interviewer. I feel sure that you must write poetry. I certainly like the colour of your necktie very much. Good-bye."

[11] Max Beerbohm responded to this appeal and sent four books, including his own *Works* and *The Happy Hypocrite* (1896). See p. 575.

Your handwriting, in your last, was so dreadful that it looked as if you were writing a three-volume novel on the terrible spread of communistic ideas among the rich, or in some other way wasting a youth that always has been, and always will remain, quite full of promise. If I wrong you in ascribing it to such a cause you must make allowances for the morbidity produced by long imprisonment. But do write clearly. Otherwise it looks as if you had nothing to conceal.

There is much that is horrid, I suppose, in this letter. But I had to blame you to yourself, not to others. Read my letter to More. F. Harris comes to see me on Saturday, I hope. Remember me to Arthur Clifton and his wife, who, I find, is so like Rossetti's wife—the same lovely hair—but of course a sweeter nature, though Miss Siddal is fascinating, and her poem AI.[1] Ever yours   OSCAR

P.S. The names of the mystical books in *En Route* fascinate me. Try and get some of them for me when I go out. Also, try and get me a good life of St Francis of Assisi.

French Books[2]

Flaubert: [*La*] *Tentation* [*de Saint Antoine*].
           Trois Contes.
           Salammbô.
Mérimée: Novels.
Anatole France: *Thaïs* [1890] and his latest works.
Pierre Louÿs: Novel [*Aphrodite*, 1896].
La Jeunesse: Novel [*L'Imitation de Notre-Maître Napoléon*, 1897].
Maeterlinck: Complete.
Baudelaire: [*Les*] *Fleurs du Mal.*
Strindberg: Last plays.
Ibsen: Translation ([*Little*] *Eyolf.* [*John Gabriel*] *Borkman*).
Montaigne.
Gautier: *Émaux et Camées.*
French Bible (University Press).
French-English Dictionary.
Some mystical books.
[Gilbert] Murray: [*History of Ancient*] *Greek Literature* [1897].
Quarterly Review for April.

---

[1] This poem, "A Year and a Day" by Rossetti's wife Elizabeth Siddal, is printed on pp. 176–77 of the first volume of *Dante Gabriel Rossetti, His Family-Letters* (1895.)

[2] Some of the items on this list have been scored through lightly in ink or pencil. This may conceivably have been done by the prison authorities (as has been suggested), but it looks much more as if Ross had struck out, at different times, in different ways, and with different pens and pencils, those items he obtained. Moreover, the publication dates of some of the books, and the objects at the end of the list, make it clear that these were the books and objects that Wilde hoped would be waiting for him when he left prison, so that the authorities cannot have been concerned.

[D.G.] Hogarth on Alexander the Great (Murray) [*Philip and Alexander of Macedon*, 1897].

Quo Vadis? (Dent) (Translation of novel by Sienkiewicz) [1896].

English

Epic and Romance [by W. P. Ker, 1897].

St William of Norwich [: *Life and Miracles* by Thomas of Monmouth. Now first edited from unique MS. by Augustus Jessopp and M. R. James, 1896].

Ancient Ideals [by H. O. Taylor, 1896].

Wagner's Letters to Roeckel (Arrowsmith) [1887].

[J. A.] Symonds: *Italian By-ways* [1883].

[Franz] Hettinger on Dante. Translated by Father [H. S.] Bowden[1] (Burns & Oates) [1896].

Mrs Mark Pattison: *Renaissance [of Art] in France* [1879].

Dom [Francis Aidan] Gasquet: *Historical Essays [The Old English Bible and other Essays*, 1897].

Yeats: *The Secret Rose* [1897].

A. E. W. Mason: *The Philanderers* (Macmillan) [1897]. Also his previous novel [*The Courtship of Morrice Buckler*, 1896].

A Bible.

Flinders Petrie on Egypt [*Egyptian Decorative Art*, 1895]. Any good book on Ancient Egypt.

Translation of Hafiz, and of oriental love-poetry.

Arthur Morrison: article in *Nineteenth Century* on Prisons and Sir Edmund Du Cane's reply. Also Arthur Morrison's Criminology series.[2]

Spanish-French Conversation Book.

Calderon: [*El*] *Mágico Prodigioso* ⎫ translated.
       [*La*] *Devoción de la Cruz* ⎭

[1] There exists (MS. Clark) a letter from Father Bowden to Wilde, written from the Oratory, London, on 15 April 1878, from which it is clear that Wilde had visited him on the previous day to ask for advice about the possibility of joining the Roman Catholic Church.

[2] Wilde was confusing the novelist Arthur Morrison (1863–1945), author of *Tales of Mean Streets* (1894), with the Rev. William Douglas Morrison (1852–1943), who was a prison chaplain 1883–98. He had published *Crime and its Causes* (1891) and *Juvenile Offenders* (1896). This was the third volume of a criminology series of which he was general editor. The other two volumes were *The Female Offender* by Cesare Lombroso and Gulielmo Ferrero (1895) and *Criminal Sociology* by Enrico Ferri (1895). Morrison was chaplain at Wandsworth when Wilde was there. I can find nothing of his in the *Nineteenth Century*, but Sir Edmund Du Cane (1830–1903), who had been Chairman of the Prison Commissioners 1877–95, had contributed two articles to the paper: "The Prison Committee Report" (August 1895) and "The Unavoidable Uselessness of Prison Labour" (October 1896): neither mentions Morrison by name. Morrison had published an article called "Are Our Prisons a Failure?" in the *Fortnightly Review* of April 1894, and another called "Prisons and Prisoners" in the same paper for May 1898, in which, without mentioning Wilde's name, he described the earlier part of Wilde's imprisonment.

Spanish Grammar.

Silver brushes—my brother. Bag also.
White ties, made up.
English manuscript books. Pencils. Foolscap paper.
Despatch-box! Where is it? Very Important.

Guide-Book to the Morbihan, Finisterre district. Quimper, Vannes.
Guide-Book to Pyrenees.
See is there near Boulogne any small place to go to. Not more than an
    hour and a half.

Reviews of *Salome*.
Salome itself.

Humphreys.

To More Adey

MS. Clark

7 *April 1897*   *[H.M. Prison] Reading*

My dear More, I am sending a letter of great importance to Robbie which
he will show you. It deals primarily with my divorce-suit. I have been
thrust into a very false position by my friends, and have to suffer for it.
I see (for reasons stated at greater length to Robbie) nothing now but to
submit, and to return beforehand my life-interest, as a sort of parting-
gift, so as not to leave my exit from the marriage-tie too ignominious and
unworthy.

    The primary fault was Robbie's in not carrying out my own wishes and
my wife's, conveyed to him in my letter of March 1896. Also, there has
been a complete misapprehension of my wife's character, which is strong
and simple, and of Mr Hargrove's. The latter has been regarded as a
solicitor of the Humphreys type, one who would bluster, and threaten, and
lie. He really is a man of the highest character and position and whatever
he said he would do he will carry out. To put me up to fight him and Sir
George Lewis was childish.

    As for buying the life-interest, Mr Hargrove would raise £5000 to-
morrow for my wife if she wanted it. He was the family solicitor of her
grandfather, and owes much of his own wealth—which is very considerable
—to Mr Horatio Lloyd. Everything has been wrong. So wrong indeed
have things been that it looks to me as if Alfred Douglas had been directing
the operations, desirous to "score off" Mr Hargrove, or my wife, or both.
His sole idea seems to be to "score off" people by sacrificing me. Please
let me know am I right in discerning some of his sinister small nature in
the whole transaction?

    At any rate, when you have read my letter to Robbie, will you seriously
consider the position into which I have been led, and don't, I beg you,
write to me again about defending the case. If a man gets drunk, whether

he does so on white wine or red matters little, and if a man has perversities of passion there is no use his denying particular details in a civil court, whatever he may do in a criminal one: and just as there are several counts in my indictment for things done by someone else, so I will be divorced I have no doubt for things I have never done, and I dare say with people I have never seen. I have to submit. I see nothing else for it.

It, of course, breaks entirely every link with my children. There was indeed no link left but my wife's kindness to me. After the divorce, I suppose I shall never see them. And when I think it is all over a paltry £150 or £200 a year I really feel ashamed. My friends seem not to have realised that what I wanted was access to my children, and their affection and my wife's. I shall await your letter with interest.

With regard to your letter about Alfred Douglas, I see of course that I must clearly ascertain what he and his family are going to do. On the occasion of my bankruptcy, which it was disgraceful of them to allow, I received through you and others a promise from Percy that £500 was to be at my disposal on my release, it being considered by him and his brother that it would be better to give the money to me instead of to their father. This promise will, I suppose, I don't doubt, be carried out, and as my release takes place in a few weeks and I am anxious to arrange my life for the next couple of years, will you kindly write to Percy and ask him to let you have the money for me. It must not go into Leverson's hands, as he would probably use it for his own purposes or in his business. I wish you to have it.

I also think it right that Percy should know a little of the mere outlines of my unfortunate acquaintance with his brother. The friendship began in May 1892 by his brother appealing to me in a very pathetic letter to help him in terrible trouble with people who were blackmailing him. I hardly knew him at the time. I had known him eighteen months, but had only seen him four times in that space. I was, however, I admit, touched by his letter, and his appeal, and did at once get him out of his trouble at considerable difficulty and annoyance to myself. Alfred Douglas was very grateful, and practically never left me for three years—not till he had got me into prison. I wish Percy to know of my incessant efforts to break off a friendship so ruinous to me artistically, financially, and socially.

In December 1893 I went so far as to fly abroad and leave a false address to try and escape from him. During the whole time he was in Egypt I refused to write to him or take any notice of his incessant letters and telegrams. It was only on his rushing back to Paris and sending me a telegram that seemed to threaten suicide that I consented even to see him. To get him out of my life was one of the objects of my life. I completely failed to accomplish it. Nothing that I could do could keep him out of my house.

As regards money, let Percy know that I spent on A. D. and with him more than £5000 in two years and a half, exclusive of bills. This I did not do as a pleasure to myself. I was forced to. I never remember on any one occasion from May 1892 to April 1895, the date of my arrest, A. D. having any money at all from either his father or his mother. He came to me for everything, nor is it any exaggeration to say that from his morning shave to his midnight hansom I was obliged to pay for every single item in his day's expenditure. He refused to have his meals at home and insisted on having them with me at the most expensive restaurants. He arrived at twelve o'clock every morning, and practically he never left me till after midnight. It was ruinous to me in every way, but I could not get rid of him. Explain to Percy that I never gave his brother large sums of money. His name hardly appears in my cheque-book. Where it does it was simply because when he was away or abroad he used to draw cheques on his own bank where his account was always overdrawn and telegraph to me to implore me to cover it by lodging to his account the amount so that his cheque might be honoured. The real expense was his support, left entirely to me.

Also, pray explain to Percy that the night A. D. arrived from Algiers I implored him to let us tell him (Percy) the truth. He absolutely refused, and insisted on the comedy of his father's delusions. Also, let Percy know the exact circumstances of my entering the absurd action. A. D. had brought to my hotel a companion of his own, one whose age, appearance, public and private profession, rendered him the most unsuitable companion possible for me in the terribly serious position in which I was placed. On my remonstrating with him, and asking him to let his companion return to his home, he made a violent scene, and preferring the society of his companion to mine retired at once to another hotel, where I subsequently had to pay the bill for them both, I need hardly say.

From his new quarters he began to bombard me with revolting letters. On the Thursday I went to my club and found Queensberry's hideous card. I returned at once to the hotel where I found a no less loathsome letter from Alfred Douglas. I felt I stood between Caliban and Sporus, and that I was in hideous danger from both of them, and, just as I had bolted from the son in December '93 to Paris, so I determined to bolt at once, to Paris again, from father as well as son. Unfortunately the bill for the ten days Alfred Douglas had planted himself on me, with his companion at the close of the period, was £148, and the hotel people would not allow my luggage to be removed till I had paid the bill in full, which I could not do. At that moment A. D. arrived, saw his father's card, and by taunts of cowardice and terror drove me to the fatal step. I stumbled like an ox into the shambles. My last straw for clutching to was the expense. I told Humphreys I had no money. A. D. at once interfered, said that his family would pay the whole expense, and be too delighted to do so. Humphreys, keen for a scandalous case, and scenting money, closed at once. I was brought in a four-wheeler by both of them to apply for a warrant, and here I am in prison. I think Percy should know these facts, as from Robbie's letter to me the Queensberry family seem to be talking foolishly about the case. So please write to Percy, and ask him from me to fulfil his promise.

Also, I want you to write to Leverson from me. During the time I was out on bail a sum of money was given to me by a friend to be of use to me in any way possible. I, not liking to have a large sum of money on me, asked Leverson and Reggie Turner to be trustees of this. They consented. Leverson personally took charge of the money. I gave Leverson a piece of paper on which my friend had written "I desire this money to be employed for your own personal use and that of your children as you may direct." These were the conditions of the trust. Leverson accepted it, but told me it would be better, more convenient, only to have one trustee, and that he had arranged with Reggie to retire. I was surprised, but made no objection.

On my way to Court to receive my sentence he began asking me in the carriage to repay him £250, the balance of £500 he had advanced to Alfred Douglas and myself for the first trial. I was astonished and wounded at his selecting such a moment to worry me over a debt, and told him that I could not discuss business then, and that the money held in trust was to be applied for my mother's wants primarily, and then, if it was necessary, for my children. He did disburse on my behalf to my mother some £280 or so: my children, my wife told me, required nothing. He now comes and proposes to deduct his debt of £250 before he hands over the balance. I cannot allow this for a single moment. He has to hand over the trust-money intact to me. He has no right to touch it for any claim of his own. He must know quite well that his proposing to pay himself in full, when my other creditors are receiving nothing, is an entire breach of the Bank-ruptcy Laws. This money was not given to me to pay my debts. It was given to me because I was at the time bankrupt and ruined, to be held in trust for me by a friend. Leverson first through you proposed to pay himself and to lend me an equivalent sum. I declined this entirely. When he came here, he calmly told me that "money was tight in the City" and that he could not let me have the money that belonged to me! As if I cared whether money was tight in the City, or knew what it meant. I suppose it means that he was speculating with trust-money. That is a dangerous amusement. As a business man he should know better.

Kindly write to him and copy out what I have said and ask him to let me have the proper balance of the money entrusted to his care for my use. Of his original loan he has already had fifty per cent: the only one of my creditors who has had anything. For him to swoop down illegally and propose to collar the balance is not to be thought of. Nor will he do so. Of course, if he tried to do so I would never speak to him again or consent to see him, and would let everyone publicly and privately know of his dishonourable conduct. I would also take other measures.[1]

There is also another matter: he bought for me at my sale my own portrait,[2] the picture of A. D. I commissioned Will Rothenstein to do, and Shannon's pastel of the Moon. He may want to be paid for these, as he said they were a present to me from himself and his wife. If so, let him deduct from what is due to me his claim. The three things themselves I wish very much could be lodged somewhere for me—in a little garret

---

[1] For the injustice of this and other attacks on Ernest Leverson, see his letter on pp. 551–552.   [2] By Harper Pennington (now in Clark).

in Hornton Street, or anywhere—so that I can get them when I want. Can you do this at once?

The Sphinx has (1) *The Duchess of Padua.* (2) The manuscript of *La Sainte Courtisane.* (3) A bundle of A. D.'s letters. Would you give her from me my kind regards and most affectionate wishes and ask her to let Robbie have them, as I want them all three as soon as I am released. This is a horrid letter, but how am I to write on horrid things but horridly? Ever yours   OSCAR

To Thomas Martin[1]
MS. Clark

[*Circa April 1897*]

My dear friend, What have I to write about except that if you had been an officer in Reading Prison a year ago my life would have been much happier. Everyone tells me I am looking better—and happier.

That is because I have a good friend who gives me the *Chronicle,* and *promises* me ginger biscuits![2]   O. W.

.   .   .   .   .

You must get me his address some day—he is such a good fellow. Of course I would not for worlds get such a friend as you are into *any danger.* I quite understand your feelings.

The *Chronicle* is capital today. You must get A S/2 to come out and clean on Saturday morning and I will give him my note then myself.

.   .   .   .   .

I hope to write about prison life and to try and change it for others, but it is too terrible and ugly to make a work of art of. I have suffered too much in it to write plays about it.

.   .   .   .   .

So sorry you have no key. Would like a long talk with you. Any more news?

To the Home Secretary
MS. H.O.

22 April 1897   *H.M. Prison, Reading*

To the Right Honourable Her Majesty's Principal Secretary of State for the Home Department.

[1] Thomas Martin, a native of Belfast, came to Reading as a warder some seven weeks before Wilde's release. He was always kind to Wilde and constantly broke the regulations to bring him extra food, as well as the *Daily Chronicle* and other papers. He contributed a chapter to Sherard's *Life of Oscar Wilde* (1906). These are examples of the surreptitious notes, written on odd scraps of paper, which Wilde passed to him in prison.

[2] At the bottom of this note Martin wrote in pencil: "Your ungrateful I done more than promise."

The Petition of the above-named prisoner humbly sheweth[1] that the petitioner was sentenced to two years' imprisonment on the 20th May, 1895,[2] and that his term of imprisonment will expire on the 19th of next May, four weeks from the date of this petition.

That the petitioner is extremely anxious to avoid the notoriety and annoyance of newspaper interviews and descriptions on the occasion of his release, the date of which is of course well known. Many English, French and American papers have already announced their intention of attending the ceremony of his release, for the purpose of seeking and publishing interviews with him on the question of the treatment he has been subjected to in prison, the real circumstances that led to his original trial, and the like. The petitioner is anxious to avoid any intrusion of the kind threatened, as he considers that such interviews at such a moment would be from every point of view unseemly. He desires to go abroad quietly without attracting public attention, and his petition is that he may be released on the Saturday preceding the 19th May—Saturday the 15th in fact—so that he may go abroad unobserved and incognito.

The petitioner would beg to be allowed to mention that he was for three weeks confined in Holloway Prison before his first trial: that he was then released on bail, and surrendered to his bail to stand his trial a second time: the second trial resulting in his conviction. The petitioner will accordingly have had more than two years' detention should he be released on the 15th May as his prayer is.

The petitioner, however, is most anxious that he should not under any circumstances be transferred to another prison from the one in which he is at present confined. The ordeal he underwent in being brought in convict dress and handcuffed by a mid-day train from Clapham Junction to Reading was so utterly distressing, from the mental no less than the emotional point of view, that he feels quite unable to undergo any similar exhibition to public gaze, and he feels it his duty to say that he was assured by the former Governor of Reading Prison that he would not under any circumstances be again submitted to so terrible an experience.

Should the petitioner's request to be released on the 15th May be granted, Mr Frank Harris, the Editor of the *Saturday Review*, who has kindly invited the petitioner to go on a driving-tour in the Pyrenees with him, would at once proceed abroad with him, crossing the Channel either in a yacht, or by night, so as to avoid observation and annoyance.

And your petitioner will ever pray etc.   OSCAR WILDE

---

[1] As before, the words up to here are printed.
[2] Actually 25 May, but Wilde's sentence ran, as the custom is, from the first day of the Sessions (20 May 1895). Remission for good conduct was allowed only to prisoners undergoing penal servitude (three years or more).

To More Adey

MS. Clark

1 May [1897]   *The Prison, Reading*

My dear More, It was a great relief to me getting your letter, though of
course it is a bitter disappointment to me not to see you and Robbie here
today. I have been anxiously waiting all the week for some notice of your
coming. Hansell has taken no notice of the two last letters I wrote him,
so it is only through you that I have ascertained that he has received the
second. Of the fate of the first letter—one still more important—I know
nothing. I always thought solicitors, even if they would not answer letters,
acknowledged their receipt, but Hansell does not even do that. Of course
he may be afraid that he will not be paid, but I assured him on his visit
here that his costs would be paid in full, and, after all, acknowledging the
receipt of a letter is not an expensive item, as the charge is limited by the
Law Institute.

The inability to ascertain whether my letters reach him, or, if they do,
whether he will act, or has acted, on my instructions, keeps me in a state
of mental distress and anxiety, that for many reasons is not good for me.
Going out of prison is a terrible ordeal, and mental trouble makes me
possibly exaggerate, certainly realise, its terrors. When I go out I think I
had better have another solicitor: someone who will answer letters. If
I don't have someone, my affairs will always be in a dreadful state,
and business-worries are the worst enemies of sanity. It is in the
Theban market-place not on the hillside of Parnassus that men become
lunatick.

I hope you and Robbie will come and see me as soon as possible. You
will have to get an order, of course. If you apply to the Prison Commissioners I do not think they can refuse you, if you state that it is an
interview necessary to make arrangements for my going out. Pray ask that
the interview be in a private room, and for the space of one hour. As
regards Ricketts, if you have mentioned the matter to him, I suppose he
must come, but I am so upset by Hansell and business-affairs generally
that I am now not keen on seeing him. I am very fond of him, but I may
want to talk of other matters than books. Still, as he seems anxious to come,
let him come, and let the order be for three. My business-affairs perhaps
you will write out on a sheet of paper for me to see clearly. I read better
than I listen, and your handwriting is hieratic in its clearness and style.
The thing I want is to know everything quite clearly as it really is. That
is what one wants to know in prison. What kills one is uncertainty, with
its accompanying anxiety and distress.

At the present moment, for instance, I am in great trouble because I
cannot get any answer from the Home Secretary with regard to the date
of my release. I sent a petition last Thursday week to him to ask to be
released on Saturday the 15th on the ground of the anxiety of the newspapers to revive public interest in my ruin and its cause by interviewing me
and the like, and also for other reasons. The *Morning* newspaper has

already been here making enquiries and preparations, and of course others will be in readiness. No notice has been taken of the petition, and I suppose I shall be kept in this horrible suspense till the evening of the 18th, when I shall no doubt be informed that the petition has been refused. Or perhaps the news will be broken to me on the morning of the 19th before my release. It is a hideous method of dealing with people who are in distress and misery, but I believe it is entirely in accordance with the ordinary rules of the Office. To me I confess the prospect of being pursued by interviewers is horrible, especially considering the terrible change in my appearance. I know, of course, that I have become brutalised and horrible in appearance: punishment produces that effect: nor have I, I need hardly say, any vanity left of any kind: but the consciousness of being degraded of aspect and grotesque is dreadful, and I am anxious to avoid the coarse pen and pencil of the English journalist, always so keen to inflict pain or excite ridicule by means of offensive personalities.

I have not much hope that the Home Secretary will accede to my request for privacy in my leaving prison, as regards the day and moment. They brought me down here handcuffed and in convict dress by a mid-day train, mobbed and hooted at every station, and I can't expect them to care very much about my feelings on release, or to sympathise with my desire for privacy. Still I wish they would convey to me even the usual verbal "No" that is the stereotyped formula of answer to all requests. I can make no plans till I know one way or the other.

As regards Frank Harris, I feel now that I would like two or three days before starting on the expedition, so as to pull myself together and be able to control my emotions, which at present I am quite incapable of doing. I mean, I could go to Boulogne, say, for three days, and then join Frank on his way to Paris: that is what I think of doing now: going from here to Folkestone: then to Boulogne, for three days. Or do you think Boulogne too public? I could cross by night, and have a private room in the hotel. Frank is a great intellectual strain, and I want to collect myself first.

With regard to the other things in your letter:

(1) I would be much obliged if Ernest Leverson would hand over to you the balance of the money placed in his hands for my use. With regard to my picture, the picture of A. D. and the Moon, bought for me at my sale, he will of course deduct what was paid for them.[1] I had asked Hansell to keep and take charge of any monies coming to me, but I don't think that would do, as it would be a terrible inconvenience for me to have whatever little money I may have to start with in the hands of a solicitor who took no notice of my letters. So would you be my banker, till I see what I can do? I must find out about banking under an assumed name. It sounds to me rather questionable. Upon the other hand, to bank under my own name is impossible. Tell Leverson that I am much obliged to him for his kindness in keeping this money for me, and I hope to thank him some day in person.

[1] See note 2, p. 527.

(2) With regard to Percy Douglas, I beg that you will at once write to him. I clearly understood from you, from Humphreys, and from Leverson, that he had set aside for me the sum that should have gone to pay his father's costs, at least £500 or £600 of it, his reason being that it would be better for *me* to have the money on my release than for his father to have it. I differed from this view, but the matter was arranged without consulting me. Humphreys, I remember, took special credit for the arrangement, and, I suppose for this, charged his £150 fee. It would be rather grotesque if now, after paying the £150, I found that Percy would not carry out his side of the agreement. In any case, I want to know the facts. Will he, or will he not, carry out his promise? What is the distressing thing to me is the uncertainty. A fact is a thing one can face, but mental anxiety is a mood I can't bear up under. Pray find out at once from Percy whether he intends to keep his word or not. I hoped all this would have been settled three months ago, so that on going out I might at any rate be at peace in some measure, but it seems to have been considered advisable to keep all the harassing business of money and the like for my last fortnight in prison as a sort of preparation for my facing the world with dignity and self-reliance. I can hardly hope you will have an answer from Percy before I see you, as I must not see you later than Saturday 8th. It is a great distress to me. I may add that I entirely differ from you and Robbie on the whole question of the duty of the Douglas family towards me. If Alfred Douglas had forged my name to a bill—*il en était bien capable*—I would of course have paid the bill. I suppose the family would not have considered themselves under any obligation to repay me? Because he has ruined my life completely, does he and his family propose to treat the whole thing as a sentimental reminiscence to be served up with the *liqueurs* after dinner? They have got to make some reparation. You, two months ago, suppressed a message I desired should be conveyed to Alfred Douglas, on the ground that I should "allow them spontaneously to do what they ought." (I quote from your letter.) Well, they have had two months for the spontaneous action. Indeed they have had two years to prepare it, a sufficiently long time for "spontaneity" surely? I merely want to know Percy's answer, "yes" or "no." Pray get it. Is he, or is he not, going to carry out his promise? I want to know exactly where I stand, and not to go out in doubt, perplexity, and uncertainty of my future for the next year or so.

(3) The people who disposed of my fur coat[1] have also, or should have, my two rugs, one a fur rug, the other a travelling rug: two portmanteaus, one brown leather with my initials, the other black: my large double hat-box. Would you write to them to ask them for these things, or to know what has become of them. I simply want to know. If they have pawned them, very well, I shall know that. If not, I can get them. I also want to know where and when my fur coat was pawned. These people will probably try to annoy me: they have already tried to do so lately: I want their letters kept, just for my protection. Last March year—fourteen months

[1] See note 1, p. 517.

532

ago now—I wrote to Robbie to ask him to try and find out about my fur coat. He would give me no answer till February 28th of this year. I was kept in suspense all the time. If I had only been told in March 1896 the truth I might have had the coat traced. Now I suppose it is too late. For fourteen months I was worried over a fur coat, about which I could get no answer. Pray see now that all I want is to know the truth about things and people.

I want to know about Percy, one way or the other; about my things, one way or the other. You and Robbie have often in your letters stated that enough money would be forthcoming to enable me to live "for eighteen months or two years." The same statement, in a more elaborate, possibly more exaggerated form, was made to Mr Hargrove by Mr Holman. As I am within two weeks of my release almost, please on the occasion of your visit let me know clearly and definitely the circumstances, what money there is. I have deferred asking the question till now. Now I must know. If you could realise how anxious I am to know clearly what I have to face on leaving prison you would understand an anxiety that I suppose seems to you difficult to explain.

I do not know whether Wotton-under-Edge is the name of a town or of your mother's place, so I send this to Hornton Street to be forwarded.[1] As this involves a delay, perhaps the visit had better be postponed till Wednesday week. By that time you will have had an answer from Percy, and also from the people of the fur coat. You have not yet told me whether they sold it or pawned it, and if we can trace it. Please ask them the simple question *from me*, and state I am anxious to trace it, and also about my other things.

Pray thank the Lady of Wimbledon for her charming and gracious message. I hope there may be "beautiful work" some day again, but these business affairs so harass me that it seems to me sometimes that all my ill-starred life will now be passed in sordid and unseemly details of the mere food and raiment of life. I am most grateful to the Sphinx for the books. Pray let her know. The Governor, who is most sympathetic about my going out and full of kindness, suggests my driving off to Twyford, about six miles from here. There I might breakfast and change my clothes. Thence to Folkestone. This sounds possible. I hope to see you Wednesday week, or sooner if you have answers: but I do want to be rid of the endless doubt, distress, and anxiety. I can bear any certainty at all. With many thanks, ever yours   OSCAR WILDE

[1] Adey's family home was called Under-the-Hill, and it stood near Wotton-under-Edge in Gloucestershire. These two names always amused Wilde and his friends. Aubrey Beardsley's *Under the Hill* and Lord Henry Wotton in *The Picture of Dorian Gray* were named after them.

To More Adey
MS. Clark

My dear More, Many thanks for your letter. Hansell has written at last and forwarded a draft of the agreement to be drawn up between my wife and myself. It is couched in legal language, and of course quite unintelligible to me. The only thing I can make out is the close, where it is laid down that I am to be deprived of my £150 if I know any "disreputable" people. As good people, as they are grotesquely termed, *will* not know me, and I am not to be *allowed* to know wicked people, my future life, as far as I can see at present, will be passed in comparative solitude. I have written to Hansell that artists and the criminal classes are the only people who will know me, and that the conditions would place him, if seriously insisted on, in an absurd position: but what I want now is a legal condonation from my wife of the past, so as not to have it raked up again and again. For the rest, to have been divorced would have been horrible of course, but now that the children are publicly taken from me by a Judge's order, and it is decided that I am unfit to be with Cyril, I am very disheartened: all I want is peace: all I ever wanted was peace: I loathe legal worries.

I don't know when you are coming: it had better be soon: I hope you have written to the *Commissioners* for permission to have the private room and a visit of an hour in duration: in the case of a special visit the Governor has no authority to grant these privileges himself, otherwise he would have gladly done so.

As to Ricketts, I see his presence troubles you: well, I thought, as he had applied so often, it was not for me to refuse a kindly offer from an artist of whom I am very fond, but I think that after half-an-hour I will ask Ricketts to leave us together to talk business: he will quite understand that I have lots of tedious and uninteresting things to settle. So then you and I and Robbie will have half-an-hour for everything.

As regards clothes etc: Robbie kindly said he would get me a blue-serge suit from Doré and an ulster: this I suppose he has done. Frank Harris also offered me some kindnesses of the same kind, so I have already written to him to say what I want in the way of other clothes, *and boots*, and to ask for the things to be sent to you, not later than Thursday 13th. Hats I ought to have a lot of, but I suppose they have disappeared: Heath, Albert Gate, was my hatter, and understands my needs: I would like a brown hat, and a grey hat, soft felt, seaside things. Would you, if there is time, get me *eighteen* collars made after the pattern you have, or say two dozen. Also, order me two dozen white handkerchiefs, and a dozen with coloured borders. Also some neckties: some dark blue with white spots and diapers, and some of whatever is being worn for summer wear. I also want eight pair of socks, coloured summer things; my size in gloves is 8¼, as my hand is so broad, but my socks need only be for an 8 glove in proportion. Also, I want two or three sets of plain mother-of-pearl (by the way I want to make "nacred" an English word) studs—nacred studs: you know how difficult they are to get abroad. Also, some nice French soap, Houbigant's if you can get it: Pritchard of King Street, St James's, used to have it for me: either "Peau d'Espagne" or "Sac de Laitue" would do: a case of three. Also, some scent; Canterbury Wood Violet I would like, and some "Eau de Lubin" for the toilet, a large bottle. Also some of Pritchard's tooth-powder, and a medium toothbrush. My hair has become very grey: I am under the impression that it is quite white, but I believe that is an exaggeration: there is a wonderful thing called Koko Marikopas, to be got at 233 Regent Street, which is a wonderful hair-tonic: the name alone seems worth the money, so please get a large bottle. I want, for psychological reasons, to feel entirely physically cleansed of the stain and soil of prison life, so these things are all—trivial as they may sound—really of great importance. I don't know if there are any night-shirts? If not, please order me half a dozen; the size of my collar will show how wide the neck should be, also, the sleeve of my shirt for length of arm: the actual length—well, I am six feet, and I like long shirts. I like them made with a turn-down collar, and a breast-pocket for a handkerchief: coloured border to collar and cuffs. If "the dreadful people" don't give up my two rugs, will you buy me one—a travelling Scotch rug, with a good fringe: *not* a tartan, of course: nor a shepherd's-plaid pattern: but the sort of fleecy striped thing. I feel I here convey no idea. All these, if possible, out of the wonderful £25: pray keep envelope of the latter, that I may try to guess from whose generous hand it has come.[1]

As for Reggie Turner, please tell him from me how charmed and touched I am by his delightful present:[2] it is most sweet and generous of him, and I accept his gift with gratitude and delight: in fact I must thank him in person, if he will let me: I hope he will come to see me between the date of my leaving here, and my starting with Frank Harris. My plans are as follows. I have had no reply from the Home Secretary, I need hardly say; and as Hansell proposes to come on Saturday the 15th with the deeds for my signature, it makes it very troublesome. I must alter Hansell's date, I suppose. In any case my idea is this. If I am kept, as I suppose I shall be, till the 19th, I wish a carriage to be here at six o'clock: by 6.15 I will be ready. The carriage, by the Governor's permission, is to drive into the prison: it is to be a closed one. In this I go to *Twyford*, six miles off: there breakfast and change, and make my way to Folkestone, Twyford being on main line. Cross over by night-boat to Boulogne, and sleep there. Stay either at Boulogne, or in the immediate vicinity by the sea, for four or five days to recruit. Then join Frank Harris and go to the Pyrenees. So you see Reggie Turner could come to Boulogne, on the Thursday. Ask him to. Of course he is to keep all this a dead secret. Also, on no account is Alfred Douglas to be told. I will see him after my voyage with Frank Harris and receive from him my letters and what is left of my presents. But not before. For him to appear at Boulogne would be horrible. I could not stand it.

[1] The donor was Adey himself.   [2] A dressing-case.

Bobbie wrote to me that Leverson would hand over the money all right: it should be about £450. If you or Bobbie would keep it for me I would be much obliged. Out of his original loan of £500 Leverson has already had £250: he must wait a little for the balance. I hope you will have received the money from him by the time I see you.

As regards Humphreys, I am under the impression that I left there my dressing bag containing my silver brushes and a suit of clothes and things: would you find out? and if so, the brushes and razors I would like. Razors and shaving things, by the way, are a necessity to be procured in England. If the bag with the silver brushes is not at Humphreys, it must be with the people who sold my furs, and they should be asked for it. They also have a dark ulster of mine.

I wish you would see if you could get me a travelling basket with strap for books: one that could go under the seat of a railway carriage: Lady Brownlow[1] gave me one, of green wicker that was charming, but I don't know where it is now. In Bond Street, or at the Stores, I fancy you could get one. They are most useful. I will let Robbie know when he comes what English books I would like.

On the strength of Percy's promise to pay £500, Humphreys claims from me £150 for the expenses of Bankruptcy. I don't know if Leverson has paid this. Percy said he would pay half. It has to be paid, so if Percy does not pay half, I must pay it all through Leverson. Leverson will of course keep back what is necessary for Humphreys's bill.

I am still anxious to know if my bags with letters have been removed from Humphreys. I would like them to be at Hornton Street.

I am very sorry to hear Robbie has not been well. When I wrote to him about people giving me books, I meant that many literary people had sent messages through him, and I would have been touched by their giving me one of their books on my release: Stuart Merrill, Lugné-Poe, and the like. It was a whim I had. I don't know if Reggie ever hears from Charlie Hickey? If he does I wish he would ask Charlie to write to me (under cover to Reggie) and tell me how he is, and where. I have pleasant memories of him.

If the Twyford scheme is all right, perhaps this would be a good programme. Breakfast at Twyford: luncheon at Richmond with Frank Harris: dinner at Folkestone: supper at Boulogne. I would like to see Frank before my going to the Pyrenees. I wonder am I to see you on Saturday? I still suspect you of wishing to incarcerate me in a Trappist monastery, and will tax you with it in Robbie's presence. With thousand thanks, Ever yours

OSCAR WILDE

Friday [7 *May*]

The answer has just come from the Home Secretary. It is the customary refusal.   O. W.

---

[1] Adelaide (1844–1917), daughter of the eighteenth Earl of Shrewsbury and Talbot, married (1868) the third Earl Brownlow (1844–1921).

To More Adey

MS. Clark

12 May[1] 1897   *Reading Prison*

My dear More, I have received from the Governor your document and read it, with great pain, I need hardly say. To begin with, with regard to money-matters.

You and Robbie both assured me by letter and personally that enough money had been subscribed for me to enable me to live in comfort for "eighteen months or two years." I believed this. When one is in prison face to face with the realities of life one believes what is said to one. I now understand that there is no such sum at all, that all there is is £50, from which Hansell's[2] and Holman's charges have to be deducted, so that nothing of any import will be left.

Let me say frankly that it was extremely wrong of you and Robbie to have made such a statement to me. It was wrong, unkind, and injudicious. Mr Holman also made a formal statement to Mr Hargrove that a considerable sum of money was to be placed at my disposal on my release. Mr Hargrove communicated this to my wife, and it conditioned her action with regard to refusing to increase her offer of £150 a year to £200. She wrote to me at Christmas telling me that she had received this information from Mr Holman through Mr Hargrove, and she very strongly urged me "to purchase an annuity" with the sum of money in question. Mr Holman had represented it as a large sum. Subsequently, after I had mentioned to you that I was indebted to Mrs Napier[3] for £150 (used to pay off the first instalment of Leverson's loan) Mr Holman declared through you (your letter lies before me) that this sum should be repaid "*at once*" to Mrs Napier. I demurred, on the ground that I would sooner repay such a debt on my release personally, but suppose I had said "yes"? Where was the money to come from? I naturally supposed that it was from the money you and Robbie had for me, to enable me to live without pecuniary anxiety for "eighteen months or two years" at least. Did you, who strongly backed up Holman's suggestion, propose that it should come from the little money set apart for my use of which Leverson had got hold? That would have left me penniless. Where *was* it to come from?

At the same interview, when you urged me to authorise the payment of my debt to Mrs Napier, I asked Robbie to go to Brussels and engage a flat for me. I said I would like a studio, sleeping-room, kitchen etc. I naturally believed there was money forthcoming for me in your hands, and proposed to spend some of it in renting a good flat with studio in Brussels, which would have cost about £100 or £120 a year. Robbie listened quite seriously, and promised to do what I wished, as soon as I had definitely decided. Why was I not told that there was no money at

---

[1] Wilde wrote "April"—an indication of his mental agitation.

[2] Arthur D. Hansell, of the firm of Stoker & Hansell, solicitors, whom Wilde had engaged to protect his interests in connection with his marriage settlement.

[3] See note 1, p. 419.

all? That the statement made by you and Robbie to me, and by Mr Holman to my wife's solicitor, was utterly untrue in every detail? What advantage was gained by deceiving me and my wife? Why did you do it? What one wants in prison is the truth. You no doubt meant it to please me. So did Robbie. Mr Holman's object I don't know. Had the thing been done by others I would say it was a heartless, stupid and offensive hoax.

It has been done by others. On April 7th Frank Harris came to see me. He had come of his own accord, and in the two applications he had made for leave to see me had stated that it was on "financial business." When I saw him he was most cordial and friendly, told me that he had made a very large sum of money—some £23,000 in South Africa—and that he had come to put his cheque-book at my disposal. I was greatly touched, I admit, at his spontaneous and unsolicited kindness, and told him that if I were set free from money anxieties I thought I could produce some good art. He said he had come for the purpose of doing so, and would send me a cheque for £500 before my release. I admit that, in my unnerved state, I was very deeply moved at his generous present, and made no attempt to conceal my feelings, which were indeed beyond my control. I now learn that he has sent a verbal message through you to say he is very sorry but cannot do it. Of course nothing would induce me to go on this driving-tour with him after that. I hardly suppose he expects it. Would you kindly write to him that you gave me his message and that I was a good deal distressed, as I had unfortunately received similar messages from every-one else who had been kind enough to promise me money, and that I found myself in such a painful and parlous state as regards my finances that I could not think of any pleasant pleasure excursion such as he had proposed till I had in some way settled my affairs and seen a possible future. This will end the driving-tour, and there is nothing in the message that could hurt his feelings, so pray give it in my own words. In fact Frank Harris has no feelings. It is the secret of his success. Just as the fact that he thinks that other people have none either is the secret of the failure that lies in wait for him somewhere on the way of Life.

As regards Percy Douglas, who comes next in *his* refusal to carry out his promise, I remember you asked me to allow him spontaneously to break with the evil "traditions of the Queensberry family." I am afraid he has spontaneously shown that he is *bien le fils de son père*. One of the notes of the Queensberry character is that they are quite unscrupulous about money affairs, and extremely mean about them. On the occasion of my bankruptcy Percy stated that instead of paying off his father's costs he would reserve the money for me, as he thought it would be much better for me to have it for myself than for his father to enjoy it. I protested strongly against this view. Outside of Queensberry I had no debts of any size. I owed the Savoy £86 and Lewis the jeweller £42! These came next. However, I was not consulted. I was told that Percy had insisted on his arrangement, and that the money, or £600 of it, was to be kept for me. I believed it. I never doubted it. Humphreys, on the strength of it, sends me in a bill for £150! I supposed my friends would naturally have got the money from Percy Douglas and kept it for me: perhaps put it into something that bears a little interest—Consols or something mysterious. Of course that is not done, and when Percy is asked to fulfil his promise, he gets out of it like Frank Harris does, but to show the generosity of his nature offers to pay *half* the solicitor's bill! I suppose the unfortunate man has spent the money on drink really. People like that give me a sense of nausea. I loathe the promise-makers. I could be humble and grateful to a beggar who gave me half of the crust out of his wallet, but the rich, the ostentatious, the false who ask one to a rich banquet and then when one is hungry and in want shut the door of house and heart against one and tell one to go elsewhere—I have nothing but contempt for them. The Frank Harrises of life are a dreadful type. I hope to see no more of them.

If anyone comes to you with promises and offers of help for me, tell them to give what they can give—if it be a piece of bread I could thank them—but don't let them promise anything. I won't have any more *promises*. People think that because one is in prison they can treat one as they choose. They should try to realise that where there is sorrow there is holy ground. They should know that sorrow is the most sensitive of all created things.

You see the state I am in. You saw it yesterday. I quiver in every nerve with pain. I am wrecked with the recurring tides of hysteria. I can't sleep. I can't eat. Why? Because on every side there comes in nothing but the tidings of evil, of indifference, of pretence. You and Robbie meant to please me, to comfort me, by inventing the story of the fund adequate for "eighteen months or two years" of existence free from all monetary worries. I lived on the hopes of it. Then there was £600 from Percy— £500 from Frank Harris—and what do I find at the end of it all, *absolutely nothing!* My wife has most kindly given orders that I am to get my first quarter of my little £150 a year on the day I leave prison. I thank God for having put the thought in her beautiful heart. At the end of it all I shall owe to her my first cup of tea or dish of food. It will taste all the sweeter to me for it.

As regards Leverson—well, of course I understand now why you did not allow me to read the paper of statement yesterday. Robbie in his letter of Monday stated that Leverson had at last consented to hand over my money intact, minus what was paid for my mother out of it. From your statement I see this is not the case. He insists on claiming a right to repay himself, alone of all my creditors, in full, and to keep back £250. This is, of course, outrageous. The money was given to me, *after I had been served with a bankruptcy notice*, to be of use to me personally and to my children. On the occasion of my foolishly entrusting it to Leverson I gave him the title-deed of the trust, a piece of paper on which was written "This is for your use and your children's." I told Leverson I wished Reggie Turner to be co-trustee with him. For Leverson to come now and claim alone of all my creditors to be paid 100 per cent and have his pound of flesh is simple fraud and dishonesty. If he desired to rank as a creditor he should have put in his claim when I was bankrupt. I do not allow him to take this money. His account is to be as follows. He received £880: he disbursed for my mother's use at my request £280. I believe when Holman was so anxious for me to pay off all my debts in full from a fund that did not exist Arthur Clifton got £50: Humphreys claimed £150, of which Douglas of Hawick consents to pay half, viz. £75: so Leverson owes me about £475: will you please let me know *by return* why Robbie said Leverson would pay in full. I mean, was this an invention of Robbie's to please me, like the other, more serious one? Or had Leverson said so? Pray let me know this, and Leverson's private address. I will write to him myself. On hearing from him, if it be unsatisfactory, I will consult my solicitor. I detest fraud, when united to gross sentimentality, and wordy, vulgar expressions of devotion. Please answer by return.[1]

The other reason I regret your not having let me see the statement is about Robbie's meeting me. On February 27th, when you and Robbie were here, he told me he was going to meet me outside the prison. I begged him not to, but he insisted. I think that for many reasons, social, emotional, and others, it is much better he should not meet me. Yesterday I told him not to come to the prison, but to be at Twyford waiting for me. I consider it much better he should meet me abroad. My inability to go to Boulogne has rather upset me. It looks an evil omen, as though Alfred Douglas stood between me and the sun. Dieppe is relaxing, fashionable, and I am too well known there. I now see Havre is the best. There is a place close to Havre which is said to be *bracing*. I forget its name. Carlos Blacker[2] used to be there a great deal.

Under these circumstances, it would be best to drive from here to *Mortimer*, which is on the Basingstoke line. At Mortimer I will breakfast and change. Something was said about Reggie. Would Reggie mind being at Mortimer, and bringing my things? All I want is that when I arrive a room should be ready for me to change in, and that breakfast should be served quickly. I would like all my luggage at Mortimer, as the chances of my suits *fitting* are questionable, so I would like a possibility of selection. As I no doubt shall be very much upset and hysterical, would you ask your doctor for any *nerve-sedative*. Nerves are not treated in prison. From Mortimer to Southampton there are many trains no doubt. I await with

[1] These accusations were baseless and Wilde's turning against his friend and benefactor was simply a manifestation of the distorted obsession about money which overcame him at this time (see his own words on page 580.) Leverson was not a rich man. It was not he but his wife who was Wilde's close friend, and it is clear from his letter on page 551 and elsewhere that throughout he treated Wilde with the utmost fairness and generosity.

[2] Carlos Blacker (1859-1928) was an Englishman of independent means who lived mostly abroad, especially in Paris, where he took a passionate interest in the Dreyfus case. He was an excellent talker, friend, correspondent and linguist, learning a new language every two years. In his old age he learned Hebrew, so that if he went to Heaven he could talk to God in His own language. A letter from Blacker to Wilde, dated 16 January 1893 (MS. Clark), suggests that Blacker had some financial interest in the original production of *Lady Windermere's Fan*.

anxiety your answer about Leverson, about his address, and about Reggie. Robbie I hope to find at Havre, or rather he can follow. I don't know how often the boat runs now, but of course he can reach Havre in many ways. I write in great distress, because I am in great distress. Ever yours OSCAR

Kindly let me have Reggie Turner's address by return.

To Robert Ross
MS. Clark

13 May[1] [1897]   *H.M. Prison, Reading*

My dear Robbie, I am sorry that the last visit was such a painful and unsatisfactory one. To begin with I was wrong to have Ricketts present: he meant to be cheering, but I thought him trivial: everything he said, including his remark that he supposed time went very fast in prison (a singularly unimaginative opinion, and one showing an entirely inartistic lack of sympathetic instinct), annoyed me extremely. Then your letter of Sunday had of course greatly distressed me. You and More had both assured me that there was enough money waiting for me to enable me to live comfortably and at ease for "eighteen months or two years." I now find that there is exactly £50 for that purpose, and that out of this have to come the costs of two solicitors who have already had long interviews with Mr Hargrove and incurred much expense! The balance is for me!

My dear Robbie, if the £50 covers the law-costs I shall be only too pleased. If there is any balance remaining I don't want to know anything about it. Pray don't offer it to me. Even in acts of charity there should be some sense of humour. You have caused me the greatest pain and disappointment by foolishly telling me a complete untruth. How much better for me had you said to me, "Yes, you will be poor, and there are worse things than poverty. You have got to learn how to face poverty;" simply, directly, and straightforwardly. But when a wretched man is in prison, the people who are outside either treat him as if he was dead, and dispose of his effects, or treat him as if he was a lunatic, and pretend to carry out his wishes and don't, or regard him as an idiot, to be humoured, and tell him silly and unnecessary lies, or look on him as a thing so low, so degraded, as to have no feelings at all, a thing whose entire life, in its most intimate relations with wife and child, and with all that wife and child represent to a ruined man, is to be bandied about like a common shuttlecock in a vulgar game, in which victory or failure are of really little interest, as it is not the life of the players that is at stake, but only someone else's life.

I am afraid that you don't realise what my wife's character and conduct have been towards me. You don't seem to understand her. From the very

[1] Wilde again wrote "April" by mistake, and in view of remarks in the next letter to Adey, 15 May seems a more likely date for this one.

541

first she forgave me, and was sweet beyond words to me. After my seeing her here when we had arranged everything between us, and I was to have £200 a year during her life, and *one third* if I survived her, and our arrangements about the children and their transference to her guardianship had been made, so far as her expressing her desire to have nothing done in a public court but to have everything done privately between us was concerned, I wrote to you to say that all opposition to my wife's purchase of my life-interest was to be withdrawn, as she had been very sweet to me and I was quite satisfied with her offer, and I expressly stated that I begged that my friends would do nothing of any kind that would imperil the reconciliation and affection between myself and my wife.

You wrote at once to say that my wishes would be carried out, and that my friends would never dream of doing anything that would endanger my friendly relation with my wife. I believed you, and trusted you. You did not tell me the truth, you and my friends did not carry out my directions, and what is the result? Instead of £200 a year I have £150. Instead of one third of the interest, which on the death of my wife's mother will amount to about £1500 a year, I have no more than a bare £150 to the end of my days. My children will have £600 or £700 a year *apiece*. Their father will remain a pauper.

But that is not all. That is merely the common money side. My children are taken from me by an order of the court. I am legally no longer their father. I have no right to speak to them. If I try to communicate with them I can be put into prison for contempt of court. My wife also is of course wounded with me for what she considers a breach of faith on my part. On Monday I sign here a deed of separation of the most painfully stringent kind and of the most humiliating conditions. If I try to communicate with my wife against her will, or without her leave, I lose my wretched £150 a year at once. My life is to be ruled after a pattern of respectability. My friends are to be such as a respectable solicitor would approve of. *I owe this, Robbie, to your not telling me the truth, and not carrying out my instructions. I merely wanted my friends not to interfere.* I did not ask them to do anything. I begged them to do nothing.

More tells me that every single thing he did, he did with the sanction and advice of your brother Aleck, whom he describes as a "sober businesslike" person. Was Aleck aware that I distinctly forbade my friends to bid against my wife for my life-interest? That it was against my directions? Was it by his advice that you wrote me the letter containing the fatal untruth that has caused all this annoyance, loss, and misery? *"I have acted throughout under the advice of Aleck"* are More's words.

And the grotesque thing about it all is that I now discover, when it is too late to do anything, that the entire proceedings have been done at *my* expense, that *I* have had to pay for Holman, whose advice and opinions have been worthless and pernicious, and that the whole cost has fallen upon *me*: so that out of £150 given to More Adey *"for my use"* and aid nothing now remains at all but I suppose about £1. 10. 6.

Don't you see what a wonderful thing it would have been for me had you been able to hand me the £150 on my going out on Wednesday? How welcome such a sum would have been! Of what incalculable value! Now the whole thing, without my permission being asked, is spent in a stupid and ill-advised attempt to arrange my relations with my wife against my wife's wishes, in making discord, in promoting estrangement. My soul and the soul of my wife met in the valley of the shadow of death: she kissed me: she comforted me: she behaved as no woman in history, except my own mother perhaps, could have behaved. You and my other friends have so little imagination, so little sympathy, so little power of appreciating what was beautiful, noble, lovely and of good report that you can think of nothing better—you, More Adey and, I am told, your brother Aleck— than to rush in between us with an entirely ignorant solicitor and part us first and then make mischief between us.

And all this you do with my own money without telling me. You pose as the generous friends. When I asked More Adey where the money was to come from for all the expense, he smiled very sweetly and mysteriously and said "Don't trouble, dear Oscar, it will all be right. You have good friends." I now find that it was *my* money paying for everything. Let us be quite frank. Do you think, Robbie, that if More Adey had candidly told me that he had been given (by strangers to him and to me, he says) this £150 "*for my use*," that I would have *allowed* him to spend it in going to law with my wife? I should have told him to keep it for me when I went out. More says, or will say, that the money was to be spent at his "discretion:" quite so: but for *my* use, and I, and not More Adey, am the proper judge of what is for my use. The money was spent stupidly, wrongly, unjustly, and to my irreparable injury. As a result of More Adey's use of my money I find myself with a seriously diminished income, with my children taken away by the law, and separated from my wife on harsh and unseemly terms. And not till the whole sum has been expended am I informed that the money was mine.

I have written bitterly about Frank Harris, because he came down to make gorgeous offers of his cheque-book to any extent I required and then sent a verbal message to say he had changed his mind, but what shall I say of More Adey, you, and Aleck, who expend £150 of my own money, money given for my use, in a litigation against which I protested from the beginning, begun against my orders, and with difficulty ended at my entreaties? I see no excuse at all for More Adey and you all spending my money in this way, or in any way without consulting me. I would like to know if Aleck approved of this behaviour towards me.

I asked in one of my letters if Alfred Douglas had been directing these operations. I am sorry I did so. It was unjust. It was unjust to unfortunate Alfred Douglas. He once played dice with his father for my life, and lost. I don't think he would again do so. In the whole of this law-business my life has been gambled for and staked on the board with utter recklessness. In the centre of it all has been a man whom I don't know, but who I now understand has secretly been my solicitor for more than a year, a man of the name of Holman. Flaubert once made *la Bêtise Humaine* incarnate in two retired solicitors or solicitors' clerks called *Bouvard et Pécuchet*.[1] The opinions of this man Holman, my secret solicitor, if collected as Holmaniana would prove a serious rival to Flaubert's grotesques. For sheer crass stupidity, they, if correctly reported, are perfectly astounding. The reckless gambling with my life has had, if a tragedy to me, at least its comic choragus in Holman, the leader of the Dunces.

Just recall events. The result of my directions about my wife being allowed to purchase my life-interest being disobeyed was, as you remember, that I received a letter from Mr Hargrove saying that in consequence of the opposition to my wife it had been determined to reduce my allowance to £150 a year for life. That this sum itself was conditional on my friends at once withdrawing their opposition. Failing this Mr Hargrove said he would be obliged to deprive me of my children, my wife, and my income.

The tidings fell on me like a thunderbolt. I was aghast. I had been under the impression that my wife had bought the interest, or that at any rate everything had been arranged for her so doing, in the preceding March. I am told that everything has been done by friends in my real interest, and that if I will only trust in them everything will be right. I am forced by them into the fatal false position that proved my ruin. "We all," writes More Adey, "beg you not to surrender your legal rights over your wife and your children." What absurd nonsense. I had *no* rights over my wife and my children. That is not a right which a formal application by a solicitor's clerk can deprive one of in twenty minutes. You should read Carlyle. A right is an articulated might.

Mr Holman, I was told, was specially strong on the subject of my not surrendering my "legal rights over my wife and children." Mr Hargrove warns me, warns More Adey, warns Holman. I am told that Holman considers that "Mr Hargrove is merely trying to frighten you by threats. That he has no intention of carrying them out." Poor Holman! His psychological estimate of Mr Hargrove was sadly to seek. My friends, reckless, as it was with my life and my money they were gambling, procure from the Receiver my life-interest at the cost of £75. To achieve this, they think of two *clever* lies, as they fancy them to be. Holman tells Mr Hargrove that a large sum of money is at my disposal, and that I am in no want of money at all. It is supposed—*O sancta simplicitas!*—that this will overawe Mr Hargrove and prevent him bidding against you! The sole result is that Mr Hargrove tells my wife that he has it on the authority of Holman that I am going to be in no want of money, so that there is not the smallest necessity for increasing the £150. So my wife writes to me at Christmas and advises me to invest the money in an annuity, so as to increase my income! She naturally supposed that it was about £3,000: something that one could buy an annuity with. So did I. I find that the entire sum was £150, of which everything except about thirty-five shillings has to go in law-expenses.

---

[1] Gustave Flaubert (1821–80) spent the last nine years of his life writing his satirical novel *Bouvard et Pécuchet*, but he never finished it, and it was published as a considerable fragment in 1881.

The other clever lie is to pretend to Mr Hargrove that you are not my agents but quite independent people, while assuring the Registrar of Bankruptcy that you are really my agents. As for me, you tell me that you are acting independently, but I find it is with my money. More Adey really expected Mr Hargrove to believe in the ridiculous comedy. So did Holman. I need hardly say that Mr Hargrove was not taken in for a single moment. He directed all his attacks on me. That is why More Adey and Holman and you were so brave. Nothing could exceed the heroism with which you exposed me to danger.

Of course there was always the peril in your eyes that my wife and I might come to a private agreement together, as we wished to do. So I am earnestly begged to promise to sign no private agreement of any kind. One of the best Holmaniana I have is that "any such agreement would be illegal and not binding." Can one conceive such a stupid opinion! It is however urged on me from every side. Finally I am induced to solemnly promise that I will not sign any private agreement without warning Holman first. It may seem odd to you but my one desire was to have all my arrangements with my wife quite private, the terms to be arranged between ourselves. But for your interference this would have been accomplished.

Finally the fight began. More writes a triumphant letter. He has secured the life-interest, and demanded at the point of the bayonet "£200 during your wife's life, and one third after her death should you survive her." There was a slight want of imagination in the terms, as they were exactly what my wife had offered and I had accepted in March. My friends, thinking to extort more, had disobeyed my instructions. Consequently my terms are reduced. Then my friends come down to the original offer. Mr Hargrove takes no notice at all of the purchase of the life-interest. He had warned Holman and More Adey. They had disregarded his warnings. Why did he take no notice?

He took no notice because he had in his pocket Inderwick's[1] clear statement that on my divorce my marriage-settlement would be broken. I had written on this point to Holman. No notice was taken at all. The point was considered of no importance. Yet it was the pivot of the whole thing. My interest depended on my wife's good will. If she divorced me it returned to her. Mr Hargrove proceeded to have it returned to her, poor Holman and More Adey not having the smallest idea of what he was aiming at, or understanding one little iota of the whole situation. Their entire incapacity to realise the position is utterly astonishing, and incredible.

Mr Hargrove, there being no necessity to take the smallest notice of anyone who has bought my life-interest, suddenly deprives me of my children. This and the death of my mother are the two terrible things of my prison-life, of all my life. Holman didn't care, they were not his children. More was not interested. Even you, who were fond of them, of whom they were fond, who knew my idolatrous love of Cyril, even you took no notice. You never wrote me a line to say you were sorry at such a tragedy coming on me. You were absolutely indifferent. To me it was a

[1] Frederic Andrew Inderwick, Q.C. (1836–1904).

blow appalling. I shall never get over it. That a Court of Law should decide that I am unfit to be with my own children is so terrible that to expunge it from the scroll of History and of Life I would gladly remain in this lonely cell for two more years—oh! for ten years if needs be. I don't care to live if I am so degraded that I am unfit to be with my own child.

What does Holman say? Well, I have received a message from More Adey to say "Holman declares himself very well satisfied so far." Can one conceive such nonsense! But he gives Holman's sapient reasons.

(1) "No costs were given against me." As regards this, the costs could not have been more than £3. 10. and no one gives costs against a bankrupt. I have no estate.

(2) "An account is to be furnished of the progress of the education of my children twice a year to me." As to this, it is quite untrue. The Court naturally requires an account to be handed in by the guardians for the Court's information. I get no account. I can employ a Queen's Counsel and make an application to know if Cyril is learning to cipher, or if Vyvyan's spelling is improved. That is all.

(3) "I have liberty to make an application if I like." Certainly, but only on points of common ordinary law: viz. if I heard that the children were badly fed, or insufficiently clothed. What a privilege! Do you think they are likely to be?

(4) "Mr Holman is of opinion that this action shows that Mr Hargrove will *not* apply for a divorce." This is a typical specimen of Holmaniana. If he knew anything about law or equity this ignorant and absurd solicitor would know that it was absolutely necessary for my wife to apply for and gain a divorce once she had charge of the children. Why? Because she had to make an affidavit that she could adequately provide for the suitable education of my children before the Court would even listen to an application to remove them from me. She was pledged to secure the life-interest. By buying it you had forced her to do so. Step by step More Adey forced my wife to bring the divorce suit. She had no option. She struggled for two years not to do it. It was reserved for my friends to force it on her. Try and realise that, my dear Robbie, and you will understand my feelings. But, you and More Adey say now, "You are *not* deprived of access to your children." This is solemnly written down in the statement left here on Tuesday last. It is true that through a technical error it is not specified that I am to have no access, but perhaps you would like to hear a letter from Hansell on the subject, dated *April 10th.* He writes as follows: "The Court does not expressly forbid access. But it is understood that should you try to make any attempt to communicate with them an order would be issued expressly restraining you." Note the words: "*any attempt to communicate with them.*" Are you satisfied now?

But, you said with triumphant emphasis on Tuesday, Holman says that the order of the Court does not restrain you abroad! This is an excellent bit of Holmaniana. Of course it does not. The bye-laws of the Reading Vestry are not binding on the green water-streets of Venice. The laws passed by the English Parliament do not bind the inhabitants of France. But who ever said they did? If I try to see the children two things happen.

(1) I lose my entire income, as the children being in charge of my wife it comes under the head of "molestation or annoyance."

(2) She at once is forced to deprive the boys of the advantage of a foreign education, to remove them to England to the jurisdiction of the Court. In England, if I try to write to them even, I can be put in prison for contempt of court. Do you understand all this? Is it dawning on you what More Adey and you and my friends have done?

The most shameful conduct on More Adey's part and the part of my friends was when my wife proceeded to the divorce. You were utterly regardless of me and my safety and position. You simply were gambling with my life. My father used to have a story about an English landlord who wrote from the Carlton to his Irish agent and said "Don't let the tenants imagine that by shooting you they will at all intimidate me." More Adey and you took up exactly the same position with regard to me. You did not care what happened.

Do you think I am writing mere rhetoric? Let me quote to you your friend More Adey's letter conveying to me the news that George Lewis was going to divorce me on appalling charges of a new and more infamous character. "*We,*" he says, "your friends" that is—"we will have nothing whatever to do with your relations to your wife and we will not be *influenced by threats of a divorce, a matter in which we have no concern.*"! . . .[1]

There are your friend's words: that is the attitude of you, More Adey, and your brother Aleck, apparently. You were all keen to repeat the Queensberry scandal and affair. First a civil trial, with me cross-examined by Carson. Then a report by the judge to the Treasury. I am divorced, and re-tried and sent to prison! That is what you were working for. Oh! but, says More Adey, when we advised you to resist and meet the "tainted" evidence we didn't mean it. We meant that you might "have time to get abroad." So the great scheme was that I should be divorced on hideous grounds, and should live in exile. As my divorce would annul my settlement I would of course have had no income at all. And when I was skulking abroad More Adey would have written to me and said, "We have succeeded in all we aimed at: you have now no longer (1) any wife (2) any children (3) any income (4) any possibility of ever coming to London to produce a play. Mr Holman says he is very well satisfied on the whole."

My dear Robbie, if that had happened, how would you have compared yourself, as a friend of mine, with wretched Alfred Douglas? I can only tell you that he would have shown up very well beside you. And really now that I reflect on your conduct and More Adey's to me in this matter I feel I have been unjust to that unfortunate young man.

In point of fact, Robbie, you had better realise that of all the incompetent people on the face of God's earth in any matter requiring wisdom, common

[1] Wilde's dots.

sense, straightforwardness, ordinary intelligence, More Adey is undoubtedly the chief. I have written to him a letter about himself which I
beg you will at once go and study. He is cultivated. He is sympathetic. He
is kind. He is patient. He is gentle. He is affectionate. He is full of charming emotional qualities. He is modest—too much so—about his intellectual attainments. I value his opinion of a work of art far more than he does
himself. I think he should have made, and still can make, a mark in literature. But in matters of business he is the most solemn donkey that ever
stepped. He has neither memory, nor understanding, nor capacity to
realise a situation, or appreciate a point. His gravity of manner makes his
entire folly mask as wisdom. Every one is taken in. He is so serious in
manner that one believes he can form an intellectual opinion. He can't.
He is *extremely dense* in all matters requiring lucidity or imagination or
instinct. In business matters he is *stupid*. The harm he has done me is
irreparable, and he is as pleased as possible with himself. Now I have
realised this, I feel it right, Robbie, that you should know it. If you have
ever thought him sensible, give up the idea. He is incapable, as I have
written to him, of managing the domestic affairs of a tom-tit in a hedge for
a single afternoon. He is a *stupid man*, in practical concerns.

You are a dear affectionate, nice, loving fellow: but of course in all
matters requiring business faculty utterly foolish. I didn't expect advice
from you. I would have as soon expected it from Cyril. I merely expected
the truth. I was quite disappointed. You have behaved very wrongly.

More gets my letter when you get this. He is to go to Leverson's *at
once*. His accepting a *post-dated* cheque is really too idiotic. My plans he
will tell you. Come when you like to this place near Havre. You shall
be as welcome as a flower, and attacked till you know yourself. You have
a heavy *atonement* before you. Kindly show Aleck this letter. Ever yours

o. w.

Of course it is understood that Alfred Douglas is not to be at Havre.
You must write to him and say that I will receive any letter from him
through you, but that he is not to attempt to see me, till I allow him. I
believe he desires to return my letters and presents personally. He can do
so, later on, in a month.

To More Adey

MS. Clark

Saturday night [*15 May 1897*]   [*H.M. Prison, Reading*]
[*Postmark 16 May 1897*]

My dear More, I was greatly disappointed at not seeing Hansell today.
Monday is so late that I fear he will be of little service to me beyond getting
my signature to the deed arranging the terms of separation from my wife.
From your letter and statement I see you have *not* been informed about
this deed. You state that you have by all this terrible legal business
succeeded in your *great object*, namely that my wife and I can "arrange our

548

own terms and our own affairs privately as we wish on my release." There is of course no truth in the idea at all. The question of the children has been settled by the Court ultimately and finally. They are taken from me, and, on my wife's death, should that terrible event occur, they will belong to Adrian Hope.

As regards our own personal relations, all that is settled on the strictest terms by this deed. If I attempt to write to her without her permission or reside near her against her wishes I at once lose my sole income, £3 a week. I am to keep away. If we make friends and live together I am to lose the income, just as much as if I annoyed her. The matter is out of my wife's control. The agreement is between a Miss Wight, whom I have never seen, with a Mr Holman, of whom I only know by hearsay. I don't fancy my wife will be called on to sign the deed.

As regards Percy: you say there was no one at the time of my Bankruptcy to whom he could have paid the money, that he consequently had to keep it himself, and so spent it. But was I so friendless that no one would take charge of £600 for me? Had Percy asked me I could have selected a person. It is astonishing to me that none of my friends thought of it.

With regard to the £50, balance of my £150 in your hands, I fear you have not read or understood my letter. Of course *my* two solicitors (I now find *I* have two) must be paid out of it. What I said in my letter to you was that their costs would probably amount to a sum so close on £50 that it would not be worth while to hand me the balance, which could not be more than thirty shillings at the most. I say that again. Pray understand it. It is quite clear surely. Why do you say that if I wish it you and Robbie will be responsible for paying Holman and Hansell? *Do read my letter carefully. There is no difficulty about it.* I need not say that, had you told me, as you should have, that you had £150 for me, and for my use, I should have absolutely prohibited you from squandering it away into a useless, annoying, and meaningless litigation. *It was very wrong of you not to tell me:* you must learn to recognise this and feel it.

With regard to Holman having told Mr Hargrove that there was a large sum of money waiting for me with you on my release, I cannot understand how you can doubt it. Mr Hargrove is perfectly truthful and made the statement to my wife who acted on it. It was a most improper statement for Holman to make. *You told me about it yourself with pride.* I asked you how it was that Mr Hargrove had not bid for the life-interest, but allowed it to go for such a purely nominal sum as £75. You said that Mr Holman had "bluffed" Mr Hargrove by saying that there was unlimited money at my disposal. You said it yourself. I remarked that I did not think it probable that Mr Hargrove was "bluffed" by Mr Holman or by anyone else, and that I thought his conduct very curious. I suppose you know now why Mr Hargrove did not bid against you? I presume you know that? It was because he had in his pocket the opinion of Inderwick the Q.C. to the effect that on my being divorced my settlement, and consequently my prospective interest in it, was not worth seventy-five brass pennies. The value of my life-interest depended on my wife's good will. I wrote to Mr

Holman asking him to ascertain whether or not my marriage-settlement would stand after a divorce. As it was the one central pivot of the case, the one thing worth knowing, naturally no notice at all was taken of my point or question. *Holman did make the statement to Mr Hargrove, and it was most improper of him.*

I learn now from you and Robbie that when you stated to me that there was money waiting for me sufficient to keep me for a year and a half or two years you were referring to the fact that I had deposited some money myself with Leverson! Surely I knew that as well as you did? I knew it much better. Robbie wrote to me—I have his letter—and said, "*I have reason to know* that sufficient money will be forthcoming for you to live comfortably for eighteen months or two years." His explanation is that he referred to the fact that Leverson had some money of mine! Really the answers I get are idiotic. The entire correspondence of you and Robbie with me should be published. The best title would be *Letters from two Idiots to a Lunatic,* I should fancy.

My dear More, the time is come when you should recognise one thing: that is that in all business matters even of the simplest kind your judgment is utterly incompetent, your opinion either foolish or perverted, and your capacity to understand the most ordinary circumstances of actual life absolutely *nil*. You are a man of singular culture: of grave and castigated taste in style: you can discern the intellectual architecture of work that seems to others flamboyant or fantastic by an immediate sympathy of recognition: to discern the classical element in contemporary work is your function, one that you should more fully recognise than you do. You have not in literature ever tried to do yourself justice. In your nature you are most sympathetic. You would love to help others. You are patient to excess. Your forbearance is beautiful. But you have not got enough common sense to manage the affairs of a tom-tit in a hedge. Everything that you do is wrong and done in the wrong manner. Robbie is better as a guide, for if he is quite irrational he has the advantage of being always illogical, so he occasionally comes to a right conclusion. But you not merely are equally irrational, but are absolutely logical: you start always from the wrong premises, and arrive logically at the wrong conclusion. As soon as I see in your letter, 1, 2, 3, I know you have been doing something utterly foolish and are giving utterly foolish reasons.

Of your accepting a post-dated cheque from Leverson it is useless to speak. A boy of ten years of age would know that a post-dated cheque is not a legal tender. *It is the one thing you should not have done.* You have given me so much trouble and so mismanaged my affairs that you have, not as a reparation, for that is out of your power, but simply as an attempt to show your regret, to do a few things for me.

On receipt of this go to Leverson *at once*. Get from him £200 either in notes or in an open cheque, payable to bearer. (If he *writes* the word "bearer" across the word "order" in the cheque see that he initials the word.) Lodge £100 in your bank for me: the other £100 convert into five £10 notes: nine £5: gold. Buy a pocket-book for me in Bond Street, a good one with silver clasps, suitable for carrying money, *not too thick*: one that I could carry in a breast-pocket: put the notes into it.

On receipt of this letter again, telegraph to Reggie Turner to see you somewhere. He must come here with you. The Home Secretary will now most probably release me on *Tuesday*: so be here with Reggie on Tuesday morning or afternoon, and see the Governor. Engage at Mortimer by wire rooms, after you come here. The interviewers are already at Reading, and Queensberry will probably come on the Tuesday also, so as to be ready. I hope through my good and kind friend, as I must call him, the Governor, to be allowed to escape on Tuesday about 6 o'clock. Of course there will be people waiting then, to see me transferred to Wormwood Scrubs, as the newspapers announced I would be: still, there won't be so many.

Remember: go to Leverson at once: see him at breakfast in presence of his wife: do not go away without the £200. Wire to Reggie. He will no doubt have things to communicate. *All* my effects are to be brought down here: *all* my clothes: kindly do not mismanage anything. Bring the £100 for me with you. Let Reggie take care of it. Put it in his charge. Ever yours   O. W.

The moment you get the money from Leverson *wire* here: wire to the Governor: don't put my name in the telegram. I am myself writing to Leverson.[1]

[1] Wilde wrote to Ernest Leverson on 16 May. That letter has not come to light, but Leverson's answer survives (MS. Clark). It is dated 17 May 1897:

My dear Oscar, Many thanks for your letter of yesterday and for the kind expressions of friendship towards my wife and myself contained therein. I assure you that you are never absent from our thoughts: your name wakes the same echo that it ever did and your future happiness is our most ardent desire.

Now to answer your letter. As I hope to see you on Wednesday I shall be brief and businesslike.

First you complain of my having given More Adey a post-dated cheque. This was for *your* protection. You wanted the money on the 19th, I dated my cheque the 18th inst. It has been recalled and I have handed More £80 in bank notes and an open cheque for £111. 11. 6.

You will recollect that you yourself in the brougham coming back from the Old Bailey insisted on my repaying myself the £250. Anyhow, although I put this in the account, this sum will be at your disposal.

I think your memory betrays you when you state that you asked me to hand over balance to More Adey on the occasion of my last visit to you. I have no recollection of such a request, nor have either Robbie nor More Adey.

I think, dear Oscar, you will remember how when you handed me this money I begged you not to speak about it. Through your indiscretion in this respect (pardonable I admit) I have been caused much extra trouble and annoyance. Your wife, Mrs Willie, the Humphreys and others got to know of it. I did not venture to make this lament to you earlier, as I appreciated your sufferings and did not wish to add to them at the time by any complaint of mine.

You wrote in the early days to Humphreys to look to me for their costs. Their first bill was 200 guineas. I got this reduced to 150 guineas, which I regret I have had to pay. Percy Douglas had agreed to pay half, but he is totally unable to pay this or anything. He is more to be pitied than blamed. He is completely without means for the present. Things have gone against him financially.

Now here is the account of my stewardship:

To Reginald Turner

MS. Hyde (D. & M.)

[Postmark 17 May 1897]   [H.M. Prison, Reading]

[On envelope] Private and *Immediate*

My dear Reggie, This is a contraband letter—my first and my last. I have found a mode of getting it out of prison unread and unseen. I send it to you because your kind and sweet and generous affection for me, as evinced in your lovely present of which I have received the tidings, has so touched me and so charmed me that I must write specially and freely to you.

I cannot tell you how good and dear it was of you in my eyes. Other people came forward with promises of large sums of money—Percy Douglas was to have £600 at my disposal: Frank Harris put his cheque-book at my disposal: Robbie and More Adey assured me they had enough money for me for two years to live on in comfort: every one of them has backed out. Leverson had in his charge some trust-money for me; he now says he must keep it to pay for £250 lent by him for the costs of my first trial: he appears as the creditor for his pound of flesh, utterly hard and dishonest. You, dear Reggie, simply quietly and thoughtfully go and get me a beautiful and useful thing. You make no noise beforehand: you blow no lying trumpets like Frank Harris: you don't pose as the generous friend:

	£	s	d
Handed you in Bank Notes	120		
Paid Humphreys in May '95 at your request	150		
Repaid myself	250		
Paid Mrs W. Wilde	50		
„ Lady Wilde	80		
Funeral Expenses [Lady Wilde's]	41.	5.	0
Rent 146 Oakley Street	39.	13.	6
Paid Humphreys	157.	10.	0
Cheque to balance handed More Adey	111.	11.	6
	£1000.	0.	0

In addition I have handed More Adey £80 in Bank Notes, as an instalment of the fresh loan which I am glad to make you. When you want more I hope you will come to me; as long as it is in my power you may always *rely on* me.

I have also sent the following articles to More which I bought at your sale and at various times and which I hope you will accept from me:

> Your two portraits
> Bosie's portrait
> Jewellery, stick etc.

Also a quantity of papers and manuscripts which were offered for sale and which I bought to prevent going to inquisitive people. Shannon's pastel I had given to Frank Harris as he admired it so much, but he has or will return it to you.

Now I don't think there is anything more about business, further explanations must be reserved till we meet.

I am looking forward with the greatest pleasure and eagerness to seeing you on Wednesday.

Hoping to find you well. With love and best wishes from Ada and myself. Your sincere friend as ever   ERNEST D. LEVERSON

you simply do a sweet kind action, unostentatiously, and you are the only one who really has helped me on my going out. I can't tell you how touched I am: I shall never forget it.

The person who has sent me money to pay for my food and expenses on going out is my dear sweet wife, and you have bought me my travelling bag: and now I want yourself; I want you, if you can, to be ready to meet me when I go out, at Mortimer, a place six miles from here. I am ill, and unnerved. Already the American interviewer and the English journalist have arrived in Reading: the Governor of the Prison has just shown me a letter from an American interviewer stating that he will be here with a carriage on Wednesday morning for me, and offering any sum I like if I will breakfast with him! Is it not appalling? I who am maimed, ill, altered in appearance so that no one can hardly recognise me, broken-hearted, ruined, disgraced—a leper, and a pariah to men—I am to be gibbeted for the pleasure of the public of two worlds!

The Home Secretary, an ignorant man, has refused to let me go out one half hour before the time! So I want to escape somewhere where I can find *you*—my good, dear, simple-hearted friend—and I beg you to keep yourself in readiness. Go to More Adey who knows my movements. My intention is to go to *Mortimer*, thence to Southampton, then to Havre, to some seaside place. I beg you, dear Reggie, to come with me. I shall never forget it if you do. I want someone whom I can trust.

More Adey was given £150 for my use. He and Robbie have spent it all but 30/- in legal expenses for making me quarrel with my wife. The annoying thing is that they both write to me that they are thoroughly satisfied with the result! I only heard yesterday that it was my money they had been expending. They had always pretended it was their own. So I want you, because you are simple and straightforward and I can trust you. There is someone else I often think of, a dear good little fellow to me always, with a sweet heart and a sweet nature, one of the dearest boys in the whole world—Charlie Hickey: to me he was always the best of friends: if those whom I loved had been like him I would not be here. I heard by chance the other day that he always asked after me in his letters. I never doubted that: I know he has often thought of me: I felt it many times: I would give anything to see Charlie again. When you write to him, which I hope you do often, tell him how dearly I love him, and tell him from me in my words quoted from this scrawled letter just what I have said of you, and what you have done: copy it out, to oblige me. Charlie will learn what you have done for me with every feeling except that of surprise. He knows you have a heart of gold, and when one is in trouble, Reggie, you don't know how one loves sincerity, truth, reality. All that is false, and pretentious, and doublefaced one loathes. I wish you and I and Charlie could be in a little seaside place all together. You both suit the sun and the sea because you are real, and sweet, and true. We must often talk about Charlie: I hate his being in America: I wish he could return, and mind you let him know that he is to write to me under cover to you.

I won't tell you all I have suffered, dear Reggie—the eternal silence, the hunger, the sleeplessness, the cruelty, the harsh and revolting punishments, the utter despair, the ignoble dress and loathsome mode of life. It would only distress you and break Charlie's heart. I must remember that a good friend is a new world. I must be with nice sweet real people. So if you can I know you will be at Mortimer on Wednesday morning. It is just possible that I may be let out on *Tuesday afternoon*. Be in telegraphic communication with More Adey. I also will telegraph to you, if I am allowed. Don't let More Adey say anything in any letter to me that will suggest you have received a letter from me, or there will be an awful tragedy. Keep the thing quiet.

There are many good nice fellows here. I have seven or eight friends: they are capital chaps: of course we can't speak to each other, except a word now and then at exercise, but we are great friends. *They* take their punishment so well, so cheerfully: *I* go out with an adder in my heart, and an asp in my tongue, and every night I sow thorns in the garden of my soul. But you will do me good. If I don't see you on Wednesday I shall be so disappointed. No one must give me the dressing-bag but yourself.

Ever, dear good Reggie, your affectionate and very grateful friend

OSCAR

To Thomas Martin
MS. Clark

[*17 May 1897*][1]   [*H.M. Prison, Reading*]

Please find out for me the name of A.2.11. Also: the names of the children who are in for the rabbits, and the amount of the fine. Can I pay this, and get them out? If so I will get them out tomorrow. Please, dear friend, do this for me. I must get them out. Think what a thing for me it would be to be able to help three little children. I would be delighted beyond words. If I can do this by paying the fine, tell the children that they are to be released tomorrow by a friend, and ask them to be happy, and not to tell anyone.

To Reginald Turner
MS. Hyde (D. & M.)

[*Postmark 17 May 1897*]   *H.M. Prison, Reading*

My dear Reggie, I write to you by kind permission of the Governor to tell you that I am to be transferred to Pentonville Prison tomorrow evening and shall be released from there. I am bound to say that the transference is to be executed under humane conditions as regards dress and not being handcuffed. Otherwise I confess I would have refused such an ordeal.

[1] For dating, see p. 568. A.2.11. was a half-witted soldier called Prince (see pp. 572–574 and 586–587). By paying their fines Wilde secured the release of these three children, who had been convicted of snaring rabbits. Warder Martin gave a biscuit to one of the children who was crying, and was dismissed the service in consequence (see pp. 568–572).

I want you, dear Reggie, to come to Pentonville Prison on Wednesday morning, to have a carriage waiting for me and to take me to some hotel in the vicinity, or wherever you think there is a quiet place. At the hotel I want to find all my clothes, your dressing-bag to which I look forward with joy and gratitude, a room to dress in, and a sitting-room. In fact, dear Reggie, you had better go yourself to an hotel tomorrow evening, and sleep there. I can dress in your room, and breakfast in a sitting-room adjoining. I daresay a hansom would do, but a little brougham with blinds might be best: you must decide. I would like coffee for breakfast, as I have been living on cocoa, and don't think I could taste tea.

The being in London, the place I wished to avoid, is terrible: but we learn humility in prison, and I have consented to go. I dare say it is best.

I suppose I had better go to Southampton on Wednesday, by some station, if possible not a big London one: I mean Vauxhall better than Waterloo etc. So get a carriage for the drive through London. There are of course only two ways by which I can travel: either third-class, which I need hardly say, dear Reggie, I don't mind a scrap: or first-class in a *reserved* carriage: it is unnecessary to explain why: you will see that while I can sit at ease with the poor, I could not with the rich: for me to enter a first-class carriage containing other people would be dreadful: they would not like it, and I would know they would not. That would distress me. So, if you can reserve a first-class carriage to Southampton, do so.

I hope that Leverson will surrender my money, and that I will have it. It is now 12.30, and he apparently has not done so. It is my own money, Reggie! He was to be the trustee of it! Can you conceive such cruelty and fraud as to try to steal it from me? I am learning bitter lessons. If however he can be got to disgorge this money he has apparently embezzled, engage a first-class carriage in any name you choose—*Mr Melmoth*[1] is my name: so let it be that. If the train stops at Vauxhall well and good: if not, I must drive to Waterloo and simply walk into the carriage and draw down the blinds.

I am told that there is an anxiety I should cross over by the day-boat to Havre: certainly: I prefer it. I did not know there was one. Engage by telegram a private cabin for Mr Melmoth: at Havre no doubt I can stay the night.

I am so distressed by the conduct of More Adey towards me in spending without my knowledge and consent the £150 he was given for my use in a hideous litigation that nearly ended in my being divorced and so left penniless either to live in exile or to be rearrested, that I could not travel with him: I will see him if he wishes at whatever hotel I go to. Robbie I will expect at Havre in two or three days. You are the only friend I have,

---

[1] From the "Wandering Jew" hero of *Melmoth the Wanderer* (1820) by the Irish writer Charles Robert Maturin (1782–1824), who was Wilde's great-uncle. Robert Ross and More Adey had collaborated in an anonymous biographical introduction to a new edition of the novel in 1892, and Ross suggested this alias to Wilde. The Christian name Sebastian was probably in memory of the martyred saint (cf. sonnet, p. 42).

Reggie, with whom I would like to go away. I will be gentle to you because I am grateful to you. With the others I know I shall be bitter. They have put an adder into my heart and an asp under my tongue.

If you will consent to come away with me you will be doing a service beyond words to a very heart-broken man. If you can do all this

(1) get my things,
(2) fix on a hotel, engage a carriage, have my rooms ready,
(3) meet me at Pentonville,
(4) come away with me to Havre, and stay a week with me,

well, you will be the best of dear boys. Nobody will ever shoot a tongue of scorn at you for having been kind to me. If they did, I know you would not care.

I have written to More Adey to acquaint him with the change of plan, and to ask him to hand over to you whatever money Leverson parts with *in toto*: even if it is only £175, that is something. Spare no expense, dear Reggie: I want to get away comfortably and quietly: and we will take with us £100. The rest keep for me.

If you consent to do this, kindly wire to the Governor here: "Consent Reginald Turner." If Leverson has parted with my money, please add "money received:" if he has not, well, I fear I must stay in London. I may receive £37 from my lawyer, from my wife, who has sweetly thought of its being of use to me. But I can't go abroad for three months on £37. More Adey wrote to me on Saturday: "Do not worry yourself, dear Oscar, about money affairs. It is all right. You will have £37 on the day of your release." Can you conceive a man being so tactless, so dull of wit, so unimaginative! It drives me frantic.

Send me a letter under cover to the Governor of Pentonville Prison: in this state what you have done. Ask him in a personal letter to hand it to me on my arrival. Try and find a hotel with a good *bathroom* close to bedroom: this most essential. Ever yours   OSCAR

P.S. Have just seen my solicitor. I do not like the idea of going to Stewart Headlam's at all.[1] I don't know him very well, and I am afraid of strangers. Please will you consider the possibility of a hotel: some quiet place— Euston Road or anywhere like that. I would much prefer it. Thank Stewart Headlam from me, but tell him I am very nervous and ill and upset. If you really wish it I will go to his house: but I would sooner not. Any quiet hotel would be better for me. I am ready to go to Southampton with you—or Dieppe, if that is preferred. But the special carriage must be got,

[1] The Rev. Stewart Duckworth Headlam (1847–1924), educated at Eton and Cambridge, had been for many years a vicar in the East End of London, but his Socialism and religious unorthodoxy cost him his position in the Church. He founded the Guild of St Michael, and the Church and Stage Guild, and was for a dozen years editor of and chief contributor to the *Church Reformer*. He was now living at 31 Upper Bedford Place, Bloomsbury. He had private means, and, although he scarcely knew Wilde, had gone bail for him in 1895 because he thought the case was being prejudged (see note 3, p. 394) and now offered his house as temporary asylum.

and special cabin. Come to Pentonville at *6.30* with a closed brougham: that will be the hour: drive in to the yard.[1]

To More Adey
MS. Clark

[*Postmark 17 May 1897*]   *H.M. Prison, Reading*

Dear More, It is right to tell you that the Home Secretary against my earnest entreaties is to send me to London, the one place I wished to avoid. I am to be transferred to Pentonville tomorrow, the day announced in the papers for my transference to Wormwood Scrubs. The transference is to be conducted with humanity. I am to wear my own clothes, and not to be handcuffed. My clothes are so dreadful that I wish I had thought of having clothes here, but it will have to stand as it is.

[1] Turner answered (MS. Clark):

My dear Oscar, I shall not be able to meet you, as More and Headlam are going to do that and have made all the necessary arrangements for your going away, and I ought frankly to tell you that I am very glad you will be in such good hands that you will not need me in addition, for were my presence to be made known by any means to my people my allowance would be stopped, and that I could not afford.

And now, dear Oscar, you must allow me to say something to you about More and Bobbie, as you have written to me about them. The most beautiful thing I have ever known is Bobbie's devotion to you. He has never had any other thought than of you; never once, for one minute, has he forgotten you; he has only looked forward to one thing, the time when he would be able to talk to you freely and affectionately again. It is very rare to find such complete devotion, and I fear, dear Oscar, that you have gone very near to breaking his heart. He and I are going to Dieppe together tonight and we shall see you tomorrow, and I feel certain that then all differences and bitterness will be forgotten, but I am certain that when you come to talk over what has been done for you, you will see that all has been in the best way when one remembers the terribly difficult position.

There may have been some mistakes and you may have been over-burdened with unnecessary details, but they have done nothing but what is good for you, and with regard to your wife they have done nothing which cannot be undone in two days if you and she be willing. They have never used any money for any other purpose than what it was given them for, though I feel that it is shameful for me to attempt to excuse the actions of such dear and devoted friends as More and Bobbie are to you. There have been, I know, bitter cruel disappointments for you, but neither Bobbie nor More are in any way responsible for them. You speak of the little bag I have got you. It fills me with shame and sorrow that I have done and been able to do so little for you in comparison with the great things More and Bobbie have done for so long and so unostentatiously. Dear Oscar, in a day or two crooked things will be put straight and you will be able to understand that what is worrying you now was inevitable. With regard to other friends, not so devoted, try to be patient with them and you will probably find that things, if not so good as you expected, are not so bad as they might be.

Charlie always asks after you most affectionately and I hope to have a letter for you from him very shortly.

Dear Oscar, we all believe that the greatest triumphs of your life have yet to come. You will be happy and renowned, but try, in this time, so terrible for your nerves, to be yourself, great, wonderful, noble. I am yours very affectionately

REGINALD TURNER

I have written to Reggie to ask him to meet me and go abroad with me. I am so hurt with you and Robbie—not so much for what you have done, but for your failing to realise what you have done, your lack of imagination, which shows lack of sympathy, your blindness to your astounding conduct in spending money without my consent that would have been of priceless service to me—that if you came abroad with me it would only distress us both: I could talk to you of nothing but of the mode in which you very nearly repeated down to the smallest detail the whole of the Queensberry episode: forcing me into a civil trial, into a loathsome divorce, to be followed either by my arrest, in case I followed your advice and resisted the "tainted evidence," or by my eternal exile, in case I followed your other advice and got "safe abroad:" in both cases being condemned to sheer pauperism, as the marriage settlement being broken *ipso facto* on my divorce, my prospective interest in it after my wife's death should I survive her would be absolutely *nil*. An order of the Court would have been obtained at once.

This, my dear More, is what you were preparing for me. If after a week you care to come to Havre and give me some explanation, I shall be delighted to see you. I hope Robbie will come with you.

5 o'clock

I have seen Hansell and signed the deed of separation. I do not really like going to Stewart Headlam's, as I don't care much about it. I know him but slightly, and a hotel would be better.

I have written to Reggie Turner to ask him to go and stay at a hotel so that I could go to his rooms and change: I mean a quiet hotel somewhere near Euston Road. Of course if it is impossible, it is impossible. But if Reggie engages rooms I can go there and change and breakfast. Only Reggie will have to sleep at the hotel.

Of course I really will be glad to see you the morning of my release, and I know you have taken a great deal of trouble about it. So come either to the prison with Reggie or to his rooms if that is more convenient. But we must not talk about business.

Receiving no telegram about Leverson is terrible. I am utterly upset.

I think you will agree with me that I have fully carried out your advice about Leverson and been most patient with him. It seems the wrong way to treat him. I feel sure that a man of that kind should be strongly dealt with. Your method at any rate has been a terrible failure.

I hear now that Dieppe has been fixed on. I am so well known there that I dislike it, and the air is relaxing, but I suppose one can move on. I am told Robbie is to be there. Very well, but you yourself would find little pleasure in my society. I feel so bitterly about so many things, that I forget many other acts of simple kindness that did me good not harm. I admit you have had endless trouble, but then you must remember I asked you through Robbie to leave my wife and myself alone: we were on terms of affection, and I was grateful to her. The rushing in to try to get more money for me was wrong. It has resulted in less money, and in a separation and the deprivation of my children, the last quite appalling.

Your intentions were always good and kind: your heart was always ready to vibrate in true sympathy: but your judgment was wrong: and the worse the results the worse your advice got. It was a miracle I escaped the divorce, the exile, the entire abandonment.

However, for your real heart-actions, your unwearying good nature, and desire to help me, I thank you very deeply. In a week I hope to be in a sweeter mood and to have lost some of my present bitterness. Then let us meet and talk about literature, in which your instinct is always right, your judgment castigated and serene, your sympathies intellectual. I hope you will hand all money to Reggie. As soon as Leverson has paid let me know. I of course cannot leave England without the money, and I don't want to have to go to his house for it. Ever yours   OSCAR

To Robert Ross
MS. Clark

[*17 May 1897*]   *H.M. Prison, Reading.*

Dear Robbie, I now hear that Dieppe has again been decided on. I dislike it as I am so well known there, but I can move on I suppose. I believe you are to be there. Very well, it will give me pleasure to see you, but it is much better that More should not be with us, as I know I could not restrain myself from discussing the terrible position in which I have been placed through his want of practical intelligence, and legal knowledge, and through his entirely mistaking the keynote of the situation.

He has been very patient, and in many ways has done kind things to me in a very sweet way, but the interference in my affairs with my wife was a grave error. My wishes should have been carried out to the letter. I merely asked people not to interefere. The result is quite awful.

I wish also that he would not write to me to say that I need be under no apprehension at all of being in want of money, as Mr Hansell will have £37 for me. It is grotesque. He might just as well remind me that I am entitled to a gratuity of 10/- from the Prison. What is £37 to me at this moment? What will I hope last me, with economy, one week. If it does I shall be satisfied.

With you, while your initial error had fatal consequences, of course you have no business capacity. I would not like you if you had, so I can't blame you except in two instances of not telling me the truth. I hope abroad to talk about lovely things. We have been friends for many years, and I know your affection and appreciation of me.

If at Dieppe you can find a place ten miles off by rail where we could go —a little quiet place—please do so. I am well known at all the Dieppe hotels, and of course my arrival will be telegraphed to London.

Please ask Aleck to write to me and tell me exactly his share in the disastrous expenditure of the £150 if he had any.

Hansell told me that the money had been collected by you and More Adey. More Adey has written to say it was entrusted to him by a stranger to himself and me. I would like to know the truth. Hansell seemed quite surprised when I told him what More Adey had written to me. Any money you had collected for me, Robbie, you should have told me about.

I see you then at Dieppe. Ever yours   OSCAR

PART SEVEN

BERNEVAL

1897

PART SEVEN
Berneval: 1897

Wilde left Reading on the evening of 18 May 1897. Before he left the Governor handed him the manuscript of his long letter to Douglas (see p. 512). Only two reporters were at the gates to see him go. Dressed in plain clothes and accompanied by two prison officers, he was driven in a cab to Twyford station, where they took the London train. They left it at Westbourne Park and travelled on by cab to Pentonville prison, where Wilde spent the night.

At 6.15 next morning he was fetched in a cab by More Adey and Stewart Headlam. They managed to avoid the press, and drove straight to Headlam's house, 31 Upper Bedford Place, Bloomsbury, where Wilde changed and breakfasted. Soon afterwards he was visited by Ernest and Ada Leverson, who recorded the scene[1]:

The drawing-room was full of Burne-Jones and Rossetti pictures, Morris wallpaper and curtains, in fact an example of the decoration of the early 'eighties, very beautiful in its way, and very like the aesthetic rooms Oscar had once loved.

We all felt intensely nervous and embarrassed. We had the English fear of showing our feelings, and at the same time the human fear of not showing our feelings.

He came in, and at once he put us at our ease. He came in with the dignity of a king returning from exile. He came in talking, laughing, smoking a cigarette, with waved hair and a flower in his buttonhole, and he looked markedly better, slighter, and younger than he had two years previously. His first words were, "Sphinx, how marvellous of you to know exactly the right hat to wear at seven o'clock in the morning to meet a friend who has been away! You can't have got up, you must have sat up." He talked on lightly for some time, then wrote a letter, and sent it in a cab to a Roman Catholic Retreat, asking if he might retire there for six months. While waiting he walked up and down, and said: "The dear Governor, such a delightful man, and his wife is charming. I spent happy hours in their garden, and they asked me to spend the summer with them. They thought I was the gardener." He began to

[1] *Letters to the Sphinx from Oscar Wilde, with Reminiscences of the Author* by Ada Leverson (1930).

laugh. "Unusual, I think? but I don't feel I can. I feel I want a change of scene."

"Do you know one of the punishments that happen to people who have been 'away'? They are not allowed to read *The Daily Chronicle*! Coming along I begged to be allowed to read it in the train. 'No!' Then I suggested I might be allowed to read it upside down. This they consented to allow, and I read all the way *The Daily Chronicle* upside down, and never enjoyed it so much. It's really the only way to read newspapers."

The man returned with the letter. We all looked away while Oscar read it. They replied that they could not accept him in the Retreat at his impulse of the moment. It must be thought over for at least a year. In fact they refused him.

Then he broke down and sobbed bitterly.

The rest of Wilde's journey to freedom has been described by Ross[1]:

According to the arrangements he was to come over by the morning boat to Dieppe where Reggie Turner and myself had got rooms for him at the Hôtel Sandwich. Wilde talked so much and insisted on seeing so many people that he missed the train, so in the afternoon went down with Adey to Newhaven, waited till late afternoon and crossed by the night boat.

We met them at half past four in the morning, a magnificent spring morning such as Wilde anticipated in the closing words of *De Profundis*. As the steamer glided into the harbour Wilde's tall figure, dominating the other passengers, was easily recognised from the great crucifix on the jetty where we stood. That striking beacon was full of significance for us. Then we began running to the landing stage and Wilde recognised us and waved his hand and his lips curled into a smile. His face had lost all its coarseness and he looked as he must have looked at Oxford in the early days before I knew him and as he only looked again after death. A good many people, even friends, thought his appearance almost repulsive, but the upper part of his face was extraordinarily fine and intellectual.

There was the usual irritating delay and then Wilde with that odd elephantine gait which I have never seen in anyone else stalked off the boat. He was holding in his hand a large sealed envelope. "This, my dear Bobbie, is the great manuscript about which you know. More has behaved very badly about my luggage and was anxious to deprive me of the blessed bag which Reggie gave me." Then he broke into great Rabelaisian sort of laughter. The manuscript was of course *De Profundis*.

All Wilde's luggage was new and marked S.M. as he had decided to adopt the name of Sebastian Melmoth: it was Turner's gift to him. He used to chaff a great deal about it and for the next few days in arguments with Turner always said "I can never forget that you gave me

[1] In the unfinished and unpublished preface (MS. Clark) to his projected collection of Wilde's letters to him (see p. xxv).

a bag." This does not sound very amusing and I only mention the incident as illustrating the childish spirits in which Wilde was at the moment.

Wilde talked until nine o'clock when I insisted on going to lie down. We all met at twelve for *déjeuner*, all of us exhausted except Wilde. In the afternoon we drove to Arques[-la-Bataille] and sat down on the ramparts of the castle. He enjoyed the trees and the grass and country scents and sounds in a way I had never known him do before, just as a street-bred child might enjoy them on his first day in the country: but of course there was an adjective for everything—"monstrous," "purple," "grotesque," "gorgeous," "curious," "wonderful." It was natural to Wilde to be artificial as I have often said and that is why he was suspected of insincerity. I mean when he wrote of serious things, of art, ethics or religion, of pain or of pleasure. Wilde in love of the beautiful was perfectly, perhaps too, sincere and not the least of his errors was a suspicion of simple things. *Simplicity* is one of the objections he urges against prisons (cf. letters).

During that day and for many days afterwards he talked of nothing but Reading Prison and it had already become for him a sort of en-chanted castle of which Major Nelson was the presiding fairy. The hideous machicolated turrets were already turned into minarets, the very warders into benevolent Mamelukes and we ourselves into Paladins welcoming Cœur de Lion after his captivity. Of every prison warder he could tell some good story. I remember asking if he met any Freemasons in prison. Wilde knew of my great prejudice against Freemasonry, especially English Freemasonry, and at once rose to the occasion. "Yes, it was very terrible. As I was walking round the yard one day I noticed that one of the men awaiting trial was signalling to me by masonic signs. I paid no attention until he made me the sign of the widow's son which no mason can ignore. He managed to convey a note to me. I found he was in for fraud of some kind and was anxious that I should get my friends to petition for his release. He was quite mad, poor fellow. As he would always insist on signalling and I was afraid the warders would get to notice it, I persuaded Major Nelson to let me wear black goggles until he was convicted and sent to Portland."

Telegram: To Robert Ross

MS. Hyde (D. & M.)

19 May 1897   *Newhaven*

Arriving by night boat. Am so delighted at prospect of seeing you and Reggie. You must not mind the foolish unkind letters. More has been such a good friend to me and I am so grateful to you all I cannot find words to express my feelings. You must not dream of waiting up for us. In the morning we will meet. Please engage rooms for us at your hotel. When I

565

see you I shall be quite happy, indeed I am happy now to think I have such wonderful friendship shown to me.   SEBASTIAN MELMOTH

To Ada Leverson
MS. Clark

[*20 May 1897*]   *Hôtel Sandwich, Dieppe*

Dear Sphinx, I was so charmed with seeing you yesterday morning that I must write a line to tell you how sweet and good it was of you to be of the very first to greet me. When I think that Sphinxes are minions of the moon, and that you got up early before dawn, I am filled with wonder and joy.

I often thought of you in the long black days and nights of my prison-life, and to find you just as wonderful and dear as ever was no surprise. The beautiful are always beautiful.

This is my first day of real liberty, so I try to send you a line, and with kind regards to dear Ernest whom I was pleased to see again, ever affectionately yours   OSCAR WILDE

I am staying here as Sebastian Melmoth—not Esquire but Monsieur Sebastien Melmoth.[1] I have thought it better that Robbie should stay here under the name of Reginald Turner, and Reggie under the name of R. B. Ross. It is better that they should not have their own names.

To Frank Harris
MS. Yale

[*Circa 20 May 1897*]   *Hôtel Sandwich, Dieppe*

My dear Frank, Just a line to thank you for your great kindness to me, for the lovely clothes, and for the generous cheque.

You have been a real good friend to me, and I shall never forget your kindness: to remember such a debt as mine to you—a debt of kind fellowship—is a pleasure.

About our tour, later on let us think about it. My friends have been so kind to me here that I am feeling happy already. Ever yours

OSCAR WILDE

If you write to me please do so under cover to R. B. Ross, who is here with me.

To Mrs Bernard Beere
MS Clark

[*Circa 22 May 1897*]   *Hôtel Sandwich, Dieppe*

My dear good beautiful Friend, Your letter has given me so much pleasure. I knew you would always be sweet and good to me—far more now, if that

---

[1] Wilde occasionally wrote Sebastien, but more often Sebastian.

566

were possible, than ever, for now I need sympathy, and know its value: a kind word to me now is as lovely to me as a flower is, and love can heal all wounds.

I cannot write much for I am nervous—dazed with the wonder of the wonderful world: I feel as if I had been raised from the dead. The sun and the sea seem strange to me.

But, dear Bernie, although my life looks ruined to the outer world, to me it is not so. I know you will like to hear that somehow I feel that out of it all—out of the silence, the solitary life, the hunger, the darkness, the pain, the abandonment, the disgrace—out of these things I may get some good. I was living a life unworthy of an artist. It was wrong of me. Worse things might have happened to your old friend, dear, than two years' hard labour—terrible though they were. At least I hope to grow to feel so. Suffering is a terrible fire; it either purifies or destroys: perhaps I may be a better fellow after it all. Do write to me here—Monsieur Sebastian Melmoth is my name now to the world. With love and gratitude, ever yours   OSCAR

To A. M. Lugné-Poe

de la part de M. Sebastien Melmoth[1]

Lundi, le 24 Mai 1897   *Hôtel Sandwich, Dieppe*

L'auteur de *Salomé* prie le Tétrarque de Judée de lui faire l'honneur de déjeuner avec lui demain matin à midi.[2]

To More Adey

MS. Clark

[*Postmark 25 May 1897*]   *Hôtel Sandwich, Dieppe*

My dear More, Lugné-Poe breakfasted with us this morning, and I was quite charmed with him: I had no idea he was so young, and so handsome. I expected a curious *maladif* edition of the great poet whom America put to death on a clearly-proved charge of having written poems entirely composed of those three wonderful things Romance, Music, and Sorrow.[3]

I earnestly impressed on him the importance of writing no interview, and giving no details of my strange name, my place of sojourn, my altered appearance, and the like: but I know how tempted people are to write for

---

[1] Many of the letters from Dieppe and Berneval (and later) are thus headed, but to save space I have not repeated the words.

[2] Lugné-Poe had played the part of Herod, Tetrarch of Judaea, in the first production of *Salome* (see note 3, p. 399). The text of this letter is taken from *Acrobaties*.

[3] Edgar Allan Poe (1809–49), whose name Lugné-Poe had in fact added to his own name of Lugné when he entered the theatrical profession. He did not himself accent the name, but gradually the French began to print it Poë and finally he seems to have acquiesced.

567

their own pleasure about others, thoughtlessly and without care. So would you see him, if possible, and impress on him that ten lines on me will be enough?

What I want him to say is how grateful I was and am to France for their recognition of me as an artist in the day of my humiliation, and how my better treatment in an English prison was due to the French men of letters.

We miss you very much, and I could not say to you one hundredth part of the gratitude and affection I feel for you. Ever yours   OSCAR

To the Editor of the Daily Chronicle

27 May [1897][1]   *[Dieppe]*

Sir, I learn with great regret, through the columns of your paper, that the warder Martin, of Reading Prison, has been dismissed by the Prison Commissioners for having given some sweet biscuits to a little hungry child. I saw the three children myself on the Monday preceding my release. They had just been convicted, and were standing in a row in the central hall in their prison dress, carrying their sheets under their arms previous to their being sent to the cells allotted to them. I happened to be passing along one of the galleries on my way to the reception room, where I was to have an interview with a friend. They were quite small children, the youngest—the one to whom the warder gave the biscuits—being a tiny little chap, for whom they had evidently been unable to find clothes small enough to fit. I had, of course, seen many children in prison during the two years during which I was myself confined. Wandsworth Prison especially contained always a large number of children. But the little child I saw on the afternoon of Monday the 17th, at Reading, was tinier than any one of them. I need not say how utterly distressed I was to see these children at Reading, for I knew the treatment in store for them. The cruelty that is practised by day and night on children in English prisons is incredible, except to those that have witnessed it and are aware of the brutality of the system.

People nowadays do not understand what cruelty is. They regard it as a sort of terrible mediæval passion, and connect it with the race of men like Eccelino da Romano,[2] and others, to whom the deliberate infliction of pain gave a real madness of pleasure. But men of the stamp of Eccelino are

[1] This letter was thus dated when it appeared in the *Daily Chronicle*, under the heading THE CASE OF WARDER MARTIN, SOME CRUELTIES OF PRISON LIFE, on 28 May, but it was presumably begun on or soon after the 24th, when the *Daily Chronicle* printed a letter from Warder Martin recounting the circumstances of his dismissal (see note p. 554) and added an editorial comment: "We are, of course, unable to verify our correspondent's statement, but we print his letter."

On the 28th Wilde's letter was backed up by two leading articles, and another letter from Martin, discussing the Home Secretary's denial (in reply to a question from Michael Davitt) that the facts were as Martin had stated them.

[2] Ghibelline leader (1194–1259). His cruelties earned him a place in Dante's *Inferno*.

merely abnormal types of perverted individualism. Ordinary cruelty is simply stupidity. It is the entire want of imagination. It is the result in our days of stereotyped systems of hard-and-fast rules, and of stupidity. Wherever there is centralisation there is stupidity. What is inhuman in modern life is officialism. Authority is as destructive to those who exercise it as it is to those on whom it is exercised. It is the Prison Board, and the system that it carries out, that is the primary source of the cruelty that is exercised on a child in prison. The people who uphold the system have excellent intentions. Those who carry it out are humane in intention also. Responsibility is shifted on to the disciplinary regulations. It is supposed that because a thing is the rule it is right.

The present treatment of children is terrible, primarily from people not understanding the peculiar psychology of a child's nature. A child can understand a punishment inflicted by an individual, such as a parent or guardian, and bear it with a certain amount of acquiescence. What it cannot understand is a punishment inflicted by society. It cannot realise what society is. With grown people it is, of course, the reverse. Those of us who are either in prison or have been sent there, can understand, and do understand, what that collective force called society means, and whatever we may think of its methods or claims, we can force ourselves to accept it. Punishment inflicted on us by an individual, on the other hand, is a thing that no grown person endures, or is expected to endure.

The child consequently, being taken away from its parents by people whom it has never seen, and of whom it knows nothing, and finding itself in a lonely and unfamiliar cell, waited on by strange faces, and ordered about and punished by the representatives of a system that it cannot understand, becomes an immediate prey to the first and most prominent emotion produced by modern prison life—the emotion of terror. The terror of a child in prison is quite limitless. I remember once in Reading, as I was going out to exercise, seeing in the dimly lit cell right opposite my own a small boy. Two warders—not unkindly men—were talking to him, with some sternness apparently, or perhaps giving him some useful advice about his conduct. One was in the cell with him, the other was standing outside. The child's face was like a white wedge of sheer terror. There was in his eyes the terror of a hunted animal. The next morning I heard him at breakfast-time crying, and calling to be let out. His cry was for his parents. From time to time I could hear the deep voice of the warder on duty telling him to keep quiet. Yet he was not even convicted of whatever little offence he had been charged with. He was simply on remand. That I knew by his wearing his own clothes, which seemed neat enough. He was, however, wearing prison socks and shoes. This showed that he was a very poor boy, whose own shoes, if he had any, were in a bad state. Justices and magistrates, an entirely ignorant class as a rule, often remand children for a week, and then perhaps remit whatever sentence they are entitled to pass. They call this "not sending a child to prison." It is, of course, a stupid view on their part. To a little child, whether he is in prison on remand or after conviction is not a subtlety of social position he can comprehend. To him the horrible thing is to be there at all. In the eyes of humanity it should be a horrible thing for him to be there at all.

This terror that seizes and dominates the child, as it seizes the grown man also, is of course intensified beyond power of expression by the solitary cellular system of our prisons. Every child is confined to its cell for twenty-three hours out of the twenty-four. This is the appalling thing. To shut up a child in a dimly lit cell, for twenty-three hours out of the twenty-four, is an example of the cruelty of stupidity. If an individual, parent or guardian, did this to a child, he would be severely punished. The Society for the Prevention of Cruelty to Children would take the matter up at once. There would be on all hands the utmost detestation of whomsoever had been guilty of such cruelty. A heavy sentence would, undoubtedly, follow conviction. But our own actual society does worse itself, and to the child to be so treated by a strange abstract force, of whose claims it has no cognisance, is much worse than it would be to receive the same treatment from its father or mother, or someone it knew. The inhuman treatment of a child is always inhuman, by whomsoever it is inflicted. But inhuman treatment by society is to the child the more terrible because there is no appeal. A parent or guardian can be moved, and let out a child from the dark lonely room in which it is confined. But a warder cannot. Most warders are very fond of children. But the system prohibits them from rendering the child any assistance. Should they do so, as Warder Martin did, they are dismissed.

The second thing from which a child suffers in prison is hunger. The food that is given to it consists of a piece of usually badly-baked prison bread and a tin of water for breakfast at half-past seven. At twelve o'clock it gets dinner, composed of a tin of coarse Indian meal stirabout, and at half-past five it gets a piece of dry bread and a tin of water for its supper. This diet in the case of a strong grown man is always productive of illness of some kind, chiefly, of course, diarrhœa, with its attendant weakness. In fact in a big prison astringent medicines are served out regularly by the warders as a matter of course. In the case of a child, the child is, as a rule, incapable of eating the food at all. Anyone who knows anything about children knows how easily a child's digestion is upset by a fit of crying, or trouble and mental distress of any kind. A child who has been crying all day long, and perhaps half the night, in a lonely dimly-lit cell, and is preyed upon by terror, simply cannot eat food of this coarse, horrible kind. In the case of the little child to whom Warder Martin gave the biscuits, the child was crying with hunger on Tuesday morning, and utterly unable to eat the bread and water served to it for its breakfast. Martin went out after the breakfasts had been served, and bought the few sweet biscuits for the child rather than see it starving. It was a beautiful action on his part, and was so recognised by the child, who, utterly unconscious of the regulation of the Prison Board, told one of the senior warders how kind this junior warder had been to him. The result was, of course, a report and a dismissal.

I know Martin extremely well, and I was under his charge for the last seven weeks of my imprisonment. On his appointment at Reading he had charge of Gallery C, in which I was confined, so I saw him constantly. I was struck by the singular kindness and humanity of the way in which he spoke to me and to the other prisoners. Kind words are much in prison, and a pleasant "Good-morning" or "Good-evening" will make one as happy as one can be in prison. He was always gentle and considerate. I happen to know another case in which he showed great kindness to one of the prisoners, and I have no hesitation in mentioning it. One of the most horrible things in prison is the badness of the sanitary arrangements. No prisoner is allowed under any circumstances to leave his cell after half-past five p.m. If, consequently, he is suffering from diarrhœa, he has to use his cell as a latrine, and pass the night in a most fetid and unwholesome atmosphere. Some days before my release Martin was going the rounds at half-past seven with one of the senior warders for the purpose of collecting the oakum and tools of the prisoners. A man just convicted, and suffering from violent diarrhœa in consequence of the food, as is always the case, asked the senior warder to allow him to empty the slops in his cell on account of the horrible odour of the cell and the possibility of illness again in the night. The senior warder refused absolutely; it was against the rules. The man had to pass the night in this dreadful condition. Martin, however, rather than see this wretched man in such a loathsome predicament, said he would empty the man's slops himself, and did so. A warder emptying a prisoner's slops is, of course, against the rules, but Martin did this act of kindness to the man out of the simple humanity of his nature, and the man was naturally most grateful.

As regards the children, a great deal has been talked and written lately about the contaminating influence of prison on young children. What is said is quite true. A child is utterly contaminated by prison life. But the contaminating influence is not that of the prisoners. It is that of the whole prison system—of the governor, the chaplain, the warders, the lonely cell, the isolation, the revolting food, the rules of the Prison Commissioners, the mode of discipline, as it is termed, of the life. Every care is taken to isolate a child from the sight even of all prisoners over sixteen years of age. Children sit behind a curtain in chapel, and are sent to take exercise in small sunless yards—sometimes a stone-yard, sometimes a yard at the back of the mills—rather than that they should see the elder prisoners at exercise. But the only really humanising influence in prison is the influence of the prisoners. Their cheerfulness under terrible circumstances, their sympathy for each other, their humility, their gentleness, their pleasant smiles of greeting when they meet each other, their complete acquiescence in their punishments, are all quite wonderful, and I myself learned many sound lessons from them. I am not proposing that the children should not sit behind a curtain in chapel, or that they should take exercise in a corner of the common yard. I am merely pointing out that the bad influence on children is not, and could never be, that of the prisoners, but is, and will always remain, that of the prison system itself. There is not a single man in Reading Gaol that would not gladly have done the three children's punishment for them. When I saw them last it was on the Tuesday following their conviction. I was taking exercise at half-past eleven with about twelve other men, as the three children passed near us, in charge of a warder, from the damp, dreary stone-yard in which they had been at their exercise. I saw the greatest pity and sympathy in the eyes of my companions as they looked at them. Prisoners are, as a class, extremely kind and sympathetic to each other. Suffering and the community of suffering makes people kind, and day after day as I tramped the yard I used to feel with pleasure and comfort what Carlyle calls somewhere "the silent rhythmic charm of human companionship."[1] In this, as in all other things, philanthropists and people of that kind are astray. It is not the prisoners who need reformation. It is the prisons.

Of course no child under fourteen years of age should be sent to prison at all. It is an absurdity, and, like many absurdities, of absolutely tragic results. If, however, they are to be sent to prison, during the daytime they should be in a workshop or schoolroom with a warder. At night they should sleep in a dormitory, with a night-warder to look after them. They should be allowed exercise for at least three hours a day. The dark, badly ventilated, ill-smelling prison cells are dreadful for a child, dreadful indeed for anyone. One is always breathing bad air in prison. The food given to children should consist of tea and bread-and-butter and soup. Prison soup is very good and wholesome. A resolution of the House of Commons could settle the treatment of children in half an hour. I hope you will use your influence to have this done. The way that children are treated at present is really an outrage on humanity and common sense. It comes from stupidity.

Let me draw attention now to another terrible thing that goes on in English prisons, indeed in prisons all over the world where the system of silence and cellular confinement is practised. I refer to the large number of men who become insane or weak-minded in prison. In convict prisons this is, of course, quite common; but in ordinary gaols also, such as that I was confined in, it is to be found.

About three months ago I noticed amongst the prisoners who took exercise with me a young man who seemed to me to be silly or half-witted. Every prison, of course, has its half-witted clients, who return again and again, and may be said to live in the prison. But this young man struck me as being more than usually half-witted on account of his silly grin and idiotic laughter to himself, and the peculiar restlessness of his eternally twitching hands. He was noticed by all the other prisoners on account of the strangeness of his conduct. From time to time he did not appear at exercise, which showed me that he was being punished by confinement to his cell. Finally, I discovered that he was under observation, and being watched night and day by warders. When he did appear at exercise he always seemed hysterical, and used to walk round crying or laughing. At chapel he had to sit right under the observation of two warders, who carefully watched him all the time. Sometimes he would bury his head in his

[1] Quotation untraced.

572

hands, an offence against the chapel regulations, and his head would be immediately struck by a warder so that he should keep his eyes fixed permanently in the direction of the Communion-table. Sometimes he would cry—not making any disturbance—but with tears streaming down his face and an hysterical throbbing in the throat. Sometimes he would grin idiot-like to himself and make faces. He was on more than one occasion sent out of chapel to his cell, and of course he was continually punished. As the bench on which I used to sit in chapel was directly behind the bench at the end of which this unfortunate man was placed I had full opportunity of observing him. I also saw him, of course, at exercise continually, and I saw that he was becoming insane, and was being treated as if he was shamming.

On Saturday week last I was in my cell at about one o'clock occupied in cleaning and polishing the tins I had been using for dinner. Suddenly I was startled by the prison silence being broken by the most horrible and revolting shrieks, or rather howls, for at first I thought some animal like a bull or a cow was being unskilfully slaughtered outside the prison walls. I soon realised, however, that the howls proceeded from the basement of the prison, and I knew that some wretched man was being flogged. I need not say how hideous and terrible it was for me, and I began to wonder who it was who was being punished in this revolting manner. Suddenly it dawned upon me that they might be flogging this unfortunate lunatic. My feelings on the subject need not be chronicled; they have nothing to do with the question.

The next day, Sunday 16th, I saw the poor fellow at exercise, his weak, ugly, wretched face bloated by tears and hysteria almost beyond recognition. He walked in the centre ring along with the old men, the beggars, and the lame people, so that I was able to observe him the whole time. It was my last Sunday in prison, a perfectly lovely day, the finest day we had had the whole year, and there, in the beautiful sunlight, walked this poor creature—made once in the image of God—grinning like an ape, and making with his hands the most fantastic gestures, as though he was playing in the air on some invisible stringed instrument, or arranging and dealing counters in some curious game. All the while these hysterical tears, without which none of us ever saw him, were making soiled runnels on his white swollen face. The hideous and deliberate grace of his gestures made him like an antic. He was a living grotesque. The other prisoners all watched him, and not one of them smiled. Everybody knew what had happened to him, and that he was being driven insane—was insane already. After half an hour he was ordered in by the warder, and I suppose punished. At least he was not at exercise on Monday, though I think I caught sight of him at the corner of the stone-yard, walking in charge of a warder.

On the Tuesday—my last day in prison—I saw him at exercise. He was worse than before, and again was sent in. Since then I know nothing of him, but I found out from one of the prisoners who walked with me at exercise that he had had twenty-four lashes in the cookhouse on Saturday afternoon, by order of the visiting justices on the report of the doctor. The howls that had horrified us all were his.

This man is undoubtedly becoming insane. Prison doctors have no knowledge of mental disease of any kind. They are as a class ignorant men. The pathology of the mind is unknown to them. When a man grows insane, they treat him as shamming. They have him punished again and again. Naturally the man becomes worse. When ordinary punishments are exhausted, the doctor reports the case to the justices. The result is flogging. Of course the flogging is not done with a cat-of-nine-tails. It is what is called birching. The instrument is a rod; but the result on the wretched half-witted man may be imagined.

His number is, or was, A.2.11. I also managed to find out his name. It is Prince. Something should be done at once for him. He is a soldier, and his sentence is one of court-martial. The term is six months. Three have yet to run. May I ask you to use your influence to have this case examined into, and to see that the lunatic prisoner is properly treated?[1]

No report of the Medical Commissioners is of any avail. It is not to be trusted. The medical inspectors do not seem to understand the difference between idiocy and lunacy—between the entire absence of a function or organ and the diseases of a function or organ. This man A.2.11 will, I have no doubt, be able to tell his name, the nature of his offence, the day of the month, the date of the beginning and expiration of his sentence, and answer any ordinary simple question; but that his mind is diseased admits of no doubt. At present it is a horrible duel between himself and the doctor. The doctor is fighting for a theory. The man is fighting for his life. I am anxious that the man should win. But let the whole case be examined into by experts who understand brain-disease, and by people of humane feelings who have still some common sense and some pity. There is no reason that the sentimentalist should be asked to interfere. He always does harm.

The case is a special instance of the cruelty inseparable from a stupid system, for the present Governor of Reading is a man of gentle and humane character, greatly liked and respected by all the prisoners. He was appointed in July last, and though he cannot alter the rules of the prison system he has altered the spirit in which they used to be carried out under his predecessor. He is very popular with the prisoners and with the warders. Indeed he has quite altered the whole tone of the prison life. Upon the other hand, the system is of course beyond his reach so far as altering its rules is concerned. I have no doubt that he sees daily much of what he knows to be unjust, stupid, and cruel. But his hands are tied. Of course I have no knowledge of his real views of the case of A.2.11, nor, indeed, of his views on our present system. I merely judge him by the complete change he brought about in Reading Prison. Under his predecessor the system was carried out with the greatest harshness and stupidity.

I remain, sir, your obedient servant   OSCAR WILDE

[1] For earlier reference to Prince, see note p. 554.

To Reginald Turner

MS. Hyde (D. & M.)

[*Postmark 27 May 1897*]   *Hôtel de la Plage, Berneval-sur-Mer,*
                                                                      Dieppe

My dear Reggie, Thank you so much for the charming books: the poems
are wonderfully fresh and buoyant: the guide-book to Berkshire is very
lax in style, and it is difficult to realise that it is constructed on any metrical
system. The matter, however, is interesting, and the whole book no doubt
symbolic.

This is my first day here. Robbie and I arrived last night. The dinner
was excellent, and we tried to eat enough for eight as we occupy so many
rooms. However we soon got tired. Only the imagination of man is
limitless. The appetite seems curiously bounded. This is one of the many
lessons I have learnt.

I have just read Max's *Happy Hypocrite*,[1] beginning at the end, as one
should always do. It is quite wonderful, and to one who was once the
author of *Dorian Gray*, full of no vulgar surprises of style or incident.

The population came at dawn to look at my dressing-case. I showed it
to them, piece of silver by piece of silver. Some of the old men wept for
joy. Robbie detected me at Dieppe in the market place of the sellers of
perfumes, spending all my money on orris-root and the tears of the
narcissus and the dust of red roses. He was very stern and led me away.
I have already spent my entire income for two years. I see now that this
lovely dressing-case with its silver vials thirsty for distilled odours will
gradually lead me to the perfection of poverty. But it seemed to me to be
cruel not to fill with rose-petals the little caskets shaped so cunningly in
the form of a rose.

Dear Reggie, it was a great delight seeing you, and I shall never forget
your kindness or the beauty of your friendship. I hope before the summer
ends to see you again. Do write to me from time to time, and remember me
to the Sphinx, and all those who do not know her secret. I know it of
course. The open secret of the Sphinx is Ernest. Ever yours

                                                                      OSCAR WILDE

To Max Beerbohm

MS. Reichmann

[*Circa 28 May 1897*]   *Hôtel de la Plage, Berneval-sur-Mer*

My dear Max, I cannot tell you what a real pleasure it was to me to find
your delightful present waiting for me on my release from prison, and to
receive the charming and sweet messages you sent me. I used to think
gratitude a heavy burden for one to carry. Now I know that it is something
that makes the heart lighter. The ungrateful man seems to me to be one
who walks with feet and heart of lead. But when one has learnt, however
inadequately, what a lovely thing gratitude is, one's feet go lightly over

[1] First published by John Lane in 1896. See note 11, p. 521.

sand or sea, and one finds a strange joy revealed to one, the joy of counting up, not what one possesses, but what one owes. I hoard my debts now in the treasury of my heart, and, piece of gold by piece of gold, I range them in order at dawn and at evening. So you must not mind my saying that I am grateful to you. It is simply one of certain new pleasures that I have discovered.

The Happy Hypocrite is a wonderful and beautiful story, though I do not like the cynical directness of the name. The name one gives to one's work, poem or picture—and all works of art are either poems or pictures, and the best both at once—is the last survival of the Greek Chorus. It is the only part of one's work in which the artist speaks directly in his own person, and I don't like you wilfully taking the name given by the common spectators, though I know what a joy there is in picking up a brickbat and wearing it as a buttonhole. It is the origin of the name of all schools of art. Not to like anything you have done is such a new experience to me that, not even for a silver dressing-case full of objects of exquisite inutility such as dear Reggie in his practical thoughtfulness provided for me on my release, shall I surrender my views. But in years to come, when you are a very young man, you will remember what I have said, and recognise its truth, and, in the final edition of the work, leave the title unchanged. Of that I feel certain. The gift of prophecy is given to all who do not know what is going to happen to themselves.

The implied and accepted recognition of *Dorian Gray* in the story cheers me. I had always been disappointed that my story had suggested no other work of art in others. For whenever a beautiful flower grows in a meadow or lawn, some other flower, so like it that it is differently beautiful, is sure to grow up beside it, all flowers and all works of art having a curious sympathy for each other. I feel also on reading your surprising and to me quite novel story how useless it is for gaolers to deprive an artist of pen and ink. One's work goes on just the same, with entrancing variations.

In case you should feel anxious about me, let me assure you frankly that the difference in colour between the two sheets of paper that compose this letter is the result not of poverty, but of extravagance. Do send me a line, to my new name. Sincerely yours   OSCAR WILDE

To Robert Ross

MS. Clark

[*28 May 1897*]   *Hôtel de la Plage, Berneval-sur-Mer*

My dear Robbie, This is my first day alone, and of course a very unhappy one. I begin to realise my terrible position of isolation, and I have been rebellious and bitter of heart all day. Is it not sad? I thought I was accepting everything so well and so simply, and I have had moods of rage passing over my nature, like gusts of bitter wind or storm spoiling the sweet corn, or blasting the young shoots. I found a little chapel, full of the most fantastic saints, so ugly and Gothic, and painted quite gaudily—some of them with smiles carved to a *rictus* almost, like primitive things—but they all seemed to me to be idols. I laughed with amusement when I saw them. Fortunately there was a lovely crucifix in a side-chapel—not a Jansenist one, but with wide-stretched arms of gold. I was pleased at that, and wandered then by the cliffs where I fell asleep on the warm coarse brown sea-grass. I had hardly any sleep last night. Bosie's revolting letter was in the room, and foolishly I had read it again and left it by my bedside. My dream was that my mother was speaking to me with some sternness, and that she was in trouble. I quite see that whenever I am in danger she will in some way warn me. I have a real terror now of that unfortunate ungrateful young man with his unimaginative selfishness and his entire lack of all sensitiveness to what in others is good or kind or trying to be so. I feel him as an evil influence, poor fellow. To be with him would be to return to the hell from which I do think I have been released. I hope never to see him again.

For yourself, dear sweet Robbie, I am haunted by the idea that many of those who love you will and do think it selfish of me to allow you and wish you to be with me from time to time. But still they might see the difference between your going about with me in my days of gilded infamy—my Neronian hours, rich, profligate, cynical, materialistic—and your coming to comfort me, a lonely dishonoured man, in disgrace and obscurity and poverty. How lacking in imagination they are! If I were rich again and sought to repeat my former life I don't think you would care very much to be with me. I think you would regret what I was doing, but now, dear boy, you come with the heart of Christ, and you help me intellectually as no one else can or ever could do. You are helping me to save my soul alive, not in the theological sense, but in the plain meaning of the words, for my soul was really dead in the slough of coarse pleasures, my life was unworthy of an artist: you can heal me and help me. No other friend have I now in this beautiful world. I want no other. Yet I am distressed to think that I will be looked on as careless of your own welfare, and indifferent of your good. You are made to help me. I weep with sorrow when I think how much I need help, but I weep with joy when I think I have you to give it to me.

I do hope to do some work in these six weeks, that when you come I shall be able to read you something. I know you love me, but I want to have your respect, your sincere admiration, or rather, for that is a word of ill-omen, your sincere appreciation of my effort to recreate my artistic life. But if I have to think that I am harming you, all pleasure in your society will be tainted for me. With you at any rate I want to be free of any sense of guilt, the sense of spoiling another's life. Dear boy, I couldn't spoil your life by accepting the sweet companionship you offer me from time to time. It is not for nothing that I named you in prison St Robert of Phillimore.[1] Love can canonise people. The saints are those who have been most loved.

[1] In *Letters to the Sphinx* Ada Leverson recorded Wilde's improvisation of this fable:
Saint Robert of Phillimore
There was a certain Saint, who was called Saint Robert of Phillimore. Every

I only made one mistake in prison in things that I wrote of you or to you in my book. My poem should have run, "When I came out of prison *you* met me with garments, with spices, with wise counsel. You met me with love."[1] Not others did it, but you. I really laugh when I think how true in detail the lines are.

8.30. I have just received your telegram.[2] A man bearded, no doubt for purposes of disguise, dashed up on a bicycle, brandishing a blue telegram. I knew it was from you. Well, I am really pleased, and look forward to the paper. I do think it will help. I now think I shall write my prison article for the *Chronicle*. It is interested in prison-reform, and the thing would not look an advertisement.

Let me know your opinion. I intend to write to Massingham.[3] Reading between the lines of your telegram I seem to discern that you are pleased. The telegram was much needed. They had offered me serpent for dinner! A serpent cut up, in an umber-green sauce! I explained that I was not a *mangeur de serpents*[4] and have converted the *patron*. No serpent is now to be served to any guest. He grew quite hot over it. What a good thing it is that I am an experienced ichthyologist!

I enclose a lot of letters. Please put money orders in them and send them off. Put those addressed to the prison in a larger envelope, each of them, addressed by yourself, if possible legibly. They are my debts of honour, and I must pay them. Of course you must read the letters. Explain to Miss Meredith[5] that letters addressed C.3.3,[6] 24 Hornton Street are for you. The money is as follows. Of course it is a great deal but I thought I would have lots:

Jackson	£1.
Fleet	£1. 10.

---

night, while the sky was yet black, he would rise from his bed and, falling on his knees, pray to God that He, of His great bounty, would cause the sun to rise and make bright the earth. And always, when the sun rose, Saint Robert knelt again and thanked God that this miracle had been vouchsafed. Now, one night, Saint Robert, wearied by the vast number of more than usually good deeds that he had done that day, slept so soundly that when he awoke the sun had already risen, and the earth was already bright. For a few moments Saint Robert looked grave and troubled, but presently he fell down on his knees and thanked God that, despite the neglectfulness of His servant, He had yet caused the sun to rise and make bright the earth.

[1] Wilde's words ran:

> When I came out of prison some met me with garments
> and spices and others with wise counsel.
> You met me with love.

They were later intended as a second dedication to *The Ballad of Reading Gaol*, but were removed at the proof stage (see note 3, p. 678).

[2] Announcing the *Daily Chronicle* publication of Wilde's letter of 27 May.

[3] Henry William Massingham (1860–1924) was editor of the *Daily Chronicle* (1895–99) and of the *Nation* (1907–23).

[4] Like the lesser breeds without the city walls of Carthage in Flaubert's *Salammbô*, ch. iv.   [5] More Adey's housekeeper at 24 Hornton Street.

[6] Wilde's number in Reading Gaol, indicating the third cell on the third floor of Block C.

Ford	£2. 10	
Stone	£3.	
× Eaton	£2.	The letters must go *at once*.
× Cruttenden	£2.	At least those marked ×
Bushell	£2. 10.	
× Millward	£2 10.	
Groves[1]	£3. 10.	
	——	
	£20. 10.	
W. Smith	£2.	

How it mounts up! But now I have merely Jim Cuthbert December 2, Jim Huggins October 9, and Harry Elvin November 6. They can keep. On second thoughts I have sent only one to the prison. Please be careful not to mix the letters. They are all *nuanced*.

I want some pens, and some red ties. The latter for literary purposes of course.

I wrote to Courtenay Thorpe[2] this morning: also to Mrs Stannard and sent her flowers.[3]

More forwards me a poem from Bosie—a love-lyric! It is absurd.

Tardieu[4] has written mysteriously warning me of dangerous friends in Paris. I hate mystery: it is so obvious.

Keep Romeike on the war-trail.

The *Figaro* announced me bicycling at Dieppe! They always confuse you and me. It really is delightful. I will make no protest. You are the best half of me.

I am very tired, and the rain is coming down. You will be glad to hear

---

[1] Groves, who was a warder, replied from Reading on 2 June (MS. Clark):

Dear Friend, In answer to yours at hand I hardly know how to thank you enough for your kindness which I shall never forget. Shall endeavour to get something in the way of household goods so as I can whenever I see it think of you. So glad to hear your Friends are still by you which no doubt is a pleasure. As I often told you, you would find good Friends as ever.

Glad to say we are all in the best of health. Mitchell arrives home tonight after ten days leave which has wonderfully improved his health.

With wishing you good health and happiness I will close with the best of Friendship. Yours   G. GROVES

N.B. As soon as things go smooth will talk on other subjects, but at present things are out of place. Hope you can quite understand *me*.

[2] English actor (1854–1927). Played much Ibsen. On 10 May 1897 he "accomplished the remarkable feat of playing Helmer [in *A Doll's House*, with Janet Achurch] in the afternoon and the Ghost in [Nutcombe Gould's] *Hamlet* in the evening, and doing both better than we have seen them done before." (Bernard Shaw, *Dramatic Opinions and Essays*, vol. 2, p. 260.) See note 2, p. 381.

[3] Henrietta Eliza Vaughan Palmer (1856–1911) married Arthur Stannard in 1884. She was a prolific and popular novelist under the pseudonym John Strange Winter. Her novel *Bootle's Baby* (1885) sold in enormous numbers. Ruskin referred to her as "the author to whom we owe the most finished and faithful rendering ever yet given of the character of the British soldier." She was first President of the Writers Club (1892) and gave as her recreations "the study of hair and skin culture." At this time she and her husband were living in Dieppe.   [4] See note 1, p. 417.

that I have not been planting *cacao* in plantain swamps, and that "Lloyd" is not now sitting on the verandah, nor is "Fanny" looking after the "labour-boys," and that of "Belle" I know nothing.[1] So now, dear Colvin (what an awful pen!) I mean dear Robbie, good night.

With all love and affection, yours   OSCAR

To an Unidentified Correspondent[2]

[*Circa 28 May 1897*]   c/o Stoker and Hansell, 14 Gray's Inn Square,
[*Berneval-sur-Mer*]

My dear Friend, I send you a line to show you that I haven't forgotten you. We were old friends in gallery C.3, were we not? I hope you are getting on well and in employment.

Don't, like a good little chap, get into trouble again. You would get a terrible sentence. I send you £2 just for luck. I am quite poor myself now, but I know you will accept it just as a remembrance. There is also 10/- which I wish you would give to a little dark-eyed chap who had a month in, I think, C.4.14. He was in from February 6th to March 6th— a little chap from Wantage, I think, and a jolly little fellow. We were great friends. If you know him give it to him from C.3.3.

I am in France by the sea, and I suppose I am getting happy again. I hope so. It was a bad time for me, but there were many good fellows in Reading. Send me a line c/o my solicitors to my own name. Your friend
C.3.3

To Major J. O. Nelson[3]
MS. Berg

[*28 May 1897*]   *Hôtel de la Plage, Berneval-sur-Mer*

Dear Major Nelson, I had of course intended to write to you as soon as I had safely reached French soil, to express, however inadequately, my real feelings of what you must let me term, not merely sincere, but *affectionate* gratitude to you for your kindness and gentleness to me in prison, and for the real care that you took of me at the end, when I was mentally upset and in a state of very terrible nervous excitement. You must not mind my using the word "gratitude." I used to think gratitude a burden to carry. Now I know that it is something that makes the heart lighter. The un- grateful man is one who walks slowly with feet and heart of lead. But when one knows the strange joy of gratitude to God and man the earth

---

[1] A parody of Robert Louis Stevenson's *Vailima Letters* to Sidney Colvin. (See also pp. 520 and 584). The references are to Stevenson's step-son, wife and step- daughter.

[2] Presumably either Ford, Bushell or Millward (see previous letter). The text of this letter is taken from the *Newbury Express* of 1 July 1897.

[3] The Governor of Reading Prison. See note 3, p. 488.

becomes lovelier to one, and it is a pleasure to count up, not one's wealth but one's debts, not the little that one possesses, but the much that one owes.

I abstained from writing, however, because I was haunted by the memory of the little children, and the wretched half-witted lad who was flogged by the doctor's orders. I could not have kept them out of my letter, and to have mentioned them to you might have put *you* in a difficult position. In your reply you *might* have expressed sympathy with my views —I think you would have—and then on the appearance of my public letter you might have felt as if I had, in some almost ungenerous or thoughtless way, procured your private opinion on official things, for use as corroboration.

I longed to speak to you about these things on the evening of my departure, but I felt that in my position as a prisoner it would have been wrong of me to do so, and that it would or might have put you in a difficult position afterwards, as well as at the time. I only hear of my letter being published by a telegram from Mr Ross, but I hope they have printed it in full, as I tried to express in it my appreciation and admiration of your own humane spirit and affectionate interest in *all* the prisoners under your charge. I did not wish people to think that any exception had been specially made for me. Such exceptional treatment as I received was by order of the Commissioners. You gave me the same kindness as you gave to everyone. Of course I made more demands, but then I think I had really more needs than others, and I lacked often their cheerful acquiescence.

Of course I side with the prisoners: I was one, and I belong to their class now. I am not a scrap ashamed of having been in prison. I am horribly ashamed of the materialism of the life that brought me there. It was quite unworthy of an artist.

Of Martin, and the subjects of my letter, I of course say nothing at all, except that the man who could change the system—if any one man can do so—is yourself. At present I write to ask you to allow me to sign myself, once at any rate in life, your sincere and grateful friend

OSCAR WILDE

To Robert Ross
MS. Clark

[*29–30 May 1897*]   *Hôtel de la Plage, Berneval-sur-Mer*

My dear Robbie, Your letter is quite admirable, but, dear boy, don't you see how right *I* was to write to the *Chronicle*? All good impulses are right. Had I listened to some of my friends I would never have written.

I am sending a postscript to Massingham—of some importance: if he publishes it, send it to me.

I have also asked him if he wishes my prison experiences, and if he would share in a syndicate. I think now, as the length of my letter is so great, that I could do *three* articles on Prison Life. Of course much will be psychological and introspective: and one will be on Christ as the Precursor of the Romantic Movement in Life, that lovely subject which was revealed to me when I found myself in the company of the same sort of people Christ liked, outcasts and beggars.[1]

I am terrified about Bosie. More writes to me that he has been practically interviewed about me! It is awful. More, desiring to spare me pain, I suppose, did not send me the paper, so I have had a wretched night.

Bosie can almost ruin me. I earnestly beg that some entreaty be made to him not to do so a second time. His letters to me are infamous.

I have heard from my wife. She sends me photographs of the boys—such lovely little fellows in Eton collars—but makes no promise to allow me to see them: she says *she* will see me, twice a year, but I want my boys.[2] It is a terrible punishment, dear Robbie, and oh! how well I deserve it. But it makes me feel disgraced and evil, and I don't want to feel that. Let me have the *Chronicle* regularly. Also write often. It is very good for me to be alone. I am working. Dear Robbie, ever yours   OSCAR

To Robert Ross

MS. Clark

Monday Night, 31 May [*1897*]   [*Hôtel de la Plage, Berneval-sur-Mer*]

My dearest Robbie, I have decided that the only way in which to get boots properly is to go to France to receive them. The *douane* charged three francs! How could you frighten me as you did? The next time you order boots please come to Dieppe to get them sent to you. It is the only way, and it will be an excuse for seeing me.

I am going tomorrow on a pilgrimage. I always wanted to be a pilgrim, and I have decided to start early tomorrow to the shrine of Notre Dame de Liesse. Do you know what Liesse is? It is an old word for joy. I suppose the same as Letizia, *laetitia*. I just heard of the shrine, or chapel, tonight, *by chance*, as you would say, from the sweet woman of the *auberge*, a perfect dear, who wants me to live always at Berneval! She says Notre Dame de Liesse is wonderful, and helps everyone to the secret of joy. I do not know how long it will take me to get to the shrine, as I must walk. But, from what she tells me, it will take at least six or seven minutes to get there, and as many to come back. In fact the chapel of Notre Dame de Liesse is just fifty yards from the hotel! Isn't it extraordinary? I intend to start after I have had my coffee, and then to bathe. Need I say that this is a miracle? I wanted to go on a pilgrimage, and I find the little grey stone chapel of Our Lady of Joy is brought to me. It has probably been waiting for me all these purple years of pleasure, and now it comes to meet me with Liesse as its message. I simply don't know what to say. I wish you were not so

---

[1] The only further prose writing of Wilde's about his prison experiences was a second letter to the *Daily Chronicle* in March 1898 (see p. 722).

[2] On 24 May Constance Wilde wrote from Italy to her brother: "O has written me a letter full of penitence and I have answered it," and on 5 August: "Oscar wanted me to bring the boys to Dieppe, and then wanted to come to me, but I think Mr Blacker has persuaded him to wait and come to me at Nervi when I am settled."

hard to poor heretics,[1] and would admit that even for the sheep who has no shepherd there is a Stella Maris to guide it home. But you and More, especially More, treat me as a Dissenter. It is very painful, and quite unjust.

Yesterday I attended Mass at ten o'clock and afterwards bathed. So I went into the water without being a Pagan. The consequence was that I was *not* tempted by either Sirens, or Mermaidens, or any of the green-haired following of Glaucus. I really think that this is a remarkable thing. In my pagan days the sea was always full of tritons blowing conches, and other unpleasant things. Now it is quite different. And yet you treat me as the President of Mansfield College: and after I had canonised you, too![2]

Dear boy, I wish you would tell me if your religion makes you happy. You conceal your religion from me in a monstrous way. You treat it like writing in the *Saturday Review* for Pollock, or dining in Wardour Street off the fascinating dish that is served with tomatoes and makes men mad. I know it is useless asking you. So don't tell me.

I felt an outcast in chapel yesterday—not really, but a little in exile. I met a dear farmer in a cornfield, and he gave me a seat in his *banc* in church: so I was quite comfortable. He now visits me twice a day, and as he has no children, and is rich, I have made him promise to adopt *three*—two boys and a girl. I told him that if he wanted them, he would find them. He said he was afraid that they would turn out badly. I told him everyone did that. He really has promised to adopt three orphans! He is now filled with enthusiasm at the idea. He is to go to the *curé* and talk to him. He told me that his own father had fallen down in a fit one day as they were talking together, and that he had caught him in his arms, and put him to bed, where he died, and that he himself had often thought how dreadful it was that if he had a fit there was no one to catch him in his arms. It is quite clear that he must adopt orphans, is it not?

I feel that Berneval is to be my home. I really do. Notre Dame de Liesse will be sweet to me, if I go on my knees to her, and she will advise me. It is extraordinary being brought here by a white horse that was a native of the place, and knew the road, and wanted to see its parents, now of advanced years. It is also extraordinary that I knew Berneval existed, and was arranged for me.

M. Bonnet wants to build me a chalet![3] 1,000 metres of ground (I don't know how much that is, but I suppose about 100 miles) and a chalet with a studio, a balcony, a *salle-à-manger*, a huge kitchen, and three bedrooms, a view of the sea, and trees—all for 12,000 francs, £480. If I can write a play I am going to have it begun. Fancy one's own lovely house and grounds in France for £480! No rent of any kind. Pray consider this, and approve, if you think right. Of course not till I have done my play.

---

[1] Ross and Adey were both Roman Catholics.

[2] Mansfield is a Congregationalist college at Oxford, established in 1889. For the canonisation of Ross, see note p. 577.

[3] O. J. Bonnet was the *patron* of the Hôtel de la Plage, and also the local estate agent.

An old gentleman lives here in the hotel. He dines alone in his rooms, and then sits in the sun. He came here for two days, and has stayed two years. His sole sorrow is that there is no theatre. Monsieur Bonnet is a little heartless about this, and says that as the old gentleman goes to bed at eight o'clock, a theatre would be of no use to him. The old gentleman says he only goes to bed at eight o'clock because there is no theatre. They argued the point yesterday for an hour. I side with the old gentleman, but Logic sides with Monsieur Bonnet, I believe.

I had a sweet letter from the Sphinx. She gives me a delightful account of Ernest subscribing to Romeike while his divorce suit was running, and not being pleased with some of the notices.[1] Considering the growing appreciation of Ibsen I must say that I am surprised the notices were not better, but nowadays everybody is jealous of everyone else, except, of course, husband and wife. I think I shall keep this last remark of mine for my play.

Have you got back my silver spoon from Reggie?[2] You got my silver brushes out of Humphreys, who is bald, so you might easily get my spoon out of Reggie, who has so many, or used to have. You know my crest is on it. It is a bit of Irish silver, and I don't want to lose it. There is an excellent substitute called Britannia metal, very much liked at the Adelphi and elsewhere. Wilson Barrett writes, "I prefer it to silver." It would suit dear Reggie admirably. Walter Besant writes, "I use none other." Mr Beerbohm Tree also writes, "Since I have tried it I am a different actor. My friends hardly recognise me." So there is obviously a demand for it.

I am going to write a Political Economy in my heavier moments. The first law I lay down is "Wherever there exists a demand, there is *no* supply." This is the only law that explains the extraordinary contrast between the soul of man, and man's surroundings. Civilizations continue because people hate them. A modern city is the exact opposite of what everyone wants. Nineteenth-century dress is the result of our horror of the style. The tall hat will last as long as people dislike it.

Dear Robbie, I wish you would be a little more considerate, and not keep me up so late talking to you. It is very flattering to me and all that, but you should remember that I need rest. Goodnight. You will find some cigarettes and some flowers by your bedside. Coffee is served *below* at eight o'clock. Do you mind? If it is too early for you, I don't at all mind lying in bed an extra hour. I hope you will sleep well. You should, as Lloyd is *not* on the verandah.[3]

Tuesday morning [1 June 1897]. 9.30.

The sea and sky one opal, no horrid drawing-master's line between them,

---

[1] Ernest Leverson had recently been cited as co-respondent in a divorce case. On the evening of the trial Ada Leverson, to show her loyalty, sat with him in the front of a box at a fashionable theatre.

[2] In the notes to *After Reading* this is explained as "some saying of Wilde's which Reginald Turner is supposed to have repeated as his own."

[3] See note 1, p. 580.

just one fishing boat, going slowly, and drawing the wind after it. I am going to bathe.

Six o'clock

Bathed and have seen a chalet here, which I wish to take for the season —quite charming: a splendid view: a large writing-room; a dining-room, and three lovely bedrooms, besides servant's room, also a huge balcony.

I don't know the *scale* of my drawing. But the rooms are *larger* than the plan is.

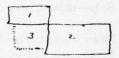

1. *Salle-à-manger*   All on ground floor, with steps
2. *Salon*   from balcony to ground.
3. Balcony

The rent for the season or year is what do you think—*£32*. Of course I must have it: I will take my meals here, separate and reserved table: it is within two minutes' walk. Do tell me to take it: when you come again your room will be waiting for you. All I need is a *domestique*. The people here are most kind.

I made my pilgrimage. The interior of the chapel is of course a modern horror, but there is a black image of Notre Dame de Liesse. The chapel is as tiny as an undergraduate's room at Oxford. I hope to get the *curé* to celebrate Mass in it soon. As a rule the service is only held there in July–August: but I want to see a Mass quite close.

There is also another thing I must write to you about.

I adore this place. The whole country is lovely, and full of forest and deep meadow. It is simple and healthy. If I live in Paris I may be doomed to things I don't desire. I am afraid of big towns. Here I get up at 7.30. I am happy all day. I go to bed at ten o'clock. I am frightened of Paris. I want to live here.

I have seen the terrain. It is the best here, and the only one left. I must build a house. If I could build a chalet for 12,000 francs—*£500*, and live in a home of my own, how happy I would be. I must raise the money somehow. It would give me a home, quiet, retired, healthy, and near England. If I lived in Egypt I know what my life would be. If I lived in the South of Italy I know I should be idle, and worse. I want to live here. Do think over this, and send me over the architect.[1] Monsieur Bonnet is excellent, and is ready to carry out my ideas. I want a little chalet of wood and plastered walls, the wooden beams showing, and the white squares of plaster diapering the framework, like, I regret to say, Shakespeare's house: like old English sixteenth-century farmers' houses. So your architect has me waiting for him, as he is waiting for me.

Do you think this idea absurd?

[1] John Fothergill (see note 2, p. 623).

I got the *Chronicle*: many thanks. I see the writer on Prince—A.2.11—
does not mention my name; foolish of her; it is a woman.[1]

I, as you, the poem of my days, are away, am forced to write poetry.
I have begun something that I think will be very good.[2]

I breakfast tomorrow with the Stannards: what a great passionate
splendid writer John Strange Winter is! How little people understand
her work! *Bootle's Baby* is *une œuvre symboliste*: it is really only the style
and the subject that are wrong. Pray never speak lightly of *Bootle's
Baby*—indeed, pray never speak of it at all; I never do. Ever yours

OSCAR

Please send a *Chronicle* to my wife, Mrs C. M. Holland, Maison Benguerel,
Bevaix, près de Neuchâtel, just marking it, and if my second letter appears,
mark that. Also one to Mrs Arthur Stannard, 28 Rue de la Halle-au-Blé,
Dieppe. Also, cut out the letter and enclose it in an envelope to Mr
Arthur Cruttenden, Poste Restante, G.P.O. Reading, with just these lines:

Dear Friend, The enclosed will interest you. There is also another
letter waiting in the Post Office for you from me, with a little money.
Ask for it, if you have not got it. Yours sincerely   C.3.3

I have no one but you, dear Robbie, to do anything. Of course the letter
to Reading must go *at once*, as my friends come out on *Wednesday* morning
early.

To Michael Davitt[3]

MS. Davitt

[*Late May or early June 1897*]   *Hôtel de la Plage, Berneval-sur-Mer*
Private and Confidential

Dear Mr Davitt, I have been sent a cutting from a Liverpool paper which
states that you intend to ask a question about the treatment of A.2.11 in
Reading prison. I do not of course know if this is true, but I sincerely
hope that you are *in some way* stirring in the matter. No one knows better
than yourself how terrible life in an English prison is and what cruelties
result from the stupidity of officialism, and the immobile ignorance of
centralisation. *You* suffered for what was done by someone else.[4] I, in that

[1] On 31 May the *Daily Chronicle* printed a letter on Prince by E. Livingston
Prescott, the pen-name of Edith Katharine Spicer-Jay, novelist (d. 1901).

[2] *The Ballad of Reading Gaol.*

[3] Irish writer and Socialist politician (1846–1906). Suffered frequent imprisonment for Fenian, Land League and similar activities. Several times elected to
Parliament. His published works include *Leaves from a Prison Diary* (1885). He
had already, on 25 and 27 May, asked two questions in the House of Commons
about the dismissal of Warder Martin.

[4] In 1870 Davitt had been sentenced to fourteen years' imprisonment for treason.
The "someone else," Arthur Forrester (1850–95), seems to have been anxious to
murder a supposed traitor in the Fenian ranks. Davitt wrote him a letter which
the jury took to be an incitement to murder, though modern historians disagree.
Davitt served seven years and was then released on a ticket-of-leave, which was
several times withdrawn when his political activities became troublesome.

respect more unfortunate, for a life of senseless pleasure and hard materialism and a mode of existence unworthy of an artist, and still more unworthy
of my mother's son. But you know what prison-life is, and that there is no
exaggeration in what I say. Everything that I state about the treatment of
A.2.11 is absolutely true. With my own punishment I have nothing to do,
except so far as it is the type of what is inflicted on much better, nicer
fellows than myself. I have no bitterness at all, but I have learnt pity: and
that is worth learning, if one has to tramp a yard for two years to learn it.

In any case I don't think they will flog A.2.11 again, and that is something. But of course I am quite powerless to do any more. I merely wrote
as any other of the prisoners might have written, who had a pen he could
use, and found a paper sufficiently large-minded to publish his letter. But
with the letter I am forced to stop. It is part of my punishment—the new
part that I have to face, and am facing very cheerfully and without any
despair or making any complaint. I prefix to this letter *my name* for the
present, and my address: but my letter requires no answer. It is simply
the expression of a hope. I remain, yours faithfully   OSCAR WILDE
P.S. Enclosed letter has just been forwarded to me, through my solicitor.
A.2.11 has apparently been flogged again—see postscript. I think it is
simply revolting. After you have read the chap's letter, of course tear it
up. I have his address.

To Thomas Martin[1]

[*Circa 1 June 1897*]   [*Berneval-sur-Mer*]
I must begin by scolding you thoroughly for a piece of carelessness on
your part. I told you I had changed my name, and wrote out most carefully for you my new name and address—in spite of this you write to me on
the envelope as Oscar Wilde, Esqre, Care of Sebastian Melmoth. Now,
this was silly of you. I changed my name so as not to be bothered, and
then you go and write to me as Oscar Wilde. You must be careful and
thoughtful about things. Just as much trouble is caused by carelessness as
by crime, my friend. . . . I have spoken highly of your character and
intellect. Let me beg of you to deserve all I have said of you. You have, I
think, a good chance of a good place, so you must be as sound and straightforward and as good a fellow as possible.

To Ada Leverson

MS. Clark

[? *1 June 1897*][2]   *Hôtel de la Plage, Berneval-sur-Mer*
My dear Sphinx, Thanks for your charming letter.
    I knew about the rape of *The Duchess of Padua*: it is of course a ten-act

[1] Text from *The Life of Oscar Wilde* by R. H. Sherard (1906).
[2] Although this letter answers one dated "June," it is difficult to place it later
than 1 June, since the *Daily Chronicle* correspondence about Wilde's letter was all in
May.

587

tragedy now: the last five acts in prose. I know you are just as sorry as I am. We simply must be sorry together. I still hope she is only hiding in some carved chest, or behind green-blue tapestries on which hunters blow silent horns. You have a lovely voice: so perhaps if you called to her three times she would come out. If so, pray call four times.[1]

Your date of your letter is only "June": a date quite accurate enough when a golden rose is writing. When however the golden rose, instead of merely chronicling her own petals, insists on stating: "there is a notice of your letter in the *Daily Chronicle* of *today*," and asks me have I seen it, I am troubled. If you can remember what day it was, would you let me see the notice. I am in the Public Press sometimes "the ex-convict," which is too obvious: sometimes "*le poète-forçat*," which I like, as it puts me into good company: sometimes I am "Mr Oscar Wilde," a phrase I remember: sometimes "the man Wilde," a phrase I don't. So I like to know how I am spoken of. To be spoken of, and not to be spoken to, is delightful.

I would love to see you, I need hardly say.

Perhaps Ernest may reconsider the position he takes up with regard to my money. If so, I hope he will write to me.

Today is hot heart of summer: but all the wind is in the trees: the sea is a burning-glass. Ever affectionately yours   OSCAR

To Lord Alfred Douglas

MS. Clark

[? *2 June 1897*][2]   *Hôtel de la Plage, Berneval-sur-Mer*

My dear Boy, If you *will* send me back beautiful letters, with bitter ones of your own, of course you will never remember my address. It is as above.

Of Lugné-Poe, of course, I know nothing except that he is singularly handsome, and seems to me to have the personality of a good actor, for personality does not require intellect to help it: it is a dynamic force of its own, and is often as superbly unintelligent as the great forces of nature, like the lightning that shook at sudden moments last night over the sea that slept before my window.

The production of *Salome* was the thing that turned the scale in my favour, as far as my treatment in prison by the Government was concerned, and I am deeply grateful to all concerned in it. Upon the other hand I could not give my next play for nothing, as I simply do not know how I shall live after the summer is over unless I at once make money. I am in a terrible and dangerous position, for money that I had been assured was set aside for me was not forthcoming when I wanted it. It was a horrible disappointment: for I have of course begun to live as a man of letters should

---

[1] Presumably either the manuscript or a corrected copy of *The Duchess of Padua* (see p. 528) had been lost or stolen while in Mrs Leverson's keeping.

[2] This must be the letter mentioned in the one to Ross of 3 June (p. 591), so I have given it this approximate date.

live—that is with a private sitting-room and books and the like. I can see no other way of living, if I am to write, though I can see many others, if I am not.

If then Lugné-Poe can give me no money, of course I shall not consider myself bound to him. But the play in question—being religious in surroundings and treatment of subject[1]—is not a play for a *run*, at all. Three performances are the most I think I could expect. All I want is to have my artistic reappearance, and my own rehabilitation through art, in *Paris*, not in London. It is a homage and a debt I owe to that great city of art.

If anyone else with money would take the play, and let Lugné-Poe play the part, I would be more than content. In any case I am not bound, and, what is of more import, the play is not written! I am still trying to finish my necessary correspondence, and to express suitably my deep gratitude to all who have been kind to me.

As regards *Le Journal*, I would be charmed to write for it, and will try and get it regularly. I do not like to *abonner* myself at the office as I am anxious that my address should not be known. I think I had better do it at Dieppe, from where I get the *Echo de Paris*.

I hear the *Jour* has had a sort of interview—a false one—with you.[2] This is very distressing: as much, I don't doubt, to you as to me. I hope however that it is not the cause of the duel you hint at. Once you get to fight duels in France, you have to be *always* doing it, and it is a nuisance. I do hope that you will always shelter yourself under the accepted right of any English gentleman to decline a duel, unless of course some personal fracas or public insult takes place. Of course you will never dream of fighting a duel for *me*: that would be awful, and create the worst and most odious impression.

Always write to me about your art and the art of others. It is better to meet on the double peak of Parnassus than elsewhere. I have read your poems with great pleasure and interest:[3] but on the whole your best work is to me still the work you did two years and a half ago—the ballads, and bits of the play. Of course your own personality has had for many reasons to express itself *directly* since then, but I hope you will go on to forms more remote from actual events and passions. One can really, as I say in *Intentions*, be far more subjective in an *objective* form than in any other way.[4] If I were asked of myself as a dramatist, I would say that my unique position was that I had taken the Drama, the most objective form known to art, and made it as personal a mode of expression as the Lyric or the Sonnet, while enriching the characterisation of the stage, and enlarging— at any rate in the case of *Salome*—its artistic horizon. You have real

[1] Perhaps *Ahab and Isabel* or *Pharaoh*. See note 4, p. 649.
[2] This interview, signed Adolphe Possien, appeared on 28 May on the front page of *Le Jour*. In it Douglas described Wilde's sufferings in prison and blamed English hypocrisy. The editorial comment was hostile, declaring that in Paris the name of Oscar Wilde was synonymous with *"pathologie passionnelle."*
[3] Presumably the published *Poems* of 1896. See note 1, p. 417.
[4] "The Critic as Artist," Part II.

sympathy with the Ballad. Pray again return to it. The Ballad is the true origin of the romantic Drama, and the true predecessors of Shakespeare are not the tragic writers of the Greek or Latin stage, from Aeschylus to Seneca, but the ballad-writers of the Border. In such a ballad as *Gilderoy* one has the prefiguring note of the romance of *Romeo and Juliet*, different though the plots are. The recurring phrases of *Salome*, that bind it together like a piece of music with recurring *motifs*, are, and were to me, the artistic equivalent of the refrains of old ballads. All this is to beg you to write ballads.

I do not know whether I have to thank you or More for the books from Paris, probably both. As I have divided the books, so you must divide the thanks.

I am greatly fascinated by the *Napoléon* of La Jeunesse.[1] He must be most interesting. André Gide's book fails to fascinate me.[2] The egoistic note is, of course, and always has been to me, the primal and ultimate note of modern art, but *to be an Egoist one must have an Ego*. It is not everyone who says "I, I" who can enter into the Kingdom of Art. But I love André personally very deeply, and often thought of him in prison, as I often did of dear Reggie Cholmondeley, with his large faun's eyes and honey-sweet smile. Give him my fondest love.[3] Ever yours   OSCAR

Kindly forward enclosed card to Reggie, with my address. Tell him to keep *both* a secret.

To Mrs Bernard Beere

MS. Yale

[*Circa 2 June 1897*]   *Hôtel de la Plage, Berneval-sur-Mer*

My dear good Friend, I am installed here in a little inn by the sea. It is very nice, and there is no one in the whole hotel, so I am quite alone. I am still filled with wonder at the beauty of the world, and with gratitude to God for still considering me worthy to enjoy it, or perhaps I should say making me worthy of such a privilege.

Do write to me, and tell me all about yourself, and your artistic plans.

[1] *L'Imitation de Notre-Maître Napoléon* by Ernest Horry Cohen La Jeunesse (1874–1917) appeared in 1897 (see p. 522). He had already published in 1896 "*un livre irrespectueux et bizarre*" called *Les Nuits, les Ennuis et les Ames de nos plus notoires Contemporains*, in which he parodied Daudet, Bourget, Anatole France (whose secretary he had been), Loti, Coppée and Huysmans. His biographer wrote: "*Sa vie s'écoula dans les cafés et sur le boulevard où il promenait l'étrange silhouette, popularisée par les caricaturistes, d'un bohème négligé, aux doigts chargés de bagues, assidu des absinthes sacramentelles, noctambule gaspillant dans des brilliantes causeries avec Alphonse Allais, Alfred Jarry, Jean de Mitty, Oscar Wilde, un abondant savoir, un esprit mordant, une faconde extraordinaire.*" He published some brief recollections of Wilde in the *Revue Blanche* of 15 December 1900, and in his book *Cinq ans chez les Sauvages* (1901).   [2] *Les Nourritures Terrestres* (1897).

[3] Thomas Tatton Reginald Cholmondeley (1865–1902), fourth son of the Hon. Thomas Grenville Cholmondeley and grandson of the first Lord Delamere. He lived mostly in Paris.

Have you any plays going? I know you are reciting, and envy those who hear that wonderful rich voice of yours that Browning, and indeed all poets, used to admire so much, and can watch your lithe panther-like grace of movement, and become dominated by the exquisite tyranny of your personality.

However, I think of you every day, and the sea-birds, whom the wind here blows about like white flowers, seem aware of the fact, and are, apparently, quite indignant about it, if screaming counts as a sign!

Send me a photograph of yourself, if you can. I want to look at your shadow: and please like and store as a secret my new name. Your affectionate friend   SEBASTIAN MELMOTH

To Robert Ross
MS. Clark

Wednesday [*2 June 1897*]   [*Berneval-sur-Mer*]

Dear Robbie, I have to pay half the rent of my chalet now, and also to pay other things. Kindly send me £40. I must establish myself.

I have determined to finish the *Florentine Tragedy*, and to get £500 for it—from somewhere. America perhaps. I will answer your letter tomorrow.

Bosie has written, for him nicely—on literature and my play. Ever yours
OSCAR

To Lord Alfred Douglas
MS. Clark

Thursday [*3 June 1897*] *2.30*   [*Hôtel de la Plage, Berneval-sur-Mer*]

My dear Boy, I have just received three copies of *Le Jour*, that I ordered from Dieppe; not knowing what day the supposed interview with you had taken place, I had ordered the numbers for Friday, Saturday, and Sunday.

The interview is quite harmless, and I am really sorry you took any notice of it. I *do* hope it is not with the low-class journalist that you are to fight, if that absurd experience is in store for you. If you ever fight in France let it be with someone who *exists*. To fight with the dead is either a vulgar farce or a revolting tragedy.

Let me know by telegram if anything has happened. The telegraph office is at Dieppe, but they send out on swift bicycles men in fantastic dresses of the middle-*class* age, who blow horns all the time so that the moon shall hear them. The costume of the *moyen-age* is lovely but the dress of the middle-*class* age is dreadful.

Let me beg one thing of you. Please *always* let me see *anything* that appears about myself in the Paris papers—good or bad, but especially the *bad*. It is a matter of vital import to me to know the attitude of the community. All mystery enrages me, and when dear More wrote to say that a false interview with you of no importance had been published, I hired a *voiture* at once and galloped to Dieppe to try and find it, and ordered, as I have told you, three separate numbers. It wrecks my nerves to think of things appearing on me that are kept from me. If More had enclosed it in his letter, I would have been happy and satisfied. As it was, I was really unnerved. The smallest word about me tells.

If *Le Journal* would publish my letter to the *Daily Chronicle* it would be a great thing for me. I hope you have seen it.

Ernest Dowson,[1] Conder,[2] and Dal Young[3]—what a name—are coming out to dine and sleep: at least I know they dine, but I believe they don't sleep. Ever yours   OSCAR

To Robert Ross
MS. Clark

Thursday 3 June
2.45 p.m. (Berneval time)
Latitude and Longitude not marked on the sea
A.D. *1897*

Dear Robbie, The entirely business-like tone of your letter just received makes me nervous that you are a prey of terrible emotions, and that it is merely a form of the calm that hides a storm. Your remark also that my letter is "undated," while as a reproach it wounds me, also seems to denote a change in your friendship towards me. I have now put the date and other facts at the head of my letter.

I get no cuttings from Paris, which makes me irritable when I hear of things appearing. Not knowing the day of the false interview with Bosie I ordered, fortunately, copies of the paper for *three successive days*: they have just arrived, and I see an impertinent *démenti* of Bosie's denial.

Bosie has also written to me to say he is on the eve of a duel! I suppose about this. They said his costume was *ridicule*. I have written to him to beg him *never* to fight duels, as once one does it one has to go on. And though it is not dangerous, like our English cricket or football is, still it is a tedious game to be always playing.

Besides, to fight with the common interviewer is to fight with the dead, a thing either farcical or tragic.

Ernest Dowson, Conder, and Dal Young come out here this afternoon to dine and sleep—at least I know they dine, but I believe they never sleep.

[1] English poet (1867–1900). He had met Wilde in 1890, and with Robert Sherard visited him at Oakley Street in the dark days between his trials.

[2] Charles Conder (1868–1909), English artist, who had lived in Australia. He became famous for his designs for fans and for his delicate water-colours painted on silk. Wilde much admired his work, and Rothenstein records his saying: "Dear Conder! With what exquisite subtlety he goes about persuading someone to give him a hundred francs for a fan, for which he was fully prepared to pay three hundred!"

[3] Dalhousie Young (1866–1921) was an English composer and pianist. A pupil of Leschetizky and Paderewski, he made his debut in Rome 1893, and in London 1895. Very soon after Wilde's conviction Young, then a stranger, had the courage

592

I think the *Chronicle* are nervous. They have not answered yet or anything. Of course with them I am all right, if they take my work. *Who is my Receiver?* I want his name and address. Ever yours   OSCAR

To Reginald Turner

MS. Hyde (D. & M.)

[*Postmark 3 June 1897*]   *Hôtel de la Plage, Berneval-sur-Mer*

My dear Reggie, I am charmed to think that you are having your usual holiday in the Law Courts. I always like to know that young people are enjoying themselves. But life has also, my dear boy, little seemingly-unimportant duties, and it is these little duties, trivial as they may seem to many, that really make life tedious. Amongst your duties of this kind is to *write to me*, from time to time.

Remember that I know *nothing* now, except through the newspapers, and they arrive only three times a day from London and Paris, so I am absolutely ignorant of what is going on in the world.

Do write to me like a good fellow. You are hiding all news of my dear Charlie from me, which is unkind, as I *did* introduce you to him, Reggie. I admit you forced me to do it, but I did it, and in those days you were, or sought to be, the Boy-Snatcher of Clements Inn. Also I want to know about your work, and your story. Write me a letter *about yourself entirely*. Then it is sure to be long, and written with interest, affection, and admiration. At least it should be if you took *my* view of the subject. Pray do so. I like you to regard *all* things from *my* point of view. In *other* matters I like my friends to be free from my tyrannous personality. I am very happy, dear Reggie, and my dressing-case has been blessed by the *curé*, a good old man. Always yours   OSCAR

To Selwyn Image[1]

MS. Clark

[*Postmark 3 June 1897*]   *Hôtel de la Plage, Berneval-sur-Mer*

My dear Image, Thank you so much for your charming and most welcome

---

to publish a pamphlet entitled *Apologia pro Oscar Wilde*, dated 31 May 1895, and ending

> To sum up shortly: I do not see any evidence that Mr Wilde's love for beauty was a pose; and if there were such evidence it would not affect me in the least. His books do not seem to me to contain any element that is morbid or immoral. I can find no trace of bad influence in his friendships; and for the question of his life, as he was convicted (rightly or wrongly, it makes no difference) of breaking a law, he is being punished for breaking a law.
>
> As regards sin, even if we know, or think we know what a man has done, we know nothing about the motive or the manner; and under these circumstances, any outside judgment is a mere impertinence.

[1] Artist, poet and clergyman (1849–1930). Slade Professor of Fine Art, Oxford 1910–16.

letter. The last message that reached me, when the prison-door closed ultimately on me, was from you—to tell me that there would be many people who would be kind and nice and gentle to me when I came out: and I often used to think of this in my dreadful life in gaol. Well, it has turned out quite true. I used to estimate my friends by their number: now I know that to everyone who has even *one* friend, God has given *two* worlds. And I have really many—far more, I am sure, than I deserve—and it is always nice to have a little more than one deserves.

Of course it has been a very awful tragedy, but still I have no bitterness in my heart against society. I accept everything. I really—strange as it may sound to you, just at first, from lips like mine—I really am not ashamed of having been in prison. I am thoroughly ashamed of having led a life quite unworthy of an artist. I do not accept the British view that Messalina is better than Sporus:[1] these things are matters of temperament, and both are equally vile, because sensual pleasures wreck the soul: but all my profligacy, extravagance, and worldly life of fashion and senseless ease, were wrong for an artist. If I have good health, and good friends, and can wake the creative instinct in me again, I may do something more in art yet. If I do so, I shall owe much to good kind fellows like yourself. I have learnt in prison-cells to be grateful. That, *for me*, is a great discovery. With many thanks, sincerely yours   OSCAR WILDE

To Arthur L. Humphreys

MS. Berg

[? *3 June 1897*]   *Hôtel de la Plage, Berneval-sur-Mer*

My dear Humphreys, I send you a few words to express my sincere thanks to you for the kind messages of sympathy that often reached me from you through my friends, and also for the books you so generously and thoughtfully sent me. I need not tell you *what* books were to me in prison: passionately as I loved literature from boyhood, to excess many said of me, I had no idea that some day that one supreme art would save both mental and physical life for me: and the knowledge that many of those books were a gift from a good fellow like yourself, made me touch and handle them with as much pleasure as though they had been, each of them, the hand of a friend: indeed each of them *was* to me the hand of a friend, and lifted me from the mire of despair and pain where I had, for a whole year, been lying.

Let me say a few things about myself. It may sound for the moment strange to you from lips like mine, but I am now not ashamed of having been in prison: I am thoroughly ashamed of having led a life unworthy of an artist, and a great one. I do not interest myself in that British view of morals that sets Messalina above Sporus: both pleasures are matters of

---

[1] Messalina was the faithless and depraved wife of the Emperor Claudius, and Sporus the effeminate favourite of the Emperor Nero, with whom, according to Suetonius, he went through a form of marriage.

temperament, and like all sensual pleasures lack nobility and slay the soul: but my reckless pursuit of mundane pleasure, my extravagance, my senseless ease, my love of fashion, my whole attitude towards life, all these things were wrong for an artist. I am glad to say I am not an embittered man: on the contrary, I am very happy. I have learnt gratitude—a new lesson for me—and a certain amount of humility as regards myself, and I don't desire riches or wild profligacy any more. I want peace, and have found it, and perhaps some day may do a work of art that you may take pleasure in. If you send me a line, note pray my *name* and address at top of this letter. Your sincere and grateful friend   OSCAR WILDE

To Lord Alfred Douglas

MS. Clark

Friday, 4 June [1897] 2.30   [*Hôtel de la Plage, Berneval-sur-Mer*]

My dear Boy, I have just got your letter, but Ernest Dowson, Dal Young, and Conder are here, so I cannot read it, except the last three lines. I love the last words of anything: the end in art is the beginning. Don't think I don't love you. Of course I love you more than anyone else. But our lives are irreparably severed, as far as meeting goes. What is left to us is the knowledge that we love each other, and every day I think of you, and I know you are a poet, and that makes you doubly dear and wonderful. My friends here have been most sweet to me, and I like them all very much. Young is the best of fellows, and Ernest has a most interesting nature. He is to send me some of his work.

We all stayed up till three o'clock; very bad for me, but it was a delightful experience. Today is a day of sea-fog, and rain—my first. Tomorrow I go with fishers to fish, but I will write to you tonight.

Ever, dear boy, with fondest love   OSCAR

To Robert Ross

MS. Clark

[? *5 June 1897*]   [*Hôtel de la Plage, Berneval-sur-Mer*]

My dear Robbie, I have taken the villa: but I have to pay £17. 10 down: the rest in October. I cannot understand why you don't see how much cheaper it is for me to have a villa, than to live here; also I do not work well in a hotel. You had better let me have £100: I will keep it at Dieppe. It has been to me a great inconvenience being without any money, as till I pay £17. 10 they will not warm or paper the villa for me. So now I have to wait I suppose for a week more: unless the £40 is payable at sight. So if you have sent me £40, as I hope through my telegram of this morning, kindly send £60 also: then I shall always be able to draw directly on my money without worrying you. I have engaged a servant at 35 francs a month, a nice simple fellow who thinks it a godsend. He will clean my room, and clothes, and make my coffee. I will have my meals here.

595

Bosie telegraphs daily. This is an exaggeration, but I made him wire about the duel, which has ended well—*no* duel. Dal Young was here on Thursday, and stayed the night, with Dowson and Conder. Ever yours

OSCAR

To Dalhousie Young[1]

[? *5 June 1897*]   *Hôtel de la Plage, Berneval-sur-Mer*

My dear Young, Of course I feel very lonely after you and my other good friends have gone away. I have no mourning, but I wear my red tie "with a difference."[2]

It was to me the most delightful experience to receive your visit, and I am very grateful to you all for your pleasant and kindly companionship. I remember saying to you on Thursday night that when any man has even *one* friend God has given him two worlds to live in, and that is what I feel, what I know about friendship. Perhaps some day I may have the privilege of meeting your wife, who, I know, has spoken of me with sweetness of pity and gentleness of word. That will be something to look forward to, like the roses of deep summer or the red gold of the August corn.

Now I want you to advise me. I feel that here I have found, as it were, a home, and that to go farther afield looking for something better would be utterly ungrateful of me. You see how nice and kind everyone here is to me, and how simple and peaceful a life may be waiting for me in this little garden by the sea. It is so close to England, that from time to time my friends may make a "pilgrimage to the sinner"—the best form of pilgrimage perhaps, for kind hearts—and though no miracles may be accorded to them, yet they will be able to work miracles themselves, for to help any human being, even to be able to do so, is a miracle compared to which the blooming of the dry staff of the Pope when Tannhäuser knelt before him is, in my eyes, nothing.[3] And while everything seems to help and heal me, from the honeysuckle that makes the air Arabia for me, to the moon that draws the refluent tides in such strange music to her feet, yet nothing can help or heal like the hand of a friend, and I seem to have far more now than I ever had, I suppose because I have, of course, far less, but know the wonderful beauty of friendship from a new standpoint and see it with changed eyes.

It seems then to me that if I can get a nice chalet built here in a garden of my own, and be in my own home, as it would be, and lord of my own maimed life, I would be able to do beautiful work and speak to the world again on an instrument that has, I think, gained other strings, and become wider in possibility of range and effect. The price would be for the whole thing, freehold, the house built according to my views, with a great room to write in, and two large balconies to sun in, a *salle-à-manger*, three bedrooms, a kitchen and servants' room, offices and cellar, £500, which seems to me, whose views are no doubt tainted by the purple of my past, absurdly

---

[1] Text from *Resurgam* (1917).   [2] *Hamlet*, Act IV, scene 5.
[3] See note 4, p. 821.

cheap. Now I want you to consider how this is to be done. If the money were got, on mortgage, and I paid 7 per cent for it, it would be only £35 a year, and where could I find anything cheaper than a lovely little chalet of my own, with its trees and garden, and kind nice neighbours, and the sea making music for me at the end of the white chalk ravine, and peace, and the sense of not being a wanderer—for £35 a year? And, really, if I write a good play, and get it produced and have a success, there are certainly £3000 to £5000 waiting for me. The money one makes by plays is quite absurd, and now that I wish to live differently, £3000 would be a real fortune. Of course I would then pay off the mortgage, and be, not king over others—I am tired of being that—but a king without subjects, *un roi dans le désert*, lord over my own soul only, over my own soul at last. Think over this like a good fellow, and tell me your views, and offer to your wife my thanks for many sweet kindnesses about me whose echo at any rate has reached me. Sincerely yours   OSCAR WILDE

To Ernest Dowson

MS. Martin

[? *5 June 1897*]   *Hôtel de la Plage, Berneval-sur-Mer*

Cher Monsieur le Poète, It was most kind of you coming to see me, and I thank you very sincerely and gratefully for your pleasant companionship and the many gentle ways by which you recalled to me that, once at any rate, I was a Lord of Language, and had myself the soul of a poet. Of course I am lonely after the departure of my three good friends—le Poète, le Philosophe, and le Peintre—but I have no mourning-suit, so all I can do is to wear my red tie "with a difference"!

I am breakfasting with the Stannards at Dieppe on Wednesday, and will be at the Café Suisse at *3.15*. If you happen to be there it would be kind of you to introduce me to Jean who has the boats or knows about them. I have a wild desire for the sea. I feel that water purifies, and that in nature there is, for me at any rate, healing power.

Of course don't put yourself out to come in from your forest—but if you happen to be in Dieppe, I would like to be introduced to Jean.

There is a sea-mist today, and my fishermen have not come up the chalk ravine to search for me. I long to get your poems. The sea's "restless chime"[1] makes me hungry for poetry. Sincerely yours   OSCAR WILDE

To Robert Ross

MS. Clark

Saturday, 5 June [*1897*]   [*Hôtel de la Plage, Berneval-sur-Mer*]

My dear Robbie, I propose to *live* at Berneval. I will *not* live in Paris, nor in Algiers, nor in southern Italy. Surely a house for a year, if I choose to

---

[1] Cf. note 1, p. 600.

continue there, at £32 is absurdly cheap! I could not live cheaper at a
hotel. You are penny foolish and pound foolish—a dreadful state for any
financier to be in. I told M. Bonnet that my banker was *M. Ross et Cie,
Banquiers célèbres de Londres*: and now you suddenly show me that you
have really no place among the great financial people, and are afraid of
any investment over £31. 10. It is merely the extra 10/- that baffles you.
As regards people living on me in the extra bedrooms: dear boy, there is no
one who would stay with me but you, and you will pay your own bill at
the hotel for meals, and as for your room the charge will be nominally
2 fr. 50 a night, but there will be *lots* of extras, such as *bougie, bain*, and hot
water: all cigarettes smoked in the bedrooms are charged extra: washing is
extra: and if any one does not take the extras, of course he is charged more.
*Bain 25 c. Pas de bain 50 c. Cigarette dans la chambre-à-coucher, 10 c. pour
chaque cigarette. Pas de cigarettes dans la chambre-à-coucher, 20 c. chaque
cigarette*. This is the *système* in all good hotels. If Reggie comes, of course
he will pay a little more. I cannot forget that he gave me a dressing-case.
Sphinxes pay a hundred per cent more than anyone else. They always did
in ancient Egypt. Architects, on the other hand, are taken at a reduction.
I have special terms for architects.[1]

But seriously, Robbie, if anyone stayed with me, of course they would
pay their *pension* at the hotel. They would have to: except architects. A
modern architect, like modern architecture, doesn't pay. But then I only
know one architect, and you are hiding him somewhere from me. I am
beginning to believe that he is as extinct as the Dado, of which now only
fossil remains are found, chiefly in the vicinity of Brompton, where they
are sometimes discovered by workmen excavating. They are usually
embedded in the old Lincrusta-Walton strata, and are rare consequently.[2]

I visited *M. le Curé* today: he has a charming house in a *jardin potager*:
he showed me over the church: tomorrow I sit in the choir by his special
invitation. He showed me all his vestments: tomorrow he really will be
charming in his red. He knows I am a heretic, and believes that Pusey is
still alive. He says that God will convert England on account of England's
kindness to the *prêtres exilés* at the time of the Revolution. It is to be the
reward of that sea-lashed island. Stained-glass windows are wanted in the
church: he only has six: fourteen more are needed. He gets them at 300
francs (£12) a window in Paris! I was nearly offering half a dozen, but
remembered you, and so only gave him something *pour ses pauvres*. You
had a narrow escape, Robbie. You should be thankful.

I hope the £40 is on its way, and that the £60 will follow. I am going

---

[1] See note 2, p. 623.

[2] In 1877 Frederick Walton invented a raised-surface wall-covering which became
very popular and is still manufactured. The name Lincrusta is a compound of the
Latin *linum* (flax) and *crusta* (relief), and its chief ingredient is solidified linseed
oil. In *Son of Oscar Wilde* Vyvyan Holland records that in the smoking-room at
16 Tite Street "the walls were covered with the peculiar wallpaper of that era
known as Lincrusta-Walton and had a William Morris pattern of dark red and dull
gold; when you poked it with your finger, it popped and split, and your finger
might even go through, so this was not much encouraged."

to hire a boat. It will save walking, and so be an economy in the end. Dear Robbie, I must start well. If the life of St Francis awaits me I shall not be angry. Worse things might happen. Ever yours OSCAR

To Robert Ross
MS. Clark

Sunday evening, 6 June [1897] [*Hôtel de la Plage, Berneval-sur-Mer*]

Dear Robbie, By all means. If Edward Strangman[1] will let me know I will make arrangements. He of course will stay here the night. There is no way of getting back to Dieppe. The hotel is quite comfortable, as you know. Let him come *on his way* to Paris, if possible. I hope something will come of it, though of course I would sooner have a new play of mine, as my new *début*.

I went to Mass at ten o'clock and to Vespers at three o'clock. The old *curé* is now devoted to me. I really don't know whether I should tell him that I am in great disgrace. I think I must do so tomorrow. He called at five o'clock and insisted on going for a walk by the sea with me. He thinks me *volontaire* but extremely *good*. It is quite distressing.

I am really in wonderful health. My days are largely occupied with letter-writing, but I can't help that. I get exercise at intervals.

I am very sorry, but you must put a £1 Postal Order or whatever it is called into enclosed letter, and send it. *Read the letter*, and you will see I must do it. It makes me sick to think that A.2.11 has been flogged again. It fills me with despair.

Till I get the money the *chalet* is vacant. I wait tomorrow's post. Don't be nervous. I have many irons, and a huge fire. But to work I must be isolated. In a few weeks the English will land here. I am afraid. Ever yours OSCAR

To Lord Alfred Douglas
MS. Clark

Sunday night, 6 June [1897] [*Hôtel de la Plage, Berneval-sur-Mer*]

My dearest Boy, I must give up this *absurd* habit of writing to you every day. It comes of course from the strange new joy of talking to you daily. But next week I must make a resolution to write to you only every *seven* days, and then on the question of the relations of the sonnet to modern life, and the importance of your writing romantic ballads, and the strange beauty of that lovely line of Rossetti's, suppressed till lately by his brother,

---

[1] Irish. Born 1866. Educated at Pembroke College, Oxford. Called to the Bar (Inner Temple) 1898. Friend of Rothenstein and Conder.

where he says that "the sea ends in a sad blueness beyond rhyme."[1] Don't you think it lovely? "In a sad *blueness* beyond rhyme." *Voilà "l'influence du bleu dans les arts,"* with a vengeance!

I am so glad you went to bed at seven o'clock. Modern life is terrible to vibrating delicate frames like yours: a rose-leaf in a storm of hard hail is not so fragile. With us who are modern it is the *scabbard* that wears out the sword.

Will you do this for me? Get *Le Courier de la Presse* to procure a copy of *Le Soir*, the *Brussels* paper, somewhere between the 26th and the 31st of May last, which has an article on my letter to the *Chronicle*, a translation of it, I believe, and notices. It is of vital importance for me to have it as soon as possible. My *Chronicle* letter is to be published as a pamphlet with a postscript, and I need the *Soir*.[2] I don't want to write myself for it, for obvious reasons. Dear boy, I hope you are still sweetly asleep: you are so absurdly sweet when you are asleep. I have been to Mass at ten o'clock and to Vespers at three o'clock. I was a little bored by a sermon in the morning, but Benediction was delightful. I am seated in the Choir! I suppose sinners should have the high places near Christ's altar? I know at any rate that Christ would not turn me out.

Remember, after a few days, only *one letter a week*. I *must* school myself to it.

En attendant, yours with all love   OSCAR,
Poète-forçat

To Reginald Turner

MS. Hyde (D. & M.)

[? *7 June 1897*]   *Hôtel de la Plage, Berneval-sur-Mer*

My dear Reggie, It is all very well giving me a lovely silver dressing-case, and meeting me at Dieppe, and behaving like an angel: but what is the result? Simply that I come to you to ask you to do something more. I can't help it. Why do you insist on behaving like an angel, if you object to my treating you as one?

[1] On 28 September 1849 D. G. Rossetti included in a letter from abroad to his brother William a short poem called "At Boulogne. Upon the Cliffs: Noon," which begins:

> The sea is in its listless chime,
>   Like Time's lapse rendered audible;
>   The murmur of the earth's large shell.
> In a sad blueness beyond rhyme

It ends.

W. M. Rossetti omitted the poem from the *Collected Works* of 1886, but printed it in the *Family-Letters* of 1895.

[2] Wilde's *Daily Chronicle* letter of 28 May was reprinted by Murdoch & Co as a pamphlet called *Children in Prison and Other Cruelties of Prison Life*, and prefaced by a brief publisher's note dated February 1898.

Read *first* enclosed letter, before you go any further. It is necessary that you should do so. This is vital. Also it is Act I.

Have you read it?
(Interval of five minutes. No band: only a cigarette.)

If so, what do you say to such a nice simple sweet letter from *Jim Cuthbert's pal* who came out on June the 2nd, and found a little £2, *no more*, waiting for him at the Post Office from me? You see what a good chap he is: he was one of my great friends in Reading; he and Jim Cuthbert and Harry Elvin were *my* pals: hearts of gold.

Now I have asked him to come and stay a week here with me, so that he may have a holiday after eighteen months' hard labour.

His offence, I told you. He was a soldier, dined too well, or perhaps too badly, and "made hay" in the harness room of the regimental stables: the sort of thing one was "gated" for at Oxford, or fined £5 for by the Proctor. He has never taken anything by fraud or by violence. He is a good chap, and has a nice sweet nature.

I had better say candidly that he is not "a beautiful boy." He is twenty-nine years of age, but looks a little older, as he inherits hair that catches silver lines early: he has also a slight, but still *real*, moustache. I am thankful and happy to be able to say that I have no feeling for him, nor could have, other than affection and friendship. He is simply a manly simple fellow, with the nicest smile and the pleasantest eyes, and I have no doubt a confirmed "*mulierast*," to use Robbie's immortal phrase.

So you see my feelings towards him. It is sad to have to explain them, but it is only fair to you.

Now Robbie has whatever little money I possess, but he is very severe on me for having sent some money to four chaps released last week. He says I can't afford it. But, dear Reggie, I must look after my prison-friends, if my good friends, like you, look after me.

I have a cheque for £40, but it will take a week to cash it, as I cannot go to Dieppe till Wednesday, and of course, as the bank does not know me, the cheque will have to be cleared in London before I touch the money here. So Monday is the earliest I can realise.

I want you then to lend me £6. *10.* till next week, if you possibly can.

Arthur Cruttenden requires clothes—a blue-serge suit, a pair of brown leather boots, some shirts, and a hat. This will cost money, and his ticket here will cost something.

So I have written to him to tell him that a good friend of mine—a Jim Cuthbert of the name of R. Turner—will send him from me £6. 10., so that he can get clothes, and be here on Saturday afternoon next, for a week. I hope in the meantime to get him a place, when his holidays with me end.

Of course if you would not mind being good to a friend of mine, it would be very sweet of you if you would let him come to see you on Friday morning. He will show you, by my orders, my letter to him, and you can tell him some good place in the Strand to go to, for clothes etc., and also clear up any mysteries about any details of dress and apparel. If you can do this, *just send him £1 to come up with*, and let him have the £5. 10 when he arrives. Tell him that it, the £5. 10, is waiting for him, and that he must bring up whatever he has already in the way of clothes.

He is not English: he is American: but has no accent at all. He always wrapped up well at night in his native land.

You don't know, Reggie, what a pleasure it is to me to think I shall have the chance of being kind to a chap who has been in trouble with me. I look forward to it with tears of joy and gratitude.

Of course if you can't see him, simply send him the money: but I would like you to see him, and to say some kind words to him. We all come out of prison as sensitive as children.

Next week you shall have the £6. 10. I simply dare not tell Robbie to give it, because he scolds me, and I hate giving him pain. I know he is right, but still I have £200 left, and £3 a week, and in a few months I shall be making money, I hope.

Send me a line at once to say if you can do all this: and if Cruttenden can go on Saturday, see that he learns about trains, and send me a wire to inform me, so that I may meet him all right at Dieppe.

If you will do this, I will give you back the dressing-case: at least I will keep it for you always: it is the same thing.

I anxiously await a letter from you. I know that, *if you can*, you will let A. C. call on you on Friday morning. It would so please him, and so fascinate me. Ever yours   OSCAR

P.S. Of course send me back Arthur Cruttenden's letter. I wouldn't part with it for many £6. 10.: nor indeed show it to anyone but you, *and Robbie* if he wouldn't lecture me about giving away among *four* fellow-prisoners and *four* warders (*including* £5 to Martin) the sum of £20! Huge I know for me, but still it is little for kindness shown. I may not have the chance again. I only know five chaps now in Reading Gaol. By the end of the year—on December 2 in fact—all my friends, thank God, will be free men, as I am. So unless I do a little *now*, I shall lose my chance.

Dear Reggie, if you will manage all this for me and A. C. you will, in some other way than the mere repayment of the £6. 10 next week, reap a harvest of deep gold in the heart of the great world. I know it. I have been taught it in cell C.3.3.

To Robert Ross

MS. Clark

Tuesday morning. 9.30
8 June [1897]   [*Hôtel de la Plage, Berneval-sur-Mer*]
My dear Robbie, On receipt of your cheque yesterday I went at once in a

voiture to Dieppe. Need I say that the banks were all closed? They always are in France, and no one seems to mind. It was a *Pentecôte* festival. So back I had to come with the cheque. Tomorrow I breakfast at the Stannards, and will give the cheque to the bank. Of course they will take *three* days to clear it, so I shall not be able to get the money till *Monday* next, the *14th*, at earliest. You see I wrote for it on Thursday the *3rd*. So it takes ten days to get money! In the meanwhile I cannot have even a fire lit in the chalet. I have to pay half the rent down: so I shall not be able to get into it for about a fortnight, as the sitting room has to be papered, at the proprietor's expense of course. The salt air and salt wind have left it in fluttering strips. Now you see how right I am to want my money *here*. The want of it simply overwhelms me with expense, so let me have the £60.

Don't think, dear Robbie, I am going to depend on you or other good friends. I have great schemes on. But I require my house. Overhead here is a lady with two children, perfect darlings, and their racket is appalling. There is no peace except in one's own home.

This is a scrawl. Ever yours   OSCAR

Postcard: To More Adey
MS. Clark

Tuesday, 8 June [1897]   *Berneval-sur-Mer*

Dear More, Thanks so much for the wonderful *Littré*,[1] and the books. You are simply too kind and good to me for words. I am very well, and have just written a severe letter to Robbie. The weather is grey, but I love the soft salt air. The *D.C.* letter has produced, I think, the best effect. Will you let me have a *Saturday Review*? Ever yours   S. M.

Postcard: To Robert Ross
MS. Clark

[Postmark 8 June 1897]   *[Berneval-sur-Mer]*

Cheque No. 2 just arrived. Thanks so much. The letter is of course from Ernest Eaton, Prospect Place, Chalvey, Slough. He was only visiting Reading for *two months*: a very nice fellow. Send him the *Chronicle marked*: I have promised it to him: please do this. All well.   S. M.

Postcard: To Reginald Turner
MS. Hyde (D. & M.)

Tuesday evening, 8 June [1897]   *Berneval-sur-Mer*

Dear Reggie, Thanks for your charming letter, just received. I hope you

[1] Emile Littré's great *Dictionnaire de la Langue Française* originally appeared 1863–69. An abridged edition was issued 1876.

received my huge envelope quite safe, and that you have been able to see *A. C.* and to advance what I asked.

Please send back *A.C.*'s letter to me, *by return*. I like it so much that I am lonely without it. A Pilgrimage to the Sinner is being organised by Will Rothenstein this week. He brings, as his offering, silent songs on stone.[1] S. M.

Postcard: To Robert Ross
MS. Clark

Tuesday evening, 8 June [1897] *Berneval-sur-Mer*

Dear Robbie, I am greatly distressed to learn from your letter that you received *three* letters from me on *one* morning. How awful! Of course it is the result of the "English Sunday." I will no longer write to you in the temporal vicinity of that day. I will simply send you twice a week my *Berneval, Day by Day*. (If the *Daily Chronicle* cares, you might arrange for simultaneous publication in their columns.) Will Rothenstein is organising a Pilgrimage to the Sinner this week. He brings, as his offering, silent songs on stone. S. M.

To Will Rothenstein
MS. Rothenstein

Wednesday [Postmark 9 June 1897] *Hôtel de la Plage, Berneval-sur-Mer*

My dear good Friend, I cannot tell you how pleased I was to get your kind and affectionate letter yesterday, and I look forward with real delight to the prospect of seeing you, though it be only for a day. I am going into Dieppe to breakfast with the Stannards, who have been most kind to me, and I will send you a telegram from there. I do hope you can come tomorrow by the day boat, so that you and your friend can dine and sleep here. There is no one in this little inn but myself, but it is most comfortable, and the chef—there is a real chef—is an artist of great distinction; he walks in the evening by the sea to get ideas for the next day. Is it not sweet of him? I have taken a chalet for the whole season for £32, so I shall be able I hope to work again, and write plays or something.

I know, dear Will, you will be pleased to know that I have not come out of prison an embittered or disappointed man. On the contrary: in many ways I have gained much. I am not really ashamed of having been in prison: I often was in more shameful places: but I *am* really ashamed of having led a life unworthy of an artist. I don't say that Messalina is a better companion than Sporus, or that the one is all right and the other all wrong: I know simply that a life of definite and studied materialism, and a philosophy of appetite and cynicism, and a cult of sensual and senseless ease, are bad things for an artist: they narrow the imagination, and dull the

[1] Whistler's definition of lithographs.

more delicate sensibilities. I was all wrong, my dear boy, in my life. I was not getting the best out of me. *Now* I think that with good health and the friendship of a few good simple nice fellows like yourself, and a quiet mode of living, with isolation for thought, and freedom from the endless hunger for pleasures that wreck the body and imprison the soul—well, I think I may do things yet that you all may like. Of course I have lost much, but still, my dear Will, when I reckon up all that is *left* to me, the sun and the sea of this beautiful world; its dawns dim with gold and its nights hung with silver; many books, and all flowers, and a few good friends; and a brain and body to which health and power are not denied—really I am *rich* when I count up what I still have: and as for money, my money did me horrible harm. It wrecked me. I hope just to have enough to enable me to live simply and write well.

So remember that you will find me in many respects very happy, and of course, by your sweetness in coming to see me, you will bring me happiness along with you.

As for the silent songs on stone, I am charmed at the prospect of having something of yours. It is awfully good of you to think of it. I have had many sweet presents, but none I shall value more than yours.

You ask me if you can bring me anything from London. Well, the salt soft air kills my cigarettes, and I have no box in which to keep them. If you are in a millionaire condition and could bring me a box for keeping cigarettes in, it would be a great boon. At Dieppe there is nothing between a trunk and a *bonbonnière*. I do hope to see you tomorrow (Thursday) for dinner and sleep. If not, well Friday morning. I am up now at eight o'clock regularly!

I hope you never forget that *but for me* you would not be *Will* Rothenstein: *Artist*. You would simply be *William* Rothenstein, *R.A.* It is one of the most important facts in the history of art.

I look forward greatly to knowing Strangman. His translating *Lady Windermere* is delightful. Your sincere and grateful friend

OSCAR WILDE

Postcard: To Robert Ross
MS. Clark

Thursday, 10 June [1897]   [*Berneval-sur-Mer*]

Thanks, dear Robbie, for your letter. Dal Young is a dear simple nice fellow. I am very fond of him, and grateful to him. The ties have arrived. The excitement at Berneval is great in consequence.   S. M.

Postcard: To Robert Ross
MS. Clark

Friday 3.30 [Postmark 11 June 1897]   *Café Suisse, Dieppe*

Dear Robbie, Will Rothenstein and Strangman arrived yesterday: Strangman is a charming sweet fellow: he has just left for Paris. W. R. stops till tomorrow. The weather is lovely. I bathed this morning. The chalet will be ready on Wednesday. Your room has a balcony and a bed. Please use postcards when you have "no news." They are so private.   s. m.

Postcard: To Reginald Turner
MS. Hyde (D. & M.)

Sunday, 13 June [*1897*]   *Berneval-sur-Mer*

Dear Reggie, *Thank you so much for your kindness*. A. C. arrived yesterday all right at 3.30 p.m. I introduced him to Will Rothenstein. He is very nice, and gentle, but not very well. He lost two stone at Reading! He is a simple and grateful fellow. I have just come back from Mass with him, and am sending him out to walk this afternoon, as I have to write letters.
                                                                s. m.

Postcard: To Robert Ross
MS. Clark

Sunday, 13 June [*1897*]   [*Hôtel de la Plage, Berneval-sur-Mer*]

Dear Robbie, Thank you so much for red ties and scarlet sonnets. I move in to my chalet on Wednesday.

I observed a slight tendency to Mrs Daubeny's ailments:[1] but you are all right now. Have just seen a *première communion*, very sweet, and flowerlike with children. The *curé's* hopes are at their highest. *Sed non sum dignus.*   s. m.

To Frank Harris
MS. Texas

13 June 1897   *Hôtel de la Plage, Berneval-sur-Mer*

My dear Frank, I know you do not like writing letters, but still I think you might have written me a line in answer, or acknowledgement of my letter to you from Dieppe. I have been thinking of a story to be called "The Silence of Frank Harris."[2]

I have, however, heard during the last few days that you do not speak of me in the friendly manner I would like. This distresses me very much.

I am told that you are hurt with me because my letter of thanks to you was not sufficiently elaborated in expression. This I can hardly credit. It

---

[1] The wife of Archdeacon Daubeny in *A Woman of No Importance* never appears, but is described at different times as suffering from headaches, deafness, gout, defective memory and an inability to eat solid food.

[2] A reference to a best-selling novel of 1886 called *The Silence of Dean Maitland* by Maxwell Gray.

seems so unworthy of a big strong nature like yours, that knows the realities of life. I told you I was grateful to you for your kindness to me. Words, *now*, to me signify *things*, actualities, real emotions, realised thoughts. I learnt in prison to be grateful. I used to think gratitude a burden. Now I know that it is something that makes life lighter as well as lovelier for one. I am grateful for a thousand things, from my good friends down to the sun and the sea. But I cannot say more than that I am grateful. I cannot make phrases about it. For *me* to use such a word shows an enormous development in my nature. Two years ago I did not know the feeling the word denotes. Now I know it, and I am thankful that I have learnt that much, at any rate, by having been in prison. But I must say again that I no longer make *roulades* of phrases about the deep things I feel. When I write directly to you I speak directly. Violin-variations don't interest me. I am grateful to you. If that does not content you, then you do not understand, what you of all men should understand, how sincerity of feeling expresses itself. But I dare say the story told of you is untrue. It comes from so many quarters that it probably is.

I am told also that you are hurt because I did not go on the driving-tour with you. You should understand that in telling you that it was impossible for me to do so, I was thinking as much of *you* as of myself. To think of the feelings and happiness of others is not an entirely new emotion in my nature. I would be unjust to myself and my friends, if I said it was. But I think of those things far more than I used to do. If I had gone with you, you would not have been happy, nor enjoyed yourself. Nor would I. You must try to realise what two years' cellular confinement is, and what two years of absolute silence mean to a man of my intellectual power. To have survived at all—to have come out sane in mind and sound of body— is a thing so marvellous to me, that it seems to me sometimes, not that the age of miracles is over, but that it is only just beginning; and that there are powers in God, and powers in man, of which the world has up to the present known little.

But while I am cheerful, happy, and have sustained to the full that passionate interest in life and art that was the dominant chord of my nature, and made all modes of existence and all forms of expression utterly fascinating to me always—still, I need rest, quiet, and often complete solitude. Friends have come to see me here for a day, and have been delighted to find me like my old self, in all intellectual energy and sensitiveness to the play of life, but it has always proved afterwards to have been a strain upon a nervous force, much of which has been destroyed. I have now no *storage* of nervous force. When I expend what I have, in an afternoon, nothing remains. I look to quiet, to a simple mode of existence, to nature in all the infinite meanings of an infinite word, to charge the cells for me. Every day, if I meet a friend, or write a letter longer than a few lines, or even read a book that makes, as all fine books do, a direct claim on me, a direct appeal, an intellectual challenge of any kind, I am utterly exhausted in the evening, and often sleep badly. And yet it is *three* whole weeks since I was released.

Had I gone with you on the driving-tour, where we would have of necessity been in immediate contact with each other from dawn to sunset, I would have certainly broken off the tour the third day, probably broken down the second. You would have then found yourself in a painful position: your tour would have been arrested at its outset; your companion would have been ill without doubt; perhaps might have needed care and attendance, in some little remote French village. You would have given it to me, I know. But I felt it would have been wrong, stupid, and thoughtless of me to have started an expedition doomed to swift failure, and perhaps fraught with disaster and distress. You are a man of dominant personality; your intellect is exigent, more so than that of any man I ever knew; your demands on life are enormous; you require response, or you annihilate. The pleasure of being with you is in the clash of personality, the intellectual battle, the war of ideas. To survive you one must have a strong brain, an assertive ego, a dynamic character. In your luncheon-parties, in old days, the remains of the guests were taken away with the *débris* of the feast. I have often lunched with you in Park Lane and found myself the only survivor. I might have driven on the white roads, or through the leafy lanes, of France with a fool, or with the wisest of all things, a child; with you it would have been impossible. You should thank me sincerely for having saved you from an experience that each of us would have always regretted.

Will you ask me why then, when I was in prison, I accepted with grateful thanks your offer? My dear Frank, I don't think you will ask so thoughtless a question. The prisoner looks to liberty as an immediate return to all his ancient energy, quickened into more vital forces by long disuse. When he goes out, he finds he has still to suffer. His punishment, as far as its effects go, lasts intellectually and physically, just as it lasts socially. He has still to pay. One gets no receipt for the past when one walks out into the beautiful air.

There is also a third thing. The Leversons kindly bought for me and presented to me my own life-size portrait of myself by Harper Pennington, and some other things, including a large pastel by my dear friend Shannon. These things they promised to store, or keep for me during my imprisonment. I knew, and realised with some natural amusement, that Leverson considered that Shannon's beautiful pastel might be demoralising to the female servants of his household. He told me so with tears in his eyes; his wife with laughter in hers. I was quite conscious of the very painful position of a man who had in his house a life-sized portrait, which he could not have in his drawing-room as it was obviously, on account of its *subject*, demoralising to young men, and possibly to young women of advanced views, and a pastel of the Moon, no less demoralising to housemaids on account of the *treatment* of the subject. I often felt the strongest sympathy with Leverson: a sentimentalist confronted with a fact either in Life or Art is a tragic spectacle to gods and men. Accordingly, the week before my release, as a slight token of my sympathy with him, I wrote to my friends to ask them to engage a small room in Hornton Street, Kensington, at my expense, where for a few shillings a week I could store the art of

Pennington and of Shannon, in a seclusion where they would be as harmless as Art can be. I considered it, I may say, a plain act of manners and morals to do so. I asked them to relieve Leverson from his terrible charge: a portrait that was a social incubus, and a pastel dangerous to chambermaids.

I have now spent the whole of my Sunday afternoon—the first real day of summer we have had—in writing to you this long letter of explanation.

I have written directly and simply, and I need not tell the author of *Elder Conklin* that sweetness and simplicity of expression take more out of one than fiddling harmonies on one string. I felt it my duty to write, but it has been a distressing one. It would have been *better* for me to have lain in the brown grass on the cliff, or to have walked slowly by the sea. It would have been *kinder* of you to have written to me directly about whatever harsh or bitter or hurt feelings you may have about me. It would have saved me an afternoon of strain, and tension.

But I have something more to say. It is pleasanter to me, now, to write about others, than about myself.

The enclosed is from a brother prisoner of mine: released June 4th. Pray read it; you will see his age, offence, and aim in life.

If you can give him a trial, do so. If you see your way to this kind action, and write to him to come and see you, kindly state in your letter that it is about a situation. He may think otherwise that it is about the flogging of A.2.11, a thing that does not interest *you*, and about which *he* is a little afraid to talk.

If the result of this long letter will be that you will help this fellow-prisoner of mine to a place in your service, I shall consider my afternoon better spent than any afternoon for the last two years, and three weeks.

In any case I have now written to you fully on all things as reported to me.

I again assure you of my gratitude for your kindness to me during my imprisonment, and on my release, and am always your sincere friend and admirer   OSCAR WILDE

With regard to Lawley.[1] All soldiers are neat, and smart, and make capital servants. He would be a good *groom*; he is, I believe, a Third Hussars man. He was a quiet well-conducted chap in Reading always.

Postcard: To Robert Ross
MS. Clark

Tuesday, 15 June [1897]   [*Berneval-sur-Mer*]

Dear Robbie, You have never told me anything about the type-writer, or my letter: pray let there be no further conspiracies. I feel apprehensive. It is only by people writing to me the worst that I can know the best.

Also, could all the remainder of my money be transferred to Dieppe? I thought *you* had it all. But you say not.

[1] Or possibly Langley.

The *New Review* portrait of the Queen is wonderful.[1] I am going to hang it on the walls of the chalet. Every poet should gaze at the portrait of his Queen, all day long. s. m.

To Lord Alfred Douglas
MS. Clark

Tuesday, 15 June [1897] *Berneval-sur-Mer*

My own dear Boy, Who posts your letters? Does anyone? Or do you ever really know the day of the month? I rarely do myself, and Ernest Dowson, who is here, never.

The reason of these tedious questions is that last night, on coming from Arques-la-Bataille, where I had been breakfasting with Ernest, I found a letter from you *dated June 11* (that is last *Friday*) but *posted* June *13* (last Sunday). I have kept the envelope for you.

You ask me in it to let you come on Saturday: but, dear honey-sweet boy, I have already asked you to come then: so we both have the same desire, as usual.

Your name is to be Jonquil du Vallon.

Will you write *at once* to Edward Strangman, Hôtel Terminus, Gare St Lazare, to say you would like to see him and have news of me. He is a very gentle, rather shy chap: Irish by race, Oxford by culture: a friend of Will Rothenstein and Robbie, and a good friend of mine: he has just sent me lovely books I needed: pray let him know that I was so touched and pleased by his visit.

I suppose I shall hear at length from you today: the *facteur* comes at twelve o'clock and leaves at once, so all I can ever write in immediate response is a green-gray postcard. Only wine will induce the *facteur* to wait. Nothing else has any influence with him. Always devotedly yours

OSCAR

To Lord Alfred Douglas
MS. Clark

Wednesday, 16 June [1897] *Berneval-sur-Mer*

My dear Boy, I am upset with the idea that you don't get my letters, or that the post goes wrong, or something. I daresay it is all absurd, but your last three letters dated the 10th, 11th, and 12th (whereas we are now at the 16th) contain no references to things I asked you, especially as regards our meeting.

I have asked you to come here on Saturday. I have a bathing costume

---

[1] A reproduction of William Nicholson's famous woodcut of Queen Victoria with her dog was issued with the June 1897 issue of the *New Review*. André Gide remembered it pinned to the wall in the chalet.

for you, but you had better get one in Paris. Also bring me a lot of books, and cigarettes. I cannot get good cigarettes here or at Dieppe.

The weather is very hot, so you will want a straw hat and flannels. I hope you will get quietly out of Paris. On arriving at Dieppe, take a good *voiture* and tell him to drive to the Hotel *Bonnet*, Berneval-sur-Mer, and go by the road by *Puys*, not by the *grande route* which is a straight line of white dust.

If you want a café at Dieppe on arriving, go to the Café Suisse.

It takes an hour and a half to get here, so arrive if you can at Dieppe about three o'clock and be here at five o'clock.

I hope to be in my chalet by Saturday: so you will stay with me there. I have a little walled-in place in the garden of the hotel where I have *déjeuner* and *dîner*—a *bosquet* of trees.

On Sunday I go to Mass, in a dark blue suit.

You must not have your letters sent on under your own name. It might do me serious harm. I still suggest—for the third time—Jonquil du Vallon, but any name you like will do.

Pray do not fail to write at once on receipt of this, and be careful of the date. Your *last* letter is dated the *12th*: which was last *Saturday*.

It is lovely here today, and I am going to bathe at 10.30. Yesterday I drove Ernest Dowson back to Arques. I like him immensely.

Thanks for the *Soir*. You ask me other questions in your letter that I have answered in letters of my own to you: but I don't know if they reach you. I will wait for today's post, and write again tomorrow.

Bring also some perfumes and nice things from the sellers of the dust of roses.

Also bring yourself. Ever yours   OSCAR

To Reginald Turner
MS. Hyde (D. & M.)

Wednesday, 16 July [actually June] [1897]   *Berneval-sur-Mer*

Dear Reggie, Arthur Cruttenden returns tomorrow: and will come and see you, as you kindly said you would see him, on *Friday*. He will call between eleven and twelve a.m. and perhaps you will leave a letter with the porter to say what hour he can find you.

He is a very simple nice fellow, and has been gentle and unassuming and grateful.

I am going to try to help him, through a friend of mine, to re-enter business: he was brought up as a saddler, and did very well while his father was alive. He will tell you his prospects. Of course I don't know if I shall be able to get him any start, but I can only try.

He will bring you a letter from me.

The weather has been charming. We breakfasted with Ernest Dowson at Arques-la-Bataille on Monday, and then Ernest drove back with us and dined and slept here.

Do you remember the pretty girl at the little café by the river at St Martin l'Église, where we drove together, with Robbie and More on bicycles behind us? We went there again yesterday, and she asked after you and my other friends with passionate interest.

Ernest had an *absinthe* under the apple-trees!

With many thanks. Sincerely yours   OSCAR

To Reginald Turner

MS. Hyde (D. & M.)

Wednesday [*16 June 1897*] *1.15. p.m.*   *Café Suisse, Dieppe*

Dear Reggie, I write to you a little line to present Arthur Cruttenden to you. He will tell you all the Berneval news. He really is a nice simple fellow, and a good musician, I find. He sings, and writes songs. I hope you will be able to see him as a friend of mine. He is very sensitive to kindness.

Do write to me soon. Sincerely yours   OSCAR

This paper is so splendid that I choose it specially to write to you on.

To Ernest Dowson

MS. Martin

[? *16 June 1897*]   *Café Suisse, Dieppe*

My dear Ernest, I arrived safe, under a cold white moon, at one o'clock in the morning. My servant was asleep, so I woke him up and enquired about his early life, which, as I expected, was quite uninteresting.

There is a fatality about our being together that is astounding—or rather quite probable. Had I stayed at Arques I should have given up all hopes of ever separating from you. Why are you so persistently and perversely wonderful?

Do I see you tomorrow? Try to come over. I hope Thompson and Socrates (*his* Socrates) will come. It was delightful meeting 'Varsity men again: I like them both so much. But I intend to send them both to Oxford, especially Thompson.

Come with vine-leaves in your hair.[1]

I suppose I shall see you in ten minutes from this. I am looking out for the green costume that goes so well with your dark hyacinth locks.

I decided this morning to take a *Pernod*. The result was marvellous. At 8.30 I was dead. Now I am alive, and all is perfect, except your absence.

Tout à toi   SEBASTIAN MELMOTH

---

[1] Like Eilert Lövborg, see Ibsen's *Hedda Gabler*, end of Act II.

To Lord Alfred Douglas
MS. Clark

Thursday, 17 June [1897] 2 o'clock p.m.   *Café Suisse, Dieppe*

My dearest Boy, I have been obliged to ask my friends to leave me, as I am so upset and distressed in nerve by my solicitor's letter, and the apprehension of serious danger, that simply I must be alone. I find that any worry utterly destroys my health, and makes me horrid and irritable and unkind, though I hate to be so.

Of course at present it is impossible for us to meet. I have to find out what grounds my solicitor has for his sudden action, and of course if your father—or rather Q, as I only know him and think of him—if Q came over and made a scene and scandal it would utterly destroy my possible future and alienate all my friends from me. I owe to my friends everything, including the clothes I wear, and I would be wretched if I did anything that would separate them from me.

So simply we must write to each other: about the things we love, about poetry and the coloured arts of our age, and that passage of ideas into images that is the intellectual history of art. I think of you always, and love you always, but chasms of moonless night divide us. We cannot cross it without hideous and nameless peril.

Later on, when the alarm in England is over, when secrecy is possible, and silence forms part of the world's attitude, we may meet, but at present you see it is impossible. I would be harassed, agitated, nervous. It would be no joy for me to let you see me as I am now.

You must go to some place where you can play golf and get back your lily and rose. Don't, like a good boy, telegraph to me unless on a matter of vital import: the telegraph office is seven miles off, and I have to pay the *facteur,* and also reply, and yesterday with three separate *facteurs,* and three separate replies, I was *sans le sou,* and also mentally upset in nerve. Say please to Percy that I will accept a bicycle with many thanks for his kindness: I want to get it here, where there is a great champion who teaches everyone, and has English machines: it will cost £15. If Percy will send me £15 to enclosed name and address in a cheque, it will make me very happy. Send him my card.

Ever yours (rather maimed and mutilated)   OSCAR

Postcard: To Robert Ross
MS. Clark

Friday, 18 June [1897]   *Berneval-sur-Mer*

Dear Robbie, Cheque arrived safe this morning. I don't know how to thank you and More for your wonderful kindness, and care of my life and interests. So I write on a postcard, as all expression is forbidden by the Postal Authorities. The postcard is the only mode of silence left to us. Will write to you tomorrow. A. D. is not here, nor is he to come. S. M.

To Robert Ross

MS. Clark

Saturday, 19 June [1897] 10.30 a.m.   [*Berneval-sur-Mer*]

My dear Robbie, I took advantage of the Postcard System yesterday to thank you for the cheque, and for all the wonderful kindness you and More have shown me. So is reticence in art taught to one.

I have not received my cheque from Hansell yet. I suspect that he is keeping it for Hansell.

I suppose you know that Hansell has resigned his position, and will not act for me any more. He writes a mysterious letter about "private information." I suppose he has heard that Bosie wishes to see me. I have now put off Bosie indefinitely. I have been so harassed, and indeed frightened, at the thought of a possible scandal or trouble. The French papers describe me going about at Longchamps with Bosie at horse-races! So that must suffice for evil tongues.

Thanks for B.2.3's letter. He was a good fellow, though not one of my intimate friends: we never talked, but I saw him daily. It is most kind of you to say you will let him have £1, but I must add 10/- of my own. My friends are good to me, and I must help others a little: so will you place 30/- in enclosed letter and send it. Of course read all letters that come for me, or that I send you.

As regards Dixon, of course he should stay in London: it would be cheaper for him: let him have a room in Hornton Street—*not* at 24, of course, but hard by: and report on Dixon: I have never seen him, so my interest is abstract.[1]

I get into the chalet on Monday now: it is the Chalet Bourgeat: but always address "Berneval-sur-Mer" simply, as the *facteur* comes at 12.30 while I am breakfasting *here*, and I read my budget over my coffee. It is very annoying that he cannot wait to get my replies. Nothing in the world will induce him to wait, except wine. And that he drains with such speed that a couple of postcards is all I can ever get off.

The books have not yet come: I expect them today. I wish you would send me A. E. W. Mason's *Philanderers* (Macmillan)—he is an old friend.[2]

I have been so worried—Bosie wiring all day long, and Hansell throwing up my interests—that I am not well. I simply cannot stand worry.

I hope you are all right again. I am sure that you are "wonderfully cheerful! wonderfully cheerful!"[3] Ever yours   OSCAR

[1] It is clear from p. 624 that Dixon was being considered as a possible typist for *De Profundis*.

[2] Alfred Edward Woodley Mason (1865–1948) had been an undergraduate at Trinity College, Oxford, acting the part of Heracles in the O.U.D.S. production of the *Alcestis* of Euripides, when he first met Wilde in the summer of 1887. In London in 1894 Wilde had entertained him and given him sound advice about his first novel. *The Philanderers*, his third, was published in May 1897.

[3] Archdeacon Daubeny's description of his wife despite her disabilities (*A Woman of No Importance*, Act III).

Postcard: To More Adey

MS. Clark

Monday, 21 June [1897]   [*Berneval-sur-Mer*]

Dear More, I have much to write to you about, but I merely now send you
a line to ask you if you have received—some two weeks since—a letter
addressed to the Lady of Wimbledon, sent to your care at Hornton Street—
a large brown envelope. I have not heard from her, and am afraid my
letter may have gone astray. Of course I am not *entitled* to hear from her,
but all I want to know is if she got it. Otherwise how ungrateful a churl
I must seem to that gracious and wonderful personality.   S. M.

Postcard: To Robert Ross

MS. Clark

Monday, 21 June [1897]   [*Berneval-sur-Mer*]

Dear Robbie, Just a line to wish you a very happy Jubilee, and many of
them.[1] I fear I cannot hope to live long enough to see more than five or
six more myself, but with you it is different. I don't know the exact route
of the procession, but I suppose the dear Queen passes by Upper Phillimore Gardens and will look up and see you waving the flags of no nations.
Of course we are having "Queen's weather" here. It began today. Yesterday nothing but the prayers at *Vêpres* prevented it from snowing.   S. M.

To Will Rothenstein

MS. Rothenstein

Monday, 21 June [1897]   *Berneval-sur-Mer*

Dear Will, Thank you so much for your nice friendly letter. Your visit
here was a great and very real delight to me. The cigarette-box is I fancy
now in Dieppe, where I hope to find it today. I am sure it will be *all* that
I want, and *more* than I deserve, which is a delightful position for anyone.
It was very good of you to remember it.

I hope today also to get some of your songs on stone framed in *passe-
partout* for my *chalet*: I have not yet got in, as the walls had to be papered.

Ernest Dowson has been most charming, and stayed three days here
with me. He and I dine with Thaulow the Swedish painter in Dieppe on
Wednesday.[2]

Your breathing a word about the final word of criticism on Marie

---

[1] Queen Victoria's Diamond Jubilee was celebrated on 22 June 1897.

[2] Fritz Thaulow (1847–1906) was in fact a Norwegian landscape-artist and
designer. A description of this dinner in the form of a conversation-piece, translated
from the Norwegian of Christian Krogh, who was also present, appeared in the *New
Age* of 10 December 1908.

Corelli[1] was of course disgraceful: but I know the temptation was irresistible: I don't mind so much, as long as it gets to her ears!

Give my kindest regards to Llewellyn Hacon (do I rightly spell his wonderful name?)[2] I was much touched by what you told me of his sympathy, and interest in me. Ever, dear Will, your sincere friend

OSCAR WILDE

To Reginald Turner
MS. Hyde (D. & M.)

21 June [1897]   *Berneval-sur-Mer*

My dear Reggie, I have not yet heard whether you have seen Arthur Cruttenden. I hope so. You, I hope, know and understand that I would not ask you to see any fellow of bad character. Nothing would induce me to do so.

Of course all you said to me, dear Reggie, was quite true: but you must understand that I have the deepest desire to try and be of a little help to other fellows who were in trouble with me. I used to be utterly reckless of young lives: I used to take up a boy, love him "passionately," and then grow bored with him, and often take no notice of him. That is what I regret in my past life. Now I feel that if I can really help others it will be a little attempt, however small, at expiation. To be of real assistance to even one of them would give me joy beyond what I can express to you.

By December 6th all my friends will be out of gaol. Indeed I have only two left there, Jim Cuthbert and Harry Elvin, so my chances are limited.

I cannot thank you enough for your prompt loan, and enclose a cheque: but I am always, for that and other kindnesses, your debtor.

Tomorrow I entertain twelve little *gamins* of Berneval-le-Grand at cakes and strawberries *pour le Jubilé de la Reine*! I wish you could be here. Ever yours

OSCAR

To Ernest Dowson
MS. Martin

Monday, 21 June [1897]   *[Berneval-sur-Mer]*

My dear Ernest, I arrived, not safe, but very unsafe, at Berneval in pouring rain at 10.30. There was only one lantern to the *voiture*, so one wheel of the carriage was always in the air. On my arrival I found André Gide, who had come from Paris to see me.

---

[1] Pen-name of Mary Mackay, best-selling English novelist (1864–1924). Her latest successes had been *The Sorrows of Satan* (1895) and *The Mighty Atom* (1896).

[2] William Llewellyn Hacon (1860–1910) was at Balliol College, Oxford, 1879–83, and was called to the Bar in 1885. He was a friend of Ricketts and Shannon, lent Ricketts £1000 to start the Vale Press, and managed it for him, selling its productions At the Sign of the Dial.

Madame Bonnet made me drink *two* hot grogs, so I came to life at 11.15 and had a wonderful evening. André left yesterday at eleven o'clock. He was most charming, and had heard of you and your work.

All my invitations to my Jubilee Garden Party were issued yesterday through Marcel, the little grandson of Madame Darcy of the Café de la Paix, Berneval-le-Grand. He supervised the invitations, and struck off several names on the perfectly right grounds that he did not like them. The list was strictly limited to twelve: as the garden only holds *six* at the most, I felt that *twelve* would be sufficient: I hate crowds. Today I go in to order strawberries. I still hope you may come. A green coat always lights up a garden so well. I intend to wear my turquoise-coloured shirt.

Finally I have found my overcoat! A dear woman at Belleville picked it up on the road. So I now "know *Joseph*" again.[1]

Wednesday, at any rate, at three o'clock Café Suisse. Wear your blue tie. Ever yours

OSCAR

To Lord Alfred Douglas
MS. Clark

Wednesday, 23 June [1897]   *Café Suisse, Dieppe*

My darling Boy, Thanks for your letter received this morning. My *fête* was a huge success: fifteen *gamins* were entertained on strawberries and cream, apricots, chocolates, cakes, and *sirop de grenadine*. I had a huge iced cake with *Jubilé de la Reine Victoria* in pink sugar just rosetted with green, and a great wreath of red roses round it all. Every child was asked beforehand to choose his present: they all chose instruments of music!!!

> 6 accordions
> 5 trompettes
> 4 clairons.

They sang the Marseillaise and other songs, and danced a *ronde*, and also played "God save the Queen:" they said it was "God save the Queen," and I did not like to differ from them. They also all had flags which I gave them. They were most gay and sweet. I gave the health of *La Reine d'Angleterre*, and they cried "*Vive la Reine d'Angleterre*"!!!! Then I gave "*La France, mère de tous les artistes*," and finally I gave *Le Président de la République*: I thought I had better do so. They cried out with one accord "*Vivent le Président de la République et Monsieur Melmoth*"!!! So I found my name coupled with that of the President. It was an amusing experience as I am hardly more than a month out of gaol.

They stayed from 4.30 to seven o'clock and played games: on leaving I gave them each a basket with a jubilee cake frosted pink and inscribed, and *bonbons*.

They seem to have made a great demonstration in Berneval-le-Grand, and to have gone to the house of the Mayor and cried "*Vive Monsieur le*

[1] Cf. *Genesis*, xxxvii, 3, and *Exodus*, i, 8.

617

Maire! Vive la Reine d'Angleterre. Vive Monsieur Melmoth!" I tremble at my position.

Today I have come in with Ernest Dowson to dine with the painter Thaulow, a giant with the temperament of Corot. I sleep here and go back tomorrow.

I will write tomorrow on things. Ever, dearest boy, yours OSCAR

To Ernest Dowson

MS. Martin

[? *24 June 1897*]   *Café Suisse, Dieppe*

My dear Ernest, Do come here at once: Monsieur Meyer is presiding over a morning meal of absinthe, and we want you.

I am a wreck of course, but *la belle sœur* is like the moon.

You were wonderful and charming all last night. Ever yours OSCAR

Postcard: To Robert Ross

MS. Clark

Monday [*Postmark 28 June 1897*]   [*Berneval-sur-Mer*]

Dear Robbie, Bosie has sent me a long indictment of you and panegyric of himself, to which I will reply tomorrow. You can understand in what tone I shall answer him. But for you, dear friend, I don't know in what black abyss of want I would have been. I should not write this on a postcard; but my handwriting is as illegible as yours is. S. M.

Postcard: To Ernest Dowson

MS. Martin

Monday [*Postmark 28 June 1897*]   [*Postmark Dieppe*]

Dear Ernest, I must see you: so I propose to breakfast at St Martin L'Église tomorrow at *11.30* and you *must* come: take a *voiture* and be there. I want to have a poet to talk to, as I have had lots of bad news since you left me. Do try, like a good chap, to be there, and wear a *blue* tie. I want to be consoled. SEBASTIAN MELMOTH

To Ernest Dowson

MS. Martin

Wednesday. 6.30 [? *30 June 1897*]   *Café Suisse, Dieppe*

Dear Ernest, I write a little line, whose only excuse is its entire illegibility, to tell you how charming you are (at Berneval) and how much I like *your* friend, *and mine*, the dear Achille.[1] He is a most noble and splendid fellow, and I feel happy to have his esteem and friendship.

Tonight I am going to read your poems—your lovely lyrics—words with wings *you* write always. It is an exquisite gift, and fortunately rare in an age whose prose is more poetic than its poetry.

Do come soon and see me.

The youthful costermonger returns on Friday, with the price of a pony and cart in his pocket. I had given him a *costume bleu* but I hope he will survive it. The effects, up to this, are not so promising as I could wish. But he *means well*!

His calling you Ernest was awful. It is the effect of vegetables on the mind.

I am now going to write poetry, as soon as the "coster" leaves me. Poor fellow, I hope he will be all right.

You and Achille and Achille's friend and I must *all* be at Berneval together. I am making arrangements.

Give to Achille my sincere friendship: you have it, and other things, always.   S. M.

To Robert Ross
MS. Clark

6 July [*1897*]   [*Chalet Bourgeat*] *Berneval-sur-Mer*

Dearest Robbie, I have had no time to write lately, but I have written a long letter—of twelve foolscap pages—to Bosie, to point out to him that I owe everything to you and your friends, and that whatever life I have as an artist in the future will be due to you. He has now written to me a temperate letter, saying that Percy will fulfil his promises when he is able. Of course he will. But the occasion of his ability is certainly distant, and my wants were pressing.

I also wrote to him about his calling himself a *grand seigneur* in comparison to a dear sweet wonderful friend like you, his superior in all fine things. I told him how grotesque, ridiculous, and vulgar such an attempt was.

I long to see you. When are you coming over? I have a lovely bedroom for More, and a small garret for you, with my heart waiting in it for you.

The photograph of Constance has arrived. It was most sweet of you to send it. She writes to me every week.

Ernest Dowson is here for a few days: he leaves tomorrow. He stays at Arques-la-Bataille.

Could you send me my pictures? Would it cost much? I long for them.

Today is stormy and wet. But my chalet is delightful, and when I pass through Berneval-le-Grand they still cry "*Vivent Monsieur Melmoth et la Reine d'Angleterre!*" It is an astonishing position.

With best love. Ever yours   OSCAR

I hope *you* will be firm with Bosie.

[1] Presumably Achille Fromentin (see p. 625).

To More Adey

MS. Clark

6 July [*1897*]   [*Chalet Bourgeat*] *Berneval-sur-Mer*

My dear More, I don't know how to thank you for the lovely books that keep arriving here. It is really most kind and sweet of you, and all that I can say is that I treasure in my heart and my affection my countless debts of gratitude to you. I had no claim on you, and you have been to me the most wonderful of friends, the most generous, the most forbearing. I do hope you will come and see me here. I have *two* bedrooms, a beautiful one with a balcony for you, and a nice, somewhat dark, garret for Robbie! Pray let me know how you are. I heard of your being ill at the time of the Jubilee, which I thought brilliant of you. Few others were so thoughtful. Bosie is bombarding from a distance. I have written to him very plainly about his conduct to Robbie. Sincerely and affectionately your friend

OSCAR WILDE[1]

To Lord Alfred Douglas

MS. Clark

Wednesday, 7 [*July 1897*]   *Café Suisse, Dieppe*

My darling Boy, I received your letters all right, and have half-written my answer.

I write now on nicer things just to know how you are, and why you stay at a place that bores you. I hear from Ernest Dowson that Montigny-sur-Loire is lovely, and full of dear brilliant artists and sweet people. Stuart Merrill lives at Marlotte, only three miles off, and of course is charming and sympathetic. I hate to know you are lonely, or in danger of *ennui*, that enemy of modern life.

I am waiting here for a new servant, sent to me from Avesnes. I have not yet seen him, but I hope he will be nice. He is to come here to find me. Brutes, bald and bearded, have arrived, and Ernest Dowson says he is sure my servant is among them. It is so awful that I am going to deny I am M. Sebastian Melmoth.

Tell me about your days. Is Gaston in waiting? Are you writing anything? Whom have you met?

Tomorrow I am going to write my poem.[2] I will send it to you. With my love, dearest boy, ever your   OSCAR

Do you know Hugues Rebell? He has just sent me his book, *Nichina*.[3] Also Tristan Klingsor?[4] who sends poems. His name is so lovely, I fear I shall be disappointed with his work. In fact I am.

[1] On the envelope is a note in Ross's hand: "Please let me know if this letter contains anything important or if he acknowledges any of the books that have been sent him. Robbie."   [2] *The Ballad of Reading Gaol.*

[3] See note 3, p. 392. *Nichina: Mémoires inédits de Lorenzo Vendramin* was published in 1897.

[4] Pseudonym of Tristan Leclère (b. 1874), French writer, painter and musician.

To Carlos Blacker

MS. Blacker

12 July 1897   [*Chalet Bourgeat*] *Berneval-sur-Mer*

My dear old Friend, I need not tell you with what feelings of affection and gratitude I read your letter. You were always my staunch friend and stood by my side for many years.

Often in prison I used to think of you: of your chivalry of nature, of your limitless generosity, of your quick intellectual sympathies, of your culture so receptive, so refined. What marvellous evenings, dear Carlos, we used to have! What brilliant dinners! What days of laughter and delight! To you, as to me, conversation—that τερπνὸν κακόν as Euripides calls it[1]—that sweet sin of phrases—was always among the supreme arts of life, and we tired many a moon with talk, and drank many a sun to rest with wine and words. You were always the truest of friends and the most sympathetic of companions. You will, I know, wish to hear about me, and what I am doing and thinking.

Well, I am in a little chalet, with a garden, over the sea. It is a nice chalet with two great balconies, where I pass much of my day and many of my nights. Berneval is a tiny place consisting of a hotel and about twenty chalets: the people who come here are *des bons bourgeois* as far as I can see. The sea has a lovely beach, to which one descends through a small ravine, and the land is full of trees and flowers, quite like a bit of Surrey: so green and shady. Dieppe is ten miles off. Many friends, such as Will Rothenstein, the artist, Conder, who is a sort of Corot of the sunlight, Ernest Dowson, the poet, and others have come to see me for a few days: and next month I hope to see Ricketts and Shannon, who decorated all my books for me, dear Robbie Ross, and perhaps some others. I learnt many things in prison that were terrible to learn, but I learnt some good lessons that I needed. I learnt gratitude: and though, in the eyes of the world, I am of course a disgraced and ruined man, still every day I am filled with wonder at all the beautiful things that are left to me: loyal and loving friends: good health: books, one of the greatest of the many worlds God has given to each man: the pageant of the seasons: the loveliness of leaf and flower: the nights hung with silver and the dawns dim with gold. I often find myself strangely happy. You must not think of me as being morbidly sad, or wilfully living in sadness, that sin which Dante punishes so terribly. My desire to live is as intense as ever, and though my heart is broken, hearts are made to be broken: that is why God sends sorrow into the world. The hard heart is the evil thing of life and of art. I have also learnt sympathy with suffering. To me, suffering seems now a sacramental thing, that makes those whom it touches holy. I think I am in many respects a much better fellow than I was, and I now make no more exorbitant claims on life: I accept everything. I am sure it is all right. I was living a life unworthy of an artist, and though I do not hold with the British view of morals that sets Messalina above Sporus, I see that any materialism in life coarsens

[1] *Hippolytus*, 384.

621

the soul, and that the hunger of the body and the appetites of the flesh desecrate always, and often destroy.

Of course I am troubled about money, because the life of a man of letters—and I hope to be one again—requires solitude, peace, books and the opportunity of retirement. I have, as I daresay you know, only £3 a week: but dear Robbie Ross and some other friends got up privately a little subscription for me to give me a start. But of course they are all quite poor themselves, and though they gave largely from their store, their store was small, and I have had to buy everything, so as to be able to live at all.

I hope to write a play soon, and then if I can get it produced I shall have money—far too much I dare say: but as yet I have not been able to work. The two long years of silence kept my soul in bonds. It will all come back, I feel sure, and then all will be well.

I long to see you, dear friend. Could you come here with your wife? Or to Dieppe? The hotel here is a charming little *auberge* with a capital cook: everything very wholesome and clean, and daintily served besides. I must talk over my future, for I believe that God still holds a future for me, only I must be wise, and must see my way.

Will you do this? It would help me very much to see you—more than I can say.

And now, dear friend, I must end my letter. I have only said a little in it, but writing is strangely difficult for me from long disuse.

Write to me as Monsieur Sebastian Melmoth. It is my new name. I enclose a card. Pray offer my homage to your wife, and believe me, ever gratefully and affectionately yours   OSCAR WILDE

Postcard: To Robert Ross

MS. Clark

Monday [*Postmark 12 July 1897*]   [*Postmark Dieppe*]

Dear Robbie, Don't mind about Dixon: he is absurd. Let me know about More: is he better? I never hear from you, but Bosie says you have apologised!! Is this true? I intend to write today, which accounts for the illegible scrawl I send you.   S. M.

Postcard: To Robert Ross

MS. Clark

Wednesday, 14 July [*1897*]   [*Berneval-sur-Mer*]

Hansell's letter most satisfactory, except his communicating with Hargrove, which means of course a possible estrangement between myself and Mrs Holland. If he is arbiter, he is arbiter. To inform them of his decision, previous to events contingent or not contingent, seems like giving himself away.

Your letters are as usual underpaid: I paid 50 c. yesterday: and one franc last week. Do buy a paper-weight. As you are clearly £2 in pocket by Ellis not calling at the P.O., you might send me a 25/- Waterbury watch.[1] I have no clock or watch, and the sun is always hours in advance. I rely on the unreliable moon.   S. M.

Postcard: To Robert Ross
MS. Clark

Monday [*Postmark 19 July 1897*] (*Postcard No. 1*)   [*Berneval-sur-Mer*]

Dear Robbie, What delightful news! I will expect you on August 1st. Bring dear More, if he can come. If not, bring the architect of the moon.[2] I have a lot of work on hand for *you* to do: literary work of course. Where *is* my Waterbury? I never know the time.   S. M.

Postcard: To Robert Ross
MS. Clark

Monday, 19 July [*1897*] (*Postcard No. 2*)   [*Berneval-sur-Mer*]

Dear Robbie, I should think that £50 would be enough for the insurance of my pictures. I hope to get them soon, as my chalet is bare of beauty in art with the exception of a *Vierge en bois sculpté* from the boat of an old fisherman—a lovely thing, and storm-vexed.   S. M.

Postcard: To More Adey
MS. Clark

Monday, 19 July [*1897*]   *Berneval-sur-Mer*

My dear More, Could you come over here with Robbie on August 1st? I mean, would you be well enough? Or are you going to your people? I shall be quite happy with Robbie, but of course, if you came, it would be delightful. I am still at my poem! Poetry is a difficult art, but I like most of what I have done.   S. M.

---

[1] A cheap and popular watch, manufactured at Waterbury, Connecticut. Cf. *The Picture of Dorian Gray*, chap xix: "Basil was very popular, and always wore a Waterbury watch. Why should he have been murdered?"

[2] John Rowland Fothergill (1876–1957) had studied at the Slade and was a friend of Ross, Rothenstein and other artists. At this time he was a student at the London School of Architecture, and his copy of *The Ballad of Reading Gaol* (now in the possession of his son) is inscribed "To Rowland Fothergill, the Architect of the Moon, with the compliments of the author O. W." He later spent twelve years as an archaeologist, helping his American friend Edward Perry Warren (1864–1928) to form the collection of classical antiquities in the Boston Museum of Fine Arts, and finally achieved fame as an innkeeper in England.

623

To Robert Ross

MS. Clark

20 July [1897]   *Chalet Bourgeat, Berneval-sur-Mer*

My dearest Robbie, Your excuse of "domesticity" is of course most treacherous: I have missed your letters very much. Pray write at least twice a day, and write at length. You now only write about Dixon. As regards him, tell him that the expense of bringing him to London is too heavy. I don't think I would like the type-written manuscript[1] sent to him. It might be dangerous. Better to have it done in London, scratching out Bosie's name, mine at the close, and the address. Mrs Marshall can be relied on.

The pictures, as I said, insure for £50.

As regards Bosie, I feel you have been, as usual, forbearing and sweet, and too good-tempered. What he must be made to feel is that his vulgar and ridiculous assumption of social superiority must be retracted and apologised for. I have written to him to tell him that *quand on est gentil-homme on est gentilhomme*, and that for him to try and pose as your social superior because he is the third son of a Scotch marquis and you the third son of a commoner is offensively stupid. There is no difference between gentlemen. Questions of titles are matters of heraldry—no more. I wish you would be strong on this point; the thing should be thrashed out of him. As for his coarse ingratitude in abusing you, to whom, as I have told him, I owe any possibility I have of a new and artistic career, and indeed of life at all, I have no words in which to express my contempt for his lack of imaginative insight, and his dullness of sensitive nature. It makes me quite furious. So pray write, when next you do so, quite calmly, and say that you will not allow any nonsense of social superiority and that if he cannot understand that gentlemen are gentlemen and no more, you have no desire to hear again from him.

I expect you on August the First: also, the architect.

The poem is nearly finished. Some of the verses are awfully good.

Wyndham comes here tomorrow to see me: for the adaptation of Scribe's *Le Verre d'Eau*: which of course you have to do. Bring *Esmond* with you, and any Queen Anne chairs you have: just for the style.[2]

I am so glad More is better.

The sketch of Frank Harris in *John Johns* is superb. Who wrote the book? It is a wonderful indictment.[3] Ever yours   OSCAR

---

[1] Of the letter known as *De Profundis* (see note 1, p. 614).

[2] *Le Verre d'Eau* (1840), a comedy by Eugène Scribe (1791–1861), is set at the Court of Queen Anne in London. Wilde's plan to translate and adapt it for Charles Wyndham came to nothing.

[3] *The Adventures of John Johns*, a novel by Frederic Carrel (1869–1928), published in February 1897. The central character was clearly based on Frank Harris.

Postcard: To Robert Ross

MS. Clark

20 July [*1897*]   [*Berneval-sur-Mer*]

Just closed up my letter without this important request. Will you kindly insert once in *The Times*, once in the *Daily Telegraph*, and three times in the *Manchester Guardian*, the following:

"M. Jules Hammond, late of the Foreign Legion serving in Tonkin, is earnestly requested to communicate with M. Achille Fromentin, 84th Regiment, Avesnes, Nord. Two medals are waiting for M. Jules Hammond at the Gendarmerie, Calais."

You will do a great service to one of my best friends.   S. M.[1]

To an Unidentified Correspondent[2]

MS. Clark

20 July [*1897*]   *Berneval-sur-Mer*

I have not yet heard from you which books were from your generous and gracious hand: the rose-petals are waiting to mark them.

Could you get me something in London I want very much?

Do you know that Japanese cloth of gold, made I believe of *papier mâché*, with no design on it, or with one very close to the fabric and unimportant, *not too bright*, rather dull?

If so, would you get me a piece about two yards square? I want a background to put some lithographs in *passe-partout* on—things by Shannon and Will Rothenstein—and wall-papers are dreary or hopeless. I feel that for white drawings a gold background is vital. I will nail it up on the wall, and look at the "songs in stone."

If you can do this for me, it would be most kind of you. Please send it over here, and let me know the cost, of course: I don't fancy it will be much. If gold cannot be got, could you get me a good brown in some rough material, but remember the drawings are on *white* paper. Your sincere friend   SEBASTIAN MELMOTH

Postcard: To Reginald Turner

MS. Hyde (D. & M.)

20 July [*1897*]   [*Berneval-sur-Mer*]

Mr Sebastian Melmoth would like to hear from Mr Turner on any important or unimportant matter, as soon as possible.

---

[1] The notice appeared at the top of the Personal Column of *The Times* on 22 July.

[2] Although this letter appeared in *After Reading*, in which all the other letters are addressed to Ross, it was obviously written to someone Wilde knew less well. He had already written twice to Ross on 20 July.

Postcard: To Reginald Turner

MS. Hyde (D. & M.)

[Postmark 22 July 1897]   *[Berneval-sur-Mer]*

Dear Reggie, Could you get me a little clock, for my writing table: a sort of nickel Waterbury affair. I want it to *go*: to keep time: I fancy about £1. 10 or so. I will send you a cheque on receipt. Do get it for me. Army and Navy Stores, or elsewhere: and send it at once; I never know the time now.

Pray do this before you leave.   S. M.

Postcard: To Robert Ross

MS. Clark

22 July [1897]   *Berneval-sur-Mer*

No letter from you today. I suspect that domesticity is dominating: also no Waterbury! Do send me one. The *douane* is perfectly easy. A nickel watch is what I long for. Silver is bimetallic. I never know the time, and my poem goes all wrong consequently, though it aims at eternity. Also the pictures don't arrive. I feel some other influence is ruling a youth full of promises. Wyndham is to arrive, he says, today. So you must begin to be Queen Anne style at once.   S. M.

Postcard: To Robert Ross

MS. Clark

Friday [Postmark 23 July 1897]   *[Berneval-sur-Mer]*

Just had a wire from Wyndham to say he comes over today to see me, but must leave tonight again.

Please send my pictures at once. I cannot leave them in London. Ask Chapman[1] if the pastel would not be safer without the glass. The glass is the only danger, and I can get one at Dieppe, but I am wretched without my things, and want to have my chalet like "*le home.*" Please do this.   S. M.

Postcard: To Robert Ross

MS. Clark

Saturday [Postmark 24 July 1897]   *[Berneval-sur-Mer]*

Dear Robbie, I saw Wyndham yesterday: he came for three hours, and now I feel I can do the play pretty well, as he leaves me *carte blanche* to pull it about as I like. You are quite right about Congreve. Fortunately

---

[1] Chapman Brothers were, and still are, frame-makers and picture-cleaners in King's Road, Chelsea.

he is among the books you gave me. But I like Wardour Street English very much. The cast Wyndham proposes is splendid, and if *you* work hard *I* shall have a great success. I am preparing a *salon de lecture* for you.

S. M.

To Robert Ross

MS. Clark

26 July [*1897*]   *Berneval-sur-Mer*

My dear Robbie, I wish you would not be so unkind about my pictures. I cannot go on storing them in London; it is childish. I want them here where I live. People were sweet enough to buy them in for me, and it would be ungracious and absurd to leave them in some warehouse or garret in England: they were given to me that I should have them. I have asked the frame-maker here, and he says that if paper is gummed or pasted over the glass, it will be all right. I do hope they will come this week.

Mind you arrive by the *day-boat*: 3.30 in the afternoon.

Also, do stay a long time. I have a great deal of work for you to do. *Le Verre d'Eau* must be reconstructed entirely.

I hope dear More is all right again.

I saw Aubrey at Dieppe on Saturday: he was looking very well, and in good spirits. I hope he is coming out here tomorrow to dine.[1] Smithers, the publisher, was with him: very intoxicated but amusing.[2]

Dear boy, I long for your arrival here. Ever yours   OSCAR

---

[1] This seems to refute the often-repeated accusation that Beardsley "cut" Wilde when they met in Dieppe. On the other hand there is no evidence that he accepted Wilde's invitation to dinner. Beardsley was staying at the Hôtel Sandwich with his mother, who strongly disapproved of Wilde, as did probably most of the other English people in the hotel. Moreover, Beardsley was in the last stages of consumption, and on 19 December he wrote to Smithers from Menton:

> By all means bring forth the *Peacock*. I will contribute cover and what you will, and also be editor, that is if it is *quite agreed that Oscar Wilde contributes nothing to the magazine, anonymously, pseudonymously or otherwise.*

The proposed periodical the *Peacock* never appeared.

[2] In 1891 Smithers (see p. 221) had abandoned the law in Sheffield and set up in London as bookseller and publisher. Although he was known to trade in pornography, and was reported as saying "I'll publish anything that the others are afraid of," he published, besides Wilde's last three books, the poems of Ernest Dowson and Arthur Symons, the *Savoy*, much of Aubrey Beardsley's work, and the first collected drawings of Max Beerbohm, who long afterwards described him as "a strange and rather depressing person, a north-countryman, known to have been engaged in the sale of disreputable books." Robert Ross considered him "the most delightful and irresponsible publisher I ever met." His private life was uncontrolled, and he is believed to have died of drink and drugs.

To Carlos Blacker

MS. Blacker

Thursday, 29 July [1897]   *Café Suisse, Dieppe*

Dear Friend, I am terribly distressed about what you tell me about Constance. I had no idea it was so serious.[1]

Of course she could not come here. I see that. She would require the attendance of a maid, and I have only my man-servant, and the journey would be too much.

Do you think I should go and see her in about three weeks? I really think it would be better for her to see me, and have it over. I would only stay a couple of days. I think that she is afraid I am fearfully altered. I don't think I am in appearance. My friends say I am not. Just try and advise me.

I am so glad she is with you and your charming, brilliant wife.

For myself, I really am quite heart-broken. Nemesis seems endless.

With many thanks, dear old friend, ever yours   OSCAR

To Reginald Turner

MS. Hyde (D. & M.)

Saturday [Postmark 31 July 1897]   *Berneval-sur-Mer*

My dear Reggie, The most lovely clock has arrived, and I hear it is from you. It is most sweet of you to give it to me, and you will be pleased, and perhaps astonished, to hear that though it is quite beautiful, and has a lovely face and wonderful slim restless hands, yet it is strangely punctual in all its habits, business-like in its methods, of ceaseless industry, and knows all that the sun is doing. I hope you will come here and see it. It has been greatly admired by all the inhabitants. Come any time you like. I am not responsible for the architecture of the chalet: all that I am responsible for at Berneval are the sunsets and the sea.

I don't know if you are with Bosie, but send this to his care.[2] Affectionately yours   OSCAR

To Carlos Blacker

MS. Blacker

[Postmark 4 August 1897]   *Café Suisse, Dieppe*

My dear Friend, I am simply heart-broken at what you tell me. I don't mind my life being wrecked—that is as it should be—but when I think of poor Constance I simply want to kill myself. But I suppose I must live

---

[1] Constance Wilde was already suffering from the creeping spinal paralysis which was soon to kill her.

[2] This letter is addressed to Reginald Turner, c/o Lord Alfred Douglas, Villa Myosotis, Villeville-sur-Mer, Calvados.

through it all. I don't care. Nemesis has caught me in her net: to struggle is foolish. Why is it that one runs to one's ruin? Why has destruction such a fascination? Why, when one stands on a pinnacle, must one throw oneself down? No one knows, but things are so.

Of course I think it would be much better for Constance to see me, but you think not. Well, you are wiser. My life is spilt on the sand—red wine on the sand—and the sand drinks it because it is thirsty, for no other reason.

I wish I could see you. Where I shall be in September I don't know. I don't care. I fear we shall never see each other again. But all is right: the gods hold the world on their knees. I was made for destruction. My cradle was rocked by the Fates. Only in the mire can I know peace. Ever yours   OSCAR

To Leonard Smithers

TS. Ross (A. L.)

4 August 1897   *Berneval-sur-Mer*
Strictly Private

My dear Smithers, The wonderful parcel, the prize-packet in fact, of books has just arrived, and I must send you a line at once to tell you how beautiful they are and how nice it is of you to send them to me.

I hope very much that some day I shall have something that you will like well enough to publish.

I am just off to breakfast at Martin l'Église, and tonight on my return I will look at your wonderful productions by starlight: the moon just at present is not to be relied on: indeed she never is.

Your generosity in not including Symons is much appreciated.[1] Good-bye till Saturday. Don't land with vine-leaves in your hair:[2] let us keep them for later on.

I have not had a word from Ernest Dowson, I hope he has been to see you. Sincerely yours   OSCAR WILDE

To W. R. Paton[3]

MS. Paton

[? *Early August 1897*]   *Berneval-sur-Mer*

My dear Paton, Thank you for your kind and friendly letter. I have often heard from others of your sympathy and unabated friendship.

I don't dream of social rehabilitation, nor do I want it, but I *do* want to do artistic work again, and hope to do so.

---

[1] The cause of Wilde's jokingly contemptuous attitude towards Arthur Symons (see note 2, p. 276) is unknown, but it persisted at any rate until Symons's favourable review of *The Ballad of Reading Gaol* in March 1898. See p. 716.

[2] See note, p. 612.

[3] See note 2, p. 78.

629

I have had many offers for plays, but up to this have done nothing. The shock of alien freedom is still on me, but I have many good friends, and the world is still full of beauty for me.

I have written a long poem, which, if published, I will send you. It is a new style for me, full of actuality and life in its directness of message and meaning.

I hope you are happy, and finding Greek things every day. Ever yours

OSCAR WILDE

To Ernest Dowson
MS. Martin

Tuesday, 9 [actually 10] August [1897] [*Berneval-sur-Mer*]

My dear Ernest, I send you your letters. I have not of course read them! But I have cut open the envelopes on account of the postal arrangements. I also send you your *cahiers*.[1]

I hope you will be able to send me what you owe me in a few days, as I have no money. Your bill with Monsieur Bonnet was £11, and then in Dieppe of course there were huge expenses, and I also lent you money. It comes to £19, which I hope to receive within a week, as I cannot pay Monsieur Bonnet and he is getting offensively tedious.

I have lost many pleasures in life. One is the pleasure of playing a host's part. I have not the means: nor do I know how to live at all.

Vincent O'Sullivan[2] came here on Sunday and dined: he spoke of you with much affection, in which I joined I need not tell you. Ever yours

O. W.

To Reginald Turner
MS. Hyde (D. & M.)

Tuesday 10 August [1897] [*Dieppe*]

My dear Reggie, Will you come over here on Saturday next, by the afternoon boat? Robbie is here, and we want you so much. It is quite quiet and the weather is charming. Also last night acrobats arrived. Smithers, the publisher and owner of Aubrey, comes over on Sunday and we all dine with him: then we go to Berneval.

I do not know if you know Smithers: he is usually in a large straw hat, has a blue tie delicately fastened with a diamond brooch of the impurest water—or perhaps wine, as he never touches water: it goes to his head at once. His face, clean-shaven as befits a priest who serves at the altar whose God is Literature, is wasted and pale—not with poetry, but with poets,

---

[1] Dowson had returned to England in the middle of July.

[2] Irish-American poet and novelist (1868–1940). He spent most of his life in France. His *Aspects of Wilde* (1936) is one of the most perceptive and reliable books on the subject.

who, he says, have wrecked his life by insisting on publishing with him. He loves first editions, especially of women: little girls are his passion. He is the most learned erotomaniac in Europe. He is also a delightful companion, and a dear fellow, very kind to me.

You will on arrival proceed without delay to the *Café Suisse*, where Robbie and I will be waiting for you.

If you don't come I shall be quite wretched. I long to see you again. Ever yours   OSCAR

Postcard: To Reginald Turner

MS. Hyde (D. & M.)

Wednesday, 11 August [*1897*]   [*Postmark Dieppe*]

Dear Reggie, I hope you got my letter all right, and that we shall see you on Saturday. By my elaborate description of Smithers you are certain not to recognise him. Bring over your play, and let me hear it. Ever yours
O. W.

To Will Rothenstein

MS. Rothenstein

14 August 1897   *Berneval-sur-Mer*

My dear Will, I don't know if the enclosed will suit. If so, pray use it.[1] Also don't forget to come and see me as soon as possible. I simply long for your delightful companionship. Robbie Ross and Sherard are here at present: the latter goes away today. We all go to Dieppe to dine with Smithers. Ever yours   O. W.

He founded a school, and has survived all his disciples. He has always thought too much about himself, which is wise; and written too much about others, which is foolish. His prose is the beautiful prose of a poet, and his poetry the beautiful poetry of a prose-writer. His personality is insistent. To converse with him is a physical no less than an intellectual recreation. He is never forgotten by his enemies, and often forgiven by his friends. He has added several new words to the language, and his style is an open secret. He has fought a good fight, and has had to face every difficulty except popularity.

!!! !!!

To Reginald Turner

MS. Hyde (D. & M.)

[? *Mid-August 1897*]   *Café des Tribunaux, Dieppe*

My dear Reggie, I woke up this morning with a dreadful cold—voice quite

[1] Rothenstein's book *English Portraits* (1898) consisted of twenty-four lithographed drawings, with a brief note on each sitter. These were anonymous and by different hands; Wilde had been asked to describe W. E. Henley.

gone, and endless coughing—so I cannot see you from the pier as I had hoped.[1]

I dined last night with a curious fellow called Hubert Byron,[2] who is living here with a gold-haired pianist, and a violet-haired secretary. The latter is very beautiful. It was an Hellenic evening.

Love to Eugene. Ever yours   OSCAR

To Ernest Dowson
MS. Martin

18 August [*1897*]   *Berneval-sur-Mer*

My dear Ernest, I think your translating *Aphrodite*[3] a capital idea: I do hope you will get someone to make good terms for you. Why not Smithers? The Bacchic, the Dionysiac!

You should make a lot of money by royalties. The book, if well puffed, might be a great *succès*.

Robbie Ross is here with me, and Sherard left on Saturday. Smithers is devoted, and breakfasts here every Monday. I like him immensely. He is a most interesting and, in some respects, a charming personality.

I have not yet finished my poem, but I hope to do so soon. I wrote four splendid stanzas yesterday. I am going to try and get a lot of money for it from the *New York World*. Robert Sherard will, he says, arrange it for me.

Vincent O'Sullivan has been twice here to dine. I *now* like him. At first I loathed him.

As for the cheque: I know, dear Ernest, you will send it as soon as you can. I scramble on somehow, and hope to survive the season. After that, Tunis, rags, and hashish! Ever yours   OSCAR

To Will Rothenstein
MS. Rothenstein

Friday [? *20 August 1897*]   *Café Suisse* [*Dieppe*]

Dearest Will, I knew you would get nervous. I told you so. Therefore either let me have back my appreciation of W. E. H., which will be useful to me in a thing I have been asked to do—*Artistic London,* notes on notabilities and mediocrities. *Or,* if you still want it, get someone else to do Henley from the *outside* point of view, just the account of what he has done. His editorship of the periodicals, his plays with R. L. S. etc.

[1] Turner was landing at Dieppe on his way to stay at Bois Guillaume, near Rouen, whence he wrote on 24 August to Max Beerbohm (MS. Reichmann): "I may go to Berneval at the end of my stay here when the 'quality' have left Dieppe."
[2] Unidentified.
[3] By Pierre Louÿs. (See note 6, p. 298.) Dowson did not translate it into English.

Mine you will call

W. E. Henley
by
A Private Admirer

the other

W. E. Henley
by
A National Observer.

Of course *mine* must come *last*: and the "National Observer" must confine himself to the *facts* of his life. This is the only solution.

I have nearly finished my own poem; and like it awfully. Ever yours

OSCAR

To Leonard Smithers

MS. Clark

Sunday, 22 August 1897   *Chalet Bourgeat, Berneval-sur-Mer*

My dear Smithers, I look forward to seeing you on Saturday, and thank you for your kind letters.

Your wife, whose sweetness and kindness to me I shall never forget, came out to tea on Wednesday: the Stannards and Dal and others were here. I don't think you will do much with Dal's art, but Anquetin is a different thing:[1] however *Les Trois Mousquetaires* is too *obvious*, and Stanley Weyman has rewritten Dumas for the British public—I must say, very well indeed. From what Thaulow tells me (I dined on Friday with him) Anquetin's art is at his best with nymph and satyr; he is a sort of erotic Michael Angelo. Would an edition of Beckford be any use? Perhaps you have already done one.

Will Rothenstein, as I expected, is too nervous to publish my little appreciation of Henley. He says he is the editor of "a *paying* magazine." That seems a degrading position for any man to occupy. I have recommended Symons: he will do just what is unnecessary: it is his *métier*.

I enclose you a letter for Daly, which you can read. I don't feel really at liberty to take his money, though I would like it. I have never done that sort of thing, and I can't begin. It is merely the weakness of the criminal classes that makes me refuse.

Conder is now a *vineyard*: the Youngs are very serious about him, and there is a moral atmosphere about Dieppe that you should come over and dissipate. Sincerely yours   OSCAR WILDE

---

[1] Louis Anquetin (1861–1932), French painter. A close friend of Conder, whom he greatly influenced.

633

To Augustin Daly

MS. Harvard

22 August 1897   *Chalet Bourgeat, Berneval-sur-Mer*

Dear Mr Daly, I am very much flattered by your kind offer, and I would like extremely to write a play some day for that brilliant and fascinating genius, Ada Rehan, whose own art is supreme on the English-speaking stage: it is rare to find such a personality combined with such perfection of artistic effect and method.

But I have great claims on me—from George Alexander, and from Wyndham—and though they are not legal claims, I feel bound, perhaps for that very reason, to regard them as paramount at present, and if I took your money, I know I would simply have to return it in three months.

But I will always remember your offer, and, later on, I hope to think out something that you will like. I am not yet in train for work, and have only done a poem, unfinished up to today. Later on I hope to get back the concentration of will-power that conditions and governs art, and to produce something good again.

In any case let me thank you again for your generous offer, by which I am much touched: and, believe me, truly yours   OSCAR WILDE

I enclose a card with my *name* here, and address, in case you have occasion to write.

To Mrs Leonard Smithers

F. Keller

Monday, 23 [August] 1897   *Berneval-sur-Mer*

Dear Mrs Smithers, Thank you so much for the great sweetness and kindness you have shown me during your stay at Dieppe. I hope to see you again somewhere, either in London or Paris, and to have before that done something good in art.

I had a charming letter from your husband yesterday, and look forward to seeing him on Saturday. Believe me, very sincerely yours

OSCAR WILDE

To Robert Ross

MS. Clark

Tuesday, 24 August [1897]   *Berneval-sur-Mer*

My dearest Robbie, Thanks for the cheque. I have sent it to the Dieppe bank.

My poem is still unfinished, but I have made up my mind to finish it this afternoon, and send it to be type-written. Once I see it, even type-written, I shall be able to correct it: *now* I am tired of the manuscript.

Do you think this verse good? I fear it is out of harmony, but wish you were here to talk about it. I miss you dreadfully, dear boy.

> The Governor was strong upon
> The Regulation Act:
> The Doctor said that Death was but
> A scientific fact;
> And twice a day the Chaplain called
> And left a little Tract.

It is, of course, about the condemned man's life before his execution. I have got in "latrine:" it looks beautiful.

Since Bosie wrote that he could not afford forty francs to come to Rouen to see me, he has never written. Nor have I. I am greatly hurt by his meanness and lack of imagination. Ever yours   OSCAR

To Leonard Smithers[1]

24 August 1897   *Dieppe*

Will you do me a great favour and have the poem I send you type-written for me, and bring it over with you on Saturday, or, if you cannot come, send it by post to Sebastian Melmoth, c/o Hôtel Sandwich, Dieppe, where I shall be? I want it done on good paper, *not* tissue paper, and bound in a brown paper cover. It is not yet finished, but I want to see it type-written. I am sick of my manuscript.[2]

To Will Rothenstein
MS. Rothenstein

24 August 1897   *Berneval-sur-Mer*

My dear Will, Of course I only did it to oblige you.[3] My name was not to be appended, nor was there to be any honorarium of any kind. It was to

[1] The text of this fragment is taken from Mason (p. 410), quoting from Glaenzer.
[2] On 2 September Smithers answered from London (text from Mason, p. 410):

My dear Wilde, I yesterday sent you back your poem. I showed it to Aubrey and he seemed to be much struck by it. He promised at once to do a frontispiece for it—in a manner which immediately convinced me that he will never do it. He has got tired already of *Mlle de Maupin* and talks of *Casanova* instead. It seems hopeless to try and get any connected work out of him of any kind.

I left Conder on Tuesday night in a worse state than I have ever yet seen him. He got a small cheque on Tuesday morning and we devoted the whole of Tuesday to spending it. His bill at the Sandwich bar is now colossal.

My leg has become so painful that it is an impossibility for me to walk, our appointment for Rouen must therefore stand another week.

At your convenience send me either the typewritten copy or the manuscript of your poem, for me to send you a proof. Yours very sincerely
                                                    LEONARD SMITHERS
[3] See note p. 631. The note on W. E. Henley was eventually written by Max Beerbohm.

oblige you I did it, but with me, as with you, as with all artists, one's work *est à prendre ou à laisser*. I couldn't go into the details of coarse and notorious facts. I know Henley edited the *National Observer*, and was a very bitter and in some respects a cowardly journalist in his conduct. I get the *National Review*[1] regularly, and its dullness and stupidity are beyond words. I am only concerned with the essence of the man, not with his accidents, miry or other.

When I said of W. E. H. that his prose was the prose of a poet, I paid him an undeserved compliment. His prose is jerky, spasmodic, and he is incapable of the beautiful architecture of a long sentence, which is the fine flower of prose-writing, but I praised him for the sake of antithesis: "his poetry is the beautiful poetry of a prose-writer:" that refers to Henley's finest work: the Hospital Poems, which are in *vers libres*, and *vers libres* are prose. The author by dividing the lines shows you the rhythm he wishes you to follow. But all that one is concerned with is *literature*. Poetry is not finer than prose, nor prose finer than poetry. When one uses the words poetry and prose, one is merely referring to certain technical modes of word-music, melody and harmony one might say, though they are not exclusive terms, and though I praised Henley too much, too extravagantly, when I said his prose was the beautiful prose of a poet, the latter part of the sentence is a subtle aesthetic appreciation of his *vers libres*, which W. E. H., if he has any critical faculty left, would be the first to appreciate! You seem to me to have misunderstood the sentence. Mallarmé would understand it. But the matter is of no importance. Everybody is greedy of common panegyrics, and W. E. H. would much sooner have a long list of his literary failures chronicled with dates.

I am still here, though the wind blows terribly. Your lovely lithographs are on my walls, and you will be pleased to hear that I do not propose to ask you to alter them, though I am *not* the editor of a "paying publication."

I am delighted to hear the Monticelli is sold, though Obach does not say for how much.[2] Dal Young is coming out here tomorrow and I will tell him. He seems to be under the impression that he bought it. Of course I know nothing about the facts of the case.

Robbie Ross had to go back to England on Thursday last, and I fear will not be able to come again this year.

I don't know where I shall go myself. I am not in the mood to do the work I want, and I fear I shall never be. The intense energy of creation has been kicked out of me. I don't care now to struggle to get back what, when I had it, gave me little pleasure. Ever yours   O. W.

---

[1] A slip for the *New Review*, which Henley edited from 1895 to 1898.
[2] A picture by the French painter Adolphe Joseph Thomas Monticelli (1824–86), which had belonged to Wilde. At the Tite Street sale (see note 2, p. 394) Rothenstein bought it for £8, and now sold it for Wilde's benefit. Obach was a picture-dealer in Cockspur Street, London. His business, founded in 1855, was in 1911 merged with that of Messrs Colnaghi.

To Lord Alfred Douglas

MS. Clark

Tuesday, 7.30 [? 31 August 1897]   *Café Suisse, Dieppe*

My own Darling Boy, I got your telegram half an hour ago, and just send you a line to say that I feel that my only hope of again doing beautiful work in art is being with you. It was not so in old days, but now it is different, and you can really recreate in me that energy and sense of joyous power on which art depends. Everyone is furious with me for going back to you, but they don't understand us. I feel that it is only with you that I can do anything at all. Do remake my ruined life for me, and then our friendship and love will have a different meaning to the world.

I wish that when we met at Rouen we had not parted at all.[1] There are such wide abysses now of space and land between us. But we love each other. Goodnight, dear. Ever yours   OSCAR

Postcard: To Will Rothenstein

MS. Rothenstein

2 September [1897]   *Berneval-sur-Mer*

My dear Will, Thanks so much for the cheque for £15 which was most welcome.[2] When will you come and see me? I think of going south, if I can manage it, in a fortnight. Ever yours   OSCAR

To Leonard Smithers

MS. Private

[4 September 1897]

My dear Smithers, The poem arrived quite safe, and I am very much obliged to you for sending it to me.[3]

As regards Aubrey, I wish you could get him to make a definite reply; there is no use his hedging. If he will do it, it will be a great thing: if not, why not try some of the *jeunes Belges*—Khnoppf for example.[4] I want something curious—a design of Death and Sin walking hand in hand, very severe, and mediaeval. Also, for the divisions between the separate parts of each canto of the ballad, I want not asterisks, nor lines, but a little design of three flowers, or some decorative motive, simple and severe: then there are five or six initial letters—H: F: I: I: I: T. I hope to really finish the poem by Tuesday next. I have had to add several verses.

[1] This fateful meeting seems to have taken place on August 28–29. In his *Autobiography* Douglas wrote: "Poor Oscar cried when I met him at the station. We walked about all day arm in arm, or hand in hand, and were perfectly happy."
[2] Part of the proceeds of the sale of the Monticelli (see note 2, p. 636).
[3] See note 2, p. 635.
[4] Fernand Khnoppf (1858–1921), Belgian painter, engraver and sculptor. He was a great admirer of the Pre-Raphaelites.

I am off to *Rouen*—Hôtel d'Angleterre—I wish to goodness you were with me.

I have not seen Conder or my twenty francs, and Ernest Dowson is quite silent. I have also just lent a French poet forty francs to take him back to Paris. He is very grateful, and says he will send me a sonnet in three days! Personally I am penniless, so you should come to Rouen to give me food. Ever yours   O. W.

To Robert Ross
MS. Clark

4 September 1897   *Café Suisse, Dieppe*

My dearest Robbie, The pictures arrived safe.

I am delighted you have come back, as you will now be able to join me in *Rouen*—Hôtel d'Angleterre. I go in half an hour. I simply cannot stand Berneval. I nearly committed suicide there last Thursday—I was so bored.

I have not yet finished my poem! I really want you. I have got in about the kiss of Caiaphas: it is very good.

I am going at Rouen to try to rewrite my *Love and Death—Florentine Tragedy*.

Yes: I saw Bosie, and of course I love him as I always did, with a sense of tragedy and ruin. He was on his best behaviour, and very sweet.

Do come to Rouen at once. Ever yours   OSCAR

To Will Rothenstein
MS. Rothenstein

[? *4 September 1897*]   *Café Suisse, Dieppe*

Dear Will, I am going to *Rouen*—Hôtel d'Angleterre—for a week. The weather at Berneval is too British for anything.

Do try and come for a few days. Reggie Turner is there, and you need not make a lithograph of him.   OSCAR

To Carlos Blacker
MS. Blacker

Monday [*Postmark 6 September 1897*]   *Grand Hôtel de France, Rouen*

My dear Carlos, The weather has been so dreadful at Berneval that I have come here, where the weather is much worse. I cannot stay in the North of Europe; the climate kills me. I don't mind being alone when there is sunlight, and a *joie de vivre* all about me, but my last fortnight at Berneval has been black and dreadful, and quite suicidal. I have never been so unhappy. I am trying to get some money to go to Italy, and hope to be able to find my way to Sicily, but the expenses of travelling are frightening. I don't suppose I shall see you before I go, as I think you said you could

638

Ernest Dowson

Carlos Blacker
by Johnston Forbes-Robertson

not come to France before the end of September, and the journey from Basle is, I suppose, very long and tedious.

I am greatly disappointed that Constance has not asked me to come and see the children. I don't suppose now I shall ever see them. Ever yours

OSCAR

Write to me at Berneval-sur-Mer.

To Carlos Blacker

MS. Blacker

Monday [Postmark 13 September 1897]   *Café des Tribunaux, Dieppe*

My dear Carlos, I leave here tomorrow for Paris, and will then I hope start for Italy, if I can raise the money.

My address in Paris is Sebastian Melmoth, Hôtel d'Espagne, Rue Taitbout. I cannot write here: the cold weather, the *ennui*, the dreary English, are all paralysing.

I have been obliged to decline Wyndham's offer. I simply have no heart to write clever comedy, and I feel it is best to tell him so. It is a great disappointment to me, but it cannot be helped.

If I cannot write in Italy, where can I write? It is my only chance.

You are really wrong in your views on the question of my going there. It is not perversity but unhappiness that makes me turn my steps to the South. I will write fully to you later on. Ever yours   OSCAR

To Dalhousie Young[1]

14 September 1897   *Café des Tribunaux, Dieppe*

My dear Young, I shall be in Paris tomorrow for three or four days; Sebastian Melmoth, Hôtel d'Espagne, Rue Taitbout, and would like to see you. I would also like to make some agreement about the libretto of *Daphnis and Chloe*, if you still desire it.[2]

I would ask you £100 down, and £50 *on production*, and I could go to work on it at once. I am on my way to Italy, where I hope to give myself up entirely to literature. Here there are too many people I know. Hoping to see you, believe me, sincerely yours   OSCAR WILDE

To Leonard Smithers

MS. Taylor

Tuesday [Postmark 14 September 1897]   *Café des Tribunaux, Dieppe*

My dear Smithers, It has been a great blow not seeing you again. I hope your leg is better.

[1] Text from *Resurgam* (1917).
[2] There is no record of such an opera or other work by Dalhousie Young.

I leave here for Paris tomorrow—address Sebastian Melmoth, Hôtel d'Espagne, Rue Taitbout, Paris—and from there I want to get on to Naples, in three days. At Naples I intend to finish my poem, and begin my play. I have now only three stanzas to add to the poem, and I intend, by the advice of Clyde Fitch, to ask the *New York Journal* for £200. In the meanwhile I am, of course, fearfully hard up. I suppose you are the same, but could you advance me £20 on my poem? I think I am sure to get at least £100 from the New York paper. They offered £1000 for an interview, so for poetry they could not give less than £100. If you can do this I would of course tell Pinker[1] to hand you over whatever sum he gets for the poem, and you could send me the balance. But if you can do this, will you let me have the £20 *at once*, to Paris. I don't want to stay in Paris: I want to get away to Italy, but must have money. Sincerely yours   OSCAR WILDE

Postcard: To Reginald Turner

MS. Hyde (D. & M.)

Wednesday [Postmark 15 September 1897]   *Dieppe*

Am leaving today for Hôtel d'Espagne, Rue Taitbout, Paris. Then, in three days, Hôtel Grande Bretagne, Naples. Do write to me. How is Eugene? Why does he not acknowledge his *portefeuille*?   S. M.

---

[1] James Brand Pinker (1863–1922), one of the first of the literary agents.

PART EIGHT

NAPLES

1897-98

PART EIGHT
Naples: 1897-98

The only record of Wilde's journey from Berneval to Naples is that given by Vincent O'Sullivan in his *Aspects of Wilde* (1936):

One day at the end of that summer, after he had come to Paris, I received a letter from him. He asked if I was in Paris, and if I were would I come to see him.

The next day I went about twelve o'clock to the address given—an hotel in the rue du Helder, just off the Boulevard. He was expecting a friend of his named Rowland Strong.[1] After waiting about a quarter of an hour, seeing that Strong did not turn up, he left a letter for him and we went out to lunch.

In the cab, I asked him who was Rowland Strong? He said he was an English journalist—the Paris correspondent, I think he said, of some London paper, and, what he seemed to think more important, a descendant on his mother's side of Chateaubriand. He seemed in very good spirits and launched out into a description of Strong's valet, an elderly man, who, he said, was the extreme type of the English well-trained servant. When Strong heard that Verlaine was dying, as he did not care to go himself to the mean street and the squalid abode, he sent this man to get news. The valet returned imperturbable.

"Well?" asked Strong.

"I saw the gentleman, sir, and he died immediately."

As Wilde finished this story we arrived at the restaurant, a restaurant chosen by himself, which still exists at the moment of writing, up a flight of stairs over a passage giving on the Boulevard Montmartre, having somehow survived the drastic overhauling of Paris since the war. It was a kind of restaurant where nobody would recognize Wilde, and he did not want to be recognized.

Towards the end of the meal he said that he was rather troubled—as well as I remember, he said he was "passing through a crisis." It seemed that some friends of his family in England wanted him to go into a mountain village and write plays. This, it may be said in passing, was

---

[1] 1865–1924. Paris correspondent of the *New York Times*, *Observer* and *Morning Post*. Said to have been a fervent anti-Semite. Author of successful book, *Where and How to Dine in Paris* (1900). Brother of T. Banks Strong (1861–1944), Bishop of Oxford 1925–37.

a most stupid suggestion which took no account of the havoc wrought in his brain and nerves by his trial and imprisonment. What he required was to forget, to be stimulated, distracted from his black thoughts. How could he find that in a mountain village? It would have continued the penal cell. He himself was inclined to go to Italy.

He talked of all this for some time, giving details, some of which it was hard for me to follow from lack of knowledge of the elements of the matter. So far as I remember, the main difficulty was that his wife's friends and relations wanted to keep him from rejoining Lord Alfred Douglas, who was at Naples. Then he added: "I am not telling all this to you because I want advice. I have thought it all out and I would not take advice from anyone." I assured him that nothing was farther from my thoughts than to offer him advice. That indeed was so, both because I should have thought it presumptuous to offer advice to a man so much beyond me both in years and achievement, and also because it was utterly indifferent to me what he did or where he went.

Finally he declared: "I shall go to Italy tonight. Or rather, I would go, but I am in an absurd position. I have no money."

Upon leaving the restaurant we drove to the Banque de Paris et des Pays-Bas in the rue d'Antin where I had an account. He stayed in the cab and I brought him out the sum he wanted. It is one of the few things I look back on with satisfaction. It is not every day that one has the chance of relieving the anxiety of a genius and a hero. I think he left Paris the same evening; certainly very soon.

To Robert Ross

MS. Clark

Tuesday, 21 September 1897   *Hôtel Royal des Étrangers, Naples*

My dearest Robbie, Your letter has reached me here.

My going back to Bosie was psychologically inevitable: and, setting aside the interior life of the soul with its passion for self-realisation at all costs, the world forced it on me.

I cannot live without the atmosphere of Love: I must love and be loved, whatever price I pay for it. I could have lived all my life with you, but you have other claims on you—claims you are too sweet a fellow to disregard—and all you could give me was a week of companionship. Reggie gave me three days, and Rowland[1] a sextette of suns, but for the last month at Berneval I was so lonely that I was on the brink of killing myself. The world shuts its gateway against me, and the door of Love lies open.

When people speak against me for going back to Bosie, tell them that he offered me love, and that in my loneliness and disgrace I, after three months' struggle against a hideous Philistine world, turned naturally to him. Of course I shall often be unhappy, but still I love him: the mere fact that he wrecked my life makes me love him. "*Je t'aime parce que tu m'as perdu*" is

[1] John Rowland Fothergill (see note 2, p. 623).

644

the phrase that ends one of the stories[1] in *Le Puits de Sainte Claire*—Anatole France's book—and it is a terrible symbolic truth.

We hope to get a little villa or apartments somewhere, and I hope to do work with him. I think I shall be able to do so. I think he will be kind to me; I only ask that. So do let people know that my only hope of life or literary activity was in going back to the young man whom I loved before with such tragic issue to my name.

No more today. Ever yours   OSCAR

To Dalhousie Young[2]

Tuesday, 21 September 1897   *Hôtel Royal des Étrangers, Naples*

My dear Young, I do not know if your letter and cheque have gone astray, or if they have not yet been sent. I left my address with the hotel people in Paris, but nothing has as yet arrived, so I have just telegraphed to you.

Naples is grey with pouring rain, as elsewhere, I believe, but I am beginning to work. I hope you will send me some idea, or example, of the sort of recitative prose will suit best for music, also how many voices—kind of voices—you propose to use.[3] I think of this:

Daphnis—Tenor
Shepherd—Baritone
Priest of Venus—Bass
Chloe—Soprano
Venus—Contralto

and, besides the general chorus permanent on the stage, a chorus of treble voices—shepherd-lads, who would come on about half through the opera (when Chloe is deserted by Daphnis, they beg her to return to the sheepfold). Does this commend itself to you?

I enclose you one of the lyrics, so that you can begin. I fancy I could finish the thing in six weeks, but if you have not sent me yet the £100 agreed on, pray do so, as I am living here without any money, and want to move into apartments at Posilippo as soon as possible.

I often think of our charming evenings at Dieppe, and of your wife's kindness and your own to me, and look forward to seeing you both again next year unless you come out here before that.

Pray give my kind regards to Mrs Young. Believe me, ever yours

OSCAR WILDE

---

[1] "*L'Humaine Tragédie.*" The book was published in 1895.
[2] Text from *Resurgam*.
[3] For the proposed *Daphnis and Chloe* (see note 2, p. 639). It seems clear, from the references on pp. 646 and 755, that at least some of the lyrics were to have been written by Douglas.

Postcard: To Robert Ross

MS. Clark

Wednesday, 22 [September] 1897   *Naples*

A lovely day: we are going to Posilippo. I am quite happy. Hope you got my letter of yesterday, and that you will tell people what I asked you to tell them. Please write soon, and tell me all the news.   S. M.

To Dalhousie Young[1]

Wednesday, 22 September 1897   *Hôtel Royal des Étrangers, Naples*

My dear Young, Your telegram arrived last night, and I am much obliged to you for your quick response. The "critical situation" was, of course, our entire lack of money. The £100 will solve the difficulty and give me the chance to work.

I forgot to say in my letter of yesterday that, of course, you must have at least *one* ballet, and shepherd dance, so you can work at that without words, as soon as you have set the lyric to music. I hope you like the lyric. I think it quite lovely.

With regard to the copyright of the words: when they are published *with* the music, the profits, if any, should be Bosie's and mine, and, of course, he reserves the right to publish his lyrics in his next volume; in fact, they are a gift to me, so, while I use them, I cannot sell them.

Today the weather is charming, and we are going to Posilippo. Ever yours   OSCAR WILDE

Do you take the *Saturday Review*? If so, I wish you would let me see it after you have done with it. I can find no English paper here except the *Morning Post*.

To Stanley V. Makower[2]

MS. Bridge

22 September 1897   *Hôtel Royal des Étrangers, Naples*

My dear Stanley, I think your book intensely interesting: a most subtle analysis of the relations between music and a soul: I know nothing else in literature where this *motif* is treated with anything like your skill of analysis and power of presentation.

[1] Text from *Resurgam*.

[2] Stanley Victor Makower (1872–1911), English writer and music critic. As an undergraduate he helped Oswald Sickert and Edward Marsh to edit the *Cambridge Observer* (see note 2, p. 313). He was a member of the *Yellow Book* group, contributing stories and one of the earliest studies of Yvette Guilbert. His first novel, *The Mirror of Music* (1895), which had appeared in John Lane's Keynotes series, is the book in question here. In the *Musician* of 30 June 1897 Ernest Newman wrote "Finer even than Balzac's portraiture of the musical mind is that of Mr Stanley V. Makower in *The Mirror of Music*." Makower's other novels were *Cecilia* (1897) and *The Outward Appearance* (1912).

It is a very remarkable book, and should be translated into French. I wish you would send a copy to Henry Davray,[1] 33 Avenue d'Orléans, Paris. He has just translated Meredith's *Essay on Comedy* for the *Mercure de France*, and is a charming fellow besides being a good English scholar.

I hope you are writing more. How is dear Oswald?[2] I often think of those charming days on which I saw you both: you were both so sweet and nice to me.

I intend to winter here, if all goes well. I love the place: it is, to me, full of Dorian and Ionian airs.

My poem I have not yet sent off, and I find it difficult to recapture the mood and manner of its inception. It seems alien to me now—real passions so soon become unreal—and the actual facts of one's life take different shape and remould themselves strangely. Still, it must be finished. Then I turn to the Drama.

I hope you will still write me a line sometime to tell me of your work and yourself, and that Oswald will do the same. My address will be always Sebastian Melmoth. Sincerely yours   OSCAR WILDE

To Carlos Blacker
MS. Blacker

Thursday, 23 September [*1897*]   *Hôtel Royal des Étrangers, Naples*

My dear Carlos, Your letter was forwarded to me here from Paris. I will go and see Constance in October.

I know that all you have written to me about my coming here comes from the sympathy and loyalty of your great generous heart, and I am sorry that my being here gives you pain. It gives pain to most of my friends: but I cannot help it: I must remake my maimed life on my own lines. Had Constance allowed me to see my boys, my life would, I think, have been quite different. But this she would not do. I don't in any way venture to blame her for her action, but every action has its consequence.

I waited three months. At the expiration of that long, lonely time, I had to take my life into my own hands.

I intend to winter here. Perhaps live here. Much depends of course on my ability to write again.

You must not, dear Carlos, pass harsh judgments on me, whatever you may hear. It is not for pleasure that I come here, though pleasure, I am glad to say, walks all round. I come here to try to realise the perfection of my temperament and my soul. We have all to choose our own methods. I have chosen mine. My friends in England are greatly distressed. Still, they are good friends to me: and will remain so, most of them at any rate. You must remain so too. Ever yours   OSCAR

[1] French author, journalist, anglophile and translator from the English (1873–1944). For many years he was in charge of foreign literature in the *Mercure de France*. His *Oscar Wilde: La Tragédie Finale* was published in 1928.

[2] Sickert. See p. 313.

To Reginald Turner

MS. Hyde (D. & M.)

[*Postmark 23 September 1897*] *Hôtel Royal des Étrangers, Naples*

My dear Reggie, Bosie and I came here on Monday: we met at Aix: and spent a day at Genoa.

Much that you say in your letter is right, but still you leave out of consideration the great love I have for Bosie. I love him, and have always loved him. He ruined my life, and for that very reason I seem forced to love him more: and I think that now I shall do lovely work. Bosie is himself a poet, far the first of all the young poets of England, an exquisite artist in lyric and ballad. It is to a poet that I am going back. So when people say how dreadful of me to return to Bosie, do say *no*—say that I love him, that he is a poet, and that, after all, whatever my life may have been ethically, it has always been *romantic*, and Bosie is my romance. My romance is a tragedy of course, but it is none the less a romance, and he loves me very dearly, more than he loves or can love anyone else, and without him my life was dreary.

So stick up for us, Reggie, and be nice.

I had a charming letter from Eugene, for which thank him. Ever yours

OSCAR

Postcard: To Robert Ross

MS. Clark

Saturday, 25 September [*1897*] [*Naples*]

Dear Robbie, An Italian here (age twenty-five), a writer, is anxious to translate *Salome*. I have no copy, nor has Bosie. Would you *lend* me yours? It would be very good of you, and I would return it honourably. I hope to have *Salome* played here in the winter.

To Dalhousie Young[1]

Saturday, 25 September 1897 *Hôtel Royal des Étrangers, Naples*

My dear Young, I have given you a great deal of trouble, but I did not like a cheque in my own name. Of course, people already know here who I am, but I would not like to approach a strange banker with my own name on a cheque. Also, as you said the cheque would be your wife's, I did not like my name to be in her pass-book, or go through her account or yours, for that matter. Besides all these reasons—absurd I daresay—a cheque at Naples takes ten or eleven days to cash, and I am at a hotel of absurd prices, which I am anxious to leave at once. We have taken a villa at Posilippo—the Villa Giudice, Via Posilippo, Napoli—where pray write for the future. I enclose cheque, which for fear of accidents I have defaced.

[1] Text from *Resurgam*.

I was greatly relieved to get your telegram last night, and hope to touch the money on Monday; tomorrow the office is closed. Believe me, truly yours OSCAR WILDE

To Robert Ross

MS. Clark

Friday [1 October 1897]　　　　　　*Villa Giudice, Posilippo, Naples*

Dearest Robbie, I have not answered your letters, because they distressed me and angered me, and I did not wish to write to *you* of all people in the world in an angry mood. You have been such a good friend to me. Your love, your generosity, your care of me in prison and out of prison are the most lovely things in my life. Without you what would I have done? As you remade my life for me you have a perfect right to say what you choose to me, but I have no right to say anything to you except to tell you how grateful I am to you, and what a pleasure it is to feel gratitude and love at the same time for the same person.

I daresay that what I have done is fatal, but it had to be done. It was necessary that Bosie and I should come together again; I saw no other life for myself. For himself he saw no other: all we want now is to be let alone, but the Neapolitan papers are tedious and wish to interview me, etc. They write nicely of me, but I don't want to be written about. I want peace— that is all. Perhaps I shall find it.

Now to literature. Of course I want you to help me.

I have sent Smithers my poem with directions for a type-written copy to be sent at once to *you*: please send me any suggestions and criticisms that occur to you.

Also, see Smithers, and *Pinker*: Pinker lives at Effingham House. I must have £300 at least—more, if possible. The poem is to be published simultaneously in the *New York Journal* and by *Smithers*. I think bits of the poem very good now, but I will never again out-Kipling Henley.

Bosie has written three lovely sonnets, which I have called "The Triad of the Moon"—they are quite wonderful.[1] He has sent them to Henley. I have also got him to send his sonnet on Mozart to the *Musician*.[2]

Tomorrow I begin the *Florentine Tragedy*. After that I must tackle *Pharaoh*.[3]

We have a lovely villa over the sea; and a nice piano. I take lessons in Italian conversation from Rocco three times a week.

My handwriting is now dreadful, as bad as yours. Ever yours　OSCAR

[1] They were included in Douglas's second volume of poems, *The City of the Soul* (1899), which was published anonymously.

[2] A weekly magazine which ran only from 12 May to 17 November 1897. No poem by Douglas appeared in it. For the sonnet on Mozart, see p. 657.

[3] André Gide reported that when he visited Wilde at Berneval he was shown the chalet; "*C'est là qu'il veut écrire ses drames*; *son* Pharaon *d'abord, puis un* Achab et Jésabel (*Il prononce* Isabelle) *qu'il raconte merveilleusement.*" Nothing of either play seems ever to have got on to paper. One of Wilde's unwritten prose-poems (see note 3, p. 809) is about Jezebel.

To Reginald Turner

MS. Hyde (D & M.)

[? *Circa 1 October 1897*][1]   [*Naples*]

Dear Reggie, Could you get me a loan of a *Salome*? A young Italian poet wishes to translate it, and I have no copy. I hope to have it produced here in the winter. You and Eugene must come out for the first night.

I will return the copy at once. I will have it type-written, so that it will not pass into the young poet's hands, as poets return nothing but love—and not always that.

I have sent my poem at last to Smithers. Do call on him and discuss things with him. I want it published simultaneously in the *New York Journal* and by Smithers. I am going to ask huge sums from America.

The weather is charming, and we hope to go to Capri for a few days. Our address is Villa Giudice, Posilippo, Napoli.

Robbie has written me three unkind and detestable letters, but he is such a dear, and I love him so much, that I have accepted them meekly. Ever yours   OSCAR

To Leonard Smithers

MS. Private

Friday [?*1 October 1897*]   *Villa Giudice, Posilippo*
[*Postmark of receipt 11 October 1897*]

Dear Smithers, Your letter has just arrived, and as the enclosure seems to have slipped out I wired at once to you to ask you to *telegraph* the £20 through Cook's office. I do hope you will do so. The crisis is of a grave and usual character—were it unique I would not feel so agitated.

I have decided long ago that I would not send my poem to the *Chronicle*, as it is far too long for a paper. It is now 600 lines almost, so Symons need not prophesy—he is unnecessary.

I am going to ask £300 for my poem from America! It is well worth it. Do at once send me specimen type.

Also have you good initial letters? Let me see them. By spacing the intervals of the poem well I think it will be almost a book. Wherever a space occurs one should have a fresh page—begin a fresh page.

One can always fall back on vegetable parchment for a cover; it is rather nice really, and is very good for jam and poetry.

How *can* you keep on asking is Lord Alfred Douglas in Naples? You know quite well he is—we are together. He understands me and my art, and loves both. I hope never to be separated from him. He is a most delicate and exquisite poet, besides—far the finest of all the young poets in England. You have got to publish his next volume; it is full of lovely

---

[1] This letter is in an envelope postmarked 8 October 1897, but its contents suggest an earlier date.

lyrics, flute-music and moon-music, and sonnets in ivory and gold. He is witty, graceful, lovely to look at, loveable to be with. He has also ruined my life, so I can't help loving him—it is the only thing to do.

My wife's letter came too late. I had waited four months in vain, and it was only when the children had gone back to school that she asked me to come to her—whereas what I want is the love of my children. It is now irretrievable, of course. But in questions of the emotions and their romantic qualities, unpunctuality is fatal.

I dare say I may have more misfortunes yet. Still, I can write as well, I think, as I used to write. Half as well would satisfy me.

With regard to the postal arrangements in France, I am still of opinion that one *can*. The bet holds good, for the third time now. Ever yours

OSCAR WILDE

To Leonard Smithers

TS. ROSS (A. L.)

Sunday [? *3 October 1897*][1]   *Villa Giudice, Posilippo*

My dear Smithers, I have heard nothing from Cook yet, but I have no doubt at all that you have done what I asked you. You see how wonderful my confidence in you is.

You must remember that I am not asking you for an ordinary loan of money at all. I am asking for a small advance on my poem which you are about to publish.

When you asked me my terms at Dieppe I said I would be ready to leave the question to you. You said you would give me the entire profits of the book. This offer, I may say, was made before, not after, dinner at the Café des Tribunaux. I said I could not agree to that, as I did not think it was fair to you or business-like in any way, but that I would take half the profits. This was agreed to.

At that time I proposed to publish first in some paper, but since then I decided not to, so you have now the perfect virginity of my poem for the satyrs of the British public to ravish. Previous publication would of course have damaged your sale. People will not pay half a crown for what they can buy for a penny. Why, I cannot understand, but it is so everywhere except perhaps at Naples.

So after having refused to take advantage of your generosity in offering me the entire profits, and also having let you have the virginity of the poem unsoiled by any liaison with the newspapers, I don't think I am really asking a great favour in saying that I wish you to advance me £20 on account. It is an ordinary thing to do, as I have already given you a

[1] The typescript copy from which this text is taken is dated 14 October 1897, but Mason, who prints (p. 411) extracts of it from Glaenzer, dates it 2 October. Glaenzer, who dates the letter 9 October, says that Wilde headed the letter Sunday, and I have therefore chosen the nearest Sunday to Mason's date, which seems to me the most likely.

certain *quid pro quo*, by assigning half the profits of the book, and leaving you to be its first producer. I give you a clear market and offer you a virgin who has never even been engaged to Arthur Symons—harmless though such a thing would have been in the sight of all sensible people.[1]

The fact is, my dear Smithers, I really don't think you are business-like: it is a painful thing to have to say of anyone: but in your case it is sadly true. I hope you won't mind my having spoken frankly about it.

In case then you have not grasped the idea that an advance of £20 on my poem is really a thing that I have a perfect right to expect on business grounds, pray do so at once. Application to you for a personal and private loan may, and I have no doubt will, follow later on, but up to the present our relations have been merely the usual ones of poet and publisher, with the usual complete victory of the latter. I also, such is my generosity of nature, send you enclosed *four* more verses of great power and romantic-realistic suggestion.[2] Twenty-four lines in all, each worth a guinea, in any of the market-places for poetry. Will you kindly give them at once to the type-writer and ask her to insert them in Part II of the poem: after the sixth stanza, the one ending "has each a sin to pay." They come in there splendidly and improve Part II, as it was a little too short compared to the others.

Your telegraphic address is still too long, and costs a heap of money. Leonardo, London, would be enough.

I hope you have seen Pinker and that in his business capacity he carried out the extraordinary promise of his name. Also, I hope that you have already written to me on the question of having an illustrated *second* edition of the poem. The *Musician*, editor Robin Grey,[3] wants to publish the whole poem before you do so in book form, but I have refused, though they offered large sums. So you see what sacrifices I make for you. I refuse money from others in order that you may have the first fruits of my poem, and yet you have not, up to the present, consented to advance me less than half of what the *Musician* offered me: and there is a tone of levity in your letters—at least in the business part of them—that pains me.

I do hope you will be serious now; it will help you in your business more than you know. Sincerely yours   OSCAR WILDE

To Robert Ross

MS. Clark

Sunday [? *3 October 1897*][4]   *Villa Giudice, Posilippo*

My dear Robbie, I hope you have received a type-written copy of the poem by this. I have just sent Smithers four more stanzas, for insertion—one of

---

[1] See note 1, p. 629.

[2] The four stanzas beginning "The oak and elm have pleasant leaves," and ending "His sightless soul may stray."

[3] Robin Grey edited the *Musician* during its brief life, and published selections from his writings in it as *Studies in Music* (1901).

[4] So dated in *After Berneval*, and clearly written soon after the preceding letter.

them very good—in the romantic vein that you don't quite approve of, but that on the whole will I think make a balance in the poem. I can't be always "banging the tins." Here it is:

> It is sweet to dance to violins
> When Life and Love are fair:
> To dance to flutes, to dance to lutes,
> Is delicate and rare:
> But it is not sweet with nimble feet
> To dance upon the air.

On the whole I like the poem now, except the second and third stanzas of Part III. I can't get that part right.

I am awaiting a thunderbolt from my wife's solicitor. She wrote me a terrible letter, but a foolish one, saying "*I forbid you*" to do so and so: "I will not *allow* you" etc.: and "I *require* a distinct promise that you will not" etc.[1] How can she really imagine that she can influence or control my life? She might just as well try to influence and control my art. I could not live such an absurd life—it makes one laugh. So I suppose she will now try to deprive me of my wretched £3 a week. Women are so petty, and Constance has no imagination. Perhaps, for revenge, she will have another trial: then she certainly may claim to have for the first time in her life influenced me. I wish to goodness she would leave me alone. I don't meddle with her life. I accept the separation from the children: I acquiesce. Why does she want to go on bothering me, and trying to ruin me? Another trial would, of course, entirely destroy me. On the whole, dear Robbie, things are dark with storm.

The solitude of our life here is wonderful, and no one writes to either of us. It is lucky that we love each other, and would be quite happy if we had money, but of course Bosie is as penniless as usual—indeed he has nothing at all to speak of, and unless Pinker gets me £300 we will not be able to get food. Up to the present I have paid for almost everything.

Do stir Pinker to acts of daring. Tell him that £500 is the proper price.[2]

Smithers is displaying levity in his business-relations with me: it is very annoying.

It is very curious that none of the English colony here have left cards on us. Fortunately we have a few simple friends amongst the poorer classes.

[1] Constance's letter has perished, but on 26 September 1897 she wrote to Carlos Blacker (MS. Blacker):

I have today written a note to Oscar saying that I required an immediate answer to my question whether he had been to Capri or whether he had met anywhere that appalling individual. I also said that he evidently did not care much for his boys since he neither acknowledged their photos which I sent him nor the remembrances that *they* sent him. I hope it was not too hard of me to write this, but it was quite necessary.

[2] A letter from Ross to Smithers (text from Stetson sale catalogue, 1920) headed "Wednesday evening" [? 6 October 1897] reads: "I received this evening a very vague letter from Melmoth. He asks me to see Pinker, though in what capacity he does not say, except that he must have £300 at least for the poem . . . I do not think his work has any market value, but I may be quite wrong."

653

When do you go to America?

Give my love to Reggie.

I expect a long letter from you about my poem. Pray go through it carefully, and note what you don't like. Ever yours   OSCAR

To Robert Ross
MS. Clark

Thursday [? *7 October 1897*]   *Villa Giudice, Posilippo*

My dear Robbie, Thank you so much for your telegram. I am delighted to think you are to see Pinker. I really think £500 should be *asked*, and £300 taken: and will send you a wire tomorrow to that effect. It is a *coup* that may come off. If it does, of course, I shall be all right for the winter. The winters here are so hot that I look forward with some apprehension to them, as I have nothing but very thick clothes, and cannot afford a new outfit.

Smithers has been behaving very badly, and now talks of an edition of 600 copies at 2/6!

If the thing goes at all, it should certainly sell 1500 copies, at that price. If on the other hand 500 is the probable sale, it should be 5/-. Smithers knows all about bad wine and bad women, but on books he is sadly to seek.

Let me know by wire all progress. Ever yours   OSCAR

To Robert Ross
MS. Clark

Friday [*8 October 1897*][1]   *Villa Giudice, Posilippo*

My dear Robbie, Thanks so much for your letter. Smithers took my letter a little too seriously. It was unfair of him, as I certainly did not take his advice seriously, though he gave me a great deal of it, with reference to my wife, through the medium of his type-writer. He is a very good fellow, and most kind to me.

With much of your criticism I agree. The poem suffers under the difficulty of a divided aim in style. Some is realistic, some is romantic: some poetry, some propaganda. I feel it keenly, but as a whole I think the production interesting: that it is interesting from more points of view than one is artistically to be regretted.

With regard to the adjectives, I admit there are far too many "dreadfuls" and "fearfuls." The difficulty is that the objects in prison have no shape or form. To take an example: the shed in which people are hanged is a little shed with a glass roof, like a photographer's studio on the sands at Margate. For eighteen months I thought it *was* the studio for photographing prisoners. There is no adjective to describe it. I call it "hideous"

---

[1] So dated in *After Berneval*.

654

Naples 1897

On the back of a copy
of the lower photograph
which he sent to Turner
Wilde wrote: "A young
unmitred Bishop *in
partibus*"

Oscar Wilde and Lord Alfred Douglas at Naples, 1897

because it became so to me after I knew its use. In itself it is a wooden, oblong, narrow shed with a glass roof.

A cell again may be described *psychologically*, with reference to its effect on the soul: in itself it can only be described as "whitewashed" or "dimly-lit." It has no shape, no contents. It does not exist from the point of view of form or colour.

In point of fact, describing a prison is as difficult artistically as describing a water-closet would be. If one had to describe the latter in literature, prose or verse, one could merely say it was well, or badly, papered: or clean or the reverse: the horror of prison is that everything is so simple and commonplace in itself, and so degrading, and hideous, and revolting in its effect.

The *Musician* expressed a great desire to publish the poem: I refused then: now I think I would accept *any* English paper. If the *Musician* would offer £50, it would be a great thing. But, of course, I would prefer the *Sunday Sun*, or *Reynolds*. If the *Saturday* will take it, well and good. I can't offer it myself, but Smithers might.

It is very annoying that I cannot get a copy of the poem. I sent it exactly two weeks ago, and until I get it I cannot pull it together. I write daily on the subject to Smithers. He takes no notice. I am not reproaching him for this: I am merely stating a fact.

I am going to retain the opening of Part IV, but to cut out three stanzas at opening of Part III.

As regards the spirits, I think the *grotesqueness* of the scene to a certain degree makes their speech possible, but Bosie agrees with you: though we do not hold your views on the Ghost in *Hamlet*: there is so little parallel between lyrical and dramatic poetry or method.

I have had no money at all for three days, so cannot buy note-paper. This is *your* foolscap. Ever yours   OSCAR

To Ernest Dowson
MS. Martin

Monday [? *11 October 1897*]   *Villa Giudice, Posilippo*

Dear Ernest, Thank you very much for your nice letter. My poem is finished at last, and is now with Smithers. I have added a good deal to it.

What you owe me is between £18 and £20—whichever you choose. I am thinking of telegraphing to you today to wire it, or as much as you can afford, through Cook's agency. They wire money like angels, and cheques and P.O. orders are difficult to cash. If I can find the money, I will, for at present I am quite penniless, and Smithers has not behaved well to me at all. I wanted a paltry £20 in advance for my poem—secured on its sale and the American rights—and for three weeks he has put me off with silly promises, never realised of course. I feel it, because when he offered me the entire profits in a moment of dramatic generosity I refused to take his offer, and insisted on his sharing half. Also, I have refused an offer from the

Musician to publish the poem, as I felt that previous publication would spoil Smithers's edition. So I made all these sacrifices, and at the end he refuses a petty sum in advance. Smithers is personally charming, but at present I simply am furious with him, and intend to remain so, till he sends me the money.

I am delighted to hear you have finished your novel[1] and are writing stories. I have begun today the tragedy in one act I told you about at Berneval, with the passages about clothes in it.[2] I find the architecture of art difficult now. It requires sustained effort, but I must do it.

The Neapolitan papers have turned out to be the worst form of American journalism. They fill columns with me, and write interviews of a fictitious character. I wish the world would let me alone, and really I thought that at Naples I would be at peace. I dare say they will tire of this nonsense soon.

I hope you will do a good thing with *Aphrodite*,[3] and that when you make lots of money, you will be able to find time to come to Naples, which I know you would like. The museum is full, as you know, of lovely Greek bronzes. The only bother is that they all walk about the town at night. However, one gets delicately accustomed to that—and there are compensations. Ever yours   OSCAR WILDE

To Reginald Turner
MS. Hyde (D. & M.)

Thursday, 14 October [1897]   *Villa Giudice, Posilippo*

Dear Reggie, I have not heard yet from you about lending me a copy of *Salome*. If you can't do this, would you try to get me one through Humphreys or Smithers or some other publisher? I will pay whatever it costs.

But at the close of the month there arrives here the best Italian company of actors there is. They have already played the *Cristo* of Bovio;[4] a religious drama, of course, and would like to do *Salome*. It would help me here greatly to have it done, as the papers have been rather offensive, and I want to assert myself here as *an artist*. Once I do that, they will leave me alone. So do try and get it for me.

I have finished the great poem—six hundred lines now. I hope it will make a good effect. I like much of it myself. Much is, I feel, for a harsher instrument than the languorous flute *I* love.

Do write to me soon. Bosie sends his love. Ever yours   OSCAR

---

[1] Presumably *Adrian Rome* (1899), which Dowson wrote in collaboration with Arthur Moore.

[2] Perhaps one of the two plays mentioned by Gide (see note 4, p. 649).

[3] See note 3, p. 632.

[4] *Cristo alla festa di Purim* by Giovanni Bovio (1841–1903), although a philosophical dialogue rather than a play, enjoyed a wide success in the theatre.

To Stanley V. Makower

MS. Bridge

14 October [1897]   *Villa Giudice, Posilippo*

My dear Stanley, Alfred Douglas has shown me your letter to him, with its nice message to me. The hope you express that my poem will be published without designs or drawings will be fulfilled. It is to be brought out for 2/6, quite simply. Later on, if the poem is a success I hope to have an edition illustrated: I have a longing for visible symbols to reinterpret my realism in the spirit with which I think it is informed.

The rest of your letter, however, pained me and distressed me a good deal: because it showed that you did not understand or appreciate, in the very smallest way, the reason why he sent you his sonnet on Mozart. He was charmed and fascinated by much in your book, which I had lent him, and wrote to you to express his pleasure in your work, and, as a sign of his pleasure in it, sent you a sonnet of his own, not as a corpse for a callous dissecting table, but as a flower to gild one grey moment in a London day.[1]

He is a little in years, and a little in literature, your senior. His beautiful book of poems was published I think some time before your novel: and his poems place him at once quite in the front of all the young poets of

---

[1] Douglas had written from the Villa Giudice on 2 October (MS. Bridge):

Dear Mr Makower, Oscar Wilde thinks that you would like the enclosed sonnet about Mozart and wants me to send it to you, so at the risk of boring you very much I do so. Of course it should be headed by the whole of the first thirteen bars of the trio in question, but I was too lazy to write it all out. I must tell you that I read your book *The Mirror of Music* and thought it quite wonderful. I have read no book so good for a very long time. Believe me, yours truly

ALFRED DOUGLAS

Trio. Ah, taci ingiusto core! (From *Don Giovanni*).

 et cet: till

O wonderful delightful melody!
O drops of clear white water! pearls and stars,
Strung on a silver string! no passion mars
Thy perfect beauty. Realised agony
In its excess leaves me both cold and free,
Nor can I ever bleed at pictured scars;
But I have never heard those thirteen bars
But that my tears paid tribute unto thee.

The beauty of perfection makes me weep
With helpless ecstasy. O rare Mozart!
Prince of the sweet untroubled countenance.
Exquisite shepherd that hast, for flock of sheep,
Live troops of notes that run and trip and dance
In the green pastures of eternal art.

Alfred Douglas

England: I know no young poet who is in any way his equal, or even near to him: and the elder poets are, of course, *hors concours*, through their mediocrity and the harsh music of their hoarse throats. So for you to take upon yourself to pull his sonnet to bits: to reconstruct it, while admitting yourself that you "have no knowledge of this form of poetry," was unnecessary, as unasked: nor was so intrusive a recklessness really atoned for by your concluding remark that in spite of everything you considered the poem "full of promise." Full of promise is an expression quite meaningless in even the most elementary art-criticism.

As regards the unknown friend whose standard of poetry is so high that he will not publish, I am sorry to find this antiquated type, if it exists, reappearing in modern life. I was in hopes he had disappeared as completely as he has been found out. Not to publish shows simply a lack of the vitality of creative interest. There is no instance I know of, in literature, of any good poet who did not publish his work. I see in the self-restraint of the supposed high standard merely the self-restraint of the impotent, and the chastity of the eunuch.

Had you read and admired Alfred Douglas's volume of poems and sent him your own book as a present you would, believe me, have received a more gracious answer than the one you have sent him.

I may say finally that Alfred Douglas was merely amused at your letter: the one who was pained was myself, as I had the pleasure—and it was a great pleasure—of knowing you personally and had often spoken to him about you, and it was a grief to me to find that, even without meaning it, you could be ungracious, and lacking in recognition of a charming compliment from a poet of the highest distinction. Sincerely yours

OSCAR WILDE

To Reginald Turner
MS. Hyde (D. & M.)

Friday [*15 October 1897*]　　　　　　　　*Villa Giudice* [*Posilippo*]
[*Postmark 16 October 1897*]

Dear Reggie, Thank you so much for sending me the copy of *Salome*, and please tell the Sphinx how kind it was of her to part with such a treasure.

If it is acted at Naples, it will really be, if successful, a great thing for me here. I simply now, from all the letters I get from England, seem utterly isolated, and people who have nothing to do with my life write long tedious letters to me informing me that I have wrecked my life for the second time.

Of the worldly-success point-of-view I really cannot say: it may be so: but I myself feel that I am happier with Bosie than I could be if all my laurels were given back to me. Somehow, he is my life: of course, he is unchanged: he is just what he was: kinder, and more considerate in a thousand ways: but still the same wilful, fascinating, irritating, destructive, delightful personality. If we had money, we would be all right, but he is in his usual state, and I have raised on prospective work all I can. Our sole hope of food is in Pinker and *The Ballad of Reading Gaol,* for which I ask £500! I hope to get £300, at least. I now think of beginning my play for George Alexander, but I cannot see myself writing comedy. I suppose it is all in me somewhere, but I don't seem to feel it. My sense of humour is now concentrated on the grotesqueness of tragedy.

I have extracted, after three weeks of telegrams, £10 from Smithers! It is absurd. However, with it we go to Capri for three days. I want to lay a few simple flowers on the tomb of Tiberius. As the tomb is of someone else really, I shall do so with the deeper emotion.

I don't at all approve of Max collaborating with anyone.[1] He is too individual a genius. I am pleased to hear that his brother is still acting, and hope he will have a success, some day. I read Max on Clement Scott lately—his last appreciation.[2] It was very dainty and witty. England has more subjects for art than any other country: I suppose that is the reason it has fewer artists.

Pray write whenever you have something better to do. Ever yours

OSCAR

To Leonard Smithers
MS. Clark

Saturday, 16 October [1897]   *Posilippo [Postmark Capri]*

My dear Smithers, It is a pleasing reflection for me to think that I have one duty left in life—that of writing to you daily—and that I perform it duly and cheerfully.

I suppose that Sherard was in his cups at the Authors' Club.[3] He was

[1] This may conceivably refer to the two plays in which Max Beerbohm collaborated: *Caesar's Wife* (adapted from Paul Hervieu's *L'Énigme*) with Frank Harris, and *The Fly on the Wheel* with S. Murray Carson. They were both produced in London in 1902.

[2] Max Beerbohm had published an ironical review of *Sisters by the Sea*, a book of essays by Clement Scott, in the *Saturday Review* of 4 September 1897, under the heading "An Appreciation."

[3] Sherard's account of this incident (*Oscar Wilde: The Story of an Unhappy Friendship*, 1902, p. 258) runs:

A few days later it became known that Oscar Wilde had resumed the friendship which had brought disaster and ruin upon him.

I heard of it in London, one afternoon when I was in the smoking-room of a literary club. With no other purpose than to distress me, two men, who were both the worse for liquor, called on me there and triumphantly announced that Oscar Wilde had gone to the Villa G[iudice], and had there taken up his permanent abode.

I said it was a great and an unfortunate mistake on his part; that his action would everywhere be misconstrued; that his traducers and enemies would be justified in the eyes of the world, and many sympathies would be alienated.

A lying account of my words was immediately transmitted to Naples, and some days later I received from my friend a letter which distressed me greatly, for it showed me in what an unhappy state of mind he was.

He then prints the fragment which follows this letter.

in his grenadine all the time he was at Berneval with me. I have written to him, without of course mentioning your name, simply to ask him when he takes upon himself to censure my life not to talk so loud that I can hear him at Naples. It is inartistic to play Tartuffe as if it was Termagant.

I am delighted to hear O'Sullivan is coming to Naples, and hope he will come soon. I had a charming breakfast with him in Paris.

The reason you should publish Lord Alfred Douglas's poems is that it will ensure you a niche in the History of English Literature. To be the herald of such music would be fame. I am pained to think that you might throw away such a wonderful chance in life.

I am anxious about Pinker. Of course *he* does not give the money—he only asks for it—and takes ten per cent. Robbie Ross has promised to wire to me how the negotiations promise.

Your £10 has made a great difference in my simple household, and this morning the servants are singing like larks. Ever yours   OSCAR WILDE

To R. H. Sherard[1]

[*Circa 16 October 1897*]   *Naples*

When you wish to talk morality—always an amusement—and to attack me behind my back, don't, like a good fellow, talk so loud, as the reverberation reaches from the [Authors'] Club to Naples; also, it is easy—far too easy—for you to find an audience that does not contain any friends of mine; before them, play Tartuffe in the style of Termagant to your heart's content; but when you do it in the presence of friends of mine, you expose yourself to rebuke and contempt, and of course I hear all about it.

To Vincent O'Sullivan

MS. Bodley

19 October 1897   *Villa Giudice, Posilippo*

Dear Vincent O'Sullivan, I am delighted to hear from Smithers that there is really some chance of your being at Naples this winter, and look forward with the greatest pleasure, I need hardly say, to seeing you again.

I have also heard incidentally of something that happened at the Authors' Club last week: and I cannot express to you adequately how deeply touched I was by the position you took up with regard to me, and by the dignity and, I cannot help saying, justice of your rebuke to Sherard. I feel it all the more as, in old days of high position and the like, I had not had the privilege of counting you amongst my intimate friends. I hope, however, you will not consider yourself bound to tilt at every blundering windmill that whistles on the high hill of Folly: you would have no time left in which to write jewelled verse or strange and subtly-coloured prose.

[1] The text of this fragment is taken from Sherard (see note 3, p. 659).

Whatever future may be in store for me depends entirely on my art, and the possibility of my art coming again into touch with life. I have no inclination to propitiate Tartuffe, nor indeed is that monster ever to be propitiated.

Pray let me know when your next volume comes out. In your poetry you seem to be a Catholic, in your prose a Pagan. Is this a mood, or a principle of music? Both are equally important in art. Sincerely yours

OSCAR WILDE

To Robert Ross

MS. Clark

Tuesday, 19 October [1897]   *Hôtel Royal des Étrangers, Naples*

My dear Robbie, Thank you so much for all the trouble you have taken.

I now think that as an edition of 500 at 2/- (100 for reviews, author etc.) would only fetch £40, which would only just cover expenses of paper, printing, etc., with £10 for advertisements, and leave nothing at all for me, that I had better publish in an English newspaper. I suggest *Reynolds*: it circulates among the lower orders, and the criminal classes, and so ensures me my right audience for sympathy. Also, it has always been nice to me, and about me.[1] Pinker might approach them. I still think they would give £100, and that if the *New York Journal* bites at the bait—my metaphor is drawn from fishing[2]—it should give £250 or £300. But I may be disappointed.

You are quite right in saying that the poem should end at "outcasts always mourn," but the propaganda, which I desire to make, begins there. I think I shall call the whole thing *Poésie et Propagande* or *Dichtung und Wahrheit*. I have added two stanzas since I wrote: one I like.

> For man's grim Justice goes its road,
>   And may not swerve aside:
> It slays the weak, it slays the strong;
>   It has a deadly stride:
> With iron heel it slays the strong,
>   This monstrous parricide!

Bosie is at Capri. I came back yesterday, as there was scirocco and rain. He dines with Mrs Snow.[3] We both lunched with Dr Munthe, who has a lovely villa and is a great connoisseur of Greek things. He is a wonderful personality.[4]

[1] *Reynolds* and the *Daily Chronicle* were the only papers that reported Wilde's trials impartially.

[2] Cf. Canon Chasuble and Miss Prism in *The Importance of Being Earnest*, Act II.

[3] An American lady living on Capri. Norman Douglas wrote in *Looking Back* (1934) that "a vision of her helped me to portray the Duchess" of San Martino in *South Wind* (1917).

[4] Axel Munthe (1857–1949), Swedish doctor and author of *The Story of San Michele* (1929).

661

I hope you will not go to Canada. What am I to do without you in London? Ever yours OSCAR

To Ernest Dowson

MS. Martin

Tuesday, 19 October 1897 *Hôtel Royal des Étrangers, Naples*

My dear Ernest, Why you should have given Smithers the £10 to send to me I cannot understand. You should have sent it to me yourself. I have heard nothing about it. I asked you in my telegram to wire what you owe me through Cook; had you done this, or sent even a portion of it, I would not be in the absurd position in which I am placed. There is no reason that Smithers should receive the money. The person to receive it is myself. The whole business is most irritating and silly. I am now going to telegraph to Smithers.

If you see Davray, as of course you are sure to do, will you tell him that I have received no drawing of any kind from Herrmann,[1] and that consequently I have to bring out my poem without design of any kind, as I cannot wait too long. Later on, if the poem is a success, I may bring out an adorned edition, but I know nothing of Herrmann's views at all.

Do try and pull yourself together, and close an annoying money-account —a thing I hate, because it is so painfully new to me. Ever yours

OSCAR

To Reginald Turner

MS. Hyde (D. & M.)

19 October [1897] *Hôtel Royal des Étrangers, Naples*

Dearest Reggie, I hear from Robbie that you have provided one Murphy, who is to be interested in *The Ballad of Reading Gaol*—a representative.[2] This is excellent, and I am much obliged to you.

I have just written to Robbie to say that I think of publishing with *Reynolds'* paper, simultaneously with America. *Reynolds* is an organ that appeals directly to the criminal classes, so my audience is gathered together for me.

Then there is the *Sunday Sun*. Do you think T. P. O'Connor would publish it? If he did, it would be a great thing—better, of course, than *Reynolds*. I have written to Pinker about it.

The translation[3] is in the hands of Rocco—a poet here—who knows French well. I hope it will be all right.

[1] Paul Herrmann (b. 1864) was a German artist who settled in Paris in 1895 and used the name Henri Héran. He had been introduced to Wilde by Davray and had offered to illustrate *The Ballad*. In a letter to Wilde (MS. Clark), dated 22 January 1898 and written in French from Paris, he says he is enclosing a sketch for a frontispiece which he proposes to execute as *"une eau-forte en quatre couleurs,"* but this never appeared.

[2] Unidentified, except that he seems to have been the London representative of the *New York Journal*.   [3] Of *Salome*.

The French papers describe me as living, broken down in health, in the lovely villa of the son of Lord Douglas!

I am to receive twelve copies of the poem from Smithers. Of course you are to have a presentation copy, and Bobbie, and More. The rest are for the Governor, Chaplain, Warders, and Prisoners of Reading Gaol. Ever yours   OSCAR

To Leonard Smithers
MS. Texas

Tuesday, 19 October 1897   *Hôtel Royal des Étrangers, Naples*

Dear Smithers, As an edition of 500—of which 100 will go to press, author, etc. practically—will only just pay expenses, and leave me £20 in your debt, I now think that it would be better after all to publish the poem in a paper. It is too long for the *Chronicle*, and Frank Harris has been so offensive to me and about me that I don't think negotiations possible with him.

My idea is *Reynolds*. It has, for some odd reason, always been nice to me, and used to publish my poems when I was in prison, and write nicely about me. Also, it circulates widely amongst the criminal classes, to which I now belong, so I shall be read by my peers—a new experience for me. I have written to Robbie Ross about the matter.

There are, I think, still 400 people left amongst the lovers of poetry to buy our edition up.

I have had a letter from Ernest Dowson to say he gave you £10 of his debt to me to send to me. This seems improbable, as I have heard nothing of it from you, but I have no doubt he "means well."

I am eagerly waiting for the type-written copies. Truly yours
                                                                        OSCAR WILDE

To More Adey
MS. Clark

19 October [1897]   *Villa Giudice, Posilippo*

My dear More, It is ages since I heard from you, and Robbie's statement that you had become a country gentleman was bewildering. I hope it merely means that you have become a shepherd and are piping many songs to one lost sheep.

I have not yet involved you in my negotiations with Pinker about the current price of poetry in America, and the demand for ballads. Pray fling yourself at once into the whole affair. I am sure you could influence Pinker. Also please tell Robbie that I now think the *Sunday Sun* if it still exists would be the best paper for me to publish in in London—that is, if T. P. O'Connor would consent to publish. I think he might. He has a literary sense.

663

This paper is so absurdly thin that I think I had better write on one side only.

As soon as I get rid of *The Ballad* I am going to begin my comedy, but at present *The Ballad* still dominates.

Is there any chance of your coming to Naples? Bosie and I would like immensely to see you again. I am getting rather astonishing in my Italian conversation. I believe I talk a mixture of Dante and the worst modern slang. Ever yours   OSCAR

To Stanley V. Makower

MS. Bridge

Thursday, 21 October [*1897*]   *Villa Giudice, Posilippo*

My dear Stanley, You have borne my bomb-shell with sweetness of temper and delightful resignation: I felt sure you would: indeed I would not have written to you so strongly had I not been sure that you would understand the whole thing, and accept it as you have done. We will now think no more and talk no more of what in its origin was a mere misunderstanding on your part.

I am awaiting type-written proofs of my poem from Smithers, after which I hope in a short time to see it published. I am also supervising an Italian version of *Salome*, which is being made here by a young Neapolitan poet. I hope to produce it on the stage here, if I can find an actress of troubling beauty and flute-like voice. Unfortunately most of the tragic actresses of Italy—with the exception of Duse—are stout ladies, and I don't think I could bear a stout Salome.

Pray remember me to Oswald, and believe me, sincerely yours

OSCAR WILDE

To Leonard Smithers[1]

22 October 1897   *Posilippo*

In the desert of my life you raised up the lovely mirage of the great sum of £20. You said that its conversion into a reality was a matter of days. On the faith of this I took a lovely villa on the Bay of Naples which I cannot inhabit as I have to take all my meals at the hotel. This is the simple truth . . .

Your letter received today is dated *Monday* last—and Dowson wrote to me that he had given you £10 for me on Saturday. What does this mean? Will you write to him and ask an explanation? It seems a disgraceful thing for him to have said. I will write to him about it myself.

[1] The text of this fragment is taken from *The Real Oscar Wilde* by R. H. Sherard.

To Ernest Dowson

MS. Martin

[*22 October 1897*]   *Villa Giudice, Posilippo*

My dear Ernest, I have just received a letter from Smithers dated *last Monday*; he says nothing in it of having received any money from you for me. From the date of your letter you seem to have entrusted him with this £10 on Saturday or Friday last. I have written to him again on the subject. Would you kindly write yourself. There seems something strange —almost improbable—in his retaining money entrusted to him for me.

However, Psychology is in its infancy, as a science. I hope, in the interests of Art, it will always remain so. Ever yours   OSCAR

To Leonard Smithers

MS. Princeton

Friday. 2.30 [*22 October 1897*]   *Villa Giudice* [*Posilippo*]
[*Postmark 23 October 1897*]

My dear Smithers, I like the last specimen of type. I think that larger might be a mistake. So, as far as I am concerned, I am quite content to have it. The type seems crisp and clean. I suppose it is as *black* as one can get? Perhaps a shade *thicker* would be well.

I hope to get my type-written copies this week. I cannot work without them. And every day is of importance.

You say to me "I suppose you have received Dowson's £10 by this time." All I have had from him is a letter stating that he gave it to you for me on Saturday last. It is clear that he did nothing of the kind, and I think his saying so disgraceful and meaningless.

As the type is to be kept standing, I think a *second* edition would be better. And I am pleased to think 3/6 a possible price. At any rate a *first* edition of 500. The rest I must leave to you. Of course a second *un*-illustrated edition of 500 would be on same terms. I mention that because in our agreement the copyright for a second edition reverts to me: and it would be fairer to continue same terms, as the poem will be from same type. Ever yours   O. W.

To Leonard Smithers

MS. Taylor

Friday [*Postmark 22 October 1897*]   *Villa Giudice* [*Posilippo*]

LETTER NO 2.

My dear Smithers, I have just heard from Robbie Ross: he gives me a terrific scolding for my conduct to you and hugely disapproves of my letters to you: however, I have already told you I am very sorry, and you will make allowances for a man of wrecked nerves and life on the brink of many abysses. Also, I think you took my letters *a little* too seriously.

As regards Pinker. Robbie says Pinker is not to be trusted. This, of course, is a great blow. And in this case do not, of course, let him take away a copy till he gets a definite offer. Pray in fact treat the whole affair as if you were the owner of the American copyright. There is in New York my own agent for my plays—a woman of the highest position—agent for Sardou, and indeed all the dramatists—*Miss Marbury*. Her address you can find at Low's American Exchange, Trafalgar Square, or c/o Low's Exchange, New York would find her. She is in touch with everything of journalistic position in New York. In case Pinker gets no offer, and that Murphy can do nothing, it would be best to send Miss Marbury the manuscript and let her get terms.

The *Paris* edition of the *New York Herald* might publish simultaneously with a New York paper, and also some London Sunday paper. If I could secure simultaneous publication in the *New York Journal*, the Sunday edition of the *New York Herald in Paris*, and the *Sunday Sun* in London, it would bring in a good deal of money. The next day, a Monday, you might publish.

I do hope you will let me have my two copies at once. I have received from Robbie Ross, whose literary instinct and judgment has always influenced me, a lot of suggestions, and will accept half of them.

I have no note-paper, and no money to buy any, so I write to you on foolscap.

If you write to Miss Marbury, please say that you are my representative and entitled to conclude all agreements with reference to this work. Low has a telegraphic code that is very useful. A single expletive conveys volumes. Ever yours   OSCAR WILDE

To Ernest Dowson
MS. Martin

[*Circa 26 October 1897*]   *Villa Giudice, Posilippo*

Dear Ernest, The fault was the fault of the post: they took twelve days to deliver Smithers's letter.[1]

I am much obliged to you for what you have sent me. I am afraid I wrote irritably to you, but I have been terribly worried by the want of money—the most sordid and hungry of wants.

I hope your translation will be a great success, though of course I like you to do your own original work best.

The negotiations over my poem still drag on: as yet no offer, and no money in consequence. Still I keep on building castles of fairy gold in the air: we Celts always do.

---

[1] Sherard prints (*The Real Oscar Wilde*, p. 76) a statement of Smithers's account with Dowson, from which it appears that Smithers sent off Dowson's £10 on 14 October. I have dated this letter accordingly.

Pray let me know how you are getting on in Paris, and whom you see
Ever yours   OSCAR
I have retaken my own name, as my incognito was absurd.

To Leonard Smithers
MS. Taylor

Wednesday [27 October 1897]   *Villa Giudice, Posilippo*

My dear Smithers, Your letter with Ernest's £10 and the manuscript[1] were
only delivered on Monday last! The post is disgraceful here. It was very
kind of you to secure the £10 for me, and I am much obliged. It has
amongst other things enabled me to buy some writing paper of the cheaper
kind. Next week I hope to be able to buy a pen.

As regards *Reynolds*, I dare say you will think me very unpractical and
all that, but I candidly confess that if I have to choose between *Reynolds*
and Smithers, I choose Smithers.

Upon the other hand I think the *Sunday Sun* a good idea, if T. P.
O'Connor would consent.

I will return the proof tomorrow. I have had to make many alterations.
Pinker seems an absurdity, so far. I think Miss Marbury the best chance.

You are taking a great deal of trouble for me, and I will never forget it,
or your many other kindnesses to me. Sincerely yours   OSCAR WILDE

To Robert Ross
MS. Clark

Thursday [28 October 1897]   *Villa Giudice, Posilippo*

Dear Robbie, I have sent Smithers the corrected copy.[2] I don't think I
can do much more with the poem. All your suggestions were very interesting, but, of course, I have not taken them all: "black dock's dreadful
pen" for instance is my own impression of the place in which I stood: it is
burned into my memory.

As regards page 13, "goes for ever through the land with the red feet
of Cain," I have altered that, not on account of Hood,[3] but because I use
Cain later on, and he is too big to be used twice with effect.

But do you think that in the corrected version I should have for the last
line "And binds it with a chain"? Otherwise it is too like the end of *The
Sphinx*.[4]

---

[1] The typed fair copies of *The Ballad*, for which Wilde had been clamouring.
[2] The typed fair copy recorrected.
[3]   He told how murderers walk the earth
                Beneath the curse of Cain.
                        ("The Dream of Eugene Aram")
[4] The last line of *The Sphinx* runs:
    And weeps for every soul that dies, and weeps for every soul in vain.
                                        [*Footnote continues overleaf.*

667

I fear I have built air-castles of false gold on my dreams of America. My hope now is in Miss Marbury, who is on the spot. But I should like Murphy, if he has authority, to see the poem. He represents the greatest paper in America. You will consider the point. Ever yours OSCAR

To Leonard Smithers
MS. Vander Poel

Friday [? 29 October 1897]   *Villa Giudice, Posilippo*

My dear Smithers, On page 10 of type-written copy I have inserted a verse at top of page, beginning "The moaning wind." In line 5 of this verse, instead of "O wind of woe" please put "O *moaning* wind." I use "woe" later on in an important line.

On page *17*, line 4 of first stanza, I now wish to have "*gibe*" the old and grey: not "strike," which was my last correction.

Also page 16, stanza 3, I now wish the stanza to be exactly as it was type-written. I am not satisfied with it, but I cannot better it.

Also page *10*, inserted verse at top, line *three*, I wish

> *Till* like a wheel of turning steel
> We *felt* the *minutes* crawl.

All these corrections show my anxiety to have as few corrections as possible in the *printed* proof, and yet you say I know as much about business as a chrysanthemum!

Your letter has just come.

(1) Certainly: both sides of page: the other method is really inartistic: blank *spaces* are lovely, but blank *pages* are otiose.

(2) I have always felt that to publish in a newspaper would quite spoil our book. It was merely the terror of getting nothing from the new, and I hope the last, Republic[1] that made me suggest the *Police News* as my proper organ.

(3) By all means have 1200 at 3/6, and the type no 2 pleases me. I am quite satisfied with it.

(4) This is merely an appeal to your quite inexhaustible good nature.

Reggie Turner suggests "syndicating" the poem in America. He says that in this way a large sum could be got. Would you consider how you could help me to do this? I have full confidence in Miss Marbury, a brilliant delightful woman, who is anxious to help me. Don't you think I had better give up Pinker? Miss Marbury might syndicate for a date fixed by you—say at end of November.

Pray in your relations with Miss Marbury treat the poem as your own

---

and the revised stanza of *The Ballad* ends:

> And makes it bleed great gouts of blood,
> And makes it bleed in vain!

[1] i.e. the U.S.A.

property, as far as all American rights go. I enclose an absurd document to enable you to assert these rights. I call it absurd, because it has no stamp, and I have always believed in stamps as legal things. But Miss Marbury will understand the "chrysanthemum" method of business.

You said you would publish *An Ideal Husband*. That is delightful of you. The manuscript is in Lewis Waller's possession, type-written. I will write to him for it. He has no rights except for production. Would you, as I don't know his address, send him enclosed letter. My own manuscript—as all my things—disappeared at the seizure of my house.

(5) Reggie Turner says that he *repeated* a stanza of the poem to Murphy, and that he said that had he known the poem was so good he would have communicated with the *New York Journal* in a different strain!

Surely Murphy, an accredited agent, might have been allowed to see the work. How else could he propose to buy it? But obviously to syndicate is the thing, and only Miss Marbury can do this.

(6) The whole business about the post shows clearly that, as I have always said, to telegraph money through *Cook* is the only way. In this manner one gets the money in three hours. A registered letter takes *eleven* days to arrive. I beg you to use Cook.

(7) Would you ask *Shannon* to design the cover of *An Ideal Husband*. He did the others, and they form a series. I want same colour and treatment.

Pray excuse this brief letter.[1] Ever yours   OSCAR WILDE

To Robert Ross

MS. Clark

Saturday, 30 October 1897   *Villa Giudice, Posilippo*

My dear Robbie, I hear from Smithers that you are in Durham, and that from that point of vantage you have expressed your disapproval of my proposal to publish in an English newspaper of any kind.

I quite see that it would spoil the book, and, as you know, always intended to publish directly with the good Smithers. But he wrote several times to me to say he did not mind a bit the thing appearing elsewhere, and the desire of money and of a wide audience made me reconsider my decision, but now I feel that it may be better to leave it entirely with Smithers.

Reggie suggests syndicating the poem. This, of course, Pinker should have done. I now rely on Miss Marbury, with whom the poem will be quite safe. Will you kindly tell Smithers that I have written to Lewis Waller to ask him to send Smithers a copy of *An Ideal Husband*. Ever yours

       OSCAR

---

[1] The original covers sixteen pages.

To Reginald Turner

MS. Hyde (D. & M.)

Saturday [*Postmark 30 October 1897*]   *Villa Giudice, Posilippo*

My dear Reggie, I am very sorry Murphy was not shown the poem. I don't see how, without seeing it, he could be expected to procure an offer from his paper.

Of course to syndicate it would be the best, and I have written to Smithers to ask him to try and do this through Miss Marbury, my theatrical agent at New York. Pinker seems an absurdity. It was simply the fatal attraction of his name that made me pin my faith to him.

I now want you to do me a favour. I want you to lend me £2. 10. I have one friend left in Reading, the one I liked best; a very handsome young soldier of twenty years of age—Harry Elvin. I promised him I would leave a letter at the Post Office for him and he would be greatly disappointed not to hear from me, as we always walked together, and had long chats.

So will you put P.O. orders into the enclosed letter for £2. 10. and I will pay you as soon as I get some money from America. You were kind enough to lend me money before, so I hope you will be as kind again. H. E. comes out on November 6th, so the letter should be sent off *at once*.

I read the *Morning Post* on Carton's play: it seems a rubbishy thing for George Alexander to be sympathetic in.[1]

I began my play the other day, but the comedy troubles me, and I must settle my American poem first.

The weather is lovely here, and if we had money we would be all right, but the daily financial crisis is wearying.

Denis Browne,[2] whom you know, had luncheon here yesterday; he was very witty, and talkative: I told him your "Is that quite healthy?"—*à-propos* of Wordsworth's grave—and he was delighted to have a new story to take back to the Embassy.[3]

Why do you say the *Anti-Philistine* is horrid?[4] Of course all cries of

---

[1] George Alexander had produced *The Tree of Knowledge*, a play in five acts by R. C. Carton, at the St James's Theatre on 25 October.

[2] Probably Beauchamp D. Browne, who was an honorary attaché at the British Embassy in Rome 1896–99.

[3] In *An Innkeeper's Diary* (1931) John Fothergill related how when he was "nineteen and straight from our Lake District fastness," he found himself, "shy and tender," at a dinner-party. "Ross's sister, Mrs Ethel Jones, took pity on me and talked to me about my home. 'We live at Grasmere,' I told her, and, seeing a chance to get in a literary touch, added 'quite near Wordsworth's grave,' but unhappily a silence had just dropped upon the party and Reggie Turner called out from the other end, 'And don't you find it very unhealthy?' "

[4] A pocket-sized sixpenny monthly containing poems and *belles lettres*, of which only four issues appeared (June–September 1897). It was published by John and Horace Cowley, and its contributors included Ambrose Bierce, Edgar Saltus, Joaquin Miller, Gertrude Atherton and J. H. Skrine. The name Callan does not occur in it, but may have been the real name of someone writing under a pseudonym. The four issues were later bound in cloth and sold as a book.

Leonard Smithers

The
Ballad of Reading Gaol
By
C. 3. 3.

Leonard Smithers
Royal Arcade London W
Mdcccxcviii

Title-page of the First Edition

revolt are harsh—Peace is the note of Art as of Religion—but it is on the right road. Besides, I like one of the writers, young Callan, very much. His style is somewhat colourless but he has purple hair. Ever yours

OSCAR

To Leonard Smithers

MS. Yale

Thursday night [? *4 November 1897*]   *Villa Giudice, Posilippo*

My dear Smithers, Your telegram has just been delivered but, my dear fellow, *why* did you not wire the money through Cook's office last Monday as I asked you to do? It is the best, cheapest, and most easy mode of sending money abroad. Had you done so I would have had the money on Monday afternoon, and the utter and ridiculous penury of the last four days would have been staved off.

I suppose I shall receive your money tomorrow, or Saturday. I hope it is not a cheque, as they take nine days to cash a cheque on London here. Do please always in the future, if you have any money to send me, wire it through Cook.

I calculate the expenses incurred by waiting for this £20 at £34 up to the present, as it was promised three weeks ago. The mental anxiety cannot be calculated. I suppose you think that mental anxiety is good for poets. It is not the case, when pecuniary worries are concerned. Sincerely yours

OSCAR WILDE

To Robert Ross

MS. Clark

Monday [*8 November 1897*]   *Villa Giudice, Posilippo*

My dear Robbie, The £9 you so kindly announced is a miracle of a very wonderful kind: I am telegraphing to you for it: it is really most sweet and generous of you to have set it aside for me.

I see that the difficulties about America are terrible. It is a sort of dreadful shock to me to find that there is such a barrier between me and the public. I must reconsider my position, as I cannot go on living here as I am doing, though I know that there is no such thing as changing one's life: one merely wanders round and round within the circle of one's own personality.

I am very pleased at what you say of the poem now. The reason I altered "red Hell" into "hidden Hell" was that it seemed violent, but I now wish to go back to it. Will you alter it in the copy for me?

On page *8* line 4 I have written "*arid*" vigil, but I do not like it, because the vigil was rich in psychological experiences. I see nothing now but "*ceaseless,*" or "*endless,*" the latter for choice.

Today the *Musician* is to make me an offer; unless it is a good one I shall not take it. But I have almost given up hope about America, and must make money somehow. Of course the *Musician* must wait for simultaneous publication, if there is to be one.

I am still a little loth to lose the opening of Canto Three, but I suppose it must go.

I hear from Reggie of your "wit-combats" with Cowley! Pray let me know about him. I love details about asses.

More has appealed to me "in the name of Beauty and Art" to surrender my £3 a week, but I don't think I dare to. What should I live on? Besides I understood that it was a regular legal agreement—not a *favour*. That was the point you and More insisted on to me always. I need not tell you that Bosie could not give me three *shillings* a week. He has not enough for his own wants. So I don't think I should play Quixote. To tilt with death is worse than to tilt with windmills. Ever yours   OSCAR

To Reginald Turner
MS. Hyde (D. & M.)

11 November [1897]   *Villa Giudice, Posilippo*

My dear Reggie, This is to introduce to you our friend Ashton,[1] who has been in Naples for a month, and of whom we have seen, I am glad to say, a great deal. He is a most charming and delightful fellow, and has been a very good friend to me, so I am anxious for you to know him.

I was and am much obliged to you for your kindness about Harry Elvin. I have not heard from him yet, but I expect a letter daily. I am quite sorry I cannot see him: we were always great friends. Ever yours   OSCAR

To Robert Ross
MS. Clark

Tuesday, 16 November 1897   *Villa Giudice, Posilippo*

My dear Robbie, I received this afternoon a letter from Hansell to say he was going to decide that I was to be deprived of my absurd income because I was with Bosie. I don't suppose that anything will prevent him from doing this, but I felt it due to myself and to Bosie to write to him a letter of protest, on the ground that I do not think it just or socially-speaking accurate to describe Bosie as a "disreputable person." After all, no charge was made against him at any of my trials, nor anything proved, or attempted to be proved.

Nor do I think that it is fair to say that I have created a "public scandal" by being with him. If newspapers chronicle the fact, that is their business; I can't help that. If I were living here with you they would chronicle my

[1] Enclosed in this letter is a visiting-card inscribed "*Mr I. D. W. Ashton. Piccadilly Club, W.*" Further than that I have failed to trace him. Meyerfeld says that he was nicknamed Sir John, and this is corroborated by the complementary references to him and St Malo on pp. 766 and 767. See also p. 739.

being here with equal venom and vulgarity: or if I were living with someone of unblemished reputation and unassailable position. I think I should only be held accountable for any scandal caused by my getting into trouble with the law. My existence is a scandal. But I do not think I should be charged with creating a scandal by continuing to live: though I am conscious that I do so. I cannot live alone, and Bosie is the only one of my friends who is either able or willing to give me his companionship. If I were living with a Naples renter I would I suppose be all right. As I live with a young man who is well bred and well born, and who has been charged with no offence, I am deprived of all possibility of existence.

This is the point I have made to Hansell. I merely tell it to you, not that you should worry about a pre-judged matter, but because I tell you everything: you tried your best to create a possible life for me, but it was one my own temperament could not suffer. I could not live alone, and so inevitably I took the love and companionship that was offered to me. It seemed to me to be the only gate to any life, but I did it conscious of all the new ruin it might bring on me. I was not blind to what I was doing. You know what beautiful, wise, sensible schemes of life people bring to one: there is nothing to be said against them: except that they are not for oneself.

But don't think I am complaining: I wish merely to tell you what has occurred. I suppose you knew it already. I myself felt it was coming.

You have not written to me for ages except about the worrying business of my unsaleable poem. You had, I know, great worry about it. I had no idea that there were such barriers between me and publication in America. I thought I would romp in, and secure a good lump sum. It is curious how vanity helps the successful man, and wrecks the failure. In old days half of my strength was my vanity.

Please let me know what books are being published, and what is going on. I sometimes see English papers, but not often. They are so dear. I read all about Carton's play—an absurd production.[1]

I wish you could come out here for a little. I suppose it is impossible but, of course, we are terribly isolated. I dare say Paris would have been better, but Bosie said he could not winter there.

I have written to Ernest Leverson for some of my money, but I don't know if anything will come of it. Of course do not say anything to him about it.

George Ives has sent me his poems[2]—of course without an inscription. His caution is amusing. He means well, which is the worst of it.

Give my love to Reggie. Ever yours, dearest Robbie   OSCAR

---

[1] See note 1, p. 670.
[2] *A Book of Chains* (1897), published anonymously and containing poems about prisons, as well as prose-poems in the Wilde manner.

To Ada Leverson

MS. Clark

16 November 1897   *Villa Giudice, Posilippo*

My dear Ada, I have never answered your many sweet and brilliant letters because I have been so hurt and wounded at Ernest's conduct to me in retaining money entrusted to him for my use. It has nothing to do with you at all, and you yourself told me how deeply you regretted his proposed action towards me,[1] but still, I could not write to you with the freedom and affection I would like while I felt so bitterly about Ernest. I have now, after waiting five months for the letter you said he was writing to me, written to him myself. I deferred doing so, as I know how strongly he dislikes parting with money—even the money of other people—till I was absolutely penniless, and in want. But now, as the absurd income I had—£3 a week —has been stopped by my trustees because I am here with Bosie, the only friend I have who either is able or willing to be with me, I am forced to do so, and I find that I cannot get my poem—a long poem of 700 lines— accepted even by the most revolting New York paper. So I am face to face with starvation, not in any rhetorical sense, but as an ugly fact. Of course Bosie, as you know, has only £25 a month, and naturally that is not enough for his own wants. He cannot, financially, help me with either the smallest sum or the most meagre assistance. He simply has not got the money.

These are the circumstances under which I have written very strongly to Ernest to say that of the money of mine that he has at any rate £100 must be telegraphed at once to me through Cook's agency: there is nothing else for him to do.

For yourself, dear Sphinx, I have always the deepest love and admiration, and Bosie and I often talk over your delightful sayings, and your brilliant and beautiful personality—unique, troubling, and imaginative.

I will send you your *Salome* tomorrow. I must have it done up properly. It was most kind of you to lend it.

I have no good news to tell you. I am in such distress and misery, but it is pleasant to tell you that I am always your affectionate and devoted admirer   OSCAR[2]

---

[1] i.e. the repayment of half the loan, see p. 683.

[2] This is the last known surviving letter to Ada Leverson, but it is clear that Wilde preserved his affection for her to the last. Her copy of *The Ballad of Reading Gaol* (1898) was inscribed "To the Sphinx of Pleasure from the Singer of Pain," and her copy of *The Importance of Being Earnest* (1899): "To the wonderful Sphinx, to whose presence on the first night the success of this comedy was entirely due, from her friend, her admirer, who wrote it, Oscar Wilde."

To Leonard Smithers

MS. Yale

Tuesday 16 [November 1897]   *Villa Giudice, Posilippo*

My dear Smithers, Do remember that what is comedy to you may be the reverse of comic to others.

Since I received your letter in which you said "I expect that before the arrival of this letter you will have received the £10," I have been down twice *a day* to Naples to Cook's office, and have just returned from a third visit now—5.30. Of course there was nothing, and I am really so ashamed of my endless enquiries about a sum of £10 to be telegraphed from London. Perhaps you only wrote what you did to give me hope, but, my dear fellow, hope constantly disappointed makes one's bread bitter, especially as I have just heard from *my own* solicitor to say that as I am in Naples with Alfred Douglas he is going to give his decision that I am leading an infamous life, and so deprive me of my sole income—£38 a quarter! For one's own solicitor this seems a little strong. Unluckily he has it in his power to stop my wretched allowance, and is going to do so,[1] and as I see my poem is a very unsaleable affair I simply have starvation or suicide before me—the latter, as I dislike pain, for choice. Alfred Douglas has no money, not enough for his own wants, and cannot do anything, even temporarily, for me.

I am anxious however to correct my proofs before retiring from a world of injustice and wrong and annoyance. So do let me have them. You said you would send them last Wednesday—as yet no sign of them.

I should not like to die without seeing my poem as good as I can make a poem, whose subject is all wrong, and whose treatment too personal. I hope to receive the proofs this week. As regards the cover, do what you like—the simpler the better.

I won't write any more about America. I have no hopes: but I do trust you will copyright it in the States: there is a *chance*—just a chance—of a big sale.

The weather is entrancing, but in my heart there is no sun. Ever yours

                                                                o. w.

---

[1] On 18 November Constance Wilde wrote to her brother: "I have stopped O's allowance as he is living with Lord Alfred Douglas, so in a short time war will be declared! His legal friends in London make no defence and so far make no opposition, as it was always understood that if he went back to that person his allowance would stop. They have bought a villa at Naples and are living there together."

To Leonard Smithers

MS. Private

Friday, 19 [November 1897]   *Villa Giudice, Posilippo*

My dear Smithers, Your letter announcing proofs just received. I expect the latter this afternoon.

With regard to the description of a prison doctor: the passage in which it occurs does not refer to a particular execution, but to executions in general. I was not present at the Reading execution, nor do I know anything about it. I am describing a general scene with general types. The Governor of Reading for instance was a "mulberry-faced Dictator:"[1] a great red-faced, bloated Jew who always looked as if he drank, and did so: his name was Isaacson; he did not, could not have had a "*yellow* face" of Doom or anything else. Brandy was the flaming message of his pulpy face. By "Caiaphas" I do not mean the present Chaplain of Reading: he is a good-natured fool, one of the silliest of God's silly sheep: a typical clergyman in fact. I mean any priest of God who assists at the unjust and cruel punishments of man.

I will change *one* word so as to avoid being misunderstood. I will put "while *some* coarse-mouthed doctor" etc. That simply describes the *type* of prison-doctor in England. As a class they are brutes, and excessively cruel.

The Chiswick Press is idiotic.[2]

I hope you sent Miss Marbury the poem. Otherwise she cannot get offers. If you have not, perhaps better wait till the proofs arrive. But I suppose America is a foolish dream as far as buying my poem goes.

I still go to Cook's every day to enquire if there is a telegram of £10 for me. For four days I have had no cigarettes, no money to buy them, or notepaper. I wish you would make an effort. Ever yours   o. w.

To Leonard Smithers

MS. Houghton

Friday, 19 [November] 1897   *Villa Giudice, Posilippo*

My dear Smithers, Your telegram has just arrived: and I am very much obliged to you for your kindness, as in the midst of my hideous worries the lack of any money at all was paralysing. Now, I can really think about my position, and form some judgment as to whether it is worth while fighting on against the hideous forces of the world. Personally I don't think it is, but Vanity, that great impulse, still drives me to think of a possible future of self-assertion. It seems absurd to be beaten by the want of money. And

[1] A reference to Sulla, the Roman dictator, whose face was said to resemble a mulberry sprinkled with meal.
[2] The Chiswick Press, the printers of *The Ballad of Reading Gaol*, were clearly nervous of being involved in a libel action by the Reading doctor. Their name did not appear in *The Ballad* until the seventh edition.

yet I feel that every problem in life must be solved on its own conditions. And Financial Problems can be solved only by Finance. Genius, Art, Romance, Passion, and the like are useless when the point at issue is one of figures. A solution for an algebraic problem is not to be found in the sense of Beauty, however developed.

The proofs also have arrived:[1] in old days of power and personality I always insisted that my proofs should be sent to me on the paper to be ultimately used. Otherwise I would not have been able to judge of the look of a page. Of course the paper of these proofs is awful, and the whole thing looks to me mean in consequence. The type is good: though I think the ?'s lacking in style, and the stops, especially the full-stops, characterless. But setting this aside, the whole thing looks too meagre for a 3/6 book. When one remembers what thick cloth-bound volumes the public buys nowadays for 3/6 or 2/6, it seems to me that they will think twice before they pay 3/6 for what looks like a thin sixpenny pamphlet, lacking in all suggestion of permanence of form. The public is largely influenced by the *look* of a book. So are we all. It is the only artistic thing about the public.

I had intended that wherever there was a break (marked by a leaf) in my poem, a *new* page should begin. This would give the book thickness and an air of responsibility. Whether it would really look well, I cannot say: you are, of course, the better judge. Failing this, it really would be better to print on alternate leaves, as you suggested. As it stands, it is not adequate to 3/6.

The drawback of beginning a new page at every break is that it makes the poem look piecemeal, and robs it of the impression of continuous unity of development. The advantage is the increase of the number of pages. I really think that printing on alternate pages is the best. You say this will necessitate a cloth binding. Well, let us have one. A plain olive-green, or cinnamon cloth, with a white back gold-lettered.[2] The colours, nowadays, in cloths are lovely.

The title-page is not good. (I hope, by the way, you have a double proof?) The "By C.3.3" is far too small. Also, as a general rule in art, I think that the less the type is changed on a page the better. Too many types spoil the looking. Nor do I care for, or indeed stand, the placing of the "By C.3.3."

Why not

The

Ballad of Reading Gaol

By

C.3.3.[3]

Indeed place "By C.3.3." quite at the side, so as to draw down the type-design to the publisher's lines and fill the page. As a rule in English books the publisher's name looks a sudden intrusion into a page more candid without it, whereas it should be part of it all.

[1] The first printed proofs.   [2] This suggestion was carried out.
[3] For the final lay-out of the title-page, see plate facing p. 671.

I would suggest the same type for the full title and the suggestion of the author. The publisher's name and address, of course, smaller.

The type for the Dedication is *revolting*. It is like a bad brass by Gilbert Scott.[1] There need be no suggestion of a Pugin tombstone about it.[2] Joy and Assertion are its notes.

At the close of each Canto a leaf is out of place. It marks transition, not finality.

The "In Memoriam" page is an example of what I mean by the in-artistic effect of changing type: it looks like a page of specimen-types for a printer's apprentice. It should be quite simple, and no tombstone Gothic about the words "In Memoriam." On the whole I think now that the combination of Latin and English is wrong. What do you say to this? (not in tombstone-type)

In Memory
of
R. J. M.
late of H.M. Dragoon Guards.
Died in H.M. Prison, Reading
July 13
1896.[3]

Or, shall we put "Her Majesty's" in full? Perhaps not, as it would go badly with Gaol or Prison: though the official address on prison note-paper (paper of a loathsome blue colour) is *H.M. Prison*. Perhaps "Died in Reading Gaol, Berkshire" would suit the title better. It would not suggest that there was any sneer in the title.

[1] George Gilbert Scott (1811–78), English architect and "restorer" of churches. He was knighted for designing the Albert Memorial in Kensington Gardens.

[2] Augustus Welby Northmore Pugin (1812–52), an English architect of French extraction, was one of the leaders of the neo-Gothic movement. He helped Sir Charles Barry to design the new Houses of Parliament 1837–43.

[3] Apparently Wilde's original plan was to disguise the identity and circumstances of the man he was commemorating, but he changed his mind, and the final dedication read:

In Memoriam
C. T. W.
Sometime Trooper of the Royal Horse Guards.
Obiit H.M. Prison, Reading, Berkshire,
July 7th, 1896.

Charles Thomas Wooldridge, aged 30, was hanged in Reading Gaol on 7 July 1896 for the murder of his wife. A full account of the murder and execution from the *Reading Mercury* of 10 July is printed by Mason, pp. 426–27.

The additional dedication (see note 1, p. 578) was now removed. On 16 November Ross had written to Smithers (text from American Art Association catalogue, 18 April 1929):

I want to write to you about the dedication. Please do not tell Oscar my views or quote my views to him as it will merely irritate him and at all events while the poem is in progress he must be kept in good humour . . . I think the dedication with or without initials is ROT and at all events quite unsuitable to a poem of that sort . . . I am convinced that dear Oscar meant to tell me and Douglas and two or three other people that each was intended. That only amuses me.

Do you think "Hanged in Reading Gaol" would either be too like G. R. Sims,[1] or give away the plot of the poem?

Or do you think that the words "In Memory of R. J. M." would be enough? I now, sometimes, think so. It would excite interest, without giving away the plot. It is a difficult point. Please consult with Robbie. Alfred Douglas thinks that if I don't put that R. J. M. died in Reading Prison people might think that it was all imaginary. This is a sound objection.

As regards the doctor, I have written to you today. To sacrifice the stanza on the dung-heap of the Chiswick Press would be absurd. Would you kindly say that the description is generic, and that the Reading doctor is a thin sallow man with an aquiline nose, and that the description is imaginary, just like the yellow face of the Governor, or the Caiaphas-chaplain. It does not occur in any description of Reading Gaol. It is abstract. The only people I have libelled in the poem are the Reading warders. They were—most of them—as good as possible to me. But to poetry all must be sacrificed, even warders.

Robbie has written me a very acrimonious letter to assure me that he never showed you any letters of mine, except passages on business. But you wrote to me "Is it *kind* or *just* of you to write to Ross that I dictated to my type-writer advice about your wife and your conduct to her?" So Robbie must have thought my remarks on the subject of a business-character. They really were not. But Robbie is on horseback at present. He can ride everything, except Pegasus.

I hope to send you the proofs tomorrow. Do you think that copy-righting *portions* of the poem will prevent the piracy of quotation in the papers? I don't. I think the only chance is to go for a big thing and to publish the poem in America at one dollar. This of course would rank as general expenses. So you would have half the profits in America, and they *may be* great. But the moment you publish in England, the American papers, under pretence of criticism, will publish the whole affair. That is certain.

I now think that we must wait till after Christmas. If we are to secure America we must. And the 1st of January would not be a bad date. Consider the point.

You suggest "gray" instead of "grey" in one passage. But I have "grey" everywhere else. Is there any rule about it? I only know that Dorian *Gray* is a classic, and deservedly. Excuse this brief letter.[2] I am in a hurry to buy cigarettes—the first for four days. Sincerely yours

OSCAR WILDE

---

[1] George Robert Sims (1847–1922) was a prolific and very successful playwright, journalist and versifier, particularly as Dagonet in the *Referee*. His melodramas *The Lights of London* (1881) and *Harbour Lights* (1885) had long runs, and his ballad beginning "It is Christmas Day in the Workhouse" was a great favourite.

[2] The original covers eight quarto pages.

To Robert Ross

MS. Clark

Friday, 19 [November] 1897   *Villa Giudice, Posilippo*

My dear Robbie, Of course I received with gratitude and wonder the £9. I wrote to you some days ago to say so. But our post is so bad that letters take four or five days. I would have wired my thanks, only I feared you would think it extravagant.

The only reason I mentioned your having read my letter—the private parts of it—to Smithers, was that he wrote to me a private letter in his own handwriting saying "Is it *kind* or *just* of you to say to Ross that I dictated to my type-writer advice about Mrs Wilde and your relations to her? I carefully suppressed her name." Of course my remarks to you were of the nature of enforced repartee. But Bosie says that the words "cruel and unfounded charge" in your letter are a joke, a *scie* of old standing. So I daresay you are not serious. But tragedy and comedy are so mixed in my life now that I lose the sense of difference.

The poem as printed looks like a sixpenny pamphlet. I have written to Smithers to say that if he wishes to ask 3/6 he should make it look, as a book, to be worth at least 9d. This can be done by different pagination.

"*Grey* Hunger and Green Thirst" might seem an echo of Swinburne's "Green Pleasure and Grey Grief."[1]

By the way, is there any difference between "grey" and "gray"? I believe there is, but I don't know what it is. In *one* place in the poem Smithers suggests "*gray*." In others he leaves "grey." Perhaps he is seeing red. I believe they are sympathetic colours in spectroscope investigations.

The point of the doctor is childish. The description is generic. It is a type. The account of the execution is not the account of the Reading scene; it is general. I am going to put in "*some* coarse-faced doctor." Pray assure Smithers that this is adequate. It *is* adequate.

I don't like using "*another's* vigil" because I end the verse by the words "*another's* terror," and taking that as my cue begin a new stanza by "*another's* guilt." Three times is too much. But I won't have "arid." I now put "endless."

I am writing to More and to Adrian Hope about this monstrous attempt to leave me to starve because I live with the only human being—amongst gentlemen—who will live with me, and of course Hansell's attitude is out-rageous. He writes to me that he holds "any member of the Queensberry family" as coming under the category of "disreputable person." I should like to know Percy's views on that subject. They might leave a lasting impression on Hansell. I always distrusted Hansell, but I did not think he would strain the meaning of a legal document to ruin his own client. He might leave that to Hargrove et Cie. But my views are for More, who will of course show you my letter. Ever yours   OSCAR

---

[1] "Green pleasure or grey grief" occurs in "A Match" in Swinburne's *Poems and Ballads* (1866). Wilde changed his phrase to read "lean Hunger and green Thirst."

680

To More Adey
MS. Clark

Sunday [Postmark 21 November 1897]   *Villa Giudice, Posilippo*

My dear More, I cannot tell you the utter astonishment with which I read your letter.

You tell me that you, and Bobbie, on being asked whether Bosie was "a disreputable person" felt bound at once to say yes: and that you declared that my wife was acting "strictly within her legal rights according to the agreement" in depriving me of my allowance, because I have the pleasure of Bosie's companionship, the only companionship in the world open to me.

In what way, my dear More, is Bosie more disreputable than either you or Robbie?

When you came to see me at Reading in November 1895, my wife, on being informed of this by my sister-in-law, wrote to me a most violent letter, in which she said—I quote from her letter now before me—"I hear with horror that Mr More Adey has been to see you. Is this your promise to lead a new life? What am I to think of you if you still have intercourse with your old infamous companions? I require you to assure me that you will never see him again, or any people of that kind" etc. etc.

That is my wife's view of you, based on the information supplied to her by George Lewis about you, and Robbie, and other friends of mine. My wife also knows what Robbie's life is and has been.

May I ask, if you had come to give me the pleasure of your companionship in my lonely life, whether Robbie would have at once agreed that you were a "disreputable person" and that I had forfeited all claim to my allowance in consequence?

If Robbie had lived with me, would you have taken the same course? I simply don't know how to describe my feelings of utter amazement and indignation.

As for Hansell, he calmly writes to me that he considers "*any member* of the Queensberry family" is "a disreputable person." Conceive such ignorance, such impertinence. If Lord Douglas of Hawick offered me the shelter of his roof I was to be left a pauper!

Hansell is bound to decide according to the legal agreement: it is his duty to do so. I say nothing about his failing in his duty to me as a client. That would only give him pleasure. But simply as an arbitrator, in a question of life and death practically, he utterly ignores the wording of the agreement, and gives a decision entirely illegal, entirely unjust, in order, I suppose, to curry favour with Mr Hargrove, or to experience for the first time in his life the priggish pleasure of what he ignorantly thinks is a moral attitude.

When he tells me in black and white that if Percy came and stayed with me he would regard me as living with a disreputable person, he shows his entire disregard of the legal agreement of whose clauses he was stupidly made arbitrator.

As for you and Robbie calmly acquiescing in this monstrous injustice,

I do not know what to think about either of you. I simply cannot comprehend it, nor can I write, today, any more about it. Ever yours OSCAR

To Reginald Turner

MS. Hyde (D. & M.)

Sunday [21 November 1897]   *Villa Giudice, Posilippo*

My dear Reggie, I am very sorry to say that I cannot at present repay you the £2. 10 you so kindly lent me for Harry Elvin. I had hoped to do so this week, out of my quarterly allowance, but I am informed by my solicitor and by More and Robbie that *they have all unanimously* decided that Bosie comes under the *legal* definition of "a disreputable person" (the words used in my deed of separation with my wife) and that consequently I am to be deprived of my sole income, the wretched £3 a week, that stands between me and starvation.

For More and Robbie to have done this—More and Robbie of all people in the world!—is so astounding that I cannot comment on the fact. I simply state it.

"I said at once," says More, "that your wife was acting strictly within her legal rights according to the agreement, when I was asked whether your friends wished to oppose your wife's action in withdrawing your allowance." Can you imagine such a thing?

As for my solicitor, he takes a still more generous and genial view. "I consider *every member* of the Queensberry family disreputable" is his view in his own words!!!

More and Robbie have certainly played an incomprehensible part in the affair. Would you some day inform them that in a legal document words have to be interpreted in a legal sense: and not by private feelings of whatever kind they may be. A disreputable person is a person against whom some shameful charge has been legally proved. I am disreputable, legally, but Bosie is no more so than More.

I don't wish, dear Reggie, to mix you up in this matter, but you know enough law to be able to point out to More and Robbie that they have done a most unjust and illegal thing. They don't understand that legal documents are things that have to be carefully, rightly interpreted, and they think that by calmly throwing me and my legal rights overboard they have done a very splendid, chivalrous thing, whereas what they have done is unfair, stupid, and utterly unjust.

I don't mind being a Don Quixote, but it is rather hard that my life should depend on two Sancho Panzas.

Of course, as not merely my own solicitor, but the friends who arranged the agreement and supervised it, have decided that Bosie is legally "a disreputable person" I can do nothing, but I have written to Adrian Hope, the guardian of my children, to protest against the conduct of my solicitor and of More and Robbie. I have left on record at any rate a very strong protest against their unfair treatment of me, and possibly Adrian Hope may refuse to take advantage of the fact that those who held my interests in their hands had not my interest in their hearts, nor were intellectually able to decide rightly on the legal meaning of words.

I am delighted that you had nothing to do with the affair. You are still on your usual pedestal in my heart. Ever yours   o. w.

To Robert Ross
MS. Clark

[*Circa 23 November 1897*]   *Villa Giudice, Posilippo*

My dear Robbie, I have not heard yet from Hansell or Adrian Hope, nor do I know whether they will answer me or not.

Do you think that if I engaged not to *live* with Bosie—in the same house —that that would be regarded as a concession of any kind? To say that I would never see him or speak to him again would of course be childish— out of the question—but I am quite ready, and so will Bosie be, to say that we would not live in the same house again, if that would be regarded as an equitable concession. Or do you think that everything is over, and that my wife will hear of nothing that would enable me to live?

It is a dreary sordid tragedy, but I do think they should see that it is absurd to say that my wife cannot be expected to give me money to live with Bosie. How I spend my money is surely a question for myself. If my wife became a teetotaller, would she have a right to say she would not give me money to spend on wine? If she objected to smoking, would I have to give up cigarettes?

Besides, the income was purchased and sold for a consideration. You often said to me in your letters "You have now as a *right* what before you only had as a favour." I am not reproaching you, but pointing out that it turns out that after all I have it at the whim of my wife.

With regard to Leverson, his statement is quite untrue. On my way to Court, the last day, to be sentenced, he asked me whether he might take his £250 out of the trust-money. I said that I could not possibly assent to that as the money was not given me to pay my debts, and I did not know what my mother's wants would be, that she was the person to be considered first. I think his conduct utterly dreadful, and dishonourable, and his taking no notice of my letter unpardonably insolent. I am going to write to him again.

I suppose Smithers has received the proofs by this time. Pray look over them carefully. I may have omitted something, or passed over an error.

The actor-manager here, Cesare Rossi,[1] was astounded with *Salome*, but said he had no actress who could possibly touch the part. I am going to try Duse, but have not much hope.

My books have come from Dieppe by long sea, but I have not the money

---

[1] Italian actor (1829–98) who ended his career as director of the Fiorentini Theatre in Naples.

to get them out, so I have to do without them for the present; it is a great nuisance.

The *Gil Blas* has an interview with me which I send you.[1] Ever yours
OSCAR

To Robert Ross

MS. Clark

Thursday [25 November 1897][2]   *Villa Giudice, Posilippo*

My dear Robbie, Thanks for writing to me. The situation is appalling.

I will begin by a few literary notes. I have put back the stanzas I expunged, because I think they are dramatically necessary for the narrative. I think people will want to know what the man did after his conviction, so the narrative is improved, though the poetry is not good, but while it is possible to correct a good verse, it is almost impossible to correct a bad one.

I have put "The Governor was *strict* upon The Regulations Act." I now think that "strong" is better. The verse is meant to be colloquial— G. R. Sims at best—and when one is going for a coarse effect, one had better be coarse. So please restore *"strong."*

You did not like "The man in red who reads the Law," because you said it reminded you of the "man in blue" for a policeman. The reminiscence it brought to me was the *"Voilà ! l'homme rouge qui passe"* of Hugo's *Marion De Lorme*,[3] and I like the expression, but "who reads *one's doom"* would I think be better. Will you alter this for me? Unless you think I have fiddled too often on the string of Doom.[4]

Smithers has been very kind and has sent me £5. He promises another this week; but it has not yet arrived. I think after Christmas would be better for publication: I am hardly a Christmas present.

What astonishes and interests me about my present position is that the moment the world's forces begin to persecute anyone they *never leave off.* This seems to me a historical fact, as well as an interesting psychological problem. To leave off persecution is to admit that one has been wrong, and the world will never do that. Also, the world is angry because their punishment has had no effect. They wished to be able to say "We have done a capital thing for Oscar Wilde: by putting him in prison we have put a stop to his friendship with Alfred Douglas and all that that implies." But now they find that they have not had that effect, that they merely treated me

---

[1] This interview, signed Gideon Spilett, appeared in *Gil Blas* on 22 November. In it Wilde discoursed wittily on a number of topics including contemporary literature. Of Verlaine he said: *"La statue du héros doit être sur le champ de bataille de sa vie,"* i.e. in the Café François Premier, rather than the Luxembourg.

[2] So dated in *After Berneval.*

[3] The last line of Hugo's verse-drama of the time of Louis XIII, first produced in 1831. It is cried by the heroine and refers to Cardinal Richelieu, under whose edict her lover has just been executed for fighting a duel.

[4] Presumably Ross did, for the line was not altered.

684

barbarously, but did not influence me, they simply ruined me, so they are furious.

I have written to Adrian Hope, but have not yet heard anything. To Hansell I have written violently. Of dear More I have made a holocaust: it had to be. But he will survive any pyre: in the ashes his heart—*cor cordium*—will be found untouched.[1]

I will write tomorrow, but for the future cannot afford stamps! Ever yours   OSCAR

To More Adey

MS. Clark

Saturday [Postmark 27 November 1897]   *Villa Giudice, Posilippo*

My dear More, I have not yet heard anything from you in answer to my letter. But Hansell has written to me stating that his decision is irrevocable.

I now want to know if there cannot be a compromise made. I am quite ready to agree not to live in the same house with Bosie again. Of course to promise to cut him, or not to speak to him, or not to associate with him, would be absurd. He is the only friend with whom I can be in contact, and to live without some companion is impossible. I had silence and solitude for two years: to condemn me now to silence and solitude would be barbarous.

It is not a matter of much importance, but I never wrote to my wife that I was going "to keep house with Alfred Douglas." I thought "keep house" was only a servant-girl's expression.

My wife wrote me a very violent letter on September 29 last saying: "I *forbid* you to see Lord Alfred Douglas. I forbid you to return to your filthy, insane life. I forbid you to live at Naples. I will not allow you to come to Genoa." I quote her words.

I wrote to her to say that I would never dream of coming to see her against her will, that the only reason that would induce me to come to see her was the prospect of a greeting of sympathy with me in my misfortunes, and affection, and pity. That for the rest, I only desired peace, and to live my own life as best I could. That I could not live in London, or, as yet, in Paris, and that I certainly hoped to winter at Naples. To this I received no answer.

I do think that, if we engage not to live together, I might be still left the wretched £3 a week—so little, but still something. How on earth am I to live?

Do, if possible, try to arrange something. I know you all think I am wilful, but it is the result of the nemesis of character, and the bitterness of life. I was a problem for which there was no solution. Ever yours

OSCAR

[1] A reference to Shelley's funeral pyre and the inscription on his tomb. Cf. p. 40.

To Leonard Smithers

MS. Taylor

Sunday [? *28 November 1897*]   *Posilippo*

Dear Smithers, Do try and make the Chiswick Press less mad and less maddening. I now have "While *some* coarse-mouthed doctor straddles by, with *a* flattened bulldog nose, fingering *the* watch" etc. If they ask you is there no offence in it, say it is simply miching mallecho, but to say it with style wear sables.[1] However, if they kick, I cannot sacrifice the lines about the watch, so I enclose a feeble substitute, but I shall be outraged and perhaps outrageous if it is used.[2]

I wish you would start a Society for the Defence of Oppressed Personalities: at present there is a gross European concert headed by brutes and solicitors against us. It is really ridiculous that after my entire life has been wrecked by Society, people should still propose to exercise social tyranny over me, and try to force me to live in solitude—the one thing I can't stand. I lived in silence and solitude for two years in prison. I did not think that on my release my wife, my trustees, the guardians of my children, my few friends, such as they are, and my myriad enemies would combine to force me by starvation to live in silence and solitude again. After all in prison we had food of some kind: it was revolting, and made as loathsome as possible on purpose, and quite inadequate to sustain life in health. Still, there *was* food of some kind. The scheme now is that I am to live in silence and solitude and have no food at all. Really, the want of imagination in people is appalling. This scheme is put forward on moral grounds! It is proposed to leave me to die of starvation, or to blow my brains out in a Naples urinal. I never came across anyone in whom the moral sense was dominant who was not heartless, cruel, vindictive, log-stupid, and entirely lacking in the smallest sense of humanity. Moral people, as they are termed, are simple beasts. I would sooner have fifty unnatural vices than one unnatural virtue. It is unnatural virtue that makes the world, for those who suffer, such a premature Hell.

All this has, of course, direct reference to my poem: and indeed is the usual way in which poets write to publishers.

I have decided to put back the opening of Canto *Three*, because it is dramatically necessary for the telling of the story. The reader wants to know where the condemned man was, and what he was doing. I wish it were better, but it *isn't* and can't be. I think it aids the narrative immensely. So stick it in. For the rest I think I have corrected enough. The

[1] Cf. *Hamlet*, Act III, scene 2.
[2] This stanza finally read:

> He does not rise in piteous haste
>   To put on convict-clothes,
> While some coarse-mouthed Doctor gloats, and notes
>   Each new and nerve-twitched pose,
> Fingering a watch whose little ticks
>   Are like horrible hammer-blows.

686

popularity of the poem will be largely increased by the author's painful death by starvation. The public love poets to die in that way. It seems to them dramatically right. Perhaps it is. Ever yours   O. W.

To More Adey
MS. Princeton

Sunday [? *28 November 1897*][1]   *Villa Giudice, Posilippo*

My dear More, I am sorry my letter gave you pain: very sorry indeed: but then your action gave me still greater pain: not that I suggest or think that any protest from you would have prevented my wife from doing what she has done: but that I do think you would have been entitled to say that you did not regard Bosie as a "disreputable person" in the legal meaning of the word in a legal document. I was hurt at your saying to me that you felt bound to admit that "Mrs Wilde was acting strictly within her legal rights according to the agreement." I do not think that that is the case. Though had there been no agreement, and my wife was merely making me an allowance of her own free will, I quite admit that her action would have been natural, from the point of view of the passions and emotions of human nature, and popular, from the point of view of social approval by ordinary people. It seemed to me that you gave up unnecessarily and prematurely: a protest from you would not have stopped the confiscation, but it would have enabled me to make a stronger protest to Adrian Hope than I have done.

At present my own friends have given away my position. I am fighting without support. And, as you knew what Hansell's decision would probably, if not certainly be, you might have, and I think should have, said that the terms of the agreement did not *legally* apply to Bosie.

You can understand I feel sore about it, and the position in which I have placed myself makes me bitter.

At present I don't know what to do. Bosie will probably go back to Paris. I see nothing to do but to stay on here, and try to get to literary work. Of course I am depressed by the difficulty of reaching an audience; the adventures of my American poem have been a terrible blow to my ambition, my vanity, and my hopes.

Perhaps Adrian Hope may recommend my wife to continue the allowance on condition of my not ever again living in the same house as Bosie, and we are both ready to accept the inevitable, forced now on him as well as on me. We have no option. Whether Adrian Hope will help me, I don't know. Ever yours   OSCAR

---

[1] This letter is in an envelope endorsed by Adey "Melmoth 18 December 98," but its contents place it beyond doubt at the end of November 1897.

To Leonard Smithers[1]

30 November [1897]   *Villa Giudice [Posilippo]*

Robbie Ross has sent me a copy of a letter he has written you, in which
he states that he finds he has no longer my confidence in business matters,
and so does not wish to be connected with my affairs. I . . . assure you that
Robbie writes under a complete misapprehension . . . Robbie has done
everything for me in business that anyone on earth could do, and his own
generosity and unwearying kindness are beyond any expression of praise on
my part, though, I am glad to say, not beyond my powers of gratitude . . .
It would be fairer of him to say that it is too much worry to go on, than
that he finds he has not my confidence. Such a statement is childish.

To Leonard Smithers
MS. Taylor

Tuesday [? 30 November 1897]   *Villa Giudice, Posilippo*

My dear Smithers, Your letter just received.

I am very glad you are going to print on one side only: my suggestion
of a new page after each closing stanza was merely in case you did not
wish to print on one side only. But I was always conscious it would give a
casual piecemeal air to the work.

As regards the cover, I am quite content with paper; we must see how it
all makes up. Also as regards price, your judgment is of course better
than mine. I am myself in favour of 2/6.

Do send a copy at once to Miss Marbury, and Reynolds:[2] they *cannot*
get an offer unless the poem is read: and I don't think that a New York
paper of standing would pirate, any more than the editor of a magazine.
All my plays went to Miss Marbury. She is a woman of the highest position, and would not allow any nonsense. So pray let her have a copy at
once. Reynolds I don't know, but he can have access to hers. I think that
£5 would copyright the poem in the States: I used to copyright my plays
for £20 each, through Miss Marbury. She does all that sort of work.

With regards to the notes of interrogation, I really think that it would
be best to discuss vital points like this *en tête-à-tête*, so I hope you will
come out to Naples and see me.

As I have lost my entire income, of course I cannot live with Alfred
Douglas any more. He has only just enough for himself. So he is going
back to Paris, and I shall be alone here. I do not know if, now that we are
going to separate, there is any likelihood of my income being restored to

[1] The text of this fragment is taken from Glaenzer. On 25 November Ross had
written to Smithers (text from the Stetson sale catalogue, 1920):

> I regret to inform you that I have ceased to be on intimate terms with Oscar
> Wilde or to enjoy his confidence in business or any other matter . . . Alfred
> Douglas has written to a common friend that I have tried to prevent any con-
> siderable sum being obtained for the poem.

[2] Paul Reynolds (1864–1944), American literary agent, worked closely with
Elisabeth Marbury. She handled plays and he did not.

me. I unluckily have now no one to plead my cause aright. I have alienated all my friends, partly through my own fault, partly through theirs. The Paris *Journal* has a sympathetic paragraph to say I am starving at Naples, but French people subscribe nothing but sonnets when one is alive, and statues when one is not.

With regard to Daly, it would be very kind of you if you would write to him and say that I will begin a comedy for him for £100 down, and £100 for each completed act, the royalties to be such as I received for my last American play. Miss Marbury will let him know the contract. This would of course see me through the winter.

As regards the ownership of the publishing rights of my plays, the Bankruptcy trustee made no claim on them at all: they are not amongst my assets. Robbie will tell you who the trustee is. He is, I believe, very friendly disposed, and will make no claim: it would be absurd.

I still think that, to secure American copyright, it would be best to publish after Christmas, though Miss Marbury could copyright the thing in a week for you.

I hope Robbie is not behaving so unkindly as his letter to me suggested. After all it is on me that the whole tragedy has fallen: and it is mere sentimentality for the spectators to claim the crown of thorns as theirs, on the ground that their feelings have been harrowed.

You give me no news about the verse about the doctor. I think that with my alteration ("some" etc.) it should stand, but other alternatives were given.

My handwriting—once Greek and gracious—is now illegible: I am very sorry: but I really am a wreck of nerves. I don't eat, or sleep: I live on cigarettes. Ever yours   O. W.

To Leonard Smithers[1]

[? *Circa 2 December 1897*]   [*Naples*]

I think this is necessary on the grounds of narrative. And the standard by which the poem is to be judged is not that of lyrical beauty, but of realistic presentation and actuality, at least by a sane critic, if there is one outside Bedlam.

I don't think that a proof is necessary. Robbie, *still* a *literary* friend, would I am sure correct the proof for me, or for you. To send proofs here is a matter of nine days for return.

As regards the ultimate shape, do consider seriously the impossibility of asking 3/6 for a meagre pamphlet. I think no one, except a damned and chosen few, would buy it; they would be content with reviews and pirated quotation.

---

[1] The text of this fragment is taken from the Kern sale catalogue (1929).

To Henry D. Davray[1]

[Received 4 December 1897]   *Villa Giudice [Posilippo]*

Je ne sais si vous avez reçu une lettre que je vous ai écrit il y a quelque temps à propos du projet de dessins de votre brillant et intéressant ami pour mon poème. Mon éditeur de Londres désire publier le poème en une édition populaire à bon marché, et ensuite, si c'est un succès, essayer d'en faire faire par un bon artiste une édition de luxe. Je ne crois pas maintenant que le poème puisse paraître avant Noël. Naturellement je vous en enverrai un exemplaire.

To Robert Ross

MS. Clark

Monday [6 December 1897][2]   *Villa Giudice [Posilippo]*

My dear Robbie, I know that it would have been impossible for you to have prevented Hansell's decision: what hurt me was that no effort was made, and I still hold that More was wrong in saying that my wife was "acting strictly within her rights according to the legal agreement." Hansell is of the same opinion. He writes to me that he gave his decision, not on the grounds of the written agreement, but on the understanding that existed that I was not to live with Bosie.

He told me at *Reading* that he would decide so. At that time I did not want ever to see Bosie again, so I didn't mind. Afterwards was a different thing. I then had a right to claim that the strictest *legal* interpretation should be put on the wording of a very elaborate agreement. Bosie is of course a gilded pillar of infamy in this century, but whether he is *legally* disreputable is another question.

I knew that I was running a fearful risk of losing my income by being with Bosie. I was warned on all sides: my eyes were not blinded: still I was a good deal staggered by the blow: one may go to a dentist of one's own free will, but the moment of tooth-extraction is painful: and More's acquiescence in Mr Hargrove's refusal to pay Mr Holman wounded me, and I shot poisoned arrows back. Arthur Clifton is trying to arrange some terms with Adrian Hope, and I of course engage never to live in the same house as Bosie again. I hope Arthur will do this, but Adrian Hope has never answered my letter to him. I have not much hope, however. Things have come to a crash of a terrible character. You have done wonderful things for me, but the Nemesis of circumstances, the Nemesis of character, have been too strong for me—and as I said to More I think I was a problem for which there was no solution. Money alone could have helped me, not to solve, but to avoid solving the difficulty.

As for your letter to Smithers, I don't think you should have taken up

---

[1] The text of this fragment is taken from the editorial commentary to Davray's translation of *The Ballad of Reading Gaol* (1927 edition). The original may well have been in English. The artist was Héran (Herrmann), see note 1, p. 662.

[2] So dated in *After Berneval.*

such an attitude about me in consequence of some phrase in a letter of someone else's, with which I had nothing to do. You wrote to Smithers "I *hope* you will *refuse* to publish Oscar Wilde's poem if he insists on publishing first in a paper." The question of Smithers's publishing in book-form something that had appeared in a periodical was a question for him. What you meant of course was that you hoped Smithers would induce me to consent not to publish in a periodical: in point of fact Smithers wrote to me seven weeks ago that he did not care twopence whether I published previously or not. He did this in an answer to a letter of mine in which I told him that I had refused an offer from the *Musician*, on the ground that it would spoil Smithers's book. Bosie did not, and does not, see why, if I got £25 or £50 from a paper for the poem, you should try to induce Smithers to refuse to publish in book-form. Such things are constantly done. In any case it was a matter for Smithers to decide, and he had previously assured me that he did not care a scrap. This was the meaning of Bosie's no doubt too vivacious expression, and there is no offence in its substance, while, as for the form, I don't think that in the correspondence of either of you Form has been the predominant note, or the sense of Beauty the indwelling spirit. In any case it has nothing to do with me. I hope Smithers will show you all my letters to him in which you are mentioned. I am greatly and rightly pained at your writing to him that our intimate friendship is over, and that you find you have no longer my confidence in business matters. The former is a question at any rate for yourself: the latter statement is unjust, unwarranted, and unkind.

And on the whole I do think you make wonderfully little allowance for a man like myself, now ruined, broken-hearted, and thoroughly unhappy. You stab me with a thousand phrases: if one phrase of mine shrills through the air near you, you cry out that you are wounded to death. Ever yours

OSCAR

To Leonard Smithers

MS. Yale

Monday [Postmark 6 December 1897]   *Villa Giudice, Posilippo*

My dear Smithers, I am very glad you have heard from Miss Marbury, but do send her the poem. Her suggestion of *illustration* is of course out of the question. Pray tell her from me that I feel it would entirely spoil any beauty the poem has, and not add anything to its psychological revela-tions. The horror of prison-life is the contrast between the grotesqueness of one's aspect, and the tragedy in one's soul. Illustrations would emphasise the former, and conceal the latter. Of course I refer to realistic illustration.

I am quite broken-hearted about Bobbie's attitude towards me, and the way he has written of me to Alfred Douglas. But nothing can ever spoil the memory of his wonderful devotion to me, or rob me of the pleasure of being deeply grateful to him for the love he showed me. Alfred Douglas is on his way to Paris.

I wonder if you would *abonner* me at the *Daily Chronicle* office for a *month*: English papers here cost *fourpence*! It would be very good of you if you would see that I get the *D.C.* for at any rate four weeks— *à mon compte, bien entendu*—but *you* will have to pay in advance.

I received today Vincent O'Sullivan's poems:[1] they are beautifully bound and printed: I like the *format* of the book intensely, and I think the poems better than his former ones—more concentrated in motive, better thought-out, more fully realised, but in what a midnight his soul seems to walk! And what maladies he draws from the moon! When I have read them more carefully I am going to write to him.

I have seen the *Academy* with its lists of Immortals.[2] It is very funny what sort of people are proposed. But it is difficult no doubt to make out a list. Personally I cannot make up my mind as to whether the Duke of Argyll or Jerome K. Jerome has the better claims—I think the former. The unread is always better than the unreadable.

I await the revises, and promise you not to "make my quietus with a bare bodkin"[3] till I have returned them. After that, I think of retiring. But first I would like to dine with you here. To leave life as one leaves a feast is not merely philosophy but romance. Ever yours   O. W.

To Leonard Smithers
TS. Clark

Friday [? *10 December 1897*]   *Villa Giudice, Posilippo*

My dear Smithers, The £5, like manna from heaven, arrived safe. Many thanks for your endless kindness.

[1] *The Houses of Sin*, published by Smithers in 1897. O'Sullivan's *Poems* had been issued by Elkin Mathews in 1896. Smithers answered on 10 December: "I am glad you like the way I have produced O'Sullivan's poems."

[2] On 6 November 1897 the *Academy* printed the following list of suggested members for an Academy of Letters, "based upon a consensus of opinion gathered from the staff":

> John Ruskin, W. E. Gladstone, Herbert Spencer, Duke of Argyll, A. C. Swinburne, George Meredith, John Morley, Thomas Hardy, James Bryce, Sir G. O. Trevelyan, Leslie Stephen, George Macdonald, R. D. Blackmore, Rudyard Kipling, Aubrey de Vere, R. C. Jebb, Dr Salmon, W. W. Skeat, Dr J. A. H. Murray, W. P. Ker, W. E. H. Lecky, S. R. Gardiner, Bishop Creighton, Bishop Stubbs, Rev. Aidan Gasquet, W. E. Henley, Andrew Lang, William Archer, H. D. Traill, Edmund Gosse, Mrs Meynell, Mrs Humphry Ward, Francis Thompson, W. B. Yeats, Henry James, Austin Dobson, J. M. Barrie, A. W. Pinero, W. S. Gilbert, 'Lewis Carroll.'

This produced a flood of letters in the issue of 13 November. Gladstone said that he was too old to discuss the matter, but many readers and literary men suggested alternative names. Both H. G. Wells and Bernard Shaw suggested the inclusion of Wilde's name. Wells also asked, "Why does the Duke of Argyll always figure in this sort of thing? His name has been before me from my earliest years, and from my earliest years I have been trying in vain to discover his connexion with literature!" Nobody in fact suggested Jerome K. Jerome, though the correspondence continued briskly on 20 November, with another letter from Shaw.

[3] *Hamlet*, Act III, sc. 1.

I am delighted with the *size* of the book, as shown in the Van Gelder paper. If the public get the book for 2/6, nicely bound, they are fortunate. Of course when you see the general effect you will fix the price. Perhaps 3/- might do. I don't know what discount you give to booksellers.

The title-page, all in same type (excluding publisher's name), will be all right.

As regards the dedication: I wish to introduce the fact of his having been a Guardsman. He was, I believe, in the Second Life Guards (*Blues*), so it would run:

In Memoriam
Trooper of H.M. Second Life Guards
Obiit . . . etc.

But I know nothing about the technicality of uniforms. Do the Life Guards (*Blues*) wear blue uniforms? I cannot alter my poem if they do— to *me* his uniform was red. Only if they wear *blue* we had perhaps better omit the regiment. Could you ask some one? I believe they all wear red.

I like the two H.M.'s for the dedication. Also be sure it is the Second Life Guards. A newspaper file will tell everything.

The last page of all, page 31, is dreadfully placed. I see you have ordered two more leads. That will bring the text up higher on the page, but I think it would look well to add the pseudonym C.3.3 at the end. It would fill up the page and be, I think, a literary adjunct. It would explain the fact that the pseudonym is not a mere literary caprice, but the actual name for eighteen months of the man who wrote the poem. It should be the same type, I think, as the capital R in Reading Gaol. Same size, or one size larger if you like. Personally I like economy in type.

You ask me to make it up with Robbie. My dear fellow, I would gladly go on my knees from here to Naples if Robbie would be nice to me. I was upset and distressed at everything that had happened, and wrote bitterly— not about anything that was said about me but about what was acquiesced in about someone else. In my deed of separation with my wife a clause was inserted to say that if I lived with any disreputable person, in such a way as to cause public scandal, I was to lose my income. My wife's advisers said that Alfred Douglas was a "disreputable person," and More Adey wrote to me that he and Robbie felt bound to admit that my wife was "acting strictly within the terms of her legal agreement." I was hurt at More Adey and Robbie acquiescing at once in this view.

I do not deny that Alfred Douglas is a gilded pillar of infamy, but I do deny that he can be properly described in a legal document as a disreputable person, and I felt that some little stand might have been made by his friends and mine, for both Robbie and More Adey have been on friendly terms with Alfred Douglas and been with him in Paris. Indeed Robbie spent two months in Capri with him last year. Of course they could not have prevented my wife doing what she wished, but they could have protested, and that protest would have helped me. *Hinc illae lachrymae.* Which, however, have been more of my shedding than Robbie's. To me the loss of his affection is irreparable. I really now have not one friend, of all my old friends, left in the world.

Robbie's refusal to interest himself in my poem I feel is inartistic of him —my work as a poet is separate from my life as a man—and as for my life, it is one ruined, unhappy, lonely and disgraced. All pity, or the sense of its beauty, seems to me dead in the world. Two months ago, before this last worry began, Robbie wrote to me "Remember always that you committed the unpardonable and vulgar error of being found out."

This is the attitude of the world in its relation to me. I think it is one harsh, ignoble and pharisaic. But I wrote to Robbie at once that I would accept everything he said about me—that I could not write bitterly to him in return. When he seemed to me to acquiesce with unnecessary alacrity in the proposed definition of L. A. D. I protested. However I still hope that Robbie may be kind to me again. I am deeply sorry I gave him pain, but, like most people, he only realises the pain he gets and not the pain he gives.

You have been kind enough to ask me if you could help me to get back my income. I fear not. Arthur Clifton, an old friend of mine and of my wife's, wrote to me three weeks ago to say that if I would leave A. D. an arrangement could be made. I have parted from Alfred Douglas, and written to Arthur Clifton to say so, three letters, but none of my letters have been answered. I also wrote to another old friend, Adrian Hope, the guardian of my children and their cousin. He has taken no notice. The fact is that when a man has had two years of hard labour, people, quite naturally, treat him as a pariah dog. This is a social truth that I realise every day. I don't complain about it. There is no use complaining about facts. *Je constate le fait, c'est tout.* It comes from the decay of imagination in the race, caused by the pressure of an artificial and mechanical Society. And, after all, when my own wife leaves me to die of starvation in Naples, without taking the smallest interest in the matter, I don't see why I should expect old friends to take the trouble to even answer or acknowledge my letters.

But let us return to the poem. "There's life in Art, take refuge there," says Goethe—slightly misquoted by Arnold.[1]

I do not like "*callous* doctor."

(1) The term "callous man of science" etc. has been used to death.

(2) Callous people do not gloat: to gloat is to imply a morbid, passionate interest. "Coarse-mouthed" is much better—it goes with "gloat."

Do you think you might, to give the book a *cachet*, prefix a note that 25 large paper copies are printed, of which 22 are for sale, say at 10/6, and also that the edition is limited to 500 copies? When there is a demand, we can put second edition on the next 500. Also the fact of the poem being copyrighted in the States under Act of Congress must be mentioned. I think

---

[1] *The end is everywhere,*
Art still has truth, take refuge there!

are the words put into Goethe's mouth by Matthew Arnold in his "Memorial Verses", written in 1850 after the death of Wordsworth.

that *some* large paper copies could be sold. I am sure of it. But of course the cover should be slightly different.

I am sending off this letter today, but the proofs I keep until tomorrow as I cannot do up parcels and am not going to Naples.

I hope O'Sullivan will arrive soon. I suppose, however, he will stop and say his prayers at Rome.

I will be greatly obliged if you can get me a copy of *Dorian Gray* and send it to me. There is a Neapolitan poet, and good English scholar, who wants to translate it, and I want the Italians to realise that there has been more in my life than a love for Narcissus, or a passion for Sporus: fascinating though both may be.

Eleanora Duse is now reading *Salome*. There is a chance of her playing it. She is a fascinating artist though nothing to Sarah.

Pray write constantly, especially when there is no necessity to do so. Ever yours   o. w.

To Leonard Smithers
MS. Private

Saturday [11 December 1897]   *Villa Giudice [Posilippo]*
[Postmark 12 December 1897]

My dear Smithers, A holograph letter from you is indeed a curiosity of literature, and I treasure it for its manner no less than for its matter.

As for dear Robbie, if he will kindly send me out a pair of his oldest boots I will blacken them with pleasure, and send them back to him with a sonnet. I have loved Robbie all my life, and have not the smallest intention of giving up loving him. Of all my old friends he is the one who has the most beautiful nature; had my other friends been like him, I would not be the pariah-dog of the nineteenth century. But natures like his are not found twice in a life-time.

When dear Robbie heavily bombarded me (an unfair thing, as un-fortified places are usually respected in civilised war) I bore it with patriarchal patience. I admit, however, that when he seemed to me slightly casual about someone else, I sent up a rocket of several colours. I am sorry I did so. But what is there in my life for which I am not sorry? And how useless it all is! My life cannot be patched up. There is a doom on it. Neither to myself, nor others, am I any longer a joy. I am now simply an ordinary pauper of a rather low order: the fact that I am also a pathological problem in the eyes of German scientists is only interesting to German scientists: and even in their works I am tabulated, and come under the law of *averages*! *Quantum mutatus*![1]

Now to the title-page, which I enclose. The *C.3.3* is not good. It is too thin. It should be as black and thick as the title. There may be some difficulty about the numerals, but the *C* seems to me much thinner than the *G* in "Gaol."

---

[1] *Quantum mutatus ab illo* (How changed). Virgil, *Aeneid*, II, 274.

Also, your name is too large. I am not discussing the relative values of publisher and poet, as the poet's name is not mentioned. But the title of the poem is the foremost thing. By printing your name in the same type, or near it, the printers have spoiled the page. There is no balance, and it looks as if the poem was by Leonard Smithers.

It was much better in the second proof. You have marked on that that your name is to be "one size larger type." They seem to have made it three sizes larger. Personally, I think that there should be simply *two* types —one for the title and pseudonym, the other for publisher and address and date. If you wish a third type, take the one of L.S. in the title-page of O'Sullivan's book. Also, surely the spacing of the full title should be equalised. There seems to me too much white between

Gaol

→

By

→

3.

I do think it would look better together, made more of a block of. In any case your name is evidently out of all proportion—I speak typographically.

I think that you had better send me no more proofs of the poem. I have the *maladie de perfection* and keep on correcting. I know I have got it now to a fairly high standard, but I don't want to polish for ever. So *after you get* the proofs, I think you yourself could see that all my corrections were carried out, and let me have merely the title-page and "In Memoriam" page. This is out of regard for your time and pocket. I would also like to see the cover.

I think that if you try and get in your name and address on the back, where the lettering is to be, it will be too crowded. I propose simply "The Ballad of Reading Gaol." But you will see yourself. However, I see your name is all right on O'Sullivan's back.

Robbie has just sent me the *Weekly Sun*. I do not know if this is a sign of forgiveness or the reverse. Ever yours   OSCAR WILDE

To More Adey

MS. Clark

Monday, 13 December [*1897*]   *Villa Giudice, Posilippo*

My dear More, I must thank you very sincerely for your kindness in sending me the cheque, and I am really sorry that you should have again been bothered by my affairs.[1] I am very much grieved that I wrote to you

---

[1] Copies of letters in More Adey's hand (MS. Holland) read:

9 December 1897   *24 Hornton Street*
Dear Oscar, I enclose a cheque for £100, the amount I have just received from Lady Queensberry. She says she will pay the second hundred to me in a week or ten days. I write in great haste to catch the post. Ever yours   MORE

as I did, but I was upset, irritable, and horrid. All I said to Adrian Hope was that I considered that Bosie's actual position socially was in no way inferior to that of any of my friends, and I still think so. He holds his own with Society with amazing success. That was all I said.

But I hope you will forgive me for the petulance with which I wrote to you. After all, you can understand what a wreck of all fine things I am. In old days I was judged by a different standard from others: I should be equally so judged now: only now the standard has to be *lower*, not higher. Gratefully yours   OSCAR

---

6 January 1898   *Under the Hill, Wotton-under-Edge*
My dear Oscar, I have only just heard of your return to Naples. I had been waiting to write at length until I knew your address, as you did not mention what it would be at Taormina. However I did write a very short letter to you at the Poste Restante there, on the chance of its reaching you, just to tell you that your second £100 has been paid in to me, and awaits your disposal in my bank. [For further references to this sum of £200, see note 3, p. 714 and p. 717.] I came to Wotton-under-Edge the week before Christmas and shall be here until the end of the month. More Adey, Wotton-under-Edge is the telegraphic address and is enough for letters also. I have given directions for the usual weekly papers to be sent you from town at the end of the week, and any others that may contain news of interest.

It is rather late for me to say anything about the recent misunderstandings and disturbances, but while they were going on, and the atmosphere both here and with you was so electric, it was useless for me to say anything. Meanwhile however, I was doing everything I could possibly think of, to mitigate to both you and Bosie the unpleasantness of the situation and leave you freedom of action. You interpreted a sentence of mine about Mrs Wilde's having acted strictly within her legal rights, to mean that I had somehow admitted that Bosie was a disreputable character. I made no admissions about Bosie of any kind. His character did not enter into the question at all. The question was merely one of fact—whether you and he were living together or not. This question had been laid before the arbitrator, without my knowledge, before my interview with Holman took place. I had nothing to do with it. The one interview is all the communication I had with Holman. With Hansell I have had none at all since he ceased to act as your solicitor. Mrs Wilde did act strictly within her legal rights by appealing to the arbitrator according to the agreement; your friends, as the other parties to it, had therefore nothing to do but submit to his decision. There was no ground on which to oppose Mrs Wilde; it would have been a purely vexatious opposition, worse than useless to you, and we had no money to pay solicitors for carrying on a fruitless correspondence merely to gain time. But I did what little I could by absolutely refusing to interfere with you in concert with your wife's advisers, and by urging that you ought to be left to act on your own judgment. I then asked Arthur Clifton to urge the same thing to Hope personally.

I write merely of myself, but of course all your friends did anything they could too. I did not believe when you and Bosie answered my first letter that you could suppose for long that I had given away either his reputation or your interests, even if you supposed so at the moment, which I scarcely believed you really did. I heard nothing at all about your letter to Hope in which you mentioned me, except what you or Bosie wrote to me or our common friends here. I asked Clifton not to mention it to Hope, out of any consideration for me, if he should be seeing him again. But he had not seen him up to the time when I received your last letter and is not likely to have done so since. I thought at first that it was unkind of you to write to Hope about me in the tone in which your letters from Posilippo implied you had, but I preferred to believe that you had done so

697

To Leonard Smithers

MS. Taylor

9 January 1898   *31 Santa Lucia [Naples]*

My dear Smithers, The revise has never arrived, and I have waited from day to day for it. To wait longer would be foolish.[1]

I am sure it is all right. As regards your suggestion, or request, that I should revert to "in God's sweet world again," instead of "for weal or woe again" (Canto Two somewhere), certainly. Pray mark the correction yourself. Second thoughts in art are always, or often, worst.[2]

The C.3.3 I enclose seems excellent. The C. T. W. of the In Memoriam page was better larger, as before. "*trooper*" (same page) should have a *capital T*.

I *think* that "*in* the Royal Horse Guards" should be "*of* the R.H.G." I don't know, however; you might ask. "*Of*" seems nicer. The cover etc. I leave to you.

The post here is impossible, so pray bring it all out as soon as possible, without further consultation. I, as all poets, am safe in your hands.

As regards America, I think it would be better now to publish there *without* my name. I see it is my *name* that terrifies. I hope an edition of some kind will appear. I cannot advise about what should be done, but it seems to me that the withdrawal of my name is essential in America as elsewhere. And the public like an open secret. Half of the success of Marie Corelli is due to the no doubt unfounded rumour that she is a woman. In other respects pray do as you like about America, but do see that there is *some* edition.[3]

---

under the influence of great worry and annoyance, or more probably had not written so bitterly as the letters seemed to imply. Your last letter puts quite a different complexion on your letter to Hope; at any rate you are right, if I had anything to forgive you, I have forgiven it long ago. It is very nice of our common friends to defend me, often, I daresay, when they may really think that I have done or written something foolish, but, though I am grateful to them, I do not believe in the efficacy of vicarious justification. I refer to these matters because you have continued to do so, that I may not seem to refuse, from some senseless motive of pride or resentment, to justify myself. If I cannot entirely realise, I sympathise most affectionately with you in the fearful *bouleversement* of your whole life from the brilliant position you held before, through all your terrible misfortunes, into the dullness of your present isolation. I hope and believe that it may yet rise to something higher and greater even than what it attained to before. No one but you, with your astounding personality, could have come out of such a furnace of suffering as you did.

I have heard nothing of you since you wrote to me last. Do write soon about beautiful plays and poems and nice new friends and your plans. It was nice going to Taormina with the Russian Elder, it would have been horrid for you left at Posilippo alone. Ever your friend   MORE ADEY

[1] Smithers's letter of 29 December 1897, enclosing a further proof of the title-sheet, is printed by Mason, pp. 413–14.

[2] This correction was not made until the second edition. At Harvard is the copy of the first edition corrected for the second (see note 1, p. 703). Most of the corrections (including some not noted by Mason) are in Wilde's hand, but this particular one is in Smithers's.

[3] On 12 January Smithers wrote to Elisabeth Marbury asking her to get the best

I have had many misfortunes since I wrote to you—influenza, the robbery, during my absence in Sicily, of *all* my clothes etc. by a servant whom I left at the villa, ill-health, loneliness, and general *ennui* with a tragi-comedy of an existence, but I want to see my poem out before I take steps. Ever yours

O. W.

To Leonard Smithers[1]

[*Postmark 7 February 1898*]   *31 Santa Lucia* [*Naples*]

I am really charmed with the book. It is quite right, except the final signature of C.3.3 (page 31). That is awful; it should have been cut. In the remote case of a second edition, please have one cut. The cover is very nice, and the paper excellent. The title-page is a masterpiece—one of the best I have ever seen. I am really so cheerfully grateful to you, my dear fellow, for the care and trouble you have taken.

I have sent you the title-pages. Robbie Ross will give you the addresses, except Alfred Douglas's, which is Hôtel Bellevue, Mentone.

American serial price possible for *The Ballad*, with or without Wilde's name. On 25 January she replied from New York (text from Mason, pp. 415–16): "Nobody here seems to feel any interest in the poem, and this morning I received from the *Journal* their final offer, which, alas, is only $100," though in her memoirs, *My Crystal Ball* (1923), she claims to have got an offer of $250 from the *New York World*. In the event no American serial publication took place. The first American book-edition was published by Benjamin R. Tucker of New York in 1899.

[1] The text of this incomplete letter is taken from the American Art Association catalogue, 5 and 6 November 1923, supplemented by the Kern sale catalogue (1929). On 26 January Smithers had written from London (text from Mason, p. 416):

My dear Wilde, *The Ballad* is with the binder. I enclose you samples of the cloth in which it is to be bound: the white cloth is for its back, and the cinnamon coloured cloth is for its sides. The little fold will show you the thickness of the book; and I have pencilled on it a lettering which I propose to put on the back of the book—this lettering is to be in type similar in character to that on the title page. I have instructed the binders to send me twenty copies of the title sheet, which will be forwarded to you (probably tomorrow) for you to write inscriptions on them. You will then please return them to me, and I will see that the copies all go out to their respective owners, after they are bound up. I should like you to give me the addresses of such people as I am not likely to know, so that their copies can reach them. Immediately the book is bound I will send you a copy of it, which I beg of you not to allow to leave your possession until the day of publication—of course, as regards this, I am simply waiting for Miss Marbury's success in selling the book. Failing this success within the next fortnight, I shall beg of her to have the book set up in the States, and copyrighted at my expense. I would send you a sample copy of the book, which I have received today from the binder; but as it is not yet in a complete state, with its white and cinnamon back on it, I must remember the old proverb, which says that children should never see things half finished. So I will hold it back until it has got its binding on it.

I hope you are happy and well. Since I last wrote to you I have neglected absinthe, and have drunk whiskey and water, but I have distinctly seen the error of my ways, and have gone back to absinthe. I hear that you are within an ace of completing your play, *Pharaoh*. Yours very sincerely   LEONARD SMITHERS
Dowson sends his love, and he is gushing over the poem at the present moment.

To Leonard Smithers

MS. Lohman

Wednesday [*9 February 1898*]   *31 Santa Lucia* [*Naples*]
[*Postmark 11 February 1898*]

My dear Smithers, There are many addresses, I fear, that Robbie Ross may not know.

Major Nelson, Governor, H.M. Prison, Reading.

Mr George Groves, Officer, H.M. Prison, Reading, Berks.

Fritz Thaulow, Villa des Orchidées, Dieppe, France.

Mrs Ernest Leverson, 4 Deanery Street, Park Lane.

Robin Grey is the editor of the *Musician*. I don't know his address.

Oswald Sickert is in Pembroke Gardens, Kensington—forget number.

Stanley Makower is, I think, Pembroke Square, Kensington.[1]

I shall be in Paris on Sunday next. It is my only chance of working. I miss an intellectual atmosphere, and am tired of Greek bronzes. I don't know my address, but will send it to you, and hope to see you next week. My chief object in going to Paris is to dine with you, I need hardly say.

My life has gone to great ruin here, and I have no brains now, or energy. I hope to make an effort in Paris.

I am very much touched by your kindness in not putting advertising of your books at the end of mine. It is a detestable habit, and most inartistic.

Be sure and come to Paris next week. I shall be in the Quartier Latin somewhere. Ever yours   OSCAR WILDE

P.S. I don't know Robbie Ross's address—it used to be Phillimore Gardens —but it is three months since he last wrote to me, so perhaps he has left. Kindly show this postscript to Robbie.

---

[1] Wilde's list of recipients for copies of *The Ballad* (MS. Clark) reads "Oswald Sickert, Stanley Makower, Robbie, Reggie, More, Rowland Fothergill, Nelson, George Groves, Thaulow, Dowson, Rothenstein, Ricketts, Robin Grey, Max B., V. O'Sullivan, York Powell [see note 3, p. 789], Lamotte, L. Irving [see note 1, p. 704], G. B. Shaw, Archer, Harland [see note 4, p. 731], Leverson, Massingham, Headlam."

Digby Holden Ross Harwick La Motte (1861–1946) was educated at Rugby and Trinity College, Oxford. He was an assistant master at St Paul's School 1886– 1934, famous as teacher and eccentric.

PART NINE

PARIS

1898-1900

Paris: 1898-1900

The exact date of Wilde's return to Paris is not known, but he may well have carried out the intention expressed in the last letter and reached Paris on Sunday, 13 February, the day on which Smithers published *The Ballad of Reading Gaol*.

To Leonard Smithers

MS. Private

[*18 February 1898*]   *Hôtel de Nice, Rue des Beaux-Arts, Paris*

My dear Smithers, I sent you off the corrected copy[1] *yesterday* (Thursday): it only arrived on *Wednesday night*. I hope you have received it, and not gone to press without it. I really am distressed at your want of faith in the poem, and only printing 400 to start.[2]

And also, *do advertise*. I am told that no advertisements of any consequence have appeared. It is just possible that there may be a great popular sale, but if *you* don't assert the book, the press may ignore it.[3]

Also, why not print some copies on some special paper—*not* Japanese; that you have done. I want to distribute about ten copies in Paris, and don't like to give second editions to people.[4] Please send Frank Harris a copy, with a *printed* slip, "with the compliments of the author." Mark the package "*private*."

I am very glad you are coming over *alone*. I don't want to be bored with Mrs Dowson.[5] Ernest is charming, but I would sooner be with you alone, or with him along with you. Wire your arrival.

[1] For the second edition of *The Ballad*, which contained a number of verbal corrections (mostly printed in Mason pp. 417–419, but see note 2, p. 698). This edition (1000 copies) was printed on 24 February and issued before the end of the month.

[2] Smithers had eventually capitulated and printed another 400, so that the first edition of *The Ballad* consisted of 800 copies at 2/6, plus thirty numbered copies printed on Japanese vellum at 21/-.

[3] Smithers had in fact advertised *The Ballad* in the *Athenaeum* of 12 February, and on 19 February he took another large space there to announce the second edition as "ready next week."

[4] Smithers fell in with this suggestion, and the third edition of *The Ballad* (March 1898) consisted of 99 copies signed by the author at 10/6.

[5] This reference is inexplicable in any literal sense. Ernest Dowson never married, and his mother had died in 1895.

As regards addresses:

Fritz Thaulow, Villa des Orchidées, Dieppe.

Laurence Irving,[1] Lyceum Theatre.

Oswald Sickert (somewhere in Pembroke Gardens, Kensington—look in directory—I think *12*)

W. Archer, I suppose the *Daily Chronicle*. I don't know his address.

Would you kindly send a copy, with a *printed* slip "compliments of the author," to Stephen Phillips,[2] c/o John Lane, Bodley Head. Also, one to Rev. Arthur[3] Morrison, Assistant Chaplain, Wandsworth Prison, Wandsworth. I think the editor of the local Reading paper should have a copy. I don't know its name. Also, some Irish papers. *Dublin.*

Pray thank Arthur Symons from me for his kind offer, and say how gratified I should be to be reviewed by him. I hope the *Saturday* will have an article by him.[4]

I would like a copy sent to Oscar Browning Esq., King's College, Cambridge, with a slip inside.

Please let me have all notices. The *Chronicle* meant well, but there is more in the poem than a pamphlet on prison-reform.[5]

On the whole I think we are going on very well. Ever yours   O. W.

To Frank Harris[6]

[Circa 18 February 1898]   *Paris*

Dear Frank, I have never forgotten your kindness to me when I was in prison and I hope you will accept from me a copy of *The Ballad of Reading Gaol* as a slight sign of recognition on my part. There may be some verses in it that may please or interest you . . .

I don't know if you come to Paris as often as you used; if you do I need not say how much I would like to see you.

---

[1] Actor, manager and author (1871–1914). Younger son of Sir Henry.

[2] English poet and dramatist (1864–1915). His *Poems* (1897) had been widely praised and read. Le Gallienne quotes Wilde's saying to him: "Ah, Stephen, my sins are of scarlet and purple, but your sins are of white marble!"

[3] A slip for W. D. (see note 2, p. 523).

[4] Arthur Symons had written to Smithers (text from the Stetson sale catalogue, 1920):

I see by your advertisement in the *Athenaeum* that you are publishing Wilde's poem. I need scarcely say that if I could do anything that would be of service to Wilde, now that he is making his first attempt to return to literature, I should be only too glad to do it.

[5] On 15 February the *Daily Chronicle* had devoted two thirds of a column on the leader page to *The Ballad*, criticising it favourably but concentrating on the horrors of prison life which it portrayed.

[6] The text of this incomplete letter is taken from Maggs's catalogue 306 (1913).

To Robert Ross

MS. Clark

[? *18 February 1898*]   *Hôtel de Nice*

My dearest Robbie, Thanks so much for the cuttings.

Smithers is absurd, only printing 400 copies, to begin with, and not advertising. I fear he has missed a popular "rush." He is so fond of "suppressed" books that he suppresses his own. Don't tell him this from me. I have written to him.

It is very unfair of people being horrid to me about Bosie and Naples. A patriot put in prison for loving his country loves his country, and a poet in prison for loving boys loves boys. To have altered my life would have been to have admitted that Uranian[1] love is ignoble. I hold it to be noble— more noble than other forms. Ever yours   OSCAR

To Robert Ross

MS. Clark

Sunday [? *20 February 1898*][2]   [*Paris*]

Dear Robbie, Certainly: it would be very kind of you to give Smithers the names of the people who should have copies. I have asked him to print slips for insertion "with the compliments of the author." Arthur Clifton, of course, and Dal Young, and anyone else you can think of. I have sent O. B.[3] one at King's.

Miss Frances Forbes-Robertson should have one. Do you know her address? I suppose I would have no right to send *Miss Schuster* one? It is a great pity. I would like Sydney Grundy to have a copy.[4]

I fear that the press will boycott the work. It is very bitter and unfair, but I have not much hope of recognition.

Who *are* the people who object to my having been with Bosie at Naples, and spent my days with Heliogabalus, and my nights with Antinous?[5] I mean are they people who were *ever* my friends? Or are they simply those to whom Uranian love is horrible? If the latter, I cannot care. If the former, I do.

---

[1] i.e. homosexual. The word was apparently first used in this sense by the Austrian writer Karl Heinrich Ulrichs (1825–95). It was derived from the Greek Uranos (Heaven) in the belief that such love was of a higher order than ordinary love, and referred to Plato's *Symposium* (181 C). In 1896 André Raffalovich published a book in French called *Uranisme et Unisexualité*, containing a chapter on Wilde which had been separately published in 1895.

[2] In *After Berneval* this letter is dated 13 February, but its contents indicate a later date.   [3] Oscar Browning.

[4] Dramatist (1848–1914). On 8 April 1895, three days after Wilde's arrest, Grundy wrote a letter to the *Daily Telegraph*, protesting against the removal of Wilde's name from the programmes and play-bills of *The Importance of Being Earnest* at the St James's Theatre.

[5] The boy-favourite of the Emperor Hadrian. Cf. *The Sphinx*, stanza 17:

You heard from Adrian's gilded barge the laughter of Antinous.

I am sending my wife a copy.[1]

I have hardly seen anyone in Paris. I am waiting to distribute *twelve* copies to my friends here, Henri Bauër, Mirbeau,[2] and others.

A poem gives one *droit de cité*, and shows that one is still an artist.

There was an M.P. who was nice about me, through Miss Schuster; I forget his name. Would you have a copy sent to him also, with a slip?[3]

I have had a charming letter from Cunninghame Graham,[4] but, except you and Reggie, none of the people to whom I sent copies have written to me. The lack of imagination in people is astonishing. I wish I could see you. I see no one here, but a young Irishman called Healy, a poet.[5] Ever yours   OSCAR

What does Aleck think of *The Ballad*?

To Robert Ross

MS. Clark

Monday [*21 February 1898*][6]   [*Paris*]

My dear Robbie, Thanks for all your letters, and cuttings.

I have written to Smithers to tell him that you will give him a list of people to whom I wish copies to be sent, and Smithers has some printed slips "from the author" or "with the compliments of the author" done for me, which he will insert.

Will you kindly do this for me? The books are to be entered to *my* account, of course. I have written to Smithers to tell him so.

---

[1] On 19 February Constance Wilde wrote to her brother (MS Holland):

I am frightfully upset by this wonderful poem of Oscar's, of which so far I have only seen the extracts in the *D.C.* I hear that it was sold out the day it was published and that orders are pouring in, and that is a good thing as it means money! It is frightfully tragic and makes one cry.

[2] Octave Henri Marie Mirbeau (1850–1917), French author and journalist. During the early part of Wilde's imprisonment Mirbeau defended him in the French press. His novel *Le Journal d'une Femme de Chambre* (1900) contains a brief caricature of Wilde in the character of Sir Harry Kimberly.

[3] Almost certainly Richard Burdon Haldane (1856–1928), Liberal M.P. 1885–1911. (Later Secretary of State for War, Viscount and twice Lord Chancellor.) In his *Autobiography* (1929) he describes how, as a member of the Home Office committee investigating prisons, he visited Wilde in Wandsworth Gaol and advised him to use his prison experiences as a subject for literature. Haldane persuaded the Home Secretary to transfer Wilde to Reading and obtained books for him. He duly received his copy of *The Ballad*. The only other M.P. who showed sympathy was Ernest Flower (1865–1926), philanthropist and Conservative M.P. for Bradford West 1895–1906, who made "serious representations" to the Home Secretary about Wilde's condition during his imprisonment.

[4] Robert Bontine Cunninghame Graham (1852–1936), the most picturesque Scot of his time, traveller, poet, horseman, scholar, Scottish Nationalist, laird and Socialist, author of many volumes of stories, essays and sketches.

[5] Chris Healy, then a free-lance Paris correspondent. His *Confessions of a Journalist* (1904) contains a brief account of Wilde's conversation at this time.

[6] So dated in *After Berneval*.

Wyndham, George Alexander, and Lewis Waller should have copies. Also Mrs Bernard Beere—Church Cottage, Marylebone Road—and Selwyn Image, and *all* your list.

Dear good Ashton is here—quite wonderful and improbable. I am going to write to Constance to say that really now my income, such as it is, must be restored. Bosie and I are irrevocably parted—we can never be together again—and it is absurd to leave me to starve. Will you suggest this to her, if you write? Ever yours   O. W.

To Will Rothenstein

MS. Rothenstein

[*Late February 1898*]   *Hôtel de Nice*

My dear Will, I cannot tell you how touched I am by your letter, and by all you say of my poem. Why on earth don't you write literary criticisms for papers? I wish *The Ballad* had fallen into your hands. No one has said things so *sympathiques*, so full of delicate insight, so large, from the point of view of art, as you. Your letter has given me more pleasure, more pride, than anything has done since the poem appeared.

Yes: it is something to have made a "sonnet out of skilly" (Cunninghame Graham will explain to you what skilly is.[1] You must never know by personal experience). And I *do* think the whole affair "realised," and that is triumph.

I hope you will be in Paris some time this spring, and come and see me.

I see by the papers that you are still making mortals immortal, and I wish you were working for a Paris newspaper, that I could see your work making *kiosques* lovely. Ever yours   OSCAR

To Frank Harris

MS. Texas

[*Late February 1898*]   *Hôtel de Nice*

My dear Frank, I cannot express to you how deeply touched I am by your letter: it is *une vraie poignée de main*. I simply long to see you, and to come again in contact with your strong, sane, wonderful personality.

I cannot understand about the poem. My publisher tells me that, as I had begged him to do, he sent the two *first* copies to the *Saturday* and the *Chronicle*, and he also tells me that Arthur Symons told him he had written specially to you to ask you to allow him to do a *signed* article. I suppose publishers are untrustworthy. They certainly always look it. I hope *some* notice will appear, as your paper, or rather yourself, is a great force in

[1] Cunninghame Graham had been imprisoned for six weeks at Pentonville for his part in the Trafalgar Square riots of 1887. Some account of his prison experiences is to be found in the sketch "Sursum Corda" in his book *Success* (1902). Skilly was a kind of thin gruel given to prisoners.

London, and when you speak men listen. I, of course, feel that the poem is too autobiographical and that *real* experiences are alien things that should never influence one, but it was wrung out of me, a cry of pain, the cry of Marsyas, not the song of Apollo. Still, there are some good things in it. I feel as if I had made a sonnet out of skilly! And that is something.

When you return from Monte Carlo please let me know. I long to dine with you.

As regards a comedy, my dear Frank, I have lost the mainspring of life and art, *la joie de vivre*; it is dreadful. I have pleasures, and passions, but the joy of life is gone. I am going under: the morgue yawns for me. I go and look at my zinc-bed there. After all, I had a wonderful life, which is, I fear, over. But I must dine once with you first. Ever yours   O. W.

To Leonard Smithers

MS. Clark

[*Postmark 25 February 1898*][1]   *Hôtel de Nice*

My dear Smithers, We have waited for you for hours. Surely you have not left Paris? It seems impossible, as the city wears its wonted air of joy. Please see about the leaflet, and the Author's Edition with a cover by Ricketts—a new colour and a *remarque* in gold.[2] The *D.T.*, by the influence of Reggie Turner, has been forced to notice the book, but grudgingly and badly.[3] Do send me all the papers that have notices tomorrow. I have hopes of the *Academy*.

Will you kindly send me *six* copies of the Second Edition. It was a great delight seeing you, and I must thank you for all your kindness to me. Maurice[4] sends his kindest regards. We met by chance this morning, and I hope to see him again this evening. Ever yours   O. W.

To Leonard Smithers[5]

[*Postmark 28 February 1898*]   [*Paris*]

I am still looking for you in Paris. Are you here, or in London? Please be serious, and let me know. In the Author's Edition I would like the dedication inserted.[6] It would give an interest to the edition, and an air of psychological mystery. Robbie has written to me about to whom I should send copies—people who have been kind to me and about me.

[1] So dated in the American Art Association catalogue of 9 February 1927. When the letter reached Clark it was in an envelope postmarked 11 May 1898, which cannot belong to it.

[2] The signed edition of *The Ballad* (see note 4, p. 703) was bound in purple and white linen, with a leaf-design by Ricketts stamped in gold.

[3] The *Daily Telegraph*, for which Turner was now working, reviewed *The Ballad* briefly on 23 February.

[4] Maurice Gilbert, one of Wilde's closest and most devoted friends during these last years. Except that his father was English and his mother French, I have failed to discover anything about him.

[5] The text of this incomplete letter is taken from the American Art Association catalogue of 9 February 1927.   [6] See note 1, p 578.

He will bring you the list. Please enter them to my account. Also, do send me some money ... I have just twenty-two francs left. I long to hear about America. There are great possibilities there for a *coup*. Do try and work some papers for more reviews: they help immensely.   O. W.

To Henry D. Davray
MS. Princeton

[*Circa 1 March 1898*]   *Hôtel de Nice*

My dear Mr Davray, I must write a line to you to tell you again how touched and gratified I am by your appreciation of my *Ballad*, and by the interest you take in it.[1] I would greatly like to have it published with a translation by you, for no French man of letters can render English as you can, and either in a review or as a separate volume. I fancy that a review is the more feasible. Perhaps you will ask Vallette about the matter.[2] I long to hear about the Odéon: it would help me very much if my work was recited there.

As soon as I get rooms I am going to begin a new play: which I hope you will like.

Pray offer to Madame Davray the expression of my homage, and believe me, truly yours   OSCAR WILDE

To Robert Ross
MS. Clark

Wednesday [? *2 March 1898*]   [*Paris*]

My dear Robbie, A thousand thanks for all the trouble you are taking for me. You, although a dreadful *low-Church* Catholic, as a little Christian sit in the snow-white rose.[3] Christ did not die to save people, but to teach people how to save each other. This is, I have no doubt, a grave heresy, but it is also a fact.

I have *not* read your letter to Constance. I would sooner leave it to you. You have the tact of affection and kindness, and I would sooner return it unread.

The facts of Naples are very bald and brief.

Bosie, for four months, by endless letters, offered me a *"home."* He offered me love, affection, and care, and promised that I should never want for anything. After four months I accepted his offer, but when we met at *Aix* on our way to Naples I found that he had no money, no plans, and had forgotten all his promises. His one idea was that I should raise money for us both. I did so, to the extent of £*120*. On this Bosie lived, quite happy. When it came to his having, of course, to repay his own *share*, he

[1] A long review of *The Ballad* by Davray appeared in the *Mercure de France* for April. Wilde may have seen it beforehand, and in any case the April issue was probably on sale sometime in March.

[2] Alfred Vallette (1858–1935) founded the *Mercure de France* 1889–90 and edited it until his death. He married the novelist Rachilde.   [3] See note p. 486.

became terrible, unkind, mean, and penurious, except where his own pleasures were concerned, and when my allowance ceased, he left.

With regard to the £500, which he said was "a debt of honour" etc. he has written to me to say that he admits that it is a debt of honour, but that "lots of gentlemen don't pay their debts of honour," that it is "quite a common thing," and that no one thinks anything the worse of them.

I don't know what you said to Constance, but the bald fact is that I accepted the offer of a "*home*," and found that I was expected to provide the money, and that when I could no longer do so, I was left to my own devices.

It is, of course, the most bitter experience of a bitter life; it is a blow quite awful and paralysing, but it had to come, and I know it is better that I should never see him again. I don't want to. He fills me with horror. Ever yours   o. w.

To Frank Harris

MS. Texas

[? *Circa 3 March 1898*]   *Hôtel de Nice*

My dear Frank, You have been so good and generous to me that I hate to have to ask you to be generous again. But I am entirely without money, and if you could let me have £5 you would be doing me a great kindness. I have had no money from my trustees for six months, and am trying to get back my little £3 a week, through Robbie Ross, always a good friend to me, but there are delays, and in the meanwhile I drift in ridiculous impecuniosity, without a sou. So, if you can, do something.

I long to see you here, and to have the dinner you asked me to at *Reading*. Ever yours   OSCAR WILDE

To Leonard Smithers[1]

[*Postmark 3 March 1898*]   *Paris*

Very well: no dedication for the Author's Edition. You are always wise and prudent (about other people's affairs). Please send the money you promise for tomorrow in a bank-note, as no banks are open on Sunday, and I may not get it till too late on Saturday . . . I [don't] think the poem will suffer from a French edition, with translation, either in a book or a review . . . I am not at all well and also am very unhappy, but dear Robbie Ross is bestirring himself in my interests, like the good chap he is. There is going to be a recitation in a French translation of some of my poems in prose at the Odéon—at a literary matinée. Maurice has won twenty-five games of bezique and I twenty-four: however, as he has youth, and I have only genius, it is only natural that he should beat me.

OSCAR WILDE

[1] The text of this incomplete letter is taken from the American Art Association catalogue of 9 February 1927.

To Leonard Smithers[1]

If we could have an edition at Boston or New York of even three hundred copies, I think that would be a start. I know you will work your best for it. Please send me the *Academy*. I have not seen it . . . I rely on your sending me a little money tomorrow. I have only succeeded in getting twenty francs from the concierge, and I am in a bad way. Do you really think that 10/- is enough for the Author's Edition? I should have thought 15/- was the least. Could you find out who wrote the *Sunday Special*[2] notice? . . . The *Athenaeum* advertisement is splendid.[3]   OSCAR

To Leonard Smithers

MS. Clark

Saturday [*Postmark 5 March 1898*]   [*Postmark Paris*][4]

Dear Smithers, This is all the proprietor of the café can do in the way of advertising the book, and hiding[5] the "*pen*"—it is not bad for a beginning.

The cheque, a thousand thanks for it, arrived safe, and, with reckless confidence, the banker cashed it. Maurice took it to the bank, so I dare say it was on account of his *beaux yeux*. He grows dearer to me daily, and we now dine at a restaurant for two francs! It is an excellent place, *seulement il est défendu de manger*.

The sheets[6] have not yet arrived; I expect them tonight.

I think 10/6 for copies signed by the author too little. My signature should be worth more than Japanese paper. Think of this point.

What could you print 250 copies with a French translation on the opposite page for? I think that they would go well here. Please let me know. Vallette would place them, and Davray do the translation.

Maurice says he is too old to play marbles, and I am too young to begin, so we bezique our youthful lives away. Ever yours   O. W.

---

[1] The text of this incomplete letter is taken from the American Art Association catalogue of 9 February 1927.

[2] A Sunday newspaper which ran from December 1897 till December 1903. On 13 February 1898 (publication day) it had published the first and most enthusiastic review of *The Ballad*, the anonymous reviewer claiming that "not since the first publication of 'The Ancient Mariner' have the English public been proffered such a weird, enthralling and masterly ballad-narration."

[3] A large advertisement in the issue of 5 March, announcing the fourth edition of *The Ballad*.

[4] This letter is written on café paper with an engraving of a pen-nib, through which Wilde has drawn two strokes, adding alongside: "*The Ballad of Reading Gaol. Price 3 francs.*"

[5] This word might conceivably be "having," but Wilde's two lines could be said to be hiding the pen (a slang term for penitentiary).

[6] The unbound copies or "sheets" of the signed (third) edition of *The Ballad*. See note 4, p. 703.

To Leonard Smithers

MS. Clark

Monday [*Postmark 7 March 1898*]   [*Postmark Paris*]

My dear Smithers, I am very glad you went to Margate, which, I believe, is the *nom-de-plume* of Ramsgate. It is a quiet nice spot not vulgarised by crowds of literary people. I hope it has done you and your companions good.

I sent off the sheets yesterday. Maurice sent them off; he was most kind and wrote nearly all the signatures, as I, I don't know why, was rather tired. He writes much better than I do, so his copies should fetch 30/- at least.

I have read *Henley*—it is very coarse and vulgar, and entirely lacking in literary or gentlemanly instinct.[1] He is so proud of having written *vers libres* on his scrofula that he is quite jealous if a poet writes a lyric on his prison.

Will you kindly send Henry Davray, 33 Avenue d'Orléans, Paris, a copy of the second edition *at once*: and also another to *me*. I want to see the corrections, and Davray must have for his translation the (so far) ultimate form of the great work.

It is to appear in the *Mercure de France* for the First of April, a day on which all poems should be published.

But, if it would not cost much, I think a small (300) edition, with a French version, might sell well here. I will speak to Vallette tomorrow about it.[2]

I suppose Symons will be in *next* week's *Saturday*.

The *Academy* arrived all right; it is a heavy judicial charge.[3] People don't understand that criticism is prejudice, because to understand one must love, and to love one must have passion. It is only the unimaginative who are ever fair. But I am glad they noticed it.

Would you have copies sent to: Rev. Page Hopps,[4] Leicester; the Baron von Gloeden,[5] Taormina, Sicily; Illustrio Signor Alberto Stopford,[6]

[1] Henley's unsympathetic review of *The Ballad* appeared anonymously in the *Outlook* of 5 March.

[2] Davray's translation, *La Ballade de la Geôle de Reading*, appeared in the May issue of the *Mercure de France* and the proposed volume publication took place in the autumn. Later Davray made translations of five of Wilde's six prose-poems (see note 4, p. 356), which appeared in the *Revue Blanche* of 1 May 1899.

[3] A long, pompous and patronising review of *The Ballad* had appeared in the *Academy* of 26 February. The anonymous critic complained that Wilde was "not as whole-souled a battler for truth as he should be," and compared the poem to Thomas Hood's "Dream of Eugene Aram:" "Hood's work is, we think, the finer of the two: it has more concentration, its author had more nervous strength, was a more dexterous master of words, was superior to morbidity and hysteria."

[4] See p. 168.

[5] A German who settled at Taormina in the nineties and died there in 1931. He acquired some reputation for his photographs of Sicilian youths posed "noble and nude and antique" in the guise of Theocritan goatherds or shepherds.

[6] Albert Henry Stopford (b. 1860), great-grandson of the third Earl of Courtown, was prominent in London society until he moved to the Continent.

Taormina, Sicily; Laurence Housman Esq.,[1] c/o Grant Richards, Publisher; all with the printed slip of "author's compliments."

Do you think the religious papers would review it? I think it would be worth while trying. Ever yours

o. w.

To Henry D. Davray

MS. Yale

Monday [*7 March 1898*]   *Hôtel de Nice*

My dear Davray, I am delighted that my poem is to appear with a translation by you, and will go and see Vallette tomorrow morning. I have told my publisher to send you a copy of the Second Edition which contains some corrections. You will receive it on Wednesday. I will also bring Vallette a copy, so that he can have it set up in type.

I need not say with what pleasure I would see your translation. Of course, there are many words, relating to prison life, for which the proper French *prison* equivalents must be found: words that, though not *argot*, are still *technical*. I am always free, so pray let me know when I can see you, on the completion of the poem.

I have written to my publisher to suggest his printing *250* copies with your translation on the opposite page, to appear simultaneously with the *Mercure*, and to bear, of course, the name of the *Mercure* on it—on the title-page—as well as that of the London publisher. Your sincere friend

OSCAR WILDE

To Frank Harris[2]

[*Circa 7 March 1898*]   *Hôtel de Nice*

Just a line to thank you for your generosity, and the sweet way in which you make your generosity dear to one. Many can do acts of kindness, but to be able to do them without wounding those who are helped in their trouble is given only to a few, to a few big, sane, large natures like yours.

I long to see you and catch health and power from your presence and personality.

---

[1] English author (1867-1959), who wrote to Allan Wade on 12 November 1954: "When Wilde came out of jail I sent him a copy of my book *All Fellows*, hoping that he would find in it something to suit his condition. Presently I got a letter from him saying: 'By the same post that brought me your book of *All Fellows* I received from your brother A. E. H. a copy of his poems, *A Shropshire Lad*. So you two brothers have between you given me a taste of that rare thing called happiness'. I think those are almost the exact words." In his dialogue *Echo de Paris* (1923) Laurence Housman recorded an impression of Wilde's conversation in Paris during his last years.

[2] The text of this incomplete letter is taken from Maggs's catalogue 269 (1911), supplemented by the Anderson Galleries catalogue of 19 November 1931.

The *Mercure de France* is going to publish my poem here with a prose translation by a young poet who knows English, so I have something to think of besides things that are dreary or dreadful. And I am starting on a play, so perhaps there is something for me in the future.

To Leonard Smithers

MS. Clark

Wednesday [*Postmark 9 March 1898*]　　　　　　　　　[*Postmark Paris*]

My dear Smithers, Without my morning letter from you life would be dreadful—*is* dreadful—except for Maurice, who is sweeter than ever.

Why don't you write to me? Why not tell me if you will do a French edition, to be launched by Vallette? I don't think there is money in it, but I think that at five francs we should clear expenses.

Also send me the *Referee*, if the attack has appeared. I am rather languid and want a tonic.[1]

Galignani has five lines this morning to say that the poem is "*wonderfully weird.*" It is not worth while sending to you.

Will you send a copy to the *Guardian*? I used to know the editor very well: he is Irish, and quite a man of letters. His interest in curates is feigned.[2] Ever yours　　　　　　　　　　　　　　　　　　o. w.

To Carlos Blacker

MS. Blacker

[*Postmark 9 March 1898*]　　　　　　　　　　　　　*Hôtel de Nice*

My dear Carlos, I cannot express to you how thrilled and touched by emotion I was when I saw your handwriting last night. Please come and see me tomorrow (Thursday) at five o'clock if you possibly can: if not, pray make some other appointment: I want particularly to see you, and long to shake you by the hand again, and to thank you for all the sweet and wonderful kindness you and your wife have shown to Constance and the boys.[3]

---

[1] The *Referee* noticed *The Ballad* briefly on 6 March.

[2] Daniel Conner Lathbury (1831–1922) was editor of the *Guardian*, a Liberal and High Church paper, from 1883 to 1899. See p. 265.

[3] On 4 March Constance Wilde had written to Blacker (MS. Blacker):

Oscar is or at least was at the Hôtel de Nice, Rue des Beaux-Arts. Would it be at all possible for you to go and see him there, or is it asking too much of you? He has, as you know, behaved exceedingly badly both to myself and my children and all possibility of our living together has come to an end, but I am interested in him, as is my way with anyone that I have once known. Have you seen his new poem, and would you like a copy, as if so I will send you one? His publisher lately sent me a copy which I conclude came from him. Can you find this out for me, and if you do see him tell him that I think *The Ballad* exquisite, and I hope that the great success it has had in London at all events will urge him on to write more. I hear that he does nothing now but drink and I heard that he had left Lord A. and had received £200 from Lady Q. on condition that he did not see him again, but of course this may be untrue. Is Lord A. in Paris? Do what seems right to you.

For other references to this £200, see note p. 694 and p. 717.

714

I am living here quite alone: in one room, I need hardly say, but there is an armchair for you. I have not seen Alfred Douglas for three months: he is I believe on the Riviera. I don't think it probable that we shall ever see each other again. The fact is that if he is ever with me again he loses £10 a month of his allowance, and as he has only £400 a year he has adopted the wise and prudent course of conduct.

I am so glad my poem has had a success in England. I have had for some weeks a copy for you—of the first edition—by me, which I long to present to you.

It appears with a French translation in the *Mercure de France* for April, and I hope to have it published in book form also, in a limited edition of course, but it is my *chant de cygne*, and I am sorry to leave with a cry of pain—a song of Marsyas, not a song of Apollo; but Life, that I have loved so much—too much—has torn me like a tiger, so when you come and see me, you will see the ruin and wreck of what once was wonderful and brilliant, and terribly improbable. But the French men of letters and artists are kind to me, so I spend my evenings reading the *Tentation* by Flaubert. I don't think I shall ever write again: *la joie de vivre* is gone, and that, with will-power, is the basis of art.

When you come ask for Monsieur Melmoth. Ever yours   OSCAR

To Otho Holland Lloyd
MS. Clark

[*Circa 15 March 1898*]   *Hôtel de Nice*

My dear Otho, I am so glad you received the copy of the poem I sent you. I could not write your name in it, as I was away in Naples.

I am glad to say it has been a great success, and they are now printing the *fifth* edition, but I only get 3d. a copy so it will not come to much.[1] It was a mistake selling it at 2/6. It is, *as far as the paper goes*, too cheap. The poetry is another question.

However, it is a good thing to have written it, and a good thing to have had it published, and I am greatly touched by what you say about it.

My kind regards to Mary.[2] Sincerely yours   OSCAR

To Frank Harris
MS. Texas

[*Circa 15 March 1898*]   *Hôtel de Nice*

My dear Frank, It gave me great pleasure to find that the most sensitive

---

[1] The fifth edition of *The Ballad* (1000 copies) was printed on 17 March. The fourth edition (1200 copies) had been printed on 4 March, and the sixth edition (1000) followed on 21 May. The Chiswick Press records show that Smithers's bill for the composition, corrections and printing of all six editions (including the Japanese vellum for thirty copies) came to £42. 1. 9.

[2] Lloyd's second wife, whom he had married in 1888.

715

and intellectual appreciation of my poem appeared in your paper. I am greatly touched by Symons's article; it is most admirably phrased, and its mode of approach is artistic and dignified. A thousand thanks to you, and to him.[1]

When do you arrive?

I have a *faim de loup* for your presence, and for dinner. I am eating the *vache enragée* with a vengeance, which perhaps accounts for my Greek handwriting having become a scrawl.[2]

I wish you would let me have the *Saturday* from time to time: papers are so dear here. Ever yours   OSCAR

To Leonard Smithers[3]

[Postmark 15 March 1898]   *Hôtel de Nice*

A thousand thanks for the £4: it was most kind of you to think of it. I have been rather unhappy and troubled, so have not written, but I hope to get all right this week . . . I was greatly pleased with Symons's article; it is admirably written, and most . . . artistic in its mode of approval . . . I don't think I should answer Henley. I think it would be quite vulgar. What does it matter! He is simply jealous. He made his scrofula into *vers libres*, and is furious because I have made a sonnet out of "skilly." Besides, there are only two forms of writers in England, the unread and the unreadable. Henley belongs to the former class. (You can send this aphorism to the *Sunday Special*.)

To Robert Ross

MS. Clark

[Postmark 17 March 1898]   *Hôtel de Nice*

My dear Robbie, Thanks for your letter.

My wife wrote to Carlos Blacker that she had sent you £40 for me, but she has evidently changed her mind.[4] I think it is absurd my not having

---

[1] Arthur Symons's review of *The Ballad* appeared in the *Saturday Review* on 12 March. He later revised it and included it with other reviews of Wilde's books and essays on his work in *A Study of Oscar Wilde* (1930).

[2] *Manger de la vache enragée* is a slang term meaning to go hungry.

[3] Text from Mason (p. 420), quoting Glaenzer.

[4] On 10 March Constance Wilde had written to Blacker (MS. Blacker):

I naturally would not have asked you to see Oscar, if I had thought there was any chance of your meeting that person whom I know that very naturally you loathe. I heard long ago that Oscar was not with him, and that he is on the Riviera with his mother, and that his allowance stops if he ever lives with O. again. The result of your writing to O. is that he has written to me more or less demanding money as of right. Fortunately for him, hearing that he was in great straits, I had yesterday, or rather the day before, sent him £40 through Robbie Ross. He says that I owe him £78 and hopes that I will send it. I know that he

the arrears of my allowance—nearly £80—now due to me, and lopping me from £150 to £120 is of course absurd also. However, it is something, and I am glad to get it.

It is quite untrue that I received £200 from Lady Q. on condition of not living with Bosie.[1]

Bosie owed me £500. He admitted this a debt of honour, and got his brother to formally guarantee it etc. He paid me £200 of this, but I have had no communication with that mischievous foolish woman; I simply received less than half of what Bosie owes me. I know that Bosie made terms with his mother, but that is not my concern. In paying debts of honour people cannot make terms. So pray tell my wife that it is quite untrue, or that you know nothing about it. The former statement would be the true one.

As soon as the £10 arrives I am going to see how to live on it. I must try and invent some scheme of poverty, and have found a restaurant where for 80 francs a month one can get nothing fit to eat—two chances a day—so shall *abonner* myself there. But you don't realise what a problem it is, to live on 250 francs a month. However, I must try.

Today is the *Mi-Carême*, a detestable day of clowns and confetti, so I am writing in a *café*, where I get this paper for nothing.

I am charmed with Symons's article in the *Saturday*.

My writing has gone to bits—like my character. I am simply a self-conscious nerve in pain. Ever yours   o. w.

To Leonard Smithers
MS. Berg

[*Postmark 17 March 1898*]   *Hôtel de Nice*

My dear Smithers, Can you give me any idea of the prospective profits of my poem? I suppose we can depend on a sale of 4000 copies, some of which are dearer than the others. I don't care to be always worrying you for money, but of course I see no prospect for me except advances, not on problematic successes, but on an achieved sale.

Of course you have to wait for the booksellers' accounts, but still as the money is assured I should like to have some if I have not already over-drawn, which I cannot believe.

My handwriting has gone to bits, because I am nervous and unhappy. I never could understand mathematics, and life is now a mathematical problem. When it was a romantic one, I solved it—too well. Ever yours
                                                            o. w.

---

is in great poverty, but I don't care to be written to as though it were my fault. He says that he loved too much and that that is better than hate! This is true abstractedly, but his was an unnatural love, a madness that I think is worse than hate. I have no hatred for him, but I confess that I am afraid of him.
[1] See note p. 694 and note 3, p. 714.

To Carlos Blacker

MS. Blacker

[*Circa 17 March 1898*]   *Hôtel de Nice*

My dear Friend, A thousand thanks for your good kindly letter. I do hope
to see you soon. I have heard from Robbie Ross. It seems that my wife
will not pay the arrears of my allowance—£80—nor any portion of it.
She says she will let me have £10 a month: that is all she promises, and
she has as yet sent nothing.[1]

In the meanwhile I am in dreadful straits, as I was forced to pay my

---

[1] On 20 March Constance Wilde wrote to Blacker (MS. Blacker):

I did send £40 to Mr Ross, but he would not, and I expect rightly did not, send
more than £10 at a time to him. I enclose you letters that I have had from Robbie
which at any rate are truthful, which I know that Oscar is not. The actual sum
that I owe him, if you call it owing, is at the rate of £12. 10. a month. £62. 10.
and not £80. This is counting it from the month of November when I stopped
giving him his allowance to the end of this present month. I have said that I
would give him £10 a month, so at the most I owe him little more than £20! By
his own account to me he received £30 from Smithers, and he seems to have had
money since. Also he had £10 of mine which he more than ignores in his letter
to you, for he says that he has had nothing from me. Oscar is so pathetic and such
a born actor, and I am hardened when I am away from him. No words will
describe my horror of that BEAST, for I will call him nothing else, A. D. Fancy
Robbie receiving abusive letters from him, and you know perfectly well that they
are sent with Oscar's knowledge and consent. I do not wish him dead, but considering how he used to go on about Willie's extravagance and about his cruelty
in forcing his mother to give him money, I think that he might leave his wife and
children alone. I beg that you will not let him know that you have seen these
letters, only I wish you to realize that he knew perfectly well that he was forfeiting
his income, small as it was, in going back to Lord A., and that it is absurd of him
to say now that I acted without his knowledge. He owes, I am certain, more than
£60 in Paris, and if I pay money now he will think that he can write to me at any
time for more. I have absolutely no-one to fall back upon, and I will not get into
debt for anyone. The boys' expenses will go on increasing until they are grown
up and settled, and I *will* educate them and give them what they reasonably
require. As Oscar will not bargain or be anything but exceedingly extravagant,
why should *I* do with my money what is utterly foreign to my nature? If I were
living on someone else's money, it would be a different thing and pride would
make me do even what I hate. But Oscar has no pride. When he had this disastrous law-suit, he borrowed £50 from me, £50 from my cousin, and £100 from
my aunt. The £50 I repaid my cousin, the £100 never has been, and I suppose
never will be, repaid. I was left penniless, and borrowed £150 from Burne-Jones,
and I have never borrowed a penny since. I still owe money in London which I
am trying to pay, but all these things are nothing to Oscar as long as someone
supports him! I paid all my tradespeople immediately and I had £60 advanced
to me out of my settlement to pay for the boys' education. You will say in the
face of all this why did I ask you to go and see him in Paris? Well, I thought
you would have nothing to do with his money affairs, and I strongly advise you
to leave them alone. I knew that you were not in your own house, and therefore
could not ask him to dinner, and I was silly enough to think that you would
merely give him the intellectual stimulus he needed. I don't know what name he
is living under in Paris. Is it his own or the name he took when he left England?
If he was fixed anywhere, I could make an arrangement to pay 10 francs a day
for his board to the hotel, not to him, for I know that he would never pay it.

hotel bill with the money you kindly lent me. I don't know what to do, and I have pawned everything I had. It was very kind of you writing to my wife, but I have a sort of idea she really wants me to be dead. It is a horrible and persistent thought, and I daresay she would be relieved to hear you had recognised me at the Morgue. Ever yours   OSCAR

To Leonard Smithers

MS. Clark

[*Circa 18 March 1898*]   [*Paris*]

My dear Smithers, I was greatly shocked to read of poor Aubrey's death.[1] Superbly premature as the flowering of his genius was, still he had immense development, and had not sounded his last stop. There were great possibilities always in the cavern of his soul, and there is something macabre and tragic in the fact that one who added another terror to life should have died at the age of a flower.

You never write now. I know nothing of *yesterday's* sales!! What were they? I suppose you have seen enclosed? All *Galignani's* said was "wonderfully weird verses."

The book has had quite a sale here at Brentano's and Galignani's, so if you print a leaflet let them each have one.

When do you come over? I hear Miss D'Or is looking pale and sad, but on such topics I only speak at second-hand.

Maurice is well and begs to be remembered. Ever yours   O. W.

To Robert Ross

MS. Clark

Friday [? *18 March 1898*]   [*Paris*]

My dear Robbie, Many thanks for the cheque, which I received this morning. The absurd money-changer, blind to his own interests, declared that he did not know your name! So I have to wait till Monday to touch the gold, but I have borrowed twenty francs from the concierge, so am all right.

I wish you could come over—for three days at any rate.

Bosie is, I believe, going to Venice, but I have not heard from him for ages. What do you think of his going back to London? He tells me he returns there with his mother in May. I think it is premature. I mean of course from the point of view of "social recognition" which he desires so much, and, *I* fear, so much in vain. It is not his past, but his future, that people so much object to, I am afraid.

I suppose you know that he made his mother leave the hotel at Mentone because the proprietor refused to publish his name among the fashionable arrivals. They have rooms now, I believe.

[1] Aubrey Beardsley died of consumption at Mentone on 16 March 1898, aged twenty-five.

719

The reviews you sent me are excellent, and really the Press has behaved very well, and Henley's hysterical personalities have done no harm, but rather the contrary. I am quite obliged to him for playing the rôle of the *Advocatus Diaboli* so well. Without it my beatification as a saint would have been impossible, but I shall now live as the Infamous St Oscar of Oxford, Poet and Martyr. My niche is just below that of the Blessed St Robert of Phillimore, Lover and Martyr—a saint known in *Hagiographia* for his extraordinary power, not in resisting, but in supplying temptations to others. This he did in the solitude of great cities, to which he retired at the comparatively early age of eight.[1] Ever yours   O. W.

To Frank Harris
MS. Texas

[*Circa 20 March 1898*]   *Hôtel de Nice*

My dear Frank, The *Saturday* arrived last night, and I read your article on Shakespeare with intense interest, and this morning I got your letter.[2] I am much obliged for your kind promise to let me have the *Saturday* regularly, and I will duly acquaint the office with any change of name, address, or personal appearance. To read it keeps me in touch with you, and though you do not blow through all the horns and flutes, or beat on *all* the drums, still I feel you are there, just as in the old days there was always the aroma of poor old Lady Pollock's weak tea and literary twaddle —the "five o'clock" of their reminiscences and butter.[3] I envy you your phrase the "rose-mist of passion." You should save it for a sonnet.

I wish you would have a good article on Aubrey Beardsley—as a personality. Robbie Ross knew him intimately. Ever yours   OSCAR

To Leonard Smithers [4]

[*Postmark 20 March 1898*]   *Paris*

I quite understand how you feel about poor Aubrey. Still you, and you alone, recreated his art for him, gave him a new and greater position, and for such generous and enthusiastic service to art and to an artist you will have your reward in Heaven—at least you will never have it in this world . . .

---

[1] See note p. 577.

[2] The first instalment of "The True Shakespeare—an Essay in Realistic Criticism" by Frank Harris appeared in the *Saturday Review* of 19 March 1898. It included the phrase quoted by Wilde. This essay formed the basis of Harris's book *The Man Shakespeare* (1909).

[3] Juliet Creed (d. 1899) married (1844) William Frederick Pollock (1815–88), who became second Baronet 1870. A friend of Macready and deeply interested in the theatre, she recommended Ellen Terry to Irving as leading lady. Her second son was W. H. Pollock (see note 1, p. 168).

[4] The text of this incomplete letter is taken from Maggs's catalogue 343 (1916).

Have Smith's bookstalls taken the poem? If not, do work it—and supply them with a placard.

Could you have a leaflet with criticisms put into the leaves of a good magazine? like Pears' soap, and other more useful things. I think it would be possible; in any case it would irritate the reader. The *Athenaeum* advertisement is admirable;[1] I feel like Lipton's tea.   O.W.

To George Ives
MS. Texas

[*Postmark 21 March 1898*]   *Hôtel de Nice*

My dear George, Thanks so much for your letter. Your charming friend came to see me one morning at the hotel, and was most delightful. I hope to see him again in a few days. He seems quite fascinated by Paris.

Thanks so much for ordering my book: it is now in its fifth edition. Smithers has put a flaming advertisement into the *Athenaeum*, headed

"3000 copies sold in three weeks."

When I read it I feel like Lipton's tea!

Yes: I have no doubt we shall win, but the road is long, and red with monstrous martyrdoms. Nothing but the repeal of the Criminal Law Amendment Act would do any good. That is the essential. It is not so much public opinion as public officials that need educating. Ever yours
OSCAR

To Carlos Blacker
MS. Blacker

Tuesday night [? *22 March 1898*]   *Hôtel de Nice*

My dear Carlos, My once Greek and gracious hand-writing has been so wrecked by long disuse and troubled nerves that I always feel that my letters to you are hieroglyphs that Paton should *not* discover, and that Sayce would be unable to translate.[2]

Still, I cannot help writing to you to tell you that I have had a letter from Robbie Ross in which he says that, in consequence of your letter to Constance, she has written to him more kindly about me, and has sent him £30, for me.[3]

Whether this is meant as my income for the next three months, or as a restitution of my forfeited income, Robbie Ross does not know. But at any rate I have something on which I can take a couple of rooms, and I hope to begin to write.

All this, as much else, I owe to you, my dear friend. Ever yours O. W.

[1] It appeared on 19 March.
[2] For Paton and Sayce, see pp. 78 and 22.
[3] It seems clear that when Ross learned that Wilde knew Constance had sent £40, and not just £10, he sent Wilde the remaining £30, which he had previously intended to eke out prudently.

To the Editor of the Daily Chronicle[1]

23 March [1898]   [*Paris*]

Sir, I understand that the Home Secretary's Prison Reform Bill is to be read this week for the first or second time, and as your journal has been the one paper in England that has taken a real and vital interest in this important question, I hope that you will allow me, as one who has had long personal experience of life in an English gaol, to point out what reforms in our present stupid and barbarous system are urgently necessary.

From a leading article that appeared in your columns about a week ago, I learn that the chief reform proposed is an increase in the number of inspectors and official visitors, that are to have access to our English prisons.

Such a reform as this is entirely useless. The reason is extremely simple. The inspectors and justices of the peace that visit prisons come there for the purpose of seeing that the prison regulations are duly carried out. They come for no other purpose, nor have they any power, even if they had the desire, to alter a single clause in the regulations. No prisoner has ever had the smallest relief, or attention, or care from any of the official visitors. The visitors arrive not to help the prisoners, but to see that the rules are carried out. Their object in coming is to ensure the enforcement of a foolish and inhuman code. And, as they must have some occupation, they take very good care to do it. A prisoner who has been allowed the smallest privilege dreads the arrival of the inspectors. And on the day of any prison inspection the prison officials are more than usually brutal to the prisoners. Their object is, of course, to show the splendid discipline they maintain.

The necessary reforms are very simple. They concern the needs of the body and the needs of the mind of each unfortunate prisoner. With regard to the first, there are three permanent punishments authorised by law in English prisons:

1. Hunger.
2. Insomnia.
3. Disease.

The food supplied to prisoners is entirely inadequate. Most of it is revolting in character. All of it is insufficient. Every prisoner suffers day and night from hunger. A certain amount of food is carefully weighed out ounce by ounce for each prisoner. It is just enough to sustain, not life exactly, but existence. But one is always racked by the pain and sickness of hunger.

The result of the food—which in most cases consists of weak gruel, badly-baked bread, suet, and water—is disease in the form of incessant

---

[1] This letter appeared in the *Daily Chronicle*, under the heading DON'T READ THIS IF YOU WANT TO BE HAPPY TODAY, on 24 March, when the House of Commons began the debate on the second reading of the Prison Bill. This, which introduced some of the improvements suggested by Wilde, became law in August as the Prison Act.

diarrhœa. This malady, which ultimately with most prisoners becomes a permanent disease, is a recognised institution in every prison. At Wandsworth Prison, for instance—where I was confined for two months, till I had to be carried into hospital, where I remained for another two months—the warders go round twice or three times a day with astringent medicines, which they serve out to the prisoners as a matter of course. After about a week of such treatment it is unnecessary to say the medicine produces no effect at all. The wretched prisoner is then left a prey to the most weakening, depressing, and humiliating malady that can be conceived; and if, as often happens, he fails, from physical weakness, to complete his required revolutions at the crank or the mill he is reported for idleness, and punished with the greatest severity and brutality. Nor is this all.

Nothing can be worse than the sanitary arrangements of English prisons. In old days each cell was provided with a form of latrine. These latrines have now been suppressed. They exist no longer. A small tin vessel is supplied to each prisoner instead. Three times a day a prisoner is allowed to empty his slops. But he is not allowed to have access to the prison lavatories, except during the one hour when he is at exercise. And after five o'clock in the evening he is not allowed to leave his cell under any pretence, or for any reason. A man suffering from diarrhœa is consequently placed in a position so loathsome that it is unnecessary to dwell on it, that it would be unseemly to dwell on it. The misery and tortures that prisoners go through in consequence of the revolting sanitary arrangements are quite indescribable. And the foul air of the prison cells, increased by a system of ventilation that is utterly ineffective, is so sickening and unwholesome that it is no uncommon thing for warders, when they come in the morning out of the fresh air and open and inspect each cell, to be violently sick. I have seen this myself on more than three occasions, and several of the warders have mentioned it to me as one of the disgusting things that their office entails on them.

The food supplied to prisoners should be adequate and wholesome. It should not be of such a character as to produce the incessant diarrhœa that, at first a malady, becomes a permanent disease.

The sanitary arrangements in English prisons should be entirely altered. Every prisoner should be allowed to have access to the lavatories when necessary, and to empty his slops when necessary. The present system of ventilation in each cell is utterly useless. The air comes through choked-up gratings, and through a small ventilator in the tiny barred window, which is far too small, and too badly constructed, to admit any adequate amount of fresh air. One is only allowed out of one's cell for one hour out of the twenty-four that compose the long day, and so for twenty-three hours one is breathing the foulest possible air.

With regard to the punishment of insomnia, it only exists in Chinese and English prisons. In China it is inflicted by placing the prisoner in a small bamboo cage; in England by means of the plank bed. The object of the plank bed is to produce insomnia. There is no other object in it, and it invariably succeeds. And even when one is subsequently allowed a hard mattress, as happens in the course of imprisonment, one still suffers from insomnia. For sleep, like all wholesome things, is a habit. Every prisoner who has been on a plank bed suffers from insomnia. It is a revolting and ignorant punishment.

With regard to the needs of the mind, I beg that you will allow me to say something.

The present prison system seems almost to have for its aim the wrecking and the destruction of the mental faculties. The production of insanity is, if not its object, certainly its result. That is a well ascertained fact. Its causes are obvious. Deprived of books, of all human intercourse, isolated from every humane and humanising influence, condemned to eternal silence, robbed of all intercourse with the external world, treated like an unintelligent animal, brutalised below the level of any of the brute-creation, the wretched man who is confined in an English prison can hardly escape becoming insane. I do not wish to dwell on these horrors; still less to excite any momentary sentimental interest in these matters. So I will merely, with your permission, point out what should be done.

Every prisoner should have an adequate supply of good books. At present, during the first three months of imprisonment, one is allowed no books at all, except a Bible, prayer-book, and hymn-book. After that, one is allowed one book a week. That is not merely inadequate, but the books that compose an ordinary prison library are perfectly useless. They consist chiefly of third-rate, badly-written, religious books, so-called, written apparently for children, and utterly unsuitable for children or for anyone else. Prisoners should be encouraged to read, and should have whatever books they want, and the books should be well chosen. At present the selection of books is made by the prison chaplain.

Under the present system a prisoner is only allowed to see his friends four times a year, for twenty minutes each time. This is quite wrong. A prisoner should be allowed to see his friends once a month, and for a reasonable time. The mode at present in vogue of exhibiting a prisoner to his friends should be altered. Under the present system the prisoner is either locked up in a large iron cage or in a large wooden box, with a small aperture, covered with wire netting, through which he is allowed to peer. His friends are placed in a similar cage, some three or four feet distant, and two warders stand between, to listen to, and, if they wish, stop or interrupt the conversation such as it may be. I propose that a prisoner should be allowed to see his relatives or friends in a room. The present regulations are inexpressibly revolting and harassing. A visit from our relatives or friends is to every prisoner an intensification of humiliation and mental distress. Many prisoners, rather than support such an ordeal, refuse to see their friends at all. And I cannot say I am surprised. When one sees one's solicitor, one sees him in a room with a glass door, on the other side of which stands the warder. When a man sees his wife and children, or his parents, or his friends, he should be allowed the same privilege. To be exhibited, like an ape in a cage, to people who are fond of one, and of whom one is fond, is a needless and horrible degradation.

Every prisoner should be allowed to write and receive a letter at least once a month. At present one is allowed to write only four times a year. This is quite inadequate. One of the tragedies of prison life is that it turns a man's heart to stone. The feelings of natural affection, like all other feelings, require to be fed. They die easily of inanition. A brief letter, four times a year, is not enough to keep alive the gentler and more humane affections by which ultimately the nature is kept sensitive to any fine or beautiful influences that may heal a wrecked and ruined life.

The habit of mutilating and expurgating prisoners' letters should be stopped. At present, if a prisoner in a letter makes any complaint of the prison system, that portion of his letter is cut out with a pair of scissors. If, upon the other hand, he makes any complaint when he speaks to his friends through the bars of the cage, or the aperture of the wooden box, he is brutalised by the warders, and reported for punishment every week till his next visit comes round, by which time he is expected to have learned, not wisdom, but cunning, and one always learns that. It is one of the few things that one does learn in prison. Fortunately, the other things are, in some instances, of higher import.

If I may trespass on your space for a little longer, may I say this? You suggested in your leading article that no prison chaplain should be allowed to have any care or employment outside the prison itself. But this is a matter of no moment. The prison chaplains are entirely useless. They are, as a class, well-meaning, but foolish, indeed silly, men. They are of no help to any prisoner. Once every six weeks or so a key turns in the lock of one's cell door, and the chaplain enters. One stands, of course, at attention. He asks one whether one has been reading the Bible. One answers "Yes" or "No," as the case may be. He then quotes a few texts, and goes out and locks the door. Sometimes he leaves a tract.

The officials who should not be allowed to hold any employment outside the prison, or to have any private practice, are the prison doctors. At present the prison doctors have usually, if not always, a large private practice, and hold appointments in other institutions. The consequence is that the health of the prisoners is entirely neglected, and the sanitary condition of the prison entirely overlooked. As a class I regard, and have always from my earliest youth regarded, doctors as by far the most humane profession in the community. But I must make an exception for prison doctors. They are, as far as I came across them, and from what I saw of them in hospital and elsewhere, brutal in manner, coarse in temperament, and utterly indifferent to the health of the prisoners or their comfort. If prison doctors were prohibited from private practice they would be compelled to take some interest in the health and sanitary condition of the people under their charge.

I have tried to indicate in my letter a few of the reforms necessary to our English prison system. They are simple, practical, and humane. They are, of course, only a beginning. But it is time that a beginning should be made, and it can only be started by a strong pressure of public opinion formularised in your powerful paper, and fostered by it.

But to make even these reforms effectual, much has to be done. And the first, and perhaps the most difficult task is to humanise the governors of prisons, to civilise the warders and to Christianise the chaplains. Yours, etc.   THE AUTHOR OF "THE BALLAD OF READING GAOL"

To Robert Ross
MS. Clark

[? *Circa 25 March 1898*]   [*Paris*]

My dear Robbie, A thousand thanks for cheque. Would you find out from Constance whether it is meant for *arrears*, or whether I am to live on it for four months? I wrote to her two days ago, and I don't think I would like to write again. She does not like my letters, I fear. I mean that my writing to her at all distresses her. So, at least, I fancy. So you could find out, as I want to take an *apartment* with two rooms—one for writing, one for insomnia (both in fact for insomnia).

I don't know if Bosie will really go to London, but I understand your apprehensions. Personally, I think it would be wiser for him to wait till he is sixty. Ashton seems quite devoted to the Sphinx: he is clearly caught in the net of her jade eyes. Ever yours   OSCAR

To Carlos Blacker
MS. Blacker

Friday [*Postmark 25 March 1898*]   [*Paris*]

My dear Carlos, A thousand thanks for your great kindness. Really you have saved my life for me, for a little at any rate, and your friendship and interest give me hope. I do hope to see you soon. Could we dine together at some little restaurant; the Café du Cardinal is excellent—I dined there twice with my publisher—or *Foyot* in the Quartier Latin, just you and I together, and talk about divine and beautiful things?

I have had some more reviews from England, all good and sympathetic. Ever gratefully and affectionately yours   O. W.

Postcard: To Robert Ross
MS. Clark

[*Postmark 28 March 1898*]   [*Postmark Paris*]

Dear Robbie, My new address is at Hôtel d'Alsace, Rue des Beaux-Arts. Much better, and half the price. Have been ill, through an accident, for five days, but am better.[1]   S. M.

---

[1] It seems probable that the accident happened on 25 March, and that "five days" is an exaggeration.

Petit Bleu: To Carlos Blacker

MS. Blacker

[? *28 March 1898*]   *Hôtel d'Alsace, Rue des Beaux-Arts*

Dear Carlos, I had a horrid accident in a fiacre three days ago, and cut my mouth terribly. Could you come and see me this afternoon, any time you like—at *three*, if that will suit you? I have moved to the Hôtel d'Alsace— same street, much cleaner. Ever yours   OSCAR

To Carlos Blacker

MS. Blacker

Monday [*28 March 1898*]   *Hôtel d'Alsace*

My dear Carlos, Thanks for your *petit bleu*. I am so sorry you can't come to see me, as I have not been out since Friday, except one night when I was dragged out to meet *Esterhazy* at dinner! The Commandant was astonishing. I will tell you all he said some day. Of course he talked of nothing but Dreyfus *et Cie*.[1]

What happened to me was simply that through the horse coming down I was thrown almost through the front window of a fiacre, and cut my lower lip almost in two. It was quite dreadful, and, of course, a hideous shock to my nerves. It is so horrible to have no one to look after one, or to see one, when one is cooped up in a wretched hotel. I hope to go out tomorrow.

I had a very nice letter from Constance yesterday. Ever yours   o. w.

To Robert Ross

MS. Clark

[*Circa 30 March 1898*]   *Hôtel d'Alsace*

My dear Robbie, What day do you come over? I really am recovering from my cab-accident quite swiftly in consequence of the tidings of your coming.

I saw Davray's translation of *Reading Gaol* yesterday, and went over part of it with him. It is a very difficult thing to translate, as, unluckily and oddly, Davray has never been in prison, so knows nothing of prison-terms. "We banged the tins" appeared as "*On battait le fer blanc*"![2] I still have to work for days over it.

---

[1] Commandant Marie-Charles Ferdinand Walsin-Esterhazy (1847–1923) was the man who forged the famous document, known as the *bordereau*, for which Captain Alfred Dreyfus was sentenced to exile on Devil's Island. Davray reports Wilde as saying of Esterhazy: "*C'est lui qui est l'auteur du bordereau, il me l'a avoué . . . Esterhazy est bien plus intéressant que Dreyfus qui est innocent. On a toujours tort d'être innocent. Pour être criminel, il faut de l'imagination et du courage . . . Mais c'est fâcheux qu'Esterhazy ne soit jamais allé en prison.*"

[2] In the printed translation this has become "*On heurtait les gamelles.*"

How splendid Stephen Phillips's poem in the *D.C.*! It shows how much *truer* Imagination is than Observation.[1]

If you see Smithers, please ask him to write sometimes to me. Ever yours O. W.

Postcard: To Reginald Turner

MS. Hyde (D. & M.)

[*Postmark 30 March 1898*] Hôtel d'Alsace

Dear Reggie, When are you coming over to see me? The weather is lovely.
S. M.

To Leonard Smithers[2]

[? *April 1898*] Hôtel d'Alsace

My dear Smithers, I don't know how *The Ballad* is going. As it has been twice quoted in the House[3] I should have thought you would have had a good advertisement of it in the *Chronicle*, or somewhere else, but I suppose Marie Corelli monopolises your attention.[4]

I am very ill, and have had to call in doctors. I wish to goodness you would write. Ever yours O. W.

To Henry D. Davray[5]

[*April 1898*] [Paris]

Mon cher Davray, Merci pour l'épreuve; le poème se lit admirablement.

Je voudrais vous demander s'il n'y a pas (page 2) de mot pour le surplis blanc porté par un prêtre: est-ce que "enrobé de blanc" suggère l'idée d'un vêtement? Il va sans dire que ce n'est pas une soutane: c'est le surplis de linge blanc que le prêtre catholique porte à la messe sous la chasuble.

(page 2) *And binds one with three leathern thongs,* etc. est-ce que "vous ligote" ne serait pas mieux, et "votre gorge n'ait plus," etc.? Je veux dire que c'est une sorte de chose qui pourrait arriver à tout le monde.

[1] Stephen Phillips's poem "The Torturers," "suggested by a letter to the *Daily Chronicle* from the author of *The Ballad of Reading Gaol*," appeared in the *Daily Chronicle* on 28 March 1898. It was reprinted in Phillips's *New Poems* (1908).

[2] The text of this incomplete letter is taken from Maggs's catalogue 266 (1911), supplemented by a facsimile of the last page in Sherard's *Life of Oscar Wilde* (1906).

[3] On 28 March 1898, on the second day of the second reading of the Prison Bill, John Redmond (1856–1918, M.P. for Waterford and subsequently leader of the united Irish Parliamentary Party) quoted a stanza of *The Ballad* while attacking the Bill. I can find no second quotation in Hansard.

[4] O'Sullivan says that Smithers longed to publish a best-seller and used to suggest opening negotiations with Marie Corelli.

[5] Text from *Oscar Wilde, La Tragédie Finale* by Henry D. Davray (1928).

(page 4) est-ce que "réprouvé" est bon pour *outcast*? "Déshérité" ne vaudrait-il pas mieux? Lord Byron était un *outcast*.

(page 6) *we did not care*: est-ce que "qu'importe" rend tout à fait cela?

(page 6) *fool and knave*: est-ce que "dupe" ne vaudrait pas mieux? Par *fool* je veux dire quelqu'un qui a été bafoué et dupé par la vie.

(page 6) *went feet we could not hear*. Je veux dire: des fantômes et des spectres allaient et venaient avec des pieds silencieux; nous en éprouvions la sensation sans les entendre.

(page 7) ici encore je crois que "dupe" vaut mieux qu' "insensé": *the fool, the fraud, the knave.*

(page 4) *we said no* word, *we had no* word *to say*: ne pourriez-vous répéter "mot"?

(page 7) "sacrés grotesques," *the damned grotesques*, comme un juron.

(page 9) *the cry the silent marshes hear*, etc. Certainement pas bruit. C'est le cri du lépreux: "le cri."

(page 11) *Flowers have been known to heal*, etc. Cela veut dire "parfois." Ce n'est pas "on sait": c'est plutôt "quelquefois." Je veux dire: Il y a eu des exemples de fleurs qui . . . etc.

(page 11) *The wretched man*: Je veux dire le malheureux, le ruiné, le naufragé. Est-ce que "le misérable" exprime tout cela? J'emploie le mot avec pitié. Sans doute Hugo a écrit *Les Misérables*, aussi peut-être est-ce bien?

(page 12) *his mourners will be outcast men And outcasts always mourn*. Ne pourriez-vous donner l'effet de la répétition de *mourners* et *mourn*? Pourquoi pas: "sans cesse les rejetés pleurent"?

J'ai mis une croix, sur le côté de la page, là où je fais une suggestion. Je suis grandement satisfait de l'effet de l'ensemble. C'est admirablement fait, par un admirable et parfait artiste.

Telegram: To Robert Ross

MS. Clark

[*Postmark 12 April 1898*]   *Paris*

Constance is dead.[1] Please come tomorrow and stay at my hotel. Am in great grief.   OSCAR[2]

[1] Constance Wilde died at Genoa on 7 April 1898, aged forty, and was buried in the Protestant cemetery there.

[2] Ross responded to this call, and on 17 April he wrote to Smithers from the Hôtel Voltaire (MS. Clark):

My dear Smithers, I ought to have written to you ages ago, but it is quite impossible with Oscar to get anything done. I have however read two of the manuscripts and will present you with written opinions on Wednesday when I shall come and see you. I return on Tuesday.

You will have heard of Mrs Wilde's death. Oscar of course did not feel it at all. It is rather appalling for him as his allowance ceases and I do not expect his wife's trustees will continue it. He is in very good spirits and does not consume too many. He is hurt because you never write. I explained you had been ill and rather worried with the domesticities of publishing.

Telegram: To Otho Holland Lloyd

MS. Holland

[*Postmark 12 April 1898*]   [*Postmark Paris*]

Am overwhelmed with grief. It is the most terrible tragedy. Am writing.

OSCAR

Petit Bleu: To Carlos Blacker

MS. Blacker

[*Postmark 12 April 1898*]   [*Postmark Paris*]

My dear Carlos, I suppose you have heard the terrible news. Constance is dead.

I would like to see you tomorrow (Wednesday) at any hour you like. Ever yours   OSCAR

To Carlos Blacker

MS. Blacker

[*12 or 13 April 1898*]   [*Paris*]

My dear Carlos, It is really awful. I don't know what to do. If we had only met once, and kissed each other.

It is too late. How awful life is. How good you were to come at once. I have gone out as I don't dare to be by myself. Ever yours   OSCAR

When I arrived the Mauritius [presumably Maurice Gilbert] was not here but has since turned up. I do wish you had been here. Next time we must come together as it would be amusing to compare notes.

I met Davray at dinner with Frank Harris. He understands every other thing that Oscar says. I also told him you were beset with worries and as usual said all that was charming. I hope you will not be angry. You are so fearfully candid. Oscar has only seen Douglas once. I went to see his lordship. He is less interested in other people than ever before, especially Oscar. So I really think that alliance will die a natural death.

Oscar is very amusing as usual but is very abstracted at times. He says that *The Ballad of Reading Gaol* doesn't describe his prison life, but his life at Naples with Bosie and that all the best stanzas were the immediate result of his existence there.

"A man's face is his autobiography. A woman's face is her work of fiction."

Did you hear what he said to someone who objected that the guardsman could not have worn a *scarlet* coat as he was in the Blues? He emended the lines:

"He did not wear his *azure* coat
For blood and wine are *blue*."

I am told there were flaming notices of dear Aubrey in the *Figaro* and elsewhere. It is a pity we did not get them.

Oscar says he will give me full leave to write *your* biography. Always yours

ROBBIE ROSS

730

Petit Bleu: to Henry D. Davray

MS. Sterling

Thursday [Postmark 14 April 1898]   *[Postmark Paris]*

My dear Davray, If you come to *Foyot's* Restaurant at 2.30 this afternoon I can have the pleasure of introducing Frank Harris to you.[1] Ever yours

OSCAR WILDE

To Robert Ross

MS. Clark

[Late April 1898]   *[Paris]*

My dear Robbie, The copybooks are, of course, far too lovely to write in, but I look at them with joy, and "feel literary longings in me."[2] It was very kind of you to send them.

Edmond de Goncourt begs to be remembered with love to you. He adores his sash and your memory.[3]

Harland is here.[4] I dined with him and his wife at Pousset's last night. Remembering your delightful imitations I could not help shouting with laughter from time to time. "Isn't he *wonderful*, Aline?" reappeared every five minutes, but they were both very nice. I dine with him again on Saturday.

The *Revue Blanche* has a capital notice of my poem, and Fénéon, the editor, has written me a charming letter begging me to go and see them all.[5]

Bosie is very angelic and quiet. It did him a great deal of good being trampled on by Maurice. Whistler and I met face to face the other night, as I was entering Pousset's to dine with the Thaulows. How old and weird he looks! Like Meg Merrilies.[6] Ever yours   OSCAR

Letter-card: To Leonard Smithers

MS. Yale

[Postmark 1 May 1898]   *[Postmark Paris]*

Thank you very much for cheque. Have you settled yet with America? If not, please do. 12½ per cent is quite enough.

Come over as soon as possible. Ever yours   O. W.

[1] Davray collaborated in translating Harris's *Life and Confessions of Oscar Wilde* into French (two vols, 1928).   [2] Cf. *Antony and Cleopatra*, Act V, sc. 2.

[3] The nickname of a boy called Edmond. The famous Edmond de Goncourt (see note 3, p. 144) had died in 1896.

[4] Henry Harland (1861–1905), American novelist and editor of the *Yellow Book*. O'Sullivan described him as "a sort of lemonade Henry James." He married (1884) an American girl called Aline Merriam.

[5] A review of *The Ballad* appeared in the *Revue Blanche* of 15 April. It was written by Laurence Jerrold (1873–1918), grandson of the author of *Mrs Caudle's Curtain Lectures*. He spent most of his life in Paris, where he represented the *Daily Telegraph* for more than twenty years. He translated some of Walt Whitman's poems into French. Félix Fénéon (1861–?1943) edited the *Revue Blanche*, which ran from 1891 to 1903.

[6] The half-crazy gipsy woman of Walter Scott's *Guy Mannering* (1815).

To Robert Ross

MS. Clark

[*Circa 1 May 1898*] [*Paris*]

My dear Robbie, More paper has arrived! How good you are. I really must begin "The Sphere."[1]

I enclose you Hargrove's letter: it seems conclusive. Will you show it to Holman? My allowance should begin *now*—May the 1st—but did Holman not understand the circumstances? There was clearly no necessity to write to Adrian at all. He is bound to pay.

Bosie has not gone into his flat yet, but I chose some nice furniture for him at Maples.[2] He will move in tomorrow, I hope. He apparently goes to races every day, and loses of course. As I wrote to Maurice today, he has a faculty of spotting the loser, which, considering that he knows nothing at all about horses, is perfectly astounding.

Ernest[3] has been in Paris again. He invited Bosie to dinner at the Café Anglais—but did not even come to see me. He avoids me with the artificial modesty of the debtor.

Edmond is very smart, and directs his little band of brigands on the Boulevard with great success. His book, *Les Chevaliers du Boulevard*, is begun, but he says he finds poetry very difficult. That promises well for his future as an artist.

I dined with the Thaulows the other night, and on Saturday I went to the *vernissage* at the Salon.[4] Rodin's statue of Balzac is superb—just what a *romancier* is, or should be. The leonine head of a fallen angel, with a dressing-gown. The head is gorgeous, the dressing-gown an entirely unshaped cone of white plaster. People howl with rage over it. A lady who had gazed in horror on it had her attention directed to Rodin himself who was passing by.[5] She was greatly surprised at his appearance. "*Et pourtant il n'a pas l'air méchant*" was her remark.

Do you love Maurice? Ever yours OSCAR

To Leonard Smithers[6]

2 May 1898 *Paris*

Do you think that a shilling edition (on grey paper but not in blunt type) would sell?—of *The Ballad*. I think so. I suppose the type still stands, so the expense is small. The cover should be grey with red letters—vermilion—and at the end we might have a good selection of press

---

[1] A short story which Wilde never wrote. Frank Harris adapted and published it in his *Unpath'd Waters* (1913), under the title "The Irony of Chance (after O.W.)." See also p. 408.

[2] The London store had opened a Paris branch in 1883. [3] Leverson.

[4] The Salon exhibition was open from 1 May to 30 June, and the *vernissage* or private view took place on Saturday, 30 April. [5] Auguste Rodin (1840-1917).

[6] The text of this incomplete letter is taken from the American Art Association catalogue of 9 February 1927.

notices. If someone like Davitt would write a preface it would add to it very much. Could you get an estimate of 1000 copies at 1/-? The poem should still be on one side only of the paper, I think, unless the paper is too bad to bear the test of a blank surface. I sent Robbie the *Revue Blanche* for you to look at . . .

Would you kindly let me have eight copies of *The Ballad*, and a copy of *Dorian Gray* also, as soon as possible.

To Leonard Smithers
MS. Vander Poel

[*Circa 4 May 1898*]   [*Paris*]

My dear Smithers, I am delighted to see that you *don't* know your "Browning". I hope you never will. But, to avoid any discussion on printing, let me remind you of the lines

> "Or some scrofulous French novel
> *On grey paper with blunt type*,
> Once you glance in it, you grovel
> Neck and crop in Satan's gripe."

It is out of a poem called, I think, "A Spanish Cloister," and I quote the last two lines inaccurately, I am glad to say.[1]

I am quite prepared for sixpence a copy, but please get estimates, so as to be sure that there will be a margin. Your estimate of 10,000 copies is flattering, but is it safe? I would like the cover to be grey, not black.[2]

I don't know what you mean by talking of Ricketts's "design," and the advisability of using it. A badly-drawn leaf flung casually on a cover is not a design at all. It is a mistake—nothing more.

I don't know who would be the right man for a preface, perhaps T. P. O'Connor. It should be largely on prison-reform. Perhaps John Burns[3] would be better. Don't you know anyone who could sound them? Or can you suggest a good writer of such a preface?

Let us have good paper, not what Robbie calls "*home-made* paper"! but something decent.

With regard to the press-notices, I merely want the assertion of the poem's reception. You remember the doubt there was about it, and how when you printed only 400 copies of the first edition the cocks in the Arcade crew thirty-three times.[4]

The accounts of the two editions should be *separate*: they are different affairs.

[1] See stanza viii of Browning's *Soliloquy of the Spanish Cloister*.
[2] This plan for a shilling or sixpenny edition of *The Ballad* came to nothing.
[3] Labour politician (1858–1943). He was arrested and imprisoned with Cunninghame Graham in 1887 (see note p. 707). President of the Board of Trade, 1914. He resigned from the Cabinet on the outbreak of war.
[4] Smithers's publishing office was then in the Royal Arcade, Old Bond Street.

Could you send a paragraph to the papers to say that *The Ballad* has been translated into French by M. Henry Davray and appears in the current number of the *Mercure de France*: and that it will shortly appear in book-form in Paris, the English on one side, the French on the other.

Have you a copy of Aubrey's drawing of Mlle de Maupin?[1] There is a young Russian here, who is a great amateur of Aubrey's art, who would love to have one. He is a great collector, and rich. So you might send him a copy and name a price, and also deal with him for drawings by Aubrey. His name is Serge de Diaghilew, Hôtel St James, Rue St Honoré, Paris.[2]

If you don't feel up to charging much for the Mlle de Maupin, which I suppose is inexpensive, you might send it to him for nothing, and propose a deal. I said to him I would get you to send him one, but do what you think is in your own interest. If you want a guinea—and what gentleman does not?—and the price is a guinea, by all means enclose your account. In any case he wants it, and can pay.

Your delay in coming over is painful. Also, you must make friends with Conder: it is absurd not to know the unknowable. Ever yours   o. w.

Type-write Alexander's copy and send it to me. This will save great expense in printing etc.[3]

To Robert Ross
MS. Clark

[*Circa 4 May 1898*]   [*Paris*]

My dear Robbie, I hope you received Hargrove's letter all right. I clearly am entitled to my quarter, which was always paid in advance. It came due on May 1st, Constance having paid for April. I hope Holman will act rightly and behave well.

Conder is over here, very vague and mist-like. The *Revue Blanche* I sent you, please show to Smithers, and let him have it, for the press-notices.

I want someone to write a preface for the sixpenny edition of *The Ballad*. Do you approve? And what do you think of Davitt, or John Burns? It should be a prison-reform preface.

I also would like the press-notices included, to show the reception of the poem. Do you see any objection?

Also, are you in love with Maurice? Ever yours   o.w.

[1] Beardsley had begun to illustrate Gautier's *Mademoiselle de Maupin* for Smithers, but completed only six drawings (which Smithers reproduced by photogravure and sold in a portfolio). These included a water-colour drawing of the heroine, intended as a frontispiece, of which Smithers sold coloured photogravure reproductions, 100 copies at a guinea, and a further 30 at higher prices.

[2] This remarkable man (1872–1929), who was to change the art of ballet throughout the world, was at this time simply a member of the Russian intelligentsia, dabbling in painting and a new artistic review. He had met Beardsley at Dieppe.

[3] Presumably the only available copy of *The Importance of Being Earnest*, from which Smithers could print, was George Alexander's prompt copy.

To Carlos Blacker

MS. Blacker

[6 or 7 May 1898] *Hôtel d'Alsace*

My dear Carlos, I am very sorry to trouble you again, but I have received no money this month and if you could let me have fifty francs it would be an inestimable service.

I have heard nothing from Frank Harris at all, and Mr Hargrove makes difficulty about paying my quarterly allowance for three months, which is unjust. It began on May 19th 1897, and should be always paid on corresponding date, should it not?

Bobbie is trying to manage it, but in the meanwhile I am without a penny. Sincerely yours OSCAR

To Robert Ross

MS. Clark

Sunday [8 May 1898][1] *[Paris]*

My dear Robbie, Something must be done. Friday and Saturday I had not a penny, and had to stay in my room, and as they only give breakfast at the hotel, *not* dinner, I was dinnerless. My quarter is really due the 18th May: it began the 18th May and was always paid in advance. The November allowance was suppressed, but the February was paid by my wife, and the May is due on the 18th.

In any case, as I would like it always paid through you, could *you* get someone to advance the money, so as to be paid now, and when it *is* paid you simply hand over the cheque.

I enclose what seems a legal document. I judge solely from its want of style. Armed with this, surely, dear Robbie, you could get me £30 at least, if not £38. 10. I am quite off my balance with want and worries, and have also had to have an operation on my throat, unpaid for yet, except in pain.[2] Ever yours OSCAR

To Carlos Blacker

MS. Blacker

Sunday [8 May 1898] *Café de l' Univers [Paris]*

My dear Carlos, Thank you so much for the fifty francs. I had been three

---

[1] So dated in *After Berneval*.

[2] In a note headed "Tuesday night [10 May 1898]" Ross wrote to Smithers (text from American Art Association catalogue of 18 April 1929):

> I had a fearful letter from poor Oscar who seems in a dreadful state of poverty even allowing for slight exaggeration. He says he had no dinner on Friday or Saturday. If you could sell the 'Réjane' for me at once send Oscar £5 as soon as possible . . . Tell Oscar that a 'friend' is sending the money. There is no need to mention my name.

days without any money at all, and as I cannot get more than breakfast at my hotel, was in a very bad way. I also had to have my throat operated on, so have had a very dreadful time. The operation itself was all right, as I was drenched with cocaine, but afterwards it was very painful, as the light food I was ordered—minces and the like—I of course could not get.

My allowance is really due the 18th of May: it began the 18th May last year and should go on as usual. My wife paid the amount due in February, but I hear the trustees want to defer paying for three months. It is very brutal of them.

I have now made over the allowance to Robbie Ross, and have asked him to try and raise the first quarter, £37. 10, for me. All the cheques will pass through his hands, and his receipt is to be the equivalent of mine. The cheques also are to be made payable to him, so I hope he will be able to manage it.

Did you send me an unsigned telegram saying you would call between 3 and 4? I waited in till 6.30, when I got your kind and welcome letter. Ever yours   O. W.

To Leonard Smithers
MS. Taylor

[Circa 8 May 1898]   *[Paris]*

My dear Smithers, Nothing has arrived this morning. I hope to get a little from you in the course of the day, as I am in a very bad way, and had no dinner on Friday and Saturday last.

The "format" of the *play* should be identical—in type, paper, setting, margin, etc.—with the format of the other plays, and Shannon should do a similar cover, same cloth, same colour, and similar design.

It should be out early in June, so as to have at least six weeks' run for its money.

Kindly get from the St James's a play-bill, and date of production. I reproduce the cast always.

I await the type-written copy with eagerness. Of course I cut out nearly all the stage-directions.

Let me know about Smith's bookstalls, and *The Ballad*. It seems to me that the whole thing largely depends on him. Also, get a good distributor —and traveller. The provinces must be made to rise like one man. Ever yours   O. W.

To Leonard Smithers[1]

[Postmark 9 May 1898]   *Paris*

You are so accustomed to bringing out books limited to an edition of

---

[1] The text of this fragment is taken from the Spoor sale catalogue (1939). It is there dated 13 May 1898, but seems likely to have exchanged envelopes with the letter on p. 740.

three copies, one for the author, one for yourself, and one for the Police, that I really feel you are sinking beneath your standard in producing a six-penny edition of anything. Perhaps, as I want the poem to reach the poorer classes, we might give away a cake of Maypole soap with each copy: I hear it dyes people the most lovely colours, and is also cleansing.[1]

To Carlos Blacker

MS. Clark

Monday [*9 May 1898*]   *Hôtel d'Alsace*

My dear Carlos, The dreadful and grotesque way in which I am living cannot go on as it is doing, and I write to know if you can manage this for me.

I have directed that my quarterly allowance of £37. 10. 0 is to be paid directly to Robbie Ross, and that *his* receipt is to be a full discharge to the trustees of any claims of mine.

This sum is properly due next week, but may not be paid till *July*. In either case could you advance it to me, and Robbie will, on receipt of my quarter's allowance, send you the cheque. On the other side, or rather on a separate piece of paper, I have written an order on Robbie which, if you can do this for me, you will send him.

I am sorry to be such a source of trouble to you, but you are the only old friend I have in Paris. Truly yours   O. W.

To Robert Ross

MS. Clark

Tuesday, [*10 May 1898*][2]   [*Paris*]

My dear Robbie, Thanks for the letter of the wicked Holman. By reading between the lines I can discern passionate remorse underlying the apparent coldness.

Personally, as the allowance was from the first paid *in advance*, I cannot understand how the trustees can possibly take on themselves to alter an arrangement made by my wife. I have written, in my nicest style, to Hargrove on the subject.

I have had a very bad time lately, and for two days had not a penny in my pocket, so had to wander about, filled with a wild longing for *bock* and cigarettes: it was really like journeying through Hell. I was in the "Circle of the Boulevards," one of the worst in the Inferno, and I could only get breakfast here, not dinner, so was dinnerless.

[1] A contemporary advertisement runs:

MAYPOLE SOAP
FOR HOME DYEING
DYES ANY COLOUR
WON'T WASH OUT OR FADE.

[2] So dated in *After Berneval*.

737

I hope to get a type-written copy of *Bunbury*[1] soon, and to work on it. In type, size, paper, and the like, it should be identical with the other plays, and Shannon should do the cover.

The chance of a popular edition of *The Ballad* depends entirely on Smith's bookstalls.

Bosie is at Nogent, with Strong:[2] very angry because I won't join him. Best love. Ever yours   OSCAR

To Reginald Turner

MS. Hyde (D. & M.)

[*11 May 1898. Postmark 12 May 1898*]   *Hôtel d'Alsace*

My dear Reggie, How very good and kind of you; it really is most sweet of you, and you have for this, and many other generous and thoughtful actions, my affectionate love and gratitude. I have had a very bad week of it, but I think I am all right now.

I was very pleased to see your friend Eugene, and hope he is well. He seems quite devoted to you, as indeed all who really know you are. He was in excellent spirits, and seemed to be having a good time.

A kind friend took me to the Folies-Bergère last night—the dear Scheffer.[3] The acrobats were more wonderful than ever, but the audience was dreadfully mulierastic, and aged women covered with diamonds of the worst water came up and begged for *bocks*. On being refused they left with horrible imprecations.

Bosie has furnished a charming flat in the Avenue Kléber, but has spent all his money and so lives at Nogent, where it rains all day. He comes up every afternoon to look at his apartment, for his "bed is green."[4] I chose it for him at Maples. He is devoted to a dreadful little ruffian aged fourteen, whom he loves because at night, in the scanty intervals he can steal from an arduous criminal profession, he sells bunches of purple violets in front of the Café de la Paix. Also every time he goes home with Bosie he tries to rent him. This, of course, adds to his terrible fascination. We call him the "*Florifer*," a lovely name. He also keeps another boy, aged twelve! whom Bosie wishes to know, but the wise "Florifer" declines.

Reggie Cholmondely is here with Sir Tatton Sykes,[5] just back from Rome. Lady Sykes forced her way into Reggie's bedroom yesterday morning, and borrowed five francs from him.

I wish you would come over: it is absurd of you not to. Rodin's statue of Balzac is an astonishing masterpiece, a gorgeous leonine head, stuck on

---

[1] i.e. *The Importance of Being Earnest*.   [2] Rowland Strong. See note p. 643.

[3] Robert Scheffer (1864–1926), French poet and novelist. A copy of his book of poems, *La Chanson de Néos* (1897), is inscribed: "*Au grand poète Oscar Wilde. Hommage de sympathie et d'admiration.* Robert Scheffer."

[4] *The Song of Solomon*, i, 16.

[5] Fifth baronet (1826–1913), landowner and author. Married (1874) Christina, daughter of the Rt Hon. George Augustus Cavendish-Bentinck. Reggie Cholmondeley was the son of Sir Tatton's sister.

the top of a cone-shaped dressing-gown. The Philistines are mad with rage about it. I have suggested that the statue to Alphonse Daudet should consist merely of a dressing-gown, without any head at all.

How is my golden Maurice? I suppose he is wildly loved. His upper lip is more like a rose-leaf than any rose-leaf I ever saw. I fear he would not be a good secretary; his writing is not clear enough, and his eyelashes are too long, but he would be a sweet theatrophone,[1] and an entrancing phonograph.

I should go and see my doctor today, but I don't like to, as I am not feeling very well. I only care to see doctors when I am in perfect health; then they comfort one, but when one is ill they are most depressing.

Give my love to Maurice when you see him.

And, with many thanks, dear Reggie, ever affectionately yours OSCAR

To Robert Ross

MS. Clark

Wednesday [11 May 1898][2]   *[Paris]*

My dearest Robbie, Thanks so much. I have got some money now, but I hope that Carlos will advance me my allowance. I have given him an order on *you* to pay it over to him (the first instalment, of course).

He says he will do so if you say "that it is for my good." Well, it is clearly for my good to have dinner and other necessaries. Monday was really too appalling for words, and indeed I have had a very bad time. So I hope you have consented.

I am going to ask Smithers to *buy The Importance of Being Earnest*, and then I think I shall go to the country somewhere. The difficulty is that it pours with rain all day now.

As regards Bosie, he has been very nice to me indeed, but for the last week he has been at Nogent, with Strong, as he had no money at all, and I could not ask him for any. But when he had money he was very hospitable and generous in paying for things when we were together. Of course the difficulty is that Bosie when he asks me to dinner will always insist on going to a very expensive place and ordering champagne, spending about sixty francs in the whole evening. I would be quite content with a three-franc dinner, but he hates it. The last time we dined together I insisted on a three-franc dinner at a capital restaurant Conder took me to, quite close here in the Rue de l'Échelle, and it went off capitally, but this was the only occasion I managed to make him economise at all. The most revolting letters are passing between him and Sir John.[3] Bosie is very proud of his last postscript, "Abraham and his seed for ever!" (You know Sir John is the son of a Jewish singer—a wonderful and talented woman, I believe.) I am of course very sorry about the whole affair. Sir John is such a good fellow in many ways, and has been kindness itself to me. I have written to

---

[1] A telephone for transmitting stage dialogue from the theatre.
[2] So dated in *After Berneval*.   [3] See note p. 672.

739

Reggie a full account of Bosie's last love—the "*Florifer*," so-called because he hawks violets. I will write again when I hear from Carlos.

With a thousand thanks, dear Robbie, for all your sweetness to me, ever yours   OSCAR

To Leonard Smithers[1]

[Postmark 13 May 1898][2]   *[Paris]*

The 100 francs arrived yesterday morning all right and were most welcome. I see that it might be unwise to spoil our 2/6 edition so soon, but I should have thought that a cheap edition ready for bookstall by August next might do, if Smith would take it up. Also I do think sixpence too little . . . The profit is far too small . . .

I would like a good vivid cover for *The Ballad* in the shilling form, red or grey, but something striking—something that would attract and charm the eye, say a kneeling chained nude figure of sorrow in a decorative design of thorns [*rough sketch*] or hemlock or some dreadful . . . plant or an erect figure standing among thorns.

To Robert Ross

MS. Clark

[14 May 1898][3]   *Taverne F. Pousset, 14 Boulevard des Italiens [Paris]*

My dear Robbie, Yes: all that you say is true: but still, I have done a good year's work: you might remember that. Now I want to do work again, for the next year, but it is not easy to recapture the artistic mood of detachment from the accidents of life.

Of course I cannot bear being alone, and while the literary people are charming when they meet me, we meet rarely. My companions are such as I can get, and I of course have to pay for such friendships, though I am bound to say they are not *exigeants* or expensive.

Of course the allowance has to be paid to Holman *first*. All I meant was that he should send it to you, instead of to me. In that way Carlos could advance the sum required. I enclose a note for Holman.

Frank Harris has sent me nothing. I think of writing to him.

Certainly rooms at £60 a year could easily be got, and could be the most splendid thing for me. It is very good of you to think of it. The hotel is unwholesome and also difficult to write in. Pray let me know if your project comes to anything. I should like them fairly near, so as to avoid using cabs. Ever yours   OSCAR

---

[1] The text of this fragment is taken from the Spoor sale catalogue (1939).
[2] See note p. 736.
[3] So dated in *After Berneval*.

To Martin Holman

MS. Clark

14 May 1898   *Hôtel d'Alsace*

Dear Sir, I should be much obliged if you would kindly pay my allowance, as it comes due each quarter, to Mr Robert Ross, of 11 Upper Phillimore Gardens, W. His receipt will in all cases be a full receipt for any claims of mine, and I beg you to accept it as such. I remain, your obedient servant   OSCAR WILDE

To Robert Ross

MS. Clark

[Postmark 18 May 1898]   *[Postmark Paris]*

My dear Robbie, You are really the *Angelus ex machina* who has taken the place of the wicked Pagan gods in modern tragedy: the only drawback is that a modern tragedy has fifty-five acts, and that the ἄγγελος must appear in all of them.

I will write to you tomorrow at length—on many things. But your arrangement with Holman is delightful. Pray thank him from me.

Bosie wishes to be remembered. Ever yours   OSCAR

I am writing in a café where there is no ink.

To Leonard Smithers

MS. Taylor

Friday [20 May 1898][1]   *[Paris]*

My dear Smithers, As regards the French translation (with the English original) of *The Ballad*, there will be no sale for it in London, except a few copies for bibliophiles. No one wants a poem with a French translation except French people. Nor could Vallette guarantee that no copies should be introduced into England. What he wishes to do is to give you *special* terms so that you will be able to sell it at a larger profit or cheaper price than anyone else. But I don't think you would sell more than a dozen, unless you bought from Vallette some large-paper or Japanese-paper copies. There will be, I hope, a few.

The book will be brought out here at *two* francs. It will be quite unattractive in form, except its ordinary *jonquil* paper cover, so useless in English air.

I wish to goodness you would come over. Also, send me, if you can, four pounds, or even three. I am now trying to leave my hotel, and get rooms, where I can breakfast, and so stay in during the morning. Going out for breakfast is fatal to work. But do run over. Also, kindly buy the copyright of my play. Ever yours   O. W.

[1] So dated by postmark in Glaenzer.

741

To Robert Ross
MS. Clark

Friday, 20 [May 1898]   *Hôtel d'Alsace*

My dear Robbie, The idea of the rooms is too delightful, and I could get admirable rooms for what you mention. Of course unfurnished rooms are much cheaper, but then furnishing costs a lot.

I hope the £10 for May will arrive soon. I have had to pay my washerwoman and my doctor and some money Bosie lent me.

Bosie is now furious with me, because when Davray, who is or wishes to be most respectable, invited me to a café to meet a poet who desired to know me, Bosie turned up ten minutes after my arrival with *Gaston!* of all people, and placed him at Davray's table, where he gabbled about bicycles, and was generally offensive. Davray was much annoyed, and so was I. Bosie cannot understand the smallest iota of social tact, and does not see that to thrust "Giton, the boy-paederast"[1] into a literary reunion, without being invited, is vulgar. So life goes on.

Vallette (of the *Mercure*) has ultimately arranged to bring out my poem in volume form at two francs. I fear my only profit will be the profitable pleasure of looking at the daffodil paper cover. They never pay for translations of poems. I have written a poem in prose this morning, an old one, but not written out up to this.[2]

The weather is detestable. Edmond desires his *hommage* to be sent to you. Ever yours   OSCAR

To Robert Ross
MS. Clark

Tuesday, 24 May [1898]   *[Paris]*

Dear Robbie, Thanks for your letter. I hope the £10 will arrive tomorrow. It will be a sunlit moment when it does. If it doesn't I am afraid I shall be obliged to telegraph to you daily.

As regards the rooms, the difficulty about taking furnished apartments is this.

If one has *furnished* apartments one is entirely at the mercy of the *propriétaire*, who can ask one to leave whenever he chooses, and all houses in Paris where there are furnished rooms are a form of hotel. Other people live there, and might object to my living at the same address. The *propriétaire* would of course find out my real name and ask me to go.

This would not be a question of my conduct, but of my personality. Besides, he would see all my visitors, and might object to some of them. At the Rue Tronchet Bosie had great trouble because Maurice used to stay with him. The proprietor demanded Maurice's name, and said he

---

[1] Giton (here presumably used as a pun on Gaston) is one of the principal characters in the *Satyricon* of Petronius Arbiter, and the boy-friend of the narrator.
[2] Perhaps "The Poet." See note 3, p. 809.

was bound to take the names of people who passed the night in the house. He also objected to others of Bosie's visitors arriving with him at midnight and leaving at 3.15 in the morning.

Furnished apartments would be impossible for me. I am undisturbed as yet at my hotel, because it is a very poor and unsanitary place. People won't stay there as there is no drainage.

Also, I am very anxious to be able always to breakfast in, and sometimes to dine in: otherwise work is impossible. In furnished apartments one is charged hotel prices, and a furnished flat with a kitchen would cost about £80 a year at least.

If I had an unfurnished flat with a kitchen, I could have, as Bosie has, a woman to come in every morning to clean and cook, and to return, if required, at six o'clock to cook some dinner. The saving is enormous. Such breakfast as I take, a couple of eggs and a cutlet, costs very little if you buy the things yourself.

But the chief point is that, if you take unfurnished rooms, you are your own master. Your visitors go up directly to call on you; the concierge is not seen nor consulted; no one can interfere. I have been several times to see Bosie, and I have not yet seen the concierge. If Bosie could not live in the Rue Tronchet, is it likely that I could live anywhere under similar conditions?

At the present moment if the *patron* of the Hôtel d'Alsace asked me to leave, I would have to go at once. Ashton, as you know, was turned out of his hotel by a *commissaire de police* because he was intoxicated. He was in bed at the time, and asleep, and Maurice and I had to dress him and take him out of the hotel at 10.15 at night. The *Juge d'Instruction*, whom I saw personally at the Police Station, told me that the proprietor of furnished rooms could turn out any person he chose, at any time. That is the French law. In unfurnished rooms one can do as one chooses.

So you see that for *me* the only chance I have is to take unfurnished rooms. I don't take them for the purpose of riotous living—lack of money, to put it on the lowest grounds, entails chastity and sobriety—but I do not want to be disturbed, and if Edmond comes to see me at tea-time I don't want the proprietor to question me about his social status.

To suggest I should have visitors of high social position is obvious, and the reason why I cannot have them is obvious also. But, as I said, in unfurnished rooms I can live quietly and at peace. Please seriously consider this point.

Also, my dear Robbie, do not listen to stories about my being expelled from Paris; they are childish. I live a very ordinary life. I go to cafés like Pousset's where I meet artists and writers. I don't frequent places like the Café de la Paix. I dine in modest restaurants for two or three francs. My life is rather dull. I cannot flaunt or dash about: I have not got the money, nor the clothes. When I can I go to the Quartier Latin under the wing of a poet, and talk about art.

I suppose Carlos is the author of the *canard*? It is unkind of him. Ever yours   OSCAR

To Leonard Smithers[1]

[24 May 1898]   [Paris]

My dear Smithers, You are a very good fellow, and I am much obliged to you, but you must really come over and see me and also look on Rodin's wonderful statue of Balzac—a superb work of genius . . . I went to see the trial of Carrara and his wife yesterday. It was very tragic and the judge tortured them. The audience laughed when the beast in red made a point. . . .

Dear Robbie, so thoughtful for others, is making arrangements for me to live in a cheerful French *pension*, with *table-d'hôte* at 6.30 and pleasant ladies' society in the evening. I am to play dominoes. Ever yours O. W.

To Leonard Smithers

MS. Taylor

Wednesday, 24 [actually 25] May [1898]   [Paris]

My dear Smithers, I understood that my letter to *you* was to be Alexander's warrant for sending you the manuscript. I am very sorry for the mistake, and have written this morning to Alexander to send it to you at once. The *chasseur* (a rather nice-looking lad called Charles) has just posted it.

Maurice arrived this morning, looking tired and beautiful. He seems to have been a great success in London, and is full of pleasant reminiscences of the inhabitants. My friend Robert Ross especially seems to have taken quite an interest in him. He is so fond of children, and of people, like myself, who have childlike simple natures.

I wonder you don't ever publish a series—the Short Story series—composed chiefly of translations from the French. Every week in the Paris papers there appear at least two or three really capital short stories, full of wit, of observation, concentrated in style, and invariably clever in idea. They could be translated into English, and I don't fancy you would have to pay more than twenty-five francs a story. If you really think of it I would like you to have them translated by Rowland Jerrold,[2] who wrote to you about translating *Reading Gaol* into French. He is most clever, and well-bred, and well-read.

Of course the thing should be done as a series, and published in an inexpensive form. Will you think it over? I would be glad to help in the selection of the stories. I should begin by the witty ones. The French can treat any subject with wit, and where one laughs there is no immorality; immorality and seriousness begin together.

---

[1] The text of this incomplete letter is taken from the Stetson sale catalogue (1920). Xavier-Ange Carrara, an Italian (naturalised French) mushroom-grower, had with the connivance of his wife murdered a debt-collector and burned his body in a coke-oven. Their trial opened in Paris on 23 May, and next day Carrara was sentenced to death, his wife to life-imprisonment.

[2] Clearly a slip for Laurence Jerrold (see note 5, p. 731), and possibly a momentary confusion with Rowland Strong.

Of course you understand that Alexander's manuscript is to be type-written at once and the copy sent to *me*, the original returned to him. Please have it type-written on thick good paper, *not* tissue, as I cannot correct tissue, and one should not waste tissue: so at least the doctors say.

Please also write to me that you have given up your idea of coming to Paris—*then* your arrival will be a surprise. At present in consequence of your letters I expect you daily, and have done so for three months past. Ever yours

o. w.

I am thinking of writing a novel called *The Boy-Snatcher of Clements Inn*.[1] Will you ask Robbie Ross what he thinks of the title? He knows the pulse of the public.

To Robert Ross

MS. Clark

Wednesday, 24 [actually 25] May [1898]   [Paris]

My dear Robbie, No cheque this morning, but instead my sweet Maurice, *our* sweet Maurice, looking quite charming and as delightful as ever. He seemed a little *tired*, but of course that was the journey. He was full of affectionate memories of you and Reggie, and is quite devoted to you both. He also has lovely clothes, and looks as if he had fallen from Paradise. The concealment of his real address was idiotic. Why he should always have written from Drayton Gardens instead of from Clements Inn is incomprehensible. I am delighted he was with Reggie, as Ashton, when he was here last, told me he did not want to have Maurice staying with him any more, and I was afraid that Maurice, unconscious of this, was forcing himself on an unwilling host, and Ashton is *difficile* and sometimes rough in his awkward moments. I mean when he has *vine-yards* in his hair.

I was sorry to hear that Bosie had written a dreadful postcard to Ashton: it is a horrible thing to have done. I hate it because it shows he has had more than one *damnosa hæreditas* from his father.

I hope that you were able to read my letter of yesterday. Believe me that in furnished apartments I could not live. I would be asked to go.

I understand from Maurice that you think that I have boys to tea every day, and shower gold on them. My dear Robbie, I have not been visited by a single boy since the day Edmond came—in the *daytime* I mean. Of course when the moon is full I often return with Léon, to smoke a cigarette or to weave words about Life, but no one comes to see me. I am never in during the afternoon, except when I am confined to the house by a sharp attack of penury.

I hope to go looking for rooms tomorrow with Maurice. I would like them near here if possible, but the vital thing is the sanitary question. It is a real horror in life to live in an unsanitary house, especially now that summer is coming on. So I think of looking in some of the streets close to

[1] See p. 593. Reggie Turner lived at 2 Clements Inn, where Maurice Gilbert had been staying with him.

the *near* end of the Champs Elysées: there are new and well-drained houses there. As regards the idea of my pawning the furniture, of course that was a joke. If Smithers would give me £30 for the play, I could buy quite enough furniture. Bosie, on £40, is really splendidly gorgeous—an air of wealth about the chairs.

Goodbye, dear Robbie. Write soon. Ever yours   OSCAR

To Reginald Turner
MS. Hyde (D. & M.)

Wednesday [*Postmark 25 May 1898*]   [*Postmark Paris*]

My dear Reggie, Just a line to inform you of the safe arrival of our dear Maurice. He appeared, jonquil-like in aspect, a sweet narcissus from an English meadow, at ten o'clock, and was sweet and loving and loveable as ever. He was quite cut up at his parting with you and Robbie.

It is wonderful how well all flowers of the narcissus kind thrive in the old musty Law-Inns of London: there is something in the air that seems to suit them. Phillimore Gardens is excellent for wallflowers, but for Narcissus or Hyacinth the Law-Inns are best.

I have an idea for a novel about which I have written to *Smithers*, and suggested a title, which I like, but which may sound rather too melodramatic. I wish you would see Smithers, if you are in Bond Street, and ask him about it, whether he would run it or not. If he doesn't I am going to try Grant Richards. I hear he is daring, and likes to splash in great waters.[1]

How is Eugene? I think it is very unkind his not writing to me. Tell him so, and give him my love.

Bosie has grown tired of the "*Florifer*," but intends using the word in a sonnet. All romances should end in a sonnet. I suppose all romances do.

Alfred Jarry[2] has sent me a complete collection of his works. He is a most extraordinary young man, very corrupt, and his writings have sometimes the obscenity of Rabelais, sometimes the wit of Molière, and always something curious of his own. He made his *début* by producing a play called *Ubu Roi* at the Théâtre de L'Œuvre. The point of the play was that everybody said "*Merde*" to each other, all through the five acts, apparently for no reason. The play was so hooted that Jarry became famous, and the *Mercure de France* has published *Ubu Roi* in an edition de luxe. Jarry is

[1] Richards (see note 4, p. 314) had set up on his own as publisher on 1 January 1897 and had already published *Plays Pleasant and Unpleasant* by Bernard Shaw, who many years later said that Richards's autobiography should be called *The Tragedy of a Publisher who Allowed Himself to Fall in Love with Literature.*

[2] French symbolist poet and dramatist (1873–1907). His *Ubu Roi*, a prose drama, was published in June 1896 and first produced by Lugné-Poe at the Théâtre de L'Œuvre on 10 December 1896. Arthur Symons described it as "the first symbolist farce." The characters were dressed as masked marionettes, and the action was accompanied off stage by the marionette music of fairs. André Gide wrote of Jarry's "*figure ininventable . . . ce Kobold, à la face plâtrée.*"

now the rising light of the Quartier Latin. In person he is most attractive. He looks just like a very nice renter.

If you see Rowland, the architect of the moon,[1] please tell him to come over to Paris at once. You should come to take care of him of course. Ever yours
OSCAR

To Robert Ross
MS. Clark

[*Circa 28 May 1898*]   [*Paris*]

My dear Robbie, A thousand thanks for the cheque. May I ask *when* the June £10 comes due? Of course the 1st of the month; otherwise I will never be able to keep my accounts straight.

Of course nothing can be done about rooms till you decide, and have the collection for the sweet sinner of England in hand, but I still suspect you of having a flat of some kind concealed about your person. My instinct in such points is unerring.

I wish you would write and tell me how much you love Maurice. He is a great dear, and loves us all, a born Catholic in romance; he is always talking of you and Reggie.

Yesterday he and I and Bosie went to the Salon. As modern art had a chastening effect on Maurice, and he seemed sad, we went afterwards to the *Foire aux Invalides*, where Maurice won a knife, by foolishly throwing a ring over something.

Robert Sherard is here. On Wednesday he created a horrible scene in Campbell's Bar by bawling out "*À bas les juifs*," and insulting and assaulting someone whom he said was a Jew. The fight continued in the street, and Robert tried to create an Anti-Semite, Anti-Dreyfusard demonstration. He succeeded, and was ultimately felled to the ground by the Jew!

Bosie and I met him at Campbell's by chance on the next day. Campbell told him that the only reason he would consent to serve him was that Bosie and I had shaken hands with him! This rather amused me, when I remember Robert's monstrous moralising about us, and how nobody should know us. Robert looked quite dreadful, all covered with cigar-ash, stains of spilt whiskey, and mud. He was unshaven, and his face in a dreadful state. He had no money, and borrowed a franc from Bosie.

Yesterday he turned up again, and had to receive a rather insolent lecture from Campbell, who told him he preferred Jews to drunkards in his bar. He was much depressed, so of course I gave him drinks and cigarettes and all he wanted. To show his gratitude he insisted on reciting *The Ballad of Reading Gaol*, at the top of his voice, and assuring me that I was "*le plus grand maître de la littérature moderne, et le plus grand homme du monde.*" At the end he got very tedious, and lest I might love my poem less than I wish to, I went away. Poor Robert, he really is quite insane, and unbearable, except to very old friends who bear much. He begged me to

<hr />

[1] See note 2, p. 623.

747

lunch with him and to bring Maurice, but I declined, feigning temporary good health as my excuse! His asking me to bring Maurice was astounding, as when he was last in Paris he refused to call on me because M. was staying with me, and generally was offensive about a lovely and loveable friendship. He has gone to the country today; I hope he will get better. Years ago he was a very good and dear fellow.

I dined last night with Robert d'Humières, a very charming young Frenchman, whom I first met, years ago, at Frank Schuster's.[1] He had asked a poet to meet me, and I believe I was rather wonderful.

I liked the review you sent me immensely. Do you know the writer? It is a very good appreciation.

This letter seems not at all business-like, but Maurice's account of you has somewhat disturbed the severe Spartan Ideal I had formed of you lately. Ever yours   OSCAR

To Leonard Smithers[2]

[Circa 30 May 1898]   *[Paris]*

If you wish to stop the somewhat improbable sale of the French edition of *The Ballad* in London, surely copyright or registration can do it . . .

Have you asked Shannon to do you new petals for the cover of the play? The covers are the same in colour, but the little gold petals are different . . . Ever yours   O. W.

To Reginald Turner
MS. Hyde (D. & M.)

Monday, 30 May [1898]   *[Postmark Paris]*

Dear Reggie, Thanks for your letter. I am greatly distressed about your remarks about Eugene, that wonderful harvest-moon. It is clearly the fatal and unconscious influence of dear Maurice, who, as I have mentioned to my publisher in a business-letter I was writing to him, is all French lily and English rose.

I went yesterday to the *Fête des Fous*—naturally—and saw the Miracle Play. I afterwards dined with Stuart Merrill who had asked most of the actors and actresses to meet me. We had a delightful evening, and the whole Quartier Latin was bright with beauty and wine, and the students in their mediaeval costumes picturesque and improbable and gay. A meeting with *Léon*, whom I found wandering in the moonlit chasm of my little street, ended an admirable Continental Sunday. If you had only been

---

[1] (1840–1928). Brother of Adela. Wealthy music-lover and social figure. Vicomte Robert d'Humières (1869–1915, killed in action) helped Louis Fabulet (see p. 752) with his translations of Kipling, who wrote a preface to the English edition (1905) of d'Humières *L'Ile et L'Empire de Grande Bretagne* (1904).

[2] The text of this fragment is taken from the Spoor sale catalogue (1939).

with me you could have written an admirable signed article for the *D.T.*
Why were you not? Do you know Treherne, a friend of Will Rothenstein's? He is a most charming fellow.[1] Ever yours   O. W.

To Robert Ross

MS. Clark

Tuesday, 31 May [1898]   [*Postmark Paris*]

My dear Robbie, I feel we are both premature. People who count their
chickens before they are hatched act very wisely: because chickens run
about so absurdly that it is almost impossible to count them accurately:
but the question of rooms is different. And I fear you will have great
trouble in getting any promises: I am not very sanguine about it. I don't
wish to be horrid, but I think you are a little unkind in saying that you
cannot explain to people that the object of my taking unfurnished rooms is
to enable me to have boys. Boys can be had everywhere. The difficulty I
am under is my name, my personality. I might be practically turned out of
furnished rooms at a moment's notice. In unfurnished I am my own master.
Would it be quite fair to say of Reggie that he has taken a flat in Clements
Inn in order "to have boys"? Of course he could not live his life in
furnished lodgings: it would be impossible, and most dangerous. But
his object is simply to live his own life, with all that implies. But as I said,
all this is premature. If you get any serious promises, of course you will let
me know.

I saw a delightful Miracle Play on Sunday in the Quartier Latin, and
dined with a lot of the actors and four poets afterwards. They were most
nice and sympathetic, and we were all very gay on *vin ordinaire*. After all,
the only proper intoxication is conversation. Last night Antoine[2] sent me a
box to see *Les Tisserands*, the play that was suppressed in Berlin, and, for a
long time, here.[3] It is socialistic in subject-matter, and I did not care
much for it. The play was rather like a public meeting, and should be
called *The Triumph of the Supers*, but, of course, I was glad to see it.

I see that Max has become Dramatic Critic, and has begun by his
valedictory address. He is clearly entitled to his retiring pension by this
time.[4]

[1] Apsley Philip Treherne (1872–1922) was a nephew of Georgina Weldon. He
was trained as an architect and published biographies of his aunt (*A Plaintiff in
Person*, 1923) and of Spencer Perceval, as well as several novels.
[2] André Antoine (1858–1943), French actor, producer and manager. He founded
the Théâtre Libre in 1887, and in 1897 took over the Théâtre des Menus-Plaisirs,
which he renamed the Théâtre Antoine.
[3] This was a French translation, by Jean Thorel, of Gerhart Hauptmann's play,
Die Weber. A historical drama, based on the revolt of the Silesian weavers in 1844,
it was written in 1892 and banned in Germany until 1893. The French translation
was first produced by Antoine at the Théâtre Libre on 29 May 1893. The English
translation, *The Weavers*, by Mary Morrison, was published by Heinemann in 1899
and first produced at the Crystal Palace Theatre on 1 April 1901. The cast includes
forty-three named characters, as well as a crowd of weavers and rioters.
[4] Max Beerbohm's first dramatic criticism appeared in the *Saturday Review* on

With regard to *The Ballad*, I wrote to Smithers to suggest to him that simple copyright would enable him to stop the sale of the French edition, if it should be on sale. I would like you and some others to have copies, as literary curios, but I personally don't want it sold in London, as I get nothing out of it. It should be made as contraband as Tauchnitz.

On Friday I dine with the editor of *L'Ermitage*, that artistic *revue*,[1] and Maeterlinck has conveyed to me his desire to meet me. He is now in London, but is anxious I should call on his *fiancée*, Georgette Leblanc, an astonishing woman, now singing Sapho at the Opéra Comique in Calvé's place. I am told she is one of the most brilliant and strange personalities in the world.[2]

Where do you spend your summer? Is there any chance of your being in France? Conder has asked me to come and see him at a place called Bonnières between this and Rouen. He says he has found a furnished house for me, 150 francs for three months, but I am afraid of the river-air. I hope to go to the sea. Rivers are very bad for me. I need air like strong wine.

When I see Maurice I shall give him, as you ask me, your "undying love," and that despotism shall be untempered by epigrams.

I fear if I write any more that the weight of the ink will force you, or me, to pay extra postage. So, dear Robbie, a thousand thanks for all your trouble for the perverse and impossible person. Ever yours   OSCAR

To Georgina Weldon[3]

31 May 1898   *Hôtel d'Alsace*

My dear Mrs Weldon, So Philip Treherne is your nephew! When he gave me his card I wondered if he was kith and kin with that lady whom friends of mine remember as the "beautiful Miss Treherne" and whom the world will always remember as Mrs Weldon. But we talked of books and art and the idea passed from my mind. How cultivated he is! and so well bred in his nice quiet gravity and courteous ways. I enjoyed my meeting with him very much and hope he will do well in literature. At present he has perhaps

---

28 May 1898. It was headed "Why I Ought Not to have become a Dramatic Critic."

[1] Charles Edouard Ducoté, French poet and novelist (1870–1929), took over the editorship of *L'Ermitage* in 1896.

[2] Maurice Maeterlinck (1862–1949), Flemish poet, dramatist and essayist, lived for many years with the actress and singer Georgette Leblanc. Massenet's opera, *Sapho*, with libretto by Henri Cain and Arthur Bernède, based on Daudet's novel, was first produced at the Opéra Comique, Paris, on 27 November 1897, with the French soprano, Emma Calvé (1866–1942), in the title-rôle.

[3] See note 1, p. 202. The text of this letter is taken from a manuscript copy in Mrs Weldon's diary, now the property of Miss Marjory Pegram. Mrs Weldon recorded that it was in answer to a letter she wrote to Wilde on 30 May, in which she said "that, as he had given up his insane and unnatural penchants, I did not see any reason why an old lady like me should hold him at arm's distance and that, if he wished, I would see him when I came to Paris."

just a little too much appreciation of other people's work to be able to realise his own creative energy, but admiration is the portal to all great things.

Yes: I think that, aided by some splendid personalities like Davitt and John Burns, I have been able to deal a heavy and fatal blow at the monstrous prison-system of English justice. There is to be no more starvation, nor sleeplessness, nor endless silence, nor eternal solitude, nor brutal floggings. The system is exposed, and, so, doomed. But it is difficult to teach the English either pity or humanity. They learn slowly. Next, the power of Judges (an extremely ignorant set of men—ignorant, that is, of what they are doing, their power to inflict the most barbarous sentences on those who are brought before them) must be limited. A Judge, at present, will send a man to two years' hard labour or to five years' penal servitude with utter callousness, not knowing that all such sentences are sentences of death. It is the lack of imagination in the Anglo-Saxon race that makes the race so stupidly, harshly cruel. Those who are bringing about Prison Reform in Parliament are Celtic to a man. For every Celt has inborn imagination.

For myself, of course, the aim of life is to realise one's *own* personality —one's *own* nature, and now, as before, it is through Art that I realise what is in me. I hope soon to begin a new play, but poverty with its degrading preoccupation with money, the loss of many friends, the deprivation of my children, by a most unjust law, by a most unjust Judge, the terrible effects of two years of silence, solitude and ill-treatment—all these have, of course, to a large extent, killed if not entirely that great joy in living that I once had. However, I must try, and the details of Prison Reform will have to be worked out by others. I put the fly in motion but I cannot drive the wheels. It is enough for me that the thing is coming and that what I suffered will not be suffered by others. That makes me happy.

One word more. Your letter gave me great pleasure, but when you allude to my life being in some respects "unnatural and insane" you are judging of the life of another by an alien standard. Those very expressions— *unnatural and insane*—were often used of you in reference to your conduct as a wife with duties of affection, and a woman with duties of rational conduct. You know that they were unjustly so used. I know it too. But there were many who had a different estimate: there are many still who have a different estimate. They make the harsh error of judging another person's life without understanding it. Do not you—of all people—commit the same error. Charity is not a sentimental emotion: it is the only method by which the soul can attain to any knowledge—to any wisdom. Very sincerely yours   OSCAR WILDE[1]

---

[1] Mrs Weldon noted: "I replied to O. W. I wished I knew one person who had said that of me, I'd have at them. He did not reply."

To Robert Ross

MS. Clark

1 June 1898   [*Paris*]

My dear Robbie, People who repent in sackcloth are dreary, but those who repent in a suit by Doré, and intend this suit for another, are worthy of Paradise. It is most sweet of you, and the colour I would like is *blue*, like the suit I had last year.

A rather painful fact, apparent to all, must now be disclosed. Pray mention it to no one but Doré, and break it to him gently. I am distinctly stouter than I was when the last suit was made. I should say a good inch and a half. I *can* still button the old Doré suit, but it is tight, and the two lower buttons drag. I would like the same stuff, if possible; it is such good stuff, and has lasted so well.

Bosie is now inseparable from Maurice; they have gone again to Nogent. I made Maurice put a postscript into a rather silly letter, inspired by Bosie, which he sent off to you today. I think letters of that kind quite stupid and witless, but Bosie has no real enjoyment of a joke unless he thinks there is a good chance of the other person being pained or annoyed. It is an entirely English trait, the English type and symbol of a joke being the jug on the half-opened door, or the distribution of orange-peel on the pavement of a crowded thoroughfare.

I hope that the beautiful blue suit will be brought over by either you or Reggie. If not, let Smithers be told that the duty is his. I hear that the Custom House is exorbitant, and sends you papers on which they have thrown sand.

I find I have written the beginning of a letter to a French poet on the other side of this, so cannot write more. Fabulet is the author of *La Crise*, an attempt at an anarchical poem, a dull thing at best.[1] Ever yours

OSCAR

To Robert Ross

MS. Clark

[*Early June 1898*]   [*Paris*]

My dear Robbie, Thanks so much for cheque.

I hope you replaced Oxford in the right way. It is sad to think I may have of disciples "but few or none"[2] in that sweet grey city that nurtured me.

---

[1] Louis Fabulet (1862–1933), apart from *La Crise* (1896), was chiefly noted for his translations of Kipling and other English and American writers. The abortive letter to him on the back of this sheet runs: "*Cher Monsieur Fabulet, Je vous remercie bien de votre charmante lettre, et de . . .*"

[2] "Sing him thy best! for few or none
Hears thy voice right, now he is gone"
Matthew Arnold, "Memorial Verses,"
referring to Wordsworth and the river Rotha.

Georgette Leblanc, Maeterlinck's mistress, sent me seats last night for *Sapho* at the Opéra Comique. She is one of the most wonderful artists I ever saw. The music meandered aimlessly about, as Massenet's usually does, with endless false alarms of a real melody, and incessant posing of themes that are not resolved into any development, but her acting was really a marvel. Bosie was with me, and she looked at us with wonderful eyes, and on her "calls" gave us her bows to the exclusion of the rest of a crowded house. Bosie was seated next a *German* who exhaled in strange gusts the most extraordinary odours, some of them racial (it is smell that differentiates races); others connected with all kinds of trades from leather-dressing and carpentry, to vitriol-works and the keeping of an Italian warehouse; others such as are found only among "*les mangeurs des choses immondes*;"[1] others connected with gas, fuel, and candles. In the last act he became like a petroleum lamp. Bosie bore it very well indeed: but had practically to sit in my pocket.

Maurice, unfortunately under the influence of his mother, who seems to be devoted to betting, spends all his days at surburban race-courses. Of course he always wins: he is a child of the Sun, not a $\sigma\epsilon\lambda\eta\nu\iota\zeta\acute{o}\mu\epsilon\nu\sigma\varsigma$[2] as you and I are, but in spite of betting, and "spotting the winner," the curves of his mouth are more wonderful than ever. His mouth, when he talks, and he is never silent, is the most beautiful mouth I know. It has the curves of Greek art and English flowers.

Bosie preys on his *femme-de-ménage*, who now pays for everything, including cigars. When he gives his orders she "looks upon the wondering sky with unreproachful stare,"[3] she is so bewildered. She apparently thought that Bosie was going to pay for everything. Of course she finds that that is out of the question. Her psychological condition is extraordinary.

Edmond tells me he wrote you an absurd letter. I *can't* understand why he called with a young champion bicyclist. Ever yours   OSCAR

Petit Bleu: To Maurice Gilbert

MS. Clark

[Postmark 18 June 1898]   *[Nogent-sur-Marne]*

My dear Maurice, Bosie and I are at Nogent. Do come down either tonight or tomorrow *early*. I have taught them how to make *œufs à l'aurore*. Ever yours   O.

---

[1] Flaubert: *Salammbô*, ch. iv (see note 4, p. 578).

[2] Moonstruck. The word used in *Matthew*, iv. 24, for the lunatics brought to Jesus to be healed.

[3] *The Ballad of Reading Gaol*, section IV.

To Henry D. Davray[1]

[Date of receipt 20 June 1898] *[Paris]*

A thousand apologies. Here is page 11. I have only just come up from L'Idée, Le Perreux, Nogent. L'Idée is a little inn where poor poets go, like *L'Ermitage* in literature.

To Leonard Smithers

MS. Taylor

[23 June 1898][2] *[Nogent-sur-Marne]*

My dear Smithers, Please send me £10, and you will receive the manuscript with its due corrections. I don't think you can receive it if you don't, as I am quite penniless, and on the brink of expulsion from my hotel. I do not receive anything till July 1st. I hope you will make up your mind about this coming to Paris, as Robbie has a suit of clothes for me, and if you don't come I shall have to wait till I can pay the duty.

I have gone to a little inn at Nogent. Address: M. Sebastian Melmoth, L'Idée, Le Perreux, Nogent-sur-Marne, as I dare not go back to my hotel, and at Nogent I have credit.

Do please do this for me *at once.* Ever yours   O. W.

To Robert Ross

MS. Clark

Monday, 27 June [1898] *[Nogent-sur-Marne]*

My dear Robbie, I did not write to you because I really expected you and the lovely suit of clothes over here. Reggie wrote to me a fortnight ago that you were coming over to see Maurice, and would no doubt call on me and on Bosie.

I have been staying at Nogent, with Bosie. It is a lovely place, and we have had some charming days, but Bosie goes up to Paris daily, and only returns for dinner. He goes and sits in his rooms. He says it is absurd to have rooms and not to sit in them. *[400 words omitted][3]* Ever yours

OSCAR

To Robert Ross

MS. Clark

[July 1898] *L'Idée, Le Perreux, Nogent-sur-Marne*

My dear Robbie, I went up to Paris today and found the lovely suit at my hotel. It fits perfectly and is most smart and elegant. A thousand thanks

---

[1] Fragment from catalogue No. 3 of Alwin J. Scheuer, New York (1927).

[2] So dated, presumably from a postmark now lost, in *Oscar Wilde, Fragments and Memories,* by Martin Birnbaum (1920).

[3] This passage contains a bitter and irrelevant attack on a friend whose close descendants might justifiably be hurt by its publication.

for it. Dear Reggie's offerings are most welcome also: just what I wanted. I must write to him at once to thank him. [*1065 words omitted*][1]

It is a curious thing, dear little absurd Robbie, that you *now* always think that I am in the wrong. It is a morbid reaction against your former, and more rational, estimate of me.

The only thing that consoles me is that your moral attitude towards yourself is even more severe than your moral attitude towards others. Yours is the pathological tragedy of the hybrid, the Pagan-Catholic. You exemplify the beauty and the uselessness of Conscience.

When I read your, often bitter, censures of me, and your stern lectures, I think of your censures of yourself, of your awful curtain-lectures, delivered alone, listened to in silence, unanswerable merely because they are not answered, judge and prisoner the same person, yourself your own gaoler.

Why not sometimes think that I may be in the right? Why, at once, take the side of "*le triste individu*"? I often wonder what would have happened to those in pain if, instead of Christ, there had been a Christian.

As regards Dal Young I have written, or rather am going to write, to him.[2] It is a long history, but I think when you know the circumstances that you will have a different view. In any case Bosie has nothing to do with the matter. All he did was to write some lovely lyrics—for nothing, I need hardly say. Dal Young at first offered to give me a house, to have it built for me at Berneval so that I should have a home. It was to cost £700 (with a freehold of the land). This offer I declined. I thought it a piece of generous but Quixotic enthusiasm. I hardly knew him at the time. I did not think it right to accept such an offer.

Then he begged me to write him a libretto. I made out a libretto that enchanted him. For two months he was at me to promise to do it. I told him that I did not, could not, know if I could continue my literary work. He laughed at the idea. His wife, his friends urged me to accept his offer. I was asked to name a price for a libretto.

I asked £100, and £50 on production. I could hardly have asked less. The lowest literary hack in Grub Street would not write the libretto of an original classical opera for less. I asked little, because I knew he was simply anxious to show his confidence in my future by giving me a start: he wanted to help me. I had refused the gift of a house at £700. After three months I did accept what I knew in my heart was meant half as a gift, half as an encouragement. He told me to take my own time about it. He said that all he wanted was that I should know that he believed in me etc. etc.

Well, I have not done it yet. I may never do it. I don't think I shall ever write again. I told him all that. Of course it would have been more *prudent* for me to have secured the house. £700 is a good stroke of business is it not? But someway I did not like to do it; I could not have done it. It would have been wiser if I had, but I should have rather despised

[1] A further and more bitter attack on the person mentioned in note 2, p. 754, omitted for the same reason.   [2] See pp. 639 and 645-646.

myself. Ultimately I accepted a commission, and being asked to fix my own terms, fixed the lowest I could think of. I knew it was all, *at that time*, meant simply as a means of being kind to me, of helping me without humiliating me. If now I am accused of getting money from Young under false pretences, it shows me that one should never accept any sort of kindness. People regret their good actions. That is the point to which the moral sense ultimately arrives. In any case, in this matter I have done nothing that could be brought up against me, and Young should set the matter right at once if such a rumour is current.

Your postcard has just been handed to me here. Who is Steele? Is he the painter? Or has he a profile? In any case I must thank him. But there are different modes of showing gratitude.

Frank Harris was most hospitable and nice to me here. I dined with him every night, except one night when I dined with Maeterlinck and his wonderful mistress, Georgette Leblanc, the prima-donna of the Opéra Comique, a woman very like Sarah Bernhardt. They have a lovely little house, near the Bois de Boulogne—all white walls, and green furniture, and Burne-Jones photographs, heaps of books, and Dutch brass candlesticks, and copper things. He is *bon garçon*. Of course he has quite given up art. He only thinks of making life sane and healthy, and freeing the soul from the trammels of culture. Art seems to him now a malady. And the *Princesse Maleine* an absurdity of his youth. He rests his hope of humanity on the Bicycle. I dined with him the night before he left for London. You have never told me anything about *Pelléas et Mélisande*. Was it absurd?[1]

One night I made Frank Harris invite Bosie to dinner. We dined at Maire's. The bill was terrific. Bosie was childlike and sweet. Runciman[2] and Mrs Harris (No 2)[3] were of course present. Frank was wonderful on the subject of the Greek passions of Christ and Shakespeare—especially Christ. He insisted that the betrayal by Judas was the revenge of a great lover discarded for "that sentimental beast John." Rostand[4] and one of his

---

[1] *La Princesse Maleine* (1889) was Maeterlinck's first play. Octave Mirbeau's glowing review of it in the *Figaro* caused its author to be known as "the Belgian Shakespeare." *Pelléas et Mélisande* (1892) was the most successful of his early plays. It was first produced in Paris by Lugné-Poe in 1893, and in London, translated by J. W. Mackail, and with special music by Gabriel Fauré, nine matinées were given at the Prince of Wales Theatre, beginning on 21 June 1898, with Mrs Patrick Campbell, Johnston Forbes-Robertson and Martin Harvey in the leading parts.

[2] John F. Runciman (1866–1916), outspoken music critic of the *Saturday Review* under Frank Harris, and author of books on music. In 1896 he caused a storm by describing the Royal Academy of Music as "a cesspool of academic musical life." Bernard Shaw described him as "young, clever, and quite genuine, but, like many middle-class Bohemians, without a notion of public or private manners. He drank, died, and is forgotten; but he held his own among us for a time."

[3] Harris had recently eloped with an Irish beauty called Helen (Nellie) O'Hara, to whom he remained married for the rest of his life.

[4] Edmond Rostand (1868–1918), French dramatist, had scored successes with *La Princesse Lointaine* (1895), in which Sarah Bernhardt played the heroine, and *Cyrano de Bergerac* (1897), with Coquelin aîné in the title-rôle.

756

mistresses was dining at another table. He listened so attentively that I feel sure he does not understand a word of English.

Maurice is looking very ill. Bosie insists that he is consumptive, but I don't believe it. He works, or rather overworks, with Strong from 9 a.m. till 9.45 p.m. in a stuffy room. He is always sweet and nice. And the curves of his mouth are a source of endless wonder and admiration to me. Out of such a mouth I would drink Lethe in this world and in the next ambrosia.

This letter is too tedious and too long. The fault is yours. You think it good for me that you should never be on my side. The Goliaths who threaten me are always assisted by my David. Ever yours   o. w.

Write to Paris always.

Postcard: To Robert Ross

MS. Clark

[Postmark 29 July 1898]   *[Postmark Paris]*

My dear Robbie, You are quite right. *The Duchess* is unfit for publication —the only one of my works that comes under that category. But there are some good lines in it.[1]

Could you let me have my £10 cheque, so that I can cash it on Monday, the 1st August? It would be very good of you. Bosie is in Paris till Sunday. Ever yours   s. m.

To Leonard Smithers

MS. Private

Tuesday [Postmark 9 August 1898]   *[Paris]*

My dear Smithers, I am greatly distressed at not hearing from you. I have had as yet no acknowledgment of the manuscript nor the £20 I begged you to let me have in accordance with your promise made to me when you were last here.

You said that at the end of the month (July) you would be able to let me have £30. I have been now for a whole week with nothing at all. I managed to borrow twenty francs—that was all, and my hotel is clamorous for payment of my bill. I do hope that you have sent me the £20. If not, pray make an effort and telegraph it to me through Cook tomorrow. This poverty really breaks one's heart: it is so *sale*, so utterly depressing, so hopeless. Pray do what you can.

[1] When Ross published *The Duchess of Padua* in the Collected Edition of 1908 he dedicated it to Adela Schuster and wrote: "A few months before his death Mr Oscar Wilde expressed to me a regret that he had never dedicated any of his works to one from whom he had received such infinite kindness and to whom he was under obligations no flattering dedication could repay. With not very great sincerity, because I knew he was a dying man, I suggested he might still write a play or book which you would accept. He answered with truth, 'There is nothing but *The Duchess of Padua* and it is unworthy of her and unworthy of me.' "

Paris is hot and empty. Even the charming people of bad character have gone away. Perspiring English families are all that can be seen. Pray don't desert me in this crisis. I really am without food, as far as dinner goes, and have no money for even French cigarettes. If you desert me now I don't know what will become of me. Ever yours   O. W.

To Leonard Smithers

MS. Taylor

Friday [12 August 1898][1]   *[Paris]*

My dear Smithers, Thank you very much for the cheque, which was a great boon, to the *patron* of the hotel primarily, and in a secondary degree to myself. I am much obliged to you. I hope to receive my proofs soon.

It is so hot in Paris that I simply cannot write a letter. At night it is charming, but by day a tiger's mouth. If I could get away to the sea all would be well.

I saw Carrington the other night. He tells me of a wonderful book of poems you have published, and has promised to let me see it. Carrington looked twisted and hysterical. What a curious type he is![2]

The English are very unpopular in Paris now, as all those who are over here, under Cook's direction, are thoroughly respectable. There is much indignation on the Boulevards. I try to convince them that they are our worst specimens, but it is a difficult task. Ever yours   O. W.

To Frank Harris

MS. Texas

[Postmark 13 August 1898][3]   *Hôtel d'Alsace*

My dear Frank, How are you? I read your appreciation of Rodin's "Balzac" with immense pleasure,[4] and am looking forward to more Shakespeare.[5] You will of course put all your Shakespearean essays into a book, and, equally of course, I must have a copy. It is a great era in Shakespearean criticism, the first time that one has looked in the plays, not for philosophy, for there is none, but for the wonder of a great personality—something far better, and far more mysterious, than any philosophy.

[1] So dated, presumably from postmark, in *Oscar Wilde, Fragments and Memories*, by Martin Birnbaum (1920).

[2] Charles Carrington was a bookseller of doubtful honesty, working in Paris. In 1901 he republished *The Picture of Dorian Gray*, and later bought the rights from Ward Lock. During the years after Wilde's death he brought out pirated editions of *Salome* and others of Wilde's works, as well as publishing books fraudulently claiming to be Wilde's translations from the French.

[3] So dated by Harris, and, though the Rodin reference suggests an earlier month, the "streets of brass" match the ones in the next letter.

[4] The only notice of Rodin's statue that had appeared in Harris's paper, the *Saturday Review*, was a glowing tribute by D. S. M[acColl], couched in Biblical language and published on 14 May.

[5] Thirteen of Harris's Shakespeare articles (see note 2, p. 720) appeared in the

It is a great thing that you have done. I remember writing once in *Intentions* that the more objective a work of art is in form, the more subjective it really is in matter, and that it is only when you give the poet a mask that he can tell you the truth.[1] But you have shown it fully in the case of the one artist whose personality was supposed to be a mystery of deep seas, a secret as impenetrable as the secret of the moon.

Paris is terrible in its heat. I walk in streets of brass, and there is no one here. Even the criminal classes have gone to the seaside, and the *gendarmes* yawn and regret their enforced idleness. Giving wrong directions to English tourists is the only thing that consoles them.

You were most kind and generous last month in letting me have the £10: it gives me just the margin to live on and to live by. May I have it again this month? Or has gold flowed away from you? Ever yours

OSCAR

To Robert Ross

MS. Clark

Tuesday [*Postmark 16 August 1898*]   [*Postmark Paris*]

My dear Robbie, I have been suffering from a complete paralysis of epistolary power. I simply have not been able to write to anyone.

Paris is a fiery furnace. I walk in streets of brass. And even the bad boys have left for *les bains de mer*.

I dined last night with Strong, to meet Esterhazy and *la fille Pays*, who is a most charming woman—very clever and handsome. I am to dine with her and the *Commandant* on Thursday.[2]

Maurice never comes to see me. I asked him to breakfast last Sunday week and he never even answered my letter. I am sorry, for I used to like him very much.

Bosie is at Trouville still. But as the doctor won't let him bathe, and his mother won't let him baccarat, he is dreadfully bored. He goes to Aix next month.

I dined with Sarluis[3] last week. He introduced a wonderful boy with

---

Saturday Review at varying intervals between March and December 1898. None appeared during August.   [1] "The Critic as Artist," Part II.

[2] Marie (*dite* Marguérite) Pays, also known as "Four-fingered Margaret," was a registered prostitute, Esterhazy's mistress, and one of the central characters in the intrigues and forgeries of the Dreyfus Case. Like Esterhazy, she was arrested and acquitted for lack of evidence.

[3] Léonard Sarluis (1874–1949) was a Dutch-Jewish painter and book-illustrator who came to Paris in 1894 and was later naturalised. "*Au café Napolitain,*" says his biographer, "*Ernest La Jeunesse devint son fidèle mentor, Oscar Wilde son dieu; au banquet Verhaeren, on le fait monter sur la table au dessert pour que tout le monde puisse contempler ce nouveau phénomène, Rachilde l'embrasse avec effusion et, le lendemain, Jean Lorrain, dans son pêle-mêle du* Journal, *annonce qu'une sorte de chérubin hollandais vient d'arriver à Paris ayant le sourire de la Joconde, le génie de Raphaël et troublant les dames aux bandeaux plats et les messieurs à cravate volumineuse.*"

red hair like the hair of a Botticelli angel. His occupation by day is preparing the ingredients necessary for *vol-au-vents*, in a shop near the Halles. At night, attired in one of Sarluis's best suits, he looks wonderful.

Thanks very much for your suggestion to let me have my income weekly: it is the only thing to do. I must however leave my hotel, and really live as a very poor man. My hotel bill for rooms and *café-au-lait* is 100 francs a month. I must try and get rooms for 40 francs instead of 70. I don't think I shall ever really write again. Something is killed in me. I feel no desire to write. I am unconscious of power. Of course my first year in prison destroyed me body and soul. It could not have been otherwise.

I saw Cossie Lennox with his wife[1] and Harry Melvill the other night. Cossie and Harry Melvill both cut me! I felt as if I had been cut by two Piccadilly renters. For people whom one has had to give themselves moral or social airs is childish. I was very much hurt. But have quite recovered.

Give my love to dear Reggie. That harvest-moon, Eugene, loomed on me on the Boulevard the other day. He looked like a prize melon.

Do write and tell me news, when you can. Ever yours   OSCAR

To Will Rothenstein
MS. Rothenstein

[*August 1898*]   *La Maison Rouge, Hôtel, Café, Restaurant,*
          La Roche-Guyon, Seine-et-Oise

My dear Will, So sorry to miss you. I rowed down in Blunt's[2] boat, Madame Richard came to breakfast, and Conder and Blunt have gone back part of the way with her. I shall come over tomorrow about three o'clock to see you and the rose-like lady whom I admire and like so much.[3] I hear the wild-haired poet[4] has gone to Paris, but is to return, so we must have "a nicht wi' Robbie Burns" (I believe that is Scotch). Ever yours
          OSCAR

To Robert Ross
MS. Clark

[*August 1898*]   *Hôtel d'Alsace*

Dear Robbie, Where are you? I received the cheque all right, but there was no pen or ink in the *département* in which I was (Seine-et-Oise) so could not acknowledge it.

I have been with Rothenstein and Conder. They have both been very

[1] Cosmo Gordon-Lennox (see note 8, p. 521) had recently married the actress Marie Tempest (1866–1942).

[2] Arthur Cadogan Blunt (b. 1860), artist son of the Rev. Gerald Blunt, Rector of Chelsea.

[3] Alice Knewstub, whom Rothenstein was to marry in the following year.

[4] John Pringle Nichol. His father John Nichol (1833–94) had been Professor of English Literature at Glasgow 1861–89, and was a lifelong friend of Swinburne.

nice to me. The Seine is lovely, and there are wonderful backwaters, with willows and poplars, with water-lilies and turquoise kingfishers. I bathed twice a day, and spent most of my time in rowing about. Nichol, the son of the Glasgow professor, was there also—a nice fellow, but insane. He cannot think or talk, so he quotes Swinburne's *Poems and Ballads* always, instead of conversation—a capital idea, after all.

Will you let me dedicate *The Importance of Being Earnest* to you? I would so much like to write your name on the dedication-page, or, at any rate, your initials. The evening papers might disclose your identity if properly approached. Ever yours   OSCAR

To Robert Ross
MS. Clark

[*August 1898*]   *Hôtel de l'Écu, Chennevières-sur-Marne, Seine-et-Oise*

Dear Robbie, Of course I have not cashed your cheque, but I want to. I must have ten pounds at once, as my hotel *patron* comes down here, and bores me with horrible cries. *Do let me*: in advance of September. It really would be good of you. I am worried to extinction. Please wire me *yes*, and I will get the money.

I will write my life more fully tomorrow. Ever yours   OSCAR

Please write to me under my *real name*.

To Robert Ross
MS. Clark

3 October 1898   *Paris*

My dear Robbie, Thanks so much for the £17. 10, duly received.[1]

I wish you and Reggie could have stopped in Paris a night, but I hope you will pass some days here on your return. It is ages since I saw Reggie.

Bosie is back from Aix: his mother on leaving gave him £30 to go to Venice with. He of course lost it all at once at the Casino, and arrived in Paris on the proceeds of his sleeve-links. For the moment he is penniless.

Frank Harris is at St Cloud. I have breakfasted and dined with him, of course, many times, and have brought Bosie, to whom Frank is very nice. Frank has bought a hotel at Monaco, and hopes to make lots of money. He wants me to go to a place called Napoule, near Cannes, where he is going to winter. In Paris I certainly do nothing.

Charlie Owen[2] is here, and we all dined one night together. He is really

[1] In Clark is Ross's original cheque for £7. 10, dated 30 September 1898 and endorsed Sebastian Melmoth and Alfred Douglas. The remaining £10 had presumably been sent in advance, but Wilde acknowledged £17. 10 because this was the sum due to him in the last month of each quarter. In each of the two other months he received £10, thus making the total quarterly allowance £37. 10.

[2] Probably the "racing man" mentioned by Douglas in *Without Apology* (1935).

very handsome and amusing. He thinks of going to Japan, and then to winter in India.

Great rows here over Strong selling Esterhazy's confession. He is violently attacked by his old *confrères*, and Robert Sherard writes terrific diatribes.[1]

Do write, and give my love to dear Reg. Ever yours   OSCAR

To Leonard Smithers[2]

[*Postmark 18 October 1898*]

Could you lend me or send me £10? I am in great straits, and have been ill in bed for some time. Please try to do this, as I have no money. Do please tell me if I am to have proofs of my play, and when. I have been expecting to see you for days.   OSCAR

To Horace Sedger[3]

24 October 1898   *Paris*

I hereby assign and secure to you the sole and exclusive performing rights, in the United Kingdom, of the play, the scenario of which I submitted to you last night, on the following terms . . . I agree to give you my next modern play upon the same terms . . . It is understood that the casting of the play is to be subject to my approval, which shall not be unreasonably withheld. It is understood that you will endeavour to procure Mr Forbes-Robertson and Mrs Patrick Campbell for the two leading parts.   OSCAR WILDE

To Robert Ross

MS. Clark

[*Circa 23 November 1898*]   *Grand Café, 14 Boulevard des Capucines, Paris*

My dear Robbie, The clothes are quite charming—suitable to my advanced age. The trousers are too tight round the waist. That is the result of my rarely having good dinners: nothing fattens so much as a dinner at

[1] On 18 September 1898 Rowland Strong published in the *Observer* an article in which he reported Esterhazy as being in London and ready to make startling disclosures. A week later he printed a long confession in which Esterhazy admitted having written the *bordereau*. These revelations were printed in the *Temps* of 23 and 27 September, and in the *Figaro* of 4 October. Esterhazy denied everything, threatened the *Observer* with a libel action, and succeeded in getting £500 out of them.
[2] The text of this fragment is taken from the American Art Association catalogue of 9 February 1927.
[3] English theatrical manager (1853–1917). The text of this fragment is taken from the Stetson sale catalogue (1920). The scenario was the one which eventually became *Mr and Mrs Daventry*.

1 fr. 50, but the blue waistcoat is a dream.[1] Smithers I received in the same parcel. He was quite wonderful, and depraved, went with monsters to the sound of music, but we had a good time, and he was very nice.

Would it bother you if I asked you to let me have my allowance for December now? A wretched inn-keeper at Nogent to whom I owe 100 francs, out of a bill of 300, threatens to sell Reggie's dressing-case, my overcoat, and two suits, if I don't pay him by Saturday. He has been detaining the things, and now threatens a sale. It is less than a week, so perhaps you might manage it without too much worry to yourself.

Sir John was astonishing, went through a romance with an absurd Boulevard boy, who, of course, cheated him, and treated him badly. The reason was that Sir John had given him a suit of clothes—an admirable reason. To undress is romance, to dress, philanthropy. You are quite philanthropic to me, but you are also romantic—the sole instance of the lack of philosophy in clothes. Do let me have a cheque: if you can, by return.
Ever yours   OSCAR

To Robert Ross

MS. Clark

Friday [*25 November 1898*]   *Paris*

My dear Robbie, I am so sorry about my excuse. I had forgotten I had used Nogent before. It shows the utter collapse of my imagination, and rather distresses me.

Do let me know about Bosie. I suppose that London takes no notice at all: that is the supreme punishment.[2]

I have corrected two-thirds of my proofs,[3] and await the last act. I don't want to make threats, but remember that the dedication is not yet written, and I may write

To
R. B. Ross
in recognition of his good advice.

That would be terrible, so do not lecture till *after Dec. 7th*.[4]

---

[1] A letter from Ross (TS. Holland), headed "Monday evening" [? 21 November 1898] from 11 Upper Phillimore Gardens, reads:

Dear Oscar, I have just received the French version of *The Ballad*. It really looks charming and the French is so unlike the original that one has all the sensations of reading a new poem. I wish however it was a *new* book by you. I have sent off your clothes today. Let me know when they arrive. I wish Sir John had told me that he was going to Paris. He might have taken them. Please give him my love.

Smithers tells me that he is "going to send you proofs of the play." I am bound to say that I now take your side. He is quite absurd about proofs. Always yours   ROBBIE

The publication date of the French edition of *The Ballad* is unknown, but it was *"achevé d'imprimer le dix Septembre 1898"* and probably appeared within a month or so. The British Museum copy is stamped 11 April 1899.

[2] Douglas was paying his first visit to London since 1895.

[3] Of *The Importance of Being Earnest*.   [4] For the final dedication, see p. 770.

763

I see a great deal of La Jeunesse, who is more intolerable than ever, and I dined with Strong, who has reduced Maurice to a state of silent frightened idiocy. Dogma without Literature is bad for boys. Ever yours   OSCAR

To H. C. Pollitt[1]

MS. Princeton

[Postmark 26 November 1898]   *Hôtel d'Alsace*

Dear Mr Pollitt, I should like a photograph of you, of all things. Pray let me have one. There is no duty (Custom-House) except on purely British products, and I am sure you do not come under that category. So the post will safely convey me your profile.

My "trivial comedy for serious people" comes out in a few weeks, if Shannon will do as he did for my others plays—strew three gilt petals on a purple field, but I don't know if he will be idle enough. I hear rumours of industry in the Richmond vale.

You ask me what I am writing: very little: I am always worried by that mosquito, money; bothered about little things, such as hotel-bills, and the lack of cigarettes and little silver *francs*. Peace is as requisite to the artist as to the saint: my soul is made mean by sordid anxieties. It is a poor ending, but I had been accustomed to purple and gold.

I like your Christian name so much: I suppose you are your own lion?[2]
Sincerely yours   OSCAR WILDE

To Reginald Turner

MS. Hyde (D. & M.)

Saturday [Postmark 26 November 1898]   *Paris*

My dear Reggie, Thanks for your nice letter. I hope to send you another book—my play—next month. It is dedicated to Robbie, but the terms of the dedication depend on the amount of lecturing he gives me between this and Dec. 7th. At present he is a combination of the University Extension Scheme and the Reformation, but he is always a dear: and when he knocks me down with the Decalogue, I introduce Narcissus to him, as the only repartee.

I do hope you will come soon to Paris. Of course it was rash my asking our two young friends to the same table as ourselves, but you will behave better when you are here, and only go to the Grand Café in the evening: there the aristocrats are gathered together, and their clothes are so smart that to talk to them is an outward and painfully visible sign of respectability.

---

[1] Herbert Charles Pollitt (1871–1942), a native of Kendal in Westmorland, had been an undergraduate at Trinity College, Cambridge, 1889–92, and made a name there as an amateur ballet-dancer. He preferred Jerome to his own Christian names and signed himself so in his letters to Wilde. Wilde sent him inscribed copies of the French translation of *The Ballad of Reading Gaol* and of *The Importance of Being Earnest*.

[2] St Jerome, the translator of the Vulgate, is usually portrayed reading or writing with a lion seated beside him.

Do let me know about Bosie in London. Is he happy to be back? And are people kind to him? How is he behaving? He has only written to me once—a brief scrawl—not very charming.

Do you remember the young Corsican at the Restaurant Jouffroy? His position was menial, but eyes like the night and a scarlet flower of a mouth made one forget that: I am great friends with him. His name is Giorgio: he is a most passionate faun.

I expect dear Sir John tomorrow. I do hope he will arrive. He is the last great sentimentalist left to us, and clothes everybody except the naked. Ever yours

OSCAR

To Leonard Smithers[1]

[Postmark 27 November 1898]

Your good-natured disposition still will excite false hopes ... I go to Cook's twice a day, but the order you said you hoped to send on Wednesday last does not flash through the wires. As for the offer for my plays, I thought there might be a difference between advancing £20 on a poem, and purchasing for £50 two plays that have been great successes, have been admired etc, and belong to a series of published plays that were sold out almost at once.[2] Your spending £1000 in paying debts seems to me awful. I cannot understand such extravagance. Where will you end if you go on like this? Bankruptcy is always ahead for those who pay their debts. It is their punishment. I hope proofs have arrived safe, and that you will have decided on the format. Also, *do* copyright in America: "Sixty millions of people, *all* fools!" to improve, or expand, Carlyle.[3] Ever yours

O. W.

To Robert Ross

MS. Clark

2 December [1898]   *Taverne F. Pousset, 14 Boulevard des Italiens, Paris*

My dear Robbie, You are usually so kind in sending me my allowance on the 30th of the month, so that I can touch it by the 1st, that I write to say

[1] The text of this incomplete letter is taken from the American Art Association catalogue of 9 February 1927, where the last two sentences and signature are reproduced in facsimile.

[2] There exists (MS. Bodley Head) a document signed by Wilde, which runs:

Agreement made between Leonard Smithers and Oscar Wilde this 27th day of April 1899.

Oscar Wilde agrees to sell to Leonard Smithers all his right and interest in the publication in book form of *An Ideal Husband* and *The Importance of Being Earnest* for thirty pounds and acknowledges the receipt of that sum.

[3] "Consider, in fact a body of Six-hundred and fifty-eight miscellaneous persons set to consult about 'business,' with Twenty-seven millions, mostly fools, assiduously listening to them" (*Latter-Day Pamphlets*, No. VI, "Parliaments," 1850).

that nothing has yet arrived. The post often goes wrong, so I write merely to tell you.

Hylton,[1] whom you know, is here with a London lad, whose lack of aspirates reminds me of many of my former friends. He seems to be enjoying himself very much. Ashton is supposed to arrive tomorrow with his boy from St Malo.

I have corrected all the proofs of my play, but I feel sure my "woulds" and "shoulds," my "wills" and "shalls," are all wrong. Perhaps you might look at them.

Shannon will do the cover.

Love to Reggie. Ever yours   OSCAR

To Robert Ross
MS. Clark

Saturday, 3 December [1898]   [*Paris*]

My dear Robbie, Many thanks: the cheque, delayed I suppose on the Goodwin Sands by stress of storm, arrived today by the second post.

I am delighted to hear of my photograph being sold again: it shows revival of strange sympathies.

What *can* you want to lecture me about, except my past and my present, which you expressly exclude? I have no future, my dear Robbie. I don't think I am equal to intellectual architecture of thought: I have moods and moments; and Love, or Passion with the mask of Love, is my only consolation.

I hope to see Frank Harris here, but as yet have heard nothing. Sir John has not yet arrived.

La Jeunesse is publishing a new review. I am going to make an effort and try to write a poem in prose, for the first number.[2]

It is quite true that when you talk morals to me, which you do quite beautifully, I always pipe on a reed and a faun comes running out of the thicket. You at once say "What a lovely faun!" The rest is silence— that is all I said to Smithers.

In the dedication would you like your full name? Robert Baldwin Ross: or merely Robert B. Ross? I propose to insert the splendid Irish-Norman of Baldwin, which, as you know, is "Baudouin," a most noble name.

I have re-read Watts-Dunton's book. Of course it is old-fashioned in style, but the tone is nice, and the plot romantic: on the whole a capital book to give to one's parents at Christmas time.[3]

Paris is quite cold and wet, so like London that it was unnecessary for

---

[1] Unidentified.

[2] The only new reviews which Ernest La Jeunesse started at this time were *Le Sifflet*, which he edited under the pseudonym of Achille Steens, and which contained nothing but Dreyfusard caricatures; and *Ouste !*, of which only two issues appeared, also consisting entirely of caricatures.

[3] *Aylwin, a poetic romance* (1898).

Bosie to return to England. I wrote a fortnight ago to Bosie, who had told me that Percy was returning with £30,000, to ask him if Percy could now carry out his promise, and let me have the balance of the £500. Since then Bosie has not written—an ominous silence. I fear he won't do anything, after all his fine phrases. I read a notice of his rhymes[1] in the *Daily News*—rather silly. Ordinary critics always think that children are sentimental about literature: they are not: they have humour instead. Later on in life, humour goes, but laughter is the primaeval attitude towards life—a mode of approach that survives only in artists and criminals.

I have just passed the Café de la Paix: Eugene, the harvest-moon, seemed to fill up the *terrasse*.

You will be grieved to hear that Marius has had a cold.

My best love to Reggie. I wish he would let me know about Bosie in London, how he felt etc. Ever yours OSCAR

To H. C. Pollitt

MS. Princeton

3 December 1898 *Paris*

Dear Mr Pollitt, Thank you so much for the two photographs you have so kindly sent me. I like the little one, in the Norfolk suit, best: it looks young and nice: the other, the one by Hollyer, looks to me like the portrait of an Oxford Dean—troubled and affected and ineffectual: not a bit like you, I am sure. Mrs Leverson, a recognised authority for the colour of young men's hair, assured me you were quite golden, and I have always thought of you as a sort of gilt sunbeam masquerading in clothes, but, no doubt, you are Protean, and have many forms. When you come to Paris pray be golden entirely, and leave your more serious aspect in charge of Smithers, who needs, indeed, some stern monitor for his manner of living.

No: don't come to the Hôtel d'Alsace; it is a poor little Bohemian hotel, only suited for those Sybarites who are exiled from Sybaris. It would be a poor background for you, and background is so much. Go to some purple place, which will go with your hair: and bring a green window[2] with you that you may look out on life in proper fashion: attitude is all. Ever yours OSCAR WILDE

To Reginald Turner

MS. Hyde (D. & M.)

Tuesday [Postmark 6 December 1898] *Hôtel d'Alsace*

My dear Reggie, Sir John arrived long after midnight on Saturday from St Malo, after a journey of about eight hours, and four *changes de voiture*.

[1] *Tales with a Twist*, Lord Alfred Douglas's first volume of nonsense verse, published by Edward Arnold in 1898.

[2] Pollitt's Kendal home was called The Green Window.

He found his little friend Joseph with a black eye and a swollen nose, caused by intoxication and a political discussion. Joseph also left him on Sunday morning, and did not appear till the next day, having had vine-leaves in his hair. He is a little Dionysiac, and the conversation of Sir John, which is chiefly composed of good advice, drives him to drink. Tonight I dine with Sir John at Bosie's flat: Joseph is to serve, if he is sober: if not, he is to dine with us, I suppose. I am glad to say Sir John is getting cured of his infatuation: and I have begged him never again to try to have a good influence: it simply drives happy bright-eyed lads to *delirium tremens*.

Your little friend Alphonse was arrested last night for *chantage*.[1] He demanded fifteen francs, and was only given ten and a cab-fare, so on being expelled from the house he made a scene and was taken up. There is much joy amongst his friends, as his general conduct did not meet with approval. It is a pity he always wanted to behave badly; it gave him a demoniac pleasure. He was quite an imp, though attractive in love-scenes.

Hylton is here with his boy Herbert. I must say he is almost impossible. He is a sort of grown-up man with a hysterical womb, and makes scenes with Sir John like a woman with child. On the whole I don't think I can stand him much longer, though of course he professes lavish adoration of me, and perhaps feels some too.

I wish you would tell me all about Bosie in London. I hear he went to the Empire, with many vine-leaves in his gilt hair, but did not see much of anyone except you and Strangman.

Kalisaya, the American Bar near the Crédit Lyonnais,[2] is now the literary resort of myself and my friends: and we all gather there at five o'clock—Moréas, and La Jeunesse, and all the young poets. One beautiful boy of bad character—of the name of Georges—goes there too, but he is so like Antinous, and so smart, that he is allowed to talk to poets. One of the poets was the intimate friend of Émile Henry, the young anarchist who was guillotined under Carnot, and has told me wonderful things about him and his life.[3]

André Gide, one of my old friends here, has written an astonishing play on Saul, whose madness he ascribes to his hopeless love for David, and his wild jealousy of Jonathan: it is to be played at the Théâtre Antoine, but the parts of the lads are to be filled by women, which is, artistically, to be regretted.[4]

Do send me a line from time to time. Ever yours OSCAR

---

[1] Blackmail.

[2] In the Boulevard des Italiens.

[3] Marie François Sadi Carnot (1837–94) was President of the French Republic from 1887 until he was assassinated by an Italian anarchist, in revenge for the guillotining in 1893 of Émile Henry and Edouard Vaillant, who had hurled a bomb into the assembled Chamber.

[4] Gide's five-act play *Saül*, although written in 1898, was not published until 1903, and was first produced by Jacques Copeau at the Vieux-Colombier in 1922.

Postcard: To Leonard Smithers

MS. Private

[*Postmark 9 December 1898*] *Hôtel d'Alsace*

Reduced to postcards. Please wire me something tomorrow—hundred francs. Am arranging my affairs through R.R. but it takes a long time. Meanwhile things are dreadful and ridiculous. S. M.

To André Gide

MS. Doucet

[*Postmark 10 December 1898*] *Hôtel d'Alsace*

Mon cher ami, Je vous remercie beaucoup. Le traité de maximes[1] est un petit chef-d'oeuvre d'appréciation esthétique, et c'est un des premiers souvenirs que j'ai de vous. Je suis bien content de l'avoir, et je l'ai relu avec le plus vif plaisir.

Cependant au présent moment je suis très triste. Je n'ai rien reçu de mon éditeur de Londres, qui me doit de l'argent: et je suis tout à fait dans la misère. Je ne sais pas si vous pouvez m'aider, mais si vous pouviez me prêter 200 francs vous me rendriez assez heureux, et avec cela je pourrais vivre pour quelque temps. Vous voyez comme la tragédie de ma vie est devenu ignoble. La souffrance est possible, est peut-être nécessaire, mais la pauvreté, la misère—voilà ce qui est terrible. Cela salit l'âme de l'homme.
Votre ami OSCAR WILDE

To Louis Wilkinson[2]

MS. Wilkinson

[*Postmark 14 December 1898*] *Hôtel d'Alsace*

Dear Mr Wilkinson, Certainly: you can dramatise my play, but please tell me if the version is yours, and how the play is constructed.

Who acts Dorian Gray? He should be beautiful.

My work is so far in your hands that I rely on your artistic instinct that the play shall have some quality of beauty and style.

You can have four performances, and if there should be any notices of the play in papers, pray let me see them.

Your letter of last summer gave me great pleasure. Pray let me know all about yourself. Who are you? What are you doing or going to do? Send me your photograph.

[1] Probably Gide's *Réflexions sur quelques points de Littérature et de Morale* (1897).
[2] Louis Umfreville Wilkinson (b. 1881) was at this time a Radley schoolboy. He has since published many novels and other books under the name Louis Marlow. In his *Seven Friends* (1953) he quotes many of Wilde's letters to him, and confesses that he invented an "Ipswich Dramatic Society" and its wish to dramatise *The Picture of Dorian Gray*, so as to get into correspondence with Wilde, whom he never met.

Write to me at the above address, and direct the envelope to *Sebastian Melmoth*, a fantastic name that I shall explain to you some day. Sincerely yours   OSCAR WILDE

To Robert Ross

MS. Clark

Wednesday [14 December 1898]
Taverne F. Pousset, 14 Boulevard des Italiens, Paris

My dear Robbie, Just a line to say that I leave with Frank Harris for Napoule, near Cannes, tomorrow night. Frank has been most kind, and nice, and, of course, we have dined and lunched together every day at Durand's. At least I lunch at one o'clock, and dine at eight o'clock. Frank arrives at 2.30 and 9.15. It is rather a bore, and no one should make unpunctuality a formal rule, and degrade it to a virtue, but I have admirable, though lonely, meals. Frank insists on my being always at high intellectual pressure; it is most exhausting; but when we arrive at Napoule I am going to break the news to him—now an open secret—that I have softening of the brain, and cannot always be a genius. I shall send you my address tomorrow.

Ashton is with me; he is more penniless than ever, poor dear fellow; and Walter, that snub-nosed little horror, has just gone back to England, so Sir John is sad and sentimental. Ever yours   OSCAR

To Leonard Smithers

MS. Taylor

Wednesday, 14 December [1898]   *Taverne F. Pousset [Paris]*

My dear Smithers, Thanks for the enclosure of the letter.
The dedication of the play is

To
Robert Baldwin Ross:
in appreciation
in affection.

Of course Shannon's design is to be repeated on the cover as in the other editions. I think *both* sides are decorated—they should be. Of course you have a copy of *Lady Windermere* to follow?

I go with Frank Harris to Napoule, near Cannes, tomorrow, so do not send any *Chronicles* to Paris. I shall let you know the exact address tomorrow.

I suppose the book is out in January?

I hope to work in the south. In fact I am only taken on the condition of producing a masterpiece.

How is Strangman? Please give him my kind regards. Ever yours
OSCAR

To Laurence Housman

MS. Clark (R)

Wednesday, 14 December [1898]   *Taverne F. Pousset [Paris]*

My dear Housman, Thank you so much, not merely for your kindness, but for your charming letter. Style is certainly part of your character: your soul has beautiful curves and colours.

Frank Harris, late of the *Saturday Review*, a dear good friend of mine, has just arrived, and is taking me tomorrow to a lovely little place near Cannes called Napoule. I am to work there!! And to stay for a month, at the end of which I am to produce a work of art. I hope I shall be able to do something. The high sapphire wall of sea, the gold dust of the sun, the petals and perfumes of southern flowers—perhaps these may tune my soul to some note of beauty. Of course I shall write and let you know my address. Sincerely and affectionately yours   O. W.

To André Gide

MS. Doucet

[Postmark 14 December 1898]   *Taverne F. Pousset [Paris]*

Mon cher André, Je vous remercie beaucoup. Un de mes amis, le rédacteur du *Saturday Review*, à Londres, vient d'arriver à Paris, et me prend à Cannes avec lui pour un mois. Peut-être là je retrouverai mon âme.

J'espère vous voir à mon retour. Tout à vous   OSCAR

Postcard: To Leonard Smithers

MS. Private

[Circa 18 December 1898]   *Hôtel des Bains, Napoule, Cannes*

This is to show you where the poet is now living. I sent you proofs days ago. Pray acknowledge them.

The landscape and figures are by Conder: the hotel by Rothenstein.
                                                                 O. W.

Postcard: To Reginald Turner

MS. Hyde (D. & M.)

[Postmark of receipt 20 December 1898]   *Hôtel des Bains, Napoule*

Dear Reggie, I send you this to show you where I am now living. I wish you could come out. I get into Cannes in ten minutes, and there are wonderful pine-woods all about, making the air pungent. How is Sir John? And how are you?   O. W.

771

To Robert Ross

MS. Clark

Tuesday [27 December 1898]   *Hôtel des Bains, Napoule*

My dear Robbie, Would you kindly send me my January allowance through *Cook's* Agency at Cannes? I can then get it cashed at once, and if possible send it soon.

Frank Harris has, I hear, gone away. He did not come to Napoule after all, nor have I heard from him, though I wrote twice.

The weather is charming. Napoule is nice and dull. I take walks in the pine-woods.

Yesterday I was by the sea and suddenly George Alexander appeared on a bicycle. He gave me a crooked, sickly smile, and hurried on without stopping. How absurd and mean of him!

A nice fellow called Harold Mellor, who is staying at Cannes, comes over constantly to see me. He is a nephew of Mrs Jacob Bright's.[1] He has a pretty Italian boy with him. They stayed last night at Napoule, and we had plum-pudding and Mellor ordered Pommery-Greno, so I kept Christmas pleasantly, and Christmas improves by being kept a day. On the real Christmas I dined alone.

The fishing population of the Riviera have the same freedom from morals as the Neapolitans have. They are very nice. Ever yours   OSCAR

To Louis Wilkinson

MS. Hyde (H. M.)

28 December [1898]   *Hôtel des Bains, Napoule*

Dear Mr Wilkinson, Thank you so much for your long and interesting letter. I envy you going to Oxford: it is the most flower-like time of one's life. One sees the shadow of things in silver mirrors. Later on, one sees the Gorgon's head, and one suffers, because it does not turn one to stone.

I am on the Riviera, in blue and gold weather, the sun warm as wine, and apricot-coloured. The little hotel where I am staying is right on the Golfe de Juan, and all round are pine-woods with their pungent breath: the wind growing aromatic as it moves through the branches: one's feet crushing sweetness out of the fallen needles: I wish you were here.

In your second letter you tell me that you enclose your photograph for me, but no photograph was in the envelope. Your thoughts must have been in the crystal of the moon. Call them back, and let me have your portrait. Sincerely yours   OSCAR WILDE

---

[1] Harold Mellor (1868–1925) was the neurotic son of a Bolton cotton-spinner. His father died in 1893, leaving him wealthy, and he spent most of the rest of his life abroad, finally committing suicide in his villa at Cannes. His aunt Ursula Mellor married Jacob Bright (1821–99), brother of John Bright and Liberal M.P. for Manchester 1867–95 with two short intervals.

To Robert Ross
MS. Clark

28 December [1898]   *Hôtel des Bains, Napoule*

Dear Robbie, I never got the Henry James book, nor the *Volpone*. I did not like to write to you for either, as you had just given me a blue waist-coat with onyx buttons. To have asked for more would have been greedy. But I do think that Smithers should have sent me the *Volpone*.[1] I read a charming little notice of your eulogy, in the *D.T.* I think, and I want very much to see it, as you will, of course, be doing mine some day.

If you happen to have the Henry James, and can afford stamps, it would be sweet of you to send it.

I went to Nice the other day, for the afternoon. It was most pretty and gay. I met there a very nice boy whom I knew in Paris, one of the noble army of the Boulevard. He is eighteen, very elegant, and apparently a leader of fashion at Nice. At least he seemed to know everyone, and, on my leaving, accompanied me to the station, and borrowed five francs. I hope you have had a nice Christmas, and that all is well with your people.
Ever yours   OSCAR

To Mrs Leonard Smithers
MS. Clark

28 December [1898]   *Hôtel des Bains, Napoule*

Dear Mrs Smithers, Thank you so much for your charming card: I wish I could come to your party, but I am a wretched walker and would probably not arrive till midsummer.

I wish there was some chance of your coming out here: the weather is lovely—blue and gold weather—and the warm sun broods on the sea. Leonard must be quite exhausted with neglecting his business, and the rest would do him good.

I often think of your delightful visits to Berneval: if you will only come to luncheon at Napoule I promise you acrobats! And good cooking. The *chef* here is a much purer poet than John Davidson is.

I see I have made a dreadful blot on this page. It looks like a Conder fan, in its early stages, so pray excuse it; and believe me, with many thanks, sincerely yours   OSCAR WILDE

To Frank Harris
MS. Texas

Thursday [29 December 1898]   *[Napoule]*

My dear Frank, You can understand that, as you are regarded at Napoule

---

[1] For the Henry James book, see note p. 776. Smithers had recently published a de luxe edition of Ben Jonson's *Volpone*, containing a cover-design, frontispiece and five initial letters by Aubrey Beardsley, a critical essay on Ben Jonson by Vincent O'Sullivan, and a eulogy of Beardsley by Robert Ross.

as the future regenerator of the spot, much public anxiety was felt when you were seen rushing express-rate into the unknown. I myself thought that you might have been summoned to London on business, or that you were flying from Runciman. I am charmed to know it was love and affection that made you take wings.

A very nice young Englishman, whom I met by chance, has invited me to go to Nice tomorrow to see my dear Sarah in *La Tosca*. We return the next day.

Your coming is anxiously waited for by the hotel proprietor, and by the worthy Ribot, who wants to place his son, a nice youth of seventeen, in the Palace Hotel,[1] to learn his *métier*. Ribot is anxious to place on the porphyry rocks by the sea small glass-walled pavilions for eating oysters in! I told him you would not allow it.

Pray give my kind regards to your charming wife. Ever yours OSCAR

To H. C. Pollitt
MS. Princeton

[Postmark of receipt 31 December 1898]   *Hôtel des Bains, Napoule*

Dear Mr Pollitt, I have come down to the Riviera, with your photograph, of course (the nice one in the Norfolk suit), and the day is blue and gold, the sun warm like wine, and apricot-coloured: the pine-woods change the air to an aromatic: the wind that stirs their branches is pungent with keen odours: and when one walks in green aisles one crushes sweetness out of the fallen needles. Of course, *you* should be here also. I search for you daily.

It is a little fishing village, on the Golfe de Juan, close to Cannes. The inhabitants have beautiful eyes, crisp hair of a hyacinth colour, and no morals—an ideal race. At times, being morbid, I am bored by the lack of intellect: but that is a grave fault: I attribute it to Oxford. None of us survive culture.

What are you doing in the Green Window?[2] Are you writing? Or simply looking at Nature? I am on bad terms with Nature: I see in her neither intellect nor passion—the only two things that make surfaces possible for me. I allude of course to what is termed Landscape.

Send *me* a nice letter and a nice book. Sincerely yours OSCAR WILDE

To Robert Ross
MS. Clark

2 January 1899   *Napoule*

My dear Robbie, The cheque on Cook arrived this morning: many thanks. The proprietor was looking a little anxious—rather yellow in fact—but has

---

[1] Harris's hotel at Monte Carlo.
[2] See note 2, p. 767. This letter is addressed "M. Jerome Pollit, The Green Window, Kendal, Lake-Poet-District."

now quite regained his spirits, as I have told him I shall pay him this afternoon.

No sign yet of Frank Harris: it is a great bore. There is a charming fellow called Harold Mellor (sent away from Harrow at the age of fourteen for being loved by the captain of the cricket eleven) who is staying with his mother near Cannes, and comes over on his bicycle to breakfast every morning. He is about twenty-six, but looks younger. Sometimes a very pretty, slim, fair-haired Italian boy bicycles over with him. His name is *Eolo*; his father, who sold him to Harold for 200 lire, having christened all his children—seventeen in number—out of the *Mythological Dictionary*. Harold is a nice fellow, but his boy bores him. It is dreadfully sad.

He took me to Nice on Friday and we saw Sarah in *La Tosca*. I went round to see Sarah and she embraced me and wept, and I wept, and the whole evening was wonderful. I wish to goodness you would come here. I need you immensely. As regards my marrying again, I am quite sure that you will want me to marry this time some sensible, practical, plain, middle-aged boy, and I don't like the idea at all. Besides I am practically engaged to a fisherman of extraordinary beauty, age eighteen. So you see there are difficulties.

Love to Reggie. Ever yours   OSCAR

To Reginald Turner
MS. Hyde (D. & M.)

[*Postmark 3 January 1899*]   *Hôtel des Bains, Napoule*

My dear Reggie, How are you getting on? And how is Sir John? Do let me have a little news of you. Of course there is no good begging you to come out here, though there is wonderful sunshine each day. Sometimes the Mistral blows a little—it is a harsh Philistine wind—but on the whole the weather is utterly delightful.

My friend, my new friend, Harold Mellor comes here today to stay at the hotel, and tomorrow we go to Nice, for the day. A great friend of mine, a Paris boy called *le petit Georges*, is now at Nice, and I have promised to run over and see him. He is like a very handsome Roman boy, dark, and bronze-like, with splendidly chiselled nose and mouth, and the tents of midnight are folded in his eyes; moons hide in their curtains. He is visiting Nice on speculative business. It is beautiful, and encouraging, to find people who can combine romance with business—blend them indeed, and make them one.

I am in constant correspondence now with a Radley schoolboy, aged seventeen. His photograph, which he has sent me, and sends me constantly, is most beautiful. He seems to read nothing but my books, and says his one desire is to "follow in my footsteps"! But I have told him that they lead to terrible places.

I hope you are combining romance with business. Robbie seems to

775

think that you are terribly overpaid and underworked, which looks like it: but perhaps that is merely Robbie's jealousy.

Do send me a line. Ever affectionately yours   OSCAR

To Robert Ross
MS. Clark

Thursday [? 12 January 1899]   *Hôtel des Bains, Napoule*

My dear Robbie, Thanks so much for the Henry James. I think it is a most wonderful, lurid, poisonous little tale, like an Elizabethan tragedy. I am greatly impressed by it.[1] James is developing, but he will never arrive at passion, I fear.

I have been over again to Nice with Harold Mellor, for three days. It was most pretty and gay, and music everywhere. I met one beautiful person, called André, with wonderful eyes, and a little Italian, Pietro, like a young St John. One would have followed him into the desert.

Poor Sir John! However, I think he may do well in the States. The only thing I never could forgive him was his absurd love of Walter—a plain, crooked, ugly, and tedious youth—but Sir John was capital company, and a very astounding person in his capacity for pleasure, grand in his cups, and with a heart of gold.

I have received *Volpone*, and read your eulogy with great pleasure: it is admirably written. I think you have attacked the public *a little* too often. Aubrey produced his effect on them, and the effect that pleases an artist. Also, would you really say that Byzantine art is our link with the art of the East? Surely it was Greek? But it is a delightfully written eulogy, and most admirable in style, full of many very perfect phrases.

My Radley boy is called Louis Wilkinson—a horrid name—but his photograph is most interesting, and his poetry passionate and incoherent. He seems a most astonishing boy. He has dramatised *Dorian Gray*! Ever yours   OSCAR

To Reginald Turner
MS. Hyde (D. & M.)

[Postmark 19 January 1899]   *Hôtel des Bains, Napoule*

My dear Reggie, I was charmed to hear from you, but it is absurd your being in bad spirits about Life. You used to be such a light-hearted lad. The influence of the *D.T.* is obviously of the worst kind.[2]

I am still sitting on porphyry rocks, or roaming through pine-woods. Occasionally my friend Harold Mellor orders a bottle of Pommery for dinner. Then the exquisite taste of ancient life comes back to me. And twice a week I look at the shop-windows in Cannes.

[1] This must refer to "The Turn of the Screw," which was published in a volume called *The Two Magics* in October 1898.   [2] See note 3, p. 708.

The weather is lovely, and the mimosa in flower—such powdered gold-dust dancing in the sun, the dainty feather-like leaves always tremulous with joy.

I am very anxious to go to Corsica. Would you like a long Corsican knife marked "*Vendetta*"? They are deadly and inexpensive, and you have many friends. It might be useful.

If you hear any news of poor Sir John do let me know. Ever yours

OSCAR

To H. C. Pollitt

MS. Princeton

[*Postmark 19 January 1899*]   *Hôtel des Bains, Napoule*

Thank you so much for your last photograph, which has just arrived. It is not a bit like the others, so I feel sure a good likeness, and the Coan[1] robe most becoming. Your personality becomes more and more mysterious, more and more wonderful, each portrait that I receive, but indeed all my life Sphinxes have crossed and recrossed my way.

I am still wandering on porphyry rocks, fishing occasionally, and now and then just tasting the old taste of life at Nice, or Cannes. Champagne, now a strange luxury, occasionally is offered to me by devoted friends: if it is not, I always ask for it. I should be quite happy if I did not know how to read or write. My dream at present is to go to Corsica. Would you like a long Corsican knife marked "*Vendetta*"? Everyone in Corsica has them: they are deadly, and inexpensive.

Your handwriting in your last letter was quite beautiful, but are you sure that you spell your name right?[2] Sincerely yours   O. W.

To Robert Ross

MS. Clark

2 February 1899   *Napoule*

My dear Robbie, Thank you for the cheque, duly received. Your account of Henry James has much amused Frank Harris: it is a delightful story for your memorabilia.

Today, for the first time, rain—quite an Irish day. Yesterday was lovely. I went to Cannes to see the *Bataille des Fleurs*. The loveliest carriage—all yellow roses, the horses with traces and harness of violets—was occupied by an evil-looking old man, English: on the box, beside the coachman, sat his valet, a very handsome boy, all wreathed with flowers. I murmured "Imperial, Neronian Rome."

I have signed the copies of the play for Smithers, a "Japanese" for you.

---

[1] i.e. transparent (see Horace, *Satires* I, ii, 101). The island of Cos was famous for its finely-woven silks.

[2] Wilde spelt it wrong in all the four surviving letters (see note p. 774).

Smithers will show you my list: if I have forgotten anyone, let me know. Of course dear More Adey has a "large-paper:" and also Reggie.[1]

Harold Mellor will be in London at the end of the month. He is going there to get me some neckties. I have asked him to write and let you know. He is a charming fellow, very cultivated, though he finds that Literature is an inadequate expression of Life. That is quite true: but a work of Art is an adequate expression of Art; that is its aim. Only that. Life is merely the *motif* of a pattern. I hope all things are well with you. Frank Harris is upstairs, thinking about Shakespeare at the top of his voice. I am earnestly idling. Ever yours   OSCAR

To Reginald Turner
MS. Hyde (D. & M.)

[*Postmark 3 February 1899*]   *Hôtel des Bains, Napoule*

My dear Reggie, I hope you are in better spirits. Poor dear Sir John was always in the best spirits (and water): the most good-hearted of the alcoholic. Life goes on very pleasantly here. Frank Harris is of course exhausting. After our literary talk in the evening I stagger to my room, bathed in perspiration. I believe he talks the Rugby game.

Max's caricature in the *Chronicle* is a masterpiece—as far as George Moore goes: it is a most brilliant and bitter rendering of that vague formless obscene face. The Archer is *manqué*—not at all like. I showed the drawing to Frank, who was in ecstasies over the Moore, and would like to have a replica of it by Max.[2]

I am sending you, of course, a copy of my book. It was extraordinary reading the play over. How I used to toy with that tiger Life! I hope you will find a place for me amongst your nicest books, not near anything by Hichens or George Moore. I should like it to be within speaking distance of *Dorian Gray*. You will also get a copy addressed to Charlie Hickey. How is that dear boy? I wish you would import him.

There is a *Carnaval* at Nice on Sunday. I hope to run over: on Sundays there are no confetti, which is a blessing. Ever yours   OSCAR

---

[1] The exact publication date of *The Importance of Being Earnest* is not known. Mason says simply "February." The British Museum copy (one of twelve printed on Japanese vellum) is stamped 2 March. The ordinary edition (1000 copies) was priced 7/6, and the large-paper edition (100 signed copies) 21/-. The twelve signed Japanese vellum copies were for presentation only.

[2] Max Beerbohm's caricature appeared in the *Daily Chronicle* on 30 January 1899, illustrating a long letter from W. B. Yeats on "Mr Moore, Mr Archer and the Literary Theatre." It represents George Moore as a tipsy Irish peasant with a trailed coat in one hand and a shillelagh in the other. William Archer, dressed in kilt and glengarry, has one foot on Moore's coat, at which he is pointing in an admonitory way.

To Louis Wilkinson

MS. Wilkinson

[*Postmark 3 February 1899*]   *Hôtel des Bains, Napoule*

Dear Mr Wilkinson, Your photographs arrived quite safely. I don't much like the amateur one; it makes you look far too old, and a little too learned: but in the other you have the eyes of the poet, and your hair is charming. I am sure it is shot with wonderful lights, and I like the curve of its curl. William Morris, in his translation of the *Odyssey*, renders "hyacinth-like hair" as "curled like the rings of the daffodil,"[1] I remember, so perhaps that describes your curl.

Your last poem is most dainty in metre and treatment. I see you are studying the delicate *forms* of verse. That is quite right. To master one's instrument is the great thing. The "Circe" I liked too, for its colour and passion, but in form it is not quite so good. I hope you will devote yourself, with vows, to poetry. It is a sacramental thing, and there is no pain like it.

Do you love Arnold's "Thyrsis" and "The Scholar Gypsy"? The former is an exquisite little classic. Sicilian flutes are not sweeter than either.

I am sending you a book of mine: when it comes out—in about three weeks—you will get it. It is a fanciful, absurd, comedy, written when I was playing with that tiger Life. I hope it will amuse you. I am directing this to Radley. I suppose you are back there, educating the masters. Write to me soon. Your friend   O.

To Frank Harris

MS. Texas

[*Circa 15 February 1899*]   *Hôtel Terminus, Nice*

My dear Frank, I have waited in vain to hear from you, and am stuck here in this expensive hotel, where I am forced to have my meals as I am absolutely *sans le sou*, and the manager, a revolting German, comes every morning with the bill. Do, like a good chap, send over your servant or someone, or post a registered letter, with what I asked you for, £20. Otherwise I shall be in a very serious mess here, and may have trouble with the hotel.

You were kind enough to promise me three months on the Riviera, and I have had two of them, and since I arrived you have given me £30. Do let me have £20 now, and I shall go off to Switzerland on the 1st: full of pleasant memories of your great kindness, and of our charming evenings together. But, for goodness sake, send at once. Ever yours   O. W.

---

[1] "With the hair on his head crisp curling as the bloom of the daffodil" (Bk. vi, line 231). Wilde quoted this line when he reviewed the first volume of Morris's translation in the *Pall Mall Gazette* of 26 April 1887.

Telegram: To Leonard Smithers

MS. Yale

[*Postmark 15 February 1899*]   [*Nice*]

Please wire fifteen crisis. Melmoth, Hôtel Terminus, Nice.

To Frank Harris

MS. Texas

Saturday [*18 February 1899*]   *Hôtel Terminus, Nice*

My dear Frank, Many, many thanks for your enclosure and letter. The hotel had become perfectly brutal, as I had not been able to pay them anything.

I hope you don't really think I had forgotten about the money you so kindly gave me in Paris, but that I spent before coming down in paying my hotel and other bills. I was only alluding to what you had given me since our arrival, nine weeks ago. And I trust you don't think I have rushed you too much, or been recklessly extravagant.

I have again written to Smithers, my publisher, to ask him to let me have something on account of my play, just published, which I think he can hardly refuse doing: though I do not fancy the play will have anything like the success of *The Ballad*. It is so trivial, so irresponsible a comedy: and while the public liked to hear of my pain—curiosity and the auto-biographical form being elements of interest—I am not sure that they will welcome me again in airy mood and spirit, mocking at morals, and defiance of social rules. There is, or at least in their eyes there should be, such a gap between the two Oscars. I believe they would like me to edit prayers for those at sea, or to recant the gospel of the joy of life in a penny tract. They do not see that only the utterly worthless can be reformed. Permanence of temperament, the indomitable assertion of the soul (and by soul I mean the unity of mind and body), such are the things of value in anyone.

In the meanwhile I want to get out of the hotel; the prices are appalling, and for the last four days I have been obliged to have my meals there—loathsome German cooking at ten francs a day, *rien compris*—and my bedroom still at almost carnival prices. Of course when I went there I thought you would be moving into a villa at once, as you yourself did too. I gave them 200 francs this morning. But I owe nearly 100 francs more. If you could kindly lend me this, I would return it to you next week, when I am sure Smithers will let me have at least a tenner. There is a capital little hotel in the Rue d'Angleterre, where I can get *pension*, with room, for eight francs a day: in the Hôtel Terminus I feel living in a White Elephant, and being obliged to feed the monster. When I stayed there before I was Mellor's guest, so I did not know how horribly dear it was. I am sure, if you can, you will do this. I must get out of the place at once. I am delighted to see you won your libel action, but what a bore those things are.[1] Ever yours   O. W.

[1] Harris, together with the printer and publisher of the *Saturday Review*, had

To Frank Harris
MS. Texas

[*Circa 22 February 1899*]

Hôtel Terminus & Cosmopolitain, Monte Carlo

My dear Frank, I am in great trouble, and am obliged to come over to Monte Carlo and see you.

As I was, of course, unable to leave the hotel at Nice, not having enough money to pay the whole bill last Saturday, I have been forced to stay on, and to have my meals at *table-d'hôte*, though naturally at a separate table. The middle-class English who are at the hotel have objected to my presence, and this morning I was presented with my bill and requested to leave by twelve o'clock.

I declined to do this, and said I could not pay the bill today. They have given me till tomorrow at noon, and have asked me not to have my meals in the hotel, so I have come over to Monte Carlo, having raised ten francs on my ring.

You have not forgotten that you invited me to spend three months on the Riviera as your guest. My bill at Napoule for eight weeks amounted to £35, of which you gave me £30, and I cannot think that it was very extravagant of me. The choice of Napoule was yours, and £4 a week is not very extravagant. Of course at Nice it is different. My bill is forty francs a day at the hotel. You asked me to go there, and to look out for a villa for you. My one anxiety has been to leave the place, but I have not been able. Now I am turned out, and everyone at the hotel knows it. My dear Frank, you must come down and see me here for a few moments. You cannot, and you will not, abandon me. I won't go to the Palace, because it would not be good for your hotel for me to be seen there. This little place is quiet. Please come. Ever yours   o. w.

To Frank Harris
MS. Texas

[*Circa 23 February 1899*]

Hôtel des Alpes-Maritimes, Rue d'Angleterre, Nice

My dear Frank, I have, as you see from above address, left the Terminus—that horrible den of Jews, Germans, and English—and am now safely installed at a tiny hotel near the station. I only pay three francs a night for

---

been sued for libel by John Pym Yeatman on the grounds that his *History of Common Law* (1874) had been ridiculed in the paper, and his book on Shakespeare (1896) dismissed by an anonymous reviewer (John Churton Collins) as "miserable twaddle." Mr Yeatman maintained that these reviews were inspired by a clique of barristers who had already driven him from his circuit. The plaintiff conducted his own case before Lord Chief Justice Coleridge and a special jury, who after retiring for twenty minutes found for the defendants. This occurred on 14 February 1899 and was reported in next day's *Daily Chronicle*, where Wilde probably read of it. I have dated this letter accordingly.

781

my bedroom, which is a great comfort, and I sleep in peace. My last week at the Terminus my bill was left every night by my bedside, and another copy brought up with my coffee in the morning! You can fancy my state of nerves.

Are you coming over tomorrow? I hope so. If you can, do wire to me and we can dine together. Switzerland is close at hand, and I feel rather depressed at the prospect, which, I suppose, is ungrateful of me, but I dread the cold and the lack of coloured, moving, beautiful life.

Of course we have won our bets from Mellor. The "beautiful, ineffectual angel . . ." is naturally Arnold's: Dowden could never have written it. It occurs in the Essay on Byron (I have verified it).[1] We must see that we get paid. I believe Mellor still thinks it is Dowden's.

I wish you would come and talk about the Four Gospels over some good wine. Ever yours   OSCAR

To Leonard Smithers[2]

[*24 February 1899. Postmark 25 February 1899*]   *Nice*

I leave tomorrow for Geneva . . . Please send the £30 there—also a copy of the play. I have not yet seen it. I hope the large paper are finished by this. Have any other copies been sent out? I have received no acknowledgment from anyone.   O. W.

To Robert Ross
MS. Clark

Saturday [*25 February 1899*]   *Nice*

My dear Robbie, Just a line to thank you for your kindness in wiring to me, and letting me have my March allowance now. I am afraid I am a great worry to you.

I leave today for Switzerland: via Genoa, where I wish to stay a day. My address will be c/o Monsieur Harold Mellor, Gland, Canton Vaud, La Suisse. I hope to be happy there: at any rate there will be free meals, and champagne has been ordered, though the Nice doctor now absolutely forbids me to take any, on account of gout.

I am sorry my play is boycotted by the press, particularly for Smithers's sake; he has shown great pluck in bringing it out at all. However I hope some of the faithful, and all the elect, will buy copies.[3]

---

[1] "Shelley, beautiful and ineffectual angel, beating in the void his luminous wings in vain." From the preface to *Poetry of Byron*, chosen and arranged by Matthew Arnold (1881). Reprinted in *Essays in Criticism, Second Series* (1888).

[2] The text of this fragment is taken from the American Art Association catalogue of 9 February 1927.

[3] Scarcely a review of the published edition of *The Importance of Being Earnest* appeared in the press.

If you hear anything nice said about the play, write it to me: if not, invent it.

I hear with much regret that the large-paper copies have not been bound yet. I don't know if any of my friends have received copies at all: at any rate, none have written in acknowledgment.

If you are down at Oxford, do go to Radley and see Louis Wilkinson; he is most cultivated: knew FitzGerald: and was at the first night of *Lady Windermere's Fan*! I suppose in a perambulator.[1] Ever yours   O. W.

To Robert Ross

MS. Clark

[*Circa 1 March 1899*]   *Gland, Canton Vaud, Switzerland*

My dear Robbie, Thanks for your charming letter, which I found waiting for me here on my arrival from Genoa yesterday.

It was a great pleasure writing your name on the page of dedication. I only wish it was a more wonderful work of art—of higher seriousness of intent—but it has some amusing things in it, and I think the tone and temper of the whole thing bright and happy.[2]

I went to Genoa to see Constance's grave. It is very pretty—a marble cross with dark ivy-leaves inlaid in a good pattern. The cemetery is a garden at the foot of the lovely hills that climb into the mountains that girdle Genoa. It was very tragic seeing her name carved on a tomb—her surname, my name, not mentioned of course—just "Constance Mary, daughter of Horace Lloyd, Q.C." and a verse from *Revelations*. I brought some flowers. I was deeply affected—with a sense, also, of the uselessness of all regrets. Nothing could have been otherwise, and Life is a very terrible thing.

This is a pretty house on the Lake. We look over to the snows and hills of Savoy. Geneva is half an hour by rail. You are to come whenever you like. April is lovely here, I believe, and flaunts in flowers.

There is an Italian cook, also the lad Eolo, who waits at table. His father told Mellor at Spezia that he was christened Eolo because he was born on a night on which there was a dreadful wind! I think it is rather nice to have thought of such a name. An English peasant would probably have said "We called him John, sir, because we were getting in the hay at the time."[3]

There is no truth at all in Sedger's advertisement, and I am very angry about it.[4] It is quite monstrous. My only chance is a play produced

[1] Wilkinson had invented this, like the dramatisation of *Dorian Gray*, to attract Wilde's attention.

[2] The inscription in Ross's copy of *The Importance of Being Earnest* reads: "To the Mirror of Perfect Friendship: Robbie: whose name I have written on the portal of this little play. Oscar. February '99."

[3] Cf. *The Duchess of Padua*, Act II:

Duke: "Why were you called Dominick?"

First Citizen (scratching his head): "Marry, because I was born on Saint George's day."   [4] See note 3, p. 762.

anonymously. Otherwise the First Night would be a horror, and people would find meanings in every phrase.

I am going to try a bicycle. I have never forgotten the lesson you so kindly gave me: even my leg remembers it.

Do write again soon. Have I forgotten anyone to whom I should send a copy? Ever yours OSCAR

To More Adey
MS. Clark

[*March 1899*]   *Gland, Switzerland*

My dear More, I am so glad you liked the play, and that it arrived safe. As a rule Smithers suppresses all my presentation copies. I am staying, as I dare say you know, in a villa on the Lake of Geneva. There is much beauty of an obvious, old-fashioned kind—snow-capped mountains, blue sky, pine-trees and the like. But the sunlight is golden: brazen rather. I don't like my host, and the Swiss are so ugly to look at that it conveys melancholy into all my days.

I am much interested to hear of your book on Dante. I have not read Dante for ages: it is a great pity. He is the supreme modern poet: Greek tragedy deals with the elemental difficulties of life—the terrible things external to us—but in Dante are all the complexities of the modern soul. Robbie, with ostentatious modesty, has told me nothing about his story at all.

I was very happy on the Riviera—lovely weather—and at Nice beautiful people and beautiful flowers. As one nears Italy physical beauty comes running to meet one. At Nice I knew three lads like bronzes, quite perfect in form. English lads are chryselephantine. Swiss people are carved out of wood with a rough knife, most of them; the others are carved out of turnips.

I have been reading much of Maupassant lately, and I now find much tenderness in him—a great pity for life. I don't agree with the attacks on him for *brutalité* or the praise of him for it. And *Une Vie* is a masterpiece: Balzac would have been filled with wonder at it. Maupassant always thought that Flaubert was his master, lived and died under that impression, but, of course, his master was Balzac.

There are lovely walks here by the Lake, through the grounds of others: but I am a born trespasser. Prince Napoleon's villa is quite close—the one he used to have. He had lovely bronze and marble statues set everywhere, and a splendid fountain with a bronze centaur strangling a bear from whose gullet rushes the water.[1] Nyon, a little village, is three miles off. I go there on foot daily and have a *bock* and buy French papers.

I often think of your wonderful visits to me when I was in pain, and of your tenderness, and kindness to me. I fear that, in consequence, your

---

[1] Prince Napoleon (1822–91), the son of Jérome Bonaparte, spent his last years at the Château de Prangins, between Gland and Nyon.

784

stay in the Purgatorio—where the poets are—will be too brief. However, you will find Statius in heaven. I wish he was a better poet.[1] Ever yours

OSCAR

To Robert Ross

MS. Clark

Wednesday [*15 March 1899*]   *Gland, Switzerland*

My dear Robbie, Thank you very much for your thoughtfulness in wiring to me about my brother's death.[2] I suppose it had been expected for some time. I am very sorry for his wife, who, I suppose, has little left to live on. Between him and me there had been, as you know, wide chasms for many years. *Requiescat in Pace.*

I don't know what position I hold about this absurd Irish property. It comes to me by entail, but I suppose my creditors will claim it. I wish I had asked for my discharge. It was most foolish of me not to. Could you ask some solicitor what is likely to be done? If I could sell it for a fair sum, and have the money, I would give my sister-in-law something of course, but I don't know if I can sell.

I hope to write more tomorrow. I don't like Mellor very much, and would like to get away, but, at present, it is impossible. Ever yours   O. W.

To Frank Harris

MS. Texas

[*Circa 19 March 1899*]   *Gland, Switzerland*

My dear Frank, I am, as you see from above, in Switzerland with Mellor: a rather dreadful combination. The villa is pretty, and on the borders of the Lake with pretty pines about: on the other side are the mountains of Savoy and Mont Blanc: we are an hour, by a slow train, from Geneva. But Mellor is tedious, and lacks conversation: also he gives me Swiss wine to drink: it is horrid: he occupies himself with small economies, and mean domestic interests. So I suffer very much. *Ennui* is the enemy.

I want to know if you will allow me to dedicate to you my next play, *An Ideal Husband*, which Smithers is bringing out for me in the same form as the other, of which I hope you received your copy. I should so much like to write your name and a few words on the dedicatory page.[3]

---

[1] Statius (*circa* A.D. 45–96) was traditionally the first Christian poet. His shade accompanied Dante through much of Purgatory, and eventually to the Earthly Paradise.

[2] Willie Wilde died in London on 13 March 1899, aged forty-six.

[3] The dedication to *An Ideal Husband* reads: TO FRANK HARRIS / A SLIGHT TRIBUTE TO / HIS POWER AND DISTINCTION / AS AN ARTIST / HIS CHIVALRY AND NOBILITY / AS A FRIEND.

I look back with joy and regret to the lovely sunlight of the Riviera, and the charming winter you so generously and kindly gave me: it was most good of you: nor can it ever be forgotten by me.

Next week a petroleum launch is to arrive here, so that will console me a little, as I love to be on water: and the Savoy side is starred with pretty villages and green valleys.

Of course we won our bet. The phrase on Shelley is in Arnold's preface to Byron: but Mellor won't pay me![1] He suffers agony over a franc. It is very annoying as I have had no money since my arrival here. However I regard the place as a Swiss *pension*, where there is no weekly bill.

My kindest regards to your wife. Ever yours   OSCAR

To Reginald Turner
MS. Hyde (D. & M.)

[*Postmark 20 March 1899*]   *Gland, Switzerland*

My dear Reggie, Thanks so much for your letter. I am delighted you are pleased with your copy of the play. I like the play's irresponsibility and its *obiter dicta*, but it is essentially an acting play: it should have been a classic for the English Theatre, but alas! the author was struck by madness from the moon.

Did you get the copy for Charlie Hickey? I wrote his name on a fly-leaf, and sent it to Smithers to be forwarded to you.

Here the weather is bright and sunny. Across the Lake I see Mont Blanc, showing above the Savoy mountains: but it has lost the virginity of the snows: spinsters and curates climb it: its terrors are over.

The villa is pretty and comfortable: but I don't like Mellor: he is a silent, dull person, cautious, and economical: revolting Swiss wines appear at meals: he is complex without being interesting: has Greek loves, and is rather ashamed of them: has heaps of money, and lives in terror of poverty: so I regard it as a sort of Swiss *pension*, where there is no weekly bill.

I have been twice to Geneva, which is beautifully situated and full of swans and bridges, but the Swiss are really too ugly. I feel sure that the reason they have produced nobody—except sterile things like Amiel and *Obermann*[2]—is their lack of physical beauty: they never gain an impulse from the vision of perfection of form: life is robbed of its first great element: the people are formless, colourless; one longs for Italy, or England, where beauty walks in the sun.

[1] See note 1, p. 782.
[2] Henri Frédéric Amiel (1821–81) was a Swiss philosopher and critic. His posthumously published *Journal Intime* appeared in an English translation by Mrs Humphry Ward in 1885. *Obermann* (1804) was a book of philosophical letters by the French writer, Étienne Pivert de Senancour (1770–1846), who spent most of his life in Switzerland. Matthew Arnold wrote two poems in his memory.

I read a great deal, and correct the proofs of *An Ideal Husband*,[1] shortly to appear. It reads rather well, and some of its passages seem prophetic of tragedy to come.

On my way I stopped at Genoa, where I met a beautiful young actor, a Florentine, whom I wildly loved. He has the strange name of Didaco. He had the look of Romeo, without Romeo's sadness: a face chiselled for high romance. We spent three days together.

Write and tell me some of your adventures, and what new stars have crossed your way. Are you in love? If not, why not?

I don't know how long I shall stay here. I can't get away, having neither gold nor silver. I wait on Fortune, like a discarded lover. Ever yours

OSCAR

To Louis Wilkinson

MS. Wilkinson

[*Postmark 20 March 1899*]   *Gland, Switzerland*

My dear Boy, I am glad the play arrived safely, and has amused you. It is quite irresponsible, but some of the *obiter dicta* amuse me, and it was delightfully acted.

I am, as you see, in Switzerland: on the Lake of Geneva in the villa of a friend. Across the Lake, on the other side, are the mountains of Savoy, and Mont Blanc: who at sunset flushes like a rose: with shame perhaps at the prevalence of tourists: he has lost all his terrors: spinsters climb him now: and his snows are not virgin any more.

The fringes of the Lake are fledged with pines, but I don't like Switzerland: it has produced nothing but theologians and waiters; Amiel and *Obermann* are types of sterility. I attribute it all to the lack of physical beauty in the race: they are shapeless, colourless: grey of texture, and without form. The beautiful races are the great races: here they are like cavemen: no impulse born of the splendour of physical perfection has ever filled them; their cattle have more expression. *Je m'ennuie, je m'ennuie.*

So you love Shakespeare's Sonnets: I have loved them, as one should love all things, not wisely but too well. In an old *Blackwood*—of I fancy 1889—you will find a story of mine called "The Portrait of Mr W. H.," in which I have expressed a new theory about the wonderful lad whom Shakespeare so deeply loved. I think it was the boy who acted in his plays. If you come across the story, read it, and tell me what you think. So you knew FitzGerald. His *Omar* is a masterpiece of art: I feel proud that a kinsman of mine—Sir Ralph Ouseley—brought the first manuscript of Omar Kháyyám to England: to Europe perhaps: it is the beautiful Bodleian manuscript: which I suppose you have seen.[2] Affectionately yours

OSCAR

[1] It seems certain, from the letter of 26 March and other references, that it was in fact a manuscript or typescript that Wilde was correcting.

[2] It was in fact Sir William Ouseley (1767–1842) who brought this manuscript (MS. Ouseley 140) to England. It was bought by the Bodleian in 1844 as part of Sir

To Leonard Smithers[1]

[*Postmark 20 March 1899*]   [*Gland*]

I am sending you off the manuscript.[2] I think it reads very well now. Corrections are a great trouble—worse than a new play: I am quite exhausted . . . Shaw's copy should go to his publishers' care. Do have them sent off at once. No money from you. This is dreadful. Do let me have £5 at once. Mellor carries out the traditions of the ancient misers. If I ask him to lend me five francs, he grows yellow and takes to his bed. I discover some new fault in him daily. The way he grows on one is awful—and he gives me Swiss wine to drink. I look on you as owing me £25, so really £5 by return is nothing, but do send it at once.

o. w.

To Robert Ross

MS. Clark

Tuesday [*21 March 1899*][3]   *Gland, Switzerland*

My dear Robbie, Thank you so much for your long letter. For the first time in my life I was glad that your handwriting was illegible, so I was able to miss a lot, or rather forced to.

The position is this. Moytura is entailed on me, but not beyond me. One can only entail I believe for two lives: in this case my brother's and mine. So the place is mine to sell, and should fetch £3000 or a little more. It is beautifully situated, and there are lovely trees etc.

As regards my bankruptcy, if my *trustees* heard of it, they would no doubt try to seize it. I fancy I had best remain passive, and receive the rents, such as they are. My brother was bankrupt, and received the rents. Why should not I? The only thing is to ascertain *how* the rents are paid, whether through an agent or not. This my sister-in-law would be able to tell you. I would be ready to give her £40 a year, if I received £140 (gross), as she has a child. The whole affair is a great bore. I wonder whether a private sale would be illegal. Of course, what one wants is a solicitor who will be able to show how one can escape the law. In gaining legal possession of an entailed estate I wonder has one to go to a Court of Probate? I wonder does the Court of Bankruptcy take cognizance of any-

---

William's collection, and from E. B. Cowell's copy of it Edward FitzGerald made his own copy. It was not Louis Wilkinson but his father who had known Fitz-Gerald. They were neighbours in Suffolk.

[1] The text of this incomplete letter is taken from the American Art Association catalogue of 9 February 1927.   [2] Of *An Ideal Husband.*

[3] Walter Edwin Ledger, a friend and admirer of Ross (who dedicated *Miscellanies* to him), formed a large Wilde collection, which is now in the Bodleian. It includes a transcript in Ledger's hand of most of the surviving letters from Wilde to Ross. Many of them are there dated, presumably with the help of Ross. This letter bears Ledger's date.

thing without a creditor applying? But I have not much hope of anything good. However, one can try.

I dislike Mellor, because he is unsocial, taciturn, wretched company, and taking no pains to please or gratify his guest. He is very well off, but absurdly mean in everything. He gives me at dinner the most horrid Swiss *vin ordinaire*, though he has a capital cellar, and is quite amused by the fact that I don't like it. There is insanity in his family. His mother is under restraint, and his brother went mad and killed himself. His own insanity is misanthropy, and meanness. I am philosophic about it now; indeed we only meet at meals. In the evening he reads *The Times*, or sleeps —both audibly. But I should love to get away.

I never dreamed of having Smithers to bring alcoholic experience to bear on my affairs. It was a joke.

I shall write to Arthur,[1] and also to my sister-in-law. If you see her, you need not say anything about my proposal to give her £40 a year, if I get £140. There is no necessity to worry you too much. The weather here is bright and sunny, but cold; snow has fallen on the mountains. Ever yours

OSCAR

To Robert Ross
MS. Clark

Sunday [26 March 1899][2]   *Gland, Switzerland*

My dear Robbie, I am sending two acts of the new play (*Ideal Husband*) to Smithers, after corrections. When they are set up would you look over them, and see that the "wills" and "shalls" are not too Hibernian? Also, I have put in descriptions of the *dramatis personae*, and I don't much like giving physical details about the bodies whose souls, or minds, or passions, I deal with. I build up so much out of *words* that the colour of people's hair seems unimportant. So, when it is in proof, will you look over it and tell me your views?

I enclose dedications for the friends you asked me for.

The only people who have thanked me for the books I sent are you, More, Reggie, and York Powell[3]—also my Radley boy. I am rather hurt. I will send you a Japanese paper for Miss Schuster. I would like to give her my copy.

I still dislike Mellor. By the way, could you come here for a fortnight? There is a petroleum launch on the Lake, and bicycles, and the country is pretty. Ever yours   OSCAR

[1] Presumably Arthur Clifton.   [2] Ledger's date.
[3] Frederick York Powell (1850–1904), author, scholar and editor. Regius Professor of Modern History at Oxford 1894–1904. He was the only well-known person who in fact signed Adey's petition in 1895 (see note p. 408). Bernard Shaw and Stewart Headlam were prepared to sign, but, as Shaw wrote: "That would be no use, for we were two notorious cranks, and our names would by themselves reduce the petition to absurdity and do Oscar more harm than good."

To Frank Harris
MS. Texas

[*Circa 27 March 1899*]   *Gland, Switzerland*

My dear Frank, Thank you so much for your letter and its enclosure, the latter arriving, like Iris, with much comfort from the gods, as I had had no cigarettes for three days. Mellor keeps his own carefully locked up! All eccentricities are in some way or other interesting, except meanness, and Mellor is too grotesque for words.

I am so glad you are seeing land at last in your great voyage as an Elizabethan adventurer. I hope the book will be out before August. It will make a new and a great era.

I am so glad you have met Georgette Leblanc. I thought her most interesting, and full of quick sympathies. The mind mobile, the whole temperament sensitive to the colours of life as they pass. As an actress she is superb.

I read the special supplement of the *Gaulois* on *Messaline*.[1] It seems to be a great success.

Mellor is loud in his complaints about being overcharged for the wine: he drones about it at all meals, so will not have it drunk. Swiss beer is served instead! He *weeps* over the price of the Château Olivier, that lovely scented wine whose memory is fragrant. He is very lamentable and I hope to get away next week. I shall go to Genoa. Paris is too dear. Ever yours

O. W.

To Robert Ross
MS. Clark

Monday [*27 March 1899*][2]   [*Gland, Switzerland*]

My dear Robbie, I am dedicating the next play to Frank Harris: I have sent *two* dedications to Smithers: I like the second best. Will you tell me your opinion?

I have heard from Arthur: but nothing definite: the great thing is not to give information to Hargrove et Cie: they are the only enemies. I hope the thing will go over quietly.

I don't think I can come to Paris after all: Paris is so expensive. I think as soon as I can get away from this loathsome place that I shall go back to Genoa: it is better than the Boulevards.

When you let me have my allowance, will you send it through *Cook* at

---

[1] An opera in three acts by Isidore de Lara, *né* Cohen (1858–1935), with libretto by Armand Silvestre and Eugène Morand, first produced at the Casino, Monte Carlo, on 21 March 1899. An English version was staged at Covent Garden on 13 July. De Lara was a close friend of Princess Alice of Monaco. There exists a copy of Wilde's *Poems* (fifth edition, 1882) inscribed: "To my friend Isidore de Lara, the poet of the musicians, in sincere admiration and affection, Oscar Wilde, June '87." For a pen-portrait of de Lara, see Osbert Sitwell's *Noble Essences* (1950).

[2] Ledger's date.

Geneva, please: of course the sooner I get it the sooner I can leave Gland, which has become intolerable. There are pretty places near Genoa[1] where I might live for a time. Ever yours   OSCAR

To Robert Ross

MS. Clark

[*29 March 1899*][2]   *Gland, Switzerland*

My dear Robbie, Thanks so much for the cheque. I hope to be able to "*toucher*" (excellent expression) on Saturday. If so, I shall leave for Genoa on Sunday morning.

I could not stay any longer at Mellor's: he really is too insane, and impossible. I never disliked anyone so thoroughly. My visit has taught me a curious and bitter lesson. I used to rely on my personality: now I know that my personality really rested on the fiction of *position*. Having lost position, I find my personality of no avail. Mellor has treated me as I would not have treated the most dull and unimportant of the lower middle-classes. I feel very humble, besides feeling very indignant: the former being my intellectual realisation of my position, the latter an emotion that is a "survival" of old conditions.

I won't go to Paris, because I should spend all my money in no time. I can't live in Paris under £1 a day; it is impossible. Near Genoa I hope to find some little spot, and sunlight counts as half one's income.

Your news about Moytura *are* crushing. That octopus the Law! One cannot escape. I don't know what to do. Do you think that if I applied for my discharge I would get it? It depends on Hargrove. *Could he be sounded*?

Thanks so much for the *Outlook*: it is a good notice, well written.[3]

Could you not come to Genoa? *Do*: for a month. We never see each other now. My address will be Albergo di Firenze, Genoa.

Please write, and please come. Ever yours   OSCAR

To Leonard Smithers

MS. Private

[*Postmark 30 March 1899*]   *Gland*
                                    At the House of the Enemy
                                    Among the Cities of the Plain.

My dear Smithers, The £20 has not yet arrived! This is absurd. Please send it at once.

I leave on Sunday for Genoa—Albergo di Firenze. It is impossible for me to go to Paris: I have not enough money. I am going to try and find a place near Genoa, where I can live for ten francs a day (boy *compris*). The

---

[1] Wilde accidentally wrote Geneva.   [2] Ledger's date.

[3] On 18 March the *Outlook* had published a favourable review of *The Importance of Being Earnest*, without mentioning Wilde's name.

791

chastity of Switzerland has got on my nerves. Neither Sporus nor Ganymede treads these fields of snow, and Mellor is too repulsive for anything. When I got your fiver, I had no money at all, and asked him to lend me three francs to go into Geneva with. He declined, on the ground that he had made it a rule never *to lend money* to anyone! I had to get my railway-fare from the cook! On my return, to a dreary dinner with Swiss beer, he told me that he did not like people borrowing money from his servants!

On the other hand when I told him I was going away, he went into floods of tears, and said that all his friends deserted him! Tartuffe and Harpagon[1] sum him up, though on too grand a scale.

Kindly send me the £20 *in an order on Cook's at Genoa for £20.*

Pray be business-like. Mrs Brown-Potter[2] shall have her copy of the new play. Has she a lovely new hat? Ever yours   O. W.

To Robert Ross
MS. Clark

1 April [1899]   *Café du Nord, Geneva*

My dear Robbie, I have left Gland. Mellor wept at my departure, apologised, implored me to stay, and put his conduct under the aegis of the Hereditary Furies of insanity that beset his race. I really was very sorry for him, but I could not stay. However, we parted amicably on my side, and on his with protestations of admiration and remorse.

I leave tomorrow morning for Genoa—Albergo di Firenze—a small inn on the quay, rather *mal-famé* but cheap. Then I think of some little place in the environs. There is no good my going to Paris; I can't afford to live there.

The only thing I see to do now, is to see what Hargrove will do if I ask for my discharge. Of course if he insists I suppose everything will be seized.

The weather has become very hot—quite summer: I expect Italy will be delightful. Could you not come for three weeks to Genoa? I never see you. You would do me no end of good. And there is More, who is apparently sentenced to life-long imprisonment in Great Britain: cannot he get away? I should love to have you both near at hand for a little. It would be delightful. Please do this. I believe that at the holy season of Easter one is supposed to forgive all one's friends.

I hope to find at Genoa, waiting for me, a young lad, by name Edoardo Rolla, one of the sea-farers. He has fair hair, and is always in dark blue. I have written to him. After the chill virginity of Swiss Alps and snow, I long for the red flowers of life that stain the feet of summer in Italy. Ever yours   O. W.

---

[1] Molière's hypocrite and miser.   [2] See note 1, p. 830.

Postcard: To Robert Ross
MS. Clark

[*Postmark 7 April 1899*] *Santa Margherita, Ligure*[1]

Dear R, My new address is Ristorante Christofero Colombo, Santa Margherita, Ligure, Italia. I send you specimens of the views to tempt you.

S. M.

Postcard: To Robert Ross
MS. Clark

[*Postmark 7 April 1899*] [*Rapallo*]

This is just a mile from Santa Margherita along the coast: it is quite delightful.

S. M.

Postcard: To Robert Ross
MS. Clark

[*Postmark 7 April 1899*] [*Portofino*]

This is a really lovely little place: only reached by mules or boats. S. M.

Postcard: To Robert Ross
MS. Clark

[*Postmark 7 April 1899*] [*San Fruttuoso*]

Have not yet been here: but have decided to enter the *chiostro*[2]—just the place for me.

S. M.

To Robert Ross
MS. Clark

[*April 1899*] *Santa Margherita*

My dear Robbie, Is there *any* chance of your coming out here? I wish now I had gone to Paris: it is so close to you. And here I am ill and lonely.

The only thing to do as regards the Irish affairs is, I think, this.

To approach Hargrove: to ask him if he will object to my discharge: i.e. if he will withdraw his claim. If he will, there will not be much left to fight against. I don't know about Queensberry's solicitors—whether they will be hostile, or not. Could Hargrove be approached?

I wish you would write to me, dear boy. I simply loathe my life at present. Ever yours

OSCAR

---

[1] These four picture-postcards were all posted at Santa Margherita on the same day. [2] Cloister.

To Robert Ross

MS. Clark

[*April 1899*]   *Santa Margherita*

My dear Robbie, I see I cannot fight the Receiver, who represents the unintelligent violence of the Law: the only thing to do is to see what my creditors will take: the place is only worth £120 a year. If Hargrove withdrew his claim I could manage to pay the others, I suppose, five shillings in the pound. If Hargrove *won't* do so, then the whole thing will have to go. I am, as usual, quite powerless. In any case for nine months after my brother's death nothing can be done, as if he leaves male issue it goes to his son. Of course he won't have a son, but I suppose the law has to wait and see.

I am so sorry you are ill. I am wretched, which makes me sympathetic.

Whatever I do is wrong: because my life is not on a right basis. In Paris I am bad: here I am bored: the last state is the worse.

I wish I could see you. A few days with you would be a tonic. Ever yours   OSCAR

To Robert Ross

MS. Clark

[*Circa 16 May 1899*]   *Hôtel de la Néva,*[1] *Rue Montigny* [*Paris*]

My dear Robbie, Smithers's letter arrived this morning: it was, as you know, for me. I hope he will come over.

I saw Strong last night at the Horse-Shoe: he has taken Grandcourt as his secretary: I did not discuss his treatment of Maurice at all. I thought it better not. Maurice, I hope, dines with me tonight.

I was so sorry you had to go, but it was charming being with you, and it was really most sweet of you to come to Italy to save me from Santa Margherita.[2] I am quite happy in Paris.

Your little friend Henri plies up and down all day, and has the sweetest and most compromising smiles for me, especially when I am with friends.

Do write soon. Ever, with fondest love   OSCAR

---

[1] It is not known exactly when Wilde returned to Paris, but he certainly stayed first at this hotel. Smithers wrote to him there on 25 May (TS. Holland): "I have got the agreement ready to send you and am simply retaining it until I definitely know your address. Please write me *by return* and let me know if you have left the Hôtel de la Néva? I have also further proofs for you of *An Ideal Husband. I do wish* you would send me *at once* the proofs of *An Ideal Husband* and *The Ballad* as I am much embarrassed by not getting them." The proofs of *The Ballad* were those of the seventh edition, which was printed on 23 June 1899, and was the first to carry Wilde's name on the title-page.

[2] Wilde's stay at Santa Margherita had ended by Ross's rescuing him and taking him back to Paris.

To Leonard Smithers

MS. Private

[*Date of receipt 18 May 1899*]   *Grand Café, 14 Boulevard des Capucines,*
Paris

My dear Smithers, Do come over: at any rate we can discuss the matter. Of course it is largely a question of money.

When am I to have more proofs? Do let us get the book out in June at latest.[1]

Will you kindly send a copy of *The Importance of Being Earnest* to Morton Fullerton Esq.,[2] *Times* Office, 35 Boulevard des Capucines, Paris, and write in it "with the compliments of the author."

Paris is lovely today—real summer.

I did not wire to you because I expected you to come today. You should always keep your "pleasure appointments." I hope to see you tomorrow.
Ever yours   OSCAR

To Frank Harris

MS. Texas

[*Late May 1899*]   *Hôtel Marsollier, Rue Marsollier, Paris*

My dear Frank, Armand Point's[3] address is Marlotte, Seine-et-Marne, and if you will send him an impression in wax of your emerald he will be charmed to design and execute a ring for you.

How are you? And how are the automobiles and the Baryes?[4] I no longer, now that you are not here, live in purple and fine linen at Durand's: such pomp, however, should be intermittent.

If you want to read a terrible little book, order Octave Mirbeau's *Le Jardin des Supplices*: it is quite awful: a *Sadique* joy in pain pulses in it: it is very revolting to me, but, for all that, wonderful.[5] His soul seems to have wandered in fearsome places. But you, to whom fear is unknown, will face the book with courage: to me it is a sort of grey adder.

How is Shakespeare? He was a mist and you have made him marble. I wish the Golden Book would appear. Shakespeare: his soul and body.

If you are rolling in gold, and have achieved your victory over Beit and the other lost tribes of Israel, do send me a tenner.[6] Life is rather dust now, and water-wells are rare in the desert. My compliments to Mrs Harris.
Ever yours   OSCAR

---

[1] See note 1, p. 794.

[2] American journalist and author (1865–1952). From 1891 to 1911 he was Paris correspondent of *The Times*, which recorded in his obituary: "A great friend and admirer of Henry James, his English style was so closely modelled on that of James as often to involve a very drastic process of sub-editing before it was suitable for publication in a daily newspaper."   [3] French painter (1861–1949).

[4] Presumably works by Antoine Louis Barye (1796–1875), the French animal sculptor.   [5] Published 1899.

[6] Alfred Beit (1853–1906), financier, diamond-merchant, philanthropist, friend and supporter of Cecil Rhodes, made a fortune out of the development of South African diamonds. Harris had visited South Africa in 1896 and had thereafter pursued a violently anti-Rhodes policy in the *Saturday Review* and elsewhere.

To Robert Ross
MS. Clark

[*29 May 1899*]¹   *Hôtel Marsollier*

Dear Robbie, Would you kindly send me the June allowance tomorrow by
an *order* on Cook, so that I can *toucher* on the 1st? I believe you don't like
the swifter mode of telegraphing.

The unmasking of our poor Smithers has been a blow. I found out, by
chance, that he was employed by Sequale to get my play² at one fourth of
the terms Sequale had offered! It is too astonishing for words. Smithers is
merely *l'homme de paille*, paid to get round me. I have wired to him to tell
him I have found it all out, and to advise him to come over at once. Ever
yours   o. w.

To Leonard Smithers³

[*Postmark 30 May 1899*]   *Hôtel Marsollier*

You will, I trust, be here tomorrow night. I know all about your arrangement with Roberts—done to make me accept a small sum instead of
proper terms . . . "You become more interesting hourly," to quote from
*The Importance of Being Earnest.*⁴ Of course a new agreement will have to
be made . . . as you concealed from me the real circumstances. You were
merely *l'homme de paille*, a new role I hope. It is not a nice one.

To William B. Fitts⁵
MS. Harvard

31 May [*1899*]   *Hôtel Marsollier*

Dear Mr Fitts, I have drawn out in my mind the scheme of the article for
your *Review*, and I propose now to leave Paris, and go to Marlotte in the
forest of Fontainebleau, for the purpose of writing it. I have many literary
friends there, so the surroundings will be conducive to work. It is a
colonie artistique, and creation is in the air.

Upon the other hand, it is difficult for me—impossible almost—to
engage on literary work without receiving some sum down: in the present
case, one third of the honorarium agreed on. I have, as you doubtless know,

¹ Ledger's date.
² The scenario which eventually became *Mr and Mrs Daventry*. Sequale and
Roberts (see next letter) were some sort of agents through whom Smithers succeeded in getting Wilde an advance payment of £100. Roberts may conceivably
have been Sir Randal (see note 3, p. 223), who did not die until 10 October 1899.
³ Text from Mason (p. 436), quoting Glaenzer.   ⁴ Act II.
⁵ An editor on the staff of the *North American Review*. In a letter to Wilde
(MS. Clark) dated 9 May 1899 and written from the Hôtel Liverpool, Rue de
Castiglione, Paris, he expressed his "great satisfaction" at the promise of an article
from Wilde, and undertook to send £75 directly it was delivered. It never appeared.

lost all my fortune: what is left to me is quite inadequate for any mode of cultivated life.

If you can do this, without violating the traditions of your magazine, or even by violating them, I could promise you the article in a month. Believe me, truly yours   OSCAR WILDE

To Leonard Smithers
MS. Taylor

[? *1 June 1899*]   *Hôtel Marsollier*

My dear Smithers, Business relations with you have always their comedy side, so I don't think it is worth while seriously discussing the question of epistolary style. What I want to know are the facts.

Roberts has stated that you were acting for him all the while, in order to get the play on terms much less than he at first offered.

Everyone seems to have been aware of this, except the one person to whom it should have been told—myself. Even Robbie, the most careful of rising young men, in his letter to me this morning, says that while he knew nothing definitely he always understood that if you succeeded in getting the play from me on certain terms you were to receive from Roberts a share of the profits.

I told you that I did not wish Roberts to have any share in the production of my play, as he lacks experience and tact, and would inevitably play the showman. You stated this at the Bodega to Roberts in my presence. He gave a grim smile, whose import I now begin to understand.

So now tell me:

Is it Roberts, or people whom he represents, who has taken, or proposes to take rather, the Garrick Theatre for my play? This is a very important question.

What contracts, if any, have you entered into with Roberts?

You must deal quite frankly with me. It is the only way for us to do business.

You are of course aware that a personal contract cannot be altered or transferred without the consent of both parties. Roberts never had any rights over my play at all. My contract was with Sedger. As you told me you had paid Roberts £100, and that Sedger resigned all claim on me, I dealt with you. But I was under no necessity to do so. If I agree with Beerbohm Tree that he shall produce a play by me, Tree cannot transfer his contract to Dan Leno.[1]

As regards Roberts's statements that you were all the while acting for him (either with tacit or written agreement), what do you say about them? I hear he showed much of his native fun on the subject, and indeed was rather amusing. His explanation was that you had told him that I disliked him personally, and that his only chance was to get the play through you,

[1] Stage name of George Galvin (1860–1904), one of the best loved of English music-hall and pantomime comedians.

797

and that you could easily get me to agree to much lower terms. His terms, you remember, were £100 on the completion of each act—£400 in all: besides clothes, hotel bill, etc. Your terms were £25 for each act. I cannot understand why you don't see that I must know exactly the facts of the case. Your statement that my telegram to you was like the telegram of a husband to a guilty wife in a farcical comedy I forgive. Ever yours

O. W.

To Robert Ross
MS. Clark

[2 June 1899]   Hôtel Marsollier

My dear Robbie, The £10 arrived safe. Marchand was addressing the mob next door—at the Military Club—so I had to fight my way to Cook's, but by the aid of patriotic cries I succeeded in forcing a passage through the patriots.[1]

I *did* think it curious when Smithers told me that you wanted to be repaid the hotel bill at Genoa, the fifty francs at Santa Margherita, and the railway-ticket: but I concluded that there had been an earthquake in Phillimore Gardens. I also thought it odd that you never wrote to tell me that you had received it. When you give, my dear Robbie, you give. There is no one so generous, so good as you are. I have written to Smithers to send it to me at once, as I am going now to Havre. I found Fontainebleau relaxing, but I am fond of the sea. I cannot stay in Paris; it costs too much.

Bosie has [piece torn out] horse. I am very glad.

I saw Robert Sherard last night. He was very insane, and sentimental: wept over a friendship of seventeen years; upon the other hand abused all my friends in the foulest way. I had to stop him in a peremptory manner. Three times he parted from me, and three times I found him following me to other places. He and Strong have each other on the brain. They think of nothing else. It is a great bore. Robert has almost lost all his good looks. He was dreadful of aspect last night: quite dreadful.

I am very glad Will is marrying Miss Kingsley. I think it only right, and I like her immensely.[2] Your proposal to sacrifice your [piece torn out] always seemed to me [piece torn out]. Ever yours   OSCAR

[1] On 10 July 1898 Commandant J.-B. Marchand (1863–1934) and a small French force captured from the Mahdists the port of Fashoda on the Upper Nile. This action caused a state of tension between France and Great Britain, and the French force was withdrawn on 11 December. During 1899 Marchand toured France making speeches against the weakness which had led to the evacuation. He arrived in Paris with his officers on 1 June and spoke there the same day. According to *The Times* of 2 June, "It was not until 5 o'clock that the immense crowd which had surrounded the Military Club in the Avenue de l'Opéra . . . was rewarded by the appearance of the explorer . . . At present—11 o'clock—it is enormous, and more enthusiastic than ever. At every few moments it calls for Major Marchand to appear on the balcony of the club."

[2] William Rothenstein married Alice Knewstub on 11 June 1899. She had acted on the professional stage under the name of Alice Kingsley.

To Leonard Smithers

MS. Taylor

[Circa 3 June 1899]   *Grand Café, 14 Boulevard des Capucines, Paris*

My dear Smithers, After your letter of this morning I see that the statements made by Roberts here in Paris were entirely false, and I readily withdraw all I have said to you that may have wounded you.

When I first learned what Roberts had stated—that you were merely his agent etc.—I could hardly credit it, but when you wrote to me that you proposed to take a theatre at once, it seemed to me to corroborate Roberts's assertions, as I knew you could not take a theatre on your own account. I wired to you, and you replied in a very comedy strain, as if you thought it a good joke. I then certainly felt very indignant at what seemed to me treachery on your part, and wrote accordingly.

I think that it was scandalous of Roberts to say what he said.

You will be pleased to hear that I have written more than half of the Fourth Act: it is a serious, a tragic act, so I began with it. It is the comedy of Acts I and II that frightens me a little. It is difficult for *me* to laugh at life, as I used to.

I hope, if I hear from you satisfactorily, to go to Havre on Monday. The title-page is all right (*Ballad*)[1] though I don't like the form of the bracket. Ever yours   O. W.

To Leonard Smithers

MS. Taylor

Tuesday [6 June 1899][2]   *Hôtel Marsollier*

My dear Smithers, Thanks for your letter.

I hope to receive soon the title-page, dedication, and play-bill of *An Ideal Husband*. In Act II the word *décolleté* occurs: please see that the accents are put in all right.

As regards that annoying absurdity Roberts, the statements he made were made quite seriously, as far as manner goes. He said for instance to Bosie the last time he saw him "I suppose Wilde has no idea at all that I have got his play?" Bosie said he did not know, and asked me when I saw him. This is only one out of many things he said. What was I to think? I naturally thought that you had written the *bordereau*, and sold it to Schwartzkoppen-Sequale. Hence "*l'affaire Smithers.*" Now, of course, you are acquitted, and it is proved that the real traitor is Worsley-Esterhazy, assisted by Du Paty-Roberts. This I hope is clear to you.[3]

I await the cheque for £12. I don't propose to stay at Havre, but somewhere near. Blankenberghe is, or used to be, very fashionable. If the cheque comes tonight I hope to get away Thursday.

[1] Of the seventh edition.   [2] So dated by postmark in Glaenzer.
[3] Schwartzkoppen, Esterhazy and Du Paty de Clam were leading characters in the Dreyfus case.

I saw Ernest Dowson the other night: he forced me to go to the Panthéon at midnight. It was dreadful, a Café-Pandemonium.[1] The drawing on the cover of *Hunger* is like a horrible caricature of Ernest. This was, I suppose, intended.[2]

Weather here quite terrible. Ever yours   O. W.

To Robert Ross

MS. Clark

Tuesday [6 June 1899]   *Hôtel Marsollier*

My dear Robbie, Thanks for your letter. Smithers has not yet sent the cheque. He says in his letter that he will do so when he sees you.

Paris is awfully hot: quite dreadful. I long to be away.

I saw Ada Rehan and Augustin Daly the other night at the Café de la Paix, where Bosie had invited me to dine. They were most charming: her hair has turned quite white. I accused her at once of dyeing her hair white. She was delighted.

They also want me to write something for them.[3]

I have made friends with a charming American youth, expelled from Harvard for immoral conduct! He is very amusing and good-looking. Ever yours   OSCAR

---

[1] Ernest Dowson wrote to Smithers at about this time (text from Glaenzer):

I ran across Oscar last night, also Strong who shook hands with me but objected (through Oscar) to drink with me on the grounds of my relations with Sherard. Oscar quite agreed with me that this conduct was childish and levanted with me to another café. I need not say that *je m'en fous de M. Strong* as much as of Sherard.

[2] Smithers had recently published an English translation by George Egerton of *Hunger*, a Norwegian novel by Knut Hamsun. The cover design was by William Thomas Horton (1864–1919), who had contributed to the *Savoy* in 1896.

[3] Graham Robertson in his *Time Was* described Ada Rehan's account of this incident:

She and the Dalys had been dining at a restaurant and, looking up, she had seen Oscar Wilde sitting with some men at a neighbouring table and looking at her tentatively . . . "I didn't know what to do," she told me. "Mr and Mrs Daly were with me and I could not tell how they would feel about it. You never *do* know with men when they are going to feel very proper and when they are not."

"And *was* Mr Daly feeling proper?" I enquired.

"No," said poor Ada, "he wasn't. It was such a relief: if I could not have bowed I should have cried. So Mr Wilde came over and sat with us and talked so charmingly—it was just like old times—we had a lovely evening. And then, only a few days later, Mr Daly died. Arrangements had to be made and Mrs Daly was not equal to taking them in hand. I seemed to be all alone, and so confused and frightened. And then Oscar Wilde came to me and was more good and helpful than I can tell you—just like a very kind brother. I shall always think of him as he was to me through those few dreadful days."

Augustin Daly died in Paris on 7 June 1899, and I have dated this letter accordingly.

To Leonard Smithers[1]

[*Postmark 8 June 1899*]   *Paris*

Yes: it was Roberts's reiterated statements to Bosie that made the fire rage in the stubble. He spoke of it as a joke he had played on me . . . The picture on *Hunger* grows more like Ernest daily. I now hide it.

Bosie lunched with Paul Potter yesterday. Not the man who painted the cow, but an American dramatist who wrote a play, I suppose about a cow, that George Alexander produced.[2]

The luncheon at Maire's lasted from 12.30 to 5.15. Burgundy, Champagne and Cognac of 1800 were consumed in goblets. Bosie had vine-leaves in his hair and saw the moon at mid-day; the evening was agitating. Bosie is naturally in high spirits over his first review in the *Outlook*; it certainly is splendid. It arrived while we were dining together at Avenue Kléber, and we celebrated the glory of the "Great Unknown" at the Horse-Shoe Bar.[3]

Daly, who has just died, had made us a large offer for the American rights of our play. I am sorry for him; he was cultivated and charming.

To Robert Ross

MS. Clark

[*June 1899*][4]   *Hôtel Marsollier*

My dearest Robbie, Thanks so much: the £7. 10 arrived safe at 3.45.

I am delighted to hear of Bosie's great success: he sent me a copy apparently, in fact I know he did: but it has never arrived. Some lyrical postman stole it, I suppose.

Casquette is well, and has a blue suit. Edmond de Goncourt has returned from prison and shows himself on the Boulevard in a straw hat. I am still devoted to Le Premier Consul, but I also love a young Russian called Maltchek Perovinski, aged eighteen. He is quite charming, and very educated.

I dined with Stuart Merrill the other night. Ferdinand Hérold was there, and sent me subsequently a lovely edition of *La Vie et la Mort de La Sainte Vierge*, a book he compiled from apocryphal Gospels and elsewhere. It is very charming, and written in verses.[5]

---

[1] The text of this incomplete letter is taken from Maggs's catalogue 289 (1912).

[2] *The Conquerors*, a drama in four acts by Paul M. Potter, produced at the St James's Theatre on 4 April 1898. Cf. note 3, p. 824.

[3] Douglas's second volume of poems, *The City of the Soul*, had just been published anonymously by Grant Richards, and on 3 June the *Outlook* printed a glowing review headed "A Great Unknown." Its anonymous author, who was in fact Lionel Johnson, announced "Among crowds of clever versifiers here comes a poet." [4] Ledger's date.

[5] André-Ferdinand Hérold (1865–1949), French symbolist poet and novelist. *Le Livre de la Naissance, de la Vie et de la Mort de la bienheureuse Vierge-Marie* was first published in 1895.

I see a good deal of a young poet called Michaël Robas:[1] he is astonishingly handsome: we went to Montmartre the other night, to the café where Jehan Rictus,[2] the poet, recites. I was received with great honour, and everyone was presented to me. I was not allowed to pay for my *bocks*, and the *chasseur*, a lad of singular beauty, begged for my autograph in his album, which contained, he told me, the autographs of *cinquante-trois poètes, et deux meurtriers*! I graciously acceded. Ever yours   OSCAR

To Frances Forbes-Robertson
TS. Harrod

[*June 1899*]   *Hôtel Marsollier*

My dear sweet, beautiful Friend, Eric has just sent me your charming letter and I am delighted to have a chance of sending you my congratulations on your marriage, and all the good wishes of one who has always loved and admired you.[3] I met Eric by chance, and he told me he had been over to the marriage. He was as picturesque and sweet as usual, but more than usually vague. I was quite furious with him. He could not quite remember who it was you had married, or whether he was fair or dark, young or old, tall or small. He could not remember where you were married or what you wore, or whether you looked more than usually beautiful. He said there were a great many people at the wedding but could not remember their names. He remembered, however, Johnston being present. He spoke of the whole thing as a sort of landscape in a morning mist. Your husband's name he could not for the moment recall: but said he thought he had it written down at home. He went dreamily away down the Boulevard followed by violent reproaches from me, but they were no more to him than the sound of fluting: he wore the sweet smile of those who are always looking for the moon at mid-day.

So, dear Frankie, you are married, and your husband is a king of men! That is as it should be: those who wed the daughters of the gods are kings, or become so.

I have nothing to offer you but one of my books, that absurd comedy *The Importance of being Earnest*, but I send it to you in the hopes it may live on your bookshelves and be allowed to look at you from time to time. The dress is pretty, it wears Japanese vellum and belongs to a limited family of *nine* and is not on speaking terms with the popular edition: it refuses to recognise the poor relations whose value is only seven and sixpence. Such is the pride of birth. It is a lesson.[4]

[1] Unidentified, except that five mediocre sonnets in his hand, inscribed *"pour le Maître,"* are in Clark.

[2] Pseudonym of the French poet, Gabriel Randon de Saint-Arnaud (1867–1933). A copy of *The Ballad* inscribed *"Pour le poète Jehan Rictus. Sympathie, hommage, admiration.* Oscar Wilde" is in the Bibliothèque Nationale.

[3] Frances Forbes-Robertson married Henry Dawes Harrod in London on 10 April 1899. For the first three years of their married life they lived in Anglesey.

[4] This copy on Japanese vellum is inscribed: "To Frankie on her happy marriage from her old friend and comrade the Author. June '99."

Ah! how delightful it would be to be with you and your husband in your own home! But my dear child, how could I get to you? Miles of sea, miles of land, the purple of the mountains and the silver of the rivers divide us: you don't know how poor I am: I have no money at all: I live or am supposed to live on a few francs a day: a bare remnant saved from shipwreck. Like dear St Francis of Assisi I am wedded to Poverty: but in my case the marriage is not a success; I hate the bride that has been given to me. I see no beauty in her hunger and her rags: I have not the soul of St Francis: my thirst is for the beauty of life: my desire for the joy. But it was dear of you to ask me, and do tell the king of men how touched and grateful I am by the invitation you and he have sent me.

And, also sometimes, send me a line to tell me of the beauty you have found in life. I live now in echoes and have little music of my own. Your old friend   OSCAR

To W. Morton Fullerton
MS. Harvard

[*June 1899*]   *Hôtel Marsollier*

My dear Fullerton, I find myself in very great trouble owing to not getting some money I expected, from America, where it is owing to me.

Would it be an inconvenience to you to lend me 100 francs? I receive my quarterly allowance, such as it is, on July 1st, when I will be able to return it to you. At present I am quite without money, and I hope you will not mind my asking you this favour.

If you are able to do this would you send it to me, Monsieur *Sebastian Melmoth*, at the above address? Believe me, truly yours OSCAR WILDE

Telegram: To Leonard Smithers
MS. Yale

[*Postmark 23 June 1899*]   [*Postmark Havre*]

Kindly wire ten which will be repaid by Ross first July. Very urgent. Melmoth, Hotel Tortoni, Havre.

To W. Morton Fullerton[1]
MS. Harvard

Dimanche, 25 Juin [*1899*]   *Trouville*

My dear Fullerton, Thanks for your letter, which has just been forwarded

---

[1] Fullerton had answered Wilde's earlier letter as follows (MS. Clark):

23 June 1899   *35 Boulevard des Capucines*
My dear Melmoth, I am distressed to have left your touching appeal unanswered

803

to me from Paris. I am glad to say the momentary difficulty I was in has quite passed away. It was not very serious, but it is always a bore to find oneself without pocket-money. Balzac's *héros métallique* still dominates our age, as do indeed all Balzac's heroes;[1] and the French have not yet realised that the basis of all civilisation is unlimited credit. Empires only fall when they have to pay their bills: at that moment the Barbarians arrive.

But what a Johnsonian letter you have written me! "I grope at the hope that you will not have occasion to put either me or anyone else again into such a position of positive literal chagrin:" so might the great lexicographer have written (though perhaps he might have found tautology in "positive ... literal"). In so slight a matter, my dear Fullerton, sentiment need not borrow stilts.

I am glad you received my play safely, and were amused by it. It is a bit of nonsense, with style: a form of art the French are rich in, but the English sadly to seek.

So you have been in Stendhal's *patrie*. I fear I don't know where it is; I think of him as *Arrigo Beyle: Milanese*—so, I think, he wished his epitaph to run.[2]

Trouville is boring, so I return to Paris tomorrow or next day, and hope to come across you, but you must not be Johnsonian: Theocritean were better. Sincerely yours   OSCAR WILDE

---

for so long. But I have been on *congé* in the *patrie* of Stendhal, and had cogniz-ance of your *gêne* only yesterday.

You do me too much honour in asking me to come to the rescue of an artist such as you. And if I could have known of the situation three weeks ago when I had money in my pocket I should not have hesitated for a moment, especially as I had just received your play and was in the state of mind of one who says of a thing without thinking: "it is worth its weight in gold." But at present, after an expensive journey, I am unable, with the best good-will in the world, to seize the event and to accept the *rôle* in this particular comedy—I use the word in its Hellenic and Gallic sense, *bien entendu*, in the sole sense in which it exists for the admirers of *Lady Windermere's Fan* and of *The Importance of Being Earnest*. The maker of those masterpieces has too much delicacy and *esprit* not to sympathize sincerely with the regret of a man obliged to reply thus to an appeal which cer-tainly he could not have expected, and for which it was impossible for him to prepare but which is none the less precious for that. I grope at the hope that meanwhile the stress has passed, and that you will not have occasion to put, *malgré vous*, either me or anyone else again into such a position of positive literal chagrin.   Yours sincerely   W. M. FULLERTON

[1] "*Certes, personne ne fut moins avare que l'auteur de* La Comédie Humaine, *mais son génie lui faisait pressentir le rôle immense que devait jouer dans l'art ce héros métallique, plus intéressant pour la société moderne que les Grandisson, les Desgrieux, les Oswald, les Werther, les Malek-Adhel, les René, les Lara, les Waverley, les Quentin-Durward etc.*"   Gautier, "*Honoré de Balzac*," in *Portraits Contemporains* (1874) Wilde had referred to this passage in "The Truth of Masks" in *Intentions*.

[2] Marie Henri Beyle (1783–1842), the French writer who used the name Stendhal, was a native of Grenoble, but spent happy years at Milan during his youth and wrote his own epitaph: *Qui giace Arrigo Beyle Milanese: visse, scrisse, amò.*

To Leonard Smithers

MS. Private

[*Circa 25 June 1899*]   [*Havre*]

My dear Smithers, Here are the proofs. In *Act 4*—opening—you will see
"*Servant*" as one of the speaking characters. This should be altered to
"*James.*" You remember I wrote to you to hold the type over. I have cut
out the quotation from Meredith.

It has just occurred to me that perhaps you may have sent the money to
Cook's here. If so, you should have wired me to that effect. I wait all day
long at the hotel. I shall go tomorrow morning to Paris. Havre is too
awful for words. Ever yours   o. w.

To Leonard Smithers

MS. Morrison

Monday [*Postmark 26 June 1899*]   *Havre*

My dear Smithers, The £5 arrived last night, and I am leaving for Paris—
same address, Hôtel Marsollier, Rue Marsollier.

Do wire the other £5 tomorrow through Cook. I have only enough to
pay my bill and reach Paris. You will be paid on July 1st. It is only a
loan for four days. Surely you can't object. It is not a big sum to ask for.
Ever yours   o. w.

To Leonard Smithers

MS. Clark

3 July [*1899*]   *Hôtel Marsollier, Paris*

My dear Smithers, Frank Harris must have a Japanese paper: one for you:
and one for me.

Large paper: six for me.

Small paper: fifteen for me.[1]

I shall be charmed to see O'Sullivan. I shall say nothing about Kalisaya.
Ever yours   OSCAR

---

[1] The first edition of *An Ideal Husband*, which was published in July 1899,
consisted of twelve numbered presentation copies on Japanese vellum, 100 numbered
copies on Dutch handmade paper (price 21s.) and a thousand on ordinary paper
(price 7/6). Wilde's list of recipients (MS. Clark) reads: "*Large* [*Paper*]. Robbie,
Reggie, Bosie, More, Shannon. *Small* [*Paper*]. Louis Wilkinson, Kyrle Bellew,
H. H. Morell, Lewis Waller, Osman Edwards, V. O'Sullivan, Ernest Dowson,
Felix Fénéon, Ernest La Jeunesse, Langrel [see note 3, p. 814], Henri Bauër, Digby
Lamotte, Frankie, Humphreys, Lautrec, Stuart Merrill, André Gide, Hérold,
W. Blunt, Major Nelson, Davray."

To Leonard Smithers
MS. Private

[*July 1899*]   *Taverne F. Pousset, 14 Boulevard des Italiens,*
                                                                      Paris

My dear Smithers, You were a wretch to give me chloral: or was it hashish?
I prefer chloral.

I want you to send me at once £10. You can be repaid this £5 on
August 1, and £5 on September 1.

I am going now to La Varenne, on the Marne, but I must pay the hotel
here, so do send me the money.

Give my kindest regards to Mrs Falconer—and let me hear from
you. Ever yours   OSCAR

To Frank Harris
MS. Berg

[*July 1899*]   *L'Île d'Amour, Chennevières-sur-Marne*

My dear Frank, The play you let me dedicate to you is out, but the Japanese
paper copy destined for you is not yet bound, so I have told Smithers, my
publisher, 5 Old Bond Street, to send you an ordinary copy.[1] Later on you
will get a Japanese paper (one of an edition of 12 copies) and a large-paper
(one of an edition of 100). It is a real pleasure to me to see your name on
the portal of a book of mine.

How are you? I am living in a little inn on an island in the Marne,
beautifully wooded and quiet, an exquisite place, and at night-time
"silver-sweet."[2] My kind regards to your wife. Ever yours   OSCAR

Telegram: To Leonard Smithers
MS. Yale

24 July 1899   [*Postmark La Varenne-St-Hilaire*]

Please send ten here loan. Melmoth, Restaurant L'Île, Chennevières-
sur-Marne.

---

[1] Mason says *An Ideal Husband* was published in July, but the exact date is
unknown. The British Museum copy of the large-paper edition of 100 copies is
stamped 30 August. Clearly the twelve signed copies on Japanese vellum appeared
later than the ordinary edition.

[2] "How silver-sweet sound lovers' tongues by night" (*Romeo and Juliet*, Act II,
Sc. ii).

To Leonard Smithers

MS. Yale

[*26 July 1899*]   *L'Île d'Amour, Chennevières-sur-Marne*

My dear Smithers, Why don't you answer my telegram? It is quite maddening. You said you would send me some money last week. On the strength of this I came down here—a lovely spot, but the *patron* is gloomy as I have paid nothing as yet. I have put it all on you, and described you in lurid colours.

Will you now send me £10? Send it to *Betts*,[1] and I will go in on Saturday and get it. I fear the post here. It is only a loan for three days, as Saturday will be the 29th. *Please* do this.

I have at last signed all the copies, but I cannot send them till I get some money for registration. I shall bring them into Paris on Saturday, and send it off through Fleury, the bookseller.

It is extraordinary what an amount of suffering you cause me.

I enclose list of *addresses* for your clerk. Ever yours   o. w.

To Frank Harris

MS. Texas

[*Circa 26 July 1899*]   *Hôtel de l'Écu, Chennevières-sur-Marne*

My dear Frank, I don't know if you have any money going, or if the Transvaal belongs to you now or not.[2] I am in a great mess over things, and if you have £15 that you would like to throw to the poets, do send me a cheque for it. I am dreadfully worried by hotel-*patrons*—only one, but a tiger from the Hôtel Marsollier—coming down and making life horrible, and I have no money. Ever yours   OSCAR

Please write to me under *my real* name here.   OSCAR WILDE

Postcard: To Louis Wilkinson

MS. Hyde (H. M.)

[*Postmark 27 July 1899*]

Monsieur Sebastian Melmoth est à L'Île d'Amour, Chennevières-sur-Marne, Seine-et-Oise, France. Il trouve votre sonnet très, très beau; et il espère recevoir une autre lettre de vous prochainement.   o.

Postcard: To Vincent O'Sullivan

MS. Clark

Thursday [*27 July 1899. Postmark of receipt 31 July 1899*]   *L'Île d'Amour*

Your charming invitation has only just reached me—alas! too late. I shall be in Paris on Saturday, and shall breakfast at Pousset's in the Avenue de l'Opéra, close to your hotel. Perhaps you may look in.

                              SEBASTIAN MELMOTH

[1] Agents in the Rue Castiglione.   [2] See note 6, p. 795.

To Leonard Smithers

MS. Private

[*August 1899*]   *Hôtel d'Alsace, Rue des Beaux-Arts, Paris*

My dear Smithers, I am back at my old hotel: the country was too dear.

I don't know if you have received the proof-sheets yet: you have never acknowledged them. I also think you might have sent me a copy of the book when it appeared. I have only seen it at Galignani's. It looked very nice.

The address of "*Frankie*" in one of the copies is Mrs Harrod, Amlwch, Anglesey, Wales. The other addresses are I think all indicated.

Did you get my letter about Percy and the £300 which is owing to me? It is just a hope.

Also, can you let me have my September allowance in advance? £10. Robbie cannot himself advance it, and I have no money at all. I am in a dreadful state, as all my clothes are at the Hôtel Marsollier, where I owe a bill.[1] I am really in the gutter.

Do send me *at once* a cheque on Betts. Since Sunday I have only had seven francs to live on. Ever yours   OSCAR

To Leonard Smithers

MS. Yale

[*August 1899*]   *Hôtel d'Alsace*

Dear Smithers, Is this quite quite nice of you? Can you sleep at night?

Does not your conscience draw back the curtains of your bed and make mows at you?

In any case please send me the £6 of my allowance, so that I get it on Wednesday next. Please don't delay about this.

As regards the £20 for the two plays, I wish you would send it. My garments are at the Hôtel Marsollier, in pawn for £10, and I have really no clothes but an old flannel suit. £20 would enable me to have my clothes such as they are. I wish you would be serious. Ever yours   OSCAR

To Frank Harris

MS. Yale

[*August 1899*]   *Hôtel d'Alsace*

My dear Frank, The faithful Silk—still, I am glad to see, your slave and

---

[1] Wilde's clothes and other belongings had been left behind at the Hôtel Marsollier because of his inability to pay his bill there. A letter to Wilde from the proprietor demanding his money (MS. Clark) is dated 14 July 1899. Dupoirier, the proprietor of the Hôtel d'Alsace, eventually paid Wilde's debt and recovered his clothes.

secretary—has sent me the £20, in a banknote of extraordinary beauty. A thousand thanks, my dear Frank, for all your kindness and thoughtfulness and friendship towards me. I long to see you again, and to learn all about your book, your Baryes,[1] and your automobiles. I am getting my clothes today from the hotel whose evil proprietor detained them, so I shall be all right. Up to the present I have been, if not "in looped and windowed nakedness" (I quote loosely),[2] at any rate dreadfully shabby, and am more than ever in disaccord with Carlyle on the question of the relation of clothes and Society. A hole in the trousers may make one as melancholy as Hamlet, and out of bad boots a Timon may be made.

Is there any chance of your being here soon? Of course when you *do* come you will let me know. Ever yours   OSCAR

To Aimée Lowther

MS. Hillyard

[? *August 1899*]   *Hôtel d'Alsace*

My dear Aimée, It was very lucky you wrote to me, as the little poem in prose I call "The Poet" appears next week in a Paris magazine above my own signature![3] Had it *subsequently* appeared with *your* signature to it I fear the critics and the papers would have let off some vulgar fireworks. No: my dear Aimée, you must always create your own plots. "*On exécute mal ce qu'on n'a pas conçu soi-même !*" You remember that fine phrase of Charlotte Corday?[4]

Write for little Gordon Craig something about Fontainebleau.[5] The subject is of no importance: give your *real* impressions of *anything*.

It was great joy to see you the other day, looking so beautiful, and improbable, and your friendship is a blossom on the crown of thorns that my life has become. Do write to me again. Sincerely and affectionately, ever yours   O. W.

[1] See note 4, p. 795.

[2] *King Lear*, Act III, scene 4: "your looped and windowed raggedness."

[3] I have not succeeded in tracing this magazine, or any version of "The Poet" written by Wilde. A number of versions have been printed by people who heard Wilde tell the story, including André Gide, but the best known is probably that recorded by Mrs Gabrielle Enthoven (née Romaine, 1868–1950), the theatre historian and collector. At some unspecified time she wrote down from memory versions of four prose-poems which she had heard Wilde tell ("The Poet," "The Actress," "Simon of Cyrene," and "Jezebel"). She had them printed in a twelve-page pamphlet with a crinkly purple cover and ECHOES printed on the front. It is undated and bears no name of author, editor or printer. The British Museum copy, which was presented by Mrs Enthoven in 1948, contains two letters from her in which she says that only "five or six copies" were printed. One is in the collection of Mr Montgomery Hyde, and another (presented by Aimée Lowther, who was a close friend of Mrs Enthoven) used to belong to Mr Vyvyan Holland, who reprinted its contents as an appendix to his *Son of Oscar Wilde*.

[4] Quoted by Pater in his essay on Winckelmann in *Studies in the History of the Renaissance* (1873).

[5] Edward Gordon Craig (b. 1872), the son of Ellen Terry and E. W. Godwin, produced four numbers of a periodical called *The Page* between 1898 and 1901.

To Aimée Lowther

MS. Hillyard

[? *August 1899*] *Hôtel d'Alsace*

My dear Aimée, I wrote to you at Pont Street. I dare say I put the wrong number, but you are so unique that it must reach you. It was merely to tell you that the little prose-poem, "The Poet," appears, with some others by me, in one of the French magazines this month. I fear that if it appeared elsewhere the stars would fall on the head of little Gordon Craig—perhaps something worse than stars!

Write him something of your own—your own impressions of *anything*. Subject is no matter: style, treatment, vision, method—these are the important things. A day in a forest could be made as lovely as a lyric: any one day in your life could be converted into a work of art.

I have seen nothing of Claude: but I talked about you last night to a most interesting person fresh from Fontainebleau. Ever your sincere friend and admirer   OSCAR

To Robert Ross

MS. Clark

[? *Late September 1899*] *Hôtel d'Alsace*

My dear Robbie, Thank you very much: I will take care not to die on the wrong date.

Could you wire me £5 on account tomorrow? I don't know when my allowance is really due, whether this week or the next. Of course you will deduct your fiver from your cheque, but I am in great want of it. Ever yours   OSCAR

To Robert Ross

MS. Clark

[? *Late September 1899*] *Hôtel d'Alsace*

Dear Robbie, Thanks for the cheque. Do let me see you on your way through Paris.

Are you serious about a postcard dated October 7th? Would not the postmark be noticed? I, of course, will do as you like.

Reggie was wonderful here, purple and perfect. The Boulevard, I regret to say, still talks of him.

I hope to write soon to you an interesting letter. This is a scrawl. Ever yours   OSCAR

To Robert Ross

MS. Clark

[? *Early October 1899*]

Dear Robbie, When do you arrive? Do spend a couple of days at any rate here.

I enclose a cutting from the *Cri de Paris*.

On the 7th I will send you a certificate of existence and vaccination.[1]

O.W.

Petit Bleu: To Will Rothenstein

MS. Rothenstein

Wednesday [*Postmark 4 October 1899*]   *Kalisaya* [*Paris*]

Dear Will, I have heard nothing from you, so I suppose you are busy. Do let us meet before you leave. My kindest regards to your dear wife, and also to the charming Celtic poet in colour.[2]   OSCAR

To Robert Ross

MS. Clark

7 October 1899[3]   *Hôtel d'Alsace*

My dear Robbie, I have to thank you for your kindness in sending me my allowance now due: I hope to thank you in person before long.

Will Rothenstein and his wife have been here, and we dined many times together. He has secured some wonderful drawings and casts from Rodin, and was in excellent spirits. Believe me, dear Robbie, your sincere friend   OSCAR WILDE

To Louis Wilkinson

MS. Hyde (H. M.)

[*Postmark 2 November 1899*]   *Hôtel d'Alsace*

Thanks so much, my dear boy, for your photographs. They interest me, fascinate me much: not merely because they show me *you*, as you are, but because they show me what *I* was in my Oxford days. I have photographs of myself just like, so like that many of my friends think on seeing your

---

[1] Cf. "I have also in my possession, you will be pleased to hear, certificates of Miss Cardew's birth, baptism, whooping cough, registration, vaccination, confirmation, and the measles; both the German and the English variety" (*The Importance of Being Earnest*, Act III).

[2] Augustus John, whom Rothenstein had taken to see Wilde in Paris.

[3] The comparative formality of this letter makes it look like the "certificate of existence", which Ross required on the 7th of the first month in each quarter as legal proof of Wilde's survival (cf. p. 831).

photographs that they are of me, twenty years ago; the hair, the brow, the *eyes*—all strangely like. The suggestion charms me, but *you* must not, in life at any rate, trail purple palls of tragedy, or be caught in evil nets of Fate.

I like your poem "To ——" very much: the one "with a moral" much less. Have you read *Jasper Tristram*? published by *Heinemann*.[1] It is about Radley obviously: there are two boys in it, one of them like you to look at, the other like you to listen to. Our age is full of mirrors and masks: if you have not read the book, order it. The early part—half Hellenic—is charming. Affectionately yours   OSCAR

To Louis Wilkinson
MS. Wilkinson

[*Postmark of receipt 28 November 1899*]

My dear Boy, My address is Hôtel d'Alsace, Rue des Beaux-Arts, Paris. Do send me your new photograph.

Did you ever receive a copy of my last play, *An Ideal Husband*? I told my publisher to send you one to Radley. I wrote your name on the title-page.

I think your poem "Hyacinthe" (I don't like the longer title) very beautiful indeed: a most delicate work of art.

I am afraid you are going to be a poet: how tragic! How terribly tragic! In the waters of Helicon there is death—the only death worth dying. Affectionately yours   OSCAR

To Florence Waller[2]
MS. Clark

[? *December 1899*]   *Grand Café, 14 Boulevard des Capucines, Paris*

Dear Mrs Waller, Thanks so much for your letter. I heard from many of my friends how wonderfully the play went, and how really great you and your husband were in the last act. The general silence of the papers is ignoble, and unjust to you as to me.

Yes, I shall be here all the month. Last year I was on the Riviera with roses, but this year I fear I shall have to stay in the icy north. One can't get railway-tickets on credit: it is such a bore!

It will be a great pleasure to see you again. You shall retell me your triumphs. Sincerely yours   OSCAR WILDE

[1] A novel by A. W. Clarke, published in 1899. The school in the story is certainly based on Radley.

[2] Florence West (1862–1912), English actress, married Lewis Waller 1883. In 1893–94 they had toured together in *A Woman of No Importance*, and Mrs Waller appears to have given at least one more performance about now. She had in fact separated from Waller some time before this.

To Robert Ross

MS. Clark

2 January 1900   *Hôtel d'Alsace*

Dear Robbie, I have to acknowledge with thanks the two cheques you have sent me for my income for December and January, £27. 10 in all.

Paris has been cold and wet, but I had a very pleasant Christmas.

Pray remember me to your mother: I was delighted to see her looking so well when she was in Paris. Ever yours   OSCAR WILDE

To Louis Wilkinson

MS. Hyde (H. M.)

[Postmark 4 January 1900]   *Hôtel d'Alsace*

My dear Boy, I am very glad you have met my Australian friend: he is a charming fellow. Remember me to him.

So you are coming abroad. I think it is an admirable idea. Radley had nothing left to teach you, though you could have taught it much: did so, I doubt not.

I fear you would not like my hotel. I live there because I have no money ever. It is an absurd place: it is not a background: the only thing really nice in the whole hotel is your own photograph: but one cannot, or one should not, play Narcissus to a photograph: even water is horribly treacherous: the eyes of one who loves one are the only mirror.

You asked me about "Melmoth:" of course I have not changed my name: in Paris I am as well known as in London: it would be childish. But to prevent postmen having fits I sometimes have my letters inscribed with the name of a curious novel by my grand-uncle, Maturin: a novel that was part of the romantic revival of the early century, and though imperfect, a pioneer: it is still read in France and Germany: Bentley republished it some years ago. I laugh at it, but it thrilled Europe, and is played as a play in modern Spain. Write soon. Ever your friend   OSCAR

To John Farrington[1]

7 February 1900   *Paris*

I enclose two new agreements. I have accepted all Miss Rehan's conditions as I am only too pleased to have my work presented by so brilliant an artist . . .

I have placed July 1st as the date on which if the play is not completed I am to return the money advanced. . . .

I hope to receive by return your cheque, and duplicate agreement signed.

[1] Theatrical agent of the firm of Farrington & Canby Ltd, of Adelphi House, Adam Street, London. There is no direct evidence that this incomplete letter

To Louis Wilkinson

MS. Hyde (H. M.)

[*Postmark 12 February 1900*]   *Hôtel d'Alsace*

My dear Boy, I am so glad that we are seemingly quite close to each other, at any rate without the "salt unplumbed estranging sea"[1] between us. I hope you are perfecting yourself in French: to read Greek and speak French are two of the greatest pleasures in the cultivation of Life.

If you have not read Georges Eekhoud's books—he is a Flamand—order them at once: *Mes Communions* and *Le Cycle Patibulaire*. The last has a wonderful story dedicated to me.[2]

Could you come to Paris for a few days? Do, if you can.

I am very sorry that you are in correspondence with Langrel Harris.[3] He is a most infamous young swindler, who selected *me*—of all ruined people—to swindle out of money. He is clever, but little more than a professional thief. He introduced himself to me, and induced me to make myself responsible for his hotel bills, left me to pay them, and stole money besides. What the French call *"un sale individu."* Don't write to him any more, or know him. But how *did* you know him? Please tell me by return. I hope you have read Paul Adam's *Basile et Sophia*, a coloured Byzantine novel, very terrible, and curious.[4] Also get a little book called *Mémoires d'un petit Gendelettre*, with a wonderful preface by Paul Adam.[5] The

---

(text from Maggs's catalogue 449 of 1924) is to him, but there exist in Clark two letters from Farrington to Wilde about *Mr and Mrs Daventry*. The first is dated 9 July 1900 and reads:

> Dear Mr Wilde, Miss Rehan is amazed and disappointed, but accepts the alternative.
>
> Re the return of her £100 she requests me to say that she will allow you the "little time" for repayment that you ask for. Yours faithfully
>
>   JOHN FARRINGTON

The second is dated 24 November 1900:

> Dear Sir, It is now many months since you promised to return the £100 I paid on account of Miss Ada Rehan, and Miss Rehan is urging me to collect the money for her.
>
> Will you kindly send on a cheque, and greatly oblige. Yours truly
>
>   JOHN FARRINGTON

[1] With the first two words transposed this is the last line of Matthew Arnold's poem "To Marguerite—Continued." Wilkinson was now at a tutor's in Brussels.

[2] The book was published in 1896. The story in it called *"Le Tribunal au Chauffoir"* is dedicated *"À Monsieur Oscar Wilde, au Poète et au Martyr Païen, torturé aux nom de la Justice et de la Vertu Protestantes."* In it a group of derelicts and criminals in a penitentiary discuss the origin of their misfortune. The most eloquent speaker is a star-crossed homosexual.

[3] I have failed to identify this curiously named character, of whom Louis Wilkinson has no recollection.

[4] Published 1900. In the *Revue Blanche* of 15 May 1895, between Wilde's trials, Paul Adam, French novelist (1862–1920), had contributed an article called *"L'Assaut Malicieux,"* which ended: *"Nos moralistes manquent d'habileté déductive. Si nous invoquons la seule justice, il n'est point d'hésitation à connaître. Entre l'adultère et le pédéraste, c'est au second que doit échoir notre indulgence. Il lèse moins."* The Lautrec drawing reproduced facing p. 383 appeared as an illustration to this article.

[5] *Le Livre d'un Petit Gendelettre* was published in 1900. Maurice Léon shot

author, Maurice Léon, committed suicide some months ago because he found that one could rarely speak the truth about others, never about one-self. He is a strange intellectual martyr, who died not for Faith but for Doubt.

Also, do come to Paris. I am ill and unhappy. The touch of your hand might heal me. Always affectionately yours   OSCAR

I am so glad you have found out my name.

To George Ives
MS. Clark

12 February [Postmark 1900]   *Hôtel d'Alsace*

My dear George, Thank you for the article, which is very suggestive and interesting.

Do, when again, if ever, you come to Paris let me know, and also let me know your address. Don't have with *me* the silly mania for secrecy that makes you miss the value of things: to you it is of more importance to conceal your address from a friend, than to see your friend.

You called on me twice, but would not leave either your name or address with the concierge: please don't do that again: I dislike to be told that a young man—you are still young of aspect—called twice, and refused to give his name. It annoys me.

Also, when you send me a *petit bleu* to ask me to make an appointment with you, please put your address: otherwise I can't reply. I received your *dépêche* all right, but could not answer.

As regards seeing you in private in preference to seeing you in public, the matter is indifferent to me as far as the place is concerned. It is a pleasure to me to see you. I don't invite my friends to my hotel because my room is cold and uncomfortable and I dislike it. The ordinary meeting-places are clubs in London and cafés in Paris. You must not imagine that people in cafés listen to the conversation of others; nobody bothers to do anything of the kind. People in life listen primarily to their own conversation, then to the conversation of the person or persons with whom they are, if the latter are interesting.

Your proposal that I should breakfast with you in a cabaret the other side of the Arc de Triomphe, frequented, you said, only by *cochers de fiacre* was too appalling. There are seemly inexpensive restaurants in proper quarters where two gentlemen can breakfast quietly, without the noisy and vulgar surroundings of your cabmen.

Nor, finally, have you and I, when we meet, to discuss business, which

---

himself at the age of nineteen. André Gide wrote of him (reprinted in *Prétextes*, 1903): "*Pour beaucoup l'intelligence a suffi; si Léon est mort, c'est donc qu'*elle commence à ne plus suffire. *Le suicide de Léon est important: il y a peu de temps encore on ne se serait pas tué pour cela . . . Hélas! Léon n'avait pas moins à dire que plusieurs autres d'aujourd'hui* et *qui vivent.—Léon fut plus consciencieux.*"

often requires privacy of a severe kind. I like to talk to you about literature, life, the progress of thought, its power to touch the world, its practical energy—subjects of no interest to others than ourselves. It is not necessary to go to a remote cabman's shelter for such discussions.

On the whole, George, you are a great baby. One can't help being angry with you. Ever yours OSCAR

To George Ives

MS. Texas

[*Postmark 22 February 1900*] *Hôtel d'Alsace*

My dear George, Thank you very much for the book: it's powerfully written. Of course it lacks style, but between Truth and Style there is always a *désaccord*, unless one is a poet. The ideas in the book are excellent, but the mode of presentation lacks charm. The book stimulates but does not win one. But I am glad to have it.

I know you *intended* to put your address in your telegram, but the habit, the bad habit, of secretiveness made you omit it. What a warning!

I have no doubt your little eating house, where the *cochers de fiacre* go, is delightful to you, but really George, it is hardly the place to invite others to. You should keep it as a private luxury, a cheap haven of unrest.

When you come again to Paris I hope you will breakfast with *me*. I know lots of nice, quiet, seemly places, where we can talk. *Rien n'est sacré à un cocher de fiacre*. Besides, they are revolting personally.

Bosie is over here, with his brother. They are in deep mourning and the highest spirits. The English are like that.[1]

I am delighted you are interested in the cover of your book. I always *began* with the cover. Ever yours OSCAR

To Leonard Smithers

MS. Morgan

[*Circa 24 February 1900*] [*Paris*]

My dear Smithers, I am greatly distressed to hear of Ernest's death: how sudden it must have been![2] Poor wounded wonderful fellow that he was, a tragic reproduction of all tragic poetry, like a symbol, or a scene. I hope bay-leaves will be laid on his tomb, and rue, and myrtle too, for he knew what love is.

He was a sweet singer, with a note all the lovelier because it reminds us of how thrushes sang in Shakespeare's day. If he is not yet laid to rest or unrest, do put some flowers for me on his grave.

---

[1] Their father, Lord Queensberry, had died on 31 January.

[2] Ernest Dowson died in Robert Sherard's house at Catford on 23 February 1900. He was buried in the Roman Catholic part of Lewisham Cemetery on 27 February.

I have been very ill, in bed since Monday, some disease with a hybrid-Greek name: it attacks the throat and the soul.

How is Althea?[1] Has she still the green wand? Ever yours

OSCAR WILDE

To Robert Ross

MS. Clark

Wednesday [? *28 February 1900*][2]   *Hôtel d'Alsace*

My dear Robbie, How could I have written to you during the last three months considering that I have been in bed since last Monday. I am very ill and the doctor is making all kinds of experiments. My throat is a lime kiln, my brain a furnace and my nerves a coil of angry adders. I am apparently in much the same state as yourself.

Maurice—you remember Maurice?—has kindly come to see me and I've shared all my medicines with him, shown him what little hospitality I can. We are both horrified to hear that Bosie's suspicions of you are quite justified. That and your being a Protestant make you terribly *unique* (I have told Maurice how to spell the last word as I was afraid that he might have used a word which often occurs in the Protestant bible).[3]

Aleck[4] lunched with Bosie and me one day and I lunched alone with him another. He was most friendly and pleasant and gave me a depressing account of you. I see that you, like myself, have become a *neurasthenic*. I have been so for four months, quite unable to get out of bed till the afternoon, quite unable to write letters of any kind. My doctor has been trying to cure me with arsenic and strychnine but without much success, as I became poisoned through eating mussels, so you see what an exacting and tragic life I have been leading. Poisoning by mussels is very painful and when one has one's bath one looks like a leopard. Pray never eat mussels.

As soon as I get well I'll write you a long letter, though your letter asking me to stay with you in Rome never reached me.

Thanks so much for the cheque, but your letter was really too horrid. With love, ever yours   OSCAR

To Reginald Turner

MS. Hyde (D. & M.)

Friday [*Postmark 9 March 1900*]   *In Bed, Paris*

Dear Reggie, I suppose Maurice has by this time arrived. Of course his

<hr>

[1] Althea Gyles, English artist (1868–1948). She illustrated an edition of Wilde's poem "The Harlot's House," which Smithers (masquerading as the Mathurin Press) published in 1904.

[2] Although this letter was dated November 1900 by Ledger, and has long been accepted as Wilde's last surviving letter, the references to having been in bed since Monday with a bad throat tally exactly with the preceding letter, and the references to mussel-poisoning and Rome prove that it was written before Wilde's visit to Rome. It is in another hand (clearly Maurice Gilbert's) except for the last eighteen words, which are in Wilde's.   [3] Presumably eunuch.   [4] Aleck Ross.

place was by my side, as I am very ill, but he longed to see the Queen, so I gave in.[1] He has been most sweet and kind to me, quite a darling boy, and looked after me in every way. When he is away from the chilling torpedo-touch of Strong he is quite as nice as he used to be.

I hear you volunteered for the front at 5 a.m. at the Cecil,[2] intoxicated by Bosie and Perrier-Jouet '89, but subsequently felt that duty called you to stay in the Fleet Street Kopje.[3] Quite right—the pen is more dangerous than the sword.

Do write to me. Ever yours   OSCAR

"*Boucher*" has *three* years for theft. *Joseph* is still in durance. All is well.

To Charles Wyndham
MS. Albery

[? *March 1900*]   *Hôtel d'Alsace*

My dear Wyndham, I am sorry I have not been able to write to you, but I have been suffering from a sort of blood-poisoning, owing I fear to the insanitary state of my hotel, and had to go to a private hospital for ten days. I am quite well now, and am anxious to get away from my hotel as soon as I can pay them, and go into the country.

I have been re-reading *La Dame de Monsoreau*[4] with the idea of the drama, but I think that it is too tragic in idea for your theatre, and that the part of the jester would always be overshadowed by that of Bussy-d'Amboise, the real, the only hero. I don't quite know whether the Charles II play that has been submitted to you really cuts across our lines or not. It would be a far more congenial part for you than that of Chicot. And I would sooner work at that, in case you do not take the other Nell Gwynn play. Of course you could not produce two Charles II plays. Perhaps I had better try to think out an original plot, but I must get away, if possible to the south, where I could work in peace, and, of course, I have no money; my £2. 10 a week only just enables me to drag on in endless anxiety about the necessaries of daily life.

You will, I am sure, consider what you can do for me, and also give me time. Sincerely and gratefully yours   OSCAR WILDE

---

[1] On 7, 8 and 9 March 1900 Queen Victoria drove through London in an un-official victory parade to mark the turning of the tide in the Boer War (Ladysmith had been relieved on 28 February). "Everywhere the same enormous crowds and incessant demonstrations of enthusiasm," she wrote in her journal; "if possible, even beyond that of the two Jubilees."

[2] A large hotel, famous for conviviality, on the south side of the Strand. Shell-Mex House was built on its site.

[3] A Cape Dutch word, meaning a low hill, which had been much used in Boer War despatches.

[4] A historical novel of the time of Henri III by Dumas *père*, first published in eight volumes in 1846, and known in English as *Chicot the Jester*.

To Robert Ross

MS. Clark

Thursday [Late March 1900]   *Grand Café, 14 Boulevard des Capucines,*
Paris

Dear Robbie, I am so annoyed at your not writing to me every day that I must come and talk to you.

Mellor, with whom I am now friends (below zero of course) has invited me to go to Italy to the extent of £50! When that gives out I shall have to walk home, but as I want to see you, I have consented to go, and hope to be in Rome in about ten days. It will be delightful to be together again, and this time I really must become a Catholic, though I fear that if I went before the Holy Father with a blossoming rod it would turn at once into an umbrella or something dreadful of that kind. It is absurd to say that the age of miracles is past. It has not yet begun.

Your story of dear Rowland is charming. How dangerous it is to be called "John" is the moral. Anything may happen to a person called John.[1]

You have not yet broken to me the impression I produced on Aleck. I suppose it was painful. All went well till an unlucky thing occurred.

Only an hour after I, with "waving hands" like Tennyson's Vivien,[2] had evolved a new evangel of morals, dear Aleck passed before the little *café* behind the Madeleine, and saw me with a beautiful boy in grey velvet —half rough, all Hylas. Alas, the eye he turned on me was not the sightless one.[3] His smile was terrible. It was like one of Besant's novels.

I really felt it very much. At luncheon I had been singularly ethical. I am always ethical at the Café de la Paix.

Wire, or write at once to me, chez Mellor, Gland, Vaud, and tell me a good hotel. Also bed out some Narcissi. It is their season.

With best love, dear horrid irritating Robbie, yours   OSCAR

Postcard: To Reginald Turner

MS. Hyde (D. & M.)

2 April [1900]   *Palermo*

Dear Reggie, Arrived this morning. Lovely weather. Hope you are well, and Maurice also.   O. W.

---

[1] John Fothergill. See note 2, p. 623.

[2] For Merlin, overtalk'd and overworn,
Had yielded, told her all the charm, and slept.

Then, in one moment, she put forth the charm
Of woven paces and of waving hands,
And in the hollow oak he lay as dead,
And lost to life and use and name and fame.
    (*Idylls of the King*)

[3] Aleck Ross had lost the sight of one eye in early youth.

To Robert Ross

MS. Clark

16 April [*1900*]   *c/o Cook & Son, Piazza di Spagna, Rome*

My dear Robbie, I simply cannot write. It is too horrid, not *of* me, but *to* me. It is a mode of paralysis—a *cacoethes tacendi*[1]—the one form that malady takes in me.

Well, all passed over very successfully. Palermo, where we stayed eight days, was lovely. The most beautifully situated town in the world, it dreams away its life in the Conca d'Oro, the exquisite valley that lies between two seas. The lemon-groves and the orange-gardens were so entirely perfect that I became again a Pre-Raphaelite, and loathed the ordinary Impressionists, whose muddy souls and blurred intelligences would have rendered but by mud and blur those "golden lamps hung in a green night"[2] that filled me with such joy. The elaborate and exquisite detail of the true Pre-Raphaelites is the compensation they offer us for the absence of motion; Literature and Music being the only arts that are not immobile.

Then nowhere, not even at Ravenna, have I seen such mosaics. In the Cappella Palatina, which from pavement to domed ceilings is all gold, one really feels as if one was sitting in the heart of a great honeycomb *looking* at angels singing; and looking at angels, or indeed at people singing, is much nicer than listening to them. For this reason the great artists always give to their angels lutes without strings, pipes without vent-holes, and reeds through which no wind can wander or make whistlings.

Monreale you have heard of, with its cloisters and cathedral. We often drove there, the *cocchieri* most dainty finely-carved boys. In them, not in the Sicilian horses, is race seen. The most favoured were Manuele, Francesco, and Salvatore. I loved them all, but only remember Manuele.

I also made great friends with a young Seminarist who lived *in* the Cathedral of Palermo, he and eleven others in little rooms beneath the roof, like birds.

Every day he showed me all over the Cathedral, and I really knelt before the huge porphyry sarcophagus in which Frederick the Second lies. It is a sublime bare monstrous thing, blood-coloured, and held up by lions, who have caught some of the rage of the great Emperor's restless soul. At first, my young friend, Giuseppe Loverde by name, gave *me* information: but on the third day I gave information to him, and re-wrote History as usual, and told him all about the Supreme King and his Court of Poets, and the terrible book that he never wrote.[3] Giuseppe was fifteen, and most

---

[1] Craving for silence. Cf. the *scribendi cacoethes* (itch for writing) of Juvenal, Satire VII, 52.

[2] He hangs in shades the Orange bright
Like golden Lamps in a green Night.
(Andrew Marvell: "Bermudas")

[3] Frederick II (1194–1250), Roman Emperor, King of Sicily and Jerusalem, popularly known as *Stupor Mundi*. Italian poetry, according to Dante, was born

sweet. His reason for entering the Church was singularly mediaeval. I asked him why he thought of becoming a *clerico*: and how.

He answered "My father is a cook, and most poor, and we are many at home, so it seemed to me a good thing that there should be in so small a house as ours one mouth less to feed, for, though I am slim, I eat much: too much, alas! I fear."

I told him to be comforted, because God used poverty often as a means of bringing people to Him, and used riches never, or but rarely. So Giuseppe was comforted, and I gave him a little book of devotion, very pretty, and with far more pictures than prayers in it; so of great service to Giuseppe, whose eyes are beautiful. I also gave him many *lire*, and prophesied for him a Cardinal's hat, if he remained very good, and never forgot me. He said he never would: and indeed I don't think he will, for every day I kissed him behind the high altar.

At Naples we stopped three days. Most of my friends are, as you know, in prison, but I met some of nice memory, and fell in love with a Sea-God, who for some extraordinary reason is at the Regia Marina School, instead of being with Triton.

We came to Rome on Holy Thursday. H. M. left on Saturday for Gland, and yesterday,[1] to the terror of Grissell[2] and all the Papal Court, I appeared in the front rank of the pilgrims in the Vatican, and got the blessing of the Holy Father[3]—a blessing they would have denied me.

He was wonderful as he was carried past me on his throne, not of flesh and blood, but a white soul robed in white, and an artist as well as a saint —the only instance in History, if the newspapers are to be believed.

I have seen nothing like the extraordinary grace of his gesture, as he rose, from moment to moment, to bless—possibly the pilgrims, but certainly me. Tree should see him. It is his only chance.

I was deeply impressed, and my walking-stick showed signs of budding; would have budded indeed, only at the door of the chapel it was taken from me by the Knave of Spades. This strange prohibition is, of course, in honour of Tannhäuser.[4]

How did I get the ticket? By a miracle, of course. I thought it was hopeless, and made no effort of any kind. On Saturday afternoon at five o'clock Harold and I went to have tea at the Hôtel de l'Europe. Suddenly, as I was eating buttered toast, a man, or what seemed to be one, dressed like a hotel porter, entered and asked me would I like to see the Pope on Easter Day. I bowed my head humbly and said *"Non sum dignus,"* or words to that effect. He at once produced a ticket!

---

at his court, and he was suspected by the Papal party of writing a book called *De Tribus Impostoribus* (the three impostors—Moses, Jesus and Mahomet).

[1] Easter Day 1900 was on 15 April.

[2] See note 1, p. 49.   [3] Leo XIII (1810–1903), Pope from 1878.

[4] Wilde several times referred to Tannhäuser's pilgrimage as a penitent to Rome, and the blossoming of the Pope's staff (see Act III of Wagner's opera). Cf. *The Ballad of Reading Gaol*, section IV:

> Since the barren staff the pilgrim bore
> Bloomed in the great Pope's sight.

When I tell you that his countenance was of supernatural ugliness, and that the price of the ticket was thirty pieces of silver, I need say no more.

An equally curious thing is that whenever I pass the hotel, which I do constantly, I see the same man. Scientists call that phenomenon an obsession of the visual nerve. You and I know better.

On the afternoon of Easter Day I heard vespers at the Lateran: music quite lovely: at the close a Bishop in red, and with red gloves—such as Pater talks of in *Gaston de Latour*—came out on the balcony and showed us the relics.[1] He was swarthy, and wore a yellow mitre. A sinister mediaeval man, but superbly Gothic, just like the Bishops carved on stalls or on portals. And when one thinks that once people mocked at stained-glass attitudes! They are the only attitudes for the clothed. The sight of this Bishop, whom I watched with fascination, filled me with the sense of the great realism of Gothic art. Neither in Greek nor in Gothic art is there any pose. Posing was invented by bad portrait-painters, and the first person who ever posed was a stockbroker, and he has gone on ever since.

Homer talks much—a little too much—of you. He slightly suspects you of treachery, and your immediate return seems to him problematical. Your allusion to his conduct on a postcard was mysterious. How was the "revision" painful?

I have added one Pietro Branca-d'Oro to the group. He is dark, and gloomy, and I love him very much.

I send you a photograph I took on Palm Sunday at Palermo. Do send me some of yours, and love me always, and try to read this letter. It is a labour of a week to read it.

Kindest regards to your dear mother. Always   OSCAR

To Edouard Dupoirier
MS. Clark

[*Postmark 18 April 1900*][2]   *chez Cook et Fils, Rome*

Mon cher Patron, Je ne retournerai pas avant le premier juin, et par conséquence vous pouvez louer mon appartement: c'est inutile de le garder, et sans doute vous aurez beaucoup de touristes au mois de mai pour l'Exposition.

Je vous prie d'avoir la bonté de conserver toutes mes choses pour moi, comme vous l'avez fait l'année passée.

J'espère que Madame et la petite se portent bien.

Je vous remercie pour mes lettres.

Recevez mes compliments.   SEBASTIAN MELMOTH

[1] There is a bishop in *Gaston de Latour*, but the colour of his gloves is not mentioned. Wilde was probably confusing him with the Bishop of Auxerre in Pater's "Denys L'Auxerrois" (in *Imaginary Portraits*, 1887), who, "in vestments of deep red in honour of the relics, blessed the new shrine . . . At last from a little narrow chest, into which the remains [of the saint] had been almost crushed together, the bishop's red-gloved hands drew the dwindled body."

[2] So dated in Anderson Galleries catalogue 2047 (1926).

To Robert Ross
MS. Clark

Saturday [21 April 1900]   *Rome*

My dear Robbie, A thousand thanks for all your trouble. The cheque arrived safely this morning.

Of course I got your telegram, from Milan, and wrote to you at the Hôtel Cavour—a long, interesting, and of course seriously compromising letter. Should it fall into the hands of the authorities you will be immortal.

I have not seen the Holy Father since Thursday, but am bearing up wonderfully well. I am sorry to say he has approved of a dreadful handkerchief, with a portrait of himself in the middle, and basilicas at the corners. It is very curious the connection between Faith and bad art: I feel it myself. Where I see the Pope I admire Bernini: but Bernini had a certain dash and life and assertion—theatrical life, but life for all that: the handkerchief is a dead thing.[1]

By the way, did I tell you that on Easter Sunday I was completely cured of my mussel-poisoning? It is true, and I always knew I would be. Five months under a Jewish physician at Paris not merely did not heal me, but made me worse: the blessing of the Vicar of Christ made me whole. Armand Point, the French painter, a bad Botticelli-Jones artist, is here, and has promised to do me a *tabella votiva*. The only difficulty is the treatment of the mussels. They are not decorative, except the shells, and I didn't eat the shells.

I have been three times to see the great Velasquez of the Pamfili Pope: it is quite the grandest portrait in the world. The entire man is there.[2] I also go to look at that beautiful voluptuous marble boy I went to worship with you at the Museo Nazionale. What a lovely thing it is!

I have given up Armando, a very smart elegant young Roman Sporus. He was beautiful, but his requests for raiment and neckties were incessant: he really bayed for boots, as a dog moonwards. I now like Arnaldo: he was Armando's greatest friend, but the friendship is over. Armando is *un invidioso*[3] apparently, and is suspected of having stolen a lovely covertcoat in which he patrols the Corso. The coat is so delightful, and he looks so handsome in it, that, although the coat wasn't mine, I have forgiven him the theft.

Omero has never received your letter. I need not say I have not given him your London address—at least not your real one: he now believes that your real name is Edmondo Gosse, and that your address is the Savile. I also added that some of your more intimate friends prefer to write to you

---

[1] Giovanni Lorenzo Bernini (1598–1680), Italian painter, sculptor and architect, designed the palace of Pope Urban VIII and the great colonnade of St Peter's.

[2] This portrait of Pope Innocent X (1574–1655) hangs in the Doria Palace in Rome.

[3] Jealous.

as   Reginaldo Turner
                Avvocato
             The Reform Club:

but that I, from old associations, prefer to address you as

             Sir Wemyss Reid,

so I fancy there will be many interesting letters arriving in London.

Yesterday a painful thing happened. You know the terrible, the awe-inspiring effect that Royalty has on me: well, I was outside the Caffè Nazionale taking iced coffee with *gelato*—a most delightful drink—when the King drove past. I at once stood up, and made him a low bow, with hat doffed—to the admiration of some Italian officers at the next table. It was only when the King had passed that I remembered I was *Papista* and *Nerissimo*![1] I was greatly upset: however I hope the Vatican won't hear about it.

I enclose you a little cutting that appeared in Palermo while I was there. My incognito vanished in three hours, and the students used to come to the café to talk—or rather to listen. To their great delight I always denied my identity. On being asked my name, I said every man has only one name. They asked me what name that was. "Io"[2] was my answer. This was regarded as a wonderful reply, containing in it all philosophy.

Rome is burning with heat: really terrible: but at 4.30 I am going to the Borghese, to look at daisies, and drink milk: the Borghese milk is as wonderful as the Borghese daisies. I also intend to photograph Arnaldo. By the way, can you photograph cows well? I did one of cows in the Borghese so marvellous that I destroyed it: I was afraid of being called the modern Paul Potter.[3] Cows are very fond of being photographed, and, unlike architecture, don't move.

I propose to go to Orvieto tomorrow: I have never seen it, and I must revisit Tivoli. How long I shall stay here I don't know—a fortnight perhaps.

Write always to Cook's. Love to More and Reggie. Ever yours OSCAR

To Robert Ross

MS. Clark

[*22 April 1900*]   [*Rome*]

Dear little Robbie, I enclose the Sicilian cutting. I forgot it of course: it is pleasant to pluck praise in the meadows of Persephone—recognition by asphodels.

Need I say that I see the Holy Father again tomorrow? I am thrilled with the prospect of an old pleasure, and I am promised a seat for the canonisation, or beatification, on the 24th. Rome is hot, so I don't know

[1] Very black. A term in use amongst the Roman nobility, meaning ultra-Catholic. There was at this time a great antipathy between regal and Papal circles, and the Pope was known as the Prisoner in the Vatican.
[2] Italian for I.   [3] Dutch animal painter (1625–54).

that I can stay, but I would like to go. It would annoy the withered Grissell, and fill me with holy joy.

Yesterday I went to *Albano*: how lovely it is! The day was beautiful, and the silent waveless lake a mirror of turquoise. It was wise enough to reflect nothing but its own beauty: would that the same could be said of all mirrors.

Omero was with me, and Armando, forgiven for the moment. He is so absurdly like the Apollo Belvedere that I feel always as if I was Winckelmann when I am with him.[1] His lips are the same, his hair, his somewhat vulgar, because quite obvious, pride; and he also represents that decadence of the triumph of the face over the body, never seen in great Greek art. Witness the thighs of Theseus, the breasts and flanks of Hermes.

His body is slim, dandy-like, elegant, and without a single great curve. He has not come out of the womb of giant circles.

I am at the Roma, the first time for ten days. Would you were here. Do you observe that I have fallen in love with you again? Our Indian winter. Ever yours

OSCAR

To More Adey
MS. Clark

[*Postmark 26 April 1900*]　　　　　　　　　　*c/o Cook and Son, Rome*

My dear More, I hear with great regret from Robbie of the loss you have sustained.[2] You were so kind to *my* mother, so sympathetic and gentle in your delicate attentions to her up to the last, that I know you will let me express my sorrow at the death of *your* mother: it seems to me that I have almost a right to do so: for friends have all things in common.

I wish you could come out here: one is healed at Rome of every trouble: and I should like to go with you to the Vatican, where I hope you will some day walk gravely in mediaeval dress, with the gold chain of office, and guide pilgrims to the feet of the Pope.

I do nothing but see the Pope: I have already been blessed many times, once in the private Chapel of the Vatican.

He, as I wrote to Robbie, is no longer of flesh and blood: he has no taint of mortality: he is like a white soul robed in white. I spend all my money in getting tickets: for, now, as in old days, men rob the pilgrims in Rome. The robbing is chiefly done by hotel porters, or rather by real robbers disguised as hotel porters, and it is perhaps right that heretics should be mulcted, for we are not of the fold.

My position is curious: I am not a Catholic: I am simply a violent Papist. No one could be more "black" than I am. I have given up bowing to the King. I need say no more.

The weather is entrancing, and the Borghese Gardens, from which I

---

[1] Johann Joachim Winckelmann (1717–68), German archaeologist, historian and in some sense re-discoverer of Greek art. Lived for many years in Rome. Pater devoted a long chapter to him in *Studies in the History of the Renaissance* (1873).

[2] Adey's mother had died on 9 April.

have just come, too lovely for words—for prose rather, for birds sing its praises all day long. The long grass-glades are powdered with the silver and gold of meadow-flowers, and the trees tremble with music. Each leaf is as a note: the groves are symphonies.

Sicily was beautiful: and the golden chapel at Palermo—all Byzantine mosaic—the marvel of marvels: when one was in it one felt as if one was in a precious shrine, consecrated almost in a tabernacle. Naples was evil and luxurious. Rome is the one city of the soul.[1]

I am writing from a tiny café in front of the Fontana Trevi: the sound of the waters is wonderful: it soothes: it has κάθαρσις.

Robbie left me a legacy of a youthful guide, who knows nothing about Rome. Omero is his name, and I am showing him Rome.

Goodbye for the present, dear More, and believe me always affectionately yours   OSCAR

To Robert Ross
MS. Clark

Vendredi [27 April 1900][2]   [*Rome*]

Dear Robbie, Would it bore you awfully to send me my allowance in an order on Cook here? It takes a week to cash a cheque. I know it will bore you, but then you are a little saint, not, I am glad to say, in conduct, which is nothing, but in soul, which is all.

I am so glad you told me about More's loss. I had the chance of writing to him about all his sweet courteous gentle kindness to my own mother. He is so good to others, that one feels it is vulgar to praise him to himself, and to praise him to others unnecessary. I hope to see him in the Vatican, *not* as the Knave of Spades, but mediaeval, or rather Renaissance, ruff and gold chain, and the sombre splendour of black raiment: a Spanish fashion, I believe. All the people at the Vatican try to look like More: that they succeed is their fault rather than his.

Today, on coming out of the Vatican Gallery, Greek gods and the Roman middle-classes in my brain, all marble to make the contrast worse, I found that the Vatican Gardens were open to the Bohemian and the Portuguese pilgrims. I at once spoke both languages fluently, explained that my English dress was a form of penance, and entered that waste, desolate park, with its faded Louis XIV gardens, its sombre avenues, its sad woodland. The peacocks screamed, and I understood why tragedy dogged the gilt feet of each pontiff. But I wandered in exquisite melancholy for an hour. One Philippo, a student, whom I culled in the Borgia room, was with me: not for many years has Love walked in the Pope's pleasaunce.

I have been reading dear Aylmer Vallance on Burne-Jones—his decorative side. It is most delightful.[3] No more paper. Always yours   OSCAR

[1] Oh, Rome! my Country! City of the Soul!" (Byron, *Childe Harold*, 4, lxxviii).
[2] Ledger's date.
[3] *The Decorative Art of Burne-Jones*, by Aylmer Vallance, was published as the Easter Art Annual of the *Studio* in 1900.

To Robert Ross

MS. Clark

Thursday [*May 1900*]   *Rome*

Dearest Robbie, Your telegram just arrived: its deciphering was most fascinating work: we all felt like the archaeologists over the stone at the Lapis Niger: which stone I believe to be an early example of Roman humour: Fescennine licence it was called later on.[1]

I wrote to you yesterday, to the Cavour. Today is wet and stormy, but I have again seen the Holy Father. Each time he dresses differently; it is most delightful. Today over his white and purple a velvet cape edged with ermine, and a huge scarlet and gold stole. I was deeply moved as usual.

I gave a ticket to a new friend, *Dario*. I like his name so much: it was the first time he had ever seen the Pope: and he transferred to me his adoration of the successor of Peter: would I fear have kissed me on leaving the Bronze Gateway had I not sternly repelled him. I have become very cruel to boys, and no longer let them kiss me in public.

The pilgrims arrive in great black swarms: I am sure that Pharaoh was punished by a plague of them: some of them, however, go mad. Three cases yesterday. They are much envied by their more sane brethren.

I wish you would write to me about Venice: it is really absurd: is it due to Symonds? Renters in gondolas are grotesque.

How is dear More? He was missed as usual at the Vatican. Carlyle Stebbing does not suit St Peter's; its astounding proportions *increase* his size: it is most curious.[2] Write soon. Ever yours   OSCAR

To Robert Ross

MS. Clark

14 May [*1900*]   *Rome*

Dearest Robbie, You never write to me now, so I don't know if it is worth while informing you of my movements. However, I leave Rome tomorrow for Naples, thence by boat to Genoa, thence to Chambéry, where Harold Mellor awaits me, or should do so, with his automobile—and so to Paris. I suppose one of us will arrive safe; I hope it will be me.

Rome has quite absorbed me. I must winter here; it is the only city of the soul. I have been to Albano, and Nemi, and Tivoli, and seen much of Armand Point, who is really a dear fellow, gay and romantic, simple and intellectually subtle, with an inordinate passion for beauty in its most complete expression, and an inordinate love of life.

My photographs are now so good that in my moments of mental

[1] The Lapis Niger is the legendary sepulchre of Romulus in the Comitium, adjoining the Forum. In 1899 a black pavement was excavated nearby.

[2] Wilde is clearly referring to Carlisle James Scott Spedding (1852–1915), who in 1894 was appointed Private Chamberlain of the Sword and Cloak to Pope Leo XIII. Spedding is said to have been one of the greatest bores of his time.

depression (alas! not rare) I think that I was intended to be a photographer. But I shake off the mood, and know that I was made for more terrible things of which colour is an element.

Today I bade goodbye, with tears and one kiss, to the beautiful Greek boy who was found in my garden—I mean in Nero's garden. He is the nicest boy you ever introduced to me.

In the mortal sphere I have fallen in and out of love, and fluttered hawks and doves alike. How evil it is to buy Love, and how evil to sell it! And yet what purple hours one can snatch from that grey slowly-moving thing we call Time! My mouth is twisted with kissing, and I feed on fevers. The Cloister or the Café—there is my future. I tried the Hearth, but it was a failure. Ever yours   OSCAR

Write to Paris

To Robert Ross
MS. Clark

[*May-June 1900*]   *Hôtel d'Alsace, Paris*

Dearest Robbie, I have at last arrived. I stayed ten days with Harold Mellor at Gland: the automobile was delightful, but, of course, it broke down: they, like all machines, are more wilful than animals—nervous, irritable, strange things: I am going to write an article on "nerves in the inorganic world."

Frank Harris is here, also Bosie. I asked Bosie what you suggested—without naming any sum at all—after dinner. He had just won £400 at the races, and £800 a few days before, so he was in high spirits. When I spoke to him he went into paroxysms of rage, followed by satirical laughter, and said it was the most monstrous suggestion he had ever heard, that he would do nothing of the kind, that he was astounded at my suggesting such a thing, that he did not recognise I had any claim of any kind on him. He was really revolting: I was quite disgusted. I told Frank Harris about it, and he was greatly surprised: but made the wise observation "One should never ask for anything: it is always a mistake." He said I should have got someone to sound Bosie, and ask him for me. I had also the same idea, but you did not seem to like the prospect of a correspondence with Bosie where money was concerned, and I am not surprised.

It is a most horrible and really heart-breaking affair. When I remember his letters at Dieppe, his assurances of eternal devotion, his entreaties that I should always live with him, his incessant offers of all his life and belongings, his desire to atone in some way for the ruin he and his family brought on me—well, it sickens me, it gives me nausea.

The affair occurred in the Café de la Paix, so, of course, I made no scene. I said that if he did not recognise my claim there was nothing more to be said.

We dined last night with Frank Harris at Maire's. I was quite as usual, but he[1] really is, now that he has money, become mean, and narrow, and

[1] i.e. Douglas.

828

greedy. He always accused you of having the bourgeois commercial view of money, instead of the generous, chivalrous, aristocratic view, but he really has out-Heroded Herod this time. "I can't afford to spend anything except on myself" was one of his observations. I thought of you, and dear More, and all your generosity and chivalry and sacrifice for me. It is an ugly thing; it taints life.

Send me my cheque, like a good boy. Ever yours   OSCAR
I am horrified about Smithers. It really is too bad.[1]

To Robert Ross
MS. Clark

[*June 1900*]   [*Paris*]

Dear Robbie, Thanks for cheque.

Frank Harris has spoken to Bosie, who now seems to have more sense of the situation, and what he should do: his only fear was that he had spent all his money! But he cannot be serious. So if you write to him, perhaps it would be better to say how pleased you are to hear from me that he is going to arrange some scheme for me.

Why doesn't Reggie come to Paris? All his enemies are in prison— "*Le Boucher*" for robbery with violence, "Joseph" for attempted murder. Joseph was Ashton's pet boy.

Frank Harris is very wonderful and really very good and *sympathique*. He always comes two hours late for meals, but in spite of that is delightful. He keeps Bosie in order: the age of miracles is clearly not over.

The only ugly thing at the Exhibition is the public.[2] The most beautiful modern picture is Shannon's portrait of himself. I have gone several times to see it.[3] Ever yours   OSCAR

To Frank Harris
MS. Texas

20 June 1900   *Pavillon d'Armenonville, Bois de Boulogne*

My dear Frank, It is quite understood that in the case of our collaboration in the play *Love is Law*,[4] to our mutual satisfaction, all business transactions

---

[1] Smithers's financial collapse had begun, though he was not officially adjudged bankrupt until 18 September.

[2] The Paris Exhibition of 1900 was open from 14 April to 5 November.

[3] This picture, painted in 1897 and known as *A Man in a Black Shirt*, is now in the National Portrait Gallery.

[4] One of the suggested titles for the play which eventually appeared as *Mr and Mrs Daventry*. The original idea was entirely Wilde's, as written to Alexander in 1894 (see p. 360), but the final play was written by Frank Harris alone. Before and during the negotiations with Harris, Wilde had sold some sort of options on the play to Mrs Brown-Potter, Horace Sedger, Ada Rehan, Louis Nethersole, and Smithers (see p. 847). The play was first published in 1956, with a full introduction by H. Montgomery Hyde, discussing this whole perplexed matter.

are to be directed by you, with the reservation of Mrs Brown-Potter's rights,[1] to be arranged by you. Ever yours   OSCAR WILDE

To Robert Ross
MS. Clark

Wednesday [? *27 June 1900*][2]   [*Paris*]

Dear Robbie, Thanks so much for the photographs: you photograph nearly as well as I do. What an art it is! Your only rival in titles is Rossetti.

Do tell me about Reggie. Was he the victim of a painful and unfounded charge? I know such charges are constantly made, and always against innocent people.

Smithers appeared here with his new mistress. She is quite clean, and charmingly dressed. We went to the Exhibition one night. Mellor was with me. He doesn't like Mellor. He tried to explain about you: he is a pleasant, plausible *ruffiano*: and one touch of comedy sends morality and moralising sky-high. I do hope you will get back your money. Smithers attributes his ruin to Percy Douglas and Strangman!

I dined with Vincent O'Sullivan last night: he was really very pleasant, for one who treats life from the standpoint of the tomb. He was much amused at my asking him where Walter Pollock was "taking" the whiskies and waters now?

Please send me my cheque *at once*: pray do this. Love to Reg. Ever yours
OSCAR

To Robert Ross
MS. Clark

[? *Circa 29 June 1900*]   [*Paris*]

My dear Robbie, Thanks for the cheque. I enclose receipt.[3]

I am horrified at what you tell me about Grissell: its impertinence, its

---

[1] The words "Mrs Brown-Potter's rights" have been ineffectively scored through, probably by Harris. Mrs James Brown-Potter, *née* Cora Urquhart (1859–1936), was one of the first American society women to become a professional actress. In 1887 Wilde had written in the *Court and Society Review*: "With regard to Mrs Brown-Potter, as acting is no longer considered absolutely essential for success on the English stage, there is really no reason why the pretty bright-eyed lady who charmed us all last June by her merry laugh and her nonchalant ways should not—to borrow an expression from her native language—make a big book and paint the town red." She later went into management, and was one of several who bought an option on *Mr and Mrs Daventry*. On 22 March 1900 she wrote: "Dear Mr Wilde, When will you give me over my play? Don't you think I have been very patient with you about it? Let me hear from you by return post. Truly, Cora Potter."

[2] Ledger dates this letter August, but the references to photography and (in the next letter, which was clearly written within a few days) to Grissell make it more suitable to June, when Wilde had recently been in Rome. Mellor seems to have driven him back to Paris (and stayed there) at the beginning of June, and again, after Wilde's further visit to Gland, in August.

[3] Possibly an acknowledgment of Ross's cheque (MS. Clark) for £17.10.0., dated

Rome, 1900

Robert Ross and Reginald Turner

coarseness, its lack of imagination: I should really write to him if I were you. He who seven times sought and seven times received the blessing of the Holy Father is not to be excommunicated on postcards by the withered eunuch of the Vatican Latrines. (By "He" I mean myself.)

It is a curious, and therefore natural thing, but I cannot stand Christians because they are never Catholics, and I cannot stand Catholics because they are never Christians. Otherwise I am at one with the Indivisible Church.

By the way, I suppose the great revival of architecture, Gothic and Renaissance, was due simply to the fact that God found he could only live in temples made by hands: in the heart of man he could not live, he was not the first.

I have seen Maurice lately; we spent two evenings at the Exhibition. He was pale, and sweet, and gentle. He now forms part of a *ménage à trois*: none of the members sleep: the girl—a rose-like thing I hope—lies in the middle, and knows the pleasure and insecurity of the *Via Media*. Maurice won't tell me the name of the other partner, but admits he has a slight moustache. He does odd jobs for Strong, and quarrels with him incessantly. I find I am very fond of Maurice still. He is a dear fellow.

From your silence about Reggie my worst suspicions are confirmed: is it a sprightly lady-journalist who led him astray? Or was it one of those typical English women with their "fatal gift of duty"?[1]

Bosie I have not seen for a week. I feel sure he will do nothing. Boys, brandy, and betting monopolise his soul. He is really a miser: but his method of hoarding is spending: a new type.

Love to R. Ever yours   OSCAR

To Robert Ross[2]

7 July 1900   *Hôtel d'Alsace*

Dear Robbie, Thank you for the cheque which represents my quarterly income. It is very good of you to take care of this for me.

The exhibition is very delightful and all the old works of art quite wonderful. Rodin has a pavilion to himself and showed me anew all his great dreams in marble. He is by far the greatest poet in France, and has, as I was glad to tell myself, completely outshone Victor Hugo. Ever yours

OSCAR

---

27 June 1900 and endorsed Sebastian Melmoth. The official receipt may well have been the next letter, which Wilde dated 7 July, because Ross needed proof of his survival to satisfy the lawyers (cf. note 3, p. 811).

[1] Cf. "Italia! oh, Italia! thou who hast
       The fatal gift of Beauty."
                  (Byron, *Childe Harold*, 4, xlii)

[2] The original of this letter has disappeared, but it was among those which Ross showed to Meyerfeld, who translated it into German and published it in *Letzte Briefe* (1925). For this text I have translated the letter back into English.

To George Alexander

MS. Arents

[*? July 1900*]   *Hôtel d'Alsace*

My dear Aleck, It was really a great pleasure to see you again, and to receive your friendly grasp of the hand after so many years. Nor shall I forget your dear wife's charming and affectionate greeting of me. I know now how to value things like that.

With regard to your proposal to spread the payment for the plays over a certain time, I know it was dictated by sheer kindness and the thoughtfulness of an old friend.[1]

If you would send Robert Ross £20 on the first of every month for me it would be a great boon. He would send it on to me, as he looks after all my affairs. His address is R. B. Ross, 24 Hornton Street, Kensington W. I would then have before me a year free from worry, and perhaps may do something you would like. Could you do this for me?

I was delighted to see you so well, and so unchanged.

Kindest wishes to your wife. Sincerely yours   OSCAR WILDE

To Louis Wilkinson

MS. Hyde (H. M.)

[*Postmark 15 July 1900*]   *Hôtel d'Alsace*

Dear Boy, Come and see me next week. I can get you a room in my hotel.

I am not going to write to you any more: I want to see you. I have waited long enough. [*signature cut away*]

Telegram: To Louis Wilkinson

MS. Wilkinson

[*July 1900—a few days later*]   [*Paris*]

Je suis très malade. Ne venez pas cette semaine. Je vous écrirai.

OSCAR

To Robert Ross

MS. Clark

[*August 1900*]   *Hôtel d'Alsace*

Dear Robbie, You say I should have acknowledged the cheque: I didn't do so because you only wrote one line and three quarters to me, though

---

[1] At the time of Wilde's bankruptcy Alexander had bought the acting rights of *Lady Windermere's Fan* and *The Importance of Being Earnest*. He made some voluntary payments to Wilde and bequeathed the rights to Wilde's son.

you were in the country where you must have had heaps of leisure. I now beg you to send me a cheque at once, and also a long letter.

I have been with Harold Mellor at Gland: he is almost as neurasthenic as I am: but there was the automobile. I had to consult a specialist before I left Paris, I was so ill: it seems that not "mussels" but neurasthenia were the cause of my illness, which had returned with renewed violence.[1]

I am very glad my sister-in-law is to be married to Teixeira: it is an excellent idea.[2]

I hear Reggie is in France. I wish he would come here. How are you? Do let me know what you are doing, and how Max's engagement is going on. It is the only amusing engagement I ever heard of.[3] Ever yours

OSCAR

To Robert Ross
MS. Clark

Saturday, 1 September [1900]   [*Paris*]

My dear Robbie, Thanks for the cheque. Your letter is very maddening: nothing about yourself: no details, and yet you know I love middle-class tragedies, and the little squabbles that build up family life in England. I have had delightful letters from you quite in the style of Jane Austen. You, I know, are the Cinderella of your family, and lead them all a dreadful life, like your *Märchen*-prototype. You turned your dear mother's carriage into a pumpkin, and won't let your sisters wear your slippers, and always have the comfortable ingle-nook by the fire, except in summer, when you make poor Aleck sit there.

The "Mellor cure" was dull, but I got better. He is now in Paris with his slave Eolo, who like all slaves is most tyrannical. He and I, however, are great friends. I think Harold is on the verge of acute melancholia. At present he has almost arrived at total abstinence—drinks and talks mineral waters. I like people who talk wine.

So Bosie is in London: where is he staying? Do you think he has really spent all his money? It is a great pity if he has. How is dear More? And Reggie? Paris is full of second-rate tourists. German and American are the only languages one hears. It is dreadful. Ever yours   OSCAR

To Frank Harris
MS. Texas

2 September [1900]   *Hôtel d'Alsace*

My dear Frank, Since you left Paris I have not received, till this morning,

[1] A surviving letter from Mellor to Wilde (MS. Clark), written from Gland and dated 21 July 1900, runs: "Am much distressed about your illness . . . I hope to be able to receive you on Monday 30 [July]."   [2] See note 2, p. 23.

[3] Max Beerbohm was at this time engaged to an actress called Grace (or Kilseen) Conover, whom he had met while touring in America with his brother's theatrical company in 1895.

a single line from you on any subject. It is curious that your letter should have gone astray, as the post is usually all right.

I don't know that it was quite wise of you to speak to Mrs Potter: she holds the agreement for the play. I cannot, as I told you, break with her —it is impossible.

I thought, from not hearing from you, that you had given up the idea of writing the scene (the third act scene).

I first received from Kyrle Bellew £5 a week, but after five weeks he ceased payment, and the agreement lapsed in consequence.[1]

I then got £100 from Mrs Potter and a new agreement was signed.

On the completion of the play I am to receive more down, and of course, on its production, royalties.

It is a great bore that you never write. Now that you have a type-writer you might let me hear from you.

I am in my usual state, drifting along. I wish I had your concentration of purpose, and controlled intellect. My last visit to Mellor has given me melancholia. I must go no more. Ever yours   OSCAR

To Leonard Smithers[2]

[*Postmark 2 September 1900*]   *Paris*

I think that I shall take £6 and you can have £4. This would be a better arrangement.[3]

How are you getting on? Are the creditors howling? If the wolf is at the door the only thing is to ask him in to dine.

Is there any chance of your being in Paris? My dear Neapolitans have returned to Naples and I miss that brown faun with his deep woodland eyes and his sensuous grace of limb. A slim brown Egyptian, rather like a handsome bamboo walking-stick, occasionally serves me drinks at the Café d'Égypte, but he does not console me for the loss of the wanton sylvan boy of Italy.

I think *Salome* should have been published. One of Dowson's friends translated it . . . Why "*jeunes artistes*"? What has age to do with acting? The only person in the world who could act Salome is Sarah Bernhardt, that "serpent of old Nile,"[4] older than the Pyramids.

---

[1] Kyrle Bellew (see note 2, p. 104) was for a long time associated with Mrs Brown-Potter. In 1899 he had corresponded with Wilde about a possible collaboration in a play or plays.

[2] The text of this incomplete letter is taken from *Forty Years in my Bookshop* by W. T. Spencer (1923), corrected and supplemented by the American Art Association catalogue of 1 February 1928.

[3] According to the American Art Association catalogue this refers to fees or royalties on *Salome*.   [4] *Antony and Cleopatra*, Act I, scene 5.

To George Ives

MS. Texas

[*Postmark 6 September 1900*]   [*Postmark Paris*]

My dear George, I am very glad your book has been received well. I hope it will give you the position you deserve.[1]

I will be charmed to see you in Paris, but you must come to proper, seemly restaurants, not go to dreadful cabarets where *cochers-de-fiacre* resort. I hope you will never lose the sense of style in life: it keeps the barbarians away.

I know you are not rich, but I wonder could you lend me £10 till October 1st? I get my small income through Robbie Ross on the first of each month, and could ask him to pay you back direct. I am in great worry and annoyance over money, the price of my rooms has been doubled owing to the Exhibition, and my landlord presses me.

If you can do this, would you mind sending notes in a registered letter. Cheque takes ages to cash. Ever yours   OSCAR

To George Ives

MS. Texas

Saturday [*8 September 1900. Postmark 9 September 1900*]

[*Postmark Paris*]

My dear George, Many thanks: it is most kind of you.

I hope you will come over soon, and not alone: but don't conceal your charming friends: you usually hide them from me.

Your book that you promised me has never arrived: do let me have a copy.

Paris has gone back to summer weather, and the problem of how to dress is acute. One never knows what the day is going to be like.

What a charming book Edward Carpenter's *Civilisation, Cause and Cure* is: it is most suggestive. I constantly read it.[2] Ever, with my thanks, yours
OSCAR

To Frank Harris

MS. Yale

[*Circa 12 September 1900*][3]   *Hôtel d'Alsace*

My dear Frank, My *propriétaire* is worrying me to distraction, to pay my

[1] Ives's second book of poems, *Eros' Throne*, was published in 1900. The British Museum copy is stamped 15 May.

[2] First published in 1889, this book was already in its sixth edition. One of its essays, "Defence of Criminals: a Criticism of Morality," contains the sentence: "The Outcast of one age is the Hero of another."

[3] Endorsed: "Received Thursday morning, 13 September 1900."

bill, or part of it. Could you send me £20? I am quite without a sou, and I must give the landlord £15.

I suppose this is a great bore to you, but really I don't know what to do. If you can manage it, it will be a great kindness. Ever yours   OSCAR

To Frank Harris

MS. Texas

Tuesday [18 September 1900][1]   *Hôtel d'Alsace*

My dear Frank, It will be a great delight to see you, but do telegraph beforehand: if you only send a wire from Calais, I may miss it.

For the rest of your letter many, many thanks. Ever yours   OSCAR

To Frank Harris

MS. Texas

[Circa 20 September 1900]   *[Paris]*

Dear Frank, Our misunderstanding of last night came from the fact that you had proposed collaboration, and then appeared with the play finished. I have not seen a line of it, and now I think—and I dare say you will also —that there is no necessity I should. So let the matter be concluded in this way.

You buy my plot and scenario, for the terms you proposed last night:

£200 down
£500 shares in the Reserve
¼ of profits of play.

I will send Bellew his money, and of course he has no claim on you of any kind.

Will you send me a line to corroborate this, or, better still, come and see me or make an appointment for dinner.

I am writing in bed—in considerable pain. Ever yours   OSCAR

To Frank Harris

MS. Texas

26 September 1900   Élysée Palace Hôtel, Avenue des Champs Élysées

Dear Frank, In consideration of the sum of £175, of which this is an acknowledgment, and as one-fourth share of your profits from the play, I hereby assign to you absolutely the entire rights in the plot and scenario I laid before you last June. You to have full rights to deal with said plot and scenario as you choose.

The plot and scenario are those used in the play provisionally termed *Her Second Chance*.[2] Yours sincerely   OSCAR WILDE[3]

[1] Endorsed: "Received 19 September 1900."
[2] Another title for the play which eventually became *Mr and Mrs Daventry*.
[3] This letter carries 27/6 worth of official-looking stamps.

Telegram: To Frank Harris

MS. Texas

[*Postmark 11 October 1900*]   *Paris*

If you come over tomorrow come and see me first. Nethersole[1] is very impossible

OSCAR

Telegram: To Robert Ross[2]

11 October 1900   *Paris*

Operated on yesterday. Come over as soon as possible.

Telegram: To Robert Ross[2]

[? *12 October 1900*]   *Paris*

Terribly weak. Please come.

To Frank Harris

MS. Texas

Friday [? *12 October 1900*]   [*Paris*]

Dear Frank, According to our agreement you were to pay me £175 within a week. I was so certain of your keeping your word that I wrote in the agreement "£175 of which this is a receipt," and signed it.

You never sent it.

Now you send me £25 instead of £175.[3] You have no right to break the agreement. You assured me that Bellew had no claim of any kind. You made a violent scene on the subject: the scene the first night we met.

You now calmly propose to hand over £125 of my money to Bellew. I don't, I can't, allow you to do that. I shall repay Bellew the £100 I owe —not £125—when I can. I can't afford to do it now. But I insist on your carrying out your agreement with me. If I had not had implicit trust in you I should not have signed anything.

The operation I have had to undergo was a most terrible one. The surgeon's fee is 1500 francs (£60). This, by the aid of my doctor, I got reduced to 750 francs. I was obliged to give a *post-dated* cheque for next Monday. I also have to have a hospital male nurse all day, and a doctor to

---

[1] Louis Nethersole (1865–1936) was a theatrical manager and press representative. Brother of Olga (see note 3, p. 231.)

[2] Text from Ross's letter to More Adey (see p. 847).

[3] As soon as Harris announced the production of *Mr and Mrs Daventry* he was compelled to buy off some or all of the people to whom Wilde had sold options (see note 4, p. 829) and naturally withheld the £150 due to Wilde. Harris had many faults, but lack of generosity to Wilde was not one of them.

sleep at night in the room. I then have to pay my own doctor, who comes daily, and the hotel for another room; and the chemist's bill is about £20 already. I entered on these expenses as I have your signed agreement to send me £175. You send me £25! It is really too monstrous.

Your remarks on Nethersole are incredible. Of course the scenario that Nethersole bought from a scoundrel called Eliot was my scenario: that is the whole point. It was mine, and Eliot had no right to sell it, or deal with it, or adapt it, or do anything with it at all. His selling it to Nethersole was a fraud.

Nethersole was under the idea that because he had bought my scenario from a man who didn't own it he had a right to produce it! I had to explain to him elaborately that he had no such right. The scenario was mine. Had the scenario *not* been mine of course he could have done anything he chose with it.

Ultimately, though very ill, I got Nethersole to see that he had no right to use or produce my scenario, that it would be dishonest and fraudulent. You state in your letter that it is evident that my purpose in so doing was to annoy you and to bother you!!!

What do you mean by that?

Do you think I should have told Nethersole that he had a perfect right to produce my scenario in New York or elsewhere because he had bought a copy of the scenario from a swindler who stole it? That is what Nethersole wanted me to say, but what I refused to say.

As regards his sister, he told me that you had read her the play in London, and wanted her to play it. She is very clever, and popular, and I said I would certainly like her to play it, and I write to you to that effect.

If you didn't want her to play it, why did you read it to her? If you prefer some other actress, give it to the other actress. Olga Nethersole draws enormous houses in America, but you must get good terms. The terms offered by her brother were ridiculous.

In the meanwhile send me the £125 you owe me, and for which I gave you, as you know, a receipt. I want it at once. I must have it. I am astonished at your breaking your agreement. Ever yours   OSCAR

To Frank Harris
MS. Texas

[*October 1900*]   [*Paris*]

Dear Frank, Your telegram just arrived. I have no money to pay for telegrams. You have, by breaking your agreement, put me in an awful position, and I must ask you to send me £125 at once.

Smithers has no more right than Kyrle Bellew has. You told me at Durand's that Bellew had no rights, that you had taken legal opinion, and that there was no copyright in a plot.

Smithers bought my contract with Sedger—and gave me £60. When, as I did not wish him, a publisher, to have anything to do with its production,

I proposed to close with Bellew, Smithers came over to Paris and agreed to surrender whatever rights he had if I returned him the £160 out of the proceeds of the play. This was agreed between us, Miss Althea Gyles, the artist, being present. It is absurd his coming up now, especially as you assured me that even Bellew had no legal rights.

You must, if you wish to go on, assure Smithers, who is bankrupt, something out of the profits. I should think he would be glad to take £100.

But in the meanwhile you have broken your agreement with me, but it never occurred to me to ask you for a seven-day bill, or a post-dated cheque. I trusted implicitly in your word, and at the end of two weeks you send me a paltry £25 instead of the £150 owed to me. I wish to goodness you would drop the whole thing. I don't want other people to write my plays. I object to it. If they do commandeer them, I object to not being paid the very paltry price agreed on. Ever yours   OSCAR

To Frank Harris[1]

MS. Clark

[*Circa 12 November 1900*]   [*Hôtel d'Alsace*]

value, if any, a lapsed agreement with me had.

After all this, Smithers goes privately to you and blackmails you out of £100.

If my agreement with Smithers is worth the paper it is written on, it belongs to the Official Receiver: Smithers has no more right to it than Robbie Ross or R[eggie] Turner: and his raising [money] on it is an impudent fraud on you.

How you were ta[ken in] I cannot understand. [Didn't] you know Smithers was [a] bankrupt? a[nd don't] you know the A.B.C. of the bankruptcy laws?

Smithers told Robbie Ross a month ago that he was going to "blackmail" you: the word was Smithers's own. Robbie thought it was a joke, and was astounded last night to find you had fallen into the trap.

Get your solicitor to [write] at once to Smithers. [? I don't] know whether or not [you will] get your £100 back, [or whe]ther it has all gone [on whis]kies and sodas: but [it would] be a serious thing [for Smi]thers if the Official Receiver were informed of the transaction, and if you have a good solicitor, as I have no doubt you have, he, I fancy, will be able to make this wretched Smithers disgorge, without the Receiver knowing anything of the matter. But the matter should be taken in hand at once.

I don't suppose I shall get much of what he owes me out of Smithers— sixpence in the pound possibly—but Robbie has transferred to me his debt of £90, due to him by Smithers, and proved in Court, so I may get a little.

The Smithers affair with you, however, has nothing to do with *my* agreement with you.

[1] The beginning and end of this letter are missing, also a page or more from the middle, and one of the sheets is torn. It may well not have been sent (see next letter).

On September 26th you signed an agreement promising "to pay within a week" from that date the sum of £175, besides other clauses.

You explained to me that you had left your cheque-book in London, but that you would send me a cheque on your return which was fixed for the following day. You gave me £25 on account, and I, naturally accepting the word of one of my oldest and best friends, backed up by an [*a page or more missing*]

. . . operation, for most of the time suffering acute pain. Twice a day a surgeon comes to dress my wounds, which are not yet healed. I have to have a *garde-malade* to be with me night and day. The doctor calls every second day. My bill at the chemists is £35. My expenses and debts amount to about £200. And, all the while, I was almost literally without a penny, torturing myself with apprehension, getting myself into a state of fever, trying to raise small sums of money, not knowing what was going to become of me.

I would have been well a fortnight ago had you kept your word to me. It is mental trouble that has kept me back. I rarely sleep. I have taken so much morphine that it has no more effect on me than water. Chloral and opium are the only things the doctor can think of, as the surgeon declines to allow any subcutaneous injections till the wounds heal up.

All this, my dear Frank, is due to you. And let me ask you a few questions, and please give me candid answers.

When you gave me the agreement to sign, did you really intend to pay me within the week, or were you merely keen to get an agreement out of me to enable you to deal with Mrs Campbell?

Had you really forgotten your cheque-book in London? It is difficult to imagine your living in Paris—in the style and luxury that you like and are accustomed to—without a cheque-book. I don't suppose that you are like President Kruger and travel with bullion.

When did the idea of trying to make *me*, of all people, responsible for Smithers's blackmailing occur to you? It was obviously subsequent to October 3rd, on which day the payment of the £150 came ultimately due. Indeed, as far as I can make out by comparing dates with Robbie, it was a good time after my operation. It was an afterthought evidently. But not a brilliant one. Had Smithers tried it on with me, he would have had a very smart rejoinder and some good advice. But he was cautious enough to enter me in his statement of affairs as one of his creditors. He may have been the more eager to do this, as there is an awkward matter of embezzlement that Robbie is investigating.

Smithers some time ago got me to sign a paper entitling him to receive on my behalf a sum of money that was coming to me: a sum infinitesimally petty to anyone like you, but of importance to me. He said I was not business-like, and that it would be a pleasure for him to look after my affairs. As he had always posed as a great friend of mine I fell into the trap, and indeed promised him a large commission, as I did not wish to trespass on his time for nothing.

This was at the beginning of September, and since I signed the document I have heard nothing from Smithers except that I am amongst his creditors. I believe the money was paid to him, and that he kept it, but I have as yet no definite proof.

Perhaps, the latter affair being merely a digression and of no interest to you, you don't like my asking you a list of questions. If so, as I have survived the operation and the terrible five weeks of physical pain aggravated by mental anxiety, and, though still dreadfully ill, am alive and "cased" neither in lead nor deal—as dead king or dead pauper—let us bury the horrible past as far as possible, and deal with the present actual situation.

I owe about £180—the cost of my dreadful illness. It is due to doctors, surgeons, chemists, my attendant, the restaurant that sends me in my meals (no cooking being possible in the hotel), the hotel itself, whose bill will be enormous, and the incidentals of a sickroom, all of which I have had to buy.

You owe me, on our agreement of September 26th, £125.

You also owe me £25, my share of the £100 paid by Mrs Campbell.

That makes £150. (One hundred and fifty pounds.)

Then there is the question of the royalties.[1] Of these I have received no account. Of course I should get an account weekly.

From your statement I fear that, as I told you, royalties in such a tiny theatre are of little importance. From *A Woman of No Importance* at the Haymarket I used to draw £170 to nearly £200 a week.

I hope you will do your best to make Mrs Campbell try and get hold of a large smart West-end Theatre, if one can be got. The Royalty is useless as far as author's fees go.

I don't know what you are doing about America. Do try and get Frohman to take the piece.[2] He, as you know, I suppose, is the head of the Theatrical Syndicate, the trust that owns all the big theatres in the great towns. If one is not in with the trust one has to play in little theatres like the Royalty, which makes a good profit impossible. When I tell you that Ada Rehan, the most popular actress in America, was unable to go on tour because she was not in with the trust you will understand how serious the matter is. [*The rest of this letter is missing*]

---

[1] *Mr and Mrs Daventry* had opened at the Royalty Theatre on 25 October with Mrs Patrick Campbell and Fred Kerr in the title-rôles. Small parts were played by Gerald du Maurier and George Arliss. Max Beerbohm published a very favourable notice in the *Saturday Review* of 3 November, but except for J. T. Grein most of the other critics were hostile. Nevertheless the play achieved more than a hundred performances, and ran until 23 February 1901. From 11 December 1900 Max Beerbohm's one-act dramatisation of his own story *The Happy Hypocrite* was included in the bill as a curtain-raiser.

[2] Charles Frohman (1860–1915), the American impresario, who had already sponsored an American tour of *Lady Windermere's Fan* (1893) and the New York production of *The Importance of Being Earnest* (22 April 1895). His brother Daniel (1851–1941) had presented *An Ideal Husband* in New York (12 March 1895).

To Frank Harris[1]
MS. Texas

20 November 1900   *Hôtel d'Alsace*

Dear Frank, I have now been in bed for nearly ten weeks and am still
extremely ill, having had a relapse a fortnight ago. I must, however, for
many reasons write to you at once on the question of the money you owe
me. The expenses of my illness amount to close on £200 and I must beg
that you pay me immediately the sum for which you are still indebted to
me. On September 26th, nearly two months ago, you drew up an agreement in your own handwriting promising to pay me within a week from
that date the sum of £175 besides one-fourth of all profits. You explained
to me that you had left your cheque-book in London, but that you would
send me a cheque on your return, which was fixed for the following day.
You gave me £25 on account, and I naturally accepted the word of one of
my oldest friends, backed up by an agreement drawn out by yourself, not
actually signed, but I gave you a receipt for the entire sum. I no more
doubted that you would pay me in the course of a week than I doubted
of the shining of sun or moon. A week passed over without my hearing a
line from you, and finally the surgeon felt it his duty to inform me that unless
I was operated on immediately it would be too late, and that the consequences of the delay would probably be fatal. With great difficulty I
managed to raise amongst my friends, or rather the sum was raised for me
by them, the 1500 francs which was the surgeon's fee, and was duly operated on under chloroform. I then telegraphed to you to ask you to send
the money you owed me at once. All I received from you in return was
£25. You then took no further notice of the matter but left me for a whole
month in the most terrible position I have ever been in. I do not wish to
criticise your conduct towards me, I merely state the plain facts. You owe
at present, on your agreement of two months ago, the sum of £125. You
also owe me £25 additional, my share of the £100 paid over in advance by
Mrs Campbell. You told me at Durand's that this sum was not in advance
of fees. I should like to know whether this is the case or not. The play has
now been running for, I believe, three weeks and I have received no account
of the receipts or royalties. A statement of the receipts and my proportion
of author's fees should, of course, be sent to me every week. I must ask you
to at once settle up accounts, as I cannot possibly go on living in the present
manner, with two doctors and attendants, a medical nurse and all the
terrible expenses incident on a long and dangerous illness.

With regard to Smithers, I am, I need hardly say, astounded that you
should have allowed yourself to be blackmailed by him, but your proposal
to recoup yourself out of the money you owe me and to sequestrate my
small share of the profits, is of course out of the question. I could not
allow it for a moment. Smithers had an agreement with me some years ago
to write him a play within a certain given time. I was unable to carry out
my side of the agreement, and Smithers formally relinquished to me in

---

[1] Except for the last two lines, this letter is in the hand of Maurice Gilbert.

Paris any claim he had on me for the broken agreement. It is true I did not get Smithers's pronunciation in writing, but Smithers was at that time a great friend of mine, and in his case, as later on in yours, I considered the word of a friend adequate. I promised him in return to give him the publishing rights of two of my plays,[1] as well as the copyright of a poem for which illustrations were at that time being made by an artist of great ability.[2] Since that time Smithers, as you know, has become bankrupt, and I am one of his creditors. Had Smithers considered that his agreement with me was still valid he would naturally have entered it as an asset against me, but he did not do so, showing clearly that the agreement in his opinion had lapsed in reality as it had lapsed in time. His coming to you and attempting to extort money from you is really an act of blackmailing, for if my lapsed agreement with him has the value of five shillings, it belongs of course to the Official Receiver, and Smithers has no more right to deal with it or treat it as his property than the man in the street. It is unnecessary to tell you, I presume, that what Smithers has done is a most serious offence against the bankruptcy laws, and if it came to the knowledge of the Official Receiver, Smithers would find himself in a very painful, possibly criminal position. If you will put these facts before your lawyer he will tell you that I am perfectly right. And I should fancy that unless Smithers has spent the £100 he extorted from you in whiskeys and sodas, your solicitor will be able to recover the money for you. However that is your business, not mine, but as Smithers is having a very bad time with the Official Receiver, I should not fancy that he would care to risk imprisonment.

When the man Nethersole intruded here almost daily during the worst crisis of my illness and tried to blackmail me on the ground that he had managed to secure a copy of the scenario, and that a play belonged to any man who had a copy of the scenario, if under these circumstances I had been foolish enough to hand him £200, I think you would have been rather amused if I had written subsequently to you to claim the £200 from your pocket. But, without adducing parallels, your lawyer will tell you that Smithers's action is entirely illegal, and that you were very foolish to yield to it for a moment.

As for me, I regret what has occurred for your sake, but I cannot recoup you, nor should you for a moment expect me to do so. The important thing, however, is to settle up our accounts and I must beg you to send me by return the £150 you owe me, as well as any royalties that may be due.

I need not say how distressed I am that things should have turned out in this manner between us, but you must remember that the fault is in no sense mine. Had you kept your word to me, fulfilled the agreement and sent me the money that was due to me and for which I gave you a receipt which you still hold, all would have been well; and indeed I myself would have perfectly recovered two weeks ago, had it not been for the state of mental anxiety which your conduct kept me in all day long, with its

[1] See note 2, p. 765.
[2] Althea Gyles (see note 1, p. 817).

accompanying sleeplessness at night, a sleeplessness over which none of the opiates the doctors dared to order me seemed to have any effect. Today is Tuesday the 20th. I rely on receiving from you the £150 you owe me. Sincerely yours   OSCAR WILDE

EPILOGUE

Epilogue

Robert Ross to More Adey[1]

14 December 1900

On Tuesday, October 9th, I wrote to Oscar, from whom I had not heard
for some time, that I would be in Paris on Thursday, October the 18th for
a few days, when I hoped to see him. On Thursday, October 11th, I got a
telegram from him as follows: "Operated on yesterday—come over as soon
as possible." I wired that I would endeavour to do so. A wire came in
response, "Terribly weak—please come." I started on the evening of
Tuesday, October 16th. On Wednesday morning I went to see him about
10.30. He was in very good spirits; and though he assured me his sufferings were dreadful, at the same time he shouted with laughter and told
many stories against the doctors and himself. I stayed until 12.30 and
returned about 4.30, when Oscar recounted his grievances about the Harris
play. Oscar, of course, had deceived Harris about the whole matter—as
far as I could make out the story. Harris wrote the play under the impression that only Sedger had to be bought off at £100, which Oscar had
received in advance for the commission; whereas Kyrle Bellew, Louis
Nethersole, Ada Rehan, and even Smithers, had all given Oscar £100 on
different occasions, and all threatened Harris with proceedings. Harris,
therefore, only gave Oscar £50 on account, as he was obliged to square
these people first—hence Oscar's grievance. When I pointed out to him
that he was in a much better position than formerly, because Harris, at
any rate, would eventually pay off the people who had advanced money and
that Oscar would eventually get something himself, he replied in the
characteristic way, "Frank has deprived me of my only source of income by
taking a play on which I could always have raised £100."

I continued to see Oscar every day until I left Paris. Reggie and myself
sometimes dined or lunched in his bedroom, when he was always very
talkative, although he looked very ill. On October 25th my brother Aleck
came to see him, when Oscar was in particularly good form. His sister-in-
law, Mrs Willie, and her husband, Teixeira, were then passing through

[1] Text from Harris, vol. 2, pp. 595-603.

Paris on their honeymoon, and came at the same time. On this occasion he said he was "dying above his means" . . . he would never outlive the century . . . the English people would not stand him—he was responsible for the failure of the Exhibition, the English having gone away when they saw him there so well-dressed and happy . . . all the French people knew this, too, and would not stand him any more.

On October the 29th Oscar got up for the first time at mid-day, and after dinner in the evening insisted on going out—he assured me that the doctor had said he might do so and would not listen to any protest.

I had urged him to get up some days before as the doctor said he might do so, but he had hitherto refused. We went to a small café in the Latin Quarter, where he insisted on drinking absinthe. He walked there and back with some difficulty, but seemed fairly well. Only I thought he had suddenly aged in face, and remarked to Reggie next day how different he looked when up and dressed. He appeared *comparatively* well in bed. (I noticed for the first time that his hair was slightly tinged with grey. I had always remarked that his hair had never altered its colour while he was in Reading; it retained its soft brown tone. You must remember the jests he used to make about it, he always amused the warders by saying that his hair was perfectly white.)

Next day I was not surprised to find Oscar suffering with a cold and great pain in his ear; however, Dr Tucker[1] said he might go out again, and the following afternoon, a very mild day, we drove in the Bois. Oscar was much better, but complained of giddiness; we returned about 4.30. On Saturday morning, November 3rd, I met the *Panseur*[2] Hennion (Reggie always called him the *Libre Panseur*); he came every day to dress Oscar's wounds. He asked me if I was a great friend or knew Oscar's relatives. He assured me that Oscar's general condition was very serious—that he could not live more than three or four months unless he altered his way of life—that I ought to speak to Dr Tucker, who did not realise Oscar's serious state—that the ear trouble was not of much importance in itself, but a grave symptom.

On Sunday morning I saw Dr Tucker—he is a silly, kind, excellent man; he said Oscar ought to write more, that he was much better, and that his condition would only become serious when he got up and went about in the usual way. I begged him to be frank. He promised to ask Oscar if he might talk to me openly on the subject of Oscar's health. I saw him on the Tuesday following by appointment; he was very vague; and though he endorsed Hennion's view to some extent, said that Oscar was getting well now, though he could not live long unless he stopped drinking. On going to see Oscar later in the day I found him very agitated. He said he did not want to know what the doctor had told me. He said he did not care if he had only a short time to live, and then went off on to the subject of his debts, which I gather amounted to something over more than £400. He asked me to see that at all events some of them were paid if I was in a position to do so after he was dead; he suffered remorse about some of his

---

[1] The British Embassy doctor.   [2] Dresser or male nurse.

creditors. Reggie came in shortly afterwards much to my relief. Oscar told us that he had had a horrible dream the previous night—"that he had been supping with the dead." Reggie made a very typical response, "My dear Oscar, you were probably the life and soul of the party." This delighted Oscar, who became high-spirited again, almost hysterical. I left feeling rather anxious. That night I wrote to Douglas saying that I was compelled to leave Paris, that the doctor thought Oscar very ill, that ——[1] ought to pay some of his bills as they worried him very much, and the matter was retarding his recovery—a great point made by Dr Tucker. On November 2nd, All Souls' Day, I had gone to Père Lachaise with ——.[1] Oscar was much interested and asked me if I had chosen a place for his tomb. He discussed epitaphs in a perfectly light-hearted way, and I never dreamt he was so near death.

On Monday, November 12th, I went to the Hôtel d'Alsace with Reggie to say good-bye, as I was leaving for the Riviera next day. It was late in the evening after dinner. Oscar went all over his financial troubles. He had just had a letter from Harris about the Smithers claim, and was much upset; his speech seemed to me a little thick, but he had been given morphia the previous night, and he always drank too much champagne during the day. He knew I was coming to say good-bye, but paid little attention when I entered the room, which at the time I thought rather strange; he addressed all his observations to Reggie. While we were talking, the post arrived with a very nice letter from Alfred Douglas, enclosing a cheque.[2] It was partly in response to my letter I think. Oscar wept a little but soon recovered himself. Then we all had a friendly discussion, during which Oscar walked around the room and declaimed in rather an excited way. About 10.30 I got up to go. Suddenly Oscar asked Reggie and the nurse to leave the room for a minute, as he wanted to say good-bye. He rambled at first about his debts in Paris: and then he implored me not to go away, because he felt that a great change had come over him during the last few days. I adopted a rather stern attitude, as I really thought that Oscar was simply hysterical, though I knew that he was genuinely upset at my departure. Suddenly he broke into a violent sobbing, and said he would never see me again because he felt that everything was at an end. This very painful incident lasted about three-quarters of an hour.

He talked about various things which I can scarcely repeat here. Though it was very harrowing, I really did not attach any importance to my farewell, and I did not respond to poor Oscar's emotion as I ought to have done, especially as he said, when I was going out of the room, "Look out for some little cup in the hills near Nice where I can go when I am better, and where you can come and see me often." Those were the last articulate words he ever spoke to me.

I left for Nice the following evening, November 13th.[3]

---

[1] Name omitted by Harris.
[2] According to Douglas (*Autobiography*, p. 323) this was for £10.
[3] This letter is continued on p. 853.

Reginald Turner to Robert Ross

MS. Clark

Monday [*26 November 1900*]   *3 Rue Cambon, Paris*

My dear Robbie, I had today a long talk with the *patron* of the Hôtel d'Alsace. At the consultation yesterday the doctors gave very little hope of Oscar's recovery, and Tucker was very anxious that you should be sent for; I think he does not know you are not in Paris. I told the *patron* that I would see Tucker and communicate with you, and the *patron* wants you to write to him as to anyone who should be sent for in the case of Oscar getting worse. He wanted to know if his children should not be written to, but I told him that I would write to you. Certainly in the event of Oscar being at the last gasp or even dying, I do not know who to send for; someone should be there to look after his affairs, besides the business questions which may arise. I shall probably see Tucker tomorrow or the next day.

As to Oscar, he of course knows nothing of what they say, but he is beyond taking notice, his mind wanders and he sleeps. That is I think partly the result of the morphine which they inject into him, but now that is forbidden, so they are going only to pretend to inject. He welcomed me today and was pleased to see me, and we had a moment's lucid conversation, but he then relapsed into drowsiness and when he did speak seemed to wander. Of course this may be the result of drugs. I myself cannot help thinking he may yet live to furnish Frank Harris with another plot, but I may be quite wrong. What they fear is, I think, that the disease should go to the brain.

Oscar is not in want of anything as he is not sensible enough to desire anything. He is very difficult and rude, but to me he was very nice. The *patron* warned me not to be annoyed if he was rude. The *patron* is awfully good to him, but a bit of a bore. You had better write to Bosie, I think. I will do so but am not sure of his address, and I think I will send a line to Frank Harris to tell him how serious Oscar's condition is. As a matter of fact Oscar does not speak of Frank Harris, he is past that for the moment, but I think we shall be able to judge better of his condition when he has been free from morphia. Oscar asked if you had sent any details of your life at Nice. Ever yours   REG

Reginald Turner to Robert Ross

MS. Clark

27 November [*1900*]   *3 Rue Cambon* [*Paris*]

Dear Robbie, Please send directions at once as to who is to be communicated with if Oscar dies, also be prepared to wire to anyone. I am rather muddled. Tucker wired to me to warn Oscar's family and on my going to see him (Tucker) he told me Oscar might die at any minute and that his mind was gone. On coming here I found Oscar better, the mind clear and able to talk, but his utterance is thick and his eyes odd. Tucker now thinks he may get better, but thinks the chance small. I am sleeping at the Hôtel d'Alsace tonight and shall do so so long as the condition is dangerous. Tucker explained he could not have consultations with no money, so I have told him I will be responsible for all necessary expense.

In case Oscar dies I must have some advice and instructions how to act. Who is the responsible person? You ought to write to the guardian of his children if you know his address. The doctors are very nervous as they are afraid they will be called to account by someone. In this country they are very responsible, but I told Tucker he need not be afraid. He is going to write an account of the consultations and seal it and give it to you.

Is there anyone in London who ought to be told? I don't know Bosie's address, but wrote yesterday to Duke Street on the chance. I also wrote to Harris saying if he had anything soothing to say to Oscar he had better do so at once, as he might die at any moment, or might be better, in which case mental consolation would be of the utmost value.

Tucker wanted to wire to you today, but as he finds him better he said a letter would be as good.

If Oscar dies, Harris must hand over the money to you or some responsible person who will pay the debts to these people who have been so good to Oscar. He is very difficult, makes scenes and refuses to allow them to put mustard plasters on his legs. His head is kept in ice. He takes hardly any nourishment.

All the same I am of opinion that he will *not* die, at any rate at present, though of course I only go by instinct.

You had better write or wire to me at the *Hôtel Cambon*, unless you hear from me to the contrary. Telegraphic address is Hôtel Cambon, Paris.

Oscar has not asked for anybody and I don't think realises any danger, he is too ill and his mind is very weak, though it is hard to say how weak as at moments he discusses books. Ought he to have a priest or Protestant clergyman if he gets worse? Tucker is anxious. I think not unless he asks for one, but on such matters I would rather be guided by you.

I want to know:

(1) Any necessary persons' addresses.
(2) If he should have a priest if dying.
(3) If he dies, general advice.

I will send a wire if necessary. If he is at the last gasp would you come to Paris?

REG

Reginald Turner to Robert Ross

MS. Clark

Wednesday [28 November 1900]   *Hôtel d'Alsace*

My dear Robbie, I'm afraid it's all over with Oscar. He has been delirious for two or three days and gets worse. This morning a consultation of doctors after which I sent my wire to you. Another consultation tomorrow. If he is not better in three or four days he will be dead. I sat with him till 5.30 this morning. He talks nonsense the *whole* while in English and French. He recognises one more or less.

Maurice came this morning, but does not like being in the room. I am having a special nurse tonight, though they say it is not any good. Of course if he resents a strange face we shall send him away.

I think everything is being done for him that can be, but apparently nothing much can be. An operation is out of the question, as is set out in the doctors' statement. He takes no nourishment or hardly any. By turning the lights out and substituting milk for water I deceived him into drinking three glasses last night.

I don't know whether anyone will come here. Of course if he dies he must be buried in Paris and I suppose by the English clergyman. As to money he has none, but even if he dies Frank Harris will I hope give money for the bills and things.

It is very terrible to hear Oscar going on talking, and to be able to do nothing.

I have been watching alone while writing this, and have had a painful scene, one of many. Oscar tried to get out of bed, and I managed to get to the bed while holding him. He is quite gone in the mind, but recognised me again, and asked me if I could get a "Munster to cook for him"? and added that one steamboat was very like another.[1]

I think the *garde malade* ought to have been here before, but Tucker is not very quick.

I won't write more now.   REG

I fear he suffers terribly but I suppose is unconscious of it. He must have had fearful pain before the brain became affected.

I have an awful head myself, and my eye gets worse. But I think my treatment agrees with me and I shall be all right in a week or so.

Reginald Turner to Robert Ross
MS. Clark

Wednesday [28 November 1900] 5.30 p.m.   [*Hôtel d'Alsace*]

Dear Robbie, Have just sent off reply to your wire. I suppose you will understand from my first wire that if you can come to Paris you have no time to lose. Just now Oscar seems a little easier. After holding an ice bag on his head for three-quarters of an hour he said to me, "You dear little Jew, don't you think that's enough?" He talked to you about his play today, saying it was worth fifty centimes.

I think I told you there is another consultation tomorrow, after which I will send you a wire. I need not tell you that I told Tucker I would be responsible for any expenses; but as yet not a word from Frank Harris. I have written to Wallis telling him to wire Bosie of Oscar's condition.

[1] The s.s. *Munster* was one of the packet boats on the Kingstown-Holyhead route from 1865 to 1914.

Tucker thinks you are his agent, and he keeps worrying about the children. I know you will wire to whoever is necessary.

Just now he seems easier, one would say sleeping, if so I think he has a chance. You see I have had so many surprises with Oscar, that I don't want you to arrive here and curse me on finding him better, but I suppose he could hardly be worse. Of course you know how I should like you to be here, but I know that it is not easy for you. So far as being looked after is concerned you can do no more than is being done, and he is too ill to want anyone in particular. Still he might at any moment. He has not once hinted he thinks he is in danger, nor did he before the delirium began. He was only anxious to be out of pain. I fear that day he went out with me and I left him on the boulevard he had an absinthe, but I don't suppose that made much difference.

He knew Maurice, but only by name, not putting any meaning on his coming.

I fear this is a stupid letter, but really circumstances excuse that.   REG

Give me any instructions you want. I have not told More; he is moving.

6 p.m. Dr Tucker has just been. He says it is no good his writing to you as I have done so. Oscar a little better, but Tucker cannot say it means anything. We are going to have his hair cut if Oscar will allow it. His temperature keeps very high, but he understands the doctor more or less. You cannot be wrong in coming to Paris; it may be too late, but I hope you may find him better. I won't write again, only wire. But send me any instructions or advice. Tucker and the specialist made me and the *patron* sign a paper giving an account of the consultation so that his sons may see if they want to at any future time that all possible is being done for him. Tucker again asked for the address of the guardian of his children.

Oscar has just asked for letters or telegrams.

Robert Ross to More Adey
(continued from page 849)

14 December, 1900

During my absence Reggie went every day to see Oscar, and wrote me short bulletins every other day. Oscar went out several times with him driving, and seemed much better. On Tuesday, November 27th, I received the first of Reggie's letters, which I enclose (the others came after I had started), and I started back for Paris; I send them because they will give you a very good idea of how things stood. I had decided that when I had moved my mother to Mentone on the following Friday, I would go to Paris on Saturday, but on the Wednesday evening, at five-thirty, I got a telegram from Reggie saying, "Almost hopeless." I just caught the express and arrived in Paris at 10.20 in the morning. Dr Tucker and Dr Kleiss, a specialist called in by Reggie, were there. They informed me that Oscar could not live for more than two days. His appearance was very painful, he had become quite thin, the flesh was livid, his breathing heavy. He was trying to speak. He was conscious that people were in the room, and raised his hand when I asked him whether he understood. He pressed our hands. I then went in search of a priest, and after great difficulty found Father Cuthbert Dunne, of the Passionists, who came with me at once and administered Baptism and Extreme Unction—Oscar could not take the Eucharist. You know I had always promised to bring a priest to Oscar when he was dying, and I felt rather guilty that I had so often dissuaded him from becoming a Catholic, but you know my reasons for doing so. I then sent wires to Frank Harris, to Holman (for communicating with Adrian Hope) and to Douglas. Tucker called again later and said that Oscar might linger a few days. A *garde malade* was requisitioned as the nurse had been rather overworked.

Terrible offices had to be carried out into which I need not enter. Reggie was a perfect wreck.

He and I slept at the Hotel d'Alsace that night in a room upstairs. We were called twice by the nurse, who thought Oscar was actually dying. About 5.30 in the morning a complete change came over him, the lines of the face altered, and I believe what is called the death rattle began, but I had never heard anything like it before; it sounded like the horrible turning of a crank, and it never ceased until the end. His eyes did not respond to the light test any longer. Foam and blood came from his mouth, and had to be wiped away by someone standing by him all the time. At 12 o'clock I went out to get some food, Reggie mounting guard. He went out at 12.30. From 1 o'clock we did not leave the room; the painful noise from the throat became louder and louder. Reggie and myself destroyed letters to keep ourselves from breaking down. The two nurses were out, and the proprietor of the hotel had come up to take their place; at 1.45 the time of his breathing altered. I went to the bedside and held his hand, his pulse began to flutter. He heaved a deep sigh, the only natural one I had heard since I arrived, the limbs seemed to stretch involuntarily, the breathing came fainter; he passed at 10 minutes to 2 p.m. exactly.[1]

After washing and winding the body, and removing the appalling *débris* which had to be burnt, Reggie and myself and the proprietor started for the Mairie to make the official declaration. There is no use recounting the tedious experiences which only make me angry to think about. The excellent Dupoirier lost his head and complicated matters by making a mystery over Oscar's name, though there was a difficulty, as Oscar was registered under the name of Melmoth at the hotel, and it is contrary to the French law to be under an assumed name in your hotel. From 3.30 till 5 p.m. we hung about the Mairie and the Commissaire de Police offices. I then got angry and insisted on going to Gesling, the undertaker to the English

[1] On Friday, 30 November 1900. The latest medical opinion is that he died of an intercranial complication of suppurative *otitis media*, or middle-ear disease, of which his illness in prison (see p. 404) was an earlier symptom. See "The Last Illness of Oscar Wilde" by Terence Cawthorne, F.R.C.S., in the *Proceedings of the Royal Society of Medicine*, February 1959.

Embassy, to whom Father Cuthbert had recommended me. After settling matters with him I went off to find some nuns to watch the body. I thought that in Paris of all places this would be quite easy, but it was only after incredible difficulties I got two Franciscan sisters.

Gesling was most intelligent and promised to call at the Hôtel d'Alsace at 8 o'clock next morning. While Reggie stayed at the hotel interviewing journalists and clamorous creditors, I started with Gesling to see officials. We did not part till 1.30, so you can imagine the formalities and oaths and exclamations and signing of papers. Dying in Paris is really a very difficult and expensive luxury for a foreigner.

It was in the afternoon the District Doctor called and asked if Oscar had committed suicide or was murdered. He would not look at the signed certificates of Kleiss and Tucker. Gesling had warned me the previous evening that owing to the assumed name and Oscar's identity, the authorities might insist on his body being taken to the Morgue. Of course I was appalled at the prospect; it really seemed the final touch of horror. After examining the body, and, indeed, everybody in the hotel, and after a series of drinks and unseasonable jests, and a liberal fee, the District Doctor consented to sign the permission for burial. Then arrived some other revolting official; he asked how many collars Oscar had, and the value of his umbrella. (This is quite true, and not a mere exaggeration of mine.) Then various poets and literary people called, Raymond de la Tailhade, Tardieu, Charles Sibleigh, Jehan Rictus, Robert d'Humières, George Sinclair, and various English people, who gave assumed names, together with two veiled women. They were all allowed to see the body when they signed their names. . . .[1]

I am glad to say dear Oscar looked calm and dignified, just as he did when he came out of prison, and there was nothing at all horrible about the body after it had been washed. Around his neck was the blessed rosary which you gave me, and on the breast a Franciscan medal given me by one of the nuns, a few flowers placed there by myself and an anonymous friend who had brought some on behalf of the children, though I do not suppose the children know that their father is dead. Of course there was the usual crucifix, candles and holy water.

Gesling had advised me to have the remains placed in the coffin at once, as decomposition would begin very rapidly, and at 8.30 in the evening the men came to screw it down. An unsuccessful photograph of Oscar was taken by Maurice Gilbert at my request, the flashlight did not work properly. Henry Davray came just before they had put on the lid. He was very kind and nice. On Sunday, the next day, Alfred Douglas arrived, and various people whom I do not know called. I expect most of them were journalists. On Monday morning[2] at 9 o'clock, the funeral started from the hotel—we all walked to the Church of St Germain des Prés behind the hearse—Alfred Douglas, Reggie Turner and myself, Dupoirier, the proprietor of the hotel, Henri the nurse, and Jules, the servant of the hotel, Dr Hennion and Maurice Gilbert, together with two strangers whom I did

---

[1] Presumably Harris's dots.   [2] December 3.

not know. After a low mass, said by one of his *vicaires* at the altar behind the sanctuary, part of the burial office was read by Father Cuthbert. The *Suisse* told me that there were fifty-six people present—there were five ladies in deep mourning—I had ordered three coaches only, as I had sent out no official notices, being anxious to keep the funeral quiet. The first coach contained Father Cuthbert and the acolyte; the second Alfred Douglas, Turner, the proprietor of the hotel, and myself; the third contained Madame Stuart Merrill, Paul Fort, Henry Davray and Sarluis; a cab followed containing strangers unknown to me. The drive took one hour and a half; the grave is at Bagneux, in a temporary concession hired in my name—when I am able I shall purchase ground elsewhere, at Père la Chaise for choice. I have not yet decided what to do, or the nature of the monument. There were altogether twenty-four wreaths of flowers; some were sent anonymously. The proprietor of the hotel supplied a pathetic bead trophy, inscribed, "*À mon locataire*," and there was another of the same kind from the "*service de l'hôtel*," the remaining twenty-two were, of course, of real flowers. Wreaths came from, or at the request of, the following: Alfred Douglas, More Adey, Reginald Turner, Miss Schuster, Arthur Clifton, the *Mercure de France*, Louis Wilkinson, Harold Mellor, Mr and Mrs Teixeira de Mattos, Maurice Gilbert, and Dr Tucker. At the head of the coffin I placed a wreath of laurels inscribed, "A tribute to his literary achievements and distinction." I tied inside the wreath the following names of those who had shown kindness to him during or after his imprisonment, "Arthur Humphreys, Max Beerbohm, Arthur Clifton, Ricketts, Shannon, Conder, Rothenstein, Dal Young, Mrs Leverson, More Adey, Alfred Douglas, Reginald Turner, Frank Harris, Louis Wilkinson, Mellor, Miss Schuster, Rowland Strong," and by special request a friend who wished to be known as "C.B."[1]

I can scarcely speak in moderation of the magnanimity, humanity and charity of Dupoirier, the proprietor of the Hôtel d'Alsace. Just before I left Paris Oscar told me he owed him over £190. From the day Oscar was laid up he never said anything about it. He never mentioned the subject to me until after Oscar's death, and then I started the subject. He was present at Oscar's operation, and attended to him personally every morning. He paid himself for luxuries and necessities ordered by the doctor or by Oscar out of his own pocket. I hope that —— or ——[2] will at any rate pay him the money still owing. Dr Tucker is also owed a large sum of money. He was most kind and attentive, although I think he entirely misunderstood Oscar's case.

Reggie Turner had the worst time of all in many ways—he experienced all the horrible uncertainty and the appalling responsibility of which he did not know the extent. It will always be a source of satisfaction to those who were fond of Oscar, that he had someone like Reggie near him during his last days while he was articulate and sensible of kindness and attention.

[1] Presumably Carlos Blacker.
[2] Names omitted by Harris. Probably Douglas and Harris.

Father Cuthbert Dunne's Narrative [1]

MS. Burke

He [Robert Ross] took the next train back to Paris and hurried to the hotel; from there he came at once to the Avenue Hoche where he found me and requested that I should come in haste to attend a dying man. Having been told the necessary details, I went with him prepared to administer Baptism as well as Extreme Unction, with Holy Communion if possible.

As the *voiture* rolled through the dark streets that wintry night, the sad story of Oscar Wilde was in part repeated to me. When we reached the little bedroom of the hotel, the attendants were requested to leave. Robert Ross knelt by the bedside, assisting me as best he could while I administered conditional Baptism, and afterwards answering the responses while I gave Extreme Unction to the prostrate man and recited the prayers for the dying.

As the man was in a semi-comatose condition, I did not venture to administer the Holy Viaticum; still I must add that he could be roused and was roused from this state in my presence. When roused, he gave signs of being inwardly conscious. He made brave efforts to speak, and would even continue for a time trying to talk, though he could not utter articulate words. Indeed I was fully satisfied that he understood me when told that I was about to receive him into the Catholic Church and give him the Last Sacraments. From the signs he gave as well as from his attempted words, I was satisfied as to his full consent. And when I repeated close to his ear the Holy Names, the Acts of Contrition, Faith, Hope and Charity, with acts of humble resignation to the Will of God, he tried all through to say the words after me.

At a later visit, I was if anything more convinced as to his inward consciousness when, in my presence, one of the attendants offered him a cigarette which he took into his fingers and raised to his face, although, in the attempt to put it between his lips, he failed. On his head above the forehead, there was a leech on either side, put there to relieve the pressure of blood upon the brain. At these subsequent visits, he repeated the prayers with me again and each time received Absolution.

Entry No 547 in the Register of St Joseph's Church

1900: Nov. 29   To-day Oscar Wilde, lying *in extremis* at the Hôtel d'Alsace, 13 Rue des Beaux-Arts, Paris, was conditionally baptised by me.   Cuthbert Dunne.

He died the following day, having received at my hands the Sacrament of Extreme Unction.

[1] Father Cuthbert Dunne C.P. (1869–1950), a native of Dublin, was at this time attached to the Passionist Church, St Joseph's, in the Avenue Hoche, Paris. He bequeathed his papers, including this statement, to Father Edmund Burke C.P., by whose kindness it is here printed. See also Father Burke's article in the *London Magazine* of May 1961.

Reginald Turner to Max Beerbohm

MS. Reichmann

8 December 1900   *3 Rue Cambon, Paris*

My dear Max, I saw the article on you in the *World* quite by chance yesterday. You are indeed a great man, and I hope your play will come out soon. I am sure it will be a success.

Robbie went back to Menton tonight. We have had a fearful time, and I shall not forget it yet. I was Oscar's only friend in Paris when his brain was attacked and as I knew neither the address nor name of his children's guardian all I could do was to wire to Robbie. I sat up with him and did my best to help the others in nursing him, and fortunately Robbie arrived the day before he died. I have never had so horrible an experience, for poor Oscar's death was terribly distressing for the spectators, though I don't think he had any consciousness of it himself. Then it was touch and go as to whether he would be taken to the Morgue, as he had no relation or legal representative, and had been registered in an assumed name. The officials were maddening. Added to all this was the fear of being penniless, and I had not much money nor had Robbie, and my spare money was gone in specialists. His bills however are now going to be paid, or the greater part of them. I got your wreath. It was only ten francs, as we none of us had any money, but for ten francs you get very pretty flowers, and Oscar's coffin was covered with really beautiful flowers. We got one wreath of laurels which we placed at the head and tied all the cards to it.

It is certainly a good thing for Oscar that he is dead, and I confess that I was glad when I saw him quiet on his bed after a week of awful struggle and agony. I never thought to see anyone die before my eyes hour by hour and in such a way, and certainly not Oscar. I thought he would get over it till the last day, as he was so strong, but the doctor says if he had recovered his mind would have gone.

Keep these details to yourself. Do write to me, dear Max, and don't forget me amid your success. If I take an apartment you must come and stay. I suppose you are very rich just now. With love to all, yours affectionately   REG

Robert Ross to Adela Schuster

MS. Hyde (H. M.)

23 December 1900   *Hôtel Belle Vue, Mentone*

Dear Madam, Oscar Wilde began to be in failing health about a year ago. Like his brother he was inclined to take too much alcohol at times, but never regularly, and he never bore outward signs of it. In fact owing to his extraordinary constitution he was able (unfortunately perhaps) to take a great deal too much without being affected. He never became incapable. When I was with him in Genoa in the spring of 1899, just after his brother's death, I managed to frighten him so much on the subject that he quite reformed for six months. Had circumstances permitted me to be with him more than I was, I might have done something with him as he liked being ordered about by people whom he knew were fond of him.

In March and April of this year he came to Rome where I was wintering with my mother and I noticed that a great change had come over his health, but he was in very good spirits. He wanted me then to introduce him to a priest with a view to being received into the Church, and I reproach myself deeply for not having done so, but I really did not think he was quite serious. Being a Catholic myself, I really rather dreaded a relapse, and having known so many people under the influence of sudden impulse, aesthetic or other emotion become converts, then cause grave scandal by lapsing, that I told him I should never *attempt his conversion* until I thought he was serious. You, who once knew him so well, will appreciate the great difficulty. He was never quite sure himself where and when he was serious. Furthermore I did not know any priest in Rome sufficiently well to prepare for a rather grave intellectual conflict. It would have been no use getting an amiable and foolish man who would have treated him like an ordinary person and entirely ignored the strange paradoxical genius which he would have to overcome or convince. Mr Wilde was equipped moreover for controversy, being deeply read in Catholic philosophy especially of recent years. I need hardly say he made a good story out of his stay with me in Rome, and told people that whenever he wanted to be a Catholic I stood at the door with a flaming sword which only turned in *one* direction and prevented him from entering.

Shortly after his release when Mr Adey and I left him at Berneval, he made friends with a French priest and was very nearly received then, he told me, and of course you know that as a young man he was only prevented from doing so by his father and Professor Mahaffy. When I went for the priest to come to his deathbed he was quite conscious and raised his hand in response to questions and *satisfied* the priest, Father Cuthbert Dunne of the Passionists. It was the morning before he died, and for about three hours he understood what was going on (and knew I had come from the South in response to a telegram), that he was given the last sacraments. The doctors said that if he recovered consciousness in a few days, it would be a signal that the end was near.

He was in Paris from last June but had been away to Switzerland for a few weeks, and underwent a slight operation on October 10. He did not even wire for me, but on the 11th I got a telegram saying "Operated on yesterday try and come over soon." He knew that I was to pass through Paris at the end of the month. I was then in England. I came over on October 15.[1] He was looking extremely well and seeing various friends at intervals during the day, and sometimes was in the highest spirits. He was, as he always was at least twice a year, financially embarrassed, and this worried him a good deal. He was quarrelling with Frank Harris, who had really been most generous to him over the play *Mr and Mrs Daventry*. He owed about £170, most of which was due to the proprietor of the hotel, and

[1] Cf. p. 645.

859

the doctor told me that his recovery was being retarded by this circumstance. Had it been an outside debt he would not have troubled very much. I may here say that the proprietor of the Alsace was a most charitable and humane man, that he never spoke to Mr Wilde on the subject from the time of the operation, paid *himself* for luxuries and necessities ordered by the physicians, and never even spoke to me about it until after the funeral, while all the other creditors of course flocked round directly they heard the case was hopeless. I trust that Mr Harris will be able to settle the proprietor's bill at all events, as he has promised to do. I merely mention this point because there is an *unfounded* report which has been reproduced in the newspapers that Mr Wilde died in a sort of neglected and sordid way. Of course the hotel is rather a shabby little place compared to what he would have liked to stay in, but it is perfectly comfortable as I know by staying there often, and Mr Wilde wanted for *nothing* in the last weeks of his life. He had a special nurse, food sent in from a restaurant, the Embassy doctor Tucker; Hobean a well-known specialist operated, and Mr Turner and myself had in a brain specialist, Dr Kleiss, when meningitis declared itself. As long as he was allowed champagne, he had it *throughout* his illness.

To continue. I saw him every day and sometimes twice a day from October 15 till November 13th. He drove out in the Bois with me on several occasions. On November 1st the doctor took me aside and told me that although he was getting well, his general condition was serious, and that unless he pulled himself up he could not live for more than five years. I had no idea before then that such was the state of the case. I talked the next day very straightly as I always did to Mr Wilde. He of course laughed and said he could never outlive the century as the English people would not stand it, that he was already responsible for the failure of the Exhibition, as English people on seeing him there had gone away. However he made plans for coming to the South of France in order to be near me when he was better and Harris had sent him over the money due for his play. I asked a Mr Turner, an old friend of mine who had been very kind to Mr Wilde since his release, to look him up every day while I was absent and send me bulletins, and Mr Turner more than fulfilled my request.

The night before I went away, when I paid a farewell visit, I found Mr Wilde in a very excited state. He asked Mr Turner and the nurse to leave the room, and then burst into hysterical tears, saying he would never see me again. Here again I rather reproach myself, for I did not think him nearly so ill as he must have been, and I knew he had been taking morphia a good deal, and I became rather stern, as you are told always to be with people in hysteria. I simply attributed the whole scene to general weakness after his illness. As I mentioned before, he was nervous about his finances and the issue of his dispute with Harris. In this respect again, melancholy and dreadful though his death was in many ways, his poverty has been exaggerated. To *my* knowledge since January last he had £400 over and above the annuity of £150 paid from his wife's trustees through me—£300 came from the Queensberry family and £100 from a theatrical manager,[1] while his expenses in Italy were all paid by a Mr Mellor who was travelling with him and has always been most kind to him. There are so many sad and grievous circumstances in his later career, that there is no necessity for those who were interested in him to be harrowed by imaginary pictures of his poverty. The debts you will observe were very small comparatively, for him especially, out of the £170 £50 being due to the general practitioner Dr Tucker, and £96 to the proprietor of the hotel.

About five days before I left for Nice he caught a slight cold in the ear and this developed into an abscess rapidly, *causing him great pain*. No importance was attached to it by the English doctor, but the French doctor regarded it as a grave symptom. It was much better on November 13th. It was, however, the abscess which eventually produced inflammation of the brain. Mr Turner sent me several letters to Nice reporting progress and several drives in the Bois. On Sunday the 25th he did not get up, complained of giddiness and during the evening became light-headed. I think I told you the last details in my former letter. He was never able to *articulate* after my arrival. It was most fortunate that Mr Turner, whom he knew very well, was with him the whole of the last week of his life. Till Sunday 25th he was able to laugh and talk, though he got easily tired and slept a great deal and spoke constantly of coming south, so I hardly think he believed he was dying. I am thankful I arrived in time, as there was no other person there who could assume any authority or knew of his affairs. Owing to his being *registered* at his hotel under an assumed name (contrary to French law it seems) his body was nearly taken to the Morgue. The French authorities could not understand the absence of relatives or legal representatives. By great efforts and kind assistance of others I was able to prevent such a ghastly contingency. Mr Hope, the guardian of his children, for some reason or other did not communicate with me, although I wired to him directly I arrived in Paris asking for instructions in case of his death.

Please do not mention these personal matters. I blame Mr Hope very much, but I dare say he acted according to his view and of course could not be expected to take much interest in the matter. He communicated with me after everything was over and all difficulties overcome, through *my solicitor*. I think on the children's account he might have taken a little more interest, at all events when he knew Mr Wilde was dead. But on the other hand he had every reason to distrust me as a friend of the father, and suspected my motives at all times since the difficulty about the annuity. He highly disapproved of *Mrs Wilde* corresponding with me as she did, after her husband's release. I believe I told you that the grave is at Bagneux in a *temporary* concession. I shall either purchase the ground outright later on and erect a suitable monument, or move the remains to a permanent resting place. Though everyone who knew him well enough to *appreciate* his wonderful power and the sumptuous endowment of his intellect will regret his death, apart from personal affection the terrible commonplace "it was for the best" is really true in his case.

[1] Almost certainly Alexander. See note p. 832.

Two things were absolutely necessary for him, contact with comely things, as Pater says, and social position. Comely things meant for him a certain standard of living, and this, since his release, he *was able to have* except for a few weeks at a time, or perhaps months. Social position he realised after five months he could not have. Many people were kind to him, but he was too proud, or too vain, to be forgiven by those whom he regarded as social and intellectual inferiors. It galled him to have to appear grateful to those whom he did not, or would not have regarded, before the downfall. You who knew him so well in former years will understand what others will never understand I suppose. He chose therefore a Bohemian existence, entirely out of note with his genius and temperament. There was no use arguing or exhorting him. The temporary deprivation of his annuity produced no result. You cannot ask a man who started on the top rung of the ladder to suddenly start again from the lowest rung of all. Among his many fine qualities he showed in his later years was that he never blamed anyone but himself for his own disasters. He never bore any ill-will to anybody, and in a characteristic way was really surprised that anyone should bear any resentment against him. For example he really did not understand how cruel he was to his wife, but I never expect anyone to believe that.

I was not surprised by the silence of the press. Journalists could hardly say very much, and it was better to be silent than point a moral. Later on I think everyone will recognise his achievements; his plays and essays will endure. Of course you may think with others that his personality and conversation were far more wonderful than anything he wrote, so that his written works give only a pale reflection of his power. Perhaps that is so, and of course it will be impossible to reproduce what is gone for ever. I am not alas a Boswell, as some friends have kindly suggested I should become. But I only met him in '86 and only became intimate with him when he was writing *Lady Windermere*, but there were long intervals when I never saw him, and he never corresponded with me regularly until after the downfall. I stayed with him in '87 for two months and used then to write down what he said, but to tell you a *great secret* which I ought not to do, I gave him my notes and he used a great deal of them for one of his later plays which was written in a great hurry and against time as he wanted money. This of course is *private*. I think it would be a great pity myself to dwell too much on the sad and later part of his life with which I am of course more familiar, and the difficulties of collecting material for the "great period," as one may call it, would be immense. A great many people would dislike admitting their former intimacy with him, and if they have kept his letters would not care to lend them. I could only give a personal impression of him, and that really would not be of much value to the world or to his friends. You want the whole man from every side. In this letter to you I fear you will already be tired of my own views and remarks, but I wanted to try and tell you what you wanted, and it is difficult to edit out one's own personality from a hastily written letter.

Some time I should be very grateful if you allowed me to have your views as to the advisability of a memoir, and its scope or plan, and if done with discretion whether it would please and interest his friends. I would not care for it to appeal to morbid curiosity, and I remember Mr Wilde's remark "that it is always Judas who writes the biography."[1] You are in a better position to judge of this question, and to gauge the value of the interest taken in his work and career prior to the downfall.

Sincerely yours   ROBERT ROSS

A plain tombstone was later set above the grave at Bagneux, bearing these words from the twenty-ninth chapter of the Book of Job: *Verbis meis addere nihil audebant et super illos stillabat eloquium meum.*[2]

In 1909 Wilde's body was moved to the cemetery of Père Lachaise in Paris, where it rests under Epstein's monument and Wilde's own words:

> And alien tears will fill for him
> Pity's long-broken urn
> For his mourners will be outcast men,
> And outcasts always mourn.

[1] "Every great man nowadays has his disciples, and it is usually Judas who writes the biography." (Wilde in an anonymous article in the *Court and Society Review* of 20 April 1887, referring to a biographical essay on Whistler by Walter Dowdeswell in the *Art Journal.*

[2] "To my words they durst add nothing, and my speech dropped upon them." (Douai version.)

APPENDICES

APPENDICES

APPENDIX A

A Visit to Babbacombe

Campbell Dodgson to Lionel Johnson[1]

MS. B.M.

8 February 1893   *Babbacombe Cliff*

My dear Lionel, Bosie's whims have led me dancing on devious ways, many and strange, since Saturday last, and more improbable things have befallen me in these few days than usually brighten my sombre and cowlike existence in as many months. I am vastly amused at the whole thing as a spectator, while I feel that as a tutor I am the merest fraud: only nobody seems to expect anything else. My last few days at home were enlivened by continual telegrams from the Douglas family, which resulted in my going to Winchester, instead of to Salisbury, from Saturday till Monday. This I greatly enjoyed; the weather was divine, the Richardsons received me with the warmest affection, and I met no dull folk.

Then on Monday I went to Salisbury hoping to find Bosie at home: no such thing—he was still gadding about. I spent a very pleasant day with Lady Queensberry, and wandered about the Cathedral and the Close; was locked into the Cloisters, and trespassed in the Gardens of the Bishop. In the evening Bosie appeared, with a flutter of telegrams about him, and dishevelled locks, and plunged at once into editorial correspondence. This lasted all the evening, while I placidly read your Goethe and the *Westminster Gazette*.

The next day Bosie read Plato with zeal for one and a half hours. He then quietly informed me at lunch that we were going to Torquay that afternoon to stay with Oscar Wilde! I gasped amazed, but I am phlegmatic and have a strong constitution, so I bore the shock well, and resignedly

---

[1] From other letters between Dodgson and Johnson (MS. B.M.) it is clear that Johnson, who had been staying with Lady Queensberry at Salisbury, had recommended Dodgson as a tutor for Douglas, who, wrote Johnson, "wants most help in logic, Aristotle, Bacon, history." Dodgson agreed to go for a month, but on 3 February he learned that his examination for the British Museum, for which he needed at least ten days' hard preparation, was to begin on 21 February. Lady Queensberry asked him to come all the same, if only for a week, while she found another tutor.

spent the whole afternoon in repacking the portmanteau which I had just unpacked. Our departure was dramatic; Bosie was as usual in a whirl; he had no book, no money, no cigarettes and had omitted to send many telegrams of the first importance. Then, with a minimum of minutes in which to catch our train, we were required to overload a small pony chaise with a vast amount of trunks while I was charged with a fox terrier and a scarlet morocco dispatch-box, a gorgeous and beautiful gift from Oscar. After hurried farewells to the ladies, we started on a wild career, Bosie driving. I expected only to drag my shattered limbs to the Salisbury infirmary, but we arrived whole at the station.

When we had been gone an hour or so, it occurred to Bosie that he had never told Oscar we were coming, so a vast telegram was dispatched from Exeter. We finally arrived about nine o'clock and dined luxuriously. This is a lovely house, full of surprises and curious rooms, with suggestions of Rossetti at every turn. It is Lady Mount-Temple's, and is lent to Oscar Wilde. Our life is lazy and luxurious; our moral principles are lax. We argue for hours in favour of different interpretations of Platonism. Oscar implores me, with outspread arms and tears in his eyes, to let my soul alone and cultivate my body for six weeks. Bosie is beautiful and fascinating, but quite wicked. He is enchanted with Plato's sketch of democratic man, and no arguments of mine will induce him to believe in any absolute standards of ethics or of anything else. We do no logic, no history, but play with pigeons and children and drive by the sea.

Oscar sits in the most artistic of all the rooms called "Wonderland," and meditates on his next play. I think him perfectly delightful with the firmest conviction that his morals are detestable. He professes to have discovered that mine are as bad. His command of language is extraordinary, so at least it seems to me who am inarticulate, and worship Irishmen who are not. I am going back on Saturday. I shall probably leave all that remains of my religion and my morals behind me. Yours always   C.D.

868

APPENDIX B

A Few Maxims for the Instruction of the Over-Educated

By Oscar Wilde[1]

Education is an admirable thing. But it is well to remember from time to time that nothing that is worth knowing can be taught.

Public opinion exists only where there are no ideas.

The English are always degrading truths into facts. When a truth becomes a fact it loses all its intellectual value.

It is a very sad thing that nowadays there is so little useless information.

The only link between Literature and the Drama left to us in England at the present moment is the bill of the play.

In old days books were written by men of letters and read by the public. Nowadays books are written by the public and read by nobody.

Most women are so artificial that they have no sense of Art. Most men are so natural that they have no sense of Beauty.

Friendship is far more tragic than love. It lasts longer.

What is abnormal in Life stands in normal relations to Art. It is the only thing in Life that stands in normal relations to Art.

A subject that is beautiful in itself gives no suggestion to the artist. It lacks imperfection.

The only thing that the artist cannot see is the obvious. The only thing that the public can see is the obvious. The result is the Criticism of the Journalist.

[1] See note 4, p. 378. Five of these aphorisms in Wilde's hand are among nine manuscript pages of aphorisms in Clark.

Art is the only serious thing in the world. And the artist is the only person who is never serious.

To be really mediaeval one should have no body. To be really modern one should have no soul. To be really Greek one should have no clothes.

Dandyism is the assertion of the absolute modernity of Beauty.

The only thing that can console one for being poor is extravagance. The only thing that can console one for being rich is economy.

One should never listen. To listen is a sign of indifference to one's hearers.

Even the disciple has his uses. He stands behind one's throne, and at the moment of one's triumph whispers in one's ear that, after all, one is immortal.

The criminal classes are so close to us that even the policeman can see them. They are so far away from us that only the poet can understand them.

Those whom the gods love grow young.

APPENDIX C

A Visit from Mr Hargrove

Otho Holland Lloyd to Mary Lloyd[1]

MS. Holland

Monday, 9 September 1895   *Hôtel du Parc, Glion*

My darling Mary, Many thanks for your letters. I cannot afford any more
at the moment than a few lines in answer, as after dinner we cross the lake
by steamer to St Gingolph, there to spend the afternoon and take tea. This
is Miss Boxwell's birthday, so Constance wanted to do something to distinguish it a little from the rest of the week. She has had, besides, some
small presents from all of us; *Diana of the Crossways* from Constance, a
small chalet and a brown bear from Vyvyan and Cyril, from me a notebook
that cost a franc: it is one which has taken all our fancies. Constance
bought one for herself, then I bought one for Miss Boxwell and one for
you, finally Miss Boxwell made Constance take her to buy another which,
though she bought it to present to a friend, she felt it would be a great
struggle with herself to part with; so my gift came in opportunely.

To business now. At luncheon time yesterday they brought word to
Constance that a gentleman who knew her well in London, a Mr Erroll,
had telephoned from Les Avants that he would come to see her today at
five o'clock. Constance knew no such name. I suggested one of the
Rollers; Nettie Huxley has married one of the men. We waited impatiently
for the visitors' list; it came about four o'clock, and—(seven p.m.). At that
point the luncheon bell rang, and now it is nearly the dinner-hour. I was
going to say that Constance found the name of the gentleman; it was Mr
Hargrove! She gasped with horror. Could anything have been worse.
Remember that the day before the letter had gone to Oscar, in clean contradiction to all that Mr Hargrove has always advised (Dinner-bell: goodness knows when this can be finished. It cannot be posted today).

Tuesday. 9.30 a.m.

I take the first moment after breakfast to continue this most piecemeal

[1] See note 1, p. 398.

of letters. Well, yesterday morning Mr Hargrove came; he had asked to change the hour to nine o'clock. I was there at the interview; Constance had asked me to be there, so as to have someone at least to stand by her. And the first thing Mr Hargrove did was to pull out of his pocket a letter from Oscar; it was for Constance but it had been sent through Mr Hargrove. He, in her interests, had himself read it, and he said that it was one of the most touching and pathetic letters that had ever come under his eye. To cut short a long story it was clear that Mr Hargrove had come prepared to admit the possibility, in view of such a humble, penitent letter, that Constance would give forgiveness to Oscar, a thing which otherwise he would utterly have scouted. Wasn't that a deliverance? Nothing could ever have fallen more pat. So Constance, while saying nothing of my letter, showed him the letter of Mr Sherard, and told him that her mind was already made up not to proceed with the divorce. Of course Mr Hargrove pointed out to her, as he had to do, that in this case she and Oscar must go to the other side of the world with their boys and begin life quite afresh under a new name. But apparently she is ready for that. Myself I believe that in France or Spain they could find a home and friends, while schools could be found for the boys in England, and even that ultimately some ten or fifteen years later Oscar could cautiously make his way back again into England, the more so if works from his pen found readers or an audience in the meantime. All this is supposing him to come through the rest of his term, poor fellow.

And now for Constance's plans. Yesterday she wrote him a few lines to tell him that there was forgiveness for him, and that Cyril never forgets him. By the same post she wrote to the Governor saying that she would like to be allowed to have an interview with her husband, and she proposes to go over for this purpose to England in the company of Miss Boxwell whose stay is up on the 18th. She will stay in London for a week, and then will go to Yverdon for a month. For the week she is away, she will send Cyril and Vyvyan to ourselves. I think it will prove that she is acting for the best in taking him back, but only time can show.

That is bad news about your Auntie. I am certainly sorry that circumstances rendered it impossible to have her with us. We could easily otherwise have taken in her and your Auntie Edna together, which would have saved them a great deal of money. Perhaps if she lives through the winter we can arrange it for the winter following. I wonder where they are going. In any case I am very glad that she has been ordered abroad.

I enclose you 250 francs in French notes. Goodbye in much haste. Your loving husband   OTHO

Index of Recipients

Adams, William Davenport, 151
Adey, More, 347, 390, 407, 415, 418, 420, 524, 530, 534, 537, 548, 557, 567, 603, 615, 620, 623, 663, 681, 685, 687, 694, 784, 825
Ainslie, Douglas, 188
Alexander, George, 282, 308, 349, 359, 360, 368, 375, 383, 832
Allen, Grant, 286
Allen, Phoebe, 200
Allhusen, Mrs, 255
Anderson, Mary, 124, 126, 128, 130, 135, 167
Appleton, G. W., 155
Archer, William, 318, 332, 337
Arnold, Matthew, 78
Atwood, Roland, 293

Bailly, E., 324
Balcombe, Florence, 51, 54, 55, 330
Bale, Edwin, 205
Bancroft, Mrs, 66
Barraclough, Sydney, 321, 322, 323, 324
Bauër, Henri, 342
Beardsley, Aubrey, 348
Beerbohm, Max, 575
Beere, Mrs Bernard, 110, 211, 251, 355, 382, 566, 590
Bell, Edward Hamilton, 330
Benson, W. A. S., 174
Blacker, Carlos, 621, 628, 638, 639, 647, 714, 718, 721, 726, 727, 730, 735, 737
Blackie, J. S., 166
Blackwood, William, 243, 244, 245, 246, 247
Blanch, William Harnett, 349
Blanche, Jacques-Emile, 144, 145
Blunt, Wilfrid Scawen, 150
Bogue, David, 76
Boulton, Harold, 62
Bovet, Marie-Anne de, 241

Bramley, Rev. H. R., 35
Bright, R. Golding, 380
Brodrick, Hon. St John, 201
Browning, Oscar, 61, 63, 77, 247
Browning, Robert, 77

Campbell, Mrs Patrick, 353
Cantel, Jules, 294
Carte, Richard D'Oyly, 89, 103, 104
Cartwright, Charles, 285
Chanler, Amelie Rives, 237
Churchill, Lady Randolph, 341
Clegg, R., 292
Clifton, Arthur, 235
Cobden-Sanderson, T. J., 234
Combe, W. E., 324
Cook, Keningale, 39
Coquelin, Constant-Benoît, 298
Corkran, Alice, 232
Courtney, W. L., 236
Curzon, Hon. George, 151, 178, 179

Daily Chronicle, The, 263, 568, 722
Daily Telegraph, The, 283, 310
Daly, Augustin, 296, 634
Davitt, Michael, 586
Davray, Henry D., 689, 709, 713, 728, 731, 754
Dodgson, Campbell, 333
Don, Laura, 125
Douglas, Lord Alfred, 322, 326, 327, 336, 337, 340, 344, 347, 354, 355, 357, 359, 360, 362, 369, 376, 377, 383, 386, 393, 396, 397, 423–511, 588, 594, 595, 598, 610, 613, 617, 620, 637
Dowden, Edward, 228, 229
Dowson, Ernest, 600, 612, 616, 618, 630, 632, 655, 662, 665, 666
Doyle, Arthur Conan, 291
Duckworth, Gerald, 351
Dunn, James Nicol, 232, 234

873

INDEX OF RECIPIENTS

INDEX OF RECIPIENTS

INDEX OF RECIPIENTS

General Index

Where there is a footnote giving a person's main biographical particulars it will
be found on the first page mentioned after the person's name.

Art—*cont.*

262; pleasure of creating purely personal, 266; unreality in, 272; and love only two things of importance, 276; unhealthy work of defined, 289 n; useless, 292; and Nature, 301; comic footmen outside scope of W's, 377; not a mirror but a crystal, 415; Douglas the ruin of W's, 427; Sculpture, Music and Literature as, 460; and philosophy, 466; sorrow the type and test of all great, 473; no saying of Plato or Christ unsuitable for, 476; the cry of Marsyas in much modern, 490; no gulf between W and, 490; W in false colours as champion of morality in, 493; difficult entry into kingdom of, 590; influence of blue in, 600; England has more subjects for, 659; and Psychology, 665; aphorisms on, 869–870

Art and Morality
and *Dorian Gray*, 257 n

Arthur (factotum)
causes chaos by tidying up, 362

Artist
his function to invent, 259; has no ethical sympathies, 266; must educate critic, 269; all artists need protection, 311–312; revolves in a cycle of masterpieces, 372; God and other artists always a little obscure, 379; artists and criminals only people who will know W after prison, 534; W's life unworthy of, 567; reason for paucity of artists in England, 659; aphorisms on, 869–870

"Artist, The" (prose-poem)
the note of doom in, 475–476

Artistic Life
a long and lovely suicide, 183; is simple self-development, 476; Pater's attempt to reconcile with religion, 476; in relation to Conduct, W plans to write on, 484; where it leads a man, 487

Arundel print
W gives to Harding, 28

Ashton, I. D. W. ("Sir John")
introduced to Turner, 672; nicknamed Sir John, 672 n; wonderful and improbable, 707; devoted to Sphinx, 726; son of a Jewish singer, 739; turned out of hotel, 743; unwilling to put up Maurice, 745; Douglas's dreadful postcard to, 745; cheated by

boy, 763; the last great sentimentalist, 765; clothes all but the naked, 765; expected with boy from St Malo, 766; arrives from St Malo, 767; his troubles with boys, 768; Hylton makes scenes with, 768; more penniless than ever, 770; W asks after, 771, 775; leaves for U.S., 776; described by W, 776; W asks for news of, 777; always in the best spirits (and water), 778; Joseph pet boy of, 829

Asquith, H. H.
W sits in Royal Box with, 377

Atalanta
good name for magazine, 204

Athenaeum, The
correspondence on Newman in, 274; Smithers advertises *Ballad* in, 703 n, 711, 721

Athens
W visits, 34–35; Douglas stays at, 434

Atkins, Frederick
wretched and perjured, 452; Allen probably mistaken for, 493

Atlantic Ocean
disappointing, 369

Atwood, Roland
W sends necktie to, 293

Augustine, St
works of sent to W in prison, 399 n

Aurora Leigh
much the greatest work in our literature, 21; sent to Ward, 21, 22; simply "*intense*," 25; W recommends to Harding, 37; read by Harding, 42; quoted by W, 69

Austen, Jane
lack of books by in Reading Gaol, 521; Ross's letters in style of, 833

Austin, Alfred
his new volume, 463; W on, 463 n

Australia
Mrs Bernard Beere's plans for, 355; W's plays produced in, 355 n

Auteri-Manzocchi, Salvatore
crowned in Milan, 10

Authors' Club
Sherard censures W at, 659–660; O'Sullivan defends W at, 660

Authorship
W advises on, 179

Autobiography
a man's face is his, 730 n

Avenue Kléber
Douglas's flat in, 738

anxious to see at Dieppe, 582 n; on
Lincrusta-Walton, 598 n; W realises
he will never see, 639; "The Poet"
and other prose-poems published by,
809 n; gives Miss Boxwell a birthday
present, 871

Hollingshead, John
and stage scenery, 172

Holloway Prison
W imprisoned in, 389–395; W's
letters to Douglas from, 393, 396,
397, 452, 455; Douglas's visits to W
in, 448; W's three weeks in, 529

Holman, Martin
Adey's solicitor, 416; in communication with Official Receiver, 420; and
W's possible divorce, 515, 518; and
money promised for W's release, 533;
his charges, 537; his untrue statement, 538; his anxiety about W's
debt, 540; his advice worthless, 542;
a serious rival to Flaubert's grotesques, 544; the leader of the Dunces,
544; Holmaniana, 544, 545, 546; well
satisfied, 547; not seen by W, 549;
payment of, 549; W writes to, 550;
Hargrove refuses to pay, 690; Adey
interviews, 697 n; Hargrove's letter to
be shown to, 732; W hopes he will act
rightly, 734; his letter analysed, 737;
allowance to be paid to, 740; asked to
pay W's allowance to Ross, 741; Ross
wires to, 854

Holmes, Augusta
W possibly at her party, 193

Holmes, Oliver Wendell
W meets in Boston, 89, 90, 94; W
sends Poems to, 90

Homburg
W takes cure at, 316–319; Queensberry pursues Lord Rosebery to, 445

Home Secretary
W's petitions to, 401, 406, 411, 528;
Adey's petition to, 408; no answer
from, 530, 531, 535; refusal received
from, 536; and W's release, 551; an
ignorant man, 553; sends W to
Pentonville for release, 557

Homer
Odyssey sent to Cyril, 370; Morris's
Odyssey quoted, 779

Homer (boy)
talks much of Ross, 822; W gives false
names and addresses to, 823–824;
accompanies W to Albano, 825; W
shows Rome to, 826

Homosexuality
Grant Allen shies off, 375 n; form of
sexual madness, 402, 411; Bauër on
folly of punishing, 455 n; Ulrich's
phrase for, 705; Raffalovich's book
on, 705 n; the road is long, 721

Honeymoon
W's described, 156–159

Hood, Jacob
illustrates W stories, 215

Hood, Thomas
alteration in Ballad not on account of,
667; Ballad compared to "Eugene
Aram" of, 712 n

Hope, Adrian
made guardian of W's children, 499,
464 n, 548; W writes to about allowance, 680, 682, 687, 697; no answer
from, 683, 685, 694; Clifton tries to
arrange terms with, 690, 697 n;
bound to pay restored allowance,
732; Ross to write to, 851; Tucker
asks for address of, 853; Ross wires to,
854; fails to communicate with Ross,
861; blamed by Ross, 861; disapproves of Ross's corresponding
with Constance, 861

Hope, Anthony
lack of books by in Reading Gaol, 521

Hopps, Rev. J. Page
and funeral reform, 168–169; Ballad
sent to, 712

Horace
quoted by W, 250

Horne, Herbert P.
and a Chatterton memorial, 188, 189,
191, 192; his poems praised, 294;
stanza quoted, 294 n

Hornton Street
De Profundis to be typed in, 513; W's
pictures to be stored in, 528, 608; W
sends letter to, 533; W's bags to be
taken to, 536; W's letters addressed
to, 578; Adey writes from, 696 n

Horse-Shoe, The (bar)
W sees Strong at, 794; Douglas's
good review celebrated at, 801

Horton, W. T.
his drawing for cover of Hunger considered a caricature of Dowson, 800,
801

Hotel Cecil
Turner accused of enlisting at, 818

Hôtel d'Alsace, Paris
W moves to, 726; breakfast only meal
provided at, 736, 737; W's insecurity

GENERAL INDEX

Maturin, C. R.
W's great-uncle, 555 n; his book enjoyed by Rossetti, 520; W's alias taken from, 555 n, 813

Maupassant, Guy de
cited by Whibley, 268 n; reported dying, 299; W finds much tenderness in, 784; *Une Vie* a masterpiece, 784; Balzac true master of, 784

Maurice, *see* Gilbert, Maurice

Max, *see* Beerbohm, Max

Maxwell, Gerald
Bournemouth thrilled by, 231; W tries to get part for, 254; no longer playing Lord Darlington, 325

Maxwell, W. B.
W plays euchre with, 231

May, ?Arthur Dampier
W takes to Windsor, 27, 29; a friend of Godwin, 164

Maypole soap
W suggests giving away *Ballad* with, 737

McClure, S. S.
and "Lord Arthur Savile's Crime," 209; free interview refused to, 379

McInnes, John
sends W china, 151

Medhurst, Blanche
contributes to *Woman's World*, 206

Meilhac and Halévy
W sees English version of *La Boule* by, 29; W's heroine reads *Frou-Frou*, 361; W's scenario compared to *Frou-Frou*, 408 n

Meissonnier, J. L. E.
W visits exhibition of, 158

Mellish, Fuller
terrible as Charles Surface, 324

Mellor, Harold
W meets at Napoule, 772; orders champagne, 772, 776; invites W to Nice, 774; sacked from Harrow, 775; buys Eolo for 200 lire, 775; takes W to Nice, 775, 776; to visit London, 778; loses bet about quotation, 782, 786; W sends Ross address of, 782; W stays at Gland with, 783–792; W turns against, 785; tedious, 785; refuses to pay, 786; W explains his dislike of, 786; carries out traditions of ancient misers, 788; W still dislikes, 789; insanity in family of, 789; keeps his cigarettes locked up, 790; serves Swiss beer instead of wine, 790; no longer tolerable, 791; too repulsive for anything, 792; compared to Tartuffe and Harpagon, 792; weeps at W's departure, 792; invites W to Italy, 819; takes W to Sicily, Naples and Rome, 819–821; leaves Rome, 821; to meet W at Chambéry and drive him to Paris, 827; W stays ten days with, 828; Smithers dislikes, 830; his movements in 1900, 830 n; W's last visit to, 833; almost as neurasthenic as W, 833; in Paris, 833; drinks and talks mineral waters, 833; his letter to W, 833 n; W given melancholia by last visit to, 834; sends wreath to W's funeral, 856; named on laurel wreath, 856; all W's Italian expenses paid by, 861

Melmoth, Sebastian
W's adoption of as name, 555, 564; suggested by Ross, 555 n; abandoned as absurd, 667; W still registered as at death, 854

Melmoth the Wanderer
W takes name from, 555 n; loved by Rossetti, 520; Ross and Adey's introduction to, 555 n

Melvill, Harry
Happy Prince sent to, 220; cuts W in Paris, 760

Mendès, Catulle
his telegram to Goncourt, 304 n

Mentone
Douglas's behaviour at, 719; Beardsley dies at, 719 n; Ross moves his mother to, 853; Ross returns to, 857

Mercure de France, Le
Douglas's article intended for, 393 n, 453, 455, 459, 494, 511; Douglas's *Poems* published by, 400 n; compared by Douglas to *Fortnightly*, 455, 459; Davray translates Meredith for, 647; founded by Vallette, 709 n; Davray reviews *Ballad* in, 709 n; to publish French translation of *Ballad*, 712, 713, 714, 715, 734, 742; publish *Ubu Roi*, 746; send wreath to W's funeral, 856

Meredith, George
Le Gallienne's book on praised, 277; W in prison asks for books by, 423 n; W charmed by *Amazing Marriage*, 520; his *Essay on Comedy* translated by Davray, 647; in list of Immortals, 692 n; W cuts quotation from out of *Ideal Husband*, 805

GENERAL INDEX

Naples—*cont.*

forbids W to live at, 685; objections to W's association with Douglas at, 705; facts of related to Ross, 709–710; W says *Ballad* refers to life at, 730 n; W stops three days at, 821; evil and luxurious, 826; W to sail from, 827

Napoleon I

his ill-treatment of Queen of Prussia, 472; La Jeunesse's book on praised, 590

Napoleon, Prince

W visits villa of, 784

Napoule

Harris invites W to, 761; W plans to leave for, 770; W stays at, 771–779; pinewoods enjoyed at, 771, 772, 774; Harris fails to arrive at, 772

Narcissus

more in W's life than a love for, 695; the only repartee to the Decalogue, 764

National Observer, The

no review copy for, 318, 328

Nature

no good for inspiration, 174; de-moralising influence of, 207; and Art, 301; looked at too much, lived with too little, 509; neither intellect nor passion in, 774

Neilson, Julia

in *Hypatia*, 323 n; in *Woman of No Importance*, 338 n; in *Once Upon a Time*, 356 n

Nelson, Major J. O.

his coming to Reading, 488; censors W's list of books, 405 n; reads Ross's message to W, 412; W's trust in, 415–416; allows W to receive and answer Adey's letter, 418, 420; submits further list of books for W, 423 n; and writing of *De Profundis*, 424 n, 512 n, 514; most sympathetic and kind, 533; has no authority to grant special privileges, 534; gives per-mission for carriage to drive into prison, 535; hands on Adey's docu-ment, 537; "my good and kind friend," 551; shows W letter from interviewer, 553; allows letter to Turner, 554; Turner to wire to, 556; hands W MS of *De Profundis*, 563; W describes gardening for, 563; as presiding fairy in enchanted castle, 565; his humane character, 574; W's letter of gratitude to, 580–581; *Ballad*

to be sent to, 663, 700; copy of *Ideal Husband* for, 805 n

Nemesis

seems endless, 628; W caught in net of, 629; of character, 685; too strong for W, 690

Nero

W imitates *coiffure* of, 135, London amazed by *coiffure*, 148; Christ bore sins of, 477; W's Neronian hours, 577; and Messalina, 594 n; Cannes *Bataille des Fleurs* reminds W of Rome of, 777

Nesbit, E.

her poems praised, 190

Nethersole, Louis

very impossible, 837; his claim on *Mr and Mrs Daventry*, 829 n, 838, 843; pays W £100 for option, 847

Nethersole, Olga

quite wonderful in *Dean's Daughter*, 231; and *Mr and Mrs Daventry*, 838; her success in America, 838

Nettleship, Mrs

Miss Reubell wants dress by, 158

Nevill, Lady Dorothy

Lytton's death described to, 299; her birthday book, 299 n; possible con-tributor to *Woman's World*, 195, 201

Newdigate Prize

awarded to W's *Ravenna*, 52; history of, 53–54

Newhaven

W embarks at, 564; W telegraphs to Ross from, 565

Newman, Cardinal

friend of Dean Miles, 17; W's interest in, 19; a very unhappy man, 20; a good philosopher and Christian, 20; W dreams of visit to, 31; W plans visit to, 33; and Dr Charles Russell, 41 n; his fine "temper," 274; his grammar questioned, 274 n; books by sent to W in prison, 399 n; W asks for essays of, 405 n; W reads in prison, 409 n

Newman, Ernest

praises Makower's *Mirror of Music*, 646 n

New Review, The

Gosse defends W in, 323; publishes Nicholson's woodcut of Queen Vic-toria, 610; its dullness and stupidity, 636

Newspapers

written by prurient for Philistines,

GENERAL INDEX

tive art, 264; quoted, 264 n; the story only fit for C.I.D., 265; defended against *Scots Observer*, 266–267, 268–272; offensive review in *Punch*, 267; its ethical import recognised by Churches, 268; praised by *Speaker*, 268; lots of morality in, 269; 216 criticisms of, 270; classed with *La Terre*, 270; Pater's review of, 270 n; Yeats's review of, 270 n; Ricketts's cover for, 276; copy inscribed to Douglas, 281; in book form, 287 n; sold to Carrington, 287 n; discussed with Kernahan, 288–289; preface published in *Fortnightly*, 289; "preface should teach them," 290; commissioned by Stoddart, 291 n; not immoral, 292; preface quoted, 292 n; W's poor royalty on, 295; sent to Mallarmé, 297; Mallarmé's praise of, 298 n; preface quoted by W, 301; sent to Rothenstein, 302; John Gray not model for, 312 n; Huysmans and, 313; Ada Leverson's skit on, 343; W's self-identification with characters in, 352; French translation of, 417; of value still, 418; quoted by W, 464, 483, 492; the note of doom in, 475; W repeats phrase from, 509; origin of Lord Henry Wotton's name in, 533 n; and *Happy Hypocrite*, 575, 576; and Waterbury watch, 623 n; deservedly a classic, 679; possible Italian translation of, 695; W asks for copy of, 733; Carrington's editions of, 758; Wilkinson invents dramatisation of, 769 n, 776, 783 n; *Importance* to be within speaking distance of, 778

Pietro (boy)
like a young St John, 776

Pigott, E. F. S.
inept Examiner of plays, 316; bans *Salome*, 316; W very much hurt by action of, 318; his silly vulgar rule, 319

Pilcher, F.
W agrees to lecture for, 190

Pindar
quoted by W, 487

Pinero, A. W.
a brilliant dramatist, 339; presides at dinner for charity, 339 n; *Second Mrs Tanqueray* declined by Hare, 348 n; W's admiration for work of, 376; in list of Immortals, 692 n

Pinker, J. B.
and serialisation of *Ballad*, 640; Ross to see, 649; the extraordinary promise of his name, 652; Ross to stir up, 653, 654; W's sole hope of food, 659; W anxious about, 660; to approach *Reynolds*, 661, 662, 663; not to be trusted, 666; an absurdity, 667, 670; unsatisfactory, 668, 669

Pius IX, Pope
W hopes to see, 13; and Papal Infallibility, 17 n, 18

Plagiarism
Whistler accuses W of, 253; Labouchere on, 253 n; *Weekly Sun* accuses W of, 370–372

Plato
W borrows notes on, 48; to be re-read, 185; Mill's ignorance of, 237; studied by Douglas at Babbacombe, 328; quoted by W, 413; W's letter comprehensible to readers of *Symposium* of, 440; no saying of unsuitable for art, 476; W refers to *Charmides*, 483; and Christ, 483; phrase Uranian Love taken from *Symposium* of, 705 n; read by Douglas and Dodgson, 867; discussed at Babbacombe, 868

Playgoers' Club
W's speech to, 310–312

Plays by W, *see Duchess of Padua, Ideal Husband, Importance of Being Earnest, Lady Windermere's Fan, Salome, Vera,* and *Woman of No Importance*

Plunket, David
proposes W for St Stephen's Club, 31

Poe, Edgar Allan
W visits house of, 131 n; lord of romance, 169; W recommends sonnet by, 182; marvellous lord of rhythmic expression, 186; Mallarmé's translation of, 288; would have entertained Clibborn and Allen, 493; and Lugné-Poe, 567; put to death by America, 567

Poems by W (see also *Ballad of Reading Gaol, Ravenna,* and *Sphinx*)
printed in full: "Easter Day," 38; "Keats' Grave," 42; "On the Recent Massacre of the Christians in Bulgaria," 37; "On the Sale by Auction of Keats's Love Letters," 182–183; "Sonnet (written after hearing

Watson, William
his lines on banning of *Salome*, 316 n;
rebuked by Gosse, 323 n
Watts, G. F.
W sends poem to, 68; and Ellen
Terry, 159 n
Watts, Theodore
interested in Chatterton memorial,
192; W on Swinburne and, 192 n;
and grant to Lady Wilde, 228; W's
opinion of his *Aylwin*, 766
Weekly Sun, The, see *Sunday Sun, The*
Weldon, Georgina
W misses her Jubilee party, 202;
Philip Treherne nephew of, 749 n;
W writes to from Paris, 750-751
Wells, H. G.
protégé of Henley, 521; proposes W
for list of Immortals, 692 n; on Duke
of Argyll, 692 n
West Ashby
W stays at, 13-14
West, Benjamin
explained away, 170-171
Westminster, Constance, Duchess of
something too charming, 33
Weyman, Stanley
lack of books by in Reading Gaol,
521; has rewritten Dumas for English
public, 633
Wharton, J. H. T.
Oxford friend of W, 20
Whibley, Charles
attacks *Dorian Gray*, 265 n, 268, 269
Whistler, James McNeill
W banters from America, 96; W's
clever and amusing remarks on, 40;
U.S. papers sent to, 87; his telegram
to W in America, 102; one of W's
heroes, 105; Leadville miners roused
by, 111; Frances Richards introduced
to, 119; invited to Japan, 121; his
Venice etchings, 135; praises Waldo
Story, 135; and *Punch* article, 152;
Constance sound about, 155; his
breakfast party, 155 n; Miss Reubell a
friend of, 157; his Salon pictures,
157; and E. W. Godwin, 159 n; his
marriage, 160 n; warned to remain
incomprehensible, 170-171; his Ten
O'Clock Lecture, 170-171 n; his row
with W, 191; on Watts's change of
name, 192 n; accuses W of plagiarism, 253 n; W answers, 253-254;
Sturges friend of, 330 n; Rothen-

stein's continued friendship with,
338 n; W loses drawings by, 451; his
definition of lithographs, 604 n; W
meets in Paris, 731; like Meg
Merrilies, 731; W refers to Dowdeswell's essay on, 863
White, Gleeson
publishes W's villanelle, 193; his
contribution to *Woman's World*, 193 n
White, Sir Henry
W sits with in Royal Box, 377
White's Club
Douglas retires to, 493; qualification
for membership of, 503
Whitman, Walt
W sends Swinburne's letter to 99; W
meets, 99 n; W loses inscribed books
by, 451
Widowers' Houses
Shaw promises to send, 332 n; Op. 2
of the great Celtic School, 339; W's
praise of, 339; produced by Independent Theatre, 345 n
Wight, Miss
unseen signer of agreement, 549
Wilde, Constance
describes W in Dublin, 152-153;
engaged to W, 153; described to Lily
Langtry, 154, to Waldo Story, 155;
her marriage and honeymoon, 156-
159; W's only surviving letter to,
165; her note on Irving's benefit, 202;
stays with the Thursfields, 249; upset
by Herbert Vivian's articles, 256;
House of Pomegranates dedicated to,
300 n; on W's cure at Homburg,
316 n; her love of Babbacombe, 321;
visits Italy, 328, 333; on W's visit to
Algiers, 381 n; W's note to about
Cyril, 384; W's note to during trial,
386; writes to Mrs Robinson, 389 n;
W's first prison letters probably
written to, 398 n, 872; and W's life-
interest in their marriage-settlement,
398-399, 406, 409 n, 517; breaks news
of Lady Wilde's death to W, 399, 458,
517; her description of W, 399 n; in
Germany, 406; Lady Brooke with,
408 n; Adey asks W to write to, 408 n;
her proposal re marriage-settlement,
415; Lady Brooke's influence with,
417; and possible divorce, 442, 545,
547; Douglas advised to consult, 444;
gains custody of her children, 464;
told by W of Lady Queensberry and